W. JACKSON BATE
Harvard University

DAVID PERKINS
Harvard University

HARCOURT BRACE JOVANOVICH, PUBLISHERS
San Diego New York Chicago Atlanta Washington, D.C.
London Sydney Toronto

ISBN: 0-15-505588-7

Library of Congress Catalog Card Number: 85-60875

Printed in the United States of America

PREFACE

This anthology is intended for students who are being introduced to poetry at the college level.

Our hope in selecting poets and poems has been to maintain a balance between anthologies that concentrate on only a dozen or score of poets and those that present selections from two hundred or more. In the period after World War II there was a widespread desire, with which we sympathized, to strip anthologies down to relatively few writers (the "Great Authors" movement). Yet each of the present editors, in courses we gave, began to share the wish of other college teachers for a more capacious selection that would allow the teacher more individual choice. In the 1970s the pendulum swung too far, we believe, in the other direction, toward anthologies which would include something from almost every possible poet. This in time seemed to have at least three disadvantages. One was that the sheer number of poets represented naturally limits the amount that can be devoted to the greater writers. Moreover, the amount of commentary, introductory or in notes, often had to be reduced in order to allow space. A third disadvantage was that the inclusion of so many poets could produce a book too cumbersome to hold easily in the hand, and could subtly alienate the student by giving a sense of glut, even though the teacher assigned only a fraction of the poems in the book.

In trying to find a balance between extremes, our prevailing principle has been to offer teachers what is still a wide selection from which to choose, while at the same time providing a book that, in sheer bulk, would not give a student a sense of suffocation. We have offered somewhat more annotation than is generally found in anthologies of this kind. But it is intended not to interfere with the teacher's freedom in interpretation. The notes, as a rule, are concerned with information of fact, meanings of unusual or obsolete words, and allusions. The introductions have been restricted to short discussions in which we hope to distill only what will be most helpful. Biographical detail is not mentioned except when it has particular interest or relevance to the poems that follow. Brief bibliographies are provided at the end of the book because some teachers may find them useful for students who, for course purposes, should pursue further the work of some particular poet.

In addition to the usual Appendix on versification, we include another short discussion, "On Reading Poetry Aloud." College teachers often express regret that, in both elementary and secondary schools, poetry is rarely read aloud, and that students entering college have not been given guidelines which—with a little practice—might enable them to read poetry aloud more effectively and thus better appreciate it as one of the great traditional forms of human expression.

Three details should be mentioned about the order of selections offered, about dates, and about footnotes.

Poets are presented chronologically according to year of birth (and, if born in the same year, then alphabetically). The selection of poems under each is arranged according to the date of publication. When more than one poem is published in the same year, the order, within that year, is by date of composition when this is known. We have chosen this arrangement not because we believe that a chronological approach, in teaching or in reading, is the best. The reason is simply that a grouping of poets and poems by topic, genre, or other categories inevitably becomes subjective and debatable. A chronological listing leaves teachers free to choose whatever mode of selection they prefer.

Dates of publication are given at the end of each poem. Naturally an exception has had to be made, in the earlier part of the anthology, for poems that were not published until long after they were written. This is particularly true of the early ballads as well as some of the Elizabethan poems, such as Sir Walter Ralegh's poem "To His Son," which was composed about 1600 but never published until the twentieth century. In these cases the date given is the estimated year in which the poem was written.

A final explanation involves the notes. Like many other teachers, we have found that the flow of the poetry, as the student reads it, is abruptly broken by the presence either of footnote numbers in the text or by "bubbles" after words or phrases. The presence of either tends to make the reader stop and look down or aside at notes or else feel that the reading *should* have been stopped, at a crucial point, in order to glance at a note before proceeding further. The obvious answer is to provide the information in a note without distracting readers by signals in the text, and to identify the footnote reference at the bottom of the page by the number of the line and the key word or phrase involved. Samuel Johnson remarks, in a fine passage in his *Preface to Shakespeare,* that the real delight of encountering a great author comes in reading first with utter "negligence" of commentary; only afterwards, "when the pleasures of novelty have ceased," need one look at the notes.

Our acknowledgments, aside from those listed elsewhere for permission to reproduce texts, would have to include scores of teachers whose opinions and suggestions, over the years, have been valuable, both for selecting the poems most necessary for an anthology of this kind and for the sort of commentary most desired. In particular, we are grateful to Professor Charles Dunn for his help with the Chaucer selections. For assistance in preparing the manuscript we thank Anne Macaulay.

W.J.B.
D.P.

Contents

Geoffrey Chaucer

(1343–1400)

"Here," said the great English poet John Dryden, speaking of Chaucer centuries later: "Here is God's plenty." And it was fortunate for all poetry in the English language that our first major poet, Geoffrey Chaucer, in addition to his wonderful artistry in versification and phrasing, represented life with such realism and variety.

He was able to do this because of his wide experience of the world. He was a practical man of affairs and held a number of important jobs in the government. He served as a Forester, Clerk of the Works (in charge of engineering projects), Controller of the Customs and Tariffs, a Justice of the Peace, and a member of Parliament. But Chaucer also knew human nature by introspection and imaginative sympathy. Like Shakespeare, he could trace thoughts and feelings from their first germinal impulses to their fully developed expression. And with his powerful sympathetic imagination he could identify with all kinds of persons, high and low, male and female. Hence his characters, like those in Shakespeare or in great novelists such as Charles Dickens, are forever remembered as though they were living people. We see this especially in his two masterpieces. One of them is the long poem *Troilus and Cressida* (1385–86), which uses an old Greek story as a basis and tells it with such brilliant psychological insight that it is often called the "first English novel." The second is his famous *The Canterbury Tales* (largely written in 1386–1400), a long chain of twenty-four stories told by a group of pilgrims who are traveling from London to visit the shrine of St. Thomas à Becket in Canterbury. On the way they take turns at telling stories. These stories are not only interesting in themselves but also adapted to the character of the person who is narrating.

Both in his characterizations and his narratives Chaucer combines vivid realism with gusto and humor. His attitude reminds us of what Matthew Arnold said about the Greek dramatist Sophocles: he " saw life steadily, and saw it whole."

We give first the General Prologue to *The Canterbury Tales,* where Chaucer offers a preliminary group of portraits of the people who are setting off on this pilgrimage. There is a knight, a squire, a fat widow called "the Wife of Bath," a bookish scholar from Oxford (the "Clerk"), a merchant, a miller (who tells one of the famous "dirty" stories known as *fabliaux*), a demure prioress from a convent, and so on.

One of these characters is what was then called a pardoner. Such persons traveled Europe soliciting contributions for religious institutions and offered "pardons" to the donors for their sins. Pardoners were supposed to be licensed by the church to sell "pardons," but many were fraudulent. Chaucer makes his Pardoner both repulsive and dishonest. One critic has said that the Pardoner is the "lost soul" among the Canterbury pilgrims.

The Pardoner exploits the faith of his hearers in order to make money, and he selects the tale he narrates with this aim in mind. His is an archetypal tale almost as old as history. Three men set out in search of "Death," the universal enemy, resolved to kill him. They do indeed meet "Death," for they find a pile of gold, and each then plots successfully to get rid of the others in order to have all the gold himself. In different versions this story has been part of the folk culture of many different countries. It is found as one of the "Jakatas" or tales told by or about the Buddha in ancient India, and we find variations of it in our own century in Rudyard Kipling's *Second Jungle Book* and in the famous film of the 1940s, *The Treasure of the Sierra Madre*. About fifty years ago a scholar who was working in a logging camp in the western United States told the Pardoner's tale to the loggers, who were fascinated by it.

With his typically humane, complex vision, Chaucer allows us to feel that even the Pardoner is somewhat redeemed as he tells his story, simply because the tale moves even him. But Chaucer also feels and shows that the Pardoner would at once try to cover up his moment of sincere emotion; he starts again to hawk his pardons.

Chaucer was a master of language and versification. But living so long after him, we must learn how to read his English as it was spoken in his time.

The Language: Chaucer writes in what is called Middle English. It is called "Middle" because it was in use between Old English (also called "Anglo-Saxon," the language spoken in England before the Norman Conquest in 1066) and our modern English. Old English is so different it seems a completely foreign language. But the English of Chaucer can still be understood without special study. Of the several English dialects spoken in Chaucer's time, his is that of London, and it is this especially from which modern English derives.

Pronunciation: To hear Chaucer's language as it sounded in his time, we must follow three necessary rules, the third of which is more important than the others: (1) The long vowels are pronounced as they would be in French, German, and Italian: *a* is generally *ah*, as in *father; e* is pronounced like *ay*, as in *lane*; *i* is pronounced *ee*, as in *tree.* (2) Pronounce all consonants as we do now, but add another consonant sound: This is the *gh* sound in *laugh, rough,* and so on. In Middle English, the *gh* was a "gutteral," like the Scottish Lo*ch* Lomond, or the German name Ba*ch*. The word *right* or *night* would therefore sound like *richt* or *nicht*. (3) Even more important, for the music of the verse, is the final *e* at the end of Middle English words. This sound is like the *uh* sound in *the*. Always pronounce this final *e except* when the next word following begins with a vowel or an *h*. Thus, in line 5 of the Prologue, the *e* at the end of *sweete* would be pronounced. But in line 2, in the phrase "The droghte of March . . . ," the *e* in *droghte* would not be pronounced because the next word (*of*) begins with a vowel. Unless we keep this in mind, we miss the lovely liquid flow and rhythm of the verse. But readers from Shakespeare's time until that of Wordsworth and Keats did not know how to pronounce Chaucer's English, and they still admired and enjoyed Chaucer.

Our text is based on the standard British edition of Walter Skeat. Occasional changes in spelling have been made after comparison with the American editions of F. N. Robinson, J. M. Manly and Edith Rickert, and Charles Dunn, the last of whom we have followed in punctuation and capitalization. The modern translation of words appearing in the margin follow those of Charles Dunn in his *Chaucer Reader* (1952), and are reproduced with the permission of Professor Dunn and the publisher, Harcourt Brace Jovanovich. Additional explanations, particularly those of a factual nature, appear as footnotes at the bottom of the page.

from The Canterbury Tales

The General Prologue

Whan that° Aprill with his shoures soote°	When sweet
The droghte of March hath perced to the roote	
And bathed every veyne in swich licour°	such liquid
Of which vertu° engendred is the flour,	By power of which
Whan Zephirus eek° with his sweete breeth	also
Inspired hath in every holt° and heeth°	wood heath
The tendre croppes,° and the yonge sonne	shoots
Hath in the Ram his half cours y-ronne,	
And smale foweles maken° melodye	birds make

THE CANTERBURY TALES. GENERAL PROLOGUE. **5. Zephirus:** West Wind. **8. Hath . . . y-ronne:** "Has run his half course in the Ram." In late March the "young sun" of the coming spring has moved through the first half of its course through the constellation called the "Ram."

That slepen al the nyght with open eye,	
So priketh hem° Nature in hir corages,°	stirs them their hearts
Than longen° folk to goon° on pilgrymages,	Then long go
And palmeres° for to seken° straunge strondes,°	pilgrims seek strands
To ferne halwes kouthe° in sondry londes.	distant shrines known
And specially, from every shires ende	
Of Engelond, to Caunterbury they wende,	
The holy, blisful martir for to seke	
That hem hath holpen° whan that they were seeke.°	helped sick
Bifel° that in that sesoun on a day	It befell
In Southwerk at the Tabard, as I lay	
Redy to wenden on my pilgrymage	
To Caunterbury with ful devout corage,°	heart
At nyght was come into that hostelrye	
Wel nyne-and-twenty in a compaignye	
Of sondry folk by aventure y-falle°	chance fallen
In felaweshipe, and pilgrymes were they alle	
That toward Caunterbury wolden° ryde.	intended to
The chambres and the stables weren wyde,°	spacious
And wel we weren esed atte beste°;	entertained at the best
And shortly, whan the sonne was to reste,	
So hadde I spoken with hem everichon°	every one
That I was of hir° felaweshipe anon;	their
And made forward° erly for to ryse	(we) made agreement
To take oure wey ther-as° I yow devyse.°	where tell
But, nathelees,° whil I have tyme and space,	nevertheless
Er that° I ferther in this tale pace,°	Before pass
Me thynketh it acordant to resoun	
To telle yow al the condicioun	
Of ech of hem° so as it semed me,	them
And whiche they weren, and of what degree,	
And eek in what array that they were inne;	
And at a knyght than wol I first bigynne.	
A Knyght ther was, and that a worthy man,	
That, fro the tyme that he first bigan	
To riden° out, he loved chivalrye,	ride (in expeditions)
Trouthe and honour, fredom and curteisye.	
Ful worthy was he in his lordes werre,°	war
And ther-to hadde he riden, no man ferre,°	farther
As wel in Cristendom as in hethenesse,°	heathendom
And evere honoured for his worthynesse.	
At Alisaundre° he was whan it was wonne.	Alexandria (Egypt)
Ful ofte tyme he hadde the bord bigonne°	table headed

17. martir: St. Thomas à Becket (1118–1170), Archbishop of Canterbury, who had been murdered there in the Cathedral and was made a saint in 1172. **20. Southwerk:** Southwark, then a small town immediately south of London, across the Thames River; now a part of London. **Tabard:** an inn. **51–65. Alisaundre . . . Palatye:** The campaigns against the pagans listed here show the Knight was a veteran of forty years service.

Aboven alle nacions in Pruce.
In Lettow hadde he reysed,° and in Ruce,   served
No Cristen man so ofte of his degree.
In Gernade at the seege eek hadde he be°   been
Of Algezir, and riden in Belmarye.
At Lyeys was he and at Satalye
Whan they were wonne; and in the Grete° See   Mediterranean
At many a noble armee° hadde he be.   armada
At mortal batailles hadde he been fiftene,
And foghten for oure feith at Tramyssene
In lystes° thries, and ay° slayn his foo.   tournaments   always
This ilke° worthy Knyght hadde been also   same
Som tyme with the lord of Palatye°   Balat (Turkey)
Agayn° another hethen in Turkye.   Against
  And evere moore° he hadde a sovereyn prys,°   always   reputation
And, though that he were worthy, he was wys
And of his port° as meke as is a mayde.   deportment
He nevere yet no vileynye° ne sayde   anything boorish
In al his lyf unto no maner wight.°   any kind of person
He was a verray,° parfit, gentil knyght.   true
  But for to tellen yow of his array,
Hise hors° were goode, but he was nat gay.   horses
Of fustian° he wered a gypon°   rough cotton   blouse
Al bismotered° with his habergeon,°   stained   coat of mail
For he was late y-come from his viage°   journey
And wente for to doon his pilgrymage.

  With hym ther was his sone, a yong SQUIER,
A lovere and a lusty bacheler,
With lokkes crulle as° they were leyd in presse.°   curled as if   curlers
Of twenty yeer of age he was, I gesse.
  Of his stature he was of evene° lengthe,   medium
And wonderly delyvere,° and of greet strengthe;   agile
And he hadde been som tyme in chivachye°   on a raid
In Flaundres, in Artoys, and Picardye,
And born hym wel, as of so litel space,
In hope to stonden in his lady grace.
  Embrouded° was he as it were a meede°   Embroidered   meadow
Al ful of fresshe floures white and reede.
Syngynge he was or floytynge° al the day.   fluting
He was as fressh as is the month of May.
Short was his gowne with sleves longe and wyde.
Wel koude he sitte on hors and faire° ryde.   gracefully
He koude songes make and wel endite,°   compose words
Juste,° and eek° daunce, and wel purtreye,° and
  write.   Joust   also   draw

51–65. Alisaundre . . . Palatye: The place names indicate campaigns in Egypt, Prussia, Lithuania, Russia, Granada (Spain), Morocco, Armenia, Turkey, Algeria, and on the Mediterranean Sea. **80. bacheler:** a young man hoping to become a knight, meanwhile learning war and courtly manners from service to an experienced knight. **87. so litel space:** in such a short time (being so young).

So hoote he lovede that by nyghtertale° nighttime
He slepte namoore than dooth a nyghtyngale.
Curteys he was, lowely, and servysable,
And carf° biforn his fader at the table. carved

A YEMAN° hadde he and servantz namo° yeoman no more
At that tyme, for hym liste° ryde so, he liked to
And he was clad in coote and hood of grene.
A sheef of pecok arwes° bright and kene arrows
Under his belt he bar° ful thriftily.° carried neatly
Wel koude he dresse° his takel° yemanly; prepare equipment
His arwes drouped noght with fetheres lowe.
And in his hand he bar a myghty bowe.
A not° heed hadde he, with a broun visage. close-cropped
Of wodecraft wel koude° he al the usage. knew
Upon his arm he bar a gay bracer,° archer's guard
And by his syde a swerd° and a bokeler,° sword buckler
And on that° oother syde a gay daggere, the
Harneysed° wel, and sharp as poynt of spere, Mounted
A Cristofer° on his brest of silver shene.° St. Christopher bright
An horn he bar, the bawdryk° was of grene. carrying-belt
A forster° was he soothly,° as I gesse. forester truly

Ther was also a nonne, a PRIORESSE,
That of hir smylyng was ful symple° and coy.° unpretentious quiet
Hir gretteste ooth was but by Seinte Loy;
And she was cleped° Madame Eglentyne. called
Ful wel she soong° the servyce dyvyne, sang
Entuned° in hir nose ful semely,° Intoned properly
And Frenssh she spak ful faire and fetisly° elegantly
After the scole of Stratford atte Bowe,
For Frenssh of Parys was to hire unknowe.
At mete wel y-taught was she with alle;
She leet no morsel from hir lippes falle,
Ne wette hir fyngres in hir sauce depe;
Wel koude she carie a morsel, and wel kepe° take care
That no drope ne fille° upon hir brest. fell
In curteisie was set ful muchel° hir lest.° much concern
Hir over lippe wyped she so clene
That in hir coppe ther was no ferthyng° sene particle
Of grece whan she dronken hadde hir draughte.
Ful semely after hir mete she raughte,° reached
And sikerly° she was of greet desport,° certainly fun
And ful plesaunt and amyable of port,° deportment
And peyned hire to countrefete cheere
Of court, and to been estatlich° of manere, stately
And to been holden digne° of reverence. considered worthy

120. Seinte Loy: a minor saint, who had been a French bishop in early Christian days. **125–26. Stratford . . . Parys:** Her French was only that of the Stratford school in England, not of Paris itself. **139. peyned . . . cheere:** strove to imitate the behaviour.

But for to speken of hir conscience,	
She was so charitable and so pitous,°	sympathetic
She wolde wepe if that she sawe a mous	
Caught in a trappe, if it were deed or bledde.	
Of smale houndes hadde she that she fedde	
With rosted flessh, or mylk and wastel° breed;	white wheat
But soore wepte she if oon of hem were deed,	
Or if men smoot it with a yerde smerte.°	stick severely
And al was conscience and tendre herte.	
Ful semely hir wympel pynched was,	
Hir nose tretys,° hir eyen greye as glas,	shapely
Hir mouth ful smal, and ther-to softe and reed,	
But sikerly she hadde a fair forheed;	
It was almoost a spanne brood, I trowe,°	believe
For hardily° she was nat undergrowe.	undeniably
Ful fetys° was hir cloke, as I was war°;	graceful aware
Of smal coral aboute hir arm she bar°	carried
A peyre of bedes, gauded al with grene,	
An ther-on heng a brooch of gold ful shene,°	bright
On which ther was first writen a crowned A,	
And after *Amor vincit omnia.*°	Love conquers all.
Another NONNE with hire hadde she,	
That was hir chapeleyne, and preestes thre.	
A MONK ther was, a fair for the maistrye,°	an extremely fine (one)
An outridere° that lovede venerye,°	supervisor hunting
A manly man, to been an abbot able.	
Ful many a deyntee° hors hadde he in stable,	valuable
And whanne he rood, men myghte his brydel heere	
Gynglen° in a whistlynge wynd as cleere	Jingle
And eek° as loude as dooth the chapel belle	also
Ther-as° this lord was kepere of the celle.°	Where group
The reule of Seint Maure or of Seint Beneit,	
By cause that it was old and somdel streit,°	somewhat strict
This ilke° Monk leet olde thynges pace	same
And heeld after the newe world, the space.°	for the meanwhile
He yaf° nat of that text a pulled° hen	gave plucked
That seith that hunters been° nat holy men,	are
Ne that a monk, whan he is recchelees,°	not following the rules of his order
Is likned til° a fissh that is waterlees,	like to
This is to seyn,° a monk out of his cloystre.	say
But thilke° text heeld he nat worth an oystre;	that same

146. Of smale houndes: some small dogs; lap dogs that she pampered, though nuns were not supposed to have pets. **151. semely . . . pynched:** Her head-dress was gracefully fluted. **159. peyre . . . grene:** A string of beads (a rosary) had she, with every **gand** (large bead) colored green. **173. Seint Maure . . . Beneit:** St. Maurus and his predecessor, St. Benedict, who laid down rules for monks. Chaucer is saying that this monk, in charge of one of the "cells" or groups at the monastery, was less strict in enforcing the old "rule."

And I seyde his opinion was good.
What° sholde he studie and make hymselven wood°   Why himself insane
Upon a book in cloystre alwey to poure,
Or swynken° with his handes and laboure   work
As Austyn bit?° How shal the world be served?   commands
Lat Austyn have his swynk to hym reserved.
Therfore he was a prikasour° aright.   fast rider
Grehoundes he hadde as swift as fowel in flight.
Of prikyng° and of huntyng for the hare   tracking (the hare)
Was al his lust, for no cost wolde he spare.
  I seigh° his sleves purfiled° at the hond   saw trimmed
With grys,° and that the fyneste of a lond;   gray fur
And, for to festne his hood under his chyn,
He hadde of gold wroght a ful curious pyn;
A love knotte in the gretter ende ther was.
His heed was balled,° that shoon as any glas,   bald
And eek° his face as° he hadde been enoynt.   also as if anointed
He was a lord ful fat and in good poynt,°   condition
Hise eyen stepe° and rollynge in his heed,   eyes bulging
That stemed° as a forneys° of a leed,°   glowed furnace boiler
His bootes souple, his hors in greet estat.
  Now certeynly he was a fair prelat.
He was nat pale as a forpyned goost.°   tormented spirit
A fat swan loved he best of any roost.
His palfrey was as broun as is a berye.

  A FRERE° ther was, a wantowne and a merye,   friar
A lymytour,° a ful solempne° man.   limiter splendid
In alle the ordres foure is noon that kan°   knows
So muche of daliaunce° and fair langage.   flirtation
He hadde maad° ful many a mariage   arranged
Of yonge wommen at his owene cost.
  Unto his ordre he was a noble post.°   pillar
Ful wel biloved and famulier was he
With frankeleyns over-al° in his contree   rich landholders everywhere
And with worthy wommen of the toun,
For he hadde power of confessioun,
As seyde hymself, moore than a curat,°   parish priest
For of his ordre he was licenciat.
Ful swetely herde he confessioun,
And plesaunt was his absolucioun.
He was an esy man to yeve° penaunce   give
Ther-as he wiste° to have a good pitaunce.°   Where he knew gift
For unto a povre ordre for to yive°   give

187. Austyn: St. Augustine (fifth century), who had stated that monks should do manual work. **209. lymytour:** A "limiter" was a friar who had been granted an area within which he had exclusive rights to beg. **210. ordres foure:** the four orders of friars—Carmelites, Augustinians, Dominicans, and Franciscans. **220. licenciat:** one who was licensed to hear confessions.

Is signe that a man is wel y-shryve°;	confessed
For if he yaf,° he dorste make avaunt,°	gave dared to avow
He wiste° that a man was repentaunt;	knew
For many a man so hard is of his herte,	
He may not wepe, althogh hym soore smerte.°	smart
Therfore, in stede of wepynge and preyeres,	
Men moote° yeve silver to the povre freres.	ought to
His typet° was ay farsed° full of knyves	cape always stuffed
And pynnes for to yeven faire wyves.	
And certeynly he hadde a murye note.	
Wel koude he synge and pleyen on a rote°;	stringed instrument
Of yeddynges° he bar outrely° the prys.	ballads carried off completely
His nekke whit was as the flour-de-lys°;	fleur-de-lis
Ther-to° he strong was as a champioun.	In addition
He knew the tavernes wel in every toun	
And every hostiler° and tappestere°	innkeeper bar-maid
Bet than a lazar or a beggestere,	
For unto swich° a worthy man as he	such
Acorded nat, as by his facultee,°	capacity
To have with sike° lazars aqueyntaunce.	sick
It is nat honeste,° it may nat avaunce,°	proper benefit
For to deelen with no swich poraille°	such poor folk
But al with riche and selleres of vitaille.°	victuals
And, over-al ther-as° profit sholde arise,	everywhere where
Curteys he was and lowely of servyse.	
Ther was no man nowher so vertuous.	
He was the beste beggere in his hous,°	friary
For thogh a wydwe° hadde noght a sho,°	widow shoe
So plesant was his *In principio,*	
Yet wolde he have a ferthyng° er he wente.	farthing
His purchas was wel bettre than his rente.	
And rage° he koude as it were right° a whelp.	frolic just like
In lovedayes ther koude he muchel help,	
For ther he was nat lyk a cloysterer	
With a thredbare cope,° as is a poure scoler,	cloak
But he was lyk a maister° or a pope;	Master of Arts
Of double worstede was his semycope,°	short cloak
That rounded as a belle out of the presse.	
Somwhat he lipsed for his wantownesse°	playfulness
To make his Englissh sweete upon his tonge;	
And in his harpyng, whan that he hadde songe,	
Hise eyen twynkled in his heed aright	
As doon the sterres in the frosty nyght.	
This worthy lymytour was cleped° Huberd.	called

242. Bet . . . beggestere: better than a leper or a woman beggar. **254. *In principio:*** "In the beginning." These opening words of the gospel of St. John were used as a religious formula and were often spoken by friars when they encountered other people. **256. purchas . . . rente:** His pickings were better than his regular income. **258. lovedayes:** days for settling disputes by arbitration instead of in a court of law.

A MARCHANT was ther with a forked berd,	
In motelee,° and hye on hors he sat,	figured cloth
Upon his heed a Flaundryssh° bever hat,	Flemish
His bootes clasped faire and fetisly.°	elegantly
Hise resons° he spak ful solempnely,°	views impressively
Sownynge° alwey the encrees of his wynnyng.°	Relating profit
He wolde the see were kept for any thyng	
Bitwixe Middelburgh° and Orewelle.°	Middelburg (Holland) Orwell Harbor (England)
Wel koude he in eschaunge sheeldes selle.	
This worthy man ful wel his wit bisette.°	applied
Ther wiste° no wight° that he was in dette,	knew person
So estatly was he of his governaunce	
With his bargaynes and with his chevysaunce.°	manipulation
For sothe,° he was a worthy man with alle,	Truly
But, sooth to seyn,° I noot° how men hym calle.	say don't know
A CLERK° ther was of Oxenford° also	student Oxford
That unto logyk hadde longe y-go.°	long since gone
As leene was his hors as is a rake,	
And he was nat right° fat, I undertake,°	particularly vow
But looked holwe° and ther-to sobrely.	hollow
Ful thredbare was his overeste courtepy,°	outer short coat
For he hadde geten hym yet no benefice,°	ecclesiastical appointment
Ne was so worldly for to have office,	
For hym was levere° have at his beddes heed	he would rather
Twenty bookes clad in blak or reed	
Of Aristotle and his philosophie	
Than robes riche or fithele° or gay sautrie.°	fiddle psaltery (harp)
But, al be that he was a philosophre,	
Yet hadde he but litel gold in cofre,	
But al that he myghte of his frendes hente,°	get
On bookes and on lernynge he it spente,	
And bisily gan for the soules preye°	prayed *(gan . . . preye)*
Of hem that yaf° hym wher-with to scoleye.°	gave study
Of studie took he moost cure° and moost heede.	care
Noght oo° word spak he moore than was neede,	one
And that was seid in forme and reverence	
And short and quyk and ful of high sentence.°	significance
Sownynge in° moral vertu was his speche,	Tending toward
And gladly wolde he lerne and gladly teche.	
A SERGEANT OF THE LAWE, war° and wys,	wary
That often hadde been at the Parvys,	

278. Wel . . . selle: He well knew how to sell "shields" (French coins) illegally at the money-exchange. **286. unto logyk . . . y-go:** had long since gone into the study of philosophy (logic). **297–98: philosophre . . . cofre:** Besides the obvious meaning (the clerk was more interested in books and ideas than money), Chaucer is half-punning on the word "philosopher," which then, as used in the term "*natural* philosophy" as distinct from "moral philosophy," included the study of "alchemy"—the hoped-for science of turning other metals into gold. **310. Parvys:** St. Paul's porch, London, where lawyers were often consulted.

Ther was also, ful riche of excellence.	
Discreet he was and of greet reverence—	
He semed swich,° hise wordes weren so wise.	such
Justice he was ful often in assise°	local assize court
By patente° and by pleyn° commissioun.	public full
For his science and for his heigh renoun,	
Of fees and robes hadde he many oon.°	a one
So greet a purchasour° was nowher noon;	buyer of land
Al was fee symple° to hym in effect.	unrestricted possession
His purchasyng myghte nat been infect.°	invalidated
Nowher so bisy a man as he ther nas,°	was
And yet he semed bisier than he was.	
In termes hadde he caas and doomes alle	
That from the tyme of Kyng William were falle.	
Ther-to° he koude endite° and make a thyng°;	In addition compose draw up a document
Ther koude no wight pynchen° at his writyng.	person find fault
And every statut koude° he pleyn by rote.°	knew fully by heart
He rood but hoomly° in a medlee° cote,	plainly striped
Girt with a ceynt° of silk with barres smale.	belt
Of his array telle I no lenger tale.	
A Frankeleyn was in his compaignye.	
Whit was his berd as is the dayesye°;	daisy
Of his complexioun he was sangwyn.°	blood-red
Wel loved he by the morwe° a sop° in wyn.	morning piece of bread
To lyven in delyt was evere his wone,°	custom
For he was Epicurus owene sone,	
That heeld opynyoun that pleyn° delit	complete
Was verray° felicitee parfit.°	true perfect
An housholdere, and that a greet,° was he;	great (one)
Seint Julyan he was in his contree.	
His breed, his ale, was alweys after oon.°	consistently good
A bettre envyned° man was nevere noon.	wined
Withoute bake-mete° was nevere his hous	pie
Of fissh and flessh, and that so plentevous	
It snewed° in his hous of mete° and drynke,	snowed food
Of alle deyntees that men koude thynke,	
After° the sondry sesons of the yeer,	According to
So chaunged he his mete and his soper.°	supper
Ful many a fat partrich hadde he in muwe,°	coop
And many a breem and many a luce° in stuwe.°	pike pond
Wo was his cook but if° his sauce were	unless
Poynaunt° and sharp, and redy al his geere.°	Pungent utensils
His table dormaunt in his halle alway	
Stood redy covered al the longe day.	

323–24: In termes . . . falle: He knew precisely all the cases and judgments from the time of King William I (1066–87). **331. Frankeleyn:** A franklin was a wealthy country gentleman though not a nobleman. **340. Seint Julyan:** patron saint of hospitality (a way of saying that the rich Franklin was generous in his hospitality). **353–54. table . . . day:** He kept a permanent **(dormaunt)** table in his main hall (with food for any guests).

At sessions ther he was lord and sire;	
Ful ofte tyme he was knyght of the shire.°	Member of Parliament
An anlaas° and a gipser° al of silk	dagger purse
Heeng° at his girdel whit as morne° mylk.	Hung morning
A shirreve° hadde he been and a countour°;	sheriff auditor
Was nowher swich a worthy vavasour.°	squire
An HABERDASSHERE and a CARPENTER,	
A WEBBE,° a DYERE, and a TAPYCER°—	weaver tapestry-maker
And they were clothed alle in oo° lyveree	one
Of a solempne° and a greet fraternytee.°	important religious guild
Ful fressh and newe hir geere apiked° was;	trimmed
Hir knyves were chaped° noght with bras	mounted
But al with silver; wroght ful clene and wel	
Hir girdles and hir pouches everydel.°	altogether
Wel semed ech of hem a fair burgeys°	citizen
To sitten in a yeldehalle° on a deys.°	guildhall platform
Everych° for the wisdom that he kan°	Each one knows
Was shaply° for to been an alderman,	suited
For catel° hadde they ynogh and rente,°	property income
And eek° hir wyves wolde it wel assente,	also
And elles° certeyn they were to blame.	otherwise
It is ful fair to been y-cleped° "madame"	called
And goon to vigilies al bifore	
And have a mantel roialliche y-bore.°	carried
A COOK they hadde with hem for the nones°	occasion
To boille the chiknes° with the marybones,°	chickens marrowbones
And poudre-marchaunt° tart, and galyngale.°	flavoring spice
Wel koude he knowe° a draughte of Londoun ale.	judge
He koude rooste and sethe° and broille and frye,	boil
Maken mortreux,° and wel bake a pye.	stews
But greet harm was it, as it thoughte° me,	seemed to
That on his shyne a mormal° hadde he.	shin an ulcer
For blankmanger° that made he with the beste.	sweet creamed fowl
A SHIPMAN° was ther, wonyng° fer by weste;	ship owner living
For aught I woot,° he was of Dertemouthe.°	know Dartmouth
He rood upon a rouncy as he kouthe°	nag as best he could
In a gowne of faldyng° to the knee.	serge
A daggere hangynge on a laas° hadde he	lanyard
Aboute his nekke, under his arm adoun.	
The hoote somer had maad his hewe al broun.	
And certeynly he was a good felawe.	
Ful many a draughte of wyn hadde he drawe	
Fro Burdeuxward° whil that the chapman° sleep.	From Bordeaux (France) dealer
Of nyce° conscience took he no keep°;	tender heed
If that he faught and had the hyer hond,	

355. sessions . . . sire: He was a lord at the sessions of the local Justices of the Peace. **377. vigilies . . . bifore:** to festivals at the head of the procession ("al bifore") on the eves of saints' days.

By water he sente hem hoom° to every lond. — them home (overboard)
  But of his craft to rekene wel his tydes,
His stremes,° and his daungers hym bisydes,° — currents around
His herberwe,° and his moone, his lodemenage,° — harbor pilotage
Ther nas noon swich from Hulle to Cartage.° — Cartagena (Spain)
Hardy he was and wys to undertake.° — conduct an enterprise
With many a tempest hadde his berd been shake.
He knew alle the havenes as they were
Fro Gootland° to the cape of Fynystere° — Gottland (off Sweden) Finisterre (Spain)
And every cryke° in Britaigne and in Spayne. — creek
His barge y-cleped was the Mawdelayne.

  With us ther was a DOCTOUR OF PHISIK°; — medicine
In al this world ne was ther noon hym lyk,
To speke of phisik and of surgerye,
For he was grounded in astronomye.° — astrology
He kepte his pacient a ful greet deel
In houres by his magik natureel.
Wel koude he fortunen the ascendent
Of hise ymages for his pacient.
He knew the cause of every maladye,
Were it of hoot or coold or moyste or drye,
And where they engendred, and of what humour.
He was a verray,° parfit practisour.° — true practitioner
  The cause y-knowe° and of his harm the roote, — known
Anon° he yaf° the sike man his boote.° — Immediately gave remedy
Ful redy hadde he his apothecaries
To sende hym drogges and his letuaries,° — remedies
For ech of hem made oother for to wynne°; — gain
Hir° frendshipe nas nat° newe to begynne. — Their was not
  Wel knew he the olde Esculapius,
And Deiscorides, and eek Rufus,
Old Ypocras, Haly, and Galyen,
Serapion, Razis, and Avycen,
Averrois, Damascien, and Constantyn,
Bernard, and Gatesden, and Gilbertyn.
  Of his diete mesurable° was he, — moderate
For it was of no superfluitee
But of greet norissynge° and digestible. — nourishment
His studie was but litel on the Bible.
  In sangwyn° and in pers° he clad was al, — red Persian blue

415–16. kepte . . . houres: observed his patient closely in astrologically important hours. **417–18. fortunen . . . ymages:** determine the correct point of the Zodiac for using his curative images. **420–21. Were . . . humour:** According to the medical lore of Chaucer's time, the four "humours" of the body were blood, black and yellow bile, and phlegm. They involved different combinations of heat, cold, moisture, and dryness, and the disorders of the humors caused diseases. **429–34. Esculapius . . . Gilbertyn:** famous medical authorities. Five were ancient Greeks: Aesculapius, Rufus, Hippocrates, Galen, Serapion. Four were either Persians or Arabs: Hali, Rhazes, Avicenna, Averroës. The last three were medieval British physicians.

Text	Gloss
Lyned with taffata and with sendal,°	silk
And yet he was but esy° of dispence.°	cautious spending
He kepte that° he wan in pestilence.	what
For° gold in phisik is a cordial,°	Because heart-remedy
Therfore he loved gold in special.	
A good Wyf was ther of biside Bathe,	
But she was somdel° deef, and that was scathe.°	somewhat a pity
Of clooth-makyng she hadde swich an haunt,°	such a skill
She passed hem° of Ypres and of Gaunt.°	surpassed them (the Flemish weavers) Ghent
In al the parisshe, wyf ne was ther noon	
That to the offrynge bifore hire sholde goon°;	go
And if ther dide, certeyn, so wrooth was she	
That she was out of alle charitee.	
Hir coverchiefs° ful fyne were of ground°;	head-coverings texture
I dorste° swere they weyeden ten pound	would dare
That on a Sonday weren upon hir heed.	
Hir hosen weren of fyn scarlet reed,	
Ful streite y-teyd,° and shoes ful moyste and newe.	tightly tied
Boold was hir face and fair and reed of hewe,	
She was a worthy womman al hir lyve.	
Housbondes at chirche dore she hadde fyve,	
Withouten° oother compaignye in youthe—	Not to mention
But ther-of nedeth nat to speke as nouthe.°	now *(as nouthe)*
And thries° hadde she been at Jerusalem.	thrice
She hadde passed many a straunge° strem.	foreign
At Rome she hadde been, and at Boloyne,°	Boulogne (France)
In Galice° at Seint Jame,° and at Coloyne.°	Galicia James (of Compostela) Cologne
She koude° muche of wandrynge by the weye.	knew
Gat-tothed° was she, soothly° for to seye.	Gap-toothed truly
Upon an amblere esily she sat,	
Y-wympled wel,° and on hir heed an hat	Well hooded
As brood as is a bokeler° or a targe,°	buckler shield
A foot-mantel° aboute hir hipes large,	outer skirt
And on hir feet a peyre of spores sharpe.	
In felawshipe wel koude she laughe and carpe°;	talk
Of remedies° of love she knew par chaunce,	restoratives
For she koude of that art the olde daunce.	
A good man was ther of religioun	
And was a poure Persoun° of a toun,	parson
But riche he was of holy thoght and werk.	
He was also a lerned man, a clerk,°	scholar
That Cristes gospel trewely° wolde preche.	faithfully

443–44. For . . . special: Because gold was then an element in some medicines, the doctor was fond of it. Chaucer is of course being ironic. **460. chirche dore:** Marriages at the time often took place at the church door, before the marriage-mass. **473. spores:** She wore spurs because she rode astride.

His parisshens° devoutly wolde he teche. — parishioners
Benygne he was and wonder° diligent, — remarkably
And in adversitee ful pacient,
And swich he was preved ofte sithes.° — times
  Ful looth were hym to cursen° for his tithes,° — excommunicate church dues
But rather wolde he yeven° out of doute — give
Unto his poure parisshens aboute
Of his offrynge and eek of his substaunce.° — income
He koude in litel thyng have suffisaunce.
Wyd was his parisshe and houses fer asonder,
But he ne lafte° nat for reyn ne° thonder, — neglected nor
In siknesse nor in meschief,° to visite — misfortune
The ferreste° in his parisshe, muche° and lite,° — furthest (members) great small
Upon his feet, and in his hond a staf.
  This noble ensample° to his sheep he yaf,° — example gave
That first he wroghte, and afterward he taughte.
Out of the gospel he tho° wordes caughte.° — those took
And this figure° he added eek ther-to, — parallel
That if gold ruste, what sholde iren do?
For if a preest be foule on whom we truste,
No wonder is a lewed° man to ruste. — unlearned
And shame it is, if a preest take keep,° — heed
A shiten° shepherde and a clene sheep. — defiled
Wel oghte a preest ensample for to yive° — give
By his clennesse how that his sheep sholde lyve.
  He sette nat his benefice to hyre
And leet° his sheep encombred in the myre — left
And ran to Londoun unto Seinte Poules° — St. Paul's (Cathedral)
To seken hym a chauntrye for soules,
Or with a bretherhede to been withholde,
But dwelte at hoom and kepte° wel his folde — watched
So that the wolf ne made it nat myscarye.
He was a shepherde and noght a mercenarye.
  And thogh he hooly were and vertuous,
He was noght to synful men despitous,° — scornful
Ne° of his speche daungerous ne digne,° — Nor domineering or pompous
But in his techyng discreet and benigne.
To drawen folk to hevene by fairnesse,
By good ensample, this was his bisynesse.
But it° were any persone obstinat, — if there
What so° he were of heigh or lowe estat, — Whether
Hym wolde he snybben° sharply for the nonys.° — reprove occasion
  A bettre preest I trowe° that nowher noon ys. — believe
He wayted after no pompe and reverence,
Ne maked hym a spiced° conscience, — Nor assumed an over scrupulous

507. benefice to hyre: He did not, like many other priests, rent out his job in the parish to another and then go off to more lucrative positions in places like St. Paul's Cathedral in London. **510–11. seken . . . withholde:** secure an endowment to sing masses for dead souls, or to be retained as chaplain with a religious fraternity.

But Cristes loore° and his apostles twelve	teaching
He taughte, but first he folwed it hymselve.	
With hym ther was a PLOWMAN, was his brother,	
That hadde y-lad° of donge° ful many a fother.°	hauled manure load
A trewe swynkere° and a good was he,	laborer
Lyvynge in pees and parfit charitee.	
God loved he best with al his hoole herte	
At alle tymes, thogh hym gamed or smerte,°	he rejoiced or grieved
And thanne his neighebore right° as hymselve.	just as much
He wolde thresshe and ther-to dyke and delve	
For Cristes sake for every poure wight	
Withouten hire,° if it lay in his myght.	payment
His tithes payde he ful faire and wel	
Bothe of his propre swynk° and his catel.°	own work property
In a tabard° he rood, upon a mere.°	smock (unfashionable) mare
Ther was also a REVE and a MILLERE,	
A SOMNOUR and a PARDONER also,	
A MAUNCIPLE and myself; ther were namo.°	no more
The MILLER was a stout carl for the nones.°	an especially stout fellow
Ful big he was of brawn and eek of bones.	
That proved wel, for over-al ther° he cam,	everywhere
At wrastlynge he wolde have alwey the ram.°	ram (as prize)
He was short-sholdred, brood, a thikke knarre.°	knot of a fellow
Ther was no dore that he nolde° heve of harre°	would not off its hinges
Or breke it at a rennyng with his heed.	
His berd as any sowe or fox was reed°	red
And ther-to brood° as though it were a spade.	as broad
Upon the cop right° of his nose he hade	very top
A werte,° and ther-on stood a tuft of herys,°	wart hairs
Reed as the bristles of a sowes erys.°	ears
His nosethirles° blake were and wyde.	nostrils
A swerd and a bokeler bar° he by his syde.	wore
His mouth as greet was as a greet fourneys.°	furnace
He was a jangler° and a goliardeys.°	talker jester
And that was moost of synne and harlotries.	
Wel koude he stelen corn and tollen thries,°	levy a toll thrice
And yet he hadde a thombe of gold, pardee.°	certainly
A whit cote and a blew hood wered° hee.	wore
A baggepipe wel koude he blowe and sowne,°	play
And ther-with-al he broghte us out of towne.	
A gentil MAUNCIPLE° was ther of a temple°	purchasing agent law society's residence
Of which achatours° myghte take exemple	From whom buyers
For to be wys in byynge of vitaille,°	victuals
For wheither that he payde or took by taille,°	tally (of the debit)
Algate° he wayted° so in his achaat°	In any case watched buying
That he was ay biforn° and in good staat.	always ahead

543. Somnour: Summoner, who served summons to the Ecclesiastical Courts.

Now, is nat that of God a ful fair grace
That swich a lewed° mannes wit shal pace° — such an unlearned / surpass
The wisdom of an heep of lerned men!
Of maistres hadde he mo° than thries ten — more
That weren of° lawe expert and curious,° — in / ingenious
Of whiche ther were a dozeyne in that hous
Worthy to been stywardes° of rente° and lond — be stewards / income
Of any lord that is in Engelond,
To make hym lyve by his propre good° — own resources
In honour detteles, but if° he were wood,° — unless / insane
Or lyve as scarsly° as hym list° desire; — sparingly / he wishes to
And able for to helpen° al a shire — aid (legally)
In any caas that myghte falle or happe.
And yet this Maunciple sette hir aller cappe.° — on them all the dunce cap

The Reve° was a sclendre, colerik man. — estate-manager
His berd was shave as nigh° as ever he kan; — close
His heer was by his erys° ful round y-shorn; — ears
His top was dokked° lyk a preest byforn. — cut close
Ful longe were his legges and ful lene;
Ylik a staf,° ther was no calf y-sene. — Like a stick
Wel koude he kepe a gerner° and a bynne; — watch a granary
Ther was noon auditour koude on hym wynne.
Wel wiste° he by the droghte and by the reyn — knew
The yeldynge of his seed and of his greyn.
His lordes sheep, his neet,° his dayerye, — cattle
His swyn, his hors, his stoor,° and his pultrye — stock
Was hoolly in this Reves governynge,
And by his covenant yaf° the rekenynge — (he) gave
Syn° that his lord was twenty yeer of age. — Since the time
Ther koude no man brynge hym in arrerage° — arrears
Ther nas baillif, ne hierde, ne oother hyne
That he ne knew his sleighte and his covyne.
They were adrad° of hym as of the deeth. — afraid
His wonyng° was ful faire upon an heeth; — dwelling
With grene trees shadwed was his place.
He koude bettre than his lord purchace;
Ful riche he was astored pryvely.° — stocked in secret
His lord wel koude he plesen subtilly
To yeve and lene° hym of his owene good° — lend / property
And have a thank and yet° a coote and hood. — also
In youthe he hadde lerned a good myster°: — trade
He was a wel good wrighte, a carpenter.
This Reve sat upon a ful good stot,° — stallion
That was al pomely° grey and highte° Scot. — dapple / was called
A long surcote of pers° upon he hade, — overcoat of Persian blue
And by his syde he baar° a rusty blade. — wore
Of Northfolk° was this Reve of which I telle, — Norfolk

603–604. nas . . . covyne: was not overseer, shepherd, or other servant whose tricks and fraud ("sleighte" and "covyne") he didn't know.

Biside a toun men clepen Baldeswelle.° — Bawdswell
Tukked he was as is a frere° aboute; — friar
And evere he rood the hyndreste° of oure route.° — hindermost company

A SOMNOUR was ther with us in that place,
That hadde a fyr-reed cherubynnes face,
For saucefleem° he was, with eyen° narwe. — pimpled eyes
As hoot he was and lecherous as a sparwe,° — sparrow
With scaled° browes blake and piled° berd. — scabby scanty
Of his visage children were aferd.
Ther nas quyksilver, lytarge,° ne brymstoon, — lead ointment
Boras,° ceruce,° ne oille° of tartre noon, — Borax white lead cream
Ne oynement that wolde clense and byte,
That hym myghte helpen° of his whelkes° white, — could rid pustules
Nor of the knobbes sittynge on his chekes.
Wel loved he garlek, oynons, and eek lekes,
And for to drynke strong wyn reed as blood;
Thanne wolde he speke and crye as° he were wood°; — as if mad
And whan that he wel dronken hadde the wyn,
Thanne wolde he speke no word but Latyn.
A fewe termes hadde he, two or thre,
That he had lerned out of som decre.
No wonder is! He herde it al the day;
And eek ye knowen wel how that a jay
Kan clepen "Watte"° as wel as kan the Pope. — call out "Walter" (like "Polly")
But who so koude in oother thyng hym grope,° — examine
Thanne hadde he spent al his philosophie.
Ay° *"Questio, quid juris?"* wolde he crie. — Always
He was a gentil harlot° and a kynde; — an obliging rascal
A bettre felawe sholde men noght fynde.
He wolde suffre,° for a quart of wyn, — allow
A good felawe° to have his concubyn° — A rascal mistress
A twelf monthe and excuse hym atte fulle.° — fully
Ful pryvely° a fynch eek koude he pulle°; — secretively fornicate (*pulle a fynch*)
And if he foond owher° a good felawe, — found anywhere
He wolde techen hym to have noon awe
In swich caas of the ercedekenes curs° — archdeacon's curse (of excommunication)

But if° a mannes soule were in his purs, — Unless
For in his purs he sholde y-punysshed be.
"Purs is the ercedekenes helle," seyde he.
But wel I woot° he lyed right in dede; — know
Of cursyng oghte ech gilty man drede,—
For curs wol slee,° right as assoillyng° savith,— — slay absolution
And also war hym of° a *significavit.*° — beware writ for arrest
In daunger hadde he at his owene gyse

646. *Questio, quid juris*: "Question, what is the law (here, about this matter)?" **663–65. daunger . . . reed:** In his own way ("gyse") he had the young people ("gerles," referring to men and women) of the diocese in subjection ("daunger"), and he knew their secrets and was the advisor of all of them.

The yonge gerles of the diocise,	
And knew hir counseil, and was al hir reed.	
A gerland° hadde he set upon his heed,	garland
As greet as it were for an ale stake°;	alehouse sign
A bokeler hadde he maad hym of a cake.	
With hym ther rood a gentil PARDONER	
Of Rouncival, his freend and his comper,°	comrade
That streight was comen fro the court of Rome.	
Ful loude he soong, "Com hider,° love, to me."	hither
This Somnour bar° to hym a stif burdoun,°	carried strong accompaniment
Was nevere trompe° of half so greet a soun.	trumpet
This Pardoner hadde heer as yelow as wex,	
But smothe it heeng° as dooth a strike of flex.°	hung hank of flax
By ounces° henge his lokkes that he hadde,	In wisps
And ther-with he his shuldres overspradde,	
But thynne it lay by colpons oon and oon.°	in single strands
But hood, for jolitee,° wered° he noon,	jauntiness wore
For it was trussed up in his walet.	
Hym thoughte he rood al of the newe jet.°	style
Dischevelee,° save his cappe he rood al bare.	With loose hair
Swiche glarynge eyen hadde he as an hare.	
A vernycle° hadde he sowed upon his cappe,	souvenir of St. Veronica
His walet biforn hym in his lappe,	
Bret° ful of pardoun comen from Rome al hoot.°	Cram hot
A voys he hadde as smal as hath a goot.°	goat
No berd hadde he, ne nevere sholde have;	
As smothe it was as it were late y-shave.	
I trowe he were a geldyng or a mare.	
But of his craft fro Berwyk into Ware	
Ne was ther swich another pardoner,	
For in his male° he hadde a pilwe-beer°	bag pillowcase
Which that he seyde was Oure Lady veyl.	
He seyde he hadde a gobet° of the seyl°	piece sail
That Seint Peter hadde whan that he wente°	walked
Upon the see till Jesu Crist hym hente.°	caught
He hadde a croys of latoun° ful of stones,	copper alloy
And in a glas he hadde pigges bones.	
But with thise relikes, whan that he fond	
A poure persoun° dwellyng upon lond,°	parson (to aid him) the country
Upon a° day he gat hym moore moneye	one
Than that the persoun gat in monthes tweye.	
And thus with feyned flaterye and japes°	tricks
He made the persoun and the peple his apes.°	fools
But trewely to tellen, atte laste,	
He was in chirche a noble ecclesiaste.	
Wel koude he rede a lessoun or a storie,°	Bible story (*or* saint's life)
But alderbest° he song an offertorie,	best of all

698. til Jesu . . . hente: The account of Jesus catching him when Peter walked on the sea is in Matthew 14:29.

For wel he wiste° whan that song was songe,	knew
He moste° preche and wel affile° his tonge	must make smooth
To wynne silver, as he ful wel koude.	
Ther-fore he song the murierly° and loude.	more merrily
Now have I told yow soothly in a clause°	truly in brief
Th' estaat, th' array, the nombre, and eek the cause	
Why that assembled was this compaignye	
In Southwerk at this gentil hostelrye,	
That highte° the Tabard, faste° by the Belle.°	was called close Bell Inn
But now is tyme to yow for to telle	
How that we baren us° that ilke° nyght	conducted ourselves same
Whan we were in that hostelrie alyght°;	alighted
And after wol I telle of oure viage°	journey
And al the remenant of oure pilgrymage.	
But first I pray yow of youre curteisye	
That ye n' arette it nat° my vileynye°	won't blame it on boorishness
Thogh that° I pleynly speke in this matere	Even if
To telle yow hir° wordes and hir cheere,°	their behavior
Ne thogh° I speke° hir wordes proprely.°	And if repeat literally
For this ye knowen also° wel as I,	as
Who so shal telle° a tale after a man,	retell
He moot reherce° as nigh° as evere he kan	must repeat closely
Everich a° word if it be in his charge,	Every single
Al° speke he nevere so rudeliche° and large,°	Even though rudely broadly
Or ellis° he moot telle his tale untrewe,	else
Or feyne thyng,° or fynde wordes newe.	invent something
He may nat spare° al thogh he were his brother;	hold back
He moot° as wel seye o° word as another.	must one
Crist spak hymself ful brode° in holy writ,	freely
And wel ye woot,° no vileynye is it.	know
Eek Plato seith, who so kan hym rede,	
The wordes mote° be cosyn to the dede.	must
Also, I pray yow to foryeve it me,	
Al° have I nat set folk in hir degree°	Even if their order of rank
Here in this tale as that° they sholde stonde.°	just as stand
My wit is short, ye may wel understonde.	
Greet cheere made oure Hoost us everichon,°	for each of us
And to the soper sette he us anon.°	immediately
He served us with vitaille° at the beste.	victuals
Strong was the wyn, and wel to drynke us leste.°	it pleased
A semely° man oure Hoost was with alle	suitable
For to been a marchal in an halle.°	banquet hall
A large man he was, with eyen stepe.°	bulging
A fairer burgeys° was ther noon in Chepe,°	citizen Cheapside (London)
Boold of his speche, and wys, and wel y-taught,	
And of manhode hym lakked right naught.	
Eke ther-to he was right° a murye man,	truly
And after soper pleyen° he bigan	to joke

And spak of myrthe,° amonges othere thynges,	amusement
Whan that we hadde maad° oure rekenynges,°	paid bills
And seyde thus, "Now, lordynges,° trewely,	sirs
Ye been° to me right welcome, hertely,	are
For by my trouthe, if that I shal not lye,	
I saugh nat this yeer so murye a compaignye	
At ones° in this herberwe° as is now.	once lodging
Fayn° wolde I doon° yow myrthe, wiste I° how.	Gladly provide if I knew
And of a myrthe I am right now bythoght	
To doon yow ese,° and it shal coste noght.	comfort
"Ye goon to Caunterbury, God yow spede!	
The blisful martir quyte° yow youre mede°!	grant reward
And wel I woot,° as ye goon by the weye,	know
Ye shapen yow to talen° and to pleye,	intend to tell tales
For trewely confort ne° myrthe is noon°	nor none
To ryde by the weye domb as a stoon.	
And ther-fore wol I maken yow disport,°	amusement
As I seyde erst,° and doon yow som confort.	before
And if yow liketh alle by oon assent	
For to stonden at° my juggement	abide by
And for to werken° as I shall yow seye,	do
Tomorwe, whan ye riden by the weye,	
Now, by my fader° soule, that is deed,	father's
But° ye be murye, I wol yeve yow myn heed.°	Unless head
Hoold up youre hondes withouten moore speche."	
Oure conseil was nat longe for to seche.°	seek
Us thoughte it was nat worth to make it wys,°	difficult
And graunted° hym withouten moore avys°	(we) yielded to consideration
And bad hym seye his voirdit° as hym leste.°	verdict it pleased
"Lordynges," quod° he, "now herkneth° for the beste,	said listen
But taketh it not, I pray yow, in desdeyn.°	contemptuously
This is the poynt, to speken short and pleyn,	
That ech of yow, to shorte with oure weye,	
In this viage° shal telle tales tweye,°—	journey two
To Caunterburyward° I mene it so,—	toward Canterbury
And homward he shal tellen othere two	
Of aventures that whilom° have bifalle.	once upon a time
And which of yow that bereth° hym best of alle,	conducts
That is to seyn, that telleth in this caas	
Tales of best sentence° and moost solaas,°	significance delight
Shal have a soper at oure aller cost	
Here in this place, sittyng by this post,	
Whan that we come agayn fro Caunterbury.	
And, for to make yow the moore mury,	
I wol myself goodly with yow ryde	
Right at myn owene cost and be your gyde;	
And who so wole my juggement withseye°	resist
Shal paye al that we spende by the weye.	
And if ye vouchesauf that it be so,	

Tel me anoon° withouten wordes mo,°	immediately more
And I wol erly shape° me ther-fore."	prepare
This thyng was graunted, and oure othes swore	
With ful glad herte, and preyden° hym also	(we) begged
That he wolde vouchesauf for to do so,	
And that he wolde been oure governour,	
And of oure tales juge and reportour,°	critic
And sette a soper at a certeyn prys,	
And we wol reuled been at his devys°	discretion
In heigh and lough.° And thus by oon assent	In all matters
We been acorded to his juggement;	
And ther-upon the wyn was fet anoon.°	fetched immediately
We dronken, and to reste wente echon°	each one
Withouten any lenger taryynge.	
A morwe,° whan that day bigan to sprynge,	The next morning
Up roos oure Hoost and was oure aller cok°	the cock (who crowed) for us all
And gadred° us togidre° in a flok,	gathered together
And forth we riden, a° litel moore than pas,°	at a foot-pace
Unto the wateryng° of Seint Thomas,	watering-place
And there oure Hoost bigan his hors areste°	to halt
And seyde, "Lordynges, herkneth,° if yow leste.°	listen it pleases
Ye woot° youre forward° and it yow recorde.°	know agreement remember it
If evensong and morwesong acorde,°	morning-song agree
Lat se° now who shal telle the firste tale.	Let's see
As evere moot° I drynke wyn or ale,	may
Who so be rebel to my juggement	
Shal paye for al that by the wey is spent.	
Now draweth cut er that we ferrer twynne.°	lots before we further depart
He which that hath the shorteste shal bigynne.	
Sire Knyght," quod he, "my mayster and my lord,	
Now draweth cut, for that is myn acord.°	agreement
Cometh neer," quod he, "my lady Prioresse,	
And ye, sire Clerk, lat be° youre shamefastnesse,°	lay aside modesty
Ne studieth noght. Ley hond to, every man."	
Anoon° to drawen every wight bigan,	Immediately
And shortly for to tellen as it was,	
Were it by aventure° or sort° or cas,°	chance lot destiny
The sothe° is this: the cut fil° to the Knyght,	truth fell
Of which ful blithe and glad was every wight,°	person
And telle he moste° his tale, as was resoun°	must right
By forward° and by composicioun,°	agreement compact
As ye han° herd. What nedeth wordes mo?	have
And whan this goode man saugh that it was so,	
As he that wys was and obedient	
To kepe his forward by his free assent,	
He seyde, "Syn° I shal bigynne the game,	Since
What,° welcome be the cut, a° Goddes name!	Why in
Now lat us ryde, and herkneth what I seye."	
And with that word we ryden forth oure weye,	
And he bigan with right a murye° cheere	a very merry
His tale anoon° and seyde as ye may heere.	thereupon

The Pardoner's Prologue

"Lordynges," quod he, "in chirches whan I preche,	
I peyne me° to han an hauteyn° speche	take pains dominating
And rynge it out as round as gooth a belle,	
For I kan° al by rote that I telle.	know
My theme is alwey oon,° and ever was—	always one
Radix malorum est cupiditas.°	The root of evils is avarice
First I pronounce whennes that° I come,	whence
And thanne my bulles° shewe I alle and some.°	papal documents one and all
Oure lige lordes° seel on my patente,	liege lord's (bishop's)
That shewe I first, my body to warente,°	person to safeguard
That no man be so bold, ne° preest ne° clerk,	neither nor
Me to destourbe of Cristes holy werk.	
And after that thanne telle I forth my tales.	
Bulles of popes and of cardynales,	
Of patriarkes and bisshopes I shewe,	
And in Latyn I speke a wordes fewe	
To saffron with my predicacioun,°	flavor my preaching with
And for to stire hem to devocioun.	
Thanne shewe I forth my longe cristal stones°	glass cases
Y-crammed ful of cloutes° and of bones;	rags
Relikes been° they, as wenen° they echon.°	are believe each one
Thanne have I in latoun° a shulder-bon	(set) in copper alloy
Which that was of° an holy Jewes sheep.	Which was taken from
'Goode men,' I seye, 'tak of my wordes keep.°	heed
If that this boon be wasshe° in any welle,	washed
If cow, or calf, or sheep, or oxe swelle,	
That any worm hath ete or worm y-stonge,	
Taak water of that welle, and wassh his° tonge,	its
And it is hool anoon.° And forther moor,	cured at once
Of pokkes, and of scabbe, and every soor	
Shal every sheep be hool that of this welle	
Drynketh a draughte. Taak kepe,° eek, what I telle:	heed
If that the goode man that the bestes oweth	
Wol every wyke,° er that the cok hym croweth	week
Fastynge, drynken of this welle a draughte,	
As thilke° holy Jew oure eldres taughte,	that same
Hise bestes and his stoor° shal multiplie.	stock
And, sire, also it heeleth jalousie,	
For thogh a man be falle in jalous rage,	
Lat maken° with this water his potage,	Have made
And nevere shal he moore his wyf mystriste,°	mistrust
Thogh he the soothe° of hir defaute wiste,°	truth fault should know
Al° hadde she taken preestes two or thre.	Even if
'Heere is a miteyn,° eek, that ye may se.	mitten

THE PARDONER'S PROLOGUE. **23. holy . . . sheep:** taken from a sheep belonging to some "holy Jew" (one of the heroes of the Old Testament). The shoulder bone of a sheep had been used since ancient times to foretell the future. **27. worm . . . y-stonge:** that had eaten any (poisonous) worm or been stung by one.

He that his hand wol putte in this mitayn,
He shal have multiplyyng of his grayn
Whan he hath sowen, be it whete or otes,
So that° he offre pens or ellis grotes.° — Provided that else groats (four pennies)
'Goode men and wommen, o° thyng warne I yow, — one
If any wight° be in this chirche now — person
That hath doon synne horrible, that he
Dar° nat for shame of it y-shryven° be, — Dare confessed and absolved
Or any womman, be she yong or old,
That hath y-maked hir housbond cokewold,° — deceived her husband
Swich° folk shal have no power, ne no grace, — Such
To offren to my relikes in this place.
And who so fyndeth hym° out of swich blame, — himself
They wol come up and offre, a° Goddes name, — in
And I assoille° hym by the auctoritee° — absolve authority
Which that by bulle y-graunted was to me.'
By this gaude° have I wonne yeer by yeer — trick
An hundred mark° sith° I was pardoner. — marks (13*s*.4*d*.) since
I stonde lyk a clerk in my pulpet;
And whan the lewed° peple is doun y-set, — ignorant
I preche so as ye han° herd bifore, — have
And telle an hundred false japes° more. — frauds
Thanne peyne I me° to strecche forth the nekke, — I take pains
And est and west upon the peple I bekke,° — nod
As dooth a dowve° sittyng on a berne.° — dove barn
Myne handes and my tonge goon so yerne° — eagerly
That it is joye to se my bisynesse.° — industriousness
Of avarice and of swich cursednesse
Is al my prechyng, for to make hem free
To yeven hir° pens, and namely° unto me. — give their particularly
For myn entente is nat but for to wynne,° — only to gain
And no thyng° for correccioun of synne. — in no way
I rekke° nevere, whan that° they been beryed,° — care when are buried
Thogh that hir soules goon a-blakeberyed.
For certes° many a predicacioun° — certainly sermon
Comth ofte tyme of yvel entencioun,
Som for plesance° of folk and flaterye, — the satisfying
To been avanced° by ypocrisye, — advanced
And som for veyne glorie, and som for hate.
For whan I dar noon oother weyes debate,° — way contend
Thanne wol I stynge hym with my tonge smerte° — sharp
In prechyng, so that he shal nat asterte° — avoid
To been defamed falsly, if that he
Hath trespased to my bretheren or to me.
For thogh I telle noght his propre name,
Men shal wel knowe that it is the same
By signes and by othere circumstances.
Thus quyte° I folk that doon° us displesances; — repay cause
Thus spitte I out my venym under hewe° — pretext
Of holynesse, to seme holy and trewe.

But shortly myn entente I wol devyse°: — explain
I preche of no thyng but for coveityse.° — covetousness
Therfore my theme is yet, and evere was,
Radix malorum est cupiditas.
Thus kan I preche agayn° that same vice — against
Which that I use, and that is avarice.
But though myself be gilty in that synne,
Yet kan I maken oother folk to twynne° — depart
From avarice, and soore° to repente. — sorely
But that is nat my principal entente.
I preche no thyng but for coveitise.
Of this matere it oghte ynow° suffise. — enough
Thanne telle I hem ensamples many oon° — a one
Of olde stories longe tyme agoon,° — past
For lewed° peple loven tales olde. — ignorant
Swiche thynges kan they wel reporte and holde.° — remember
What! Trowe° ye that, whiles I may preche, — Believe
And wynne gold and silver for° I teche, — for what
That I wol lyve in poverte wilfully°? — willingly
Nay, nay! I thoghte it nevere, trewely.
For I wol preche and begge in sondry landes;
I wol nat do no labour with myne handes,
Ne° make baskettes and lyve ther-by, — nor
By cause I wol nat beggen ydelly.° — in vain
I wol noon of the apostles countrefete.° — imitate
I wol have moneye, wolle,° chese, and whete, — wool
Al° were it yeven of the poureste° page, — Though poorest
Or of the poureste widwe° in a village, — widow
Al sholde hir children sterve for famyne.
Nay, I wol drynke licour of the vyne
And have a joly wenche in every toun.
But herkneth, lordynges, in conclusioun.
Youre likyng is that I shal telle a tale.
Now have I dronke a draghte of corny ale,
By God, I hope I shal yow telle a thyng
That shal by resoun been at youre likyng.
For, thogh myself be a ful vicious man,
A moral tale yet I yow telle kan,
Which I am wont° to preche for to wynne.° — accustomed gain
Now, holde youre pees.° My tale I wol bigynne." — peace

The Pardoner's Tale

In Flaundres whilom° was a compaignye — Flanders once
Of yonge folk that haunteden° folye, — practiced
As° riot, hasard,° stewes,° and tavernes — Such as dicing brothels
Where-as° with harpes, lutes, and gyternes° — Where guitars
They daunce and pleyen at dees° bothe day and nyght, — dice
And ete also and drynke over hir myght,° — beyond their capacity

Thurgh which they doon° the devel sacrifise	do
Withinne that develes temple in cursed wise°	manner
By superfluytee abhomynable.	
Hir othes been° so grete and so dampnable	Their oaths are
That it is grisly for to heere hem swere;	
Oure blissed Lordes body they to-tere°;	tear apart
Hem thoughte that Jewes rente hym noght ynough!	
And ech° of hem at otheres synne lough.°	each laughed
And right anon thanne comen tombesteres,°	dancing-girls
Fetys° and smale,° and yonge frutesteres,°	Trim slender fruit-sellers
Syngeres with harpes, baudes,° wafereres,°	bawds confectioners
Whiche been the verray develes officeres,	
To kyndle and blowe the fyr of lecherye,	
That is annexed unto glotonye.	
The Holy Writ take I to my witnesse	
That luxurie° is in wyn and dronkenesse.	excess
Lo how that dronken Loth unkyndely°	unnaturally
Lay by his doghtres two unwityngly.°	unknowingly
So dronke he was, he nyste° what he wroghte.°	didn't know was doing
Herodes, whoso wel the stories soghte,	
Whan he of wyn was replet° at his feste,	overfilled
Right at his owene table he yaf° his heste°	gave order
To sleen° the Baptist John ful giltelees.	slay
Senec° seith a good word, doutelees.	Seneca
He seith he kan no difference fynde	
Bitwix a man that is out of his mynde	
And a man which that is dronkelewe,°	drunken
But that woodnesse y-fallen° in a shrewe	madness occurring
Persevereth lenger than dooth dronkenesse.	
O glotonye, ful of cursednesse,	
O cause first of oure confusioun°!	ruin
O original of oure dampnacioun,	
Til Crist hadde boght us with his blood agayn°!	redeemed (*boght . . . agayn*)
Lo how deere,° shortly for to sayn,	dearly
Aboght° was thilke° cursed vileynye.	Paid for that same
Corrupt was al this world for glotonye.	
Adam oure fader, and his wyf also,	
Fro° Paradys to labour and to wo	From
Were dryven for that vice, it is no drede.°	doubt
For whil that Adam fasted, as I rede,	
He was in Paradys; and whan that he	
Eet° of the fruyt defended° on the tree,	Ate forbidden
Anon° he was out cast to wo and peyne.	At once
O glotonye, on thee wel oghte us pleyne.°	should we complain
O, wiste° a man how manye maladies	knew
Folwen of° excesse and of glotonyes,	Follow from

THE PARDONER'S TALE. **13. Hem . . . ynough:** "It seemed to them the Jews did not rend him enough." **23. Loth:** Lot (Genesis 19:33, 35). **26. Herodes:** Herod (Matthew 14).

He wolde been the moore mesurable° — moderate
Of his diete, sittyng at his table.
Allas, the shorte throte, the tendre mouth,
Maketh that, est and west and north and south,
In erthe, in eyr, in water, men to swynke
To gete a glotoun deyntee mete and drynke.
Of this matere, O Paul, wel kanstow° trete. — can you
"Mete unto wombe,° and wombe eek unto mete, — belly
Shal God destroyen bothe," as Paulus° seith. — Paul (I *Cor.*, vi, 13)
Allas, a foul thyng is it, by my feith,
To seye this word, and fouler is the dede,
Whan man so drynketh of the white and rede° — red (wine)
That of his throte he maketh his pryvee° — privy
Thurgh thilke° cursed superfluitee. — that same
  The apostle° wepyng seith ful pitously, — Paul (*Phil.*, iii, 18, 19)
"Ther walken manye of whiche yow toold have I,—
I seye it now wepyng with pitous voys—
They been° enemys of Cristes croys, — are
Of whiche° the ende is deth; wombe is hir God." — whom
O wombe, O bely, O stynkyng cod,° — paunch
Fulfilled of donge and of corrupcioun,
At either ende of thee foul is the soun!
How greet labour and cost is thee to fynde°! — provide for
Thise cokes,° how they stampe, and streyne, and grynde, — cooks
And turnen substaunce into accident,
To fulfillen al thy likerous talent.° — unrestrained appetite
Out of the harde bones knokke they
The mary,° for they caste noght awey — marrow
That may go thurgh the golet° softe and soote.° — gullet sweet
Of spicerie of leef, and bark, and roote
Shal been his sauce y-maked, by delit
To make hym yet a newer appetit.
But, certes,° he that haunteth swiche delices° — certainly pursues such delights
Is deed whil that° he lyveth in tho° vices. — dead while those
  A lecherous thyng is wyn, and dronkenesse
Is ful of stryvyng° and of wrecchednesse. — strife
O dronke man, disfigured is thy face,
Sour is thy breeth, foul artow° to embrace, — are you
And thurgh thy dronke nose semeth the soun
As thogh thou seydest ay° "Sampsoun, Sampsoun." — always
And yet, God woot,° Sampsoun drank nevere no wyn. — knows
Thou fallest as it were a stiked swyn,° — like a stuck pig
Thy tonge is lost, and al thyn honeste cure.° — care for honor
For dronkenesse is verray sepulture° — the very burial
Of mannes wit° and his discrecioun. — understanding
In whom that drynke hath dominacioun,

93. Sampsoun . . . wyn: Samson had vowed not to drink wine.

He kan no conseil kepe, it is no drede.° — doubt
Now kepe yow fro the white and fro the rede,
And namely fro° the white wyn of Lepe — particularly from
That is to selle in Fisshstrete° or in Chepe.° — Fish Street (London) Cheapside
This wyn of Spaigne crepeth subtilly
In othere wynes growynge faste by,° — near by
Of which ther riseth swich fumositee° — such spirituous vapors
That, whan a man hath dronken draghtes thre,
And weneth° that he be at hoom in Chepe, — believes
He is in Spaigne right at the toune of Lepe,
Nat at the Rochel° ne at Burdeux° toun. — La Rochelle Bordeaux (France)
And thanne wol he seyn "Sampsoun, Sampsoun."
  But herkneth, lordynges, o° word, I yow preye, — one
That alle the sovereyn actes, dar I seye,
Of victories in the Olde Testament,
Thurgh verray God, that is omnipotent,
Were doon in abstinence and in prayere.
Looketh the Bible, and ther ye may it leere.° — learn
  Looke, Attila, the grete conquerour,
Deyde in his sleep with shame and dishonour,
Bledyng at his nose in dronkenesse.
A capitayn sholde lyve in sobrenesse.
And over al this, avyseth yow° right wel — consider
What was comaunded unto Lamwel°— — Lemuel
Nat Samuel but Lamwel, seye I.
Redeth the Bible, and fynd it expresly
Of wyn-yevyng° to hem that han justise. — wine-giving
Namoore of this, for it may wel suffise.
  And now that I have spoken of glotonye,
Now wol I yow defenden hasardrye.° — forbid dicing
Hasard is verray moder of lesynges,° — the very mother of falsehood
And of deceite, and cursed forswerynges,° — perjuries
Blaspheme of Crist, manslaughtre, and wast° also — waste
Of catel° and of tyme; and forther mo° — substance more
It is repreve° and contrarie of honour — reproach
For to ben holde° a commune hasardour. — To be held
And evere the hyer he is of estaat,
The moore is he holden desolat.
If that a prynce useth hasardrye,
In alle governaunce and policye
He is, as by commune opynyoun,
Y-holde the lasse in reputacioun.
  Stilbon, that was a wys embassadour,
Was sent to Corynthe in ful gret honour
Fro Lacedomye° to make hire° alliaunce; — Lacedaemon (in Greece) their
And whan he cam, hym happed° par chaunce — it happened to him

101–103. Lepe . . . Spaigne: The strong wines of Lepe, in Spain, were cheaper than French wines produced nearby (*faste by*) and were added to them. **122. Lamwel:** In Proverbs 31, King Lemuel is urged to avoid wine.

That alle the gretteste that were of that lond
Pleiynge atte hasard he hem fond.° — found
For which, as soone as it myghte be,
He stal° hym hoom agayn to his contree, — stole
And seyde, "Ther wol I nat lese° my name, — lose
N' I wol nat° take on me so greet defame — Nor will
Yow for to allie unto none hasardours.
Sendeth othere wise embassadours,
For, by my trouthe, me were levere° dye — I would rather
Than I yow sholde to hasardours allye.
For ye that been so glorious in honours
Shal nat allye yow with hasardours
As by my wyl ne as by my tretee."
This wise philosophre thus seyde he.
  Look eek that to the kyng Demetrius
The kyng of Parthes,° as the book seith us, — Parthia
Sente hym a paire of dees° of gold in scorn, — dice
For he hadde used hasard ther-biforn°; — previously
For which he heeld his glorie or his renoun
At no value or reputacioun.
Lordes may fynden oother manere° pley — sort of
Honeste ynow° to dryve the day awey. — enough
  Now wol I speke of oothes false and grete
A word or two, as olde bokes trete.
Greet sweryng is a thyng abhomynable.
And fals sweryng is yet moore reprevable.° — reprovable
The heighe God forbad sweryng at al.
Witnesse on Mathew°; but in special — *Matthew,* v, 34
Of sweryng seith the holy Jeremye,° — *Jeremiah,* iv, 2
"Thow shalt swere sooth° thyne othes and nat lye, — truthfully
And swere in doom° and eek in rightwisnesse.°" — judgment righteousness
But ydel° sweryng is a cursednesse. — vain
Bihoold and se that, in the firste table
Of heighe Goddes Hestes° honurable, — (Ten) Commandments
How that the Seconde Heste of hym is this:
"Take nat my name in ydel° or amys." — vain
Lo, rather he forbedeth swich sweryng
Than homycide or many a cursed thyng.
I seye that, as by ordre,° thus it standeth; — in order
This knowen, that hise Hestes understandeth,
How that the Seconde Heste of God is that.
And forther over, I wol thee telle al plat° — plainly
That vengeance shal nat parten° from his hous — depart (*Ecclesiasticus,* xxiii, 11)
That of hise othes is to° outrageous. — too
"By Goddes precious herte," and "By his nayles,"
And "By the blood of Crist that is in Hayles,° — (preserved) at Hayles (Gloucestershire)
Sevene is my chaunce, and thyn is cynk° and treye,°" — five three
"By Goddes armes, if thow falsly pleye,
This daggere shal thurgh out thyn herte go,"
This fruyt cometh of the bicched bones° two, — cursed dice

Forsweryng, ire, falsnesse, homycide.
Now, for the love of Crist, that for us dyde,
Lete° youre othes, bothe grete and smale.   Restrain
But, sires, now wol I telle forth my tale.

Thise riotoures° thre of whiche I telle,   profligates
Longe erst er pryme rong° of any belle,   before prime (9 A.M.) rang
Were set hem° in a taverne to drynke;   seated
And, as they sat, they herde a belle clynke°   clang
Biforn a cors° was caried to his° grave.   corpse (which) its
That oon° of hem gan° callen to his knave°:   One began to boy
"Go bet,°" quod° he, "and axe° redily   faster said ask
What cors is this that passeth heer forby.
And looke that thow reporte his name wel."
"Sire," quod this boy, "it nedeth° never a del.°   is necessary one bit
It was me told er ye cam heer two houres.
He was, pardee,° an old felawe° of youres,   certainly companion
And sodeynly he was y-slayn to-nyght,°   last night
Fordronke,° as he sat on his bench upright.   Very drunk
Ther cam a pryvee° theef, men clepeth° Deeth,   secretive (whom) men call
That in this contree al the peple sleeth,°   slays
And with his spere he smoot his herte a-two,
And wente his wey withouten wordes mo.
He hath a thousand slayn, this pestilence.
And, maister, er ye come in his presence,
Me thynketh that it were necessarie
For to be war of swich an adversarie.
Beth° redy for to meete hym evere moore.°   Be always
Thus taughte me my dame.° I sey namoore."   mother
"By seinte Marie," seyde this taverner,°   innkeeper
"The child seith sooth, for he hath slayn this yer,
Henne° over a myle, withinne a greet village,   Hence
Bothe man and womman, child, and hyne,° and page.   servant
I trowe° his habitacioun be there.   believe
To been avysed° greet wisdom it were,   be prepared
Er that he dide a man a dishonour."
"Ye,° Goddes armes!" quod this riotour.   Yes
"Is it swich peril with hym for to meete?
I shal hym seke by wey and eek by strete,
I make avow to Goddes digne° bones.   worthy
Herkneth, felawes. We thre been al ones.°   one
Lat ech of us holde up his hand til° oother,   to
And ech of us bicome otheres brother,°   the other's sworn brother
And we wol sleen° this false traytour Deeth.   slay
He shal be slayn, he that so manye sleeth,
By Goddes dignytee, er it be nyght."
Togidres° han thise thre hir trouthes plight°   Together pledged their faith
To lyve and dyen ech of hem for oother,
As thogh he were his owene y-bore° brother.   born

And up they stirte,° al dronken in this rage,   sprang
And forth they goon towardes that village
Of which the taverner hadde spoke biforn.
And many a grisly ooth thanne han they sworn,
And Cristes blessed body they to-rente.°   tore to pieces
Deeth shal be deed, if that they may hym hente°!   catch
When they han goon nat fully half a myle,
Right° as they wolde han treden° over a stile,   Just   have stepped
An old man and a poure° with hem mette.   poor
This olde man ful mekely hem grette°   greeted
And seyde thus, "Now, lordes, God yow se.°"   save
The proudeste of thise riotoures thre
Answerde agayn,° "What, carl°! With sory grace!°   back   churl   Curse you!
Why artow° al forwrapped° save thy face?   are you   wrapped up
Why lyvestow° so longe in so greet age?"   live you
This olde man gan looke in his visage
And seyde thus: "For I ne kan nat fynde
A man, thogh that I walked into Inde,°   India
Neither in citee ne in no village,
That wolde chaunge his youthe for myn age.
And, therfore, moot° I han myn age stille,   must
As longe tyme as it is Goddes wille.
"Ne Deeth, allas, ne wol nat han° my lyf.   have
Thus walke I lyk a restelees caytyf,°   wretch
And on the ground, which is my modres° gate,   mother's
I knokke with my staf bothe erly and late,
And seye, 'Leeve° moder, leet me in.   Dear
Lo, how I vanysshe, flessh, and blood, and skyn.
Allas, whan shul my bones been at reste?
Moder, with yow wolde I chaunge my cheste,°   clothes-chest
That in my chambre longe tyme hath be,°   been
Ye,° for an heyre clowt° to wrappe me!"   Yes   hair rag
But yet to me she wol nat do that grace,
For which ful pale and welked° is my face.   withered
"But, sires, to yow it is no curteisye
To speken to an old man vileynye
But° he trespase in word or elles° in dede.   Unless   else
In Holy Writ ye may yourself wel rede,
'Agayns° an old man, hoor° upon his heed,   Before   hoary (*Lev.*, xix, 32)
Ye sholde arise.' Wherfore I yeve yow reed°:   advice
Ne dooth° unto an old man noon harm now,   Don't do
Namoore than that ye wolde men dide to yow
In age, if that ye so longe abyde.
And God be with yow, wher° ye go° or ryde.   whether   walk
I moot go thider as° I have to go."   where
"Nay, olde cherl. By God, thow shalt nat so,"
Seyde this oother hasardour° anon.   gambler
"Thow partest° nat so lightly,° by seint John.   depart   easily
Thow spak right now of thilke° traytour Deeth,   that same
That in this contree alle oure freendes sleeth.

Have here my trouthe,° as thow art his espye,°	oath spy
Telle wher he is, or thow shalt it abye,°	pay for
By God and by the holy sacrament!	
For soothly thow art oon of his assent	
To sleen° us yonge folk, thow false theef!"	slay
"Now, sires," quod he, "if that yow be so leef°	eager
To fynde Deeth, turn up this croked wey.	
For in that grove I lafte° hym, by my fey,°	left faith
Under a tree, and ther he wol abyde.	
Nat for youre boost he wol hym° no thyng hyde.	himself
Se ye that ook°? Right ther ye shal hym fynde.	oak
God save yow, that boghte agayn° mankynde,	redeemed
And yow amende." Thus seyde this olde man.	
And everich° of thise riotoures ran	each
Til they came to that tree, and ther they founde	
Of floryns° fyne of gold y-coyned rounde	florins (coins)
Wel ny an eighte° busshels, as hem thoughte.°	Very nearly eight it seemed to
No lenger thanne° after Deeth they soughte;	then
But ech of hem so glad was of the sighte,	
For that the floryns been so faire and brighte,	
That doun they sette hem° by this precious hoord.	themselves
The worste of hem he spak the firste word.	
"Bretheren," quod he, "taak kepe° what I seye.	heed to
My wit° is greet, thogh that I bourde° and pleye.	understanding jest
This tresor hath fortune unto us yeven,°	given
In myrthe and jolitee oure lyf to lyven.	
And lightly as it cometh, so wol we spende.	
By Goddes precious dignytee, who wende°	would have believed
Today that we sholde han so fair a grace?	
But, myghte this gold be caried fro this place	
Hoom to myn hous, or ellis unto youres—	
For wel ye woot° that al this gold is oures—	know
Thanne were we in heigh felicitee.	
But, trewely, by daye it may nat be.	
Men wolde seyn° that we were theves stronge°	say violent
And for oure owene tresor doon us honge.°	have us hanged
This tresor moste y-caried be° by nyghte	must be carried
As wisly and as slyly as it myghte.	
Wherfore I rede° that cut° among us alle	advise cuts
Be drawe, and lat se° wher the cut wol falle.	let see
And he that hath the cut, with herte blithe	
Shal renne° to the toune, and that ful swithe,°	run quickly
And brynge us breed and wyn ful pryvely.°	secretly
And two of us shul kepen subtilly°	guard craftily
This tresor wel; and if he wol nat tarie,	
Whan it is nyght, we wol this tresor carie	
By oon assent wher-as us thynketh° best."	where it seems to us
That oon° of hem the cut broghte in his fest,°	The one fist
And bad hem drawe and looke wher it wol falle,	
And it fil° on the yongeste of hem alle,	fell

And forth toward the toun he wente anon.°   at once
And also° soone as that he was agon,°   as gone
That oon of hem spak thus unto that oother:
"Thow knowest wel, thow art my sworn brother.
Thy profit wol I telle thee anon.
Thow woost° wel that oure felawe is agon,   know
And heere is gold, and that ful greet plentee,
That shal departed° been among us thre.   divided
But, nathelees,° if I kan shape it so   nevertheless
That it departed were among us two,
Hadde I nat doon a freendes torn° to thee?"   turn
  That oother answerde, "I noot° how that may be.   don't know
He woot° that the gold is with us tweye.°   knows two
What shal we doon? What shal we to hym seye?"
  "Shal it be conseil°?" seyde the firste shrewe.°   secret wretch
"And I shal tellen in a wordes fewe
What we shul doon, and brynge it wel aboute."
  "I graunte," quod that oother, "out of doute,
That, by my trouthe, I wol thee nat biwreye.°"   betray
  "Now," quod the firste, "thow woost wel we be tweye,
And two of us shul strenger be than oon.
Looke, whan that he is set, that right anoon°   at once
Arys as though thow woldest with hym pleye,
And I shal ryve° hym thurgh the sydes tweye,   stab
Whil that thow strogelest with hym as in game.
And with thy daggere looke thow do the same,
And thanne shal al this gold departed be,
My deere freend, bitwixe me and thee.
Thanne may we bothe oure lustes al fulfille,
And pleye at dees° right at oure owene wille."   dice
And thus acorded been thise shrewes tweye
To sleen the thridde, as ye han herd me seye.
  This yongeste, which that wente to the toun,
Ful ofte in herte he rolleth up and doun
The beautee of thise floryns newe and brighte.
"O Lord," quod he, "if so were that I myghte
Have al this tresor to myself allone,
Ther is no man that lyveth under the trone
Of God that sholde lyve so myrie as I!"
And atte laste the feend, oure enemy,
Putte in his thoght that he sholde poyson beye,°   buy
With which he myghte sleen his felawes tweye,
For-why° the feend foond° hym in swich lyvynge   Because found
That he hadde leve° hym to sorwe brynge.   permission (from God)
For this was outrely° his ful entente,   entirely
To sleen hem bothe and nevere to repente.
And forth he goth—no lenger wolde he tarie—
Into the toun unto a pothecarie,°   apothecary
And preyed hym that he hym wolde selle
Som poysoun that he myghte his rattes quelle,°   kill

And eek ther was a polcat° in his hawe,° weasel hedge
That, as he seyde, his capouns° hadde y-slawe,° capons killed
And fayn° he wolde wreke hym,° if he myghte, gladly avenge himself
On vermyn that destroyed° hym by nyghte. annoyed
The pothecarie answerde, "And thow shalt have
A thyng that, also° God my soule save, as
In al this world ther is no creature
That ete° or dronke hath of this confiture° eaten preparation
Nat but the montaunce° of a corn° of whete, quantity grain
That he ne shal his lyf anoon forlete.° lose
Ye,° sterve° he shal, and that in lasse while Yes die
Than thow wolt goon a paas° nat but a myle, walk at footpace
The poysoun is so strong and violent."
This cursed man hath in his hond y-hent° taken
This poysoun in a box, and sith° he ran then
Into the nexte strete unto a man
And borwed of hym large botels thre,
And in the two his poyson poured he.
The thridde he kepte clene for his drynke,
For al the nyght he shoop hym for to swynke° intended to work
In cariyng of the gold out of that place.
And whan this riotour—with sory grace!°— curse him!
Hadde filled with wyn hise grete botels thre,
To hise felawes agayn repaireth he.
What nedeth it to sermone of it moore?
For right as they hadde cast° his deeth bifore, planned
Right so they han hym slayn, and that anon.
And whan that this was doon, thus spak that oon:
"Now lat us sitte, and drynke, and make us merye,
And afterward we wol his body berye."
And with that word it happed hym par cas° he happened by chance
To take the bottel ther° the poysoun was, where
And drank, and yaf° his felawe drynke also, gave
For which anon they storven° bothe two. died
But, certes,° I suppose that Avycen certainly
Wroot nevere in no canon ne in no fen
Mo wonder signes° of empoysonyng More wonderful symptoms
Than hadde thise wrecches two er hir° endyng. before their
Thus ended been thise homicides two,
And eek the false empoysonere also.
O cursed synne of alle cursednesse!
O traytours homicide! O wikkednesse!
O glotonye, luxurie, and hasardrye!
Thou blasphemour of Crist with vileynye
And othes grete of usage° and of pryde°! habit ostentation
Allas, mankynde, how may it bityde

427–28. Avycen . . . fen: Avicenna (980–1037), Arab philosopher, whose *Canon of Medicine* is divided into "fens," or sections, containing rules for medical cures, including cures for poisoning.

That to thy Creatour, which that thee wroghte°   made
And with his precious herte-blood thee boghte,
Thow art so fals and so unkynde,° allas?   unnatural
Now, goode men, God foryeve° yow youre trespas,   forgive
And ware yow fro° the synne of avarice.   beware of
Myn holy pardoun may yow alle warice,°   cure
So that ye offre nobles or sterlynges,
Or elles silver broches, spones, rynges.
Boweth youre heed under this holy bulle!
Cometh up, ye wyves! Offreth of youre wolle°!   wool
Youre name I entre here in my rolle anon;
Into the blisse of hevene shul ye gon.
I yow assoille,° by myn heigh power,   absolve
Yow that wol offre, as clene and eek as cler
As ye were born.—And lo, sires, thus I preche.
And Jesu Crist, that is oure soules leche,°   leech (physician)
So graunte yow his pardoun to receyve,
For that is best. I wol yow nat deceyve.

Epilogue

"But, sires, o° word forgat I in my tale.   one
I have relikes and pardon in my male°   wallet
As faire as any man in Engelond,
Whiche were me yeven by the Popes hond.
If any of yow wol, of° devocioun,   out of
Offren and han myn absolucioun,
Com forth anon, and kneleth here adoun,
And mekely receyveth my pardoun;
Or ellis taketh pardoun, as ye wende,°   travel
Al newe and fressh at every myles ende,
So° that ye offren, alwey newe and newe,°   Providing   again and again
Nobles or pens whiche that been goode and trewe.
It is an honour to everich° that is heer   each one
That ye mowe° have a suffisant pardoner   can
T'assoille° yow, in contree as ye ryde,   To absolve
For aventures° whiche that may bityde.   incidents
Peraventure° ther may falle oon or two   Perhaps
Doun of° his hors, and breke his nekke atwo.   off
Looke which° a seuretee° is it to yow alle   what   security
That I am in youre felaweship y-falle,°   fallen
That may assoille yow, bothe moore° and lasse,°   high   low
Whan that the soule shal fro the body passe.
I rede° that oure Hoost shal bigynne,   advise
For he is moost envoluped° in synne.   enveloped
Com forth, sire Hoost, and offre first anon,°   at once

445. nobles . . . sterlynges: "Nobles" were a coin worth 6s. 8d; "sterlynges" were silver pennies. Both coins were valuable.

And thow shalt kisse the relikes everychon,° each one
Ye,° for a grote.° Unbokele anon thy purs." Yes groat (4*d.*)
"Nay, nay!" quod he. "Thanne have I Cristes curs!
Lat be!" quod he. "It shal nat be, so thee'ch.° may I prosper (*thee ich*)
Thow woldest make me kisse thyn olde breech,
And swere it were a relyk of a seint,
Thogh it were with thy fundement depeynt.° discolored
But, by the croys which that Seint Eleyne fond,
I wolde I hadde thy coylons° in myn hond testicles
In stede of relikes or of seintuarie.° holy objects
Lat kutte hem of!° I wol thee helpe hem carie. Have them cut off!
They shul be shryned—in an hogges toord°!" turd
This Pardoner answerde nat a word;
So wrooth° he was, no word ne wolde he seye. wrathful
"Now," quod oure Hoost, "I wol no lenger pleye
With thee, ne with noon° oother angry man." nor with any
But right anon the worthy Knyght bigan,
Whan that he saugh that al the peple lough,° were laughing
"Namoore of this, for it is right ynough.
Sire Pardoner, be glad and murye° of cheere. merry
And ye, sire Hoost, that been to me so deere,
I pray yow that ye kisse the Pardoner.
And, Pardoner, I pray thee, drawe thee neer.
And, as we diden, lat us laughe and pleye."
Anon they kiste, and ryden° forth hir weye. rode

ANONYMOUS LYRICS AND BALLADS

TO 1600

For the modern reader the charm of the anonymous songs of this period—their limpid clarity and simple, haunting music—comes from the fact that, unlike most modern poems, they are not primarily an expression of the poet's private or individual emotions. In these songs (for most of them are songs meant to be sung to music) the themes, images, and musical cadences follow *conventions* that had been developed for generations and that aroused a ready response in everyone. Some of the later songs—like "Back and Side Go Bare, Go Bare," a lusty drinking song celebrating old English "Nut-Brown Ale"—were also incorporated in plays of the Elizabethan period.

489. by . . . fond: "by the cross that Saint Helena found" (Helena, mother of the Emperor Constantine, was believed to have discovered the true cross in Jerusalem in 326).

The greatest treasury of anonymous popular poetry of the time is the collection of folk ballads, most of them from Scotland or from the north of England along the Scottish border (the "border ballads"). Only a few of these folk ballads continued to be known to the literary world into the seventeenth century. But in the middle 1700s Bishop Thomas Percy found handwritten copies of many of them in an old book, and published several (with revisions to "modernize" them) in his *Reliques of Ancient English Poetry* (1765). The work made a strong impact on the Romantic poets, many of whom composed poems in partial imitation (for example, Coleridge's "Rime of the Ancient Mariner" and Keats's "La Belle Dame Sans Merci"). After Percy other scholars, searching through old manuscripts or long-forgotten books, discovered more ballads, and throughout the nineteenth century it was common for collectors to go among the people in rural areas, the American frontier, the seaports, and so forth, and record the ballads that were still sung. The standard collection of ballads is still that of the American scholar, Francis James Child, in his *English and Scottish Popular Ballads* (1882–98).

No one knows how these ballads were composed. However they originated, they were favorite songs of the common people and were passed down from generation to generation. Just as a story may be changed somewhat by each person who tells it, the ballads were gradually altered in transmission, and often they may be read in several versions. Typically the ballads tell their stories through dialogue (often through question and answer) and with a starkness or absence of detail that activates imagination and creates poignance. Many of their formal characteristics, such as their frequent repetitions and use of refrains, are related to the fact that they were sung. Most of the ballads were probably based on events that actually occurred, but they also include folklore motifs found all over Europe.

Lyrics

Sumer Is Y-cumen In

Sumer is y-cumen in,
  Lude sing, cuccu!
Groweth sed and bloweth med
  And springth the wude nu.

SUMER IS Y-CUMEN IN. **1–4. Sumer . . . nu**: "Summer is come in; Sing loudly, cuckoo! Seed grows, and the meadow blows [flowers] and the wood springs anew."

Sing, cuccu!
Awe bleteth after lamb,
Lowth after calve cu;
Bulluc sterteth, bucke ferteth.
Merie sing, cuccu!
Cuccu, cuccu,
Wel singes thu, cuccu;
Ne swik thu never nu!

Sing, cuccu, nu! Sing, cuccu!
Sing, cuccu! Sing, cuccu, nu!

Ich Am of Irlonde

Ich am of Irlonde,
Ant of the holy londe
Of Irlonde.
Gode sire, pray ich thee,
For of sainte charite,
Come ant dance wit me,
In Irlonde.

Westron Winde, When Will Thou Blow?

Westron winde, when will thou blow,
The smalle raine downe can raine?
Crist, if my love wer in my armis,
And I in my bed againe.

I Sing of a Maiden

I sing of a maiden
That is makeles;
King of alle kinges
To here sone che ches.

He cam also stille
Ther his moder was,

6–8. Awe . . . ferteth: "Ewe [female sheep] bleats after her lamb; cow [*cu*] lows after her calf. The young bull [bullock] leaps up; the buck farts [from eating the fresh grass]." **11–12. Wel . . . nu:** "Well singest thou, cuckoo. Do not ever stop [*swik*] now!" ICH AM OF IRLONDE. **1. Ich . . . Irlonde:** "I am of Ireland." **5. For of:** for the sake of. I SING OF A MAIDEN. **Title:** Like the next poem, this was an early Christmas carol. This one is about the birth of Jesus, the next is a celebrative song. **2. makeles:** matchless. **4. To . . . ches:** As her son she chose. **5. also:** so.

As dew in Aprille
  That fallith on the gras.

He cam also stille
  To his moderes bowr,
As dew in Aprille
  That fallith on the flowr.

He cam also stille
  Ther his moder lay,
As dew in Aprille
  That fallith on the spray.

Moder and maiden
  Was never non but che;
Wel may swich a lady
  Godes moder be.

Christmas Carol

Now is Yole comen wyth gentil chere—
Of myrthe and gamen he hath no pere;
In every lond wher he cometh nere
  Is myrthe and gamen, I dar wel seye.

Now is comen a messager
Of thy lord, Sir Newe Yeer;
Biddeth us alle ben myrie heer
  And make as myrie as we may.

Ther-fore every man that is heer
Synge a carole on his manere;
If he can non we shullen him lere,
  So that we ben myrie alwey.

Whoso-evere maketh hevy chere,
Were he nevere to me dere,
In a dich I wolde he were
  To drye his clothes til it were day.

Mende the fyr and make good chere!
Fill the cuppe, sire boteler!
Lat every man drynke to his fere!
  This endeth my carole wyth care awey.

19. swich: such. CHRISTMAS CAROL. **1. Yole:** Yuletide. **2. myrthe and gamen:** mirth and games. **7. myrie:** merry. **11. lere:** teach. **12. alwey:** always. **13. maketh hevy chere:** makes heavy cheer (causes gloom). **14. nevere . . . dere:** however dear he is to me. **15. dich:** ditch. **18. boteler:** butler (literally, "bottler," one in charge of bottles of wine). **19. fere:** companion.

The Sparrow-Hawk's Complaint

In what state that ever I be
Timor mortis conturbat me.

As I me walked in one morning,
I herd a bird both weep and sing;
This was the tenor of her talking:
Timor mortis conturbat me.

I asked this bird what he ment.
He said: "I am a musket gent;
For dred of deth I am nigh shent;
Timor mortis conturbat me.

"Jesu Crist, when He shuld die,
To His Fader loud gan He cry:
'Fader', He said, 'in Trinity,
Timor mortis conturbat me.'

"When I shall die know I no day;
In what place or contrey can I not say;
Therfore this song sing I may,
Timor mortis conturbat me."

I Have a Yong Suster

I have a yong suster
Fer biyonde the see;
Many ben the drueries
That she sente me.

She sente me the chery
Wythouten any ston,
And so she dide the dowve
Wythouten any bon.

She sente me the brere
Wythouten any rynde,
She bad me love my lemman
Wythouten longynge.

How sholde any chery
Ben wythouten ston?

THE SPARROW-HAWK'S COMPLAINT. **2. *Timor . . . me*:** "Fear of death distresses me." The phrase comes from the Catholic service, "Office of the Dead." **8. musket gent:** a gentle (noble) sparrow-hawk. **9. shent:** destroyed. I HAVE A YONG SUSTER. **2. Fer . . . see:** "far beyond the sea." **3. drueries:** presents. **6. ston:** stone. **7–8. the dowve . . . bon:** "the dove without any bone." **9–10. brere . . . rynde:** "briar (wild rose) without any bark." **11. lemman:** lover.

And how sholde any dowve
  Ben wythouten bon?

How sholde any brere
  Ben wythouten rynde?
How sholde I love my lemman
  Wythouten longynge?

Whan the chery was a flour,
  Than hadde it non ston;
Whan the dowve was an ey,
  Than hadde it non bon.

Whan the brere was unbred,
  Than hadde it non rynde;
Whan the mayden hath that she loveth,
  She is wythouten longynge.

Back and Side Go Bare, Go Bare

Back and side go bare, go bare,
  Both foot and hand go cold;
But, belly, God send thee good ale enough,
  Whether it be new or old.

I cannot eat but little meat,
  My stomach is not good;
But sure I think that I can drink
  With him that wears a hood.
Though I go bare, take ye no care,
  I am nothing a-cold;
I stuff my skin so full within
  Of jolly good ale and old.

Back and side go bare, go bare,
  Both foot and hand go cold;
But, belly, God send thee good ale enough,
  Whether it be new or old.

I love no roast but a nutbrown toast,
  And a crab laid in the fire;
A little bread shall do me stead,

21. flour: flower. **23. ey:** egg. **25. unbred:** unborn (still a seed). BACK AND SIDE GO BARE, GO BARE **Title:** This song is included in a comic play, *Gammer Gurton's Needle*, by William Stevenson, a Fellow of Christ's College, Cambridge, which was performed there in the 1550s and published in 1575. But it is generally assumed that Stevenson did not himself write it, and that it had long been current as an anonymous song. **8. him . . . hood:** a monk or friar, meaning, "I can drink as much as any monk (or friar)." **17. nutbrown toast:** toasted bread floating in nut-brown ale (used as a sop). **18. crab:** crab apple. **19. stead:** service.

Much bread I not desire.
No frost nor snow, no wind, I trow,
Can hurt me if I would,
I am so wrapped, and throughly lapped
Of jolly good ale and old.

Back and side go bare, & c.

And Tib my wife, that as her life
Loveth well good ale to seek,
Full oft drinks she, till ye may see
The tears run down her cheek.
Then doth she troll to me the bowl,
Even as a maltworm should,
And saith, Sweetheart, I took my part
Of this jolly good ale and old.

Back and side go bare, & c.

Now let them drink, till they nod and wink,
Even as good fellows should do;
They shall not miss to have the bliss
Good ale doth bring men to;
And all poor souls that have scoured bowls
Or have them lustily trolled,
God save the lives of them and their wives,
Whether they be young or old.

Back and side go bare, & c.

Weep You No More, Sad Fountains

Weep you no more, sad fountains;
What need you flow so fast?
Look how the snowy mountains
Heaven's sun doth gently waste!
But my Sun's heavenly eyes
View not your weeping,
That now lies sleeping,
Softly, now softly, lies
Sleeping.

Sleep is a reconciling,
A rest that peace begets;
Doth not the sun rise smiling
When fair at even he sets?
Rest you then, rest, sad eyes!
Melt not in weeping,

21. trow: trust. **23. throughly lapped:** thoroughly lapped around. **30. troll:** pass. **31. maltworm:** heavy drinker of malt (ale).

While she lies sleeping,
Softly, now softly, lies
Sleeping.

1603

Ballads

Lord Randal

1

"O where ha' you been, Lord Randal, my son?
And where ha' you been, my handsome young man?"
"I ha' been at the greenwood; mother, mak my bed soon,
For I'm wearied wi' huntin', and fain wad lie down."

2

"And wha met ye there, Lord Randal, my son?
And wha met you there, my handsome young man?"
"O I met wi' my true-love; mother, mak my bed soon,
For I'm wearied wi' huntin', and fain wad lie down."

3

"And what did she give you, Lord Randal, my son?
And what did she give you, my handsome young man?"
"Eels fried in a pan; mother, mak my bed soon,
For I'm wearied wi' huntin', and fain wad lie down."

4

"And wha gat your leavin's, Lord Randal, my son?
And wha gat your leavin's, my handsome young man?"
"My hawks and my hounds; mother, mak my bed soon,
For I'm wearied wi' huntin', and fain wad lie down."

5

"And what becam of them, Lord Randal, my son?
And what becam of them, my handsome young man?"
"They stretched their legs out and died; mother, mak my bed soon,
For I'm wearied wi' huntin', and fain wad lie down."

6

"O I fear you are poisoned, Lord Randal, my son!
I fear you are poisoned, my handsome young man!"

LORD RANDAL. **4. wad:** would.

"O yes, I am poisoned; mother, mak my bed soon,
For I'm sick at the heart, and I fain wad lie down."

7

"What d' ye leave to your mother, Lord Randal, my son?
What d' ye leave to your mother, my handsome young man?"
"Four and twenty milk kye; mother, mak my bed soon,
For I'm sick at the heart, and I fain wad lie down."

8

"What d' ye leave to your sister, Lord Randal, my son?
What d' ye leave to your sister, my handsome young man?"
"My gold and my silver; mother, mak my bed soon,
For I'm sick at the heart, and I fain wad lie down."

9

"What d' ye leave to your brother, Lord Randal, my son?
What d' ye leave to your brother, my handsome young man?"
"My houses and my lands; mother, mak my bed soon,
For I'm sick at the heart, and I fain wad lie down."

10

"What d' ye leave to your true-love, Lord Randal, my son?
What d' ye leave to your true-love, my handsome young man?"
"I leave her hell and fire; mother, mak my bed soon,
For I'm sick at the heart, and I fain wad lie down."

Edward

1

"Why does your brand sae drap wi' bluid,
        Edward, Edward,
Why does your brand sae drap wi' bluid,
    And why sae sad gang ye, O?"
"O I ha'e killed my hawk sae guid,
        Mither, mither,
O I ha'e killed my hawk sae guid,
    And I had nae mair but he, O."

2

"Your hawke's bluid was never sae reid,
        Edward, Edward,
Your hawke's bluid was never sae reid,

27. kye: kine (cattle). EDWARD. **1. brand sae drap:** sword so drip. **4. gang:** go. **9. reid:** red.

My dear son I tell thee, O."
"O I ha'e killed my reid-roan steed,
Mither, mither,
O I ha'e killed my reid-roan steed,
That erst was sae fair and free, O."

3

"Your steed was auld, and ye ha'e gat mair,
Edward, Edward,
Your steed was auld, and ye ha'e gat mair,
Some other dule ye drie, O."
"O I ha'e killed my fader dear,
Mither, mither,
O I ha'e killed my fader dear,
Alas, and wae is me, O!"

4

"And whatten penance wul ye drie for that,
Edward, Edward?
And whatten penance wul ye dree for that,
My dear son, now tell me O?"
"I'll set my feet in yonder boat,
Mither, mither,
I'll set my feet in yonder boat,
And I'll fare over the sea, O."

5

"And what wul ye do wi' your towers and your ha',
Edward, Edward?
And what wul ye do wi' your towers and your ha',
That were sae fair to see, O?"
"I'll let them stand tul they down fa',
Mither, mither,
I'll let them stand tul they down fa',
For here never mair maun I be, O."

6

"And what wul ye leave to your bairns and your wife,
Edward, Edward?
And what wul ye leave to your bairns and your wife,
Whan ye gang over the sea, O?"
"The warlde's room, let them beg thrae life,
Mither, mither,
The warlde's room, let them beg thrae life,
For them never mair wul I see, O."

20. dule: grief. **drie:** suffer. **25. whatten:** what kind of. **33. ha':** hall. **40. never mair maun:** never more must. **41. bairns:** children. **45. The warlde's room:** the world's room (the whole world). **thrae:** through.

7

"And what wul ye leave to your ain mither dear,
Edward, Edward?
And what wul ye leave to your ain mither dear,
My dear son, now tell me, O?"
"The curse of hell frae me sall ye bear,
Mither, mither,
The curse of hell frae me sall ye bear,
Sic counsels ye gave to me, O."

Barbara Allan

1

It was in and about the Martinmas time,
When the green leaves were a falling,
That Sir John Græme, in the West Country,
Fell in love with Barbara Allan.

2

He sent his man down through the town,
To the place where she was dwelling:
"O haste and come to my master dear,
Gin ye be Barbara Allan."

3

O hooly, hooly rose she up,
To the place where he was lying,
And when she drew the curtain by:
"Young man, I think you're dying."

4

"O it's I'm sick, and very, very sick,
And 'tis a' for Barbara Allan."
"O the better for me ye s' never be,
Though your heart's blood were a-spilling.

5

"O dinna ye mind, young man," said she,
"When ye was in the tavern a drinking,
That ye made the healths gae round and round,
And slighted Barbara Allan?"

53. frae me sall: from me shall. **56. Sic:** such. BARBARA ALLAN. **1. Martinmas:** Mass (or feast) of St. Martin (d. 655) on November 11. **8. Gin:** if. **9. hooly:** gently, softly. **15. s':** shall. **17. dinna ye mind:** don't you remember. **19. gae:** go.

6

He turned his face unto the wall,
  And death was with him dealing:
"Adieu, adieu, my dear friends all,
  And be kind to Barbara Allan."

7

And slowly, slowly raise she up,
  And slowly, slowly left him,
And sighing said, she could not stay,
  Since death of life had reft him.

8

She had not gane a mile but twa,
  When she heard the dead-bell ringing,
And every jow that the dead-bell geid,
  It cried, "Woe to Barbara Allan!"

9

"O mother, mother, make my bed!
  O make it saft and narrow!
Since my love died for me to-day,
  I'll die for him to-morrow."

Mary Hamilton

1

Word's gane to the kitchen,
  And word's gane to the ha',
That Marie Hamilton gangs wi' bairn
  To the hichest Stewart of a'.

2

He's courted her in the kitchen,
  He's courted her in the ha',
He's courted her in the laigh cellar,
  And that was warst of a'.

3

She's tied it in her apron
  And she's thrown it in the sea;
Says, "Sink ye, swim ye, bonny wee babe!
  You'll ne'er get mair o' me."

28. reft: deprived. **29. gane:** gone. **twa:** two. **31. jow:** beat. **geid:** gave. MARY HAMILTON. **3. gangs wi' bairn:** goes with child (is pregnant). **4. hichest:** highest. **7. laigh:** low.

4

Down then cam the auld queen,
  Goud tassels tying her hair:
"O Marie, where's the bonny wee babe
  That I heard greet sae sair?"

5

"There was never a babe intill my room,
  As little designs to be;
It was but a touch o' my sair side,
  Come o'er my fair body."

6

"O Marie, put on your robes o' black,
  Or else your robes o' brown,
For ye maun gang wi' me the night,
  To see fair Edinbro' town."

7

"I winna put on my robes o' black,
  Nor yet my robes o' brown;
But I'll put on my robes o' white,
  To shine through Edinbro' town."

8

When she gaed up the Cannogate,
  She laughed loud laughters three;
But when she cam down the Cannogate
  The tear blinded her ee.

9

When she gaed up the Parliament stair,
  The heel cam aff her shee;
And lang or she cam down again
  She was condemned to dee.

10

When she cam down the Cannogate,
  The Cannogate sae free,
Many a lady looked o'er her window,
  Weeping for this lady.

11

"Ye need nae weep for me," she says,
  "Ye need nae weep for me;

14. Goud: gold. **16. greet:** cry. **sair:** sorely. **17. intill:** in. **23. maun:** must. **25. winna:** will not. **29. gaed:** went. **32. ee:** eye. **35. or:** before.

For had I not slain mine own sweet babe,
  This death I wadna dee.

12

"Bring me a bottle of wine," she says,
  "The best that e'er ye ha'e,
That I may drink to my weil-wishers,
  And they may drink to me.

13

"Here's a health to the jolly sailors,
  That sail upon the main;
Let them never let on to my father and mother
  But what I'm coming hame.

14

"Here's a health to the jolly sailors,
  That sail upon the sea;
Let them never let on to my father and mother
  That I cam here to dee.

15

"Oh little did my mother think,
  The day she cradled me,
What lands I was to travel through,
  What death I was to dee.

16

"Oh little did my father think,
  The day he held up me,
What lands I was to travel through,
  What death I was to dee.

17

"Last night I washed the queen's feet,
  And gently laid her down;
And a' the thanks I've gotten the night
  To be hanged in Edinbro' town!

18

"Last night there was four Maries,
  The night there'll be but three;
There was Marie Seton, and Marie Beton,
  And Marie Carmichael, and me."

67. the night: tonight.

Sir Patrick Spens

1

The king sits in Dumferling town,
  Drinking the blude-reid wine:
"O whar will I get guid sailor,
  To sail this ship of mine?"

2

Up and spak an eldern knicht,
  Sat at the king's richt knee:
"Sir Patrick Spens is the best sailor
  That sails upon the sea."

3

The king has written a braid letter
  And signed it wi' his hand,
And sent it to Sir Patrick Spens,
  Was walking on the sand.

4

The first line that Sir Patrick read,
  A loud lauch lauched he;
The next line that Sir Patrick read,
  The tear blinded his ee.

5

"O wha is this has done this deed,
  This ill deed done to me,
To send me out this time o' the year,
  To sail upon the sea?

6

"Mak haste, mak haste, my mirry men all,
  Our guid ship sails the morn."
"O say na sae, my master dear,
  For I fear a deadly storm.

7

"Late, late yestre'en I saw the new moon
  Wi' the auld moon in hir arm,
And I fear, I fear, my dear master,
  That we will come to harm."

SIR PATRICK SPENS. **2. blude-reid:** blood red. **9. braid:** broad. **14. lauch:** laugh. **16. ee:** eye. **23. sae:** so.

8

O our Scots nobles were richt laith
To weet their cork-heeled shoon,
But lang or a' the play were played
Their hats they swam aboon.

9

O lang, lang may their ladies sit,
Wi' their fans into their hand,
Or ere they see Sir Patrick Spens
Come sailing to the land.

10

O lang, lang may the ladies stand
Wi' their gold kems in their hair,
Waiting for their ain dear lords,
For they'll see them na mair.

11

Half o'er, half o'er to Aberdour
It's fifty fadom deep,
And there lies guid Sir Patrick Spens
Wi' the Scots lords at his feet.

Get Up and Bar the Door

1

It fell about the Martinmas time,
And a gay time it was then,
When our goodwife got puddings to make,
And she's boiled them in the pan.

2

The wind sae cauld blew south and north,
And blew into the floor;
Quoth our goodman to our goodwife,
"Gae out and bar the door."

3

"My hand is in my hussyfskap.
Goodman, as ye may see;

29. laith: loath. **30. weet:** wet. **shoon:** shoes. **31. lang or:** long before. **32. aboon:** above. **38. kems:** combs. GET UP AND BAR THE DOOR. **1. Martinmas:** November 11. **5. sae:** so. **8. Gae:** go. **9. hussyfskap:** housewife duties.

An it should nae be barred this hundred year,
  It s' no be barred for me."

4

They made a paction 'tween them twa,
  They made it firm and sure,
That the first word whae'er should speak,
  Should rise and bar the door.

5

Then by there came two gentlemen,
  At twelve o'clock at night,
And they could neither see house nor hall,
  Nor coal nor candle-light.

6

"Now whether is this a rich man's house,
  Or whether is it a poor?"
But ne'er a word wad ane o' them speak,
  For barring of the door.

7

And first they ate the white puddings,
  And then they ate the black;
Though muckle thought the goodwife to hersel,
  Yet ne'er a word she spak.

8

Then said the one unto the other,
  "Here, man, tak ye my knife;
Do ye tak aff the auld man's beard,
  And I'll kiss the goodwife."

9

"But there's nae water in the house,
  And what shall we do then?"
"What ails ye at the pudding-broo,
  That boils into the pan?"

10

O up then started our goodman,
  An angry man was he:
"Will ye kiss my wife before my een,
  And scad me wi' pudding-bree?"

11. An: if. **12. It s' no:** it shall not. **23. wad:** would. **27. muckle:** much. **35. ails ye at:** is the trouble with. **broo:** broth. **39. een:** eyes. **40. scad:** scald.

11

Then up and started our goodwife,
  Gied three skips on the floor:
"Goodman, you've spoken the foremost word,
  Get up and bar the door."

JOHN SKELTON

(c. 1460–1529)

A clergyman and briefly tutor to Henry VIII, Skelton was a court figure. Many of his poems are satires, and some of these are composed in a special type of verse (now known as "Skeltonics"), in which a long sequence of short lines end on the same rhyme. "To Mistress Margaret Hussey," however, is a more traditional type of poem. The qualities for which Mistress Margaret is admired and the objects to which she is compared are typical in medieval poems in praise of women.

To Mistress Margaret Hussey

  Merry Margaret,
    As midsummer flower,
  Gentle as falcon
  Or hawk of the tower:
With solace and gladness,
Much mirth and no madness,
All good and no badness;
    So joyously,
    So maidenly,
    So womanly
    Her demeaning
    In every thing,
    Far, far passing
    That I can indite,
    Or suffice to write
Of Merry Margaret
  As midsummer flower,
Gentle as falcon

42. Gied: gave. TO MISTRESS MARGARET HUSSEY. **4. hawk . . . tower:** hawk that towers high in the air. **14. indite:** write.

Or hawk of the tower.
  As patient and still
And as full of good will
As fair Isaphill,
Coriander,
Sweet pomander,
Good Cassander,
Steadfast of thought,
Well made, well wrought,
Far may be sought
Ere that ye can find
So courteous, so kind
As Merry Margaret,
  This midsummer flower,
Gentle as falcon
Or hawk of the tower.

Sir Thomas Wyatt

(1503–1542)

One of the sixteenth-century poets who typified the Renaissance ideal of the "courtier," Wyatt went to Italy as a diplomat during his twenties. Entranced by the Italian poetry that had been flourishing there for two hundred years, especially the sonnets of Petrarch (Francesco Petrarca, 1304–1374), he introduced into England the fourteen-line Italian or Petrarchan sonnet, which he usually rhymed *abba abba cdcd ee* (see *sonnet* in the Appendix on Versification). This was to become an important lyrical form of the Elizabethan age, used especially for love poetry. But Wyatt's lyrics in other forms are as fine as his sonnets and more characteristic of him. Many of his poems were published after his death in the most famous of Elizabethan collections, *Tottel's Miscellany* (1557), named for the printer, Richard Tottel, who compiled this anthology of songs and sonnets; a few of Wyatt's poems remained in manuscript until our own century.

22. Isaphill: Hypsipyle, Queen of Lemnos, known for her devotion to her father and children. **23. Coriander:** herb believed to relieve pain. **24. pomander:** ball of perfumed herbs. **25. Cassander:** Cassandra, daughter of King Priam of Troy, gifted with ability to prophesy.

Whoso List to Hunt

Whoso list to hunt, I know where is an hind,
But as for me, alas, I may no more;
The vain travail hath wearied me so sore,
I am of them that furthest come behind.
Yet may I by no means my wearied mind
Draw from the deer, but as she fleeth afore
Fainting I follow; I leave off therefore,
Since in a net I seek to hold the wind.
Who list her hunt, I put him out of doubt,
As well as I, may spend his time in vain.
And graven with diamonds in letters plain,
There is written her fair neck round about,
"*Noli me tangere*, for Caesar's I am,
And wild for to hold, though I seem tame."

1557

My Galley Chargèd with Forgetfulness

My galley chargèd with forgetfulness
Thorough sharp seas in winter nights doth pass
'Tween rock and rock; and eke mine enemy, alas,
That is my lord, steereth with cruelness;
And every oar a thought in readiness,
As though that death were light in such a case.
An endless wind doth tear the sail apace
Of forced sighs, and trusty fearfulness.
A rain of tears, a cloud of dark disdain,
Hath done the wearied cords great hinderance;
Wreathed with error and eke with ignorance,
The stars be hid that led me to this pain;
Drowned is reason that should me consort,
And I remain despairing of the port.

1557

Madam, Withouten Many Words

Madam, withouten many words,
Once, I am sure ye will, or no;
And if ye will, then leave your bords,
And use your wit, and show it so.

WHOSO LIST TO HUNT. **1. list:** desires. **13. *Noli me tangere*:** "Touch me not." MADAM, WITHOUTEN MANY WORDS. **3. bords:** jokes.

And with a beck ye shall me call,
  And if of one that burneth alway,
Ye have any pity at all,
  Answer him fair with yea or nay.

If it be yea, I shall be fain;
  If it be nay, friends as before;
Ye shall another man obtain,
  And I mine own, and yours no more.

1557

They Flee from Me

They flee from me, that sometime did me seek,
With naked foot stalking in my chamber.
I have seen them, gentle, tame, and meek,
That now are wild, and do not remember
That sometime they put themselves in danger
To take bread at my hand; and now they range,
Busily seeking with a continual change.

Thanked be Fortune it hath been otherwise,
Twenty times better; but once in special,
In thin array, after a pleasant guise,
When her loose gown from her shoulders did fall,
And she me caught in her arms long and small,
And therewith all sweetly did me kiss
And softly said, "Dear heart, how like you this?"

It was no dream, I lay broad waking.
But all is turned, thorough my gentleness,
Into a strange fashion of forsaking;
And I have leave to go, of her goodness,
And she also to use newfangleness.
But since that I so kindely am served,
I fain would know what she hath deserved.

1557

My Lute, Awake!

My lute, awake! Perform the last
Labor that thou and I shall waste,
And end that I have now begun;

THEY FLEE FROM ME. **12. small**: slim. **19. newfangleness**: fickleness. **20. so kindely**: in so natural (or human) a way, as well as in the modern sense of *kindly*.

For when this song is sung and past,
My lute, be still, for I have done.

As to be heard where ear is none,
As lead to grave in marble stone,
My song may pierce her heart as soon.
Should we then sigh or sing or moan?
No, no, my lute, for I have done.

The rocks do not so cruelly
Repulse the waves continually
As she my suit and affection.
So that I am past remedy,
Whereby my lute and I have done.

Proud of the spoil that thou hast got
Of simple hearts, thorough love's shot;
By whom, unkind, thou hast them won,
Think not he hath his bow forgot,
Although my lute and I have done.

Vengeance shall fall on thy disdain
That makest but game on earnest pain.
Think not alone under the sun
Unquit to cause thy lovers plain,
Although my lute and I have done.

Perchance thee lie withered and old
The winter nights that are so cold,
Plaining in vain unto the moon.
Thy wishes then dare not be told.
Care then who list, for I have done.

And then may chance thee to repent
The time that thou hast lost and spent
To cause thy lovers sigh and swoon.
Then shalt thou know beauty but lent,
And wish and want as I have done.

Now cease, my lute. This is the last
Labor that thou and I shall waste,
And ended is that we begun.
Now is this song both sung and past;
My lute, be still, for I have done.

1557

MY LUTE, AWAKE! **7. grave**: engrave. The sense of lines 6–7 is "As to be heard when there is no ear to hear, or when lead (a soft metal) can engrave marble." **24. unquit**: unavenged. **plain**: complain. **30. list**: desires (or likes).

Forget Not Yet

Forget not yet the tried intent
Of such a truth as I have meant;
My great travail so gladly spent
Forget not yet.

Forget not yet when first began
The weary life ye know, since whan
The suit, the service none tell can;
Forget not yet.

Forget not yet the great assays,
The cruel wrong, the scornful ways,
The painful patience in denays,
Forget not yet.

Forget not yet, forget not this,
How long ago hath been and is
The mind that never meant amiss;
Forget not yet.

Forget not then thine own approved,
The which so long hath thee so loved,
Whose steadfast faith yet never moved;
Forget not this.

Henry Howard, Earl of Surrey

(1517–1547)

The most gifted of Sir Thomas Wyatt's disciples was this impetuous and politically ambitious cousin of Henry VIII's fifth wife, Catherine Howard. Following Catherine's execution, Surrey was beheaded for treason at the age of thirty. He had, however, made two important contributions to English poetry. Following Wyatt, he developed the Petrarchan or Italian sonnet into what is called the English sonnet or, sometimes, the Shakespearean sonnet (because Shakespeare's is the greatest use of it): three alternate rhyming quatrains followed by a couplet—*abab cdcd efef gg* (see *sonnet* in the Appendix on Versification).

FORGET NOT YET. **9. assays**: attempts (or trials). **11. denays**: denials.

A second contribution is that his translation of part of Virgil's *Aeneid* (1554–57) first employed in English the most important single form of verse of our poetry, blank verse, or unrhymed iambic pentameter (see *blank verse* in the Appendix on Versification). In Surrey's hands blank verse was still rather wooden, but in Marlowe and Shakespeare it became marvelously flexible for poetic drama; in the poetry of later writers from Milton through Wordsworth, Keats, Tennyson, and Frost it proved capable of immense variation.

My Friend, the Things That Do Attain

My friend, the things that do attain
The happy life be these, I find:
The riches left, not got with pain;
The fruitful ground; the quiet mind;

The equal friend; no grudge, no strife;
No charge of rule, nor governance;
Without disease, the healthy life;
The household of continuance;

The mean diet, no dainty fare;
Wisdom joined with simpleness;
The night dischargèd of all care,
Where wine the wit may not oppress;

The faithful wife, without debate;
Such sleeps as may beguile the night;
Content thyself with thine estate,
Neither wish death, nor fear his might.

1547

Love, That Doth Reign and Live Within My Thought

Love, that doth reign and live within my thought,
And built his seat within my captive breast,
Clad in the arms wherein with me he fought,
Oft in my face he doth his banner rest.
But she that taught me love and suffer pain,
My doubtful hope and eke my hot desire
With shamefast look to shadow and refrain,

LOVE, THAT DOTH REIGN. **Title**: This sonnet is translated from Petrarch, *Sonetto in Vita* 91.
6. eke: also.

Her smiling grace converteth straight to ire.
And coward Love, then, to the heart apace
Taketh his flight, where he doth lurk and plain,
His purpose lost, and dare not show his face.
For my lord's guilt thus faultless bide I pain,
Yet from my lord shall not my foot remove:
Sweet is the death that taketh end by love.

1557

Sir Walter Ralegh

(c. 1552–1618)

A courtier, soldier, and explorer as well as a poet, Sir Walter Ralegh spent most of the last fifteen years of his life in prison, having incurred the enmity of James I by his implacable hostility to Spain. In prison, where he was finally executed, he wrote a memorable prose *History of the World;* he left it unfinished because, as he characteristically observed, to come too near the present would be dangerous.

Ralegh was an intellectual and speculative man, a patron of Edmund Spenser, and one of the best of the courtier poets. "The Nymph's Reply to the Shepherd" is one of many retorts composed by various poets to Marlowe's famous poem, "The Passionate Shepherd to His Love." Ralegh's ominous, bittersweet "To His Son" was a favorite of the modern American poet, Robert Frost, who loved to recite it to his students.

The Nymph's Reply to the Shepherd

If all the world and love were young,
And truth in every shepherd's tongue,
These pretty pleasures might me move
To live with thee and be thy love.

Time drives the flocks from field to fold
When rivers rage and rocks grow cold,
And Philomel becometh dumb;
The rest complains of cares to come.

The flowers do fade, and wanton fields
To wayward winter reckoning yields;

10. plain: complain THE NYMPH'S REPLY. **7. Philomel:** the nightingale.

A honey tongue, a heart of gall,
Is fancy's spring, but sorrow's fall.

Thy gowns, thy shoes, thy beds of roses,
Thy cap, thy kirtle, and thy posies
Soon break, soon wither, soon forgotten—
In folly ripe, in reason rotten.

Thy belt of straw and ivy buds,
Thy coral clasps and amber studs,
All these in me no means can move
To come to thee and be thy love.

But could youth last and love still breed,
Had joys no date nor age no need,
Then these delights my mind might move
To live with thee and be thy love.

1600

Nature, That Washed Her Hands in Milk

Nature, that washed her hands in milk,
And had forgot to dry them,
Instead of earth took snow and silk,
At love's request to try them,
If she a mistress could compose
To please love's fancy out of those.

Her eyes he would should be of light,
A violet breath, and lips of jelly;
Her hair not black, nor overbright,
And of the softest down her belly;
As for her inside he'd have it
Only of wantonness and wit.

At love's entreaty such a one
Nature made, but with her beauty
She hath framed a heart of stone;
So as love, by ill destiny,
Must die for her whom nature gave him,
Because her darling would not save him.

But time (which nature doth despise,
And rudely gives her love the lie,
Makes hope a fool, and sorrow wise)
His hands do neither wash nor dry;
But being made of steel and rust,
Turns snow and silk and milk to dust.

14. kirtle: underskirt or petticoat. **22. date:** ending.

The light, the belly, lips, and breath,
He dims, discolors, and destroys;
With those he feeds but fills not death,
Which sometimes were the food of joys.
Yea, time doth dull each lively wit,
And dries all wantonness with it.

Oh, cruel time! which takes in trust
Our youth, our joys, and all we have,
And pays us but with age and dust;
Who in the dark and silent grave
When we have wandered all our ways
Shuts up the story of our days.

c. 1610

To His Son

Three things there be that prosper all apace
And flourish, while they are asunder far;
But on a day they meet all in a place,
And when they meet, they one another mar.
And they be these: the wood, the weed, the wag.
The wood is that that makes the gallows tree;
The weed is that that strings the hangman's bag;
The wag, my pretty knave, betokens thee.
Now mark, dear boy: while these assemble not,
Green springs the tree, hemp grows, the wag is wild;
But when they meet, it makes the timber rot,
It frets the halter, and it chokes the child.
God bless the child!

Even Such Is Time

Even such is time, which takes in trust
Our youth, our joys, and all we have,
And pays us but with age and dust,

NATURE, THAT WASHED HER HANDS. **31–36. Oh . . . days:** These lines were later revised to form the poem printed below, "Even Such Is Time." TO HIS SON. **Title:** Our version is that in the Malone manuscript 19. Another version, perhaps less authoritative and bearing no title, is the one commonly printed and has two lines added at the end in place of the short line "God bless the child!": "Then bless thee, and beware, and let us pray/ We part not with thee at this meeting day." **12. frets:** wears away. EVEN SUCH IS TIME. **Title:** Traditionally believed to have been written the night before Ralegh was executed (1618), the poem consists substantially of the last stanza of "Nature, That Washed Her Hands in Milk," printed above, with two new lines added at the end.

Who in the dark and silent grave
When we have wandered all our ways
Shuts up the story of our days,
And from which earth, and grave, and dust
The Lord shall raise me up, I trust.

1628

EDMUND SPENSER

(1552–1599)

Born in London, Spenser attended school there, then went as a poor scholar to the university at Cambridge. He was employed by a number of patrons, and he made friends among persons interested in literature, such as Sir Philip Sidney, to whom he dedicated *The Shepheardes Calender* (1579), a sequence of pastoral poems. By 1580 Spenser was at work on *The Faerie Queene.* He moved to Ireland, where he held a position in the government and acquired an estate. During a rebellion of the Irish in 1598 against English rule, Spenser's castle was burned, and he returned to England, where he died and was buried in Westminster Abbey.

Though Spenser wrote many poems of different kinds, his greatest work is *The Faerie Queene.* Like many of the most ambitious poems of the Renaissance, *The Faerie Queene* was conceived with a moral and educational aim. The poem was to represent the virtues necessary for the perfection of human nature. These virtues Spenser embodied in various questing knights, each knight illustrating one particular virtue. The knights do not, however, possess this virtue from the start, but acquire it in the course of their adventures. The knights and everything they encounter are allegorical. The Faerie Queene herself signifies "Glory" and is also meant to stand for Queen Elizabeth. The poem was published in two installments: Books I to III in 1590, and Books IV to VI in1596. The "Mutability Cantos" of the unfinished Book VII were published after Spenser died.

In addition to being an allegory, *The Faerie Queene* is the archetypal chivalric romance of English literature. Of no literary genre are the conventions more familiarly known: the heroic knight in quest of adventure; the damsel in distress whom he protects and aids; the evil knights and monsters he must overcome; the imaginary landscape with its castles, woods, caves, bowers, wayside chapels, and so forth; and the loose, episodic structure of the narrative, in which one can meet anything—a lion, hermit, dwarf, witch, Saracen, dragon—at any moment, and an adventure takes place on every page. To create his incidents Spenser ransacked literature for suggestions, borrowing especially from the classics and from Italian writers such as Ariosto and Tasso; he also drew on paintings, emblem books, the Bible, religious tradition, and folklore. The mythological allusions, which are so frequent in Spenser, were fashionable during the Renaissance, when the newly discovered Greek and Latin classics enjoyed such prestige and were known to most readers. Spenser told his story with an elaborate, sustained melodiousness previously unmatched in English poetry and he lingered on pictorial detail—so much so that to a modern reader *The Faerie Queene* may seem leisurely and dreamlike.

After 1590 Spenser was recognized by his contemporaries as the great poet of the age. For the next fifty years his reputation remained high, especially among younger poets. But during the long period from Dryden to Wordsworth (1660 to 1800), only a few scholars and poets read *The Faerie Queene*. For the Romantics, especially John Keats, he was again one of the great poets in English. But the Victorians, though they felt that they should pay lip-service to *The Faerie Queene,* really had little taste for it. This is partly because of his prolific mythological allusions, and partly because of his fondness for words (and even spellings) that were already obsolete in his own age. In the revolution of poetry associated with Ezra Pound and T. S. Eliot ("High Modernism") no one was much concerned with Spenser. Since then many things have contributed to a new appreciation of Spenser's great work—the application of Freudian depth-psychology to literature, modern studies of symbolism and myth, a more sophisticated historical understanding of Renaissance culture, a greater interest in literary forms and theory and, as a result, a more intelligent response to allegory as a method—but the revival of Spenser remains largely academic and scholarly.

In Book I, the first Canto of which is included here, the Red Cross Knight of Holiness becomes the protector of Una ("unity"—the "one" true religion) and must struggle against the wicked enchanter Archimago ("Hypocrisy"), who is trying to capture Una. The so-called "Mutability Cantos" surviving from the unfinished Book VII are also given here.

The stanza form in which Spenser writes the poem (the *Spenserian stanza*) is his own invention: a nine-line stanza consisting of two interlocking quatrains—*abab bcbc*—followed by an hexameter, or six-foot line (also called an *Alexandrine*). In the pattern of rhymes within the stanza *(abab, bcbc, c)* the *b* rhymes act as a sounding board, and the final *c* rhyme, coming when the stanza seems already completed, is like the wash of a long wave. Poets have since used the Spenserian stanza occasionally and have especially valued it as a frame for pictorial effects (see, for example, Keats's "Eve of St. Agnes"). The series of love sonnets called *Amoretti* (the word means "little loves" or, in this case, "little love poems") uses a similar kind of "interlocking" of *b* rhymes *(abab bcbc cdcd ee)* in what is still called the Spenserian sonnet. The occasion of the *Epithalamion,* or "wedding song" (literally, in Greek, it means "at the bridal chamber"), was Spenser's own marriage to his second wife, Elizabeth Boyle. The exquisite *Prothalamion* (which in Greek means "before the bridal chamber") was written to celebrate the marriages of Elizabeth and Katherine Somerset, the daughters of the Earl of Worcester.

The First Booke of the Faerie Queene

Contayning The Legende of the Knight of the Red Crosse,
or of Holinesse

Canto I

The Patron of true Holinesse,
Foule Errour doth defeate:
Hypocrisie him to entrappe,
Doth to his home entreate.

1

A Gentle Knight was pricking on the plaine,
Ycladd in mightie armes and silver shielde,
Wherein old dints of deepe wounds did remaine,
The cruell markes of many a bloudy fielde;
Yet armes till that time did he never wield:
His angry steede did chide his foming bitt,
As much disdayning to the curbe to yield:
Full jolly knight he seemd, and faire did sitt,
As one for knightly giusts and fierce encounters fitt.

2

But on his brest a bloudie Crosse he bore,
The deare remembrance of his dying Lord,

THE FAERIE QUEENE. Canto I. **1. Gentle:** well born (as in gentleman). **pricking:** riding. **2. Ycladd:** clothed. **8. jolly:** confident. **9. giusts:** jousts (tourneys).

For whose sweete sake that glorious badge he wore,
And dead as living ever him adored:
Upon his shield the like was also scored,
For soveraine hope, which in his helpe he had:
Right faithfull true he was in deede and word,
But of his cheere did seeme too solemne sad;
Yet nothing did he dread, but ever was ydrad.

3

Upon a great adventure he was bond,
That greatest Gloriana to him gave,
That greatest Glorious Queene of Faerie Lond,
To winne him worship, and her grace to have,
Which of all earthly things he most did crave;
And ever as he rode, his hart did earne
To prove his puissance in battell brave
Upon his foe, and his new force to learne;
Upon his foe, a Dragon horrible and stearne.

4

A lovely Ladie rode him faire beside,
Upon a lowly Asse more white then snow,
Yet she much whiter, but the same did hide
Under a vele, that wimpled was full low,
And over all a blacke stole she did throw,
As one that inly mournd: so was she sad,
And heavie sat upon her palfrey slow:
Seemèd in heart some hidden care she had,
And by her in a line a milke white lambe she lad.

5

So pure an innocent, as that same lambe,
She was in life and every vertuous lore,
And by descent from Royall lynage came
Of ancient Kings and Queenes, that had of yore
Their scepters stretcht from East to Westerne shore,
And all the world in their subjection held;
Till that infernall feend with foule uprore
Forwasted all their land, and them expeld:
Whom to avenge, she had this Knight from far compeld.

6

Behind her farre away a Dwarfe did lag,
That lasie seemd in being ever last,
Or wearied with bearing of her bag
Of needments at his backe. Thus as they past,

14. scored: engraved. **17. cheere:** face. **sad:** serious. **18. ydrad:** dreaded. **22. worship:** honor. **24. earne:** yearn. **31. wimpled:** folded. **45. compeld:** summoned.

The day with cloudes was suddeine overcast,
And angry Jove an hideous storme of raine
Did poure into his Lemans lap so fast,
That every wight to shrowd it did constrain,
And this faire couple eke to shroud themselves were fain.

7

Enforst to seeke some covert nigh at hand,
A shadie grove not far away they spide,
That promist ayde the tempest to withstand:
Whose loftie trees yclad with sommers pride,
Did spred so broad, that heavens light did hide,
Not perceable with power of any starre:
And all within were pathes and alleies wide,
With footing worne, and leading inward farre:
Faire harbour that them seemes; so in they entred arre.

8

And foorth they passe, with pleasure forward led,
Joying to heare the birdes sweete harmony,
Which therein shrouded from the tempest dred,
Seemed in their song to scorne the cruell sky.
Much can they prayse the trees, so straight and hy,
The sayling Pine, the Cedar proud and tall,
The vine-prop Elme, the Poplar never dry,
The builder Oake, sole king of forrests all,
The Aspine good for staves, the Cypresse funerall.

9

The Laurell, meed of mightie Conquerours
And Poets sage, the Firre that weepeth still,
The Willow worne of forlorne Paramours,
The Eugh obedient to the benders will,
The Birch for shaftes, the Sallow for the mill,
The Mirrhe sweete bleeding in the bitter wound,
The warlike Beech, the Ash for nothing ill,
The fruitfull Olive, and the Platane round,
The carver Holme, the Maple seeldom inward sound.

10

Led with delight, they thus beguile the way,
Untill the blustring storme is overblowne;
When weening to returne, whence they did stray,
They cannot finde that path, which first was showne,
But wander too and fro in wayes unknowne,

52. Lemans: lover's (here, the earth). **53. wight:** creature. **shrowd:** cover (as with a shroud). **54. eke:** also. **73. meed:** reward. **76. Eugh:** yew. **77. Sallow:** willow. **80. Platane:** plane tree. **81. Holme:** holly. **84. weening:** intending.

Furthest from end then, when they neerest weene,
That makes them doubt, their wits be not their owne:
So many pathes, so many turnings seene,
That which of them to take, in diverse doubt they been.

11

At last resolving forward still to fare,
Till that some end they finde or in or out,
That path they take, that beaten seemd most bare,
Which when by tract they hunted had throughout,
And like to lead the labyrinth about;
At length it brought them to a hollow cave,
Amid the thickest woods. The Champion stout
Eftsoones dismounted from his courser brave,
And to the Dwarfe a while his needlesse spere he gave.

12

"Be well aware," quoth then that Ladie milde,
"Least suddaine mischiefe ye too rash provoke:
The danger hid, the place unknowne and wilde,
Breedes dreadfull doubts: Oft fire is without smoke,
And perill without show: therefore your stroke
Sir knight with-hold, till further triall made."
"Ah Ladie," said he, "shame were to revoke
The forward footing for an hidden shade:
Vertue gives her selfe light, through darkenesse for to wade."

13

"Yea but," quoth she, "the perill of this place
I better wot then you, though now too late
To wish you backe returne with foule disgrace,
Yet wisedome warnes, whilest foot is in the gate,
To stay the steepe, ere forcèd to retrate.
This is the wandring wood, this Errours den,
A monster vile, whom God and man does hate:
Therefore I read beware." "Fly fly," quoth then
The fearefull Dwarfe: "this is no place for living men."

14

But full of fire and greedy hardiment,
The youthfull knight could not for ought be staide,
But forth unto the darksome hole he went,
And lookèd in: his glistring armor made
A litle glooming light, much like a shade,
By which he saw the ugly monster plaine,

92. or . . . or: either . . . or. **94. tract:** track. **95. about:** out of. **98. Eftsoones:** soon afterwards. **107. for:** on account of. **116. read:** advise. **118. hardiment:** courage.

Halfe like a serpent horribly displaide,
But th' other halfe did womans shape retaine,
Most lothsom, filthie, foule, and full of vile disdaine.

15

And as she lay upon the durtie ground,
Her huge long taile her den all overspred,
Yet was in knots and many boughtes upwound,
Pointed with mortall sting. Of her there bred
A thousand yong ones, which she dayly fed,
Sucking upon her poisonous dugs, eachone
Of sundry shapes, yet all ill favorèd:
Soone as that uncouth light upon them shone,
Into her mouth they crept, and suddain all were gone.

16

Their dam upstart, out of her den effraide,
And rushèd forth, hurling her hideous taile
About her cursèd head, whose folds displaid
Were stretcht now forth at length without entraile.
She lookt about, and seeing one in mayle
Armèd to point, sought backe to turne againe;
For light she hated as the deadly bale,
Ay wont in desert darknesse to remaine,
Where plaine none might her see, nor she see any plaine.

17

Which when the valiant Elfe perceived, he lept
As Lyon fierce upon the flying pray,
And with his trenchand blade her boldly kept
From turning backe, and forcèd her to stay:
Therewith enraged she loudly gan to bray,
And turning fierce, her speckled taile advaunst,
Threatning her angry sting, him to dismay:
Who nough aghast, his mightie hand enhaunst:
The stroke down from her head unto her shoulder glaunst.

18

Much daunted with that dint, her sence was dazd,
Yet kindling rage, her selfe she gathered round,
And all attonce her beastly body raizd
With doubled forces high above the ground:
Tho wrapping up her wrethèd sterne arownd,
Lept fierce upon his shield, and her huge traine

129. boughtes: coils. **134. uncouth:** unfamiliar. **139. entraile:** winding. **141. to point:** entirely. **142. bale:** evil. **147. trenchand:** cutting. **152. enhaunst:** raised. **158. Tho:** then.

All suddenly about his body wound,
That hand or foot to stirre he strove in vaine:
God helpe the man so wrapt in Errours endlesse traine.

19

His Lady sad to see his sore constraint,
Cride out, "Now now Sir knight, shew what ye bee,
Add faith unto your force, and be not faint:
Strangle her, else she sure will strangle thee."
That when he heard, in great perplexitie,
His gall did grate for griefe and high disdaine,
And knitting all his force got one hand free,
Wherewith he grypt her gorge with so great paine,
That soone to loose her wicked bands did her constraine.

20

Therewith she spewd out of her filthy maw
A floud of poyson horrible and blacke,
Full of great lumpes of flesh and gobbets raw,
Which stunck so vildly, that it forst him slacke
His grasping hold, and from her turne him backe:
Her vomit full of bookes and papers was,
With loathly frogs and toades, which eyes did lacke,
And creeping sought way in the weedy gras:
Her filthy parbreake all the place defilèd has.

21

As when old father Nilus gins to swell
With timely pride above the Aegyptian vale,
His fattie waves do fertile slime outwell,
And overflow each plaine and lowly dale:
But when his later spring gins to avale,
Huge heapes of mudd he leaves, wherein there breed
Ten thousand kindes of creatures, partly male
And partly female of his fruitfull seed;
Such ugly monstrous shapes elswhere may no man reed.

22

The same so sore annoyèd has the knight,
That welnigh chokèd with the deadly stinke,
His forces faile, ne can no longer fight.
Whose corage when the feend perceived to shrinke,
She pourèd forth out of her hellish sinke
Her fruitfull cursèd spawne of serpents small,
Deformèd monsters, fowle, and blacke as inke,

168. griefe: rage. **170. gorge:** neck. **180. parbreake:** vomit. **182. timely:** at the right time. **183. fattie:** rich. **185. avale:** prevail, get stronger. **189. reed:** perceive.

Which swarming all about his legs did crall,
And him encombred sore, but could not hurt at all.

23

As gentle Shepheard in sweete even-tide,
When ruddy Phoebus gins to welke in west,
High on an hill, his flocke to vewen wide,
Markes which do byte their hasty supper best;
A cloud of combrous gnattes do him molest,
All striving to infixe their feeble stings,
That from their noyance he no where can rest,
But with his clownish hands their tender wings
He brusheth oft, and oft doth mar their murmurings.

24

Thus ill bestedd, and fearfull more of shame,
Then of the certaine perill he stood in,
Halfe furious unto his foe he came,
Resolved in minde all suddenly to win,
Or soone to lose, before he once would lin;
And strooke at her with more then manly force,
That from her body full of filthie sin
He raft her hateful head without remorse;
A streame of cole black bloud forth gushèd from her corse.

25

Her scattred brood, soone as their Parent deare
They saw so rudely falling to the ground,
Groning full deadly, all with troublous feare,
Gathred themselves about her body round,
Weening their wonted entrance to have found
At her wide mouth: but being there withstood
They flockèd all about her bleeding wound,
And suckèd up their dying mothers blood,
Making her death their life, and eke her hurt their good.

26

That detestable sight him much amazde,
To see th' unkindly Impes of heaven accurst,
Devoure their dam; on whom while so he gazd,
Having all satisfide their bloudy thurst,
Their bellies swolne he saw with fulnesse burst,
And bowels gushing forth: well worthy end
Of such as drunke her life, the which them nurst;
Now needeth him no lenger labour spend,
His foes have slaine themselves, with whom he should contend.

200. welke: decline. **206. clownish:** peasant-like. **208. bestedd:** conditioned. **212. lin:** stop. **215. raft:** chopped off. **218. rudely:** harshly.

27

His Ladie seeing all, that chaunst, from farre
  Approcht in hast to greet his victorie,
  And said, "Faire knight, borne under happy starre,
  Who see your vanquisht foes before you lye;
  Well worthy be you of that Armorie,
  Wherein ye have great glory wonne this day,
  And prooved your strength on a strong enimie,
  Your first adventure: many such I pray,
And henceforth ever wish, that like succeed it may."

28

Then mounted he upon his Steede againe,
  And with the Lady backward sought to wend;
  That path he kept, which beaten was most plaine,
  Ne ever would to any by-way bend,
  But still did follow one unto the end,
  The which at last out of the wood them brought.
  So forward on his way (with God to frend)
  He passèd forth, and new adventure sought;
Long way he travellèd, before he heard of ought.

29

At length they chaunst to meet upon the way
  An aged Sire, in long blacke weedes yclad,
  His feete all bare, his beard all hoarie gray,
  And by his belt his booke he hanging had;
  Sober he seemde, and very sagely sad,
  And to the ground his eyes were lowly bent,
  Simple in shew, and voyde of malice bad,
  And all the way he prayèd, as he went,
And often knockt his brest, as one that did repent.

30

He faire the knight saluted, louting low,
  Who faire him quited, as that courteous was:
  And after askèd him, if he did know
  Of straunge adventures, which abroad did pas.
  "Ah my deare Sonne," quoth he, "how should, alas,
  Silly old man, that lives in hidden cell,
  Bidding his beades all day for his trespas,
  Tydings of warre and worldly trouble tell?
With holy father sits not with such things to mell.

245. wend: go. **250. to frend:** as a friend. **257. sad:** serious. **262. louting:** bowing. **263. quited:** replied. **267. Silly:** innocent, holy. **268. Bidding:** telling. **270. mell:** meddle.

31

"But if of daunger which hereby doth dwell,
And homebred evill ye desire to heare,
Of a straunge man I can you tidings tell,
That wasteth all this countrey farre and neare."
"Of such," said he, "I chiefly do inquere,
And shall you well reward to shew the place,
In which that wicked wight his dayes doth weare.
For to all knighthood it is foule disgrace,
That such a cursèd creature lives so long a space,"

32

"Far hence," quoth he, "in wastfull wildernesse
His dwelling is, by which no living wight
May ever passe, but thorough great distresse."
"Now," sayd the Lady, "draweth toward night,
And well I wote, that of your later fight
Ye all forwearied be: for what so strong,
But wanting rest will also want of might?
The Sunne that measures heaven all day long,
At night doth baite his steedes the Ocean waves emong.

33

"Then with the Sunne take Sir, your timely rest,
And with new day new worke at once begin:
Untroubled night they say gives counsell best."
"Right well Sir knight ye have advisèd bin,"
Quoth then that aged man; "the way to win
Is wisely to advise: now day is spent;
Therefore with me ye may take up your In
For this same night." The knight was well content:
So with that godly father to his home they went.

34

A little lowly Hermitage it was,
Downe in a dale, hard by a forests side,
Far from resort of people, that did pas
In travell to and froe: a little wyde
There was an holy Chappell edifyde,
Wherein the Hermite dewly wont to say
His holy things each morne and eventyde:
Thereby a Christall streame did gently play,
Which from a sacred fountaine wellèd forth alway.

277. weare: spend. **280. wastfull:** desertlike. **284. later:** recent. **288. baite:** feed. **295. In:** inn. **301. wyde:** distance from it. **302. edifyde:** built. **303. wont:** was accustomed.

35

Arrivèd there, the little house they fill,
  Ne looke for entertainement, where none was:
  Rest is their feast, and all things at their will;
  The noblest mind the best contentment has.
  With faire discourse the evening so they pas:
  For that old man of pleasing wordes had store,
  And well could file his tongue as smooth as glas;
  He told of Saintes and Popes, and evermore
He strowd an *Ave-Mary* after and before.

36

The drouping Night thus creepeth on them fast,
  And the sad humour loading their eye liddes,
  As messenger of Morpheus on them cast
  Sweet slombring deaw, the which to sleepe them biddes.
  Unto their lodgings then his guests he riddes:
  Where when all drownd in deadly sleepe he findes,
  He to his study goes, and there amiddes
  His Magick bookes and artes of sundry kindes,
He seekes out mighty charmes, to trouble sleepy mindes.

37

Then choosing out few wordes most horrible
  (Let none them read), thereof did verses frame,
  With which and other spelles like terrible,
  He bade awake blacke Plutoes griesly Dame,
  And cursèd heaven, and spake reprochfull shame
  Of highest God, the Lord of life and light;
  A bold bad man, that dared to call by name
  Great Gorgon, Prince of darknesse and dead night,
At which Cocytus quakes, and Styx is put to flight.

38

And forth he cald out of deepe darknesse dred
  Legions of Sprights, the which like little flyes
  Fluttring about his ever damnèd hed,
  A-waite whereto their service he applyes,
  To aide his friends, or fray his enimies:
  Of those he chose out two, the falsest twoo,
  And fittest for to forge true-seeming lyes;
  The one of them he gave a message too,
The other by him selfe staide other worke to doo.

317. humour: moisture. **318. Morpheus:** god of sleep. **320. riddes:** dispatches. **328. Plutoes . . . Dame:** Proserpine, wife of Pluto, god of the underworld. **333. Cocytus . . . Styx:** rivers in the underworld. **338. fray:** frighten.

39

He making speedy way through spersèd ayre,
And through the world of waters wide and deepe,
To Morpheus house doth hastily repaire.
Amid the bowels of the earth full steepe,
And low, where dawning day doth never peepe,
His dwelling is; there Tethys his wet bed
Doth ever wash, and Cynthia still doth steepe
In silver deaw his ever-drouping hed,
Whiles sad Night over him her mantle black doth spred.

40

Whose double gates he findeth lockèd fast,
The one faire framed of burnisht Yvory,
The other all with silver overcast;
And wakefull dogges before them farre do lye,
Watching to banish Care their enimy,
Who oft is wont to trouble gentle Sleepe.
By them the Sprite doth passe in quietly,
And unto Morpheus comes, whom drownèd deepe
In drowsie fit he findes: of nothing he takes keepe.

41

And more, to lulle him in his slumber soft,
A trickling streame from high rocke tumbling downe
And ever-drizling raine upon the loft,
Mixt with a murmuring winde, much like the sowne
Of swarming Bees, did cast him in a swowne:
No other noyse, nor peoples troublous cryes,
As still are wont t'annoy the wallèd towne,
Might there be heard: but carelesse Quiet lyes,
Wrapt in eternall silence farre from enemyes.

42

The messenger approching to him spake,
But his wast wordes returnd to him in vaine:
So sound he slept, that nought mought him awake.
Then rudely he him thrust, and pusht with paine,
Whereat he gan to stretch: but he againe
Shooke him so hard, that forced him to speake.
As one then in a dreame, whose dryer braine
Is tost with troubled sights and fancies weake,
He mumbled soft, but would not all his silence breake.

343. spersèd: dispersed. **348. Tethys:** goddess of the sea. **349. Cynthia:** Diana, moon goddess. **360. keepe:** heed. **364. sowne:** sound. **365. swowne:** swoon. **367. still:** always. **371. wast:** wasted. **376. dryer braine:** Those who slept badly were thought to have too little moisture in the brain.

43

The Sprite then gan more boldly him to wake,
And threatned unto him the dreaded name
Of Hecate: whereat he gan to quake,
And lifting up his lumpish head, with blame
Halfe angry askèd him, for what he came.
"Hither," quoth he, "me Archimago sent,
He that the stubborne Sprites can wisely tame,
He bids thee to him send for his intent
A fit false dreame, that can delude the sleepers sent."

44

The God obayde, and calling forth straight way
A diverse dreame out of his prison darke,
Delivered it to him, and downe did lay
His heavie head, devoide of carefull carke,
Whose sences all were straight benumbd and starke.
He backe returning by the Yvorie dore,
Remounted up as light as chearefull Larke,
And on his litle winges the dreame he bore
In hast unto his Lord, where he him left afore.

45

Who all this while with charmes and hidden artes,
Had made a Lady of that other Spright,
And framed of liquid ayre her tender partes
So lively, and so like in all mens sight,
That weaker sence it could have ravisht quight
The maker selfe for all his wondrous witt,
Was nigh beguilèd with so goodly sight:
Her all in white he clad, and over it
Cast a blacke stole, most like to seeme for Una fit.

46

Now when that ydle dreame was to him brought
Unto that Elfin knight he bad him fly,
Where he slept soundly void of evill thought
And with false shewes abuse his fantasy,
In sort as he him schoolèd privily:
And that new creature borne without her dew
Full of the makers guile, with usage sly

381. Hecate: goddess of the dead. **384. Archimago:** archmagician. **385. Sprites:** spirits. **387. sent:** sense perception. **389. diverse:** varied. **391. carke:** burden. **393. Yvorie dore:** the Ivory Gate through which false dreams come, while true ones come from the gate of horn (Homer's *Odyssey,* XIX, 562*ff.*). **405. Una:** Latin for *one* or *unity;* meaning "the one true faith." **410. In sort:** in such a manner. **411. her dew:** her due (born in a natural way).

He taught to imitate that Lady trew,
Whose semblance she did carrie under feignèd hew.

47

Thus well instructed, to their worke they hast,
And comming where the knight in slomber lay
The one upon his hardy head him plast,
And made him dreame of loves and lustfull play
That nigh his manly hart did melt away,
Bathèd in wanton blis and wicked joy:
Then seemèd him his Lady by him lay,
And to him playnd, how that false wingèd boy
Her chast hart had subdewd, to learne Dame pleasures toy.

48

And she her selfe of beautie soveraigne Queene
Faire Venus seemde unto his bed to bring
Her, whom he waking evermore did weene
To be the chastest flowre, that ay did spring
On earthly braunch, the daughter of a king,
Now a loose Leman to vile service bound:
And eke the Graces seemèd all to sing,
Hymen iô Hymen, dauncing all around,
Whilst freshest Flora her with Yvie girlond crownd.

49

In this great passion of unwonted lust,
Or wonted feare of doing ought amis,
He started up, as seeming to mistrust
Some secret ill, or hidden foe of his:
Lo there before his face his Lady is,
Under blake stole hyding her bayted hooke,
And as halfe blushing offred him to kis,
With gentle blandishment and lovely looke,
Most like that virgin true, which for her knight him took.

50

All cleane dismayd to see so uncouth sight,
And halfe enragèd at her shamelesse guise,
He thought have slaine her in his fierce despight:
But hasty heat tempring with sufferance wise,
He stayde his hand, and gan himselfe advise
To prove his sense, and tempt her faignèd truth.
Wringing her hands in wemens pitteous wise,

414. hew: form. **422. playnd:** complained. **wingèd boy:** Cupid. **426. weene:** think. **427. ay:** always. **429. Leman:** lover. **432. Yvie:** ivy. **433. unwonted:** unaccustomed. **442. uncouth:** unfamiliar. **444. despight:** defiance.

Tho can she weepe, to stirre up gentle ruth,
Both for her noble bloud, and for her tender youth.

51

And said, "Ah Sir, my liege Lord and my love,
Shall I accuse the hidden cruell fate,
And mightie causes wrought in heaven above,
Or the blind God, that doth me thus amate,
For hopèd love to winne me certaine hate?
Yet thus perforce he bids me do, or die.
Die is my dew: yet rew my wretched state
You, whom my hard avenging destinie
Hath made judge of my life or death indifferently.

52

"Your owne deare sake forst me at first to leave
My Fathers kingdome." There she stopt with teares;
Her swollen hart her speach seemd to bereave,
And then againe begun, "My weaker yeares
Captived to fortune and frayle worldly feares,
Fly to your faith for succour and sure ayde:
Let me not dye in languor and long teares."
"Why Dame," quoth he, "what hath ye thus dismayd?
What frayes ye, that were wont to comfort me affrayd?"

53

"Love of your selfe," she said, "and deare constraint
Lets me not sleepe, but wast the wearie night
In secret anguish and unpittied plaint,
Whiles you in carelesse sleepe are drownèd quight."
Her doubtfull words made that redoubted knight
Suspect her truth: yet since no'untruth he knew,
Her fawning love with foule disdainefull spight
He would not shend, but said, "Deare dame I rew,
That for my sake unknowne such griefe unto you grew.

54

"Assure your selfe, it fell not all to ground;
For all so deare as life is to my hart,
I deeme your love, and hold me to you bound;
Ne let vaine feares procure your needlesse smart,
Where cause is none, but to your rest depart."
Not all content, yet seemd she to appease
Her mournefull plaintes, beguilèd of her art,

449. can she: began to. **ruth:** pity. **454. blind god:** Cupid. **amate:** daunt, confound. **469. deare:** dire. **473. redoubted:** dreaded. **476. shend:** put to shame. **483. appease:** stop.

And fed with words, that could not chuse but please,
So slyding softly forth, she turnd as to her ease.

55

Long after lay he musing at her mood,
Much grieved to thinke that gentle Dame so light,
For whose defence he was to shed his blood.
At last dull wearinesse of former fight
Having yrockt a sleepe his irkesome spright,
That troublous dreame gan freshly tosse his braine,
With bowres, and beds, and Ladies deare delight:
But when he saw his labour all was vaine,
With that misformèd spright he backe returned againe.

Book VII. Two Cantos of Mutabilitie

Canto VI

Proud Change (not pleasd, in mortall things,
beneath the Moon, to raigne)
Pretends, as well of Gods, as Men,
to be the Soveraine.

1

What man that sees the ever-whirling wheele
Of Change, the which all mortall things doth sway,
But that thereby doth find, and plainly feele,
How MUTABILITY in them doth play
Her cruell sports, to many mens decay?
Which that to all may better yet appeare,
I will rehearse that whylome I heard say,
How she at first her selfe began to reare,
Gainst all the Gods, and th' empire sought from them to beare.

2

But first, here falleth fittest to unfold
Her antique race and linage ancient,
As I have found it registred of old,
In Faery Land mongst records permanent:
She was, to weet, a daughter by descent
Of those old Titans, that did whylome strive

494. he: Archimago. MUTABILITY CANTOS Canto VI. **2. sway:** govern. **5. decay:** ruin. **6. that:** so that. **14. to weet:** to wit (that is to say). **15. Titans:** the original, primeval race of Gods in Greek mythology who preceded the Olympian gods of whom Zeus was king. **whylome:** once.

With Saturnes sonne for heavens regiment.
Whom, though high Jove of kingdome did deprive,
Yet many of their stemme long after did survive.

3

And many of them, afterwards obtained
Great power of Jove, and high authority;
As Hecatè, in whose almighty hand,
He plac't all rule and principality,
To be by her disposèd diversly,
To Gods, and men, as she them list divide:
And drad Bellona, that doth sound on hie
Warres and allarums unto Nations wide,
That makes both heaven and earth to tremble at her pride.

4

So likewise did this Titanesse aspire,
Rule and dominion to her selfe to gaine;
That as a Goddesse, men might her admire,
And heavenly honours yield, as to them twaine.
At first, on earth she sought it to obtaine;
Where she such proofe and sad examples shewed
Of her great power, to many ones great paine,
That not men onely (whom she soone subdewed)
But eke all other creatures, her bad dooings rewed.

5

For she the face of earthly things so changed,
That all which Nature had establisht first
In good estate, and in meet order ranged,
She did pervert, and all their statutes burst:
And all the worlds faire frame (which none yet durst
Of Gods or men to alter or misguide)
She altered quite, and made them all accurst
That God had blest; and did at first provide
In that still happy state for ever to abide.

6

Ne shee the lawes of Nature only brake,
But eke of Justice, and of Policie;
And wrong of right, and bad of good did make,
And death for life exchangèd foolishlie;
Since which, all living wights have learned to die,
And all this world is woxen daily worse.

16. regiment: rule. **21. Hecatè:** goddess of witches and that aspect of the moon deity concerned with the underworld. **24. list:** wished to. **30. admire:** wonder at. **39. meet:** appropriate. **50. wights:** creatures. **51. woxen:** grown.

O pittious worke of MUTABILITIE!
By which, we all are subject to that curse,
And death in stead of life have suckèd from our Nurse.

7

And now, when all the earth she thus had brought
To her behest, and thrallèd to her might,
She gan to cast in her ambitious thought,
T' attempt the empire of the heavens hight,
And Jove himself to shoulder from his right.
And first, she past the region of the ayre,
And of the fire, whose substance thin and slight,
Made no resistance, ne could her contraire,
But ready passage to her pleasure did prepaire.

8

Thence, to the Circle of the Moone she clambe,
Where Cynthia raignes in everlasting glory,
To whose bright shining palace straight she came,
All fairely deckt with heavens goodly story;
Whose silver gates (by which there sate an hory
Old aged Sire, with hower-glasse in hand,
Hight Tyme) she entred, were he liefe or sory;
Ne staide till she the highest stage had scand,
Where Cynthia did sit, that never still did stand.

9

Her sitting on an Ivory throne shee found,
Drawne of two steeds, th' one black, the other white,
Environd with tenne thousand starres around,
That duly her attended day and night;
And by her side, there ran her Page, that hight
Vesper, whom we the Evening-starre intend:
That with his Torche, still twinkling like twylight,
Her lightened all the way where she should wend,
And joy to weary wandring travailers did lend:

10

That when the hardy Titanesse beheld
The goodly building of her Palace bright,
Made of the heavens substance, and up-held
With thousand Crystall pillors of huge hight,
Shee gan to burne in her ambitious spright,
And t' envie her that in such glorie raigned.

57. cast: resolve. **62. contraire:** oppose. **64. clambe:** climbed. **67. story:** architecture. **70. Hight:** called. **liefe:** willing. **71. Ne:** nor. **stage:** floor. **scand:** reached. **78. intend:** call. **80. wend:** go.

Eftsoones she cast by force and tortious might,
Her to displace; and to her self to have gained
The kingdome of the Night, and waters by her wained.

11

Boldly she bid the Goddesse downe descend,
And let her selfe into that Ivory throne;
For, shee her selfe more worthy thereof wend,
And better able it to guide alone:
Whether to men, whose fall she did bemone,
Or unto Gods, whose state she did maligne,
Or to th' infernall powers, her need give lone
Of her faire light, and bounty most benigne,
Her selfe of all that rule shee deemèd most condigne.

12

But shee that had to her that soveraigne seat
By highest Jove assigned, therein to beare
Nights burning lamp, regarded not her threat,
Ne yielded ought for favour or for feare;
But with sterne countenaunce and disdainfull cheare,
Bending her hornèd browes, did put her back:
And boldly blaming her for comming there,
Bade her attonce from heavens coast to pack,
Or at her peril bide the wrathfull Thunders wrack.

13

Yet nathemore the Giantesse forbare:
But boldly preacing-on, raught forth her hand
To pluck her downe perforce from off her chaire;
And there-with lifting up her golden wand,
Threatened to strike her if she did with-stand.
Where-at the starres, which round about her blazed,
And eke the Moones bright wagon, still did stand,
All beeing with so bold attempt amazed,
And on her uncouth habit and sterne looke still gazed.

14

Meane-while, the lower World, which nothing knew
Of all that chauncèd here, was darkned quite;
And eke the heavens, and all the heavenly crew
Oh happy wights, now unpurvaide of light,

88. tortious: evil. **90. wained:** diminished (the tides of the ocean, subject to the moon's influence). **93. wend:** considered. **99. condigne:** worthy. **104. cheare:** mood. **109. nathemore:** not at all. **110. raught:** reached. **111. perforce:** by force. **121. unpurvaide of:** not supplied with.

Were much afraid, and wondred at that sight;
Fearing least Chaos broken had his chaine,
And brought againe on them eternall night:
But chiefely Mercury, that next doth raigne,
Ran forth in haste, unto the king of Gods to plaine.

15

All ran together with a great out-cry,
To Joves faire Palace, fixt in heavens hight;
And beating at his gates full earnestly,
Gan call to him aloud with all their might,
To know what meant that suddaine lack of light.
The father of the Gods when this he heard,
Was troubled much at their so strange affright,
Doubting least Typhon were againe upreared,
Or other his old foes, that once him sorely feared.

16

Eftsoones the sonne of Maia forth he sent
Downe to the Circle of the Moone, to knowe
The cause of this so strange astonishment,
And why shee did her wonted course forslowe,
And if that any were on earth belowe
That did with charmes or Magick her molest,
Him to attache, and downe to hell to throwe:
But, if from heaven it were, then to arrest
The Author, and him bring before his presence prest.

17

The wingd-foot God, so fast his plumes did beat,
That soone he came where-as the Titanesse
Was striving with fair Cynthia for her seat:
At whose strange sight, and haughty hardinesse,
He wondred much, and fearèd her no lesse.
Yet laying feare aside to doe his charge,
At last, he bade her, with bold stedfastnesse,
Cease to molest the Moone to walke at large,
Or come before high Jove, her dooings to discharge.

123. least: lest. **125. Mercury . . . next:** The planet Mercury (named after the messenger of the gods) was thought at the time to be the next higher sphere of the heavens after the moon. **126. plaine:** complain. **134. Typhon:** a monster born of Earth and Tartarus; confined beneath Mt. Aetna, from which he sent up volcanic fire. **135. feared:** frightened. **136. Eftsoones:** at once. **sonne of Maia:** Mercury. **139. forslowe:** delay. **142. attache:** capture. **144. prest:** rapidly. **148. hardinesse:** boldness. **150. charge:** assignment. **152. molest:** hinder. **153. discharge:** justify.

18

And there-with-all, he on her shoulder laid
His snaky-wreathèd Mace, whose awfull power
Doth make both Gods and hellish fiends affraid;
Where-at the Titanesse did sternely lower,
And stoutly answered, that in evill hower
He from his Jove such message to her brought,
To bid her leave faire Cynthias silver bower;
Sith shee his Jove and him esteemèd nought,
No more than Cynthia's selfe; but all their kingdoms sought.

19

The Heavens Herald staid not to reply,
But past away, his doings to relate
Unto his Lord; who now in th' highest sky,
Was placèd in his principall Estate,
With all the Gods about him congregate:
To whom when Hermes had his message told,
It did them all exceedingly amate,
Save Jove; who, changing nought his count'nance bold,
Did unto them at length these speeches wise unfold:

20

"Harken to mee awhile yee heavenly Powers;
Ye may remember since th' Earth's cursèd seed
Sought to assaile the heavens eternall towers,
And to us all exceeding feare did breed:
But how we then defeated all their deed,
Yee all doe knowe, and them destroièd quite;
Yet not so quite, but that there did succeed
An off-spring of their bloud, which did alite
Upon the fruitfull earth, which doth us yet despite.

21

"Of that bad seed is this bold woman bred,
That now with bold presumption doth aspire
To thrust faire Phoebe from her silver bed,
And eke ourselves from heavens high Empire,
If that her might were match to her desire:
Wherefore, it now behoves us to advise

155. snaky-wreathèd Mace: the caduceus (rod with two snakes wrapped around it), which had magic powers. **169. amate:** dismay. **173. since:** before this time. **cursèd seed:** the Titans. **179. off-spring:** The Titans, it was prophesied, would be destroyed, and humankind engendered from their blood. **180. despite:** despise. **186. advise:** think over.

What way is best to drive her to retire;
Whether by open force, or counsell wise,
Areed ye sonnes of God, as best ye can devise."

22

So having said, he ceast; and with his brow,
His black eye-brow, whose doomefull dreaded beck
Is wont to wield the world unto his vow,
And even the highest Powers of heaven to check,
Made signe to them in their degrees to speake:
Who straight gan cast their counsell grave and wise.
Meane-while, th' Earths daughter, thogh she nought did reck
Of Hermes message, yet gan now advise
What course were best to take in this hot bold emprize.

23

Eftsoones she thus resolved; that whilst the Gods,
After return of Hermes Embassie,
Were troubled, and amongst themselves at ods,
Before they could new counsels re-allie,
To set upon them in that extasie;
And take what fortune time and place would lend:
So, forth she rose, and through the purest sky
To Joves high Palace straight cast to ascend
To prosecute her plot: Good on-set boads good end.

24

Shee there arriving, boldly in did pass;
Where all the Gods she found in counsell close,
All quite unarmed, as then their manner was.
At sight of her they suddaine all arose,
In great amaze, ne wist what way to chose.
But Jove, all fearlesse, forced them to aby;
And in his soveraine throne, gan straight dispose
Himselfe more full of grace and Majestie,
That mote encheare his friends, and foes mote terrifie.

25

That, when the haughty Titanesse beheld,
All were she fraught with pride and impudence,
Yet with the sight thereof was almost queld;

189. Areed: advise. **191. beck:** movement. **192. wont:** accustomed. **vow:** will. **194. degrees:** ranks. **195. cast:** consider. **198. emprize:** enterprise. **202. re-allie:** form once again. **203. extasie:** bewilderment. **209. close:** secret. **212. ne wist:** nor knew. **213. aby:** stay. **214. dispose:** arrange. **216. mote:** might. **218. All were she:** Although she was.

And inly quaking, seemed as reft of sense,
And void of speech in that drad audience;
Untill that Jove himself, herself bespake:
"Speake thou fraile woman, speake with confidence,
Whence art thou, and what doost thou here now make?
What idle errand hast thou, earth's mansion to forsake?"

26

Shee, halfe confusèd with his great commaund,
Yet gathering spirit of her natures pride,
Him boldly answered thus to his demaund:
"I am a daughter, by the mothers side
Of her that is Grand-mother magnifide
Of all the Gods, great Earth, great Chaos child.
But by the fathers (be it not envide)
I greater am in bloud, whereon I build,
Then all the Gods, though wrongfully from heaven exiled.

27

"For Titan, as ye all acknowledge must,
Was Saturnes elder brother by birth-right,
Both sonnes of Uranus: but by unjust
And guilefull meanes, through Corybantès slight,
The younger thrust the elder from his right:
Since which, thou Jove, injuriously hast held
The Heavens rule from Titans sonnes by might;
And them to hellish dungeons downe hast feld:
Witnesse ye Heavens the truth of all that I have teld."

28

Whilst she thus spake, the Gods that gave good care
To her bold words, and markèd well her grace,
Beeing of stature tall as any there
Of all the Gods, and beautifull of face,
As any of the Goddesses in place,
Stood all astonied, like a sort of Steeres
Mongst whom, some beast of strange and forraine race,
Unwares is chaunc't, far straying from his peeres:
So did their ghastly gaze bewray their hidden feares.

221. drad: dread. **224. make:** do. **238. Corybantès slight:** *Slight* is trickery. The reference is to a myth that Saturn would devour his children when born lest the prophecy prove true that one of them would depose him. The Corybantes (attendants to the "Great Mother" in Eastern cults) distracted Saturn when one of his children was born and gave him a stone to eat instead of the child. **239. younger . . . elder:** The young Zeus (Jove) deposed Saturn. **242. feld:** thrown. **248. in place:** there. **249. sort:** herd. **252. bewray:** reveal.

29

Till having pauzed awhile, Jove thus bespake;
"Will never mortall thoughts ceasse to aspire,
In this bold sort, to Heaven claime to make,
And touch celestiall seates with earthly mire?
I would have thought, that bold Procrustès hire,
Or Typhons fall, or proud Ixions paine,
Or great Prometheus, tasting of our ire,
Would have suffized, the rest for to restraine;
And warned all men by their example to refraine;

30

"But now, this off-scum of that cursèd fry,
Dare to renew the like bold enterprize,
And chalenge th' heritage of this our skie;
Whom what should hinder, but that we likewise
Should handle as the rest of her allies,
And thunder-drive to hell?" With that, he shooke
His Nectar-deawèd locks, with which the skyes
And all the world beneath for terror quooke,
And eft his burning levin-brond in hand he tooke.

31

But when he lookèd on her lovely face,
In which, faire beames of beauty did appeare,
That could the greatest wrath soone turne to grace
(Such sway doth beauty even in Heaven beare)
He staide his hand; and having changed his cheare,
He thus againe in milder wise began;
"But ah! if Gods should strive with flesh yfere,
Then shortly should the progeny of Man
Be rooted out, if Jove should doe still what he can.

32

"But thee faire Titans child, I rather weene,
Through some vaine errour or inducement light,
To see that mortall eyes have never seene;

257. Procrustes hire: *Hire* here means punishment. The reference is to Procrustes, who forced his guests to fit the beds he provided by stretching them if they were too short, or cutting off their legs if they were too tall. His punishment was that he was made to fit his own bed, in the same way, by Theseus. **258. Typhons:** See line 134. **Ixion:** a king who was bound to a constantly revolving fiery wheel for attempting to seduce Zeus's wife, Hera. **259. Prometheus:** Because he stole fire from the gods and gave it to men, Zeus punished him by having him chained, while an eagle daily plucked at his liver. **269. quooke:** quaked. **270. eft:** then. **levin-brond:** lightning flash. **274. sway:** power. **275. cheare:** mood. **277. flesh yfere:** against flesh. **279. still:** always. **280. weene:** think. **281. light:** frivolous. **282. that:** what.

Or through ensample of thy sisters might,
Bellona; whose great glory thou dost spight,
Since thou hast seene her dreadfull power belowe,
Mongst wretched men, dismaide with her affright,
To bandie Crownes, and Kingdomes to bestowe;
And sure thy worth, no less then hers doth seem to showe.

33

"But wote thou this, thou hardy Titanesse,
That not the worth of any living wight
May challenge ought in Heavens interesse;
Much lesse the Title of old Titans Right:
For we by Conquest of our soveraine might,
And by eternall doome of Fates decree,
Have wonne the Empire of the Heavens bright;
Which to our selves we hold, and to whom wee
Shall worthy deeme partakers of our blisse to bee.

34

"Then cease thy idle claime thou foolish gerle,
And seeke by grace and goodnesse to obtaine
That place from which by folly Titan fell;
There-to thou maist perhaps, if so thou faine
Have Jove thy gratious Lord and Soveraigne."
So, having said, she thus to him replide,
"Ceasse Saturnes sonne, to seeke by proffers vaine
Of idle hopes t' allure me to thy side,
For to betray my Right, before I have it tride.

35

"But thee, O Jove, no equall Judge I deeme
Of my desert, or of my dewfull Right;
That in thine owne behalfe maist partiall seeme:
But to the highest him, that is behight
Father of Gods and men by equall might;
To weet, the God of Nature, I appeale."
There-at Jove wexèd wroth, and in his spright
Did inly grudge, yet did it well conceale;
And bade Dan Phoebus Scribe her Appellation seale.

284. Bellona: goddess of war. **spight:** envy. **287. bandie:** toss about. **289. wote:** know. **301. faine:** wish. **306. For to:** in order to. **307. equall:** open-minded (or objective). **308. dewfull:** due. **315. Dan Phoebus Scribe:** Phoebus (Apollo) was called scribe, or secretary, to the gods because he was also god of poetry. **Appellation:** appeal.

36

Eftsoones the time and place appointed were,
Where all, both heavenly Powers, and earthly wights,
Before great Natures presence should appeare,
For triall of their Titles and best Rights:
That was, to weet, upon the highest hights
Of Arlo-hill (Who knowes not Arlo-hill?)
That is the highest head, in all mens sights,
Of my old father Mole, whom Shepheards quill
Renowmèd hath with hymmes fit for a rurall skill.

37

And, were it not ill fitting for this file,
To sing of hilles and woods, mongst warres and Knights,
I would abate the sternenesse of my stile,
Mongst these sterne stounds to mingle soft delights;
And tell how Arlo through Dianaes spights
(Being of old the best and fairest Hill
That was in all this holy-Islands hights)
Was made the most unpleasant, and most ill.
Meane while, O Clio, lend Calliope thy quill.

38

Whylome, when Ireland florishèd in fame
Of wealths and goodnesse, far above the rest
Of all that beare the British Islands name,
The Gods then used, for pleasure and for rest,
Oft to resort there-to, when seemed them best:
But none of all there-in more pleasure found,
Then Cynthia; that is soveraine Queene profest
Of woods and forrests, which therein abound,
Sprinkled with wholsom waters, more then most on ground.

39

But mongst them all, as fittest for her game,
Either for chace of beasts with hound or boawe,
Or for to shroude in shade from Phoebus flame,
Or bathe in fountaines that doe freshly flowe,
Or from high hilles, or from the dales belowe,
She chose this Arlo; where she did resort
With all her Nymphes enrangèd on a rowe,
With whom the woody Gods did oft consort:
For with the Nymphes, the Satyres love to play and sport.

325. file: story. **328. stounds:** conflicts. **333. Clio . . . Calliope:** The poet asks Clio, the muse of history, to now give her pen to his own inspiration—Calliope, the muse of epic poetry. **340. Cynthia:** Diana, goddess of the moon and of hunting. **profest:** acknowledged. **343. game:** play. **351. Satyres:** minor wood gods, given to drink and lust.

40

Amongst the which, there was a Nymph that hight
Molanna; daughter of old father Mole,
And sister unto Mulla, faire and bright:
Unto whose bed false Bregog whylome stole,
That Shepheard Colin dearely did condole,
And made her lucklesse loves well knowne to be.
But this Molanna, were she not so shole,
Were no lesse faire and beautifull then shee:
Yet as she is, a fairer flood may no man see.

41

For, first, she springs out of two marble Rocks,
On which, a grove of Oakes high mounted growes,
That as a girlond seemes to deck the locks
Of som faire Bride, brought forth with pompous showes
Out of her bowre, that many flowers strowes:
So, through the flowry Dales she tumbling downe,
Through many woods, and shady coverts flowes,
That on each side her silver channell crowne,
Till to the Plaine she come, whose Valleyes shee doth drowne.

42

In her sweet streames, Diana used oft,
After her sweatie chace and toilsome play,
To bathe her selfe; and after, on the soft
And downy grasse, her dainty limbes to lay
In covert shade, where none behold her may:
For much she hated sight of living eye.
Foolish God Faunus, though full many a day
He saw her clad, yet longèd foolishly
To see her naked mongst her Nymphes in privity.

43

No way he found to compasse his desire,
But to corrupt Molanna, this her maid,
Her to discover for some secret hire:
So, her with flattering words he first assaid;
And after, pleasing gifts for her purvaid,
Queene-apples, and red Cherries from the tree,
With which he her allurèd and betraid
To tell what time he might her Lady see
When she her selfe did bathe, that he might secret bee.

353–56. Molanna: the river Behanna in Ireland, renamed by Spenser as a combination of *Mole* and *Behanna*. **Mulla:** the name of the nearby river Awbeg. **Bregog:** a third river, mentioned in Spenser's poem "Colin Clout Comes Home Again." **356. condole:** lament. **358. shole:** shallow. **364. pompous:** splendid. **379. compasse:** accomplish. **381. discover:** reveal. **hire:** bribe. **384. Queene-apples:** quinces.

44

There-to hee promist, if shee would him pleasure
With this small boone, to quit her with a better;
To weet, that where-as shee had out of measure
Long loved the Fanchin, who by nought did set her,
That he would undertake, for this to get her
To be his Love, and of him likèd well:
Besides all which, he vowed to be her debter
For many moe good turnes then he would tell:
The least of which, this little pleasure should excell.

45

The simple maid did yield to him anone;
And eft him placèd where he close might view
That never any saw, save onely one;
Who, for his hire to so foole-hardy dew,
Was of his hounds devoured in Hunters hew.
Tho as her manner was on sunny day,
Diana, with her Nymphes about her, drew
To this sweet spring; where, doffing her array,
She bathed her lovely limbes, for Jove a likely pray.

46

There Faunus saw that pleasèd much his eye,
And made his hart to tickle in his brest,
That for great joy of some-what he did spy,
He could him not contain in silent rest,
But breaking forth in laughter, loud profest
His foolish thought. A foolish Faune indeed,
That couldst not hold thy selfe so hidden blest,
But wouldest needs thine own conceit areed.
Babblers unworthy been of so divine a meed.

47

The Goddesse, all abashèd with that noise,
In haste forth started from the guilty brooke;
And running straight where-as she heard his voice,
Enclosed the bush about, and there him tooke,
Like darrèd Larke; not daring up to looke
On her whose sight before so much he sought.
Thence, forth they drew him by the hornes, and shooke
Nigh all to peeces, that they left him nought;
And then into the open light they forth him brought.

389. quit: reward. **391. Fanchin:** the river Funsheon, into which the Behanna (Molanna) flows. **nought . . . her:** set no store by her. **399. that:** that which. **400. hire:** punishment. **401. hew:** slaughter. **402. Tho:** then. **405. pray:** prey. **412. so:** thus. **413. areed:** declare. **414. meed:** reward. **419. darrèd:** trapped.

48

Like as an huswife, that with busie care
Thinks of her Dairie to make wondrous gaine,
Finding where-as some wicked beast unware
That breakes into her Dayr'house, there doth draine
Her creaming pannes, and frustrate all her paine;
Hath in some snare or gin set close behind,
Entrappèd him, and caught into her traine,
Then thinkes what punishment were best assigned,
And thousand deathes deviseth in her vengefull mind:

49

So did Diana and her maydens all
Use silly Faunus, now within their baile;
They mocke and scorne him, and him foule miscall;
Some by the nose him pluckt, some by the taile,
And by his goatish beard some did him haile:
Yet he, poore soule, with patience all did beare;
For, nought against their wils might countervaile:
Ne ought he said, what ever he did heare;
But hanging downe his head, did like a Mome appeare.

50

At length, when they had flouted him their fill,
They gan to cast what penaunce him to give.
Some would have gelt him, but that same would spill
The Wood-gods breed, which must for ever live:
Others would through the river him have drive,
And duckèd deepe; but that seemed penaunce light;
But most agreed and did this sentence give,
Him in Deares skin to clad; and in that plight,
To hunt him with their hounds, him selfe save how hee might.

51

But Cynthia's selfe, more angry then the rest,
Thought not enough, to punish him in sport,
And of her shame to make a gamesome jest;
But gan examine him in straighter sort,
Which of her Nymphes, or other close consort,
Him thither brought, and her to him betraid?
He, much affeard, to her confessèd short,
That 'twas Molanna which her so bewraid.
Then all attonce their hands upon Molanna laid.

424. huswife: housewife. **426. unware:** secretly. **429. gin:** trap. **430. traine:** trap. **434. baile:** custody. **435. miscall:** revile. **437. haile:** pull. **441. Mome:** fool. **444. gelt:** castrated. **that same would spill:** that castration would destroy. **454. straighter:** stricter. **455. consort:** companions.

52

But him, according as they had decreed,
With a Deeres-skin they covered, and then chast
With all their hounds that after him did speed;
But he more speedy, from them fled more fast
Then any Deere: so sore him dread aghast.
They after followed all with shrill outcry,
Shouting as they the heavens would have brast:
That all the woods and dales where he did flie,
Did ring againe, and loud reeccho to the skie.

53

So they him followed till they weary were,
When, back returning to Molann' againe,
They, by commaundment of Diana, there
Her whelmed with stones. Yet Faunus, for her pain,
Of her beloved Fanchin did obtaine,
That her he would receive unto his bed.
So now her waves passe through a pleasant Plaine,
Till with the Fanchin she her selfe doe wed,
And, both combined, themselves in one faire river spred.

54

Nath'lesse, Diana, full of indignation,
Thence-forth abandoned her delicious brooke;
In whose sweet streame, before that bad occasion,
So much delight to bathe her limbes she tooke:
Ne onely her, but also quite forsooke
All those faire forrests about Arlo hid,
And all that Mountaine, which doth over-looke
The richest champian that may else be rid,
And the faire Shure, in which are thousand Salmons bred.

55

Them all, and all that she so deare did way,
Thence-forth she left; and parting from the place,
There-on an heavy haplesse curse did lay,
To weet, that Wolves, where she was wont to space,
Should harboured be, and all those Woods deface,
And Thieves should rob and spoile that Coast around.
Since which, those Woods, and all that goodly Chase,
Doth to this day with Wolves and Thieves abound:
Which too-too true that lands in-dwellers since have found.

466. brast: burst. **472. whelmed . . . stones:** filled it with stones (indicating how shallow the river was). **485. champian:** field. **rid:** seen. **486. Shure:** the river Suir in Ireland. **487. way:** esteem. **490. space:** roam. **492. Coast:** area. **493. Chase:** hunting ground.

Canto VII

Pealing, from Jove, to Natur's Bar,
bold Alteration pleades
Large Evidence: but Nature soone
her righteous Doome areads.

1

Ah! whither doost thou now thou greater Muse
Me from these woods and pleasing forrests bring?
And my fraile spirit (that dooth oft refuse
This too high flight, unfit for her weake wing)
Lift up aloft, to tell of heavens King
(Thy soveraine Sire) his fortunate successe,
And victory, in bigger noates to sing,
Which he obtained against that Titanesse,
That him of heavens Empire sought to dispossesse.

2

Yet sith I needs must follow thy behest,
Doe thou my weaker wit with skill inspire,
Fit for this turne, and in my feeble brest
Kindle fresh sparks of that immortall fire,
Which learned minds inflameth with desire
Of heavenly things: for, who but thou alone,
That art yborne of heaven and heavenly Sire,
Can tell things doen in heaven so long ygone;
So farre past memory of man that may be knowne.

3

Now, at the time that was before agreed,
The Gods assembled all on Arlo hill;
As well those that are sprung of heavenly seed,
As those that all the other world doe fill,
And rule both sea and land unto their will:
Onely th' infernall Powers might not appeare:
Aswell for horror of their count'naunce ill,
As for th' unruly fiends which they did feare;
Yet Pluto and Proserpina were present there.

Canto VII. Quatrain. **Pealing:** appealing. **Alteration:** Mutability. **areads:** makes judgment. **1. greater Muse:** Clio, muse of history. **3. refuse:** turn back from. **6. Sire:** Zeus, grandfather of the Muses. **10. sith:** since. **12. turne:** performance. **20. Arlo hill:** near Spenser's home at Kilcolman Castle, Ireland. **22. other world:** the earth. **27. Pluto . . . Proserpina:** King and Queen of the Underworld.

4

And thither also came all other creatures,
What-ever life or motion doe retaine,
According to their sundry kinds of features;
That Arlo scarsly could them all containe;
So full they fillèd every hill and Plaine:
And had not Natures Sergeant (that is Order)
Them well disposèd by his busie paine,
And raungèd farre abroad in every border,
They would have causèd much confusion and disorder.

5

Then forth issewed (great goddesse) great dame Nature,
With goodly port and gracious Majesty:
Being far greater and more tall of stature
Then any of the gods or Powers on hie:
Yet certes by her face and physnomy,
Whether she man or woman inly were,
That could not any creature well descry:
For, with a veile that wimpled every where,
Her head and face was hid, that mote to none appeare.

6

That some doe say was so by skill devized,
To hide the terror of her uncouth hew,
From mortall eyes that should be sore agrized
For that her face did like a Lion shew,
That eye of wight would not indure to view:
But others tell that it so beautious was,
And round about such beames of splendor threw,
That it the Sunne a thousand times did pass,
Ne could be seene, but like an image in a glass.

7

That well may seemen true: for, well I weene
That this same day, when she on Arlo sat,
Her garment was so bright and wondrous sheene,
That my fraile wit cannot devize to what
It to compare, nor finde like stuffe to that,
As those three sacred Saints, though else most wise,
Yet on mount Thabor quite their wits forgat,
When they their glorious Lord in strange disguise
Transfigured sawe; his garments so did daze their eyes.

41. physnomy: face. **44. wimpled:** folded up. **47. uncouth hew:** unfamiliar appearance. **48. agrized:** terrified. **53. pass:** surpass. **57. sheene:** beautiful. **60–63. Saints . . . eyes:** John, James, and Peter saw Christ transfigured on a mountain (Matthew 17:1–8).

8

In a fayre Plaine upon an equal Hill,
  She placèd was in a pavilion;
  Not such as Crafts-men by their idle skill
  Are wont for Princes states to fashion:
  But th' earth her self of her owne motion,
  Out of her fruitfull bosome made to growe
  Most dainty trees; that, shooting up anon,
  Did seeme to bow their bloosming heads full lowe,
For homage unto her, and like a throne did shew.

9

So hard it is for any living wight,
  All her array and vestiments to tell,
  That old Dan Geffrey (in whose gentle spright
  The pure well head of Poesie did dwell)
  In his *Foules parley* durst not with it mel,
  But it transferd to Alane, who he thought
  Had in his *Plaint of kindes* described it well:
  Which who will read set forth so as it ought,
Go seek he out that Alane where he may be sought.

10

And all the earth far underneath her feete
  Was dight with flowres, that voluntary grew
  Out of the ground, and sent forth odours sweet;
  Tenne thousand mores of sundry sent and hew,
  That might delight the smell, or please the view:
  The which, the Nymphes, from all the brooks thereby
  Had gatherèd, which they at her foot-stoole threw;
  That richer seemed then any tapestry,
That Princes bowres adorne with painted imagery.

11

And Mole himselfe, to honour her the more,
  Did deck himself in freshest faire attire,
  And his high head, that seemeth alwaies hore
  With hardned frosts of former winters ire,
  He with an Oaken girlond now did tire,
  As if the love of some new Nymph late seene,
  Had in him kindled youthfull fresh desire,
  And made him change his gray attire to greene:
Ah gentle Mole! such joyance hath thee well beseene.

66. idle: vain. **67. states:** thrones. **75. Dan:** Sir. **75–79. Geffrey . . . well:** Geoffrey Chaucer, who in his *Parliament of Fowls* (lines 316–18) refers to a work by Alanus de Insulis as *Pleynt of Kind* (Complaint of Nature). **77. mel:** meddle. **83. dight:** ornamented. **voluntary:** uncultivated. **85. mores:** plants. **95. girlond:** garland. **tire:** attire or adorn. **99. beseene:** ornamented.

12

Was never so great joyance since the day,
  That all the gods whylome assembled were,
  On Haemus hill in their divine array,
  To celebrate the solemne bridall cheare,
  Twixt Peleus, and dame Thetis pointed there:
  Where Phoebus self, that god of Poets hight,
  They say did sing the spousall hymne full cleere,
  That all the gods were ravisht with delight
Of his celestiall song, and Musicks wondrous might.

13

This great Grandmother of all creatures bred
  Great Nature, ever young yet full of eld,
  Still mooving, yet unmovèd from her sted;
  Unseene of any, yet of all beheld;
  Thus sitting in her throne as I have teld,
  Before her came dame Mutabilitie;
  And being lowe before her presence feld,
  With meek obaysance and humilitie,
Thus gan her plaintif Plea, with words to amplifie:

14

"To thee O greatest goddesse, onely great,
  An humble suppliant loe, I lowely fly
  Seeking for Right, which I of thee entreat;
  Who Right to all dost deal indifferently,
  Damning all Wrong and tortious Injurie,
  Which any of thy creatures doe to other
  (Oppressing them with power, unequally)
  Sith of them all thou art the equall mother,
And knittest each to each, as brother unto brother.

15

"To thee therefore of this same Jove I plaine,
  And of his fellow gods that faine to be,
  That challenge to themselves the whole worlds raign:
  Of which, the greatest part is due to me,
  And heaven it selfe by heritage in Fee:
  For, heaven and earth I both alike do deeme,
  Sith heaven and earth are both alike to thee;
  And, gods no more than men thou doest esteeme:
For, even the gods to thee, as men to gods do seeme.

104. Peleus . . . Thetis: parents of Achilles. **pointed:** appointed. **110. eld:** age. **111. sted:** place. **115. feld:** felled. **118. onely:** uniquely. **121. indifferently:** impartially. **122. tortious:** wicked. **128. faine:** pretend. **129. challenge:** claim. **131. in Fee:** legally.

16

"Then weigh, O soveraigne goddesse, by what right
These gods do claime the worlds whole soverainty;
And that is onely dew unto thy might
Arrogate to themselves ambitiously:
As for the gods owne principality,
Which Jove usurpes unjustly; that to be
My heritage, Jove's self cannot deny,
From my great Grandsire Titan, unto mee,
Derived by dew descent; as is well knowen to thee.

17

"Yet mauger Jove, and all his gods beside,
I doe possesse the worlds most regiment,
As, if ye please it into parts divide,
And every parts inholders to convent,
Shall to your eyes appeare incontinent.
And first, the Earth (great mother of us all)
That only seems unmoved and permanent,
And unto Mutability not thrall;
Yet is she changed in part, and eeke in generall.

18

"For, all that from her springs, and is ybredde,
How-ever fayre it flourish for a time,
Yet see we soone decay; and, being dead,
To turne again unto their earthly slime:
Yet, out of their decay and mortall crime,
We daily see new creatures to arize;
And of their Winter spring another Prime,
Unlike in forme, and changed by strange disguise:
So turne they still about, and change in restlesse wise.

19

"As for her tenants; that is, man and beasts,
The beasts we daily see massàcred dy,
As thralls and vassalls unto mens beheasts:
And men themselves doe change continually
From youth to eld, from wealth to poverty,
From good to bad, from bad to worst of all.
Ne doe their bodies only flit and fly:
But eeke their minds (which they immortall call)
Still change and vary thoughts, as new occasions fall.

138. that: that which. **145. mauger:** despite. **146. regiment:** rule. **148. inholders:** tenants. **convent:** call together. **149. incontinent:** immediately. **158. crime:** corruption. **160. Prime:** spring (of the year).

20

"Ne is the water in more constant case;
  Whether those same on high, or these belowe.
  For, th' Ocean moveth stil, from place to place;
  And every River still doth ebbe and flowe:
  Ne any Lake, that seems most still and slowe,
  Ne Poole so small, that can his smoothnesse holde,
  When any winde doth under heaven blowe;
  With which, the clouds are also tost and rolled;
Now like great Hills; and, streight, like sluces, them unfold.

21

"So likewise are all watry living wights
  Still tost, and turnèd, with continuall change,
  Never abyding in their stedfast plights.
  The fish, still floting, doe at randon range,
  And never rest; but evermore exchange
  Their dwelling places, as the streames them carrie:
  Ne have the watry foules a certaine grange,
  Wherein to rest, ne in one stead do tarry;
But flitting still doe flie, and still their places vary.

22

"Next is the Ayre: which who feeles not by sense
  (For, of all sense it is the middle meane)
  To flit still? and, with subtill influence
  Of his thin spirit, all creatures to maintaine,
  In state of life? O weake life! that does leane
  On thing so tickle as th' unsteady ayre;
  Which every howre is changed, and altred cleane
  With every blast that bloweth fowle or faire:
The faire doth it prolong; the fowle doth it impaire.

23

"Therein the changes infinite beholde,
  Which to her creatures every minute chaunce;
  Now, boyling hot: streight, friezing deadly cold:
  Now, faire sun-shine, that makes all skip and daunce:
  Streight, bitter storms and balefull countenance,
  That makes them all to shiver and to shake:
  Rayne, hayle, and snowe do pay them sad penance,
  And dreadful thunder-claps (that make them quake)
With flames and flashing lights that thousand changes make.

173. same on high: the clouds. **175. still:** always. **180. streight:** immediately. **184. floting:** swimming. **187. grange:** dwelling. **188. stead:** place. **191. meane:** medium. **195. tickle:** unstable.

24

"Last is the fire: which, though it live for ever,
Ne can be quenchèd quite; yet, every day,
Wee see his parts, so soone as they do sever,
To lose their heat, and shortly to decay;
So, makes himself his owne consuming pray.
Ne any living creatures doth he breed:
But all, that are of others bredd, doth slay;
And, with their death, his cruell life dooth feed;
Nought leaving but their barren ashes, without seede.

25

"Thus, all these fower (the which the ground-work bee
Of all the world, and of all living wights)
To thousand sorts of Change we subject see.
Yet are they changed (by other wondrous slights)
Into themselves, and lose their native mights;
The Fire to Aire, and th' Ayre to Water sheere,
And Water into Earth: yet Water fights
With Fire, and Aire with Earth approaching neere:
Yet all are in one body, and as one appeare.

26

"So, in them all raignes Mutabilitie;
How-ever these, that Gods themselves do call,
Of them doe claime the rule and soverainty:
As, Vesta, of the fire aethereall;
Vulcan, of this, with us so usuall;
Ops, of the earth; and Juno of the Ayre;
Neptune, of Seas; and Nymphes, of Rivers all.
For, all those Rivers to me subject are:
And all the rest, which they usurp, be all my share.

27

"Which to approven true, as I have told,
Vouchsafe, O goddesse, to thy presence call
The rest which doe the world in being hold:
As, times and seasons of the yeare that fall:
Of all the which, demand in generall,
Or judge thy selfe, by verdit of thine eye,
Whether to me they are not subject all."
Nature did yeeld thereto; and by-and-by,
Bade Order call them all, before her Majesty.

217. fower: four. **220. slights:** tricks. **222. sheere:** clear. **230. Vulcan:** god of fire (earthly fire—hence "with us," on earth), as contrasted with Vesta, goddess of heavenly fire. **235. approven:** prove. **237. hold:** maintain.

28

So, forth issewed the Seasons of the yeare;
First, lusty Spring, all dight in leaves of flowres
That freshly budded and new bloosmes did beare
(In which a thousand birds had built their bowres
That sweetly sung, to call forth Paramours):
And in his hand a javelin he did beare,
And on his head (as fit for warlike stoures)
A guilt engraven morion he did weare;
That as some did him love, so others did him feare.

29

Then came the jolly Sommer, being dight
In a thin silken cassock coloured greene,
That was unlynèd all, to be more light:
And on his head a girlond well beseene
He wore, from which as he had chauffèd been
The sweat did drop; and in his hand he bore
A boawe and shaftes, as he in forrest greene
Had hunted late the Libbard or the Bore,
And now would bathe his limbes, with labor heated sore.

30

Then came the Autumne all in yellow clad,
As though he joyèd in his plentious store,
Laden with fruits that made him laugh, full glad
That he had banisht hunger, which to-fore
Had by the belly oft him pinchèd sore.
Upon his head a wreath that was enrold
With eares of corne, of every sort he bore:
And in his hand a sickle he did holde,
To reape the ripened fruits the which the earth had yold.

31

Lastly, came Winter cloathed all in frize,
Chattering his teeth for cold that did him chill,
Whil'st on his hoary beard his breath did freese;
And the dull drops that from his purpled bill
As from a limbeck did adown distill.
In his right hand a tippèd staffe he held,
With which his feeble steps he stayèd still:
For, he was faint with cold, and weak with eld;
That scarse his loosèd limbes he hable was to weld.

250. stoures: conflicts. **251. morion:** helmet. **257. chauffèd:** heated. **260. Libbard:** leopard. **Bore:** boar. **270. yold:** yielded. **271. frize:** heavy wood cloth. **274. bill:** nose.

32

These, marching softly, thus in order went,
  And after them, the Monthes all riding came;
  First, sturdy March with brows full sternly bent,
  And armèd strongly, rode upon a Ram,
  The same which over Hellespontus swam:
  Yet in his hand a spade he also hent,
  And in a bag all sorts of seeds ysame,
  Which on the earth he strowèd as he went,
And fild her womb with fruitfull hope of nourishment.

33

Next came fresh Aprill full of lustyhed,
  And wanton as a Kid whose horne new buds:
  Upon a Bull he rode, the same which led
  Europa floting through th' Argolick fluds:
  His hornes were gilden all with golden studs
  And garnishèd with garlonds goodly dight
  Of all the fairest flowres and freshest buds
  Which th' earth brings forth, and wet he seemed in sight
With waves, through which he waded for his love's delight.

34

Then came faire May, the fayrest mayd on ground,
  Deckt all with dainties of her seasons pryde,
  And throwing flowres out of her lap around:
  Upon two brethrens shoulders she did ride,
  The twinnes of Leda; which on eyther side
  Supported her like to their soveraine Queene.
  Lord! how all creatures laught, when her they spide,
  And leapt and daunc't as they had ravisht beene!
And Cupid selfe about her fluttred all in greene.

35

And after her, came jolly June, arrayd
  All in greene leaves, as he a Player were;
  Yet in his time, he wrought as well as playd,

279. loosèd: weak. **weld:** control. **280. softly:** slowly. **282. First . . . March:** March was the first month of the year in the old (Julian) calendar until the Gregorian calendar was adopted in England in 1752. **283–84. Ram . . . swam:** The ram refers to the constellation Aries (the Ram) prominent in March as well as to the story of the winged ram of the Golden Fleece, which carried Helle across the Hellespont until she fell off and was drowned (whence the name Hellespont). **285. hent:** held. **286. ysame:** together. **289. lustyhed:** health (lustiness). **291–92. Bull . . . fluds:** Zeus, in the form of a bull, swam with Europa to Crete across the Greek waters (*Argolick fluds*). **297 love's:** Europa's. **302. twinnes of Leda:** Castor and Pollux, the Gemini. **305. ravisht:** caught up in delight. **308. Player:** actor. **309. wrought:** worked.

That by his plough-yrons mote right well appeare:
Upon a Crab he rode, that him did beare
With crooked crawling steps an uncouth pase,
And backward yode, as Bargemen wont to fare
Bending their force contrary to their face,
Like that ungracious crew which faines demurest grace.

36

Then came hot July boyling like to fire,
That all his garments he had cast away:
Upon a Lyon raging yet with ire
He boldly rode and made him to obay:
It was the beast that whylome did forray
The Nemaean forrest, till th' Amphytrionide
Him slew, and with his hide did him array;
Behinde his back a sithe, and by his side
Under his belt he bore a sickle circling wide.

37

The sixt was August, being rich arrayd
In garment all of gold downe to the ground
Yet rode he not, but led a lovely Mayd
Forth by the lilly hand, the which was cround
With eares of corne, and full her hand was found;
That was the righteous Virgin, which of old
Lived here on earth, and plenty made abound;
But, after Wrong was loved and Justice solde,
She left th' unrighteous world and was to heaven extold.

38

Next him, September marchèd eeke on foote;
Yet was he heavy laden with the spoyle
Of harvests riches, which he made his boot,
And him enricht with bounty of the soyle:
In his one hand, as fit for harvests toyle,
He held a knife-hook; and in th' other hand
A paire of waights, with which he did assoyle
Both more and lesse, where it in doubt did stand,
And equall gave to each as Justice duly scanned.

310. plough-yrons: plowshare. **311. Crab:** Cancer, where the sun starts moving "backward" toward the south after June 21. **313. yode:** went. **318–21. Lyon . . . Amphytrionide:** The constellation Leo (the Lion) is identified with the Nemean lion killed by Hercules, son of Amphitryon. **330. Virgin:** Astraea, goddess of Justice. **333. extold:** raised. **336. boot:** booty. **340. assoyle:** determine. **342. scanned:** measured.

39

Then came October full of merry glee:
  For, yet his noule was totty of the must,
  Which he was treading in the wine-fats see,
  And of the joyous oyle, whose gentle gust
  Made him so frollick and so full of lust:
  Upon a dreadfull Scorpion he did ride,
  The same which by Dianaes doom unjust
  Slew great Orion: and eeke by his side
He had his ploughing share, and coulter ready tyde.

40

Next was November, he full grosse and fat,
  As fed with lard, and that right well might seeme;
  For, he had been a fatting hogs of late,
  That yet his browes with sweat, did reek and steem,
  And yet the season was full sharp and breem;
  In planting eeke he took no small delight:
  Whereon he rode, not easie was to deeme;
  For it a dreadfull Centaure was in sight,
The seed of Saturne and faire Naïs, Chiron hight.

41

And after him, came next the chill December:
  Yet he through merry feasting which he made,
  And great bonfires, did not the cold remember;
  His Saviours birth his mind so much did glad:
  Upon a shaggy-bearded Goat he rode,
  The same wherewith Dan Jove in tender yeares,
  They say, was nourisht by th' Idaean mayd;
  And in his hand a broad deepe boawle he beares;
Of which, he freely drinks an health to all his peeres.

42

Then came old January, wrappèd well
  In many weeds to keep the cold away;
  Yet did he quake and quiver like to quell,
  And blowe his nayles to warme them if he may:
  For, they were numbd with holding all the day

344. noule . . . must: his head was befuddled (*totty*) with the wine-mash (*must*). **345. see:** pool (sea). **346. gust:** taste. **347. lust:** pleasure. **348–50. Scorpion . . . Orion:** Diana sent a scorpion to kill the hunter Orion. **351. coulter:** cutting edge of plow. **356. breem:** bitter. **359–60. Centaure . . . Chiron:** Charon, the centaur, was the child of Saturn and Naïs. **365. Goat:** Capricorn, who nourished Zeus when he was hiding from Saturn. **367. Idaean mayd:** nymph of Mt. Ida, Crete. **372. quell:** die.

An hatchet keene, with which he fellèd wood,
And from the trees did lop the needlesse spray:
Upon an huge great Earth-pot steane he stood;
From whose wide mouth, there flowèd forth the Romane floud.

43

And lastly, came cold February, sitting
In an old wagon, for he could not ride;
Drawne of two fishes for the season fitting,
Which through the flood before did softly slyde
And swim away: yet had he by his side
His plough and harnesse fit to till the ground,
And tooles to prune the trees, before the pride
Of hasting Prime did make them burgein round:
So past the twelve Months forth, and their dew places found.

44

And after these, there came the Day, and Night,
Riding together both with equall pase,
Th' one on a Palfrey blacke, the other white;
But Night had covered her uncomely face
With a black veile, and held in hand a mace,
On top whereof the moon and stars were pight,
And sleep and darknesse round about did trace:
But Day did beare, upon his scepters hight,
The goodly Sun, encompast all with beamès bright.

45

Then came the Howres, faire daughters of high Jove,
And timely Night, the which were all endewed
With wondrous beauty fit to kindle love;
But they were Virgins all, and love eschewed,
That might forslack the charge to them foreshewed
By mighty Jove; who did them Porters make
Of heavens gate (whence all the gods issued)
Which they did dayly watch, and nightly wake
By even turnes, ne ever did their charge forsake.

46

And after all came Life, and lastly Death;
Death with most grim and griesly visage seene,
Yet is he nought but parting of the breath;
Ne ought to see, but like a shade to weene,

376. spray: branch. **377. steane:** urn. **378. Romane floud:** Tiber River at Rome. **386. burgein:** bud. **393. pight:** placed. **398. timely:** passing. **endewed:** endowed. **401. forslack:** cause neglect of.

Unbodièd, unsouled, unheard, unseene.
But Life was like a faire young lusty boy,
Such as they faine Dan Cupid to have beene,
Full of delightfull health and lively joy,
Deckt all with flowres, and wings of gold fit to employ.

47

When these were past, thus gan the Titanesse:
"Lo, mighty mother, now be judge and say,
Whether in all thy creatures more or lesse
CHANGE doth not raign and beare the greatest sway:
For, who sees not, that Time on all doth pray?
But Times do change and move continually.
So nothing here long standeth in one stay:
Wherefore, this lower world who can deny
But to be subject still to Mutabilitie?"

48

Then thus gan Jove: "Right true it is, that these
And all things else that under heaven dwell
Are chaunged of Time, who doth them all disseise
Of being: But, who is it (to me tell)
That Time himselfe doth move and still compell
To keepe his course? Is not that namely wee
Which poure that vertue from our heavenly cell,
That moves them all, and makes them changèd be?
So them we gods doe rule, and in them also thee."

49

To whom, thus Mutability: "The things
Which we see not how they are moved and swayd,
Ye may attribute to your selves as Kings,
And say they by your secret powre are made:
But what we see not, who shall us perswade?
But were they so, as ye them faine to be,
Moved by your might, and ordred by your ayde;
Yet what if I can prove, that even yee
Your selves are likewise changed, and subject unto mee?

50

"And first, concerning her that is the first,
Even you faire Cynthia, whom so much ye make

409. weene: understand. **426. of Time:** by time. **disseise:** deprive. **430. vertue:** power. **heavenly cell:** planet. **442. her . . . first:** the moon, the orbit of which is closest to the earth. The gods throughout the next several lines are mentioned as planets. In the Ptolemaic system, the nearest to earth was the moon, and then, in order, Mercury, Venus, the Sun, Mars, Jupiter, and Saturn.

Joves dearest darling, she was bred and nurst
On Cynthus hill, whence she her name did take:
Then is she mortall borne, how-so ye crake;
Besides, her face and countenance every day
We changèd see, and sundry forms partake,
Now hornd, now round, now bright, now brown and gray:
So that *as changefull as the Moone* men use to say.

51

"Next, Mercury, who though he lesse appeare
To change his hew, and alwayes seeme as one;
Yet, he his course doth altar every yeare,
And is of late far out of order gone:
So Venus eeke, that goodly Paragone,
Though faire all night, yet is she darke all day;
And Phoebus self, who lightsome is alone,
Yet is he oft eclipsèd by the way,
And fills the darkned world with terror and dismay.

52

"Now Mars that valiant man is changèd most:
For, he some times so far runs out of square,
That he his way doth seem quite to have lost,
And cleane without his usuall sphere to fare;
That even these Star-gazers stonisht are
At sight thereof, and damne their lying bookes:
So likewise, grim Sir Saturne oft doth spare
His sterne aspect, and calme his crabbèd lookes:
So many turning cranks these have, so many crookes.

53

"But you Dan Jove, that only constant are,
And King of all the rest, as ye do clame,
Are you not subject eeke to this misfare?
Then let me aske you this withouten blame,
Where were ye borne? some say in Crete by name,
Others in Thebes, and others other-where;
But wheresoever they commènt the same,
They all consent that ye begotten were,
And borne here in this world, ne other can appeare.

445. Cynthus hill: on the Greek island of Delos, birthplace of Apollo and Diana. **446. crake:** boast. **457. Phoebus . . . alone:** Phoebus (the Sun), who alone gives his own light. **468. cranks:** twists. **crookes:** bends. **471. misfare:** mishap. **475. commènt:** invent. **477. ne other:** not otherwise.

54

"Then are ye mortall borne, and thrall to me,
Unlesse the kingdome of the sky yee make
Immortall, and unchangeable to bee;
Besides, that power and vertue which ye spake,
That ye here worke, doth many changes take,
And your owne natures change: for, each of you
That vertue have, or this, or that to make,
Is checkt and changèd from his nature trew,
By others opposition or obliquid view.

55

"Besides, the sundry motions of your Spheares,
So sundry waies and fashions as clerkes faine,
Some in short space, and some in longer yeares;
What is the same but alteration plaine?
Onely the starrie skie doth still remaine:
Yet do the Starres and Signes therein still move,
And even it self is moved, as wizards saine.
But all that moveth, doth mutation love:
Therefore both you and them to me I subject prove.

56

"Then since within this wide great Universe
Nothing doth firme and permanent appeare,
But all things tost and turnèd by transverse:
What then should let, but I aloft should reare
My Trophee, and from all, the triumph beare?
Now judge then (O thou greatest goddesse trew!)
According as thy selfe doest see and heare,
And unto me addoom that is my dew;
That is the rule of all, all being ruled by you."

57

So having ended, silence long ensewed,
Ne Nature to or fro spake for a space,
But with firme eyes affixt, the ground still viewed.
Meane while, all creatures, looking in her face,
Expecting th' end of this so doubtfull case,
Did hang in long suspence what would ensew,
To whether side should fall the soveraigne place:
At length, she looking up with chearefull view,
The silence brake, and gave her doome in speeches few.

486. By . . . view: referring to the astrological belief that each planet bestows a particular "virtue" on the earth. **488. clerkes:** scholars. **faine:** imagine. **493. wizards saine:** wisemen say. **498. by transverse:** haphazardly. **499. let:** prevent. **503. addoom that:** decide what. **506. space:** time. **511. whether:** which. **513. doome:** judgment.

58

"I well consider all that ye have sayd,
And find that all things stedfastnes doe hate
And changèd be: yet being rightly wayd
They are not changèd from their first estate;
But by their change their being doe dilate:
And turning to themselves at length againe,
Doe worke their owne perfection so by fate:
Then over them Change doth not rule and raigne;
But they raigne over change, and doe their states maintaine.

59

"Cease therefore daughter further to aspire,
And thee content thus to be ruled by me:
For thy decay thou seekst by thy desire;
But time shall come that all shall changèd bee,
And from thenceforth, none no more change shall see."
So was the Titaness put downe and whist,
And Jove confirmed in his imperiall see.
Then was that whole assembly quite dismist,
And Natur's selfe did vanish, wither no man wist.

from Amoretti

Sonnet 75

One day I wrote her name upon the strand,
But came the waves and washèd it away:
Agayne I wrote it with a second hand,
But came the tyde, and made my paynes his pray.
"Vayne man," sayd she, "that doest in vaine assay,
A mortall thing so to immortalize,
For I my selve shall lyke to this decay,
And eek my name bee wypèd out lykewize."
"Not so," quod I, "let baser things devize
To dy in dust, but you shall live by fame:
My verse your vertues rare shall eternize,
And in the hevens wryte your glorious name.
Where whenas death shall all the world subdew,
Our love shall live, and later life renew."

516. wayd: weighed. **518. dilate:** evolve. **528. whist:** silenced. **529. see:** throne. **531. wist:** knew. AMORETTI. Sonnet 75. **1. strand:** seashore. **4. pray:** prey. **8. eek:** also. **9. quod:** quoth. **devize:** make plans.

Sonnet 79

Men call you fayre, and you doe credit it,
For that your selfe ye dayly such doe see:
But the trew fayre, that is the gentle wit,
And vertuous mind, is much more praysd of me.
For all the rest, how ever fayre it be,
Shall turne to nought and loose that glorious hew:
But onely that is permanent and free
From frayle corruption, that doth flesh ensew.
That is true beautie: that doth argue you
To be divine and borne of heavenly seed:
Derived from that fayre Spirit, from whom al true
And perfect beauty did at first proceed.
He onely fayre, and what he fayre hath made:
All other fayre, lyke flowres, untymely fade.

Epithalamion

Ye learned sisters which have oftentimes
Beene to me ayding, others to adorne:
Whom ye thought worthy of your gracefull rymes,
That even the greatest did not greatly scorne
To heare theyr names sung in your simple layes,
But joyèd in theyr prayse.
And when ye list your owne mishaps to mourne,
Which death, or love, or fortunes wreck did rayse,
Your string could soone to sadder tenor turne,
And teach the woods and waters to lament
Your dolefull dreriment.
Now lay those sorrowfull complaints aside,
And having all your heads with girland crownd,
Helpe me mine owne loves prayses to resound,
Ne let the same of any be envìde:
So Orpheus did for his owne bride,
So I unto my selfe alone will sing,
The woods shall to me answer and my Eccho ring.

Early before the worlds light giving lampe,
His golden beame upon the hils doth spred,
Having disperst the nights unchearefull dampe,
Doe ye awake, and with fresh lustyhed

Sonnet 79. **1. credit:** believe. **6. hew:** form. **8. ensew:** follow. EPITHALAMION. **Title:** "A Wedding Song" (literally, in Greek, "at the bridal chamber"). **1. sisters:** the Muses. **9. tenor:** mood. **11. dreriment:** sorrow ("dreary-ment"). **15. of:** by. **16. Orpheus:** a poet and musician whose music could charm beasts and move trees. **22. lustyhed:** health (lustiness).

Go to the bowre of my belovèd love,
My truest turtle dove,
Bid her awake; for Hymen is awake,
And long since ready forth his maske to move,
With his bright Tead that flames with many a flake,
And many a bachelor to waite on him,
In theyr fresh garments trim.
Bid her awake therefore and soone her dight,
For lo the wishèd day is come at last,
That shall for al the paynes and sorrowes past,
Pay to her usury of long delight:
And whylest she doth her dight,
Doe ye to her of joy and solace sing,
That all the woods may answer and your eccho ring.

Bring with you all the Nymphes that you can heare
Both of the rivers and the forrests greene:
And of the sea that neighbours to her neare,
Al with gay girlands goodly wel beseene.
And let them also with them bring in hand,
Another gay girland
For my fayre love of lillyes and of roses,
Bound truelove wize with a blew silke riband.
And let them make great store of bridale poses,
And let them eeke bring store of other flowers
To deck the bridale bowers.
And let the ground whereas her foot shall tread,
For feare the stones her tender foot should wrong
Be strewed with fragrant flowers all along,
And diapred lyke the discolored mead.
Which done, doe at her chamber dore awayt,
For she will waken strayt,
The whiles doe ye this song unto her sing,
The woods shall to you answer and your Eccho ring.

Ye Nymphes of Mulla which with carefull heed,
The silver scaly trouts doe tend full well,
And greedy pikes which use therein to feed,
(Those trouts and pikes all others doo excell)
And ye likewise which keepe the rushy lake,
Where none doo fishes take,
Bynd up the locks the which hang scatterd light,
And in his waters which your mirror make,
Behold your faces as the christall bright,

23. bowre: chamber. **25. Hymen:** god of marriage. **27. Tead:** ceremonial torch at weddings. **flake:** spark. **30. dight:** dress. **33. usury:** interest. **35. solace:** comfort. **37. that . . . heare:** that can hear you. **45. poses:** posies. **51. discolored mead:** multicolored meadow. **56. Mulla:** Spenser's name for the River Awbeg, near his home in Ireland. **61. take:** catch.

That when you come whereas my love doth lie,
No blemish she may spie.
And eke ye lightfoot mayds which keepe the deere,
That on the hoary mountayne use to towre,
And the wylde wolves which seeke them to devoure,
With your steele darts doo chace from comming neer
Be also present heere,
To helpe to decke her and to help to sing,
That all the woods may answer and your eccho ring.

Wake, now my love, awake; for it is time,
The Rosy Morne long since left Tithones bed,
All ready to her silver coche to clyme,
And Phoebus gins to shew his glorious hed.
Hark how the cheerefull birds do chaunt theyr laies
And carroll of loves praise.
The merry Larke hir mattins sings aloft,
The thrush replyes, the Mavis descant playes,
The Ouzell shrills, the Ruddock warbles soft,
So goodly all agree with sweet consent,
To this dayes merriment.
Ah my deere love why doe ye sleepe thus long,
When meeter were that ye should now awake,
T' awayt the comming of your joyous make,
And hearken to the birds lovelearnèd song,
The deawy leaves among.
For they of joy and pleasance to you sing,
That all the woods them answer and theyr eccho ring.

My love is now awake out of her dreame,
And her fayre eyes like stars that dimmèd were
With darksome cloud, now shew theyr goodly beams
More bright then Hesperus his head doth rere.
Come now ye damzels, daughters of delight,
Helpe quickly her to dight,
But first come ye fayre houres which were begot
In Joves sweet paradice, of Day and Night,
Which doe the seasons of the yeare allot,
And al that ever in this world is fayre
Doe make and still repayre.
And ye three handmayds of the Cyprian Queene,
The which doe still adorne her beauties pride,
Helpe to addorne my beautifullest bride:
And as ye her array, still throw betweene
Some graces to be seene,

68. towre: climb high. **80. mattins:** morning prayer. **81. Mavis:** thrush. **descant:** melody. **82. Ouzell:** blackbird. **Ruddock:** robin. **86. meeter:** more fitting. **87. make:** mate. **95. Hesperus:** evening star. **97. dight:** adorn. **102. still repayre:** continually change. **103. Cyprian Queene:** Venus.

And as ye use to Venus, to her sing,
The whiles the woods shal answer and your eccho ring.

Now is my love all ready forth to come,
Let all the virgins therefore well awayt,
And ye fresh boyes that tend upon her groome
Prepare your selves; for he is comming strayt.
Set all your things in seemely good aray
Fit for so joyfull day,
The joyfulst day that ever sunne did see.
Faire Sun, shew forth thy favourable ray,
And let thy lifull heat not fervent be
For feare of burning her sunshyny face,
Her beauty to disgrace.
O fayrest Phoebus, father of the Muse,
If ever I did honour thee aright,
Or sing the thing, that mote thy mind delight,
Doe not thy servants simple boone refuse,
But let this day let this one day be myne,
Let all the rest be thine.
Then I thy soverayne prayses loud wil sing,
That all the woods shal answer and theyr eccho ring.

Harke how the Minstrels gin to shrill aloud
Their merry Musick that resounds from far,
The pipe, the tabor, and the trembling Croud,
That well agree withouten breach or jar.
But most of all the Damzels doe delite,
When they their tymbrels smyte,
And thereunto doe daunce and carrol sweet,
That all the sences they doe ravish quite,
The whyles the boyes run up and downe the street,
Crying aloud with strong confusèd noyce,
As if it were one voyce.
Hymen iô Hymen, Hymen they do shout,
That even to the heavens theyr shouting shrill
Doth reach, and all the firmament doth fill,
To which the people standing all about,
As in approvance doe thereto applaud
And loud advaunce her laud,
And evermore they *Hymen Hymen* sing,
That al the woods them answer and theyr eccho ring.

Loe where she comes along with portly pace
Lyke Phoebe from her chamber of the East,
Arysing forth to run her mighty race,
Clad all in white, that seemes a virgin best.

108. use: do. **114. aray:** order. **118. lifull:** full of life. **120. disgrace:** mar. **124. boone:** request. **131. tabor:** small drum. **Croud:** fiddle. **132. jar:** discord. **134. tymbrels:** tambourines. **145. laud:** praise. **151. seemes:** befits.

So well it her beseemes that ye would weene
Some angell she had beene.
Her long loose yellow locks lyke golden wyre,
Sprinckled with perle, and perling flowres a tweene,
Doe lyke a golden mantle her attyre,
And being crownèd with a girland greene,
Seeme lyke some mayden Queene.
Her modest eyes abashèd to behold
So many gazers, as on her do stare,
Upon the lowly ground affixèd are.
Ne dare lift up her countenance too bold,
But blush to heare her prayses sung so loud,
So farre from being proud.
Nathlesse doe ye still loud her prayses sing.
That all the woods may answer and your eccho ring.

Tell me ye merchants daughters did ye see
So fayre a creature in your towne before,
So sweet, so lovely, and so mild as she,
Adornd with beautyes grace and vertues store,
Her goodly eyes lyke Saphyres shining bright,
Her forehead yvory white,
Her cheekes lyke apples which the sun hath rudded,
Her lips lyke cherryes charming men to byte,
Her brest like to a bowle of creame uncrudded,
Her paps lyke lyllies budded,
Her snowie necke lyke to a marble towre,
And all her body lyke a pallace fayre,
Ascending uppe with many a stately stayre,
To honors seat and chastities sweet bowre.
Why stand ye still ye virgins in amaze,
Upon her so to gaze,
Whiles ye forget your former lay to sing,
To which the woods did answer and your eccho ring.

But if ye saw that which no eyes can see,
The inward beauty of her lively spright,
Garnisht with heavenly guifts of high degree,
Much more then would ye wonder at that sight,
And stand astonisht lyke to those which red
Medusaes mazeful hed.
There dwels sweet love and constant chastity,
Unspotted fayth and comely womanhood,
Regard of honour and mild modesty,
There vertue raynes as Queene in royal throne,
And giveth lawes alone.
The which the base affections doe obay,

155. perling: winding. **173. rudded:** reddened. **175. uncrudded:** uncurdled. **186. spright:** spirit. **189. red:** saw. **196. base:** lower.

And yeeld theyr services unto her will,
Ne thought of thing uncomely ever may
Thereto approch to tempt her mind to ill.
Had ye once seene these her celestial threasures,
And unrevealèd pleasures,
Then would ye wonder and her prayses sing,
That al the woods should answer and your eccho ring.

Open the temple gates unto my love,
Open them wide that she may enter in,
And all the postes adorne as doth behove,
And all the pillours deck with girlands trim,
For to recyve this Saynt with honour dew,
That commeth in to you.
With trembling steps and humble reverence,
She commeth in, before th' almighties vew,
Of her ye virgins learne obedience,
When so ye come into those holy places,
To humble your proud faces:
Bring her up to th' high altar, that she may
The sacred ceremonies there partake,
The which do endlesse matrimony make,
And let the roring Organs loudly play
The praises of the Lord in lively notes,
The whiles with hollow throates
The Choristers the joyous Antheme sing,
That al the woods may answere and their eccho ring.

Behold whiles she before the altar stands
Hearing the holy priest that to her speakes
And blesseth her with his two happy hands,
How the red roses flush up in her cheekes,
And the pure snow with goodly vermill stayne,
Like crimsin dyde in grayne,
That even th' Angels which continually
About the sacred Altare doe remaine,
Forget their service and about her fly,
Ofte peeping in her face that seemes more fayre,
The more they on it stare.
But her sad eyes still fastened on the ground,
Are governèd with goodly modesty,
That suffers not one looke to glaunce awry,
Which may let in a little thought unsownd.
Why blush ye love to give to me your hand,
The pledge of all our band?
Sing ye sweet Angels, Alleluya sing,
That all the woods may answere and your eccho ring.

206. behove: is proper. **227. vermill:** vermillion. **228. in grayne:** into the grain of the cloth (fast colors). **234. sad:** serious. **239. band:** bond.

Now al is done; bring home the bride againe,
Bring home the triumph of our victory,
Bring home with you the glory of her gaine,
With joyance bring her and with jollity.
Never had man more joyfull day then this,
Whom heaven would heape with blis.
Make feast therefore now all this live long day,
This day for ever to me holy is,
Poure out the wine without restraint or stay,
Poure not by cups, but by the belly full,
Poure out to all that wull,
And sprinkle all the postes and wals with wine,
That they may sweat, and drunken be withall.
Crowne ye God Bacchus with a coronall,
And Hymen also crowne with wreathes of vine,
And let the Graces daunce unto the rest;
For they can doo it best:
The whiles the maydens doe theyr carroll sing,
To which the woods shal answer and theyr eccho ring.

Ring ye the bels, ye yong men of the towne,
And leave your wonted labors for this day:
This day is holy; doe ye write it downe,
That ye for ever it remember may.
This day the sunne is in his chiefest hight,
With Barnaby the bright,
From whence declining daily by degrees,
He somewhat loseth of his heat and light,
When once the Crab behind his back he sees.
But for this time it ill ordainèd was,
To chose the longest day in all the yeare,
And shortest night, when longest fitter weare:
Yet never day so long, but late would passe.
Ring ye the bels, to make it weare away,
And bonefiers make all day,
And daunce about them, and about them sing:
That all the woods may answer, and your eccho ring.

Ah when will this long weary day have end,
And lende me leave to come unto my love?
How slowly do the houres theyr numbers spend?
How slowly does sad Time his feathers move?
Hast thee O fayrest Planet to thy home
Within the Westerne fome:
Thy tyred steedes long since have need of rest.
Long though it be, at last I see it gloome,

244. of her gaine: of gaining her. **252. wull:** wish it. **255. coronall:** flower crown. **262. wonted:** accustomed. **266. Barnaby the bright:** St. Barnabas's day (July 11), the summer solstice in the calendar of the time. **273. late:** at last.

And the bright evening star with golden creast
Appeare out of the East.
Fayre childe of beauty, glorious lampe of love
That all the host of heaven in rankes doost lead,
And guydest lovers through the nightès dread,
How chearefully thou lookest from above,
And seemst to laugh atweene thy twinkling light
As joying in the sight
Of these glad many which for joy doe sing,
That all the woods them answer and their eccho ring.

Now ceasse ye damsels your delights forepast;
Enough is it, that all the day was youres:
Now day is doen, and night is nighing fast:
Now bring the Bryde into the brydall boures.
Now night is come, now soone her disaray,
And in her bed her lay;
Lay her in lillies and in violets,
And silken courteins over her display,
And odourd sheetes, and Arras coverlets.
Behold how goodly my faire love does ly
In proud humility;
Like unto Maia, when as Jove her tooke,
In Tempe, lying on the flowry gras,
Twixt sleepe and wake, after she weary was,
With bathing in the Acidalian brooke.
Now it is night, ye damsels may be gon,
And leave my love alone,
And leave likewise your former lay to sing:
The woods no more shal answere, nor your eccho ring.

Now welcome night, thou night so long expected,
That long daies labour doest at last defray,
And all my cares, which cruell love collected,
Hast sumd in one, and cancellèd for aye:
Spread thy broad wing over my love and me,
That no man may us see,
And in thy sable mantle us enwrap,
From feare of perrill and foule horror free.
Let no false treason seeke us to entrap,
Nor any dread disquiet once annoy
The safety of our joy:
But let the night be calme and quietsome,
Without tempestuous storms or sad afray:
Lyke as when Jove with fayre Alcmena lay,
When he begot the great Tirynthian groome:

303. display: spread out. **304. odourd:** perfumed. **Arras:** tapestry. **307. Maia:** one of the Pleiades, beloved of Zeus, mother of Hermes. **316. defray:** pay back. **328. Alcmena:** mother of Hercules, the *Tirynthian groome* of the next line.

Or lyke as when he with thy selfe did lie,
And begot Majesty.
And let the mayds and yongmen cease to sing:
Ne let the woods them answer, nor theyr eccho ring.

Let no lamenting cryes, nor dolefull teares,
Be heard all night within nor yet without:
Ne let false whispers, breeding hidden feares,
Breake gentle sleepe with misconceivèd dout.
Let no deluding dreames, nor dreadful sights
Make sudden sad affrights;
Ne let housefyres, nor lightnings helpelesse harmes,
Ne let the Pouke, nor other evill sprights,
Ne let mischìvous witches with theyr charmes,
Ne let hob Goblins, names whose sence we see not,
Fray us with things that be not.
Let not the shriech Oule, nor the Storke be heard:
Nor the night Raven that still deadly yels,
Nor damnèd ghosts cald up with mighty spels,
Nor griesly vultures make us once affeard:
Ne let th' unpleasant Quyre of Frogs still croking
Make us to wish theyr choking.
Let none of these theyr drery accents sing;
Ne let the woods them answer, nor theyr eccho ring.

But let stil Silence trew night watches keepe,
That sacred peace may in assurance rayne,
And tymely sleep, when it is tyme to sleepe,
May poure his limbs forth on your pleasant playne,
The whiles an hundred little wingèd loves,
Like divers fethered doves,
Shall fly and flutter round about your bed,
And in the secret darke, that none reproves,
Their prety stealthes shal worke, and snares shal spread
To filch away sweet snatches of delight,
Conceald through covert night.
Ye sonnes of Venus, play your sports at will,
For greedy pleasure, carelesse of your toyes,
Thinks more upon her paradise of joyes,
Then what ye do, albe it good or ill.
All night therefore attend your merry play,
For it will soone be day:
Now none doth hinder you, that say or sing,
Ne will the woods now answer, nor your Eccho ring.

Who is the same, which at my window peepes?
Or whose is that faire face, that shines so bright?

337. dout: fear. **341. Pouke:** Puck. **344. Fray:** terrify. **346. still:** always. **348. griesly:** horrible. **357. loves:** cupids.

Is it not Cinthia, she that never sleepes,
But walkes about high heaven al the night?
O fayrest goddesse, do thou not envỳ
My love with me to spy:
For thou likewise didst love, though now unthought,
And for a fleece of woll, which privily,
The Latmian shephard once unto thee brought,
His pleasures with thee wrought.
Therefore to us be favorable now;
And sith of wemens labours thou hast charge,
And generation goodly dost enlarge,
Encline thy will t' effect our wishfull vow,
And the chast wombe informe with timely seed,
That may our comfort breed:
Till which we cease our hopefull hap to sing,
Ne let the woods us answere, nor our Eccho ring.

And thou great Juno, which with awful might
The lawes of wedlock still dost patronize,
And the religion of the faith first plight
With sacred rites hast taught to solemnize:
And eeke for comfort often callèd art
Of women in their smart,
Eternally bind thou this lovely band,
And all thy blessings unto us impart.
And thou glad Genius, in whose gentle hand,
The bridale bowre and geniall bed remaine,
Without blemish or staine,
And the sweet pleasures of theyr loves delight
With secret ayde doest succour and supply,
Till they bring forth the fruitfull progeny,
Send us the timely fruit of this same night.
And thou fayre Hebe, and thou Hymen free,
Grant that it may so be.
Til which we cease your further prayse to sing,
Ne any woods shal answer, nor your Eccho ring.

And ye high heavens, the temple of the gods,
In which a thousand torches flaming bright
Doe burne, that to us wretched earthly clods,
In dreadful darknesse lend desirèd light;
And all ye powers which in the same remayne,
More then we men can fayne,
Poure out your blessing on us plentiously,
And happy influence upon us raine,
That we may raise a large posterity,

378. unthought: thought otherwise. **379. woll:** wool. **380. Latmian shephard:** Endymion, beloved of Diana. **386. informe:** give life to. **395. smart:** labor. **398. Genius:** patron of sex and procreation. **405. Hebe:** wife of Hercules, patron of youth.

Which from the earth, which they may long possesse,
With lasting happinesse,
Up to your haughty pallaces may mount,
And for the guerdon of theyr glorious merit
May heavenly tabernacles there inherit,
Of blessed Saints for to increase the count.
So let us rest, sweet love, in hope of this,
And cease till then our tymely joyes to sing,
The woods no more us answer, nor our eccho ring.

Song made in lieu of many ornaments,
With which my love should duly have bene dect,
Which cutting off through hasty accidents,
Ye would not stay your dew time to expect,
But promist both to recompens,
Be unto her a goodly ornament,
And for short time an endlesse moniment.

1595

Prothalamion

Calme was the day, and through the trembling ayre,
Sweete breathing Zephyrus did softly play
A gentle spirit, that lightly did delay
Hot Titans beames, which then did glyster fayre:
When I whom sullein care,
Through discontent of my long fruitlesse stay
In Princes Court, and expectation vayne
Of idle hopes, which still doe fly away,
Like empty shaddowes, did aflict my brayne,
Walkt forth to ease my payne
Along the shoare of silver streaming Themmes,
Whose rutty Bancke, the which his River hemmes,
Was paynted all with variable flowers,
And all the meades adornd with daintie gemmes,
Fit to decke maydens bowres,
And crowne their Paramours,
Against the Brydale day, which is not long:
  Sweete Themmes runne softly, till I end my Song.

There, in a Meadow, by the Rivers side,
A flocke of Nymphes I chauncèd to espy,
All lovely Daughters of the Flood thereby,

428. dect: decked (dressed up). **430. expect:** await. **433. moniment:** monument. PROTHALAMION. **Title:** "Before the Bridal Chamber." **2. Zephyrus:** the West Wind. **4. Titans:** sun's. **18. Themmes:** the River Thames.

With goodly greenish locks all loose untyde,
As each had bene a Bryde,
And each one had a little wicker basket,
Made of fine twigs entraylèd curiously,
In which they gathered flowers to fill their flasket:
And with fine Fingers, cropt full feateously
The tender stalkes on hye.
Of every sort, which in that Meadow grew,
They gathered some; the Violet pallid blew,
The little Dazie, that at evening closes,
The virgin Lillie, and the Primrose trew,
With store of vermeil Roses,
To decke their Bridegromes posies,
Against the Brydale day, which was not long:
  Sweete Themmes runne softly, till I end my Song.

With that, I saw two Swannes of goodly hewe,
Come softly swimming downe along the Lee;
Two fairer Birds I yet did never see:
The snow which doth the top of Pindus strew,
Did never whiter shew,
Nor Jove himselfe when he a Swan would be
For love of Leda, whiter did appeare:
Yet Leda was they say as white as he,
Yet not so white as these, nor nothing neare;
So purely white they were,
That even the gentle streame, the which them bare,
Seemed foule to them, and bad his billowes spare
To wet their silken feathers, least they might
Soyle their fayre plumes with water not so fayre,
And marre their beauties bright,
That shone as heavens light,
Against their Brydale day, which was not long:
  Sweete Themmes runne softly, till I end my Song.

Eftsoones the Nymphes, which now had Flowers their fill,
Ran all in haste, to see that silver brood,
As they came floating on the Christal Flood.
Whom when they sawe, they stood amazèd still,
Their wondring eyes to fill,
Them seemed they never saw a sight so fayre,
Of Fowles so lovely, that they sure did deeme
Them heavenly borne, or to be that same payre
Which through the Skie draw Venus silver Teeme,

26. flasket: basket. **27. feateously:** adroitly. **33. vermeil:** vermillion. **38. Lee:** small river flowing into the Thames. **40. Pindus:** mountain range in Greece containing Mount Parnassus, home of the Muses. **43. Leda:** woman wooed by Zeus in the shape of the swan (see Yeats's "Leda and the Swan"). **55. Eftsoones:** soon afterwards. **63. Teeme:** team or pair of swans that drew the chariot of Venus.

For sure they did not seeme
To be begot of any earthly Seede,
But rather Angels or of Angels breede:
Yet were they bred of Somers-heat they say,
In sweetest Season, when each Flower and weede
The earth did fresh aray,
So fresh they seemed as day,
Even as their Brydale day, which was not long:
  Sweete Themmes runne softly, till I end my Song.

Then forth they all out of their baskets drew,
Great store of Flowers, the honour of the field,
That to the sense did fragrant odours yeild,
All which upon those goodly Birds they threw,
And all the Waves did strew,
That like old Peneus Waters they did seeme,
When downe along by pleasant Tempes shore
Scattred with Flowres, through Thessaly they streeme,
That they appeare through Lillies plenteous store,
Like a Brydes Chamber flore:
Two of those Nymphes, meane while, two Garlands bound,
Of freshest Flowres which in that Mead they found,
The which presenting all in trim Array,
Their snowie Foreheads therewithall they crownd,
Whil'st one did sing this Lay,
Prepared against that Day,
Against their Brydale day, which was not long:
  Sweete Themmes runne softly, till I end my Song.

Ye gentle Birdes, the worlds faire ornament,
And heavens glorie, whom this happie hower
Doth leade unto your lovers blisfull bower,
Joy may you have and gentle hearts content
Of your loves couplement:
And let faire Venus, that is Queene of love,
With her heart-quelling Sonne upon you smile,
Whose smile they say, hath vertue to remove
All Loves dislike, and friendships faultie guile
For ever to assoile.
Let endlesse Peace your steadfast hearts accord,
And blessed Plentie wait upon your bord,
And let your bed with pleasures chast abound,
That fruitfull issue may to you afford,
Which may your foes confound,
And make your joyes redound,
Upon your Brydale day, which is not long:
  Sweete Themmes run softly, till I end my Song.

67. Somers-heat: Spenser puns on the names of Elizabeth and Katherine Somerset, whose marriages he is celebrating. **78. Peneus:** river in Thessaly, Greece. **84. Mead:** meadow. **100. assoile:** absolve.

So ended she; and all the rest around
To her redoubled that her undersong,
Which said, their bridale daye should not be long.
And gentle Eccho from the neighbour ground,
Their accents did resound.
So forth those joyous Birdes did passe along,
Adowne the Lee, that to them murmurde low,
As he would speake, but that he lackt a tong
Yeat did by signes his glad affection show,
Making his streame run slow.
And all the foule which in his flood did dwell
Gan flock about these twaine, that did excell
The rest, so far, as Cynthia doth shend
The lesser starres. So they enrangèd well,
Did on those two attend,
And their best service lend,
Against their wedding day, which was not long:
  Sweete Themmes run softly, till I end my song.

At length they all to mery London came,
To mery London, my most kyndly Nurse,
That to me gave this Lifes first native sourse:
Though from another place I take my name,
An house of auncient fame.
There when they came, whereas those bricky towres,
The which on Themmes brode agèd backe doe ryde,
Where now the studious Lawyers have their bowers
There whylome wont the Templer Knights to byde,
Till they decayd through pride:
Next whereunto there standes a stately place,
Where oft I gaynèd giftes and goodly grace
Of that great Lord, which therein wont to dwell,
Whose want too well now feeles my freendles case:
But Ah here fits not well
Olde woes but joyes to tell
Against the bridale daye, which is not long:
  Sweete Themmes runne softly, till I end my Song.

Yet therein now doth lodge a noble Peer,
Great Englands glory and the Worlds wide wonder,
Whose dreadfull name, late through all Spaine did thunder,
And Hercules two pillors standing neere,

110. redoubled . . . undersong: repeated her undersong or refrain. **112. Eccho:** nymph of woods and hills. **121. shend:** outshine. **122. enrangèd:** arranged. **130. place . . . name:** probably from the Spencers of Northamptonshire. **132–35. bricky towres . . . byde:** The Temple in London was formerly occupied by the Knights Templar until they were suppressed in the fourteenth century; it was then handed over to law students (the "Inns of Court"). **145. Peer:** Earl of Essex, who returned in 1596 from capturing Cadiz in Spain.

Did make to quake and feare:
Faire branch of Honor, flower of Chevalrie,
That fillest England with thy triumphs fame,
Joy have thou of thy noble victorie,
And endlesse happinesse of thine owne name
That promiseth the same:
That through thy prowesse and victorious armes,
Thy country may be freed from forraine harmes:
And great Elisaes glorious name may ring
Through al the world, fild with thy wide Alarmes,
Which some brave muse may sing
To ages following,
Upon the Brydale day, which is not long:
  Sweete Themmes runne softly, till I end my Song.

From those high Towers, this noble Lord issuing,
Like Radiant Hesper when his golden hayre
In th'Ocean billowes he hath Bathèd fayre,
Descended to the Rivers open vewing,
With a great traine ensuing.
Above the rest were goodly to bee seene
Two gentle Knights of lovely face and feature
Beseeming well the bower of anie Queene,
With gifts of wit and ornaments of nature,
Fit for so goodly stature:
That like the twins of Jove they seemed in sight,
Which decke the Bauldricke of the Heavens bright.
They two forth pacing to the Rivers side,
Received those two faire Brides, their Loves delight,
Which at th'appointed tyde,
Each one did make his Bryde,
Against their Brydale day, which is not long:
  Sweete Themmes runne softly, till I end my Song.

1596

157. Elisaes: Elizabeth's. **164. Hesper:** evening star. **173. twins of Jove:** Castor and Pollux, the constellation called the Gemini. **174. Bauldricke:** belt of the Zodiac, which includes the Gemini.

Sir Philip Sidney

(1554–1586)

Universally regarded as the perfect English Renaissance gentleman, Sidney traveled widely, served as an ambassador and a soldier (he was killed in the Netherlands in a battle with the Spanish when he was thirty-two), and wrote poetry that often speaks directly to the heart. His series of love sonnets called *Astrophel and Stella* (1591), meaning "Star-Lover and Star," was the first of the famous Elizabethan *sonnet sequences.* Such sequences were written by Samuel Daniel, Michael Drayton, William Shakespeare, and several other poets. Sidney is also remembered for his long prose romance, *Arcadia* (1590–93), and for his eloquent defense of poetry as a form of writing in *An Apology for Poetry* (1593), the first important work of literary criticism in English.

from Astrophel and Stella

1

Loving in truth, and fain in verse my love to show,
That she dear she might take some pleasure of my pain,
Pleasure might cause her read, reading might make her know,
Knowledge might pity win, and pity grace obtain,
I sought fit words to paint the blackest face of woe:
Studying inventions fine, her wits to entertain,
Oft turning others' leaves, to see if thence would flow
Some fresh and fruitful showers upon my sunburned brain.
But words came halting forth, wanting Invention's stay;
Invention, Nature's child, fled stepdame Study's blows:
And others' feet still seemed but strangers in my way.
Thus, great with child to speak, and helpless in my throes,
Biting my truant pen, beating myself for spite:
"Fool," said my Muse to me, "look in thy heart, and write."

31

With how sad steps, Oh Moon, thou climb'st the skies,
How silently, and with how wan a face!
What, may it be that even in heav'nly place
That busy archer his sharp arrows tries?

ASTROPHEL AND STELLA. **1. 1. fain:** wishing. **31. 4. archer:** Cupid.

Sure, if that long-with-love-acquainted eyes
Can judge of love, thou feel'st a lover's case;
I read it in thy looks: thy languished grace,
To me that feel the like, thy state descries.
Then even of fellowship, Oh Moon, tell me,
Is constant love deemed there but want of wit?
Are beauties there as proud as here they be?
Do they above love to be loved, and yet
Those lovers scorn whom that love doth possess?
Do they call virtue there ungratefulness?

39

Come sleep, Oh sleep, the certain knot of peace,
The baiting place of wit, the balm of woe,
The poor man's wealth, the prisoner's release,
Th' indifferent judge between the high and low;
With shield of proof shield me from out the prease
Of those fierce darts Despair at me doth throw;
Oh make in me those civil wars to cease;
I will good tribute pay, if thou do so.
Take thou of me smooth pillows, sweetest bed,
A chamber deaf to noise and blind to light,
A rosy garland and a weary head;
And if these things, as being thine by right,
Move not thy heavy grace, thou shalt in me,
Livelier than elsewhere, Stella's image see.

Thomas Lodge

(c. 1558–1625)

Lodge wrote pamphlets, fiction, plays, and poems. Some of his work was composed to pass the time on long sea voyages. In the latter part of his life he was converted to Roman Catholicism and became a doctor, and his writings thereafter were either on medical topics or were translations of philosophical and religious works. In Lodge's time the term madrigal usually referred to a lyric sung by several voices in counterpoint without instrumental accompaniment.

39. 2. baiting place: refreshment stop. **4. indifferent:** impartial. **5. proof:** proven strength. **prease:** press, crowd.

Rosalind's Madrigal

Love in my bosom like a bee
  Doth suck his sweet;
Now with his wings he plays with me,
  Now with his feet.
Within mine eyes he makes his nest,
His bed amidst my tender breast;
My kisses are his daily feast,
And yet he robs me of my rest.
  Ah, wanton, will ye?

And if I sleep, then percheth he
  With pretty flight,
And makes his pillow of my knee
  The livelong night.
Strike I my lute, he tunes the string;
He music plays if so I sing;
He lends me every lovely thing;
Yet cruel he my heart doth sting.
  Whist, wanton, still ye!

Else I with roses every day
  Will whip you hence,
And bind you, when you long to play,
  For your offense.
I'll shut mine eyes to keep you in,
I'll make you fast it for your sin,
I'll count your power not worth a pin.
Alas! what hereby shall I win
  If he gainsay me?

What if I beat the wanton boy
  With many a rod?
He will repay me with annoy,
  Because a god.
Then sit thou safely on my knee,
And let thy bower my bosom be;
Lurk in mine eyes, I like of thee.
O Cupid, so thou pity me,
  Spare not, but play thee!

1590

ROSALIND'S MADRIGAL. **Title:** This madrigal is from Lodge's prose romance, *Rosalind* (1590), the plot of which Shakespeare used for his play *As You Like It.*

Chidiock Tichborne

(1558–1586)

In the early years of Queen Elizabeth's reign the dispute between Catholics and Protestants in England was heated. Several of the nobility plotted to replace Elizabeth with a Catholic monarch, and many of them were executed as a result. Tichborne was one of these. He was condemned for treason and placed in the Tower of London. There, the night before he was executed, he wrote a moving letter to his wife Agnes, which is still preserved along with these three beautiful stanzas which he also wrote that same night. The poem, when it became generally known, was set to music with a haunting melody, and published in three popular collections of madrigals (1594, 1604, 1606).

Tichborne's Elegy

Written with his own hand
in the tower before his execution

My prime of youth is but a frost of cares,
My feast of joy is but a dish of pain,
My crop of corn is but a field of tares,
And all my good is but vain hope of gain;
The day is past, and yet I saw no sun,
And now I live, and now my life is done.

My tale was heard and yet it was not told,
My fruit is fallen and yet my leaves are green,
My youth is spent and yet I am not old,
I saw the world and yet I was not seen;
My thread is cut and yet it is not spun,
And now I live, and now my life is done.

I sought my death and found it in my womb,
I looked for life and saw it was a shade,
I trod the earth and knew it was my tomb,
And now I die, and now I was but made;
My glass is full, and now my glass is run,
And now I live, and now my life is done.

1586

TICHBORNE'S ELEGY. **3. tares:** weeds. **11. thread . . . spun:** alluding to the Parcae (or Three Fates) who spun the thread of each person's life and cut it when death was due. **17. glass:** hourglass.

SAMUEL DANIEL

(1562–1619)

One of the most respected writers of his time, Daniel excelled in history, criticism, and drama, as well as verse. He was in favor at the court and briefly held the position of Poet Laureate along with several other honorific offices. These were evidently not very demanding of his time, since it is said that Daniel would "lie hid for some months together" in his house, "the more retiredly to enjoy the company of the Muses, and then would appear in public to converse with his friends." He later moved to the country. *Delia,* from which all our selections are taken, was a sequence of sonnets to that lady, whose identity is not known. It was the first of Daniel's volumes of poetry and very popular in the Elizabethan age.

from Delia

32

But love whilst that thou mayst be loved again,
Now whilst thy May hath filled thy lap with flowers,
Now whilst thy beauty bears without a stain,
Now use the summer smiles, ere winter lowers.
And whilst thou spread'st unto the rising sun
The fairest flower that ever saw the light,
Now joy thy time before thy sweet be done,
And, Delia, think thy morning must have night,
And that thy brightness sets at length to west,
When thou wilt close up that which now thou shew'st;
And think the same becomes thy fading best
Which then shall most inveil and shadow most.
  Men do not weigh the stalk for what it was,
  When once they find her flower, her glory, pass.

45

Care-charmer Sleep, son of the sable Night,
Brother to Death, in silent darkness born.
Relieve my languish and restore the light;
With dark forgetting of my cares, return.
And let the day be time enough to mourn
The shipwreck of my ill-adventured youth;
Let waking eyes suffice to wail their scorn
Without the torment of the night's untruth.

Cease, dreams, th' imagery of our day desires,
To model forth the passions of the morrow;
Never let rising sun approve you liars,
To add more grief to aggravate my sorrow.
Still let me sleep, embracing clouds in vain,
And never wake to feel the day's disdain.

46

Let others sing of knights and paladins
In aged accents of untimely words,
Paint shadows in imaginary lines
Which well the reach of their high wits records;
But I must sing of thee and those fair eyes.
Authentic shall my verse in time to come,
When yet th' unborn shall say, "Lo where she lies,
Whose beauty made him speak that else was dumb."
These are the arks, the trophies I erect,
That fortify thy name against old age;
And these thy sacred virtues must protect
Against the dark and time's consuming rage.
Though th' error of my youth they shall discover,
Suffice, they show I lived and was thy lover.

1592

Michael Drayton

(1563–1631)

Drayton wrote pastorals, satires, poems on English history, and a long poetic survey of Great Britain, its legends, wonders, and heroes, which he called *Poly-Olbion* (Part I, 1612; Part II, 1622). (The title comes from the Greek, meaning "many blessings." Drayton probably intended a pun on the ancient Celtic name for England, "Albion," meaning the "many-sided England.") The lyrics for which Drayton is now remembered are chiefly those of his sonnet sequence, *Idea*. The most famous of these sonnets, "Since there's no help . . .," expresses a simple intensity and idealism in love and thus contrasts sharply with the more complicated emotions voiced, for example, in John Donne's love poems. Drayton and Donne were contemporaries, but Drayton was carrying the attitudes and feelings of the Elizabethan age into the rather

DELIA. **46. 2. untimely:** out of date.

different period that followed the death of Queen Elizabeth in 1603. With the new century the tone of intellectual life gradually became less confident and aspiring, growing instead more troubled, skeptical, satirical, and occasionally cynical.

from Idea

6

How many paltry, foolish, painted things,
That now in coaches trouble every street,
Shall be forgotten, whom no poet sings,
Ere they be well wrapped in their winding-sheet?
Where I to thee eternity shall give,
When nothing else remaineth of these days,
And queens hereafter shall be glad to live
Upon the alms of thy superfluous praise.
Virgins and matrons reading these my rhymes
Shall be so much delighted with thy story
That they shall grieve they lived not in these times,
To have seen thee, their sex's only glory.
  So shalt thou fly above the vulgar throng,
  Still to survive in my immortal song.

61

Since there's no help, come let us kiss and part;
Nay, I have done, you get no more of me,
And I am glad, yea glad with all my heart
That thus so cleanly I myself can free;
Shake hands forever, cancel all our vows,
And when we meet at any time again,
Be it not seen in either of our brows
That we one jot of former love retain.
Now at the last gasp of love's latest breath,
When, his pulse failing, passion speechless lies,
When faith is kneeling by his bed of death,
And innocence is closing up his eyes,
  Now if thou wouldst, when all have given him over,
  From death to life thou mightst him yet recover.

63

Truce, gentle love, a parley now I crave,
Methinks 'tis long since first these wars begun;
Nor thou nor I the better yet can have;

IDEA. **63. 1. parley:** conference between enemies over terms of peace.

Bad is the match where neither party won.
I offer free conditions of fair peace,
My heart for hostage that it shall remain;
Discharge our forces, here let malice cease,
So for my pledge thou give me pledge again.
Or if no thing but death will serve thy turn,
Still thirsting for subversion of my state,
Do what thou canst, raze, massacre, and burn,
Let the world see the utmost of thy hate;
I send defiance, since if overthrown,
Thou vanquishing, the conquest is mine own.

1619

CHRISTOPHER MARLOWE

(1564–1593)

One of the greatest English dramatists, Marlowe was killed in a quarrel at a tavern when he was only twenty-nine. In such plays as *Tamburlaine* (1587) and *Dr. Faustus* (1589) he transformed blank verse, first introduced by Surrey (see Introduction to Surrey), into a flexible and eloquent medium for poetic drama. In "The Passionate Shepherd to His Love" Marlowe, who like almost every writer of his time was versed in the Latin classics, adopts pastoral conventions: The speaker is a shepherd and the rural world he describes is idyllic. The pleasure of such poetry lies partly in the acknowledged unreality of the pastoral life it describes. It offers delightful rural images to wealthy, sophisticated city dwellers, the only part of the population able to read in the ancient world and in the Renaissance. The appeal, in other words, lies partly in recognizing the poet's artistic skill in using well-established conventions and partly in the unreal but happy world he describes. The theme of persuasion to love was also a conventional one in poetry.

The Passionate Shepherd to His Love

Come live with me and be by love,
And we will all the pleasures prove
That valleys, groves, hills, and fields,
Woods, or steepy mountain yields.

And we will sit upon the rocks,
Seeing the shepherds feed their flocks,

By shallow rivers to whose falls
Melodious birds sing madrigals.

And I will make thee beds of roses
And a thousand fragrant posies,
A cap of flowers, and a kirtle
Embroidered all with leaves of myrtle;

A gown made of the finest wool
Which from our pretty lambs we pull;
Fair lined slippers for the cold,
With buckles of the purest gold;

A belt of straw and ivy buds,
With coral clasps and amber studs:
And if these pleasures may thee move,
Come live with me, and be my love.

The shepherds' swains shall dance and sing
For thy delight each May morning:
If these delights thy mind may move,
Then live with me and be my love.

1600

William Shakespeare

(1564–1616)

The greatest poet in English—perhaps in any language—is especially associated with the poetic drama: tragedies such as *Hamlet, King Lear*, and *Macbeth*; comedies such as *As You Like It* or *Much Ado About Nothing*; and historical plays such as *Richard II* or *Henry IV*. Yet if the *Sonnets* were a minor effort for Shakespeare, they are still among the finest short poems ever written. The greater number of the sonnets (1–126) are addressed to a young man. The remaining sonnets (127–152) are to a "dark lady." No one really knows who the "fair young man" or the "dark lady" may have been, although many candidates have been suggested and new arguments erupt from time to time. There have also been many attempts to find a story in the sonnets, for readers have often assumed that these poems were written in response to experiences Shakespeare underwent, and they have tried through the sonnets to find out about Shakespeare's private life. However, except for two examples that appeared in an earlier anthology, Shakespeare's sonnets were first published in 1609 by a printer who had probably not obtained the manuscript from Shakespeare. (Volumes of poems were often copied out by hand in the Elizabethan age, and these manuscripts were passed from one friend to another, with new copies being transcribed in the process.) This book is now our only source for Shakespeare's sonnets, and we do not know if it contains all the sonnets Shakespeare wrote or how it was put together. The sequence of sonnets in the original book is now usually followed in reprintings, but this sequence is not necessarily that in which the sonnets were written, or that in which Shakespeare wanted them to be read. It might just as probably be accidental. Nothing we know about Shakespeare's life from other sources throws any light on the personal experiences and emotions the sonnets may reflect, and we cannot be sure that they reflect anything personal. Many Elizabethan sonnets drew their subject matter more from what was conventional and expected in such poems than from the writer's experiences. If Shakespeare seems less conventional than other Elizabethan sonneteers, it may be because he was a better poet and therefore able to make whatever he imagined seem intensely real. Obviously he did this in his plays to a supreme degree. Consequently, although it is usually agreed that sonnets 1–126 are addressed to a young man, we cannot in fact be sure that this is true—or even that there was only one young man. An attempt to find a story of Shakespeare's life in the sonnets is hopeless.

We are equally uncertain as to when the sonnets were composed. At least some of them had been written by 1598, since in that year one contemporary referred to Shakespeare's "sugred Sonnets among his private friends." On the basis of stylistic similarities between the sonnets and Shakespeare's dramas and other poems, scholars have usually felt that the sonnets were composed between 1593 and 1609 (most of them between 1593 and 1596).

Many of the greatest sonnets deal with the themes of time and mutability—the changes that life inevitably will bring in our emotions, personal relations, circumstances in every way, and of course in our bodies as we move toward old age and death. The poet tries to rear defences against time. The young man, he says, must father children, for in some sense his children will continue his being after he is dead (sonnet 12). Or the mighty art of the poet will outlast time, forever revealing the beauty and goodness which inspires the poems (sonnets 18, 55, 60). Or, as in the great sonnet 116, the poet's love will last through all the vicissitudes of his life; no matter how the feelings of the loved person may alter towards him, nothing can make his love change. Yet in other sonnets the speaker knows that youth and beauty inexorably pass, that lovers change toward each other, that death is inevitable—in short, that in one form or another "Time will come and take my love away" (sonnet 64). Knowing that the person he loves may eventually leave him, Shakespeare touchingly shows how deeply he loves by justifying this desertion in advance, as in sonnet 49 or more bitterly in sonnet 87. Other sonnets simply declare his devotion (sonnets 109 and 110). In the powerful sonnet 129 he analyses with concentrated, shocking repugance the working of lust; in sonnet 146 he implicitly places the sonnets within a larger religious perspective, one not previously brought into the sonnets. Some of these themes—the power of the poet's art to outlast time, or the more general theme of mutability—were common in Renaissance poetry. But Shakespeare expresses them with a realistic sense of the complexity of the human heart, a power and range of reflective thought, and an imaginative richness no other poet could equal.

In addition to the *Sonnets*, we also include many of the songs from Shakespeare's plays and the difficult "The Phoenix and the Turtle," which was published in a collection of lyrics by various poets. The songs are wonderful when read as lyrics, but are still more moving if one also hears the music; of course they also have special meanings and fulfill special structural purposes in their original context in the plays. The magical "Full Fathom Five" in *The Tempest*, for example, is sung on an island by a voice in the air to Prince Ferdinand. It tells him that his father, with whom he has been shipwrecked and from whom he is separated, has been drowned. But this statement turns out to be false; the prince and his father are to be reunited. Moreover, the song describes drowning as though it were not a horrible death but an almost peaceful change of being ("a sea-change/ Into something rich and strange"). Thus the song prefigures and symbolizes a change in moral character that will take place in these shipwrecked characters. Three hundred years later, T. S. Eliot used these implications in his poem, *The Waste Land*, in which he alluded to this song.

Sonnets

12

When I do count the clock that tells the time
And see the brave day sunk in hideous night,
When I behold the violet past prime
And sable curls all silvered o'er with white,
When lofty trees I see barren of leaves,
Which erst from heat did canopy the herd,
And summer's green all girded up in sheaves
Borne on the bier with white and bristly beard;
Then of thy beauty do I question make
That thou among the wastes of time must go,

Since sweets and beauties do themselves forsake
And die as fast as they see others grow;
  And nothing 'gainst Time's scythe can make defense
  Save breed, to brave him when he takes thee hence.

15

When I consider everything that grows
Holds in perfection but a little moment,
That this huge stage presenteth nought but shows
Whereon the stars in secret influence comment;
When I perceive that men as plants increase,
Cheerèd and checked even by the selfsame sky,
Vaunt in their youthful sap, at height decrease,
And wear their brave state out of memory:
Then the conceit of this inconstant stay
Sets you most rich in youth before my sight,
Where wasteful Time debateth with Decay
To change your day of youth to sullied night;
  And, all in war with Time for love of you,
  As he takes from you, I ingraft you new.

18

Shall I compare thee to a summer's day?
Thou art more lovely and more temperate:
Rough winds do shake the darling buds of May,
And summer's lease hath all too short a date:
Sometimes too hot the eye of heaven shines,
And often is his gold complexion dimmed;
And every fair from fair sometimes declines,
By chance or nature's changing course untrimmed;
But thy eternal summer shall not fade,
Nor lose possession of that fair thou ow'st;
Nor shall death brag thou wander'st in his shade,
When in eternal lines to time thou grow'st:
  So long as men can breathe, or eyes can see,
  So long lives this, and this gives life to thee.

29

When, in disgrace with fortune and men's eyes,
I all alone beweep my outcast state,
And trouble deaf heaven with my bootless cries,
And look upon myself, and curse my fate,

SONNETS. **15. 7. vaunt:** boast. **sap:** vigor. **8. brave:** splendid. **9. conceit:** idea (conception). **18. 4. lease:** allotted time. **11. shade:** oblivion. **29. 3. bootless:** useless.

Wishing me like to one more rich in hope,
Featured like him, like him with friends possessed,
Desiring this man's art and that man's scope,
With what I most enjoy contented least;
Yet in these thoughts myself almost despising,
Haply I think on thee—and then my state,
Like to the lark at break of day arising
From sullen earth, sings hymns at heaven's gate;
  For thy sweet love remembered such wealth brings
  That then I scorn to change my state with kings.

30

When to the sessions of sweet silent thought
I summon up remembrance of things past,
I sigh the lack of many a thing I sought,
And with old woes new wail my dear time's waste:
Then can I drown an eye, unused to flow,
For precious friends hid in death's dateless night,
And weep afresh love's long since canceled woe,
And moan th' expense of many a vanished sight:
Then can I grieve at grievances foregone,
And heavily from woe to woe tell o'er
The sad account of fore-bemoanèd moan,
Which I new pay as if not paid before.
  But if the while I think on thee, dear friend,
  All losses are restored and sorrows end.

44

If the dull substance of my flesh were thought,
Injurious distance should not stop my way;
For then, despite of space, I would be brought,
From limits far remote, where thou dost stay.
No matter then although my foot did stand
Upon the farthest earth removed from thee;
For nimble thought can jump both sea and land
As soon as think the place where he would be.
But, ah, thought kills me that I am not thought,
To leap large lengths of miles when thou art gone,
But that, so much of earth and water wrought,
I must attend time's leisure with my moan,
  Receiving naught by elements so slow
  But heavy tears, badges of either's woe.

7. scope: intellectual range. **10. Haply:** perhaps. **12. sullen:** gloomy. **30. 4. wail:** bewail. **6. dateless:** endless. **9. foregone:** former. **44. 2. Injurious:** harmful, spiteful. **4. where:** to where. **11. wrought:** made. **14. either's woe:** the unhappiness of both of us.

49

Against that time, if ever that time come,
When I shall see thee frown on my defects,
Whenas thy love hath cast his utmost sum,
Called to that audit by advised respects;
Against that time when thou shalt strangely pass
And scarcely greet me with that sun, thine eye,
When love, converted from the thing it was,
Shall reasons find of settled gravity:
Against that time do I ensconce me here
Within the knowledge of mine own desert,
And this my hand against myself uprear
To guard the lawful reasons on thy part.
  To leave poor me thou hast the strength of laws,
  Since why to love I can allege no cause.

53

What is your substance, whereof are you made,
That millions of strange shadows on you tend?
Since every one hath, every one, one shade,
And you, but one, can every shadow lend.
Describe Adonis, and the counterfeit
Is poorly imitated after you.
On Helen's cheek all art of beauty set,
And you in Grecian tires are painted new.
Speak of the spring and foison of the year:
The one doth shadow of your beauty show,
The other as your bounty doth appear,
And you in every blessèd shape we know.
  In all external grace you have some part,
  But you like none, none you, for constant heart.

55

Not marble nor the gilded monuments
Of princes shall outlive this pow'rful rime,
But you shall shine more bright in these contents
Than unswept stone, besmeared with sluttish time.
When wasteful war shall statues overturn,
And broils root out the work of masonry,

49. 3. cast . . . sum: made its reckoning. **4. advised respects:** informed considerations. **5. strangely:** like a stranger. **9. ensconce:** fortify **53. 5. Adonis:** the beautiful youth loved by Venus. **counterfeit:** imitation or picture. **7. Helen:** Helen of Troy. **8. tires:** attires. **9. foison:** autumn. **55. 4. sluttish:** dirty.

Nor Mars his sword nor war's quick fire shall burn
The living record of your memory.
'Gainst death and all oblivious enmity
Shall you pace forth; your praise shall still find room
Even in the eyes of all posterity
That wear this world out to the ending doom.
So, till the judgment that yourself arise,
You live in this, and dwell in lovers' eyes.

60

Like as the waves make towards the pebbled shore,
So do our minutes hasten to their end;
Each changing place with that which goes before,
In sequent toil all forwards do contend.
Nativity, once in the main of light,
Crawls to maturity, wherewith being crowned,
Crooked eclipses 'gainst his glory fight,
And Time that gave doth now his gift confound.
Time doth transfix the flourish set on youth
And delves the parallels in beauty's brow,
Feeds on the rarities of nature's truth,
And nothing stands but for his scythe to mow:
And yet to times in hope my verse shall stand,
Praising thy worth, despite his cruel hand.

64

When I have seen by Time's fell hand defaced
The rich proud cost of outworn buried age;
When sometime lofty towers I see down-razed,
And brass eternal slave to mortal rage;
When I have seen the hungry ocean gain
Advantage on the kingdom of the shore,
And the firm soil win of the watery main,
Increasing store with loss, and loss with store;
When I have seen such interchange of state,
Or state itself confounded to decay,
Ruin hath taught me thus to ruminate,
That time will come and take my love away.
This thought is as a death, which cannot choose
But weep to have that which it fears to lose.

7. Mars his sword: Mars's sword (Mars was the god of war). **9. all oblivious enmity:** oblivion the enemy of all. **60. 4. sequent:** successive. **contend:** make battle. **13. times in hope:** to future, hoped for times. **64. 1. fell:** cruel. **2. cost:** outlay.

71

No longer mourn for me when I am dead
Than you shall hear the surly sullen bell
Give warning to the world that I am fled
From this vile world, with vilest worms to dwell:
Nay, if you read this line, remember not
The hand that writ it; for I love you so,
That I in your sweet thoughts would be forgot,
If thinking on me then should make you woe.
Oh, if, I say, you look upon this verse
When I perhaps compounded am with clay,
Do not so much as my poor name rehearse,
But let your love even with my life decay;
  Lest the wise world should look into your moan,
  And mock you with me after I am gone.

73

That time of year thou mayst in me behold
When yellow leaves, or none, or few, do hang
Upon those boughs which shake against the cold,
Bare ruined choirs, where late the sweet birds sang.
In me thou see'st the twilight of such day
As after sunset fadeth in the west;
Which by and by black night doth take away,
Death's second self, that seals up all in rest.
In me thou see'st the glowing of such fire,
That on the ashes of his youth doth lie,
As the deathbed whereon it must expire,
Consumed with that which it was nourished by.
  This thou perceiv'st, which makes thy love more strong,
  To love that well which thou must leave ere long.

87

Farewell: thou art too dear for my possessing,
And like enough thou know'st thy estimate.
The charter of thy worth gives thee releasing;
My bonds in thee are all determinate.
For how do I hold thee but by thy granting,
And for that riches where is my deserving?
The cause of this fair gift in me is wanting,

71. 13. wise: cynical, disdaining sentiment. **73. 4. choirs:** part of the church where services are sung. **87. 3. charter:** deed, or agreement on paper. **4. bonds:** claims. **determinate:** ended. **7. wanting:** lacking.

And so my patent back again is swerving.
Thyself thou gav'st, thy own worth then not knowing,
Or me, to whom thou gav'st it, else mistaking;
So thy great gift, upon misprision growing,
Comes home again, on better judgment making.
  Thus have I had thee as a dream doth flatter,
  In sleep a king, but waking no such matter.

94

They that have power to hurt and will do none,
That do not do the thing they most do show,
Who, moving others, are themselves as stone,
Unmovèd, cold, and to temptation slow;
They rightly do inherit heaven's graces
And husband nature's riches from expense;
They are the lords and owners of their faces,
Others but stewards of their excellence.
The summer's flower is to the summer sweet,
Though to itself it only live and die,
But if that flower with base infection meet,
The basest weed outbraves his dignity:
  For sweetest things turn sourest by their deeds;
  Lilies that fester smell far worse than weeds.

97

How like a winter hath my absence been
From thee, the pleasure of the fleeting year!
What freezings have I felt, what dark days seen!
What old December's bareness everywhere!
And yet this time removed was summer's time,
The teeming autumn, big with rich increase,
Bearing the wanton burden of the prime,
Like widowed wombs after their lords' decease:
Yet this abundant issue seemed to me
But hope of orphans and unfathered fruit;
For summer and his pleasures wait on thee,
And, thou away, the very birds are mute;
  Or, if they sing, 'tis with so dull a cheer
  That leaves look pale, dreading the winter's near.

11. upon misprision growing: based on a mistake. **94. 2. show:** seem able to do. **7. owners . . . faces:** possess the qualities they show. **8. stewards:** underlings, who wait on them or work for them. **97. 5. removed:** when I was away. **6. teeming:** fertile, productive. **increase:** harvest. **7. wanton burden:** harvest of its wanton productivity. **prime:** spring. **10. hope of orphans:** hope with no true parentage (or cause).

104

To me, fair friend, you never can be old,
For as you were when first your eye I eyed,
Such seems your beauty still. Three winters cold
Have from the forests shook three summers' pride,
Three beauteous springs to yellow autumn turned
In process of the seasons have I seen,
Three April perfumes in three hot Junes burned,
Since first I saw you fresh, which yet are green.
Ah, yet doth beauty, like a dial hand,
Steal from his figure, and no pace perceived;
So your sweet hue, which methinks still doth stand,
Hath motion, and mine eye may be deceived;
  For fear of which, hear this, thou age unbred:
  Ere you were born was beauty's summer dead.

106

When in the chronicle of wasted time
I see descriptions of the fairest wights,
And beauty making beautiful old rime
In praise of ladies dead and lovely knights;
Then, in the blazon of sweet beauty's best,
Of hand, of foot, of lip, of eye, of brow,
I see their antique pen would have expressed
Even such a beauty as you master now.
So all their praises are but prophecies
Of this our time, all you prefiguring;
And, for they looked but with divining eyes,
They had not skill enough your worth to sing:
  For we, which now behold these present days,
  Have eyes to wonder, but lack tongues to praise.

107

Not mine own fears, nor the prophetic soul
Of the wide world, dreaming on things to come,
Can yet the lease of my true love control,
Supposed as forfeit to a confined doom.
The mortal moon hath her eclipse endured,
And the sad augurs mock their own presage;

104. 7. burned: Like incense, the flowers of April are burned in the hot summer. **13. unbred:** not yet born. **106. 2. wights:** persons. **10. prefiguring:** picturing in advance. **11. for . . . but:** except that they had looked with. **107. 3. lease:** term. **4. Supposed . . doom:** assumed to be subject to a limited time. **5. mortal . . . endured:** The eclipse of the moon had been associated with the death of Queen Elizabeth (1603). **6. augurs:** prophets.

Incertainties now crown themselves assured,
And peace proclaims olives of endless age.
Now with the drops of this most balmy time
My love looks fresh, and Death to me subscribes,
Since, spite of him, I'll live in this poor rime,
While he insults o'er dull and speechless tribes:
  And thou in this shalt find thy monument
  When tyrants' crests and tombs of brass are spent.

109

O, never say that I was false of heart,
Though absence seemed my flame to qualify;
As easy might I from myself depart
As from my soul, which in thy breast doth lie.
That is my home of love: if I have ranged,
Like him that travels I return again,
Just to the time, not with the time exchanged,
So that myself bring water for my stain.
Never believe, though in my nature reigned
All frailties that besiege all kinds of blood,
That it could so preposterously be stained
To leave for nothing all thy sum of good;
  For nothing this wide universe I call
  Save thou, my rose; in it thou art my all.

110

Alas, 'tis true I have gone here and there
And made myself a motley to the view,
Gored mine own thoughts, sold cheap what is most dear,
Made old offenses of affections new.
Most true it is that I have looked on truth
Askance and strangely; but, by all above,
These blenches gave my heart another youth,
And worse essays proved thee my best of love.
Now all is done, have what shall have no end:
Mine appetite I never more will grind
On newer proof, to try an older friend,
A god in love, to whom I am confined.
  Then give me welcome, next my heaven the best,
  Even to thy pure and most most loving breast.

8. olives: olive branches (symbol of peace). **109. 7. Just:** punctually. **10. blood:** human flesh. **110. 2. motley:** dress worn by a jester. **4. affections new:** new love affairs violating older love and trust. **7. blenches:** turnings aside. **8. worse essays:** worse attempts.

116

Let me not to the marriage of true minds
Admit impediments. Love is not love
Which alters when it alteration finds,
Or bends with the remover to remove:
Oh, no! it is an ever-fixèd mark,
That looks on tempests and is never shaken;
It is the star to every wandering bark,
Whose worth's unknown, although his height be taken.
Love's not Time's fool, though rosy lips and cheeks
Within his bending sickle's compass come;
Love alters not with his brief hours and weeks,
But bears it out even to the edge of doom.
  If this be error and upon me proved,
  I never writ, nor no man ever loved.

129

Th' expense of spirit in a waste of shame
Is lust in action; and till action, lust
Is perjured, murderous, bloody, full of blame,
Savage, extreme, rude, cruel, not to trust;
Enjoyed no sooner but despisèd straight:
Past reason hunted, and no sooner had,
Past reason hated, as a swallowed bait,
On purpose laid to make the taker mad:
Mad in pursuit, and in possession so;
Had, having, and in quest to have, extreme;
A bliss in proof, and proved, a very woe;
Before, a joy proposed; behind, a dream.
  All this the world well knows; yet none knows well
  To shun the heaven that leads men to this hell.

130

My mistress' eyes are nothing like the sun;
Coral is far more red than her lips' red;
If snow be white, why then her breasts are dun;
If hairs be wires, black wires grow on her head.
I have seen roses damasked, red and white,
But no such roses see I in her cheeks;

116. 5. mark: sea-mark. **8. worth's . . . taken:** whose worth cannot be calculated, though the height of the star can be estimated. **129. 1–2. Th' expense . . . action:** Lust, acted out, uses up the vital power or spirit in a shameful waste. **2–4. till action . . . trust:** Until it is acted out, the appetite leading one to lust is untrustworthy, self-regarding, prone to lie, "rude" (brutal), and so on. **11. in proof . . . woe:** in the process of testing, pleasant, but, when "proved" (tested), unpleasant. **130. 5. damasked:** mixed red and white.

And in some perfumes is there more delight
Than in the breath that from my mistress reeks.
I love to hear her speak, yet well I know
That music hath a far more pleasing sound;
I grant I never saw a goddess go;
My mistress, when she walks, treads on the ground.
And yet, by heaven, I think my love as rare
As any she belied with false compare.

138

When my love swears that she is made of truth,
I do believe her, though I know she lies,
That she might think me some untutored youth,
Unlearnèd in the world's false subtleties.
Thus vainly thinking that she thinks me young,
Although she knows my days are past the best,
Simply I credit her false-speaking tongue:
On both sides thus is simple truth suppressed.
But wherefore says she not she is unjust?
And wherefore say not I that I am old?
Oh, love's best habit is in seeming trust,
And age in love loves not to have years told.
Therefore I lie with her and she with me,
And in our faults by lies we flattered be.

146

Poor soul, the center of my sinful earth,
Fooled by these rebel powers that thee array,
Why dost thou pine within and suffer dearth,
Painting thy outward walls so costly gay?
Why so large cost, having so short a lease,
Dost thou upon thy fading mansion spend?
Shall worms, inheritors of this excess,
Eat up thy charge? Is this thy body's end?
Then, soul, live thou upon thy servant's loss,
And let that pine to aggravate thy store;
Buy terms divine in selling hours of dross;

8. reeks: exudes strong odor. **14. any she:** any woman. **belied:** misrepresented. **compare:** comparison (with the sun, snow, and so on). **138. 6. past the best:** past youth and into middle age. **11. best habit . . . trust:** The best thing love can do is to appear to trust. **13. lie:** a pun, means both to lie, in the sense of telling falsehood, and also to lie in bed with. **146. 1. earth:** body. **2. Fooled by:** This is a conjecture. The original printed version simply repeated the last three words of the previous line. The sense is that the soul is being deceived by the rebellious flesh that encloses ("arrays") it. **4. Painting:** ornamenting (putting on costly clothes). **9. servant's:** the body's. **10. aggravate:** increase. **11. terms divine:** immortality in heaven. **hours of dross:** hours of waste (on earth).

Within be fed, without be rich no more.
So shalt thou feed on death, that feeds on men,
And death once dead, there's no more dying then.

1609

The Phoenix and the Turtle

Let the bird of loudest lay,
On the sole Arabian tree,
Herald sad and trumpet be,
To whose sound chaste wings obey.

But thou shrieking harbinger,
Foul precurrer of the fiend,
Augur of the fever's end,
To this troop come thou not near!

From this session interdict
Every fowl of tyrant wing,
Save the eagle, feathered king:
Keep the obsequy so strict.

Let the priest in surplice white,
That defunctive music can,
Be the death-divining swan,
Lest the requiem lack his right.

And thou treble-dated crow,
That thy sable gender mak'st
With the breath thou giv'st and tak'st,
'Mongst our mourners shalt thou go.

Here the anthem doth commence:
Love and constancy is dead,
Phoenix and the turtle fled
In a mutual flame from hence.

So they loved as love in twain
Had the essence but in one;

THE PHOENIX AND THE TURTLE. **Title:** The phoenix was a mythical bird that died in flames and was then reborn from its own ashes. It thus symbolized immortality. The turtle was an abbreviated form of turtledove, a symbol of love. **1. lay:** song. **2. sole Arabian tree:** The only tree of its kind in which the phoenix can nest. **5. harbinger:** the screech owl. **6. precurrer:** precursor (preceding the devil). **7. Augur . . . end:** prophet of death. **9. interdict:** prohibit, condemn. **10. fowl . . . wing:** bird of prey. **14. defunctive music can:** can furnish funeral music. **15. death-divining swan:** The swan, prophetically aware that it is about to die, sings its last song. **17. treble-dated crow:** long-lived (equal to three usual lives). **18. sable gender:** black offspring. **19. With the breath:** The crow was supposed to conceive its young through its beak. **25–26. So they . . . one:** They so loved that, though two, they were in essence one.

Two distincts, division none:
Number there in love was slain.

Hearts remote, yet not asunder;
Distance, and no space was seen
'Twixt this turtle and his queen;
But in them it were a wonder.

So between them love did shine
That the turtle saw his right
Flaming in the phoenix' sight:
Either was the other's mine.

Property was thus appalled,
That the self was not the same;
Single nature's double name
Neither two nor one was called.

Reason, in itself confounded,
Saw division grow together,
To themselves yet either neither,
Simple were so well compounded;

That it cried, "How true a twain
Seemeth this concordant one!
Love hath reason, reason none,
If what parts can so remain."

Whereupon it made this threne
To the phoenix and the dove,
Co-supremes and stars of love,
As chorus to their tragic scene.

Threnos

Beauty, truth, and rarity,
Grace in all simplicity,
Here enclosed in cinders lie.

27. distincts: distinct people. **28. Number . . . slain:** The mere idea of "number" (more than one person) was obliterated. **29. Hearts remote:** hearts separated in space. **32. But:** except. **it were:** it would be. **34. right:** right of love. **36. mine:** its very own. **37–38. Property . . . same:** The mere idea of "property" (personal possession) found itself defied by the idea that there were not divided private selves in this union. **39–40. Single . . . called:** The single unity of the two was something that was neither just two or just one. **41–42. Reason . . . together:** Reason, which distinguishes and divides in order to analyze, is confused because here the two parts unite and coalesce. **43–44. either . . . compounded:** Each loses its identity as it becomes merged with the other as the "simple" (individual unit) becomes so completely combined with the other. **46. concordant:** harmonious. **48. If . . . remain:** if what divides or parts into two can remain one. **49. threne:** threnody (funeral song). **55. enclosed . . . lie:** enclosed among the ashes (cinders) in the funeral urn (line 65).

Death is now the phoenix' nest;
And the turtle's loyal breast
To eternity doth rest,

Leaving no posterity:
'Twas not their infirmity,
It was married chastity.

Truth may seem, but cannot be;
Beauty brag, but 'tis not she:
Truth and Beauty buried be.

To this urn let those repair
That are either true or fair;
For these dead birds sigh a prayer.

When Daisies Pied

Spring

When daisies pied and violets blue
  And ladysmocks all silver-white
And cuckoobuds of yellow hue
  Do paint the meadows with delight,
The cuckoo then, on every tree,
Mocks married men; for thus sings he,
          Cuckoo;
Cuckoo, cuckoo: Oh word of fear,
Unpleasing to a married ear!

When shepherds pipe on oaten straws,
  And merry larks are plowmen's clocks,
When turtles tread, and rooks, and daws,
  And maidens bleach their summer smocks,
The cuckoo then, on every tree,
Mocks married men; for thus sings he,
          Cuckoo;
Cuckoo, cuckoo: Oh word of fear,
Unpleasing to a married ear!

60. infirmity: sterility. **61. married chastity:** though married, yet remaining chaste. **62. seem:** seem to exist. **63. brag . . . she:** Beauty may boast, but it will not be real beauty, which instead lies buried here. WHEN DAISIES PIED. **Title:** "Pied" means varied in color. These two songs conclude Shakespeare's early comedy, *Love's Labour's Lost* (1595). **2. ladysmocks:** spring flowers of the cress family. **12. turtles:** turtledoves. **tread:** come together in mating.

Winter

When icicles hang by the wall
  And Dick the shepherd blows his nail
And Tom bears logs into the hall,
  And milk comes frozen home in pail,
When blood is nipped and ways be foul,
Then nightly sings the staring owl,
        Tu-who;
Tu-whit, tu-who: a merry note,
While greasy Joan doth keel the pot.

When all aloud the wind doth blow,
  And coughing drowns the parson's saw,
And birds sit brooding in the snow,
  And Marian's nose looks red and raw,
When roasted crabs hiss in the bowl,
Then nightly sings the staring owl,
        Tu-who;
Tu-whit, tu-who: a merry note
While greasy Joan doth keel the pot.

1595

Under the Greenwood Tree

  Under the greenwood tree
  Who loves to lie with me,
  And turn his merry note
  Unto the sweet bird's throat,
Come hither, come hither, come hither:
    Here shall he see
    No enemy
But winter and rough weather.

  Who doth ambition shun
  And loves to live i' the sun,
  Seeking the food he eats,
  And pleased with what he gets,
Come hither, come hither, come hither:
    Here shall he see
    No enemy
But winter and rough weather.

1599

20. blows . . . nail: breathes on his fingernails to warm them. **27. keel:** stir while boiling. **32. crabs:** crab apples. UNDER THE GREENWOOD TREE. **Title:** From *As You Like It* (1599), II.5.

Blow, Blow, Thou Winter Wind

Blow, blow, thou winter wind,
Thou art not so unkind
As man's ingratitude;
Thy tooth is not so keen,
Because thou art not seen,
Although thy breath be rude.
Heigh-ho! sing, heigh-ho! unto the green holly:
Most friendship is feigning, most loving mere folly:
Then, heigh-ho, the holly!
This life is most jolly.

Freeze, freeze, thou bitter sky,
That dost not bite so nigh
As benefits forgot:
Though thou the waters warp,
Thy sting is not so sharp
As friend remembered not.
Heigh-ho! sing, . . .

1599

It Was a Lover and His Lass

It was a lover and his lass,
With a hey, and a ho, and a hey nonino,
That o'er the green corn field did pass
In springtime, the only pretty ring time,
When birds do sing, hey ding a ding, ding:
Sweet lovers love the spring.

Between the acres of the rye,
With a hey, and a ho, and a hey nonino,
These pretty country folks would lie,
In springtime, . . .

This carol they began that hour,
With a hey, and a ho, and a hey nonino,
How that a life was but a flower
In springtime, . . .

And therefore take the present time,
With a hey, and a ho, and a hey nonino;
For love is crownèd with the prime
In springtime, . . .

1599

BLOW, BLOW, THOU WINTER WIND. **Title:** From *As You Like It* (1599), II.7. IT WAS A LOVER AND HIS LASS. **Title:** From *As You Like It* (1599), V.3.

Oh Mistress Mine

Oh mistress mine! where are you roaming?
Oh! stay and hear; your true love's coming,
  That can sing both high and low.
Trip no further, pretty sweeting;
Journeys end in lovers meeting,
  Every wise man's son doth know.

What is love? 'tis not hereafter;
Present mirth hath present laughter;
  What's to come is still unsure:
In delay there lies no plenty;
Then come kiss me, sweet and twenty,
  Youth's a stuff will not endure.

1602

When That I Was and a Little Tiny Boy

When that I was and a little tiny boy,
  With hey, ho, the wind and the rain,
A foolish thing was but a toy,
  For the rain it raineth every day.

But when I came to man's estate,
  With hey, ho, . . .
'Gainst knaves and thieves men shut their gate,
  For the rain, . . .

But when I came, alas! to wive,
  With hey, ho, . . .
By swaggering could I never thrive,
  For the rain, . . .

But when I came unto my beds,
  With hey, ho, . . .
With toss-pots still had drunken heads,
  For the rain, . . .

A great while ago the world begun,
  With hey, ho, . . .
But that's all one, our play is done,
  And we'll strive to please you every day.

1602

OH MISTRESS MINE. **Title:** From *Twelfth Night* (1602), II.3. WHEN THAT I WAS. **Title:** From *Twelfth Night* (1602), sung by the clown at the end of the play.

Hark! Hark! the Lark

Hark, hark! the lark at heaven's gate sings,
  And Phoebus 'gins arise,
His steeds to water at those springs
  On chaliced flowers that lies;
And winking Mary-buds begin
  To ope their golden eyes:
With every thing that pretty is,
  My lady sweet, arise:
  Arise, arise!

1610?

Fear No More the Heat o' the Sun

Fear no more the heat o' the sun,
  Nor the furious winter's rages;
Thou thy worldly task hast done,
  Home art gone, and ta'en thy wages:
Golden lads and girls all must,
As chimney-sweepers, come to dust.

Fear no more the frown o' the great;
  Thou art past the tyrant's stroke;
Care no more to clothe and eat;
  To thee the reed is as the oak:
The scepter, learning, physic, must
All follow this, and come to dust.

Fear no more the lightning flash,
  Nor the all-dreaded thunder stone;
Fear not slander, censure rash;
  Thou hast finished joy and moan:
All lovers young, all lovers must
Consign to thee, and come to dust.

1610?

Full Fathom Five

Full fathom five thy father lies;
  Of his bones are coral made;

HARK! HARK!. **Title:** From *Cymbeline* (1610?), II.3. **2. Phoebus:** Apollo (the sun). **4. chaliced:** cup-shaped. FEAR NO MORE. **Title:** From *Cymbeline* (1610?), IV.2. **14. thunder stone:** thunderbolt. FULL FATHOM FIVE. **Title:** From *The Tempest* (1611), I.2.

Those are pearls that were his eyes:
  Nothing of him that doth fade,
But doth suffer a sea change
Into something rich and strange.
Sea nymphs hourly ring his knell:
  Ding-dong.
Hark! now I hear them—Ding-dong, bell.

1611

THOMAS CAMPION

(1567–1620)

A student of both law and medicine, Campion carried over the habits of analysis learned in these professions into music and versification. He wrote an excellent essay on verse technique, called *Observations on the Art of English Poetry* (1602), and was a talented musical composer. In writing poetry his hope, as he said, "was to couple my work and notes [music] lovingly together."

Among his aims as a poet was to discover in English the equivalent of the Greek and Latin "quantitative meter" (see Appendix on Versification). Instead of basing his meter on the alternation of accented and unaccented syllables—the usual stress-syllabic meters of English—he tried to use the ancient classical meter based on "quantity," that is, on "long" vowels (vowels that take longer to pronounce) in relation to "short" ones. This form of versification is rarely successful in English—dozens of poets have tried it—simply because of the nature of the language. But Campion wrote lovely poems in the attempt. His nearest approach to successful quantitative meter is "Rose-Cheeked Laura," in which accent is somewhat muted in favor of the length of the vowel sounds.

My Sweetest Lesbia

My sweetest Lesbia, let us live and love,
And though the sager sort our deeds reprove,

MY SWEETEST LESBIA. **Title:** Adapted and partly translated from a poem of the Latin poet Catullus (87 B.C.–54 B.C.) addressed to his beloved, Lesbia.

Let us not weigh them. Heaven's great lamps do dive
Into their west, and straight again revive,
But soon as once set is our little light,
Then must we sleep one ever-during night.

If all would lead their lives in love like me,
Then bloody swords and armor should not be;
No drum nor trumpet peaceful sleeps should move,
Unless alarm came from the camp of love.
But fools do live, and waste their little light,
And seek with pain their ever-during night.

When timely death my life and fortune ends,
Let not my hearse be vexed with mourning friends,
But let all lovers, rich in triumph, come
And with sweet pastimes grace my happy tomb;
And Lesbia, close up thou my little light,
And crown with love my ever-during night.

1601

When to Her Lute Corinna Sings

When to her lute Corinna sings,
Her voice revives the leaden strings,
And doth in highest notes appear
As any challenged echo clear;
But when she doth of mourning speak,
Ev'n with her sighs the strings do break.

And as her lute doth live or die,
Led by her passion, so must I:
For when of pleasure she doth sing,
My thoughts enjoy a sudden spring,
But if she doth of sorrow speak,
Ev'n from my heart the strings do break.

1601

When Thou Must Home

When thou must home to shades of underground,
And there arrived, a new admirèd guest,
The beauteous spirits do engirt thee round,
White Iope, blithe Helen, and the rest,

WHEN THOU MUST HOME. **4. Iope:** daughter of Aelus, renowned for her beauty. **blithe Helen:** Helen of Troy, called "blithe" (cheerfully frivolous) because she was fickle as well as beautiful.

To hear the stories of thy finished love
From that smooth tongue whose music hell can move,

Then wilt thou speak of banqueting delights,
Of masques and revels which sweet youth did make,
Of tourneys and great challenges of knights,
And all these triumphs for thy beauty's sake;
When thou hast told these honors done to thee,
Then tell, Oh tell, how thou didst murther me.

1601

Rose-cheeked Laura

Rose-cheeked Laura, come,
Sing thou smoothly with thy beauty's
Silent music, either other
Sweetly gracing.

Lovely forms do flow
From concent divinely framed;
Heav'n is music, and thy beauty's
Birth is heavenly.

These dull notes we sing
Discords need for helps to grace them;
Only beauty purely loving
Knows no discord,

But still moves delight,
Like clear springs renewed by flowing,
Ever perfect, ever in them-
Selves eternal.

1602

ROSE-CHEEKED LAURA. **6. concent:** notes uniting in harmony.

Thomas Nashe

(1567–1601)

One of the most haunting lyrics in English poetry, "A Litany in Time of Plague" was written, strangely enough, by a man noted otherwise for his vituperative and even slanderous satiric works and for a picaresque tale of rogue life called *The Unfortunate Traveler* (1594). He wrote this poem during the London plague of 1592, when he was twenty-five, and included it a few years later in a comedy called *Summer's Last Will and Testament* (1600), published just before he himself died.

A Litany in Time of Plague

Adieu, farewell, earth's bliss;
This world uncertain is;
Fond are life's lustful joys;
Death proves them all but toys;
None from his darts can fly;
I am sick, I must die.
  Lord, have mercy on us!

Rich men, trust not in wealth,
Gold cannot buy you health;
Physic himself must fade.
All things to end are made,
The plague full swift goes by;
I am sick, I must die
  Lord, have mercy on us!

Beauty is but a flower
Which wrinkles will devour;
Brightness falls from the air;
Queens have died young and fair;
Dust hath closed Helen's eye.
I am sick, I must die.
  Lord, have mercy on us!

Strength stoops unto the grave,
Worms feed on Hector brave;

A LITANY IN TIME OF PLAGUE. **3. fond:** foolish. **4. toys:** trifles. **19. Helen:** of Troy. **23. Hector:** Trojan hero in the *Iliad.*

Swords may not fight with fate,
Earth still holds ope her gate.
"Come, come!" the bells do cry.
I am sick, I must die.
  Lord, have mercy on us.

Wit with his wantonness
Tasteth death's bitterness;
Hell's executioner
Hath no ears for to hear
What vain art can reply.
I am sick, I must die.
  Lord, have mercy on us.

Haste, therefore, each degree,
To welcome destiny;
Heaven is our heritage,
Earth but a player's stage;
Mount we unto the sky.
I am sick, I must die.
  Lord, have mercy on us.

1600

JOHN DONNE

(1572–1631)

The son of a well-to-do ironmonger, Donne had important patrons and was rising in the world when in 1601 he made a secret marriage which temporarily wrecked his career. In 1615 he was ordained an Anglican priest, and within a few years he became Dean of St. Paul's Cathedral in London, where his sermons increased his fame. In addition to poetry he wrote a great deal of religious prose. Most of his poems circulated in manuscript during his lifetime, but were not printed until after his death.

By the end of his life Donne had become an important influence on other poets, who admired his colloquial voice and complicated, intellectual wit. Most poets of the previous, Elizabethan generation had striven for melodic sweetness of sound and smoothly flowing rhythm. After the turn of the century many readers and poets began to find these qualities old-fashioned and artificial. The poetry of Donne, which was partly responsible for this change of taste, was very different, as one may easily see by comparing the opening lines of "The Canonization" ("For God's sake hold your tongue . . . ") with the start of any poem by Spenser or of most by Shakespeare. The difference lies both in the blunt vocabulary and syntax and in the rhythmic movement, which in Donne is more broken and irregular. In every respect Donne's poetry is much closer to the way people actually spoke. But we should keep in mind that even in the earlier generation a rough, direct speech was ordinary and expected in poetic satires, and Donne's innovation was partly that he used the diction and rhythm of satire in lyric poetry.

Donne's complicated "wit" has been much admired at some times and condemned at others. In "A Valediction: Forbidding Mourning," for example, he compares two lovers, one of whom is about to travel, to the two legs of a compass. One of the compass legs remains fixed in one point, and the other moves, but the fixed leg leans toward the other:

> And though it in the center sit,
>   Yet when the other far doth roam,
> It leans and hearkens after it,
>   And grows erect, as that comes home.

This comparison is developed for twelve lines. In "A Valediction: Of Weeping" he compares tears to worlds and then to a deluge drowning the world; in the "Hymn to God My God, in My Sickness," where he speaks of himself on his death bed, he describes his body as a map and his doctors as geographers bent over the map and studying it. Such comparisons are often called *conceits.* The things compared to each other at first seem very dissimilar (a man's body and a map), and hence the likeness Donne finds may be described as unexpected, ingenious, remote, or (more pejoratively) far-fetched. Donne often continues and develops a conceit through several lines, finding more and more points of resemblance between the things compared. And like Donne's poetry generally, the terms of Donne's comparisons may be learned, requiring readers to know the astronomy, medical lore, alchemy, or theology of Donne's time.

Whether such conceits are poetically effective has been much debated, and three great poets and critics must be heard on the subject. In a *Discourse Concerning the Original and Progress of Satire* (1693) John Dryden said that Donne "affects the metaphysics . . . and perplexes the minds of the fair sex with nice [overly refined] speculations of philosophy, when he should engage their hearts." Here Dryden's objection is that Donne's poetry activates intellect more than it does emotion, and that this is inappropriate in love poetry. The concept of *propriety*—of what is proper in a certain genre or type of poetry—is the central consideration shaping Dryden's judgment on this point. When he speaks, in *An Essay of Dramatic Poesy* (1668), of Donne's satires instead of his love poems, Dryden praises Donne's intellectual strength: "he gives us deep thoughts in common language."

About a hundred years later Samuel Johnson remembered these remarks of Dryden when, in his *Lives of the Poets* (1779), he came to discuss the conceited style of a minor follower of Donne, Abraham Cowley. Johnson speaks of Donne and his followers as "a race of writers that may be termed the metaphysical poets," and describes the kind of "wit" found in their poetry as a "*discordia concors* [harmonious discord]; a combination of dissimilar images, or discovery of occult resemblances in things apparently unlike." Johnson goes on to consider at more length the same issues Dryden had raised. The thoughts and emotions expressed by the "metaphysical poets" were, says Johnson, unnatural and insincere. "Their courtship was void of fondness and their lamentation of sorrow. Their wish was only to say what they hoped had never been said before." Trying to be poets of "wit" they "yoked" together by violence the "most heterogenous ideas." Yet, Johnson adds, "great labor directed by great abilities is never wholly lost: if they frequently threw away their wit upon false conceits, they likewise sometimes struck out unexpected truth." And for Johnson it was a great merit of the "metaphysical poets" that they never fell into smooth, commonplace insipidity. "To write on their plan it was at least necessary to read and think."

These remarks of Dryden and of Johnson established the term "metaphysical poets" as the usual name for Donne and his followers. But even by Johnson's time their poetry was not much read or even remembered, and this continued to be the case throughout the nineteenth century. In the twentieth century, however, a revival of interest and appreciation took place, and for at least two decades, from the 1930s to the 1950s, the poetry of Donne was a major influence on modern poetry. This revival was especially fostered by critical essays T. S. Eliot published in the 1920s. Remarking that Johnson was a "very dangerous" critic to disagree with, Eliot nevertheless defined "metaphysical wit," including the conceit, in a favorable way. He argued that the remote comparisons of "metaphysical" poetry express a healthy wholeness and nimbleness of mind. They show the poet's mind "constantly amalgamating disparate" experiences and "forming new wholes" out of them. "Metaphysical wit" is not cynical, Eliot observed, but "may be confused with cynicism by the tender-minded. . . . It is confused with cynicism because it implies a constant inspection and criticism of experience. It involves, probably, a recognition, implicit in the expression of every experience, of other kinds of experience which are possible."

Thus Eliot called attention to the ironical quality of "metaphysical wit." Whatever the "metaphysical" poet asserts or feels he may also qualify, for he keeps in mind other considerations that would tend to undermine his assertion or emotion. Donne's "The Relic" is a love poem, yet it begins with a reference to death and the grave—in other words, to aspects of experience most people would not associate with love.

> When my grave is broke up again
> Some second guest to entertain
> (For graves have learned that woman-head
> To be to more than one a bed) . . .

In Elizabethan graveyards a grave was often opened in order to make room for another body, and Donne's witty conceit compares graves in this respect to a woman's bed. Thus the poem assumes that women are generally unfaithful, yet it goes on to affirm that Donne and the woman he loves are completely devoted and faithful to each other, and that their love is therefore a "miracle." Donne is being humorously witty while also expressing with utmost seriousness the depth and completeness of his love.

Song

Go and catch a falling star,
  Get with child a mandrake root,
Tell me where all past years are,
  Or who cleft the Devil's foot,
Teach me to hear mermaids singing,
Or to keep off envy's stinging,
    And find
    What wind
Serves to advance an honest mind.

If thou beest born to strange sights,
  Things invisible to see,
Ride ten thousand days and nights,
  Till age snow white hairs on thee.
Thou, when thou return'st, wilt tell me
All strange wonders that befell thee,
    And swear
    Nowhere
Lives a woman true, and fair.

If thou find'st one, let me know,
  Such a pilgrimage were sweet;

SONG. **2. mandrake root:** plant roughly resembling the human body, with two roots like human legs. Donne mentions impregnating it as an example of extreme impossibility. **5. mermaids singing:** here identified with the Sirens, whose song no one but Odysseus ever heard and survived.

Yet do not, I would not go,
  Though at next door we might meet;
Though she were true when you met her,
And last till you write your letter,
      Yet she
      Will be
False, ere I come, to two, or three.

1633

The Sun Rising

  Busy old fool, unruly sun,
  Why dost thou thus,
Through windows and through curtains call on us?
Must to thy motions lovers' seasons run?
  Saucy pedantic wretch, go chide
  Late school boys and sour prentices,
 Go tell court huntsmen that the king will ride,
 Call country ants to harvest offices;
Love, all alike, no season knows nor clime,
Nor hours, days, months, which are the rags of time.

  Thy beams, so reverend and strong
  Why shouldst thou think?
I could eclipse and cloud them with a wink,
But that I would not lose her sight so long;
  If her eyes have not blinded thine,
  Look, and tomorrow late tell me,
 Whether both th' Indias of spice and mine
 Be where thou leftst them, or lie here with me.
Ask for those kings whom thou saw'st yesterday,
And thou shalt hear, All here in one bed lay.

  She's all states, and all princes, I,
  Nothing else is.
Princes do but play us; compared to this,
All honor's mimic, all wealth alchemy.
  Thou, sun, art half as happy as we,
  In that the world's contracted thus;
 Thine age asks ease, and since thy duties be
 To warm the world, that's done in warming us.
Shine here to us, and thou art everywhere;
This bed thy center is, these walls, thy sphere.

1633

THE SUN RISING. **17. both . . . mine:** both the Indies: the East and the West—the first, a source of spice, the second thought to be a source of gold (hence *mine,* for *goldmine*). **24. alchemy:** imitation gold.

The Canonization

For God's sake hold your tongue, and let me love,
  Or chide my palsy, or my gout,
My five gray hairs, or ruined fortune, flout,
  With wealth your state, your mind with arts improve,
    Take you a course, get you a place,
    Observe His Honor, or His Grace,
Or the King's real, or his stampèd face
  Contèmplate; what you will, approve,
  So you will let me love.

Alas, alas, who's injured by my love?
  What merchant's ships have my sighs drowned?
Who says my tears have overflowed his ground?
  When did my colds a forward spring remove?
    When did the heats which my veins fill
    Add one more to the plaguy bill?
Soldiers find wars, and lawyers find out still
  Litigious men, which quarrels move,
  Though she and I do love.

Call us what you will, we're made such by love;
  Call her one, me another fly,
We're tapers too, and at our own cost die,
  And we in us find th' eagle and the dove.
    The phoenix riddle hath more wit
    By us: we two being one, are it.
So, to one neutral thing both sexes fit.
  We die and rise the same, and prove
  Mysterious by this love.

We can die by it, if not live by love,
  And if unfit for tombs and hearse
Our legend be, it will be fit for verse;
  And if no piece of chronicle we prove,
    We'll build in sonnets pretty rooms;
    As well a well-wrought urn becomes
The greatest ashes, as half-acre tombs;
  And by these hymns, all shall approve
  Us canonized for love:

THE CANONIZATION. **5. course:** career. **place:** appointment. **6. Observe:** be attentive to. **7. stampèd face:** face stamped in coins. **8. approve:** try. **13. forward:** early. **15. one more:** one more person. **plaguy bill:** list of those dead of the plague. **17. quarrels move:** stir up quarrels. **20. fly:** butterfly (like a moth, attracted by the flame of a candle to its death). **22. eagle . . . dove:** symbols of power and gentleness. **23–27. phoenix . . . love:** The way the phoenix becomes immortal, rising from its own ashes, is shown with more "wit" (aptness) by us; for we die (in the older use of the term for sexual consummation), then revive in order to die again.

And thus invoke us: You whom reverend love
  Made one another's hermitage;
You, to whom love was peace, that now is rage;
  Who did the whole world's soul contract, and drove
    Into the glasses of your eyes
    (So made such mirrors, and such spies,
That they did all to you epitomize)
  Countries, towns, courts: Beg from above
  A pattern of your love!

1633

The Anniversary

    All kings and all their favorites,
    All glory of honors, beauties, wits,
The sun itself, which makes times, as they pass,
Is elder by a year, now, than it was
When thou and I first one another saw:
All other things to their destruction draw,
    Only our love hath no decay;
This, no tomorrow hath, nor yesterday;
Running it never runs from us away,
But truly keeps his first, last, everlasting day.

    Two graves must hide thine and my corse;
    If one might, death were no divorce:
Alas, as well as other princes, we
(Who prince enough in one another be)
Must leave at last in death, these eyes, and ears,
Oft fed with true oaths, and with sweet salt tears;
    But souls where nothing dwells but love
(All other thoughts being inmates) then shall prove
This, or a love increasèd there above,
When bodies to their graves, souls from their graves remove.

    And then we shall be throughly blest,
    But we no more than all the rest;
Here upon earth, we're kings, and none but we
Can be such kings, nor of such subjects be;
Who is so safe as we, where none can do
Treason to us, except one of us two?
    True and false fears let us refrain,

40. contract: possibly a printer's error, never corrected, for "extract," which, in alchemy, applies to the process of distilling. THE ANNIVERSARY. **3. times:** seasons. **they:** refers to the kings and favorites. **11. corse:** corpse. **18. inmates:** temporary lodgers. **19. this:** the fact that death is not a permanent separation. **21. throughly:** thoroughly.

Let us love nobly, and live, and add again
Years and years unto years, till we attain
To write threescore, this is the second of our reign.

1633

A Valediction: Of Weeping

Let me pour forth
My tears before thy face whilst I stay here,
For thy face coins them, and thy stamp they bear,
And by this mintage they are something worth,
For thus they be
Pregnant of thee;
Fruits of much grief they are, emblems of more;
When a tear falls, that Thou falls which it bore,
So thou and I are nothing then, when on a diverse shore.

On a round ball
A workman that hath copies by, can lay
An Europe, Afric, and an Asia,
And quickly make that, which was nothing, all,
So doth each tear
Which thee doth wear,
A globe, yea world, by that impression grow,
Till thy tears mixed with mine do overflow
This world; by waters sent from thee, my heaven dissolvèd so.

O more than moon,
Draw not up seas to drown me in thy sphere;
Weep me not dead, in thine arms, but forbear
To teach the sea what it may do too soon.
Let not the wind
Example find
To do me more harm than it purposeth;
Since thou and I sigh one another's breath,
Whoe'er sighs most is cruelest, and hastes the other's death.

1633

A VALEDICTION: OF WEEPING. **9. diverse shore:** on a different shore. **13. make . . . all:** can make, on a blank globe, which was *nothing,* a map of the whole world *(all).*

A Nocturnal upon St. Lucy's Day, Being the Shortest Day

'Tis the year's midnight, and it is the day's,
Lucy's, who scarce seven hours herself unmasks;
  The sun is spent, and now his flasks
  Send forth light squibs, no constant rays;
    The world's whole sap is sunk;
The general balm th' hydroptic earth hath drunk,
Whither, as to the bed's-feet, life is shrunk,
Dead and interred; yet all these seem to laugh,
Compared with me, who am their epitaph.

Study me then, you who shall lovers be
At the next world, that is, at the next spring:
  For I am every dead thing,
  In whom love wrought new alchemy.
    For his art did express
A quintessence even from nothingness,
From dull privations, and lean emptiness;
He ruined me, and I am re-begot
Of absence, darkness, death; things which are not.

All others, from all things, draw all that's good,
Life, soul, form, spirit, whence they being have;
  I, by love's limbeck, am the grave
  Of all that's nothing. Oft a flood
    Have we two wept, and so
Drowned the whole world, us two; oft did we grow
To be two chaoses, when we did show
Care to aught else; and often absences
Withdrew our souls, and made us carcasses.

But I am by her death (which word wrongs her)
Of the first nothing the elixir grown;
  Were I a man, that I were one
  I needs must know; I should prefer,
    If I were any beast,
Some ends, some means; yea plants, yea stones detest,
And love; all, all some properties invest;
If I an ordinary nothing were,
As shadow, a light and body must be here.

But I am none; nor will my Sun renew.
You lovers, for whose sake the lesser sun
  At this time to the Goat is run

A NOCTURNAL UPON ST. LUCY'S DAY. **Title:** St. Lucy's Day (December 13) was the winter solstice, the shortest day of the year, in the old or Julian calendar used in England until the Gregorian calendar (our present one) was adopted in 1752.

To fetch new lust, and give it you,
Enjoy your summer all;
Since she enjoys her long night's festival,
Let me prepare towards her, and let me call
This hour her Vigil, and her Eve, since this
Both the year's, and the day's deep midnight is.

1633

A Valediction: Forbidding Mourning

As virtuous men pass mildly away,
And whisper to their souls to go,
Whilst some of their sad friends do say
The breath goes now, and some say, No;

So let us melt, and make no noise,
No tear-floods, nor sigh-tempests move,
'Twere profanation of our joys
To tell the laity our love.

Moving of th' earth brings harms and fears,
Men reckon what it did and meant;
But trepidation of the spheres,
Though greater far, is innocent.

Dull sublunary lovers' love
(Whose soul is sense) cannot admit
Absence, because it doth remove
Those things which elemented it.

But we by a love so much refined
That our selves know not what it is,
Inter-assurèd of the mind,
Care less, eyes, lips, and hands to miss.

Our two souls therefore, which are one,
Though I must go, endure not yet
A breach, but an expansion,
Like gold to airy thinness beat.

If they be two, they are two so
As stiff twin compasses are two;

A VALEDICTION: FORBIDDING MOURNING. **8. laity:** common people. **9. Moving . . . earth:** earthquakes. **11–12. trepidation . . . innocent:** The vibration of the planets in their spheres, according to the old Ptolemaic astronomy, caused general variations in the universe. This, says Donne, though a "greater" thing than earthquakes, causes less damage to our lives. **13. sublunary:** on the earth (literally, *sub luna*, "beneath the moon"). **14. sense:** sensuality. **admit:** permit. **16. elemented:** composed the elements of. **26. compasses:** not a magnetic compass, but the instrument, with two "feet" (one fixed in the center, the other holding a pen or pencil), for drawing circles.

Thy soul, the fixed foot, makes no show
  To move, but doth, if th' other do.

And though it in the center sit,
  Yet when the other far doth roam,
It leans and hearkens after it,
  And grows erect, as that comes home.

Such wilt thou be to me, who must
  Like th' other foot, obliquely run;
Thy firmness makes my circle just,
  And makes me end where I begun.

1633

The Ecstasy

Where, like a pillow on a bed,
  A pregnant bank swelled up to rest
The violet's reclining head,
  Sat we two, one another's best.
Our hands were firmly cèmented
  With a fast balm, which thence did spring.
Our eye-beams twisted, and did thread
  Our eyes upon one double string;
So to'intergraft our hands, as yet
  Was all the means to make us one;
And pictures in our eyes to get
  Was all our propagation.
As 'twixt two equal armies, Fate
  Suspends uncertain victory,
Our souls (which to advance their state,
  Were gone out) hung 'twixt her and me.
And whilst our souls negotiate there,
  We like sepulchral statues lay;
All day the same our postures were,
  And we said nothing all the day.
If any, so by love refined
  That he soul's language understood,
And by good love were grown all mind,
  Within convenient distance stood,
He (though he knew not which soul spake,
  Because both meant, both spake the same)
Might thence a new concoction take,

32. as that: as that other foot. THE ECSTASY. **Title:** In Greek, *extasis* means "a stepping out." Religious writers applied it to the state in which the soul leaves the body and finds union with God. **11. get:** beget. The reflection of oneself in the eyes of another was called a "baby." **27. concoction:** purification by heat.

And part far purer than he came.
This ecstasy doth unperplex,
We said, and tell us what we love;
We see by this it was not sex;
We see we saw not what did move;
But as all several souls contain
Mixture of things, they know not what,
Love these mixed souls doth mix again,
And makes both one, each this and that.
A single violet transplant,
The strength, the colour, and the size
(All which before was poor, and scant)
Redoubles still, and multiplies.
When love, with one another so
Interinanimates two souls,
That abler soul, which thence doth flow,
Defects of loneliness controls.
We then, who are this new soul, know,
Of what we are composed, and made,
For, th' atomies of which we grow,
Are souls, whom no change can invade.
But O alas, so long, so far
Our bodies why do we forbear?
They're ours, though they're not we; we are
Th' intelligences, they the spheres.
We owe them thanks because they thus,
Did us to us at first convey,
Yielded their forces, sense, to us,
Nor are dross to us, but allay.
On man heaven's influence works not so
But that it first imprints the air,
So soul into the soul may flow,
Though it to body first repair.
As our blood labors to beget
Spirits as like souls as it can,
Because such fingers need to knit
That subtle knot which makes us man:
So must pure lovers' souls descend
To affections, and to faculties
Which sense may reach and apprehend;
Else a great Prince in prison lies.

33. several: separate, individual. **44. Defects . . . controls:** corrects the defects (or imperfections) of loneliness. **47. atomies:** atoms. **51–52. we . . . spheres:** We are the spirits that (in Ptolemaic astronomy) control the spheres (our bodies). **56. allay:** alloy. **57–58. heaven's influence . . . air:** Angels were thought to take the form of air in their influence on people. **62. Spirits:** Vapors rising from the blood were thought to connect body with soul. **63. need:** are necessary.

To our bodies turn we then, that so
  Weak men on love revealed may look;
Love's mysteries in souls do grow,
  But yet the body is his book.
And if some lover, such as we,
  Have heard this dialogue of one,
Let him still mark us; he shall see
  Small change when we're to bodies gone.

1633

The Funeral

Whoever comes to shroud me, do not harm
    Nor question much
That subtle wreath of hair which crowns my arm;
Thy mystery, the sign you must not touch,
    For 'tis my outward soul,
Viceroy to that, which then to heaven being gone,
    Will leave this to control,
And keep these limbs, her provinces, from dissolution.

For if the sinewy thread my brain lets fall
    Through every part
Can tie those parts and make me one of all;
These hairs, which upward grew, and strength and art
    Have from a better brain,
Can better do it; except she meant that I
    By this should know my pain,
As prisoners then are manacled, when they're condemned to die.

Whate'er she meant by it, bury it with me,
    For since I am
Love's martyr, it might breed idolatry,
If into other's hands these relics came;
    As 'twas humility
To afford to it all that a soul can do,
    So 'tis some bravery,
That since you would save none of me, I bury some of you.

1633

THE FUNERAL. **6. Viceroy:** prime minister; left to rule in place of the soul (the real ruler of the body), which has gone to heaven. **9. sinewy thread:** network of nerves.

The Relic

When my grave is broke up again
Some second guest to entertain
(For graves have learned that woman-head
To be to more than one a bed),
And he that digs it, spies
A bracelet of bright hair about the bone,
Will he not let us alone,
And think that there a loving couple lies,
Who thought that this device might be some way
To make their souls, at the last busy day,
Meet at this grave, and make a little stay?

If this fall in a time, or land,
Where mis-devotion doth command,
Then he that digs us up, will bring
Us to the Bishop and the King,
To make us relics; then
Thou shalt be a Mary Magdalen, and I
A something else thereby;
All women shall adore us, and some men;
And since at such time, miracles are sought,
I would have that age by this paper taught
What miracles we harmless lovers wrought.

First, we loved well and faithfully,
Yet knew not what we loved, nor why,
Difference of sex no more we knew,
Than our guardian angels do;
Coming and going, we
Perchance might kiss, but not between those meals;
Our hands ne'er touched the seals,
Which nature, injured by late law, sets free:
These miracles we did; but now, alas,
All measure and all language I should pass,
Should I tell what a miracle she was.

1633

THE RELIC. **2. second guest:** Graves were often used again because of the shortage of space. **3. woman-head:** womanhood. **10. busy day:** Day of Judgment. **13. mis-devotion:** false worship (referring to the Catholic veneration of relics, which was denounced by many Protestants). **17. Mary Magdalen:** who was taken in adultery and forgiven by Jesus (Luke 7:36–50). Commonly used as a name for a harlot who has repented. **21. this paper:** this poem. **27–28. Coming . . . meals:** Only in greeting and leaving would we kiss, the kiss being the food ("meals") of our souls. **29–30. Our hands . . . free:** We never took part in physical intercourse, which nature would not restrain, but which is restrained by our modern laws.

Elegy XIX To His Mistress Going to Bed

Come, madam, come, all rest my powers defy,
Until I labor, I in labor lie.
The foe oft-times, having the foe in sight,
Is tired with standing though he never fight.
Off with that girdle, like heaven's zone glittering,
But a far fairer world encompassing.
Unpin that spangled breastplate which you wear,
That th' eyes of busy fools may be stopped there.
Unlace yourself, for that harmonious chime
Tells me from you that now it is bed time.
Off with that happy busk, which I envy,
That still can be, and still can stand so nigh.
Your gown, going off, such beauteous state reveals,
As when from flowry meads th' hill's shadow steals.
Off with that wiry coronet and show
The hairy diadem which on you doth grow:
Now off with those shoes, and then safely tread
In this love's hallowed temple, this soft bed.
In such white robes, heaven's angels used to be
Received by men; thou, Angel, bring'st with thee
A heaven like Mahomet's Paradise; and though
Ill spirits walk in white, we easily know
By this these angels from an evil sprite:
Those set our hairs, but these our flesh upright.
  License my roving hands, and let them go
Before, behind, between, above, below.
O my America! my new-found-land,
My kingdom, safeliest when with one man manned,
My mine of precious stones, my empery,
How blest am I in this discovering thee!
To enter in these bonds is to be free;
There where my hand is set, my seal shall be.
  Full nakedness! All joys are due to thee,
As souls unbodied, bodies unclothed must be
To taste whole joys. Gems which you women use
Are like Atlanta's balls, cast in men's views,
That when a fool's eye lighteth on a gem,
His earthly soul may covet theirs, not them.
Like pictures, or like books' gay coverings made
For lay-men, are all women thus arrayed;

ELEGY XIX. **5. heaven's zone:** belt on the constellation Orion. **7. breastplate:** stomacher, or covering for the chest. **11. busk:** corset. **21. Mahomet's Paradise:** the Paradise of the Mohammedans was associated with sensuous pleasure. **29. empery:** empire. **36. Atlanta's balls:** The swift Atalanta agreed to marry Hippomenes if he could outrace her. As he ran, he threw into her path golden apples, which she stopped to pick up and, therefore, lost the race.

Themselves are mystic books, which only we
(Whom their imputed grace will dignify)
Must see revealed. Then, since that I may know,
As liberally as to a midwife, show
Thyself: cast all, yea, this white linen hence,
There is no penance due to innocence.
  To teach thee, I am naked first; why then,
What needst thou have more covering than a man?

1669

from Holy Sonnets

7

At the round earth's imagined corners, blow
Your trumpets, angels; and arise, arise
From death, you numberless infinities
Of souls, and to your scattered bodies go;
All whom the flood did, and fire shall, o'erthrow,
All whom war, dearth, age, agues, tyrannies,
Despair, law, chance hath slain, and you whose eyes
Shall behold God, and never taste death's woe.
But let them sleep, Lord, and me mourn a space;
For, if above all these, my sins abound,
'Tis late to ask abundance of Thy grace
When we are there. Here on this lowly ground,
Teach me how to repent; for that's as good
As if Thou hadst sealed my pardon with Thy blood.

1633

10

Death, be not proud, though some have callèd thee
Mighty and dreadful, for thou are not so;
For those whom thou think'st thou dost overthrow
Die not, poor Death, nor yet canst thou kill me.
From rest and sleep, which but thy pictures be,
Much pleasure; then from thee much more must flow,
And soonest our best men with thee do go,
Rest of their bones, and soul's delivery.

42. Whom . . . dignify: we whom the grace of the Bible's books will make worthy of salvation. **47. than:** then. HOLY SONNETS. **7. 1. imagined corners:** referring to the words in the Bible, "I saw four angels standing on the four corners of the earth" (Revelation 7:1), the "corners" being of course imaginary for the "round earth." **5. flood . . . fire:** all that the great flood of Noah's time had killed, and all that the fire (the final conflagration at the end of the world) shall destroy. **8. death's woe:** allusion to Luke 9:27.

Thou art slave to fate, chance, kings, and desperate men,
And dost with poison, war, and sickness dwell,
And poppy or charms can make us sleep as well
And better than thy stroke; why swell'st thou then?
One short sleep past, we wake eternally
And death shall be no more; Death, thou shalt die.

1633

14

Batter my heart, three-personed God; for You
As yet but knock, breathe, shine, and seek to mend;
That I may rise and stand, o'erthrow me, and bend
Your force to break, blow, burn, and make me new.
I, like an usurped town, to another due,
Labor to admit You, but O, to no end;
Reason, Your viceroy in me, me should defend,
But is captìved, and proves weak or untrue.
Yet dearly I love You, and would be lovèd fain,
But am betrothed unto Your enemy.
Divorce me, untie or break that knot again;
Take me to You, imprison me, for I,
Except You enthrall me, never shall be free,
Nor ever chaste, except You ravish me.

1633

Hymn to God My God, in My Sickness

Since I am coming to that holy room
  Where, with Thy choir of saints for evermore,
I shall be made Thy music; as I come
  I tune the instrument here at the door,
  And what I must do then, think here before.

Whilst my physicians by their love are grown
  Cosmographers, and I their map, who lie
Flat on this bed, that by them may be shown
  That this is my southwest discovery
  Per fretum febris, by these straits to die,

I joy, that in these straits, I see my West;
  For, though their currents yield return to none,

14. 1. three-personed God: the Trinity (Father, Son, and Holy Ghost). A HYMN TO GOD MY GOD. **Title:** Written not in the illness before his death (1631), as was commonly thought, but during a serious illness in 1623. **9. southwest discovery:** Magellan's discovery of the straits near Cape Horn that bear his name, which permitted him to sail into the Pacific. **10. *Per fretum febris*:** through straits of fever.

What shall my West hurt me? As West and East
  In all flat maps (and I am one) are one,
  So death doth touch the resurrection.

Is the Pacific Sea my home? Or are
  The Eastern riches? Is Jerusalem?
Anyan, and Magellan, and Gibraltar,
  All straits, and none but straits, are ways to them,
  Whether where Japhet dwelt, or Cham, or Shem.

We think that Paradise and Calvary,
  Christ's cross, and Adam's tree, stood in one place;
Look, Lord, and find both Adams met in me;
  As the first Adam's sweat surrounds my face,
  May the last Adam's blood my soul embrace.

So, in his purple wrapped, receive me, Lord;
  By these his thorns give me his other crown;
And, as to others' souls I preached Thy word,
  Be this my text, my sermon to mine own;
  Therefore that he may raise the Lord throws down.

1635

BEN JONSON

(1572–1637)

In the first half of the seventeenth century the great rival poet to Donne was Jonson. And just as there was a "metaphysical" school of poets who followed Donne or somewhat resembled him in style, there were also the "sons of Ben"—poets who took the style of Jonson as their model—some of whom are called the "cavalier" poets. (The term "metaphysical" was not, however, used by the poets it now applies to, whereas the "sons of Ben" bestowed this term upon themselves.) Among the poets included in this anthology, Henry King, George Herbert, Abraham Cowley, Andrew Marvell, and Henry Vaughan are conventionally included among the "metaphysicals;" the

13–15. As west . . . resurrection: Like the left (west) and right (east) sides of a flat map, which would touch each other if joined, so death and resurrection touch each other. **18. Anyan:** the Bering Straits. **Magellan . . . Gibraltar:** the straits of Magellan and Gibraltar. **20. Japhet . . . Shem:** sons of Noah, whose inheritances were Europe (Japhet), Africa (Cham or Ham), and Asia (Shem).

"sons of Ben" number Robert Herrick, Edmund Waller, Sir John Suckling, and Richard Lovelace, although some of these more resemble grandsons. But when two powerful, somewhat contrasted styles develop at the same time, the poets who follow immediately are normally influenced by both styles at once and combine them in various ways. This is exactly what happened in the seventeenth century. A poet such as Marvell shares something of the wit and complicated irony of Donne's poetry, but also has the classically smooth and polished form typical of Jonson's lyrics. Of course, there were many other models besides Donne and Jonson, and while every poet learns from others, every good poet is also original.

After some years at Westminster School, Jonson was briefly a bricklayer, a soldier, and then an actor. Eventually he became one of the foremost playwrights of our language and—with *Every Man in His Humor* (1598)—the founder of a new type of comedy (the *comedy of humors*) which was to have a long career on the English stage. After the death of Queen Elizabeth he was employed by the new court of James I as the chief creator of the type of theatrical entertainment known as *masques*—brief, usually allegorical scripts to be performed with lavish scenery and music. Fine as they are, his poems and songs were only a small part of his creative effort.

Jonson wrote his poems in prose before he versified them, a practice which suggests the large role played in his creativity by rational self-criticism and revision. He was immensely learned in classical (especially Latin) literature, and many of his songs and epitaphs are based on some classical poem or prose passage, although Jonson always made these borrowings his own. In a more general sense he also modeled his poetry on the classical. He strove for terseness with weight of meaning, but, unlike Donne, was also careful to be immediately understandable. He was closely attentive to formal and rhetorical aspects of his poems—such as versification, figures of speech, and sequence of statements—and achieved at his best a perfect smoothness and ease. He can also seem rather cool emotionally. In the famous "Song: To Celia," for example, Jonson did not mean his exaggerations to be understood as completely sincere; he was exhibiting his art in a traditional type of classical lyric. In the poem "On My First Son," however, the emotion is direct and moving, yet still kept within bounds of reason and of artistic taste and form.

Jonson was a literary critic as well as a poet, and the poems to John Donne and to William Shakespeare reflect this preoccupation. The poem to Shakespeare is more generous to that author than Jonson always was, since elsewhere he said that "Shaksperr wanted [lacked] Arte." Three of the lyrics included here are from theatrical works: "Queen and

Huntress" is from *Cynthia's Revels* (1600), V. 6, and is sung by Hesperus, the evening star, to Cynthia (Diana), goddess of the moon, who represents Queen Elizabeth; "Come, My Celia" is from the comedy *Volpone* (1606), III. 7, in which the wicked Volpone sings it to Celia in his attempt to seduce her; and "Still to Be Neat" is from *Epicoene, or the Silent Woman* (1609), I. 1.

Queen and Huntress

Queen and huntress, chaste and fair,
Now the sun is laid to sleep,
Seated in thy silver chair,
State in wonted manner keep;
Hesperus entreats thy light,
Goddess excellently bright.

Earth, let not thy envious shade
Dare itself to interpose;
Cynthia's shining orb was made
Heaven to clear, when day did close.
Bless us then with wishèd sight,
Goddess excellently bright.

Lay thy bow of pearl apart,
And thy crystal-shining quiver;
Give unto the flying hart
Space to breathe, how short soever.
Thou that mak'st a day of night,
Goddess excellently bright.

1600

Come, My Celia

Come, my Celia, let us prove,
While we can, the sports of love;
Time will not be ours forever;
He at length our good will sever.
Spend not then his gifts in vain.
Suns that set may rise again;
But if once we lose this light,
'Tis with us perpetual night.
Why should we defer our joys?

QUEEN AND HUNTRESS. **10. clear:** make bright.

Fame and rumor are but toys.
Cannot we delude the eyes
Of a few poor household spies,
Or his easier ears beguile,
So removèd by our wile?
'Tis no sin love's fruit to steal;
But the sweet thefts to reveal,
To be taken, to be seen,
These have crimes accounted been.

1606

Still to Be Neat

Still to be neat, still to be dressed,
As you were going to a feast;
Still to be powdered, still perfumed;
Lady, it is to be presumed,
Though art's hid causes are not found,
All is not sweet, all is not sound.

Give me a look, give me a face
That makes simplicity a grace;
Robes loosely flowing, hair as free;
Such sweet neglect more taketh me
Then all th' adulteries of art.
They strike mine eyes, but not my heart.

1609

To the Reader

Pray thee, take care, that tak'st my book in hand,
To read it well: that is, to understand.

1616

On My First Daughter

Here lies, to each her parents' ruth,
Mary, the daughter of their youth;
Yet all heaven's gifts being heaven's due,

STILL TO BE NEAT. **5. art's:** artifice's. **10. taketh:** captivates. **11. adulteries:** adulterations. ON MY FIRST DAUGHTER. **1. ruth:** pity, grief.

It makes the father less to rue.
At six months' end she parted hence
With safety of her innocence;
Whose soul heaven's queen, whose name she bears,
In comfort of her mother's tears,
Hath placed amongst her virgin-train:
Where, while that severed doth remain,
This grave partakes the fleshly birth;
Which cover lightly, gentle earth!

1616

On My First Son

Farewell, thou child of my right hand, and joy;
My sin was too much hope of thee, loved boy:
Seven years thou wert lent to me, and I thee pay,
Exacted by thy fate, on the just day.
O could I lose all father now! for why
Will man lament the state he should envy,
To have so soon 'scaped world's and flesh's rage,
And, if no other misery, yet age?
Rest in soft peace, and asked, say, "Here doth lie
Ben Jonson his best piece of poetry."
For whose sake henceforth all his vows be such
As what he loves may never like too much.

1616

To John Donne

Who shall doubt, Donne, where I a poet be,
When I dare send my epigrams to thee?
That so alone canst judge, so alone dost make;
And, in thy censures, evenly dost take
As free simplicity to disavow
As thou hast best authority t' allow.
Read all I send, and if I find but one

ON MY FIRST SON. **1. right hand:** the meaning in English of the Hebrew name Benjamin, the name of Jonson's son who had died of the plague then decimating Londoners. **4. just day:** the seventh birthday of the boy (1603), thus completing the seven years term he was lent the father. TO JOHN DONNE. **1. where:** whether.

Marked by thy hand, and with the better stone,
My title's sealed. Those that for claps do write,
Let pui'nies, porters, players praise delight,
And, till they burst, their backs like asses load:
A man should seek great glory, and not broad.

1616

Epitaph on Salomon Pavy, a Child of Queen Elizabeth's Chapel

Weep with me, all you that read
  This little story,
And know, for whom a tear you shed,
  Death's self is sorry.
'Twas a child, that so did thrive
  In grace and feature,
As Heaven and Nature seemed to strive
  Which owned the creature.
Years he numbered scarce thirteen
  When Fates turned cruel,
Yet three filled zodiacs had he been
  The stage's jewel,
And did act, what now we moan,
  Old men so duly,
As, sooth, the Parcae thought him one,
  He played so truly.
So, by error, to his fate
  They all consented;
But viewing him since (alas, too late)
  They have repented.
And have sought, to give new birth,
  In baths to steep him;
But, being so much too good for earth,
  Heaven vows to keep him.

1616

8. stone: The Romans marked fortunate days with a white stone. **9. claps:** applause. **10. pui'nies:** puisnies, juniors or inferiors (pronounced *punies*). EPITAPH ON SALOMON PAVY. **Title:** Pavy was a boy (d. 1602) who had acted in plays of Jonson performed at the court by a troop of boy actors called "The Children of the Chapel." **11. zodiacs:** years. **15. Parcae:** the Fates. **22. steep him:** as Aeson, father of Jason, was made young by a bath prepared by Jason's wife, Medea.

Epitaph on Elizabeth, L. H.

Woudst thou hear what man can say
In a little? Reader, stay.
Underneath this stone doth lie
As much beauty as could die;
Which in life did harbor give
To more virtue than doth live.
If at all she had a fault,
Leave it buried in this vault.
One name was Elizabeth;
Th' other, let it sleep with death:
Fitter, where it died, to tell,
Than that it lived at all. Farewell.

1616

Song: To Celia

Drink to me only with thine eyes,
And I will pledge with mine;
Or leave a kiss but in the cup,
And I'll not look for wine.
The thirst that from the soul doth rise,
Doth ask a drink divine:
But might I of Jove's nectar sup,
I would not change for thine.
I sent thee late a rosy wreath,
Not so much honoring thee,
As giving it a hope, that there
It could not withered be.
But thou thereon did'st only breathe,
And sent'st it back to me;
Since when it grows and smells, I swear,
Not of itself, but thee.

1616

EPITAPH ON ELIZABETH, L. H. **Title:** Probably Elizabeth, Lady Hatton, the wife of Sir Edward Coke.

To the Memory of My Beloved, the Author Mr. William Shakespeare

And what he hath left us

To draw no envy, Shakespeare, on thy name,
Am I thus ample to thy book and fame,
While I confess thy writings to be such
As neither man nor Muse can praise too much.
'Tis true, and all men's suffrage. But these ways
Were not the paths I meant unto thy praise:
For silliest ignorance on these may light,
Which, when it sounds at best, but echoes right;
Or blind affection, which doth ne'er advance
The truth, but gropes, and urgeth all by chance;
Or crafty malice might pretend this praise,
And think to ruin where it seemed to raise.
These are as some infamous bawd or whore
Should praise a matron. What could hurt her more?
But thou art proof against them, and, indeed,
Above th' ill fortune of them, or the need.
I therefore will begin. Soul of the age!
The applause! delight! the wonder of our stage!
My Shakespeare, rise; I will not lodge thee by
Chaucer or Spenser, or bid Beaumont lie
A little further to make thee a room:
Thou art a monument without a tomb,
And art alive still while thy book doth live,
And we have wits to read and praise to give.
That I not mix thee so, my brain excuses,
I mean with great, but disproportioned Muses;
For, if I thought my judgment were of years,
I should commit thee surely with thy peers,
And tell how far thou didst our Lyly outshine,
Or sporting Kyd, or Marlowe's mighty line.
And though thou hadst small Latin and less Greek,
From thence to honor thee I would not seek
For names, but call forth thund'ring Aeschylus,

TO THE MEMORY OF . . . WILLIAM SHAKESPEARE. **Title:** Jonson's poem was prefixed to the famous First Folio edition of Shakespeare's plays (1623). **2. ample:** liberal. **5. suffrage:** consent. **7. silliest:** in the old sense of simplest or most innocent. **13. as:** as if. **20–21. Chaucer . . . room:** referring to the Poet's Corner in Westminster Abbey, where these poets are buried close together. Shakespeare himself was buried in Holy Trinity Church, Stratford-upon-Avon. **26. disproportioned:** not comparable. **27. of years:** taking a long view. **29–35. tell . . . Accius:** I would not compare you with your contemporaries, like Marlowe and the others, good as they were, but with the great Greek dramatists, Aeschylus, Sophocles, and Euripides, and the Latin ones, Pacucius, Accius, and Seneca, who was born in Cordova, Spain ("him of Cordova").

Euripides, and Sophocles to us,
Pacuvius, Accius, him of Cordova dead,
To life again, to hear thy buskin tread
And shake a stage; or, when thy socks were on,
Leave thee alone for the comparison
Of all that insolent Greece or haughty Rome
Sent forth, or since did from their ashes come.
Triumph, my Britain; thou hast one to show
To whom all scenes of Europe homage owe.
He was not of an age, but for all time!
And all the Muses still were in their prime
When like Apollo he came forth to warm
Our ears, or like a Mercury to charm.
Nature herself was proud of his designs,
And joyed to wear the dressing of his lines,
Which were so richly spun, and woven so fit,
As, since, she will vouchsafe no other wit:
The merry Greek, tart Aristophanes,
Neat Terence, witty Plautus now not please,
But antiquated and deserted lie,
As they were not of Nature's family.
Yet must I not give Nature all; thy Art,
My gentle Shakespeare, must enjoy a part.
For though the poet's matter Nature be,
His Art doth give the fashion; and that he
Who casts to write a living line must sweat
(Such as thine are) and strike the second heat
Upon the muses' anvil; turn the same,
And himself with it, that he thinks to frame,
Or for the laurel he may gain a scorn;
For a good poet's made as well as born.
And such wert thou! Look how the father's face
Lives in his issue, even so the race
Of Shakespeare's mind and manners brightly shines
In his well-turnèd and true-filèd lines,
In each of which he seems to shake a lance,
As brandished at the eyes of ignorance.
Sweet swan of Avon, what a sight it were
To see thee in our waters yet appear,
And make those flights upon the banks of Thames
That so did take Eliza and our James!
But stay; I see thee in the hemisphere
Advanced and made a constellation there!
Shine forth, thou star of poets, and with rage

36–37. buskin . . . socks: the "boot," worn by ancient actors of tragedy, and the light shoe worn by actors of comedy. **42. scenes:** stages. **51. Aristophanes:** Greek comic dramatist. **52. Terence . . . Plautus:** Latin comic writers. **58. that he:** that man. **63. for:** in place of. **69. shake a lance:** pun on Shakespeare's name. **74. take Eliza . . . James:** captivate Queen Elizabeth and James I.

Or influence chide or cheer the drooping stage,
Which, since thy flight from hence, hath mourned like night,
And despairs day, but for thy volume's light.

1623

JOHN FLETCHER

(1579–1625)

Fletcher was primarily a playwright and collaborated with his friend, Francis Beaumont (1584–1616), in a large number of plays, in which—as in most Elizabethan plays—songs were included to be sung at particular occasions in the play. He also collaborated with Shakespeare.

The most famous of Fletcher's songs, by far, is "Take, Oh, Take Those Lips Away." In writing it Fletcher simply added a second stanza to a song composed by Shakespeare for his play *Measure for Measure* (IV. 1) and printed in the First Folio edition of Shakespeare's plays (1623). Fletcher used the song in his play, *The Bloody Brother* (1639). This incorporating of poems by others into one's own work was relatively common at the time.

Take, Oh, Take Those Lips Away

Take, oh, take those lips away
That so sweetly were forsworn
And those eyes, like break of day,
Lights that do mislead the morn;
But my kisses bring again,
Seals of love, though sealed in vain.

Hide, oh, hide those hills of snow,
Which thy frozen bosom bears,
On whose tops the pinks that grow
Are of those that April wears;
But first set my poor heart free,
Bound in those icy chains by thee.

1639

78. influence: of the stars.

JOHN WEBSTER

(1580–1625)

Webster was a great tragic dramatist, whose plays create a brooding terror. He had deep psychological insight into the darker moods of the human psyche. Webster, said T. S. Eliot, "was much possessed by death / And saw the skull beneath the skin." The songs we include are from his most famous plays: "Call for the Robin Redbreast," from *The White Devil* (1612), and "Hark, Now Everything Is Still," from *The Duchess of Malfi* (written in 1613–14 but not published until 1623).

Call for the Robin Redbreast and the Wren

Call for the robin redbreast and the wren,
Since o'er shady groves they hover,
And with leaves and flowers do cover
The friendless bodies of unburied men.
Call unto his funeral dole
The ant, the field mouse, and the mole,
To rear him hillocks that shall keep him warm,
And, when gay tombs are robbed, sustain no harm;
But keep the wolf far thence, that's foe to men,
For with his nails he'll dig them up again.

1612

Hark, Now Everything Is Still

Hark, now everything is still;
The screech owl and the whistler shrill
Call upon our dame aloud,
And bid her quickly don her shroud.
Much you had of land and rent;
Your length in clay's now competent.
A long war disturbed your mind;
Here your perfect peace is signed.
Of what is 't fools make such vain keeping?

CALL FOR THE ROBIN REDBREAST. **5. dole:** SORROW.

Sin their conception, their birth weeping,
Their life a general mist of error,
Their death a hideous storm of terror.
Strew your hair with powders sweet,
Don clean linen, bathe your feet,
And, the foul fiend more to check,
A crucifix let bless your neck.
'Tis now full tide, 'tween night and day,
End your groan and come away.

1623

WILLIAM BROWNE

(c. 1591–1643?)

This gentle poet of the Devonshire countryside dedicated most of his poetic effort to a series of scenes, songs, and stories called *Britannia's Pastorals* (1613–16). One poem in particular keeps his memory alive. This is the beautifully grave and condensed epitaph he wrote on Mary Herbert, the mother of the Earl of Pembroke and the sister of Sir Philip Sidney, who died in 1621. For a long time it was considered too good (especially the lovely first stanza) to have been written by Browne, and was mistakenly attributed to Ben Jonson.

On the Countess Dowager of Pembroke

Underneath this sable hearse
Lies the subject of all verse:
Sidney's sister, Pembroke's mother.
Death, ere thou hast slain another
Fair and learn'd and good as she,
Time shall throw a dart at thee.

Marble piles let no man raise
To her name, for after-days
Some kind woman, born as she,
Reading this, like Niobe
Shall turn marble, and become
Both her mourner and her tomb.

1623

ROBERT HERRICK

(1591–1674)

One of the finest lyrical poets of the seventeenth century, Herrick was reared in a family of goldsmiths or jewelers. But instead of following the family business, he went to college in Cambridge. After graduating he spent approximately twelve years in London, where he was friendly with Ben Jonson and other poets and courtiers, and he himself acquired some reputation as a poet, although he had as yet published nothing. By 1627 he had become a clergyman, and two years later he became vicar of a country village in Devonshire in the west of England.

His poems are artful, graceful, witty, and charming. They are modeled on those of Ben Jonson and of the classical poets whom Jonson also so much admired. Julia and the other mistresses to whom he addressed his love poems were imaginary. As a result of the victory of the Puritans in the English Civil War, he was expelled from his vicarage in 1647. Returning to London, he published his one volume of poems (1648). Most of his lyrics involve traditional themes of Roman and Renaissance poetry—love and the fleeting brevity of time, the idyllic charm of country living—but he could express these themes with a lightness and freshness that make his work quite individual. Often he wrote on very slight subjects—his cat, his little spaniel, his attempt to stop drinking wine—and these poems are pleasant and elegant trifles.

The finest of his lyrics are the two poems about Julia and especially "Corinna's Going A-Maying." "To the Virgins, to Make Much of Time" is no less famous, and was probably the most popular poem of the second half of the seventeenth century. It is a perfect example of the Cavalier style that was fashionable at the time, and of the so-called *carpe diem* theme that was especially common then. The phrase *carpe diem*, from one of Horace's *Odes* (I. XI, 8), means "snatch the day"—in other words, enjoy the present moment while you can. Another famous example is Marvell's "To His Coy Mistress."

The Argument of His Book

I sing of brooks, of blossoms, birds, and bowers,
Of April, May, of June, and July flowers.
I sing of Maypoles, hock carts, wassails, wakes,
Of bridegrooms, brides, and of their bridal cakes.
I write of youth, of love, and have access
By these to sing of cleanly wantonness.
I sing of dews, of rains, and, piece by piece,
Of balm, of oil, of spice, and ambergris.
I sing of times trans-shifting, and I write
How roses first came red and lilies white.
I write of groves, of twilights, and I sing
The court of Mab and of the fairy king.
I write to hell; I sing (and ever shall)
Of heaven, and hope to have it after all.

1648

Delight in Disorder

A sweet disorder in the dress
Kindles in clothes a wantonness.
A lawn about the shoulders thrown
Into a fine distraction;
An erring lace, which here and there
Enthralls the crimson stomacher;
A cuff neglectful, and thereby
Ribbons to flow confusedly;
A winning wave, deserving note,
In the tempestuous petticoat;
A careless shoestring, in whose tie
I see a wild civility;
Do more bewitch me than when art
Is too precise in every part

1648

THE ARGUMENT OF HIS BOOK. **Title:** "Argument" in the sense of summary of the subject matter. **3. hock carts:** hay carts. **wakes:** celebrations at the church. **6. cleanly wantonness:** innocent carelessness and gaiety. **9. trans-shifting:** impermanence. **12. Mab:** Queen of the fairies. **fairy king:** Oberon, husband of Mab. DELIGHT IN DISORDER. **3. lawn:** linen scarf. **6. stomacher:** laced coat covering the breast and belly.

Corinna's Going A-Maying

Get up! get up for shame! the blooming morn
Upon her wings presents the god unshorn.
  See how Aurora throws her fair
  Fresh-quilted colors through the air:
  Get up, sweet slug-a-bed, and see
  The dew bespangling herb and tree.
Each flower has wept and bowèd toward the east
Above an hour since, yet you not dressed;
  Nay, not so much as out of bed?
  When all the birds have matins said,
  And sung their thankful hymns, 'tis sin,
  Nay, profanation to keep in,
Whenas a thousand virgins on this day
Spring, sooner than the lark, to fetch in May.

Rise, and put on your foliage, and be seen
To come forth, like the springtime, fresh and green,
  And sweet as Flora. Take no care
  For jewels for your gown or hair;
  Fear not; the leaves will strew
  Gems in abundance upon you;
Besides, the childhood of the day has kept,
Against you come, some orient pearls unwept;
  Come and receive them while the light
  Hangs on the dew-locks of the night,
  And Titan on the eastern hill
  Retires himself, or else stands still
Till you come forth. Wash, dress, be brief in praying:
Few beads are best when once we go a-Maying.

Come, my Corinna, come; and, coming, mark
How each field turns a street, each street a park
  Made green and trimmed with trees; see how
  Devotion gives each house a bough
  Or branch: each porch, each door ere this,
  An ark, a tabernacle is,
Made up of whitethorn neatly interwove,
As if here were those cooler shades of love.
  Can such delights be in the street
  And open fields, and we not see 't?
  Come, we'll abroad; and let's obey

CORINNA'S GOING A-MAYING. **3. Aurora:** goddess of dawn. **14. fetch . . . May:** get hawthorn blossoms, used as decoration on May Day and symbolizing fertility. **17. Flora:** goddess of flowers. **22. orient:** Eastern. **25. Titan:** the sun. **28. beads:** prayers (said to beads in the rosary).

The proclamation made for May,
And sin no more, as we have done, by staying;
But, my Corinna, come, let's go a-Maying.

There's not a budding boy or girl this day
But is got up and gone to bring in May;
A deal of youth, ere this, is come
Back, and with whitethorn laden home.
Some have dispatched their cakes and cream
Before that we have left to dream;
And some have wept, and wooed, and plighted troth,
And chose their priest, ere we can cast off sloth.
Many a green-gown has been given,
Many a kiss, both odd and even;
Many a glance, too, has been sent
From out the eye, love's firmament;
Many a jest told of the keys betraying
This night, and locks picked; yet we're not a-Maying.

Come, let us go while we are in our prime,
And take the harmless folly of the time.
We shall grow old apace, and die
Before we know our liberty.
Our life is short, and our days run
As fast away as does the sun;
And, as a vapor or a drop of rain
Once lost, can ne'er be found again;
So when or you or I are made
A fable, song, or fleeting shade,
All love, all liking, all delight
Lies drowned with us in endless night.
Then while time serves, and we are but decaying,
Come, my Corinna, come, let's go a-Maying.

1648

To the Virgins, to Make Much of Time

Gather ye rosebuds while ye may,
Old time is still a-flying;
And this same flower that smiles today
Tomorrow will be dying.

The glorious lamp of heaven, the sun,
The higher he's a-getting,
The sooner will his race be run,
And nearer he's to setting.

That age is best which is the first,
When youth and blood are warmer;

But being spent, the worse, and worst
  Times still succeed the former.

Then be not coy, but use your time,
  And, while ye may, go marry;
For, having lost but once your prime,
  You may forever tarry.

1648

To Daffodils

Fair Daffodils, we weep to see
  You haste away so soon:
As yet the early-rising sun
  Has not attained his noon.
    Stay, stay,
  Until the hasting day
    Has run
  But to the evensong;
And, having prayed together, we
  Will go with you along.

We have short time to stay as you;
  We have as short a spring;
As quick a growth to meet decay,
  As you or anything.
    We die,
  As your hours do, and dry
    Away
  Like to the summer's rain;
Or as the pearls of morning's dew,
  Ne'er to be found again.

1648

His Prayer to Ben Jonson

When I a verse shall make,
  Know I have prayed thee,
For old religion's sake,
  Saint Ben, to aid me.

Make the way smooth for me,
  When I, thy Herrick,
Honoring thee, on my knee
  Offer my lyric.

Candles I'll give to thee,
  And a new alter;
And thou, Saint Ben, shalt be
  Writ in my psalter.

1648

The Night-Piece, to Julia

Her eyes the glow-worm lend thee;
The shooting stars attend thee;
  And the elves also,
  Whose little eyes glow
Like the sparks of fire, befriend thee.

No will-o'-the-wisp mis-light thee;
No snake or slow-worm bite thee;
  But on, on thy way,
  Not making a stay,
Since ghost there's none to affright thee.

Let not the dark thee cumber;
What though the moon does slumber?
  The stars of the night
  Will lend thee their light,
Like tapers clear without number.

Then, Julia, let me woo thee,
Thus, thus to come unto me;
  And when I shall meet
  Thy silv'ry feet,
My soul I'll pour into thee.

1648

Upon Julia's Clothes

Whenas in silks my Julia goes,
Then, then, methinks, how sweetly flows
That liquefaction of her clothes.

Next, when I cast mine eyes, and see
That brave vibration, each way free,
O, how that glittering taketh me!

1648

THE NIGHT-PIECE. **7. slow-worm:** a type of lizard with a snakelike body. **11. cumber:** hinder.

An Ode for Him

Ah, Ben!
Say how or when
Shall we, thy guests,
Meet at those lyric feasts
Made at the Sun,
The Dog, the Triple Tun,
Where we such clusters had
As made us nobly wild, not mad;
And yet each verse of thine
Outdid the meat, outdid the frolic wine.

My Ben!
Or come again,
Or send to us
Thy wit's great overplus;
But teach us yet
Wisely to husband it,
Lest we that talent spend,
And having once brought to an end
That precious stock, the store
Of such a wit the world should have no more.

1648

Henry King

(1592–1669)

Henry King was a clergyman and became Bishop of Chichester. He was, like Herrick, removed from his position by the Puritans during the Civil War, and thenceforth was supported by friends until the Puritan Commonwealth collapsed and Charles II returned to power in 1660. At this time King again became a Bishop. "The Exequy," his most famous poem, is an elegy for his wife, Anne Berkeley, who died around 1624 at the age of twenty-four.

AN ODE FOR HIM. **5–6 Sun . . . Tun:** London taverns of the time.

The Exequy

Accept, thou shrine of my dead saint,
Instead of dirges, this complaint;
And for sweet flowers to crown thy hearse,
Receive a strew of weeping verse
From thy grieved friend, whom thou might'st see
Quite melted into tears for thee.

Dear loss! since thy untimely fate
My task hath been to meditate
On thee, on thee; thou art the book,
The library whereon I look,
Though almost blind. For thee, loved clay,
I languish out, not live, the day,
Using no other exercise
But what I practice with mine eyes;
By which wet glasses I find out
How lazily time creeps about
To one that mourns: this, only this,
My exercise and business is.
So I compute the weary hours
With sighs dissolvèd into showers.

Nor wonder if my time go thus
Backward and most preposterous;
Thou hast benighted me, thy set
This eve of blackness did beget,
Who wast my day, though overcast
Before thou hadst thy noontide passed;
And I remember must in tears,
Thou scarce hadst seen so many years
As day tells hours. By thy clear sun
My love and fortune first did run;
But thou wilt never more appear
Folded within my hemisphere,
Since both thy light and motion
Like a fled star is fallen and gone;
And 'twixt me and my soul's dear wish
An earth now interposèd is,
Which such a strange eclipse doth make
As ne'er was read in almanac.

I could allow thee for a time
To darken me and my sad clime;
Were it a month, a year, or ten,
I would thy exile live till then,

THE EXEQUY. **Title:** funeral rite. **23. set:** setting. **53. calcine:** burn to dust. **101. bottom:** boat. **106. van:** vanguard.

And all that space my mirth adjourn,
So thou wouldst promise to return;
And putting off thy ashy shroud,
At length disperse this sorrow's cloud.

But woe is me! the longest date
Too narrow is to calculate
These empty hopes; never shall I
Be so much blest as to descry
A glimpse of thee, till that day come
Which shall the earth to cinders doom,
And a fierce fever must calcine
The body of this world—like thine,
My little world! That fit of fire
Once off, our bodies shall aspire
To our souls' bliss; then we shall rise
And view ourselves with clearer eyes
In that calm region where no night
Can hide us from each other's sight.

Meantime, thou hast her, earth: much good
May my harm do thee. Since it stood
With heaven's will I might not call
Her longer mine, I give thee all
My short-lived right and interest
In her whom living I loved best;
With a most free and bounteous grief
I give thee what I could not keep.
Be kind to her, and prithee look
Thou write into thy doomsday book
Each parcel of this rarity
Which in thy casket shrined doth lie.
See that thou make thy reckoning straight,
And yield her back again by weight;
For thou must audit on thy trust
Each grain and atom of this dust,
As thou wilt answer Him that lent,
Not gave thee, my dear monument.

So close the ground, and 'bout her shade
Black curtains draw; my bride is laid.

Sleep on, my love, in thy cold bed,
Never to be disquieted!
My last good-night! Thou wilt not wake
Till I thy fate shall overtake;
Till age, or grief, or sickness must
Marry my body to that dust
It so much loves; and fill the room
My heart keeps empty in thy tomb.
Stay for me there; I will not fail
To meet thee in that hollow vale.

And think not much of my delay;
I am already on the way,
And follow thee with all the speed
Desire can make, or sorrows breed.
Each minute is a short degree,
And every hour a step towards thee.
At night when I betake to rest,
Next morn I rise nearer my west
Of life, almost by eight hours' sail,
Than when sleep breathed his drowsy gale.
Thus from the sun my bottom steers,
And my day's compass downward bears;
Nor labor I to stem the tide
Through which to thee I swiftly glide.

'Tis true, with shame and grief I yield,
Thou like the van first took'st the field,
And gotten hast the victory
In thus adventuring to die
Before me, whose more years might crave
A just precèdence in the grave.
But hark! my pulse like a soft drum
Beats my approach, tells thee I come;
And slow howe'er my marches be,
I shall at last sit down by thee.
The thought of this bids me go on,
And wait my dissolution
With hope and comfort. Dear (forgive
The crime), I am content to live
Divided, with but half a heart,
Till we shall meet and never part.

1657

George Herbert

(1593–1633)

A member of an aristocratic family, Herbert went to Trinity College, Cambridge, where he continued to hold various offices until he was about thirty-four, although he spent much of his time in London. He is said to have been a worldly and ambitious courtier, but he was also religious, and after many vicissitudes and a prolonged spiritual crisis he became a priest in the Anglican Church. For the last three years of his life he was the pastor of a small country parish. Most of his poems probably were written at this time. They were not published in his lifetime, although they circulated as manuscripts among his friends.

All his poetry is religious and was undoubtedly conceived by him as an offering to God. His poems give, among other more important things, a very appealing image of the way of life and devout faith of a country clergyman in his time. But his mind and spiritual life are anything but simple. His poems explore with utmost subtlety, introspective self-awareness, and honesty the emotions—the feelings of unworthiness, the sense of awful distance between the soul and God—that always assail sensitive persons in their quest for union with the divine. Yet his poems are also a mode of prayer, and the fears that assail him are always overcome by religious faith and love.

His poem "Jordan" partly expresses the view of poetry that shapes his style—a plain, directly sincere language appropriate for speaking to God. But Herbert was a consummate artist, and because he wished to offer God nothing but his best, he labored all the harder to perfect his poems; their limpidity, economy, proportion, and grace did not come from spontaneous expression of the heart but from many revisions. With this classical craftsmanship Herbert also possessed a marvelous vein of metaphysical wit. The comparison in "Virtue" of a "sweet and virtuous soul" to "seasoned timber" is as surprizing and apt as any comparison in Donne.

Just before his death, Herbert sent the manuscript of his book of poems to a friend, Nicholas Ferrar, requesting that "if he can think it may turn to the advantage of any dejected poor soul, let it be made public; if not, let him burn it; for I and it are less than the least of God's mercies." Published in 1633, Herbert's *The Temple* was widely read and greatly admired in the seventeenth century, but gradually thereafter dropped out of notice. Critical praise from Coleridge, who read virtually everything, and a religious revival within the Anglican Church (the so-called Oxford Movement) led some readers to Herbert in the nineteenth century; but not until some sixty years ago was his poetry again seriously admired by a large number of readers.

Easter Wings

Lord, who createdst man in wealth and store,
Though foolishly he lost the same,
Decaying more and more
Till he became
Most poor:
With thee
O let me rise
As larks, harmoniously,
And sing this day thy victories:
Then shall the fall further the flight in me.

My tender age in sorrow did begin;
And still with sicknesses and shame
Thou didst so punish sin,
That I became
Most thin.
With thee
Let me combine,
And feel this day thy victory;
For, if I imp my wing on thine,
Affliction shall advance the flight in me.

1633

Jordan (I)

Who says that fictions only and false hair
Become a verse? Is there in truth no beauty?
Is all good structure in a winding stair?
May no lines pass, except they do their duty
Not to a true, but painted chair?

Is it no verse, except enchanted groves
And sudden arbors shadow course-spun lines?
Must purling streams refresh a lover's loves?
Must all be veiled while he that reads, divines,
Catching the sense at two removes?

EASTER WINGS. **1. store:** abundance. **19. imp:** regraft feathers on falcons or hawks to help them fly better (a word used in falconry). JORDAN (I). **Title:** Herbert occasionally wrote two or more lyrics with the same title (marked I, II, and so on), as in "Temper (I)" and "Love (III)." Jordan is the river that the Israelites crossed to enter the Promised Land and in which Jesus was baptized. Herbert is here contrasting it, as a religious symbol, with ancient Greek pastoral poetry, thought to be inspired by the springs of Helicon. **5. painted chair:** the throne of kings. Herbert is asking: Is the only good poetry that which bows to the thrones of earthly kings as contrasted with the Heavenly King? **6–8. groves . . . streams:** "stock" images in classical pastoral poetry.

Shepherds are honest people; let them sing:
Riddle who list, for me, and pull for prime:
I envy no man's nightingale or spring;
Nor let them punish me with loss of rhyme,
Who plainly say, *My God, My King*.

1633

The Temper (I)

How should I praise thee, Lord! how should my rhymes
Gladly engrave thy love in steel,
If what my soul doth feel sometimes,
My soul might ever feel!

Although there were some forty heavens, or more,
Sometimes I peer above them all;
Sometimes I hardly reach a score;
Sometimes to hell I fall.

O rack me not to such a vast extent;
Those distances belong to thee:
The world's too little for thy tent,
A grave too big for me.

Wilt thou meet arms with man, that thou dost stretch
A crumb of dust from heaven to hell?
Will great God measure with a wretch?
Shall he thy stature spell?

O let me, when thy roof my soul hath hid,
O let me roost and nestle there;
Then of a sinner thou art rid,
And I of hope and fear.

Yet take thy way; for, sure, thy way is best:
Stretch or contract me, thy poor debtor:
This is but tuning of my breast,
To make the music better.

Whether I fly with angels, fall with dust,
Thy hands made both, and I am there.
Thy power and love, my love and trust,
Make one place everywhere.

1633

12. Riddle . . . prime: Let other poets write ingenious poetry ("riddles") as though it were a game ("pull for prime" means to draw the winning card in the game of "primero"). THE TEMPER (I). **Title:** The word is used in the sense of balance, equipoise; the poem is essentially a prayer for this quality. **16. spell:** comprehend.

Virtue

Sweet day, so cool, so calm, so bright,
  The bridal of the earth and sky:
The dew shall weep thy fall tonight;
    For thou must die.

Sweet rose, whose hue, angry and brave,
  Bids the rash gazer wipe his eye:
Thy root is ever in its grave,
    And thou must die.

Sweet spring, full of sweet days and roses,
  A box where sweets compacted lie;
My music shows ye have your closes,
    And all must die.

Only a sweet and virtuous soul,
  Like seasoned timber, never gives;
But though the whole world turn to coal,
    Then chiefly lives.

1633

Life

I made a posy, while the day ran by:
"Here will I smell my remnant out, and tie
    My life within this band."
But Time did beckon to the flowers, and they
By noon most cunningly did steal away,
    And withered in my hand.

My hand was next to them, and then my heart;
I took, without more thinking, in good part
    Time's gentle admonition;
Who did so sweetly death's sad taste convey,
Making my mind to smell my fatal day,
    Yet sugaring the suspicion.

VIRTUE. **5. angry and brave:** red and full of splendor. **10. sweets:** perfumes. **11. closes:** close of a musical cadence. **15. world . . . coal:** though the whole world, in the last day, burns to ashes.

Farewell dear flowers, sweetly your time ye spent,
Fit, while ye lived, for smell or ornament,
And after death for cures.
I follow straight without complaints or grief,
Since, if my scent be good, I care not if
It be as short as yours.

1633

The Collar

I struck the board and cried, "No more;
I will abroad!
What? shall I ever sigh and pine?
My lines and life are free, free as the road,
Loose as the wind, as large as store.
Shall I be still in suit?
Have I no harvest but a thorn
To let me blood, and not restore
What I have lost with cordial fruit?
Sure there was wine
Before my sighs did dry it; there was corn
Before my tears did drown it.
Is the year only lost to me?
Have I no bays to crown it,
No flowers, no garlands gay? All blasted?
All wasted?
Not so, my heart; but there is fruit,
And thou hast hands.
Recover all thy sigh-blown age
On double pleasures: leave thy cold dispute
Of what is fit and not. Forsake thy cage,
Thy rope of sands,
Which petty thoughts have made, and made to thee
Good cable, to enforce and draw,
And be thy law,
While thou didst wink and wouldst not see.
Away! take heed;
I will abroad.
Call in thy death's-head there; tie up thy fears.
He that forbears

LIFE. **15. cures:** rose-leaves were used in medicines. THE COLLAR. **Title:** the yoke of religious discipline. **1. board:** table. **5. store:** abundance. **6. in suit:** in attendance, suing for favor. **9. cordial:** giving health or life. **14. bays:** laurel crown of honor. **22. rope of sands:** The rope tying you down is made only of sand—is nothing, that is, except the product of your own imagination. **29. death's head:** referring to the ancient practice of bringing a skull to feasts to remind you to have a good time while you are alive, before you too are a skull.

To suit and serve his need,
Deserves his load."
But as I raved and grew more fierce and wild
At every word,
Methought I heard one calling, *Child!*
And I replied, *My Lord.*

1633

The Pulley

When God at first made man,
Having a glass of blessings standing by,
"Let us," said he, "pour on him all we can.
Let the world's riches, which dispersèd lie,
Contract into a span."

So strength first made a way;
Then beauty flowed, then wisdom, honor, pleasure.
When almost all was out, God made a stay,
Perceiving that, alone of all his treasure,
Rest in the bottom lay.

"For if I should," said he,
"Bestow this jewel also on my creature,
He would adore my gifts instead of me,
And rest in Nature, not the God of Nature;
So both should losers be.

"Yet let him keep the rest,
But keep them with repining restlessness.
Let him be rich and weary, that at least,
If goodness lead him not, yet weariness
May toss him to my breast."

1633

Discipline

Throw away thy rod,
Throw away thy wrath:
O my God,
Take the gentle path.

For my heart's desire
Unto thine is bent:
I aspire
To a full consent.

THE PULLEY. **Title:** What will draw us to God.

Not a word or look
I affect to own,
But by book,
And thy book alone.

Though I fail, I weep:
Though I halt in pace,
Yet I creep
To the throne of grace.

Then let wrath remove;
Love will do the deed:
For with love
Stony hearts will bleed.

Love is swift of foot;
Love's a man of war,
And can shoot,
And can hit from far.

Who can 'scape his bow?
That which wrought on thee,
Brought thee low,
Needs must work on me.

Throw away thy rod;
Though man frailties hath,
Thou art God:
Throw away thy wrath.

1633

Love (III)

Love bade me welcome: yet my soul drew back,
Guilty of dust and sin.
But quick-eyed Love, observing me grow slack
From my first entrance in,
Drew nearer to me, sweetly questioning
If I lacked anything.

"A guest," I answered, "worthy to be here":
Love said, "You shall be he."
"I, the unkind, ungrateful? Ah, my dear,
I cannot look on thee."
Love took my hand, and smiling did reply,
"Who made the eyes but I?"

DISCIPLINE. **22. a man of war:** echoing a phrase in a song of Moses (Exodus 15:3): "The Lord is a man of war," but also alluding to Cupid, god of love, with his bow and arrow.

"Truth, Lord; but I have marred them; let my shame
Go where it doth deserve."
"And know you not," says Love, "who bore the blame?"
"My dear, then I will serve."
"You must sit down," says Love, "and taste my meat."
So I did sit and eat.

1633

Edmund Waller

(1606–1687)

Waller came from a wealthy family and was a member of Parliament. He managed with some difficulty to maintain his position throughout the vicissitudes of the English Civil War, although he was banished by the Puritans for a period of seven years. More than any of his contemporaries he developed the closed heroic couplet (see Appendix on Versification) that Dryden, Pope, Johnson, and many other poets of the next century would use so brilliantly. Waller's poems in this form, however, are insipid. He is remembered now only for the lovely "Song" that begins "Go, lovely rose!"; for the fine, grave couplet in the poem entitled "Of the Last Verses in the Book,"

The soul's dark cottage, battered and decayed,
Lets in new light through chinks that time has made;

and for a very witty reply to Charles II, who had just been restored as monarch after the years of Oliver Cromwell's dictatorship. Waller had earlier written a *Panegyric* to Cromwell and now composed a similar poem extravagantly praising King Charles. When the king pointed out that the poem to himself was inferior as poetry to the one for Cromwell, Waller replied, "Sire, we poets never succeed so well in writing truth as in fiction."

Song

Go, lovely rose!
Tell her that wastes her time and me
That now she knows,
When I resemble her to thee,
How sweet and fair she seems to be.

Tell her that's young,
And shuns to have her graces spied,
That hadst thou sprung
In deserts, where no men abide,
Thou must have uncommended died.

Small is the worth
Of beauty from the light retired;
Bid her come forth,
Suffer herself to be desired,
And not blush so to be admired.

Then die! that she
The common fate of all things rare
May read in thee;
How small a part of time they share
That are so wondrous sweet and fair!

1645

Of the Last Verses in the Book

When we for age could neither read nor write,
The subject made us able to indite;
The soul, with nobler resolutions decked,
The body stooping, does herself erect.
No mortal parts are requisite to raise
Her that, unbodied, can her Maker praise.
The seas are quiet when the winds give o'er;
So calm are we when passions are no more!
For then we know how vain it was to boast
Of fleeting things, so certain to be lost.
Clouds of affection from our younger eyes
Conceal that emptiness which age descries.
The soul's dark cottage, battered and decayed,
Lets in new light through chinks that time has made;
Stronger by weakness, wiser men become,
As they draw near to their eternal home.
Leaving the old, both worlds at once they view,
That stand upon the threshold of the new.

1686

JOHN MILTON

(1608–1674)

For three centuries the name of Milton has stood next to that of Shakespeare as one of the summits of poetry in the English language. This is primarily because of his works in what have traditionally been considered the "greater" genres of epic and drama—the epic *Paradise Lost* (1667), as well as its sequel, *Paradise Regained* (1671), and the poetic drama, *Samson Agonistes* (1671). In these poems Milton used classical literary forms to present material from the Bible and Christian cosmology and history. The poems are didactic in the sense that they express what Milton regarded as fundamental religious truth, and *Paradise Lost* is immensely capacious—its story includes the revolt of Satan and the other rebel angels, their fall into hell, and the temptation and fall of Adam and Eve in the garden of Eden; toward its end the poem looks forward prospectively through human history to the coming of Christ. This tremendous poem places Milton beside the Italian Dante, author of the *Divine Comedy*. They are the greatest epic poets since Homer and Virgil, and the supreme poetic expounders of the Christian world view.

Milton grew up in a well-to-do middle class family. He seems to have planned to enter the ministry, although he never actually did. He also prepared himself by an immense and prolonged course of reading—seven years at the university and an additional five years on his own at home—for a vocation as a poet. During this period he composed most of his shorter poems, including "On the Morning of Christ's Nativity" (1629), "L'Allegro" and "Il Penseroso" (1631), "Lycidas" (1637), two theatrical entertainments or masques, a few sonnets, and a number of poems in Latin, which was the international language of learned people.

After a trip of fifteen months to Italy, he returned to London. He intended to become a private teacher, but he was drawn into the struggle of the Parliamentarians (the Protestant dissenters, or Puritans) against the king and his followers (the Royalist party). Milton composed prose tracts defending the Puritans and a famous work, *Areopagitica* (1644), against the censorship of books. When Oliver Cromwell set up his Puritan government (Charles I had been executed), Milton served in Cromwell's government as, in effect, the Foreign Secretary. During these years Milton's writings, except for a few sonnets, consisted entirely of prose works; these dealt mainly with political questions, though he also wrote on education and the problem of divorce. In 1651, at the age of forty-three, Milton became blind; his works were henceforth dictated, often to his daughters. After the restoration of the monarchy under Charles II, Milton was briefly imprisoned and then allowed to live quietly as a private citizen. In these last years he composed the long works we mentioned at the start.

In his shorter poems as much as in his longer ones Milton was master of an inimitable rhythm, both powerful and musical, an immense, muscular strength of language, and an imagination that fused his vast learning, creating images which are profoundly allusive and moving. We see these qualities already in his Christmas poem, "On the Morning of Christ's Nativity." "Lycidas" has been regarded by most poets and other readers as the finest elegy written in English. Although it was composed for Edward King, a fellow student of Milton's who had drowned in a storm in the Irish Sea, Milton was not a close friend of King and may not even have known him at all. But friends of King were getting up a volume of poems in his honor, and asked Milton to contribute. The occasion naturally touched deep anxieties in Milton; that a promising and devoted scholar and poet had died young, before his talents and efforts could result in any real achievement, set off in Milton an inward struggle to reconcile the seeming injustice and waste of this drowning with his faith in God.

The twin poems "L'Allegro" (the "happy man") and "Il Penseroso" (the "contemplative man") are lighter in style and theme; each is packed with the images and allusions appropriate to its mood—for the cheerful man, for example, there are springtime, pleasant pastoral scenes in the countryside, stage plays, and soft music; for the contemplative man, night, philosophical study, rainy, windy weather, and deep woods. As these poems present images of natural things or country sights, they stylize them to some degree. In other words, they smooth away naturalistic particulars and create a generalized and somewhat stock image. In "L'Allegro," for example, "the milkmaid singeth blithe," the ploughman "Whistles o'er the furrowed land" as he cheerfully ploughs, and "merry bells ring." This type of imagery and, more generally, this way of evoking a particular mood by collecting images associated with it were adopted by many poets in the eighteenth century, and "Il Penseroso" founded a whole school of poetry, the so-called Graveyard School of which Thomas Gray's famous "Elegy Written in a Country Churchyard" is an example.

It is similarly typical of Milton that he should have developed what was already the well-worn, even tired form of the sonnet in an altogether new way. The sonnet had been used in thousands of Elizabethan love poems, most of them highly conventional, and in the greater part of these the structure and rhyme scheme was that of the so-called "English" sonnet, in which three alternate-rhyming quatrains are followed by a couplet (*abab cdcd efef gg*; see "sonnet" in the Appendix on Versification). Milton returned to the Italian or Petrarchan form of the sonnet (*abba abba*, with varying sestet), which allows the same rhymes to go on reverberating throughout the first eight lines. In several sonnets, moreover, he rhymed with long vowels, thereby giving his sonnets a terrific sonority. And he made a further innovation in the Italian form by carrying the sentence over from the octave (the first eight lines) into the sestet (the concluding six lines). Normally there had been a break between these two parts of the sonnet, with a new statement beginning at the start of the sestet; Milton's innovation made the sonnet a much more unified type of poem, in which the force of Milton's passion overrides the expected stop at the end of the octave. Milton also abandoned the conventional subject matter associated with the sonnet, using the form to make a brief, passionate statement on any topic. Several of his sonnets are on political occasions or themes, and these later inspired the famous patriotic sonnets of Wordsworth. (In his sonnet "Scorn Not the Sonnet," composed at a time when the English expected to be invaded by Napoleon, Wordsworth compared Milton's sonnets to trumpet blasts.)

The following selections include the major short poems, the opening of Book I of *Paradise Lost*, as well as the poignant opening to Book III of that poem, in which the blind Milton, with prayerful feeling, gives his "Invocation to Light" and asks God for inward light so that he may continue his great epic. The footnotes attempt to explain Milton's manifold allusions to classical literature, the Bible, and other sources. However, for three centuries Milton (without footnotes) has captivated readers and most of these readers have not possessed anything like Milton's learning. One must first respond directly to the narrative, the imagination, and the rhythm of the poetry; then, if one wishes to go further, one may pursue the way Milton is using the materials on which he draws.

Lycidas

In this monody the author bewails a learned friend, unfortunately drowned in his passage from Chester on the Irish seas, 1637. And by occasion foretells the ruin of our corrupted clergy, then in their height.

Yet once more, O ye laurels, and once more
Ye myrtles brown, with ivy never sere,
I come to pluck your berries harsh and crude,
And with forced fingers rude,
Shatter your leaves before the mellowing year.
Bitter constraint, and sad occasion dear,
Compels me to disturb your season due;
For Lycidas is dead, dead ere his prime,
Young Lycidas, and hath not left his peer.
Who would not sing for Lycidas? He knew
Himself to sing, and build the lofty rhyme.
He must not float upon his watery bier
Unwept, and welter to the parching wind,
Without the meed of some melodious tear.
Begin then, sisters of the sacred well
That from beneath the seat of Jove doth spring,
Begin, and somewhat loudly sweep the string.
Hence with denial vain, and coy excuse;
So may some gentle Muse
With lucky words favor my destined urn,
And as he passes turn,
And bid fair peace be to my sable shroud.
For we were nursed upon the selfsame hill,
Fed the same flock, by fountain, shade, and rill.
Together both, ere the high lawns appeared
Under the opening eyelids of the morn,
We drove afield, and both together heard
What time the grayfly winds her sultry horn,
Battening our flocks with the fresh dews of night,
Oft till the star that rose at evening bright
Toward Heaven's descent had sloped his westering wheel.
Meanwhile the rural ditties were not mute,

LYCIDAS. **Argument: Monody** elegy. **1–2. laurels . . . ivy:** These three evergreen leaves, from which the Greek poetic crowns were made, were associated with Apollo (laurel), Venus (myrtle), and Bacchus (ivy). **2. never sere:** never turning brown. **3. crude:** not yet ripe (The poet is prematurely turning to these plants, symbolic of poetic honors, because the death of King is itself premature). **6. dear:** severe (causing pain). **13. welter:** be tossed about. **14. meed:** tribute. **15–16. sisters . . . spring:** Muses, who guarded the sacred well at the foot of Mt. Helicon beneath the altar of Jove. **25. high lawns:** upland meadows. **28. What time . . . horn:** at noon. **29. Battening:** fattening. **30. the star:** Hesperus, the evening star.

Tempered to th' oaten flute,
Rough satyrs danced, and fauns with cloven heel
From the glad sound would not be absent long,
And old Damaetas loved to hear our song.
But O the heavy change, now thou art gone,
Now thou art gone, and never must return!
Thee, shepherd, thee the woods and desert caves,
With wild thyme and the gadding vine o'ergrown,
And all their echoes mourn.
The willows and the hazel copses green
Shall now no more be seen,
Fanning their joyous leaves to thy soft lays.
As killing as the canker to the rose,
Or taint-worm to the weanling herds that graze,
Or frost to flowers that their gay wardrobe wear,
When first the white thorn blows;
Such, Lycidas, thy loss to shepherd's ear.
Where were ye, nymphs, when the remorseless deep
Closed o'er the head of your loved Lycidas?
For neither were ye playing on the steep,
Where your old Bards, the famous Druids lie,
Nor on the shaggy top of Mona high,
Nor yet where Deva spreads her wizard stream:
Ay me! I fondly dream—
Had ye been there—for what could that have done?
What could the Muse herself that Orpheus bore,
The Muse herself, for her inchanting son
Whom universal Nature did lament,
When by the rout that made the hideous roar,
His gory visage down the stream was sent,
Down the swift Hebrus to the Lesbian shore?
Alas! What boots it with uncessant care
To tend the homely slighted shepherd's trade,
And strictly meditate the thankless Muse?
Were it not better done as others use,
To sport with Amaryllis in the shade,
Or with the tangles of Neaera's hair?

36. Damaetas: conventional name in pastorals for an older shepherd; here applied to a tutor (no one in particular) they might have both had at Cambridge. **40. gadding:** wandering. **45. canker:** cankerworm. **46. weanling:** young cattle (recently weaned). **48. blows:** blossoms. **53. Druids:** the poet-priests of ancient Wales. **54–55. Mona . . . stream:** Mona is an island off the northern coast of Wales, and the wandering (wizard) River Dee—here called the "Deva"—passes through Chester, from which King sailed. **56. fondly:** foolishly. **58–63. The Muse . . . shore:** What could Calliope (muse of epic poetry) do to save her son Orpheus, greatest of poets, when he was torn to pieces by the Thracian women, his bloody head thrown by them into the river Hebrus, whence it floated into the Aegean Sea and to the island of Lesbos? **64. boots:** profits. **68–69. Amaryllis . . . Neaera:** girls in Virgil's *Eclogues*, and later conventional names in pastoral poems.

Fame is the spur that the clear spirit doth raise
(That last infirmity of noble mind)
To scorn delights, and live laborious days;
But the fair guerdon when we hope to find,
And think to burst out into sudden blaze,
Comes the blind Fury with th' abhorrèd shears,
And slits the thin spun life. "But not the praise,"
Phoebus replied, and touched my trembling ears;
"Fame is no plant that grows on mortal soil,
Nor in the glistering foil
Set off to th' world, nor in broad rumor lies,
But lives and spreads aloft by those pure eyes,
And perfect witness of all-judging Jove;
As he pronounces lastly on each deed,
Of so much fame in Heaven expect thy meed."
  O fountain Arethuse, and thou honored flood,
Smooth-sliding Mincius, crowned with vocal reeds,
That strain I heard was of a higher mood.
But now my oat proceeds,
And listens to the herald of the sea
That came in Neptune's plea.
He asked the waves, and asked the felon winds,
"What hard mishap hath doomed this gentle swain?"
And questioned every gust of rugged wings
That blows from off each beakèd promontory;
They knew not of his story,
And sage Hippotades their answer brings,
That not a blast was from his dungeon strayed,
The air was calm, and on the level brine,
Sleek Panope with all her sisters played.
It was that fatal and perfidious bark
Built in th' eclipse, and rigged with curses dark,
That sunk so low that sacred head of thine.
  Next Camus, reverend sire, went footing slow,
His mantle hairy, and his bonnet sedge,
Inwrought with figures dim, and on the edge

73. guerdon: reward. **75. blind Fury:** Atropos, one of the three Fates, or "Furies." It was she who, blindly, cut the thread of a person's life after her sisters had spun and measured it. **77. Phoebus:** Apollo, god of poetry. **79. foil:** leaf of gold or silver placed under a gem to make it brighter. **84. meed:** reward. **85–86. Arethuse . . . Mincius:** The nymph Arethuse, pursued by the river god Alpheus, was turned into a fountain in order to protect her. Her lover then turned into an underground river to unite with her. The Mincius is a river in North Italy, near Mantua, Virgil's birthplace. The double allusion implies that Milton's pastoral elegy has gone underground while the "strain . . . of a higher mood" is heard above. **88. oat:** oaten pipe (symbol of pastoral song). **89–90. herald . . . plea:** The herald Triton comes at the plea of Neptune, god of the sea, to defend Neptune against being the cause of Lycidas' drowning. **96. Hippotades:** Aeolus, god of the winds. **99. Panope:** one of the sea nymphs (Nereids). **101. eclipse:** unlucky time. **103. Camus:** god of the River Cam, which flows through Cambridge.

Like to that sanguine flower inscribed with woe.
"Ah! who hath reft," quoth he, "my dearest pledge?"
Last came and last did go
The pilot of the Galilean lake,
Two massy keys he bore of metals twain
(The golden opes, the iron shuts amain).
He shook his mitered locks, and stern bespake:
"How well could I have spared for thee, young swain,
Enow of such as for their bellies' sake,
Creep and intrude, and climb into the fold!
Of other care they little reckoning make,
Than how to scramble at the shearers' feast,
And shove away the worthy bidden guest.
Blind mouths! That scarce themselves know how to hold
A sheep-hook, or have learned aught else the least
That to the faithful herdsman's art belongs!
What reeks it them? What need they? They are sped;
And when they list, their lean and flashy songs
Grate on their scrannel pipes of wretched straw.
The hungry sheep look up, and are not fed,
But swoln with wind, and the rank mist they draw,
Rot inwardly, and foul contagion spread,
Besides what the grim wolf with privy paw
Daily devours apace, and nothing said.
But that two-handed engine at the door
Stands ready to smite once, and smite no more."
  Return, Alpheus, the dread voice is past,
That shrunk thy streams; return, Sicilian muse,
And call the vales, and bid them hither cast
Their bells and flowerets of a thousand hues.
Ye valleys low where the mild whispers use,
Of shades and wanton winds, and gushing brooks,
On whose fresh lap the swart star sparely looks,
Throw hither all your quaint enameled eyes,
That on the green turf suck the honeyed showers,
And purple all the ground with vernal flowers.
Bring the rathe primrose that forsaken dies,

106. sanguine . . . woe: alluding to the hyacinth, red (sanguine) from the blood of Hyacinth, the youth Apollo accidentally killed, and "inscribed with woe" because marks on the flower seem like the Greek letters "AI" ("alas"). **109. pilot . . . lake:** St. Peter (Luke 5:2–9). **110. keys:** of heaven, given to St. Peter by Christ (Matthew 16:19). **111. amain:** with force. **112. mitered:** wearing a Bishop's mitre or crown. **114. Enow:** enough. **115. fold:** sheepfold. **124. scrannel:** feeble. **126. draw:** inhale. **128. grim wolf:** Catholicism or Anglicanism, or both. **privy paw:** secret hand. **130. two-handed engine:** No one has yet satisfactorily explained the allusion. An "engine" here would be any instrument of war, probably a sword. Milton may be referring to the sword of Divine Vengeance in Ezekiel 21:3–15. **132. Alpheus:** who turned into a river while pursuing Arethuse (see lines 85–86). **136. use:** congregate. **138. swart star:** Sirius, the Dog Star, associated with the hot days of summer that turned plants "swarthy" or brown. **142. rathe:** early.

The tufted crow-toe, and pale jessamine,
The white pink, and the pansy freaked with jet,
The glowing violet,
The musk-rose, and the well attired woodbine,
With cowslips wan that hang the pensive head,
And every flower that sad embroidery wears;
Bid amaranthus all his beauty shed,
And daffadillies fill their cups with tears,
To strew the laureate hearse where Lycid lies.
For so to interpose a little ease,
Let our frail thoughts dally with false surmise.
Ay me! Whilst thee the shores and sounding seas
Wash far away, where'er thy bones are hurled,
Whether beyond the stormy Hebrides,
Where thou perhaps under the whelming tide
Visit'st the bottom of the monstrous world;
Or whether thou, to our moist vows denied,
Sleep'st by the fable of Bellerus old,
Where the great vision of the guarded mount
Looks toward Namancos and Bayona's hold;
Look homeward angel now, and melt with ruth:
And, O ye dolphins, waft the hapless youth.
  Weep no more, woeful shepherds, weep no more,
For Lycidas your sorrow is not dead,
Sunk though he be beneath the watery floor,
So sinks the day-star in the ocean bed,
And yet anon repairs his drooping head,
And tricks his beams, and with new-spangled ore,
Flames in the forehead of the morning sky:
So Lycidas sunk low, but mounted high,
Through the dear might of him that walked the waves,
Where other groves, and other streams along,
With nectar pure his oozy locks he laves,
And hears the unexpressive nuptial song,
In the blest kingdoms meek of joy and love.

144. freaked: speckled. **149. amaranthus:** the mythical flower of Paradise, thought never to fade. **151. laureate hearse:** bier of Lycidas, covered with laurel in his honor; but a "false surmise" (line 153) since his body was never found. **156. Hebrides:** the "Western Islands" off Scotland, scene of great storms during autumn and winter. **158. monstrous world:** world of sea monsters. **159. moist vows:** tearful prayers. **160. fable . . . Bellerus:** the fabulous giant of Land's End, Cornwall; here used as a metaphor for Land's End. **161–62. great vision . . . Bayona's hold:** where St. Michael's Mount (guarded by the archangel Michael) looks across the Bay of Biscay to the strongholds of Namancos and Bayona in northern Spain. **163. Look homeward angel:** a plea to St. Michael to turn back from Spain to England and to show **ruth** (pity) for the dead Edward King. **164. dolphins:** thought in Greek times to rescue drowning people and bring them to shore. **168. day-star:** the sun. **170. tricks:** dresses up. **ore:** gold. **175. laves:** washes. **176. unexpressive nuptial song:** the inexpressible wedding song at the "marriage supper of the Lamb," the soul's union with God (Revelation 7:17).

There entertain him all the saints above,
In solemn troops and sweet societies
That sing, and singing in their glory move,
And wipe the tears forever from his eyes.
Now, Lycidas, the shepherds weep no more;
Henceforth thou art the genius of the shore,
In thy large recompense, and shalt be good
To all that wander in that perilous flood.
  Thus sang the uncouth swain to th' oaks and rills,
While the still morn went out with sandals gray;
He touched the tender stops of various quills,
With eager thought warbling his Doric lay:
And now the sun had stretched out all the hills,
And now was dropped into the western bay;
At last he rose, and twitched his mantle blue:
Tomorrow to fresh woods, and pastures new.

1637

On the Morning of Christ's Nativity

1

This is the month, and this the happy morn,
Wherein the Son of Heaven's eternal King,
Of wedded maid and virgin mother born,
Our great redemption from above did bring;
For so the holy sages once did sing,
  That he our deadly forfeit should release,
And with his Father work us a perpetual peace.

2

That glorious form, that light unsufferable,
And that far-beaming blaze of majesty,
Wherewith he wont at Heaven's high council-table
To sit the midst of Trinal Unity,
He laid aside, and, here with us to be,
  Forsook the courts of everlasting day,
And chose with us a darksome house of mortal clay.

183. genius: guardian deity of a place. **186. uncouth swain:** unlearned shepherd. **188. quills:** reed pipes. **189. Doric:** Greek rustic dialect used for pastorals. ON THE MORNING OF CHRIST'S NATIVITY. **5. holy sages:** the Prophets of the Old Testament who foretold the coming of the Messiah. **6. forfeit:** penalty for the "original sin" of Adam. **11. Trinal Unity:** the Trinity (Father, Son, and Holy Spirit).

3

Say, Heavenly Muse, shall not thy sacred vein
Afford a present to the Infant God?
Hast thou no verse, no hymn, or solemn strain,
To welcome him to this his new abode,
Now while the heaven, by the Sun's team untrod,
  Hath took no print of the approaching light,
And all the spangled host keep watch in squadrons bright?

4

See how from far upon the eastern road
The star-led wizards haste with odors sweet!
Oh run, prevent them with thy humble ode,
And lay it lowly at his blessèd feet;
Have thou the honor first thy Lord to greet,
  And join thy voice unto the Angel choir
From out his secret altar touched with hallowed fire.

The Hymn

1

It was the winter wild,
While the Heaven-born Child
All meanly wrapt in the rude manger lies;
Nature, in awe to him,
Had doffed her gaudy trim,
With her great Master so to sympathize:
It was no season then for her
To wanton with the Sun, her lusty paramour.

2

Only with speeches fair
She woos the gentle air
To hide her guilty front with innocent snow,
And on her naked shame,
Pollute with sinful blame,
The saintly veil of maiden white to throw;
Confounded, that her Maker's eyes
Should look so near upon her foul deformities.

15. Heavenly Muse: Urania, Muse of astronomy and later of heavenly inspiration. **23. wizards:** the three Wise Men from the East (Matthew 2:1). **24. prevent:** anticipate. **28. hallowed fire:** alluding to the passage in Isaiah 6:6–7, in which Isaiah becomes able to prophesy when an angel takes a live coal from the altar and touches his lips with it. **41. sinful blame:** made sinful by the Fall of Man.

3

But he, her fears to cease,
Sent down the meek-eyed Peace:
She, crowned with olive green, came softly sliding
Down through the turning sphere,
His ready harbinger,
With turtle wing the amorous clouds dividing;
And, waving wide her myrtle wand,
She strikes a universal peace through sea and land.

4

No war, or battle's sound,
Was heard the world around;
The idle spear and shield were high uphung;
The hookèd chariot stood,
Unstained with hostile blood;
The trumpet spake not to the armèd throng;
And kings sat still with awful eye,
As if they surely knew their sovran Lord was by.

5

But peaceful was the night
Wherein the Prince of Light
His reign of peace upon the earth began.
The winds, with wonder whist,
Smoothly the waters kissed,
Whispering new joys to the mild Ocean,
Who now hath quite forgot to rave,
While birds of calm sit brooding on the charmèd wave.

6

The stars, with deep amaze,
Stand fixed in steadfast gaze,
Bending one way their precious influence,
And will not take their flight,
For all the morning light,
Or Lucifer that often warned them thence;
But in their glimmering orbs did glow,
Until their Lord himself bespake, and bid them go.

48. turning sphere: the apparent motion of the heavens as the earth rotates. **50. turtle:** turtledove. **56. hookèd chariot:** war chariot with hooks sticking out from the wheel hubs to cut the wheel spokes of other chariots. **59. awful:** full of awe or reverence. **64. whist:** silent. **68. birds of calm:** halcyons, who built their nests on the sea during periods of calm. **71. influence:** the astrological belief that stars influence human life. **74. Lucifer:** the morning star. **75. orbs:** spheres.

7

And, though the shady gloom
Had given day her room,
The Sun himself withheld his wonted speed,
And hid his head for shame,
As his inferior flame
The new-enlightened world no more should need:
He saw a greater Sun appear
Than his bright throne or burning axletree could bear.

8

The shepherds on the lawn,
Or ere the point of dawn,
Sat simply chatting in a rustic row;
Full little thought they than
That the mighty Pan
Was kindly come to live with them below:
Perhaps their loves, or else their sheep,
Was all that did their silly thoughts so busy keep.

9

When such music sweet
Their hearts and ears did greet
As never was by mortal finger strook,
Divinely-warbled voice
Answering the stringèd noise,
As all their souls in blissful rapture took:
The air, such pleasure loth to lose,
With thousand echoes still prolongs each heavenly close.

10

Nature, that heard such sound
Beneath the hollow round
Of Cynthia's seat the airy region thrilling,
Now was almost won
To think her part was done,
And that her reign had here its last fulfilling:
She knew such harmony alone
Could hold all Heaven and Earth in happier union.

11

At last surrounds their sight
A globe of circular light,

85. lawn: pasture, meadow. **88. than:** then. **89. Pan:** god of shepherds; sometimes identified with Christ as the "great Shepherd." **92. silly:** innocent. **95. strook:** struck. **100. close:** of a musical cadence. **103. Cynthia's seat:** the moon.

That with long beams the shamefaced Night arrayed;
The helmèd cherubim
And sworded seraphim
Are seen in glittering ranks with wings displayed,
Harping in loud and solemn choir,
With unexpressive notes, to Heaven's new-born Heir.

12

Such music (as 'tis said)
Before was never made,
But when of old the sons of morning sung,
While the Creator great
His constellations set,
And the well-balanced world on hinges hung,
And cast the dark foundations deep,
And bid the weltering waves their oozy channel keep.

13

Ring out, ye crystal spheres,
Once bless our human ears,
If ye have power to touch our senses so;
And let your silver chime
Move in melodious time;
And let the bass of heaven's deep organ blow;
And with your ninefold harmony
Make up full consort to th' angelic symphony.

14

For, if such holy song
Enwrap our fancy long,
Time will run back and fetch the age of gold;
And speckled vanity
Will sicken soon and die;
And leprous sin will melt from earthly mold;
And Hell itself will pass away,
And leave her dolorous mansions to the peering day.

15

Yea, Truth and Justice then
Will down return to men,
Orbed in a rainbow; and, like glories wearing,
Mercy will sit between,
Throned in celestial sheen,

112–13. cherubim . . . seraphim: two of the nine orders of angels. **119. sons . . . sung:** alluding to the statement in Job 38:4–7 about the creation, when "the morning stars sang together, and all the sons of God shouted for joy." **135. age of gold:** in Greek myth the early age of happiness and innocence.

With radiant feet the tissued clouds down steering;
And Heaven, as at some festival,
Will open wide the gates of her high palace-hall.

16

But wisest Fate says no,
This must not yet be so;
The Babe lics yet in smiling infancy
That on the bitter cross
Must redeem our loss,
So both himself and us to glorify:
Yet first, to those ychained in sleep,
The wakeful trump of doom must thunder through the deep,

17

With such a horrid clang
As on Mount Sinai rang,
While the red fire and smoldering clouds outbrake:
The agèd Earth, aghast,
With terror of that blast,
Shall from the surface to the center shake,
When, at the world's last sessiön,
The dreadful Judge in middle air shall spread his throne.

18

And then at last our bliss
Full and perfect is,
But now begins; for from this happy day
Th' old Dragon under ground,
In straiter limits bound,
Not half so far casts his usurpèd sway,
And, wroth to see his kingdom fail,
Swinges the scaly horror of his folded tail.

19

The oracles are dumb;
No voice or hideous hum
Runs through the archèd roof in words deceiving.
Apollo from his shrine
Can no more divine,
With hollow shriek the steep of Delphos leaving.
No nightly trance, or breathèd spell,
Inspires the pale-eyed priest from the prophetic cell.

155. ychained: chained ("y" is an archaic, Middle English prefix to a past participle). **156. wakeful:** awakening. **158. Mount Sinai:** where Moses received the Ten Commandments, and thunder and lightning marked the occasion (Exodus 19:16). **168. Dragon:** Satan. **172. Swinges:** whips. **178. Delphos:** site of the oracle of Apollo on the slope of Mount Parnassus.

20

The lonely mountains o'er,
And the resounding shore,
A voice of weeping heard and loud lament;
From haunted spring, and dale
Edged with poplar pale,
The parting genius is with sighing sent;
With flower-inwoven tresses torn
The Nymphs in twilight shade of tangled thickets mourn.

21

In consecrated earth,
And on the holy hearth,
The Lars and Lemures moan with midnight plaint;
In urns and altars round,
A drear and dying sound
Affrights the flamens at their service quaint;
And the chill marble seems to sweat,
While each peculiar power forgoes his wonted seat.

22

Peor and Baälim
Forsake their temples dim,
With that twice-battered God of Palestine;
And moonèd Ashtaroth,
Heaven's queen and mother both,
Now sits not girt with tapers' holy shine:
The Libyc Hammon shrinks his horn;
In vain the Tyrian maids their wounded Thammuz mourn.

23

And sullen Moloch, fled,
Hath left in shadows dread
His burning idol all of blackest hue;
In vain with cymbals' ring
They call the grisly king,
In dismal dance about the furnace blue;

186. genius: local spirit or deity. **191. Lars:** Roman gods guarding particular places. **Lemures:** spirits of the dead. **194. flamens:** Roman priests. **quaint:** elaborate. **197. Peor:** Baal-Peor, chief god of the Canaanites. **Baälim:** the lesser gods (plural form of Baal) of Canaan. **199. twice-battered God:** Dagon, god of the Philistines, whose image was overturned twice when confronted with the Ark of the Covenant (I Samuel 5:1–4). **200. Ashtaroth:** Phoenician moon goddess. **203. Libyc Hammon:** Amon, Egyptian god of the sun; here called "Libyc" because of a great temple to him in the Libyan desert. **204. wounded Thammuz:** god of vegetation in Tyre who was killed by a boar. His death was celebrated annually. **205. Moloch:** Phoenician sun god to whom children were sacrificed.

The brutish gods of Nile as fast,
Iris, and Orus, and the dog Anubis, haste.

24

Nor is Osiris seen
In Memphian grove or green,
Trampling the unshowered grass with lowings loud;
Nor can he be at rest
Within his sacred chest;
Nought but profoundest Hell can be his shroud;
In vain, with timbreled anthems dark,
The sable-stolèd sorcerers bear his worshiped ark.

25

He feels from Juda's land
The dreaded Infant's hand;
The rays of Bethlehem blind his dusky eyn;
Nor all the gods beside
Longer dare abide,
Not Typhon huge ending in snaky twine:
Our Babe, to show his Godhead true,
Can in his swaddling bands control the damnèd crew.

26

So, when the Sun in bed,
Curtained with cloudy red,
Pillows his chin upon an orient wave,
The flocking shadows pale
Troop to th' infernal jail,
Each fettered ghost slips to his several grave,
And the yellow-skirted fays
Fly after the night-steeds, leaving their moon-loved maze.

27

But see! the Virgin blest
Hath laid her Babe to rest.
Time is our tedious song should here have ending:
Heaven's youngest-teemèd star

211–14. Nile . . . Memphian: gods of Egypt ("the Nile"), "brutish" because often pictured with animal heads—that of a cow for **Isis** (the moon), a hawk for **Orus** (Horus, a god of the sun), and a jackal for **Anubis** (who pronounced judgement on the dead). **Osiris,** god of resurrection and fertility, was often shown as a bull. **Memphis** was the capital of Egypt in the Early Kingdom, giving way later to Thebes (Luxor) in Upper Egypt as the capital. **223. eyn:** eyes. **226. Typhon:** hundred-headed monster killed by Zeus. **231. orient:** Eastern. **233. infernal jail:** alluding to the belief that ghosts, at dawn, had to return to the underworld. **234. several:** separate. **235. fays:** fairies. **240. youngest . . . star:** latest born (that of Bethlehem).

Hath fixed her polished car,
Her sleeping Lord with handmaid lamp attending;
And all about the courtly stable
Bright-harnessed angels sit in order serviceable.

1645

L'Allegro

Hence loathèd Melancholy
Of Cerberus and blackest midnight born,
In Stygian cave forlorn
'Mongst horrid shapes, and shrieks, and sights unholy!
Find out some uncouth cell,
Where brooding Darkness spreads his jealous wings,
And the night-raven sings;
There under ebon shades, and low-browed rocks,
As ragged as thy locks,
In dark Cimmerian desert ever dwell.
But come thou goddess fair and free,
In Heaven yclept Euphrosyne,
And by men, heart-easing Mirth,
Whom lovely Venus at a birth
With two sister Graces more
To ivy-crownèd Bacchus bore;
Or whether (as some sager sing)
The frolic wind that breathes the spring,
Zephyr, with Aurora playing,
As he met her once a-Maying,
There on beds of violets blue,
And fresh-blown roses washed in dew,
Filled her with thee, a daughter fair,
So buxom, blithe, and debonair.
Haste thee nymph, and bring with thee
Jest and youthful Jollity,
Quips and Cranks, and wanton Wiles,
Nods, and Becks, and wreathèd Smiles,
Such as hang on Hebe's cheek,

244. Bright-harnessed: in bright armor. L'ALLEGRO. **Title:** "The Happy Man." **2. Cerberus:** watchdog of the underworld. **3. Stygian:** of the river Styx, that flows through Hades. **5. uncouth:** unknown. **8. ebon:** black as ebony. **10. Cimmerian desert:** In ancient times, Cimmeria was a mythical land in the far West, across the seas, and thought of as perpetually dark. **12. yclept:** called. **Euphrosyne:** "Mirth," one of the three Graces, daughters of Zeus and Hera, not Venus and Bacchus as Milton here says. **17–19. sager . . . Aurora:** The idea that the Graces were really children of Zephyr (West Wind) and Aurora (dawn) is Milton's invention. **27. Cranks:** jokes. **28. Becks:** curtseys. **29. Hebe:** daughter of Zeus and one of his cupbearers.

And love to live in dimple sleek;
Sport that wrinkled Care derides,
And Laughter, holding both his sides.
Come, and trip it as ye go
On the light fantastic toe,
And in thy right hand lead with thee,
The mountain nymph, sweet Liberty;
And if I give thee honor due,
Mirth, admit me of thy crew
To live with her and live with thee,
In unreprovèd pleasures free;
To hear the lark begin his flight,
And, singing, startle the dull night,
From his watch-tower in the skies,
Till the dappled dawn doth rise;
Then to come in spite of sorrow,
And at my window bid good morrow,
Through the sweetbriar, or the vine,
Or the twisted eglantine.
While the cock with lively din,
Scatters the rear of darkness thin,
And to the stack, or the barn door,
Stoutly struts his dames before;
Oft listening how the hounds and horn
Cheerly rouse the slumbering morn,
From the side of some hoar hill,
Through the high wood echoing shrill.
Sometime walking not unseen
By hedgerow elms, on hillocks green,
Right against the eastern gate,
Where the great sun begins his state,
Robed in flames, and amber light,
The clouds in thousand liveries dight;
While the plowman near at hand,
Whistles o'er the furrowed land,
And the milkmaid singeth blithe,
And the mower whets his scythe,
And every shepherd tells his tale,
Under the hawthorn in the dale.
Straight mine eye hath caught new pleasures
Whilst the landscape round it measures:
Russet lawns and fallows gray,
Where the nibbling flocks do stray;
Mountains on whose barren breast
The laboring clouds do often rest;
Meadows trim with daisies pied,

50. rear: rear guard. **60. state:** regal procession. **62. dight:** clothed. **75. pied:** dappled.

Shallow brooks, and rivers wide.
Towers and battlements it sees
Bosomed high in tufted trees,
Where perhaps some beauty lies,
The cynosure of neighboring eyes.
Hard by, a cottage chimney smokes,
From betwixt two aged oaks,
Where Corydon and Thyrsis met,
Are at their savory dinner set
Of herbs, and other country messes,
Which the neat-handed Phyllis dresses;
And then in haste her bower she leaves,
With Thestylis to bind the sheaves;
Or if the earlier season lead
To the tanned haycock in the mead.
Sometimes with secure delight
The upland hamlets will invite,
When the merry bells ring round
And the jocund rebecks sound
To many a youth and many a maid,
Dancing in the checkered shade;
And young and old come forth to play
On a sunshine holiday,
Till the livelong daylight fail;
Then to the spicy nut-brown ale,
With stories told of many a feat,
How fairy Mab the junkets eat;
She was pinched and pulled, she said,
And he, by Friar's lantern led,
Tells how the drudging goblin sweat
To earn his cream-bowl, duly set,
When in one night, ere glimpse of morn,
His shadowy flail hath threshed the corn
That ten day-laborers could not end;
Then lies him down the lubber fiend,
And, stretched out all the chimney's length,
Basks at the fire his hairy strength;
And crop-full out of doors he flings
Ere the first cock his matin rings.
Thus done the tales, to bed they creep,
By whispering winds soon lulled asleep.
Towered cities please us then,

80. cynosure: "guiding star," or object of attention. **83–88. Corydon . . . Thyrsis . . . Phyllis . . . Thestylis:** conventional pastoral names. **85. messes:** meals. **91. secure:** carefree. **94. rebecks:** fiddles. **102. Mab:** queen of fairies. **eat:** ate. **104. Friar's lantern:** will-o'-the-wisp. **105. goblin:** Puck or Robin Goodfellow, for whom farmers would put out a bowl of cream at night. **110. lubber:** loutish. **111. chimney:** fireplace. **114. matin:** morning.

And the busy hum of men,
Where throngs of knights and barons bold,
In weeds of peace, high triumphs hold,
With store of ladies, whose bright eyes
Rain influence, and judge the prize
Of wit, or arms, while both contend
To win her grace, whom all commend.
Therc let Hymen oft appear
In saffron robe, with taper clear,
And pomp, and feast, and revelry,
With masque, and antique pageantry;
Such sights as youthful poets dream
On summer eves by haunted stream.
Then to the well-trod stage anon,
If Jonson's learned sock be on,
Or sweetest Shakespeare, fancy's child,
Warble his native wood-notes wild.
And ever against eating cares
Lap me in soft Lydian airs
Married to immortal verse
Such as the meeting soul may pierce
In notes, with many a winding bout
Of linkèd sweetness long drawn out,
With wanton heed, and giddy cunning,
The melting voice through mazes running;
Untwisting all the chains that tie
The hidden soul of harmony;
That Orpheus' self may heave his head
From golden slumber on a bed
Of heaped Elysian flowers, and hear
Such strains as would have won the ear
Of Pluto, to have quite set free
His half-regained Eurydice.
These delights if thou canst give,
Mirth, with thee I mean to live.

1645

120. weeds: clothes. **triumphs:** festivals. **122. influence:** of stars (here associated with the ladies' eyes). **125. Hymen:** god of marriage. **132. sock:** light shoe worn by comic actors in ancient Greece. **136. Lydian:** mode of Greek music particularly soft and sweet. **139. bout:** bend or turn. **145. Orpheus:** In Greek myth, the supreme musician who entranced Pluto, King of the Underworld, thus securing his permission to bring back his dead wife Eurydice (line 150), but only on condition that he not look back to see whether she was following. He did look back, and thus lost her. (*See also* lines 58–63 of LYCIDAS.)

Il Penseroso

Hence vain deluding Joys,
  The brood of Folly without father bred!
How little you bestead,
  Or fill the fixèd mind with all your toys!
Dwell in some idle brain,
  And fancies fond with gaudy shapes possess,
As thick and numberless
  As the gay motes that people the sunbeams,
Or likest hovering dreams,
  The fickle pensioners of Morpheus' train.
But hail thou Goddess, sage and holy,
Hail, divinest Melancholy,
Whose saintly visage is too bright
To hit the sense of human sight;
And therefore to our weaker view,
O'erlaid with black, staid Wisdom's hue.
Black, but such as in esteem,
Prince Memnon's sister might beseem,
Or that starred Ethiope queen that strove
To set her beauty's praise above
The sea nymphs, and their powers offended.
Yet thou art higher far descended;
Thee bright-haired Vesta long of yore
To solitary Saturn bore;
His daughter she (in Saturn's reign
Such mixture was not held a stain).
Oft in glimmering bowers and glades
He met her, and in secret shades
Of woody Ida's inmost grove,
While yet there was no fear of Jove.
Come pensive nun, devout and pure,
Sober, steadfast, and demure,
All in a robe of darkest grain,
Flowing with majestic train,
And sable stole of cypress lawn
Over thy decent shoulders drawn.

IL PENSEROSO. **Title:** "The Contemplative [or Melancholy] Man." **3. bestead:** profit. **4. toys:** trifles. **6. fond:** foolish. **10. pensioners:** followers. **Morpheus:** god of sleep. **14. hit:** affect. **18. Memnon's sister:** Himera, sister of the Ethiopian prince who fought in the Trojan War. **19. starred . . . queen:** Cassiopeia, who was turned into a constellation by the Nereids (sea nymphs) when she boasted that the beauty of Andromeda, her daughter, was greater than theirs. **23–24. Thee . . . bore:** Vesta, Roman goddess of household fire, was indeed the daughter of Saturn; but Milton is inventing the idea that her mother was "Melancholy." **29. Ida:** Mount Ida, in Crete, from which Saturn ruled before his son Jove replaced him (line 30). **33. grain:** color. **35. sable . . . lawn:** black garment of Cypress linen.

Come, but keep thy wonted state,
With even step and musing gait,
And looks commercing with the skies,
Thy rapt soul sitting in thine eyes:
There held in holy passion still,
Forget thyself to marble, till
With a sad leaden downward cast,
Thou fix them on the earth as fast.
And join with thee calm Peace and Quiet,
Spare Fast, that oft with gods doth diet,
And hears the Muses in a ring
Aye round about Jove's altar sing.
And add to these retired Leisure,
That in trim gardens takes his pleasure;
But first, and chiefest, with thee bring,
Him that yon soars on golden wing,
Guiding the fiery-wheelèd throne,
The cherub Contemplation;
And the mute Silence hist along
'Less Philomel will deign a song,
In her sweetest, saddest plight,
Smoothing the rugged brow of night,
While Cynthia checks her dragon yoke
Gently o'er th' accustomed oak;
Sweet bird that shunn'st the noise of folly,
Most musical, most melancholy!
Thee chantress oft the woods among,
I woo to hear thy evensong;
And missing thee, I walk unseen
On the dry smooth-shaven green,
To behold the wandering moon,
Riding near her highest noon,
Like one that had been led astray
Through the Heaven's wide pathless way;
And oft as if her head she bowed,
Stooping through a fleecy cloud.
Oft on a plat of rising ground,
I hear the far-off curfew sound,
Over some wide-watered shore,
Swinging slow with sullen roar;
Or if the air will not permit,
Some still removèd place will fit,
Where glowing embers through the room
Teach light to counterfeit a gloom
Far from all resort of mirth,
Save the cricket on the hearth,

54. cherub Contemplation: one of the cherubim (angels) whose function was the contemplation of God. **55. hist:** called. **56. Philomel:** nightingale. **59. Cynthia:** goddess of the moon, often pictured with a chariot drawn by dragons. **73. plat:** plot.

Or the bellman's drowsy charm,
To bless the doors from nightly harm;
Or let my lamp at midnight hour
Be seen in some high lonely tower,
Where I may oft outwatch the Bear,
With thrice great Hermes, or unsphere
The spirit of Plato to unfold
What worlds, or what vast regions hold
The immortal mind that hath forsook
Her mansion in this fleshly nook;
And of those demons that are found
In fire, air, flood, or underground,
Whose power hath a true consent
With planet, or with element.
Some time let gorgeous Tragedy
In sceptered pall come sweeping by,
Presenting Thebes, or Pelops' line,
Or the tale of Troy divine.
Or what (though rare) of later age
Ennobled hath the buskined stage.
But, O sad virgin, that thy power
Might raise Musaeus from his bower,
Or bid the soul of Orpheus sing
Such notes as, warbled to the string,
Drew iron tears down Pluto's cheek,
And made Hell grant what Love did seek.
Or call up him that left half told
The story of Cambuscan bold,
Of Camball, and of Algarsife,
And who had Canacee to wife,
That owned the virtuous ring and glass,
And of the wondrous horse of brass,
On which the Tarter king did ride;
And if aught else great bards beside
In sage and solemn tunes have sung,
Of tourneys and of trophies hung,
Of forests and enchantments drear,
Where more is meant than meets the ear.
Thus, Night, oft see me in thy pale career,

83. bellman's . . . charm: watchman's sleepy song as he makes his rounds at night. **87. Bear:** the constellation, the great Bear. **88. thrice great Hermes:** not the Greek god Hermes but a legendary Egyptian sage, Hermes Trismegistus ("thrice great"). **unsphere:** call back from his sphere. **93. demons:** the spirits presiding over fire, water, air, and earth ("the four elements"). **95. consent:** harmony. **98. pall:** robe. **99–100. Thebes . . . Troy:** Many of the Greek tragedies were concerned with the royal house of Thebes (Oedipus), Pelops's descendants (Agamemnon, Electra), or the Trojan War. **102. buskined:** the boot or high shoe worn by Greek actors of tragedy. **109. him:** Chaucer. His "Squire's Tale" is the unfinished story of the characters named. **113. virtuous:** endowed with power.

Till civil-suited morn appear,
Not tricked and frounced as she was wont,
With the Attic boy to hunt,
But kerchiefed in a comely cloud,
While rocking winds are piping loud,
Or ushered with a shower still,
When the gust hath blown his fill,
Ending on the rustling leaves,
With minute-drops from off the eaves.
And when the sun begins to fling
His flaring beams, me, Goddess, bring
To archèd walks of twilight groves,
And shadows brown that Sylvan loves
Of pine or monumental oak,
Where the rude ax with heavèd stroke,
Was never heard the nymphs to daunt,
Or fright them from their hallowed haunt.
There in close covert by some brook,
Where no profaner eye may look,
Hide me from day's garish eye,
While the bee with honeyed thigh,
That at her flowery work doth sing,
And the waters murmuring
With such consort as they keep,
Entice the dewy-feathered sleep;
And let some strange mysterious dream,
Wave at his wings in airy stream,
Of lively portraiture displayed,
Softly on my eyelids laid.
And as I wake, sweet music breathe
Above, about, or underneath,
Sent by some spirit to mortals good,
Or th' unseen genius of the wood.
But let my due feet never fail
To walk the studious cloister's pale,
And love the high embowèd roof,
With antic pillars massy proof,
And storied windows richly dight,
Casting a dim religious light.
There let the pealing organ blow,
To the full-voicèd choir below,
In service high, and anthems clear,
As may with sweetness, through mine ear,
Dissolve me into ectasies,

122–24. morn . . . boy: Eos, daughter of the Dawn (Aurora), dressed sedately and not "frounced" (with curled hair), loved Cephalus, the "Attic boy." **134. Sylvan:** Sylvanus, god of forests. **145. consort:** harmony. **154. genius:** local deity or spirit. **156. pale:** enclosure. **158. antic:** quaint, decorated. **159. dight:** clothed.

And bring all heaven before mine eyes.
And may at last my weary age
Find out the peaceful hermitage,
The hairy gown and mossy cell,
Where I may sit and rightly spell
Of every star that Heaven doth show,
And every herb that sips the dew
Till old experience do attain
To something like prophetic strain.
These pleasures, Melancholy, give,
And I with thee will choose to live.

1645

On Shakespeare

What needs my Shakespeare for his honored bones
The labor of an age in pilèd stones?
Or that his hallowed reliques should be hid
Under a star-ypointing pyramid?
Dear son of Memory, great heir of Fame,
What need'st thou such weak witness of thy name?
Thou in our wonder and astonishment
Hast built thyself a livelong monument.
For whilst, to th' shame of slow-endeavoring art,
Thy easy numbers flow, and that each heart
Hath from the leaves of thy unvalued book
Those Delphic lines with deep impression took,
Then thou, our fancy of itself bereaving,
Dost make us marble with too much conceiving,
And so sepùlchred in such pomp dost lie
That kings for such a tomb would wish to die.

1645

How Soon Hath Time

How soon hath Time, the subtle thief of youth,
Stoln on his wing my three and twentieth year!
My hasting days fly on with full career,
But my late spring no bud or blossom shew'th.

170. spell: meditate. ON SHAKESPEARE. **5. son of Memory:** Memory was the mother of the Muses; Shakespeare is being equated with them. **10. numbers:** verses. **11. unvalued:** invaluable. **12. Delphic:** alluding to Dephi, the home of Apollo, god of poetry. HOW SOON HATH TIME. **4. shew'th:** shows.

Perhaps my semblance might deceive the truth,
  That I to manhood am arrived so near,
  And inward ripeness doth much less appear,
  That some more timely-happy spirits endu'th.
Yet be it less or more, or soon or slow,
  It shall be still in strictest measure even
  To that same lot, however mean or high,
Toward which Time leads me, and the will of Heaven;
  All is, if I have grace to use it so,
  As ever in my great Taskmaster's eye.

1645

When I Consider How My Light Is Spent

When I consider how my light is spent
  Ere half my days in this dark world and wide,
  And that one talent which is death to hide
  Lodged with me useless, though my soul more bent
To serve therewith my Maker, and present
  My true account, lest he returning chide;
  "Doth God exact day-labor, light denied?"
  I fondly ask; but Patience to prevent
That murmur, soon replies, "God doth not need
  Either man's work or his own gifts; who best
  Bear his mild yoke, they serve him best. His state
Is kingly. Thousands at his bidding speed
  And post o'er land and ocean without rest:
  They also serve who only stand and wait."

1673

On the Late Massacre in Piedmont

Avenge, O Lord, thy slaughtered saints, whose bones
  Lie scattered on the Alpine mountains cold,
  Even them who kept thy truth so pure of old
  When all our fathers worshiped stocks and stones,
Forget not: in thy book record their groans
  Who were thy sheep and in their ancient fold

8. endu'th: endows. **10. even:** equal. WHEN I CONSIDER. **Title:** When he wrote this (1652), Milton had been completely blind for a year. **8. fondly:** foolishly. ON THE LATE MASSACRE IN PIEDMONT. **Title:** In 1655, the year in which Milton wrote this, 1700 Protestants (of the sect called the Waldensians) had been massacred in Piedmont, a region of northern Italy, by the army of the Duke of Savoy. **4. stocks and stones:** idols.

Slain by the bloody Piedmontese that rolled
Mother with infant down the rocks. Their moans
The vales redoubled to the hills, and they
To Heaven. Their martyred blood and ashes sow
O'er all th' Italian fields where still doth sway
The triple tyrant: that from these may grow
A hundredfold, who having learnt thy way
Early may fly the Babylonian woe.

1673

Methought I Saw

Methought I saw my late espousèd saint
Brought to me like Alcestis from the grave,
Whom Jove's great son to her glad husband gave,
Rescued from Death by force, though pale and faint.
Mine, as whom washed from spot of child-bed taint
Purification in the Old Law did save,
And such, as yet once more I trust to have
Full sight of her in heaven without restraint,
Came vested all in white, pure as her mind.
Her face was veiled; yet to my fancied sight
Love, sweetness, goodness, in her person shined
So clear as in no face with more delight.
But O, as to embrace me she inclined,
I waked, she fled, and day brought back my night.

1673

from Paradise Lost, Book I

Of man's first disobedience, and the fruit
Of that forbidden tree, whose mortal taste
Brought death into the world, and all our woe,

12. triple tyrant: referring to the "triple crown" worn by the Pope. **14. Babylonian woe:** typical of the Puritan tendency to equate the Catholic Church with the tyranny, vice, and luxury of ancient Babylon. METHOUGHT I SAW. **Title:** The wife to which the sonnet refers was Milton's second wife, Katherine Woodstock, who died in 1658 and whom he had never actually seen, since he had been blind for five years before their marriage. Her face is therefore "veiled" (line 10) in the dream. **2–3. Alcestis . . . Jove's great son:** In Greek myth, Alcestis died to save her husband, Admetus, and was brought back to him from the underworld by Hercules, "Jove's great son." **5–6. washed . . . save:** In the Old Testament (Leviticus 12), women underwent ritual purification after childbirth. PARADISE LOST. BOOK I. **1. disobedience:** eating of the Tree of Knowledge in the Garden of Eden.

With loss of Eden, till one greater Man
Restore us, and regain the blissful seat,
Sing, Heavenly Muse, that, on the secret top
Of Oreb or of Sinai, didst inspire
That shepherd, who first taught the chosen seed
In the beginning how the Heavens and Earth
Rose out of Chaos; or, if Sion hill
Delight thee more, and Siloa's brook that flowed
Fast by the oracle of God, I thence
Invoke thy aid to my adventurous song,
That with no middle flight intends to soar
Above th' Aonian mount, while it pursues
Things unattempted yet in prose or rhyme.
And chiefly thou, O Spirit, that dost prefer
Before all temples the upright heart and pure,
Instruct me, for thou know'st; thou from the first
Wast present, and, with mighty wings outspread,
Dove-like sat'st brooding on the vast Abyss,
And mad'st it pregnant: what in me is dark,
Illumine; what is low, raise and support;
That to the highth of this great argument
I may assert Eternal Providence,
And justify the ways of God to men.
  Say first—for Heaven hides nothing from Thy view,
Nor the deep tract of Hell—say first what cause
Moved our grand parents, in that happy state,
Favoured of Heaven so highly, to fall off
From their Creator, and transgress his will
For one restraint, lords of the world besides.
Who first seduced them to that foul revolt?
  The infernal Serpent; he it was, whose guile,
Stirred up with envy and revenge, deceived
The Mother of Mankind, what time his pride
Had cast him out from Heaven, with all his host
Of rebel Angels, by whose aid, aspiring
To set himself in glory above his peers,
He trusted to have equalled the Most High,
If he opposed; and with ambitious aim
Against the throne and monarchy of God
Raised impious war in Heaven, and battle proud,
With vain attempt. Him the Almighty Power

4. greater Man: Christ. **6. Heavenly Muse:** not the Muse now of ancient Greek epics (Calliope), but the inspiration from God himself, speaking to Moses on Oreb or Mount Sinai (alternative names for the same place). **10. Sion hill:** Zion, the hill in Jerusalem where the temple stood ("the oracle of God"), next to the stream called Siloa. **15. Aonian mount:** Helicon, haunt of the Muses. This epic, Milton is saying, intends to fly far above classical sources of inspiration because of its religious theme. **17–22. Spirit . . . pregnant:** the spirit of God, which, in creation, had "moved upon the face of the waters" (Genesis 1:2). **24. argument:** theme. **29. grand:** first (Adam and Eve).

Hurled headlong flaming from the ethereal sky,
With hideous ruin and combustion, down
To bottomless perdition; there to dwell
In adamantine chains and penal fire,
Who durst defy the Omnipotent to arms.
  Nine times the space that measures day and night
To mortal men, he with his horrid crew
Lay vanquished, rolling in the fiery gulf,
Confounded, though immortal. But his doom
Reserved him to more wrath; for now the thought
Both of lost happiness and lasting pain
Torments him; round he throws his baleful eyes,
That witnessed huge affliction and dismay,
Mixed with obdùrate pride and stedfast hate.
At once, as far as Angels ken, he views
The dismal situation waste and wild:
A dungeon horrible on all sides round
As one great furnace flamed; yet from those flames
No light; but rather darkness visible
Served only to discover sights of woe,
Regions of sorrow, doleful shades, where peace
And rest can never dwell, hope never comes
That comes to all; but torture without end
Still urges, and a fiery deluge, fed
With ever-burning sulphur unconsumed.
Such place Eternal Justice had prepared
For those rebellious; here their prison ordained
In utter darkness, and their portion set,
As far removed from God and light of Heaven,
As from the center thrice to the utmost pole.
Oh, how unlike the place from whence they fell!
There the companions of his fall, o'erwhelmed
With floods and whirlwinds of tempestuous fire,
He soon discerns, and, weltering by his side,
One next himself in power and next in crime,
Long after known in Palestine and named
Beëlzebub. To whom th' Arch-Enemy,—
And thence in Heaven called Satan,—with bold words
Breaking the horrid silence, thus began:
  "If thou beest he,—but O, how fallen! how changed
From him, who, in the happy realms of light,
Clothed with transcendent brightness, didst outshine
Myriads though bright!—if he, whom mutual league,
United thoughts and counsels, equal hope

46. ruin: fall (the original Latin sense of the word). **59. ken:** understand; as far as the angels could see. **62–63 yet . . . light:** The fires of Hell, in traditional legend, gave no light. **68. urges:** drives. **72. utter:** outer. **74. center:** earth. **pole:** axis of the universe.

And hazard in the glorious enterprise,
Joined with me once, now misery hath joined
In equal ruin; into what pit, thou seest,
From what highth fallen! so much the stronger proved
He with his thunder; and till then who knew
The force of those dire arms? Yet not for those,
Nor what the potent Victor in his rage
Can else inflict, do I repent or change,
Though changed in outward lustre, that fixed mind,
And high disdain from sense of injured merit,
That with the Mightiest raised me to contend,
And to the fierce contention brought along
Innumerable force of spirits armed,
That durst dislike his reign, and, me preferring,
His utmost power with adverse power opposed
In dubious battle on the plains of Heaven,
And shook his throne. What though the field be lost?
All is not lost; the unconquerable will,
And study of revenge, immortal hate,
And courage never to submit or yield:
And what is else not to be overcome?
That glory never shall his wrath or might
Extort from me. To bow and sue for grace
With suppliant knee, and deify his power,
Who, from the terror of this arm, so late
Doubted his empire,—that were low indeed,
That were an ignominy and shame beneath
This downfall; since, by fate, the strength of gods
And this empyreal substance cannot fail;
Since, through experience of this great event,
In arms not worse, in foresight much advanced,
We may with more successful hope resolve
To wage by force or guile eternal war,
Irreconcilable to our grand Foe,
Who now triumphs, and in th' excess of joy
Sole reigning holds the tyranny of Heaven."
  So spake th' apostate Angel, though in pain,
Vaunting aloud, but racked with deep despair;
And him thus answered soon his bold compeer:
  "O Prince! O Chief of many thronèd Powers!
That led the embattled Seraphim to war
Under thy conduct, and, in dreadful deeds
Fearless, endangered Heaven's perpetual King,
And put to proof his high supremacy,
Whether upheld by strength, or chance, or fate!
Too well I see and rue the dire event

117. empyreal substance: heavenly substance, hence indestructible. **127. compeer:** companion. **129. Seraphim:** the highest order of angels. **134. event:** outcome.

That with sad overthrow and foul defeat
Hath lost us Heaven, and all this mighty host
In horrible destruction laid thus low,
As far as gods and Heavenly essences
Can perish: for the mind and spirit remains
Invincible, and vigour soon returns,
Though all our glory extinct, and happy state
Here swallowed up in endless misery.
But what if he our Conqueror (whom I now
Of force believe almighty, since no less
Than such could have o'erpowered such force as ours)
Have left us this our spirit and strength entire,
Strongly to suffer and support our pains,
That we may so suffice his vengeful ire;
Or do him mightier service, as his thralls
By right of war, whate'er his business be,
Here in the heart of Hell to work in fire,
Or do his errands in the gloomy Deep?
What can it then avail, though yet we feel
Strength undiminished, or eternal being
To undergo eternal punishment?"
  Whereto with speedy words th' Arch-Fiend replied:—
"Fallen Cherub, to be weak is miserable,
Doing or suffering: but of this be sure—
To do aught good never will be our task,
But ever to do ill our sole delight,
As being the contrary to his high will
Whom we resist. If then his providence
Out of our evil seek to bring forth good,
Our labour must be to pervert that end,
And out of good still to find means of evil;
Which ofttimes may succeed, so as perhaps
Shall grieve him, if I fail not, and disturb
His inmost counsels from their destined aim.
But see! the angry Victor hath recalled
His ministers of vengeance and pursuit
Back to the gates of Heaven; the sulphurous hail,
Shot after us in storm, o'erblown hath laid
The fiery surge, that from the precipice
Of Heaven received us falling; and the thunder,
Winged with red lightning and impetuous rage,
Perhaps hath spent his shafts, and ceases now
To bellow through the vast and boundless Deep.
Let us not slip th' occasion, whether scorn
Or satiate fury yield it from our foe.
Seest thou yon dreary plain, forlorn and wild,

155. To: so as to. **165. still:** always. **167. fail:** mistake. **178. slip:** lose.

The seat of desolation, void of light,
Save what the glimmering of these livid flames
Casts pale and dreadful? Thither let us tend
From off the tossing of these fiery waves,
There rest, if any rest can harbour there,
And, reassembling our afflicted powers,
Consult how we may henceforth most offend
Our Enemy, our own loss how repair,
How overcome this dire calamity,
What reinforcement we may gain from hope,
If not what resolution from despair."
  Thus Satan, talking to his nearest mate,
With head uplift above the wave, and eyes
That sparkling blazed; his other parts besides
Prone on the flood, extended long and large,
Lay floating many a rood, in bulk as huge
As whom the fables name of monstrous size,
Titanian, or Earth-born, that warred on Jove,
Briareos or Typhon, whom the den
By ancient Tarsus held, or that sea-beast
Leviathan, which God of all his works
Created hugest that swim th' ocean stream;
Him, haply, slumbering on the Norway foam,
The pilot of some small night-foundered skiff
Deeming some island, oft, as seamen tell,
With fixèd anchor in his scaly rind
Moors by his side under the lee, while night
Invests the sea, and wishèd morn delays:
So stretched out huge in length the Arch-Fiend lay,
Chained on the burning lake; nor ever thence
Had risen, or heaved his head, but that the will
And high permission of all-ruling Heaven
Left him at large to his own dark designs,
That with reiterated crimes he might
Heap on himself damnation, while he sought
Evil to others, and, enraged, might see
How all his malice served but to bring forth
Infinite goodness, grace, and mercy, shewn
On Man by him seduced; but on himself
Treble confusion, wrath, and vengeance poured.
  Forthwith upright he rears from off the pool
His mighty stature; on each hand the flames
Driven backward slope their pointing spires, and rolled

186. afflicted powers: the forces overthrown. **198–200. Titanian . . . Tarsus:** like the Titans, the original gods, and the early "giants" ("earth-born"), such as Briareos, who had a hundred hands, and Typhon, who had a hundred heads and lived near Tarsus, all of whom fought against Jove. **201. Leviathan:** whale. **204. night-foundered:** disabled by the night.

In billows, leave i' the midst a horrid vale.
Then with expanded wings he steers his flight
Aloft, incumbent on the dusky air
That felt unusual weight; till on dry land
He lights—if it were land that ever burned
With solid, as the lake with liquid fire,
And such appeared in hue; as when the force
Of subterranean wind transports a hill
Torn from Pelorus, or the shattered side
Of thundering Aetna, whose combustible
And fuelled entrails thence conceiving fire,
Sublimed with mineral fury, aid the winds,
And leave a singèd bottom all involved
With stench and smoke: such resting found the sole
Of unblest feet. Him followed his next mate,
Both glorying to have scaped the Stygian flood
As gods, and by their own recovered strength,
Not by the sufferance of supernal power.
"Is this the region, this the soil, the clime,"
Said then the lost Archangel, "this the seat
That we must change for Heaven? this mournful gloom
For that celestial light? Be it so, since he
Who now is sovran can dispose and bid
What shall be right: farthest from him is best,
Whom reason hath equalled, force hath made supreme
Above his equals. Farewell, happy fields,
Where joy for ever dwells! Hail, horrors! hail,
Infernal world! and thou, profoundest Hell,
Receive thy new possessor; one who brings
A mind not to be changed by place or time.
The mind is its own place, and in itself
Can make a Heaven of Hell, a Hell of Heaven.
What matter where, if I be still the same,
And what I should be, all but less than he
Whom thunder hath made greater? Here at least
We shall be free; th' Almighty hath not built
Here for his envy, will not drive us hence:
Here we may reign secure; and in my choice
To reign is worth ambition, though in Hell:
Better to reign in Hell than serve in Heaven.
But wherefore let we then our faithful friends,
Th' associates and copartners of our loss,
Lie thus astonished on the oblivious pool,
And call them not to share with us their part

230. hue: appearance. **232. Pelorus:** mountain in Sicily. **235. Sublimed:** made incandescent. **246. sovran:** sovereign. **257. all but less than:** almost equal to. **266. astonished:** stupified. **oblivious:** causing forgetfulness.

In this unhappy mansion, or once more,
With rallied arms, to try what may be yet
Regained in Heaven, or what more lost in Hell?"

from Book III

Hail, holy Light, offspring of Heaven first-born,
Or of the Eternal coeternal beam
May I express thee unblamed? since God is light,
And never but in unapproachèd light
Dwelt from eternity, dwelt then in thee,
Bright effluence of bright essence increate.
Or hear'st thou rather pure ethereal stream,
Whose fountain who shall tell? Before the sun,
Before the Heavens thou wert, and at the voice
Of God, as with a mantle didst invest
The rising world of waters dark and deep,
Won from the void and formless infinite.
Thee I revisit now with bolder wing,
Escaped the Stygian pool, though long detained
In that obscure sojourn, while in my flight
Through utter and through middle darkness borne
With other notes than to the Orphean lyre
I sung of Chaos and eternal Night,
Taught by the Heavenly Muse to venture down
The dark descent, and up to reascend,
Though hard and rare. Thee I revisit safe,
And feel thy sovran vital lamp; but thou
Revisit'st not these eyes, that roll in vain
To find thy piercing ray, and find no dawn;
So thick a drop serene hath quenched their orbs,
Or dim suffusion veiled. Yet not the more
Cease I to wander where the Muses haunt
Clear spring, or shady grove, or sunny hill,
Smit with the love of sacred song; but chief
Thee, Sion, and the flowery brooks beneath
That wash thy hallowed feet, and warbling flow,
Nightly I visit; nor sometimes forget

BOOK III. **1. first-born:** the first thing God created. **2–6. Or . . . increate:** Milton has given a first theory of the origin of light, and he now gives a second: that it was not created but was there from the beginning, as an emanation from God Himself. **3. express:** call. **unblamed:** without being blamed for touching on holy things. **7–8. Or . . . tell:** The third theory: because light is divine, no human being is able to find an origin for it. **14. Stygian:** alluding to the Styx, the river in the dark underworld. **16. utter . . . middle:** outer (Hell) and middle darkness (Chaos). **17. Orphean lyre:** As contrasted with Orpheus, the singer of Greek legend, Milton draws on Christian inspiration. **30. Sion:** Zion, where the Temple of Jerusalem was built. **32. Nightly:** Milton composed mainly at night.

Those other two equaled with me in fate,
So were I equaled with them in renown,
Blind Thamyris and blind Maeonides,
And Tiresias and Phineus prophets old:
Then feed on thoughts, that voluntary move
Harmonious numbers, as the wakeful bird
Sings darkling, and in shadiest covert hid
Tunes her nocturnal note. Thus with the year
Seasons return; but not to me returns
Day, or the sweet approach of even or morn,
Or sight of vernal bloom, or summer's rose,
Or flocks, or herds, or human face divine;
But cloud instead, and ever-during dark
Surrounds me, from the cheerful ways of men
Cut off, and for the book of knowledge fair
Presented with a universal blank
Of Nature's works to me expunged and razed,
And wisdom at one entrance quite shut out.
So much the rather thou, celestial Light,
Shine inward, and the mind through all her powers
Irradiate, there plant eyes, all mist from thence
Purge and disperse, that I may see and tell
Of things invisible to mortal sight.

Sir John Suckling

(1609–1642)

Suckling was considered an aristocratic playboy even by his friends among the "Cavaliers," as they were called, who supported Charles I against the rising Puritans. A hard-drinking young man, noted as a profligate gamester and swordsman, he cultivated an easy and carefree manner, which is also seen in the light, half-mocking tone of his lyrics.

33–36. other two . . . Phineus: the two blind ancient poets, Homer (Maeonides) and Thamyris, and two blind prophets, Tiresius of Thebes and Phineus of Thrace. **38. numbers:** verses. **wakeful bird:** the nightingale. **39. darkling:** in the dark.

Song

Why so pale and wan, fond lover?
  Prithee, why so pale?
Will, when looking well can't move her,
  Looking ill prevail?
  Prithee, why so pale?

Why so dull and mute, young sinner?
  Prithee, why so mute?
Will, when speaking well can't win her,
  Saying nothing do 't?
  Prithee, why so mute?

Quit, quit, for shame; this will not move,
  This cannot take her.
If of herself she will not love,
  Nothing can make her:
  The devil take her!

1638

Out upon It!

Out upon it! I have loved
  Three whole days together;
And am like to love three more,
  If it prove fair weather.

Time shall molt away his wings,
  Ere he shall discover
In the whole wide world again
  Such a constant lover.

But the spite on 't is, no praise
  Is due at all to me:
Love with me had made no stays
  Had it any been but she.

Had it any been but she,
  And that very face,
There had been at least ere this
  A dozen dozen in her place.

1659

Anne Bradstreet

(c. 1612–1672)

The first significant woman poet of America, Anne Bradstreet was brought up in a well-to-do family in England. Her loving father saw to it that she received a much better education than was usually given to women at this time. At the age of sixteen she married Simon Bradstreet, and two years later she emigrated with her husband, her father, and other Puritan families to Massachusetts. She had begun writing poems when she was a girl and continued to do so in America. Without telling her, her brother-in-law took a manuscript collection of her poems to London, where they were printed in 1650. She wrote ambitious meditative poems on general themes, as well as poems that reflect more homely experiences in the new world. All her poems are saturated with her religious feeling.

The Vanity of All Wordly Things

As he said vanity, so vain say I,
Oh! vanity, O vain all under sky;
Where is the man can say, "Lo, I have found
On brittle earth a consolation sound"?
What isn't in honor to be set on high?
No, they like beasts and sons of men shall die,
And whilst they live, how oft doth turn their fate;
He's now a captive that was king of late.
What isn't in wealth great treasures to optain?
No, that's but labor, anxious care, and pain.
He heaps up riches, and he heaps up sorrow,
It's his today, but who's his heir tomorrow?
What then? Content in pleasures canst thou find?
More vain than all, that's but to grasp the wind.
The sensual senses for a time they please,
Meanwhile the conscience rage, who shall appease?
What isn't in beauty? No that's but a snare,
They're foul enough today, that once were fair.
What is't in flow'ring youth, or manly age?
The first is prone to vice, the last to rage.
Where is it then, in wisdom, learning, arts?

THE VANITY OF ALL WORLDLY THINGS. **1. he:** Solomon, or the Preacher in Ecclesiastes: "Vanity of vanities, saith the Preacher, . . . all is vanity." (1:2).

Sure if on earth, it must be in those parts;
Yet these the wisest man of men did find
But vanity, vexation of mind.
And he that knows the most doth still bemoan
He knows not all that here is to be known.
What is it then? to do as stoics tell,
Nor laugh, nor weep, let things go ill or well?
Such stoics are but stocks, such teaching vain,
While man is man, he shall have ease or pain.
If not in honor, beauty, age, nor treasure,
Nor yet in learning, wisdom, youth, nor pleasure,
Where shall I climb, sound, seek, search, or find
That *summum bonum* which may stay my mind?
There is a path no vulture's eye hath seen,
Where lion fierce, nor lion's whelps have been,
Which leads unto that living crystal fount,
Who drinks thereof, the world doth naught account.
The depth and sea have said "'tis not in me,"
With pearl and gold it shall not valued be.
For sapphire, onyx, topaz who would change;
It's hid from eyes of men, they count it strange.
Death and destruction the fame hath heard,
But where and what it is, from heaven's declared;
It brings to honor which shall ne'er decay,
It stores with wealth which time can't wear away.
It yieldeth pleasures far beyond conceit,
And truly beautifies without deceit.
Nor strength, nor wisdom, nor fresh youth shall fade,
Nor death shall see, but are immortal made.
This pearl of price, this tree of life, this spring,
Who is possessed of shall reign a king.
Nor change of state nor cares shall ever see,
But wear his crown unto eternity.
This satiates the soul, this stays the mind,
And all the rest, but vanity we find.

1650

34. ***summum bonum*****:** "the highest good."

Abraham Cowley

(1618–1667)

Cowley was a bookish, quiet-loving man who was forced by the political upheavals of his time into a more adventurous life than he could have wished for. He wrote plays, pamphlets, essays which were once widely read, and poems. He has the merit of inventing a new poetic form, the "irregular" ode or "false Pindaric" (so-called because Cowley modeled these odes on those of the ancient Greek poet, Pindar, but did not keep Pindar's strict structure. Wordsworth's "Ode: Intimations of Immortality" is the most famous poem in this form in English.) Cowley is also remembered for some outrageously extravagant and unsuccessful conceits in the "metaphysical" style. But "The Wish" is more typical of his work and was a very popular poem in the eighteenth century.

The Wish

Well then; I now do plainly see,
This busy world and I shall ne'er agree;
The very honey of all earthly joy
Does of all meats the soonest cloy;
And they, methinks, deserve my pity
Who for it can endure the stings,
The crowd, and buzz, and murmurings
Of this great hive, the city.

Ah, yet, ere I descend to the grave
May I a small house and large garden have!
And a few friends, and many books, both true,
Both wise, and both delightful too!
And since love ne'er will from me flee,
A mistress moderately fair,
And good as guardian angels are,
Only beloved, and loving me!

O fountains, when in you shall I
Myself, eased of unpeaceful thoughts, espy?
O fields! O woods! when, when shall I be made
The happy tenant of your shade?
Here's the spring-head of pleasure's flood,
Here's wealthy Nature's treasury,
Where all the riches lie that she
Has coined and stamped for good.

Pride and ambition here
Only in farfetched metaphors appear;
Here naught but winds can hurtful murmurs scatter,
And naught but Echo flatter.
The gods, when they descended, hither
From heaven did always choose their way;
And therefore we may boldly say
That 'tis the way, too, thither.

How happy here should I
And one dear she live and, embracing, die!
She who is all the world, and can exclude
In deserts, solitude.
I should have then this only fear,
Lest men, when they my pleasures see,
Should hither throng to live like me,
And so make a city here.

1647

RICHARD LOVELACE

(1618–1657)

Lovelace, like Sir John Suckling, was one of the "Cavalier" poets associated with the court of Charles I. He fought on the King's side against the Puritans in the English Civil War, and he sold all his estates to raise money for the King, later dying in destitution. His best lyrics, such as "To Althea, from Prison" and "To Lucasta, Going to the Wars," date from the time of the English Civil War. Four of the lines in these two poems have passed into the language as common aphorisms: "Stone walls do not a prison make,/ Nor iron bars a cage"; and "I could not love thee, dear, so much,/ Loved I not honor more."

To Althea, from Prison

When Love with unconfinèd wings
Hovers within my gates,
And my divine Althea brings
To whisper at the grates;
When I lie tangled in her hair
And fettered to her eye,
The gods that wanton in the air
Know no such liberty.

When flowing cups run swiftly round,
With no allaying Thames,
Our careless heads with roses bound,
Our hearts with loyal flames;
When thirsty grief in wine we steep,
When healths and draughts go free,
Fishes, that tipple in the deep,
Know no such liberty.

When, like committed linnets, I
With shriller throat shall sing
The sweetness, mercy, majesty,
And glories of my King;
When I shall voice aloud how good
He is, how great should be,
Enlargèd winds, that curl the flood,
Know no such liberty.

Stone walls do not a prison make,
Nor iron bars a cage;
Minds innocent and quiet take
That for an hermitage.
If I have freedom in my love,
And in my soul am free,
Angels alone, that soar above,
Enjoy such liberty.

1649

To Lucasta, Going to the Wars

Tell me not, sweet, I am unkind
That from the nunnery
Of thy chaste breast and quiet mind,
To war and arms I fly.

True, a new mistress now I chase,
The first foe in the field;
And with a stronger faith embrace
A sword, a horse, a shield.

Yet this inconstancy is such
As you too shall adore;
I could not love thee, dear, so much,
Loved I not honor more.

1649

TO ALTHEA, FROM PRISON. **17. committed:** kept in a cage.

ANDREW MARVELL

(1621–1678)

In the early part of his life Marvell was a tutor in various important families; he also worked with Milton in the government of Oliver Cromwell. After the restoration of the King in 1660, Marvell represented the town of Hull in Parliament.

His poetry combines the classical elegance, proportion, and clarity of the tradition of Ben Jonson with "metaphysical" wit; it is often ironical and always characterized by active, subtle thinking. His most famous poem, "To His Coy Mistress," is on a common theme of classical and Renaissance poetry, *carpe diem* (the Latin phrase means, "seize the day"). In such poems the lover pleads or, in Marvell's case, argues with his mistress to yield herself while the lovers still have youth. Such *carpe diem* poems are often lighthearted and amusing on the surface, but their emotion is always complicated by the poet's mindfulness of time remorselessly leading to old age and death; awareness of this throws an ominous shadow across the amorous pleading. Herrick's "To the Virgins, to Make Much of Time" is another example of *carpe diem*, as are Jonson's "Come, My Celia" and Campion's translation of Catullus' "My Sweetest Lesbia." Some of Shakespeare's sonnets include this theme. Marvell's poem skillfully blends tones of lightness and seriousness, and the highly logical structure of the argument and controlled, polished character of the verse counterpoint ironically with the implied dramatic situation—a lover speaking to his mistress. Except for some later satires not included in this selection, all Marvell's poems appear to have been composed during a brief period in the 1650s.

Bermudas

Where the remote Bermudas ride,
In th' ocean's bosom unespied,
From a small boat that rowed along,
The listening winds received this song:
"What should we do but sing His praise,

BERMUDAS. **Title:** We now use the singular for the main island in the group of islands off Cape Hatteras, North Carolina. They were discovered by the Spanish (1515) and colonized by the English (1612).

That led us through the watery maze
Unto an isle so long unknown,
And yet far kinder than our own?
Where He the huge sea monsters wracks,
That lift the deep upon their backs;
He lands us on a grassy stage,
Safe from the storms, and prelate's rage.
He gave us this eternal spring
Which here enamels everything,
And sends the fowls to us in care,
On daily visits through the air;
He hangs in shades the orange bright,
Like golden lamps in a green night,
And does in the pomegranates close
Jewels more rich than Ormus shows;
He makes the figs our mouths to meet,
And throws the melons at our feet;
But apples plants of such a price,
No tree could ever bear them twice;
With cedars, chosen by His hand,
From Lebanon, He stores the land;
And makes the hollow seas, that roar,
Proclaim the ambergris on shore;
He cast (of which we rather boast)
The Gospel's pearl upon our coast,
And in these rocks for us did frame
A temple, where to sound His name.
O! let our voice His praise exalt,
Till it arrive at heaven's vault,
Which, thence (perhaps) rebounding, may
Echo beyond the Mexique Bay."
Thus sung they in the English boat,
An holy and a cheerful note;
And all the way, to guide their chime,
With falling oars they kept the time.

1681

9. sea monsters: whales. **wracks:** tosses on shore. **12. prelate's rage:** the tyranny of the Bishops of the Church of England, to escape which many Puritans and other dissenters emigrated to America. **20. Ormus:** the city of Hormuz on the Persian Gulf, famous for its export of jewels. **23. apples:** pineapples. **28. proclaim:** exhibit. **ambergris:** secretion of the sperm whale, used in perfumes.

To His Coy Mistress

Had we but world enough, and time,
This coyness, lady, were no crime.
We would sit down, and think which way
To walk, and pass our long love's day.
Thou by the Indian Ganges' side
Shoudst rubies find; I by the tide
Of Humber would complain. I would
Love you ten years before the flood,
And you should, if you please, refuse
Till the conversion of the Jews.
My vegetable love should grow
Vaster than empires and more slow;
An hundred years should go to praise
Thine eyes, and on thy forehead gaze;
Two hundred to adore each breast,
But thirty thousand to the rest;
An age at least to every part,
And the last age should show your heart.
For, lady, you deserve this state,
Nor would I love at lower rate.
But at my back I always hear
Time's wingèd chariot hurrying near;
And yonder all before us lie
Deserts of vast eternity.
Thy beauty shall no more be found;
Nor, in thy marble vault, shall sound
My echoing song; then worms shall try
That long-preserved virginity,
And your quaint honor turn to dust,
And into ashes all my lust:
The grave's a fine and private place,
But none, I think, do there embrace.
Now therefore, while the youthful hue
Sits on thy skin like morning dew,
And while thy willing soul transpires
At every pore with instant fires,
Now let us sport us while we may,
And now, like amorous birds of prey,
Rather at once our time devour
Than languish in his slow-chapped power.

TO HIS COY MISTRESS. **7. Humber:** river in north England. **7–8. I would . . . flood:** I could start my loving of you ten years before the great Flood of Noah's time. **10. conversion . . . Jews:** till the end of time (the implication being that the Jews will never surrender their traditional faith). **11. vegetable:** constantly growing, unconsciously, like a plant. **19. state:** honor. **29. quaint:** strange and old-fashioned. **35. transpires:** exhales. **36. instant:** urgent. **40. slow-chapped:** slow-jawed (that is, slowly devouring).

Let us roll all our strength and all
Our sweetness up into one ball,
And tear our pleasures with rough strife
Thorough the iron gates of life:
Thus, though we cannot make our sun
Stand still, yet we will make him run.

1681

The Definition of Love

My love is of a birth as rare
As 'tis, for object, strange and high;
It was begotten by Despair
Upon Impossibility.

Magnanimous Despair alone
Could show me so divine a thing,
Where feeble Hope could ne'er have flown
But vainly flapped its tinsel wing.

And yet I quickly might arrive
Where my extended soul is fixed;
But Fate does iron wedges drive,
And always crowds itself betwixt.

For Fate with jealous eye does see
Two perfect loves, nor lets them close;
Their union would her ruin be,
And her tyrannic power depose.

And therefore her decrees of steel
Us as the distant poles have placed
(Though Love's whole world on us doth wheel),
Not by themselves to be embraced,

Unless the giddy heaven fall,
And earth some new convulsion tear,
And, us to join, the world should all
Be cramped into a planisphere.

42–44. ball . . . gates: like a cannon-ball tearing through the iron bars of a gate. THE DEFINITION OF LOVE. **14. close:** come together. **15–16. union . . . depose:** Their union, in this perfect way, would defy the tyranny of Fate. **19. Though . . . wheel:** though we are the axis on which Love's world turns. **20. Not . . . embraced:** Since the poles are at opposite ends of the axis, they cannot touch each other. **24. planisphere:** flat map onto which a sphere is projected.

As lines, so loves oblique may well
Themselves in every angle greet;
But ours, so truly parallel,
Though infinite, can never meet.

Therefore the love which us doth bind,
But Fate so enviously debars,
Is the conjunction of the mind,
And opposition of the stars.

1681

The Mower Against Gardens

Luxurious man, to bring his vice in use,
  Did after him the world seduce,
And from the fields the flowers and plants allure,
  Where Nature was most plain and pure.
He first enclosed within the gardens square
  A dead and standing pool of air,
And a more luscious earth for them did knead,
  Which stupefied them while it fed.
The pink grew then as double as his mind;
  The nutriment did change the kind.
With strange perfumes he did the roses taint;
  And flowers themselves were taught to paint.
The tulip white did for complexion seek,
  And learned to interline its cheek;
Its onion root they then so high did hold,
  That one was for a meadow sold:
Another world was searched through oceans new,
  To find the Marvel of Peru;
And yet these rarities might be allowed
  To man, that sovereign thing and proud,
Had he not dealt between the bark and tree,
  Forbidden mixtures there to see.
No plant now knew the stock from which it came;
  He grafts upon the wild the tame,

25. oblique: slanting, not parallel, and thus likely to intersect. **31–32. conjunction . . . opposition:** The terms are taken from astronomy. "Through the mind, our love will bring us together even though physically we are kept apart." THE MOWER AGAINST GARDENS. **1. luxurious:** lecherous, lustful. **bring . . . use:** make his vice profitable. **15–16. onion . . . sold:** referring to the Dutch "tulip craze" of the 1630s when a single "onion-shaped" bulb could be sold at great price. **18. Marvel of Peru:** *mirabilis Peruviana,* a plant discovered in the early 1600s.

That the uncertain and adulterate fruit
  Might put the palate in dispute.
His green seraglio has its eunuchs too,
  Lest any tyrant him outdo;
And in the cherry he does Nature vex,
  To procreate without a sex.
'Tis all enforced, the fountain and the grot,
  While the sweet fields do lie forgot,
Where willing Nature does to all dispense
  A wild and fragrant innocence;
And fauns and fairies do the meadows till
  More by their presence than their skill.
Their statues polished by some ancient hand,
  May to adorn the gardens stand;
But, howsoe'er the figures do excel,
  The Gods themselves with us do dwell.

1681

The Mower to the Glowworms

Ye living lamps, by whose dear light
The nightingale does sit so late,
And studying all the summer night,
Her matchless songs does meditate;

Ye country comets, that portend
No war nor prince's funeral,
Shining unto no higher end
Than to presage the grass's fall;

Ye glowworms, whose officious flame
To wandering mowers shows the way,
That in the night have lost their aim,
And after foolish fires do stray;

Your courteous lights in vain you waste,
Since Juliana here is come,
For she may mind hath so displaced
That I shall never find my home.

1681

THE MOWER TO THE GLOWWORMS. **5–6. Comets . . . funeral:** referring to the belief that comets generally indicated wars, the death of kings, or public disasters. **9. officious:** dutiful. **12. foolish fires:** will-o'-the-wisp.

The Garden

How vainly men themselves amaze
To win the palm, the oak, or bays,
And their incessant labors see
Crowned from some single herb, or tree,
Whose short and narrow-vergèd shade
Does prudently their toils upbraid;
While all flowers and all trees do close
To weave the garlands of repose!

Fair Quiet, have I found thee here,
And Innocence, thy sister dear?
Mistaken long, I sought you then
In busy companies of men.
Your sacred plants, if here below,
Only among the plants will grow;
Society is all but rude
To this delicious solitude.

No white nor red was ever seen
So amorous as this lovely green.
Fond lovers, cruel as their flame,
Cut in these trees their mistress' name:
Little, alas, they know or heed
How far these beauties hers exceed!
Fair trees, wheresoe'er your barks I wound,
No name shall but your own be found.

When we have run our passion's heat,
Love hither makes his best retreat.
The gods, that mortal beauty chase,
Still in a tree did end their race:
Apollo hunted Daphne so,
Only that she might laurel grow;
And Pan did after Syrinx speed,
Not as a nymph, but for a reed.

What wondrous life is this I lead!
Ripe apples drop about my head;
The luscious clusters of the vine
Upon my mouth do crush their wine;
The nectarine and curious peach
Into my hands themselves do reach;

THE GARDEN. **1. amaze:** bewilder, perplex. **2. palm . . . bays:** honors for, respectively, war, politics, and poetry. **5. narrow-vergèd:** confined in small space. **7. close:** unite. **15. rude:** uncultivated. **29–32. Apollo . . . reed:** When Apollo pursued Daphne, she was changed into a laurel. When Pan pursued Syrinx, she was transformed into a reed. **37. curious:** choice.

Stumbling on melons, as I pass,
Insnared with flowers, I fall on grass.

Meanwhile the mind, from pleasure less,
Withdraws into its happiness;
The mind, that occan where each kind
Does straight its own resemblance find;
Yet it creates, transcending these,
Far other worlds and other seas,
Annihilating all that's made
To a green thought in a green shade.

Here at the fountain's sliding foot,
Or at some fruit tree's mossy root,
Casting the body's vest aside,
My soul into the boughs does glide:
There, like a bird, it sits and sings,
Then whets and combs its silver wings,
And, till prepared for longer flight,
Waves in its plumes the various light.

Such was that happy garden-state,
While man there walked without a mate:
After a place so pure and sweet,
What other help could yet be meet!
But 'twas beyond a mortal's share
To wander solitary there:
Two paradises 'twere in one
To live in paradise alone.

How well the skillful gardener drew
Of flowers and herbs this dial new,
Where, from above, the milder sun
Does through a fragrant zodiac run;
And as it works, th' industrious bee
Computes its time as well as we!
How could such sweet and wholesome hours
Be reckoned but with herbs and flowers?

1681

41–42. pleasure . . . happiness: getting less pleasure through the body and the senses, finds happiness through the mind and soul. **43–44. ocean . . . find:** referring to the belief that the sea contained an animal corresponding to each land animal. **47–48. Annihilating . . . shade:** reducing the material world to nothing compared to that of the human imagination. **51. vest:** covering. **54. whets:** whets its beak. **66. dial:** sundial made of flowering plants.

HENRY VAUGHAN

(1621–1695)

A disciple of George Herbert, Vaughan is valued today especially for a mystical vein within his religious emotion. It is not simply that he longs to free himself from the mortal world. In some poems he goes further and speaks of intimations of "glory," as though he had intuitional experience of a heavenly world beyond earthly life. In "The Retreat" he anticipates Wordsworth's "Ode: Intimations of Immortality" in his feelings about infancy and childhood (both Wordsworth and Vaughan were influenced by Neoplatonic myths which tell how the soul comes to earth from a prior home in heaven). "Peace" is closer to the vein of Herbert, but illustrates what a skilled artist Vaughan could be in this vein of simple, carefully worked, and deeply felt speech.

The Retreat

Happy those early days! when I
Shined in my angel infancy.
Before I understood this place
Appointed for my second race,
Or taught my soul to fancy aught
But a white, celestial thought;
When yet I had not walked above
A mile or two from my first love,
And looking back, at that short space,
Could see a glimpse of His bright face;
When on some gilded cloud or flower
My gazing soul would dwell an hour,
And in those weaker glories spy
Some shadows of eternity;
Before I taught my tongue to wound
My conscience with a sinful sound,
Or had the black art to dispense
A several sin to every sense,
But felt through all this fleshly dress
Bright shoots of everlastingness.
  O, how I long to travel back,
And tread again that ancient track!

THE RETREAT. **18. several:** separate.

That I might once more reach that plain
Where first I left my glorious train,
From whence th' enlightened spirit sees
That shady city of palm trees.
But, ah! my soul with too much stay
Is drunk, and staggers in the way.
Some men a forward motion love;
But I by backward steps would move,
And when this dust falls to the urn,
In that state I came, return.

1650

They Are All Gone into the World of Light!

They are all gone into the world of light!
  And I alone sit lingering here;
Their very memory is fair and bright,
  And my sad thoughts doth clear.

It glows and glitters in my cloudy breast
  Like stars upon some gloomy grove,
Or those faint beams in which this hill is dressed
  After the sun's remove.

I see them walking in an air of glory,
  Whose light doth trample on my days;
My days, which are at best but dull and hoary,
  Mere glimmering and decays.

O holy hope, and high humility,
  High as the heavens above!
These are your walks, and you have showed them me
  To kindle my cold love.

Dear, beauteous death! the jewel of the just,
  Shining nowhere but in the dark;
What mysteries do lie beyond thy dust,
  Could man outlook that mark!

He that hath found some fledged bird's nest may know
  At first sight if the bird be flown;
But what fair well or grove he sings in now,
  That is to him unknown.

And yet, as angels in some brighter dreams
  Call to the soul when man doth sleep,

25–26. spirit . . . trees: referring to what Moses saw when allowed to look from Mount Pisgah down into the Promised Land (Deuteronomy 34:3). THEY ARE ALL GONE. **20. mark:** boundary, limit. **21. fledged:** feathered (that is, grown up).

So some strange thoughts transcend our wonted themes,
  And into glory peep.

If a star were confined into a tomb,
  Her captive flames must needs burn there;
But when the hand that locked her up gives room,
  She'll shine through all the sphere.

O Father of eternal life, and all
  Created glories under Thee!
Resume Thy spirit from this world of thrall
  Into true liberty!

Either disperse these mists, which blot and fill
  My perspective still as they pass;
Or else remove me hence unto that hill
  Where I shall need no glass.

1655

Peace

My soul, there is a country
  Far beyond the stars,
Where stands a wingèd sentry
  All skillful in the wars:
There, above noise and danger,
  Sweet Peace sits crown'd with smiles,
And One born in a manger
  Commands the beauteous files.
He is thy gracious friend.
  And—O my soul awake!—
Did in pure love descend,
  To die here for thy sake.
If thou canst get but thither,
  There grows the flower of Peace,
The rose that cannot wither,
  Thy fortress and thy ease.
Leave, then, thy foolish ranges,
  For none can thee secure,
But One who never changes,
  Thy God, thy life, thy cure.

1655

35. Resume: take back. **38. perspective:** telescope. PEACE. **17. ranges:** wanderings.

John Dryden

(1631–1700)

Dryden, more than anyone else, established a mode of poetry that was to remain dominant for almost a century from the 1660s to the 1760s. It has continued to delight readers who enjoy a quality of "wit" and intellectual sharpness in poetry, and has especially fascinated later poets because of its polished technique.

We call this kind of writing the "High Neoclassic Mode." "Neoclassicism" means simply a "new classicism," a new emergence of qualities that had inspired the literature and art of ancient Greece and Rome. This "New Classicism" became the prevailing mode in France during the seventeenth century and was brought over to England during the Restoration (the return of the monarchy from France to England in 1660 after the English Civil War). It focussed on particular aspects and ideals of the "classical" and tried to carry them even further. These included ideals of "correctness" in language and versification, strictness of form, a crisp neatness of phrase, a clever and learned use of allusions and references, and a combination of clarity with sophisticated grace and elegance. At the same time there was the classical ideal of the poet as a moral "teacher." Types of poems that lent themselves to such "teaching" were "didactic" poems (essays in verse, like Pope's *Essay on Man,* selections of which are printed later in this anthology) and satire, where the thought was to castigate "vices and follies" for the sake of moral improvement.

The metrical form that proved most congenial to the English, when they took over the "Neoclassic" ideals, was the heroic couplet. Poetry written in couplets rhymes every two lines, and the term "heroic" in this context did not imply anything particularly heroic, but only that the meter or "line" was iambic pentameter (see Appendix on Versification). This was known as the "heroic line" because it had been the standard verse-line both for the great Elizabethan dramas, like those of Shakespeare, and for the epic, like Milton's *Paradise Lost.* As used by Dryden, Pope, and other neoclassic poets, the heroic couplet often became a self-contained unit. This certainly has limitations in narrative verse or in the lyrical expression of emotions. But the snap of the heroic couplet makes it marvellously suitable for epigrams and other condensed, polished statements of wit and wisdom, and it is especially effective in satire.

Dryden was not only a poet: He was a general man-of-letters and one of the pivotal figures in the history of literature in our language. He established a new prose style, beautifully simplified and elegant, for the century that followed. He wrote admirable essays in literary criticism that are still studied with respect. He also wrote many plays, though these are now read only by writers and critics.

But it is really as a poet that we value Dryden most today, and especially—together with Pope—as one of the supreme poets who wrote satire in English. One of his brilliant achievements as a satirist was his development of the "satiric portrait." These portraits occur in his poems when he suddenly stops the flow of narrative and describes a character, as in the two portraits we select here from *Absalom and Achitophel* (1681). *Mac Flecknoe* (1679), which we give entire, is perhaps the most hilarious short poetic satire in English. Here he conceived the idea of taking as a hero a hapless, now forgotten writer named Thomas Shadwell and having him crowned, as the prototype of dullness, by a dull predecessor named Flecknoe. This idea was picked up and developed later in Pope's *The Dunciad* (1743). The Olympian irony that Dryden can heap on his victim can be illustrated by a couplet (lines 19–20) in which Dryden compares Shadwell to other bad poets:

> The rest to some faint meaning make pretense,
> But Shadwell never deviates into sense.

For Shadwell could not reply, "Yes, I do at times deviate into sense." Nor could he say, "No, I don't deviate into sense."

At their best, it has been said, Dryden's couplets have the sound of a large bronze coin flung down upon marble. And that clang and resonance are found in his odes, including "Song for St. Cecilia's Day." But Dryden was also capable of moments of pathos, and these are all the more poignant because of the firm classical control of his language, as in his elegy "To the Memory of Mr. Oldham," a poet who had died young. Dryden, like Pope, is admittedly an acquired taste. But his poetry will never lose its appeal to readers who wish to supplement the Romantics and their modern successors with another and different example of what poetry can do.

from Absalom and Achitophel

Some by their friends, more by themselves thought wise,
Opposed the power to which they could not rise.
Some had in courts been great, and thrown from thence,
Like fiends were hardened in impenitence;
Some, by their monarch's fatal mercy, grown
From pardoned rebels kinsmen to the throne,
Were raised in power and public office high;
Strong bands, if bands ungrateful men could tie.
  Of these the false Achitophel was first;
A name to all succeeding ages cursed:
For close designs, and crooked counsels fit;
Sagacious, bold, and turbulent of wit;
Restless, unfixed in principles and place;
In power unpleased, impatient of disgrace:
A fiery soul, which, working out its way,
Fretted the pygmy body to decay,
And o'er-informed the tenement of clay.
A daring pilot in extremity;
Pleased with the danger, when the waves went high,
He sought the storms; but, for a calm unfit,
Would steer too nigh the sands, to boast his wit.
Great wits are sure to madness near allied,
And thin partitions do their bounds divide;
Else why should he, with wealth and honor blest,
Refuse his age the needful hours of rest?
Punish a body which he could not please,
Bankrupt of life, yet prodigal of ease?
And all to leave what with his toil he won,
To that unfeathered two-legged thing, a son;
Got, while his soul did huddled notions try;
And born a shapeless lump, like anarchy.
In friendship false, implacable in hate,
Resolved to ruin or to rule the state.

. . .

ABSALOM AND ACHITOPHEL. **Title:** The background of this famous political satire is the event in English history known as the "Monmouth Rebellion" (1679–83). King Charles II had no legitimate children, and many Protestants were worried that, after his death, the throne would pass to his brother, James, a Catholic. The young Duke of Monmouth, widely regarded as the illegitimate son of Charles II, attempted to win popular support among Protestants to ensure himself as Charles's heir. In this, his chief encourager was the Earl of Shaftesbury. The plan, after some minor military skirmishes, was defeated. Dryden applies to the "Monmouth Rebellion" the story in the Bible of the young Absalom's rebellion against his father, King David (in I Samuel: 13–18). Here David represents Charles II, Absalom is Monmouth, and Achitophel, Absalom's evil adviser, is the Earl of Shaftesbury. The most brilliant lines of the poem are those in the two famous "satiric portraits" printed here: the portrait of the "false Achitophel" (Shaftesbury), and that of Zimri (the Duke of Buckingham). **153. wit:** imagination. **158. o'er-informed . . . clay:** was too large for and over-filled his body. **163. wits:** geniuses. **171. huddled:** confused.

Such were the tools; but a whole Hydra more
Remains, of sprouting heads too long to score.
Some of their chiefs were princes of the land:
In the first rank of these did Zimri stand;
A man so various, that he seemed to be
Not one, but all mankind's epitome:
Stiff in opinions, always in the wrong;
Was everything by starts, and nothing long;
But, in the course of one revolving moon,
Was chemist, fiddler, statesman, and buffoon:
Then all for women, painting, rhyming, drinking,
Besides ten thousand freaks that died in thinking.

Mac Flecknoe

Or a satire upon the true-blue protestant poet, T. S.

All human things are subject to decay,
And when fate summons, monarchs must obey.
This Flecknoe found, who, like Augustus, young
Was called to empire, and had governed long;
In prose and verse, was owned, without dispute,
Through all the realms of Nonsense, absolute.
This aged prince, now flourishing in peace,
And blest with issue of a large increase,
Worn out with business, did at length debate
To settle the succession of the state;
And, pondering which of all his sons was fit
To reign, and wage immortal war with wit,
Cried: "'Tis resolved; for nature pleads that he
Should only rule, who most resembles me.

541. tools: Dryden has been speaking of members of the Monmouth conspiracy, many of them tools of Shaftesbury. **Hydra:** In Greek mythology a beast with nine heads; whenever one head was chopped off, two more heads would replace it. **545. various:** Dryden is laughing at the numerous activities in which the superficial Buckingham (Zimri) occupied himself—chemistry, music, mistresses, painting, drinking, and serving as patron to a number of "freaks" that he considered intellectuals. MAC FLECKNOE. **Title:** One of the most luminous comic satires in all literature, the poem is an attack on the then popular but now forgotten playwright Thomas Shadwell (1640–1692). The vain and swaggering Shadwell liked to consider himself the heir of the great playwright Ben Jonson. But Dryden portrays him as actually the son of Richard Flecknoe ("Mac" means "son of"), a poet who wrote a great deal of tedious poetry, and who is here used as a symbol or prototype of "Dullness." Flecknoe is looking for an heir who is dull enough to be a worthy successor to himself. **3. Augustus:** The first Roman Emperor, Augustus ruled for forty years and then had to face the problem of finding a successor, as Flecknoe is having to do. **12. wit:** intellect generally, especially imaginative genius.

Sh—— alone my perfect image bears,
Mature in dullness from his tender years:
Sh—— alone, of all my sons, is he
Who stands confirmed in full stupidity.
The rest to some faint meaning make pretense,
But Sh—— never deviates into sense.
Some beams of wit on other souls may fall,
Strike through, and make a lucid interval;
But Sh——'s genuine night admits no ray,
His rising fogs prevail upon the day.
Besides, his goodly fabric fills the eye,
And seems designed for thoughtless majesty:
Thoughtless as monarch oaks that shade the plain,
And, spread in solemn state, supinely reign.
Heywood and Shirley were but types of thee,
Thou last great prophet of tautology.
Even I, a dunce of more renown than they,
Was sent before but to prepare thy way;
And, coarsely clad in Norwich drugget, came
To teach the nations in thy greater name.
My warbling lute, the lute I whilom strung,
When to King John of Portugal I sung,
Was but the prelude to that glorious day,
When thou on silver Thames didst cut thy way,
With well-timed oars before the royal barge,
Swelled with the pride of thy celestial charge;
And big with hymn, commander of a host,
The like was ne'er in Epsom blankets tossed.
Methinks I see the new Arion sail,
The lute still trembling underneath thy nail.
At thy well-sharpened thumb from shore to shore
The treble squeaks for fear, the basses roar;
Echoes from Pissing Alley Sh—— call,
And Sh—— they resound from Aston Hall.
About thy boat the little fishes throng,
As at the morning toast that floats along.
Sometimes, as prince of thy harmonious band,
Thou wield'st thy papers in thy threshing hand.

15. Here, and throughout the poem, "Sh——" stands for Shadwell. **25. fabric:** body (alluding to his fat, unwieldy shape). **29. Heywood . . . Shirley:** Prolific dramatists of the generation before, considered old-fashioned and dull in Dryden's time; cited as earlier "types," or models, of Shadwell's work. **33. drugget:** coarse woolen cloth used to cover furniture. **35. whilom:** for a while. **36. King John:** claimed by Flecknoe as his patron. **42. Epsom . . . tossed:** a reference to two of Shadwell's plays, *Epsom Wells* and *The Virtuoso.* In the latter, one of the characters is tossed in a blanket. **43. Arion:** Greek poet, whose songs charmed a dolphin into following his ship. When robbers threw him into the sea, the dolphin saved him. Dryden is sarcastically referring to Shadwell's pride in himself as a musician. **47. Pissing Alley:** popular name for a disreputable small street near the scene here. **50. toast:** sewage.

St. André's feet ne'er kept more equal time,
Not ev'n the feet of thy own *Psyche's* rhyme;
Though they in number as in sense excel:
So just, so like tautology, they fell,
That, pale with envy, Singleton forswore
The lute and sword, which he in triumph bore,
And vowed he ne'er would act Villerius more."
Here stopped the good old sire, and wept for joy
In silent raptures of the hopeful boy.
All arguments, but most his plays, persuade,
That for anointed dullness he was made.
  Close to the walls which fair Augusta bind
(The fair Augusta much to fears inclined),
An ancient fabric raised to inform the sight,
There stood of yore, and Barbican it hight:
A watchtower once; but now, so fate ordains,
Of all the pile an empty name remains.
From its old ruins brothel houses rise,
Scenes of lewd loves, and of polluted joys,
Where their vast courts the mother-strumpets keep,
And, undisturbed by watch, in silence sleep.
Near these a Nursery erects its head,
Where queens are formed, and future heroes bred;
Where unfledged actors learn to laugh and cry,
Where infant punks their tender voices try,
And little Maximins the gods defy.
Great Fletcher never treads in buskins here,
Nor greater Jonson dares in socks appear;
But gentle Simkin just reception finds
Amidst this monument of vanished minds:
Pure clinches the suburbian Muse affords,
And Panton waging harmless war with words.
Here Flecknoe, as a place to fame well known,
Ambitiously designed his Sh——'s throne;
For ancient Dekker prophesied long since,
That in this pile would reign a mighty prince,

53. St. André: a dancing master who helped to stage Shadwell's opera *Psyche* (line 54). **57. Singleton:** operatic singer of the time. **59. Villerius:** a role in William Davenant's opera, *The Siege of Rhodes*. **64. Augusta:** London. The "fears" are of political plots. **67. Barbican:** a section of London with ruins (line 70) of old fortifications, which had become the seat of brothels. **74. Nursery:** school for actors, scene of the coronation of Shadwell. **77. punks:** prostitutes. **78. Maximin:** Roman emperor noted for his cruelty; a bombastic character in Dryden's play *Tyrannic Love*. **79–81. Fletcher . . . buskins . . . socks . . . Simkin:** The dramatist John Fletcher was a contemporary of Shakespeare and Ben Jonson. Buskins were a symbol of tragedy (from the name given the boots worn by actors in Greek tragedies), contrasted with "socks" (low shoes) worn by comic actors. Dryden is saying that neither Fletcher nor Jonson would have had a place in this acting school, which was more receptive to the clown Simkin. **83. clinches:** puns. **84. Panton:** a celebrated punster. **87. Dekker:** Elizabethan dramatist.

Born for a scourge of wit, and flail of sense;
To whom true dullness should some *Psyches* owe,
But worlds of *Misers* from his pen should flow;
Humorists and *Hypocrites* it should produce,
Whole Raymond families, and tribes of Bruce.
  Now Empress Fame had published the renown
Of Sh——'s coronation through the town.
Roused by report of Fame, the nations meet,
From near Bunhill, and distant Watling Street.
No Persian carpets spread the imperial way,
But scattered limbs of mangled poets lay;
From dusty shops neglected authors come,
Martyrs of pies, and relics of the bum.
Much Heywood, Shirley, Ogilby there lay,
But loads of Sh—— almost choked the way.
Bilked stationers for yeomen stood prepared,
And Herringman was captain of the guard.
The hoary prince in majesty appeared,
High on a throne of his own labors reared.
At his right hand our young Ascanius sate,
Rome's other hope, and pillar of the state.
His brows thick fogs, instead of glories, grace,
And lambent dullness played around his face.
As Hannibal did to the altars come,
Sworn by his sire a mortal foe to Rome,
So Sh—— swore, nor should his vow be vain,
That he till death true dullness would maintain;
And, in his father's right, and realm's defense,
Ne'er to have peace with wit, nor truce with sense.
The king himself the sacred unction made,
As king by office, and as priest by trade.
In his sinister hand, instead of ball,
He placed a mighty mug of potent ale;
Love's Kingdom to his right he did convey,

90–92. *Psyches . . . Misers . . . Humorists . . . Hypocrites*: plays or operas by Shadwell. **97. Bunhill . . . Watling Street:** Both are near the "Nursery," and suggest the limited area of Shadwell's fame. **101. Pies . . . bum:** unsold books used in bakeries and as toilet paper. **102. Heywood, Shirley, Ogilby:** John Heywood was a fifteenth-century dramatist, James Shirley a seventeenth-century dramatist, and John Ogilby a mediocre translator of Homer and Virgil. **104–105. bilked stationers . . . Herringman:** Publishers, bilked (left in the lurch) because they had invested too much in bad writers like Shadwell, are serving as his guard of honor, with Shadwell's publisher, Henry Herringman, as their captain. **108. Ascanius:** son of Aeneas, as Shadwell is the heir of Flecknoe. Dryden is here parodying passages in Virgil's *Aeneid*. **112–13. Hannibal . . . mortal foe:** Hannibal, the great Carthaginian foe of Rome, was sworn as a boy to be its mortal enemy. **118. sacred Unction:** sacred oil with which the king is anointed. **120–22. sinister . . . ball . . . right:** British kings, when crowned, hold in their left (or sinister) hand a globe, and in the right a sceptre. Here, instead of the ball, Shadwell holds a mug of ale, instead of a sceptre, a rolled up manuscript of Flecknoe's dull play, *Love's Kingdom*.

At once his scepter, and his rule of sway;
Whose righteous lore the prince had practiced young,
And from whose loins recorded *Psyche* sprung.
His temples, last, with poppies were o'erspread,
That nodding seemed to consecrate his head.
Just at that point of time, if fame not lie,
On his left hand twelve reverend owls did fly.
So Romulus, 'tis sung, by Tiber's brook,
Presage of sway from twice six vultures took.
The admiring throng loud acclamations make,
And omens of his future empire take.
The sire then shook the honors of his head,
And from his brows damps of oblivion shed
Full on the filial dullness: long he stood,
Repelling from his breast the raging god;
At length burst out in this prophetic mood:
"Heavens bless my son, from Ireland let him reign
To far Barbadoes on the western main;
Of his dominion may no end be known,
And greater than his father's be his throne;
Beyond *Love's Kingdom* let his stretch his pen!"
He paused, and all the people cried, "Amen."
Then thus continued he: "My son, advance
Still in new impudence, new ignorance.
Success let others teach, learn thou from me
Pangs without birth, and fruitless industry.
Let *Virtuosos* in five years be writ;
Yet not one thought accuse thy toil of wit.
Let gentle George in triumph tread the stage,
Make Dorimant betray, and Loveit rage;
Let Cully, Cockwood, Fopling, charm the pit,
And in their folly show the writer's wit.
Yet still thy fools shall stand in thy defense,
And justify their author's want of sense.
Let 'em be all by thy own model made
Of dullness, and desire no foreign aid;
That they to future ages may be known,
Not copies drawn, but issue of thy own.
Nay, let thy men of wit too be the same,
All full of thee, and differing but in name.
But let no alien S–dl–y interpose,
To lard with wit thy hungry *Epsom* prose.
And when false flowers of rhetoric thou wouldst cull,
Trust nature, do not labor to be dull;
But write thy best, and top; and, in each line,

126. poppies: opium poppies, inducing sleep to those nearby. **134. honors:** locks. **135. damps:** vapors. **151–53. George . . . Fopling:** Sir George Etherege, comic dramatist of the time; the names in the next two lines are those of characters in his plays. **163. S–dl–y:** Sir Charles Sedley, who contributed lines to Shadwell's *Epsom Wells*.

Sir Formal's oratory will be thine:
Sir Formal, though unsought, attends thy quill,
And does thy northern dedications fill.
Nor let false friends seduce thy mind to fame,
By arrogating Jonson's hostile name.
Let father Flecknoe fire thy mind with praise,
And uncle Ogilby thy envy raise.
Thou art my blood, where Jonson has no part:
What share have we in nature, or in art?
Where did his wit on learning fix a brand,
And rail at arts he did not understand?
Where made he love in Prince Nicander's vein,
Or swept the dust in *Psyche's* humble strain?
Where sold he bargains, 'whip-stitch, kiss my arse,'
Promised a play and dwindled to a farce?
When did his Muse from Fletcher scenes purloin,
As thou whole Eth'rege dost transfuse to thine?
But so transfused as oils on waters flow,
His always floats above, thine sinks below.
This is thy province, this thy wondrous way,
New humors to invent for each new play:
This is that boasted bias of thy mind,
By which one way, to dullness, 'tis inclined;
Which makes thy writings lean on one side still,
And, in all changes, that way bends thy will.
Nor let thy mountain-belly make pretense
Of likeness; thine's a tympany of sense.
A tun of man in thy large bulk is writ,
But sure thou'rt but a kilderkin of wit.
Like mine, thy gentle numbers feebly creep;
Thy tragic Muse gives smiles, thy comic sleep.
With whate'er gall thou sett'st thyself to write,
Thy inoffensive satires never bite.
In thy felonious heart though venom lies,
It does but touch thy Irish pen, and dies.
Thy genius calls thee not to purchase fame
In keen iambics, but mild anagram.
Leave writing plays, and choose for thy command
Some peaceful province in acrostic land.
There thou may'st wings display and altars raise,
And torture one poor word ten thousand ways.
Or, if thou wouldst thy different talents suit,

168. Sir Formal: character in Shadwell's *The Virtuoso*. **170. northern dedications:** dedications by Shadwell to his patron, Duke of Newcastle, in northern England. **179. Nicander:** one of the lovers of Psyche in Shadwell's opera of that name. **181. sold . . . bargains:** replied indecently (slang). **188. New . . . play:** Shadwell boasted he had done this for each new play. **194. likeness:** to Ben Jonson. **195. tun:** large wine cask; pun on "ton." **196. kilderkin:** a fourth of a tun. **202. Irish:** wild and heady. **204. iambics:** satire; from the meter in which Greek satire was written.

Set thy own songs, and sing them to thy lute."
He said: but his last words were scarcely heard
For Bruce and Longville had a trap prepared,
And down they sent the yet declaiming bard.
Sinking he left his drugget robe behind,
Borne upwards by a subterranean wind.
The mantle fell to the young prophet's part,
With double portion of his father's art.

1682

To the Memory of Mr. Oldham

Farewell, too little, and too lately known,
Whom I began to think and call my own:
For sure our souls were near allied, and thine
Cast in the same poetic mould with mine.
One common note on either lyre did strike,
And knaves and fools we both abhorred alike.
To the same goal did both our studies drive;
The last set out the soonest did arrive.
Thus Nisus fell upon the slippery place,
While his young friend performed and won the race.
O early ripe! to thy abundant store
What could advancing age have added more?
It might (what nature never gives the young)
Have taught the numbers of thy native tongue.
But satire needs not those, and wit will shine
Through the harsh cadence of a rugged line:
A noble error, and but seldom made,
When poets are by too much force betrayed.
Thy generous fruits, though gathered ere their prime,
Still showed a quickness, and maturing time
But mellows what we write to the dull sweets of rhyme.
Once more, hail and farewell; farewell, thou young,
But ah too short, Marcellus of our tongue;
Thy brows with ivy, and with laurels bound;
But fate and gloomy night encompass thee around.

1684

TO THE MEMORY OF MR. OLDHAM. **Title:** John Oldham, a young poet, died a year before Dryden wrote these lines. In his satires, Oldham had cultivated a vigorous and rugged style with less regard for smoothness of versification, as Dryden says (lines 13–16), than had now become the fashion. **9. Nisus:** a racer, in Virgil's *Aeneid,* who slipped near the end of a race, but tripped a rival Sicilian runner so that his friend Euryalus could win. **14. numbers:** versification or meter. **20. quickness:** liveliness. **23. Marcellus:** nephew of the Emperor Augustus, who was expected to succeed his uncle, but, like Oldham, died young.

A Song for St. Cecilia's Day

1

From harmony, from heavenly harmony
This universal frame began:
When Nature underneath a heap
Of jarring atoms lay,
And could not heave her head,
The tuneful voice was heard from high:
"Arise, ye more than dead."
Then cold, and hot, and moist, and dry,
In order to their stations leap,
And Music's power obey.
From harmony, from heavenly harmony
This universal frame began:
From harmony to harmony
Through all the compass of the notes it ran,
The diapason closing full in man.

2

What passion cannot Music raise and quell!
When Jubal struck the corded shell,
His listening brethren stood around,
And, wondering, on their faces fell
To worship that celestial sound.
Less than a god they thought there could not dwell
Within the hollow of that shell
That spoke so sweetly and so well.
What passion cannot Music raise and quell!

3

The trumpet's loud clangor
Excites us to arms,
With shrill notes of anger,
And mortal alarms.
The double double double beat
Of the thundering drum
Cries: "Hark! the foes come;
Charge, charge, 'tis too late to retreat."

A SONG FOR ST. CECILIA'S DAY. **Title:** Patron saint of music and early Christian martyr; usually pictured as playing the organ (for example, line 52). On her day, November 22, public concerts were given, and original works were commissioned. Dryden's ode was later put to music by G. F. Handel (1739). **15. diapason:** combination of all notes (and in an organ major "stops") into harmony. **17. Jubal:** described in the Bible as "the father of all such as handle the harp and organ" (Genesis, 4:21).

4

The soft complaining flute
In dying notes discovers
The woes of hopeless lovers,
Whose dirge is whispered by the warbling lute.

5

Sharp violins proclaim
Their jealous pangs, and desperation,
Fury, frantic indignation,
Depth of pains, and height of passion,
For the fair, disdainful dame.

6

But O! what art can teach,
What human voice can reach,
The sacred organ's praise?
Notes inspiring holy love,
Notes that wing their heavenly ways
To mend the choirs above.

7

Orpheus could lead the savage race;
And trees unrooted left their place,
Sequacious of the lyre;
But bright Cecilia raised the wonder higher:
When to her organ vocal breath was given,
And angel heard, and straight appeared,
Mistaking earth for heaven.

GRAND CHORUS

As from the power of sacred lays
The spheres began to move,
And sung the great Creator's praise
To all the blest above;
So, when the last and dreadful hour
This crumbling pageant shall devour,
The trumpet shall be heard on high,
The dead shall live, the living die,
And Music shall untune the sky.

1687

48. Orpheus: In classical myth, he was able to charm stones and trees and to tame beasts by the beauty of music played on a lyre. **50. Sequacious of:** following. **61. Trumpet:** Dryden echoes the passage in the Bible describing the sound of the trumpet at the resurrection of the dead (I Corinthians, 15:52).

from The Secular Masque

Chorus on the New Year

All, all, of a piece throughout:
Thy chase had a beast in view;
Thy wars brought nothing about;
Thy lovers were all untrue.
'Tis well an old age is out,
And time to begin a new.

THOMAS TRAHERNE

(1637–1674)

One of the last of the "metaphysical" poets, Traherne lived the quiet life of a country clergyman until his early death at age thirty-seven. His poems remained unknown for over two centuries. They were finally discovered in manuscript in 1897, and were identified in 1910 as Traherne's. His major theme—the innocence, purity, and visionary inspiration of childhood—was in conflict with the religious belief of his own time in "original sin," and is much closer to the attitude towards the child found in the Romantics, especially Blake and Wordsworth. So is his confidence in the essential goodness of the human heart and in the immanence of God in nature.

The Salutation

These little limbs,
These eyes and hands which here I find,
These rosy cheeks wherewith my life begins,
Where have ye been? behind
What curtain were ye from me hid so long?
Where was, in what abyss, my speaking tongue?

When silent I
So many thousand, thousand years
Beneath the dust did in a chaos lie,

How could I smiles or tears,
Or lips or hands or eyes or ears perceive?
Welcome ye treasures which I now receive.

I that so long
Was nothing from eternity,
Did little think such joys as ear or tongue
To celebrate or see:
Such sounds to hear, such hands to feel, such feet,
Beneath the skies on such a ground to meet.

New burnished joys,
Which yellow gold and pearls excel!
Such sacred treasures are the limbs in boys,
In which a soul doth dwell;
Their organized joints and azure veins
More wealth include than all the world contains.

From dust I rise,
And out of nothing now awake;
These brighter regions which salute mine eyes,
A gift from God I take.
The earth, the seas, the light, the day, the skies,
The sun and stars are mine if those I prize.

Long time before
I in my mother's womb was born,
A God, preparing, did this glorious store,
The world, for me adorn.
Into this Eden so divine and fair,
So wide and bright, I come His son and heir.

A stranger here
Strange things doth meet, strange glories see;
Strange treasures lodged in this fair world appear,
Strange all and new to me;
But that they mine should be, who nothing was,
That strangest is of all, yet brought to pass.

Wonder

How like an angel came I down!
How bright are all things here!
When first among His works I did appear,
Oh, how their glory me did crown!
The world resembled His eternity,
In which my soul did walk;
And everything that I did see
Did with me talk.

The skies in their magnificence,
The lively, lovely air,
Oh, how divine, how soft, how sweet, how fair!
The stars did entertain my sense,
And all the works of God, so bright and pure,
So rich and great did seem,
As if they must endure
In my esteem.

A native health and innocence
Within my bones did grow;
And while my God did all His glories show,
I felt a vigor in my sense
That was all spirit. I within did flow
With seas of life, like wine;
I nothing in the world did know
But 'twas divine.

Harsh ragged objects were concealed,
Oppression's tears and cries,
Sins, griefs, complaints, dissensions, weeping eyes
Were hid, and only things revealed
Which heavenly spirits and the angels prize.
The state of innocence
And bliss, not trades and poverties,
Did fill my sense.

The streets were paved with golden stones;
The boys and girls were mine,
Oh, how did all their lovely faces shine!
The sons of men were holy ones,
In joy and beauty they appeared to me,
And everything which here I found,
While like an angel I did see,
Adorned the ground.

Rich diamond and pearl and gold
In every place was seen;
Rare splendors, yellow, blue, red, white, and green,
Mine eyes did everywhere behold.
Great wonders clothed with glory did appear,
Amazement was my bliss,
That and my wealth was everywhere;
No joy to this!

Cursed and devised proprieties,
With envy, avarice,
And fraud, those fiends that spoil even Paradise,
Flew from the splendor of mine eyes;
And so did hedges, ditches, limits, bounds:

WONDER. **49. devised proprieties:** bequeathed properties.

I dreamed not aught of those,
But wandered over all men's grounds,
And found repose.

Proprieties themselves were mine,
And hedges, ornaments;
Walls, boxes, coffers, and their rich contents
Did not divide my joys, but all combine.
Clothes, ribbons, jewels, laces, I esteemed
My joys by others worn:
For me they all to wear them seemed
When I was born.

EDWARD TAYLOR

(c. 1644–1729)

Born in England, Taylor emigrated to the United States and became a clergyman in Westfield, Massachusetts. He requested that none of his poems be published, and when he died his manuscript was deposited in the library of Yale University. His work first became known in 1937, when some of his poems were printed. He was a religious poet in the style of the English "metaphysical" school represented by John Donne and George Herbert, and is usually considered the finest American poet of the colonial period.

Upon Wedlock, and Death of Children

A curious knot God made in paradise,
And drew it out enameled neatly fresh.
It was the truelove knot, more sweet than spice
And set with all the flowers of grace's dress.
It's wedding knot, that ne'er can be untied;
No Alexander's sword can it divide.

UPON WEDLOCK, AND DEATH OF CHILDREN. **2. enameled:** having varied colors. **6. Alexander's sword:** An oracle had said that whoever could untie the Gordian knot would rule Asia (the knot had been intricately tied by Gordius, King of Phrygia). Alexander the Great simply cut it with his sword.

The slips here planted, gay and glorious grow,
  Unless an hellish breath do singe their plumes.
Here primrose, cowslips, roses, lilies blow
  With violets and pinks that void perfumes:
  Whose beauteous leaves o'er laid with honey-dew,
  And chanting birds chirp out sweet music true.

When in this knot I planted was, my stock
  Soon knotted, and a manly flower out brake.
And after it my branch again did knot;
  Brought out another flower its sweet breathed mate.
  One knot gave one t'other the t'other's place;
  Whence chuckling smiles fought in each other's face.

But oh! a glorious hand from glory came
  Guarded with angels, soon did crop this flower
Which almost tore the root up of the same
  At that unlooked for, dolesome, darksome hour.
  In prayer to Christ perfumed it did ascend,
  And angels bright did it to heaven tend.

But pausing on't, this sweet perfumed my thought,
  Christ would in glory have a flower, choice, prime,
And having choice, chose this my branch forth brought.
  Lord take't. I thank thee, thou takest aught of mine,
  It is my pledge in glory; part of me
  Is now in it, Lord, glorified with thee.

But praying o'er my branch, my branch did sprout
  And bore another manly flower, and gay;
And after that another, sweet, brake out,
  The which the former hand soon got away.
  But oh! the tortures, vomit, screechings, groans,
  And six weeks fever would pierce hearts like stones.

Grief o'er doth flow, and nature fault would find
  Were not thy will, my spell charm, joy, and gem;
That as I said, I say, take, Lord, they're thine.
  I piecemeal pass to glory bright in them.
  I joy, may I sweet flowers for glory breed,
  Whether thou getst them green, or let them seed.

1937

10. void: emit. **13. stock:** stem.

Housewifery

Make me, O Lord, thy spinning wheel complete.
  Thy holy word my distaff make for me.
Make mine affections thy swift flyers neat,
  And make my soul thy holy spool to be.
  My conversation make to be thy reel,
  And reel the yarn thereon spun on thy wheel.

Make me thy loom then, knit therein this twine;
  And make thy holy spirit, Lord, wind quills.
Then weave the web thyself. The yarn is fine.
  Thine ordinances make my fulling mills.
  Then dye the same in heavenly colors choice,
  All pinked with varnished flowers of paradise.

Then clothe therewith mine understanding, will,
  Affections, judgment, conscience, memory,
My words, and actions, that their shine may fill
  My ways with glory and thee glorify.
  Then mine apparel shall display before ye
  That I am clothed in holy robes for glory.

1939

Anne Finch, Countess of Winchilsea

(1661–1720)

Anne Finch and her husband were courtiers devoted to the cause of James II. They retired to the country when the King was deposed in 1688, and Mr. Finch eventually succeeded to the title of Earl of Winchilsea. In 1701 she published "The Spleen," a poem describing the fashionable illness of that name from which she believed she suffered, and this was virtually the only poem of hers read throughout the eighteenth century. But she also published many poems, derived

HOUSEWIFERY. **1. spinning wheel:** The metaphors throughout the stanza refer to parts of the spinning wheel. The distaff holds the bunch of wool or flax that is to be spun. Flyers regulate the spinning and, with the spool, twist the fibers together. The completed thread is then wound on the reel. **8. quills:** spools or bobbins. **10. fulling mills:** where cloth is pressed and cleansed with soap or fuller's earth. **12. pinked:** adorned. **varnished:** polished, shining.

from Milton's "L'Allegro" and "Il Penseroso," in which she expressed her pleasure in the peace and beauty of nature. These were noticed and praised by Wordsworth in 1815, and this established her reputation. Besides "A Nocturnal Reverie," printed here, her most interesting poem is the long "Petition for an Absolute Retreat."

A Nocturnal Reverie

In such a night, when every louder wind
Is to its distant cavern safe confined;
And only gentle Zephyr fans his wings,
And lonely Philomel, still waking, sings;
Or from some tree, famed for the owl's delight,
She, hollowing clear, directs the wanderer right:
In such a night, when passing clouds give place,
Or thinly veil the heavens' mysterious face;
When in some river, overhung with green,
The waving moon and trembling leaves are seen;
When freshened grass now bears itself upright,
And makes cool banks to pleasing rest invite,
Whence springs the woodbind, and the bramble-rose,
And where the sleepy cowslip sheltered grows;
Whilst now a paler hue the foxglove takes,
Yet checkers still with red the dusky brakes.
When scattered glow-worms, but in twilight fine,
Show trivial beauties watch their hour to shine;
Whilst Salisbury stands the test of every light,
In perfect charms, and perfect virtue bright:
When odors, which declined repelling day,
Through temperate air uninterrupted stray;
When darkened groves their softest shadows wear,
And falling waters we distinctly hear;
When through the gloom more venerable shows
Some ancient fabric, awful in repose,
While sunburnt hills their swarthy looks conceal,
And swelling haycocks thicken up the vale:
When the loosed horse now, as his pasture leads,
Comes slowly grazing through the adjoining meads,
Whose stealing pace, and lengthened shade we fear,
Till torn-up forage in his teeth we hear:
When nibbling sheep at large pursue their food,
And unmolested kine rechew the cud;

A NOCTURNAL REVERIE. **4. Philomel:** nightingale. **16. brakes:** thickets. **19. Salisbury:** Anne Tufton, Countess of Salisbury; a famous beauty. **21. odors . . . day:** odors of the countryside, which the hot "repelling" rays of the sun repressed. **26. fabric:** building.

When curlews cry beneath the village walls,
And to her straggling brood the partridge calls;
Their shortlived jubilee the creatures keep,
Which but endures, whilst tyrant man does sleep;
When a sedate content the spirit feels,
And no fierce light disturbs, whilst it reveals;
But silent musings urge the mind to seek
Something, too high for syllables to speak;
Till the free soul to a composedness charmed,
Finding the elements of rage disarmed,
O'er all below a solemn quiet grown,
Joys in the inferior world, and thinks it like her own:
In such a night let me abroad remain,
Till morning breaks, and all's confused again;
Our cares, our toils, our clamors are renewed,
Or pleasures, seldom reached, again pursued.

1713

Jonathan Swift

(1667–1745)

Swift was probably the greatest satirist in the whole of literature. No child who reads his *Gulliver's Travels* (abridged, of course) is aware of this. Rudyard Kipling, speaking of the fate of *Gulliver,* said that "Swift turned on the glare of a volcano only to light a child to bed."

All of Swift's more powerful satires are in prose. He had attempted, as a youth, to compose poems. But when his relative, the great John Dryden, said, "Cousin Swift, you will never be a poet," Swift abandoned any serious attempt to write poetry. Yet he continued to write mocking satiric verses which are read and anthologized simply because he was so great in other ways. The poem "The Lady's Dressing Room" is included in order to show a side of Swift which is quite typical of him. What used to be called the scatological (that is, "dirty") poems of Swift were meant as a savage parody of the tame, neoclassic "pastoral" poems of the time.

35. curlews: shore birds.

A Description of the Morning

Now hardly here and there a hackney-coach
Appearing, show'd the ruddy morn's approach.
Now Betty from her master's bed had flown,
And softly stole to discompose her own.
The slipshod prentice from his master's door,
Had par'd the dirt, and sprinkled round the floor.
Now Moll had whirl'd her mop with dext'rous airs,
Prepar'd to scrub the entry and the stairs.
The youth with broomy stumps began to trace
The kennel-edge, where wheels had worn the place.
The small-coal man was heard with cadence deep,
'Till drown'd in shriller notes of chimney-sweep.
Duns at his lordship's gate began to meet,
And brickdust Moll had scream'd through half a street.
The turnkey now his flock returning sees,
Duly let out a-nights to steal for fees:
The watchful bailiffs take their silent stands;
And school-boys lag with satchels in their hands.

1709

A Description of A City Shower

[In Imitation of Virgil's Georgics]

Careful observers may foretell the hour
(By sure prognostics) when to dread a show'r:
While rain depends, the pensive cat gives o'er
Her frolics, and pursues her tail no more.
Returning home at night, you'll find the sink
Strike your offended sense with double stink.
If you be wise, then go not far to dine,
You'll spend in coach-hire more than save in wine.
A coming show'r your shooting corns presage,
Old aches throb, your hollow tooth will rage.
Sauntring in coffee-house is Dulman seen;
He damns the climate, and complains of spleen.

A DESCRIPTION OF THE MORNING. **3–7. Betty . . . Moll:** servants. **10. kennel-edge:** curb of the street. **11. small-coal:** charcoal. **13. Duns:** bill collectors. **14. brickdust Moll:** woman selling brickdust for sharpening knives. **15. turnkey:** jailer. **17. bailiffs:** deputies to the sheriff. A DESCRIPTION OF A CITY SHOWER. **3. depends:** impends. **5. sink:** sewer. **12. spleen:** melancholy.

Meanwhile the South rising with dabbled wings,
A sable cloud a-thwart the welkin flings,
That swill'd more liquor than it could contain,
And like a drunkard gives it up again.
Brisk Susan whips her linen from the rope,
While the first drizzling show'r is borne aslope,
Such is that sprinkling which some careless quean
Flirts on you from her mop, but not so clean.
You fly, invoke the gods; then turning, stop
To rail; she singing, still whirls on her mop.
Nor yet the dust had shunn'd th' unequal strife,
But aided by the wind, fought still for life;
And wafted with its foe by violent gust,
'Twas doubtful which was rain, and which was dust.
Ah! where must needy poet seek for aid,
When dust and rain at once his coat invade;
His only coat! where dust confus'd with rain;
Roughen the nap, and leave a mingled stain.

Now in contiguous drops the flood comes down,
Threat'ning with deluge this *devoted* town.
To shops in crowds the daggled females fly,
Pretend to cheapen goods, but nothing buy.
The Templar spruce, while ev'ry spout's a-broach,
Stays till 'tis fair, yet seems to call a coach.
The tuck'd-up sempstress walks with hasty strides,
While streams run down her oil'd umbrella's sides.
Here various kinds by various fortunes led,
Commence acquaintance underneath a shed.
Triumphant Tories, and desponding Whigs,
Forget their feuds, and join to save their wigs.
Box'd in a chair the beau impatient sits,
While spouts run clatt'ring o'er the roof by fits;
And ever and anon with frightful din
The leather sounds, he trembles from within.
So when Troy chair-men bore the wooden steed,
Pregnant with Greeks impatient to be freed,
(Those bully Greeks, who, as the moderns do,
Instead of paying chair-men, run them thro.)
Laocoon struck the outside with his spear,
And each imprison'd hero quaked for fear.

13. South: south wind. **14. welkin:** sky. **19. quean:** wench. **32. devoted:** condemned. **33. daggled:** spattered. **34. cheapen:** bargain for, lower the price. **35. Templar:** law student at the Temple (residence for lawyers). **a-broach:** running. **43. chair:** sedan chair. **46. leather:** leather top of the chair. **51–52. Laocoon . . . fear:** When Laocoon struck the side of the Trojan horse, which was made of wood, he frightened the Greek soldiers hiding inside the body.

Now from all parts the swelling kennels flow,
And bear their trophies with them as they go:
Filth of all hues and odours seem to tell
What street they sail'd from, by their sight and smell.
They, as each torrent drives, with rapid force
From Smithfield, or St. Pulchre's shape their course,
And in huge confluent join at Snow-hill ridge,
Fall from the conduit prone to Holborn-bridge.
Sweepings from butchers' stalls, dung, guts, and blood,
Drown'd puppies, stinking sprats, all drench'd in mud,
Dead cats and turnip-tops come tumbling down the flood.

1710

The Lady's Dressing Room

Five hours, (and who can do it less in?)
By haughty Celia spent in dressing;
The goddess from her chamber issues,
Arrayed in lace, brocades and tissues.
Strephon, who found the room was void,
And Betty otherwise employed,
Stole in, and took a strict survey,
Of all the litter as it lay;
Whereof, to make the matter clear,
An inventory follows here.
And first a dirty smock appeared,
Beneath the armpits well besmeared.
Strephon, the rogue, displayed it wide,
And turned it round on every side.
On such a point few words are best,
And Strephon bids us guess the rest,
But swears how damnably the men lie,
In calling Celia sweet and cleanly.
Now listen while he next produces
The various combs for various uses,
Filled up with dirt so closely fixt,
No brush could force a way betwixt.
A paste of composition rare,
Sweat, dandruff, powder, lead and hair;
A forehead cloth with oil upon't
To smooth the wrinkles on her front;

53. kennels: gutters. **58–60. Smithfield . . . Holborn-bridge:** The sewage flowed past Smithfield, receiving the refuse and offal from the butcher shops there, into Fleet Ditch at Holborn Bridge. **62. sprats:** herring. THE LADY'S DRESSING ROOM. **5. Strephon:** pastoral name for a shepherd who was also a dreaming lover, here used mockingly of the lover. **24. lead:** used to make hair shiny.

Here alum flower to stop the steams,
Exhaled from sour unsavory streams,
There night-gloves made of Tripsy's hide,
Bequeathed by Tripsy when she died,
With puppy water, beauty's help
Distilled from Tripsy's darling whelp;
Here gallypots and vials placed,
Some filled with washes, some with paste,
Some with pomatum, paints and slops,
And ointments good for scabby chops.
Hard by a filthy basin stands,
Fouled with the scouring of her hands;
The basin takes whatever comes
The scrapings of her teeth and gums,
A nasty compound of all hues,
For here she spits, and here she spews.
But oh! it turned poor Strephon's bowels,
When he beheld and smelled the towels,
Begummed, bemattered, and beslimed
With dirt, and sweat, and earwax grimed.
No object Strephon's eye escapes,
Here petticoats in frowzy heaps;
Nor be the handkerchiefs forgot
All varnished o'er with snuff and snot.
The stockings why should I expose,
Stained with the marks of stinking toes;
Or greasy coifs and pinners reeking,
Which Celia slept at least a week in?
A pair of tweezers next he found
To pluck her brows in arches round,
Or hairs that sink the forehead low,
Or on her chin like bristles grow.
   The virtues we must not let pass,
Of Celia's magnifying glass.
When frighted Strephon cast his eye on't
It showed visage of a giant.
A glass that can to sight disclose,
The smallest worm in Celia's nose,
And faithfully direct her nail
To squeeze it out from head to tail;
For catch it nicely by the head,
It must come out alive or dead.
   Why Strephon will you tell the rest?
And must you needs describe the chest?
That careless wench! no creature warn her
To move it out from yonder corner;
But leave it standing full in sight

29. Tripsy: a dog. **33. gallypots:** jars for medicine or cosmetics. **53. pinners:** hair pins.

For you to exercise your spite.
In vain the workman showed his wit
With rings and hinges counterfeit
To make it seem in this disguise
A cabinet to vulgar eyes;
For Strephon ventured to look in,
Resolved to go through thick and thin;
He lifts the lid, there needs no more,
He smelled it all the time before.
As from within Pandora's box,
When Epimetheus op'd the locks,
A sudden universal crew
Of human evils upwards flew;
He still was comforted to find
That Hope at last remained behind;
So Strephon lifting up the lid,
To view what in the chest was hid.
The vapors flew from out the vent,
But Strephon cautious never meant
The bottom of the pan to grope,
And foul his hands in search of Hope.
O never may such vile machine
Be once in Celia's chamber seen!
O may she better learn to keep
Those "secrets of the hoary deep!"
  As mutton cutlets, prime of meat,
Which though with art you salt and beat
As laws of cookery require,
And toast them at the clearest fire;
If from adown the hopeful chops
The fat upon a cinder drops,
To stinking smoke it turns the flame
Pois'ning the flesh from whence it came,
And up exhales a greasy stench,
For which you curse the careless wench;
So things, which must not be expressed,
When plumped into the reeking chest,
Send up an excremental smell
To taint the parts from whence they fell.
The petticoats and gown perfume,
Which waft a stink round every room.
Thus finishing his grand survey,
Disgusted Strephon stole away
Repeating in his amorous fits,
Oh! Celia, Celia, Celia shits!

83–84. Pandora . . . Epimetheus: Because Prometheus stole fire from the gods to bring it to mankind, Zeus, in revenge, created Pandora and sent her to earth with a box that contained all the ills that could happen. In some versions, Epimetheus, her husband, opened the box. In others, Pandora herself did so.

But Vengeance, goddess never sleeping,
Soon punished Strephon for his peeping;
His foul imagination links
Each Dame he sees with all her stinks:
And, if unsavory odors fly,
Conceives a lady standing by:
All women his description fits,
And both ideas jump like wits:
By vicious fancy coupled fast,
And still appearing in contrast.
I pity wretched Strephon blind
To all the charms of female kind;
Should I the queen of love refuse,
Because she rose from stinking ooze?
To him that looks behind the scene,
Satira's but some pocky quean.
When Celia in her glory shows,
If Strephon would but stop his nose
(Who now so impiously blasphemes
Her ointments, daubs, and paints and creams,
Her washes, slops, and every clout,
With which he makes so foul a rout)
He soon would learn to think like me,
And bless his ravished sight to see
Such order from confusion sprung,
Such gaudy tulips raised from dung.

1730

Isaac Watts

(1674–1748)

A clergyman in one of the Protestant sects that dissented from the established Church of England, Watts wrote prose treatises, poems in English and in Latin, and over six hundred hymns, of which many are still sung.

Our God, Our Help

Our God, our help in ages past,
  Our hope for years to come,
Our shelter from the stormy blast,
  And our eternal home:

Under the shadow of thy throne
  Thy saints have dwelt secure;
Sufficient is thine arm alone,
  And our defense is sure.

Before the hills in order stood
  Or earth received her frame,
From everlasting thou art God,
  To endless years the same.

Thy word commands our flesh to dust,
  "Return, ye sons of men";
All nations rose from earth at first,
  And turn to earth again.

A thousand ages in thy sight
  Are like an evening gone;
Short as the watch that ends the night
  Before the rising sun.

The busy tribes of flesh and blood,
  With all their lives and cares,
Are carried downwards by thy flood,
  And lost in following years.

Time, like an ever-rolling stream,
  Bears all its sons away;
They fly forgotten, as a dream
  Dies at the opening day.

Like flowery fields the nations stand,
  Pleased with the morning light;
The flowers beneath the mower's hand
  Lie withering e'er 'tis night.

Our God, our help in ages past,
  Our hope for years to come,
Be thou our guard while troubles last,
  And our eternal home.

1719

Alexander Pope

(1688–1744)

Pope, along with Dryden, is one of the two greatest poets in English who write in the "High Neoclassic Mode." Like Dryden, he used the heroic couplet, with its snap, its clean economy of language, its aphoristic condensation into succinct wisdom or "wit." And like Dryden, he expressed in verse both intellectual discourse and, through satire, a criticism of society.

Pope's "Essay on Man" (1733–34), which tries to present the human situation in the "Cosmos" as a whole, is the finest of the "didactic," or deliberately instructive, poems of the eighteenth century. His "The Rape of the Lock" (1714), which uses the stylistic devices of the old epics to narrate a trifling occurrence in the polite social world of the time (a suitor cuts off a lock of a lady's hair), is a brilliant "mock-heroic" poem.

Of all Pope's satires, the jewel is the "Epistle to Dr. Arbuthnot" (1735), an "apology" or self-defense that he wanted to have prefixed as a "prologue" to his satires. Part of the satiric wit lies in the establishment of his own character: he poses as a virtuous man who does not really want to satirize other people but is forced to do so because he is attacked by them. In justifying himself he uses dialogue with telling effect; a friend (designated here as "A") raises issues that might have been embarrassing—why is the poet in writing his satires so personal?—which allows Pope to answer these objections. Three of his most memorable satiric portraits are in this poem—that of Joseph Addison, called Atticus (lines 193–214), Bufo (lines 231–48), and the vicious portrait of Lord Hervey, called Sporus (lines 305–33). Some of the minor poets he attacks here, like a great many more in his "Dunciad" (1743), are forever preserved like flies in amber.

In the generation after Pope (the "Age of Johnson"—the second half of the eighteenth century), satire began to fall out of fashion. The emotions it expresses, such as contempt and anger, no longer seemed appropriate to poetry. For nineteenth-century taste the poetry of Dryden and Pope was also too "intellectual," too much in pursuit of "wit." But modern poets—rejecting nineteenth-century, sentimental taste—once again admire Dryden and Pope for their realism, concern for public issues, wit, and polished craftsmanship.

The Rape of the Lock

An heroi-comical poem
Dedication to Mrs. Arabella Fermor

MADAM,—It will be in vain to deny that I have some regard for this piece, since I dedicate it to you. Yet you may bear me witness, it was intended only to divert a few young ladies, who have good sense and good humour enough to laugh not only at their sex's little unguarded follies, but at their own. But as it was communicated with the air of a secret, it soon found its way into the world. An imperfect copy having been offered to a bookseller, you had the good-nature for my sake to consent to the publication of one more correct: this I was forced to before I had executed half my design, for the machinery was entirely wanting to complete it.

The machinery, Madam, is a term invented by the critics to signify that part which the Deities, Angels, or Dæmons are made to act in a Poem: for the ancient Poets are in one respect like many modern ladies: let an action be never so trivial in itself, they always make it appear of the utmost importance. These machines I determined to raise on a very new and odd foundation, the Rosicrucian doctrine of Spirits.

I know how disagreeable it is to make use of hard words before a lady; but 'tis so much the concern of a Poet to have his works understood, and particularly by your sex, that you must give me leave to explain two or three difficult terms.

The Rosicrucians are a people I must bring you acquainted with. The best account I know of them is in a French book called *Le Comte de Gabalis*, which, both in its title and size, is so like a novel that many of the fair sex have read it for one by mistake. According to these gentlemen, the four elements are inhabited by Spirits which they call Sylphs, Gnomes, Nymphs and Salamanders. The Gnomes, or Dæmons of Earth, delight in mischief; but the Sylphs, whose habitation is in the air, are the best-conditioned creatures imaginable. For

THE RAPE OF THE LOCK. **Title:** Probably the most brilliant "mock-heroic" poem in English, this is based on a real incident. The young Robert Lord Petre playfully snipped off a lock of hair of a celebrated beauty, Arabella Fermor, whom he hoped to marry. She either was or pretended to be angry. Relations between her family and Petre's became strained. Petre's relative, John Caryll (line 3), asked Pope to write a poem that would treat the matter as a joke so that the families could see it in perspective and resume good relations. The result is *The Rape of the Lock*, written in a parody of the high "epic" style. The rape of Helen of Troy in the *Iliad* is parodied in the rape of the lock of hair from Belinda (Arabella Fermor). Homer's famous description of the shield of Achilles is echoed in that of Belinda's petticoat. Virgil's description of the journey of Aeneas up the Tiber is parodied in that of Belinda's up the Thames. In place of the gods in Greek and Latin epics, Pope invents the minute "sylphs," as supernatural agents. The epigram, from a Latin poet of the first century, reads: "I was loathe, Belinda, to violate your locks; but it pleases me to pay this tribute to your prayers."

they say any mortals may enjoy the most intimate familiarities with these gentle Spirits, upon a condition very easy to all true adepts, an inviolate preservation of chastity.

As to the following Cantos, all the passages of them are as fabulous as the vision at the beginning, or the transformation at the end (except the loss of your hair, which I always mention with reverence). The human persons are as fictitious as the airy ones; and the character of Belinda, as it is now managed, resembles you in nothing but in beauty.

If this Poem had as many graces as there are in your person, or in your mind, yet I could never hope it should pass through the world half so uncensured as you have done. But let its fortune be what it will, mine is happy enough, to have given me this occasion of assuring you that I am, with the truest esteem, Madam, your most obedient, humble Servant,

A. Pope

Nolueram, Belinda, tuos violare capillos;
Sed juvat, hoc precibus me tribuisse tuis.

—Martial

Canto I

What dire offence from amorous causes springs,
What mighty contests rise from trivial things,
I sing—This verse to Caryll, Muse! is due:
This, ev'n Belinda may vouchsafe to view;
Slight is the subject, but not so the praise,
If she inspire, and he approve my lays.
  Say what strange motive, goddess! could compel
A well-bred lord to assault a gentle belle?
O say what stranger cause, yet unexplored,
Could make a gentle belle reject a lord?
In tasks so bold, can little men engage,
And in soft bosoms dwells such mighty rage?
  Sol through white curtains shot a tim'rous ray,
And oped those eyes that must eclipse the day:
Now lap-dogs give themselves the rousing shake,
And sleepless lovers, just at twelve awake:
Thrice rung the bell, the slipper knock'd the ground,
And the press'd watch return'd a silver sound.
Belinda still her downy pillow press'd,
Her guardian sylph prolong'd the balmy rest:
'Twas he had summon'd to her silent bed
The morning-dream that hover'd o'er her head;

CANTO I. **13. sol:** the sun. **curtains:** of the bed. **18. press'd watch:** a "repeater watch," which, when a stem was pressed, sounded the hour and the quarter-hours.

A youth more glittering than a birth-night beau,
(That ev'n in slumber caused her cheek to glow)
Seem'd to her ear his winning lips to lay,
And thus in whispers said, or seem'd to say:
"Fairest of mortals, thou distinguish'd care
Of thousand bright inhabitants of air!
If e'er one vision touch thy infant thought,
Of all the nurse and all the priest have taught;
Of airy elves by moonlight shadows seen,
The silver token, and the circled green,
Or virgins visited by angel powers,
With golden crowns and wreaths of heavenly flowers;
Hear and believe! thy own importance know,
Nor bound thy narrow views to things below.
Some secret truths, from learned pride conceal'd,
To maids alone and children are reveal'd:
What, though no credit doubting wits may give?
The fair and innocent shall still believe.
Know, then, unnumbered spirits round thee fly,
The light militia of the lower sky:
These, though unseen, are ever on the wing,
Hang o'er the box, and hover round the ring.
Think what an equipage thou hast in air,
And view with scorn two pages and a chair.
As now your own, our beings were of old,
And once inclosed in woman's beauteous mould;
Thence, by a soft transition, we repair
From earthly vehicles to these of air.
Think not, when woman's transient breath is fled,
That all her vanities at once are dead;
Succeeding vanities she still regards,
And though she plays no more, o'erlooks the cards.
Her joy in gilded chariots, when alive,
And love of ombre, after death survive.
For when the fair in all their pride expire,
To their first elements their souls retire:
The sprites of fiery termagants in flame
Mount up, and take a Salamander's name.
Soft yielding minds to water glide away,
And sip, with nymphs, their elemental tea.
The graver prude sinks downward to a gnome,

23. birth-night beau: courtier dressed for the royal "birthnight," the celebration of the evening before the monarch's birthday. **32. token:** coin left by an elf. **circled green:** fairy dancing-circle on the grass. **44. box:** theater box. **ring:** carriage-drive in Hyde Park, London. **46. chair:** sedan chair. **55. chariots:** carriages. **56. ombre:** card game of the time. **58. first elements:** In early Greek thought, the four original elements, of which everything was later composed, were fire, earth, air, and water. **59. termagants:** shrews. **60. Salamander:** small lizards formerly thought to live in fire.

In search of mischief still on earth to roam.
The light coquettes in sylphs aloft repair,
And sport and flutter in the fields of air.
"Know further yet; whoever fair and chaste
Rejects mankind, is by some sylph embraced:
For spirits, freed from mortal laws, with ease
Assume what sexes and what shapes they please.
What guards the purity of melting maids,
In courtly balls, and midnight masquerades,
Safe from the treach'rous friend, the daring spark,
The glance by day, the whisper in the dark,
When kind occasion prompts their warm desires,
When music softens, and when dancing fires?
'Tis but their sylph, the wise celestials know,
Though honour is the word with men below.
"Some nymphs there are, too conscious of their face,
For life predestined to the gnome's embrace.
These swell their prospects and exalt their pride,
When offers are disdain'd and love denied:
Then gay ideas crowd the vacant brain,
While peers, and dukes, and all their sweeping train,
And garters, stars, and coronets appear,
And in soft sounds, 'Your Grace' salutes their ear.
'Tis these that early taint the female soul,
Instruct the eyes of young coquettes to roll,
Teach infant cheeks a bidden blush to know,
And little hearts to flutter at a beau.
"Oft when the world imagine women stray,
The sylphs through mystic mazes guide their way,
Through all the giddy circle they pursue,
And old impertinence expel by new.
What tender maid but must a victim fall
To one man's treat, but for another's ball?
When Florio speaks, what virgin could withstand,
If gentle Damon did not squeeze her hand?
With varying vanities, from ev'ry part,
They shift the moving toy-shop of their heart;
Where wigs with wigs, with sword-knots sword-knots strive,
Beaux banish beaux, and coaches coaches drive.
This erring mortals levity may call,
Oh, blind to truth! the sylphs contrive it all.
"Of these am I, who thy protection claim,
A watchful sprite, and Ariel is my name.
Late, as I ranged the crystal wilds of air,
In the clear mirror of thy ruling star

73. spark: showy man of the town. **85. garters . . . coronets:** emblems of noble rank. **86. Your Grace:** title given a Duke or Duchess. **101. sword-knots:** ribbons tied to hilts of swords.

I saw, alas! some dread event impend,
Ere to the main this morning sun descend;
But heaven reveals not what, or how, or where:
Warn'd by the sylph, oh, pious maid, beware!
This to disclose is all thy guardian can:
Beware of all, but most beware of man!"
He said; when Shock, who thought she slept too long,
Leap'd up, and waked his mistress with his tongue.
'Twas then, Belinda, if report say true,
Thy eyes first open'd on a billet-doux;
Wounds, charms, and ardours, were no sooner read,
But all the vision vanish'd from thy head.
And now, unveil'd, the toilet stands display'd
Each silver vase in mystic order laid.
First, robed in white, the nymph intent adores,
With head uncover'd, the cosmetic powers.
A heav'nly image in the glass appears,
To that she bends, to that her eyes she rears;
Th' inferior priestess, at her altar's side,
Trembling, begins the sacred rites of pride.
Unnumber'd treasures ope at once, and here
The various offerings of the world appear;
From each she nicely culls with curious toil,
And decks the goddess with the glitt'ring spoil.
This casket India's glowing gems unlocks,
And all Arabia breathes from yonder box.
The tortoise here and elephant unite,
Transform'd to combs, the speckled and the white.
Here files of pins extend their shining rows,
Puffs, powders, patches, Bibles, billet-doux.
Now awful beauty puts on all its arms;
The fair each moment rises in her charms,
Repairs her smiles, awakens every grace,
And calls forth all the wonders of her face:
Sees by degrees a purer blush arise,
And keener lightnings quicken in her eyes.
The busy sylphs surround their darling care,
These set the head, and those divide the hair,
Some fold the sleeve, while others plait the gown;
And Betty's praised for labours not her own.

Canto II

Not with more glories, in th' ethereal plain,
The sun first rises o'er the purpled main,

115. Shock: common name for lap-dogs (from "shocks" of hair). **118. billet-doux:** love letter. **121. toilet:** dressing table. **134. Arabia:** perfumes from Arabia. **147. plait:** fold. **148. Betty:** stock name for a maid.

Than, issuing forth, the rival of his beams
Launch'd on the bosom of the silver Thames.
Fair nymphs and well-dress'd youths around her shone,
But every eye was fix'd on her alone.
On her white breast a sparkling cross she wore,
Which Jews might kiss, and infidels adore.
Her lively looks a sprightly mind disclose,
Quick as her eyes, and as unfix'd as those:
Favours to none, to all she smiles extends;
Oft she rejects, but never once offends.
Bright as the sun, her eyes the gazers strike,
And, like the sun, they shine on all alike.
Yet graceful ease, and sweetness void of pride,
Might hide her faults, if belles had faults to hide:
If to her share some female errors fall,
Look on her face, and you'll forget them all.
  This nymph, to the destruction of mankind,
Nourish'd two locks, which graceful hung behind
In equal curls, and well conspired to deck
With shining ringlets the smooth ivory neck.
Love in these labyrinths his slaves detains,
And mighty hearts are held in slender chains.
With hairy springes we the birds betray,
Slight lines of hair surprise the finny prey,
Fair tresses man's imperial race insnare,
And beauty draws us with a single hair.
  Th' adventurous baron the bright locks admired;
He saw, he wish'd, and to the prize aspired.
Resolved to win, he meditates the way,
By force to ravish, or by fraud betray;
For when success a lover's toil attends,
Few ask, if fraud or force attain'd his ends.
  For this, ere Phœbus rose, he had implored
Propitious Heaven, and every power adored:
But chiefly Love—to Love an altar built,
Of twelve vast French romances, neatly gilt.
There lay three garters, half a pair of gloves;
And all the trophies of his former loves:
With tender billet-doux he lights the pyre,
And breathes three amorous sighs to raise the fire.
Then prostrate falls, and begs with ardent eyes
Soon to obtain, and long possess the prize:
The powers gave ear, and granted half his prayer,
The rest, the winds dispersed in empty air.
  But now secure the painted vessel glides,
The sun-beams trembling on the floating tides;
While melting music steals upon the sky,

CANTO II. **25. springes:** traps.

And soften'd sounds along the waters die;
Smooth flow the waves, the zephyrs gently play,
Belinda smiled, and all the world was gay.
All but the sylph—with careful thoughts oppress'd,
Th' impending woe sat heavy on his breast.
He summons straight his denizens of air;
The lucid squadrons round the sails repair;
Soft o'er the shrouds aërial whispers breathe,
That seem'd but zephyrs to the twain beneath.
Some to the sun their insect-wings unfold,
Waft on the breeze, or sink in clouds of gold;
Transparent forms, too fine for mortal sight,
Their fluid bodies half dissolved in light.
Loose to the wind their airy garments flew,
Thin glittering textures of the filmy dew,
Dipp'd in the richest tincture of the skies,
Where Light disports in ever-mingling dyes;
While ev'ry beam new transient colours flings,
Colours that change whene'er they wave their wings.
Amid the circle on the gilded mast,
Superior by the head, was Ariel placed;
His purple pinions op'ning to the sun,
He raised his azure wand, and thus begun:
"Ye sylphs and sylphids, to your chief give ear;
Fays, fairies, genii, elves, and dÆmons, hear:
Ye know the spheres, and various tasks assign'd
By laws eternal to the aërial kind.
Some in the fields of purest ether play,
And bask and whiten in the blaze of day.
Some guide the course of wand'ring orbs on high,
Or roll the planets through the boundless sky.
Some less refined beneath the moon's pale light
Pursue the stars that shoot athwart the night,
Or suck the mists in grosser air below,
Or dip their pinions in the painted bow,
Or brew fierce tempests on the wintry main,
Or o'er the glebe distil the kindly rain.
Others on earth o'er human race preside,
Watch all their ways, and all their actions guide:
Of these the chief the care of nations own,
And guard with arms divine the British throne.
"Our humbler province is to tend the fair,
Not a less pleasing, though less glorious care;
To save the powder from too rude a gale,
Nor let the imprison'd essences exhale;
To draw fresh colours from the vernal flowers;

55. denizens: inhabitants (or specifically here) "naturalized aliens." **56. repair:** collect together. **84. bow:** rainbow. **86. glebe:** field.

To steal from rainbows, ere they drop in showers,
A brighter wash; to curl their waving hairs,
Assist their blushes and inspire their airs;
Nay, oft, in dreams, invention we bestow,
To change a flounce, or add a furbelow.
"This day, black omens threat the brightest fair
That e'er deserved a watchful spirit's care;
Some dire disaster, or by force, or slight;
But what, or where, the Fates have wrapp'd in night.
Whether the nymph shall break Diana's law,
Or some frail china jar receive a flaw;
Or stain her honour or her new brocade;
Forget her prayers, or miss a masquerade;
Or lose her heart, or necklace, at a ball;
Or whether Heaven has doom'd that Shock must fall.
Haste, then, ye spirits! to your charge repair:
The flutt'ring fan be Zephyretta's care;
The drops to thee, Brillante, we consign;
And, Momentilla, let the watch be thine;
Do thou, Crispissa, tend her fav'rite lock;
Ariel himself shall be the guard of Shock.
"To fifty chosen sylphs, of special note,
We trust th' important charge, the petticoat:
Oft have we known that seven-fold fence to fail,
Though stiff with hoops, and arm'd with ribs of whale;
Form a strong line about the silver bound,
And guard the wide circumference around.
"Whatever spirit, careless of his charge,
His post neglects, or leaves the fair at large,
Shall feel sharp vengeance soon o'ertake his sins,
Be stopp'd in vials, or transfix'd with pins;
Or plunged in lakes of bitter washes lie,
Or wedged whole ages in a bodkin's eye:
Gums and pomatums shall his flight restrain,
While clogg'd he beats his silken wings in vain:
Or alum styptics with contracting power
Shrink his thin essence like a rivell'd flower:
Or, as Ixion fix'd, the wretch shall feel
The giddy motion of the whirling mill,
In fumes of burning chocolate shall glow,
And tremble at the sea that froths below!"
He spoke; the spirits from the sails descend;
Some, orb in orb, around the nymph extend;

105. Diana's law: law of chastity. **113. drops:** earrings. **115. Crispissa:** The sylphid is named thus from the word "crisp," meaning to curl hair. **128. bodkin:** a large needle. **129. pomatums:** ointments. **131. styptics:** astringents to stop bleeding. **132. rivell'd:** shriveled. **133. Ixion:** In greek myth, Ixion was punished for daring to love the goddess Hera by being bound to a constantly revolving wheel.

Some thrid the mazy ringlets of her hair;
Some hang upon the pendants of her ear:
With beating hearts the dire event they wait,
Anxious and trembling for the birth of Fate.

Canto III

Close by those meads, for ever crown'd with flowers,
Where Thames with pride surveys his rising towers,
There stands a structure of majestic frame,
Which from the neighb'ring Hampton takes its name.
Here Britain's statesmen oft the fall foredoom
Of foreign tyrants, and of nymphs at home;
Here thou, great ANNA! whom three realms obey,
Dost sometimes counsel take—and sometimes tea.
  Hither the heroes and the nymphs resort,
To taste awhile the pleasures of a court;
In various talk th' instructive hours they pass'd,
Who gave the ball, or paid the visit last;
One speaks the glory of the British Queen,
And one describes a charming Indian screen;
A third interprets motions, looks, and eyes;
At every word a reputation dies.
Snuff, or the fan, supply each pause of chat,
With singing, laughing, ogling, *and all that.*
  Meanwhile, declining from the noon of day,
The sun obliquely shoots his burning ray;
The hungry judges soon the sentence sign,
And wretches hang that jurymen may dine;
The merchant from th' Exchange returns in peace,
And the long labours of the toilet cease.
Belinda now, whom thirst of fame invites,
Burns to encounter two adventurous knights,
At ombre singly to decide their doom;
And swells her breast with conquests yet to come.
Straight the three bands prepare in arms to join,
Each band the number of the sacred nine.
Soon as she spreads her hand, th' aërial guard
Descend, and sit on each important card:
First Ariel perch'd upon a Matadore,
Then each according to the rank he bore;
For sylphs, yet mindful of their ancient race,
Are, as when women, wondrous fond of place.
  Behold, four Kings in majesty revered,

CANTO III. **4. Hampton:** Hampton Court, one of the royal residences. **7. Anna:** Queen Anne. **three realms:** England, Scotland, and Ireland. **23. Exchange:** stock exchange. **29. arms:** combat. **33. Matadore:** the highest valued cards in Ombre are called matadores.

With hoary whiskers and a forky beard;
And four fair Queens, whose hands sustain a flower,
Th' expressive emblem of their softer power;
Four knaves in garbs succinct, a trusty band;
Caps on their heads, and halberts in their hand;
And party-colour'd troops, a shining train,
Drawn forth to combat on the velvet plain.
  The skilful nymph reviews her force with care:
"Let Spades be trumps!" she said, and trumps they were.
  Now move to war her sable Matadores,
In show like leaders of the swarthy Moors.
Spadillio first, unconquerable lord!
Led off two captive trumps, and swept the board.
As many more Manillio forced to yield,
And march'd a victor from the verdant field.
Him Basto follow'd; but his fate more hard
Gain'd but one trump, and one plebeian card.
With his broad sabre next, a chief in years,
The hoary Majesty of Spades appears,
Puts forth one manly leg, to sight reveal'd,
The rest, his many-colour'd robe conceal'd.
The rebel Knave, who dares his prince engage,
Proves the just victim of his royal rage.
Ev'n mighty Pam, that kings and queens o'erthrew,
And mow'd down armies in the fights of Lu,
Sad chance of war! now destitute of aid,
Falls undistinguish'd by the victor Spade!
  Thus far both armies to Belinda yield;
Now to the baron fate inclines the field.
His warlike Amazon her host invades,
Th' imperial consort of the crown of Spades.
The Club's black tyrant first her victim dyed,
Spite of his haughty mien, and barb'rous pride:
What boots the regal circle on his head,
His giant limbs, in state unwieldy spread;
That long behind he trails his pompous robe,
And, of all monarchs, only grasps the globe?
  The baron now his Diamonds pours apace;
Th' embroider'd King who shows but half his face,
And his refulgent Queen, with powers combined
Of broken troops an easy conquest find.
Clubs, Diamonds, Hearts, in wild disorder seen,
With throngs promiscuous strow the level green.
Thus when dispersed a routed army runs,
Of Asia's troops, and Afric's sable sons,

41. succinct: girded up. **42. halberts:** spears with battleaxes attached. **49. Spadillio:** ace of spades. **51. Manillio:** deuce of spades. **53. Basto:** ace of clubs. **61. Pam:** jack of clubs, which, in the game of Loo (Lu), is the paramount trump.

With like confusion different nations fly,
Of various habit, and of various dye,
The pierced battalions disunited fall,
In heaps on heaps; one fate o'erwhelms them all.
  The Knave of Diamonds tries his wily arts,
And wins (oh shameful chance!) the Queen of Hearts.
At this, the blood the virgin's cheek forsook,
A livid paleness spreads o'er all her look;
She sees, and trembles at th' approaching ill,
Just in the jaws of ruin, and Codille.
And now (as oft in some distemper'd state)
On one nice trick depends the gen'ral fate.
An Ace of Hearts steps forth: the King unseen
Lurk'd in her hand, and mourn'd his captive Queen:
He springs to vengeance with an eager pace,
And falls like thunder on the prostrate Ace.
The nymph exulting fills with shouts the sky;
The walls, the woods, and long canals reply.
  O thoughtless mortals! ever blind to fate,
Too soon dejected, and too soon elate.
Sudden, these honours shall be snatch'd away,
And cursed for ever this victorious day.
  For lo! the board with cups and spoons is crown'd,
The berries crackle, and the mill turns round:
On shining altars of Japan they raise
The silver lamp; the fiery spirits blaze:
From silver spouts the grateful liquors glide,
While China's earth receives the smoking tide:
At once they gratify their scent and taste,
And frequent cups prolong the rich repast.
Straight hover round the fair her airy band;
Some, as she sipp'd the fuming liquor fann'd,
Some o'er her lap their careful plumes display'd,
Trembling, and conscious of the rich brocade.
Coffee (which makes the politician wise,
And see through all things with his half-shut eyes)
Sent up in vapours to the baron's brain
New stratagems, the radiant lock to gain.
Ah cease, rash youth! desist ere 'tis too late,
Fear the just gods, and think of Scylla's fate!
Changed to a bird, and sent to flit in air,
She dearly pays for Nisus' injured hair!
  But when to mischief mortals bend their will,

92. Codille: a set in which the principal player is outmatched. **106. berries:** coffee beans being ground in the small coffee mill. **107. altars of Japan:** lacquered ("japanned") tables. **110. China's earth:** porcelain. **122. Scylla's fate:** For her lover, King Minos of Crete, Scylla cut off a lock of her father's hair on which the safety of his kingdom (Megara) depended. As punishment she was transformed into a bird constantly pursued by an eagle.

How soon they find fit instruments of ill!
Just then, Clarissa drew with tempting grace
A two-edged weapon from her shining case:
So ladies, in romance, assist their knight,
Present the spear, and arm him for the fight.
He takes the gift with reverence and extends
The little engine on his fingers' ends;
This just behind Belinda's neck he spread,
As o'er the fragrant steams she bends her head.
Swift to the lock a thousand sprites repair,
A thousand wings, by turns, blow back the hair;
And thrice they twitch'd the diamond in her ear;
Thrice she look'd back, and thrice the foe drew near.
Just in that instant, anxious Ariel sought
The close recesses of the virgin's thought:
As on the nosegay in her breast reclin'd,
He watch'd th' ideas rising in her mind,
Sudden he view'd, in spite of all her art,
An earthly lover lurking at her heart.
Amazed, confused, he found his power expired,
Resign'd to fate, and with a sigh retired.
The peer now spreads the glitt'ring forfex wide,
T' inclose the lock; now joins it, to divide.
Ev'n then, before the fatal engine closed,
A wretched sylph too fondly interposed;
Fate urged the shears, and cut the sylph in twain,
(But airy substance soon unites again)
The meeting points the sacred hair dissever
From the fair head, for ever, and for ever!
  Then flash'd the living lightning from her eyes,
And screams of horror rend th' affrighted skies.
Not louder shrieks to pitying Heaven are cast,
When husbands or when lap-dogs breathe their last;
Or when rich China vessels, fall'n from high,
In glitt'ring dust and painted fragments lie;
  "Let wreaths of triumph now my temples twine,
(The victor cried) the glorious prize is mine!
While fish in streams, or birds delight in air,
Or in a coach and six the British fair,
As long as *Atalantis* shall be read,
Or the small pillow grace a lady's bed,
While visits shall be paid on solemn days,
When numerous wax-lights in bright order blaze,
While nymphs take treats, or assignations give,
So long my honour, name, and praise shall live!"
What Time would spare, from steel receives its date,

145. power expired: Ariel no longer has power to protect Belinda. She is now falling in love with the Baron. **165. Atalantis:** a novel based on scandals of the time. **168. wax-lights:** candles. **171. date.** end.

And monuments, like men, submit to fate!
Steel could the labour of the gods destroy,
And strike to dust th' imperial towers of Troy;
Steel could the works of mortal pride confound,
And hew triumphal arches to the ground.
What wonder then, fair nymph! thy hairs should feel
The conquering force of unresisted steel?

Canto IV

But anxious cares the pensive nymph oppress'd,
And secret passions labour'd in her breast.
Not youthful kings in battle seized alive,
Not scornful virgins who their charms survive,
Not ardent lovers robb'd of all their bliss,
Not ancient ladies when refused a kiss,
Not tyrants fierce that unrepenting die,
Not Cynthia when her manteau's pinn'd awry,
E'er felt such rage, resentment, and despair,
As thou, sad virgin! for thy ravish'd hair.
  For, that sad moment, when the sylphs withdrew,
And Ariel weeping from Belinda flew,
Umbriel, a dusky, melancholy sprite,
As ever sullied the fair face of light,
Down to the central earth, his proper scene,
Repair'd to search the gloomy Cave of Spleen.
  Swift on his sooty pinions flits the gnome,
And in a vapour reach'd the dismal dome.
No cheerful breeze this sullen region knows,
The dreaded east is all the wind that blows.
Here in a grotto, shelter'd close from air,
And screen'd in shades from day's detested glare,
She sighs for ever on her pensive bed,
Pain at her side, and Megrim at her head.
Two handmaids wait the throne: alike in place,
But diff'ring far in figure and in face.
Here stood Ill-nature like an ancient maid,
Her wrinkled form in black and white array'd;
With store of prayers, for mornings, nights, and noons,
Her hand is fill'd; her bosom with lampoons.
  There Affectation, with a sickly mien,
Shows in her cheek the roses of eighteen,
Practised to lisp, and hang the head aside,
Faints into airs, and languishes with pride,
On the rich quilt sinks with becoming woe,

173. labour . . . gods: The walls of Troy were thought to have been built by the gods Apollo and Poseidon. CANTO IV. **8. manteau:** a loose upper garment. **13. Umbriel:** a name derived from the Latin word for shadow *(umbra)*. **16. Spleen:** melancholy or ill humor. **24. Megrim:** migraine headache.

Wrapp'd in a gown, for sickness, and for show.
The fair ones feel such maladies as these,
When each new night-dress gives a new disease.
  A constant vapour o'er the palace flies;
Strange phantoms rising as the mists arise;
Dreadful, as hermits' dreams in haunted shades,
Or bright, as visions of expiring maids.
Now glaring fiends, and snakes on rolling spires,
Pale spectres, gaping tombs, and purple fires:
Now lakes of liquid gold, Elysian scenes,
And crystal domes, and angels in machines.
  Unnumber'd throngs on every side are seen
Of bodies changed to various forms by Spleen.
Here living tea-pots stand, one arm held out,
One bent; the handle this, and that the spout:
A pipkin there, like Homer's tripod walks;
Here sighs a jar, and there a goose-pie talks:
Men prove with child, as powerful fancy works,
And maids turn'd bottles call aloud for corks.
  Safe pass'd the gnome through this fantastic band,
A branch of healing spleen-wort in his hand.
Then thus address'd the power: "Hail, wayward Queen!
Who rule the sex to fifty from fifteen;
Parent of vapours, and of female wit,
Who give th' hysteric or poetic fit;
On various tempers act by various ways,
Make some take physic, others scribble plays;
Who cause the proud their visits to delay,
And send the godly in a pet to pray;
A nymph there is, that all thy power disdains,
And thousands more in equal mirth maintains.
But oh! if e'er thy gnome could spoil a grace,
Or raise a pimple on a beauteous face,
Like citron waters matrons' cheeks inflame,
Or change complexions at a losing game;
If e'er with airy horns I planted heads,
Or rumpled petticoats, or tumbled beds,
Or caused suspicion when no soul was rude,
Or discomposed the head-dress of a prude,
Or e'er to costive lap-dog gave disease,
Which not the tears of brightest eyes could ease;
Hear me, and touch Belinda with chagrin,
That single act gives half the world the spleen."

43. spires: spirals. **48. various forms:** hallucinations induced by the "spleen." **51. pipkin:** earthen pot. **52. goose-pie:** Pope says he actually knew a lady who, afflicted by the spleen, imagined herself to be a goose pie. **56. spleen-wort:** a fern supposed curative to the spleen. **69. citron waters:** brandy made from lemon rind. **71. planted heads:** made men think they were cuckolded.

The Goddess with a discontented air
Seems to reject him, though she grants his prayer.
A wondrous bag with both her hands she binds,
Like that where once Ulysses held the winds;
There she collects the force of female lungs,
Sighs, sobs, and passions, and the war of tongues.
A vial next she fills with fainting fears,
Soft sorrows, melting griefs, and flowing tears.
The gnome rejoicing bears her gifts away,
Spreads his black wings, and slowly mounts to day.
Sunk in Thalestris' arms the nymph he found,
Her eyes dejected, and her hair unbound.
Full o'er their heads the swelling bag he rent,
And all the furies issued at the vent.
Belinda burns with more than mortal ire,
And fierce Thalestris fans the rising fire;
"O wretched maid!" she spread her hands, and cried,
(While Hampton's echoes, "Wretched maid!" replied)
"Was it for this you took such constant care
The bodkin, comb, and essence to prepare?
For this your locks in paper durance bound?
For this with torturing irons wreathed around?
For this with fillets strain'd your tender head,
And bravely bore the double loads of lead?
Gods! shall the ravisher display your hair,
While the fops envy and the ladies stare?
Honour forbid! at whose unrivall'd shrine
Ease, pleasure, virtue, all our sex resign.
Methinks already I your tears survey,
Already hear the horrid things they say,
Already see you a degraded toast,
And all your honour in a whisper lost!
How shall I then your helpless fame defend?
'Twill then be infamy to seem your friend!
And shall this prize, th' inestimable prize,
Exposed through crystal to the gazing eyes,
And heighten'd by the diamond's circling rays,
On that rapacious hand for ever blaze?
Sooner shall grass in Hyde Park Circus grow,
And wits take lodgings in the sound of Bow;
Sooner let earth, air, sea, to Chaos fall,
Men, monkeys, lap-dogs, parrots, perish all!"
She said; then raging to Sir Plume repairs,

82. Ulysses . . . winds: In the *Odyssey* Aeolus, god of the winds, helps Ulysses to contain them all in a bag. **89. Thalestris:** a queen of the Amazons. **98. essence:** perfume. **101. fillets:** bands. **102. lead:** strips of lead to hold curler papers. **117. Circus:** carriage course in Hyde Park (the "Ring" in Canto I, line 44). **118. Bow:** unfashionable area near Bow church in the center of London. **121. Sir Plume:** Sir George Browne, a cousin of Arabella Fermor.

And bids her beau demand the precious hairs:
(Sir Plume of amber snuff-box justly vain,
And the nice conduct of a clouded cane)
With earnest eyes, and round, unthinking face,
He first the snuff-box open'd, then the case,
And then broke out—"My Lord, why, what the devil!
Z—ds! damn the lock! 'fore Gad, you must be civil!
Plague on't! 'tis past a jest—nay prithee, pox!
Give her the hair"—he spoke, and rapp'd his box.
"It grieves me much (replied the peer again)
Who speaks so well should ever speak in vain,
But by this lock, this sacred lock, I swear,
(Which never more shall join its parted hair;
Which never more its honours shall renew,
Clipp'd from the lovely head where late it grew)
That while my nostrils draw the vital air,
This hand, which won it, shall for ever wear."
He spoke, and speaking, in proud triumph spread
The long-contended honours of her head.
  But Umbriel, hateful gnome! forbears not so;
He breaks the vial whence the sorrows flow.
Then see! the nymph in beauteous grief appears,
Her eyes half-languishing, half-drowned in tears;
On her heaved bosom hung her drooping head,
Which, with a sigh, she raised; and thus she said:
  "For ever cursed be this detested day,
Which snatch'd my best, my fav'rite curl away!
Happy! ay ten times happy had I been,
If Hampton Court these eyes had never seen!
Yet am I not the first mistaken maid,
By love of courts to numerous ills betray'd.
Oh had I rather unadmired remain'd
In some lone isle, or distant northern land;
Where the gilt chariot never marks the way,
Where none learn ombre, none e'er taste bohea!
There kept my charms conceal'd from mortal eye,
Like roses that in deserts bloom and die.
What moved my mind with youthful lords to roam?
Oh had I stayed, and said my prayers at home!
'Twas this the morning omens seem'd to tell:
Thrice from my trembling hand the patch-box fell;
The tott'ring china shook without a wind;
Nay, Poll sat mute, and Shock was most unkind!
A sylph too warn'd me of the threats of Fate,

124. nice: precise, skilled. **clouded cane:** a fashionable cane of dark color. **128. Z—ds:** *zounds,* a contraction for *God's wounds.* **140. honours:** ornaments. **156. bohea:** a variety of fine tea. **162. patch-box:** for small ornamental patches that fashionable ladies put on their faces. **164. Poll:** a parrot.

In mystic visions, now believed too late!
See the poor remnants of these slighted hairs!
My hands shall rend what e'en thy rapine spares:
These in two sable ringlets taught to break,
Once gave new beauties to the snowy neck;
The sister-lock now sits uncouth, alone,
And in its fellow's fate foresees its own;
Uncurl'd it hangs, the fatal shears demands,
And tempts, once more, thy sacrilegious hands.
Oh hadst thou, cruel! been content to seize
Hairs less in sight, or any hairs but these!"

Canto V

She said: the pitying audience melt in tears;
But Fate and Love had stopp'd the baron's ears.
In vain Thalestris with reproach assails,
For who can move when fair Belinda fails?
Not half so fix'd the Trojan could remain,
While Anna begg'd and Dido raged in vain.
Then grave Clarissa graceful waved her fan;
Silence ensued, and thus the nymph began:
"Say, why are beauties praised and honoured most,
The wise man's passion, and the vain man's toast?
Why deck'd with all that land and sea afford?
Why angels call'd, and angel-like adored?
Why round our coaches crowd the white-gloved beaux?
Why bows the side-box from its inmost rows?
How vain are all these glories, all our pains,
Unless good sense preserve what beauty gains;
That men may say, when we the front-box grace,
'Behold the first in virtue as in face!'
Oh! if to dance all night, and dress all day,
Charm'd the small-pox, or chased old age away;
Who would not scorn what housewife's cares produce,
Or who would learn one earthly thing of use?
To patch, nay, ogle, might become a saint,
Nor could it sure be such a sin to paint
But since, alas! frail beauty must decay,
Curl'd or uncurl'd, since locks will turn to grey;
Since painted, or not painted, all shall fade,
And she who scorns a man must die a maid;
What then remains, but well our power to use,
And keep good-humour still, whate'er we lose?
And trust me, dear, good-humour can prevail,

CANTO V. **5–6. Trojan . . . Dido:** Aeneas left Dido in Carthage to go on to Italy, although she and her sister Anna begged him to stay. **14–17. side-box . . . front-box:** Ladies preferred front boxes at the theater, in order to be viewed; gentlemen preferred side boxes.

When airs, and flights, and screams, and scolding fail.
Beauties in vain their pretty eyes may roll;
Charms strike the sight, but merit wins the soul."
  So spoke the dame, but no applause ensued;
Belinda frown'd, Thalestris call'd her prude.
"To arms, to arms!" the fierce virago cries,
And swift as lightning to the combat flies.
All side in parties, and begin th' attack:
Fans clap, silks rustle, and tough whalebones crack;
Heroes' and heroines' shouts confusedly rise,
And bass and treble voices strike the skies.
No common weapons in their hands are found,
Like Gods they fight, nor dread a mortal wound.
  So when bold Homer makes the Gods engage,
And heavenly breasts with human passions rage;
'Gainst Pallas, Mars; Latona, Hermes arms;
And all Olympus rings with loud alarms;
Jove's thunder roars, Heaven trembles all around,
Blue Neptune storms, the bellowing deeps resound:
Earth shakes her nodding towers, the ground gives way,
And the pale ghosts start at the flash of day!
  Triumphant Umbriel on a sconce's height
Clapp'd his glad wings, and sate to view the fight:
Propp'd on their bodkin spears, the sprites survey
The growing combat, or assist the fray.
  While through the press enraged Thalestris flies,
And scatters death around from both her eyes,
A beau and witling perish'd in the throng,
One died in metaphor, and one in song.
"O cruel nymph! a living death I bear,"
Cried Dapperwit, and sunk beside his chair.
A mournful glance Sir Fopling upwards cast,
"Those eyes are made so killing,"—was his last.
Thus on Mæander's flowery margin lies
Th' expiring swan, and as he sings he dies.
  When bold Sir Plume had drawn Clarissa down,
Chloe stepp'd in, and kill'd him with a frown;
She smiled to see the doughty hero slain,
But, at her smile, the beau revived again.
  Now Jove suspends his golden scales in air,
Weighs the men's wits against the lady's hair:
The doubtful beam long nods from side to side;
At length the wits mount up, the hairs subside.
  See fierce Belinda on the baron flies,
With more than usual lightning in her eyes:

37. virago: a manlike woman. **53. sconce:** candlestick. **65. Mæander:** winding river in Asia Minor (from which comes the verb, "to meander"). **71. scales:** Jupiter (Jove) weighed the fortunes of war in golden scales.

Nor fear'd the chief th' unequal fight to try,
Who sought no more than on his foe to die.
But this bold lord with manly strength endued,
She with one finger and a thumb subdued:
Just where the breath of life his nostrils drew,
A charge of snuff the wily virgin threw;
The gnomes direct, to every atom just,
The pungent grains of titillating dust.
Sudden, with starting tears each eye o'erflows,
And the high dome re'echoes to his nose.
"Now meet thy fate," incensed Belinda cried,
And drew a deadly bodkin from her side.
(The same, his ancient personage to deck,
Her great-great-grandsire wore about his neck,
In three seal rings; which after, melted down,
Form'd a vast buckle for his widow's gown:
Her infant grandame's whistle next it grew,
The bells she jingled, and the whistle blew;
Then in a bodkin graced her mother's hairs,
Which long she wore, and now Belinda wears.)
"Boast not my fall, (he cried) insulting foe!
Thou by some other shalt be laid as low.
Nor think, to die dejects my lofty mind:
All that I dread is leaving you behind!
Rather than so, ah let me still survive,
And burn in Cupid's flames—but burn alive."
"Restore the lock!" she cries; and all around
"Restore the lock!" the vaulted roofs rebound.
Not fierce Othello in so loud a strain
Roar'd for the handkerchief that caused his pain.
But see how oft ambitious aims are cross'd,
And chiefs contend till all the prize is lost!
The lock, obtain'd with guilt, and kept with pain,
In every place is sought, but sought in vain:
With such a prize no mortal must be blest,
So Heaven decrees! with Heaven who can contest?
Some thought it mounted to the lunar sphere,
Since all things lost on earth are treasured there.
There heroes' wits are kept in pond'rous vases,
And beaux' in snuff-boxes and tweezer-cases.
There broken vows, and death-bed alms are found,
And lovers' hearts with ends of riband bound,
The courtier's promises, and sick man's prayers,
The smiles of harlots, and the tears of heirs,
Cages for gnats, and chains to yoke a flea,
Dried butterflies, and tomes of casuistry.
But trust the Muse—she saw it upward rise,

85–86. Sudden . . . nose: His sneeze cancels his boast in Canto IV, lines 133–38.

Though mark'd by none but quick, poetic eyes:
(So Rome's great founder to the heavens withdrew,
To Proculus alone confess'd in view)
A sudden star, it shot through liquid air,
And drew behind a radiant trail of hair.
Not Berenice's locks first rose so bright,
The heavens bespangling with dishevell'd light.
The sylphs behold it kindling as it flies,
And pleased pursue its progress through the skies.
  This the beau-monde shall from the Mall survey,
And hail with music its propitious ray.
This the blest lover shall for Venus take,
And send up vows from Rosamonda's lake.
This Partridge soon shall view in cloudless skies,
When next he looks through Galileo's eyes;
And hence th' egregious wizard shall foredoom
The fate of Louis, and the fall of Rome.
  Then cease, bright nymph! to mourn thy ravish'd hair,
Which adds new glory to the shining sphere!
Not all the tresses that fair head can boast
Shall draw such envy as the lock you lost.
For, after all the murders of your eye,
When, after millions slain, yourself shall die;
When those fair suns shall set, as set they must,
And all those tresses shall be laid in dust;
This lock, the Muse shall consecrate to fame,
And 'midst the stars inscribe Belinda's name.

1712–14

from An Essay on Man

Epistle I

Awake, my St. John! leave all meaner things
To low ambition and the pride of kings.
Let us (since life can little more supply
Than just to look about us, and to die)

125–26. Rome's . . . view: On his death Romulus, founder of Rome, was said to have been snatched up and carried to heaven. **129. Berenice's locks:** Her hair, cut off and given as an offering in the temple for her husband's safe return, was said to have been turned into a constellation by Jupiter. **133. Mall:** fashionable strolling place in St. James's Park, London. **136. Rosamonda's Lake:** pond in St. James's Park. **137. Partridge:** John Partridge, an astrologer, was constantly predicting the downfall of both the Pope and King Louis of France. **138. Galileo's eyes:** the telescope, which was invented by Galileo. AN ESSAY ON MAN. **Title:** The poem is written in the form of four Epistles, or verse-letters, to Henry St. John, Lord Bolingbroke.

Expatiate free o'er all this scene of man;
A mighty maze! but not without a plan:
A wild, where weeds and flowers promiscuous shoot;
Or garden, tempting with forbidden fruit.
Together let us beat this ample field,
Try what the open, what the covert yield!
The latent tracts, the giddy heights explore
Of all who blindly creep, or sightless soar;
Eye Nature's walks, shoot folly as it flies,
And catch the manners living as they rise:
Laugh where we must, be candid where we can;
But vindicate the ways of God to man.
  I. Say first, of God above, or man below,
What can we reason, but from what we know?
Of man, what see we but his station here,
From which to reason, or to which refer?
Through worlds unnumbered, though the God be known,
'Tis ours to trace him only in our own.
He, who through vast immensity can pierce,
See worlds on worlds compose one universe,
Observe how system into system runs,
What other planets circle other suns,
What varied being peoples every star,
May tell why Heaven has made us as we are.
But of this frame the bearings and the ties,
The strong connections, nice dependencies,
Gradations just, has thy pervading soul
Look'd through? or can a part contain the whole?
  Is the great chain, that draws all to agree,
And drawn, supports, upheld by God or thee?
  II. Presumptous man! the reason wouldst thou find,
Why form'd so weak, so little, and so blind?
First, if thou canst, the harder reason guess,
Why form'd no weaker, blinder, and no less?
Ask of thy mother earth, why oaks are made
Taller and stronger than the weeds they shade?
Or ask of yonder argent fields above,
Why Jove's satellites are less than Jove?
  Of systems possible, if 'tis confess'd,
That Wisdom infinite must form the best,
Where all must full, or not coherent be,
And all that rises, rise in due degree;
Then in the scale of reas'ning life, 'tis plain,
There must be, somewhere, such a rank as man:

EPISTLE I. **9–10. beat . . . open . . . covert:** hunting terms. **13. walks:** movements. **15. candid:** generous. **25. system:** solar system. **33. chain:** the "Great Chain of Being," in which all parts of the universe are held (see line 237.) **45. full . . . coherent:** Each link in the chain of being must be filled for the chain to function.

And all the question (wrangle e'er so long)
Is only this, if God has placed him wrong?
  Respecting man, whatever wrong we call,
May, must be right, as relative to all.
In human works, though labour'd on with pain,
A thousand movements scarce one purpose gain;
In God's, one single can its end produce;
Yet serves to second too some other use.
So man, who here seems principal alone,
Perhaps acts second to some sphere unknown,
Touches some wheel, or verges to some goal;
'Tis but a part we see, and not a whole.
  When the proud steed shall know why man restrains
His fiery course, or drives him o'er the plains;
When the dull ox, why now he breaks the clod,
Is now a victim, and now Egypt's god:
Then shall man's pride and dulness comprehend
His actions', passions', being's use and end;
Why doing, suff'ring, check'd, impell'd; and why
This hour a slave, the next a deity.
  Then say not man's imperfect, Heaven in fault;
Say rather, man's as perfect as he ought:
His knowledge measured to his state and place;
His time a moment, and a point his space.
If to be perfect in a certain sphere,
What matter, soon or late, or here or there?
The blest to-day is as completely so,
As who began a thousand years ago.
  III. Heaven from all creatures hides the book of Fate,
All but the page prescribed, their present state:
From brutes what men, from men what spirits know:
Or who could suffer being here below?
The lamb thy riot dooms to bleed to-day,
Had he thy reason, would he skip and play?
Pleased to the last, he crops the flowery food,
And licks the hand just raised to shed his blood.
Oh blindness to the future! kindly given,
That each may fill the circle mark'd by Heaven:
Who sees with equal eye, as God of all,
A hero perish, or a sparrow fall,
Atoms or systems into ruin hurl'd,
And now a bubble burst, and now a world.
  Hope humbly then; with trembling pinions soar;
Wait the great teacher, Death; and God adore.
What future bliss, He gives not thee to know,
But gives that hope to be thy blessing now.
Hope springs eternal in the human breast:

64. Egypt's god: The bull represented the Egyptian god Apis. **81. riot:** wasteful living.

Man never Is, but always To be blest.
The soul, uneasy, and confined from home,
Rests and expatiates in a life to come.
  Lo, the poor Indian! whose untutor'd mind
Sees God in clouds, or hears Him in the wind;
His soul, proud Science never taught to stray
Far as the solar-walk, or milky-way;
Yet simple Nature to his hope has given,
Behind the cloud-topp'd hill, and humbler Heaven,
Some safer world in depth of woods embraced,
Some happier island in the watery waste,
Where slaves once more their native land behold,
No fiends torment, no Christians thirst for gold.
To Be, contents his natural desire,
He asks no angel's wings, no seraph's fire;
But thinks, admitted to that equal sky,
His faithful dog shall bear him company.
  IV. Go, wiser thou! and in thy scale of sense,
Weigh thy opinion against Providence;
Call imperfection what thou fanciest such,
Say, here He gives too little, there too much:
Destroy all creatures for thy sport or gust,
Yet cry, If man's unhappy, God's unjust;
If man alone engross not Heaven's high care,
Alone made perfect here, immortal there:
Snatch from his hand the balance and the rod,
Re-judge his justice, be the god of God.
In pride, in reas'ning pride, our error lies;
All quit their sphere, and rush into the skies.
Pride still is aiming at the blest abodes,
Men would be angels, angels would be gods.
Aspiring to be gods, if angels fell,
Aspiring to be angels, men rebel:
And who but wishes to invert the laws
Of Order, sins against the Eternal Cause.

. . .

  VI. What would this man? Now upward will he soar,
And little less than angel, would be more;
Now looking downwards, just as grieved appears,
To want the strength of bulls, the fur of bears.
Made for his use all creatures if he call,
Say what their use, had he the powers of all?

97. from home: away from its true home, Heaven. **108. gold:** as when the Spaniards, in quest of gold, plundered the Aztecs of Mexico and the Incas of Peru. **110. fire:** seraphs were thought of as fiery spirits. **117. gust:** appetite.

Nature to these, without profusion, kind,
The proper organs, proper powers assign'd;
Each seeming want compensated of course,
Here with degrees of swiftness, there of force;
All in exact proportion to the state;
Nothing to add, and nothing to abate.
Each beast, each insect, happy in its own:
Is Heaven unkind to man, and man alone?
Shall he alone, whom rational we call,
Be pleased with nothing, if not blest with all?
  The bliss of man (could pride that blessing find)
Is not to act or think beyond mankind;
No powers of body or of soul to share,
But what his Nature and his state can bear.
Why has not man a microscopic eye?
For this plain reason, man is not a fly.
Say what the use, were finer optics given,
To inspect a mite, not comprehend the heaven?
Or touch, if tremblingly alive all o'er.
To smart and agonise at every pore?
Or quick effluvia darting through the brain,
Die of a rose in aromatic pain?
If Nature thunder'd in his opening ears,
And stunn'd him with the music of the spheres,
How would he wish that Heaven had left him still
The whisp'ring zephyr, and the purling rill?
Who finds not Providence all good and wise,
Alike in what it gives and what denies?
  VII. Far as creation's ample range extends,
The scale of sensual, mental powers ascends:
Mark how it mounts to man's imperial race,
From the green myriads in the peopled grass:
What modes of sight betwixt each wide extreme,
The mole's dim curtain, and the lynx's beam:
Of smell, the headlong lioness between,
And hound sagacious on the tainted green:
Of hearing, from the life that fills the flood,
To that which warbles through the vernal wood?
The spider's touch, how exquisitely fine!
Feels at each thread, and lives along the line:
In the nice bee, what sense so subtly true
From poisonous herbs extracts the healing dew?

181. of course: the natural course of events. **195. optics:** eyesight. **199. effluvia:** streams of particles carrying sense impressions to the brain. **212. beam:** stream of light striking the eye. According to legend, the lynx could see through objects. **213–14. headlong lioness . . . green:** The lion, with a relatively poor sense of smell, hunts game by rushing at it when it hears a noise; whereas, to the hound, with its acute sense of smell, the grass is "tainted" with the odor of the prey it seeks. **219. nice:** discriminating.

How instinct varies in the grov'ling swine,
Compared, half-reasoning elephant, with thine!
'Twixt that, and reason, what a nice barrier;
For ever separate, yet for ever near!
Remembrance and reflection, how allied;
What thin partitions sense from thought divide;
And middle natures, how they long to join,
Yet never pass the insuperable line!
Without this just gradation could they be
Subjected, these to those, or all to thee?
The powers of all subdued by thee alone,
Is not thy reason all these powers in one?
  VIII. See, through this air, this ocean, and this earth,
All matter quick, and bursting into birth.
Above, how high, progressive life may go!
Around, how wide! how deep extend below!
Vast chain of being! which from God began,
Natures ethereal, human, angel, man,
Beast, bird, fish, insect, what no eye can see,
No glass can reach; from infinite to thee,
From thee to nothing.

. . .

  All are but parts of one stupendous whole,
Whose body Nature is, and God the soul;
That, changed through all, and yet in all the same;
Great in the earth, as in the ethereal frame;
Warms in the sun, refreshes in the breeze,
Glows in the stars, and blossoms in the trees;
Lives through all life, extends through all extent;
Spreads undivided, operates unspent!
Breathes in our soul, informs our mortal part,
As full, as perfect, in a hair as heart:
As full, as perfect in vile man that mourns,
As the rapt seraph that adores and burns:
To him no high, no low, no great, no small;
He fills, He bounds, connects, and equals all.
  X. Cease then, nor order imperfection name:
Our proper bliss depends on what we blame.
Know thy own point: this kind, this due degree
Of blindness, weakness, Heaven bestows on thee.
Submit.—In this, or any other sphere,
Secure to be as blest as thou canst bear:
Safe in the hand of one Disposing Power,
Or in the natal, or the mortal hour.

223. barrier: pronounced *bareer.* **234. quick:** alive. **280. equals:** equalizes.

All Nature is but art, unknown to thee;
All chance, direction, which thou canst not see;
All discord, harmony not understood;
All partial evil, universal good:
And, spite of pride, in erring reason's spite,
One truth is clear, Whatever is, is right.

Epistle to Dr. Arbuthnot

Or, prologue to the satires

P. Shut, shut the door, good John! fatigued, I said;
Tie up the knocker, say I'm sick, I'm dead.
The Dog-star rages! nay 'tis past a doubt,
All Bedlam, or Parnassus, is let out:
Fire in each eye, and papers in each hand,
They rave, recite, and madden round the land.
  What walls can guard me, or what shades can hide?
They pierce my thickets, through my grot they glide,
By land, by water, they renew the charge,
They stop the chariot, and they board the barge.
No place is sacred, not the church is free,
Ev'n Sunday shines no Sabbath-day to me:
Then from the Mint walks forth the man of rhyme,
Happy! to catch me, just at dinner-time.
  Is there a parson, much bemused in beer,
A maudlin poetess, a rhyming peer,
A clerk, foredoom'd his father's soul to cross,
Who pens a stanza, when he should engross?
Is there, who, lock'd from ink and paper, scrawls
With desperate charcoal round his darken'd walls?
All fly to Twit'nam, and in humble strain
Apply to me, to keep them mad or vain.

EPISTLE TO DR. ARBUTHNOT. **Title:** Written as a dialogue between Pope (P.) and Arbuthnot (A.), later published as Pope's *Prologue to the Satires*, the poem is both a justification of his satires and also a model, in miniature, of his technique as a satirist in poetry. Dr. John Arbuthnot, a friend of Pope and of other famous writers of the time, was the physician to Queen Anne and himself a gifted author. **1. John:** Pope's servant. **2. knocker:** muffled when someone in the house was sick. **3. Dog-star:** Sirius, which appears in the heat of the summer when dogs often went mad (the "dog days"). **4. Bedlam:** lunatic asylum. **Parnassus:** home of the Muses. Pope is here throwing together lunatics and scribbling writers as all of the same type. **8. grot:** a grotto on the grounds of Pope's place at Twickenham. **13. Mint:** sanctuary for debtors. On Sundays, debtors could walk anywhere free from arrest. Pope is saying that Sunday is not a true Sabbath for him since then the debtors leave the Mint and descend on him for favors and a free meal. **18. stanza:** love poem. **engross:** copy legal documents. **21. Twit'nam:** Twickenham.

Arthur, whose giddy son neglects the laws,
Imputes to me and my damn'd works the cause:
Poor Cornus sees his frantic wife elope,
And curses wit, and poetry, and Pope.
  Friend to my life! (which did not you prolong,
The world had wanted many an idle song)
What drop or nostrum can this plague remove?
Or which must end me, a fool's wrath or love?
A dire dilemma! either way I'm sped,
If foes, they write, if friends, they read me dead.
Seized and tied down to judge, how wretched I!
Who can't be silent, and who will not lie:
To laugh, were want of goodness and of grace,
And to be grave, exceeds all power of face.
I sit with sad civility, I read
With honest anguish, and an aching head;
And drop at last, but in unwilling ears,
This saving counsel,—"Keep your piece nine years."
  "Nine years!" cries he, who, high in Drury Lane,
Lull'd by soft zephyrs through the broken pane,
Rhymes ere he wakes, and prints before Term ends,
Obliged by hunger, and request of friends:
"The piece, you think, is incorrect? why take it,
I'm all submission; what you'd have it, make it."
  Three things another's modest wishes bound,
My friendship, and a prologue, and ten pound.
  Pitholeon sends to me: "You know his grace,
I want a patron; ask him for a place."
Pitholeon libell'd me—"But here's a letter
Informs you, Sir, 'twas when he knew no better.

23. Arthur: Arthur Moore, whose son was a minor poet who had plagiarized from Pope. **25. Cornus:** cuckold. **29. drop or nostrum:** medicines. **40. Keep . . . years:** Pope quotes (and puns on) Horace's advice to poets not to rush into publication, but keep the poem nine years in order to reconsider it. The pun concealed here would be "keep your peace"—that is, stay quiet. **41. high in Drury Lane:** up in an attic (because of poverty) in the theater district filled with run-down houses. **42. zephyrs:** west winds. Pope is parodying fashionable pastoral poetry of the time, in which such winds are called zephyrs. Here the implication is that the attic room is in such poor shape that the windows are broken. **43. Rhymes . . . wakes:** is so obsessed with scribbling verses that he starts writing before he is fully awake. **Term:** rushes into print before the close of the law term (the period when courts of law met and the lawyers were in town; therefore a favorite period for publishing books). **44. hunger . . . friends:** These poets are really writing for money, but pretend to publish only because friends "request" it (a common excuse in Prefaces of the time: "I publish these verses, which I had written for myself and a few friends, because my friends insist that I share these poems with a larger audience"). **48. friendship . . . ten pound:** They say they want my friendship. But even more they want me to write a laudatory Prologue to their play or verses; and still more they want cash from me. **49. Pitholeon:** a minor poet of the ancient world; meant to apply to a modern minor poet, Leonard Welsted, who had attacked Pope.

Dare you refuse him? Curll invites to dine,
He'll write a journal, or he'll turn divine."
Bless me! a packet. "'Tis a stranger sues,
A virgin tragedy, an orphan Muse."
If I dislike it, "Furies, death and rage!"
If I approve, "Commend it to the stage."
There (thank my stars) my whole commission ends,
The players and I are, luckily, no friends;
Fired that the house reject him, "'Sdeath! I'll print it,
And shame the fools—Your interest, Sir, with Lintot."
Lintot, dull rogue! will think your price too much:
"Not, Sir, if you revise it, and retouch."
All my demurs but double his attacks:
At last he whispers, "Do; and we go snacks."
Glad of a quarrel, strait I clap the door:
Sir, let me see your works and you no more.
'Tis sung, when Midas' ears began to spring
(Midas, a sacred person and a king),
His very minister who spied them first
(Some say his queen) was forced to speak or burst:
And is not mine, my friend, a sorer case,
When every coxcomb perks them in my face?
A. Good friend, forbear! you deal in dangerous things,
I'd never name queens, ministers, or kings:
Keep close to ears, and those let asses prick,
'Tis nothing—— P. Nothing? if they bite and kick?
Out with it, DUNCIAD! let the secret pass,
That secret to each fool, that he's an ass:
The truth once told (and wherefore should we lie?)
The Queen of Midas slept, and so may I.
You think this cruel? Take it for a rule,
No creature smarts so little as a fool.
Let peals of laughter, Codrus! round thee break,
Thou unconcerned canst hear the mighty crack:
Pit, box, and gallery in convulsions hurl'd,
Thou stand'st unshook amidst a bursting world.

53. Curll: Edmund Curll, a publisher of scandalous works, who will be interested in getting a new scandalous attack on Pope. **54. journal . . . divine:** He'll start bringing out a scandal-sheet; or he'll become a clergyman and start preaching, thus spreading his bad opinions more widely under the guise of being a religious spokesman. **56. virgin . . . orphan:** the first (virgin) tragedy written by a new writer; inspired by a Muse who has no parents, no tradition. **62. Lintot:** Pope's publisher. **66. go snacks:** divide the profits. **69. Midas' ears:** King Midas's ears were turned into those of an ass because, when asked to judge who played music better, Pan or Apollo, he gave the prize to Pan. Seeing these ears, which Midas tried to cover with a big cap, his queen (or minister, in some versions) could not keep it a secret but had to whisper it in a hole near the river, where the reeds picked up the sound and began to say, "Midas has ass's ears," thus explaining the whispering sounds that reeds make in the wind. **74. perks:** thrusts forward in a pushy way. **85. Codrus:** any minor poet (from a Latin poet laughed at in Roman satire).

Who shames a scribbler? break one cobweb through,
He spins the slight, self-pleasing thread anew:
Destroy his fib or sophistry, in vain,
The creature's at his dirty work again,
Throned in the centre of his thin designs,
Proud of a vast extent of flimsy lines!
Whom have I hurt? has poet yet, or peer,
Lost the arch'd eyebrow, or Parnassian sneer?
And has not Colley still his lord, and whore?
His butchers Henley, his Freemasons Moore?
Does not one table Bavius still admit?
Still to one bishop Philips seem a wit?
Still Sappho—— A. Hold! for God's sake—you'll offend:
No names—be calm—learn prudence of a friend.
I too could write, and I am twice as tall;
But foes like these—— P. One flatterer's worse than all.
Of all mad creatures, if the learn'd are right,
It is the slaver kills, and not the bite.
A fool quite angry is quite innocent:
Alas! 'tis ten times worse when they repent.
  One dedicates in high heroic prose,
And ridicules beyond a hundred foes:
One from all Grub Street will my fame defend,
And, more abusive, calls himself my friend.
This prints my letters, that expects a bribe,
And others roar aloud, "Subscribe, subscribe!"
  There are, who to my person pay their court:
I cough like Horace, and, though lean, am short.
Ammon's great son one shoulder had too high—
Such Ovid's nose,—and, "Sir! you have an eye."
Go on, obliging creatures, make me see
All that disgraced my betters met in me.
Say, for my comfort, languishing in bed,
"Just so immortal Maro held his head";
And, when I die, be sure you let me know
Great Homer died three thousand years ago.

89. cobweb: Pope compares minor poets to a spider, which keeps automatically spinning out webs when the webs are broken. **94. lines:** lines of poetry, here compared with the threads of cobwebs. **97. Colley:** Colley Cibber, poet laureate, hero of Pope's *Dunciad*. **98. Henley:** preacher, popular with the butchers of London. **Moore:** James Moore-Smythe, who preached to the freemasons. **99. Bavius:** a minor poet (originally a Roman versifier who attacked Virgil and Horace). **100. Philips:** Ambrose Philips, who wrote bad pastoral poems (see line 179) and attacked Pope. **101. Sappho:** under the name of the Greek poetess, Pope here is referring to Lady Mary Wortley Montague, with whom he is now on bad terms. **103. twicc as tall:** Pope was less than five feet tall. **111. Grub Street:** home of literary hacks. **114. subscribe:** Books were often sold by subscription. **116. lean:** Horace was also short like Pope, but plump, whereas Pope was thin. **117. Ammon's . . . son:** Alexander the Great, whom the priests of the god Amon, in Egypt, hailed as Amon's son. **high:** one of Alexander's shoulders was higher than the other. **122. Maro:** Virgil.

Why did I write? what sin to me unknown
Dipp'd me in ink, my parents', or my own?
As yet a child, nor yet a fool to fame,
I lisp'd in numbers, for the numbers came.
I left no calling for this idle trade,
No duty broke, no father disobey'd:
The Muse but served to ease some friend, not wife,
To help me through this long disease, my life;
To second, ARBUTHNOT! thy art and care,
And teach the being you preserved to bear.
But why then publish? Granville the polite,
And knowing Walsh, would tell me I could write;
Well-natured Garth inflamed with early praise,
And Congreve loved, and Swift endured my lays;
The courtly Talbot, Somers, Sheffield read,
Even mitred Rochester would nod the head,
And St. John's self (great Dryden's friends before)
With open arms received one poet more.
Happy my studies, when by these approved!
Happier their author, when by these beloved!
From these the world will judge of men and books,
Not from the Burnets, Oldmixons, and Cookes.
Soft were my numbers; who could take offence
While pure description held the place of sense?
Like gentle Fanny's was my flowery theme,
A painted mistress, or a purling stream.
Yet then did Gildon draw his venal quill;
I wish'd the man a dinner, and sate still.
Yet then did Dennis rave in furious fret;
I never answer'd—I was not in debt.
If want provoked, or madness made them print,
I waged no war with Bedlam or the Mint.
Did some more sober critic come abroad—
If wrong, I smiled; if right, I kiss'd the rod.
Pains, reading, study, are their just pretence,
And all they want is spirit, taste, and sense.
Commas and points they set exactly right,

126. Dipp'd: baptized. **135–41. Granville . . . St. John:** well-known writers and patrons who had been friends of Pope. **146. Burnets . . . Cookes:** minor authors who had attacked Pope. **149. Fanny:** nickname for Lord Hervey, satirized below as "Sporus" (lines 305–33). **150. purling stream:** Pope is saying that, when he began to write, he had composed only pretty pastoral verse, not verse of intellectual content. Why should these people have attacked him, he asks?. **151–52. Gildon . . . dinner:** Charles Gildon, who had attacked the *Rape of the Lock*. Pope implies Gildon had no real reason, but only wrote his attack for money (hence Pope says he wished him a free dinner, and did not reply). **153–54. Dennis . . . debt:** John Dennis, an enemy, who Pope implies also wrote only for money. **156. Bedlam . . . mint:** the lunatic hospital and the Mint where money was coined. **161. Commas and points:** punctuation argued about and settled by textual editors with no real interest in what is valuable about a poem.

And 'twere a sin to rob them of their mite;
Yet ne'er one sprig of laurel graced these ribalds,
From slashing Bentley down to piddling Tibbalds:
Each wight, who reads not, and but scans and spells,
Each word-catcher, that lives on syllables,
Even such small critics, some regard may claim,
Preserved in Milton's or in Shakespeare's name.
Pretty! in amber to observe the forms
Of hairs, or straws, or dirt, or grubs, or worms!
The things we know are neither rich nor rare,
But wonder how the devil they got there.
  Were others angry—I excused them too;
Well might they rage, I gave them but their due.
A man's true merit 'tis not hard to find;
But each man's secret standard in his mind,
That casting-weight pride adds to emptiness,
This, who can gratify, for who can guess?
The bard whom pilfer'd Pastorals renown,
Who turns a Persian tale for half-a-crown,
Just writes to make his barrenness appear,
And strains from hard-bound brains, eight lines a-year;
He, who still wanting, though he lives on theft,
Steals much, spends little, yet has nothing left:
And he, who now to sense, now nonsense leaning,
Means not, but blunders round about a meaning:
And he, whose fustian's so sublimely bad,
It is not poetry, but prose ran mad:
All these, my modest satire bade translate,
And own'd that nine such poets made a Tate.
How did they fume, and stamp, and roar, and chafe!
And swear, not Addison himself was safe.
  Peace to all such! but were there one whose fires
True genius kindles, and fair fame inspires;
Blest with each talent, and each art to please,
And born to write, converse, and live with ease;
Should such a man, too fond to rule alone,
Bear, like the Turk, no brother near the throne,
View him with scornful, yet with jealous eyes,
And hate for arts that caused himself to rise;
Damn with faint praise, assent with civil leer,
And, without sneering, teach the rest to sneer;

164. Bentley . . . Tibbald: Richard Bentley, classical scholar, who tried to amend the text of Milton's *Paradise Lost*; and Lewis Theobald, editor of Shakespeare (see line 168). **177. casting-weight:** tipping the scales. **179–80. The bard . . . crown:** Ambrose Philips (see line 100), who wrote pseudo "Persian Tales" in verse; half a crown was the usual price paid for a harlot. **190. Tate:** Nahum Tate, poet and playwright. **193. one:** Joseph Addison (called "Atticus" here). **198. Turk:** The Turkish sultans were often said to have killed off all members of their family who might be rivals to the throne.

Willing to wound, and yet afraid to strike,
Just hint a fault, and hesitate dislike;
Alike reserved to blame, or to commend,
A timorous foe, and a suspicious friend;
Dreading e'en fools, by flatterers besieged,
And so obliging, that he ne'er obliged;
Like Cato, give his little senate laws,
And sit attentive to his own applause;
While wits and Templars every sentence raise,
And wonder with a foolish face of praise—
Who but must laugh, if such a man there be?
Who would not weep, if Atticus were he?
  What though my name stood rubric on the walls,
Or plaster'd posts, with claps, in capitals?
Or smoking forth, a hundred hawkers load,
On wings of winds came flying all abroad?
I sought no homage from the race that write;
I kept, like Asian monarchs, from their sight:
Poems I heeded (now be-rhym'd so long)
No more than thou, great George! a birthday song.
I ne'er with wits or witlings pass'd my days,
To spread about the itch of verse and praise;
Nor like a puppy daggled through the town
To fetch and carry sing-song up and down;
Nor at rehearsals sweat, and mouth'd, and cried,
With handkerchief and orange at my side;
But sick of fops, and poetry, and prate,
To Bufo left the whole Castalian state.
  Proud as Apollo on his forked hill,
Sate full-blown Bufo, puff'd by every quill;
Fed with soft dedication all day long,
Horace and he went hand in hand in song.
His library (where busts of poets dead
And a true Pindar stood without a head)
Received of wits an undistinguish'd race,
Who first his judgment asked, and then a place:

209. Cato: Roman hero of Addison's play of that name. **211. Templars:** lawyers (called that because they lived in the Inner and the Middle Temple, a group of buildings in London that had once belonged to the Knights Templar). **215–16. rubric . . . capitals:** Publishers often advertised new books in red (rubric) print, in capital letters on posters ("claps"). **222. George:** King George I. It was a custom for poets, seeking favor, to write birthday poems for the King. Pope is comparing himself to the King in this way. He is saying that, like the King, he has been "be-rhymed so long"—had so many poems dedicated to him—that he pays no attention to them anymore. **225. daggled:** traipsed. **228. orange:** sold (like candy today) at theaters, usually to less sophisticated people in the audience (the "unwashed"). Pope is saying that he didn't go to new plays (rehearsals), weeping at their sentimental scenes with his handkerchief and orange in his hand. **230. Bufo:** Lord Halifax, possibly Bubb Doddington, would-be patron of the arts; "Bufo" is Latin for "toad." **Castalian:** a spring sacred to Apollo and the Muses. **231. forked hill:** Mount Parnassus.

Much they extoll'd his pictures, much his seat,
And flatter'd every day, and some days eat:
Till grown more frugal in his riper days,
He paid some bards with port, and some with praise,
To some a dry rehearsal was assign'd,
And others (harder still) he paid in kind.
Dryden alone (what wonder?) came not nigh,
Dryden alone escaped this judging eye:
But still the great have kindness in reserve,
He help'd to bury whom he help'd to starve.
  May some choice patron bless each grey goose quill!
May every Bavius have his Bufo still!
So when a statesman wants a day's defence,
Or Envy holds a whole week's war with Sense,
Or simple pride for flattery makes demands,
May dunce by dunce be whistled off my hands!
Bless'd be the great! for those they take away,
And those they left me—for they left me GAY;
Left me to see neglected Genius bloom,
Neglected die, and tell it on his tomb:
Of all thy blameless life the sole return
My verse, and QUEENSBERRY weeping o'er thy urn!
  Oh let me live my own, and die so too!
(To live and die is all I have to do:)
Maintain a poet's dignity and ease,
And see what friends, and read what books I please:
Above a patron, though I condescend
Sometimes to call a minister my friend.
I was not born for courts or great affairs:
I pay my debts, believe, and say my prayers;
Can sleep without a poem in my head,
Nor know if Dennis be alive or dead.
  Why am I ask'd what next shall see the light?
Heavens! was I born for nothing but to write?
Has life no joys for me? or (to be grave)
Have I no friend to serve, no soul to save?
"I found him close with Swift"—"Indeed? no doubt"
(Cries prating Balbus) "something will come out."
'Tis all in vain, deny it as I will:
"No, such a genius never can lie still";
And then for mine obligingly mistakes
The first lampoon Sir Will or Bubo makes.
Poor guiltless I! and can I choose but smile,

248. starve: Bufo gave nothing to Dryden when alive, but contributed to his funeral expenses. **249. quill:** pen. **256–60. Gay . . . Queensberry:** John Gay, noted poet and friend of Pope. The Duke and Duchess of Queensberry were patrons of Gay. **276. Balbus:** Roman lawyer. **280. Sir Will . . . Bubo:** Sir William Yonge and Bubb Doddington, opponents of Pope.

When every coxcomb knows me by my style?
Cursed be the verse, how well soe'er it flow,
That tends to make one worthy man my foe,
Give Virtue scandal, Innocence a fear,
Or from the soft-eyed virgin steal a tear!
But he who hurts a harmless neighbour's peace,
Insults fall'n worth, or beauty in distress,
Who loves a lie, lame slander helps about,
Who writes a libel, or who copies out;
That fop, whose pride affects a patron's name,
Yet absent, wounds an author's honest fame;
Who can your merit selfishly approve,
And show the sense of it without the love;
Who has the vanity to call you friend,
Yet wants the honour, injured, to defend;
Who tells whate'er you think, whate'er you say,
And if he lie not, must at least betray;
Who to the dean and silver bell can swear,
And sees at Canons what was never there;
Who reads, but with a lust to misapply,
Makes satire a lampoon, and fiction, lie;
A lash like mine no honest man shall dread,
But all such babbling blockheads in his stead.
Let Sporus tremble—— A. What? that thing of silk,
Sporus, that mere white curd of ass's milk?
Satire or sense, alas! can Sporus feel,
Who breaks a butterfly upon a wheel?
P. Yet let me flap this bug with gilded wings,
This painted child of dirt, that stinks and stings;
Whose buzz the witty and the fair annoys,
Yet wit ne'er tastes, and beauty ne'er enjoys:
So well-bred spaniels civilly delight
In mumbling of the game they dare not bite.
Eternal smiles his emptiness betray,
As shallow streams run dimpling all the way.
Whether in florid impotence he speaks,
And, as the prompter breathes, the puppet squeaks;
Or at the ear of Eve, familiar toad!
Half froth, half venom, spits himself abroad,
In puns, or politics, or tales, or lies,
Or spite, or smut, or rhymes, or blasphemies.
His wit all see-saw, between that and this,
Now high, now low, now master up, now miss,
And he himself one vile antithesis.
Amphibious thing! that acting either part,

300. Canons: ostentatious home of Duke of Chandos. **305. Sporus:** Roman hermaphrodite, beloved of Nero; here, Lord Hervey (see line 149). **319. Eve:** here, Queen Anne; Hervey is compared with Satan speaking to Eve in *Paradise Lost*, Book IV, lines 790f.

The trifling head, or the corrupted heart;
Fop at the toilet, flatterer at the board,
Now trips a lady, and now struts a lord.
Eve's tempter thus the Rabbins have express'd,
A cherub's face, a reptile all the rest.
Beauty that shocks you, parts that none will trust,
Wit that can creep, and pride that licks the dust.
  Not Fortune's worshipper, nor Fashion's fool,
Not Lucre's madman, nor Ambition's tool,
Not proud, nor servile; be one poet's praise,
That, if he pleased, he pleased by manly ways:
That flattery, even to kings, he held a shame,
And thought a lie in verse or prose the same;
That not in Fancy's maze he wander'd long,
But stoop'd to Truth, and moralised his song:
That not for Fame, but Virtue's better end,
He stood the furious foe, the timid friend,
The damning critic, half-approving wit,
The coxcomb hit, or fearing to be hit;
Laughed at the loss of friends he never had,
The dull, the proud, the wicked, and the mad;
The distant threats of vengeance on his head,
The blow unfelt, the tear he never shed;
The tale revived, the lie so oft o'erthrown,
The imputed trash, and dulness not his own;
The morals blacken'd when the writings 'scape,
The libell'd person, and the pictured shape;
Abuse, on all he loved, or loved him, spread,
A friend in exile, or a father dead;
The whisper, that to greatness still too near,
Perhaps yet vibrates on his sovereign's ear—
Welcome for thee, fair Virtue! all the past:
For thee, fair Virtue! welcome even the last!
  A. But why insult the poor, affront the great?
  P. A knave's a knave, to me, in every state;
Alike my scorn, if he succeed or fail,
Sporus at court, or Japhet in a jail,
A hireling scribbler, or a hireling peer,
Knight of the post corrupt, or of the shire;
If on a pillory, or near a throne,
He gain his prince's ear, or lose his own.
  Yet soft by nature, more a dupe than wit,
Sappho can tell you how this man was bit:
This dreaded satirist Dennis will confess
Foe to his pride, but friend to his distress:

330. Rabbins: rabbis. **332. parts:** talents. **335. Lucre's:** money's. **363. Japhet:** Japhet Crook, a forger. **365. Knight . . . post:** one who earned his living by giving false evidence. **371. distress:** Pope had helped him when he was poor.

So humble, he has knocked at Tibbald's door,
Has drunk with Cibber, nay has rhymed for Moore.
Full ten years slander'd, did he once reply?
Three thousand suns went down on Welsted's lie;
To please a mistress one aspersed his life;
He lash'd him not, but let her be his wife:
Let Budgell charge low Grub Street on his quill,
And write whate'er he pleased, except his will;
Let the two Curlls of town and court abuse
His father, mother, body, soul, and Muse.
Yet why? that father held it for a rule,
It was a sin to call our neighbour fool:
That harmless mother thought no wife a whore:
Hear this, and spare his family, James Moore!
Unspotted names, and memorable long!
If there be force in virtue, or in song.
  Of gentle blood (part shed in honour's cause,
While yet in Britain honour had applause)
Each parent sprung—— A. What fortune, pray?—— P. Their own,
And better got, than Bestia's from the throne.
Born to no pride, inheriting no strife,
Nor marrying discord in a noble wife,
Stranger to civil and religious rage,
The good man walk'd innoxious through his age.
No courts he saw, no suits would ever try,
Nor dared an oath, nor hazarded a lie.
Unlearn'd, he knew no schoolman's subtle art,
No language, but the language of the heart.
By nature honest, by experience wise,
Healthy by temperance, and by exercise,
His life, though long, to sickness pass'd unknown,
His death was instant, and without a groan.
O grant me thus to live, and thus to die!
Who sprung from kings shall know less joy than I.
  O friend! may each domestic bliss be thine!
Be no unpleasing melancholy mine:
Me, let the tender office long engage,
To rock the cradle of reposing age,
With lenient arts extend a mother's breath,
Make languor smile, and smooth the bed of death.
Explore the thought, explain the asking eye,
And keep awhile one parent from the sky!
On cares like these if length of days attend,
May Heaven, to bless those days, preserve my friend,

375. suns: Pope alluded to the advice in the Bible, "Let not the sun go down on your wrath" (Ephesians 4:26). **380. two Curlls:** Edmund Curll, the publisher (see line 53 above) and, at the court, Lord Hervey. **391. Bestia:** a dishonest Roman Consul; here, the Duke of Marlborough. **412. explain:** make intelligible.

Preserve him social, cheerful, and serene,
And just as rich as when he served a queen,
A. Whether that blessing be denied or given,
Thus far was right, the rest belongs to Heaven.

1735

The Universal Prayer

Father of all! in every age,
In every clime adored,
By saint, by savage, and by sage,
Jehovah, Jove, or Lord!

Thou Great First Cause, least understood:
Who all my sense confined
To know but this—that thou art good,
And that myself am blind:

Yet gave me, in this dark estate,
To see the good from ill;
And binding Nature fast in fate,
Left free the human will.

What conscience dictates to be done,
Or warns me not to do,
This, teach me more than Hell to shun,
That, more than Heaven pursue.

What blessings thy free bounty gives,
Let me not cast away;
For God is paid when man receives,
To enjoy is to obey.

Yet not to earth's contracted span,
Thy goodness let me bound,
Or think thee Lord alone of man,
When thousand worlds are round:

Let not this weak, unknowing hand
Presume thy bolts to throw,
And deal damnation round the land,
On each I judge thy foe.

If I am right, thy grace impart,
Still in the right to stay;
If I am wrong, oh teach my heart
To find that better way.

417. just as rich: Arbuthnot refused to profit from having been Physician to Queen Anne, and continued to earn the same income as before. THE UNIVERSAL PRAYER. **5. First Cause:** the original creator and cause of the universe. **26. bolts:** allusion to the thunderbolts Zeus used as a weapon.

Save me alike from foolish pride,
  Or impious discontent,
At aught thy wisdom has denied,
  Or aught thy goodness lent.

Teach me to feel another's woe,
  To hide the fault I see;
That mercy I to others show,
  That mercy show to me.

Mean though I am, not wholly so
  Since quickened by thy breath;
Oh lead me wheresoe'er I go,
  Through this day's life or death.

This day, be bread and peace my lot:
  All else beneath the sun,
Thou know'st if best bestowed or not,
  And let thy will be done.

To thee, whose temple is all space,
  Whose altar, earth, sea, skies!
One chorus let all being raise!
  All Nature's incense rise!

1738

Close of The Dunciad: *Book IV*

  More she had spoke, but yawned—All Nature nods:
What mortal can resist the yawn of Gods?
Churches and chapels instantly it reached;
(St. James's first, for leaden G— preached)
Then catched the schools; the hall scarce kept awake;
The convocation gaped, but could not speak:
Lost was the nation's sense, nor could be found,
While the long solemn unison went round:
Wide, and more wide, it spread o'er all the realm;
Even Palinurus nodded at the helm:
The vapour mild o'er each committee crept;
Unfinished treaties in each office slept;

CLOSE OF THE DUNCIAD. **605.** The goddess of Dullness has just finished her speech in which titles and orders of merit have been bestowed on dunces of every sort (pedants, critics, bad poets), making "one mighty Dunciad of the land." Now, through her own dullness, she is putting herself to sleep, and sleepiness is spreading everywhere—to churches, government committees, armies, navies, the arts, and the world of learning. **608. G—:** John Gilbert, preacher at St. James's Church. **610. convocation:** assembly of the clergy to discuss church matters. **611. nation's sense:** discussions in Parliament. **612. unison:** snoring in unison. **614. Palinurus:** Aeneas' pilot; here the Prime Minister, Robert Walpole.

And chiefless armies dozed out the campaign;
And navies yawned for orders on the main.
O Muse; relate, (for you can tell alone
Wits have short memories, and dunces none,)
Relate, who first, who last resigned to rest;
Whose heads she partly, whose completely, blest;
What charms could faction, what ambition lull,
The venal quiet, and entrance the dull;
Till drowned was sense, and shame, and right, and wrong—
O sing, and hush the nations with thy song!

. . .

In vain, in vain—the all-composing hour
Resistless falls: the Muse obeys the pow'r.
She comes! she comes! the sable throne behold
Of Night primeval and of Chaos old!
Before her, fancy's gilded clouds decay,
And all its varying rainbows die away.
Wit shoots in vain its momentary fires,
The meteor drops, and in a flash expires.
As one by one, at dread Medea's strain,
The sick'ning stars fade off th' ethereal plain;
As Argus' eyes by Hermes' wand opprest,
Closed one by one to everlasting rest;
Thus at her felt approach, and secret might,
Art after art goes out, and all is night,
See skulking Truth to her old cavern fled,
Mountains of casuistry heaped o'er her head!
Philosophy, that leaned on Heaven before,
Shrinks to her second cause, and is no more.
Physic of metaphysic begs defence,
And metaphysic calls for aid on sense!
See mystery to mathematics fly!
In vain! they gaze, turn giddy, rave, and die.
Religion blushing veils her sacred fires,
And unawares morality expires.

628. Resistless: irresistibly. **630. Night . . . Chaos:** the original state of the universe before the creative ordering of the cosmos takes place (for example, in Milton's *Paradise Lost*, Book I, line 543, "Chaos and old Night"). **635–36. Medea's . . . stars:** Medea, in Seneca's play of that name, calls on the heavens to avenge her; because she is a magician, they obey her, and the stars become sick, dim, and slide off the "plain" of the sky. **637. Argus' . . . eyes:** Argus, who had a hundred eyes, was sent by Juno to watch Jupiter, whom she suspected to be in love with Io. Jupiter then asked Mercury (Hermes) to charm him asleep, and his eyes closed one by one. **641. Truth . . . cavern:** alluding to the remark of Democritus that truth lay at the bottom of a deep well. **644. second cause:** For Aristotle, the First Cause of all things is God. Mere material elements comprise a Second Cause. Pope is saying that philosophy gives up on seeking the First Cause and is lazily retreating to the Second. **645. Physic:** natural science. **647. mystery:** Divine revelation leaves the inspired word of God for mathematical speculation.

For public flame, nor private, dares to shine,
Nor human spark is left, nor glimpse divine!
Lo! thy dread empire, Chaos! is restored;
Light dies before thy uncreating word;
Thy hand, great Anarch! lets the curtain fall,
And universal darkness buries all.

1742

SAMUEL JOHNSON

(1709–1784)

Johnson is one of the heroes of literature. James Boswell's famous *Life of Johnson* (1791), one of the most fascinating records we have of anyone's conversations, has made him almost a household name for generations. After first learning about him through Boswell, readers go on to discover that he is one of the supreme writers on human nature and human experience, and one of the great literary critics. His "Preface to Shakespeare" (1765) and his *Lives of the Poets* (1779–81) are landmarks in the history of literary criticism.

Johnson was also a poet, at least on the side. "The Vanity of Human Wishes" has been praised by modern poets such as T. S. Eliot and Robert Lowell as one of the finest poems in the English language. It must also be admitted that it is one of the most difficult of the major English poems. Johnson takes the already compressed heroic couplet used by Dryden and Pope and compresses it with even more allusive density, but also with more powerful effect. His poem is written as an "imitation"—a popular form in the eighteenth century, in which Greek or Latin poems are paraphrased and modernized to apply to the eighteenth-century world. His model in "The Vanity of Human Wishes" is the Tenth Satire of the Latin poet Juvenal. In Johnson's hands the poem ceases in some ways to be a "satire." Instead it turns with compassion on the general condition of man, picturing short-lived human beings who are fired by ambition and hope and then doomed to face disappointment, rivalry, illness, and finally death. In depictions of one famous person after another—from the fields of politics, war, science, literature—we are shown

654. uncreating word: God's "creating word" had been "Let there be light" (Genesis, 1); now the word is the opposite of creation—"Let there be darkness."

that (as Johnson says elsewhere) "none are to be envied." The only hope we have is religious: to turn with faith to God. In this poem the savage indignation of the neoclassic satirists, the anger at the fact that things must be as they are in life, is very actively present. But it is blunted and transmuted by Johnson's charity and sympathy.

The two other poems included here are very different in tone and style. The brief elegy "On the Death of Dr. Levet"—a lay physician who treated the poorest Londoners, and who had lived for years in Johnson's house—is written in the simple but controlled style for which the Latin poet Horace was a great model in Johnson's day. The last poem, which is still not widely known, is an English version of one of Horace's odes about the brevity of human life. Johnson wrote it shortly before he died. In the seasons of the year winter is followed by spring. But when the human being enters his own winter of old age, there is no spring ahead. This ode has been translated scores of times. But no translation has been closer than Johnson's to Horace's serene and mellow acceptance of the fact that process, change, and disappearance are inevitable. The serenity of acceptance can be compared with that of Keats's last great lyric poem, "To Autumn."

The Vanity of Human Wishes

The tenth satire of Juvenal imitated

Let observation with extensive view,
Survey mankind, from China to Peru;
Remark each anxious toil, each eager strife,
And watch the busy scenes of crouded life;
Then say how hope and fear, desire and hate,
O'erspread with snares the clouded maze of fate,
Where wav'ring man, betray'd by vent'rous pride,
To tread the dreary paths without a guide,
As treach'rous phantoms in the mist delude,
Shuns fancied ills, or chases airy good;
How rarely reason guides the stubborn choice,
Rules the bold hand, or prompts the suppliant voice;
How nations sink, by darling schemes oppress'd,
When vengeance listens to the fool's request.

THE VANITY OF HUMAN WISHES. **Title:** Johnson's own title for his imitation of Juvenal, Satire X. **13–14. darling schemes:** pet schemes or plans. The harm done to a nation when a spirit of vengeance and outrage leads a government to listen to pet schemes suggested by fools.

Fate wings with ev'ry wish th' afflictive dart,
Each gift of nature, and each grace of art,
With fatal heat impetuous courage glows,
With fatal sweetness elocution flows,
Impeachment stops the speaker's pow'rful breath,
And restless fire precipitates on death.
  But scarce observ'd, the knowing and the bold
Fall in the gen'ral massacre of gold;
Wide-wasting pest! that rages unconfin'd,
And crouds with crimes the records of mankind;
For gold his sword the hireling ruffian draws,
For gold the hireling judge distorts the laws;
Wealth heap'd on wealth, nor truth nor safety buys,
The dangers gather as the treasures rise.
  Let hist'ry tell where rival kings command,
And dubious title shakes the madded land,
When statutes glean the refuse of the sword,
How much more safe the vassal than the lord;
Low skulks the hind beneath the rage of pow'r,
And leaves the wealthy traytor in the Tow'r,
Untouch'd his cottage, and his slumbers sound,
Tho' confiscation's vultures hover round.
  The needy traveller, serene and gay,
Walks the wild heath, and sings his toil away.
Does envy seize thee? crush th' upbraiding joy,
Increase his riches and his peace destroy;
Now fears in dire vicissitude invade,
The rustling brake alarms, and quiv'ring shade,
Nor light nor darkness bring his pain relief,
One shews the plunder, and one hides the thief.
  Yet still one gen'ral cry the skies assails,
And gain and grandeur load the tainted gales;
Few know the toiling statesman's fear or care,
Th' insidious rival and the gaping heir.
  Once more, Democritus, arise on earth,
With chearful wisdom and instructive mirth,
See motley life in modern trappings dress'd,
And feed with varied fools th' eternal jest:
Thou who couldst laugh where want enchain'd caprice,
Toil crush'd conceit, and man was of a piece;
Where wealth unlov'd without a mourner dy'd,
And scarce a sycophant was fed by pride;

15. fate wings . . . dart: Our wishes often provide the feathers for the arrows or darts that afflict and hurt us. **20. precipitates:** hastens. **30. dubious title:** doubtful or disputed ownership. **33. hind:** peasant. **39–40. envy . . . destroy:** If you envy him, give him more money, and his inner peace will soon be destroyed. **42. brake:** thicket. **46. gain . . . gales:** prayers for gain and grandeur pervade and "taint" the air. **49. Democritus:** Greek philosopher who laughed at human follies and was called the "laughing philosopher."

Where ne'er was known the form of mock debate,
Or seen a new-made mayor's unwieldy state;
Where change of fav'rites made no change of laws,
And senates heard before they judg'd a cause;
How wouldst thou shake at Britain's modish tribe,
Dart the quick taunt, and edge the piercing gibe?
Attentive truth and nature to descry,
And pierce each scene with philosophic eye.
To thee were solemn toys or empty shew,
The robes of pleasure and the veils of woe:
All aid the farce, and all thy mirth maintain,
Whose joys are causeless, or whose griefs are vain.
  Such was the scorn that fill'd the sage's mind,
Renew'd at ev'ry glance on humankind;
How just that scorn ere yet thy voice declare,
Search every state, and canvass ev'ry pray'r.
  Unnumber'd suppliants croud Preferment's gate,
Athirst for wealth, and burning to be great;
Delusive Fortune hears th' incessant call,
They mount, they shine, evaporate, and fall.
On ev'ry stage the foes of peace attend,
Hate dogs their flight, and insult mocks their end.
Love ends with hope, the sinking statesman's door
Pours in the morning worshiper no more;
For growing names the weekly scribbler lies,
To growing wealth the dedicator flies,
From every room descends the painted face,
That hung the bright Palladium of the place,
And smok'd in kitchens, or in auctions sold,
To better features yields the frame of gold;
For now no more we trace in ev'ry line
Heroic worth, benevolence divine:
The form distorted justifies the fall,
And detestation rids th' indignant wall.
  But will not Britain hear the last appeal,
Sign her foes doom, or guard her fav'rites zeal?
Through Freedom's sons no more remonstrance rings,
Degrading nobles and controuling kings;
Our supple tribes repress their patriot throats,
And ask no questions but the price of votes;
With weekly libels and septennial ale,
Their wish is full to riot and to rail.
  In full-blown dignity, see Wolsey stand,

80. morning worshiper: petitioners for favors who attended receptions held in the mornings by great men. **84. Palladium:** symbol of protection (from Pallas Athena, a statue of whom at Troy supposedly preserved the city from capture). **93. remonstrance:** protest (from the Grand Remonstrance presented to Charles I in 1641). **97. septennial ale:** At elections for Parliament every seven years, free ale was distributed to voters by the candidates. **99. Wolsey:** Cardinal Wolsey, Lord Chancellor for Henry VIII.

Law in his voice, and fortune in his hand:
To him the church, the realm, their pow'rs consign,
Thro' him the rays of regal bounty shine,
Turn'd by his nod the stream of honour flows,
His smile alone security bestows:
Still to new heights his restless wishes tow'r,
Claim leads to claim, and pow'r advances pow'r;
Till conquest unresisted ceas'd to please,
And rights submitted, left him none to seize.
At length his sov'reign frowns—the train of state
Mark the keen glance, and watch the sign to hate.
Where-e'er he turns he meets a stranger's eye,
His suppliants scorn him, and his followers fly;
At once is lost the pride of aweful state,
The golden canopy, the glitt'ring plate,
The regal palace, the luxurious board,
The liv'ried army, and the menial lord.
With age, with cares, with maladies oppress'd,
He seeks the refuge of monastic rest.
Grief aids disease, remember'd folly stings,
And his last sighs reproach the faith of kings.
  Speak thou, whose thoughts at humble peace repine,
Shall Wolsey's wealth, with Wolsey's end be thine?
Or liv'st thou now, with safer pride content,
The wisest justice on the banks of Trent?
For why did Wolsey near the steeps of fate,
On weak foundations raise th' enormous weight?
Why but to sink beneath misfortune's blow,
With louder ruin to the gulphs below?
  What gave great Villiers to th' assassin's knife,
And fixed disease on Harley's closing life?
What murder'd Wentworth, and what exil'd Hyde,
By kings protected, and to kings ally'd?
What but their wish indulg'd in courts to shine,
And pow'r too great to keep, or to resign?
  When first the college rolls receive his name,
The young enthusiast quits his ease for fame;
Through all his veins the fever of renown
Burns from the strong contagion of the gown;

129. Villiers: George Villiers, Duke of Buckingham, killed by an assassin jealous of his success. **130–131. Harley . . . Hyde:** Robert **Harley,** Earl of Oxford, Tory leader under Queen Anne, fell from power and was put in prison. Thomas **Wentworth,** Earl of Strafford, an adviser to Charles I, was executed. Edward **Hyde,** Earl of Clarendon, was impeached and exiled. **138. Burns . . . gown:** Scholars attending Oxford or Cambridge put on academic gowns on becoming students. The ambition that fills their veins, on wearing the gowns, is compared to the Greek fable of the shirt of Nessus, which, when worn, burned the skin but could not be taken off without tearing the flesh.

O'er Bodley's dome his future labours spread,
And Bacon's mansion trembles o'er his head.
Are these thy views? proceed, illustrious youth,
And virtue guard thee to the throne of Truth!
Yet should thy soul indulge the gen'rous heat,
Till captive Science yields her last retreat;
Should Reason guide thee with her brightest ray,
And pour on misty Doubt resistless day;
Should no false Kindness lure to loose delight,
Nor Praise relax, nor Difficulty fright;
Should tempting Novelty thy cell refrain,
And Sloth effuse her opiate fumes in vain;
Should Beauty blunt on fops her fatal dart,
Nor claim the triumph of a letter'd heart;
Should no Disease thy torpid veins invade,
Nor Melancholy's phantoms haunt thy shade;
Yet hope not life from grief or danger free,
Nor think the doom of man revers'd for thee:
Deign on the passing world to turn thine eyes,
And pause awhile from letters, to be wise;
There mark what ills the scholar's life assail,
Toil, envy, want, the patron, and the jail.
See nations slowly wise, and meanly just,
To buried merit raise the tardy bust.
If dreams yet flatter, once again attend,
Hear Lydiat's life, and Galileo's end.
  Nor deem, when learning her last prize bestows,
The glitt'ring eminence exempt from foes;
See when the vulgar 'scape, despis'd or aw'd,
Rebellion's vengeful talons seize on Laud.
From meaner minds, tho' smaller fines content,
The plunder'd palace or sequester'd rent;
Mark'd out by dangerous parts he meets the shock,
And fatal Learning leads him to the block:
Around his tomb let Art and Genius weep,
But hear his death, ye blockheads, hear and sleep.
  The festal blazes, the triumphal show,
The ravish'd standard, and the captive foe,
The senate's thanks, the gazette's pompous tale,
With force resistless o'er the brave prevail.

139. Bodley's dome: the Bodleian Library at Oxford, around the walls of which the young scholar imagines his future books will be spread. **140. Bacon's . . . head:** referring to a tradition that if a scholar greater than Friar Roger Bacon passed underneath them, Bacon's rooms, built on an arch over the bridge, would fall on him. **164. Lydiat . . . Galileo:** Thomas Lydiat, the famous Oxford mathematician, lived in poverty; Galileo, the Italian astronomer, was imprisoned for heresy and died blind. **168. Laud:** William Laud, Archbishop of Canterbury, executed by the Puritans in 1645. **170. sequester'd:** confiscated. **171. parts:** talents. **174. sleep:** Fools can rest secure since they lack his gifts. **177. gazette:** court newspaper.

Such bribes the rapid Greek o'er Asia whirl'd,
For such the steady Romans shook the world;
For such in distant lands the Britons shine,
And stain with blood the Danube or the Rhine;
This pow'r has praise, that virtue scarce can warm,
Till fame supplies the universal charm.
Yet Reason frowns on War's unequal game,
Where wasted nations raise a single name,
And mortgag'd states their grandsires wreaths regret,
From age to age in everlasting debt;
Wreaths which at last the dear-bought right convey
To rust on medals, or on stones decay.
  On what foundation stands the warrior's pride,
How just his hopes let Swedish Charles decide;
A frame of adamant, a soul of fire,
No dangers fright him, and no labours tire;
O'er love, o'er fear, extends his wide domain,
Unconquer'd lord of pleasure and of pain;
No joys to him pacific scepters yield,
War sounds the trump, he rushes to the field;
Behold surrounding kings their pow'r combine,
And one capitulate, and one resign;
Peace courts his hand, but spreads her charms in vain;
"Think nothing gain'd," he cries, 'till nought remain,
"On Moscow's walls till Gothic standards fly,
"And all be mine beneath the polar sky."
The march begins in military state,
And nations on his eye suspended wait;
Stern Famine guards the solitary coast,
And Winter barricades the realms of Frost;
He comes, not want and cold his course delay;—
Hide, blushing Glory, hide Pultowa's day:
The vanquish'd hero leaves his broken bands,
And shews his miseries in distant lands;
Condemn'd a needy supplicant to wait,
While ladies interpose, and slaves debate.
But did not Chance at length her error mend?
Did no subverted empire mark his end?
Did rival monarchs give the fatal wound?
Or hostile millions press him to the ground?
His fall was destin'd to a barren strand,
A petty fortress, and a dubious hand;

179. rapid Greek: Alexander the Great. **182. Danube . . . Rhine:** Troops of the Duke of Marlborough fought battles near these rivers in 1704. **183. pow'r . . . warm:** Praise has a power to motivate courage that mere love of virtue cannot kindle. **192. Charles:** King Charles XII of Sweden, noted for his military skill. **210. Pultowa:** Charles was defeated there by Peter the Great of Russia. **214. ladies . . . debate:** Charles fled to Turkey, staying there while his sister in Sweden debated with friends concerning whether or not to allow him to return. **220. dubious hand:** a doubtful or unknown assassin.

He left the name, at which the world grew pale,
To point a moral, or adorn a tale.
  All times their scenes of pompous woes afford,
From Persia's tyrant to Bavaria's lord.
In gay hostility, and barb'rous pride,
With half mankind embattled at his side,
Great Xerxes comes to seize the certain prey,
And starves exhausted regions in his way;
Attendant Flatt'ry counts his myriads o'er,
Till counted myriads sooth his pride no more;
Fresh praise is try'd till madness fires his mind,
The waves he lashes, and enchains the wind;
New pow'rs are claim'd, new pow'rs are still bestow'd,
Till rude resistance lops the spreading god;
The daring Greeks deride the martial show,
And heap their vallies with the gaudy foe;
Th' insulted sea with humbler thoughts he gains,
A single skiff to speed his flight remains;
Th' incumber'd oar scarce leaves the dreaded coast
Through purple billows and a floating host.
  The bold Bavarian, in a luckless hour,
Tries the dread summits of Cesarean pow'r,
With unexpected legions bursts away,
And sees defenceless realms receive his sway;
Short sway! fair Austria spreads her mournful charms,
The queen, the beauty, sets the world in arms;
From hill to hill the beacons rousing blaze
Spreads wide the hope of plunder and of praise;
The fierce Croatian, and the wild Hussar,
And all the sons of ravage croud the war;
The baffled prince in honour's flatt'ring bloom
Of hasty greatness finds the fatal doom,
His foes derision, and his subjects blame,
And steals to death from anguish and from shame.
  Enlarge my life with multitude of days,
In health, in sickness, thus the suppliant prays;
Hides from himself his state, and shuns to know,
That life protracted is protracted woe.
Time hovers o'er, impatient to destroy,
And shuts up all the passages of joy:
In vain their gifts the bounteous seasons pour,
The fruit autumnal, and the vernal flow'r,
With listless eyes the dotard views the store,
He views, and wonders that they please no more;
Now pall the tasteless meats, and joyless wines,

224. Persia's tyrant: Xerxes, Emperor of Persia, defeated by the Greeks. **Bavaria's lord:** Charles Albert, Elector of Bavaria, who hoped to head the Holy Roman Empire. **246. queen:** Maria Theresa of Austria. **249. Hussar:** cavalryman from Hungary.

And Luxury with sighs her slave resigns.
Approach, ye minstrels, try the soothing strain,
Diffuse the tuneful lenitives of pain:
No sounds alas would touch th' impervious ear,
Though dancing mountains witness'd Orpheus near;
Nor lute nor lyre his feeble pow'rs attend,
Nor sweeter musick of a virtuous friend,
But everlasting dictates croud his tongue,
Perversely grave, or positively wrong.
The still returning tale, and ling'ring jest,
Perplex the fawning niece and pamper'd guest,
While growing hopes scarce awe the gath'ring sneer,
And scarce a legacy can bribe to hear;
The watchful guests still hint the last offence,
The daughter's petulance, the son's expence,
Improve his heady rage with treach'rous skill,
And mould his passions till they make his will.
  Unnumber'd maladies his joints invade,
Lay siege to life and press the dire blockade;
But unextinguish'd Avarice still remains,
And dreaded losses aggravate his pains;
He turns, with anxious heart and cripled hands,
His bonds of debt, and mortgages of lands;
Or views his coffers with suspicious eyes,
Unlocks his gold, and counts it till he dies.
  But grant, the virtues of a temp'rate prime
Bless with an age exempt from scorn or crime;
An age that melts with unperceiv'd decay,
And glides in modest Innocence away;
Whose peaceful day Benevolence endears,
Whose night congratulating Conscience cheers;
The gen'ral fav'rite as the gen'ral friend:
Such age there is, and who shall wish its end?
  Yet ev'n on this her load Misfortune flings,
To press the weary minutes flagging wings:
New sorrow rises as the day returns,
A sister sickens, or a daughter mourns.
Now kindred Merit fills the sable bier,
Now lacerated Friendship claims a tear.
Year chases year, decay pursues decay,
Still drops some joy from with'ring life away;
New forms arise, and diff'rent views engage,
Superfluous lags the vet'ran on the stage,
Till pitying Nature signs the last release,
And bids afflicted worth retire to peace.
  But few there are whom hours like these await,

268. lenitives: softeners. **270. Orpheus:** the legendary musician whose songs could cause hills and trees to move. **281. improve:** increase. **308. vet'ran:** the elderly.

Who set unclouded in the gulphs of fate.
From Lydia's monarch should the search descend,
By Solon caution'd to regard his end,
In life's last scene what prodigies surprise,
Fears of the brave, and follies of the wise?
From Marlb'rough's eyes the streams of dotage flow,
And Swift expires a driv'ler and a show.
  The teeming mother, anxious for her race,
Begs for each birth the fortune of a face:
Yet Vane could tell what ills from beauty spring;
And Sedley curs'd the form that pleas'd a king.
Ye nymphs of rosy lips and radiant eyes,
Whom Pleasure keeps too busy to be wise,
Whom Joys with soft varieties invite,
By day the frolick, and the dance by night,
Who frown with vanity, who smile with art,
And ask the latest fashion of the heart,
What care, what rules your heedless charms shall save,
Each nymph your rival, and each youth your slave?
Against your fame with fondness hate combines,
The rival batters, and the lover mines.
With distant voice neglected Virtue calls,
Less heard and less, the faint remonstrance falls;
Tir'd with contempt, she quits the slipp'ry reign,
And Pride and Prudence take her seat in vain.
In croud at once, where none the pass defend,
The harmless Freedom, and the private Friend.
The guardians yield, by force superior ply'd;
By Int'rest, Prudence; and by Flatt'ry, Pride.
Now beauty falls betray'd, despis'd, distress'd,
And hissing Infamy proclaims the rest.
  Where then shall Hope and Fear their objects find?
Must dull Suspence corrupt the stagnant mind?
Must helpless man, in ignorance sedate,
Roll darkling down the torrent of his fate?
Must no dislike alarm, no wishes rise,
No cries attempt the mercies of the skies?
Enquirer, cease, petitions yet remain,
Which heav'n may hear, nor deem religion vain.
Still raise for good the supplicating voice,

313. Lydia's monarch: Croesus, the wealthy King to whom Solon had said that no man could say he was securely happy till his life was over. He was deposed by Cyrus, Emperor of Persia. **317. Marlb'rough:** The Duke of Marlborough was paralyzed in his last years. **318. Swift . . . show:** Jonathan Swift, in his senility, was shown to visitors by his servants for a fee. **319. race:** progeny. **321. Vane:** Anne Vane, mistress of Frederick, Prince of Wales, was later deserted by him. **322. Sedley:** Catherine Sedley, mistress of James II, was deserted by him when he reached the throne. **332. mines:** military term, meaning to dig tunnels beneath a fortress or building and fill them with explosives. **344. Suspence:** hesitation and inaction. **346. darkling:** in the dark.

But leave to heav'n the measure and the choice,
Safe in his pow'r, whose eyes discern afar
The secret ambush of a specious pray'r.
Implore his aid, in his decisions rest,
Secure whate'er he gives, he gives the best.
Yet when the sense of sacred presence fires,
And strong devotion to the skies aspires,
Pour forth thy fervours for a healthful mind,
Obedient passions, and a will resign'd;
For love, which scarce collective man can fill;
For patience sov'reign o'er transmuted ill;
For faith, that panting for a happier seat,
Counts death kind Nature's signal of retreat:
These goods for man the laws of heav'n ordain,
These goods he grants, who grants the pow'r to gain;
With these celestial wisdom calms the mind,
And makes the happiness she does not find.

1749

On the Death of Dr. Robert Levet

Condemn'd to hope's delusive mine,
  As on we toil from day to day,
By sudden blasts, or slow decline,
  Our social comforts drop away.

Well tried through many a varying year,
  See LEVET to the grave descend;
Officious, innocent, sincere,
  Of ev'ry friendless name the friend.

Yet still he fills affection's eye,
  Obscurely wise, and coarsely kind;
Nor, letter'd arrogance, deny
  Thy praise to merit unrefin'd.

When fainting nature call'd for aid,
  And hov'ring death prepar'd the blow,
His vig'rous remedy display'd
  The power of art without the show.

361–62. love . . . ill: for love so great that mankind as a whole could hardly suffice it (in short, it transcends mankind, and turns to God); and for patience that, standing sovereign over ills, transmutes them into something else. ON THE DEATH OF DR. ROBERT LEVET. **7. Officious:** dutiful in his good offices to others.

In misery's darkest cavern known,
  His useful care was ever nigh,
Where hopeless anguish pour'd his groan,
  And lonely want retir'd to die.

No summons mock'd by chill delay,
  No petty gain disdain'd by pride,
The modest wants of ev'ry day
  The toil of ev'ry day supplied.

His virtues walk'd their narrow round,
  Nor made a pause, nor left a void;
And sure th' Eternal Master found
  The single talent well employ'd.

The busy day, the peaceful night,
  Unfelt, uncounted, glided by;
His frame was firm, his powers were bright,
  Tho' now his eightieth year was nigh.

Then with no throbbing fiery pain,
  No cold gradations of decay,
Death broke at once the vital chain,
  And free'd his soul the nearest way.

1783

Translation of Horace Odes IV, vii *(Diffugere nives)*

The snow dissolv'd no more is seen,
The fields, and woods, behold, are green,
The changing year renews the plain,
The rivers know their banks again.
The spritely Nymph and naked Grace
The mazy dance together trace.
The changing year's successive plan
Proclaims mortality to Man.
Rough Winter's blasts to Spring give way,
Spring yields to Summer's sovereign ray,
Then Summer sinks in Autumn's reign
And Winter chills the World again.
Her losses soon the Moon supplies,
But wretched Man, when once he lies
Where Priam and his Sons are laid,

28. single talent: allusion to the "parable of the talents," in which the single talent, well employed, is rewarded (Matthew 25:14–30). TRANSLATION OF HORACE *ODES* IV, vii *(Diffugere nives);* the Latin means "the snow has fled." **15. Priam:** King of Troy, father of Hector and Paris in the *Iliad.*

Is nought but Ashes and a Shade.
Who knows if Jove who counts our Score
Will toss us in a morning more?
What with your friend you nobly share,
At least you rescue from your heir.
Not you, Torquatus, boast of Rome,
When Minos once has fix'd your doom,
Or Eloquence, or splendid birth,
Or Virtue shall replace on earth.
Hyppolytus unjustly slain
Diana calls to life in vain,
Nor can the might of Theseus rend
The chains of hell that hold his friend.

1784

THOMAS GRAY

(1716–1771)

Gray's "Elegy Written in a Country Churchyard" became immensely popular after it was published in 1751. During the next century and a half it was one of the half-dozen most famous poems in the English language. Everyone read it, or parts of it, at school. Many of the lines from it sank into the heart permanently, such as "Full many a flower is born to blush unseen," "The paths of glory lead but to the grave," or "Far from the madding crowd's ignoble strife" (a line that Thomas Hardy used for the title of a famous novel). The poem was loved by American Presidents, such as Thomas Jefferson and Abraham Lincoln, by ordinary men and women in all walks of life, and even by hard-bitten miners and prospectors in the frontier West.

Although it is very much the product of the eighteenth century in its classical restraint of phrasing and purity of language, the elegy also has qualities that readers prized in the nineteenth century. It is a brooding meditation on human destiny in which individual lives are seen within a

21. Torquatus: Roman Consul. **22. Minos:** judge of the dead. **25–26. Hippolytus . . . Diana:** In Greek myth, Hippolytus, a famous hunter, was beloved by the goddess Artemis (Diana). When he was killed, Artemis tried vainly to have him restored to life. **27–28. Theseus . . . friend:** Theseus and his friend Pirithous went to Hades to rescue Proserpine. Theseus was helped to escape by Hercules, but Pirithous was kept there by Pluto, King of the Underworld.

vast perspective of time. It is suffused with a powerful, nostalgic sense of the brevity of life and the loneliness every human being can feel. And its imagery is of the simple, accessible kind that readers in the eighteenth century (in a lovely word modern criticism could profitably revive) called "the *familiar.*" As Samuel Johnson said of the poem, "The *Church-Yard* abounds with images which find a mirror in every mind, and with sentiments to which every bosom returns an echo."

Gray lived the quiet life of a scholar in the University of Cambridge, where he studied ancient and medieval history and literature. Although his masterpiece is the *Elegy*, his other poems also have lines that are still almost proverbial, such as, in the "Ode on a Distant Prospect of Eton College," the lines, "where ignorance is bliss/ 'Tis folly to be wise."

Ode on a Distant Prospect of Eton College

Ἄνθρωπος · ἱκανὴ πρόφασις εἰς τὸ δυσ τυχεῖν.
Menander

Ye distant spires, ye antique towers,
That crown the watery glade,
Where grateful Science still adores
Her Henry's holy Shade;
And ye, that from the stately brow
Of Windsor's heights the expanse below
Of grove, of lawn, of mead survey,
Whose turf, whose shade, whose flowers among
Wanders the hoary Thames along
His silver-winding way:

Ah, happy hills! ah, pleasing shade!
Ah, fields beloved in vain!
Where once my careless childhood strayed,
A stranger yet to pain!
I feel the gales that from ye blow
A momentary bliss bestow,
As, waving fresh their gladsome wing,
My weary soul they seem to soothe,
And, redolent of joy and youth,
To breathe a second spring.

ODE ON A DISTANT PROSPECT OF ETON COLLEGE. **Title:** Eton School, founded by Henry VI, is on the Thames near Windsor Castle. **Epigraph: Menander:** Greek poet. The line quoted means: "I am a man, which is reason enough for being unhappy." **3. Science:** learning. **4. Henry:** Henry VI. **6. Windsor's heights:** Windsor Castle. **19. redolent:** sweet smelling.

Say, Father Thames, for thou hast seen
Full many a sprightly race
Disporting on thy margent green
The paths of pleasure trace;
Who foremost now delight to cleave
With pliant arm thy glassy wave?
The captive linnet which enthrall?
What idle progeny succeed
To chase the rolling circle's speed,
Or urge the flying ball?

While some on earnest business bent
Their murmuring labors ply
'Gainst graver hours, that bring constraint
To sweeten liberty;
Some bold adventurers disdain
The limits of their little reign,
And unknown regions dare descry;
Still as they run they look behind;
They hear a voice in every wind,
And snatch a fearful joy.

Gay hope is theirs, by fancy fed,
Less pleasing when possessed;
The tear forgot as soon as shed,
The sunshine of the breast;
Theirs buxom health of rosy hue,
Wild wit, invention ever new,
And lively cheer of vigor born;
The thoughtless day, the easy night,
The spirits pure, the slumbers light,
That fly the approach of morn.

Alas, regardless of their doom,
The little victims play!
No sense have they of ills to come,
Nor care beyond to-day!
Yet see how all around 'em wait
The ministers of human fate,
And black Misfortune's baleful train!
Ah, show them where in ambush stand
To seize their prey the murderous band!
Ah, tell them they are men!

These shall the fury Passions tear,
The vultures of the mind,
Disdainful Anger, pallid Fear,

23. margent: shore. **27. linnet:** songbird. **enthrall:** imprison. **28. succeed:** follow the previous generation. **29. circle:** hoop. **45. buxom:** lively.

And Shame that skulks behind;
Or pining Love shall waste their youth,
Or Jealousy with rankling tooth,
That inly gnaws the secret heart,
And Envy wan, and faded Care,
Grim-visaged comfortless Despair,
And Sorrow's piercing dart.

Ambition this shall tempt to rise,
Then whirl the wretch from high,
To bitter Scorn a sacrifice,
And grinning Infamy.
The stings of Falsehood those shall try,
And hard Unkindness' altered eye,
That mocks the tear it forced to flow;
And keen Remorse with blood defiled,
And moody Madness laughing wild
Amid severest woe.

Lo, in the vale of years beneath
A grisly troop are seen,
The painful family of Death,
More hideous than their queen:
This racks the joints, this fires the veins,
That every laboring sinew strains,
Those in the deeper vitals rage;
Lo, Poverty, to fill the band,
That numbs the soul with icy hand,
And slow-consuming Age.

To each his sufferings; all are men,
Condemned alike to groan—
The tender for another's pain,
The unfeeling for his own.
Yet, ah! why should they know their fate,
Since sorrow never comes too late,
And happiness too swiftly flies?
Thought would destroy their paradise.
No more; where ignorance is bliss,
'Tis folly to be wise.

1747

71. this: this one. **75. those:** those other ones.

Ode on the Death of a Favorite Cat, Drowned in a Tub of Goldfishes

'Twas on a lofty vase's side,
Where China's gayest art had dyed
  The azure flowers that blow;
Demurest of the tabby kind,
The pensive Selima, reclined,
  Gazed on the lake below.

Her conscious tail her joy declared;
The fair round face, the snowy beard,
  The velvet of her paws,
Her coat, that with the tortoise vies,
Her ears of jet, and emerald eyes,
  She saw; and purred applause.

Still had she gazed; but 'midst the tide
Two angel forms were seen to glide,
  The genii of the stream:
Their scaly armor's Tyrian hue
Through richest purple to the view
  Betrayed a golden gleam.

The hapless nymph with wonder saw:
A whisker first and then a claw,
  With many an ardent wish,
She stretched in vain to reach the prize.
What female heart can gold despise?
  What cat's averse to fish?

Presumptuous maid! with looks intent
Again she stretched, again she bent,
  Nor knew the gulf between.
(Malignant Fate sat by and smiled)
The slippery verge her feet beguiled,
  She tumbled headlong in.

Eight times emerging from the flood
She mewed to every watery god,
  Some speedy aid to send.
No dolphin came, no Nereid stirred;
Nor cruel Tom, nor Susan heard;
  A favorite has no friend!

From hence, ye beauties, undeceived,
Know, one false step is ne'er retrieved,

ODE ON THE DEATH OF A FAVORITE CAT. **16. Tyrian:** purple. **34. dolphin:** In Greek myth, a dolphin rescued the singer Arion. **Nereid:** sea nymph. **35. Tom . . . Susan:** servants.

And be with caution bold.
Not all that tempts your wandering eyes
And heedless hearts, is lawful prize;
Nor all that glisters, gold.

1748

Elegy Written in a Country Churchyard

The curfew tolls the knell of parting day,
The lowing heard wind slowly o'er the lea,
The ploughman homeward plods his weary way,
And leaves the world to darkness and to me.

Now fades the glimmering landscape on the sight,
And all the air a solemn stillness holds,
Save where the beetle wheels his droning flight,
And drowsy tinklings lull the distant folds;
Save that from yonder ivy-mantled tower
The moping owl does to the moon complain
Of such as, wandering near her secret bower,
Molest her ancient solitary reign.

Beneath those rugged elms, that yew-tree's shade,
Where heaves the turf in many a moldering heap,
Each in his narrow cell forever laid,
The rude forefathers of the hamlet sleep.

The breezy call of incense-breathing morn,
The swallow twittering from the straw-built shed,
The cock's shrill clarion, or the echoing horn,
No more shall rouse them from their lowly bed.

For them no more the blazing hearth shall burn,
Or busy housewife ply her evening care:
No children run to lisp their sire's return,
Or climb his knees the envied kiss to share.

Oft did the harvest to their sickle yield;
Their furrow oft the stubborn glebe has broke;
How jocund did they drive their team afield!
How bowed the woods beneath their sturdy stroke!

Let not Ambition mock their useful toil,
Their homely joys, and destiny obscure;
Nor Grandeur hear with a disdainful smile
The short and simple annals of the poor.

ELEGY WRITTEN IN A COUNTRY CHURCHYARD. **16. rude:** rustic. **19. horn:** hunting horn. **26. glebe:** soil or field.

The boast of heraldry, the pomp of power,
  And all that beauty, all that wealth e'er gave,
Awaits alike the inevitable hour:
  The paths of glory lead but to the grave.

Nor you, ye proud, impute to these the fault,
  If Memory o'er their tomb no trophies raise,
Where through the long-drawn aisle and fretted vault
  The pealing anthem swells the note of praise.

Can storied urn or animated bust
  Back to its mansion call the fleeting breath?
Can Honor's voice provoke the silent dust,
  Or Flattery soothe the dull, cold ear of Death?

Perhaps in this neglected spot is laid
  Some heart once pregnant with celestial fire;
Hands that the rod of empire might have swayed,
  Or waked to ecstasy the living lyre.

But Knowledge to their eyes her ample page,
  Rich with the spoils of time, did ne'er unroll;
Chill Penury repressed their noble rage,
  And froze the genial current of the soul.

Full many a gem of purest ray serene,
  The dark unfathomed caves of ocean bear:
Full many a flower is born to blush unseen,
  And waste its sweetness on the desert air.

Some village Hampden, that with dauntless breast
  The little tyrant of his fields withstood;
Some mute, inglorious Milton here may rest,
  Some Cromwell, guiltless of his country's blood.

The applause of listening senates to command,
  The threats of pain and ruin to despise,
To scatter plenty o'er a smiling land,
  And read their history in a nation's eyes,

Their lot forbade: nor circumscribed alone
  Their growing virtues, but their crimes confined;
Forbade to wade through slaughter to a throne,
  And shut the gates of mercy on mankind;

The struggling pangs of conscious truth to hide,
  To quench the blushes of ingenuous shame,
Or heap the shrine of Luxury and Pride
  With incense kindled at the Muse's flame.

39. fretted: ornamented. **41. urn:** funeral urn for ashes. **animated:** lifelike (as if breathing). **43. provoke:** call forth. **53. serene:** bright. **57. Hampden:** John Hampden, statesman and patriot who opposed Charles I.

Far from the madding crowd's ignoble strife,
  Their sober wishes never learned to stray;
Along the cool, sequestered vale of life
  They kept the noiseless tenor of their way.

Yet even these bones from insult to protect,
  Some frail memorial still erected nigh,
With uncouth rhymes and shapeless sculpture decked,
  Implores the passing tribute of a sigh.

Their name, their years, spelt by the unlettered Muse,
  The place of fame and elegy supply;
And many a holy text around she strews,
  That teach the rustic moralist to die.

For who, to dumb forgetfulness a prey,
  This pleasing anxious being e'er resigned,
Left the warm precincts of the cheerful day,
  Nor cast one longing lingering look behind?

On some fond breast the parting soul relies,
  Some pious drops the closing eye requires;
E'en from the tomb the voice of Nature cries,
  E'en in our ashes live their wonted fires.

For thee who, mindful of the unhonored dead,
  Dost in these lines their artless tale relate;
If chance, by lonely contemplation led,
  Some kindred spirit shall inquire thy fate,—

Haply some hoary-headed swain may say,
  "Oft have we seen him at the peep of dawn
Brushing with hasty steps the dews away,
  To meet the sun upon the upland lawn.

"There at the foot of yonder nodding beech
  That wreathes its old fantastic roots so high,
His listless length at noontide would he stretch,
  And pore upon the brook that babbles by.

"Hard by yon wood, now smiling as in scorn,
  Muttering his wayward fancies he would rove;
Now drooping, woeful-wan, like one forlorn,
  Or crazed with care, or crossed in hopeless love.

"One morn I missed him on the customed hill,
  Along the heath, and near his favorite tree;
Another came; nor yet beside the rill,
  Nor up the lawn, nor at the wood was he;

90. drops: tears.

"The next, with dirges due, in sad array,
  Slow through the church-way path we saw him borne.
Approach and read (for thou canst read) the lay,
  Graved on the stone beneath yon aged thorn."

THE EPITAPH

Here rests his head upon the lap of earth,
  A youth to Fortune and to Fame unknown;
Fair Science frowned not on his humble birth,
  And Melancholy marked him for her own.

Large was his bounty, and his soul sincere;
  Heaven did a recompense as largely send:
He gave to Misery (all he had), a tear;
  He gained from Heaven ('twas all he wished) a friend.

No farther seek his merits to disclose,
  Or draw his frailties from their dread abode,
(There they alike in trembling hope repose,)
  The bosom of his Father and his God.

1751

William Collins

(1721–1759)

All of his friends referred to him as "poor Collins." For this exquisite lyric poet had a radically unhappy life. The son of an impoverished hat-maker, he was able to attend Oxford, wrote verse that poets and general readers have always admired, collapsed mentally in his thirties, and literally wasted away.

The tiny "Ode Written in the Beginning of the Year 1746" was thought by Robert Frost to be the finest poem of its length (twelve lines) in the English language. The "Ode on the Poetical Character"—by far the most "difficult" poem Collins wrote—seemed to Coleridge, who was steeped in the history of English poetry, one of the most powerful and winning poems written since the time of Shakespeare and Milton. The "Ode to Evening," gem-like, suggestive, yet restrained in phrasing, is one of the classic lyrics in English.

Ode Written in the Beginning of the Year 1746

How sleep the brave who sink to rest
By all their country's wishes blest!
When Spring, with dewy fingers cold,
Returns to deck their hallowed mold,
She there shall dress a sweeter sod
Than Fancy's feet have ever trod.

By fairy hands their knell is rung,
By forms unseen their dirge is sung;
There Honor comes, a pilgrim gray,
To bless the turf that wraps their clay,
And Freedom shall awhile repair,
To dwell a weeping hermit there!

1746

Ode on the Poetical Character

1

As once, if not with light regard,
I read aright that gifted bard
(Him whose school above the rest
His loveliest Elfin Queen has blest),
One, only one, unrivaled fair,
Might hope the magic girdle wear,
At solemn tourney hung on high,
The wish of each love-darting eye;
Lo! to each other nymph in turn applied,
As if, in air unseen, some hovering hand,
Some chaste and angel-friend to virgin-fame,
With whispered spell had burst the starting band,
It left unblest her loathed dishonored side;
Happier, hopeless fair, if never
Her baffled hand with vain endeavor
Had touched that fatal zone to her denied!
Young Fancy thus, to me divinest name,
To whom, prepared and bathed in Heaven,
The cest of amplest power is given:
To few the godlike gift assigns,
To gird their blest, prophetic loins,
And gaze her visions wild, and feel unmixed her flame!

ODE ON THE POETICAL CHARACTER. **1–6. As once . . . wear:** Collins refers to Edmund Spenser's *Faerie Queene* (Book IV, Canto V); Florimel's magic belt of chastity could be worn only by a virtuous woman (Amoret). **16. zone:** belt. **19. cest:** belt. **22. gaze:** gaze upon.

2

The band, as fairy legends say,
Was wove on that creating day,
When He who called with thought to birth
Yon tented sky, this laughing earth,
And dressed with springs, and forests tall,
And poured the main engirting all,
Long by the loved enthusiast wooed,
Himself in some diviner mood,
Retiring, sate with her alone,
And placed her on his sapphire throne,
The whiles, the vaulted shrine around,
Seraphic wires were heard to sound,
Now sublimest triumph swelling,
Now on love and mercy dwelling;
And she, from out the veiling cloud,
Breathed her magic notes aloud:
And thou, thou rich-haired Youth of Morn,
And all thy subject life was born!
The dangerous Passions kept aloof,
Far from the sainted growing woof,
But near it sate ecstatic Wonder,
Listening the deep applauding thunder,
And Truth, in sunny vest arrayed,
By whose the tarsel's eyes were made;
All the shadowy tribes of Mind
In braided dance their murmurs joined,
And all the bright uncounted Powers
Who feed on Heaven's ambrosial flowers.
Where is the bard whose soul can now
Its high presuming hopes avow?
Where he who thinks, with rapture blind,
This hallowed work for him designed?

3

High on some cliff, to Heaven up-piled,
Of rude access, of prospect wild,
Where, tangled round the jealous steep,
Strange shades o'erbrow the valley deep,
And holy genii guard the rock,
Its glooms embrown, its springs unlock,
While on its rich ambitious head
An Eden, like his own, lies spread,

29. enthusiast: one inspired by imagination. **39. Youth of Morn:** Apollo, god of the sun, poetry, and music. **42. woof:** threads (of the belt or girdle). **46. tarsel:** falcon. **50. ambrosial:** from "ambrosia" (fabled food of the gods). **54. work:** the sacred girdle or belt of poetry. **59. rock:** Mount Parnassus, home of the Muses.

I view that oak, the fancied glades among,
By which as Milton lay, his evening ear,
From many a cloud that dropped ethereal dew,
Nigh sphered in Heaven its native strains could hear;
On which that ancient trump he reached was hung:
  Thither oft, his glory greeting,
  From Waller's myrtle shades retreating,
With many a vow from Hope's aspiring tongue,
My trembling feet his guiding steps pursue;
  In vain—such bliss to one alone,
  Of all the sons of soul was known,
  And Heaven and Fancy, kindred powers,
  Have now o'erturned the inspiring bowers,
Or curtained close such scene from every future view.

1746

Ode to Evening

If aught of oaten stop, or pastoral song,
May hope, chaste Eve, to soothe thy modest ear,
  Like thy own solemn springs,
  Thy springs and dying gales,
O nymph reserved, while now the bright-haired sun
Sits in yon western tent, whose cloudy skirts,
  With brede ethereal wove,
  O'erhang his wavy bed:
Now air is hushed, save where the weak-eyed bat,
With short shrill shriek flits by on leathern wing,
  Or where the beetle winds
  His small but sullen horn,
As oft he rises 'midst the twilight path,
Against the pilgrim borne in heedless hum:
  Now teach me, maid composed,
  To breathe some softened strain,
Whose numbers, stealing through thy darkening vale,
May not unseemly with its stillness suit,
  As, musing slow, I hail
  Thy genial loved return!
For when thy folding-star arising shows
His paly circlet, at his warning lamp

62. his: Milton's (in the description of Eden in *Paradise Lost*). **69. Waller's myrtle:** Edmund Waller (1606–1687), known for his love poems as contrasted with heroic poems. (Myrtle, sacred to Venus, was the emblem of love.) ODE TO EVENING. **1. oaten stop:** shepherd's reed flute. **7. brede:** embroidery. **14. pilgrim:** wanderer. **17. numbers:** verses. **21. folding-star:** evening star, so called because it was a signal to shepherds to drive their sheep back to the fold.

The fragrant Hours, and elves
Who slept in flowers the day,
And many a nymph who wreaths her brows with sedge,
And sheds the freshening dew, and, lovelier still,
The pensive Pleasures sweet,
Prepare thy shadowy car.
Then lead, calm votaress, where some sheety lake
Cheers the lone heath, or some time-hallowed pile
Or upland fallows gray
Reflect its last cool gleam.
But when chill blustering winds, or driving rain,
Forbid my willing feet, be mine the hut
That from the mountain's side
Views wilds, and swelling floods,
And hamlets brown, and dim-discovered spires,
And hears their simple bell, and marks o'er all
Thy dewy fingers draw
The gradual dusky veil.
While Spring shall pour his showers, as oft he wont,
And bathe thy breathing tresses, meekest Eve;
While Summer loves to sport
Beneath thy lingering light;
While sallow Autumn fills thy lap with leaves;
Or Winter, yelling through the troublous air,
Affrights thy shrinking train,
And rudely rends thy robes;
So long, sure-found beneath the sylvan shed,
Shall Fancy, Friendship, Science, rose-lipped Health,
Thy gentlest influence own,
And hymn thy favorite name!

1748

Oliver Goldsmith

(1730–1774)

The lovable Goldsmith is one of those rare authors who write easily and gracefully in every form. At the start of his career he was a poor Irish boy who had drifted to London. Before he died at forty-four, he had written one of the classic English novels, *The Vicar of*

28. car: chariot. **42. breathing:** fragrant. **49. sylvan shed:** in the shelter of the forest. **50. Science:** knowledge.

Wakefield (1766), two excellent plays, including the famous *She Stoops to Conquer* (1773), numerous magazine essays of every kind, short biographies, and even a readable book about animals. As his friend Samuel Johnson said of him after his death, he "touched nothing that he did not adorn."

"The Deserted Village" was as popular in America for at least a hundred years as it was in England. Many towns in the United States were named "Auburn" after the idyllic village in Goldsmith's poem. In "The Deserted Village" Goldsmith returns to "Sweet Auburn," which he had known as a child, and remembers it as it was. He wrote the poem partly as a protest against new economic policies that were forcing people to leave the agricultural villages for the city in search of work. He is lamenting a society in which the pursuit of riches by powerful men can destroy the simple life of those villages. So moving is the strong nostalgia of the poem that it still captivates readers; modern poets like T. S. Eliot and W. H. Auden, who wrote very different kinds of poetry, have said that they could never forget this poem, which they had read in their younger days. Another reason for the respect that modern poets retain for it is the versification. Goldsmith takes the "heroic couplet" of Dryden and Pope, which they had used in satire and essayistic (or didactic) verse, and gives it a new suppleness and flexibility, with at times a haunting and melodic cadence.

When Lovely Woman Stoops to Folly

When lovely woman stoops to folly,
  And finds too late that men betray,
What charm can soothe her melancholy,
  What art can wash her guilt away?

The only art her guilt to cover,
  To hide her shame from every eye,
To give repentance to her lover,
  And wring his bosom—is to die.

1766

WHEN LOVELY WOMAN STOOPS TO FOLLY. The poem was printed in Goldsmith's novel, *The Vicar of Wakefield* (1766).

The Deserted Village

Sweet Auburn! loveliest village of the plain,
Where health and plenty cheered the laboring swain,
Where smiling spring its earliest visit paid,
And parting summer's lingering blooms delayed;
Dear lovely bowers of innocence and ease,
Seats of my youth, when every sport could please,
How often have I loitered o'er thy green,
Where humble happiness endeared each scene!
How often have I paused on every charm,
The sheltered cot, the cultivated farm,
The never-failing brook, the busy mill,
The decent church that topped the neighboring hill,
The hawthorn bush, with seats beneath the shade,
For talking age and whispering lovers made!
How often have I blessed the coming day,
When toil remitting lent its turn to play,
And all the village train, from labor free,
Led up their sports beneath the spreading tree;
While many a pastime circled in the shade,
The young contending as the old surveyed;
And many a gambol frolicked o'er the ground,
And sleights of art and feats of strength went round;
And still, as each repeated pleasure tired,
Succeeding sports the mirthful band inspired;
The dancing pair that simply sought renown,
By holding out to tire each other down;
The swain mistrustless of his smutted face,
While secret laughter tittered round the place;
The bashful virgin's sidelong looks of love,
The matron's glance that would those looks reprove—
These were thy charms, sweet village! sports like these,
With sweet succession taught even toil to please;
These round thy bowers their cheerful influence shed;
These were thy charms—but all these charms are fled.
  Sweet smiling village, loveliest of the lawn,
Thy sports are fled and all thy charms withdrawn;
Amidst thy bowers the tyrant's hand is seen,
And desolation saddens all thy green;
One only master grasps the whole domain,
And half a tillage stints thy smiling plain;
No more thy glassy brook reflects the day,
But choked with sedges works its weedy way;
Along thy glades, a solitary guest,

THE DESERTED VILLAGE. **10. cot:** cottage. **12. decent:** suitable, becoming. **40. half a tillage:** only half of the land is being tilled now.

The hollow-sounding bittern guards its nest;
Amidst thy desert walks the lapwing flies,
And tires their echoes with unvaried cries.
Sunk are thy bowers in shapeless ruin all,
And the long grass o'ertops the moldering wall;
And, trembling, shrinking from the spoiler's hand,
Far, far away, thy children leave the land.
  Ill fares the land, to hastening ills a prey,
Where wealth accumulates and men decay;
Princes and lords may flourish or may fade;
A breath can make them as a breath has made:
But a bold peasantry, their country's pride,
When once destroyed, can never be supplied.
  A time there was, ere England's griefs began,
When every rood of ground maintained its man;
For him light labor spread her wholesome store,
Just gave what life required, but gave no more:
His best companions, innocence and health;
And his best riches, ignorance of wealth.
  But times are altered; trade's unfeeling train
Usurp the land, and dispossess the swain;
Along the lawn, where scattered hamlets rose,
Unwieldy wealth and cumbrous pomp repose;
And every want to opulence allied,
And every pang that folly pays to pride.
Those gentle hours that plenty bade to bloom,
Those calm desires that asked but little room,
Those healthful sports that graced the peaceful scene,
Lived in each look, and brightened all the green—
These, far departing, seek a kinder shore,
And rural mirth and manners are no more.
  Sweet Auburn! parent of the blissful hour,
Thy glades forlorn confess the tyrant's power.
Here, as I take my solitary rounds
Amidst thy tangling walks and ruined grounds,
And, many a year elapsed, return to view
Where once the cottage stood, the hawthorn grew,
Remembrance wakes with all her busy train,
Swells at my breast, and turns the past to pain.
  In all my wanderings round this world of care,
In all my griefs—and God has given my share—
I still had hopes, my latest hours to crown,
Amidst these humble bowers to lay me down;
To husband out life's taper at the close,
And keep the flame from wasting by repose.
I still had hopes, for pride attends us still,
Amidst the swains to show my book-learned skill,

58. rood: a fourth of an acre.

Around my fire an evening group to draw,
And tell of all I felt, and all I saw;
And, as a hare whom hounds and horns pursue,
Pants to the place from whence at first she flew,
I still had hopes, my long vexations past,
Here to return—and die at home at last.
O blessed retirement, friend to life's decline,
Retreats from care, that never must be mine,
How happy he who crowns in shades like these
A youth of labor with an age of ease;
Who quits a world where strong temptations try,
And, since 'tis hard to combat, learns to fly!
For him no wretches, born to work and weep,
Explore the mine, or tempt the dangerous deep;
No surly porter stands in guilty state,
To spurn imploring famine from the gate;
But on he moves to meet his latter end,
Angels around befriending virtue's friend;
Bends to the grave with unperceived decay,
While resignation gently slopes the way;
And, all his prospects brightening to the last,
His heaven commences ere the world be past.
Sweet was the sound, when oft at evening's close
Up yonder hill the village murmur rose;
There, as I passed with careless steps and slow,
The mingling notes came softened from below;
The swain responsive as the milkmaid sung,
The sober herd that lowed to meet their young,
The noisy geese that gabbled o'er the pool,
The playful children just let loose from school,
The watch-dog's voice that bayed the whispering wind,
And the loud laugh that spoke the vacant mind—
These all in sweet confusion sought the shade,
And filled each pause the nightingale had made.
But now the sounds of population fail,
No cheerful murmurs fluctuate in the gale,
No busy steps the grass-grown footway tread,
For all the bloomy flush of life is fled;
All but yon widowed, solitary thing,
That feebly bends beside the plashy spring;
She, wretched matron, forced in age, for bread,
To strip the brook with mantling cresses spread,
To pick her wintry fagot from the thorn,
To seek her nightly shed, and weep till morn—
She only left of all the harmless train,
The sad historian of the pensive plain.
Near yonder copse, where once the garden smiled,
And still where many a garden flower grows wild,
There, where a few torn shrubs the place disclose,
The village preacher's modest mansion rose.

A man he was to all the country dear,
And passing rich with forty pounds a year;
Remote from towns he ran his godly race,
Nor e'er had changed, nor wished to change his place;
Unpractised he to fawn, or seek for power,
By doctrines fashioned to the varying hour;
Far other aims his heart had learned to prize,
More skilled to raise the wretched than to rise.
His house was known to all the vagrant train;
He chid their wanderings, but relieved their pain;
The long-remembered beggar was his guest,
Whose beard descending swept his aged breast;
The ruined spendthrift, now no longer proud,
Claimed kindred there, and has his claims allowed;
The broken soldier, kindly bade to stay,
Sat by his fire and talked the night away;
Wept o'er his wounds, or, tales of sorrow done,
Shouldered his crutch and showed how fields were won.
Pleased with his guests, the good man learned to glow,
And quite forgot their vices in their woe;
Careless their merits or their faults to scan,
His pity gave ere charity began.
  Thus to relieve the wretched was his pride,
And e'en his failings leaned to virtue's side;
But in his duty prompt at every call,
He watched and wept, he prayed and felt for all:
And, as a bird each fond endearment tries
To tempt its new-fledged offspring to the skies,
He tried each art, reproved each dull delay,
Allured to brighter worlds, and led the way.
  Beside the bed where parting life was laid,
And sorrow, guilt, and pain by turns dismayed,
The reverend champion stood. At his control
Despair and anguish fled the struggling soul;
Comfort came down the trembling wretch to raise,
And his last faltering accents whispered praise.
  At church, with meek and unaffected grace,
His looks adorned the venerable place;
Truth from his lips prevailed with double sway,
And fools who came to scoff remained to pray.
The service past, around the pious man,
With steady zeal, each honest rustic ran;
Even children followed, with endearing wile,
And plucked his gown, to share the good man's smile.
His ready smile a parent's warmth expressed,
Their welfare pleased him and their cares distressed;
To them his heart, his love, his griefs were given,
But all his serious thoughts had rest in Heaven.
As some tall cliff, that lifts its awful form,
Swells from the vale, and midway leaves the storm,

Though round its breast the rolling clouds are spread,
Eternal sunshine settles on its head.
  Beside yon straggling fence that skirts the way,
With blossomed furze unprofitably gay,
There, in his noisy mansion, skilled to rule,
The village master taught his little school.
A man severe he was, and stern to view;
I knew him well, and every truant knew;
Well had the boding tremblers learned to trace
The day's disasters in his morning face;
Full well they laughed with counterfeited glee
At all his jokes, for many a joke had he;
Full well the busy whisper, circling round,
Conveyed the dismal tidings when he frowned;
Yet he was kind, or, if severe in aught,
The love he bore to learning was in fault;
The village all declared how much he knew;
'Twas certain he could write, and cipher too;
Lands he could measure, terms and tides presage,
And even the story ran that he could gauge:
In arguing, too, the parson owned his skill,
For even though vanquished, he could argue still;
While words of learned length and thundering sound
Amazed the gazing rustics ranged around;
And still they gazed, and still the wonder grew
That one small head could carry all he knew.
  But past is all his fame. The very spot
Where many a time he triumphed is forgot.
Near yonder thorn that lifts its head on high,
Where once the sign-post caught the passing eye,
Low lies that house where nut-brown draughts inspired,
Where graybeard mirth and smiling toil retired,
Where village statesmen talked with looks profound,
And news much older than their ale went round.
Imagination fondly stoops to trace
The parlor splendors of that festive place;
The whitewashed wall, the nicely sanded floor,
The varnished clock that clicked behind the door;
The chest contrived a double debt to pay,
A bed by night, a chest of drawers by day;
The pictures placed for ornament and use,
The twelve good rules, the royal game of goose;
The hearth, except when winter chilled the day,
With aspen boughs and flowers and fennel gay;
While broken teacups, wisely kept for show,

209. terms . . . presage: estimate for rents (terms) at particular times (tides). **210. gauge:** calculate contents of barrels and crates. **211. owned:** showed. **232. rules:** of conduct, often hung in inns. **goose:** a game of dice.

Ranged o'er the chimney, glistened in a row.
  Vain transitory splendors! Could not all
Reprieve the tottering mansion from its fall?
Obscure it sinks, nor shall it more impart
An hour's importance to the poor man's heart;
Thither no more the peasant shall repair
To sweet oblivion of his daily care;
No more the farmer's news, the barber's tale,
No more the woodman's ballad shall prevail;
No more the smith his dusky brow shall clear,
Relax his ponderous strength, and lean to hear;
The host himself no longer shall be found
Careful to see the mantling bliss go round;
Nor the coy maid, half willing to be pressed,
Shall kiss the cup to pass it to the rest.
  Yes! let the rich deride, the proud disdain,
These simple blessings of the lowly train;
To me more dear, congenial to my heart,
One native charm, than all the gloss of art;
Spontaneous joys, where nature has its play,
The soul adopts, and owns their first-born sway;
Lightly they frolic o'er the vacant mind,
Unenvied, unmolested, unconfined.
But the long pomp, the midnight masquerade,
With all the freaks of wanton wealth arrayed,—
In these, ere triflers half their wish obtain,
The toiling pleasure sickens into pain;
And e'en while fashion's brightest arts decoy,
The heart distrusting asks if this be joy.
  Ye friends to truth, ye statesmen, who survey
The rich man's joys increase, the poor's decay,
'Tis yours to judge how wide the limits stand
Between a splendid and an happy land.
Proud swells the tide with loads of freighted ore,
And shouting Folly hails them from her shore;
Hoards even beyond the miser's wish abound,
And rich men flock from all the world around.
Yet count our gains: this wealth is but a name
That leaves our useful products still the same.
Not so the loss: the man of wealth and pride
Takes up a space that many poor supplied;
Space for his lake, his park's extended bounds,
Space for his horses, equipage, and hounds;
The robe that wraps his limbs in silken sloth
Has robbed the neighboring fields of half their growth;
His seat, where solitary sports are seen,
Indignant spurns the cottage from the green;

248. bliss: foaming ale.

Around the world each needful product flies,
For all the luxuries the world supplies;
While thus the land, adorned for pleasure all,
In barren splendor feebly waits the fall.
As some fair female, unadorned and plain,
Secure to please while youth confirms her reign,
Slights every borrowed charm that dress supplies,
Nor shares with art the triumph of her eyes;
But when those charms are past, for charms are frail,
When time advances and when lovers fail,
She then shines forth, solicitous to bless,
In all the glaring impotence of dress:
Thus fares the land, by luxury betrayed,
In nature's simplest charms at first arrayed;
But verging to decline, its splendors rise,
Its vistas strike, its palaces surprise;
While, scourged by famine from the smiling land,
The mournful peasant leads his humble band;
And while he sinks, without one arm to save,
The country blooms—a garden and a grave.
Where then, ah! where shall poverty reside,
To 'scape the pressure of contiguous pride?
If to some common's fenceless limits strayed,
He drives his flock to pick the scanty blade,
Those fenceless fields the sons of wealth divide,
And even the bare-worn common is denied.
If to the city sped—what waits him there?
To see profusion that he must not share;
To see ten thousand baneful arts combined
To pamper luxury, and thin mankind;
To see those joys the sons of pleasure know
Extorted from his fellow-creature's woe.
Here while the courtier glitters in brocade,
There the pale artist plies the sickly trade;
Here while the proud their long-drawn pomps display,
There the black gibbet glooms beside the way;
The dome where Pleasure holds her midnight reign,
Here, richly decked, admits the gorgeous train;
Tumultuous grandeur crowds the blazing square,
The rattling chariots clash, the torches glare.
Sure scenes like these no troubles e'er annoy!
Sure these denote one universal joy!
Are these thy serious thoughts?—Ah, turn thine eyes
Where the poor houseless shivering female lies.
She once, perhaps, in village plenty blessed,
Has wept at tales of innocence distressed;
Her modest looks the cottage might adorn,

316. artist: artisan. **318. gibbet:** gallows.

Sweet as the primrose peeps beneath the thorn;
Now lost to all—her friends, her virtue fled—
Near her betrayer's door she lays her head,
And, pinched with cold, and shrinking from the shower,
With heavy heart deplores that luckless hour,
When idly first, ambitious of the town,
She left her wheel and robes of country brown.
  Do thine, sweet Auburn, thine, the loveliest train—
Do thy fair tribes participate her pain?
E'en now, perhaps, by cold and hunger led,
At proud men's doors they ask a little bread.
  Ah, no! To distant climes, a dreary scene,
Where half the convex world intrudes between,
Through torrid tracts with fainting steps they go,
Where wild Altama murmurs to their woe.
Far different there from all that charmed before,
The various terrors of that horrid shore;
Those blazing suns that dart a downward ray,
And fiercely shed intolerable day;
Those matted woods where birds forget to sing,
But silent bats in drowsy clusters cling;
Those poisonous fields with rank luxuriance crowned,
Where the dark scorpion gathers death around;
Where at each step the stranger fears to wake
The rattling terrors of the vengeful snake;
Where crouching tigers wait their hapless prey,
And savage men more murderous still than they;
While oft in whirls the mad tornado flies,
Mingling the ravaged landscape with the skies.
Far different these from every former scene,
The cooling brook, the grassy-vested green,
The breezy covert of the warbling grove,
That only sheltered thefts of harmless love.
  Good Heaven! what sorrows gloomed that parting day
That called them from their native walks away;
When the poor exiles, every pleasure past,
Hung round their bowers, and fondly looked their last,
And took a long farewell, and wished in vain
For seats like these beyond the western main;
And, shuddering still to face the distant deep,
Returned and wept, and still returned to weep.
The good old sire the first prepared to go
To new-found worlds, and wept for others' woe;
But for himself, in conscious virtue brave,
He only wished for worlds beyond the grave.
His lovely daughter, lovelier in her tears,

344. Altama: the Altahama, a river in Georgia, where Goldsmith's friend, General Oglethorpe, had founded a colony. **355. tigers:** pumas or cougars.

The fond companion of his helpless years,
Silent went next, neglected of her charms,
And left a lover's for a father's arms.
With louder plaints the mother spoke her woes,
And blessed the cot where every pleasure rose,
And kissed her thoughtless babes with many a tear,
And clasped them close, in sorrow doubly dear;
Whilst her fond husband strove to lend relief
In all the silent manliness of grief.
  O Luxury! thou cursed by Heaven's decree,
How ill exchanged are things like these for thee!
How do thy potions, with insidious joy,
Diffuse their pleasures only to destroy!
Kingdoms by thee, to sickly greatness grown,
Boast of a florid vigor not their own:
At every draught more large and large they grow,
A bloated mass of rank, unwieldly woe;
Till, sapped their strength, and every part unsound,
Down, down they sink, and spread a ruin round.
  E'en now the devastation is begun,
And half the business of destruction done;
E'en now, methinks, as pondering here I stand,
I see the rural virtues leave the land:
Down where yon anchoring vessel spreads the sail,
That idly waiting flaps with every gale,
Downward they move, a melancholy band,
Pass from the shore, and darken all the strand.
Contented Toil, and hospitable Care,
And kind connubial Tenderness are there;
And Piety with wishes placed above,
And steady Loyalty, and faithful Love.
And thou, sweet Poetry, thou loveliest maid,
Still first to fly where sensual joys invade,
Unfit, in these degenerate times of shame,
To catch the heart, or strike for honest fame;
Dear charming nymph, neglected and decried,
My shame in crowds, my solitary pride;
Thou source of all my bliss and all my woe,
That found'st me poor at first, and keep'st me so;
Thou guide by which the nobler arts excel,
Thou nurse of every virtue, fare thee well!
Farewell! and oh! where'er thy voice be tried,
On Torno's cliffs, or Pambamarca's side,
Whether where equinoctial fervors glow,
Or winter wraps the polar world in snow,
Still let thy voice, prevailing over time,
Redress the rigors of the inclement clime;

418. Torno: Tornio River, in northern Sweden. **Pambamarca:** mountain in Ecuador.

Aid slighted truth with thy persuasive train;
Teach erring man to spurn the rage of gain;
Teach him, that states of native strength possessed,
Though very poor, may still be very blessed;
That trade's proud empire hastes to swift decay,
As ocean sweeps the labored mole away;
While self-dependent power can time defy,
As rocks resist the billows and the sky.

1770

William Cowper

(1731–1800)

A gentle, retiring man who had studied for the law, Cowper (pronounced "Cooper") had a mental breakdown in his early thirties and tried to commit suicide. Nursed back to health by the family of a clergyman, Morley Unwin, he became devoutly religious, and also turned increasingly to poetry. Among his projects were the *Olney Hymns*, named for the village where he lived with the Unwin family; these were hymns written "for the use of plain people." "The Castaway," his last important poem, was based on an actual incident in Richard Walter's *Voyage Round the World* by Admiral George Anson (1748).

from Olney Hymns

Light Shining out of Darkness

God moves in a mysterious way,
  His wonders to perform;
He plants his footsteps in the sea,
  And rides upon the storm.

Deep in unfathomable mines
  Of never failing skill,
He treasures up his bright designs,
  And works his sovereign will.

427–30. The last four lines were written by Samuel Johnson. **428. mole:** breakwater.

Ye fearful saints, fresh courage take,
  The clouds ye so much dread
Are big with mercy, and shall break
  In blessings on your head.

Judge not the Lord by feeble sense,
  But trust him for his grace;
Behind a frowning providence,
  He hides a smiling face.

His purposes will ripen fast,
  Unfolding every hour;
The bud may have a bitter taste,
  But sweet will be the flower.

Blind unbelief is sure to err,
  And scan his work in vain;
God is his own interpreter,
  And he will make it plain.

1779

The Castaway

Obscurest night involved the sky,
  The Atlantic billows roared,
When such a destined wretch as I,
  Washed headlong from on board,
Of friends, of hope, of all bereft,
His floating home forever left.

No braver chief could Albion boast
  Than he with whom he went,
Nor ever ship left Albion's coast,
  With warmer wishes sent.
He loved them both, but both in vain,
Nor him beheld, nor her again.

Not long beneath the whelming brine,
  Expert to swim, he lay;
Nor soon he felt his strength decline,
  Or courage die away;
But waged with death a lasting strife,
Supported by despair of life.

He shouted; nor his friends had failed
  To check the vessel's course,
But so the furious blast prevailed,

THE CASTAWAY. **7. braver chief:** Admiral George Anson, leader of an English expedition against the Spanish. **Albion:** England.

That, pitiless perforce,
They left their outcast mate behind,
And scudded still before the wind.

Some succor yet they could afford;
And, such as storms allow,
The cask, the coop, the floated cord,
Delayed not to bestow.
But he (they knew) nor ship, nor shore,
Whate'er they gave, should visit more.

Nor, cruel as it seemed, could he
Their haste himself condemn,
Aware that flight, in such a sea,
Alone could rescue them;
Yet bitter felt it still to die
Deserted, and his friends so nigh.

He long survives, who lives an hour
In ocean, self-upheld;
And so long he, with unspent power,
His destiny repelled;
And ever, as the minutes flew,
Entreated help, or cried, "Adieu!"

At length, his transient respite past,
His comrades, who before
Had heard his voice in every blast,
Could catch the sound no more.
For then, by toil subdued, he drank
The stifling wave, and then he sank.

No poet wept him; but the page
Of narrative sincere,
That tells his name, his worth, his age,
Is wet with Anson's tear.
And tears by bards or heroes shed
Alike immortalize the dead.

I therefore purpose not, or dream,
Descanting on his fate,
To give the melancholy theme
A more enduring date:
But misery still delights to trace
Its semblance in another's case.

No voice divine the storm allayed,
No light propitious shone,
When, snatched from all effectual aid,

24. scudded: drove along. **27. coop:** basket used in fishing; here used for rescue. **56. Descanting:** commenting.

We perished, each alone;
But I beneath a rougher sea,
And whelmed in deeper gulfs than he.

1803

Philip Freneau

(1752–1832)

Freneau came from a wealthy New York family, and at Princeton he was a college roomate of James Madison, the future President. He spent some years at sea and afterwards worked as a journalist, writing verse in support of the American Revolution. Although during his lifetime he was probably best known for his political works, he is more remembered now for his Romantic nature poems, and in "The Indian Burying Ground" reflects the Romantic interest in primitive life.

The Indian Burying Ground

In spite of all the learned have said,
I still my opinion keep;
The posture, that we give the dead,
Points out the soul's eternal sleep.

Not so the ancients of these lands—
The Indian, when from life released,
Again is seated with his friends,
And shares again the joyous feast.

His imaged birds, and painted bowl,
And venison, for a journey dressed,
Bespeak the nature of the soul,
Activity, that knows no rest.

His bow, for action ready bent,
And arrows, with a head of stone,
Can only mean that life is spent,
And not the old ideas gone.

THE INDIAN BURYING GROUND. **7. seated:** Indians frequently buried the dead in a sitting position.

Thou, stranger, that shalt come this way,
  No fraud upon the dead commit—
Observe the swelling turf, and say
  They do not lie, but here they sit.

Here still a lofty rock remains,
  On which the curious eye may trace
(Now wasted, half, by wearing rains)
  The fancies of a ruder race.

Here still an aged elm aspires,
  Beneath whose far-projecting shade
(And which the shepherd still admires)
  The children of the forest played!

There oft a restless Indian queen
  (Pale Shebah, with her braided hair)
And many a barbarous form is seen
  To chide the man that lingers there.

By midnight moons, o'er moistening dews;
  In habit for the chase arrayed,
The hunter still the deer pursues,
  The hunter and the deer, a shade!

And long shall timorous fancy see
  The painted chief, and pointed spear,
And Reason's self shall bow the knee
  To shadows and delusions herc.

1788

PHILLIS WHEATLEY

(1754–1784)

The first important black poet of America was a woman. Phillis Wheatley was brought as a slave from Africa at the age of seven, was purchased by a wealthy Boston tailor, John Wheatley, and, proving to be brilliant, quickly learned to read and write, studied English poetry, and became fluent in Latin. Her poem on the death of the English preacher, George Whitefield, made her famous. Mrs. Wheatley sent her to England where she visited well-known people. Always frail in health, she died after the birth of her third child at the age of thirty.

On Being Brought from Africa to America

'Twas mercy brought me from my pagan land,
Taught my benighted soul to understand
That there's a God, that there's a Savior too:
Once I redemption neither sought nor knew.
Some view our sable race with scornful eye,
"Their color is a diabolic dye."
Remember, Christians, Negroes, black as Cain,
May be refined, and join the angelic train.

1773

On the Death of the Rev. Mr. George Whitefield, 1770

Hail, happy saint, on thine immortal throne,
Possessed of glory, life, and bliss unknown;
We hear no more the music of thy tongue,
Thy wonted auditories cease to throng.
Thy sermons in unequaled accents flowed,
And every bosom with devotion glowed;
Thou didst in strains of eloquence refined
Inflame the heart, and captivate the mind.
Unhappy we the setting sun deplore,
So glorious once, but ah! it shines no more.

Behold the prophet in his towering flight!
He leaves the earth for heav'n's unmeasured height,
And worlds unknown receive him from our sight.
There Whitefield wings with rapid course his way,
And sails to Zion through vast seas of day.
Thy prayers, great saint, and thine incessant cries
Have pierced the bosom of thy native skies.
Thou moon hast seen, and all the stars of light,
How he has wrestled with his God by night.
He prayed that grace in every heart might dwell,
He longed to see America excel;
He charged its youth that every grace divine

ON BEING BROUGHT FROM AFRICA TO AMERICA. **5. sable:** black. **7. Cain:** sometimes thought to be the ancestor of blacks (see Genesis 4:1–15). ON THE DEATH OF THE REV. GEORGE WHITEFIELD, 1770. **Title:** Whitefield, the most famous revivalist preacher of the eighteenth century, was a follower of John Wesley. He made several trips to America and preached before audiences of 20,000 or more. This was the first poem Wheatley published. **4. wonted:** accustomed. **15. Zion:** city of God. **22. charged:** told.

Should with full luster in their conduct shine;
That Savior, which his soul did first receive,
The greatest gift that ev'n a God can give,
He freely offered to the numerous throng,
That on his lips with listening pleasure hung.

"Take Him, ye wretched, for your only good,
Take Him my dear Americans," he said,
Ye thirsty, come to this life-giving stream,
Ye preachers, take Him for your joyful theme;
Take Him my dear Americans," he said,
"Be your complaints on His kind bosom laid:
Take Him, ye Africans, He longs for you,
Impartial Savior is His title due:
Washed in the fountain of redeeming blood,
You shall be sons, and kings, and priests to God."

Great *Countess*, we Americans revere
Thy name, and mingle in thy grief sincere;
New England deeply feels, the orphans mourn,
Their more than father will no more return.

But, though arrested by the hand of death,
Whitefield no more exerts his laboring breath,
Yet let us view him in the eternal skies,
Let every heart to this bright vision rise;
While the tomb safe retains its sacred trust,
Till life divine re-animates his dust.

1773

William Blake

(1757–1827)

Beginning in his childhood, Blake saw the ordinary world in which we live in a visionary way. In the streets of London or in the fields outside it, he was confident that he could meet and talk with angels and other spirits. Inevitably many of the people who met him thought him mad, however talented. But to Blake it was the world that seemed mad: obsessed with war, scrambling for wealth, hypocritically repressive in the name of "morality," and above all, loveless.

38. Countess: Countess of Huntington, who supported Whitefield. Wheatley later visited her in England.

As soon as he could hold a pencil, he began to show skill as an artist. He was apprenticed to an engraver, studied art at the Royal Academy, set up shop as an engraver, and continued to earn his living in this craft. He usually printed and illustrated his own poems. His early "To the Muses" expresses a theme he was to develop later. In it he protests that the Muses, who in mythology presided over the arts, have deserted them, and that poets now are only mechanical and tired versifiers.

His two great collections of lyrics, *Songs of Innocence* (1789) and *Songs of Experience* (1794), portray, as Blake said in 1794, "the Two Contrary States of the Human Soul." After the initial publications of the two books, he always printed the two collections as one volume, so that the two sets of songs would be read together. "The Lamb," for example, in the *Songs of Innocence* is a counterpart to "The Tyger" in *Songs of Experience.* In "The Lamb" the speaker of the poem (who represents Innocence) believes that the Creator is like the Lamb: "He is meek, & he is mild;/ He became a little child." Thinking of the traditional epithet of Jesus as the Lamb of God, the speaker adds that the Creator was Himself called the Lamb. Is this just the expression of what the human heart wants to believe? Or is Innocence closer to the truth than Experience? Blake's *Songs of Innocence* lead us to ask such questions, but suggest no certain answers. In "The Tyger" of *Songs of Experience,* both the creature and possibly also its Creator represent qualities opposite to the meek lamb. The Creator, who is pictured as a blacksmith, forging the tiger as a smith would forge something from metal, may seem as dreadful as the tiger he creates. The question—did the Creator "smile his work to see?"—refers to the passage in Genesis, in which God, after creating the world, "saw that it was good." To the question, "Did he who made the Lamb make thee," the answer must presumably be "yes," but the speaker of this poem would find it hard to accept either "yes" or "no." If the answer were "yes," the Creator would be the source of something the speaker views as terrible. An answer of "no," however, might imply that there are two Creators. Thus the speaker seems to raise questions to which he can give no answer, and the final stanza simply repeats, though with one change, the words with which the poem begins.

In addition to early lyrics such as "To the Muses" and the *Songs of Innocence and Experience,* Blake wrote a number of narrative poems, some of them quite long. In these he set forth his system of thought in a mythology he himself invented. *The Four Zoas* was one of these so-called "prophetic books." The last of its nine "Nights"—Blake's term for the parts of his poem—has the Last Judgment for its theme, and describes the destruction of the fallen world and the return of existence to the ideal state that Blake called Eternity. The first extract printed here narrates the beginning of the Last Judgment. We also include a pastoral section from the middle of the poem; here a feminine figure called Vala expresses her emotions of joy, gratitude, love, and dependence.

The famous lyric from the Preface to *Milton* (a prophetic book named after the great English epic poet, John Milton) also involves the Biblical theme of the Last Judgment and the coming of the New Jerusalem. The magic of the poem lies partly in the coalescence of the Biblical with the locally familiar; the New Jerusalem of the Biblical book of Revelation will be built in "England's green & pleasant Land." The destruction that accompanies the Last Judgment is conceived as a battle in which the poet will engage—but the battle will take place in the mind ("Mental Fight"). The revolution Blake envisions would transform society, but essentially it would be a revolution in mind and imagination.

Song

How sweet I roam'd from field to field,
  And tasted all the summer's pride,
'Till I the prince of love beheld,
  Who in the sunny beams did glide!

He shew'd me lillies for my hair,
  And blushing roses for my brow;
He led me through his gardens fair,
  Where all his golden pleasures grow.

With sweet May dews my wings were wet,
  And Phoebus fir'd my vocal rage;
He caught me in his silken net,
  And shut me in his golden cage.

He loves to sit and hear me sing,
  Then, laughing, sports and plays with me;
Then stretches out my golden wing,
  And mocks my loss of liberty.

1783

SONG. **10. Phoebus:** Apollo, god of muses, poetry, and the sun.

To the Muses

Whether on Ida's shady brow,
  Or in the chambers of the East,
The chambers of the sun, that now
  From antient melody have ceas'd;

Whether in Heav'n ye wander fair,
  Or the green corners of the earth,
Or the blue regions of the air,
  Where the melodious winds have birth;

Whether on chrystal rocks ye rove,
  Beneath the bosom of the sea
Wand'ring in many a coral grove,
  Fair Nine, forsaking Poetry!

How have you left the antient love
  That bards of old enjoy'd in you!
The languid strings do scarcely move!
  The sound is forc'd, the notes are few!

1783

The Lamb

  Little Lamb, who made thee?
  Dost thou know who made thee?
Gave thee life, & bid thee feed
By the stream & o'er the mead;
Gave thee clothing of delight,
Softest clothing, wooly, bright;
Gave thee such a tender voice,
Making all the vales rejoice?
  Little Lamb, who made thee?
  Dost thou know who made thee?

  Little Lamb, I'll tell thee,
  Little Lamb, I'll tell thee:
He is callèd by thy name,
For He calls himself a Lamb.
He is meek, & he is mild;
He became a little child.
I a child, & thou a lamb,
We are callèd by his name.
  Little Lamb, God bless thee!
  Little Lamb, God bless thee!

1789

TO THE MUSES. **1. Ida:** mountain in Crete. **12. Fair Nine:** the nine Muses.

The Little Black Boy

My mother bore me in the southern wild,
And I am black, but O! my soul is white;
White as an angel is the English child,
But I am black, as if bereav'd of light.

My mother taught me underneath a tree,
And, sitting down before the heat of day,
She took me on her lap and kissed me,
And, pointing to the east, began to say:

"Look on the rising sun: there God does live,
And gives his light, and gives his heat away;
And flowers and trees and beasts and men receive
Comfort in morning, joy in the noonday.

"And we are put on earth a little space,
That we may learn to bear the beams of love;
And these black bodies and this sunburnt face
Is but a cloud, and like a shady grove.

"For when our souls have learn'd the heat to bear,
The cloud will vanish; we shall hear his voice,
Saying: 'Come out from the grove, my love & care,
And round my golden tent like lambs rejoice.'"

Thus did my mother say, and kissed me;
And thus I say to little English boy.
When I from black and he from white cloud free,
And round the tent of God like lambs we joy,

I'll shade him from the heat till he can bear
To lean in joy upon our father's knee;
And then I'll stand and stroke his silver hair,
And be like him, and he will then love me.

1789

The Chimney Sweeper

When my mother died I was very young,
And my father sold me while yet my tongue
Could scarcely cry "'weep! 'weep! 'weep! 'weep!"
So your chimneys I sweep, & in soot I sleep.

There's little Tom Dacre, who cried when his head,
That curl'd like a lamb's back, was shav'd: so I said

THE CHIMNEY SWEEPER. **3. 'weep:** the child's lisping way of uttering his cry, for jobs, as he walks the street—"sweep."

"Hush, Tom! never mind it, for when your head's bare
You know that the soot cannot spoil your white hair."

And so he was quiet, & that very night,
As Tom was a-sleeping, he had such a sight!—
That thousands of sweepers, Dick, Joe, Ned, & Jack,
Were all of them lock'd up in coffins of black.

And by came an Angel who had a bright key,
And he open'd the coffins & set them all free;
Then down a green plain leaping, laughing, they run,
And wash in a river, and shine in the Sun.

Then naked & white, all their bags left behind,
They rise upon clouds and sport in the wind;
And the Angel told Tom, if he'd be a good boy,
He'd have God for his father, & never want joy.

And so Tom awoke; and we rose in the dark,
And got with our bags & our brushes to work.
Tho' the morning was cold, Tom was happy & warm;
So if all do their duty they need not fear harm.

1789

from Songs of Experience

The Tyger

Tyger! Tyger! burning bright
In the forests of the night,
What immortal hand or eye
Could frame thy fearful symmetry?

In what distant deeps or skies
Burnt the fire of thine eyes?
On what wings dare he aspire?
What the hand dare seize the fire?

And what shoulder, & what art,
Could twist the sinews of thy heart?
And when thy heart began to beat,
What dread hand? & what dread feet?

What the hammer? what the chain?
In what furnace was thy brain?
What the anvil? what dread grasp
Dare its deadly terrors clasp?

When the stars threw down their spears,

THE TYGER. **17. stars . . . spears:** What Blake had in mind is unknown and much debated. The stars may be angels throwing down their spears in despair when they see that the tiger has been created.

And water'd heaven with their tears,
Did he smile his work to see?
Did he who made the Lamb make thee?

Tyger! Tyger! burning bright
In the forests of the night,
What immortal hand or eye,
Dare frame thy fearful symmetry?

1794

The Clod and the Pebble

"Love seeketh not Itself to please,
Nor for itself hath any care,
But for another gives its ease,
And builds a Heaven in Hell's despair."

So sung a little Clod of Clay,
Trodden with the cattle's feet,
But a Pebble of the brook
Warbled out these metres meet:

"Love seeketh only Self to please,
To bind another to Its delight,
Joys in another's loss of ease,
And builds a Hell in Heaven's despite."

1794

A Poison Tree

I was angry with my friend:
I told my wrath, my wrath did end.
I was angry with my foe:
I told it not, my wrath did grow.

And I water'd it in fears,
Night & morning with my tears;
And I sunned it with smiles,
And with soft deceitful wiles.

And it grew both day and night,
Till it bore an apple bright;
And my foe beheld it shine,
And he knew that it was mine,

And into my garden stole
When the night had veil'd the pole:
In the morning glad I see
My foe outstretch'd beneath the tree.

1794

The Sick Rose

O Rose, thou art sick!
The invisible worm,
That flies in the night,
In the howling storm,

Has found out thy bed
Of crimson joy,
And his dark secret love
Does thy life destroy.

1794

Ah! Sun-flower

Ah, Sun-flower! weary of time,
Who countest the steps of the Sun,
Seeking after that sweet golden clime
Where the traveller's journey is done:

Where the Youth pined away with desire,
And the pale Virgin shrouded in snow
Arise from their graves, and aspire
Where my Sun-flower wishes to go.

1794

London

I wander thro' each charter'd street,
Near where the charter'd Thames does flow,
And mark in every face I meet
Marks of weakness, marks of woe.

In every cry of every Man,
In every Infant's cry of fear,
In every voice, in every ban,
The mind-forg'd manacles I hear.

How the Chimney-sweeper's cry
Every black'ning Church appalls;
And the hapless Soldier's sigh
Runs in blood down Palace walls.

But most thro' midnight streets I hear
How the youthful Harlot's curse
Blasts the new born Infant's tear,
And blights with plagues the Marriage hearse.

1794

LONDON. **1. charter'd:** owned as private property (through deeds or "charters").

Mock On, Mock On, Voltaire, Rousseau

Mock on, Mock on, Voltaire, Rousseau:
Mock on, Mock on; 'tis all in vain!
You throw the sand against the wind,
And the wind blows it back again.

And every sand becomes a Gem
Reflected in the beams divine;
Blown back they blind the mocking Eye,
But still in Israel's paths they shine.

The Atoms of Democritus
And Newton's Particles of light
Are sands upon the Red sea shore,
Where Israel's tents do shine so bright.

1800–1803

from The Four Zoas

Night the Ninth

Then fell the fires of Eternity with loud & shrill
Sound of Loud Trumpet thundering along from heaven to heaven
A mighty sound articulate: "Awake, ye dead, & come
To Judgment from the four winds! Awake & Come away!"
Folding like scrolls of the Enormous volume of Heaven & Earth,
With thunderous noise & dreadful shakings, rocking to & fro,
The heavens are shaken & the Earth removed from its place,
The foundations of the Eternal hills discover'd:
The thrones of Kings are shaken, they have lost their robes & crowns,
The poor smite their oppressors, they awake up to the harvest,
The naked warriors rush together down to the sea shore
Trembling before the multitudes of slaves now set at liberty:
They are become like wintry flocks, like forests strip'd of leaves:
The oppressed pursue like the wind; there is no room for escape.

. . .

"Rise up, O sun, most glorious minister & light of day.
Flow on, ye gentle airs, & bear the voice of my rejoicing.

MOCK ON, MOCK ON, VOLTAIRE, ROUSSEAU. **1. Voltaire, Rousseau**. Eighteenth-century French philosophers who were, in Blake's opinion, "Deists" (believing God was known not through the Bible but through the ordered structure of the universe) and were, therefore, "mockers" of the faith. **9. Democritus:** Greek philosopher who argued that everything could be reduced to atoms of matter; hence, for Blake, another materialist. **10. Newton's Particles:** Sir Isaac Newton advanced the theory that light consisted of a stream of particles. Blake therefore views him as a materialist. THE FOUR ZOAS. **14–17. scrolls . . . discover'd:** See Revelation 6:14; Isaiah 25:3–4.

Wave freshly, clear waters flowing around the tender grass;
And thou, sweet smelling ground, put forth thy life in fruits & flowers.
Follow me, O my flocks, & hear me sing my rapturous song.
I will cause my voice to be heard on the clouds that glitter in the sun.
I will call; & who shall answer me? I will sing; who shall reply?
For from my pleasant hills behold the living, living springs,
Running among my green pastures, delighting among my trees.
I am not here alone: my flocks, you are my brethren;
And you birds that sing & adorn the sky, you are my sisters.
I sing, & you reply to my song; I rejoice, & you are glad.
Follow me, O my flocks; we will now descend into the valley.
O how delicious are the grapes, flourishing in the sun!
How clear the spring of the rock, running among the golden sand!
How cool the breezes of the valley, & the arms of the branching trees!
Cover us from the sun; come & let us sit in the shade.
My Luvah here hath plac'd me in a sweet & pleasant land,
And given me fruits & pleasant waters, & warm hills & cool valleys.
Here will I build myself a house, & here I'll call on his name,
Here I'll return when I am weary & take my pleasant rest."

So spoke the sinless soul, & laid her head on the downy fleece
Of a curl'd Ram who stretch'd himself in sleep beside his mistress,
And soft sleep fell upon her eyelids in the silent noon of day.

c. 1797–1804

Preface to MILTON

And did those feet in ancient time
Walk upon England's mountains green?
And was the holy Lamb of God
On England's pleasant pastures seen?

And did the Countenance Divine
Shine forth upon our clouded hills?
And was Jerusalem builded here
Among these dark Satanic Mills?

Bring me my Bow of burning gold:
Bring me my Arrows of desire:
Bring me my Spear: O clouds, unfold!
Bring me my Chariot of fire.

PREFACE TO "MILTON." **1. those feet:** the feet of Jesus, who, according to an ancient British legend, had visited England in the company of Joseph of Arimathea. **8. Mills:** Blake's symbol of the mechanistic and materialistic conception of the world, but also a reference to the growing importance of industrialism, especially in the English Midlands.

I will not cease from Mental Fight,
Nor shall my Sword sleep in my hand
Till we have built Jerusalem
In England's green & pleasant Land.

c. 1804

Robert Burns

(1759–1796)

During the period 1750 to 1830, Scotland became one of the world centers of culture—in medicine, science, philosophy, and a brilliant new study of literature and rhetoric. But it also cherished its native traditions, especially the legends, folksongs, and poetry of the Highlands and the Lowlands. This same period saw an immense revival of interest in medieval ballads; many poets, including Burns, wrote in the ballad form.

Scotland's most famous poet also emerged in these years: Robert Burns, the "plow-boy poet," who came from humble beginnings, and who expressed, for Scots everywhere, their feelings and language. Burns speaks immediately to the heart, whether in the high lyric gaiety and lilt of "Green Grow the Rashes" or the simple, stirring pathos of "John Anderson, My Jo" and "O, Wert Thou in the Cauld Blast." For over a century and a half some of Burn's lyrics have been part of the heritage of all English-speaking peoples, especially "Auld Lang Syne," sung throughout the Atlantic world on New Year's Eve.

To a Mouse

On turning her up in her nest with the plough, November, 1785

Wee, sleekit, cow'rin, tim'rous beastie,
O, what a panic's in thy breastie!
Thou need na start awa sae hasty,
            Wi' bickering brattle!
I wad be laith to rin an' chase thee,
            Wi' murd'ring pattle!

TO A MOUSE. **1. sleekit:** sleek. **4. bickering:** hurrying. **brattle:** scamper. **5. laith:** loath, unwilling. **6. pattle:** plowstaff (from "paddle").

I'm truly sorry man's dominion
Has broken Nature's social union,
An' justifies that ill opinion
Which makes thee startle
At me, thy poor earth-born companion,
An' fellow-mortal!

I doubt na, whiles, but thou may thieve;
What then? poor beastie, thou maun live!
A daimen icker in a thrave
'S a sma' request:
I'll get a blessin wi' the lave,
And never miss't!

Thy wee bit housie, too, in ruin!
Its silly wa's the win's are strewin!
An' naething, now, to big a new ane,
O' foggage green!
An' bleak December's winds ensuin,
Baith snell an' keen!

Thou saw the fields laid bare and waste,
An' weary winter comin fast,
An' cozie here, beneath the blast,
Thou thought to dwell,
Till crash! the cruel coulter past
Out thro' thy cell.

That wee bit heap o' leaves an' stibble
Has cost thee mony a weary nibble!
Now thou's turned out, for a' thy trouble,
But house or hald,
To thole the winter's sleety dribble,
An' cranreuch cauld!

But, Mousie, thou art no thy lane,
In proving foresight may be vain:
The best laid schemes o' mice an' men
Gang aft a-gley,
An' lea'e us nought but grief an' pain,
For promised joy.

Still thou art blest, compared wi' me!
The present only toucheth thee:
But och! I backward cast my e'e

13. whiles: sometimes. **14. maun:** must. **15. daimen:** occasional. **icker:** ear of corn. **thrave:** shock. **17. lave:** what is left. **20. silly wa's:** frail walls. **21. big:** build. **22. foggage:** moss. **24. snell:** bitter. **29. coulter:** cutter. **31. stibble:** stubble. **34. but house or hald:** without home or land. **35. thole:** endure. **36. cranreuch:** frost. **40. Gang aft a-gley:** go often awry.

On prospects drear!
An' forward, tho' I canna see,
I guess an' fear!

1786

Green Grow the Rashes

Chorus

Green grow the rashes, O;
Green grow the rashes, O;
The sweetest hours that e'er I spend,
Are spent amang the lasses, O!

There's nought but care on ev'ry han',
In ev'ry hour that passes, O:
What signifies the life o' man,
An' 'twere na for the lasses, O.
(*Chorus*)

The warly race may riches chase,
An' riches still may fly them, O;
An' though at last they catch them fast,
Their hearts can ne'er enjoy them, O.
(*Chorus*)

But gie me a canny hour at e'en,
My arms about my dearie, O;
An' warly cares, an' warly men,
May a' gae tapsalteerie, O!
(*Chorus*)

For you sae douce, ye sneer at this,
Ye're nought but senseless asses, O:
The wisest man the warl' saw,
He dearly loved the lasses, O.
(*Chorus*)

Auld nature swears, the lovely dears
Her noblest work she classes, O:
Her prentice han' she tried on man,
An' then she made the lasses, O.
(*Chorus*)

1787

GREEN GROW THE RASHES. **1. rashes:** rushes. **9. warly:** worldly. **13. canny:** pleasant. **e'en:** evening. **16. tapsalteerie:** topsy-turvy. **17. douce:** sober.

John Anderson, My Jo

John Anderson, my jo, John,
  When we were first acquent,
Your locks were like the raven,
  Your bonnie brow was brent;
But now your brow is beld, John,
  Your locks are like the snow;
But blessings on your frosty pow,
  John Anderson, my jo.

John Anderson, my jo, John,
  We clamb the hill thegither;
And mony a canty day, John,
  We've had wi' ane anither:
Now we maun totter down, John,
  And hand in hand we'll go,
And sleep thegither at the foot,
  John Anderson, my jo.

1790

Auld Lang Syne

Should auld acquaintance be forgot,
  And never brought to min'?
Should auld acquaintance be forgot,
  And days o' lang syne?

Chorus

For auld lang syne, my dear,
  For auld lang syne,
We'll tak a cup o' kindness yet,
  For auld lang syne.

We twa hae run about the braes,
  And pu'd the gowans fine;
But we've wandered mony a weary foot,
  Sin' auld lang syne.

(*Chorus*)

JOHN ANDERSON, MY JO. **1. jo:** joy (beloved one). **4. brent:** straight. **7. pow:** head. **10. clamb:** climbed. **11. canty:** merry. AULD LANG SYNE. **Title:** "Syne" is an old form of the word "since" (meaning originally "from the time past"). Scottish vernacular retains that old form. The title thus means "Old Times Long Since." **9. braes:** slopes. **10. gowans:** daisies. **13. burn:** brook or stream. **14. dine:** dinner time (noon).

We twa hae paidled i' the burn,
  From morning sun till dine;
But seas between us braid hae roared,
  Sin' auld lang syne.
(*Chorus*)

And there's a hand, my trusty fiere,
  And gie's a hand o' thine;
And we'll tak a right gude-willie waught,
  For auld lang syne.
(*Chorus*)

And surely ye'll be your pint-stowp,
  And surely I'll be mine;
And we'll tak a cup o' kindness yet,
  For auld lang syne.
(*Chorus*)

1796

O, Wert Thou in the Cauld Blast

O, wert thou in the cauld blast
  On yonder lea, on yonder lea,
My plaidie to the angry airt,
  I'd shelter thee, I'd shelter thee.
Or did misfortune's bitter storms
  Around thee blaw, around thee blaw,
Thy bield should be my bosom,
  To share it a', to share it a'.

Or were I in the wildest waste,
  Sae black and bare, sae black and bare,
The desert were a paradise,
  If thou wert there, if thou wert there.
Or were I monarch o' the globe,
  Wi' thee to reign, wi' thee to reign,
The brightest jewel in my crown
  Wad be my queen, wad be my queen.

1800

15. braid: broad. **17. fiere:** friend. **19. gude-willie waught:** good strong swallow. **21. be:** pay for. **pint-stowp:** pint mug.

WILLIAM WORDSWORTH

(1770–1850)

Wordsworth grew up in the Lake District of northwest England, a desolate but beautiful region of mountains, lakes, moors, and lonely farms. His deepest emotional experiences as a child took place when he was alone in the natural world. Some of these are described in his autobiographical poem, "The Prelude," in which uncanny memories from boyhood are integrated with philosophical ideas developed in later life. He believed that the Divine exists in the forms of nature and is expressed through them. A child reared in nature senses the presence of the Divine—for example, in the grandeur of the mountains, in the mystery and force of the winds, and in the harmony pervading a landscape—and gradually such natural forms, or the life they express, modify the soul or moral being of the growing child, impressing their character upon it. But this could not happen unless the child were sensitive and imaginative in its response to what it sees and hears in the natural world. The child, in other words, is creative: Through its own imagination it enters into and partially creates the experience to which it responds. Thus from one point of view, nature impresses itself upon the child; from another point of view, the child realizes in nature, as its deeper significance, truths it already possesses. These ideas were not uncommon in Wordsworth's generation (for example, they underlie Coleridge's "Frost at Midnight"), but Wordsworth expressed them with exceptional weight and intensity of feeling, profundity, intimacy, and vividness.

Wordsworth wrote poetry of remarkably different types. Along with the autobiographical and meditative "Prelude," his philosophical poems include two especially famous ones, "Lines Composed a Few Miles Above Tintern Abbey" and "Ode: Intimations of Immortality." "Tintern Abbey," which Wordsworth composed on a walk of four or five days in southwestern England, presents his thoughts and emotions on returning to a particular landscape for a second time. (Wordsworth mentions the medieval Tintern Abbey in the title in order to specify his vantage point—the scenic view over the valley of the river Wye from "A Few Miles Above Tintern Abbey," which was famous for its beauty.) The poem is an impassioned meditation on what this particular landscape has meant to him over the five years since he first saw it (in 1793); more generally, the poem describes his changing relationship but continuing indebtedness to nature through all his past life. Although the poem does not tell us this, we know from other sources that five years before, when Wordsworth first came to this place, he had been in a state of extreme emotional self-conflict and perhaps of psychological breakdown. He attributed his gradual recovery in part to the quiet influence of nature, and these personal circumstances underlie his emotion in the opening lines of the poem.

The "Ode: Intimations of Immortality" is an immensely powerful expression of Romantic transcendentalism, the belief that ultimate reality lies beyond the world we experience with our senses. With this theme Wordsworth typically integrates his concern (also present in "The Prelude" and in "Tintern Abbey") with changes in our imaginative life as we grow older. Although the visionary experiences of childhood do not recur in later life, Wordsworth regrets and weighs their loss against the power of conscious reflection (the "philosophic mind") that comes with maturity. The first four stanzas of the poem were written in 1802; the rest of the poem was composed two years later.

Apparently simple lyrics such as "She Dwelt Among the Untrodden Ways" and "A Slumber Did My Spirit Seal" illustrate a different side of Wordsworth's genius. In them Wordsworth fulfills, in considerable degree, the ideals of style he announced in the Preface to the Second Edition (1800) of the *Lyrical Ballads*, a famous volume jointly composed by Wordsworth and his friend Coleridge. In this Preface, Wordsworth attacked unnatural diction in the poetry of the eighteenth century, and argued that the sentiments expressed in this poetry were equally artificial. Poetry, he said, should voice elementary human feelings in words someone might actually speak. This natural language and emotion could best be "contemplated," Wordsworth said, in "humble and rustic" persons and ways of life.

Finally, in a number of sonnets composed in 1802, and in numerous other poems as well, Wordsworth addresses patriotic and public subjects. Here his style, though still personal and emotional, comes closer to that of public speech or even of oratory. The sonnets of 1802 were greatly influenced, in the handling of the form and in subject matter and emotion, by the sonnets of Milton. In its high-minded confidence that nature itself will forever inspire and "work for" the cause of liberty, and that this must eventually prevail, the sonnet "To Toussaint L'Ouverture" is typical of Romantic political idealism. If a modern poet wrote on this subject, the emotion would probably be less assured.

Lines written in Early Spring

I heard a thousand blended notes,
While in a grove I sate reclined,
In that sweet mood when pleasant thoughts
Bring sad thoughts to the mind.

To her fair works did Nature link
The human soul that through me ran;
And much it grieved my heart to think
What man has made of man.

Through primrose tufts, in that green bower,
The periwinkle trailed its wreaths;
And 'tis my faith that every flower
Enjoys the air it breathes.

The birds around me hopped and played,
Their thoughts I cannot measure:—
But the least motion which they made,
It seemed a thrill of pleasure.

The budding twigs spread our their fan,
To catch the breezy air;
And I must think, do all I can,
That there was pleasure there.

If this belief from heaven be sent,
If such be Nature's holy plan,
Have I not reason to lament
What man has made of man?

1798

Lines

Composed a few miles above Tintern Abbey, on revisiting the banks of the Wye during a tour. July 13, 1798

Five years have passed; five summers, with the length
Of five long winters! and again I hear
These waters, rolling from their mountain-springs
With a soft inland murmur. Once again
Do I behold these steep and lofty cliffs,
That on a wild secluded scene impress

LINES WRITTEN IN EARLY SPRING. **10. periwinkle:** evergreen plant with small blue flowers.
LINES . . . TINTERN ABBEY. **Title:** Tintern Abbey is the ruin of a former abbey in Monmouthshire.

Thoughts of more deep seclusion; and connect
The landscape with the quiet of the sky.
The day is come when I again repose
Here, under this dark sycamore, and view
These plots of cottage ground, these orchard tufts,
Which at this season, with their unripe fruits,
Are clad in one green hue, and lose themselves
'Mid groves and copses. Once again I see
These hedgerows, hardly hedgerows, little lines
Of sportive wood run wild; these pastoral farms,
Green to the very door; and wreaths of smoke
Sent up, in silence, from among the trees!
With some uncertain notice, as might seem
Of vagrant dwellers in the houseless woods,
Or of some Hermit's cave, where by his fire
The Hermit sits alone.
These beauteous forms,
Through a long absence, have not been to me
As is a landscape to a blind man's eye;
But oft, in lonely rooms, and 'mid the din
Of towns and cities, I have owed to them,
In hours of weariness, sensations sweet,
Felt in the blood, and felt along the heart;
And passing even into my purer mind,
With tranquil restoration—feelings too
Of unremembered pleasure; such, perhaps,
As have no slight or trivial influence
On that best portion of a good man's life,
His little, nameless, unremembered acts
Of kindness and of love. Nor less, I trust,
To them I may have owed another gift,
Of aspect more sublime; that blessed mood,
In which the burthen of the mystery,
In which the heavy and the weary weight
Of all this unintelligible world,
Is lightened—that serene and blessed mood,
In which the affections gently lead us on—
Until, the breath of this corporeal frame
And even the motion of our human blood
Almost suspended, we are laid asleep
In body, and become a living soul;
While with an eye made quiet by the power
Of harmony, and the deep power of joy,
We see into the life of things.
If this
Be but a vain belief, yet, oh! how oft—
In darkness and amid the many shapes
Of joyless daylight; when the fretful stir
Unprofitable, and the fever of the world,
Have hung upon the beatings of my heart—

How oft, in spirit, have I turned to thee,
O sylvan Wye! thou wanderer through the woods,
How often has my spirit turned to thee!
And now, with gleams of half-extinguished thought,
With many recognitions dim and faint,
And somewhat of a sad perplexity,
The picture of the mind revives again;
While here I stand, not only with the sense
Of present pleasure, but with pleasing thoughts
That in this moment there is life and food
For future years. And so I dare to hope,
Though changed, no doubt, from what I was when first
I came among these hills; when like a roe
I bounded o'er the mountains, by the sides
Of the deep rivers, and the lonely streams,
Wherever nature led—more like a man
Flying from something that he dreads than one
Who sought the thing he loved. For nature then
(The coarser pleasures of my boyish days,
And their glad animal movements all gone by)
To me was all in all.—I cannot paint
What then I was. The sounding cataract
Haunted me like a passion; the tall rock,
The mountain, and the deep and gloomy wood,
Their colors and their forms, were then to me
An appetite; a feeling and a love,
That had no need of a remoter charm,
By thought supplied, nor any interest
Unborrowed from the eye.—That time is past,
And all its aching joys are now no more,
And all its dizzy raptures. Not for this
Faint I, nor mourn nor murmur; other gifts
Have followed; for such loss, I would believe,
Abundant recompense. For I have learned
To look on nature, not as in the hour
Of thoughtless youth; but hearing oftentimes
The still, sad music of humanity,
Nor harsh nor grating, though of ample power
To chasten and subdue. And I have felt
A presence that disturbs me with the joy
Of elevated thoughts; a sense sublime
Of something far more deeply interfused,
Whose dwelling is the light of setting suns,
And the round ocean and the living air,
And the blue sky, and in the mind of man:
A motion and a spirit, that impels
All thinking things, all objects of all thought,

86. Faint: lose courage.

And rolls through all things. Therefore am I still
A lover of the meadows and the woods,
And mountains; and of all that we behold
From this green earth; of all the mighty world
Of eye, and ear—both what they half create,
And what perceive; well pleased to recognize
In nature and the language of the sense
The anchor of my purest thoughts, the nurse,
The guide, the guardian of my heart, and soul
Of all my moral being.
Nor perchance,
If I were not thus taught, should I the more
Suffer my genial spirits to decay:
For thou art with me here upon the banks
Of this fair river; thou my dearest Friend,
My dear, dear Friend; and in thy voice I catch
The language of my former heart, and read
My former pleasures in the shooting lights
Of thy wild eyes. Oh! yet a little while
May I behold in thee what I was once,
My dear, dear Sister! and this prayer I make,
Knowing that Nature never did betray
The heart that loved her; 'tis her privilege,
Through all the years of this our life, to lead
From joy to joy: for she can so inform
The mind that is within us, so impress
With quietness and beauty, and so feed
With lofty thoughts, that neither evil tongues,
Rash judgments, nor the sneers of selfish men,
Nor greetings where no kindness is, nor all
The dreary intercourse of daily life,
Shall e'er prevail against us, or disturb
Our cheerful faith, that all which we behold
Is full of blessings. Therefore let the moon
Shine on thee in thy solitary walk;
And let the misty mountain winds be free
To blow against thee: and, in after years,
When these wild ecstasies shall be matured
Into a sober pleasure; when thy mind
Shall be a mansion for all lovely forms,
Thy memory be as a dwelling place
For all sweet sounds and harmonies; oh! then,
If solitude, or fear, or pain, or grief
Should be thy portion, with what healing thoughts
Of tender joy wilt thou remember me,
And these my exhortations! Nor, perchance—

113. genial: inborn and enlivening. **115. fair river:** the Wye. **116. Friend:** his sister, Dorothy Wordsworth.

If I should be where I no more can hear
Thy voice, nor catch from thy wild eyes these gleams
Of past existence—wilt thou then forget
That on the banks of this delightful stream
We stood together; and that I, so long
A worshiper of Nature, hither came
Unwearied in that service; rather say
With warmer love—oh! with far deeper zeal
Of holier love. Nor wilt thou then forget
That after many wanderings, many years
Of absence, these steep woods and lofty cliffs,
And this green pastoral landscape, were to me
More dear, both for themselves and for thy sake!

1798

from The Prelude

Book I

Fair seedtime had my soul, and I grew up
Fostered alike by beauty and by fear:
Much favored in my birthplace, and no less
In that belovèd Vale to which erelong
We were transplanted—there were we let loose
For sports of wider range. Ere I had told
Ten birthdays, when among the mountain slopes
Frost, and the breath of frosty wind, had snapped
The last autumnal crocus, 'twas my joy
With store of springes o'er my shoulder hung
To range the open heights where woodcocks run
Along the smooth green turf. Through half the night,
Scudding away from snare to snare, I plied
That anxious visitation—moon and stars
Were shining o'er my head. I was alone,
And seemed to be a trouble to the peace
That dwelt among them. Sometimes it befell
In these night wanderings, that a strong desire
O'erpowered my better reason, and the bird
Which was the captive of another's toil
Became my prey; and when the deed was done
I heard among the solitary hills

THE PRELUDE, BOOK I. **304. Vale:** valley; Esthwaite, at the head of the lake is Hawkshead, where Wordsworth had attended school. **310. springes:** snares for birds and small animals. **313. scudding:** moving swiftly, as if blown by the wind.

Low breathings coming after me, and sounds
Of undistinguishable motion, steps
Almost as silent as the turf they trod.

Nor less, when spring had warmed the cultured Vale,
Moved we as plunderers where the mother bird
Had in high places built her lodge; though mean
Our object and inglorious, yet the end
Was not ignoble. Oh! when I have hung
Above the raven's nest, by knots of grass
And half-inch fissures in the slippery rock
But ill sustained, and almost (so it seemed)
Suspended by the blast that blew amain,
Shouldering the naked crag, oh, at that time
While on the perilous ridge I hung alone,
With what strange utterance did the loud dry wind
Blow through my ear! the sky seemed not a sky
Of earth—and with what motion moved the clouds!

Dust as we are, the immortal spirit grows
Like harmony in music; there is a dark
Inscrutable workmanship that reconciles
Discordant elements, makes them cling together
In one society. How strange that all
The terrors, pains, and early miseries,
Regrets, vexations, lassitudes interfused
Within my mind, should e'er have borne a part,
And that a needful part, in making up
The calm existence that is mine when I
Am worthy of myself! Praise to the end!
Thanks to the means which Nature deigned to employ;
Whether her fearless visitings, or those
That came with soft alarm, like hurtless light
Opening the peaceful clouds; or she may use
Severer interventions, ministry
More palpable, as best might suit her aim.

One summer evening (led by her) I found
A little boat tied to a willow tree
Within a rocky cave, its usual home.
Straight I unloosed her chain, and stepping in
Pushed from the shore. It was an act of stealth
And troubled pleasure, nor without the voice
Of mountain echoes did my boat move on;
Leaving behind her still, on either side,
Small circles glittering idly in the moon,
Until they melted all into one track
Of sparkling light. But now, like one who rows,
Proud of his skill, to reach a chosen point
With an unswerving line, I fixed my view
Upon the summit of a craggy ridge,

The horizon's utmost boundary; for above
Was nothing but the stars and the gray sky.
She was an elfin pinnace; lustily
I dipped my oars into the silent lake,
And, as I rose upon the stroke, my boat
Went heaving through the water like a swan;
When, from behind that craggy steep till then
The horizon's bound, a huge peak, black and huge,
As if with voluntary power instinct,
Upreared its head. I struck and struck again,
And growing still in stature the grim shape
Towered up between me and the stars, and still,
For so it seemed, with purpose of its own
And measured motion like a living thing,
Strode after me. With trembling oars I turned,
And through the silent water stole my way
Back to the covert of the willow tree;
There in her mooring place I left my bark,
And through the meadows homeward went, in grave
And serious mood; but after I had seen
That spectacle, for many days, my brain
Worked with a dim and undetermined sense
Of unknown modes of being; o'er my thoughts
There hung a darkness, call it solitude
Or blank desertion. No familiar shapes
Remained, no pleasant images of trees,
Of sea or sky, no colors of green fields;
But huge and mighty forms, that do not live
Like living men, moved slowly through the mind
By day, and were a trouble to my dreams.

Wisdom and Spirit of the universe!
Thou Soul that art the eternity of thought,
That givest to forms and images a breath
And everlasting motion, not in vain
By day or starlight thus from my first dawn
Of childhood didst thou intertwine for me
The passions that build up our human soul;
Not with the mean and vulgar works of man,
But with high objects, with enduring things—
With life and nature—purifying thus
The elements of feeling and of thought,
And sanctifying, by such discipline,
Both pain and fear, until we recognize
A grandeur in the beating of the heart.

373. pinnace: small sailboat. **378–80. peak . . . Upreared:** He faces the shore of the lake as he rows. While he is close to the shore, a cliff hides the higher hills behind it. As he moves out into the lake, this distance permits him to see over this cliff and the huge peak beyond it emerges.

Nor was this fellowship vouchsafed to me
With stinted kindness. In November days,
When vapors rolling down the valley made
A lonely scene more lonesome, among woods,
At noon and 'mid the calm of summer nights,
When, by the margin of the trembling lake,
Beneath the gloomy hills homeward I went
In solitude, such intercourse was mine;
Mine was it in the fields both day and night,
And by the waters, all the summer long.

And in the frosty season, when the sun
Was set, and visible for many a mile
The cottage windows blazed through twilight gloom,
I heeded not their summons: happy time
It was indeed for all of us—for me
It was a time of rapture! Clear and loud
The village clock tolled six—I wheeled about,
Proud and exulting like an untired horse
That cares not for his home. All shod with steel,
We hissed along the polished ice in games
Confederate, imitative of the chase
And woodland pleasures—the resounding horn,
The pack loud chiming, and the hunted hare.
So through the darkness and the cold we flew,
And not a voice was idle; with the din
Smitten, the precipices rang aloud;
The leafless trees and every icy crag
Tinkled like iron; while far distant hills
Into the tumult sent an alien sound
Of melancholy not unnoticed, while the stars
Eastward were sparkling clear, and in the west
The orange sky of evening died away.
Not seldom from the uproar I retired
Into a silent bay, or sportively
Glanced sideway, leaving the tumultuous throng,
To cut across the reflex of a star
That fled, and, flying still before me, gleamed
Upon the glassy plain; and oftentimes,
When we had given our bodies to the wind,
And all the shadowy banks on either side
Came sweeping through the darkness, spinning still
The rapid line of motion, then at once
Have I, reclining back upon my heels,
Stopped short; yet still the solitary cliffs
Wheeled by me—even as if the earth had rolled
With visible motion her diurnal round!

450. reflex: reflection.

Behind me did they stretch in solemn train,
Feebler and feebler, and I stood and watched
Till all was tranquil as a dreamless sleep.

Book VI

The only track now visible was one
That from the torrent's further brink held forth
Conspicuous invitation to ascend
A lofty mountain. After brief delay
Crossing the unbridged stream, that road we took,
And clomb with eagerness, till anxious fears
Intruded, for we failed to overtake
Our comrades gone before. By fortunate chance,
While every moment added doubt to doubt,
A peasant met us, from whose mouth we learned
That to the spot which had perplexed us first
We must descend, and there should find the road,
Which in the stony channel of the stream
Lay a few steps, and then along its banks;
And, that our future course, all plain to sight,
Was downwards, with the current of that stream.
Loth to believe what we so grieved to hear,
For still we had hopes that pointed to the clouds,
We questioned him again, and yet again;
But every word that from the peasant's lips
Came in reply, translated by our feelings,
Ended in this,—*that we had crossed the Alps.*

Imagination—here the Power so called
Through sad incompetence of human speech,
That awful Power rose from the mind's abyss
Like an unfathered vapour that enwraps,
At once, some lonely traveller. I was lost;
Halted without an effort to break through;
But to my conscious soul I now can say—
"I recognise thy glory:" in such strength
Of usurpation, when the light of sense
Goes out, but with a flash that has revealed
The invisible world, doth greatness make abode,
There harbours whether we be young or old.
Our destiny, our being's heart and home,
Is with infinitude, and only there;
With hope it is, hope that can never die,
Effort, and expectation, and desire,
And something evermore about to be.

BOOK VI. **592–616. Imagination . . . plain:** The imaginative insight expressed here arose not while Wordsworth was actually crossing the Alps but fourteen years later, as he was writing the poem.

Under such banners militant, the soul
Seeks for no trophies, struggles for no spoils
That may attest her prowess, blest in thoughts
That are their own perfection and reward,
Strong in herself and in beatitude
That hides her, like the mighty flood of Nile
Poured from his fount of Abyssinian clouds
To fertilise the whole Egyptian plain.

She Dwelt Among the Untrodden Ways

She dwelt among the untrodden ways
  Beside the springs of Dove,
A Maid whom there were none to praise
  And very few to love;

A violet by a mossy stone
  Half hidden from the eye!
—Fair as a star, when only one
  Is shining in the sky.

She lived unknown, and few could know
  When Lucy ceased to be;
But she is in her grave, and, oh,
  The difference to me!

1800

A Slumber Did My Spirit Seal

A slumber did my spirit seal;
  I had no human fears:
She seemed a thing that could not feel
  The touch of earthly years.

No motion has she now, no force;
  She neither hears nor sees;
Rolled round in earth's diurnal course,
  With rocks, and stones, and trees.

1800

A SLUMBER DID MY SPIRIT SEAL. **7. diurnal:** daily.

To Toussaint L'Ouverture

Toussaint, the most unhappy man of men!
Whether the whistling Rustic tend his plough
Within thy hearing, or thy head be now
Pillowed in some deep dungeon's earless den;—
O miserable Chieftain! where and when
Wilt thou find patience! Yet die not; do thou
Wear rather in thy bonds a cheerful brow:
Though fallen thyself, never to rise again,
Live, and take comfort. Thou hast left behind
Powers that will work for thee; air, earth, and skies;
There's not a breathing of the common wind
That will forget thee; thou hast great allies;
Thy friends are exultations, agonies,
And love, and man's unconquerable mind.

1803

My Heart Leaps up When I Behold

My heart leaps up when I behold
  A rainbow in the sky:
So was it when my life began;
So is it now I am a man;
So be it when I shall grow old,
  Or let me die!
The Child is father of the Man;
And I could wish my days to be
Bound each to each by natural piety.

1807

Ode

Intimations of immortality from recollections of early childhood

The Child is father of the Man;
And I could wish my days to be
Bound each to each by natural piety.

TO TOUSSAINT L'OUVERTURE. **Title:** Toussaint L'Ouverture was leader of the struggle of Haiti for independence from France. He was captured, held in prison (at the time of this sonnet), and died there a year later.

1

There was a time when meadow, grove, and stream,
The earth, and every common sight,
        To me did seem
    Appareled in celestial light,
The glory and the freshness of a dream.
It is not now as it hath been of yore—
        Turn whereso'er I may,
          By night or day,
The things which I have seen I now can see no more.

2

        The Rainbow comes and goes,
        And lovely is the Rose,
        The Moon doth with delight
Look round her when the heavens are bare,
        Waters on a starry night
        Are beautiful and fair;
  The sunshine is a glorious birth;
  But yet I know, where'er I go,
That there hath passed away a glory from the earth.

3

Now, while the birds thus sing a joyous song,
  And while the young lambs bound
        As to the tabor's sound,
To me alone there came a thought of grief:
A timely utterance gave that thought relief,
        And I again am strong:
The cataracts blow their trumpets from the steep;
No more shall grief of mine the season wrong;
I hear the Echoes through the mountains throng,
The Winds come to me from the fields of sleep,
        And all the earth is gay;
            Land and sea
      Give themselves up to jollity,
        And with the heart of May
      Doth every Beast keep holiday—
        Thou Child of Joy,
Shout round me, let me hear thy shouts, thou happy
        Shepherd-boy!

ODE: INTIMATIONS OF IMMORTALITY. **21. tabor:** small drum often used to accompany a pipe.

4

Ye blessèd Creatures, I have heard the call
Ye to each other make; I see
The heavens laugh with you in your jubilee;
My heart is at your festival,
My head hath its coronal,
The fullness of your bliss, I feel—I feel it all.
Oh, evil day! if I were sullen
While Earth herself is adorning,
This sweet May morning,
And the Children are culling
On every side,
In a thousand valleys far and wide,
Fresh flowers; while the sun shines warm,
And the Babe leaps up on his Mother's arm—
I hear, I hear, with joy I hear!
—But there's a Tree, of many, one,
A single Field which I have looked upon,
Both of them speak of something that is gone:
The Pansy at my feet
Doth the same tale repeat:
Whither is fled the visionary gleam?
Where is it now, the glory and the dream?

5

Our birth is but a sleep and a forgetting:
The Soul that rises with us, our life's Star,
Hath had elsewhere its setting,
And cometh from afar:
Not in entire forgetfulness,
And not in utter nakedness,
But trailing clouds of glory do we come
From God, who is our home:
Heaven lies about us in our infancy!
Shades of the prison-house begin to close
Upon the growing Boy,
But he
Beholds the light, and whence it flows,
He sees it in his joy;
The Youth, who daily farther from the east
Must travel, still is Nature's Priest,
And by the vision splendid
Is on his way attended;
At length the Man perceives it die away,
And fade into the light of common day.

40. coronal: crown of flowers worn by shepherds in pastoral poetry.

6

Earth fills her lap with pleasures of her own;
Yearnings she hath in her own natural kind,
And, even with something of a Mother's mind,
And no unworthy aim,
The homely Nurse doth all she can
To make her foster child, her Inmate Man,
Forget the glories he hath known,
And that imperial palace whence he came.

7

Behold the Child among his newborn blisses,
A six-years' Darling of a pygmy size!
See, where 'mid work of his own hand he lies,
Fretted by sallies of his mother's kisses,
With light upon him from his father's eyes!
See, at his feet, some little plan or chart,
Some fragment from his dream of human life,
Shaped by himself with newly-learnèd art;
A wedding or a festival,
A mourning or a funeral;
And this hath now his heart,
And unto this he frames his song;
Then will he fit his tongue
To dialogues of business, love, or strife;
But it will not be long
Ere this be thrown aside,
And with new joy and pride
The little Actor cons another part;
Filling from time to time his "humorous stage"
With all the Persons, down to palsied Age,
That Life brings with her in her equipage;
As if his whole vocation
Were endless imitation.

8

Thou, whose exterior semblance doth belie
Thy Soul's immensity;
Thou best Philosopher, who yet dost keep
Thy heritage, thou Eye among the blind,
That, deaf and silent, read'st the eternal deep,
Haunted forever by the eternal mind—
Mighty Prophet! Seer blest!
On whom those truths do rest,
Which we are toiling all our lives to find,

104. "humorous stage": quoted from the Elizabethan poet Samuel Daniel, in the dedication of his *Musophilus* (1599).

In darkness lost, the darkness of the grave;
Thou, over whom thy Immortality
Broods like the Day, a Master o'er a Slave,
A Presence which is not to be put by;
Thou little Child, yet glorious in the might
Of heaven-born freedom on thy being's height,
Why with such earnest pains dost thou provoke
The years to bring the inevitable yoke,
Thus blindly with thy blessedness at strife?
Full soon thy Soul shall have her earthly freight,
And custom lie upon thee with a weight,
Heavy as frost, and deep almost as life!

9

O joy! that in our embers
Is something that doth live,
That nature yet remembers
What was so fugitive!
The thought of our past years in me doth breed
Perpetual benediction: not indeed
For that which is most worthy to be blest;
Delight and liberty, the simple creed
Of Childhood, whether busy or at rest,
With new-fledged hope still fluttering in his breast—
Not for these I raise
The song of thanks and praise;
But for those obstinate questionings
Of sense and outward things,
Fallings from us, vanishings;
Blank misgivings of a Creature
Moving about in worlds not realized,
High instincts before which our mortal Nature
Did tremble like a guilty Thing surprised;
But for those first affections,
Those shadowy recollections,
Which, be they what they may,
Are yet the fountain light of all our day,
Are yet a master light of all our seeing;
Uphold us, cherish, and have power to make
Our noisy years seem moments in the being
Of the eternal Silence: truths that wake,
To perish never;
Which neither listlessness, nor mad endeavor,
Nor Man nor Boy,
Nor all that is at enmity with joy,
Can utterly abolish or destroy!
Hence in a season of calm weather
Though inland far we be,

Our Souls have sight of that immortal sea
Which brought us hither,
Can in a moment travel thither,
And see the Children sport upon the shore,
And hear the mighty waters rolling evermore.

10

Then sing, ye Birds, sing, sing a joyous song!
And let the young Lambs bound
As to the tabor's sound!
We in thought will join your throng,
Ye that pipe and ye that play,
Ye that through your hearts today
Feel the gladness of the May!
What though the radiance which was once so bright
Be now forever taken from my sight,
Though nothing can bring back the hour
Of splendor in the grass, of glory in the flower;
We will grieve not, rather find
Strength in what remains behind;
In the primal sympathy
Which having been must ever be;
In soothing thoughts that spring
Out of human suffering;
In the faith that looks through death,
In years that bring the philosophic mind.

11

And O, ye Fountains, Meadows, Hills, and Groves,
Forebode not any severing of our loves!
Yet in my heart of hearts I feel your might;
I only have relinquished one delight
To live beneath your more habitual sway.
I love the Brooks which down their channels fret,
Even more than when I tripped lightly as they;
The innocent brightness of a new-born Day
Is lovely yet;
The clouds that gather round the setting sun
Do take a sober coloring from an eye
That hath kept watch o'er man's mortality;
Another race hath been, and other palms are won.
Thanks to the human heart by which we live,
Thanks to its tenderness, its joys, and fears,
To me the meanest flower that blows can give
Thoughts that do often lie too deep for tears.

1807

It Is a Beauteous Evening, Calm and Free

It is a beauteous evening, calm and free,
The holy time is quiet as a Nun
Breathless with adoration; the broad sun
Is sinking down in its tranquility;
The gentleness of heaven broods o'er the Sea:
Listen! the mighty Being is awake,
And doth with his eternal motion make
A sound like thunder—everlastingly.
Dear Child! dear Girl! that walkest with me here,
If thou appear untouched by solemn thought,
Thy nature is not therefore less divine:
Thou liest in Abraham's bosom all the year,
And worship'st at the Temple's inner shrine,
God being with thee when we know it not.

1807

Composed upon Westminster Bridge, September 3, 1802

Earth has not anything to show more fair:
Dull would he be of soul who could pass by
A sight so touching in its majesty;
This City now doth, like a garment, wear
The beauty of the morning; silent, bare,
Ships, towers, domes, theaters, and temples lie
Open unto the fields, and to the sky;
All bright and glittering in the smokeless air.
Never did sun more beautifully steep
In his first splendor, valley, rock, or hill;
Ne'er saw I, never felt, a calm so deep!
The river glideth at his own sweet will:
Dear God! the very houses seem asleep;
And all that mighty heart is lying still!

1807

IT IS A BEAUTEOUS EVENING. **12. Abraham's bosom:** a place near heaven where the souls of the blest go before their final vision of God (*see* Luke 16:19–31); used more generally for a state of happiness in the other world.

London, 1802

Milton! thou shouldst be living at this hour:
England hath need of thee: she is a fen
Of stagnant waters: altar, sword, and pen,
Fireside, the heroic wealth of hall and bower,
Have forfeited their ancient English dower
Of inward happiness. We are selfish men;
Oh! raise us up, return to us again;
And give us manners, virtue, freedom, power.
Thy soul was like a Star, and dwelt apart;
Thou hadst a voice whose sound was like the sea:
Pure as the naked heavens, majestic, free,
So didst thou travel on life's common way,
In cheerful godliness; and yet thy heart
The lowliest duties on herself did lay.

1807

The World Is Too Much with Us; Late and Soon

The world is too much with us; late and soon,
Getting and spending, we lay waste our powers;
Little we see in Nature that is ours;
We have given our hearts away, a sordid boon!
This Sea that bares her bosom to the moon,
The winds that will be howling at all hours,
And are up-gathered now like sleeping flowers,
For this, for everything, we are out of tune;
It moves us not.—Great God! I'd rather be
A Pagan suckled in a creed outworn;
So might I, standing on this pleasant lea,
Have glimpses that would make me less forlorn;
Have sight of Proteus rising from the sea;
Or hear old Triton blow his wreathèd horn.

1807

THE WORLD IS TOO MUCH WITH US. **13–14. Proteus . . . Triton:** sea gods. Proteus could take any shape he wished. Triton is usually pictured as a man from the chest upward and a fish from the belly downward. He is generally shown blowing a horn of shell (wreathed in the contours).

Nuns Fret Not at Their Convent's Narrow Room

Nuns fret not at their convent's narrow room;
And hermits are contented with their cells;
And students with their pensive citadels;
Maids at the wheel, the weaver at his loom,
Sit blithe and happy; bees that soar for bloom,
High as the highest Peak of Furness-fells,
Will murmur by the hour in foxglove bells:
In truth the prison, unto which we doom
Ourselves, no prison is: and hence for me,
In sundry moods, 'twas pastime to be bound
Within the Sonnet's scanty plot of ground;
Pleased if some Souls (for such there needs must be)
Who have felt the weight of too much liberty,
Should find brief solace there, as I have found.

1807

Scorn Not the Sonnet; Critic, You Have Frowned

Scorn not the sonnet; critic, you have frowned,
Mindless of its just honors; with this key
Shakespeare unlocked his heart; the melody
Of this small lute gave ease to Petrarch's wound;
A thousand times this pipe did Tasso sound;
With it Camöens soothed an exile's grief;
The sonnet glittered a gay myrtle leaf
Amid the cypress with which Dante crowned
His visionary brow; a glow-worm lamp,
It cheered mild Spenser, called from Faeryland
To struggle through dark ways; and, when a damp
Fell round the path of Milton, in his hand

NUNS FRET NOT AT THEIR CONVENT'S NARROW ROOM. **6. Furness-fells:** mountains in Furness, near the area where Wordsworth lived in the Lake Country. SCORN NOT THE SONNET. **4. Petrarch's wound:** Petrarch (1304–1374) was an Italian poet who wrote in the sonnet form; his "wound" is his love for his mistress Laura, as expressed in his sonnets. **5. Tasso:** Torquato Tasso, Italian poet. **6. Camöens:** Luis de Camöens, Portuguese poet, who had to spend much of his life as a soldier overseas. **8–12. Dante . . . Milton:** In addition to his epic, *The Divine Comedy,* Dante wrote some love sonnets to Beatrice (the myrtle leaf here mentioned was a symbol of love); Spenser, in addition to *The Faerie Queene* and other longer poems, wrote the series of love sonnets called *Amoretti;* and Milton, whose sonnets Wordsworth admired most and took as a model, wrote great "public sonnets," powerful in their rhetoric and trumpet-like in sound.

The thing became a trumpet; whence he blew
Soul-animating strains—alas, too few!

1827

I Wandered Lonely as a Cloud

I wandered lonely as a cloud
That floats on high o'er vales and hills,
When all at once I saw a crowd,
A host, of golden daffodils;
Beside the lake, beneath the trees,
Fluttering and dancing in the breeze.

Continuous as the stars that shine
And twinkle on the milky way,
They stretched in never-ending line
Along the margin of a bay:
Ten thousand saw I at a glance,
Tossing their heads in sprightly dance.

The waves beside them danced; but they
Outdid the sparkling waves in glee;
A poet could not but be gay,
In such a jocund company;
I gazed—and gazed—but little thought
What wealth the show to me had brought:

For oft, when on my couch I lie
In vacant or in pensive mood,
They flash upon that inward eye
Which is the bliss of solitude;
And then my heart with pleasure fills,
And dances with the daffodils.

1807

The Solitary Reaper

Behold her, single in the field,
Yon solitary Highland Lass!
Reaping and singing by herself;
Stop here, or gently pass!
Alone she cuts and binds the grain,
And sings a melancholy strain;
O listen! for the Vale profound
Is overflowing with the sound.

No Nightingale did ever chaunt
More welcome notes to weary bands
Of travelers in some shady haunt,
Among Arabian sands;
A voice so thrilling ne'er was heard
In springtime from the Cuckoo bird,
Breaking the silence of the seas
Among the farthest Hebrides.

Will no one tell me what she sings?—
Perhaps the plaintive numbers flow
For old, unhappy, far-off things,
And battles long ago;
Or is it some more humble lay,
Familiar matter of today?
Some natural sorrow, loss, or pain,
That has been, and may be again?

Whate'er the theme, the Maiden sang
As if her song could have no ending;
I saw her singing at her work,
And o'er the sickle bending—
I listened, motionless and still;
And, as I mounted up the hill,
The music in my heart I bore,
Long after it was heard no more.

1807

Surprised by Joy—Impatient as the Wind

Surprised by joy—impatient as the Wind
I turned to share the transport—Oh! with whom
But thee, deep buried in the silent tomb,
That spot which no vicissitude can find?
Love, faithful love, recalled thee to my mind—
But how could I forget thee? Through what power,
Even for the least division of an hour,
Have I been so beguiled as to be blind
To my most grievous loss!—That thought's return
Was the worst pang that sorrow ever bore,
Save one, one only, when I stood forlorn,
Knowing my heart's best treasure was no more;
That neither present time, nor years unborn
Could to my sight that heavenly face restore.

1815

THE SOLITARY REAPER. **17. what she sings:** Her song is in Gaelic (Erse). SURPRISED BY JOY. **3. thee:** Wordsworth's daughter, Caroline, who had died three years before.

After-Thought

I thought of Thee, my partner and my guide,
As being past away.—Vain sympathies!
For, backward, Duddon! as I cast my eyes,
I see what was, and is, and will abide;
Still glides the Stream, and shall for ever glide;
The Form remains, the Function never dies;
While we, the brave, the mighty, and the wise,
We Men, who in our morn of youth defied
The elements, must vanish;—be it so!
Enough, if something from our hands have power
To live, and act, and serve the future hour;
And if, as toward the silent tomb we go,
Through love, through hope, and faith's transcendent
dower,
We feel that we are greater than we know.

1820

Sir Walter Scott

(1771–1832)

Scott is remembered for his novels—the colorful historical novels like *Ivanhoe* (1819) and *Quentin Durward* (1823), and those about Scottish life, such as *Rob Roy* (1817) and *The Heart of Midlothian* (1818). Some of the best of his short lyrics appeared in the novels. The following song is sung by a character in one of the novels—the crazy old Madge Wildfire in *The Heart of Midlothian.*

Proud Maisie

Proud Maisie is in the wood
Walking so early;
Sweet Robin sits on the bush,
Singing so rarely.

AFTER-THOUGHT. **Title:** This is the last of a series of sonnets, *The River Duddon,* in which the poet follows the course of the river from its source in the hills to its entrance into the sea. **1. Thee:** the River Duddon.

"Tell me, thou bonny bird,
  When shall I marry me?"—
"When six braw gentlemen
  Kirkward shall carry ye."

"Who makes the bridal bed,
  Birdie, say truly?"—
"The gray-headed sexton
  That delves the grave duly.

"The glow-worm o'er grave and stone
  Shall light thee steady,
The owl from the steeple sing,
  'Welcome, proud lady.'"

1818

Samuel Taylor Coleridge

(1772–1834)

Coleridge had three different careers as a writer. During his twenties and early thirties, he wrote poems that are among the treasures of English literature. Then by his mid-thirties he turned to the criticism of literature, especially Shakespeare, with such brilliance of insight that he ranks among the four or five greatest critics in the history of literature. By the time he was fifty, he had become entirely absorbed in philosophy and religion—for which he had been preparing all his life, reading widely in metaphysics, psychology, and science as well as literature in several languages. In all three of these careers, his self-confidence was hampered by an addiction to opium, which he began taking during a severe illness as a young man. At that time little was known about drug addiction, and Coleridge was never able to free himself completely, though he struggled heroically against it, often in great pain and despair.

His most famous poems are those dealing with the supernatural, especially "The Rime of the Ancient Mariner" and "Kubla Khan." Yet, surprisingly, the supernatural was not really the subject matter about which he wanted most to write. His own bent was for the kind of poetry we see in his "Conversation Poems," of which "Frost at Midnight" is an

PROUD MAISIE. **7. braw:** handsome. **8. Kirkward:** churchward.

example: a poetry in quiet blank verse, in which the poet becomes a friend talking to friends. Here the poet's musings, as he sits before the fire, become focussed on his infant son, Hartley, lying in a nearby cradle. He thinks back to his own childhood in the city, and expresses his confidence that the sleeping baby will grow up amid the forms of nature and under their benign influence.

But when Coleridge and his friend Wordsworth decided to bring out a volume of poems together—the famous *Lyrical Ballads* (1798)—Coleridge felt that Wordsworth could write this kind of "natural" meditative verse better than himself, and that, in order to do something different, he would take up the "supernatural" for his subject. The most notable example was "The Rime of the Ancient Mariner," which, like most great poems, is not about one but several things. It is a poem about geographical, psychological, and religious exploration and discovery; about guilt, remorse, penance, and redemption; and about the relation of human beings to the universe and to God. It is saturated with a sense of the mystery of human life and the human conscience. The ship that carries the Mariner enters a sea no one else has ever explored. His thoughtless slaying of the albatross brings him into contact with forces that he might otherwise never have encountered. The poem ends with the Mariner trying to draw a moral from his experience, but he is a simple man, and his moral ("He prayeth best, who loveth best/All things both great and small"), though not wrong, seems not fully adequate to the experiences he narrates. The poem, in short, is left open for every reader to interpret. We should also notice the form of the poem. Its stanza is essentially that of the old ballads, though with some variations. At the time Coleridge was growing up (1772–1800) there was a new interest in ballads, which were associated with the middle ages and Renaissance and with the folk rather than the learned classes. By using the ballad stanza and archaic words ("eftsoons" for "at once," "weal" for "good"), Coleridge was trying to give the atmosphere and tone of a time remote from his own age.

"Kubla Khan," one of the most magnificent poems ever written on the theme of poetic inspiration, was composed by Coleridge in a lonely farm house as he was gradually waking from an opium dream. He had been reading an account of Marco Polo's thirteenth-century visit to China, where he met the emperor, Kubla. The ode, "Dejection," like many of the greatest lyrics of the Romantic period, enacts a drama of intellectual discovery. Coleridge wrote the poem after hearing the opening stanzas of Wordsworth's "Ode: Intimations of Immortality." Like Wordsworth in the "Ode," Coleridge is aware that he no longer feels all that he formerly had in response to the natural world. As he tries to account for this change, he realizes that "we *receive* but what we *give.*" We must, in other words, ourselves be creative, giving to nature—the world outside us—the meaning and life it has for us. But how can we be creative in this way if the fountain of hope and joy within us is dry? The seventh stanza of the poem, going further, dramatizes that in a state of "dejection" (we might now call it psychological depression) our creativity can become a torment to us, for the imagination produces images of horror. With this thought the poet tries to come to some kind of internal peace by turning his thoughts from himself to another person, by asking a blessing for another. In other words, he "sends his soul abroad," to adapt Coleridge's phrase in line 18, in sympathy and love.

After Coleridge's death "Limbo" and "On Donne's Poetry" were found in his notebooks. We do not know why he had not published them. If we assume that Coleridge himself had experienced the state he calls "positive Negation" or Limbo, the revelation of his suffering may have seemed too personal for publication. In their packed metaphors both poems somewhat anticipate modern poetic idiom, and in "On Donne's Poetry" Coleridge prizes in Donne what was most valued in Donne and his followers by T.S. Eliot and other critics and poets who revived "metaphysical poetry" in the 1920s and 1930s.

The Rime of the Ancient Mariner

Facile credo, plures esse Naturas invisibiles quam visibiles in rerum universitate. Sed horum omnium familiam quis nobis enarrabit? et gradus et cognationes et discrimina et singulorum munera? Quid agunt? quae loca habitant? Harum rerum notitiam semper ambivit ingenium humanum, nunquam attigit. Juvat, interea, non diffiteor, quandoque in animo, tanquam in tabulà, majoris et melioris mundi imaginem contemplari: ne mens assuefacta hodiernae vitae minutiis se contrahat nimis, et tota subsidat in pusillas cogitationes. Sed veritati interea in-

THE RIME OF THE ANCIENT MARINER. **Motto:** "I readily believe that there are more invisible than visible things in the universe. But who shall describe for us their families, their ranks, relationships, distinguishing features, and functions? What do they do? Where do they live? The human mind has always circled about knowledge of these things, but never attained it. I do not doubt, however, that it is sometimes good to contemplate in the mind, as in a picture, the image of a greater and better world; otherwise the intellect, habituated to the petty things of daily life, may too much contract itself, and wholly sink down to trivial thoughts. But meanwhile we must be vigilant for truth and keep proportion, that we may distinguish the certain from the uncertain, day from night."

vigilandum est, modusque servandus, ut certa ab incertis, diem a nocte, distinguamus.
[Thomas Burnet, Archaeologiae Philosophicae (1692), p. 68].

Argument

How a Ship having passed the Line was driven by storms to the cold Country towards the South Pole; and how from thence she made her course to the tropical Latitude of the Great Pacific Ocean; and of the strange things that befell; and in what manner the Ancyent Marinere came back to his own Country.

Part I

An ancient Mariner meeteth three Gallants bidden to a wedding feast, and detaineth one.

It is an ancient Mariner,
And he stoppeth one of three.
—"By thy long gray beard and glittering eye,
Now wherefore stopp'st thou me?

The Bridegroom's doors are opened wide,
And I am next of kin;
The guests are met, the feast is set:
May'st hear the merry din."

He holds him with his skinny hand,
"There was a ship," quoth he.
"Hold off! unhand me, graybeard loon!"
Eftsoons his hand dropped he.

The Wedding Guest is spellbound by the eye of the old seafaring man, and constrained to hear his tale.

He holds him with his glittering eye—
The Wedding Guest stood still,
And listens like a three years' child:
The Mariner hath his will.

The Wedding Guest sat on a stone:
He cannot choose but hear;
And thus spake on that ancient man,
The bright-eyed Mariner.

"The ship was cheered, the harbor cleared,
Merrily did we drop
Below the kirk, below the hill,
Below the lighthouse top.

The Mariner tells how the ship sailed southward with a good wind and fair weather, till it reached the line.

The Sun came up upon the left,
Out of the sea came he!
And he shone bright, and on the right
Went down into the sea.

Thomas Burnet: Anglican clergyman, 1635–1715. **12. Eftsoons:** at once. **23. kirk:** church.

Higher and higher every day,
Till over the mast at noon—"
The Wedding Guest here beat his breast,
For he heard the loud bassoon.

The Wedding Guest heareth the bridal music; but the Mariner continueth his tale.

The bride hath paced into the hall,
Red as a rose is she;
Nodding their heads before her goes
The merry minstrelsy.

The Wedding Guest he beat his breast,
Yet he cannot choose but hear;
And thus spake on that ancient man,
The bright-eyed Mariner.

The ship driven by a storm toward the South Pole.

"And now the STORM-BLAST came, and he
Was tyrannous and strong;
He struck with his o'ertaking wings,
And chased us south along.

With sloping masts and dipping prow,
As who pursued with yell and blow
Still treads the shadow of his foe,
And forward bends his head,
The ship drove fast, loud roared the blast,
And southward aye we fled.

And now there came both mist and snow,
And it grew wondrous cold:
And ice, mast-high, came floating by,
As green as emerald.

The land of ice, and of fearful sounds where no living thing was to be seen.

And through the drifts the snowy clifts
Did send a dismal sheen:
Nor shapes of men nor beasts we ken—
The ice was all between.

The ice was here, the ice was there,
The ice was all around:
It cracked and growled, and roared and howled,
Like noises in a swound!

Till a great sea bird, called the Albatross, came through the snow-fog, and was received with great joy and hospitality.

At length did cross an Albatross,
Thorough the fog it came;
As if it had been a Christian soul,
We hailed it in God's name.

It ate the food it ne'er had eat,
And round and round it flew.
The ice did split with a thunder-fit;
The helmsman steered us through!

30. over . . . noon: The ship has reached the equator. **62. swound:** swoon.

And lo! the Albatross proveth a bird of good omen, and followeth the ship as it returned northward through fog and floating ice.

And a good south wind sprung up behind;
The Albatross did follow,
And every day, for food or play,
Came to the mariners' hollo!

In mist or cloud, on mast or shroud,
It perched for vespers nine;
Whiles all the night, through fog-smoke white,
Glimmered the white Moon-shine."

The ancient Mariner inhospitably killeth the pious bird of good omen.

"God save thee, ancient Mariner!
From the fiends, that plague thee thus!—
Why look'st thou so?"—With my crossbow
I shot the ALBATROSS.

Part II

The Sun now rose upon the right:
Out of the sea came he,
Still hid in mist, and on the left
Went down into the sea.

And the good south wind still blew behind,
But no sweet bird did follow,
Nor any day for food or play
Came to the mariners' hollo!

His shipmates cry out against the ancient Mariner, for killing the bird of good luck.

And I had done a hellish thing,
And it would work 'em woe:
For all averred, I had killed the bird
That made the breeze to blow.
Ah wretch! said they, the bird to slay,
That made the breeze to blow!

But when the fog cleared off, they justify the same, and thus make themselves accomplices in the crime.

Nor dim nor red, like God's own head,
The glorious Sun uprist:
Then all averred, I had killed the bird
That brought the fog and mist.
'Twas right, said they, such birds to slay,
That bring the fog and mist.

The fair breeze continues; the ship enters the Pacific Ocean, and sails northward, even till it reaches the Line.

The fair breeze blew, the white foam flew,
The furrow followed free;
We were the first that ever burst
Into that silent sea.

The ship hath been suddenly becalmed.

Down dropped the breeze, the sails dropped
down,
'Twas sad as sad could be;

76. vespers: service of evening worship. **83. upon the right:** The ship has now rounded Cape Horn and is sailing north into the Pacific.

And we did speak only to break
The silence of the sea!

All in a hot and copper sky,
The bloody Sun, at noon,
Right up above the mast did stand,
No bigger than the Moon.

Day after day, day after day,
We stuck, nor breath nor motion;
As idle as a painted ship
Upon a painted ocean.

And the Albatross begins to be avenged.

Water, water, everywhere,
And all the boards did shrink;
Water, water, everywhere,
Nor any drop to drink.

The very deep did rot: O Christ!
That ever this should be!
Yea, slimy things did crawl with legs
Upon the slimy sea.

About, about, in reel and rout
The death-fires danced at night;
The water, like a witch's oils,
Burnt green, and blue and white.

A Spirit had followed them; one of the invisible inhabitants of this planet, neither departed souls nor angels; concerning whom the learned Jew, Josephus, and the Platonic Constantinopolitan, Michael Psellus, may be consulted. They are very numerous, and there is no climate or element without one or more.

And some in dreams assurèd were
Of the Spirit that plagued us so;
Nine fathom deep he had followed us
From the land of mist and snow.

And every tongue, through utter drought,
Was withered at the root;
We could not speak, no more than if
We had been choked with soot.

The shipmates, in their sore distress, would fain throw the whole guilt on the ancient Mariner: in sign whereof they hang the dead sea bird round his neck.

Ah! well-a-day! what evil looks
Had I from old and young!
Instead of the cross, the Albatross
About my neck was hung.

Part III

There passed a weary time. Each throat
Was parched, and glazed each eye.
A weary time! a weary time!
How glazed each weary eye,

127. reel and rout: whirling, dashing movements. **128. death-fires:** St. Elmo's fire, electricity in the air causing the appearance of lights in the rigging. Sailors regarded it as an omen of death.

The ancient Mariner beholdeth a sign in the element afar off.

When looking westward, I beheld
A something in the sky.

At first it seemed a little speck,
And then it seemed a mist;
It moved and moved, and took at last
A certain shape, I wist.

A speck, a mist, a shape, I wist!
And still it neared and neared:
As if it dodged a water sprite,
It plunged and tacked and veered.

At its nearer approach, it seemeth him to be a ship; and at a dear ransom he freeth his speech from the bonds of thirst.

With throats unslaked, with black lips baked,
We could nor laugh nor wail;
Through utter drought all dumb we stood!
I bit my arm, I sucked the blood,
And cried, A sail! a sail!

A flash of joy;

With throats unslaked, with black lips baked,
Agape they heard me call:
Gramercy! they for joy did grin,
And all at once their breath drew in,
As they were drinking all.

And horror follows. For can it be a ship that comes onward without wind or tide?

See! see! (I cried) she tacks no more!
Hither to work us weal;
Without a breeze, without a tide,
She steadies with upright keel!

The western wave was all aflame.
The day was well nigh done!
Almost upon the western wave
Rested the broad bright Sun;
When that strange shape drove suddenly
Betwixt us and the Sun.

It seemeth him but the skeleton of a ship.

And straight the Sun was flecked with bars,
(Heaven's Mother send us grace!)
As if through a dungeon grate he peered
With broad and burning face.

And its ribs are seen as bars on the face of the setting Sun.

Alas! (thought I, and my heart beat loud)
How fast she nears and nears!
Are those *her* sails that glance in the Sun,
Like restless gossameres?

The Specter-Woman and her Deathmate, and no other on board the skeleton ship.

Are those *her* ribs through which the Sun
Did peer, as through a grate?
And is that Woman all her crew?
Is that a DEATH? and are there two?
Is DEATH that woman's mate?

152. wist: knew. **164. Gramercy:** great thanks (from Old French *grand merci*). **168. weal:** good or happiness.

Like vessel, like crew!

Her lips were red, *her* looks were free,
Her locks were yellow as gold:
Her skin was as white as leprosy,
The Nightmare LIFE-IN-DEATH was she,
Who thicks man's blood with cold.

Death and Life-in-Death have diced for the ship's crew, and she (the latter) winneth the ancient Mariner.

The naked hulk alongside came,
And the twain were casting dice;
"The game is done! I've won! I've won!"
Quoth she, and whistles thrice.

No twilight within the courts of the Sun.

The Sun's rim dips; the stars rush out:
At one stride comes the dark;
With far-heard whisper, o'er the sea,
Off shot the specter-bark.

At the rising of the Moon,

We listened and looked sideways up!
Fear at my heart, as at a cup,
My lifeblood seemed to sip!
The stars were dim, and thick the night,
The steersman's face by his lamp gleamed
white;
From the sails the dew did drip—
Till clomb above the eastern bar
The hornèd Moon, with one bright star
Within the nether tip.

One after another,

One after one, by the star-dogged Moon,
Too quick for groan or sigh,
Each turned his face with ghastly pang,
And cursed me with his eye.

His shipmates drop down dead.

Four times fifty living men,
(And I heard nor sigh nor groan)
With heavy thump, a lifeless lump,
They dropped down one by one.

But Life-in-Death begins her work on the ancient Mariner.

The souls did from their bodies fly—
They fled to bliss or woe!
And every soul, it passed me by,
Like the whizz of my cross-bow!

Part IV

The Wedding Guest feareth that a Spirit is talking to him;

"I fear thee, ancient Mariner!
I fear thy skinny hand!
And thou art long, and lank, and brown,
As is the ribbed sea-sand.

188. a Death: a skeleton. **209. clomb:** climbed. **212. star-dogged Moon:** a star following the moon was, among sailors, another omen of disaster.

I fear thee and thy glittering eye,
And thy skinny hand, so brown."—

But the ancient Mariner assureth him of his bodily life, and proceedeth to relate his horrible penance.

Fear not, fear not, thou Wedding Guest!
This body dropped not down.

Alone, alone, all, all alone,
Alone on a wide wide sea!
And never a saint took pity on
My soul in agony.

He despiseth the creatures of the calm,

The many men, so beautiful!
And they all dead did lie:
And a thousand thousand slimy things
Lived on; and so did I.

And envieth that *they* should live, and so many lie dead.

I looked upon the rotting sea,
And drew my eyes away;
I looked upon the rotting deck,
And there the dead men lay.

I looked to heaven, and tried to pray;
But or ever a prayer had gushed,
A wicked whisper came, and made
My heart as dry as dust.

I closed my lids, and kept them close,
And the balls like pulses beat,
For the sky and the sea, and the sea and the sky
Lay like a load on my weary eye,
And the dead were at my feet.

But the curse liveth for him in the eye of the dead men.

The cold sweat melted from their limbs,
Nor rot nor reek did they:
The look with which they looked on me
Had never passed away.

An orphan's curse would drag to hell
A spirit from on high;
But oh! more horrible than that
Is the curse in a dead man's eye!

Seven days, seven nights, I saw that curse,

In his loneliness and fixedness he yearneth towards the journeying Moon, and the stars that still sojourn, yet still move onward; and everywhere the blue sky belongs to them, and is their appointed rest, and their native country and their own natural homes, which they enter unannounced, as lords that are certainly expected and yet there is a silent joy at their arrival.

And yet I could not die.
The moving Moon went up the sky,
And nowhere did abide:
Softly she was going up,
And a star or two beside—

Her beams bemocked the sultry main,
Like April hoar-frost spread;
But where the ship's huge shadow lay,
The charmèd water burnt alway
A still and awful red.

Beyond the shadow of the ship,
I watched the water snakes:
They moved in tracks of shining white,
And when they reared, the elfish light
Fell off in hoary flakes.

By the light of the Moon he beholdeth God's creatures of the great calm.

Within the shadow of the ship
I watched their rich attire:
Blue, glossy green, and velvet black,
They coiled and swam; and every track
Was a flash of golden fire.

Their beauty and their happiness.

O happy living things! no tongue
Their beauty might declare:
A spring of love gushed from my heart,
And I blessed them unaware:
Sure my kind saint took pity on me,
And I blessed them unaware.

He blesseth them in his heart.

The spell begins to break.

The self-same moment I could pray;
And from my neck so free
The Albatross fell off, and sank
Like lead into the sea.

Part V

Oh sleep! it is a gentle thing,
Beloved from pole to pole!
To Mary Queen the praise be given!
She sent the gentle sleep from Heaven,
That slid into my soul.

By grace of the holy Mother, the ancient Mariner is refreshed with rain.

The silly buckets on the deck,
That had so long remained,
I dreamt that they were filled with dew;
And when I awoke, it rained.

My lips were wet, my throat was cold,
My garments all were dank;
Sure I had drunken in my dreams,
And still my body drank.

I moved, and could not feel my limbs:
I was so light—almost
I thought that I had died in sleep,
And was a blessèd ghost.

He heareth sounds and seeth strange sights and commotions in the sky and the element.

And soon I heard a roaring wind:
It did not come anear;
But with its sound it shook the sails,
That were so thin and sere.

275. elfish: bewitched. **297. silly:** useless.

The upper air burst into life!
And a hundred fire-flags sheen,
To and fro they were hurried about!
And to and fro, and in and out,
The wan stars danced between.

And the coming wind did roar more loud,
And the sails did sigh like sedge;
And the rain poured down from one black cloud;
The Moon was at its edge.

The thick black cloud was cleft, and still
The Moon was at its side:
Like waters shot from some high crag,
The lightning fell with never a jag,
A river steep and wide.

The bodies of the ship's crew are inspirited, and the ship moves on;

The loud wind never reached the ship,
Yet now the ship moved on!
Beneath the lightning and the Moon
The dead men gave a groan.

They groaned, they stirred, they all uprose,
Nor spake, nor moved their eyes;
It had been strange, even in a dream,
To have seen those dead men rise.

The helmsman steered, the ship moved on;
Yet never a breeze up-blew;
The mariners all 'gan work the ropes,
Where they were wont to do;
They raised their limbs like lifeless tools—
We were a ghastly crew.

The body of my brother's son
Stood by me, knee to knee:
The body and I pulled at one rope,
But he said nought to me.

But not by the souls of the men, nor by demons of earth or middle air, but by a blessèd troop of angelic spirits, sent down by the invocation of the guardian saint.

"I fear thee, ancient Mariner!"
Be calm, thou Wedding Guest!
'Twas not those souls that fled in pain,
Which to their corses came again,
But a troop of spirits blest:

For when it dawned—they dropped their arms,
And clustered round the mast;
Sweet sounds rose slowly through their mouths,
And from their bodies passed.

319. sedge: rushes that border streams and ponds. **325. jag:** zig-zag. **348. corses:** corpses.

Around, around, flew each sweet sound,
Then darted to the Sun;
Slowly the sounds came back again,
Now mixed, now one by one.

Sometimes a-dropping from the sky
I heard the sky-lark sing;
Sometimes all little birds that are,
How they seemed to fill the sea and air
With their sweet jargoning!

And now 'twas like all instruments,
Now like a lonely flute;
And now it is an angel's song,
That makes the heavens be mute.

It ceased; yet still the sails made on
A pleasant noise till noon,
A noise like of a hidden brook
In the leafy month of June,
That to the sleeping woods all night
Singeth a quiet tune.

Till noon we quietly sailed on,
Yet never a breeze did breathe:
Slowly and smoothly went the ship,
Moved onward from beneath.

The lonesome Spirit from the South Pole carries on the ship as far as the Line, in obedience to the angelic troop, but still requireth vengeance.

Under the keel nine fathom deep,
From the land of mist and snow,
The spirit slid: and it was he
That made the ship to go.
The sails at noon left off their tune,
And the ship stood still also.

The Sun, right up above the mast,
Had fixed her to the ocean:
But in a minute she 'gan stir,
With a short uneasy motion—
Backwards and forwards half her length
With a short uneasy motion.

Then like a pawing horse let go,
She made a sudden bound:
It flung the blood into my head,
And I fell down in a swound.

The Polar Spirit's fellow demons, the invisible inhabitants of the element, take part in his wrong; and two of them relate, one to the other, that penance long and

How long in that same fit I lay,
I have not to declare;
But ere my living life returned,
I heard and in my soul discerned
Two voices in the air.

362. jargoning: twittering. **394. not to declare:** cannot say.

heavy for the ancient Mariner hath been accorded to the Polar Spirit, who returneth southward.

"Is it he?" quoth one, "Is this the man?
By him who died on cross,
With his cruel bow he laid full low
The harmless Albatross.

The spirit who bideth by himself
In the land of mist and snow,
He loved the bird that loved the man
Who shot him with his bow."

The other was a softer voice,
As soft as honey-dew:
Quoth he, "The man hath penance done,
And penance more will do."

Part VI

FIRST VOICE

"But tell me, tell me! speak again,
Thy soft response renewing—
What makes that ship drive on so fast?
What is the ocean doing?"

SECOND VOICE

"Still as a slave before his lord,
The ocean hath no blast;
His great bright eye most silently
Up to the Moon is cast—

If he may know which way to go;
For she guides him smooth or grim.
See, brother, see! how graciously
She looketh down on him."

FIRST VOICE

The Mariner hath been cast into a trance; for the angelic power causeth the vessel to drive northward faster than human life could endure.

"But why drives on that ship so fast,
Without or wave or wind?"

SECOND VOICE

"The air is cut away before,
And closes from behind.

Fly, brother, fly! more high, more high!
Or we shall be belated:
For slow and slow that ship will go,
When the Mariner's trance is abated."

The supernatural motion is retarded; the Mariner awakes, and his penance begins anew.

I woke, and we were sailing on
As in a gentle weather:
'Twas night, calm night, the moon was high;
The dead men stood together.

All stood together on the deck,
For a charnel-dungeon fitter:
All fixed on me their stony eyes,
That in the Moon did glitter.

The pang, the curse, with which they died,
Had never passed away:
I could not draw my eyes from theirs,
Nor turn them up to pray.

The curse is finally expiated.

And now this spell was snapped: once more
I viewed the ocean green,
And looked far forth, yet little saw
Of what had else been seen—

Like one, that on a lonesome road
Doth walk in fear and dread,
And having once turned round walks on,
And turns no more his head;
Because he knows, a frightful fiend
Doth close behind him tread.

But soon there breathed a wind on me,
Nor sound nor motion made:
Its path was not upon the sea,
In ripple or in shade.

It raised my hair, it fanned my cheek
Like a meadow-gale of spring—
It mingled strangely with my fears,
Yet it felt like a welcoming.

Swiftly, swiftly flew the ship,
Yet she sailed softly too:
Sweetly, sweetly blew the breeze—
On me alone it blew.

And the ancient Mariner beholdeth his native country.

Oh! dream of joy! is this indeed
The lighthouse top I see?
Is this the hill? is this the kirk?
Is this mine own countree?

We drifted o'er the harbor-bar,
And I with sobs did pray—
O let me be awake, my God!
Or let me sleep alway.

The harbor-bay was clear as glass,
So smoothly it was strewn!
And on the bay the moonlight lay,
And the shadow of the Moon.

435. charnel-dungeon: bone-dungeon. When graveyards were filled up, bones from old graves were put there in order to make space for new burials.

The rock shone bright, the kirk no less,
That stands above the rock:
The moonlight steeped in silentness
The steady weathercock.

And the bay was white with silent light,
Till rising from the same,
Full many shapes, that shadows were,
In crimson colors came.

The angelic spirits leave the dead bodies,

A little distance from the prow
Those crimson shadows were:
I turned my eyes upon the deck—
Oh, Christ! what saw I there!

And appear in their own forms of light.

Each corse lay flat, lifeless and flat,
And, by the holy rood!
A man all light, a seraph-man,
On every corse there stood.

This seraph-band, each waved his hand:
It was a heavenly sight!
They stood as signals to the land,
Each one a lovely light;

This seraph-band, each waved his hand,
No voice did they impart—
No voice; but oh! the silence sank
Like music on my heart.

But soon I heard the dash of oars,
I heard the Pilot's cheer;
My head was turned perforce away
And I saw a boat appear.

The Pilot and the Pilot's boy,
I heard them coming fast:
Dear Lord in Heaven! it was a joy
The dead men could not blast.

I saw a third—I heard his voice:
It is the Hermit good!
He singeth loud his godly hymns
That he makes in the wood.
He'll shrieve my soul, he'll wash away
The Albatross's blood.

489. rood: crucifix. **490. seraph:** angel with a fiery body. **512. shrieve:** hear confession, impose penance, and give absolution.

Part VII

The Hermit of the Wood

This Hermit good lives in that wood
Which slopes down to the sea.
How loudly his sweet voice he rears!
He loves to talk with marineres
That come from a far countree.

He kneels at morn, and noon, and eve—
He hath a cushion plump:
It is the moss that wholly hides
The rotted old oak stump.

The skiff-boat neared: I heard them talk,
"Why, this is strange, I trow!
Where are those lights so many and fair,
That signal made but now?"

Approacheth the ship with wonder.

"Strange, by my faith!" the Hermit said—
"And they answered not our cheer!
The planks looked warped! and see those sails,
How thin they are and sere!
I never saw aught like to them,
Unless perchance it were

Brown skeletons of leaves that lag
My forest-brook along;
When the ivy tod is heavy with snow,
And the owlet whoops to the wolf below,
That eats the she-wolf's young."

"Dear Lord! it hath a fiendish look,"
The Pilot made reply,
"I am a-feared"—"Push on, push on!"
Said the Hermit cheerily.

The boat came closer to the ship,
But I nor spake nor stirred;
The boat came close beneath the ship,
And straight a sound was heard.

The ship suddenly sinketh.

Under the water it rumbled on,
Still louder and more dread:
It reached the ship, it split the bay;
The ship went down like lead.

The ancient Mariner is saved in the Pilot's boat.

Stunned by that loud and dreadful sound,
Which sky and ocean smote,
Like one that hath been seven days drowned

535. ivy tod: ivy bush.

My body lay afloat;
But swift as dreams, myself I found
Within the Pilot's boat.

Upon the whirl, where sank the ship,
The boat spun round and round;
And all was still, save that the hill
Was telling of the sound.

I moved my lips—the Pilot shrieked
And fell down in a fit;
The holy Hermit raised his eyes,
And prayed where he did sit.

I took the oars: the Pilot's boy,
Who now doth crazy go,
Laughed loud and long, and all the while
His eyes went to and fro.
"Ha! ha!" quoth he, "full plain I see,
The Devil knows how to row."

And now, all in my own countree,
I stood on the firm land!
The Hermit stepped forth from the boat,
And scarcely he could stand.

The ancient Mariner earnestly entreateth the Hermit to shrieve him; and the penance of life falls on him.

"O shrieve me, shrieve me, holy man!"
The Hermit crossed his brow.
"Say quick," quoth he, "I bid thee say—
What manner of man art thou?"

Forthwith this frame of mine was wrenched
With a woeful agony,
Which forced me to begin my tale;
And then it left me free.

And ever and anon throughout his future life an agony constraineth him to travel from land to land;

Since then, at an uncertain hour,
That agony returns:
And till my ghastly tale is told,
This heart within me burns.

I pass, like night, from land to land;
I have strange power of speech;
That moment that his face I see,
I know the man that must hear me:
To him my tale I teach.

What loud uproar bursts from that door!
The wedding guests are there:
But in the garden-bower the bride

575. crossed: made the sign of the cross.

And bridemaids singing are:
And hark the little vesper bell,
Which biddeth me to prayer!

O Wedding Guest! this soul hath been
Alone on a wide wide sea:
So lonely 'twas, that God himself
Scarce seemèd there to be.

O sweeter than the marriage feast,
'Tis sweeter far to me,
To walk together to the kirk
With a goodly company!

To walk together to the kirk,
And all together pray,
While each to his great Father bends,
Old men, and babes, and loving friends
And youths and maidens gay!

And to teach, by his own example, love and reverence to all things that God made and loveth.

Farewell, farewell! but this I tell
To thee, thou Wedding Guest!
He prayeth well, who loveth well
Both man and bird and beast.

He prayeth best, who loveth best
All things both great and small;
For the dear God who loveth us,
He made and loveth all.

The Mariner, whose eye is bright,
Whose beard with age is hoar,
Is gone: and now the Wedding Guest
Turned from the bridegroom's door.

He went like one that hath been stunned,
And is of sense forlorn:
A sadder and a wiser man,
He rose the morrow morn.

1798

Frost at Midnight

The Frost performs its secret ministry,
Unhelped by any wind. The owlet's cry
Came loud—and hark, again! loud as before.
The inmates of my cottage, all at rest,
Have left me to that solitude, which suits
Abstruser musings: save that at my side
My cradled infant slumbers peacefully.

FROST AT MIDNIGHT. **7. infant:** Coleridge's son Hartley.

'Tis calm indeed! so calm, that it disturbs
And vexes meditation with its strange
And extreme silentness. Sea, hill, and wood,
This populous village! Sea, and hill, and wood,
With all the numberless goings-on of life,
Inaudible as dreams! the thin blue flame
Lies on my low-burnt fire, and quivers not;
Only that film, which fluttered on the grate,
Still flutters there, the sole unquiet thing.
Methinks its motion in this hush of nature
Gives it dim sympathies with me who live,
Making it a companionable form,
Whose puny flaps and freaks the idling Spirit
By its own moods interprets, everywhere
Echo or mirror seeking of itself,
And makes a toy of Thought.

But O! how oft,
How oft, at school, with most believing mind,
Presageful, have I gazed upon the bars,
To watch that fluttering *stranger!* and as oft
With unclosed lids, already had I dreamt
Of my sweet birthplace, and the old church tower,
Whose bells, the poor man's only music, rang
From morn to evening, all the hot Fair-day,
So sweetly, that they stirred and haunted me
With a wild pleasure, falling on mine ear
Most like articulate sounds of things to come!
So gazed I, till the soothing things, I dreamt,
Lulled me to sleep, and sleep prolonged my dreams!
And so I brooded all the following morn,
Awed by the stern preceptor's face, mine eye
Fixed with mock study on my swimming book:
Save if the door half opened, and I snatched
A hasty glance, and still my heart leaped up,
For still I hoped to see the *stranger's* face,
Townsman, or aunt, or sister more beloved,
My playmate when we both were clothed alike!

Dear Babe, that sleepest cradled by my side,
Whose gentle breathings, heard in this deep calm,
Fill up the interspersèd vacancies
And momentary pauses of the thought!

15. film: bits of soot fluttering on the fireplace. In a note Coleridge said that "these films are called *strangers*, and supposed to portend the arrival of some absent friend." **20. freaks:** sudden, unexpected changes. **24. school:** Christ's Hospital, London, which Coleridge had attended as a boy. **25. presageful:** foretelling. **28. birthplace:** the country town of Ottery St. Mary, in Devon. **37. stern preceptor:** James Bowyer, the stern headmaster of the school, to whose rigorous teaching Coleridge felt he owed a great debt. **43. playmate:** his sister Ann.

My babe so beautiful! it thrills my heart
With tender gladness, thus to look at thee,
And think that thou shalt learn far other lore,
And in far other scenes! For I was reared
In the great city, pent 'mid cloisters dim,
And saw nought lovely but the sky and stars.
But *thou*, my babe! shalt wander like a breeze
By lakes and sandy shores, beneath the crags
Of ancient mountain, and beneath the clouds,
Which image in their bulk both lakes and shores
And mountain crags: so shalt thou see and hear
The lovely shapes and sounds intelligible
Of that eternal language, which thy God
Utters, who from eternity doth teach
Himself in all, and all things in himself.
Great universal Teacher! he shall mold
Thy spirit, and by giving make it ask.

Therefore all seasons shall be sweet to thee,
Whether the summer clothe the general earth
With greenness, or the redbreast sit and sing
Betwixt the tufts of snow on the bare branch
Of mossy apple tree, while the nigh thatch
Smokes in the sun-thaw; whether the eave-drops fall
Heard only in the trances of the blast,
Or if the secret ministry of frost
Shall hang them up in silent icicles,
Quietly shining to the quiet Moon.

1798

Kubla Khan

Or a vision in a dream. A fragment

In Xanadu did Kubla Khan
A stately pleasure dome decree:
Where Alph, the sacred river, ran

52. cloisters: of his school. **60. eternal language:** the forms of nature. KUBLA KHAN. **Title:** Kubla Khan was the Mogul Emperor of China in the thirteenth century, and was a descendant of Genghis Khan. Coleridge gave the following account of the poem: "In the summer of the year 1797, the Author, then in ill health, had retired to a lonely farm-house between Porlock and Linton, on the Exmoor confines of Somerset and Devonshire. In consequence of a slight indisposition, an anodyne had been prescribed, from the effects of which he fell asleep in his chair at the moment that he was reading the following sentence, or words of the same substance, in 'Purchas's Pilgrimage': 'Here the Khan Kubla commanded a palace to be built, and a stately garden thereunto. And thus ten miles of fertile

Through caverns measureless to man
  Down to a sunless sea.
So twice five miles of fertile ground
Will walls and towers were girdled round:
And there were gardens bright with sinuous rills,
Where blossomed many an incense-bearing tree;
And here were forests ancient as the hills,
Enfolding sunny spots of greenery.

But oh! that deep romantic chasm which slanted
Down the green hill athwart a cedarn cover!
A savage place! as holy and enchanted
As e'er beneath a waning moon was haunted
By woman wailing for her demon lover!
And from this chasm, with ceaseless turmoil seething,
As if this earth in fast thick pants were breathing,
A mighty fountain momently was forced:
Amid whose swift half-intermitted burst
Huge fragments vaulted like rebounding hail,
Or chaffy grain beneath the thresher's flail:
And 'mid these dancing rocks at once and ever
It flung up momently the sacred river.
Five miles meandering with a mazy motion
Through wood and dale the sacred river ran,
Then reached the caverns measureless to man,
And sank in tumult to a lifeless ocean:
And 'mid this tumult Kubla heard from far
Ancestral voices prophesying war!
  The shadow of the dome of pleasure
  Floated midway on the waves;
  Where was heard the mingled measure
  From the fountain and the caves.
It was a miracle of rare device,
A sunny pleasure dome with caves of ice!

ground were inclosed with a wall.' The Author continued for about three hours in a profound sleep, at least of the external senses, during which time he has the most vivid confidence, that he could not have composed less than from two or three hundred lines; if that indeed can be called composition in which all the images rose up before him as things, with a parallel production of the correspondent expressions, without any sensation or consciousness of effort. On awaking he appeared to himself to have a distinct recollection of the whole, and taking his pen, ink, and paper, instantly and eagerly wrote down the lines that are here preserved. At this moment he was unfortunately called out by a person on business from Porlock, and detained by him above an hour, and on his return to his room, found, to his no small surprise and mortification, that though he still retained some vague and dim recollection of the general purport of the vision, yet, with the exception of some eight or ten scattered lines and images, all the rest had passed away like the images on the surface of a stream into which a stone has been cast, but, alas! without the after restoration of the latter!"

A damsel with a dulcimer
In a vision once I saw:
It was an Abyssinian maid,
And on her dulcimer she played,
Singing of Mount Abora.
Could I revive within me
Her symphony and song,
To such a deep delight 'twould win me,
That with music loud and long,
I would build that dome in air,
That sunny dome! those caves of ice!
And all who heard should see them there,
And all should cry, Beware! Beware!
His flashing eyes, his floating hair!
Weave a circle round him thrice,
And close your eyes with holy dread,
For he on honey-dew hath fed,
And drunk the milk of Paradise.

1797–98

Dejection: An Ode

Late, late yestreen I saw the new Moon,
With the old Moon in her arms;
And I fear, I fear, my master dear!
We shall have a deadly storm.
Ballad of Sir Patrick Spence

1

Well! If the bard was weather-wise, who made
The grand old ballad of Sir Patrick Spence,
This night, so tranquil now, will not go hence
Unroused by winds, that ply a busier trade
Than those which mold yon cloud in lazy flakes,
Or the dull sobbing draft, that moans and rakes
Upon the strings of this Aeolian lute,
Which better far were mute.
For lo! the New-moon winter-bright!
And overspread with phantom light,
(With swimming phantom light o'erspread
But rimmed and circled by a silver thread)
I see the old Moon in her lap, foretelling
The coming-on of rain and squally blast.

DEJECTION: AN ODE. **7. Aeolian lute:** wind-harp (after Aeolus, God of the winds); a box with strings placed at an open window, where the breeze, moving the strings, makes music.

And oh! that even now the gust were swelling,
  And the slant night shower driving loud and fast!
Those sounds which oft have raised me, whilst they awed,
    And sent my soul abroad,
Might now perhaps their wonted impulse give,
Might startle this dull pain, and make it move and live!

2

A grief without a pang, void, dark, and drear,
  A stifled, drowsy, unimpassioned grief,
  Which finds no natural outlet, no relief,
    In word, or sigh, or tear—
O Lady! in this wan and heartless mood,
To other thoughts by yonder throstle wooed,
  All this long eve, so balmy and serene,
Have I been gazing on the western sky,
  And its peculiar tint of yellow green:
And still I gaze—and with how blank an eye!
And those thin clouds above, in flakes and bars,
That give away their motion to the stars;
Those stars, that glide behind them or between,
Now sparkling, now bedimmed, but always seen:
Yon crescent Moon, as fixed as if it grew
In its own cloudless, starless lake of blue;
I see them all so excellently fair,
I see, not feel, how beautiful they are!

3

    My genial spirits fail;
    And what can these avail
To lift the smothering weight from off my breast?
  It were a vain endeavor,
    Though I should gaze forever
On that green light that lingers in the west:
I may not hope from outward forms to win
The passion and the life, whose fountains are within.

4

O Lady! we receive but what we give,
And in our life alone does Nature live:
Ours is her wedding garment, ours her shroud!
  And would we aught behold, of higher worth,
Than that inanimate cold world allowed
To the poor loveless ever-anxious crowd,
  Ah! from the soul itself must issue forth
A light, a glory, a fair luminous cloud

19. wonted: accustomed. **39. genial:** inspired or vital energy (connected with "genius").

Enveloping the Earth—
And from the soul itself must there be sent
A sweet and potent voice, of its own birth,
Of all sweet sounds the life and element!

5

O pure of heart! thou need'st not ask of me
What this strong music in the soul may be!
What, and wherein it doth exist,
This light, this glory, this fair luminous mist,
This beautiful and beauty-making power.
Joy, virtuous Lady! Joy that ne'er was given,
Save to the pure, and in their purest hour,
Life, and Life's effluence, cloud at once and shower,
Joy, Lady! is the spirit and the power,
Which wedding Nature to us gives in dower
A new Earth and new Heaven,
Undreamt of by the sensual and the proud—
Joy is the sweet voice, Joy the luminous cloud—
We in ourselves rejoice!
And thence flows all that charms or ear or sight,
All melodies the echoes of that voice,
All colors a suffusion from that light.

6

There was a time when, though my path was rough,
This joy within me dallied with distress,
And all misfortunes were but as the stuff
Whence Fancy made me dreams of happiness:
For hope grew round me, like the twining vine,
And fruits, and foliage, not my own, seemed mine.
But now afflictions bow me down to earth:
Nor care I that they rob me of my mirth;
But oh! each visitation
Suspends what nature gave me at my birth,
My shaping spirit of Imagination.
For not to think of what I needs must feel,
But to be still and patient, all I can;
And haply by abstruse research to steal
From my own nature all the natural man—
This was my sole resource, my only plan:
Till that which suits a part infects the whole,
And now is almost grown the habit of my soul.

7

Hence, viper thoughts, that coil around my mind,
Reality's dark dream!
I turn from you, and listen to the wind,
Which long has raved unnoticed. What a scream

Of agony by torture lengthened out
That lute sent forth! Thou Wind, that rav'st without,
  Bare crag, or mountain tairn, or blasted tree,
Or pine grove whither woodman never clomb,
Or lonely house, long held the witches' home,
  Methinks were fitter instruments for thee,
Mad lutanist! who in this month of showers,
Of dark-brown gardens, and of peeping flowers,
Mak'st devils' yule, with worse than wintry song,
The blossoms, buds, and timorous leaves among.
  Thou actor, perfect in all tragic sounds!
Thou mighty poet, e'en to frenzy bold!
    What tell'st thou now about?
    'Tis of the rushing of an host in rout,
  With groans, of trampled men, with smarting wounds—
At once they groan with pain, and shudder with the cold!
But hush! there is a pause of deepest silence!
  And all that noise, as of a rushing crowd,
With groans, and tremulous shudderings—all is over—
  It tells another tale, with sounds less deep and loud!
    A tale of less affright,
    And tempered with delight,
As Otway's self had framed the tender lay—
    'Tis of a little child
    Upon a lonesome wild,
Not far from home, but she hath lost her way:
And now moans low in bitter grief and fear,
And now screams loud, and hopes to make her mother hear.

8

'Tis midnight, but small thoughts have I of sleep:
Full seldom may my friend such vigils keep!
Visit her, gentle Sleep! with wings of healing,
  And may this storm be but a mountain birth,
May all the stars hang bright above her dwelling,
  Silent as though they watched the sleeping Earth!
    With light heart may she rise,
    Gay fancy, cheerful eyes,
  Joy lift her spirit, joy attune her voice;
To her may all things live, from pole to pole,
Their life the eddying of her living soul!
  O simple spirit, guided from above,
Dear Lady! friend devoutest of my choice,
Thus mayest thou ever, evermore rejoice.

1802

100. tairn: pool. **106. devils' yule:** a devil's Christmas (a winter storm in spring, and therefore unnatural or devilish). **120. Otway:** Thomas Otway, a seventeenth-century poet noted for his tender pathos. **129. mountain birth:** a local storm confined to a mountain.

Limbo

The sole true Something—This! In Limbo's Den
It frightens Ghosts, as here Ghosts frighten men.
Thence cross'd unseiz'd—and shall some fated hour
Be pulveris'd by Demogorgon's power,
And given as poison to annihilate souls—
Even now it shrinks them—they shrink in as Moles
(Nature's mute monks, live mandrakes of the ground)
Creep back from Light—then listen for its sound;—
See but to dread, and dread they know not why—
The natural alien of their negative eye.
'Tis a strange place, this Limbo!—not a Place,
Yet name it so;—where Time and weary Space
Fettered from flight, with night-mare sense of fleeing,
Strive for their last crepuscular half-being;—
Lank Space, and scytheless Time with branny hands
Barren and soundless as the measuring sands,
Not mark'd by flit of Shades,—unmeaning they
As moonlight on the dial of the day!
But that is lovely—looks like Human Time,—
An Old Man with a steady look sublime,
That stops his earthly task to watch the skies;
But he is blind—a Statue hath such eyes;—
Yet having moonward turn'd his face by chance,
Gazes the orb with moon-like countenance,
With scant white hairs, with foretop bald and high,
He gazes still,—his eyeless face all eye;—
As 'twere an organ full of silent sight,
His whole face seemeth to rejoice in light!
Lip touching lip, all moveless, bust and limb—
He seems to gaze at that which seems to gaze on him!
No such sweet sights doth Limbo den immure,
Wall'd round, and made a spirit-jail secure,
By the mere horror of blank Naught-at-all,
Whose circumambience doth these ghosts enthral.
A lurid thought is growthless, dull Privation,
Yet that is but a Purgatory curse;
Hell knows a fear far worse,
A fear—a future state;—'tis positive Negation!

1817

LIMBO. **Title:** Limbo, traditionally located on the edge of Hell, was the abode of pagans who died before Christ and of unbaptized infants; more loosely, a state of neither being nor non-being, but something between. **14. crepuscular:** of or like twilight; applied more specifically to insects and birds that become active then.

On Donne's Poetry

With Donne, whose muse on dromedary trots,
Wreathe iron pokers into true-love knots;
Rhyme's sturdy cripple, fancy's maze and clue,
Wit's forge and fire-blast, meaning's press and screw.

1836

WALTER SAVAGE LANDOR

(1775–1864)

Landor wrote dramas, long poems, and several volumes of wonderfully readable *Imaginary Conversations* (1824–53), the latter consisting of dialogues in which famous characters of history are shown conversing with each other. But Landor is now best remembered for the terse lyrics he wrote in emulation of Greek and Roman classics. In the way they combine extreme brevity, point, and polish of style with controlled emotional intensity, they recall some poems of Ben Jonson but are otherwise almost unique in English poetry. Although not popular when they were written, the poems have since been greatly admired by poets especially. Landor's poetic style strangely contrasts with his uninhibited, impetuous behavior. He was a powerfully built man, and one story tells about his lifting an unruly servingman and tossing him out of a window facing Landor's garden. He then exclaimed, "Great God, I forgot the flowers."

Rose Aylmer

Ah what avails the sceptered race,
  Ah what the form divine!
What every virtue, every grace!
  Rose Aylmer, all were thine.
Rose Aylmer, whom these wakeful eyes

ROSE AYLMER. **Title:** daughter of Baron Aylmer (hence "sceptered race" for noble family). She had died in Calcutta at the age of twenty-one. Landor's poem was later carved on her tomb.

May weep, but never see,
A night of memories and of sighs
I consecrate to thee.

1806

Death Stands Above Me, Whispering Low

Death stands above me, whispering low
I know not what into my ear:
Of his strange language all I know
Is, there is not a word of fear.

1853

Dying Speech of an Old Philosopher

I strove with none, for none was worth my strife:
Nature I loved, and, next to Nature, Art:
I warmed both hands before the fire of Life;
It sinks; and I am ready to depart.

1853

THOMAS MOORE

(1779–1852)

The son of a Dublin grocer, Moore acquired an immense reputation in his own time. The Irish regarded him almost as their national poet, and some of his longer narrative poems sold widely wherever English was read. Now he is remembered primarily for a handful of lyrics from his *Irish Melodies* (1808–34), many of them written to go with traditional Irish airs, though, for some of them, he wrote his own music. Two of these lyrics continue to be sung, and even to be learned at school by children: "The Harp that Once through Tara's Halls" (Tara, northwest of Dublin, was the seat of ancient Irish kings) and "Believe Me, if All Those Endearing Young Charms."

The Harp that Once through Tara's Halls

The harp that once through Tara's halls
  The soul of music shed,
Now hangs as mute on Tara's walls
  As if that soul were fled.—
So sleeps the pride of former days,
  So glory's thrill is o'er,
And hearts that once beat high for praise
  Now feel that pulse no more!

No more to chiefs and ladies bright
  The harp of Tara swells;
The chord alone that breaks at night
  Its tale of ruin tells.
Thus freedom now so seldom wakes,
  The only throb she gives
Is when some heart indignant breaks,
  To show that still she lives.

1834

Believe Me, if All Those Endearing Young Charms

Believe me, if all those endearing young charms,
  Which I gaze on so fondly today,
Were to change by tomorrow, and fleet in my arms,
  Like fairy gifts fading away,
Thou wouldst still be adored, as this moment thou art,
  Let thy loveliness fade as it will,
And around the dear ruin each wish of my heart
  Would intwine itself verdantly still.

It is not while beauty and youth are thine own,
  And my cheeks unprofaned by a tear,
That the fervor and faith of a soul can be known,
  To which time will but make thee more dear;
No, the heart that has truly loved never forgets,
  But as truly loves on to the close,
As the sunflower turns on her god, when he sets,
The same look which she turned when he rose.

1834

George Gordon, Lord Byron

(1788–1824)

Byron was the most famous poet of his time, not only in England but in Europe and throughout the Atlantic world. He seemed to have everything: genius, wealth, aristocratic rank, and beauty. Rumors of his wild moods and sexual profligacy made him seem the more glamorous to many persons. After his death in Greece, where he was fighting on the side of the Greeks in their revolt against Turkish rule, he was celebrated as a heroic battler for political freedom.

Byron wrote dramas, narrative poems, lyrics, and, in *Childe Harold's Pilgrimage,* a verse account of his travels through Europe and the Near East. All these works have enormous verve, but Byron's complicated personality is most fully expressed in his comic masterpiece, *Don Juan.* This long narrative poem (which Byron left unfinished) alludes to the old legend in which Don Juan is a diabolic seducer, but in keeping with Byron's comic and satiric intentions, the poem portrays Don Juan as a well meaning, somewhat passive young man pursued by women. Byron also invented a worldly-wise narrator to tell Juan's story, and the narrator's disillusioned commentaries and changing moods make him as splendid a creation as Don Juan himself. No brief selection from *Don Juan* can adequately represent so huge and various a poem, but we include the famous conclusion to the first Canto and a portion from the second. In the latter extract Juan has been shipwrecked on an Aegean island and has met the beautiful Haidee, a pirate's daughter. Our selection from Byron also includes some of the lyrics that show his rhetorical flair and grasp of melody and cadence.

Maid Of Athens, ere We Part

Ζώη μοῡ, σᾶς ἀγαπῶ.

Maid of Athens, ere we part,
Give, oh give me back my heart!
Or, since that has left my breast,

MAID OF ATHENS. The Greek motto used also as a refrain after each stanza means: "My life, I love you."

Keep it now, and take the rest!
Hear my vow before I go,
Ζώη μοῦ, σᾶς ἀγαπῶ.

By those tresses unconfined,
Woo'd by each Ægean wind;
By those lids whose jetty fringe
Kiss thy soft cheeks' blooming tinge;
By those wild eyes like the roe,
Ζώη μοῦ, σᾶς ἀγαπῶ.

By that lip I long to taste;
By that zone-encircled waist;
By all the token-flowers that tell
What words can never speak so well;
By love's alternate joy and woe,
Ζώη μοῦ, σᾶς ἀγαπῶ.

Maid of Athens, I am gone:
Think of me, sweet! when alone.
Though I fly to Istambol,
Athens holds my heart and soul:
Can I cease to love thee? No!
Ζώη μοῦ, σᾶς ἀγαπῶ.

1812

She Walks in Beauty

She walks in beauty, like the night
  Of cloudless climes and starry skies;
And all that's best of dark and bright
  Meet in her aspect and her eyes:
Thus mellow'd to that tender light
  Which heaven to gaudy day denies.

One shade the more, one ray the less,
  Had half impaired the nameless grace
Which waves in every raven tress,
  Or softly lightens o'er her face;
Where thoughts serenely sweet express
  How pure, how dear their dwelling-place.

And on that cheek, and o'er that brow,
  So soft, so calm, yet eloquent,
The smiles that win, the tints that glow,
  But tell of days in goodness spent,
A mind at peace with all below,
  A heart whose love is innocent!

1815

SHE WALKS IN BEAUTY. **1. She:** Lady Wilmot Horton, a relative by marriage, whom Byron met at a ball the night before he wrote this.

The Destruction of Sennacherib

The Assyrian came down like the wolf on the fold,
And his cohorts were gleaming in purple and gold;
And the sheen of their spears was like stars on the sea,
When the blue wave rolls nightly on deep Galilee.

Like the leaves of the forest when summer is green,
That host with their banners at sunset were seen:
Like the leaves of the forest when autumn hath blown,
That host on the morrow lay wither'd and strown.

For the Angel of Death spread his wings on the blast,
And breathed in the face of the foe as he pass'd;
And the eyes of the sleepers wax'd deadly and chill,
And their hearts but once heaved, and forever grew still!

And there lay the steed with his nostril all wide,
But through it there roll'd not the breath of his pride;
And the foam of his gasping lay white on the turf,
And cold as the spray of the rock-beating surf.

And there lay the rider distorted and pale,
With the dew on his brow, and the rust on his mail:
And the tents were all silent, the banners alone,
The lances unlifted, the trumpet unblown.

And the widows of Ashur are loud in their wail,
And the idols are broke in the temple of Baal;
And the might of the Gentile, unsmote by the sword,
Hath melted like snow in the glance of the Lord!

1815

Stanzas for Music

There's not a joy the world can give like that it takes away,
When the glow of early thought declines in feeling's dull decay;
'Tis not on youth's smooth cheek the blush alone, which fades so fast,
But the tender bloom of heart is gone, ere youth itself be past.

Then the few whose spirits float above the wreck of happiness
Are driven o'er the shoals of guilt or ocean of excess:
The magnet of their course is gone, or only points in vain
The shore to which their shiver'd sail shall never stretch again.

THE DESTRUCTION OF SENNACHERIB. **Title:** For the story, see II Kings, 18–19.

Then the mortal coldness of the soul like death itself comes down;
It cannot feel for others' woes, it dare not dream its own;
That heavy chill has frozen o'er the fountain of our tears,
And though the eye may sparkle still, 'tis where the ice appears.

Though wit may flash from fluent lips, and mirth distract
    the breast,
Through midnight hours that yield no more their former hope
    of rest;
'Tis but as ivy-leaves around the ruin'd turret wreath,
All green and wildly fresh without, but worn and gray beneath.

Oh could I feel as I have felt,—or be what I have been,
Or weep as I could once have wept o'er many a vanish'd scene;
As springs in deserts found seem sweet, all brackish though
    they be,
So, midst the wither'd waste of life, those tears would flow to me.

1816

Prometheus

Titan! to whose immortal eyes
  The sufferings of mortality,
  Seen in their sad reality,
Were not as things that gods despise;
What was thy pity's recompense?
A silent suffering, and intense;
The rock, the vulture, and the chain,
All that the proud can feel of pain,
The agony they do not show,
The suffocating sense of woe,
  Which speaks but in its loneliness,
And then is jealous lest the sky
Should have a listener, nor will sigh
  Until its voice is echoless.

Titan! to thee the strife was given
  Between the suffering and the will,
  Which torture where they cannot kill;
And the inexorable Heaven,
And the deaf tyranny of Fate,
The ruling principle of Hate,
Which for its pleasure doth create
The things it may annihilate,
Refused thee even the boon to die:
The wretched gift eternity

PROMETHEUS. **Title:** Prometheus stole fire from the gods in order to give it to mankind.

Was thine—and thou hast borne it well.
All that the Thunderer wrung from thee
Was but the menace which flung back
On him the torments of thy rack;
The fate thou didst so well foresee,
But would not to appease him tell;
And in thy silence was his sentence,
And in his soul a vain repentance,
And evil dread so ill dissembled,
That in his hand the lightnings trembled.

Thy Godlike crime was to be kind,
  To render with thy precepts less
  The sum of human wretchedness,
And strengthen man with his own mind;
But baffled as thou wert from high,
Still in thy patient energy,
In the endurance, and repulse
  Of thine impenetrable spirit,
Which Earth and Heaven could not convulse,
  A mighty lesson we inherit:
Thou art a symbol and a sign
  To mortals of their fate and force;
Like thee, man is in part divine,
  A troubled stream from a pure source;
And man in portions can foresee
His own funereal destiny;
His wretchedness, and his resistance,
And his sad unallied existence:
To which his spirit may oppose
Itself—and equal to all woes,
  And a firm will, and a deep sense,
Which even in torture can descry
  Its own concenter'd recompense,
Triumphant where it dares defy,
And making death a victory.

1816

So We'll Go No More A-Roving

So, we'll go no more a-roving
  So late into the night,
Though the heart be still as loving,
  And the moon be still as bright.

26. Thunderer: Zeus (or Jupiter). **29. fate . . . foresee:** Prometheus foresaw the downfall of Zeus.

For the sword outwears its sheath,
  And the soul outwears the breast,
And the heart must pause to breathe,
  And love itself have rest.

Though the night was made for loving,
  And the day returns too soon,
Yet we'll go no more a-roving
  By the light of the moon.

1817

from Don Juan

FRAGMENT

On the back of the Poet's MS. of Canto I.

I would to heaven that I were so much clay,
  As I am blood, bone, marrow, passion, feeling—
Because at least the past were pass'd away—
  And for the future—(but I write this reeling,
Having got drunk exceedingly to-day,
  So that I seem to stand upon the ceiling)
I say—the future is a serious matter—
And so—for God's sake—hock and soda-water!

from Canto the First

CCXIV

No more—no more—Oh! never more on me
  The freshness of the heart can fall like dew,
Which out of all the lovely things we see
  Extracts emotions beautiful and new,
Hived in our bosoms like the bag o' the bee.
  Think'st thou the honey with those objects grew?
Alas! 't was not in them, but in thy power
To double even the sweetness of a flower.

CCXV

No more—no more—Oh! never more, my heart,
  Canst thou be my sole world, my universe!
Once all in all, but now a thing apart,

DON JUAN. FRAGMENT. **8. hock:** Rhine wine (from German *Hochheimer*). Hock and soda water were frequently drunk to relieve a hangover.

Thou canst not be my blessing or my curse:
The illusion's gone for ever, and thou art
Insensible, I trust, but none the worse,
And in thy stead I've got a deal of judgment
Though heaven knows how it ever found a lodgment.

CCXVI

My days of love are over; me no more
The charms of maid, wife, and still less of widow,
Can make the fool of which they made before,—
In short, I must not lead the life I did do;
The credulous hope of mutual minds is o'er,
The copious use of claret is forbid too,
So for a good old-gentlemanly vice,
I think I must take up with avarice.

CCXVII

Ambition was my idol, which was broken
Before the shrines of Sorrow, and of Pleasure;
And the two last have left me many a token
O'er which reflection may be made at leisure;
Now, like Friar Bacon's brazen head, I've spoken
"Time is, Time was, Time 's past":—a chymic treasure
Is glittering youth, which I have spent betimes—
My heart in passion, and my head on rhymes.

CCXVIII

What is the end of fame? 't is but to fill
A certain portion of uncertain paper:
Some liken it to climbing up a hill,
Whose summit, like all hills, is lost in vapor;
For this men write, speak, preach, and heroes kill,
And bards burn what they call their "midnight taper,"
To have, when the original is dust,
A name, a wretched picture, and worse bust.

CCXIX

What are the hopes of man? Old Egypt's King
Cheops erected the first pyramid
And largest, thinking it was just the thing
To keep his memory whole, and mummy hid:
But somebody or other rummaging,
Burglariously broke his coffin's lid:
Let not a monument give you or me hopes,
Since not a pinch of dust remains of Cheops.

1733. Bacon's . . . head: a brass head that could speak, made by Friar Roger Bacon. **1752. Cheops:** builder of the Great Pyramid.

CCXX

But I, being fond of true philosophy,
  Say very often to myself, "Alas!
All things that have been born were born to die,
  And flesh (which Death mows down to hay) is grass;
You've passed your youth not so unpleasantly,
  And if you had it o'er again—'t would pass—
So thank your stars that matters are no worse,
And read your Bible, sir, and mind your purse."

CCXXI

But for the present, gentle reader! and
  Still gentler purchaser! the bard—that's I—
Must, with permission, shake you by the hand,
  And so your humble servant, and good-bye!
We meet again, if we should understand
  Each other; and if not, I shall not try
Your patience further than by this short sample—
'T were well if others followed my example.

CCXXII

"Go, little book, from this my solitude!
  I cast thee on the waters—go thy ways!
And if, as I believe, thy vein be good,
  The world will find thee after many days."
When Southey's read, and Wordsworth understood,
  I can't help putting in my claim to praise—
The four first rhymes are Southey's, every line:
For God's sake, reader! take them not for mine!

1819

from Canto the Second

CLXXVII

It was a wild and breaker-beaten coast,
  With cliffs above, and a broad sandy shore,
Guarded by shoals and rocks as by an host,
  With here and there a creek, whose aspect wore
A better welcome to the tempest-tost;
  And rarely ceased the haughty billow's roar,
Save on the dead long summer days, which make
The outstretch'd ocean glitter like a lake.

1769–72. "Go . . . days": quoted from the last stanza of Robert Southey's *Epilogue to the Lay of the Laureate.* "Don Juan" was dedicated—in a mocking spirit—to Southey, who had become poet laureate in 1813.

CLXXVIII

And the small ripple spilt upon the beach
  Scarcely o'erpass'd the cream of your champagne,
When o'er the brim the sparkling bumpers reach,
  That spring-dew of the spirit! the heart's rain!
Few things surpass old wine; and they may preach
  Who please,—the more because they preach in vain,—
Let us have wine and woman, mirth and laughter,
Sermons and soda-water the day after.

CLXXIX

Man, being reasonable, must get drunk;
  The best of life is but intoxication:
Glory, the grape, love, gold, in these are sunk
  The hopes of all men, and of every nation;
Without their sap, how branchless were the trunk
  Of life's strange tree, so fruitful on occasion:
But to return,—Get very drunk; and when
You wake with headache, you shall see what then.

CLXXX

Ring for your valet—bid him quickly bring
  Some hock and soda-water, then you'll know
A pleasure worthy Xerxes the great king;
  For not the blest sherbet, sublimed with snow,
Nor the first sparkle of the desert-spring,
  Nor Burgundy in all its sunset glow,
After long travel, ennui, love, or slaughter,
Vie with that draught of hock and soda-water.

Percy Bysshe Shelley

(1792–1822)

Ever since his early death, Shelley has been for many readers the quintessence of the "Romantic Poet." Even his death seemed typical of his dauntless spirit. He drowned when he sailed his small boat out into the Mediterranean Sea even though a storm was predicted and he could not swim. He was only twenty-nine. He had lived only for his ideals. He looked forward to a time when society would be transformed, when all men and women would not only be equal in the ordinary sense but would all manifest the divine spirit. Naturally he viewed existing social institutions—monarchy, the church, private property—as repressive, and felt that the ideal society could come about only after their overthrow. But he also believed that a true and lasting revolution could not be brought about by violence.

His poetry is pervaded by his idealism. He attempts to show readers that human nature and society can and must be redeemed, and he presents images of the ideal possibilities, images that will motivate us, Shelley believes, to work to make them real. Frequently he falls into deep melancholy and is close to despair at the obstacles to his hope. He based his hopes on the English empirical philosophy of his age, for this philosophy taught that we can change human character and behavior by changing the social institutions that shape them. Shelley was also entranced by the Greek philosopher, Plato, for whom the ultimate realities or true forms of existence lay beyond the mortal world in which we live. Even while we are still in the mortal world, Plato argued, we can know and be inspired by these true forms, and many of Plato's followers taught that at moments these forms descend into human consciousness, revealing themselves and causing an irresistable love for them. This is a theme of Shelley's "Hymn to Intellectual Beauty" and "Ode to the West Wind." In the latter poem, the ultimate Platonic reality is symbolized in the west wind; its sudden descent—which can bring about the total change, as from winter to spring—is what the poem anticipates and celebrates.

Shelley would never have approved a discussion of poetry that focussed mainly on style and form. But in the arts, as the generations pass, we begin to pay less attention to the particular "message" and consider more the splendor and power with which it is put, whether in words, painting, or music. Thus what now seems most wonderful in the "Ode to the West Wind" is the power or sweep in expression. Using masterfully a confined and somewhat classical form of stanza called *terza rima* (three lines rhyming *a b a,* followed by a line that picks up the middle rhyme, *b,* and uses it to continue *b c b,* and so forth), Shelley's headlong intensity mounts through a series of clauses to the climactic prayer to the wind in Stanza V. Actors and other people familiar with the art of recitation have found that because of its sustained intensity and sweep, reading this magnificent poem aloud is an enormous challenge.

Hymn to Intellectual Beauty

I

The awful shadow of some unseen Power
  Floats though unseen among us,—visiting
  This various world with as inconstant wing
As summer winds that creep from flower to flower,—
Like moonbeams that behind some piny mountain shower,
    It visits with inconstant glance
    Each human heart and countenance;
Like hues and harmonies of evening,—
    Like clouds in starlight widely spread,—
    Like memory of music fled,—
    Like aught that for its grace may be
Dear, and yet dearer for its mystery.

II

Spirit of BEAUTY, that dost consecrate
  With thine own hues all thou dost shine upon
  Of human thought or form,—where art thou gone?
Why dost thou pass away and leave our state,
This dim vast vale of tears, vacant and desolate?
    Ask why the sunlight not for ever
    Weaves rainbows o'er yon mountain-river,
Why aught should fail and fade that once is shown,
    Why fear and dream and death and birth
    Cast on the daylight of this earth
    Such gloom,—why man has such a scope
For love and hate, despondency and hope?

III

No voice from some sublimer world hath ever
  To sage or poet these responses given—
  Therefore the names of Demon, Ghost, and Heaven,
Remain the records of their vain endeavour,
Frail spells—whose uttered charm might not avail to sever,
    From all we hear and all we see,
    Doubt, chance, and mutability.
Thy light alone—like mist o'er mountains driven,
    Or music by the night-wind sent
    Through strings of some still instrument,
    Or moonlight on a midnight stream,
Gives grace and truth to life's unquiet dream.

HYMN TO INTELLECTUAL BEAUTY. **Title:** Beauty as perceived solely by the mind, through spiritual insight, without the need of the senses. **25–26. No . . . responses:** Revealed religion gives no answers to the questions in lines 13–17.

IV

Love, Hope, and Self-esteem, like clouds depart
  And come, for some uncertain moments lent.
  Man were immortal, and omnipotent,
Didst thou, unknown and awful as thou art,
Keep with thy glorious train firm state within his heart.
    Thou messenger of sympathies,
    That wax and wane in lovers' eyes—
Thou—that to human thought art nourishment,
    Like darkness to a dying flame!
    Depart not as thy shadow came,
    Depart not—lest the grave should be,
Like life and fear, a dark reality.

V

While yet a boy I sought for ghosts, and sped
  Through many a listening chamber, cave and ruin,
  And starlight wood, with fearful steps pursuing
Hopes of high talk with the departed dead.
I called on poisonous names with which our youth is fed;
  I was not heard—I saw them not—
  When musing deeply on the lot
Of life, at that sweet time when winds are wooing
    All vital things that wake to bring
    News of birds and blossoming,—
    Sudden, thy shadow fell on me;
I shrieked, and clasped my hands in ecstasy!

VI

I vowed that I would dedicate my powers
    To thee and thine—have I not kept the vow?
    With beating heart and streaming eyes, even now
I call the phantoms of a thousand hours
Each from his voiceless grave: they have in visioned bowers
    Of studious zeal or love's delight
    Outwatched with me the envious night—
They know that never joy illumed my brow
    Unlinked with hope that thou wouldst free
    This world from its dark slavery,
    That thou—O awful LOVELINESS,
Wouldst give whate'er these words cannot express.

41. train: company. **53. poisonous names:** trying to summon spirits of the dead through "black magic."

VII

The day becomes more solemn and serene
When noon is past—there is a harmony
In autumn, and a lustre in its sky,
Which through the summer is not heard or seen,
As if it could not be, as if it had not been!
Thus let thy power, which like the truth
Of nature on my passive youth
Descended, to my onward life supply
Its calm—to one who worships thee,
And every form containing thee,
Whom, SPIRIT fair, thy spells did bind
To fear himself, and love all human kind.

1817

Ozymandias

I met a traveller from an antique land
Who said: Two vast and trunkless legs of stone
Stand in the desert . . . Near them, on the sand,
Half sunk, a shattered visage lies, whose frown,
And wrinkled lip, and sneer of cold command,
Tell that its sculptor well those passions read
Which yet survive, stamped on these lifeless things,
The hand that mocked them, and the heart that fed:
And on the pedestal these words appear:
"My name is Ozymandias, king of kings:
Look on my works, ye Mighty, and despair!"
Nothing beside remains. Round the decay
Of that colossal wreck, boundless and bare
The lone and level sands stretch far away.

1818

Song to the Men of England

I

Men of England, wherefore plough
For the lords who lay ye low?
Wherefore weave with toil and care
The rich robes your tyrants wear?

OZYMANDIAS. **6–8. passions . . . fed:** expressions of passions that survive the hand of the artist that imitated or mocked them, as well as the heart of the king that fed them.

II

Wherefore feed, and clothe, and save,
From the cradle to the grave,
Those ungrateful drones who would
Drain your sweat—nay, drink your blood?

III

Wherefore, Bees of England, forge
Many a weapon, chain, and scourge,
That these stingless drones may spoil
The forced produce of your toil?

IV

Have ye leisure, comfort, calm,
Shelter, food, love's gentle balm?
Or what is it ye buy so dear
With your pain and with your fear?

V

The seed ye sow, another reaps;
The wealth ye find, another keeps;
The robes ye weave, another wears;
The arms ye forge, another bears.

VI

Sow seed,—but let no tyrant reap;
Find wealth,—let no impostor heap;
Weave robes,—let not the idle wear;
Forge arms,—in your defence to bear.

VII

Shrink to your cellars, holes, and cells;
In halls ye deck another dwells.
Why shake the chains ye wrought? Ye see
The steel ye tempered glance on ye.

VIII

With plough and spade, and hoe and loom,
Trace your grave, and build your tomb,
And weave your winding-sheet, till fair
England be your sepulchre.

1819

Ode to the West Wind

I

O wild West Wind, thou breath of Autumn's being,
Thou, from whose unseen presence the leaves dead
Are driven, like ghosts from an enchanter fleeing,

Yellow, and black, and pale, and hectic red,
Pestilence-stricken multitudes: O thou,
Who chariotest to their dark wintry bed

The wingèd seeds, where they lie cold and low,
Each like a corpse within its grave, until
Thine azure sister of the Spring shall blow

Her clarion o'er the dreaming earth, and fill
(Driving sweet buds like flocks to feed in air)
With living hues and odours plain and hill:

Wild Spirit, which art moving everywhere;
Destroyer and preserver; hear, oh, hear!

II

Thou on whose stream, mid the steep sky's commotion,
Loose clouds like earth's decaying leaves are shed,
Shook from the tangled boughs of Heaven and Ocean,

Angels of rain and lightning: there are spread
On the blue surface of thine aëry surge,
Like the bright hair uplifted from the head

Of some fierce Maenad, even from the dim verge
Of the horizon to the zenith's height,
The locks of the approaching storm. Thou dirge

Of the dying year, to which this closing night
Will be the dome of a vast sepulchre,
Vaulted with all thy congregated might

Of vapours, from whose solid atmosphere
Black rain, and fire, and hail will burst: oh, hear!

III

Thou who didst waken from his summer dreams
The blue Mediterranean, where he lay,
Lulled by the coil of his crystalline streams,

ODE TO THE WEST WIND. **9. sister:** Zephyr, the West Wind that brings the spring. **10. clarion:** trumpet call. **21. Maenad:** frenzied women dancers who worshipped Dionysus, god of fertility and wine.

Beside a pumice isle in Baiae's bay,
And saw in sleep old palaces and towers
Quivering within the wave's intenser day,

All overgrown with azure moss and flowers
So sweet, the sense faints picturing them! Thou
For whose path the Atlantic's level powers

Cleave themselves into chasms, while far below
The sea-blooms and the oozy woods which wear
The sapless foliage of the ocean, know

Thy voice, and suddenly grow gray with fear,
And tremble and despoil themselves: oh, hear!

IV

If I were a dead leaf thou mightest bear;
If I were a swift cloud to fly with thee;
A wave to pant beneath thy power, and share

The impulse of thy strength, only less free
Than thou, O uncontrollable! If even
I were as in my boyhood, and could be

The comrade of thy wanderings over Heaven,
As then, when to outstrip thy skiey speed
Scarce seemed a vision; I would ne'er have striven

As thus with thee in prayer in my sore need.
Oh, lift me as a wave, a leaf, a cloud!
I fall upon the thorns of life! I bleed!

A heavy weight of hours has chained and bowed
One too like thee: tameless, and swift, and proud.

V

Make me thy lyre, even as the forest is:
What if my leaves are falling like its own!
The tumult of thy mighty harmonies

Will take from both a deep, autumnal tone,
Sweet though in sadness. Be thou, Spirit fierce,
My spirit! Be thou me, impetuous one!

Drive my dead thoughts over the universe
Like withered leaves to quicken a new birth!
And, by the incantation of this verse,

32. pumice: porous stone produced by volcanoes. **Baiae:** district west of Naples. **57. lyre:** Aeolian lyre, on which the wind plays by stirring the strings.

Scatter, as from an unextinguished hearth
Ashes and sparks, my words among mankind!
Be through my lips to unawakened earth

The trumpet of a prophecy! O, Wind,
If Winter comes, can Spring be far behind?

1820

The Cloud

I bring fresh showers for the thirsting flowers,
    From the seas and the streams;
I bear light shade for the leaves when laid
    In their noonday dreams.
From my wings are shaken the dews that waken
    The sweet buds every one,
When rocked to rest on their mother's breast,
    As she dances about the sun.
I wield the flail of the lashing hail,
    And whiten the green plains under,
And then again I dissolve it in rain,
    And laugh as I pass in thunder.

I sift the snow on the mountains below,
    And their great pines groan aghast;
And all the night 'tis my pillow white,
    While I sleep in the arms of the blast.
Sublime on the towers of my skiey bowers,
    Lightning my pilot sits;
In a cavern under is fettered the thunder,
    It struggles and howls at fits;
Over earth and ocean, with gentle motion,
    This pilot is guiding me,
Lured by the love of the genii that move
    In the depths of the purple sea;
Over the rills, and the crags, and the hills,
    Over the lakes and the plains,
Wherever he dream, under mountain or stream,
    The Spirit he loves remains;
And I all the while bask in Heaven's blue smile,
    Whilst he is dissolving in rains.

The sanguine Sunrise, with his meteor eyes,
    And his burning plumes outspread,
Leaps on the back of my sailing rack,
    When the morning star shines dead;
As on the jag of a mountain crag,
    Which an earthquake rocks and swings,

THE CLOUD. **20. at fits:** fitfully. **33. rack:** thin, high-flying clouds.

An eagle alit one moment may sit
In the light of its golden wings.
And when Sunset may breathe, from the lit sea beneath,
Its ardours of rest and of love,
And the crimson pall of eve may fall
From the depth of Heaven above,
With wings folded I rest, on mine aëry nest,
As still as a brooding dove.

That orbed maiden with white fire laden,
Whom mortals call the Moon,
Glides glimmering o'er my fleece-like floor,
By the midnight breezes strewn;
And wherever the beat of her unseen feet,
Which only the angels hear,
May have broken the woof of my tent's thin roof,
The stars peep behind her and peer;
And I laugh to see them whirl and flee,
Like a swarm of golden bees,
When I widen the rent in my wind-built tent,
Till the calm rivers, lakes, and seas,
Like strips of the sky fallen through me on high,
Are each paved with the moon and these.

I bind the Sun's throne with a burning zone,
And the Moon's with a girdle of pearl;
The volcanoes are dim, and the stars reel and swim,
When the whirlwinds my banner unfurl.
From cape to cape, with a bridge-like shape,
Over a torrent sea,
Sunbeam-proof, I hang like a roof,—
The mountains its columns be.
The triumphal arch through which I march
With hurricane, fire, and snow,
When the Powers of the air are chained to my chair,
Is the million-coloured bow;
The sphere-fire above its soft colours wove,
While the moist Earth was laughing below.

I am the daughter of Earth and Water,
And the nursling of the Sky;
I pass through the pores of the ocean and shores;
I change, but I cannot die.
For after the rain when with never a stain
The pavilion of Heaven is bare,
And the winds and sunbeams with their convex gleams
Build up the blue dome of air,
I silently laugh at my own cenotaph,

51. woof: fabric. **58. these:** the stars. **59. zone:** belt. 79. **convex:** rays of light curved by the atmosphere. **81. cenotaph:** monument honoring someone buried elsewhere.

And out of the caverns of rain,
Like a child from the womb, like a ghost from the tomb,
I arise and unbuild it again.

1820

To a Skylark

Hail to thee, blithe Spirit!
Bird thou never wert,
That from Heaven, or near it,
Pourest thy full heart
In profuse strains of unpremeditated art.

Higher still and higher
From the earth thou springest
Like a cloud of fire;
The blue deep thou wingest,
And singing still dost soar, and soaring ever singest.

In the golden lightning
Of the sunken sun,
O'er which clouds are bright'ning,
Thou dost float and run;
Like an unbodied joy whose race is just begun.

The pale purple even
Melts around thy flight;
Like a star of Heaven,
In the broad daylight
Thou art unseen, but yet I hear thy shrill delight,

Keen as are the arrows
Of that silver sphere,
Whose intense lamp narrows
In the white dawn clear
Until we hardly see—we feel that it is there.

All the earth and air
With thy voice is loud,
As, when night is bare,
From one lonely cloud
The moon rains out her beams, and Heaven is overflowed.

What thou art we know not;
What is most like thee?
From rainbow clouds there flow not
Drops so bright to see
As from thy presence showers a rain of melody.

TO A SKYLARK. **22. silver sphere:** morning star.

Like a Poet hidden
  In the light of thought,
Singing hymns unbidden,
  Till the world is wrought
To sympathy with hopes and fears it heeded not:

Like a high-born maiden
  In a palace-tower,
Soothing her love-laden
  Soul in secret hour
With music sweet as love, which overflows her bower:

Like a glow-worm golden
  In a dell of dew,
Scattering unbeholden
  Its aëreal hue
Among the flowers and grass, which screen it from the view:

Like a rose embowered
  In its own green leaves,
By warm winds deflowered,
  Till the scent it gives
Makes faint with too much sweet those heavy-wingèd thieves:

Sound of vernal showers
  On the twinkling grass,
Rain-awakened flowers,
  All that ever was
Joyous, and clear, and fresh, thy music doth surpass:

Teach us, Sprite or Bird,
  What sweet thoughts are thine:
I have never heard
  Praise of love or wine
That panted forth a flood of rapture so divine.

Chorus Hymeneal,
  Or triumphal chant,
Matched with thine would be all
  But an empty vaunt,
A thing wherein we feel there is some hidden want.

What objects are the fountains
  Of thy happy strain?
What fields, or waves, or mountains?
  What shapes of sky or plain?
What love of thine own kind? what ignorance of pain?

With thy clear keen joyance
  Langour cannot be:

55. thieves: the warm winds in line 53. **61. Sprite:** spirit. **66. Hymeneal:** in celebration of marriage.

Shadow of annoyance
Never came near thee:
Thou lovest—but ne'er knew love's sad satiety.

Waking or asleep,
Thou of death must deem
Things more true and deep
Than we mortals dream,
Or how could thy notes flow in such a crystal stream?

We look before and after,
And pine for what is not:
Our sincerest laughter
With some pain is fraught;
Our sweetest songs are those that tell of saddest thought.

Yet if we could scorn
Hate, and pride, and fear;
If we were things born
Not to shed a tear,
I know not how thy joy we ever should come near.

Better than all measures
Of delightful sound,
Better than all treasures
That in books are found,
Thy skill to poet were, thou scorner of the ground!

Teach me half the gladness
That thy brain must know,
Such harmonious madness
From my lips would flow
The world should listen then—as I am listening now.

1820

To—

Music, when soft voices die,
Vibrates in the memory—
Odours, when sweet violets sicken,
Live within the sense they quicken.

Rose leaves, when the rose is dead,
Are heaped for the beloved's bed;
And so thy thoughts, when thou art gone,
Love itself shall slumber on.

1824

A Lament

I

O world! O life! O time!
On whose last steps I climb,
  Trembling at that where I had stood before;
When will return the glory of your prime?
    No more—Oh, never more!

II

Out of the day and night
A joy has taken flight;
  Fresh spring, and summer, and winter hoar,
Move my faint heart with grief, but with delight
    No more—Oh, never more!

1824

The World's Great Age Begins Anew

The world's great age begins anew,
  The golden years return,
The earth doth like a snake renew
  Her winter weeds outworn:
Heaven smiles, and faiths and empires gleam,
Like wrecks of a dissolving dream.

A brighter Hellas rears its mountains
  From waves serener far;
A new Peneus rolls his fountains
  Against the morning star.
Where fairer Tempes bloom, there sleep
Young Cyclads on a sunnier deep.

A loftier Argo cleaves the main,
  Fraught with a later prize;
Another Orpheus sings again,
  And loves, and weeps, and dies.
A new Ulysses leaves once more
Calypso for his native shore.

THE WORLD'S GREAT AGE BEGINS ANEW. **Title:** The poem is a chorus from Shelley's play "Hellas." **3. snake:** shedding its skin, a symbol of regeneration. **4. weeds:** clothes. **9. Peneus:** river in Greece famous for its beauty. **11. Tempe:** valley of the Peneus. **12. Cyclads:** islands in the Aegean Sea. **13. Argo:** the ship in which Jason sailed in search of the Golden Fleece. **15. Orpheus:** Greek musician, whose singing allowed his wife Eurydice to be released from Hades provided he did not look at her before they returned to earth. But he did look and thus lost her.

Oh, write no more the tale of Troy,
  If earth Death's scroll must be!
Nor mix with Laian rage the joy
  Which dawns upon the free:
Although a subtler Sphinx renew
Riddles of death Thebes never knew.

Another Athens shall arise,
  And to remoter time
Bequeath, like sunset to the skies,
  The splendour of its prime;
And leave, if nought so bright may live,
All earth can take or Heaven can give.

Saturn and Love their long repose
  Shall burst, more bright and good
Than all who fell, than One who rose,
  Than many unsubdued:
Not gold, not blood, their altar dowers,
But votive tears and symbol flowers.

Oh, cease! must hate and death return?
  Cease! must men kill and die?
Cease! drain not to its dregs the urn
  Of bitter prophecy.
The world is weary of the past,
Oh, might it die or rest at last!

1822

A Dirge

Rough wind, that moanest loud
  Grief too sad for song;
Wild wind, when sullen cloud
  Knells all the night long;
Sad storm, whose tears are vain,
Bare woods, whose branches strain,
Deep caves and dreary main,—
  Wail, for the world's wrong!

1824

21. Laian: Oedipus, not knowing who he was, killed his father Laius of Thebes.

William Cullen Bryant

(1794–1878)

A poet of the Romantic movement in the United States, Bryant was born in Massachusetts in a log farmhouse on the edge of the wilderness. His father, a doctor, saw to it that his son received a good education. As a schoolboy Bryant was impressed by the stately meditative poetry of England in the eighteenth century, such as Gray's *Elegy*, with its themes of mortality and the uncertainties of life. Then, when he was sixteen, he read Wordsworth, and was deeply moved by Wordsworth's concept of nature as a manifestation and expression of God. Both influences may be seen in his poem "Thanatopsis" (meaning "meditation on death"), the first version of which was written when he was seventeen and studying law in western Massachusetts (he expanded the poem a few years later). The quiet control and dignified phrasing of the blank verse, modeled after Wordsworth, brought him rapid acclaim from readers who could not believe that so mature a poem had been written by someone so young. His later poems continued to reflect his Wordsworthian approach to nature.

Bryant's fame as a poet had a number of causes. His *Poems* (1821) contained the best verse published in America up to that time, and Americans were eager for a poet of their own. He conferred a poetical quality, so to speak, on American landscape, Indian legends, history, and ways of life by using them as subjects of poetry. His high-minded faith appealed to readers who, like himself, had abandoned rigorous Puritan beliefs but retained a religious cast of mind. (Bryant had been brought up as a Calvinist, but his dogmatic commitment had weakened in early manhood.) In the later years of his long life he represented to a younger generation, born around 1850, the virtuous simplicity of an earlier time that now seemed past.

It was difficult to make a living from poetry in the young America of his time, and Bryant eventually became a very successful newspaper editor in New York City. He used his influence to advance liberal causes, especially the abolition of slavery.

Thanatopsis

To him who in the love of Nature holds
Communion with her visible forms, she speaks
A various language; for his gayer hours
She has a voice of gladness, and a smile
And eloquence of beauty, and she glides
Into his darker musings, with a mild
And gentle sympathy, that steals away
Their sharpness, ere he is aware. When thoughts
Of the last bitter hour come like a blight
Over thy spirit, and sad images
Of the stern agony, and shroud, and pall,
And breathless darkness, and the narrow house,
Make thee to shudder, and grow sick at heart;—
Go forth under the open sky, and list
To Nature's teachings, while from all around—
Earth and her waters, and the depths of air,—
Comes a still voice—Yet a few days, and thee
The all-beholding sun shall see no more
In all his course; nor yet in the cold ground,
Where thy pale form was laid, with many tears,
Nor in the embrace of ocean shall exist
Thy image. Earth, that nourished thee, shall claim
Thy growth, to be resolv'd to earth again;
And, lost each human trace, surrend'ring up
Thine individual being, shalt thou go
To mix forever with the elements,
To be a brother to th' insensible rock
And to the sluggish clod, which the rude swain
Turns with his share, and treads upon. The oak
Shall send his roots abroad, and pierce thy mould.
Yet not to thy eternal resting place
Shalt thou retire alone—nor couldst thou wish
Couch more magnificent. Thou shalt lie down
With patriarchs of the infant world—with kings,
The powerful of the earth—the wise, the good,
Fair forms, and hoary seers of ages past,
All in one mighty sepulchre.—The hills
Rock-ribb'd and ancient as the sun,—the vales
Stretching in pensive quietness between;
The venerable woods—rivers that move
In majesty, and the complaining brooks
That make the meadows green; and pour'd round all,
Old ocean's grey and melancholy waste,—

THANATOPSIS. **Title:** "Meditation on Death." **28. swain:** farmer.

Are but the solemn decorations all
Of the great tomb of man. The golden sun,
The planets, all the infinite host of heaven,
Are shining on the sad abodes of death,
Through the still lapse of ages. All that tread
The globe are but a handful to the tribes
That slumber in its bosom.—Take the wings
Of morning—and the Barcan desert pierce,
Or lose thyself in the continuous woods
Where rolls the Oregan, and hears no sound,
Save his own dashings—yet—the dead are there,
And millions in those solitudes, since first
The flight of years began, have laid them down
In their last sleep—the dead reign there alone.—
So shalt thou rest—and what if thou shalt fall
Unnoticed by the living—and no friend
Take note of thy departure? All that breathe
Will share thy destiny. The gay will laugh
When thou art gone, the solemn brood of care
Plod on, and each one as before will chase
His favourite phantom; yet all these shall leave
Their mirth and their employments, and shall come,
And make their bed with thee. As the long train
Of ages glide away, the sons of men,
The youth in life's green spring, and he who goes
In the full strength of years, matron, and maid,
The bow'd with age, the infant in the smiles
And beauty of its innocent age cut off,—
Shall one by one be gathered to thy side,
By those, who in their turn shall follow them.
So live, that when thy summons comes to join
The innumerable caravan, that moves
To the pale realms of shade, where each shall take
His chamber in the silent halls of death,
Thou go not, like the quarry-slave at night,
Scourged to his dungeon, but sustain'd and sooth'd
By an unfaltering trust, approach thy grave,
Like one who wraps the drapery of his couch
About him, and lies down to pleasant dreams.

1821

51–53. Barcan . . . Oregan: the Barcan Desert is in Libya. The Oregan (early spelling of Oregon) was the Columbia River.

To a Waterfowl

Whither, 'midst falling dew,
While glow the heavens with the last steps of day,
Far, through their rosy depths, dost thou pursue
Thy solitary way?

Vainly the fowler's eye
Might mark thy distant flight, to do thee wrong,
As, darkly seen against the crimson sky,
Thy figure floats along.

Seek'st thou the plashy brink
Of weedy lake, or marge of river wide,
Or where the rocking billows rise and sink
On the chafèd ocean side?

There is a Power, whose care
Teaches thy way along that pathless coast,—
The desert and illimitable air,—
Lone wandering, but not lost,

All day thy wings have fanned,
At that far height, the cold thin atmosphere;
Yet stoop not, weary, to the welcome land,
Though the dark night is near.

And soon that toil shall end,
Soon shalt thou find a summer home, and rest,
And scream among thy fellows; reeds shall bend,
Soon, o'er thy sheltered nest.

Thou'rt gone, the abyss of heaven
Hath swallowed up thy form, yet, on my heart
Deeply hath sunk the lesson thou hast given,
And shall not soon depart.

He, who, from zone to zone,
Guides through the boundless sky thy certain flight,
In the long way that I must trace alone,
Will lead my steps aright.

1818

TO A WATERFOWL. **9. plashy:** marshy.

John Keats

(1795–1821)

Keats, who died at the age of twenty-five, was the youngest of the great poets of the world. His life has always fascinated because of the brilliance of his development in so brief a time. He started with few advantages. His father, who managed stables for carriage-horses, was killed in an accident when Keats, the oldest of four children, was eight, and a few years later his mother died of tuberculosis, the same disease that was later to prove fatal to Keats and his brothers. Money left by their grandfather could have helped the Keats children, but it was largely withheld from them by an unscrupulous guardian. Keats was able, however, to get enough to start studying medicine at Guy's Hospital in London. While there he wrote poetry that was by no means precocious. But his reading of great poets of the past, especially Shakespeare and Milton, helped him within a mere two years to become self-corrective and to learn to write poetry of so high a quality that it has haunted the imagination of readers over the past century and a half and of all later poets. His writing continued at this high level for another year and a half until, at the age of twenty-four, he became too ill to write.

The sonnet "On First Looking into Chapman's Homer" is one of the famous expressions of literary discovery. A friend, Charles Cowden Clarke, showed Keats one evening the translation of Homer by the Elizabethan poet, George Chapman. Suddenly a new world opened for Keats. He saw a poetry that need not be cute or sentimental, as the fashionable magazine-verse of his time was, but had vigor, power, and range. So excited was he, as he walked across London Bridge on his way back to the Hospital late at night, that he composed this sonnet in his head. The sonnet "On Sitting Down to Read *King Lear* Once Again" is another expression of his habit, when he began a major poem, of attuning his mind to the highest poetry by reading some great work of the past—in this case, Shakespeare's *King Lear*.

"The Eve of St. Agnes" was composed as a release after a difficult period when he had been nursing his dying brother, Tom Keats. "La Belle Dame sans Merci," written in the ballad form, develops a theme familiar in Keats, the doomed union of a mortal and an immortal. Almost immediately after this magical short ballad came the famous odes. The "Ode to Psyche" is a kind of credo, in which Keats affirms a belief that had grown on him. He thought that the great poets of the past whom he so much admired, such as Spenser and Milton, had in their epic sweep still left relatively unexplored the "inner life" of the human mind. He would himself now turn to the "inner life," as he thought Wordsworth was doing. He found a symbol of this in Psyche, the classical goddess representing the "soul" or the "mind" who appears as a goddess only late in the history of classical myth. The twin odes, the "Ode to a Nightingale" and the "Ode on a Grecian Urn," present, among other things, a kind of drama of the human heart longing to escape from the brevity of mortal life through identification with something that, as a symbol, seems to have immortality: the song of the nightingale and the Grecian urn that has endured for so many centuries. The identification Keats strives for can never be fully achieved, for the symbols have a different life of their own into which human beings cannot fully enter. The nightingale flies away; the Grecian urn is at last recognized as an inanimate object made of marble. Both odes begin in a state of intense response (to the nightingale or the urn), move into a culminating moment of almost complete self-forgetfulness, and return with some sorrow to ordinary reality. But in both poems the symbols can continue to impart to the imagination at least hints and suggestions of something beyond us, and serve, as Keats says of the Grecian urn, as "a friend to man."

The "Ode on Melancholy" and the final ode, "To Autumn," also deal with mortality and the human longing to transcend it. The first expresses the belief that the deepest melancholy comes in realizing that nothing cherished in this world by the human heart can last; hence, the greater the joy we feel, the profounder is the regret that the joy cannot remain with us. "To Autumn," the last of the odes, is a serene acceptance of the fact that all life is process (gradual transition) against a background of finality and death. Autumn is pictured as a deity who presides over the twofold aspect of Autumn: its ripeness, with growth reaching its climax, and, secondly, its harvesting, when the mature growth is cut and gathered before the winter comes. But this benevolent deity is also responsive to the longing of the human heart to postpone the end of things—Autumn-as-harvester is now stopping or slowing its work; it is "sitting careless on a granary floor," or drowsing on a "half-reap'd furrow," its hook sparing the next swath, or halting to watch the slow pressing of apples into cider as the long hours pass. Then the ode moves from the personified figure of "Autumn" to images of life still untouched by any thought of death—the red-breasts, the hedge-crickets, the swallows "gathering" only to migrate. In short, process and the inevitability of an end are not denied. But the process is slowed up, as if to help the human heart to accept it with the realization (to use a phrase Keats liked in

Shakespeare's *King Lear*) that "Ripeness is all": "Men must endure," Shakespeare wrote, "Their going hence, even as their coming hither:/ Ripeness is all."

On First Looking into Chapman's Homer

Much have I travell'd in the realms of gold,
And many goodly states and kingdoms seen;
Round many western islands have I been
Which bards in fealty to Apollo hold.
Oft of one wide expanse had I been told
That deep-brow'd Homer ruled as his demesne;
Yet did I never breathe its pure serene
Till I heard Chapman speak out loud and bold:
Then felt I like some watcher of the skies
When a new planet swims into his ken;
Or like stout Cortez when with eagle eyes
He star'd at the Pacific—and all his men
Look'd at each other with a wild surmise—
Silent, upon a peak in Darien.

1817

When I Have Fears

When I have fears that I may cease to be
Before my pen has glean'd my teeming brain,
Before high-piled books, in charactery,
Hold like rich garners the full ripen'd grain;
When I behold, upon the night's starr'd face,
Huge cloudy symbols of a high romance,
And think that I may never live to trace
Their shadows, with the magic hand of chance;
And when I feel, fair creature of an hour,
That I shall never look upon thee more,
Never have relish in the faery power
Of unreflecting love;—then on the shore
Of the wide world I stand alone, and think
Till love and fame to nothingness do sink.

1817

ON FIRST LOOKING INTO CHAPMAN'S HOMER. **6. demesne:** realm. **11. Cortez:** Keats mistakenly ascribes Balboa's discovery to Cortez. **14. Darien:** isthmus of Panama. WHEN I HAVE FEARS. **3. charactery:** writing (characters).

The Eve of St. Agnes

I

St. Agnes' Eve—Ah, bitter chill it was!
The owl, for all his feathers, was a-cold;
The hare limp'd trembling through the frozen grass,
And silent was the flock in woolly fold:
Numb were the Beadsman's fingers, while he told
His rosary, and while his frosted breath,
Like pious incense from a censer old,
Seem'd taking flight for heaven, without a death,
Past the sweet Virgin's picture, while his prayer he saith.

II

His prayer he saith, this patient, holy man;
Then takes his lamp, and riseth from his knees,
And back returneth, meagre, barefoot, wan,
Along the chapel aisle by slow degrees:
The sculptur'd dead, on each side, seem to freeze,
Emprison'd in black, purgatorial rails:
Knights, ladies, praying in dumb orat'ries,
He passeth by; and his weak spirit fails
To think how they may ache in icy hoods and mails.

III

Northward he turneth through a little door,
And scarce three steps, ere Music's golden tongue
Flatter'd to tears this aged man and poor;
But no—already had his deathbell rung:
The joys of all his life were said and sung:
His was harsh penance on St. Agnes' Eve:
Another way he went, and soon among
Rough ashes sat he for his soul's reprieve,
And all night kept awake, for sinners' sake to grieve.

IV

That ancient Beadsman heard the prelude soft;
And so it chanc'd, for many a door was wide,
From hurry to and fro. Soon, up aloft,
The silver, snarling trumpets 'gan to chide:
The level chambers, ready with their pride,
Were glowing to receive a thousand guests:

THE EVE OF ST. AGNES. **Title:** St. Agnes is the patron saint of virgins. During St. Agnes' Eve (the night of January 20), a maiden who performed certain rites could have a vision of her future husband. **5–6. Beadsman . . . rosary:** a monk praying for someone, using a rosary (string of beads) on which prayers are counted. **16. orat'ries:** chapels adjoining a church.

The carvèd angels, ever eager-eyed,
Star'd, where upon their heads the cornice rests,
With hair blown back, and wings put cross-wise on their breasts.

V

At length burst in the argent revelry,
With plume, tiara, and all rich array,
Numerous as shadows haunting faerily
The brain, new stuff'd, in youth, with triumphs gay
Of old romance. These let us wish away,
And turn, sole-thoughted, to one Lady there,
Whose heart had brooded, all that wintry day,
On love, and wing'd St. Agnes' saintly care,
As she had heard old dames full many times declare.

VI

They told her how, upon St. Agnes' Eve,
Young virgins might have visions of delight,
And soft adorings from their loves receive
Upon the honey'd middle of the night,
If ceremonies due they did aright;
As, supperless to bed they must retire,
And couch supine their beauties, lilly white;
Nor look behind, nor sideways, but require
Of Heaven with upward eyes for all that they desire.

VII

Full of this whim was thoughtful Madeline:
The music, yearning like a God in pain,
She scarcely heard: her maiden eyes divine,
Fix'd on the floor, saw many a sweeping train
Pass by—she heeded not at all: in vain
Came many a tiptoe, amorous cavalier,
And back retir'd; not cool'd by high disdain,
But she saw not: her heart was otherwhere:
She sigh'd for Agnes' dreams, the sweetest of the year.

VIII

She danc'd along with vague, regardless eyes,
Anxious her lips, her breathing quick and short:
The hallow'd hour was near at hand: she sighs
Amid the timbrels, and the throng'd resort
Of whisperers in anger, or in sport;
'Mid looks of love, defiance, hate, and scorn,

37. argent revelry: revellers dressed in silver colored clothes. **67. timbrels:** small drums.

Hoodwink'd with faery fancy; all amort,
Save to St. Agnes and her lambs unshorn,
And all the bliss to be before to-morrow morn.

IX

So, purposing each moment to retire,
She linger'd still. Meantime, across the moors,
Had come young Porphyro, with heart on fire
For Madeline. Beside the portal doors,
Buttress'd from moonlight, stands he, and implores
All saints to give him sight of Madeline,
But for one moment in the tedious hours,
That he might gaze and worship all unseen;
Perchance speak, kneel, touch, kiss—in sooth such things have been.

X

He ventures in: let no buzz'd whisper tell:
All eyes be muffled, or a hundred swords
Will storm his heart, Love's fev'rous citadel:
For him, those chambers held barbarian hordes,
Hyena foemen, and hot-blooded lords,
Whose very dogs would execrations howl
Against his lineage: not one breast affords
Him any mercy, in that mansion foul,
Save one old beldame, weak in body and in soul.

XI

Ah, happy chance! the agèd creature came,
Shuffling along with ivory-headed wand,
To where he stood, hid from the torch's flame,
Behind a broad hall-pillar, far beyond
The sound of merriment and chorus bland:
He startled her; but soon she knew his face,
And grasp'd his fingers in her palsied hand,
Saying, "Mercy, Porphyro! hie thee from this place;
They are all here to-night, the whole blood-thirsty race!

XII

"Get hence! get hence! there's dwarfish Hildebrand;
He had a fever late, and in the fit
He cursèd thee and thine, both house and land:
Then there's that old Lord Maurice, not a whit
More tame for his gray hairs—Alas me! flit!
Flit like a ghost away."—"Ah, Gossip dear,

70. Hoodwink'd: blinded. **all amort:** as if dead. **71. St. Agnes . . . lambs:** Two lambs were sacrificed on St. Agnes' Day, their wool afterwards spun and woven by nuns. **77. Buttress'd:** shielded. **90. beldame:** woman. **105. Gossip:** old female retainer.

We're safe enough; here in this arm-chair sit,
And tell me how"—"Good Saints! not here, not here;
Follow me, child, or else these stones will be thy bier."

XIII

He follow'd through a lowly archèd way,
Brushing the cobwebs with his lofty plume,
And as she mutter'd "Well-a—well-a-day!"
He found him in a little moonlight room,
Pale, lattic'd, chill, and silent as a tomb.
"Now tell me where is Madeline," said he,
'O tell me, Angela, by the holy loom
Which none but secret sisterhood may see,
When they St. Agnes' wool are weaving piously."

XIV

"St. Agnes! Ah! it is St. Agnes' Eve—
Yet men will murder upon holy days:
Thou must hold water in a witch's sieve,
And be liege-lord of all the Elves and Fays,
To venture so: it fills me with amaze
To see thee, Porphyro!—St. Agnes' Eve!
God's help! my lady fair the conjuror plays
This very night: good angels her deceive!
But let me laugh awhile, I've mickle time to grieve."

XV

Feebly she laugheth in the languid moon,
While Porphyro upon her face doth look,
Like puzzled urchin on an aged crone
Who keepeth clos'd a wond'rous riddle-book,
As spectacled she sits in chimney nook.
But soon his eyes grew brilliant, when she told
His lady's purpose; and he scarce could brook
Tears, at the thought of those enchantments cold,
And Madeline asleep in lap of legends old.

XVI

Sudden a thought came like a full-blown rose,
Flushing his brow, and in his painèd heart
Made purple riot: then doth he propose
A stratagem, that makes the beldame start:
"A cruel man and impious thou art:
Sweet lady, let her pray, and sleep, and dream

120. witch's sieve: bewitched so that water cannot go through it. **124. conjuror:** magician. **126. mickle:** much.

Alone with her good angels, far apart
From wicked men like thee. Go, go!—I deem
Thou canst not surely be the same that thou didst seem."

XVII

"I will not harm her, by all saints I swear,"
Quoth Porphyro: "O may I ne'er find grace
When my weak voice shall whisper its last prayer,
If one of her soft ringlets I displace,
Or look with ruffian passion in her face:
Good Angela, believe me by these tears;
Or I will, even in a moment's space,
Awake, with horrid shout, my foemen's ears,
And beard them, though they be more fang'd than wolves and bears."

XVIII

"Ah! why wilt thou affright a feeble soul?
A poor, weak, palsy-stricken, churchyard thing,
Whose passing-bell may ere the midnight toll;
Whose prayers for thee, each morn and evening,
Were never miss'd."—Thus plaining, doth she bring
A gentler speech from burning Porphyro;
So woful, and of such deep sorrowing,
That Angela gives promise she will do
Whatever he shall wish, betide her weal or woe.

XIX

Which was, to lead him, in close secrecy,
Even to Madeline's chamber, and there hide
Him in a closet, of such privacy
That he might see her beauty unespied,
And win perhaps that night a peerless bride,
While legion'd faeries pac'd the coverlet,
And pale enchantment held her sleepy-eyed.
Never on such a night have lovers met,
Since Merlin paid his Demon all the monstrous debt.

XX

"It shall be as thou wishest," said the Dame:
"All cates and dainties shall be storèd there
Quickly on this feast-night: by the tambour frame
Her own lute thou wilt see: no time to spare,
For I am slow and feeble, and scarce dare

156. passing-bell: tolled at a person's death (or passing). **158. plaining:** complaining. **171. Merlin . . . debt:** wizard in Arthurian tales; he was the son of a demon, who paid the debt for his existence by doing evil deeds. **173. cates:** delicacies. **174. feast:** held each year for St. Agnes. **tambour frame:** embroidery frame for the small drum.

On such a catering trust my dizzy head.
Wait here, my child, with patience; kneel in prayer
The while: Ah! thou must needs the lady wed,
Or may I never leave my grave among the dead."

XXI

So saying, she hobbled off with busy fear.
The lover's endless minutes slowly pass'd;
The dame return'd, and whisper'd in his ear
To follow her; with aged eyes aghast
From fright of dim espial. Safe at last,
Through many a dusky gallery, they gain
The maiden's chamber, silken, hush'd, and chaste;
Where Porphyro took covert, pleas'd amain.
His poor guide hurried back with agues in her brain.

XXII

Her falt'ring hand upon the balustrade,
Old Angela was feeling for the stair,
When Madeline, St. Agnes' charmèd maid,
Rose, like a mission'd spirit, unaware:
With silver taper's light, and pious care,
She turn'd, and down the agèd gossip led
To a safe level matting. Now prepare,
Young Porphyro, for gazing on that bed;
She comes, she comes again, like ring-dove fray'd and fled.

XXIII

Out went the taper as she hurried in;
Its little smoke, in pallid moonshine, died:
She clos'd the door, she panted, all akin
To spirits of the air, and visions wide:
No uttered syllable, or, woe betide!
But to her heart, her heart was voluble,
Paining with eloquence her balmy side;
As though a tongueless nightingale should swell
Her throat in vain, and die, heart-stifled, in her dell.

XXIV

A casement high and triple-arch'd there was,
All garlanded with carven imag'ries
Of fruits, and flowers, and bunches of knot-grass,
And diamonded with panes of quaint device,
Innumerable of stains and splendid dyes,
As are the tiger-moth's deep-damask'd wings;

188. amain: greatly. **198. fray'd:** alarmed.

And in the midst, 'mong thousand heraldries,
And twilight saints, and dim emblazonings,
A shielded scutcheon blush'd with blood of queens and kings.

XXV

Full on this casement shone the wintry moon,
And threw warm gules on Madeline's fair breast,
As down she knelt for heaven's grace and boon;
Rose-bloom fell on her hands, together prest,
And on her silver cross soft amethyst,
And on her hair a glory, like a saint:
She seem'd a splendid angel, newly drest,
Save wings, for heaven:—Porphyro grew faint:
She knelt, so pure a thing, so free from mortal taint.

XXVI

Anon his heart revives: her vespers done,
Of all its wreathèd pearls her hair she frees;
Unclasps her warmèd jewels one by one;
Loosens her fragrant boddice; by degrees
Her rich attire creeps rustling to her knees:
Half-hidden, like a mermaid in sea-weed,
Pensive awhile she dreams awake, and sees,
In fancy, fair St. Agnes in her bed,
But dares not look behind, or all the charm is fled.

XXVII

Soon, trembling in her soft and chilly nest,
In sort of wakeful swoon, perplex'd she lay,
Until the poppied warmth of sleep oppress'd
Her soothèd limbs, and soul fatigued away;
Flown, like a thought, until the morrow-day;
Blissfully haven'd both from joy and pain;
Clasp'd like a missal where swart Paynims pray;
Blinded alike from sunshine and from rain,
As though a rose should shut, and be a bud again.

XXVIII

Stol'n to this paradise, and so entranced,
Porphyro gazed upon her empty dress,
And listen'd to her breathing, if it chanced
To wake into a slumberous tenderness;
Which when he heard, that minute did he bless,
And breath'd himself: then from the closet crept,

216. scutcheon: coat of arms. **218. gules:** color red in heraldry; here applied to the stained glass. **241. Clasp'd . . . pray:** shut tight as a Christian prayer book would be among paynims (pagans).

Noiseless as fear in a wide wilderness,
And over the hush'd carpet, silent, stept,
And 'tween the curtains peep'd, where, lo!—how fast she slept.

XXIX

Then by the bed-side, where the faded moon
Made a dim, silver twilight, soft he set
A table, and, half anguish'd, threw thereon
A cloth of woven crimson, gold, and jet:—
O for some drowsy Morphean amulet!
The boisterous, midnight, festive clarion,
The kettle-drum, and far-heard clarinet,
Affray his ears, though but in dying tone:—
The hall door shuts again, and all the noise is gone.

XXX

And still she slept an azure-lidded sleep,
In blanchèd linen, smooth, and lavender'd,
While he from forth the closet brought a heap
Of candied apple, quince, and plum, and gourd;
With jellies soother than the creamy curd,
And lucent syrops, tinct with cinnamon;
Manna and dates, in argosy transferr'd
From Fez; and spicèd dainties, every one,
From silken Samarcand to cedar'd Lebanon.

XXXI

These delicates he heap'd with glowing hand
On golden dishes and in baskets bright
Of wreathèd silver: sumptuous they stand
In the retired quiet of the night,
Filling the chilly room with perfume light.—
"And now, my love, my seraph fair, awake!
Thou art my heaven, and I thine eremite:
Open thine eyes, for meek St. Agnes' sake,
Or I shall drowse beside thee, so my soul doth ache."

XXXII

Thus whispering, his warm, unnerved arm
Sank in her pillow. Shaded was her dream
By the dusk curtains:—'twas a midnight charm
Impossible to melt as icèd stream:

250. Noiseless as fear: quiet as a person full of fear. **257. Morphean amulet:** Morpheus, god of sleep, whose spirit has entered an amulet, a stone, or other object that has spiritual power. **266. soother:** smoother. **267. tinct:** tinctured. **269. Fez:** city in Morocco. **270. Samarcand:** in Asia, where many caravans started. **Lebanon:** famous for its great cedar trees. **276. seraph:** angel. **277. eremite:** hermit.

The lustrous salvers in the moonlight gleam;
Broad golden fringe upon the carpet lies:
It seem'd he never, never could redeem
From such a stedfast spell his lady's eyes;
So mus'd awhile, entoil'd in woofèd phantasies.

XXXIII

Awakening up, he took her hollow lute,—
Tumultuous,—and, in chords that tenderest be,
He play'd an ancient ditty, long since mute,
In Provence call'd, "La belle dame sans mercy:"
Close to her ear touching the melody;—
Wherewith disturb'd, she utter'd a soft moan:
He ceased—she panted quick—and suddenly
Her blue affrayed eyes wide open shone:
Upon his knees he sank, pale as smooth-sculptured stone.

XXXIV

Her eyes were open, but she still beheld,
Now wide awake, the vision of her sleep:
There was a painful change, that nigh expell'd
The blisses of her dream so pure and deep,
At which fair Madeline began to weep,
And moan forth witless words with many a sigh;
While still her gaze on Porphyro would keep;
Who knelt, with joinèd hands and piteous eye,
Fearing to move or speak, she look'd so dreamingly.

XXXV

"Ah, Porphyro!" said she, "but even now
Thy voice was at sweet tremble in mine ear,
Made tuneable with every sweetest vow;
And those sad eyes were spiritual and clear:
How chang'd thou art! how pallid, chill, and drear!
Give me that voice again, my Porphyro,
Those looks immortal, those complainings dear!
Oh leave me not in this eternal woe,
For if thou diest, my Love, I know not where to go."

XXXVI

Beyond a mortal man impassion'd far
At these voluptuous accents, he arose,
Ethereal, flush'd, and like a throbbing star
Seen mid the sapphire heaven's deep repose;

284. salvers: dishes. **288. woofèd:** woven. **292. Provence:** troubadour area in southern France. **"La belle dame . . . ":** title of poem by Alain Chartier ("the beautiful lady without mercy"). See Keats's poem of the same title.

Into her dream he melted, as the rose
Blendeth its odour with the violet,—
Solution sweet: meantime the frost-wind blows
Like Love's alarum pattering the sharp sleet
Against the window-panes; St. Agnes' moon hath set.

XXXVII

'Tis dark: quick pattereth the flaw-blown sleet:
"This is no dream, my bride, my Madeline!"
'Tis dark: the icèd gusts still rave and beat:
"No dream, alas! alas! and woe is mine!
Porphyro will leave me here to fade and pine.—
Cruel! what traitor could thee hither bring?
I curse not, for my heart is lost in thine,
Though thou forsakest a deceivèd thing;—
A dove forlorn and lost with sick unprunèd wing."

XXXVIII

"My Madeline! sweet dreamer! lovely bride!
Say, may I be for aye thy vassal blest?
Thy beauty's shield, heart-shap'd and vermeil dyed?
Ah, silver shrine, here will I take my rest
After so many hours of toil and quest,
A famish'd pilgrim,—sav'd by miracle.
Though I have found, I will not rob thy nest
Saving of thy sweet self; if thou think'st well
To trust, fair Madeline, to no rude infidel.

XXXIX

"Hark! 'tis an elfin-storm from faery land,
Of haggard seeming, but a boon indeed:
Arise—arise! the morning is at hand;—
The bloated wassaillers will never heed:—
Let us away, my love, with happy speed;
There are no ears to hear, or eyes to see,—
Drown'd all in Rhenish and the sleepy mead:
Awake! arise! my love, and fearless be,
For o'er the southern moors I have a home for thee."

XL

She hurried at his words, beset with fears,
For there were sleeping dragons all around,
At glaring watch, perhaps, with ready spears—
Down the wide stairs a darkling way they found.—

323. alarum: alarm signal. **325. flaw-blown:** storm blown. **333. unprunèd:** rumpled. **336. vermeil:** vermillion. **344. haggard:** wild. **349. Rhenish:** wine from the Rhine valley. **mead:** fermented honey.

In all the house was heard no human sound.
A chain-droop'd lamp was flickering by each door;
The arras, rich with horseman, hawk, and hound,
Flutter'd in the besieging wind's uproar;
And the long carpets rose along the gusty floor.

XLI

They glide, like phantoms, into the wide hall;
Like phantoms, to the iron porch, they glide;
Where lay the Porter, in uneasy sprawl,
With a huge empty flaggon by his side:
The wakeful bloodhound rose, and shook his hide,
But his sagacious eye an inmate owns:
By one, and one, the bolts full easy slide:—
The chains lie silent on the footworn stones;—
The key turns, and the door upon its hinges groans.

XLII

And they are gone: aye, ages long ago
These lovers fled away into the storm.
That night the Baron dreamt of many a woe,
And all his warrior-guests, with shade and form
Of witch, and demon, and large coffin-worm,
Were long be-nightmar'd. Angela the old
Died palsy-twitch'd, with meagre face deform;
The Beadsman, after thousand aves told,
For aye unsought for slept among his ashes cold.

1820

Bright Star

Bright star, would I were stedfast as thou art—
Not in lone splendour hung aloft the night
And watching, with eternal lids apart,
Like nature's patient, sleepless Eremite,
The moving waters at their priestlike task
Of pure ablution round earth's human shores,
Or gazing on the new soft-fallen mask
Of snow upon the mountains and the moors—
No—yet still stedfast, still unchangeable,
Pillow'd upon my fair love's ripening breast,
To feel for ever its soft fall and swell,

358. arras: tapestries or curtains. **377. aves:** prayers; from *Ave Maria* ("Hail Mary").
BRIGHT STAR. **4. Eremite:** hermit.

Awake for ever in a sweet unrest,
Still, still to hear her tender-taken breath,
And so live ever—or else swoon to death.

1819

La Belle Dame sans Merci

O, what can ail thee, knight-at-arms,
  Alone and palely loitering?
The sedge has wither'd from the lake,
  And no birds sing.

O, what can ail thee, knight-at-arms,
  So haggard and so woe-begone?
The squirrel's granary is full,
  And the harvest's done.

I see a lilly on thy brow,
  With anguish moist and fever dew,
And on thy cheeks a fading rose
  Fast withereth too.

I met a lady in the meads,
  Full beautiful—a faery's child,
Her hair was long, her foot was light,
  And her eyes were wild.

I made a garland for her head,
  And bracelets too, and fragrant zone;
She look'd at me as she did love,
  And made sweet moan.

I set her on my pacing steed,
  And nothing else saw all day long,
For sidelong would she bend and sing
  A faery's song.

She found me roots of relish sweet,
  And honey wild, and manna dew,
And sure in language strange she said
  "I love thee true."

She took me to her elfin grot,
  And there she wept and sigh'd full sore,
And there I shut her wild wild eyes
  With kisses four.

LA BELLE DAME SANS MERCI. **Title:** "The beautiful lady without mercy." Taken from the title of a medieval poem by Alain Chartier (see "Eve of St. Agnes," line 292). **13. meads:** meadows. **18. zone:** girdle.

And there she lullèd me asleep,
  And there I dream'd—Ah! woe betide!
The latest dream I ever dream'd
  On the cold hill side.

I saw pale kings and princes too,
  Pale warriors, death-palc were they all;
They cried, "La Belle Dame sans Merci
  Hath thee in thrall!"

I saw their starved lips in the gloam,
  With horrid warning gapèd wide,
And I awoke, and found me here,
  On the cold hill's side.

And this is why I sojourn here,
  Alone and palely loitering,
Though the sedge is wither'd from the lake,
  And no birds sing.

1820

Ode to Psyche

O Goddess! hear these tuneless numbers, wrung
  By sweet enforcement and remembrance dear,
And pardon that thy secrets should be sung
  Even into thine own soft-conchèd ear:
Surely I dreamt to-day, or did I see
  The wingèd Psyche with awaken'd eyes?
I wander'd in a forest thoughtlessly,
  And, on the sudden, fainting with surprise,
Saw two fair creatures, couchèd side by side
  In deepest grass, beneath the whisp'ring roof
  Of leaves and trembled blossoms, where there ran
      A brooklet, scarce espied:

'Mid hush'd, cool-rooted flowers, fragrant-eyed,
  Blue, silver-white, and budded Tyrian,
They lay calm-breathing on the bedded grass;

ODE TO PSYCHE. **Title:** Psyche, from the Greek word for soul or mind, was made a goddess in late classical times (hence she is described in line 24 as "latest born" of the Olympian hierarchy of gods). In the story Keats is using, Venus, goddess of love, has become jealous of Psyche, drives her from her home, and sends her son Cupid to make her (the "soul") fall in love with a deformed creature. But Cupid, seeing Psyche, falls in love with her himself. Eventually he becomes united with her (that is, love becomes united with mind, and proves to be the salvation of the mind). The thought behind the poem is that the poetry of the future must turn more to the mind and the inner life. **4. conchèd:** shell-like. **14. Tyrian:** purple.

Their arms embracèd, and their pinions too;
Their lips touch'd not, but had not bade adieu,
As if disjoinèd by soft-handed slumber,
And ready still past kisses to outnumber
At tender eye-dawn of aurorean love:
The wingèd boy I knew;
But who wast thou, O happy, happy dove?
His Psyche true!

O latest born and loveliest vision far
Of all Olympus' faded hierarchy!
Fairer than Phoebe's sapphire-region'd star,
Or Vesper, amorous glow-worm of the sky;
Fairer than these, though temple thou hast none,
Nor altar heap'd with flowers;
Nor virgin-choir to make delicious moan
Upon the midnight hours;
No voice, no lute, no pipe, no incense sweet
From chain-swung censer teeming;
No shrine, no grove, no oracle, no heat
Of pale-mouth'd prophet dreaming.

O brightest! though too late for antique vows,
Too, too late for the fond believing lyre,
When holy were the haunted forest boughs,
Holy the air, the water, and the fire;
Yet even in these days so far retir'd
From happy pieties, thy lucent fans,
Fluttering among the faint Olympians,
I see, and sing, by my own eyes inspired.
So let me be thy choir, and make a moan
Upon the midnight hours;
Thy voice, thy lute, thy pipe, thy incense sweet
From swingèd censer teeming;
Thy shrine, thy grove, thy oracle, thy heat
Of pale-mouth'd prophet dreaming.

Yes, I will be thy priest, and build a fane
In some untrodden region of my mind,
Where branchèd thoughts, new grown with pleasant pain,
Instead of pines shall murmur in the wind:
Far, far around shall those dark-cluster'd trees
Fledge the wild-ridgèd mountains steep by steep;
And there by zephyrs, streams, and birds, and bees,
The moss-lain Dryads shall be lull'd to sleep;
And in the midst of this wide quietness

20. aurorean: dawning. **25. hierarchy:** the array of classical gods. **26. Phoebe's . . . star:** the moon, of which Phoebe (Diana) was goddess. **27. Vesper:** evening star. **37. fond:** not only affectionate but in the older sense of "foolish." **41. fans:** wings. **50. fane:** temple. **56. zephyrs:** breezes. **57. Dryads:** tree nymphs.

A rosy sanctuary will I dress
With the wreath'd trellis of a working brain,
  With buds, and bells, and stars without a name,
With all the gardener Fancy e'er could feign,
  Who breeding flowers, will never breed the same:
And there shall be for thee all soft delight
  That shadowy thought can win,
A bright torch, and a casement ope at night,
  To let the warm Love in!

1820

Ode to a Nightingale

I

My heart aches, and a drowsy numbness pains
  My sense, as though of hemlock I had drunk,
Or emptied some dull opiate to the drains
  One minute past, and Lethe-wards had sunk:
'Tis not through envy of thy happy lot,
  But being too happy in thine happiness,—
    That thou, light-wingèd Dryad of the trees,
        In some melodious plot
  Of beechen green, and shadows numberless,
    Singest of summer in full-throated ease.

II

O, for a draught of vintage! that hath been
  Cool'd a long age in the deep-delvèd earth,
Tasting of Flora and the country green,
  Dance, and Provençal song, and sunburnt mirth!
O for a beaker full of the warm South,
  Full of the true, the blushful Hippocrene,
    With beaded bubbles winking at the brim,
        And purple-stainèd mouth;
  That I might drink, and leave the world unseen,
    And with thee fade away into the forest dim:

III

Fade far away, dissolve, and quite forget
  What thou among the leaves hast never known,
The weariness, the fever, and the fret

67. Love: Cupid. ODE TO A NIGHTINGALE. **2. hemlock:** poisonous herb. **4. Lethe-wards:** towards Lethe, the river of forgetfulness in Hades. **7. Dryad:** tree nymph. **13. Flora:** goddess of flowers. **16. Hippocrene:** fountain of Muses on Mount Helicon; a drink from it gave inspiration.

Here, where men sit and hear each other groan;
Where palsy shakes a few, sad, last gray hairs,
Where youth grows pale, and spectre-thin, and dies;
Where but to think is to be full of sorrow
And leaden-eyed despairs,
Where Beauty cannot keep her lustrous eyes,
Or new Love pine at them beyond to-morrow.

IV

Away! away! for I will fly to thee,
Not charioted by Bacchus and his pards,
But on the viewless wings of Poesy,
Though the dull brain perplexes and retards:
Already with thee! tender is the night,
And haply the Queen-Moon is on her throne,
Cluster'd around by all her starry Fays;
But here there is no light,
Save what from heaven is with the breezes blown
Through verdurous glooms and winding mossy ways.

V

I cannot see what flowers are at my feet,
Nor what soft incense hangs upon the boughs,
But, in embalmèd darkness, guess each sweet
Wherewith the seasonable month endows
The grass, the thicket, and the fruit-tree wild;
White hawthorn, and the pastoral eglantine;
Fast fading violets cover'd up in leaves;
And mid-May's eldest child,
The coming musk-rose, full of dewy wine,
The murmurous haunt of flies on summer eves.

VI

Darkling I listen; and, for many a time
I have been half in love with easeful Death,
Call'd him soft names in many a musèd rhyme,
To take into the air my quiet breath;
Now more than ever seems it rich to die,
To cease upon the midnight with no pain,
While thou art pouring forth thy soul abroad
In such an ecstasy!
Still wouldst thou sing, and I have ears in vain—
To thy high requiem become a sod.

32. Bacchus . . . pards: god of wine, whose chariot was drawn by leopards. **33. viewless:** invisible. **37. Fays:** fairies. **46. eglantine:** sweetbriar. **51. Darkling:** in the dark.

VII

Thou wast not born for death, immortal Bird!
No hungry generations tread thee down;
The voice I hear this passing night was heard
In ancient days by emperor and clown:
Perhaps the self-same song that found a path
Through the sad heart of Ruth, when, sick for home,
She stood in tears amid the alien corn;
The same that oft-times hath
Charm'd magic casements, opening on the foam
Of perilous seas, in faery lands forlorn.

VIII

Forlorn! the very word is like a bell
To toll me back from thee to my sole self!
Adieu! the fancy cannot cheat so well
As she is fam'd to do, deceiving elf.
Adieu! adieu! thy plaintive anthem fades
Past the near meadows, over the still stream,
Up the hill-side; and now 'tis buried deep
In the next valley-glades:
Was it a vision, or a waking dream?
Fled is that music:—Do I wake or sleep?

1820

Ode on a Grecian Urn

I

Thou still unravish'd bride of quietness,
Thou foster-child of silence and slow time,
Sylvan historian, who canst thus express
A flowery tale more sweetly than our rhyme:
What leaf-fring'd legend haunts about thy shape
Of deities or mortals, or of both,
In Tempe or the dales of Arcady?
What men or gods are these? What maidens loth?
What mad pursuit? What struggle to escape?
What pipes and timbrels? What wild ecstasy?

64–70. ancient . . . forlorn: The associations reach back to the historical past of emperor and "clown" (peasant) through biblical legend, in the story of Ruth, to the world of magic and fancy removed from human life and thus "forlorn." ODE ON A GRECIAN URN. **3. Sylvan:** woodland. **7. Tempe . . . Arcady:** pastoral areas in Greece.

II

Heard melodies are sweet, but those unheard
  Are sweeter; therefore, ye soft pipes, play on;
Not to the sensual ear, but, more endear'd,
  Pipe to the spirit ditties of no tone:
Fair youth, beneath the trees, thou canst not leave
  Thy song, nor ever can those trees be bare;
    Bold Lover, never, never canst thou kiss,
Though winning near the goal—yet, do not grieve;
  She cannot fade, though thou hast not thy bliss,
    For ever wilt thou love, and she be fair!

III

Ah, happy, happy boughs! that cannot shed
  Your leaves, nor ever bid the Spring adieu;
And, happy melodist, unwearied,
  For ever piping songs for ever new;
More happy love! more happy, happy love!
  For ever warm and still to be enjoy'd,
    For ever panting, and for ever young;
All breathing human passion far above,
  That leaves a heart high-sorrowful and cloy'd,
    A burning forehead, and a parching tongue.

IV

Who are these coming to the sacrifice?
  To what green altar, O mysterious priest,
Lead'st thou that heifer lowing at the skies,
  And all her silken flanks with garlands drest?
What little town by river or sea shore,
  Or mountain-built with peaceful citadel,
    Is emptied of this folk, this pious morn?
And, little town, thy streets for evermore
  Will silent be; and not a soul to tell
    Why thou art desolate, can e'er return.

V

O Attic shape! Fair attitude! with brede
  Of marble men and maidens overwrought,
With forest branches and the trodden weed;
  Thou, silent form, dost tease us out of thought
As doth eternity: Cold Pastoral!
  When old age shall this generation waste,
    Thou shalt remain, in midst of other woe

13. sensual: sensuous (the physical sense of hearing). **35. little town:** not pictured on the urn. The poet imagines it as a town from which these figures came, and "desolate" because they can never return to it. **41. Attic:** from Attica (Athens). **brede:** braid.

Than ours, a friend to man, to whom thou say'st,
"Beauty is truth, truth beauty,—that is all
Ye know on earth, and all ye need to know."

1820

Ode on Melancholy

I

No, no, go not to Lethe, neither twist
Wolf's-bane, tight-rooted, for its poisonous wine;
Nor suffer thy pale forehead to be kiss'd
By nightshade, ruby grape of Proserpine;
Make not your rosary of yew-berries,
Nor let the beetle, nor the death-moth be
Your mournful Psyche, nor the downy owl
A partner in your sorrow's mysteries;
For shade to shade will come too drowsily,
And drown the wakeful anguish of the soul.

II

But when the melancholy fit shall fall
Sudden from heaven like a weeping cloud,
That fosters the droop-headed flowers all,
And hides the green hill in an April shroud;
Then glut thy sorrow on a morning rose,
Or on the rainbow of the salt sand-wave,
Or on the wealth of globèd peonies;
Or if thy mistress some rich anger shows,
Emprison her soft hand, and let her rave,
And feed deep, deep upon her peerless eyes.

III

She dwells with Beauty—Beauty that must die;
And Joy, whose hand is ever at his lips
Bidding adieu; and aching Pleasure nigh,

49–50. Beauty . . . know: The text above prints the entire last two lines as a statement made by the urn. Some texts print it as though only the words, "Beauty is truth, truth beauty" are said by the urn, thus implying that the remaining comment ("that is all . . . ") is made by the poet to the reader. The consensus now is that the poet does not obtrude himself in this way. Rather the urn, speaking in its own special character as a work of art, is expressing this belief. ODE ON MELANCHOLY. **1–10. Lethe . . . soul:** Keats here lists traditional symbols: **Lethe**, the river of forgetfulness in Hades; **Proserpine**, wife of Pluto, ruler of the underworld; **yew-berries**, since yews were often planted in graveyards; the Egyptian scarab **beetle**, often placed in coffins; **death-moth**, which bore marks like a skull. He is saying that these are not nearly so melancholy in association as is the beautiful in life, since a true perception of the beautiful is crossed by our knowledge that it cannot last; and it is in that realization that the deepest melancholy is found. **21. She:** not the "mistress" but Melancholy itself.

Turning to Poison while the bee-mouth sips:
Ay, in the very temple of delight
Veil'd Melancholy has her sovran shrine,
Though seen of none save him whose strenuous tongue
Can burst Joy's grape against his palate fine;
His soul shall taste the sadness of her might,
And be among her cloudy trophies hung.

1820

To Autumn

I

Season of mists and mellow fruitfulness,
Close bosom-friend of the maturing sun;
Conspiring with him how to load and bless
With fruit the vines that round the thatch-eves run;
To bend with apples the moss'd cottage-trees,
And fill all fruit with ripeness to the core;
To swell the gourd, and plump the hazel shells
With a sweet kernel; to set budding more,
And still more, later flowers for the bees,
Until they think warm days will never cease,
For Summer has o'er-brimm'd their clammy cells.

II

Who hath not seen thee oft amid thy store?
Sometimes whoever seeks abroad may find
Thee sitting careless on a granary floor,
Thy hair soft-lifted by the winnowing wind;
Or on a half-reap'd furrow sound asleep,
Drows'd with the fume of poppies, while thy hook
Spares the next swath and all its twinèd flowers:
And sometimes like a gleaner thou dost keep
Steady thy laden head across a brook;
Or by a cyder-press, with patient look,
Thou watchest the last oozings hours by hours.

30. trophies: symbols of victory. TO AUTUMN. **Title:** In a letter to a friend (Sept. 21, 1819), Keats mentions the background of this poem and adds: "How beautiful the season is now— How fine the air. A temperate sharpness about it . . . I never lik'd stubble fields so much as now— Aye, better than the chilly green of the spring. Somehow a stubble plain looks warm—in the same way that some pictures look warm—this struck me so much in my Sunday's walk that I composed upon it." **15. winnowing:** blowing the grain from the chaff.

III

Where are the songs of Spring? Ay, where are they?
  Think not of them, thou hast thy music too,—
While barrèd clouds bloom the soft-dying day,
  And touch the stubble-plains with rosy hue;
Then in a wailful choir the small gnats mourn
  Among the river sallows, borne aloft
    Or sinking as the light wind lives or dies;
And full-grown lambs loud bleat from hilly bourn;
  Hedge-crickets sing; and now with treble soft
  The red-breast whistles from a garden-croft;
    And gathering swallows twitter in the skies.

1820

Ralph Waldo Emerson

(1803–1882)

As a schoolboy Emerson showed no particular gifts as a scholar or writer. He grew up in genteel poverty, attended Harvard, became a schoolmaster, and then a minister. Even for Unitarian Boston, Emerson's religious views were very liberal, and he resigned his ministry in 1832. After a tour of Europe he settled in Concord, Massachusetts, living on a legacy from his wife, who had died of tuberculosis. He meditated, kept diaries, lectured, composed poetry, and expressed his sensitivity to landscape and his idealistic musings in the prose of *Nature* (1836). *Essays* (1841) reached a larger public and established his reputation. As time passed and more books appeared, he was read as a spiritual teacher and prophet, and his influence gradually became enormous.

The best of Emerson is to be found in his prose, where a greater rhythmic flexibility and a freer tradition allowed him to write more closely to the inspiration of his impulse. Moreover, he thought poetry came spontaneously, and when he found, as most poets have, that only part of a poem would come that way, he lacked whatever enables a poet to compose almost as well by slow stitches and revision as by spontaneous expression. Inevitably, then, his poems seldom end as well as they begin, or vice versa. But "The Rhodora" is perfect throughout, and "Concord Hymn," "The Snowstorm," "Brahma," and "Days" are fine in their remarkably different kinds.

28. sallows: willows. **30. bourn:** region. **32. croft:** a small fenced plot of ground.

Concord Hymn

Sung at the completion of The Battle Monument, July 4, 1837

By the rude bridge that arched the flood,
Their flag to April's breeze unfurled,
Here once the embattled farmers stood
And fired the shot heard round the world.

The foe long since in silence slept;
Alike the conqueror silent sleeps;
And Time the ruined bridge has swept
Down the dark stream which seaward creeps.

On this green bank, by this soft stream,
We set to-day a votive stone;
That memory may their deed redeem,
When, like our sires, our sons are gone.

Spirit, that made those heroes dare
To die, and leave their children free,
Bid Time and Nature gently spare
The shaft we raise to them and thee.

1837

The Rhodora

On being asked, Whence is the flower?

In May, when sea-winds pierced our solitudes,
I found the fresh Rhodora in the woods,
Spreading its leafless blooms in a damp nook,
To please the desert and the sluggish brook.
The purple petals, fallen in the pool,
Made the black water with their beauty gay;
Here might the red-bird come his plumes to cool,
And court the flower that cheapens his array.
Rhodora! if the sages ask thee why
This charm is wasted on the earth and sky,
Tell them, dear, that if eyes were made for seeing,
Then Beauty is its own excuse for being:
Why thou wert there, O rival of the rose!
I never thought to ask, I never knew;
But, in my simple ignorance, suppose
The self-same Power that brought me there brought you.

1839

CONCORD HYMN. **Title:** The Battle Monument commemorates the battles of Concord and Lexington on April 19, 1775.

The Problem

I like a church; I like a cowl;
I love a prophet of the soul;
And on my heart monastic aisles
Fall like sweet strains, or pensive smiles;
Yet not for all his faith can see
Would I that cowled churchman be.

Why should the vest on him allure,
Which I could not on me endure?

Not from a vain or shallow thought
His awful Jove young Phidias brought,
Never from lips of cunning fell
The thrilling Delphic oracle;
Out from the heart of nature rolled
The burdens of the Bible old;
The litanies of nations came,
Like the volcano's tongue of flame,
Up from the burning core below,
The canticles of love and woe;
The hand that rounded Peter's dome
And groined the aisles of Christian Rome
Wrought in a sad sincerity;
Himself from God he could not free;
He builded better than he knew;
The conscious stone to beauty grew.

Know'st thou what wove yon woodbird's nest
Of leaves, and feathers from her breast?
Or how the fish outbuilt her shell,
Painting with morn each annual cell?
Or how the sacred pine-tree adds
To her old leaves new myriads?
Such and so grew these holy piles,
Whilst love and terror laid the tiles.
Earth proudly wears the Parthenon,
As the best gem upon her zone;
And Morning opes with haste her lids,
To gaze upon the Pyramids;
O'er England's abbeys bends the sky,

THE PROBLEM. **10. Phidias:** Athenian sculptor (fifth century B.C.) who carved the statuary for the Parthenon (line 33). His masterpiece was a statue of Zeus (Jove). **12. Delphic:** oracle of Apollo at Delphi, where the sybils (priestesses) gave prophecies. **19. hand . . . dome:** Michelangelo, who designed the dome of St. Peter's and the vaulted "groined" ceilings of some Roman buildings. **29. pine:** sacred to Dionysus, the Greek god of fertility. **33. Parthenon:** the great temple on the Acropolis dedicated to Athena and designed by Phidias (line 10).

As on its friends, with kindred eye;
For out of Thought's interior sphere,
These wonders rose to upper air;
And Nature gladly gave them place,
Adopted them into her race,
And granted them an equal date
With Andes and with Ararat.

These temples grew as grows the grass;
Art might obey, but not surpass.
The passive Master lent his hand
To the vast soul that o'er him planned;
And the same power that reared the shrine
Bestrode the tribes that knelt within.
Ever the fiery Pentecost
Girds with one flame the countless host,
Trances the heart through chanting choirs,
And through the priest the mind inspires.
The word unto the prophet spoken
Was writ on tables yet unbroken;
The word by seers or sibyls told,
In groves of oak, or fanes of gold,
Still floats upon the morning wind,
Still whispers to the willing mind.
One accent of the Holy Ghost
The heedless world hath never lost.
I know what say the fathers wise,
The Book itself before me lies,
Old Crysostom, best Augustine,
And he who blent both in his line,
The younger *Golden Lips* or mines,
Taylor, the Shakespeare of divines.
His words are music in my ear,
I see his cowled portrait dear;
And yet, for all his faith could see,
I would not the good bishop be.

1840

44. Ararat: mountain in Turkey where Noah's ark landed (Genesis 8:4). **51. Pentecost:** seventh Sunday after Easter. The day when the Holy Spirit descended on the Apostles. **56. tables . . . unbroken:** The stone tablets (or "tables") on which God had written the Ten Commandments were broken by Moses when he found the Israelites worshipping the golden calf (Exodus 32:1–20). **65. Crysostom:** St. John Chrysostom, one of the Greek Fathers of the Church, called "Chrysostom" ("golden lips") because of his eloquence as an orator. **Augustine:** famous early church Father (354–430) best known for his *City of God* and *Confessions*. **68. Taylor:** Jeremy Taylor (1613–1667).

The Snowstorm

Announced by all the trumpets of the sky,
Arrives the snow, and, driving o'er the fields,
Seems nowhere to alight: the whited air
Hides hills and woods, the river, and the heaven,
And veils the farmhouse at the garden's end.
The sled and traveler stopped, the courier's feet
Delayed, all friends shut out, the housemates sit
Around the radiant fireplace, enclosed
In a tumultuous privacy of storm.

  Come see the north wind's masonry.
Out of an unseen quarry evermore
Furnished with tile, the fierce artificer
Curves his white bastions with projected roof
Round every windward stake, or tree, or door.
Speeding, the myriad-handed, his wild work
So fanciful, so savage, nought cares he
For number or proportion. Mockingly,
On coop or kennel he hangs Parian wreaths;
A swan-like form invests the hidden thorn;
Fills up the farmer's lane from wall to wall,
Maugre the farmer's sighs; and, at the gate,
A tapering turret overtops the work.
And when his hours are numbered, and the world
Is all his own, retiring, as he were not,
Leaves, when the sun appears, astonished Art
To mimic in slow structures, stone by stone,
Built in an age, the mad wind's night-work,
The frolic architecture of the snow.

1841

Grace

How much, preventing God! how much I owe
To the defenses thou hast round me set:
Example, custom, fear, occasion slow,
These scornèd bondmen were my parapet.
I dare not peep over this parapet
To gauge with glance the roaring gulf below,
The depths of sin to which I had descended,
Had not these me against myself defended.

1842

THE SNOWSTORM. **18. Parian:** like the white marble of Paros, a Greek island. **21. Maugre:** notwithstanding.

Brahma

If the red slayer think he slays,
  Or if the slain think he is slain,
They know not well the subtle ways
  I keep, and pass, and turn again.

Far or forgot to me is near;
  Shadow and sunlight are the same;
The vanished gods to me appear;
  And one to me are shame and fame.

They reckon ill who leave me out;
  When me they fly, I am the wings;
I am the doubter and the doubt,
  And I the hymn the Brahmin sings.

The strong gods pine for my abode,
  And pine in vain the sacred Seven,
But thou, meek lover of the good!
  Find me, and turn thy back on heaven.

1857

Days

Daughters of Time, the hypocritic Days,
Muffled and dumb like barefoot dervishes,
And marching single in an endless file,
Bring diadems and fagots in their hands.
To each they offer gifts after his will,
Bread, kingdom, stars, and sky that holds them all.

I, in my pleached garden, watched the pomp,
Forgot my morning wishes, hastily
Took a few herbs and apples, and the Day
Turned and departed silent. I, too late,
Under her solemn fillet saw the scorn.

1857

BRAHMA. **Title:** Brahma is the highest god or spirit in Hinduism, according to which the universe originated from Brahma, is the manifestation of Brahma, and will ultimately return to Brahma. **13. strong gods:** Indra (sky), Agni (fire), and Yama (death), which, like mortals, seek final reunion with the supreme god, Brahma. **14. sacred Seven:** the highest saints of Hinduism. DAYS. **2. dervishes:** Moslem religious order, sworn to poverty. **4. fagots:** bundles of sticks for firewood. **7. pleached:** entwined. **11. fillet:** headband.

Terminus

It is time to be old,
To take in sail:
The god of bounds,
Who sets to seas a shore,
Came to me in his fatal rounds,
And said: "No more!
No farther shoot
Thy broad ambitious branches, and thy root.
Fancy departs: no more invent;
Contract thy firmament
To compass of a tent.
There's not enough for this and that,
Make thy option which of two;
Economize the failing river,
Not the less revere the Giver,
Leave the many and hold the few.
Timely wise accept the terms,
Soften the fall with wary foot;
A little while
Still plan and smile,
And—fault of novel germs—
Mature the unfallen fruit.
Curse, if thou wilt, thy sires,
Bad husbands of their fires,
Who, when they gave thee breath,
Failed to bequeath
The needful sinew stark as once,
The Baresark marrow to thy bones,
But left a legacy of ebbing veins,
Inconstant heat and nerveless reins,
Amid the Muses, left thee deaf and dumb,
Amid the gladiators, halt and numb."

As the bird trims her to the gale,
I trim myself to the storm of time,
I man the rudder, reef the sail,
Obey the voice at Eve obeyed at prime:
"Lowly faithful, banish fear,
Right onward drive unharmed;
The port, well worth the cruise, is near,
And every wave is charmed."

1867

TERMINUS. **Title:** Terminus was the Roman god of boundaries and landmarks. **28. Baresark:** berserk.

ELIZABETH BARRETT BROWNING

(1806–1861)

Some of the most poignant love lyrics in English are in the *Sonnets from the Portuguese* (1850), written by Elizabeth Barrett while she was being courted by Robert Browning, whom she met in 1845 when she was thirty-nine. She was living the secluded life of an invalid, and had written poetry ever since she was a girl. By the time she met Browning she was considered one of the foremost living poets, excelled only by Wordsworth and Tennyson, but her new happiness released a higher level of talent, and it is mainly through these sonnets that she is remembered. The sonnets, of which there are forty five, were originally intended to be private. But Browning, who thought them the finest sonnets since Shakespeare's, felt it would be wrong to withhold them from the world. The title, implying that they were a translation from Portuguese originals, was chosen to disguise their personal reference. Mrs. Browning was ardently sympathetic with liberal causes, and these furnished the subjects of most of her other poems. Her long narrative poem, *Aurora Leigh* (1857), was extremely popular in its day.

Sonnets from the Portuguese

1

I thought once how Theocritus had sung
  Of the sweet years, the dear and wished-for years,
  Who each one in a gracious hand appears
To bear a gift for mortals, old or young:
And, as I mused it in his antique tongue,
  I saw, in gradual vision through my tears,
  The sweet, sad years, the melancholy years,
Those of my own life, who by turns had flung
A shadow across me. Straightway I was 'ware,
  So weeping, how a mystic Shape did move
Behind me, and drew me backward by the hair;
  And a voice said in mastery, while I strove,—
"Guess now who holds thee?"—"Death," I said. But, there,
  The silver answer rang,—"Not Death, but Love."

SONNETS FROM THE PORTUGUESE. 1. **1. Theocritus:** Greek pastoral poet (third century B.C.). The reference is to his "Idyll 15".

43

How do I love thee? Let me count the ways.
I love thee to the depth and breadth and height
My soul can reach, when feeling out of sight
For the ends of Being and ideal Grace.
I love thee to the level of everyday's
Most quiet need, by sun and candle-light.
I love thee freely, as men strive for Right;
I love thee purely, as they turn from Praise.
I love thee with the passion put to use
In my old griefs, and with my childhood's faith.
I love thee with a love I seemed to lose
With my lost saints—I love thee with the breath,
Smiles, tears, of all my life!—and, if God choose,
I shall but love thee better after death.

1850

A Musical Instrument

What was he doing, the great god Pan,
  Down in the reeds by the river?
Spreading ruin and scattering ban,
Splashing and paddling with hoofs of a goat,
And breaking the golden lilies afloat
  With the dragonfly on the river.

He tore out a reed, the great god Pan,
  From the deep cool bed of the river;
The limpid water turbidly ran,
And the broken lilies a-dying lay,
And the dragonfly had fled away,
  Ere he brought it out of the river.

High on the shore sat the great god Pan
  While turbidly flowed the river;
And hacked and hewed as a great god can,
With his hard bleak steel at the patient reed,
Till there was not a sign of the leaf indeed
  To prove it fresh from the river.

He cut it short, did the great god Pan
  (How tall it stood in the river!),
Then drew the pith, like the heart of a man,

A MUSICAL INSTRUMENT. **1. Pan:** Greek god of fertility, woods, and flocks. Pictured as half-goat, half-man, he is associated with rural or pastoral music. He lustfully pursued the nymph Syrinx. The other nymphs, trying to hide her, turned her into a bed of reeds. From the reeds Pan plucked one and made his flute. **3. ban:** bad influence.

Steadily from the outside ring,
And notched the poor dry empty thing
In holes, as he sat by the river.

"This is the way," laughed the great god Pan
(Laughed while he sat by the river),
"The only way, since gods began
To make sweet music, they could succeed."
Then, dropping his mouth to a hole in the reed,
He blew in power by the river.

Sweet, sweet, sweet, O Pan!
Piercing sweet by the river!
Blinding sweet, O great god Pan!
The sun on the hill forgot to die,
And the lilies revived, and the dragonfly
Came back to dream on the river.

Yet half a beast is the great god Pan,
To laugh as he sits by the river,
Making a poet out of a man;
The true gods sigh for the cost and pain—
For the reed which grows nevermore again
As a reed with the reeds in the river.

1860

HENRY WADSWORTH LONGFELLOW

(1807–1882)

Like Oliver Wendell Holmes and John Greenleaf Whittier, Longfellow was long regarded as one of the American "household poets," and he was the most popular of them. Yet he was an astonishingly learned man. In fact, no American before him had so wide a sweep of literary culture. He knew a dozen languages, and taught the poetic literature of several ancient and modern countries at Harvard, always paying close attention to techniques of versification. In his poetry he adapted these techniques to native American themes. His success in doing this can be seen in the famous long narrative poems, especially "Hiawatha" (1854), a tale of American Indians in the meter of the Finnish folk epic; "Evangeline" (1847), which uses the classical epic meter, dactylic hexameter, to tell how French settlers in Nova Scotia were forced to leave Canada and ended up in Louisiana; and his story of the Pilgrims, *The Courtship of Miles Standish* (1858). His translation of Dante's

Divine Comedy is still regarded as one of the three or four best translations of Dante into English. Yet his facility in versifying, which enabled him to do so much work that was important to the cultural life of his time, lowered his reputation in the 1930s. Readers influenced by Modernist critical standards expected a denser idiom than Longfellow's, and it seems unlikely that he will ever recover the large audience he once possessed. Yet he remains an accomplished poet. Whoever reads through him is continually surprized by felicities, and all of his lyrics are skillful and moving.

Mezzo Cammin

Written at Boppard on the Rhine August 25, 1842, just before leaving for home

Half of my life is gone, and I have let
 The years slip from me and have not fulfilled
 The aspiration of my youth, to build
 Some tower of song with lofty parapet.
Not indolence, nor pleasure, nor the fret
 Of restless passions that would not be stilled,
 But sorrow, and care that almost killed,
 Kept me from what I may accomplish yet;
Though, halfway up the hill, I see the Past
 Lying beneath me with its sounds and sights,
 A city in the twilight dim and vast,
With smoking roofs, soft bells, and gleaming lights,
 And hear above me on the autumnal blast
The cataract of Death far thundering from the heights.

1846

The Fire of Driftwood

Devereux Farm, near Marblehead

We sat within the farmhouse old,
 Whose windows, looking o'er the bay,
Gave to the sea-breeze damp and cold,
 An easy entrance, night and day.

MEZZO CAMMIN. **Title:** from the opening of Dante's *Inferno* ("In the middle of the journey of our life"). Longfellow is now thirty-five, half of the Biblical allotment of three score and ten years. **7. sorrow . . . killed:** his first wife had died seven years before. THE FIRE OF DRIFTWOOD. **Title:** written after a day spent at the farm of a friend, near Marblehead, on the Atlantic coast north of Boston.

Not far away we saw the port,
The strange, old-fashioned, silent town,
The lighthouse, the dismantled fort,
The wooden houses, quaint and brown.

We sat and talked until the night,
Descending, filled the little room;
Our faces faded from the sight,
Our voices only broke the gloom.

We spake of many a vanished scene,
Of what we once had thought and said,
Of what had been, and might have been,
And who was changed, and who was dead;

And all that fills the hearts of friends,
When first they feel, with secret pain,
Their lives thenceforth have separate ends,
And never can be one again;

The first slight swerving of the heart,
That words are powerless to express,
And leave it still unsaid in part,
Or say it in too great excess.

The very tones in which we spake
Had something strange, I could but mark;
The leaves of memory seemed to make
A mournful rustling in the dark.

Oft died the words upon our lips,
As suddenly, from out the fire
Built of the wreck of stranded ships,
The flames would leap and then expire.

And, as their splendor flashed and failed,
We thought of wrecks upon the main,
Of ships dismasted, that were hailed
And sent no answer back again.

The windows, rattling in their frames,
The ocean, roaring up the beach,
The gusty blast, the bickering flames,
All mingled vaguely in our speech;

Until they made themselves a part
Of fancies floating through the brain,
The long-lost ventures of the heart,
That send no answers back again.

O flames that glowed! O hearts that yearned!
They were indeed too much akin,
The driftwood fire without that burned,
The thoughts that burned and glowed within.

1849

Snowflakes

Out of the bosom of the Air,
Out of the cloud-folds of her garments shaken,
Over the woodlands brown and bare,
Over the harvest-fields forsaken,
Silent, and soft, and slow
Descends the snow.

Even as our cloudy fancies take
Suddenly shape in some divine expression,
Even as the troubled heart doth make
In the white countenance confession,
The troubled sky reveals
The grief it feels.

This is the poem of the air,
Slowly in silent syllables recorded;
This is the secret of despair,
Long in its cloudy bosom hoarded,
Now whispered and revealed
To wood and field.

1863

Chaucer

An old man in a lodge within a park;
The chamber walls depicted all around
With portraitures of huntsman, hawk, and hound,
And the hurt deer. He listeneth to the lark,
Whose song comes with the sunshine through the dark
Of painted glass in leaden lattice bound;
He listeneth and he laugheth at the sound,
Then writeth in a book like any clerk.
He is the poet of the dawn, who wrote
The Canterbury Tales, and his old age
Made beautiful with song; and as I read
I hear the crowing cock, I hear the note
Of lark and linnet, and from every page
Rise odors of plowed field or flowery mead.

1873

CHAUCER. **8. clerk:** used in the Middle Ages, and in Chaucer, for a scholar. MILTON. **11. Maeonides:** Homer, who, like Milton, was blind.

Milton

I pace the sounding sea-beach and behold
  How the voluminous billows roll and run,
  Upheaving and subsiding, while the sun
  Shines through their sheeted emerald far unrolled
And the ninth wave, slow gathering fold by fold
  All its loose-flowing garments into one,
  Plunges upon the shore, and floods the dun
  Pale reach of sands, and changes them to gold.
So in majestic cadence rise and fall
  The mighty undulations of thy song,
  O sightless Bard, England's Maeonides!
And ever and anon, high over all
  Uplifted, a ninth wave superb and strong,
  Floods all the soul with its melodious seas.

1873

John Greenleaf Whittier

(1807–1892)

Whittier came from a Massachusetts Quaker family, and, like other Quakers, was violently opposed to slavery. His work as an editor and writer for antislavery publications was supplemented by prose fiction dealing with New England history and especially by numerous poems, originally modeled after the Scottish poet Robert Burns, in which he portrayed rural life. His best poems are narratives too long to be included in anthologies. Particularly valued for its American country setting and characters is his cycle of verse tales, *The Tent on the Beach* (1867).

Proem

    I love the old melodious lays
Which softly melt the ages through,
    The songs of Spenser's golden days,
    Arcadian Sidney's silvery phrase,
Sprinkling our noon of time with freshest morning dew.

Yet, vainly in my quiet hours
To breathe their marvelous notes I try;
I feel them, as the leaves and flowers
In silence feel the dewy showers,
And drink with glad still lips the blessing of the sky.

The rigor of a frozen clime,
The harshness of an untaught ear,
The jarring words of one whose rhyme
Beat often Labor's hurried time,
Or Duty's rugged march through storm and strife, are here.

Of mystic beauty, dreamy grace,
No rounded art the lack supplies;
Unskilled the subtle lines to trace,
Or softer shades of Nature's face,
I view her common forms with unanointed eyes.

Nor mine the seer-like power to show
The secrets of the heart and mind;
To drop the plummet-line below
Our common world of joy and woe,
A more intense despair or brighter hope to find.

Yet here at least an earnest sense
Of human right and weal is shown;
A hate of tyranny intense,
And hearty in its vehemence,
As if my brother's pain and sorrow were my own.

O Freedom! if to me belong
Nor mighty Milton's gift divine,
Nor Marvell's wit and graceful song,
Still with a love as deep and strong
As theirs, I lay, like them, my best gifts on thy shrine!

1847

Ichabod!

So fallen! so lost! the light withdrawn
Which once he wore!
The glory from his gray hairs gone
Forevermore!

Revile him not—the Tempter hath
A snare for all;
And pitying tears, not scorn and wrath,
Befit his fall!

ICHABOD. **Title:** Hebrew for "inglorious." Whittier refers to Daniel Webster who, in compromise, supported the pro-slavery advocates of the Fugitive Slave Law.

Oh! dumb be passion's stormy rage,
When he who might
Have lighted up and led his age,
Falls back in night.

Scorn! would the angels laugh, to mark
A bright soul driven,
Fiend-goaded, down the endless dark,
From hope and heaven!

Let not the land once proud of him,
Insult him now,
Nor brand with deeper shame his dim,
Dishonored brow.

But let its humbled sons, instead,
From sea to lake,
A long lament, as for the dead,
In sadness make.

Of all we loved and honored, nought
Save power remains—
A fallen angel's pride of thought,
Still strong in chains.

All else is gone; from those great eyes
The soul has fled:
When faith is lost, when honor dies,
The man is dead!

Then, pay the reverence of old days
To his dead fame;
Walk backward, with averted gaze,
And hide the shame!

1850

Abraham Davenport

In the old days (a custom laid aside
With breeches and cocked hats) the people sent
Their wisest men to make the public laws.
And so, from a brown homestead, where the Sound
Drinks the small tribute of the Mianas,
Waved over by the woods of Rippowams,
And hallowed by pure lives and tranquil deaths,
Stamford sent up to the councils of the State
Wisdom and grace in Abraham Davenport.

ABRAHAM DAVENPORT. **4–6. Sound . . . Rippowams:** Long Island Sound, into which the Mianas and Rippowams rivers flow. **8. Stamford:** Connecticut town nearby.

'Twas on a May-day of the far old year
Seventeen hundred eighty, that there fell
Over the bloom and sweet life of the Spring,
Over the fresh earth and the heaven of noon,
A horror of great darkness, like the night
In day of which the Norland sagas tell,
The Twilight of the Gods. The low-hung sky
Was black with ominous clouds, save where its rim
Was fringed with a dull glow, like that which climbs
The crater's sides from the red hell below.
Birds ceased to sing, and all the barnyard fowls
Roosted; the cattle at the pasture bars
Lowed, and looked homeward; bats on leathern wings
Flitted abroad; the sounds of labor died;
Men prayed, and women wept, all ears grew sharp
To hear the doom-blast of the trumpet shatter
The black sky, that the dreadful face of Christ
Might look from the rent clouds, not as He looked
A loving guest at Bethany, but stern
As Justice and inexorable Law.

Meanwhile in the old State House, dim as ghosts,
Sat the lawgivers of Connecticut,
Trembling beneath their legislative robes.
"It is the Lord's Great Day! Let us adjourn,"
Some said; and then, as if with one accord,
All eyes were turned to Abraham Davenport.
He rose, slow cleaving with his steady voice
The intolerable hush. "This well may be
The Day of Judgment which the world awaits;
But be it so or not, I only know
My present duty, and my Lord's command
To occupy till He come. So at the post
Where He hath set me in His providence,
I choose, for one, to meet Him face to face,
No faithless servant frightened from my task,
But ready when the Lord of the harvest calls;
And therefore, with all reverence, I would say,
Let God do His work, we will see to ours.
Bring in the candles." And they brought them in.

Then by the flaring lights the Speaker read,
Albeit with husky voice and shaking hands,
An act to amend an act to regulate
The shad and alewive fisheries. Whereupon
Wisely and well spake Abraham Davenport,

16. Twilight . . . Gods: final destruction of the gods in Norse mythology. **25. trumpet:** the trumpet of the Last Judgment (I Corinthians 15:51–52). **28. Bethany:** In Bethany, Jesus was gentle to the woman who poured out precious oil for him that the disciple felt should be used for the poor (Matthew 26:3–13). **52. alewive:** New England fish related to the herring.

Straight to the question, with no figures of speech
Save the ten Arab signs, yet not without
The shrewd dry humor natural to the man:
His awe-struck colleagues listening all the while,
Between the pauses of his argument,
To hear the thunder of the wrath of God
Break from the hollow trumpet of the cloud.

And there he stands in memory to this day,
Erect, self-poised, a rugged face, half seen
Against the background of unnatural dark,
A witness to the ages as they pass,
That simple duty hath no place for fear.

1866

EDWARD FITZGERALD

(1809–1883)

The *Rubáiyát of Omar Khayyam* was a favorite poem for reading aloud among college students in both England and America during the late Victorian period—in fact, until World War I. Several modern poets, including T. S. Eliot, Wallace Stevens, and Robert Lowell, have said that it was one of the first poems to catch their imagination as they were growing up, and Ezra Pound was so fond of it when young that he was later to name his son "Omar."

The reason for the poem's appeal does not lie merely in its simple message—"Eat, drink, and be merry, for tomorrow we die"—and in its exotic imagery of the Near East. As the poem questions and meditates upon the mystery of human existence, it has a complex, bittersweet tone and an almost Biblical simplicity and universality of metaphor and illustration.

Omar Khayyam (1050–1123) was a Persian astronomer and poet. The form he used for his quatrains (called *rubais*) was traditional in Persian poetry. The first two lines establish the rhyme; then the third, with a different ending, lifts the stanza or quatrain like a wave rising, until the verse falls back into the dominant rhyme in the last line. Fitzgerald freely translated the work and rearranged the order of the quatrains at different times, making four different versions (1859, 1868, 1872, 1879).

55. Arab signs: the ten Arabic numerals.

The Rubáiyát of Omar Khayyám of Naishápúr

1

Wake! For the Sun, who scattered into flight
The Stars before him from the Field of Night,
  Drives Night along with them from Heav'n, and strikes
The Sultán's Turret with a Shaft of Light.

2

Before the phantom of False morning died,
Methought a Voice within the Tavern cried,
  "When all the Temple is prepared within,
"Why nods the drowsy Worshipper outside?"

3

And, as the Cock crew, those who stood before
The Tavern shouted—"Open then the Door!
  "You know how little while we have to stay,
"And, once departed, may return no more."

4

Now the New Year reviving old Desires,
The thoughtful Soul to Solitude retires,
  Where the WHITE HAND OF MOSES on the Bough
Puts out, and Jesus from the Ground suspires.

5

Irám indeed is gone with all his Rose,
And Jamshýd's Sev'n-ringed Cup where no one knows;
  But still a Ruby kindles in the Vine,
And many a Garden by the Water blows.

6

And David's lips are lockt; but in divine
High-piping Pehleví, with "Wine! Wine! Wine!

THE RUBÁIYÁT. **5. False morning:** a brief light on the horizon an hour before the true dawn. **13. New Year:** In Persia this was at the start of Spring. **15–16. White . . . Jesus:** By "Moses" and "Jesus," Omar refers to two plants named in honor of them as "prophets" before Mohammed. The plant "Moses" got its name because its white blossoms reminded the Mohammedans of the incident in which Moses' hand turned white as snow (Exodus 4:6–7). The Persians believed that Jesus's power of healing came from his breath; hence here the plant is breathing health. **16. suspires:** breathes. **17. Irám:** a garden city, now sunk under the sands of Arabia. **18. Jamshýd:** Persian king, the design of whose sacred cup symbolized the ordered structure of the cosmos. **22. Pehleví:** ancient Persian language.

"Red Wine!"—the Nightingale cries to the Rose
That sallow cheek of hers to incarnadine.

7

Come, fill the Cup, and in the fire of Spring
Your Winter-garment of Repentance fling:
The Bird of Time has but a little way
To flutter—and the Bird is on the Wing.

8

Whether at Naishápúr or Babylon,
Whether the Cup with sweet or bitter run,
The Wine of Life keeps oozing drop by drop,
The Leaves of Life keep falling one by one.

9

Each Morn a thousand Roses brings, you say;
Yes, but where leaves the Rose of Yesterday?
And this first Summer month that brings the Rose
Shall take Jamshýd and Kaikobád away.

10

Well, let it take them! What have we to do
With Kaikobád the Great, or Kaikhosrú?
Let Zál and Rustum bluster as they will,
Or Hátim call to Supper—heed not you.

11

With me along the strip of Herbage strown
That just divides the desert from the sown,
Where name of Slave and Sultán is forgot—
And Peace to Mahmúd on his golden Throne!

12

A Book of Verses underneath the Bough,
A Jug of Wine, a Loaf of Bread—and Thou
Beside me singing in the Wilderness—
Oh, Wilderness were Paradise enow!

29. Naishápúr: more commonly, Nishapur; a provincial capital of Persia. Omar Khayyám lived there some of his life and is supposedly buried there. **36. Kaikobád:** founder of the great dynasty of kings that included Cyrus the Great (see line 38). **38–40. Kaikhosru . . . Hátim:** Kaikhosrú was the Persian name for Cyrus the Great (6th century B.C.), the most celebrated of Persian kings. Zál and Rustum (Sohrab and Rustum) were heroes of a Persian epic. Hátim, a Persian poet, was famous for his generosity as a host, and was constantly inviting people to lavish dinners. **44. Mahmúd:** Persian ruler who conquered India.

13

Some for the Glories of This World; and some
Sigh for the Prophet's Paradise to come;
  Ah, take the Cash, and let the Credit go,
Nor heed the rumble of a distant Drum!

14

Look to the blowing Rose about us—"Lo,
"Laughing," she says, "into the world I blow,
  "At once the silken tassel of my Purse
"Tear, and its Treasure on the Garden throw."

15

And those who husbanded the Golden grain,
And those who flung it to the winds like Rain,
  Alike to no such aureate Earth are turned
As, buried once, Men want dug up again.

16

The Worldly Hope men set their Hearts upon
Turns Ashes—or it prospers; and anon,
  Like Snow upon the Desert's dusty Face,
Lighting a little hour or two—is gone.

17

Think, in this battered Caravanserai
Whose Portals are alternate Night and Day,
  How Sultán after Sultán with his Pomp
Abode his destined Hour, and went his way.

18

They say the Lion and the Lizard keep
The Courts where Jamshýd gloried and drank deep:
  And Bahrám, that great Hunter—the Wild Ass
Stamps o'er his Head, but cannot break his Sleep.

19

I sometimes think that never blows so red
The Rose as where some buried Caesar bled;
  That every Hyacinth the Garden wears
Dropt in her Lap from some once lovely Head.

20

And this reviving Herb whose tender Green
Fledges the river-lip on which we lean—

50. Prophet's: Mohammed's. **65. Caravanserai:** inn. **70. Courts:** at Persepolis, capital of Persia in Jamshýd's time. **71. Bahrám:** Persian ruler who was lost while hunting wild asses.

Ah, lean upon it lightly! for who knows
From what once lovely Lip it springs unseen!

21

Ah, my Belovèd, fill the Cup that clears
TODAY of past Regrets and future Fears:
Tomorrow!—Why, Tomorrow I may be
Myself with Yesterday's Sev'n thousand Years.

22

For some we loved, the loveliest and the best
That from his Vintage rolling Time hath prest,
Have drunk their Cup a Round or two before,
And one by one crept silently to rest.

23

And we, that now make merry in the Room
They left, and Summer dresses in new bloom,
Ourselves must we beneath the Couch of Earth
Descend—ourselves to make a Couch—for whom?

24

Ah, make the most of what we yet may spend,
Before we too into the Dust descend;
Dust into Dust, and under Dust to lie,
Sans Wine, sans Song, sans Singer, and sans End!

25

Alike for those who for TODAY prepare,
And those that after some TOMORROW stare,
A Muezzín from the Tower of Darkness cries,
"Fools! your Reward is neither Here nor There."

26

Why, all the Saints and Sages who discussed
Of the Two Worlds so wisely—they are thrust
Like foolish Prophets forth; their Words to Scorn
Are scattered, and their Mouths are stopt with Dust.

27

Myself when young did eagerly frequent
Doctor and Saint, and heard great argument
About it and about: but evermore
Came out by the same door where in I went.

99. Muezzín: one who calls the hours of prayer from the tower of a mosque.

28

With them the seed of Wisdom did I sow,
And with mine own hand wrought to make it grow;
  And this was all the Harvest that I reaped—
"I came like Water, and like Wind I go."

29

Into this Universe, and *Why* not knowing
Nor *Whence,* like Water willy-nilly flowing;
  And out of it, as Wind along the Waste,
I know not *Whither,* willy-nilly blowing.

30

What, without asking, hither hurried *Whence?*
And, without asking, *Whither* hurried hence!
  Oh, many a Cup of this forbidden Wine
Must drown the memory of that insolence!

31

Up from Earth's Center through the Seventh Gate
I rose, and on the Throne of Saturn sate,
  And many a Knot unraveled by the Road;
But not the Master-knot of Human Fate.

. . .

91

Ah, with the Grape my fading Life provide,
And wash the Body whence the Life has died,
  And lay men shrouded in the living Leaf,
By some not unfrequented Garden-side.

92

That ev'n my buried Ashes such a snare
Of Vintage shall fling up into the Air
  As not a True-believer passing by
But shall be overtaken unaware.

93

Indeed the Idols I have loved so long
Have done my credit in this World much wrong:

119. forbidden Wine: alcohol is forbidden to strict Mohammedans. **121–22. Seventh Gate . . . Saturn:** Saturn, the seventh planet, was then considered the most remote. Hence, to be there was to be at the farthest seat of knowledge and with the widest perspective.

Have drowned my Glory in a shallow Cup,
And sold my Reputation for a Song.

94

Indeed, indeed, Repentance oft before
I swore—but was I sober when I swore?
And then and then came Spring, and Rose-in-hand
My threadbare Penitence apieces tore.

95

And much as Wine has played the Infidel,
And robbed me of my Robe of Honor—Well,
I wonder often what the Vintners buy
One half so precious as the stuff they sell.

96

Yet Ah, that Spring should vanish with the Rose!
That Youth's sweet-scented manuscript should close!
The Nightingale that in the branches sang,
Ah whence, and whither flown again, who knows!

97

Would but the Desert of the Fountain yield
One glimpse—if dimly, yet indeed, revealed,
To which the fainting Traveler might spring,
As springs the trampled herbage of the field!

98

Would but some wingèd Angel ere too late
Arrest the yet unfolded Roll of Fate,
And make the stern Recorder otherwise
Enregister, or quite obliterate!

99

Ah Love! could you and I with Him conspire
To grasp this sorry Scheme of Things entire,
Would not we shatter it to bits—and then
Remold it nearer to the Heart's Desire!

100

Yon rising Moon that looks for us again—
How oft hereafter will she wax and wane;
How oft hereafter rising look for us
Through this same Garden—and for *one* in vain!

101

And when like her, oh Sákí, you shall pass
Among the Guests Star-scattered on the Grass,
  And in your joyous errand reach the spot
Where I made One—turn down an empty Glass!
Tamám

1859

Oliver Wendell Holmes

(1809–1894)

Holmes was a professor of anatomy at the Harvard Medical School for thirty-five years, where his courses were enormously popular because of his liveliness and wit. Although literature was only a side interest, he wrote several volumes of poems and essays, as well as three novels. He was the most famous after-dinner speaker of his time. "Old Ironsides," a "classroom classic" for generations, was written in response to the decision in 1830 to dismantle the frigate *Constitution*, noted for its role in the War of 1812. The poem, reprinted in newspapers throughout the country, aroused enough public support to save the ship, which is still preserved in Boston Harbor. "The Chambered Nautilus" is remembered as Holmes's best attempt at a more fanciful and "romantic" subject.

Old Ironsides

Ay, tear her tattered ensign down!
  Long has it waved on high,
And many an eye has danced to see
  That banner in the sky;
Beneath it rung the battle shout,
  And burst the cannon's roar;—
The meteor of the ocean air
  Shall sweep the clouds no more!

405. Tamám: It is ended.

Her deck, once red with heroes' blood
Where knelt the vanquished foe,
When winds were hurrying o'er the flood
And waves were white below,
No more shall feel the victor's tread,
Or know the conquered knee;—
The harpies of the shore shall pluck
The eagle of the sea!

O better that her shattered hulk
Should sink beneath the wave;
Her thunders shook the mighty deep,
And there should be her grave;
Nail to the mast her holy flag,
Set every thread-bare sail,
And give her to the god of storms,—
The lightning and the gale!

1830

The Last Leaf

I saw him once before
As he passed by the door,
And again,
The pavement stones resound
As he totters o'er the ground
With his cane.

They say that in his prime,
Ere the pruning knife of Time
Cut him down,
Not a better man was found
By the Crier on his round
Through the town.

But now he walks the streets,
And he looks at all he meets
Sad and wan,
As he shakes his feeble head,
That it seems as if he said,
"They are gone."

The mossy marbles rest
On the lips that he has pressed
In their bloom,

THE LAST LEAF. **Title:** Holmes said the poem was suggested by the sight of Major Thomas Melville (1751–1832), one of the "Indians" of the famous Boston Tea Party of 1774 and grandfather of Herman Melville.

And the names he loved to hear
Have been carved for many a year
    On the tomb.

My grandmamma has said—
Poor old lady—she is dead
    Long ago;
That he had a Roman nose,
And his cheek was like a rose
    In the snow.

But now his nose is thin,
And it rests upon his chin
    Like a staff,
And a crook is in his back,
And a melancholy crack
    In his laugh.

I know it is a sin
For me to sit and grin
    At him here,
But the old three cornered hat,
And the breeches—and all that
      Are so queer!

And if I should live to be
That last leaf upon the tree
    In the spring,
Let them smile as I do now
At the old forsaken bough
    Where I cling.

1831

The Chambered Nautilus

This is the ship of pearl, which, poets feign,
    Sails the unshadowed main,
    The venturous bark that flings
On the sweet summer wind its purpled wings
In gulfs enchanted, where the Siren sings,
    And coral reefs lie bare,
Where the cold sea-maids rise to sun their streaming hair.

Its webs of living gauze no more unfurl;
    Wrecked is the ship of pearl!
    And every chambered cell,

THE CHAMBERED NAUTILUS. **Title:** The nautilus (from the Greek word for sailor) is a mollusk found in the Indian and South Pacific oceans. It is given its name because its webbed legs were thought to serve as a sail.

Where its dim dreaming life was wont to dwell,
As the frail tenant shaped his growing shell,
Before thee lies revealed,
Its irised ceiling rent, its sunless crypt unsealed!

Year after year beheld the silent toil
That spread his lustrous coil;
Still, as the spiral grew,
He left the past year's dwelling for the new,
Stole with soft step its shining archway through,
Built up its idle door,
Stretched in his last-found home, and knew the old no more.

Thanks for the heavenly message brought by thee,
Child of the wandering sea,
Cast from her lap, forlorn!
From thy dead lips a clearer note is born
Than ever Triton blew from wreathèd horn!
While on mine ear it rings,
Through the deep caves of thought I hear a voice that sings:

Build thee more stately mansions, O my soul,
As the swift seasons roll!
Leave thy low-vaulted past!
Let each new temple, nobler than the last,
Shut thee from heaven with a dome more vast,
Till thou at length art free,
Leaving thine outgrown shell by life's unresting sea!

1858

EDGAR ALLAN POE

(1809–1849)

The son of an actor, Poe was orphaned at the age of two. He was brought up in the family of a Virginia merchant, John Allan. As a student at the University of Virginia and later at West Point, he quarrelled with his foster father over money, and eventually lost all prospect of financial assistance. He had already begun to drink excessively. He took up a literary career, but he was unable to earn enough from his writings and also unable, because of alcoholism, to keep the editorial jobs he obtained on magazines. He lived henceforth in or close to poverty.

26. Triton: Greek sea god who blew a trumpet made of a conch shell. (See Wordsworth's "The World Is Too Much with Us," line 14.)

In prose fiction Poe's tales of horror are famous, and he created the genre of the detective story. His literary criticism greatly influenced French poets such as Charles Baudelaire and Stéphane Mallarmé. Poe held that the object of poetry is neither truth nor morality, but beauty, and that to create beauty the poet must rely on versification and on sensory, suggestive imagery. Reflective and discursive passages were inappropriate for poetry, and since an intense state of mind could be sustained only for a short time, a long poem is a "contradiction in terms." "To Helen" and "Annabel Lee" reflect Poe's love of English Romantic poets and especially of Shelley, and, like "The Raven," the latter poem particularly illustrates his experiments in verbal melody and in creating emotional states of extreme dreamlike vagueness and intensity.

To Helen

Helen, thy beauty is to me
  Like those Nicean barks of yore,
That gently, o'er a perfumed sea,
  The weary, way-worn wanderer bore
  To his own native shore.

On desperate seas long wont to roam,
  Thy hyacinth hair, thy classic face,
Thy Naiad airs have brought me home
  To the glory that was Greece
 And the grandeur that was Rome.

Lo! in yon brilliant window-niche
  How statue-like I see thee stand!
  The agate lamp within thy hand,
Ah! Psyche, from the regions which
  Are Holy Land!

1831

The Raven

Once upon a midnight dreary, while I pondered, weak and weary,
Over many a quaint and curious volume of forgotten lore—
While I nodded, nearly napping, suddenly there came a tapping,

TO HELEN. **2. Nicean:** from Nicea, in Asia Minor, associated with the god Dionysus, the "wanderer." Poe is using the word largely because of its musical sound. **8. Naiad:** water nymph.

As of some one gently rapping, rapping at my chamber door—
"'Tis some visiter," I muttered, "tapping at my chamber door—
Only this and nothing more."

Ah, distinctly I remember it was in the bleak December;
And each separate dying ember wrought its ghost upon the floor.
Eagerly I wished the morrow;—vainly I had sought to borrow
From my books surcease of sorrow—sorrow for the lost Lenore—
For the rare and radiant maiden whom the angels name Lenore—
Nameless *here* for evermore.

And the silken, sad, uncertain rustling of each purple curtain
Thrilled me—filled me with fantastic terrors never felt before;
So that now, to still the beating of my heart, I stood repeating
"'Tis some visiter entreating entrance at my chamber door—
Some late visiter entreating entrance at my chamber door;—
This it is and nothing more."

Presently my soul grew stronger; hesitating then no longer,
"Sir," said I, "or Madam, truly your forgiveness I implore;
But the fact is I was napping, and so gently you came rapping,
And so faintly you came tapping, tapping at my chamber door,
That I scarce was sure I heard you"—here I opened wide the door;—
Darkness there and nothing more.

Deep into that darkness peering, long I stood there wondering, fearing,
Doubting, dreaming dreams no mortal ever dared to dream before;
But the silence was unbroken, and the stillness gave no token,
And the only word there spoken was the whispered word, "Lenore!"
This I whispered, and an echo murmured back the word, "Lenore!"
Merely this and nothing more.

Back into the chamber turning, all my soul within me burning,
Soon again I heard a tapping somewhat louder than before.
"Surely," said I, "surely that is something at my window lattice;
Let me see, then, what thereat is, and this mystery explore—
Let my heart be still a moment and this mystery explore;—
'Tis the wind and nothing more!"

Open here I flung the shutter, when, with many a flirt and flutter,
In there stepped a stately Raven of the saintly days of yore;
Not the least obeisance made he; not a minute stopped or stayed he;
But, with mien of lord or lady, perched above my chamber door—
Perched upon a bust of Pallas just above my chamber door—
Perched, and sat, and nothing more.

THE RAVEN. **41. Pallas:** Pallas Athene, patron goddess of Athens.

Then this ebony bird beguiling my sad fancy into smiling,
By the grave and stern decorum of the countenance it wore,
"Though thy crest be shorn and shaven, thou," I said, "art sure no craven,
Ghastly grim and ancient Raven wandering from the Nightly shore—
Tell me what thy lordly name is on the Night's Plutonian shore!"
Quoth the Raven "Nevermore."

Much I marvelled this ungainly fowl to hear discourse so plainly,
Though its answer little meaning—little relevancy bore;
For we cannot help agreeing that no living human being
Ever yet was blessed with seeing bird above his chamber door—
Bird or beast upon the sculptured bust above his chamber door,
With such name as "Nevermore."

But the Raven, sitting lonely on the placid bust, spoke only
That one word, as if his soul in that one word he did outpour.
Nothing farther then he uttered—not a feather then he fluttered—
Till I scarcely more than muttered "Other friends have flown before—
On the morrow *he* will leave me, as my Hopes have flown before."
Then the bird said "Nevermore."

Startled at the stillness broken by reply so aptly spoken,
"Doubtless," said I, "what it utters is its only stock and store
Caught from some unhappy master whom unmerciful Disaster
Followed fast and followed faster till his songs one burden bore—
Till the dirges of his Hope that melancholy burden bore
Of 'Never—nevermore.'"

But the Raven still beguiling my sad fancy into smiling,
Straight I wheeled a cushioned seat in front of bird, and bust and door;
Then, upon the velvet sinking, I betook myself to linking
Fancy unto fancy, thinking what this ominous bird of yore—
What this grim, ungainly, ghastly, gaunt, and ominous bird of yore
Meant in croaking "Nevermore."

Thus I sat engaged in guessing, but no syllable expressing
To the fowl whose fiery eyes now burned into my bosom's core;
This and more I sat divining, with my head at ease reclining
On the cushion's velvet lining that the lamp-light gloated o'er,
But whose velvet-violet lining with the lamp-light gloating o'er,
She shall press, ah, nevermore!

Then, methought, the air grew denser, perfumed from an unseen censer
Swung by seraphim whose foot-falls tinkled on the tufted floor.
"Wretch," I cried, "thy God hath lent thee—by these angels he hath sent thee

47. Plutonian: Pluto, god of the underworld.

Respite—respite and nepenthe from thy memories of Lenore;
Quaff, oh quaff this kind nepenthe and forget this lost Lenore!"
    Quoth the Raven "Nevermore."

"Prophet!" said I, "thing of evil!—prophet still, if bird or devil!—
Whether Tempter sent, or whether tempest tossed thee here ashore,
Desolate yet all undaunted, on this desert land enchanted—
Oh this home by Horror haunted—tell me truly, I implore—
Is there—*is* there balm in Gilead?—tell me—tell me, I implore!"
    Quoth the Raven "Nevermore."

"Prophet!" said I, "thing of evil!—prophet still, if bird or devil!
By that Heaven that bends above us—by that God we both adore—
Tell this soul with sorrow laden if, within the distant Aidenn,
It shall clasp a sainted maiden whom the angels name Lenore—
Clasp a rare and radiant maiden whom the angels name Lenore."
    Quoth the Raven "Nevermore."

"Be that word our sign of parting, bird or fiend!" I shrieked,
    upstarting—
"Get thee back into the tempest and the Night's Plutonian shore!
Leave no black plume as a token of that lie thy soul hath spoken!
Leave my loneliness unbroken!—quit the bust above my door!
Take thy beak from out my heart, and take thy form from off my door!"
    Quoth the Raven "Nevermore."

And the Raven, never flitting, still is sitting, *still* is sitting
On the pallid bust of Pallas just above my chamber door;
And his eyes have all the seeming of a demon's that is dreaming,
And the lamp-light o'er him streaming throws his shadow on the floor;
And my soul from out that shadow that lies floating on the floor
    Shall be lifted—nevermore!

1845

Annabel Lee

It was many and many a year ago,
    In a kingdom by the sea,
That a maiden there lived whom you may know
    By the name of Annabel Lee;
And this maiden she lived with no other thought
    Than to love and be loved by me.

She was a child and *I* was a child,
    In this kingdom by the sea,
But we loved with a love that was more than love—

82. nepenthe: in classical myth, a drink to banish sorrow. **89. balm in Gilead:** medicine made from a tree in Gilead, Jordan (Jeremiah 8:22). **93. Aidenn:** Arabic for Eden.

I and my Annabel Lee—
With a love that the wingèd seraphs of Heaven
Coveted her and me.

And this was the reason that, long ago,
In this kingdom by the sea,
A wind blew out of a cloud by night
Chilling my Annabel Lee;
So that her highborn kinsmen came
And bore her away from me,
To shut her up in a sepulchre
In this kingdom by the sea.

The angels, not half so happy in Heaven,
Went envying her and me:
Yes! that was the reason (as all men know,
In this kingdom by the sea)
That the wind came out of the cloud, chilling
And killing my Annabel Lee.

But our love it was stronger by far than the love
Of those who were older than we—
Of many far wiser than we—
And neither the angels in Heaven above
Nor the demons down under the sea,
Can ever dissever my soul from the soul
Of the beautiful Annabell Lee:

For the moon never beams without bringing me dreams
Of the beautiful Annabel Lee;
And the stars never rise but I see the bright eyes
Of the beautiful Annabel Lee;
And so, all the night-tide, I lie down by the side
Of my darling, my darling, my life and my bride,
In her sepulchre there by the sea—
In her tomb by the side of the sea.

1849

ALFRED, LORD TENNYSON

(1809–1892)

By the age of twelve Tennyson had completed an epic of six thousand lines, and he continued to study and practice his art with unremitting devotion till he died. He was educated by his father, a clergyman of difficult character, who, it is said, would not allow his son to leave home for Trinity College, Cambridge, until he had recited from memory all of Horace's odes. Having lived closely within his family, Tennyson was shy about making friends at college, but gradually attracted a group of talented persons who believed in his genius. One of these was A. H. Hallam, whose death later occasioned Tennyson's greatest single poem, "In Memoriam." His father died in 1831, and Tennyson was obliged to leave college. All his life he was subject to attacks of psychological depression, and after he returned to the family home, these gradually became more severe, affecting his general health. Hallam's untimely death from a stroke in 1833 was a dreadful blow. But by 1836 he was in love with Emily Sellwood, and the couple were soon engaged, although they could not marry for lack of money.

Tennyson had published splendid collections of lyrics in 1830 and 1833, but his fame was established by the *Poems* of 1842, which included two printed here, the haunting lyric "Break, Break, Break," and the noble dramatic monologue, "Ulysses." From this time, when he was only thirty-three, until his death fifty years later, Tennyson was recognized as the great poet of the age. But in 1842 he also lost all his money in an unlucky financial speculation, and almost died of the shock. He was rescued from poverty by a government pension. In 1850 the success of "In Memoriam," together with the continuing sales of earlier volumes, made it possible for him to marry. His life henceforth fulfilled, at least outwardly, Victorian ideals and wishes. He had a happy marriage, a worthy occupation, and enormous reputation. The income from his books amounted in some years to as much as $300,000 in present-day purchasing power. The great and famous were his friends, including Thomas Carlyle, Charles Dickens, and the Prime Minister, William Gladstone. Queen Victoria was an admirer. He became Poet Laureate in 1850, after the death of Wordsworth. He was buried in Westminster Abbey.

Because he was integrated with the middle class of his time and reflected its ideals, Tennyson was very unusual among the great poets of the modern world. Since the Romantic period most poets have been critics of their society, questioning accepted images of morality and reality and proposing new ones. If we ask why Tennyson could hold a position so different from that of the Romantic quester or rebel or of the twentieth-century alienated poet of the avant-garde, one reason lies in the character of the Victorian reading public. Many middle-class persons believed in the value of literary culture and pursued it, reading good books with serious attention and pleasure. Writing for this audience, Tennyson could live up to the highest standards of his art as he understood it. Tennyson's readers expected "beauty" in poetry, by which they meant a synthesis of certain Romantic emotions and stylistic features. Poetic imagery was to offer refreshment and escape, as it may be found amid the scenery of classical myth, medieval romance, the glamorous East, folklore witcheries, and especially in nature—the dales, grain fields, escarpments, waterfalls, vistas, light effects, and other rich, varied landscape Tennyson renders. Tennyson's audience also welcomed descriptions of familiar, contemporary character and life, so long as these were humorous, idealized, or, at any rate, essentially sympathetic. Versification was to be melodious—and no English poet is more so than Tennyson, although a few other poets may please the ear more delicately. Melody and beauty were not pursued at the cost of expressiveness, for the realities and emotions impossible to represent within these terms were not considered appropriate to poetry. One wrote of love, not lust, and of courage, faith, and other virtues and ideals. An old man might be heroic, like Ulysses in Tennyson's poem, or weary like Tithonus, but certainly not senile. "In Memoriam" conveys grief's monotonous, continuing pain, but it is also inspirational; these brief elegies, which Tennyson composed at intervals over seventeen years, struggle with religious doubts and gradually move toward hope. Tennyson's poetry is saturated with regret, weariness, and death longing, but these emotions do not appall us, for as Tennyson expresses them, the beauty and melody sweeten, elevate, and console, as in the music of Tschaikovsky. The direct expression of intimate emotion was greatly valued by Tennyson's readers. Finally, these readers sought accessible, important meaning. Poetry included profound reflection on the mysteries of human existence. Its insights might be expressed in concrete symbols, but the hunger of the middle-class audience was rather for direct, intelligible generalization, a language of meditation and statement.

Break, Break, Break

Break, break, break,
  On thy cold gray stones, O Sea!
And I would that my tongue could utter
  The thoughts that arise in me.

O, well for the fisherman's boy,
  That he shouts with his sister at play!
O, well for the sailor lad,
  That he sings in his boat on the bay!

And the stately ships go on
  To their haven under the hill;
But O for the touch of a vanished hand,
  And the sound of a voice that is still!

Break, break, break,
  At the foot of thy crags, O Sea!
But the tender grace of a day that is dead
  Will never come back to me.

1842

Ulysses

It little profits that an idle king,
By this still hearth, among these barren crags,
Matched with an aged wife, I mete and dole
Unequal laws unto a savage race,
That hoard, and sleep, and feed, and know not me.
I cannot rest from travel; I will drink
Life to the lees. All times I have enjoyed
Greatly, have suffered greatly, both with those
That loved me, and alone; on shore, and when
Through scudding drifts the rainy Hyades
Vext the dim sea. I am become a name;
For always roaming with a hungry heart
Much have I seen and known—cities of men
And manners, climates, councils, governments,
Myself not least, but honored of them all,—
And drunk delight of battle with my peers,

ULYSSES. **Title:** Ulysses (Greek "Odysseus," hero of Homer's *Odyssey*), after his long journey home to Ithaca, became restless in his old age, according to Dante (*Inferno,* XXVI), and wished once again to travel. Gathering some of his followers, he set off for unknown places. **3. mete and dole:** measure out rewards and punishments. **10. Hyades:** stars in the constellation Taurus; when they rose with the sun, they were thought to indicate rain.

Far on the ringing plains of windy Troy.
I am a part of all that I have met;
Yet all experience is an arch wherethrough
Gleams that untraveled world whose margin fades
For ever and for ever when I move.
How dull it is to pause, to make an end,
To rust unburnished, not to shine in use!
As though to breathe were life! Life piled on life
Were all too little, and of one to me
Little remains; but every hour is saved
From that eternal silence, something more,
A bringer of new things; and vile it were
For some three suns to store and hoard myself,
And this gray spirit yearning in desire
To follow knowledge like a sinking star,
Beyond the utmost bound of human thought.
  This is my son, mine own Telemachus,
To whom I leave the scepter and the isle,
Well-loved of me, discerning to fulfill
This labor, by slow prudence to make mild
A rugged people, and through soft degrees
Subdue them to the useful and the good.
Most blameless is he, centered in the sphere
Of common duties, decent not to fail
In offices of tenderness, and pay
Meet adoration to my household gods,
When I am gone. He works his work, I mine.
  There lies the port; the vessel puffs her sail;
There gloom the dark, broad seas. My mariners,
Souls that have toiled, and wrought, and thought with me,
That ever with a frolic welcome took
The thunder and the sunshine, and opposed
Free hearts, free foreheads—you and I are old;
Old age hath yet his honor and his toil.
Death closes all; but something ere the end,
Some work of noble note, may yet be done,
Not unbecoming men that strove with gods.
The lights begin to twinkle from the rocks;
The long day wanes; the slow moon climbs; the deep
Moans round with many voices. Come, my friends,
'Tis not too late to seek a newer world.
Push off, and sitting well in order smite
The sounding furrows; for my purpose holds
To sail beyond the sunset, and the baths
Of all the western stars, until I die.
It may be that the gulfs will wash us down;
It may be we shall touch the Happy Isles,

63. Happy Isles: Elysium, or Islands of the Blessed, where heroes lived after death. They were thought to lie in the furthest reaches of the western seas.

And see the great Achilles, whom we knew.
Though much is taken, much abides; and though
We are not now that strength which in old days
Moved earth and heaven, that which we are, we are,
One equal temper of heroic hearts,
Made weak by time and fate, but strong in will
To strive, to seek, to find, and not to yield.

1842

Songs from The Princess

The Splendor Falls on Castle Walls

The splendor falls on castle walls
  And snowy summits old in story;
The long light shakes across the lakes,
  And the wild cataract leaps in glory.
Blow, bugle, blow, set the wild echoes flying,
Blow, bugle; answer, echoes, dying, dying, dying.

O, hark, O, hear! how thin and clear,
  And thinner, clearer, farther going!
O, sweet and far from cliff and scar
  The horns of Elfland faintly blowing!
Blow, let us hear the purple glens replying,
Blow, bugle; answer, echoes, dying, dying, dying.

O love, they die in yon rich sky,
  They faint on hill or field or river;
Our echoes roll from soul to soul,
  And grow for ever and for ever.
Blow, bugle, blow, set the wild echoes flying,
And answer, echoes, answer, dying, dying, dying.

1850

Tears, Idle Tears, I Know Not What They Mean

  Tears, idle tears, I know not what they mean,
Tears from the depth of some divine despair
Rise in the heart, and gather to the eyes,
In looking on the happy autumn-fields,
And thinking of the days that are no more.

64. Achilles: the Greek hero of the *Iliad*.

Fresh as the first beam glittering on a sail,
That brings our friends up from the underworld,
Sad as the last which reddens over one
That sinks with all we love below the verge;
So sad, so fresh, the days that are no more.

Ah, sad and strange as in dark summer dawns
The earliest pipe of half-awakened birds
To dying ears, when unto dying eyes
The casement slowly grows a glimmering square;
So sad, so strange, the days that are no more.

Dear as remembered kisses after death,
And sweet as those by hopeless fancy feigned
On lips that are for others; deep as love,
Deep as first love, and wild with all regret;
O Death in Life, the days that are no more!

1847

Now Sleeps the Crimson Petal, Now the White

Now sleeps the crimson petal, now the white;
Nor waves the cypress in the palace walk;
Nor winks the gold fin in the porphyry font.
The firefly wakens; waken thou with me.

Now droops the milk-white peacock like a ghost,
And like a ghost she glimmers on to me.

Now lies the Earth all Danaë to the stars,
And all thy heart lies open unto me.

Now slides the silent meteor on, and leaves
A shining furrow, as thy thoughts in me.

Now folds the lily all her sweetness up,
And slips into the bosom of the lake.
So fold thyself, my dearest, thou, and slip
Into my bosom and be lost in me.

1847

NOW SLEEPS THE CRIMSON PETAL. **7. Danaë:** Greek princess, locked in a tower by her father to keep away suitors. Zeus visited her in the form of a gold shower, and their offspring was the hero Perseus.

from In Memoriam A. H. H.

Obiit. MDCCCXXXIII

1

I held it truth, with him who sings
To one clear harp in divers tones,
That men may rise on stepping-stones
Of their dead selves to higher things.

But who shall so forecast the years
And find in loss a gain to match?
Or reach a hand through time to catch
The far-off interest of tears?

Let Love clasp Grief lest both be drowned,
Let darkness keep her raven gloss.
Ah, sweeter to be drunk with loss,
To dance with Death, to beat the ground,

Than that the victor Hours should scorn
The long result of love, and boast,
"Behold the man that loved and lost,
But all he was is overworn."

2

Old yew, which graspest at the stones
That name the underlying dead,
Thy fibers net the dreamless head,
Thy roots are wrapt about the bones.

The seasons bring the flowers again,
And bring the firstling to the flock;
And in the dusk of thee the clock
Beats out the little lives of men.

O, not for thee the glow, the bloom,
Who changest not in any gale,
Nor branding summer suns avail
To touch thy thousand years of gloom;

And gazing on thee, sullen tree,
Sick for thy stubborn hardihood,
I seem to fail from out my blood
And grow incorporate into thee.

IN MEMORIAM A. H. H. **Title:** In memory of Arthur Henry Hallam (1811–1833), Tennyson's closest friend. SECTION 1. **1. him who sings:** the German poet, J. W. von Goethe.

7

Dark house, by which once more I stand
  Here in the long unlovely street,
  Doors, where my heart was used to beat
So quickly, waiting for a hand,

A hand that can be clasped no more—
  Behold me, for I cannot sleep,
  And like a guilty thing I creep
At earliest morning to the door.

He is not here; but far away
  The noise of life begins again,
  And ghastly through the drizzling rain
On the bald street breaks the blank day.

11

Calm is the morn without a sound,
  Calm as to suit a calmer grief,
  And only through the faded leaf
The chestnut pattering to the ground;

Calm and deep peace on this high wold,
  And on these dews that drench the furze,
  And all the silvery gossamers
That twinkle into green and gold;

Calm and still light on yon great plain
  That sweeps with all its autumn bowers,
  And crowded farms and lessening towers,
To mingle with the bounding main;

Calm and deep peace in this wide air,
  These leaves that redden to the fall,
  And in my heart, if calm at all,
If any calm, a calm despair;

Calm on the seas, and silver sleep,
  And waves that sway themselves in rest,
  And dead calm in that noble breast
Which heaves but with the heaving deep.

19

The Danube to the Severn gave
  The darkened heart that beat no more;
  They laid him by the pleasant shore,
And in the hearing of the wave.

SECTION 7. **2. unlovely street:** Wimpole Street, London, where Hallam had lived. SECTION 11. **5. wold:** high open field. SECTION 19. **1. Danube . . . Severn:** Hallam had died at Vienna on the Danube River. He was buried near the Severn, a river in Western England.

There twice a day the Severn fills;
The salt sea-water passes by,
And hushes half the babbling Wye,
And makes a silence in the hills.

The Wye is hushed nor moved along,
And hushed my deepest grief of all,
When filled with tears that cannot fall,
I brim with sorrow drowning song.

The tide flows down, the wave again
Is vocal in its wooded walls;
My deeper anguish also falls,
And I can speak a little then.

50

Be near me when my light is low,
When the blood creeps, and the nerves prick
And tingle; and the heart is sick,
And all the wheels of being slow.

Be near me when the sensuous frame
Is racked with pangs that conquer trust;
And Time, a maniac scattering dust,
And Life, a Fury slinging flame.

Be near me when my faith is dry,
And men the flies of latter spring,
That lay their eggs, and sting and sing
And weave their petty cells and die.

Be near me when I fade away,
To point the term of human strife,
And on the low dark verge of life
The twilight of eternal day.

119

Doors, where my heart was used to beat
So quickly, not as one that weeps
I come once more; the city sleeps;
I smell the meadow in the street;

I hear a chirp of birds; I see
Betwixt the black fronts long-withdrawn
A light-blue lane of early dawn,
And think of early days and thee,

And bless thee, for thy lips are bland,
And bright the friendship of thine eyes;
And in my thoughts with scarce a sigh
I take the pressure of thine hand.

7. Wye: a tributary to the Severn.

121

Sad Hesper o'er the buried sun
  And ready, thou, to die with him,
  Thou watchest all things ever dim
And dimmer, and a glory done.

The team is loosened from the wain,
  The boat is drawn upon the shore;
  Thou listenest to the closing door,
And life is darkened in the brain.

Bright Phosphor, fresher for the night,
  By thee the world's great work is heard
  Beginning, and the wakeful bird;
Behind thee comes the greater light.

The market boat is on the stream,
  And voices hail it from the brink;
  Thou hear'st the village hammer clink,
And see'st the moving of the team.

Sweet Hesper–Phosphor, double name
  For what is one, the first, the last,
  Thou, like my present and my past,
Thy place is changed; thou art the same.

130

Thy voice is on the rolling air;
  I hear thee where the waters run;
  Thou standest in the rising sun,
And in the setting thou art fair.

What are thou then? I cannot guess;
  But though I seem in star and flower
  To feel thee some diffusive power,
I do not therefore love thee less.

My love involves the love before;
  My love is vaster passion now;
  Though mixed with God and Nature thou,
I seem to love thee more and more.

Far off thou art, but ever nigh;
  I have thee still, and I rejoice;
  I prosper, circled with thy voice;
I shall not lose thee though I die.

1850

SECTION 121. **1. Hesper:** evening star. **5. wain:** wagon. **9. Phosphor:** morning star. **17. double name:** both the morning and the evening star are the planet Venus.

Tithonus

The woods decay, the woods decay and fall,
The vapors weep their burthen to the ground,
Man comes and tills the field and lies beneath,
And after many a summer dies the swan.
Me only cruel immortality
Consumes; I wither slowly in thine arms,
Here at the quiet limit of the world,
A white-haired shadow roaming like a dream
The ever-silent spaces of the East,
Far-folded mists, and gleaming halls of morn.
Alas! for this gray shadow, once a man—
So glorious in his beauty and thy choice,
Who madest him thy chosen, that he seemed
To his great heart none other than a God!
I asked thee, "Give me immortality."
Then didst thou grant mine asking with a smile,
Like wealthy men who care not how they give.
But thy strong Hours indignant worked their wills,
And beat me down and marred and wasted me,
And though they could not end me, left me maimed
To dwell in presence of immortal youth.
Immortal age beside immortal youth,
And all I was in ashes. Can thy love,
Thy beauty, make amends, though even now,
Close over us, the silver star thy guide,
Shines in those tremulous eyes that fill with tears
To hear me? Let me go; take back thy gift.
Why should a man desire in any way
To vary from the kindly race of men,
Or pass beyond the goal of ordinance
Where all should pause, as is most meet for all?
A soft air fans the cloud apart; there comes
A glimpse of that dark world where I was born.
Once more the old mysterious glimmer steals
From thy pure brows, and from thy shoulders pure,
And bosom beating with a heart renewed.
Thy cheek begins to redden through the gloom,
Thy sweet eyes brighten slowly close to mine,
Ere yet they blind the stars, and the wild team

TITHONUS. **Title:** Aurora, goddess of the dawn, fell in love with Tithonus, a Trojan prince, and married him. Zeus granted her prayer to make Tithonus immortal. But she forgot to ask that he also would remain forever young. As a result, he continued to live, growing constantly older, and viewed his immortality as a curse. **4. swan:** noted for their long lives. **6. thine arms:** the arms of Aurora, his wife. **25. silver star:** morning star. **30. ordinance:** what is ordained for human beings. **39. wild team:** the horses that drew Aurora's chariot.

Which love thee, yearning for thy yoke, arise,
And shake the darkness from their loosened manes,
And beat the twilight into flakes of fire.
  Lo! ever thus thou growest beautiful
In silence, then before thine answer given
Departest, and thy tears are on my cheek.
  Why wilt thou ever scare me with thy tears,
And make me tremble lest a saying learnt,
In days far-off, on that dark earth, be true?
"The Gods themselves cannot recall their gifts."
  Ay me! ay me! with what another heart
In days far-off, and with what other eyes
I used to watch—if I be he that watched—
The lucid outline forming round thee; saw
The dim curls kindle into sunny rings;
Changed with thy mystic change, and felt my blood
Glow with the glow that slowly crimsoned all
Thy presence and thy portals, while I lay,
Mouth, forehead, eyelids, growing dewy-warm
With kisses balmier than half-opening buds
Of April, and could hear the lips that kissed
Whispering I knew not what of wild and sweet,
Like that strange song I heard Apollo sing,
While Ilion like a mist rose into towers.
  Yet hold me not for ever in thine East;
How can my nature longer mix with thine?
Coldly thy rosy shadows bathe me, cold
Are all thy lights, and cold my wrinkled feet
Upon thy glimmering thresholds, when the steam
Floats up from those dim fields about the homes
Of happy men that have the power to die,
And grassy barrows of the happier dead.
Release me, and restore me to the ground.
Thou seest all things, thou wilt see my grave;
Thou wilt renew thy beauty morn by morn,
I earth in earth forget these empty courts,
And thee returning on thy silver wheels.

1860

63. Ilion . . . towers: the walls and towers of Troy (or Ilion) were said to have been raised by the sound of Apollo's music.

To Virgil

Written at the request of the Mantuans
for the nineteenth centenary of Virgil's death

1

Roman Virgil, thou that singest
    Ilion's lofty temples robed in fire,
Ilion falling, Rome arising,
    wars, and filial faith, and Dido's pyre;

2

Landscape-lover, lord of language
    more than he that sang the Works and Days,
All the chosen coin of fancy
    flashing out from many a golden phrase;

3

Thou that singest wheat and woodland,
    tilth and vineyard, hive and horse and herd;
All the charm of all the Muses
    often flowering in a lonely word;

4

Poet of the happy Tityrus
    piping underneath his beechen bowers;
Poet of the poet-satyr
    whom the laughing shepherd bound with flowers;

5

Chanter of the Pollio, glorying
    in the blissful years again to be,
Summers of the snakeless meadow,
            unlaborious earth and oarless sea;

TO VIRGIL. **Title:** Mantua, in northern Italy, was the town near which Virgil was born (70 B.C.). **1–4. singest . . . Dido's pyre:** The *Aeneid* of Virgil traces the history of Aeneas from the fall of Troy through his love affair with Dido, Queen of Carthage (who, when left by him, destroys herself), to his founding of Rome. **6. Works and Days:** a poem on occupations by the Greek poet Hesiod, which anticipates Virgil's *Georgics* about country and farm life. **13. Tityrus:** shepherd in Virgil's *Eclogue* I. **15. poet-satyr:** Silenus in *Eclogue* VI. **17. Pollio:** Roman consul, friend of Virgil, celebrated in *Eclogue* IV.

6

Thou that seest Universal
Nature moved by Universal Mind;
Thou majestic in thy sadness
at the doubtful doom of human kind;

7

Light among the vanished ages;
star that gildest yet this phantom shore;
Golden branch amid the shadows,
kings and realms that pass to rise no more;

8

Now thy Forum roars no longer,
fallen every purple Caesar's dome—
Though thine ocean-roll of rhythm
sound forever of Imperial Rome—

9

Now the Rome of slaves hath perished,
and the Rome of freemen holds her place,
I, from out the Northern Island
sundered once from all the human race,

10

I salute thee, Mantovano,
I that loved thee since my day began,
Wielder of the stateliest measure
ever molded by the lips of man.

1883

Frater Ave Atque Vale

Row us out from Desenzano, to your Sirmione row!
So they rowed, and there we landed—"O venusta Sirmio!"
There to me through all the groves of olive in the summer glow,
There beneath the Roman ruin where the purple flowers grow,

27. Golden branch: a golden bough carried by Aeneas, as a gift to Proserpine, allowed him to enter the underworld safely (*Aeneid,* V, 208f.). **37. Mantovano:** citizen of Mantua. FRATER AVE ATQUE VALE. **Title:** "Brother, Hail and Farewell." The words are from an elegy by the Latin poet Catullus (c. 10) on the death of his brother. Tennyson also echoes phrases from another poem by Catullus (XXXI) on visiting Sirmio. **1. Desenzano:** town on Lake Garda, Italy. **Sirmione:** (Sirmio) peninsula near Desenzano. **2. "O venusta Sirmio":** O lovely Sirmio.

Came that "Ave atque Vale" of the poet's hopeless woe,
Tenderest of Roman poets nineteen-hundred years ago,
"Frater Ave atque Vale"—as we wandered to and fro
Gazing at the Lydian laughter of the Garda Lake below,
Sweet Catullus's all-but-island, olive-silvery Sirmio!

1885

Crossing the Bar

Sunset and evening star,
  And one clear call for me!
And may there be no moaning of the bar,
  When I put out to sea,

But such a tide as moving seems asleep,
  Too full for sound and foam,
When that which drew from out the boundless deep
  Turns again home.

Twilight and evening bell,
  And after that the dark!
And may there be no sadness of farewell,
  When I embark;

For though from out our bourne of Time and Place
  The flood may bear me far,
I hope to see my Pilot face to face
  When I have crossed the bar.

1889

Robert Browning

(1812–1889)

As a boy Browning spent much of his time reading in his father's large library. His parents encouraged his ambition to be a poet. His first published poem, *Pauline* (1833), showed his enthusiasm for Shelley. *Paracelsus* (1835) and *Sordello* (1840) were character studies, with autobiographical elements, of flawed genius in a sixteenth-century

8. Lydian: the Etruscans of the area were said to be descended from the Lydians of Asia Minor.

scientist and mystic and in a thirteenth-century troubadour. The latter poem told its story with such extreme indirection and ellipsis that Browning became notorious for obscurity. Seven plays he composed between 1837 and 1846 had little success on the stage, but contributed to his mastery of the genre for which he is famous, the short "dramatic monologue."

In 1844 a volume of poems by Elizabeth Barrett, then a poet of much larger reputation, included a flattering phrase about Browning's poetry. Greatly pleased by this notice and by her poetry, Browning wrote to Barrett, who was in turn excited to receive a letter from "the author of *Paracelsus,* the king of the mystics." The story of the courtship that followed has often been told: letters led to visits, but before he met her, Browning had declared his love by mail; after the first visit he proposed marriage; she feared lest her ill health would make her a burden; moreover, her father had forbidden his daughters to marry (and when she did, he never afterwards saw or wrote to her, and returned her letters unopened). In 1846 they married in secret and stole away to Italy, where they lived in Florence until her death in 1861.

During the sixteen years of his marriage Browning composed relatively little, although one important volume, *Men and Women* (1855), showed that his powers were still developing. He now returned to London. The public success of *The Ring and the Book* (1868–69) showed that he had at last acquired an audience. This long poem narrated a murder in seventeenth-century Rome from twelve different points of view. Additional poems appeared frequently, for though by Victorian expectations Browning was a slow producer, his rate of twenty-five to thirty lines a day was rapid by modern standards. The poems of his last twenty years frequently set forth his moral ideas and religious speculations—the immortality of the soul? the origin of evil?—and are of less interest today. But for many persons Browning was a guide and prophet, and the first of numerous Browning Societies was founded in 1881 to elucidate his doctrines.

To his contemporaries Browning appealed by his psychological insight and by the inspiration of his ethical and religious views. His colloquial diction and rhythms were harder to appreciate, and in many poems were undeniably eccentric. Victorian readers were also unused to the swift alterations of associations and feelings in his poems, and to the sudden, complex juxtapositions that result. In these respects Browning somewhat anticipated techniques of Modernist poetry, and his influence is visible in early poems of Ezra Pound and T. S. Eliot.

Browning's dramatic monologues are illustrated here by "My Last Duchess," "The Bishop Orders His Tomb at Saint Praxed's Church," and "Andrea del Sarto." Poems in this genre present the words of a character on some particular occasion. We infer the occasion from what the speaker says, and often we can also infer the reaction of the person or persons to whom he speaks, but the interest of the poem lies in the revelation of the speaker's character. Many of Browning's dramatic monologues present not only a character but also a historical period, which the "mind" or "sensibility" of the speaker embodies. Because the poet is not present in the poem but remains invisible behind it, we cannot know whether the monologue expresses the poet's own views; in many of Browning's monologues we assume that there is a very considerable distance between the author and the speaker. That a poet of dramatic monologues was viewed as a moral and religious guide is unexpected, and less naive readers, such as Henry James and Thomas Hardy, were puzzled by Browning and unsure what his "real" character and opinions might be. His dramatic monologues lead us to judge the speaker morally, but they may also leave us uncertain what judgment we are invited to pass. This, indeed, is part of their fascination.

My Last Duchess

Ferrara

That's my last duchess painted on the wall,
Looking as if she were alive. I call
That piece a wonder, now: Frà Pandolf's hands
Worked busily a day, and there she stands.
Will't please you sit and look at her? I said
"Frà Pandolf" by design, for never read
Strangers like you that pictured countenance,
The depth and passion of its earnest glance,
But to myself they turned (since none puts by
The curtain I have drawn for you, but I)
And seemed as they would ask me, if they durst,
How such a glance came there; so, not the first
Are you to turn and ask thus. Sir, 'twas not
Her husband's presence only, called that spot
Of joy into the Duchess' cheek: perhaps
Frà Pandolf chanced to say, "Her mantle laps
"Over my lady's wrist too much," or, "Paint

MY LAST DUCHESS. **Title:** The speaker is based on an actual person, Alfonso II, Duke of Ferrara, Italy. His first wife, Lucrezia, died three years after their marriage. The Duke then negotiated through an agent to marry the niece of the Count of Tyrol. Here the Duke is portrayed as speaking to the agent. **16. Frà Pandolf:** a fictional name for an artist.

"Must never hope to reproduce the faint
"Half-flush that dies along her throat": such stuff
Was courtesy, she thought, and cause enough
For calling up that spot of joy. She had
A heart—how shall I say?—too soon made glad,
Too easily impressed; she liked whate'er
She looked on, and her looks went everywhere.
Sir, 'twas all one! My favor at her breast,
The dropping of the daylight in the West,
The bough of cherries some officious fool
Broke in the orchard for her, the white mule
She rode with round the terrace—all and each
Would draw from her alike the approving speech,
Or blush, at least. She thanked men—good! but thanked
Somehow—I know not how—as if she ranked
My gift of a nine-hundred-years-old name
With anybody's gift. Who'd stoop to blame
This sort of trifling? Even had you skill
In speech—which I have not—to make your will
Quite clear to such an one, and say, "Just this
"Or that in you disgusts me; here you miss,
"Or there exceed the mark"—and if she let
Herself be lessoned so, nor plainly set
Her wits to yours, forsooth, and made excuse,
—E'en then would be some stooping; and I choose
Never to stoop. Oh sir, she smiled, no doubt,
Whene'er I passed her; but who passed without
Much the same smile? This grew; I gave commands;
Then all smiles stopped together. There she stands
As if alive. Will't please you rise? We'll meet
The company below, then. I repeat,
The Count your master's known munificence
Is ample warrant that no just pretense
Of mine for dowry will be disallowed;
Though his fair daughter's self, as I avowed
At starting, is my object. Nay, we'll go
Together down, sir. Notice Neptune, though,
Taming a sea-horse, thought a rarity,
Which Claus of Innsbruck cast in bronze for me!

1842

56. Claus: another fictional artist.

Home-Thoughts From Abroad

1

Oh, to be in England
Now that April's there,
And whoever wakes in England
Sees, some morning, unaware,
That the lowest boughs and the brushwood sheaf
Round the elm-tree bole are in tiny leaf,
While the chaffinch sings on the orchard bough
In England—now!

2

And after April, when May follows,
And the whitethroat builds, and all the swallows!
Hark, where my blossomed pear-tree in the hedge
Leans to the field and scatters on the clover
Blossoms and dewdrops—at the bent spray's edge—
That's the wise thrush; he sings each song twice over,
Lest you should think he never could recapture
The first fine careless rapture!
And though the fields look rough with hoary dew
All will be gay when noontide wakes anew
The buttercups, the little children's dower
—Far brighter than this gaudy melon-flower!

1845

The Bishop Orders His Tomb at Saint Praxed's Church

Rome, 15–

Vanity, saith the preacher, vanity!
Draw round my bed: is Anselm keeping back?
Nephews—sons mine . . . ah God, I know not! Well—
She, men would have to be your mother once,
Old Gandolf envied me, so fair she was!

THE BISHOP ORDERS HIS TOMB. **Title:** St. Praxed's Church (or, in Italian, the Church of St. Prassede) in Rome was named in honor of a Roman virgin (second century A.D.) who gave her riches to the poor. Both the Bishop and his predecessor, Gandolf, are imaginary characters, representing the sophisticated and worldly minds of Renaissance churchmen in sixteenth-century Rome. **1. Vanity . . . vanity:** an echo of the opening of the book of Ecclesiastes in the Bible ("Vanity of vanities, saith the Preacher; all is vanity").

What's done is done, and she is dead beside,
Dead long ago, and I am Bishop since,
And as she died so must we die ourselves,
And thence ye may perceive the world's a dream.
Life, how and what is it? As here I lie
In this state-chamber, dying by degrees,
Hours and long hours in the dead night, I ask,
"Do I live, am I dead?" Peace, peace seems all.
Saint Praxed's ever was the church for peace;
And so, about this tomb of mine. I fought
With tooth and nail to save my niche, ye know:
—Old Gandolf cozened me, despite my care;
Shrewd was that snatch from out the corner south
He graced his carrion with, God curse the same!
Yet still my niche is not so cramped but thence
One sees the pulpit o' the epistle-side,
And somewhat of the choir, those silent seats,
And up into the aery dome where live
The angels, and a sunbeam's sure to lurk:
And I shall fill my slab of basalt there,
And 'neath my tabernacle take my rest,
With those nine columns round me, two and two,
The odd one at my feet where Anselm stands:
Peach-blossom marble all, the rare, the ripe
As fresh-poured red wine of a mighty pulse.
—Old Gandolf with his paltry onion-stone,
Put me where I may look at him! True peach,
Rosy and flawless: how I earned the prize!
Draw close: that conflagration of my church
—What then? So much was saved if aught were missed!
My sons, ye would not be my death? Go dig
The white-grape vineyard where the oil-press stood,
Drop water gently till the surface sink,
And if ye find . . . Ah God, I know not, I! . . .
Bedded in store of rotten fig-leaves soft,
And corded up in a tight olive-frail,
Some lump, ah God, of *lapis lazuli,*
Big as a Jew's head cut off at the nape,
Blue as a vein o'er the Madonna's breast . . .
Sons, all have I bequeathed you, villas, all,
That brave Frascati villa with its bath,
So, let the blue lump poise between my knees,
Like God the Father's globe on both his hands

17. cozened: cheated. **21. epistle-side:** the right hand side as one faces the altar (from which side the Epistles of the New Testament are read). **26. tabernacle:** canopied roof under which the tomb would lie. **30. pulse:** vitality, as if blood pulsating. **31. onion-stone:** inferior green marble that peels in layers like an onion. **41. olive-frail:** olive basket. **42. *lapis lazuli:*** semiprecious bright blue stone. **46. Frascati:** Roman suburb of wealthy villas. **48. globe:** symbol of God's sovereignty over the world.

Ye worship in the Jesu Church so gay,
For Gandolf shall not choose but see and burst!
Swift as a weaver's shuttle fleet our years:
Man goeth to the grave, and where is he?
Did I say basalt for my slab, sons? Black—
'Twas ever antique-black I meant! How else
Shall ye contrast my frieze to come beneath?
The bas-relief in bronze ye promised me,
Those Pans and Nymphs ye wot of, and perchance
Some tripod, thyrsus, with a vase or so,
The Saviour at his sermon on the mount,
Saint Praxed in a glory, and one Pan
Ready to twitch the Nymph's last garment off,
And Moses with the tables . . . but I know
Ye mark me not! What do they whisper thee,
Child of my bowels, Anselm? Ah, ye hope
To revel down my villas while I gasp
Bricked o'er with beggar's moldy travertine
Which Gandolf from his tomb-top chuckles at!
Nay, boys, ye love me—all of jasper, then!
'T is jasper ye stand pledged to, lest I grieve
My bath must needs be left behind, alas!
One block, pure green as a pistachio-nut,
There's plenty jasper somewhere in the world—
And have I not Saint Praxed's ear to pray
Horses for ye, and brown Greek manuscripts,
And mistresses with great smooth marbly limbs?
—That's if ye carve my epitaph aright,
Choice Latin, picked phrase, Tully's every word,
No gaudy ware like Gandolf's second line—
Tully, my masters? Ulpian serves his need!
And then how I shall lie through centuries,
And hear the blessed mutter of the mass,
And see God made and eaten all day long,
And feel the steady candle-flame, and taste
Good strong thick stupefying incense-smoke!

49. Jesu Church: Jesuit church in Rome where the sculptured group of the Trinity contains a huge globe made of lapis lazuli. **51. Swift . . . years:** an echo of Job 7:6: "My days are swifter than a weaver's shuttle, and are spent without hope." **55. frieze:** band of sculpture. **58. tripod, thyrsus:** pagan religious objects. The tripod was a three-legged stand on which the priestess of Apollo at Delphi sat and pronounced oracles. The thyrsus, or staff wound with ivy, was a symbol of Bacchus, god of wine. Both are contrasted with Christian symbols and events (Christ's Sermon on the Mount, Saint Praxed, Moses with the tablets containing the Ten Commandments). **60–61. Pan . . . garment:** Pan, associated with lust, was often pictured pursuing nymphs. **66. travertine:** limestone, often used for cheaper buildings. **68. jasper:** a semiprecious green stone. **77. Tully:** Cicero (Marcus Tullius Cicero). **79. Ulpian:** Roman jurist, whose dry style contrasted with the eloquence of Cicero's style. **82. God . . . eaten:** the doctrine of transubstantiation, in which the bread, as the body of Christ, is eaten by the communicants.

For as I lie here, hours of the dead night,
Dying in state and by such slow degrees,
I fold my arms as if they clasped a crook,
And stretch my feet forth straight as stone can point,
And let the bedclothes, for a mortcloth, drop
Into great laps and folds of sculptor's-work:
And as yon tapers dwindle, and strange thoughts
Grow, with a certain humming in my ears,
About the life before I lived this life,
And this life too, popes, cardinals and priests,
Saint Praxed at his sermon on the mount,
Your tall pale mother with her talking eyes,
And new-found agate urns as fresh as day,
And marble's language, Latin pure, discreet,
—Aha, ELUCESCEBAT quoth our friend?
No Tully, said I, Ulpian at the best!
Evil and brief hath been my pilgrimage.
All *lapis,* all, sons! Else I give the Pope
My villas! Will ye ever eat my heart?
Ever your eyes were as a lizard's quick,
They glitter like your mother's for my soul,
Or ye would heighten my impoverished frieze,
Piece out its starved design, and fill my vase
With grapes, and add a vizor and a Term,
And to the tripod ye would tie a lynx
That in his struggle throws the thyrsus down,
To comfort me on my entablature
Whereon I am to lie till I must ask,
"Do I live, am I dead?" There, leave me, there!
For ye have stabbed me with ingratitude
To death—ye wish it—God, ye wish it! Stone—
Gritstone, a-crumble! Clammy squares which sweat
As if the corpse they keep were oozing through—
And no more *lapis* to delight the world!
Well, go! I bless ye. Fewer tapers there,
But in a row: and, going, turn your backs
—Ay, like departing altar-ministrants,
And leave me in my church, the church for peace,
That I may watch at leisure if he leers—
Old Gandolf, at me, from his onion-stone,
As still he envied me, so fair she was!

1845

87. crook: shepherd's crook, symbolic of the office of a bishop. **89. mortcloth:** funeral pall. **95. Saint . . . mount:** The Bishop's mind wanders as he is dying, and he mistakenly attributes the Sermon on the Mount to St. Praxed. **99. Elucescebat:** "He shone forth." Intended to be inelegant Latin. If the epitaph had been taken from Cicero instead of Ulpian, the word would have been more proper—*elucebat.* **108. vizor:** a mask worn by Greek and Roman actors. **Term:** a column or pillar bearing the bust of the upper part of the body. **111. entablature:** platform supporting a statue. **116. Gritstone:** a coarse sandstone used as a grindstone.

Memorabilia

1

Ah, did you once see Shelley plain,
And did he stop and speak to you
And did you speak to him again?
How strange it seems and new!

2

But you were living before that,
And also you are living after;
And the memory I started at—
My starting moves your laughter.

3

I crossed a moor, with a name of its own
And a certain use in the world no doubt,
Yet a hand's-breadth of it shines alone
'Mid the blank miles round about:

4

For there I picked up on the heather
And there I put inside my breast
A moulted feather, an eagle-feather!
Well, I forget the rest.

1855

Andrea del Sarto

Called "The Faultless Painter"

But do not let us quarrel any more,
No, my Lucrezia; bear with me for once:
Sit down and all shall happen as you wish.
You turn your face, but does it bring your heart?
I'll work then for your friend's friend, never fear,
Treat his own subject after his own way,
Fix his own time, accept too his own price,

MEMORABILIA. **Title:** The word means "things worth remembering." Browning met a man in a bookstore who mentioned having talked with Shelley. Browning said the man "burst into laughter as he observed me staring at him with blanched face . . . I still vividly remember how strangely the presence of a man who had seen and spoken with Shelley affected me." ANDREA DEL SARTO. **Title:** One of the most skillful painters of Florence, Del Sarto (1486–1531) still never fulfilled the promise of his early work. His wife, Lucrezia del Fede, was partly to blame. She encouraged him to neglect his work.

And shut the money into this small hand
When next it takes mine. Will it? tenderly?
Oh, I'll content him—but tomorrow, Love!
I often am much wearier than you think,
This evening more than usual, and it seems
As if—forgive now—should you let me sit
Here by the window with your hand in mine
And look a half-hour forth on Fiesole,
Both of one mind, as married people use,
Quietly, quietly the evening through
I might get up tomorrow to my work
Cheerful and fresh as ever. Let us try.
Tomorrow, how you shall be glad for this!
Your soft hand is a woman of itself,
And mine the man's bared breast she curls inside.
Don't count the time lost, neither; you must serve
For each of the five pictures we require:
It saves a model. So! keep looking so—
My serpentining beauty, rounds on rounds!
—How could you ever prick those perfect ears,
Even to put the pearl there! oh, so sweet—
My face, my moon, my everybody's moon,
Which everybody looks on and calls his,
And, I suppose, is looked on by in turn,
While she looks—no one's: very dear, no less.
You smile? why, there's my picture ready made,
There's what we painters call our harmony!
A common grayness silvers everything,
All in a twilight, you and I alike
—You, at the point of your first pride in me
(That's gone you know)—but I, at every point;
My youth, my hope, my art, being all toned down
To yonder sober pleasant Fiesole.
There's the bell clinking from the chapel-top;
That length of convent-wall across the way
Holds the trees safer, huddled more inside;
The last monk leaves the garden; days decrease,
And autumn grows, autumn in everything.
Eh? the whole seems to fall into a shape
As if I saw alike my work and self
And all that I was born to be and do,
A twilight-piece. Love, we are in God's hand.
How strange now, looks the life he makes us lead;
So free we seem, so fettered fast we are!
I feel he laid the fetter: let it lie!

15. Fiesole: suburb of Florence. **23–25. you must . . . model:** The face of Lucrezia keeps reappearing in the women of many of Andrea's paintings. **26. rounds:** coils of hair.

This chamber for example—turn your head—
All that's behind us! You don't understand
Nor care to understand about my art,
But you can hear at least when people speak:
And that cartoon, the second from the door
—It is the thing, Love! so such things should be—
Behold Madonna! I am bold to say.
I can do with my pencil what I know,
What I see, what at bottom of my heart
I wish for, if I ever wish so deep—
Do easily, too—when I say, perfectly,
I do not boast, perhaps: yourself are judge,
Who listened to the Legate's talk last week,
And just as much they used to say in France.
At any rate 'tis easy, all of it!
No sketches first, no studies, that's long past:
I do what many dream of, all their lives,
—Dream? strive to do, and agonize to do,
And fail in doing. I could count twenty such
On twice your fingers, and not leave this town,
Who strive—you don't know how the others strive
To paint a little thing like that you smeared
Carelessly passing with your robes afloat—
Yet do much less, so much less, Someone says,
(I know his name, no matter)—so much less!
Well, less is more, Lucrezia: I am judged.
There burns a truer light of God in them,
In their vexed beating stuffed and stopped-up brain,
Heart, or whate'er else, than goes on to prompt
This low-pulsed forthright craftsman's hand of mine.
Their works drop groundward, but themselves, I know,
Reach many a time a heaven that's shut to me,
Enter and take their place there sure enough,
Though they come back and cannot tell the world.
My works are nearer heaven, but I sit here.
The sudden blood of these men! at a word—
Praise them, it boils, or blame them, it boils too.
I, painting from myself and to myself,
Know what I do, am unmoved by men's blame
Or their praise either. Somebody remarks
Morello's outline there is wrongly traced,
His hue mistaken; what of that? or else,
Rightly traced and well ordered; what of that?
Speak as they please, what does the mountain care?
Ah, but a man's reach should exceed his grasp,
Or what's a heaven for? All is silver-gray,

57. cartoon: preparatory drawing of a painting to be made later. **65. Legate:** ambassador of the Pope. **93. Morello:** a mountain peak in the Appenines outside Florence.

Placid and perfect with my art: the worse!
I know both what I want and what might gain,
And yet how profitless to know, to sigh,
"Had I been two, another and myself,
Our head would have o'erlooked the world!" No doubt.
Yonder's a work now, of that famous youth
The Urbinate who died five years ago.
('Tis copied, George Vasari sent it me.)
Well, I can fancy how he did it all,
Pouring his soul, with kings and popes to see,
Reaching, that heaven might so replenish him,
Above and through his art—for it gives way;
That arm is wrongly put—and there again—
A fault to pardon in the drawing's lines,
Its body, so to speak: its soul is right,
He means right—that, a child may understand.
Still, what an arm! and I could alter it:
But all the play, the insight and the stretch—
Out of me, out of me! And wherefore out?
Had you enjoined them on me, given me soul,
We might have risen to Rafael, I and you!
Nay, Love, you did give all I asked, I think—
More than I merit, yes, by many times.
But had you—oh, with the same perfect brow,
And perfect eyes, and more than perfect mouth,
And the low voice my soul hears, as a bird
The fowler's pipe, and follows to the snare—
Had you, with these the same, but brought a mind!
Some women do so. Had the mouth there urged,
"God and the glory! never care for gain.
The present by the future, what is that?
Live for fame, side by side with Agnolo!
Rafael is waiting: up to God, all three!"
I might have done it for you. So it seems:
Perhaps not. All is as God over-rules.
Beside, incentives come from the soul's self;
The rest avail not. Why do I need you?
What wife had Rafael, or has Agnolo?
In this world, who can do a thing, will not;
And who would do it, cannot, I perceive:
Yet the will's somewhat—somewhat, too, the power—
And thus we half-men struggle. At the end,

102–103. Had I . . . world: If I had been a truly committed artist as well as a skilled craftsman, the combination would have made me supreme. **105. Urbinate:** Raphael (1483–1520), so called because he was born in Urbino, Italy. **106. Vasari:** author of *Lives of the Most Eminent Painters*, on which Browning is drawing for details, and himself a pupil of Andrea. **125. fowler's pipe:** whistle used in hunting by fowlers or birdcatchers. **130. Agnolo:** Michelangelo (1475–1564).

God, I conclude, compensates, punishes.
'Tis safer for me, if the award be strict,
That I am something underrated here,
Poor this long while, despised, to speak the truth.
I dared not, do you know, leave home all day,
For fear of chancing on the Paris lords.
The best is when they pass and look aside;
But they speak sometimes; I must bear it all.
Well may they speak! That Francis, that first time,
And that long festal year at Fontainebleau!
I surely then could sometimes leave the ground,
Put on the glory, Rafael's daily wear,
In that humane great monarch's golden look—
One finger in his beard or twisted curl
Over his mouth's good mark that made the smile,
One arm about my shoulder, round my neck,
The jingle of his gold chain in my ear,
I painting proudly with his breath on me,
All his court round him, seeing with his eyes,
Such frank French eyes, and such a fire of souls
Profuse, my hand kept plying by those hearts—
And, best of all, this, this, this face beyond,
This in the background, waiting on my work,
To crown the issue with a last reward!
A good time, was it not, my kingly days?
And had you not grown restless . . . but I know—
'Tis done and past; 'twas right, my instinct said;
Too live the life grew, golden and not gray,
And I'm the weak-eyed bat no sun should tempt
Out of the grange whose four walls make his world.
How could it end in any other way?
You called me, and I came home to your heart.
The triumph was—to reach and stay there; since
I reached it ere the triumph, what is lost?
Let my hands frame your face in your hair's gold,
You beautiful Lucrezia that are mine!
"Rafael did this, Andrea painted that;
"The Roman's is the better when you pray,
"But still the other's Virgin was his wife—"
Men will excuse me. I am glad to judge
Both pictures in your presence; clearer grows
My better fortune, I resolve to think.
For, do you know, Lucrezia, as God lives,

149. Francis: King Francis I of France. He had invited Andrea to his court at Fontainebleau and encouraged him to paint. When Andrea returned to Florence, he is said to have stolen money that Francis entrusted to him and to have used it to build a house for Lucrezia. **169–70. bat . . . walls:** a bat whose real world is inside the four walls of the barn of a country place (**"grange"**)

Said one day Agnolo, his very self,
To Rafael . . . I have known it all these years . . .
(When the young man was flaming out his thoughts
Upon a palace-wall for Rome to see,
Too lifted up in heart because of it)
"Friend, there's a certain sorry little scrub
Goes up and down our Florence, none cares how,
Who, were he set to plan and execute
As you are, pricked on by your popes and kings,
Would bring the sweat into that brow of yours!"
To Rafael's! And indeed the arm is wrong.
I hardly dare . . . yet, only you to see,
Give the chalk here—quick, thus the line should go!
Ay, but the soul! he's Rafael! rub it out!
Still, all I care for, if he spoke the truth,
(What he? why, who but Michel Agnolo?
Do you forget already words like those?)
If really there was such a chance, so lost,
Is, whether you're—not grateful—but more pleased.
Well, let me think so. And you smile indeed!
This hour has been an hour! Another smile?
If you would sit thus by me every night
I should work better, do you comprehend?
I mean that I should earn more, give you more.
See, it is settled dusk now; there's a star;
Morello's gone, the watch-lights show the wall,
The cue-owls speak the name we call them by.
Come from the window, love—come in, at last,
Inside the melancholy little house
We built to be so gay with. God is just.
King Francis may forgive me: oft at nights
When I look up from painting, eyes tired out,
The walls become illumined, brick from brick
Distinct, instead of mortar, fierce bright gold,
That gold of his I did cement them with!
Let us but love each other. Must you go?
That Cousin here again? he waits outside?
Must see you—you, and not with me? Those loans?
More gaming debts to pay? you smiled for that?
Well, let smiles buy me! have you more to spend?
While hand and eye and something of a heart
Are left me, work's my ware, and what's it worth?
I'll pay my fancy. Only let me sit
The gray remainder of the evening out,
Idle, you call it, and muse perfectly
How I could paint, were I but back in France,
One picture, just one more—the Virgin's face,

210. cue-owls: owl of which the name is derived from its cry: *ciù*.

Not yours this time! I want you at my side
To hear them—that is, Michel Agnolo—
Judge all I do and tell you of its worth.
Will you? Tomorrow, satisfy your friend.
I take the subjects for his corridor,
Finish the portrait out of hand—there, there,
And throw him in another thing or two
If he demurs; the whole should prove enough
To pay for this same Cousin's freak. Beside,
What's better and what's all I care about,
Get you the thirteen scudi for the ruff!
Love, does that please you? Ah, but what does he,
The Cousin! what does he to please you more?

I am grown peaceful as old age tonight.
I regret little, I would change still less.
Since there my past life lies, why alter it?
The very wrong to Francis! it is true
I took his coin, was tempted and complied,
And built this house and sinned, and all is said.
My father and my mother died of want.
Well, had I riches of my own? you see
How one gets rich! Let each one bear his lot.
They were born poor, lived poor, and poor they died:
And I have labored somewhat in my time
And not been paid profusely. Some good son
Paint my two hundred pictures—let him try!
No doubt, there's something strikes a balance. Yes,
You loved me quite enough, it seems tonight.
This must suffice me here. What would one have?
In heaven, perhaps, new chances, one more chance—
Four great walls in the New Jerusalem,
Meted on each side by the angel's reed,
For Leonard, Rafael, Agnolo and me
To cover—the three first without a wife,
While I have mine! So—still they overcome
Because there's still Lucrezia—as I choose.

Again the Cousin's whistle! Go, my Love.

1855

241. scudi: silver coin (from the Italian word for "shield," *scudo*, which appeared on the coin). **250. father . . . want:** Because of his infatuation for Lucrezia, Andrea was said to have stopped supporting his impoverished parents. **262. angel's reed:** measuring rod. **263. Leonard:** Leonardo da Vinci (1452–1519).

EMILY BRONTË

(1818–1848)

One of three sisters who all became distinguished writers, Brontë grew up in a small Yorkshire village. She attempted to make a living as a teacher, but this failed. In their isolated life she and her sisters were in the habit of writing stories for each other, and in 1847 they each published a famous novel: *Jane Eyre*, by Charlotte Brontë, *Agnes Grey*, by Anne Brontë, and Emily Brontë's powerful, uncanny *Wuthering Heights*. Before their novels the Brontë sisters brought out a joint volume of *Poems* (1846), in which Emily Brontë's were especially skillful. She died of tuberculosis. "No Coward Soul Is Mine" was written on her deathbed.

Hope

Hope was but a timid friend—
She sat without my grated den
Watching how my fate would tend
Even as selfish-hearted men.

She was cruel in her fear.
Through the bars, one dreary day,
I looked out to see her there
And she turned her face away!

Like a false guard false watch keeping
Still in strife she whispered peace;
She would sing while I was weeping,
If I listened, she would cease.

False she was, and unrelenting.
When my last joys strewed the ground
Even Sorrow saw repenting
Those sad relics scattered round;

Hope—whose whisper would have given
Balm to all that frenzied pain—
Stretched her wings and soared to heaven;
Went—and ne'er returned again!

1846

HOPE. **2. without:** outside.

No Coward Soul Is Mine

No coward soul is mine,
No trembler in the world's storm-troubled sphere!
I see Heaven's glories shine,
And Faith shines equal, arming me from Fear.

O God within my breast,
Almighty ever-present Deity!
Life, that in me hast rest
As I, undying Life, have power in thee!

Vain are the thousand creeds
That move men's hearts, unutterably vain;
Worthless as withered weeds,
Or idlest froth, amid the boundless main,

To waken doubt in one
Holding so fast by thy infinity,
So surely anchored on
The steadfast rock of Immortality.

With wide-embracing love
Thy spirit animates eternal years,
Pervades and broods above,
Changes, sustains, dissolves, creates and rears.

Though earth and moon were gone,
And suns and universes ceased to be,
And thou were left alone,
Every Existence would exist in thee.

There is not room for Death,
Nor atom that his might could render void,
Since thou art Being and Breath,
And what thou art may never be destroyed.

1850

Long Neglect Has Worn Away

Long neglect has worn away
Half the sweet enchanting smile;
Time has turned the bloom to gray;
Mold and damp the face defile.

But that lock of silky hair,
Still beneath the picture twined,
Tells what once those features were,
Paints their image on the mind.

Fair the hand that traced that line,
"Dearest, ever deem me true";
Swiftly flew the fingers fine
When the pen that motto drew.

1923

Herman Melville

(1819–1891)

Melville is one of the supreme names in American literature because of his novels, *Typee, Omoo, Redburn, Pierre,* and above all his classic *Moby Dick* (1851). In poetry his major effort was a huge two-volume narrative poem, *Clarel* (1876), about an American divinity student who makes a pilgrimage to the Holy Land. Little read for almost a century, the poem is beginning to fascinate scholars as a historical reflection of issues of the time, particularly the conflict of religious faith and skepticism, and also as an expression of Melville's own inner life. His book of Civil War poems, *Battle-Pieces* (1866), although also neglected for years, is now regarded as, next to Whitman's *Drum-Taps*, the finest of the scores of volumes of poetry concerned with the War.

The Portent

Hanging from the beam,
  Slowly swaying (such the law),
Gaunt the shadow on your green,
  Shenandoah!
The cut is on the crown
  (Lo, John Brown),
And the stabs shall heal no more.
Hidden in the cap
  Is the anguish none can draw;
So your future veils its face,
  Shenandoah!
But the streaming beard is shown
  (Weird John Brown),
The meteor of the war.

1866

THE PORTENT. **4. Shenandoah:** valley in Virginia, scene of Civil War battles. **6. John Brown:** leader of an abolitionist raid at Harpers Ferry (October, 1859), for which he was hanged.

The March into Virginia

Ending in the First Manassas (July 1861)

Did all the lets and bars appear
To every just or larger end,
Whence should come the trust and cheer?
Youth must its ignorant impulse lend—
Age finds place in the rear.
All wars are boyish, and are fought by boys,
The champions and enthusiasts of the state:
Turbid ardours and vain joys
Not barrenly abate—
Stimulants to the power mature,
Preparatives of fate.

Who here forecasteth the event?
What heart but spurns at precedent
And warnings of the wise,
Contemned foreclosures of surprise?
The banners play, the bugles call,
The air is blue and prodigal.
No berrying party, pleasure-wooed,
No picnic party in the May,
Ever went less loth than they
Into that leafy neighbourhood.
In Bacchic glee they file toward Fate,
Moloch's uninitiate;
Expectancy, and glad surmise
Of battle's unknown mysteries.

All they feel is this: 'tis glory,
A rapture sharp, though transitory,
Yet lasting in belaureled story.
So they gaily go to fight,
Chatting left and laughing right.

But some who this blithe mood present,
As on in lightsome files they fare,
Shall die experienced ere three days are spent—
Perish, enlightened by the volleyed glare;
Or shame survive, and, like to adamant,
The throe of Second Manassas share.

1866

THE MARCH INTO VIRGINIA. **Title:** At the first battle of Manassas ("Bull Run") in Virginia—a railroad junction 30 miles from Washington—the Union Army was defeated by the Confederates (July 21, 1861). **23. Moloch:** Old Testament idol to which children were sacrificed (Leviticus, 20:2–5). **36. Second Manassas:** At the second Battle of Manassas, or Bull Run, the Union Army was again defeated (August 30, 1862).

Shiloh

A Requiem (April 1862)

Skimming lightly, wheeling still,
  The swallows fly low
Over the field in clouded days,
  The forest-field of Shiloh—
Over the field where April rain
Solaced the parched one stretched in pain
Through the pause of night
That followed the Sunday fight
  Around the church of Shiloh—
The church so lone, the log-built one,
That echoed to many a parting groan
    And natural prayer
  Of dying foemen mingled there—
Foemen at morn, but friends at eve—
  Fame or country least their care:
(What like a bullet can undeceive!)
  But now they lie low,
While over them the swallows skim,
  And all is hushed at Shiloh.

1866

Greek Architecture

Not magnitude, not lavishness,
But form—the site;
Not innovating wilfulness,
But reverence for the archetype.

1891

SHILOH. **Title:** Shiloh Church in rural Tennessee. In the battle there (April 6–7, 1862), one of the fiercest of the Civil War, the Confederates defeated the Union forces.

WALT WHITMAN

(1819–1892)

The son of a carpenter, Whitman grew up in Brooklyn, New York. He spent only five years in school and acquired his education mainly from reading and working as a school teacher and journalist. He was deeply stirred by operas he attended in New York City and by the political questions of the age. As he started to experiment with the writing of poetry, he also began to form his ideas concerning how a truly American poetry might differ from the traditional poetry of Europe. He was greatly influenced by Emerson's ideal, expressed in a famous essay on "The Poet," of the American poet as one who addresses "our own times and social circumstances . . . America is a poem in our eyes." Together with the example of his own poems, the aims that Whitman announced for poetry continue to exert immense influence on American poets.

In a long, rhapsodic prose Preface to the first edition of his poems in 1855, Whitman proclaimed that "the poems distilled from other poems will probably pass away"; lasting poetry, he contended, comes from life expressed directly and at first hand. The poet floods "himself with the immediate age as with vast oceanic tides." The "United States themselves are essentially the greatest poem." By the United States Whitman meant the scale and variety of American landscape, of course, but he also meant the common people—their occupations, artifacts, thoughts, and feelings in all their diversity: "Men and women and the earth and all upon it are simply to be taken as they are . . . with perfect candor"; "genuineness" is superior to "all fiction and romance." But in the American poet whose soul is as grand as the continent, to express things in their reality is also to uncover their beauty. "The known universe has one complete lover and that is the greatest poet." Imbued with these convictions and, perhaps, inspired by mystical feelings or experiences, Whitman withdrew in 1854 to the home of his parents and composed *Leaves of Grass*, which was printed in 1855.

For the rest of his life Whitman struggled to make his great book accepted by the public. In a private letter to Whitman (which Whitman then printed in the New York *Tribune*), Emerson hailed the book as "the most extraordinary piece of wit and wisdom that America has yet contributed," but for the most part it was ignored or attacked. Whitman continued to write new poems, which were incorporated in subsequent editions. In 1862 he moved to Washington, D.C., and spent the remaining years of the Civil War visiting wounded soldiers in the hospital, comforting and helping them as best he could. After the war he stayed in Washington, working as a government clerk until 1873, when he suffered a stroke. He then moved to the home of his brother in Camden, New Jersey, where he lived until his death. In his later years he began to acquire disciples in England and the United States, but, despite spreading fame, his poetry continued to provoke violent controversy.

For its attackers, Whitman's poetry was formless, undiscriminating in its affirmation, egoistic and infantile in its naked delight in himself, anti-intellectual, anti-cultural, and amoral. Whitman's sexual frankness was shocking, although his homoerotic feelings also attracted readers who shared them. For his early admirers, Whitman was a profound, liberating teacher of democratic values. He voiced his intimacy and solidarity with the common people, presented their emotions and ways of life factually, without romanticizing or idealizing, and affirmed that they were good. He celebrated our sensuous, sexual, bodily being as well as our spiritual emotions and intuitions, and proclaimed that the two realms, which were sharply separated in the conventional morality and religion of the nineteenth century, were and should be interfused. He was mildly Bohemian, and had less to say about the discipline of work and social life than about spontaneously strolling about, footloose and free, and feeling yourself part of all you see. From this side of Whitman, a Romanticism of vagabond comradeship on the "open road" emerged in minor poets of the next generation.

As part of his democratic celebration, he deployed in poetry the spoken language of his time (although with occasional foreign phrases and nonce words), using it with a beautiful simplicity and vividness. Breaking with the meters of the past, he was the first poet in English to write extensively in free verse. His long lines, often with repeating patterns of grammar, tend to be more regular and chanting than most modern free verse, but are nevertheless marvelously sensitive and flexible in registering his changing emotions.

Section eleven of "Song of Myself" illustrates all that was most revolutionary in Whitman. The poem describes a woman watching from behind the blinds of her window a group of naked young men bathing in the ocean. The subject was morally forbidden in the literature of the middle nineteenth century and incredible in poetry, since realism was for novels and poetry was conventionally expected to idealize. Even today the woman's voyeuristic peeping could seem morally unattractive, and the means by which Whitman overwhelms such potential responses and makes us feel sympathy and compassion are typical of his art and should be studied. The details given in the poem have been carefully selected and interwoven for descriptive vividness and connotative depth, and the sequence of their presentation is highly dramatic, yet the poem seems simple, spontaneous, and completely realistic. Its language has the same qualities: such phrases as "She owns the fine house," which does she "like the best," and "where are you off to" are imbued with the rhythm and diction of colloquial speech, and "their white bellies bulge" is so direct and unglamorized as to seem startling. Since so many American poets after Whitman have followed in his tracks, his poetry cannot be as revolutionary for us as it was for his first readers. But it still continues to liberate poetry into bold innovation and sincerity, illustrating the Hindu proverb that the footprints of a god fill up with honey.

In the two long poems, "Out of the Cradle Endlessly Rocking" and "When Lilacs Last in the Dooryard Bloom'd," the themes—poetry, love, death—and the yearning, elegiac emotions are more typical of the poetry of the nineteenth century. But only the very greatest poetry then or since has been written with a comparable intensity of emotion, depth of inward exploration and intuition, and powerful, symphonic organization of themes and symbolic motifs. "When Lilacs Last in the Dooryard Bloom'd" is an elegy on President Lincoln which becomes an elegy for all the soldiers killed on both sides in the war. Sections 5 and 6, on the journey of the train that carried Lincoln's body from Washington to its place of burial in Springfield, Illinois, give an epic impression of the space and diversity of the American continent, and have often been imitated. In their emotions and symbols these two great poems are deeply interconnected.

from Song of Myself

1

I celebrate myself, and sing myself,
And what I assume you shall assume,
For every atom belonging to me as good belongs to you.

I loaf and invite my soul,
I lean and loaf at my ease observing a spear of summer grass.

My tongue, every atom of my blood, formed from this soil, this air,
Born here of parents born here from parents the same, and their parents
        the same,
I, now thirty-seven years old in perfect health begin,
Hoping to cease not till death.

Creeds and schools in abeyance,
Retiring back a while sufficed at what they are, but never forgotten,
I harbor for good or bad, I permit to speak at every hazard,
Nature without check with original energy.

6

A child said *What is the grass?* fetching it to me with full hands;
How could I answer the child? I do not know what it is any more than he.

I guess it must be the flag of my disposition, out of hopeful green stuff woven.

Or I guess it is the handkerchief of the Lord,
A scented gift and remembrancer designedly dropped,
Bearing the owner's name someway in the corners, that we may see and remark, and say *Whose?*

Or I guess the grass is itself a child, the produced babe of the vegetation.

Or I guess it is a uniform hieroglyphic,
And it means, Sprouting alike in broad zones and narrow zones,
Growing among black folks as among white,
Kanuck, Tuckahoe, Congressman, Cuff, I give them the same, I receive them the same.

And now it seems to me the beautiful uncut hair of graves.

Tenderly will I use you curling grass,
It may be you transpire from the breasts of young men,
It may be if I had known them I would have loved them,
It may be you are from old people, or from offspring taken soon out of their mothers' laps,
And here you are the mothers' laps.

This grass is very dark to be from the white heads of old mothers,
Darker than the colorless beards of old men,
Dark to come from under the faint red roofs of mouths.

O I perceive after all so many uttering tongues,
And I perceive they do not come from the roofs of mouths for nothing.

I wish I could translate the hints about the dead young men and women.
And the hints about old men and mothers, and the offspring taken soon out of their laps.

What do you think has become of the young and old men?
And what do you think has become of the women and children?

They are alive and well somewhere,
The smallest sprout shows there is really no death,
And if ever there was it led forward life, and does not wait at the end to arrest it,
And ceased the moment life appeared.

All goes onward and outward, nothing collapses,
And to die is different from what anyone supposed, and luckier.

11

Twenty-eight young men bathe by the shore,
Twenty-eight young men and all so friendly;
Twenty-eight years of womanly life and all so lonesome.

She owns the fine house by the rise of the bank,
She hides handsome and richly dressed aft the blinds
of the window.

Which of the young men does she like the best?
Ah the homeliest of them is beautiful to her.

Where are you off to, lady? for I see you,
You splash in the water there, yet stay stock still in your room.

Dancing and laughing along the beach came the twenty-ninth bather,
The rest did not see her, but she saw them and loved them.

The beards of the young men glistened with wet, it ran from their long
hair,
Little streams, passed all over their bodies.

An unseen hand also passed over their bodies,
It descended trembling from their temples and ribs.

The young men float on their backs, their white bellies bulge to the sun,
they do not ask who seizes fast to them.
They do not know who puffs and declines with pendant and bending
arch,
They do not think whom they souse with spray.

24

Walt Whitman, a kosmos, of Manhattan the son,
Turbulent, fleshly, sensual, eating, drinking and breeding,
No sentimentalist, no stander above men and women or apart from
them,
No more modest than immodest.

Unscrew the locks from the doors!
Unscrew the doors themselves from their jambs!

Whoever degrades another degrades me,
And whatever is done or said returns at last to me.

Through me the afflatus surging and surging, through
me the current and index.
I speak the password primeval, I give the sign of democracy,
By God! I will accept nothing which all cannot have their counterpart of
on the same terms.

Through me many long dumb voices,
Voices of the interminable generations of prisoners and slaves,
Voices of the diseased and despairing and of thieves and dwarfs,

SONG OF MYSELF. **203. aft:** behind. **505. afflatus:** poetic inspiration.

Voices of cycles of preparation and accretion,
And of the threads that connect the stars, and of wombs and of the father-stuff,
And of the rights of them the others are down upon,
Of the deformed, trivial, flat, foolish, despised,
Fog in the air, beetles rolling balls of dung.

Through me forbidden voices,
Voices of sexes and lusts, voices veiled and I remove the veil,
Voices indecent by me clarified and transfigured.

I do not press my fingers across my mouth,
I keep as delicate around the bowels as around the head and heart,
Copulation is no more rank to me than death is.

I believe in the flesh and the appetites,
Seeing, hearing, feeling, are miracles, and each part and tag of me is a miracle.

Divine am I inside and out, and I make holy whatever I touch or am touched from,
The scent of these armpits aroma finer than prayer,
This head more than churches, bibles, and all the creeds.

If I worship one thing more than another it shall be the spread of my own body, or any part of it,
Translucent mold of me it shall be you!
Shaded ledges and rests it shall be you!
Firm masculine colter it shall be you!
Whatever goes to the tilth of me it shall be you!
You my rich blood! your milky stream pale strippings of my life!
Breast that presses against other breasts it shall be you!
My brain it shall be your occult convolutions!
Root of washed sweet-flag! timorous pond-snipe! nest of guarded duplicate eggs! it shall be you!
Mixed tussled hay of head, beard, brawn, it shall be you!
Trickling sap of maple, fiber of manly wheat, it shall be you!
Suns so generous it shall be you!
Vapors lighting and shading my face it shall be you!
You sweaty brooks and dews it shall be you!
Winds whose soft-tickling genitals rub against me it shall be you!
Broad muscular fields, branches of live oak, loving lounger in my winding paths, it shall be you!
Hands I have taken, face I have kissed, mortal I have ever touched, it shall be you.

I dote on myself, there is that lot of me and all so luscious,
Each moment and whatever happens thrills me with joy,

512. father-stuff: semen. **530. colter:** blade at front of a plow. **531. tilth:** topsoil. **535. sweet-flag:** calamus, an aromatic grass growing near ponds.

I cannot tell how my ankles bend, nor whence the cause of my faintest wish,
Nor the cause of the friendship I emit, nor the cause of the friendship I take again.

That I walk up my stoop, I pause to consider if it really be,
A morning-glory at my window satisfies me more than the metaphysics of books.

To behold the daybreak!
The little light fades the immense and diaphanous shadows,
The air tastes good to my palate.

Hefts of the moving world at innocent gambols silently rising, freshly exuding.
Scooting obliquely high and low.

Something I cannot see puts upward libidinous prongs,
Seas of bright juice suffuse heaven.

The earth by the sky staid with, the daily close of their junction,
The heaved challenge from the east that moment over my head,
The mocking taunt, See then whether you shall be master!

52

The spotted hawk swoops by and accuses me, he complains of my gab and my loitering.

I too am not a bit tamed, I too am untranslatable,
I sound my barbaric yawp over the roofs of the world.

The last scud of day holds back for me,
It flings my likeness after the rest and true as any on the shadowed wilds,
It coaxes me to the vapor and the dusk.

I depart as air, I shake my white locks at the runaway sun,
I effuse my flesh in eddies, and drift it in lacy jags.

I bequeath myself to the dirt to grow from the grass I love,
If you want me again look for me under your boot-soles.

You will hardly know who I am or what I mean,
But I shall be good health to you nevertheless,
And filter and fiber your blood.

Failing to fetch me at first, keep encouraged,
Missing me one place search another,
I stop somewhere waiting for you.

1881

553. hefts: main parts. **1333. yawp:** yell, cry. **1334. scud:** wind-driven clouds. **1388. effuse:** pour out.

When I Heard the Learn'd Astronomer

When I heard the learn'd astronomer,
When the proofs, the figures, were ranged in columns before me,
When I was shown the charts and diagrams, to add, divide, and measure them,
When I sitting heard the astronomer where he lectured with much applause in the lecture-room,
How soon unaccountable I became tired and sick,
Till rising and gliding out I wander'd off by myself,
In the mystical moist night-air, and from time to time,
Look'd up in perfect silence at the stars.

1865

I Saw in Louisiana a Live-Oak Growing

I saw in Louisiana a live-oak growing,
All alone stood it and the moss hung down from the branches,
Without any companion it grew there uttering joyous leaves of dark green,
And its look, rude, unbending, lusty, made me think of myself,
But I wonder'd how it could utter joyous leaves standing alone there without its friend near, for I knew I could not,
And I broke off a twig with a certain number of leaves upon it, and twined around it a little moss,
And brought it away, and have placed it in sight in my room,
It is not needed to remind me as of my own dear friends,
(For I believe lately I think of little else than of them,)
Yet it remains to me a curious token, it makes me think of manly love;
For all that, and though the live-oak glistens there in Louisiana solitary in a wide flat space,
Uttering joyous leaves all its life without a friend, a lover near,
I know very well I could not.

1867

Out of the Cradle Endlessly Rocking

Out of the cradle endlessly rocking,
Out of the mocking-bird's throat, the musical shuttle,
Out of the Ninth-month midnight,

OUT OF THE CRADLE ENDLESSLY ROCKING. **3. Ninth-month:** September. In referring to the month by number, Whitman is also suggesting the number of months between human conception and birth.

Over the sterile sands and the fields beyond, where the child leaving his bed wander'd alone, bareheaded, barefoot,
Down from the shower'd halo,
Up from the mystic play of shadows twining and twisting as if they were alive,
Out from the patches of briers and blackberries,
From the memories of the bird that chanted to me,
From your memories sad brother, from the fitful risings and fallings I heard,
From under that yellow half-moon late-risen and swollen as if with tears,
From those beginning notes of yearning and love there in the mist,
From the thousand responses of my heart never to cease,
From the myriad thence-arous'd words,
From the word stronger and more delicious than any,
From such as now they start the scene revisiting,
As a flock, twittering, rising, or overhead passing,
Borne hither, ere all eludes me, hurriedly,
A man, yet by these tears a little boy again,
Throwing myself on the sand, confronting the waves,
I, chanter of pains and joys, uniter of here and hereafter,
Taking all hints to use them, but swiftly leaping beyond them,
A reminiscence sing.

Once Paumanok,
When the lilac-scent was in the air and Fifth-month grass was growing,
Up this seashore in some briers,
Two feather'd guests from Alabama, two together,
And their nest, and four light-green eggs spotted with brown,
And every day the he-bird to and fro near at hand,
And every day the she-bird crouch'd on her nest, silent, with bright eyes,
And every day I, a curious boy, never too close, never disturbing them,
Cautiously peering, absorbing, translating.
Shine! shine! shine!
Pour down your warmth, great sun!
While we bask, we two together.

Two together!
Winds blow south, or winds blow north,
Day come white, or night come black,
Home, or rivers and mountains from home,
Singing all time, minding no time,
While we two keep together.

Till of a sudden,
May-be kill'd, unknown to her mate,
One forenoon the she-bird crouch'd not on the nest,
Nor return'd that afternoon, nor the next,
Nor ever appear'd again.

23. Paumanok: Indian name for Long Island. **24. Fifth-month:** May.

And thenceforward all summer in the sound of the sea,
And at night under the full of the moon in calmer weather,
Over the hoarse surging of the sea,
Or flitting from brier to brier by day,
I saw, I heard at intervals the remaining one, the he-bird,
The solitary guest from Alabama.

Blow! blow! blow!
Blow up sea-winds along Paumanok's shore;
I wait and I wait till you blow my mate to me.

Yes, when the stars glisten'd,
All night long on the prong of a moss-scallop'd stake,
Down almost amid the slapping waves,
Sat the lone singer wonderful causing tears.

He call'd on his mate,
He pour'd forth the meanings which I of all men know.

Yes my brother I know,
The rest might not, but I have treasur'd every note,
For more than once dimly down to the beach gliding,
Silent, avoiding the moonbeams, blending myself with the shadows,
Recalling now the obscure shapes, the echoes, the sounds and sights after their sorts,
The white arms out in the breakers tirelessly tossing,
I, with bare feet, a child, the wind wafting my hair,
Listen'd long and long.

Listen'd to keep, to sing, now translating the notes,
Following you my brother.

Soothe! soothe! soothe!
Close on its wave soothes the wave behind,
And again another behind embracing and lapping, every one close,
But my love soothes not me, not me.

Low hangs the moon, it rose late,
It is lagging—O I think it is heavy with love, with love.

O madly the sea pushes upon the land,
With love, with love.

O night! do I not see my love fluttering out among the breakers?
What is that little black thing I see there in the white?

Loud! loud! loud!
Loud I call to you, my love!

High and clear I shoot my voice over the waves,
Surely you must know who is here, is here,
You must know who I am, my love.

Low-hanging moon!
What is that dusky spot in your brown yellow?
O it is the shape, the shape of my mate!
O moon do not keep her from me any longer.

Land! land! O land!
Whichever way I turn, O I think you could give me my mate back again if you only would,
For I am almost sure I see her dimly whichever way I look.

O rising stars!
Perhaps the one I want so much will rise, will rise with some of you.

O throat! O trembling throat!
Sound clearer through the atmosphere!
Pierce the woods, the earth,
Somewhere listening to catch you must be the one I want.

Shake out carols!
Solitary here, the night's carols!
Carols of lonesome love! death's carols!
Carols under that lagging, yellow, waning moon!
O under that moon where she drops almost down into the sea!
O reckless despairing carols.

But soft! sink low!
Soft! let me just murmur,
And do you wait a moment you husky-nois'd sea,
For somewhere I believe I heard my mate responding to me,
So faint, I must be still, be still to listen,
But not altogether still, for then she might not come immediately to me.

Hither my love!
Here I am! here!
With this just-sustain'd note I announce myself to you,
This gentle call is for you my love, for you.

Do not be decoy'd elsewhere,
That is the whistle of the wind, it is not my voice,
That is the fluttering, the fluttering of the spray,
Those are the shadows of leaves.

O darkness! O in vain!
O I am very sick and sorrowful.

O brown halo in the sky near the moon, drooping upon the sea!
O troubled reflection in the sea!
O throat! O throbbing heart!
And I singing uselessly, uselessly all the night.

O past! O happy life! O songs of joy!
In the air, in the woods, over fields,
Loved! loved! loved! loved! loved!
But my mate no more, no more with me!
We two together no more.

The aria sinking.
All else continuing, the stars shining,
The winds blowing, the notes of the bird continuous echoing,
With angry moans the fierce old mother incessantly moaning,
On the sands of Paumanok's shore gray and rustling,

The yellow half-moon enlarged, sagging down, drooping, the face of the sea almost touching,
The boy ecstatic, with his bare feet the waves, with his hair the atmosphere dallying,
The love in the heart long pent, now loose, now at last tumultuously bursting,
The aria's meaning, the ears, the soul, swiftly depositing,
The strange tears down the cheeks coursing,
The colloquy there, the trio, each uttering,
The undertone, the savage old mother incessantly crying,
To the boy's soul's questions sullenly timing, some drown'd secret hissing,
To the outsetting bard.

Demon or bird! (said the boy's soul,)
Is it indeed toward your mate you sing? or is it really to me?
For I, that was a child, my tongue's use sleeping, now I have heard you,
Now in a moment I know what I am for, I awake,
And already a thousand singers, a thousand songs, clearer, louder and more sorrowful than yours,
A thousand warbling echoes have started to life within me, never to die.

O you singer solitary, singing by yourself, projecting me,
O solitary me listening, never more shall I cease perpetuating you,
Never more shall I escape, never more the reverberations,
Never more the cries of unsatisfied love be absent from me,
Never again leave me to be the peaceful child I was before what there in the night,
By the sea under the yellow and sagging moon,
The messenger there arous'd, the fire, the sweet hell within,
The unknown want, the destiny of me.

O give me the clew! (it lurks in the night here somewhere,)
O if I am to have so much, let me have more!

A word then, (for I will conquer it,)
The word final, superior to all,
Subtle, sent up—what is it?—I listen;
Are you whispering it, and have been all the time, you sea-waves?
Is that it from your liquid rims and wet sands?

Whereto answering, the sea,
Delaying not, hurrying not,
Whisper'd me through the night, and very plainly before daybreak,
Lisp'd to me the low and delicious word death,
And again death, death, death, death,
Hissing melodious, neither like the bird nor like my arous'd child's heart,
But edging near as privately for me rustling at my feet,
Creeping thence steadily up to my ears and laving me softly all over,
Death, death, death, death, death.

Which I do not forget,
But fuse the song of my dusky demon and brother,
That he sang to me in the moonlight on Paumanok's gray beach,
With the thousand responsive songs at random,
My own songs awaked from that hour,
And with them the key, the word up from the waves,
The word of the sweetest song and all songs,
That strong and delicious word which, creeping to my feet,
(Or like some old crone rocking the cradle, swathed in sweet garments, bending aside,)
The sea whisper'd me.

1881

The Dalliance of the Eagles

Skirting the river road, (my forenoon walk, my rest,)
Skyward in air a sudden muffled sound, the dalliance of the eagles,
The rushing amorous contact high in space together,
The clinching interlocking claws, a living, fierce, gyrating wheel,
Four beating wings, two beaks, a swirling mass tight grappling,
In tumbling turning clustering loops, straight downward falling,
Till o'er the river pois'd, the twain yet one, a moment's lull,
A motionless still balance in the air, then parting, talons loosing,
Upward again on slow-firm pinions slanting, their separate diverse flight,
She hers, he his, pursuing.

1881

Reconciliation

Word over all, beautiful as the sky,
Beautiful that war and all its deeds of carnage must in time be utterly lost,
That the hands of the sisters Death and Night incessantly softly wash again, and ever again, this soil'd world;
For my enemy is dead, a man divine as myself is dead,
I look where he lies white-faced and still in the coffin—I draw near,
Bend down and touch lightly with my lips the white face in the coffin.

1881

THE DALLIANCE OF THE EAGLES. **2. dalliance:** amorous play.

When Lilacs Last in the Dooryard Bloom'd

1

When lilacs last in the dooryard bloom'd,
And the great star early droop'd in the western sky in the night,
I mourn'd, and yet shall mourn with ever-returning spring.
Ever-returning spring, trinity sure to me you bring,
Lilac blooming perennial and drooping star in the west,
And thought of him I love.

2

O powerful western fallen star!
O shades of night—O moody, tearful night!
O great star disappear'd—O the black murk that hides the star!
O cruel hands that hold me powerless—O helpless soul of me!
O harsh surrounding cloud that will not free my soul.

3

In the dooryard fronting an old farm-house near the white-wash'd palings,
Stands the lilac-bush tall-growing with heart-shaped leaves of rich green,
With many a pointed blossom rising delicate, with the perfume strong I love,
With every leaf a miracle—and from this bush in the dooryard,
With delicate-color'd blossoms and heart-shaped leaves of rich green,
A sprig with its flower I break.

4

In the swamp in secluded recesses,
A shy and hidden bird is warbling a song.

Solitary the thrush,
The hermit withdrawn to himself, avoiding the settlements,
Sings by himself a song.

Song of the bleeding throat,
Death's outlet song of life, (for well dear brother I know,
If thou wast not granted to sing thou would'st surely die.)

5

Over the breast of the spring, the land, amid cities,
Amid lanes and through old woods, where lately the violets peep'd from the ground, spotting the gray debris,

WHEN LILACS LAST IN THE DOORYARD BLOOM'D. **2. great star:** Venus, the evening star, later associated with Lincoln himself.

Amid the grass in the fields each side of the lanes, passing the endless grass,
Passing the yellow-spear'd wheat, every grain from its shroud in the dark-brown fields uprisen,
Passing the apple-tree blows of white and pink in the orchards,
Carrying a corpse to where it shall rest in the grave,
Night and day journeys a coffin.

6

Coffin that passes through lanes and streets,
Through day and night with the great cloud darkening the land,
With the pomp of the inloop'd flags, with the cities draped in black,
With the show of the States themselves as of crape-veil'd women standing,
With processions long and winding and the flambeaus of the night,
With the countless torches lit, with the silent sea of faces and the unbared heads,
With the waiting depot, the arriving coffin, and the sombre faces,
With dirges through the night, with the thousand voices rising strong and solemn,
With all the mournful voices of the dirges pour'd around the coffin,
The dim-lit churches and the shuddering organs—where amid these you journey,
With the tolling tolling bells' perpetual clang,
Here, coffin that slowly passes,
I give you my sprig of lilac.

7

(Nor for you, for one alone,
Blossoms and branches green to coffins all I bring,
For fresh as the morning, thus would I chant a song for you O sane and sacred death.

All over bouquets of roses,
O death, I cover you over with roses and early lilies,
But mostly and now the lilac that blooms the first,
Copious I break, I break the sprigs from the bushes,
With loaded arms I come, pouring for you,
For you and the coffins all of you O death.)

8

O western orb sailing the heaven,
Now I know what you must have meant as a month since I walk'd,
As I walk'd in silence the transparent shadowy night,
As I saw you had something to tell as you bent to me night after night,
As you droop'd from the sky low down as if to my side, (while the other stars all look'd on,)

30. blows: blossoms. **32. coffin:** After Lincoln's assassination (April 14, 1865), the funeral train, bearing his coffin, traveled from Washington to Springfield, Illinois, where he was buried. **37. flambeaus:** torches.

As we wander'd together the solemn night, (for something I know not what kept me from sleep,)
As the night advanced, and I saw on the rim of the west how full you were of woe,
As I stood on the rising ground in the breeze in the cool transparent night,
As I watch'd where you pass'd and was lost in the netherward black of the night,
As my soul in its trouble dissatisfied sank, as where you sad orb,
Concluded, dropt in the night, and was gone.

9

Sing on there in the swamp,
O singer bashful and tender, I hear your notes, I hear your call,
I hear, I come presently, I understand you,
But a moment I linger, for the lustrous star has detain'd me,
The star my departing comrade holds and detains me.

10

O how shall I warble myself for the dead one there I loved?
And how shall I deck my song for the large sweet soul that has gone?
And what shall my perfume be for the grave of him I love?

Sea-winds blown from east and west,
Blown from the Eastern sea and blown from the Western sea, till there on the prairies meeting,
These and with these and the breath of my chant,
I'll perfume the grave of him I love.

11

O what shall I hang on the chamber walls?
And what shall the pictures be that I hang on the walls,
To adorn the burial-house of him I love?

Pictures of growing spring and farms and homes,
With the Fourth-month eve at sundown, and the gray smoke lucid and bright,
With floods of the yellow gold of the gorgeous, indolent, sinking sun, burning, expanding the air,
With the fresh sweet herbage under foot, and the pale green leaves of the trees prolific,
In the distance the flowing gaze, the breast of the river, with a wind-dapple here and there,
With ranging hills on the banks, with many a line against the sky, and shadows,
And the city at hand with dwellings so dense, and stacks of chimneys,

82. Fourth-month: April. **171. askant: sideways.**

And all the scenes of life and the workshops, and the workmen homeward returning.

12

Lo, body and soul—this land,
My own Manhattan with spires, and the sparkling and hurrying tides, and the ships,
The varied and ample land, the South and the North in the light, Ohio's shores and flashing Missouri,
And ever the far-spreading prairies cover'd with grass and corn.

Lo, the most excellent sun so calm and haughty,
The violet and purple morn with just-felt breezes,
The gentle soft-born measureless light,
The miracle spreading bathing all, the fulfill'd noon,
The coming eve delicious, the welcome night and the stars,
Over my cities shining all, enveloping man and land.

13

Sing on, sing on you gray-brown bird,
Sing from the swamps, the recesses, pour your chant from the bushes,
Limitless out of the dusk, out of the cedars and pines.

Sing on dearest brother, warble your reedy song,
Loud human song, with voice of uttermost woe.

O liquid and free and tender!
O wild and loose to my soul—O wondrous singer!
You only I hear—yet the star holds me, (but will soon depart,)
Yet the lilac with mastering odor holds me.

14

Now while I sat in the day and look'd forth,
In the close of the day with its light and the fields of spring, and the farmers preparing their crops,
In the large unconscious scenery of my land with its lakes and forests,
In the heavenly aerial beauty, (after the perturb'd winds and the storms,)
Under the arching heavens of the afternoon swift passing, and the voices of children and women.
The many-moving sea-tides, and I saw the ships how they sail'd,
And the summer approaching with richness, and the fields all busy with labor,
And the infinite separate houses, how they all went on, each with its meals and minutia of daily usages,
And the streets how their throbbings throbb'd, and the cities pent—lo, then and there,
Falling upon them all and among them all, enveloping me with the rest,
Appear'd the cloud, appear'd the long black trail,
And I knew death, its thought, and the sacred knowledge of death.

Then with the knowledge of death as walking one side of me,
And the thought of death close-walking the other side of me,
And I in the middle as with companions, and as holding the hands of companions,
I fled forth to the hiding receiving night that talks not,
Down to the shores of the water, the path by the swamp in the dimness,
To the solemn shadowy cedars and ghostly pines so still.

And the singer so shy to the rest receiv'd me,
The gray-brown bird I know receiv'd us comrades three,
And he sang the carol of death, and a verse for him I love.

From deep secluded recesses,
From the fragrant cedars and the ghostly pines so still,
Came the carol of the bird.

And the charm of the carol rapt me,
As I held as if by their hands my comrades in the night,
And the voice of my spirit tallied the song of the bird.

Come lovely and soothing death,
Undulate round the world, serenely arriving, arriving,
In the day, in the night, to all, to each,
Sooner or later delicate death.

Prais'd be the fathomless universe,
For life and joy, and for objects and knowledge curious,
And for love, sweet love—but praise! praise! praise!
For the sure-enwinding arms of cool-enfolding death.

Dark mother always gliding near with soft feet,
Have none chanted for thee a chant of fullest welcome?
Then I chant it for thee, I glorify thee above all,
I bring thee a song that when thou must indeed come, come unfalteringly.

Approach strong deliveress,
When it is so, when thou hast taken them I joyously sing the dead,
Lost in the loving floating ocean of thee,
Laved in the flood of thy bliss O death.

From me to thee glad serenades,
Dances for thee I propose saluting thee, adornments and feastings for thee,
And the sights of the open landscape and the high-spread sky are fitting,
And life and the fields, and the huge and thoughtful night.

The night in silence under many a star,
The ocean shore and the husky whispering wave whose voice I know,
And the soul turning to thee O vast and well-veil'd death,
And the body gratefully nestling close to thee.

Over the tree-tops I float thee a song,
Over the rising and sinking waves, over the myriad fields and the prairies wide,
Over the dense-pack'd cities all and the teeming wharves and ways,
I float this carol with joy, with joy to thee O death.

15

To the tally of my soul,
Loud and strong kept up the gray-brown bird,
With pure deliberate notes spreading filling the night.
Loud in the pines and cedars dim,
Clear in the freshness moist and the swamp-perfume,
And I with my comrades there in the night.

While my sight that was bound in my eyes unclosed,
As to long panoramas of visions.

And I saw askant the armies,
I saw as in noiseless dreams hundreds of battle-flags,
Borne through the smoke of the battles and pierc'd with missiles I saw them,
And carried hither and yon through the smoke, and torn and bloody,
And at last but a few shreds left on the staffs, (and all in silence,)
And the staffs all splinter'd and broken.

I saw battle-corpses, myriads of them,
And the white skeletons of young men, I saw them,
I saw the debris and debris of all the slain soldiers of the war,
But I saw they were not as was thought,
They themselves were fully at rest, they suffer'd not,
The living remain'd and suffer'd, the mother suffer'd,
And the wife and the child and the musing comrade suffer'd,
And the armies that remain'd suffer'd.

16

Passing the visions, passing the night,
Passing, unloosing the hold of my comrades' hands,
Passing the song of the hermit bird and the tallying song of my soul,
Victorious song, death's outlet song, yet varying ever-altering song,
As low and wailing, yet clear the notes, rising and falling, flooding the night,
Sadly sinking and fainting, as warning and warning, and yet again bursting with joy,
Covering the earth and filling the spread of the heaven,
As that powerful psalm in the night I heard from recesses,
Passing, I leave thee lilac with heart-shaped leaves,
I leave thee there in the door-yard, blooming, returning with spring.

I cease from my song for thee,
From my gaze on thee in the west, fronting the west, communing with thee,
O comrade lustrous with silver face in the night.

Yet each to keep and all, retrievements out of the night,
The song, the wondrous chant of the gray-brown bird,
And the tallying chant, the echo arous'd in my soul,
With the lustrous and drooping star with the countenance full of woe,
With the holders holding my hand nearing the call of the bird,

Comrades mine and I in the midst, and their memory ever to keep, for
the dead I loved so well,
For the sweetest, wisest soul of all my days and lands—and this for his
dear sake,
Lilac and star and bird twined with the chant of my soul,
There in the fragrant pines and the cedars dusk and dim.

1881

MATTHEW ARNOLD

(1822–1888)

The son of a prominent clergyman and educator, Arnold reacted in his college years against his upbringing and posed as a dandy. The pose was presumably an instinctive effort to defend spontaneity of imagination and emotion against the demands of conscience, because the imperatives of moral duty and social responsibility were strongly developed in him, as they typically were in sensitive, intellectual Victorians. Gradually these duties and responsibilities shaped his life. He became an inspector of schools, visiting them and preparing reports for the government. Until late in his life his writing was done in evenings or on Sundays and holidays.

At first his literary effort was mainly in poetry, but by 1860 he had virtually stopped writing verse. To write poetry well required, he found, a sustained concentration which was hardly possible for him as a part-time author. Moreover, he sensed that his imaginative, emotional capacities were lessening. After his thirtieth birthday he felt, as he said, "three parts iced over." But perhaps the main reason why he virtually ceased to be a poet was that he could not approve of his own poetry. He did not criticize its technical qualities, which were superb, but the state of mind or vision of life it conveyed. Arnold believed that poetry must bring joy and wisdom. His own poetry, however, necessarily expressed the intellectual uncertainties and sad, elegiac emotions of his generation. In Arnold's opinion such poetry could not animate or fortify, but could only dispirit.

In literary and social criticism, on the other hand, Arnold was not voicing the illness of the age but seeking to remedy it. Although the critical power was inherently less important than the creative, it was more necessary, Arnold maintained, at the present moment of history.

He became the great literary critic of the Victorian age; his *Essays in Criticism* (1865) and *Essays in Criticism: Second Series* (1888) had a major impact on taste and on fundamental assumptions about poetry. In all his literary criticism Arnold explored the ways in which literature expressed the spirit of the society that produced it and also helped to shape that society. His literary criticism included social criticism as one of its dimensions, and in several prose works, such as the brilliant *Culture and Anarchy* (1869), Arnold engaged in this directly. His views were highly controversial, and his opponents were further exasperated by the imperturbable assurance and urbanity of his prose style, of which Arnold was one of the great masters in English.

In 1857 Arnold was elected professor of poetry at Oxford, a post he held for ten years. The position was partly honorific and did not relieve him of his work as an inspector of schools, but it testified to growing fame. His books sold well in intellectual circles, although they did not produce much income, and in 1883 he was invited to make a lecture tour in the United States. Viewed by Americans as a "prophet of culture," he was received with much curiosity and trepidation, since Americans worried that Arnold might think them cultureless. But Arnold took to the United States and made a second visit in 1886.

Arnold's poetry voices feelings of constriction, isolation, loss, and nostalgia. At times, as in "The Buried Life," he assumes that these feelings are inherent in the human condition—so existential, universal, and mysterious that we cannot know their deeper causes. But usually he felt that the emotional condition of human beings had been different in the past—in the Middle Ages when, as he says in "Dover Beach," the "Sea of Faith" was at full tide, or even in the earlier part of the nineteenth-century, when Romantic poetry could bring back, as he says of Wordsworth in "Memorial Verses," "The freshness of the early world."

Usually, then, Arnold believed that the melancholy he felt was typical of his own period in history and caused by it. To put his finger on just what underlay this illness of spirit was not easy, however. Much was to be explained by the modern weakening of religious faith, for although most Victorians still believed in God, many people who were assailed by doubts and questionings looked back regretfully to earlier ages when religious faith might have been naive and whole-hearted. "Dover Beach" is the most memorable single expression of this regret in English poetry. The difficulties of religious faith were in part attributable to the development of modern science, and the same development made it necessary to relinquish the Romantic view of nature. The countryside was still a source of refreshment and escape, but nature conceived according to geological science or Darwinian evolution could not be an object of sympathy and identification. Arnold accepted, of course, the discoveries of modern science, but he also felt that in his time the rational, logical, empirical, scientific aspects of the mind were overemphasized. More exactly, he pleaded that for psychological or spiritual health there must be an equal emphasis on imagination and emotion. A further suppression of emotional vitality and spontaneity was enforced by morality and duty. Here Arnold was pointing to what Freud would later call the "discontents" of civilization—the ways in which society necessarily forces us to suppress natural instincts, with a resulting loss of energy and will to live. The feelings of separation, isolation, or alienation Arnold expressed—of being cut off from the divine, from nature, from the past, from other persons, and from one's own deepest self—have not, needless to say, lessened since his time. That he felt them so profoundly and expressed them so clearly does not, perhaps, make him the greatest of the Victorian poets, but he remains unquestionably the most relevant to our own age.

Shakespeare

Others abide our question. Thou art free.
We ask and ask—thou smilest and art still,
Out-topping knowledge. For the loftiest hill,
Who to the stars uncrowns his majesty,

Planting his steadfast footsteps in the sea,
Making the heaven of heavens his dwelling-place,
Spares but the cloudy border of his base
To the foiled searching of mortality;

And thou, who didst the stars and sunbeams know,
Self-schooled, self-scanned, self-honored, self-secure,
Didst tread on earth unguessed at—better so!

All pains the immortal spirit must endure,
All weakness which impairs, all griefs which bow,
Find their sole voice in that victorious brow.

1849

To Marguerite

Yes! in the sea of life enisled,
With echoing straits between us thrown,
Dotting the shoreless watery wild,

We mortal millions live *alone.*
The islands feel the enclasping flow,
And then their endless bounds they know.

But when the moon their hollows lights,
And they are swept by balms of spring,
And in their glens, on starry nights,
The nightingales divinely sing;
And lovely notes, from shore to shore
Across the sounds and channels pour—

Oh! then a longing like despair
Is to their farthest caverns sent;
For surely once, they feel, we were
Parts of a single continent!
Now round us spreads the watery plain—
Oh might our marges meet again!

Who ordered, that their longing's fire
Should be, as soon as kindled, cooled?
Who renders vain their deep desire?—
A God, a God their severance ruled!
And bade betwixt their shores to be
The unplumbed, salt, estranging sea.

1852

Memorial Verses

April, 1850

Goethe in Weimar sleeps, and Greece,
Long since, saw Byron's struggle cease.
But one such death remained to come;
The last poetic voice is dumb—
We stand today by Wordsworth's tomb.

When Byron's eyes were shut in death,
We bowed our head and held our breath.
He taught us little; but our soul
Had *felt* him like the thunder's roll.
With shivering heart the strife we saw
Of passion with eternal law;
And yet with reverential awe
We watched the fount of fiery life
Which served for that Titanic strife.

MEMORIAL VERSES. **Title:** Intended as an elegy on the death of Wordsworth (April, 1850).
1–2. Weimar . . . cease: Goethe had died in Weimar in 1832, Byron in Greece in 1824.

When Goethe's death was told, we said:
Sunk, then, is Europe's sagest head.
Physician of the iron age,
Goethe has done his pilgrimage.
He took the suffering human race,
He read each wound, each weakness clear;
And struck his finger on the place,
And said: *Thou ailest here, and here!*
He looked on Europe's dying hour
Of fitful dream and feverish power;
His eye plunged down the weltering strife,
The turmoil of expiring life—
He said: *The end is everywhere;*
Art still has truth, take refuge there!
And he was happy, if to know
Causes of things, and far below
His feet to see the lurid flow
Of terror, and insane distress,
And headlong fate, be happiness.

And Wordsworth!—Ah, pale ghosts, rejoice!
For never has such soothing voice
Been to your shadowy world conveyed,
Since erst, at morn, some wandering shade
Heard the clear song of Orpheus come
Through Hades, and the mournful gloom.
Wordsworth has gone from us—and ye,
Ah, may ye feel his voice as we!
He too upon a wintry clime
Had fallen—on this iron time
Of doubts, disputes, distractions, fears.
He found us when the age had bound
Our souls in its benumbing round;
He spoke, and loosed our heart in tears.
He laid us as we lay at birth
On the cool flowery lap of earth,
Smiles broke from us and we had ease;
The hills were round us, and the breeze
Went o'er the sun-lit fields again;
Our foreheads felt the wind and rain.
Our youth returned; for there was shed
On spirits that had long been dead,
Spirits dried up and closely furled,
The freshness of the early world.

16. sagest head: Goethe was regarded by Arnold as the greatest philosophical poet of the nineteenth century. **17. iron age:** period of the Industrial Revolution (1790–1830) and, Arnold thought, of a new materialism. **38. Orpheus:** By his skill in music, Orpheus was able to make his way through Hades in search of his dead wife, Eurydice.

Ah! since dark days still bring to light
Man's prudence and man's fiery might,
Time may restore us in his course
Goethe's sage mind and Byron's force;
But where will Europe's latter hour
Again find Wordsworth's healing power?
Others will teach us how to dare,
And against fear our breast to steel;
Others will strengthen us to bear—
But who, ah! who, will make us feel?
The cloud of mortal destiny,
Others will front it fearlessly—
But who, like him, will put it by?

Keep fresh the grass upon his grave
O Rotha, with thy living wave!
Sing him thy best! for few or none
Hears thy voice right, now he is gone.

1850

The Buried Life

Light flows our war of mocking words, and yet,
Behold, with tears mine eyes are wet!
I feel a nameless sadness o'er me roll.
Yes, yes, we know that we can jest,
We know, we know that we can smile!
But there's a something in this breast,
To which thy light words bring no rest,
And thy gay smiles no anodyne.
Give me thy hand, and hush awhile,
And turn those limpid eyes on mine,
And let me read there, love! thy inmost soul.

Alas! is even love too weak
To unlock the heart, and let it speak?
Are even lovers powerless to reveal
To one another what indeed they feel?
I knew the mass of men concealed
Their thoughts, for fear that if revealed
They would by other men be met
With blank indifference, or with blame reproved;
I knew they lived and moved
Tricked in disguises, alien to the rest
Of men, and alien to themselves—and yet
The same heart beats in every human breast!

72. Rotha: a river near the churchyard in Grasmere where Wordsworth is buried.

But we, my love!—doth a like spell benumb
Our hearts, our voices?—must we too be dumb?

Ah! well for us, if even we,
Even for a moment, can get free
Our heart, and have our lips unchained;
For that which seals them hath been deep-ordained!

Fate, which foresaw
How frivolous a baby man would be—
By what distractions he would be possessed,
How he would pour himself in every strife,
And well-nigh change his own identity—
That it might keep from his capricious play
His genuine self, and force him to obey
Even in his own despite his being's law,
Bade through the deep recesses of our breast
The unregarded river of our life
Pursue with indiscernible flow its way;
And that we should not see
The buried stream, and seem to be
Eddying at large in blind uncertainty,
Though driving on with it eternally.

But often, in the world's most crowded streets,
But often, in the din of strife,
There rises an unspeakable desire
After the knowledge of our buried life;
A thirst to spend our fire and restless force
In tracking out our true, original course;
A longing to inquire
Into the mystery of this heart which beats
So wild, so deep in us—to know
Whence our lives come and where they go.
And many a man in his own breast then delves,
But deep enough, alas! none ever mines.
And we have been on many thousand lines,
And we have shown, on each, spirit and power;
But hardly have we, for one little hour,
Been on our own line, have we been ourselves—
Hardly had skill to utter one of all
The nameless feelings that course through our breast,
But they course on forever unexpressed.
And long we try in vain to speak and act
Our hidden self, and what we say and do
Is eloquent, is well—but 'tis not true!
And then we will no more be racked
With inward striving, and demand
Of all the thousand nothings of the hour
Their stupefying power;
Ah yes, and they benumb us at our call!
Yet still, from time to time, vague and forlorn,
From the soul's subterranean depth upborne

As from an infinitely distant land,
Come airs, and floating echoes, and convey
A melancholy into all our day.

Only—but this is rare—
When a beloved hand is laid in ours,
When, jaded with the rush and glare
Of the interminable hours,
Our eyes can in another's eyes read clear,
When our world-deafened ear
Is by the tones of a loved voice caressed—
A bolt is shot back somewhere in our breast,
And a lost pulse of feeling stirs again.
The eye sinks inward, and the heart lies plain,
And what we mean, we say, and what we would, we know.
A man becomes aware of his life's flow,
And hears its winding murmur; and he sees
The meadows where it glides, the sun, the breeze.

And there arrives a lull in the hot race
Wherein he doth forever chase
That flying and elusive shadow, rest.
An air of coolness plays upon his face,
And an unwonted calm pervades his breast.
And then he thinks he knows
The hills where his life rose,
And the sea where it goes.

1852

Philomela

Hark! ah, the nightingale—
The tawny-throated!
Hark, from that moonlit cedar what a burst!
What triumph! hark!—what pain!

O wanderer from a Grecian shore,
Still, after many years, in distant lands,
Still nourishing in thy bewildered brain
That wild, unquenched, deep-sunken, old-world pain—
Say, will it never heal?
And can this fragrant lawn
With its cool trees, and night,
And the sweet, tranquil Thames,

PHILOMELA. **Title:** Greek name for the nightingale. In Greek myth, Philomela was raped by the King of Thrace, who had her tongue cut out in order to prevent her from disclosing the rape. The gods then turned her into a nightingale, whose passionate song conceals a tale of violence.

And moonshine, and the dew,
To thy racked heart and brain
Afford no balm?

Dost thou tonight behold,
Here, through the moonlight on this English grass,
The unfriendly palace in the Thracian wild?
Dost thou again peruse
With hot cheeks and seared eyes
The too clear web, and thy dumb sister's shame?
Dost thou once more assay
Thy flight, and feel come over thee,
Poor fugitive, the feathery change
Once more, and once more seem to make resound
With love and hate, triumph and agony,
Lone Daulis, and the high Cephissian vale?
Listen, Eugenia—
How thick the bursts come crowding through the leaves!
Again—thou hearest?
Eternal passion!
Eternal pain!

1853

Dover Beach

The sea is calm tonight.
The tide is full, the moon lies fair
Upon the straits; on the French coast the light
Gleams and is gone; the cliffs of England stand,
Glimmering and vast, out in the tranquil bay.
Come to the window, sweet is the night-air!
Only, from the long line of spray
Where the sea meets the moon-blanched land,
Listen! you hear the grating roar
Of pebbles which the waves draw back, and fling,
At their return, up the high strand,
Begin, and cease, and then again begin,
With tremulous cadence slow, and bring
The eternal note of sadness in.

Sophocles long ago
Heard it on the Aegean, and it brought
Into his mind the turbid ebb and flow

21. too clear web: She made a picture in needlework to tell what had happened. **27. Daulis . . . Cephissian:** Daulis was a city in Phocis, the place where Philomela was transformed into a nightingale. The Cephissian vale was near it. **28. Eugenia:** not an actual person. DOVER BEACH. **15–16. Sophocles . . . Aegean:** Arnold refers to a passage in Sophocles' *Antigone*, lines 583–91.

Of human misery; we
Find also in the sound a thought,
Hearing it by this distant northern sea.

The Sea of Faith
Was once, too, at the full, and round earth's shore
Lay like the folds of a bright girdle furled.
But now I only hear
Its melancholy, long, withdrawing roar,
Retreating, to the breath
Of the night-wind, down the vast edges drear
And naked shingles of the world.

Ah, love, let us be true
To one another! for the world, which seems
To lie before us like a land of dreams,
So various, so beautiful, so new,
Hath really neither joy, nor love, nor light,
Nor certitude, nor peace, nor help for pain;
And we are here as on a darkling plain
Swept with confused alarms of struggle and flight,
Where ignorant armies clash by night.

1867

The Last Word

Creep into thy narrow bed,
Creep, and let no more be said!
Vain thy onset! all stands fast.
Thou thyself must break at last.

Let the long contention cease!
Geese are swans, and swans are geese.
Let them have it how they will!
Thou art tired; best be still.

They out-talked thee, hissed thee, tore thee?
Better men fared thus before thee;
Fired their ringing shot and passed.
Hotly charged—and sank at last.

Charge once more, then, and be dumb!
Let the victors, when they come,
When the forts of folly fall,
Find thy body by the wall!

1867

28. shingles: coarse, waterworn stones. **35. darkling:** in the dark, obscure.

Dante Gabriel Rossetti

(1828–1882)

Rossetti was the unofficial leader of a group of Victorian artists called the "Pre-Raphaelite Brotherhood." They were reacting against what they thought was an excessively elaborate style that had dominated European painting since the time of Raphael (1483–1520), in contrast to the simpler style that preceded Raphael. In particular they aimed at natural lighting, sharp accuracy in details, pure colors, and firm, clear outlines. In his earlier poems Rossetti tried to carry over some of these ideals. "The Blessed Damozel" is a good example. With its visual details and primary colors, much of it reads like the description of a painting. In fact, Rossetti himself painted various versions of the Damozel leaning out from the "gold bar of heaven." Quite different is his later sonnet sequence, "The House of Life," which is a difficult, moody, symbolic, and meditative sequence focussing especially on love.

The Blessed Damozel

The blessed damozel leaned out
  From the gold bar of Heaven;
Her eyes were deeper than the depth
  Of waters stilled at even;
She had three lilies in her hand,
  And the stars in her hair were seven.

Her robe, ungirt from clasp to hem,
  No wrought flowers did adorn,
But a white rose of Mary's gift,
  For service meetly worn;
Her hair that lay along her back
  Was yellow like ripe corn.

Herseemed she scarce had been a day
  One of God's choristers;
The wonder was not yet quite gone
  From that still look of hers;
Albeit, to them she left, her day
  Had counted as ten years.

THE BLESSED DAMOZEL. **Title:** "Damozel" is an old form of "damsel"—a young unmarried woman. **12. corn:** grain. **13. Herseemed:** It seemed to her.

(To one, it is ten years of years.
  . . . Yet now, and in this place,
Surely she leaned o'er me—her hair
  Fell all about my face. . . .
Nothing: the autumn fall of leaves.
  The whole year sets apace.)

It was the rampart of God's house
  That she was standing on;
By God built over the sheer depth
  The which is Space begun;
So high, that looking downward thence
  She scarce could see the sun.

It lies in Heaven, across the flood
  Of ether, as a bridge.
Beneath, the tides of day and night
  With flame and darkness ridge
The void, as low as where this earth
  Spins like a fretful midge.

Around her, lovers, newly met
  In joy no sorrow claims,
Spoke evermore among themselves
  Their rapturous new names;
And the souls mounting up to God
  Went by her like thin flames.

And still she bowed herself and stooped
  Out of the circling charm;
Until her bosom must have made
  The bar she leaned on warm,
And the lilies lay as if asleep
  Along her bended arm.

From the fixed place of Heaven she saw
  Time like a pulse shake fierce
Through all the worlds. Her gaze still strove
  Within the gulf to pierce
Its path; and now she spoke as when
  The stars sang in their spheres.

The sun was gone now; the curled moon
  Was like a little feather
Fluttering far down the gulf; and now
  She spoke through the still weather.
Her voice was like the voice the stars
  Had when they sang together.

(Ah sweet! Even now, in that bird's song,
  Strove not her accents there,
Fain to be hearkened? When those bells

Possessed the midday air,
Strove not her steps to reach my side
Down all the echoing stair?)

"I wish that he were come to me,
For he will come," she said.
"Have I not prayed in Heaven?—on earth,
Lord, Lord, has he not prayed?
Are not two prayers a perfect strength?
And shall I feel afraid?

"When round his head the aureole clings,
And he is clothed in white,
I'll take his hand and go with him
To the deep wells of light;
We will step down as to a stream,
And bathe there in God's sight.

"We two will stand beside that shrine,
Occult, withheld, untrod,
Whose lamps are stirred continually
With prayer sent up to God;
And see our old prayers, granted, melt
Each like a little cloud.

"We two will lie i' the shadow of
That living mystic tree
Within whose secret growth the Dove
Is sometimes felt to be,
While every leaf that His plumes touch
Saith His Name audibly.

"And I myself will teach to him,
I myself, lying so,
The songs I sing here; which his voice
Shall pause in, hushed and slow,
And find some knowledge at each pause,
Of some new thing to know."

(Alas! We two, we two, thou say'st!
Yea, one wast thou with me
That once of old. But shall God lift
To endless unity
The soul whose likeness with thy soul
Was but its love for thee?)

"We two," she said, "will seek the groves
Where the lady Mary is,
With her five handmaidens, whose names

87. Dove: traditional symbol of the Holy Ghost.

Are five sweet symphonies,
Cecily, Gertrude, Magdalen,
Margaret and Rosalys.

"Circlewise sit they, with bound locks
And foreheads garlanded;
Into the fine cloth white like flame
Weaving the golden thread,
To fashion the birth-robes for them
Who are just born, being dead.

"He shall fear, haply, and be dumb:
Then will I lay my cheek
To his, and tell about our love,
Not once abashed or weak:
And the dear Mother will approve
My pride, and let me speak.

"Herself shall bring us, hand in hand,
To Him round whom all souls
Kneel, the clear-ranged unnumbered heads
Bowed with their aureoles:
And angels meeting us shall sing
To their citherns and citoles.

"There will I ask of Christ the Lord
Thus much for him and me:—
Only to live as once on earth
With Love—only to be,
As then awhile, forever now
Together, I and he."

She gazed and listened and then said,
Less sad of speech than mild,
"All this is when he comes." She ceased.
The light thrilled towards her, filled
With angels in strong level flight.
Her eyes prayed, and she smiled.

(I saw her smile.) But soon their path
Was vague in distant spheres:
And then she cast her arms along
The golden barriers,
And laid her face between her hands,
And wept. (I heard her tears.)

1850

126. citherns and citoles: medieval musical instruments; the former similar to a guitar, the latter to a box-shaped stringed instrument.

from The House of Life

A Sonnet

A Sonnet is a moment's monument,—
Memorial from the Soul's eternity
To one dead deathless hour. Look that it be,
Whether for lustral rite or dire portent,
Of its own arduous fullness reverent:
Carve it in ivory or in ebony,
As Day or Night may rule; and let Time see
Its flowering crest impearled and orient.

A Sonnet is a coin: its face reveals
The soul—its converse, to what Power 'tis due:
Whether for tribute to the august appeals
Of Life, or dower in Love's high retinue,
It serve; or, 'mid the dark wharf's cavernous breath,
In Charon's palm it pay the toll to Death.

91. Lost on Both Sides

As when two men have loved a woman well,
Each hating each, through Love's and Death's deceit;
Since not for either this stark marriage-sheet
And the long pauses of this wedding-bell;
Yet o'er her grave the night and day dispel
At last their feud forlorn, with cold and heat;
Nor other than dear friends to death may fleet
The two lives left that most of her can tell:

So separate hopes, which in a soul had wooed
The one same Peace, strove with each other long,
And Peace before their faces perished since:
So through that soul, in restless brotherhood,
They roam together now, and wind among
Its bye-streets, knocking at the dusty inns.

1881

THE HOUSE OF LIFE: A SONNET. **4. lustral:** purifying. **14. Charon's palm:** Charon, who ferried the dead across the river Styx to Hades, was given a coin as a fee.

George Meredith

(1828–1909)

Though Meredith preferred writing poetry to novels, his fame depends much more on his fiction. He used his talents as a novelist in *Modern Love,* a sequence of fifty sixteen-line sonnets tracing the course and failure of a marriage. The poems are remarkable for their psychological insight and realism, and were in part autobiographical, for they were based on a growing estrangement between Meredith and his wife. His other poems equally reflect his quick and subtle mind, but are more conventional in subject and emotion.

Modern Love

1

By this he knew she wept with waking eyes:
That, at his hand's light quiver by her head,
The strange low sobs that shook their common bed
Were called into her with a sharp surprise,
And strangled mute, like little gaping snakes,
Dreadfully venomous to him. She lay
Stone-still, and the long darkness flowed away
With muffled pulses. Then, as midnight makes
Her giant heart of Memory and Tears
Drink the pale drug of silence, and so beat
Sleep's heavy measure, they from head to feet
Were moveless, looking through their dead black years,
By vain regret scrawled over the blank wall.
Like sculptured effigies they might be seen
Upon their marriage-tomb, the sword between;
Each wishing for the sword that severs all.

49

He found her by the ocean's moaning verge,
Nor any wicked change in her discerned;
And she believed his old love had returned,
Which was her exultation, and her scourge.
She took his hand, and walked with him, and seemed

MODERN LOVE. SONNET 1. **15. marriage-tomb:** like stone statues recumbent on a tomb. In medieval statuary for tombs, a naked sword between such figures symbolized chastity.

The wife he sought, though shadow-like and dry.
She had one terror, lest her heart should sigh,
And tell her loudly she no longer dreamed.
She dared not say, "This is my breast: look in."
But there's a strength to help the desperate weak.
That night he learned how silence best can speak
The awful things when Pity pleads for Sin.
About the middle of the night her call
Was heard, and he came wondering to the bed.
"Now kiss me, dear! it may be, now!" she said.
Lethe had passed those lips, and he knew all.

50

Thus piteously Love closed what he begat:
The union of this ever-diverse pair!
These two were rapid falcons in a snare,
Condemned to do the flitting of the bat.
Lovers beneath the singing sky of May,
They wandered once; clear as the dew on flowers:
But they fed not on the advancing hours:
Their hearts held cravings for the buried day.
Then each applied to each that fatal knife,
Deep questioning, which probes to endless dole.
Ah, what a dusty answer gets the soul
When hot for certainties in this our life!—
In tragic hints here see what evermore
Moves dark as yonder midnight ocean's force,
Thundering like ramping hosts of warrior horse,
To throw that faint thin line upon the shore!

1862

Lucifer in Starlight

On a starred night Prince Lucifer uprose.
Tired of his dark dominion, swung the fiend
Above the rolling ball, in cloud part screened,
Where sinners hugged their specter of repose.
Poor prey to his hot fit of pride were those.
And now upon his western wing he leaned,
Now his huge bulk o'er Afric's sands careened,
Now the black planet shadowed Arctic snows.

SONNET 49. **16. Lethe:** river of forgetfulness in Hades. SONNET 50. **1. closed:** the wife has died. **10. dole:** sorrow. **15. ramping:** rearing.

Soaring through wider zones that pricked his scars
With memory of the old revolt from Awe,
He reached a middle height, and at the stars,
Which are the brain of heaven, he looked, and sank.
Around the ancient track marched, rank on rank,
The army of unalterable law.

1883

EMILY DICKINSON

(1830–1886)

One of the greatest of American poets, Dickinson published only seven poems during her lifetime. The rest were left, tied together in bundles, for a later generation to discover. She lived as a recluse in the house of her father in Amherst, Massachusetts, in comfortable and genteel circumstances, and her experience and opportunities were thus quite different from those of most women in her time. Although she had no personal acquaintance with the intimacies of marriage or child rearing and little involvement in household management and social life, she did have the time and freedom to read, reflect, and write. Socially timid, her intellectual life was bold. Like many writers of her generation, in early adult life she rejected the religious faith in which she had been raised, but she continued to think and imagine in terms of it. Eternity, immortality, heaven, angels, crucifixion, and Hell remained expressive concepts and symbols for her. She was also very much of her generation in her response to nature—in other words, to moods of sunlight and weather and to the creatures (butterflies, robins, snakes) she observed in her back yard. She did not, like Wordsworth or Emerson, assume that nature was necessarily benevolent or that the divine was immanent within it. Nonetheless, the world of nature remained important to her imaginative life; she projected her feelings into it. She observed and recorded her own emotions with sensitivity and ruthless clarity, and in some satiric poems she observed her neighbors with the same penetration.

LUCIFER IN STARLIGHT. **9–10. scars . . . Awe:** the spreading sky reminds Satan of the wounds given him when, after rebelling against God, he was hurled from heaven to hell.

In her poems Dickinson used mainly the simple meter and stanza of the hymn. Frequently, however, she did not rhyme or employed off-rhyme. She composed in phrases, often using no punctuation except a dash. Her elliptical juxtaposition of phrases permitted her to present complex states of mind briefly, and is quite different from the rhetorical amplitude that was common in her time, particularly in the United States. Together with her imaginative boldness, emotional intensity, and complexity of response, this condensed presentation has made her greatly admired in the twentieth century, and her reputation is still growing.

These Are the Days When Birds Come Back

These are the days when Birds come back—
A very few—a Bird or two—
To take a backward look.

These are the days when skies resume
The old—old sophistries of June—
A blue and gold mistake.

Oh fraud that cannot cheat the Bee—
Almost thy plausibility
Induces my belief.

Till ranks of seeds their witness bear—
And softly thro' the altered air
Hurries a timid leaf.

Oh Sacrament of summer days,
Oh Last Communion in the Haze—
Permit a child to join.

Thy sacred emblems to partake—
Thy consecrated bread to take
And thine immortal wine!

1890

THESE ARE THE DAYS WHEN BIRDS COME BACK. **5. sophistries:** false reasonings (that is, deceptive in what they imply).

There's a Certain Slant of Light

There's a certain Slant of light,
Winter Afternoons—
That oppresses, like the Heft
Of Cathedral Tunes—

Heavenly Hurt, it gives us—
We can find no scar,
But internal difference,
Where the Meanings, are—

None may teach it—Any—
'Tis the Seal Despair—
An imperial affliction
Sent us of the Air—

When it comes, the Landscape listens—
Shadows—hold their breath—
When it goes, 'tis like the Distance
On the look of Death—

1890

The Soul Selects Her Own Society

The Soul selects her own Society—
Then—shuts the Door—
To her divine Majority—
Present no more—

Unmoved—she notes the Chariots—pausing—
At her low Gate—
Unmoved—an Emperor be kneeling
Upon her Mat—

I've known her—from an ample nation—
Choose One—
Then—close the Valves of her attention—
Like Stone—

1890

THERE'S A CERTAIN SLANT OF LIGHT. **3. Heft:** weight (something heaved up). **10. Seal:** an official stamp of approval or confirmation.

A Bird Came Down the Walk

A Bird came down the Walk—
He did not know I saw—
He bit an Angleworm in halves
And ate the fellow, raw,

And then he drank a Dew
From a convenient Grass—
And then hopped sidewise to the Wall
To let a Beetle pass—

He glanced with rapid eyes
That hurried all around—
They looked like frightened Beads, I thought—
He stirred his Velvet Head

Like one in danger, Cautious,
I offered him a Crumb
And he unrolled his feathers
And rowed him softer home—

Than Oars divide the Ocean,
Too silver for a seam—
Or Butterflies, off Banks of Noon
Leap, plashless as they swim.

1891

After Great Pain, a Formal Feeling Comes

After great pain, a formal feeling comes—
The Nerves sit ceremonious, like Tombs—
The stiff Heart questions was it He, that bore,
And Yesterday, or Centuries before?

The Feet, mechanical, go round—
Of Ground, or Air, or Ought—
A Wooden way
Regardless grown,
A Quartz contentment, like a stone—

This is the Hour of Lead—
Remembered, if outlived,
As Freezing persons, recollect the Snow—
First—Chill—then Stupor—then the letting go—

1929

A BIRD CAME DOWN THE WALK. **20. plashless:** splashless. AFTER GREAT PAIN. **6. Ought:** zero, nothing.

I Heard a Fly Buzz—When I Died

I heard a Fly buzz—when I died—
The Stillness in the Room
Was like the Stillness in the Air—
Between the Heaves of Storm—

The Eyes around—had wrung them dry—
And Breaths were gathering firm
For that last Onset—when the King
Be witnessed—in the Room—

I willed my Keepsakes—Signed away
What portion of me be
Assignable—and then it was
There interposed a Fly—

With Blue—uncertain stumbling Buzz—
Between the light—and me—
And then the Windows failed—and then
I could not see to see—

1896

The Heart Asks Pleasure—First

The Heart asks Pleasure—first—
And then—Excuse from Pain—
And then—those little Anodynes
That deaden suffering—

And then—to go to sleep—
And then—if it should be
The will of its Inquisitor
The privilege to die—

1890

Because I Could Not Stop for Death

Because I could not stop for Death—
He kindly stopped for me—
The Carriage held but just Ourselves—
And Immortality.

THE HEART ASKS PLEASURE. **3. Anodynes:** drugs to alleviate pain.

We slowly drove—He knew no haste
And I had put away
My labor and my leisure too,
For His Civility—

We passed the School, where Children strove
At Recess—in the Ring—
We passed the Fields of Gazing Grain—
We passed the Setting Sun—

Or rather—He passed Us—
The Dews drew quivering and chill—
For only Gossamer, my Gown—
My Tippet—only Tulle—

We paused before a House that seemed
A Swelling of the Ground—
The Roof was scarcely visible—
The Cornice—in the Ground—

Since then—'tis Centuries—and yet
Feels shorter than the Day
I first surmised the Horses' Heads
Were toward Eternity—

1890

My Life Closed Twice Before Its Close

My life closed twice before its close;
It yet remains to see
If Immortality unveil
A third event to me,

So huge, so hopeless to conceive
As these that twice befel.
Parting is all we know of heaven,
And all we need of hell.

1896

CHRISTINA ROSSETTI

(1830–1894)

Like her older brother, Dante Gabriel Rossetti, Christina was an early convert to the ideals—clarity, simplicity, and minute detail—of the "Pre-Raphaelite" movement. She captured a musical cadence close to Elizabethan and early seventeenth-century songs. Renowned for her beauty, she often modeled for her brother and other painters, but in her thirties she was cruelly afflicted with a painful disease of the thyroid (Graves' disease) from which she never wholly recovered. Always devoutly religious, she increasingly led the life of a secular nun. Her poems henceforth reflected her religious devotion, and were influenced by the religious poets of the seventeenth century, particularly George Herbert.

Song

When I am dead, my dearest,
  Sing no sad songs for me;
Plant thou no roses at my head,
  Nor shady cypress tree:
Be the green grass above me
  With showers and dewdrops wet;
And if thou wilt, remember,
  And if thou wilt, forget.

I shall not see the shadows,
  I shall not feel the rain;
I shall not hear the nightingale
  Sing on, as if in pain:
And dreaming through the twilight
  That doth not rise nor set,
Haply I may remember,
  And haply may forget.

1862

Amor Mundi

"Oh where are you going with your love-locks flowing
  On the west wind blowing along this valley track?"
"The downhill path is easy, come with me an it please ye,
  We shall escape the uphill by never turning back."

So they two went together in glowing August weather,
  The honey-breathing heather lay to their left and right;
And dear she was to dote on, her swift feet seemed to float on
  The air like soft twin pigeons too sportive to alight.

"Oh what is that in heaven where gray cloud-flakes are seven,
  Where blackest clouds hang riven just at the rainy skirt?"
"Oh that's a meteor sent us, a message dumb, portentous,
  An undeciphered solemn signal of help or hurt."

"Oh what is that glides quickly where velvet flowers grow thickly,
  Their scent comes rich and sickly?"—"A scaled and hooded worm."
"Oh what's that in the hollow, so pale I quake to follow?"
  "Oh that's a thin dead body which waits the eternal term."

"Turn again, O my sweetest,—turn again, false and fleetest:
  This beaten way thou beatest I fear is hell's own track."
"Nay, too steep for hill-mounting; nay, too late for cost-counting:
  This downhill path is easy, but there's no turning back."

1875

Algernon Charles Swinburne

(1837–1909)

An *enfant terrible* of late Victorian poetry, Swinburne shocked and delighted his first readers with poems which rejected Christianity and voiced a supposedly "pagan" or "classical" joy in life. His poems have strong, almost hypnotic rhythms and a syntax that drives forward with urgent momentum. They are extremely musical, with lavish assonance and alliteration and long, elaborate stanzas interweaving masculine and feminine rhymes. When read aloud, they can be intoxicating. Most of his famous poems were written by the time he was

AMOR MUNDI. **Title:** Latin for "Love of the World."

thirty, for Swinburne's health, which was never robust, was undermined by his alcoholism and bohemian way of life. He was compelled to spend his last thirty years in semi-reclusion, living quietly under a strict regimen.

Choruses from *Atalanta in Calydon*

When the Hounds of Spring Are on Winter's Traces

When the hounds of spring are on winter's traces,
  The mother of months in meadow or plain
Fills the shadows and windy places
  With lisp of leaves and ripple of rain;
And the brown bright nightingale amorous
Is half assuaged for Itylus,
For the Thracian ships and the foreign faces,
  The tongueless vigil, and all the pain.

Come with bows bent and with emptying of quivers,
  Maiden most perfect, lady of light,
With a noise of winds and many rivers,
  With a clamor of waters, and with might;
Bind on thy sandals, O thou most fleet,
Over the splendor and speed of thy feet;
For the faint east quickens, the wan west shivers,
  Round the feet of the day and the feet of the night.

Where shall we find her, how shall we sing to her,
  Fold our hands round her knees, and cling?
O that man's heart were as fire and could spring to her,
  Fire, or the strength of the streams that spring!
For the stars and the winds are unto her
As raiment, as songs of the harp-player;
For the risen stars and the fallen cling to her,
  And the southwest wind and the west wind sing.

For winter's rains and ruins are over,
  And all the season of snows and sins;
The days dividing lover and lover,
  The light that loses, the night that wins;
And time remembered is grief forgotten,

ATALANTA IN CALYDON. WHEN THE HOUNDS OF SPRING. **Title:** This opening hymn by the chorus in Swinburne's play is addressed to Artemis (Diana), huntress and goddess of the moon and chastity. **2. mother of months:** Artemis. **6. Itylus:** To avenge her sister, Philomela, who had been raped by the King of Thrace and was later transformed into a nightingale, Procne killed her son Itylus and fed the body to her husband.

And frosts are slain and flowers begotten,
And in green underwood and cover
  Blossom by blossom the spring begins.

The full streams feed on flower of rushes,
  Ripe grasses trammel a traveling foot,
The faint fresh flame of the young year flushes
  From leaf to flower and flower to fruit;
And fruit and leaf are as gold and fire,
And the oat is heard above the lyre,
And the hoofèd heel of a satyr crushes
  The chestnut-husk at the chestnut-root.

And Pan by noon and Bacchus by night,
  Fleeter of foot than the fleet-foot kid,
Follows with dancing and fills with delight
  The Maenad and the Bassarid;
And soft as lips that laugh and hide
The laughing leaves of the trees divide,
And screen from seeing and leave in sight
  The god pursuing, the maiden hid.

The ivy falls with the Bacchanal's hair
  Over her eyebrows hiding her eyes;
The wild vine slipping down leaves bare
  Her bright breast shortening into sighs;
The wild vine slips with the weight of its leaves,
But the berried ivy catches and cleaves
To the limbs that glitter, the feet that scare
  The wolf that follows, the fawn that flies.

Before the Beginning of Years

Before the beginning of years
  There came to the making of man
Time, with a gift of tears;
  Grief, with a glass that ran;
Pleasure, with pain for leaven;
  Summer, with flowers that fell;
Remembrance fallen from heaven,
  And madness risen from hell;
Strength without hands to smite;
  Love that endures for a breath:
Night, the shadow of light,
  And life, the shadow of death.
And the high gods took in hand

38. oat: flute made from oaten reeds. **41. Pan:** god of flocks and pastures. **Bacchus:** god of wine. **44. Maenad:** female worshipper of Bacchus. **Bassarid:** Thracian worshipper of Bacchus.

Fire, and the falling of tears,
And a measure of sliding sand
From under the feet of the years;
And froth and drift of the sea;
And dust of the laboring earth;
And bodies of things to be
In the houses of death and of birth;
And wrought with weeping and laughter,
And fashioned with loathing and love,
With life before and after
And death beneath and above,
For a day and a night and a morrow,
That his strength might endure for a span
With travail and heavy sorrow,
The holy spirit of man.
From the winds of the north and the south
They gathered as unto strife;
They breathed upon his mouth,
They filled his body with life;
Eyesight and speech they wrought
For the veils of the soul therein,
A time for labor and thought,
A time to serve and to sin;
They gave him light in his ways,
And love, and a space for delight,
And beauty and length of days,
And night, and sleep in the night.
His speech is a burning fire;
With his lips he travaileth;
In his heart is a blind desire,
In his eyes foreknowledge of death;
He weaves, and is clothed with derision;
Sows, and he shall not reap;
His life is a watch or a vision
Between a sleep and a sleep.

1865

The Garden of Proserpine

Here, where the world is quiet;
Here, where all trouble seems
Dead winds' and spent waves' riot

THE GARDEN OF PROSERPINE. **Title:** Proserpine (an English form of the Latin "Proserpina," for the Greek "Persephone") had been carried off to the underworld by Pluto to be his queen. She was allowed to return for half of the year to her mother, Ceres, at which time spring returned to the earth. When she went back to Hades, it marked the coming of the winter. In Swinburne's poem, she is associated simply with death and eternal sleep.

In doubtful dreams of dreams;
I watch the green field growing
For reaping folk and sowing,
For harvest-time and mowing,
A sleepy world of streams.

I am tired of tears and laughter,
And men that laugh and weep;
Of what may come hereafter
For men that sow to reap:
I am weary of days and hours,
Blown buds of barren flowers,
Desires and dreams and powers
And everything but sleep.

Here life has death for neighbor,
And far from eye or ear
Wan waves and wet winds labor,
Weak ships and spirits steer;
They drive adrift, and whither
They wot not who make thither;
But no such winds blow hither,
And no such things grow here.

No growth of moor or coppice,
No heather-flower or vine,
But bloomless buds of poppies,
Green grapes of Proserpine,
Pale beds of blowing rushes
Where no leaf blooms or blushes
Save this whereout she crushes
For dead men deadly wine.

Pale, without name or number,
In fruitless fields of corn,
They bow themselves and slumber
All night till light is born;
And like a soul belated,
In hell and heaven unmated,
By cloud and mist abated
Comes out of darkness morn.

Though one were strong as seven,
He too with death shall dwell,
Nor wake with wings in heaven,
Nor weep for pains in hell;
Though one were fair as roses,
His beauty clouds and closes;
And well though love reposes,
In the end it is not well.

34. corn: grain.

Pale, beyond porch and portal,
  Crowned with calm leaves, she stands
Who gathers all things mortal
  With cold immortal hands;
Her languid lips are sweeter
Than love's who fears to greet her
To men that mix and meet her
  From many times and lands.

She waits for each and other,
  She waits for all men born;
Forgets the earth her mother,
  The life of fruits and corn;
And spring and seed and swallow
Take wing for her and follow
Where summer song rings hollow
  And flowers are put to scorn.

There go the loves that wither,
  The old loves with wearier wings;
And all dead years draw thither,
  And all disastrous things;
Dead dreams of days forsaken,
Blind buds that snows have shaken,
Wild leaves that winds have taken,
  Red strays of ruined springs.

We are not sure of sorrow,
  And joy was never sure;
Today will die tomorrow;
  Time stoops to no man's lure;
And love, grown faint and fretful,
With lips but half regretful
Sighs, and with eyes forgetful
  Weeps that no loves endure.

From too much love of living,
  From hope and fear set free,
We thank with brief thanksgiving
  Whatever gods may be
That no life lives for ever;
That dead men rise up never;
That even the weariest river
  Winds somewhere safe to sea.

Then star nor sun shall waken,
  Nor any change of light:
Nor sound of waters shaken,
  Nor any sound or sight:

76. lure: used in falconry to bring the hawk back to the wrist.

Nor wintry leaves nor vernal,
Nor days nor things diurnal;
Only the sleep eternal
  In an eternal night.

1866

Austin Dobson

(1840–1921)

A civil servant in the Board of Trade, Dobson excelled, like many of the minor poets in his age, in slight but beautifully accomplished poems in difficult forms, such as the villanelle and the triolet. He was also a skillful translator. Dobson did not himself believe in the aestheticism ("art for the sake of art") shared by many English and French poets toward the end of the nineteenth century, but his "Ars Victrix" expresses the essence of that proud, uncompromising ideology better than any other single poem in English. It is a lose translation of "L'Art" by the French poet, Théophile Gautier (1811–1872).

from Rose-Leaves

A Kiss

Rose kissed me today.
  Will she kiss me tomorrow?
Let it be as it may,
Rose kissed me today.
But the pleasure gives way
  To a savor of sorrow;—
Rose kissed me today—
  Will she kiss me tomorrow?

1874

"Urceus Exit"

I intended an Ode,
  And it turned to a Sonnet.
It began *à la mode*,
I intended an Ode;

But Rose crossed the road
  In her latest new bonnet;
I intended an Ode,
  And it turned to a Sonnet.

1874

Ars Victrix

(Imitated from Théophile Gautier)

Yes; when the ways oppose—
  When the hard means rebel,
Fairer the work outgrows—
  More potent far the spell.

O Poet, then, forbear
  The loosely-sandaled verse,
Choose rather thou to wear
  The buskin—straight and terse;

Leave to the tyro's hand
  The limp and shapeless style;
See that thy form demand
  The labor of the file.

Sculptor, do thou discard
  The yielding clay—consign
To Paros marble hard
  The beauty of thy line—

Model thy Satyr's face
  In bronze of Syracuse;
In the veined agate trace
  The profile of thy Muse.

Painter, that still must mix
  But transient tints anew,
Thou in the furnace fix
  The firm enamel's hue;

ARS VICTRIX. **Title:** Latin for "Art the Victor." The poem it imitates is "L'Art" by the French poet Théophile Gautier (1811–1872). **6–8. loosely-sandaled . . . buskin:** Loose sandals ("socks") were worn by comic actors in Greek plays, whereas the formal, high "buskins" were worn by the tragic actors. **9. tyro:** beginner. **15. Paros:** Greek island famous for its marble. **18. Syracuse:** site of a Greek colony in Sicily, noted for its bronze statuary.

Let the smooth tile receive
  Thy dove-drawn Erycine;
Thy Sirens blue at eve
  Coiled in a wash of wine.

All passes. Art alone
  Enduring stays to us;
The Bust outlasts the throne—
  The Coin, Tiberius;

Even the gods must go;
  Only the lofty Rime
Not countless years o'erthrow—
  Not long array of time.

Paint, chisel, then, or write;
  But, that the work surpass,
With the hard fashion fight—
  With the resisting mass.

1876

Thomas Hardy

(1840–1928)

For many years Hardy's poems were rejected by publishers. Unable to make a name or a living as a poet, he composed the great novels that established his fame. In 1898 he brought out his first volume of verse, which of course contained poems written many years before, and thereafter his chief literary effort was in poetry. His gifts as a novelist contributed to his poems, for these occasionally portray characters very different from Hardy himself (for example, "The Ruined Maid"), and they also tell or imply stories. The latter may have an archetypal simplicity, as in "The Convergence of the Twain," which narrates how, as the steamship Titanic was being built, an iceberg was also forming in the far north that would sink the Titanic on its maiden voyage.

26. Erycine: Venus, goddess of love, whose chariot was drawn by doves. **27. Sirens:** In Homer's *Odyssey,* the Sirens' songs lured sailors to shipwreck. **32. Tiberius:** Roman emperor of the first century, who succeeded Augustus. Some of the finest Roman coins were made in his time and carry the imprint of his head.

Other poems, however, present the difficult relations of human beings with each other, as in the dreary end of a love affair in "Neutral Tones" or the haunted yet ambivalent grief of "The Voice," a poem Hardy wrote after the death of his first wife.

Yet the novelistic tendencies of Hardy's imagination were balanced by others, such as direct, lyric intensity of emotion and philosophic pathos. The latter term refers to Hardy's way of seeing events against a vast background, with the result that their emotional impact is tempered so that they become subjects of brooding reflection. The background in Hardy may be that of landscape or nature, an encompassing space in which the human appears as a small point or may even be lost altogether, like the grave of "Drummer Hodge" amid the veldt and overarching sky of South Africa. Or the background may be that of the infinite number of other events taking place at the same time, or of the long history of man in which the same things have occurred over and over, as in "Channel Firing," where the sound of guns a few months before the outbreak of the First World War brings to Hardy's imagination a thought of "Camelot, and starlit Stonehenge," still surviving reminders of warfare in the dim past. "In Time of the Breaking of Nations" presents only the "background," although the First World War was raging when the poem was composed in 1915 and is alluded to in the title. The poem pictures human life in a few timeless, elemental images which are seen from a distance and within a wide landscape. Thus in this poem human existence is assimilated to nature and takes on the reassuring qualities of silence and endurance that are suggested by the landscape itself.

Hardy wrote many poems of religious questioning or protest. In them he focussed on the problem of evil—how could a loving God have permitted the evil and suffering of existence?—and rejected Christian answers and faith. These poems naturally aroused controversy when they were first published, and much of the early critical writing on Hardy focussed on them in attack or defense. Even though many of them have a splendid boldness of imaginative conception, these somewhat naive and argumentative poems are no longer regarded as among Hardy's best. We see him now as a man pulled in opposite directions, loving, for example, the faith he rejected (see "The Oxen"). He was deeply sensitive to the complexity of human beings and of their relations with each other; but he also believed in the possibility of a simple, primordial, natural way of being—and he cherished it in imagination. His disposition was both compassionate and ironical, and the complicated interplay of these attitudes makes many of his poems difficult to interpret, although they seem simple enough on the surface. He was, in short, uncertain and divided in all his emotions and beliefs. Many of his finest poems enact the drama of a person struggling to decide what attitude to adopt. The struggle is expressed in fluctuations of feeling, which are sometimes very rapid, through the course of the poem. The unusual honesty of his mind and openness of his sensibility make such poems especially difficult and exemplary.

Hardy's diction can be quite idiosyncratic. Among his verbs one finds, for example, *to onflee, to unbloom* (meaning, not to bloom), and *to outskeleton* (meaning, to be more skeletal than); his nouns include a *Powerfuller*, a *hope-hour*, and a *roomage*. His diction has often been criticized as awkward and grotesque, but it at least reveals that Hardy was not swayed by a conventional notion of the poetic. He used or, sometimes, invented such words because they seemed exact to the meaning and feeling he wished to convey. A similar point can be made about his versification. It can be smooth and regular, particularly in his ballad stanzas; but in his favorite kind of line he mingled anapests and iambs, and his verses have frequent irregularities of every kind. His stanzaic patterns are often complicated, with lines of different length; together with the metrical irregularities and odd, variable diction, they create a sense of *ad hoc* devising and difficulties overcome. The poems lack what used to be called "finish." Rather than smooth flow, we feel in them Hardy's struggle for accurate expression.

Hardy's reputation has fluctuated somewhat in the twentieth century, but he has been greatly admired by many other poets, among them Ezra Pound, John Crowe Ransom, Robert Graves, Dylan Thomas, and W. H. Auden. In England in the 1950s and 1960s he again became a direct inspiration to younger poets such as Donald Davie and Philip Larkin.

Hap

If but some vengeful god would call to me
From up the sky, and laugh: "Thou suffering thing,
Know that thy sorrow is my ecstasy,
That thy love's loss is my hate's profiting!"

Then would I bear it, clench myself, and die,
Steeled by the sense of ire unmerited;
Half-eased in that a Powerfuller than I
Had willed and meted me the tears I shed.

HAP. **Title:** chance, in the sense of "happenstance."

But not so. How arrives it joy lies slain,
And why unblooms the best hope ever sown?
—Crass Casualty obstructs the sun and rain,
And dicing Time for gladness casts a moan. . . .
These purblind Doomsters had as readily strown
Blisses about my pilgrimage as pain.

1898

Neutral Tones

We stood by a pond that winter day,
And the sun was white, as though chidden of God,
And a few leaves lay on the starving sod;
        —They had fallen from an ash, and were gray.

Your eyes on me were as eyes that rove
Over tedious riddles of years ago;
And some words played between us to and fro
        On which lost the more by our love.

The smile on your mouth was the deadest thing
Alive enough to have strength to die;
And a grin of bitterness swept thereby
        Like an ominous bird a-wing. . . .

Since then, keen lessons that love deceives,
And wrings with wrong, have shaped to me
Your face, and the God-cursed sun, and a tree,
        And a pond edged with grayish leaves.

1898

Drummer Hodge

1

They throw in drummer Hodge, to rest
        Uncoffined—just as found:
His landmark is a kopje-crest
        That breaks the veldt around;
And foreign constellations west
        Each night above his mound.

13. purblind Doomsters: blind judges who decree our doom. DRUMMER HODGE. **Title:** The subject is an English soldier, from a village in Wessex, who was killed in Africa during the Boer War (1899–1902). **3. kopje-crest:** Afrikaans (South African Dutch) for a small hill. **4. veldt:** Afrikaans for prairie. **5. constellations west:** constellations in the western sky that can be seen only in the southern hemisphere.

2

Young Hodge the Drummer never knew—
Fresh from his Wessex home—
The meaning of the broad Karoo,
The Bush, the dusty loam,
And why uprose to nightly view
Strange stars amid the gloam.

3

Yet portion of that unknown plain
Will Hodge forever be;
His homely Northern breast and brain
Grow to some Southern tree,
And strange-eyed constellations reign
His stars eternally.

1902

The Darkling Thrush

I leant upon a coppice gate
When Frost was specter-gray,
And Winter's dregs made desolate
The weakening eye of day.
The tangled bine-stems scored the sky
Like strings of broken lyres,
And all mankind that haunted nigh
Had sought their household fires.

The land's sharp features seemed to be
The Century's corpse outleant,
His crypt the cloudy canopy,
The wind his death-lament.
The ancient pulse of germ and birth
Was shrunken hard and dry,
And every spirit upon earth
Seemed fervorless as I.

At once a voice arose among
The bleak twigs overhead
In a full-hearted evensong
Of joy illimited;

9. Karoo: barren table land. **10. Bush:** uncleared land filled with shrubs and trees. THE DARKLING THRUSH. **1. coppice gate:** gate leading to a thicket. **5. bine-stems:** stems of a climbing shrub. **10. Century's corpse:** the dead nineteenth century. The poem was written on its final day, December 31, 1900.

An aged thrush, frail, gaunt, and small,
In blast-beruffled plume,
Had chosen thus to fling his soul
Upon the growing gloom.

So little cause for carolings
Of such ecstatic sound
Was written on terrestrial things
Afar or nigh around,
That I could think there trembled through
His happy good-night air
Some blessed Hope, whereof he knew
And I was unaware.

1902

The Ruined Maid

"O 'Melia, my dear, this does everything crown!
Who could have supposed I should meet you in Town?
And whence such fair garments, such prosperi-ty?"
"O didn't you know I'd been ruined?" said she.

"You left us in tatters, without shoes or socks,
Tired of digging potatoes, and spudding up docks;
And now you've gay bracelets and bright feathers three!"
"Yes: that's how we dress when we're ruined," said she.

"At home in the barton you said 'thee' and 'thou,'
And 'thik oon,' and 'theäs oon,' and 't'other'; but now
Your talking quite fits 'ee for high compa-ny!"
"Some polish is gained with one's ruin," said she.

"Your hands were like paws then, your face blue and bleak
But now I'm bewitched by your delicate cheek,
And your little gloves fit as on any la-dy!"
"We never do work when we're ruined," said she.

"You used to call home-life a hag-ridden dream,
And you'd sigh, and you'd sock; but at present you seem
To know not of megrims or melancho-ly!"
"True. One's pretty lively when ruined," said she.

"I wish I had feathers, a fine sweeping gown,
And a delicate face, and could strut about Town!"
"My dear—a raw country girl, such as you be,
Cannot quite expect that. You ain't ruined," said she.

1902

THE RUINED MAID. **6. docks:** weeds. **9. barton:** farm. **19. megrims:** dark mood.

The Convergence of the Twain

Lines on the Loss of the Titanic

1

In a solitude of the sea
Deep from human vanity,
And the Pride of Life that planned her, stilly couches she.

2

Steel chambers, late the pyres
Of her salamandrine fires,
Cold currents thrid, and turn to rhythmic tidal lyres.

3

Over the mirrors meant
To glass the opulent
The sea-worm crawls—grotesque, slimed, dumb, indifferent.

4

Jewels in joy designed
To ravish the sensuous mind
Lie lightless, all their sparkles bleared and black and blind.

5

Dim moon-eyed fishes near
Gaze at the gilded gear
And query: "What does this vaingloriousness down here?"

6

Well: while was fashioning
This creature of cleaving wing,
The Immanent Will that stirs and urges everything

7

Prepared a sinister mate
For her—so gaily great—
A Shape of Ice, for the time far and dissociate.

THE CONVERGENCE OF THE TWAIN. **Title:** Written on the sinking of the luxury liner Titanic after it collided with an iceberg on April 15, 1912, with 1,513 casualties, including many wealthy people. **4. Steel chambers:** furnaces and boilers. **5. salamandrine:** the salamander was supposedly able to live in fire. **6. thrid:** thread (currents of ocean water thread their way through the furnaces of the boilers). **8. glass the opulent:** reflect the wealthy passengers.

8

And as the smart ship grew
In stature, grace, and hue,
In shadowy silent distance grew the Iceberg too.

9

Alien they seemed to be:
No mortal eye could see
The intimate welding of their later history,

10

Or sign that they were bent
By paths coincident
On being anon twin halves of one august event,

11

Till the Spinner of the Years
Said "Now!" And each one hears,
And consummation comes, and jars two hemispheres.

1912

Channel Firing

That night your great guns, unawares,
Shook all our coffins as we lay,
And broke the chancel window-squares,
We thought it was the Judgment-day

And sat upright. While drearisome
Arose the howl of wakened hounds:
The mouse let fall the altar-crumb,
The worms drew back into the mounds,

The glebe cow drooled. Till God called, "No;
It's gunnery practice out at sea
Just as before you went below;
The world is as it used to be:

"All nations striving strong to make
Red war yet redder. Mad as hatters
They do no more for Christès sake
Than you who are helpless in such matters.

CHANNEL FIRING. **Title:** written during gunnery practice in the English Channel just before World War I. **9. glebe cow:** cow on the pasture (land attached to a cottage).

"That this is not the judgment-hour
For some of them's a blessed thing,
For if it were they'd have to scour
Hell's floor for so much threatening. . . .

"Ha, ha. It will be warmer when
I blow the trumpet (if indeed
I ever do; for you are men,
And rest eternal sorely need)."

So down we lay again. "I wonder,
Will the world ever saner be,"
Said one, "than when He sent us under
In our indifferent century!"

And many a skeleton shook his head.
"Instead of preaching forty year,"
My neighbor Parson Thirdly said,
"I wish I had stuck to pipes and beer."

Again the guns disturbed the hour,
Roaring their readiness to avenge,
As far inland as Stourton Tower,
And Camelot, and starlit Stonehenge.

1914

The Voice

Woman much missed, how you call to me, call to me,
Saying that now you are not as you were
When you had changed from the one who was all to me,
But as at first, when our day was fair.

Can it be you that I hear? Let me view you, then,
Standing as when I drew near to the town
Where you would wait for me: yes, as I knew you then,
Even to the original air-blue gown!

Or is it only the breeze, in its listlessness
Travelling across the wet mead to me here,
You being ever dissolved to wan wistlessness,
Heard no more again far or near?

Thus I; faltering forward,
Leaves around me falling,
Wind oozing thin through the thorn from norward,
And the woman calling.

1914

35. Stourton Tower: stone tower at Stourhead, Wiltshire. **36. Camelot:** legendary seat of King Arthur's court. **Stonehenge:** prehistoric stone circle on Salisbury Plain. THE VOICE. **11. wistlessness:** state of being inattentive.

The Oxen

Christmas Eve, and twelve of the clock.
  "Now they are all on their knees,"
An elder said as we sat in a flock
  By the embers in hearthside ease.

We pictured the meek mild creatures where
  They dwelt in their strawy pen,
Nor did it occur to one of us there
  To doubt they were kneeling then.

So fair a fancy few would weave
  In these years! Yet, I feel,
If someone said on Christmas Eve,
  "Come; see the oxen kneel,

"In the lonely barton by yonder coomb
  Our childhood used to know,"
I should go with him in the gloom,
  Hoping it might be so.

1915

In Time of "The Breaking of Nations"

1

Only a man harrowing clods
  In a slow silent walk
With an old horse that stumbles and nods
  Half asleep as they stalk.

2

Only thin smoke without flame
  From the heaps of couch-grass;
Yet this will go onward the same
  Though Dynasties pass.

3

Yonder a maid and her wight
  Come whispering by:
War's annals will cloud into night
  Ere their story die.

1916

IN TIME OF "THE BREAKING OF NATIONS". **Title:** from Jeremiah 51:20: "Thou art my battle axe and weapons of war: for with thee will I break in pieces the nations; and with thee will I destroy kingdoms."

Afterwards

When the Present has latched its postern behind my tremulous stay,
  And the May month flaps its glad green leaves like wings,
Delicate-filmed as new-spun silk, will the neighbors say,
  "He was a man who used to notice such things"?

If it be in the dusk when, like an eyelid's soundless blink,
  The dewfall-hawk comes crossing the shades to alight
Upon the wind-warped upland thorn, a gazer may think,
  "To him this must have been a familiar sight."

If I pass during some nocturnal blackness, mothy and warm,
  When the hedgehog travels furtively over the lawn,
One may say, "He strove that such innocent creatures should come to
    no harm,
  But he could do little for them; and now he is gone."

If, when hearing that I have been stilled at last, they stand at the door,
  Watching the full-starred heavens that winter sees,
Will this thought rise on those who will meet my face no more,
  "He was one who had an eye for such mysteries"?

And will any say when my bell of quittance is heard in the gloom,
  And a crossing breeze cuts a pause in its outrollings,
Till they rise again, as they were a new bell's boom,
  "He hears it not now, but used to notice such things"?

1917

Robert Bridges

(1844–1930)

Preparing with serious deliberation for a literary career, Bridges first sought to acquaint himself with life through extensive travels and the practice of medicine. He then settled down in the country, and spent the rest of his life writing poems, dramas, and literary criticism. Both as a critic and a poet he was especially interested in versification, and when his friend Gerard Manley Hopkins showed him some poems in the "sprung rhythm" Hopkins was experimenting with, the fascinated Bridges at once tried the new meter. One result was the

AFTERWARDS. **1. postern:** rear gate.

beautiful "A Passer-By." Bridges uses sprung rhythm with less boldness and drama than Hopkins. "A Passer-By" also has less intellectual and emotional content than one would find in a poem of Hopkins, and is more purely an exhibit of prosodic virtuosity. This is typical of Bridges. His major work is the book-length *The Testament of Beauty*, which he began at the age of eighty-two and published in 1929. The poem reveals that his notion of "beauty" excluded intensities of emotion or thought that might distract from the melody of the lines and the pleasurable associations of the imagery.

A Passer-By

Whither, O splendid ship, thy white sails crowding,
  Leaning across the bosom of the urgent West,
That fearest nor sea rising, nor sky clouding,
  Whither away, fair rover, and what thy quest?
  Ah! soon, when Winter has all our vales opprest,
When skies are cold and misty, and hail is hurling,
  Wilt thou glide on the blue Pacific, or rest
In a summer haven asleep, thy white sails furling.

I there before thee, in the country that well thou knowest,
  Already arrivèd am inhaling the odorous air.
I watch thee enter unerringly where thou goest,
  And anchor queen of the strange shipping there,
  Thy sails for awnings spread, thy masts bare;
Nor is aught from the foaming reef to the snow-capped, grandest
  Peak, that is over the feathery palms more fair
Than thou, so upright, so stately, and still thou standest.

And yet, O splendid ship, unhailed and nameless,
  I know not if, aiming a fancy, I rightly divine
That thou hast a purpose joyful, a courage blameless,
  Thy port assured in a happier land than mine.
  But for all I have given thee, beauty enough is thine,
As thou, aslant with trim tackle and shrouding,
  From the proud nostril curve of a prow's line
In the offing scatterest foam, thy white sails crowding.

1879

Gerard Manley Hopkins

(1844–1889)

One of the greatest religious poets, Hopkins became a Jesuit priest after he was converted to Roman Catholicism by the famous Cardinal Newman. He worked in various parishes, including one in a Liverpool slum, and a few years before he died was appointed Professor of Classics at University College, Dublin. Hopkins made no attempt to publish his poems, but almost thirty years after his death, Robert Bridges brought out an edition of his lyrics (1918). His reputation spread gradually but steadily; by the end of the 1920s, Hopkins was one of the most admired poets of the nineteenth century, a strong influence on contemporary poetry.

As his letters reveal, Hopkins gave intense consideration to method or style. His poetry strikes a reader as difficult partly because, in order to get a highly concentrated intensity, he often left out words that would make his sentences grammatically easier to follow. In this use of "ellipsis," as it is called, Hopkins anticipated poets of the High Modernist mode of the 1920s. He also strove to present things with the utmost degree of particularity and concreteness. In this he was influenced by the medieval philosopher Duns Scotus. Against many philosophers who argued that the reality of anything was to be found in its general form—in the idea of it—Duns Scotus maintained that the reality was the particular, concrete being or *haecceitas* ("thisness") of the thing. To designate this Hopkins used the word "inscape," and to catch and render this "inscape" he used phrases that fuse multiple sensory perceptions.

"Pied Beauty" celebrates the creative power of God as it is manifested in the infinitely variegated particulars of existence. Seeking in this poem to describe, for example, the spots on trout, Hopkins writes "rose-moles all in stipple upon trout that swim"; in this phrase he views the trout with extreme closeness, and describes the color (rose), the round, raised shape (moles), and the thick multiplicity (stipple) of their spots. It is also typical of Hopkins that this "inscape" is caught and expressed in action—"trout that swim." In "The Windhover" he describes a falcon flying at dawn as "dapple-dawn drawn"—outlined against and drawn forth by the dawn, which is dappled (mottled) with variegated colors. Hopkins' "inscape" often includes an imaginative empathy or identification with the thing rendered, a feeling of what the thing itself must feel. In "The Windhover," for example, "dapple" is an adjective usually applied to horses, and the poem later suggests the sense of "mastery," as of a "chevalier" on a horse, with which the falcon rides the dawn.

Another principal aim of Hopkins' style was the development of the new meter he called "sprung rhythm." The advantages of this meter, Hopkins believed, lay partly in its more complicated and intense musicality, and partly in its greater dramatic expressiveness, especially as it permitted a rapid onrush or a *ralentando* of syllables. He described "sprung rhythm" in very elaborate ways, and readers have disagreed in interpreting it. For Hopkins it was essentially a way of governing the length of time taken to pronounce the syllables in a line of verse. Simplifying somewhat, we may say that in contrast to the regular feet (iamb, trochee, and so on) traditional in English verse, a metrical foot in "sprung rhythm" has one strongly stressed syllable and from one to five or more unstressed syllables. Hopkins scanned the third line of "The Windhover," for example,

> Of the rolling level underneath him steady air, and striding.

Here the accents (´) indicate the stressed syllables and the underlinings mark syllables which Hopkins called "outriders," syllables "not counted in the nominal scanning." If we ignore the "outriders," we find a fairly regular line of verse, although no one could actually say the line as Hopkins has scanned it. In general, Hopkins' "sprung rhythm" should be read with a very pronounced stress on the strong syllables in the main words and a rapid scurry over the light syllables. Above all, there should be what Hopkins called "extravagant pauses" at the end of each phrase.

In addition to "sprung rhythm" (which he did not always use), Hopkins explored many other innovations. His diction revived old English words and phrases, and he also incorporated dialect words such as "fettle" and "sillion." He invented compounds, both with and without hyphens ("rose-moles," "leafmeal"). He deployed lavish internal rhyme, alliteration, and assonance. His assonance came often in a rapid rush, as in the opening lines of "The Windhover," in which the sound ô is established in the second word ("*caug*ht"), and picked up in the next line in "dawn," "drawn," "dauphin," and "Falcon," in which Hopkins pronounced the first vowel to sound like the *au* in "caught." He also manipulated progressions of vowel sounds, as in this phrase from "Pied Beauty": "Fresh-firecoal chestnut-falls." With the exception of "chestnut," which is outside the pattern, the vowels move from the front to the back of the mouth as one pronounces this.

A principal theme running throughout all of his finest lyrics is the supreme need of the human heart, however great the struggle with ourselves, to surrender to God and to see the beauty about us (as in "God's

Grandeur" or "Pied Beauty") as the manifestation of the divine. The most splendid example of this is "The Windhover," which Hopkins said was "the best thing I ever wrote." Here the bird (the English kestrel or falcon) as it rides with powerful grace through the air is used as a symbol for Christ. The poem is saying that the self-fulfillment of the bird, as it gives itself to action and to its own unique function, is, in miniature, the same thing Christ typifies on a far greater scale ("a billion times told lovelier").

The last three sonnets printed here are from a group written toward the end of Hopkins' life. Because of the state of psychological and spiritual torment they reveal, they are often called the "terrible sonnets." But appalling as they are, they do not express a loss or weakening of Hopkins' faith. Such times of anguish are not infrequent in the religious life, and are the more common in persons of extreme religious sensitivity. Despite his suffering and temptation to despair, Hopkins never quite allows himself to despair in these sonnets; in the dramatic last two words of "I Wake and Feel the Fell of Dark . . . ," the firmness of mind with which he refuses to see himself among the "lost" is deeply moving.

Heaven-Haven

A Nun Takes the Veil

I have desired to go
Where springs not fail,
To fields where flies no sharp and sided hail
And a few lilies blow.

And I have asked to be
Where no storms come,
Where the green swell is in the havens dumb,
And out of the swing of the sea.

1918

The Habit of Perfection

Elected Silence, sing to me
And beat upon my whorlèd ear,
Pipe me to pastures still and be
The music that I care to hear.

Shape nothing, lips; be lovely-dumb:
It is the shut, the curfew sent
From there where all surrenders come
Which only makes you eloquent.

Be shellèd, eyes, with double dark
And find the uncreated light:
This ruck and reel which you remark
Coils, keeps, and teases simple sight.

Palate, the hutch of tasty lust,
Desire not to be rinsed with wine:
The can must be so sweet, the crust
So fresh that come in fasts divine!

Nostrils, your careless breath that spend
Upon the stir and keep of pride,
What relish shall the censers send
Along the sanctuary side!

O feel-of-primrose hands, O feet
That want the yield of plushy sward,
But you shall walk the golden street
And you unhouse and house the Lord.

And, Poverty, be thou the bride
And now the marriage feast begun,
And lily-coloured clothes provide
Your spouse not laboured-at nor spun.

1893

God's Grandeur

The world is charged with the grandeur of God.
  It will flame out, like shining from shook foil;
  It gathers to a greatness, like the ooze of oil
Crushed. Why do men then now not reck his rod?
Generations have trod, have trod, have trod;

THE HABIT OF PERFECTION. **10. uncreated light:** in medieval theology, a symbol of the primal energy of God. **15. can:** mug or tankard. **18. keep:** upkeep or support. **19. censers:** containers for incense. **24. unhouse and house:** take the Communion Host from the tabernacle, and receive it. **27–28. lily . . . spun:** Hopkins echoes the Sermon on the Mount: "Consider the lilies . . . they toil not, neither do they spin; And yet I say unto you, that not even Solomon in all his glory was arrayed like one of these" (Matthew 6:28–29).
GOD'S GRANDEUR. **2. shook foil:** Hopkins said of the phrase: "I mean foil in the sense of leaf or tinsel . . . Shaken goldfoil gives off broad glares like sheet lightning and also, and this is true of nothing else, owing to its zigzag dints and creasings and network of small many cornered facets, a sort of fork lightning too." **4. Crushed:** as oil from crushed olives.

And all is seared with trade; bleared, smeared with toil;
And wears man's smudge and shares man's smell: the soil
Is bare now, nor can foot feel, being shod.

And for all this, nature is never spent;
There lives the dearest freshness deep down things;
And though the last lights off the black West went
Oh, morning, at the brown brink eastward, springs—
Because the Holy Ghost over the bent
World broods with warm breast and with ah! bright wings.

1895

The Windhover

To Christ Our Lord

I caught this morning morning's minion, king-
dom of daylight's dauphin, dapple-dawn-drawn Falcon, in his riding
Of the rolling level underneath him steady air, and striding
High there, how he rung upon the rein of a wimpling wing
In his ecstasy! then off, off forth on swing,
As a skate's heel sweeps smooth on a bow-bend: the hurl and gliding
Rebuffed the big wind. My heart in hiding
Stirred for a bird,—the achieve of, the mastery of the thing!

Brute beauty and valour and act, oh, air, pride, plume, here
Buckle! AND the fire that breaks from thee then, a billion
Times told lovelier, more dangerous, O my chevalier!

THE WINDHOVER. **Title:** a kestrel, or small hawk, called the "windhover" because it hovers in the air with its head to the wind. **1. minion:** darling. **2. dauphin:** title of the eldest son of the King of France; here used generally for the heir to a royal position. **4. rein:** of a horse; the comparison is to a horse circling around its trainer at the end of a long rein. **wimpling:** rippling or undulating. **6. bow-bend:** a curve like that of a bent bow. **8. achieve:** verb used as a noun (achievement) to stress intensity of action; as in "act" for "action" in line 9. **10. Buckle:** come together closely and be fastened; also used in the sense of "crumpling"—all these things coming together "crumple" and become folded into something larger. **AND:** By printing the word in capital letters, Hopkins intends for the word to be stressed very strongly in order to emphasize that the poem is turning now from the bird to the far greater subject of Christ himself. **thee:** Christ. **10–11. fire . . . dangerous:** the red of the windhover's breast, as the bird descends, becomes infinitely more brilliant and more dangerous in the sacrificial descent of Christ. **chevalier:** knight, chivalric noble figure.

No wonder of it: shèer plòd makes plough down sillion
Shine, and blue-bleak embers, ah my dear,
Fall, gall themselves, and gash gold-vermilion.

1918

Pied Beauty

Glory be to God for dappled things—
For skies of couple-colour as a brinded cow;
For rose-moles all in stipple upon trout that swim;
Fresh-firecoal chestnut-falls; finches' wings;
Landscape plotted and pieced—fold, fallow, and plough;
And àll tràdes, their gear and tackle and trim.

All things counter, original, spare, strange;
Whatever is fickle, freckled (who knows how?)
With swift, slow; sweet, sour; adazzle, dim;
He fathers-forth whose beauty is past change:
Praise him.

1918

Felix Randal

Felix Randal the farrier, O he is dead then? my duty all ended,
Who have watched his mould of man, big-boned and hardy-handsome
Pining, pining, till time when reason rambled in it and some
Fatal four disorders, fleshed there, all contended?

Sickness broke him. Impatient, he cursed at first, but mended
Being anointed and all; though a heavenlier heart began some

12. plough down sillion: plow going down the soil through a "sillion" (an old word for the soil that is pushed up into a ridge as a plow cuts a furrow). The point of the image is that, through friction, the metal on the plow is cleansed of rust and, through use, is thus made to shine. Hopkins echoes a line in Virgil's *Georgics,* I.46: "And the plowshare glistens when rubbed by the furrow." **14. gall . . . vermillion:** The black-blue embers of a dying fire collapse with red and gold sparks, like death-wounds similar to those of Christ when crucified. PIED BEAUTY. **Title:** "Pied" in the sense of particolored, spotted, varied. **1–2. dappled . . . couple-colour . . . brinded:** variegated in blotches and streaks. **3. rose-moles . . . trout:** rose-coloured spots that are "stippled" (a form of painting with dots and flecks) on the trout. **4. chestnut-falls:** chestnuts stripped of husks after being roasted. **5. plotted and pieced:** divided into squares or fields of different colors. **fold, fallow, and plough:** three kinds of fields—pasture (fold), unseeded land (fallow), and plowed land. **6. gear . . . trim:** equipment. **7. counter:** contrary, in opposition. **spare:** rare. FELIX RANDAL. **1. farrier:** blacksmith.

Months earlier, since I had our sweet reprieve and ransom
Tendered to him. Ah well, God rest him all road ever he offended!

This seeing the sick endears them to us, us too it endears.
My tongue had taught thee comfort, touch had quenched thy tears,
Thy tears that touched my heart, child, Felix, poor Felix Randal;

How far from then forethought of, all thy more boisterous years,
When thou at the random grim forge, powerful amidst peers,
Didst fettle for the great grey drayhorse his bright and battering
sandal!

1918

Spring and Fall

To a Young Child

Màrgarèt, are you grìeving
Over Goldengrove unleaving?
Leàves, lìke the things of man, you
With your fresh thoughts care for, can you?
Àh! às the heart grows older
It will come to such sights colder
By and by, nor spare a sigh
Though worlds of wanwood leafmeal lie;
And yet you wìll weep and know why.
Now no matter, child, the name:
Sòrrow's sprìngs àre the same.
Nor mouth had, no nor mind, expressed
What heart heard of, ghost guessed:
It ìs the blight man was born for,
It is Margaret you mourn for.

1893

No Worst, There Is None

No worst, there is none. Pitched past pitch of grief,
More pangs will, schooled at forepangs, wilder wring.
Comforter, where, where is your comforting?
Mary, mother of us, where is your relief?

8. all road: in whatever way. **13. random:** haphazard, having no purpose (compared with the religious life). **14. fettle:** prepare. SPRING AND FALL. **8. wanwood:** trees in the autumn with pale ("wan") leaves. **leafmeal:** leaf by leaf (a word coined by Hopkins after the word "piecemeal," meaning piece by piece). **13. ghost:** spirit, soul. Hopkins used this older meaning of "ghost" for alliteration with "guessed." NO WORST, THERE IS NONE. **1. Pitched:** hurled. **pitch:** highest pitch of intensity (as in musical tone). **2. forepangs:** pangs previously suffered.

My cries heave, herds-long; huddle in a main, a chief
Woe, world-sorrow; on an age-old anvil wince and sing—
Then lull, then leave off. Fury had shrieked "No ling-
ering! Let me be fell: force I must be brief."

O the mind, mind has mountains; cliffs of fall
Frightful, sheer, no-man-fathomed. Hold them cheap
May who ne'er hung there. Nor does long our small
Durance deal with that steep or deep. Here! creep,
Wretch, under a comfort serves in a whirlwind: all
Life death does end and each day dies with sleep.

1918

My Own Heart Let Me More Have Pity On

My own heart let me more have pity on; let
Me live to my sad self hereafter kind,
Charitable; not live this tormented mind
With this tormented mind tormenting yet.

I cast for comfort I can no more get
By groping round my comfortless, than blind
Eyes in their dark can day or thirst can find
Thirst's all-in-all in all a world of wet.

Soul, self; come, poor Jackself, I do advise
You, jaded, let be; call off thoughts awhile
Elsewhere; leave comfort root-room; let joy size
At God knows when to God knows what; whose smile
's not wrung, see you; unforeseen times rather—as skies
Betweenpie mountains—lights a lovely mile.

1918

Thou Art Indeed Just, Lord

Justus quidem tu es, Domine, si disputem tecum: verumtamen justa loquar ad te: Quare via impiorum prosperatur? &c.

5. herds-long: coming in large numbers—in herds (like herds of sheep). **8. fell:** savage, cruel. **force:** by force. **13. comfort serves:** such comfort as may serve or be possible. MY OWN HEART. **7–8. thirst . . . wet:** as someone adrift on the ocean, surrounded by a world of water ("wet"), cannot find water to drink. **9. Jackself:** the humble self ("Jack" in the older sense of a lowly person). **11. root-room:** room for roots to grow. **11–12. size . . . what:** grow in size whenever God wills and to whatever extent God allows possible. **13. wrung:** forced out instead of coming naturally. **13–14. skies . . . mountains:** the varied shade of sky and mountains in a "pied" way (as in "Pied Beauty"). THOU ART INDEED JUST, LORD. **Title:** The epigraph is from the Vulgate (Latin) version of the Bible, Jeremiah 12:1: "Thou indeed, O Lord, art just, if I plead with thee, but yet I will speak what is just to thee: Why doth the way of the wicked prosper?"

Thou art indeed just, Lord, if I contend
With thee; but, sir, so what I plead is just.
Why do sinners' ways prosper? and why must
Disappointment all I endeavour end?
  Wert thou my enemy, O thou my friend,
How wouldst thou worse, I wonder, than thou dost
Defeat, thwart me? Oh, the sots and thralls of lust
Do in spare hours more thrive than I that spend,
Sir, life upon thy cause. See, banks and brakes
Now, leavèd how thick! lacèd they are again
With fretty chervil, look, and fresh wind shakes
Them; birds build—but not I build; no, but strain,
Time's eunuch, and not breed one work that wakes.
Mine, O thou lord of life, send my roots rain.

1893

William Ernest Henley

(1849–1903)

Despite disastrous health, Henley became an influential magazine editor. He played an active role in London literary life and aided the careers of many good writers, including Robert Louis Stevenson and Rudyard Kipling. His poems were quite diverse in theme and style, but "Invictus" sounds the note for which he was best known. It is now often omitted from anthologies, perhaps because editors are shy of including the inspirational. But, knowing the story of Henley's life, we feel that he earned his brave words. The poem used to be a favorite piece for recitation in American schools.

Invictus

Out of the night that covers me,
  Black as the Pit from pole to pole,
I thank whatever gods may be
  For my unconquerable soul.

7. thralls: slaves. **11. fretty:** interlaced with ornamental lines. **chervil:** a garden herb. **13. wakes:** becomes alive. **14. Mine:** my roots.

In the fell clutch of circumstance
  I have not winced nor cried aloud.
Under the bludgeonings of chance
  My head is bloody, but unbowed.

Beyond this place of wrath and tears
  Looms but the Horror of the shade,
And yet the menace of the years
  Finds, and shall find, me unafraid.

It matters not how strait the gate,
  How charged with punishments the scroll,
I am the master of my fate:
  I am the captain of my soul.

1888

Robert Louis Stevenson

(1850–1894)

Known mainly for his novels *(Treasure Island, Kidnapped, Dr. Jekyll and Mr. Hyde)* and poems for children *(A Child's Garden of Verses),* Stevenson was inspired in writing his "Requiem" by Fragment 149 of the ancient Greek poet, Sappho, of which his final two lines are a loose version.

Requiem

Under the wide and starry sky,
Dig the grave and let me lie.
Glad did I live and gladly die,
And I laid me down with a will.

This be the verse you grave for me:
Here he lies where he longed to be;
Home is the sailor, home from sea,
And the hunter home from the hill.

1887

A. E. Housman

(1859–1936)

Although he went up to St. John's College, Oxford, as a promising scholar, Housman deliberately failed his final examinations at the university. The reasons for this self-destructive behaviour probably lie in a severe emotional crisis arising out of his love for a friend in his last year at Oxford. He worked in the Government Patent Office, but he also found time to write and publish learned articles on classical authors. On the strength of these he was appointed Professor of Latin at the University of London and, in 1911, at Cambridge. His career was spent in teaching, in brilliant editing of a minor Roman poet, and in writing scholarly reviews, some of them of a notorious savagery. At least in later life he accepted the fact that he was homosexual, although of course in his time and place he could not have declared this openly.

Although his poems were published at long intervals in three separate volumes (in 1896, 1922, and 1936), they were almost all written within a ten-year period from 1895 to 1905. The first and most famous of these volumes, *A Shropshire Lad,* was originally published at Housman's own expense. It sold slowly until, in 1915, some poems from it were included in an anthology of poems for soldiers, which reached a large number of readers. Since then Housman has been one of the most popular poets of the twentieth century.

His poems express simple, universal emotions—love of nature, nostalgia for the past, the pathos of man's brief existence—in scenes and narratives that are easy to understand and with which the reader can readily identify. His style derives from the old ballads and from classical poetry, and both influences tend to make his expression terse and shapely. Together with his pessimism and irony, which can be savage, the formal qualities of his style keep his intense emotion from seeming sentimental. The lyrics frequently allude to the civilization of ancient Rome—its empire, far-flung armies, folk customs, and stoic attitudes. That Rome is the background, so to speak, to the scenes of contemporary rural England in the foreground contributes to the timelessness and universality of Housman's poetry.

Loveliest of Trees, the Cherry Now

Loveliest of trees, the cherry now
Is hung with bloom along the bough,
And stands about the woodland ride
Wearing white for Eastertide.

Now, of my threescore years and ten,
Twenty will not come again,
And take from seventy springs a score,
It only leaves me fifty more.

And since to look at things in bloom
Fifty springs are little room,
About the woodlands I will go
To see the cherry hung with snow.

1896

Reveille

Wake: the silver dusk returning
  Up the beach of darkness brims,
And the ship of sunrise burning
  Strands upon the eastern rims.

Wake: the vaulted shadow shatters,
  Trampled to the floor it spanned,
And the tent of night in tatters
  Straws the sky-pavilioned land.

Up, lad, up, 'tis late for lying:
  Hear the drums of morning play;
Hark, the empty highways crying
  "Who'll beyond the hills away?"

Towns and countries woo together,
  Forelands beacon, belfries call;
Never lad that trod on leather
  Lived to feast his heart with all.

Up, lad; thews that lie and cumber
  Sunlit pallets never thrive;
Morns abed and daylight slumber
  Were not meant for man alive.

Clay lies still, but blood's a rover;
  Breath's a ware that will not keep.
Up, lad: when the journey's over
  There'll be time enough to sleep.

1896

To an Athlete Dying Young

The time you won your town the race
We chaired you through the market-place;
Man and boy stood cheering by,
And home we brought you shoulder-high.

Today, the road all runners come,
Shoulder-high we bring you home,
And set you at your threshold down,
Townsman of a stiller town.

Smart lad, to slip betimes away
From fields where glory does not stay
And early though the laurel grows
It withers quicker than the rose.

Eyes the shady night has shut
Cannot see the record cut,
And silence sounds no worse than cheers
After earth has stopped the ears:

Now you will not swell the rout
Of lads that wore their honors out,
Runners whom renown outran
And the name died before the man.

So set, before its echoes fade,
The fleet foot on the sill of shade,
And hold to the low lintel up
The still-defended challenge-cup.

And round that early-laureled head
Will flock to gaze the strengthless dead,
And find unwithered on its curls
The garland briefer than a girl's.

1896

On Wenlock Edge the Wood's in Trouble

On Wenlock Edge the wood's in trouble;
  His forest fleece the Wrekin heaves;
The gale, it plies the saplings double,
  And thick on Severn snow the leaves.

ON WENLOCK EDGE. **Title:** a ridge in Shropshire next to the Severn River. **2. Wrekin:** a hill next to Wenlock.

'Twould blow like this through holt and hanger
  When Uricon the city stood:
'Tis the old wind in the old anger,
  But then it threshed another wood.

Then, 'twas before my time, the Roman
  At yonder heaving hill would stare:
The blood that warms an English yeoman,
  The thoughts that hurt him, they were there.

There, like the wind through woods in riot,
  Through him the gale of life blew high;
The tree of man was never quiet:
  Then 'twas the Roman, now 'tis I.

The gale, it plies the saplings double,
  It blows so hard, 'twill soon be gone:
To-day the Roman and his trouble
  Are ashes under Uricon.

1896

With Rue My Heart Is Laden

With rue my heart is laden
  For golden friends I had,
For many a rose-lipt maiden
  And many a lightfoot lad.

By brooks too broad for leaping
  The lightfoot boys are laid;
The rose-lipt girls are sleeping
  In fields where roses fade.

1896

"Terence, This Is Stupid Stuff . . ."

  "Terence, this is stupid stuff:
You eat your victuals fast enough;
There can't be much amiss, 'tis clear,
To see the rate you drink your beer.
But oh, good Lord, the verse you make,
It gives a chap the belly-ache.
The cow, the old cow, she is dead;

5. holt: wooded hill. **6. Uricon:** a Roman city that had once stood in the area. "TERENCE, THIS IS STUPID STUFF . . ." **Title:** Housman addresses himself thus. His original title for *A Shropshire Lad* was *The Poems of Terence Hearsay.*

It sleeps well, the hornèd head:
We poor lads, 'tis our turn now
To hear such tunes as killed the cow.
Pretty friendship 'tis to rhyme
Your friends to death before their time
Moping melancholy mad:
Come, pipe a tune to dance to, lad."

Why, if 'tis dancing you would be,
There's brisker pipes than poetry.
Say, for what were hop-yards meant,
Or why was Burton built on Trent?
Oh many a peer of England brews
Livelier liquor than the Muse,
And malt does more than Milton can
To justify God's ways to man.
Ale, man, ale's the stuff to drink
For fellows whom it hurts to think:
Look into the pewter pot
To see the world as the world's not.
And faith, 'tis pleasant till 'tis past:
The mischief is that 'twill not last.

Oh I have been to Ludlow fair
And left my necktie God knows where,
And carried halfway home, or near,
Pints and quarts of Ludlow beer:
Then the world seemed none so bad,
And I myself a sterling lad;
And down in lovely muck I've lain,
Happy till I woke again.
Then I saw the morning sky:
Heigho, the tale was all a lie;
The world, it was the old world yet,
I was I, my things were wet,
And nothing now remained to do
But begin the game anew.

Therefore, since the world has still
Much good, but much less good than ill,
And while the sun and moon endure
Luck's a chance, but trouble's sure,
I'd face it as a wise man would,
And train for ill and not for good.
'Tis true, the stuff I bring for sale
Is not so brisk a brew as ale:
Out of a stem that scored the hand
I wrung it in a weary land.
But take it: if the smack is sour,
The better for the embittered hour;
It should do good to heart and head

When your soul is in my soul's stead;
And I will friend you, if I may,
In the dark and cloudy day.

There was a king reigned in the East:
There, when kings will sit to feast,
They get their fill before they think
With poisoned meat and poisoned drink.
He gathered all that springs to birth
From the many-venomed earth;
First a little, thence to more,
He sampled all her killing store;
And easy, smiling, seasoned sound,
Sate the king when healths went round.
They put arsenic in his meat
And stared aghast to watch him eat;
They poured strychnine in his cup
And shook to see him drink it up:
They shook, they stared as white's their shirt:
Them it was their poison hurt.
—I tell the tale that I heard told.
Mithridates, he died old.

1896

Rudyard Kipling

(1865–1936)

One of the most prolific and skillful writers of his generation, Kipling produced novels, short stories, and marvelous books for children, such as the two *Jungle Books* (1894–95) and *Kim* (1901). Born in India, he was educated in England and then returned to India to work as a journalist. His early stories caught the atmosphere and ways of life of the subcontinent with unrivaled vividness. He settled eventually in England and lived as a successful author. His poems were enormously popular, for the characters and stories they presented were interesting and the verse had an irresistible swing. Moreover, readers could easily sympathize with Kipling's sense of life as ruthless competition and with his praise of hard work, prudence, discipline, duty, and the acceptance of responsibility—virtues which, in Kipling's opinion, were necessary for survival in a dangerous world.

76. Mithridates: The king of Pontus (120–63 B.C.) described earlier in this stanza.

Of such a world and the necessities it dictates, the experiences of the army in India provided a metaphor, and a great many of Kipling's poems present incidents of army life. The fine ballad on the hanging of a soldier named "Danny Deever" illustrates that while Kipling accepted the necessity of discipline, he was by no means insensitive to its tragic cost; the emotional burden of the poem is intense and ambivalent. The famous hymn "Recessional" refutes the common belief that Kipling advocated power only. Man's ineluctable responsibility for the human order must be guided by moral principle and religious faith.

Danny Deever

"What are the bugles blowin' for?" said Files-on-Parade.
"To turn you out, to turn you out," the Color-Sergeant said.
"What makes you look so white, so white?" said Files-on-Parade.
"I'm dreadin' what I've got to watch," the Color-Sergeant said.
  For they're hangin' Danny Deever, you can hear the Dead March
      play,
  The Regiment's in 'ollow square—they're hangin' him today;
  They've taken of his buttons off an' cut his stripes away,
  An they're hangin' Danny Deever in the mornin'.

"What makes the rear rank breathe so 'ard?" said Files-on-Parade.
"It's bitter cold, it's bitter cold," the Color-Sergeant said.
"What makes that front-rank man fall down?" said Files-on-Parade.
"A touch o' sun, a touch o' sun," the Color-Sergeant said.
  They are hangin' Danny Deever, they are marchin' of 'im round,
  They 'ave 'alted Danny Deever by 'is coffin on the ground;
  An' 'e'll swing in 'arf a minute for a sneakin' shootin' hound—
  O they're hangin' Danny Deever in the mornin'!

"'Is cot was right-'and cot to mine," said Files-on-Parade.
"'E's sleepin' out an' far tonight," the Color-Sergeant said.
"I've drunk 'is beer a score o' times," said Files-on-Parade.
"'E's drinkin bitter beer alone," the Color-Sergeant said.
  They are hangin' Danny Deever, you must mark 'im to 'is place,
  For 'e shot a comrade sleepin'—you must look 'im in the face;
  Nine 'undred of 'is county an' the Regiment's disgrace,
  While they're hangin' Danny Deever in the mornin'.

DANNY DEEVER. **1. Files-on-Parade:** a common soldier (a private). **2. Color-Sergeant:** the ranking noncommissioned officer of a company. **6. 'ollow square:** formation used for ceremonial occasions. **23. county:** Regiments in the British army at the time were often recruited from and named after particular counties.

"What's that so black agin the sun?" said Files-on-Parade.
"It's Danny fightin' 'ard for life," the Color-Sergeant said.
"What's that that whimpers over'ead?" said Files-on-Parade.
"It's Danny's soul that's passin' now," the Color-Sergeant said.
  For they're done with Danny Deever, you can 'ear the quickstep
      play,
  The Regiment's in column, an' they're marchin' us away;
  Ho! the young recruits are shakin', an' they'll want their beer
      today,
  After hangin' Danny Deever in the mornin'!

1890

Recessional

1897

God of our fathers, known of old,
  Lord of our far-flung battle-line,
Beneath whose awful Hand we hold
  Dominion over palm and pine—
Lord God of Hosts, be with us yet,
Lest we forget—lest we forget!

The tumult and the shouting dies;
  The Captains and the Kings depart:
Still stands Thine ancient sacrifice,
  An humble and a contrite heart.
Lord God of Hosts, be with us yet,
Lest we forget—lest we forget!

Far-called, our navies melt away;
  On dune and headland sinks the fire:
Lo, all our pomp of yesterday
  Is one with Nineveh and Tyre!
Judge of the Nations, spare us yet,
Lest we forget—lest we forget!

RECESSIONAL. **Title:** a hymn sung at the end of a service in the Church of England. **6. forget:** "Then beware lest thou forget the Lord" (Deuteronomy 6:12). **10. contrite heart:** Kipling echoes Psalms 51:17: "The sacrifices of God are a broken spirit: a broken and a contrite heart, O God, thou wilt not despise." **16. Nineveh and Tyre:** once great capitals of ancient empires. Nineveh, capital of the Assyrian Empire, is buried under the sands of the desert. Tyre was the great trading city of Phoenicia, on the eastern coast of the Mediterranean. Only a small town, built on its site, remains.

If, drunk with sight of power, we loose
  Wild tongues that have not Thee in awe,
Such boastings as the Gentiles use,
  Or lesser breeds without the Law—
Lord God of Hosts, be with us yet,
Lest we forget—lest we forget!

For heathen heart that puts her trust
  In reeking tube and iron shard,
All valiant dust that builds on dust,
  And guarding, calls not Thee to guard,
For frantic boast and foolish word—
Thy mercy on Thy People, Lord!

1899

William Butler Yeats

(1865–1939)

A descendant of English families long settled in Ireland, Yeats grew up in London and in a suburb of Dublin, and spent summers with his grandparents in Sligo on the west coast of Ireland. The landscape of the countryside around Sligo recurs in his poetry throughout his life. "The Lake Isle of Innisfree," for example, is near Sligo, and Yeats had seen there the glimmering and purple light the poem describes.

In 1889 he met the beautiful Maud Gonne and was in love with her for at least the next ten years. She would not accept him, but neither would she decisively reject him. To her Yeats addressed many famous love poems, such as "When You Are Old." Ireland was at this time ruled by Great Britain, but a nationalist revolutionary movement had developed, and Maud Gonne was wholly dedicated to this cause. Partly as a way of wooing her, Yeats agitated for the independence of Ireland. He also attempted to create an Irish national literature, one that would express the history, folklore, and imagination of the Irish people. "The Song of Wandering Aengus" is typical of many poems he composed at this time in which a private emotion—his love for Maud Gonne—is expressed through Irish mythology.

The mystical and occult elements of this poem reflect still another passion of Yeats in the 1890s. He was a devoted student of occult lore—

19–22: If, drunk . . . Law: Kipling echoes Romans 2:14.

magic, astrology, alchemy, spiritualism, theosophy, Rosicrucianism, and the like—and he believed, or wished to believe, that the symbols central to such hermetic traditions invoked spiritual realities. Moreover, he developed a technique of what he called "reverie." He would concentrate on a symbol, in hope of evoking other symbols. He did not, in such moments, seek to interpret the symbols, but simply allowed them to fill his mind, for he assumed that through such symbols he might be in touch with profound truths which the rational, interpreting part of the mind could not grasp. Such truths could not be expressed in discursive or generalizing language—only in the symbol itself—for even if it was not talismanic or magical, a symbol, such as the moon, the rose, or the cross, evoked innumerable associations and implications. Consequently, a poem containing such symbols acquired a depth and density of connotation greater than even the poet might know. "A hundred generations," Yeats said, "might write out what seemed the meaning . . . and they would write different meanings." And in a 1900 essay on Shelley he argued that "It is only by ancient symbols, by symbols that have numberless meanings besides the one or two the writer lays an emphasis upon, or the half-score he knows of," that poetry can "escape from the barrenness and shallowness of a too conscious arrangement, into the abundance and depth of Nature."

His lyrics in the 1890s had made Yeats famous and widely imitated, but gradually after 1900 he became dissatisfied with his early style, which now seemed to him vague, dreamy, and limited in mood to plaintiveness and Romantic idealism. Many things contributed to this dissatisfaction and aided him to change his style. He was manager of the Abbey Theater in Dublin and composed plays for it. Writing for the stage forced him to seek a direct, idiomatic speech. Although he was becoming disillusioned with Irish nationalist politics, his long immersion in them had given him a new idea of his own character. He no longer seemed to himself a dreamy man of contemplation and reverie, but one capable of hard, effective action. When Maud Gonne married another man in 1903, Yeats felt that in all the years of his idealistic devotion to her he had been living in a fool's dream. After this shock his emotions were much embittered. The change in his style was gradual, but by 1914 his imagery had become more concrete and realistic; his diction, syntax, and versification were closer to the spoken idiom; and his lyrics could express anger, contempt, and sardonic irony as readily as praise, reverence, devotion, or longing. Although it dates from a later period, "The Scholars" illustrates the breakthrough he had now accomplished, in which he was able to speak in poetry as from the whole man.

Lyrics of pithy, colloquial utterance were opposite to Yeats's earlier mode, the impersonal lyric of reverie that evoked symbols. But by 1917

Yeats had synthesized these two styles. The setting of "The Wild Swans at Coole," for example, is a lake at Coole Park, the home of a close friend named Lady Gregory. Yeats would actually have walked through the woods to the lake, and watched the drifting swans on the water at twilight, just as the poem describes. His diction, although slightly heightened in this poem, remains close to that of ordinary speech, and his rhythm has the slight irregularities and awkwardnesses that suggest spontaneous conversation. In these respects the poem belongs to the type of lyric Yeats called "personal utterance." Yet at the same time everything Yeats described in this apparently naturalistic scene—the swans, the water, the dry paths, the stones—was for him symbolic. Water, for example, symbolized natural, passionate life for Yeats, and dry paths an antithetical opposite associated with old age and with occult wisdom from the realm of the dead. The symbolic implications of the imagery give the poem an enormously greater depth, complexity, and intellectual excitement than it would otherwise have.

Yet if we read only "The Wild Swans at Coole," we would not fully perceive that its images are symbolic, and of course we would not understand what their implications might be. We grasp the poem more deeply, in other words, if we know many other poems by Yeats. His imagination was retentive and associative to an incredible degree, and as we read through his work, we find that the same or similar images recur, with a growing nexus of meanings and connotations. Since the poems included in this anthology are a limited selection from Yeats, they cannot fully illustrate this aspect of his poetry. But one might compare the image of the swan in "The Wild Swans at Coole" with that in "Among School Children" and "Leda and the Swan"; or of fire in "Leda and the Swan," "Sailing to Byzantium," and "Byzantium"; or of the coming of Christ in "The Magi," "The Second Coming," and "Two Songs from a Play"; or of the animal, human, aesthetic (the work of art), and supernatural in "The Magi," "The Second Coming," "Leda and the Swan," "Among School Children," "Sailing to Byzantium," and "Byzantium."

Although Yeats was already the greatest poet of his generation, his achievement reached new heights in the 1920s and 1930s. In such poems as "Byzantium" and "Two Songs from a Play," he concentrated on impersonal symbols, as he often had in the 1890s, but in other poems the symbol was only one element in a debate. In "Sailing to Byzantium," for example, the city of Byzantium symbolizes a life devoted to art and intellect and is appropriate to old age. The opposite life is that of nature and passion. Yeats chooses Byzantium, but the intense emotional drama of the poem lies in his bitter awareness that he is himself old. He must celebrate Byzantium and voyage to it, for the life of the heart and senses is now closed to him. "Young," as he says in "After Long Silence," "We loved each other and were ignorant."

Yeats married in 1917, and had much domestic happiness in his family. When Ireland became an independent country, he served for four years as a Senator. He was awarded the Nobel Prize in 1923. He was the only poet of the late Victorian world who radically transformed his style and became an even greater poet in the new age of High Modernism.

The Lake Isle of Innisfree

I will arise and go now, and go to Innisfree,
And a small cabin build there, of clay and wattles made:
Nine bean-rows will I have there, a hive for the honey-bee,
And live alone in the bee-loud glade.

And I shall have some peace there, for peace comes dropping slow,
Dropping from the veils of the morning to where the cricket sings;
There midnight's all a glimmer, and noon a purple glow,
And evening full of the linnet's wings.

I will arise and go now, for always night and day
I hear lake water lapping with low sounds by the shore;
While I stand on the roadway, or on the pavements gray,
I hear it in the deep heart's core.

1892

When You Are Old

When you are old and gray and full of sleep,
And nodding by the fire, take down this book,
And slowly read, and dream of the soft look
Your eyes had once, and of their shadows deep;

How many loved your moments of glad grace,
And loved your beauty with love false or true,
But one man loved the pilgrim soul in you,
And loved the sorrows of your changing face;

And bending down beside the glowing bars,
Murmur, a little sadly, how Love fled
And paced upon the mountains overhead
And hid his face amid a crowd of stars.

1893

THE LAKE ISLE OF INNISFREE. **Title:** a small island (the word means "Heather Island" in Irish) in a lake near Sligo in West Ireland. **2. wattles:** interwoven twigs.

The Song of Wandering Aengus

I went out to the hazel wood,
Because a fire was in my head,
And cut and peeled a hazel wand,
And hooked a berry to a thread;
And when white moths were on the wing,
And moth-like stars were flickering out,
I dropped the berry in a stream
And caught a little silver trout.

When I had laid it on the floor
I went to blow the fire aflame,
But something rustled on the floor,
And some one called me by my name:
It had become a glimmering girl
With apple blossom in her hair
Who called me by my name and ran
And faded through the brightening air.

Though I am old with wandering
Through hollow lands and hilly lands,
I will find out where she has gone,
And kiss her lips and take her hands;
And walk among long dappled grass,
And pluck till time and times are done
The silver apples of the moon,
The golden apples of the sun.

1899

The Magi

Now as at all times I can see in the mind's eye,
In their stiff, painted clothes, the pale unsatisfied ones
Appear and disappear in the blue depth of the sky
With all their ancient faces like rain-beaten stones,
And all their helms of silver hovering side by side,
And all their eyes still fixed, hoping to find once more,
Being by Calvary's turbulence unsatisfied,
The uncontrollable mystery on the bestial floor.

1914

THE SONG OF WANDERING AENGUS. **Title:** Angus Og was the ancient Irish god of love and beauty. **3. hazel wand:** In Irish myth, the hazel was the tree of knowledge. A branch of it therefore had magical properties (for example, in the use of a hazel prong to find the existence of water). THE MAGI. **Title:** a priestly caste in ancient Persia. The "three wise men," who came to worship the newly born Christ, were Magi. **7. Calvary's turbulence:** the crucifixion of Christ on Calvary. **8. mystery . . . floor:** mystery of Christ's birth in the stable at Bethlehem, "uncontrollable" because it changed history irrevocably.

Easter 1916

I have met them at close of day
Coming with vivid faces
From counter or desk among gray
Eighteenth-century houses.
I have passed with a nod of the head
Or polite meaningless words,
Or have lingered awhile and said
Polite meaningless words,
And thought before I had done
Of a mocking tale or a gibe
To please a companion
Around the fire at the club,
Being certain that they and I
But lived where motley is worn:
All changed, changed utterly:
A terrible beauty is born.

That woman's days were spent
In ignorant good will,
Her nights in argument
Until her voice grew shrill.
What voice more sweet than hers
When, young and beautiful,
She rode to harriers?
This man had kept a school
And rode our wingèd horse;
This other his helper and friend
Was coming into his force;
He might have won fame in the end,
So sensitive his nature seemed,
So daring and sweet his thought.
This other man I had dreamed
A drunken, vainglorious lout.
He had done most bitter wrong
To some who are near my heart,
Yet I number him in the song;
He, too, has resigned his part
In the casual comedy;

EASTER 1916. **Title:** An uprising of Irish Nationalists on Easter Monday, 1916, was forcibly suppressed by the British; its leaders, including the four mentioned here, were executed. **17. That woman:** Countess Constance Markiewicz (Gore-Booth was her maiden name), famous for her beauty and horsemanship, took a prominent part in the uprising. **24. This man:** Patrick Pearse, schoolteacher and poet-spokesman (hence "rode our wingèd horse"). **26. This other:** Thomas MacDonagh, writer and teacher. **31. other man:** John MacBride, who had married Maud Gonne, whom Yeats loved. MacBride was separated from her because of his drinking.

He, too, has been changed in his turn,
Transformed utterly:
A terrible beauty is born.

Hearts with one purpose alone
Through summer and winter seem
Enchanted to a stone
To trouble the living stream.
The horse that comes from the road,
The rider, the birds that range
From cloud to tumbling cloud,
Minute by minute they change;
A shadow of cloud on the stream
Changes minute by minute;
A horse-hoof slides on the brim,
And a horse plashes within it;
The long-legged moor-hens dive,
And hens to moor-cocks call;
Minute by minute they live:
The stone's in the midst of all.

Too long a sacrifice
Can make a stone of the heart.
O when may it suffice?
That is Heaven's part, our part
To murmur name upon name,
As a mother names her child
When sleep at last has come
On limbs that had run wild.
What is it but nightfall?
No, no, not night but death;
Was it needless death after all?
For England may keep faith
For all that is done and said.
We know their dream; enough
To know they dreamed and are dead;
And what if excess of love
Bewildered them till they died?
I write it out in a verse—
MacDonagh and MacBride
And Connolly and Pearse
Now and in time to be,
Wherever green is worn,
Are changed, changed utterly:
A terrible beauty is born.

1916

68. England . . . faith: England had promised Home Rule to Ireland.

The Wild Swans at Coole

The trees are in their autumn beauty,
The woodland paths are dry,
Under the October twilight the water
Mirrors a still sky;
Upon the brimming water among the stones
Are nine-and-fifty swans.

The nineteenth autumn has come upon me
Since I first made my count;
I saw, before I had well finished,
All suddenly mount
And scatter wheeling in great broken rings
Upon their clamorous wings.

I have looked upon those brilliant creatures,
And now my heart is sore.
All's changed since I, hearing at twilight,
The first time on this shore,
The bell-beat of their wings above my head,
Trod with a lighter tread.

Unwearied still, lover by lover,
They paddle in the cold
Companionable streams or climb the air;
Their hearts have not grown old;
Passion or conquest, wander where they will,
Attend upon them still.

But now they drift on the still water,
Mysterious, beautiful;
Among what rushes will they build,
By what lake's edge or pool
Delight men's eyes when I awake some day
To find they have flown away?

1917

The Scholars

Bald heads forgetful of their sins,
Old, learned, respectable bald heads
Edit and annotate the lines
That young men, tossing on their beds,
Rhymed out in love's despair
To flatter beauty's ignorant ear.

THE WILD SWANS AT COOLE. **Title:** Coole Park was the home of Yeats's friend and patroness, Lady Gregory.

All shuffle there; all cough in ink;
All wear the carpet with their shoes;
All think what other people think;
All know the man their neighbor knows.
Lord, what would they say
Did their Catullus walk that way?

1917

A Deep-Sworn Vow

Others because you did not keep
That deep-sworn vow have been friends of mine;
Yet always when I look death in the face,
When I clamber to the heights of sleep,
Or when I grow excited with wine,
Suddenly I meet your face.

1919

The Second Coming

Turning and turning in the widening gyre
The falcon cannot hear the falconer;
Things fall apart; the center cannot hold;
Mere anarchy is loosed upon the world,
The blood-dimmed tide is loosed, and everywhere
The ceremony of innocence is drowned;
The best lack all conviction, while the worst
Are full of passionate intensity.

Surely some revelation is at hand;
Surely the Second Coming is at hand.
The Second Coming! Hardly are those words out
When a vast image out of *Spiritus Mundi*
Troubles my sight: somewhere in sands of the desert
A shape with lion body and the head of a man,

THE SCHOLARS. **12. Catullus:** Latin poet, known for his fervent love lyrics. THE SECOND COMING. **Title:** The Second Coming refers traditionally to the coming of Christ as judge on the last day. According to the esoteric lore Yeats expounded in his prose work, *A Vision*, every cycle of history lasts 2000 years ("twenty centuries," line 19) and begins with the coming of a god. The god envisioned in this poem is ironically different from the figure of Christ traditionally expected and alluded to in the title. **1. gyre:** the widening spiral of the falcon's upward flight; a symbol of Yeats's cyclical view of history. The widening of the gyre also indicates the falconer's loss of control over the falcon. **12. *Spiritus Mundi*:** spirit of the world. **14. shape . . . man:** a sphinx-like creature, half lion, half man.

A gaze blank and pitiless as the sun,
Is moving its slow thighs, while all about it
Reel shadows of the indignant desert birds.
The darkness drops again; but now I know
That twenty centuries of stony sleep
Were vexed to nightmare by a rocking cradle,
And what rough beast, its hour come round at last,
Slouches towards Bethlehem to be born?

1921

Leda and the Swan

A sudden blow: the great wings beating still
Above the staggering girl, her thighs caressed
By the dark webs, her nape caught in his bill,
He holds her helpless breast upon his breast.

How can those terrified vague fingers push
The feathered glory from her loosening thighs?
And how can body, laid in that white rush,
But feel the strange heart beating where it lies?

A shudder in the loins engenders there
The broken wall, the burning roof and tower
And Agamemnon dead.
Being so caught up,
So mastered by the brute blood of the air,
Did she put on his knowledge with his power
Before the indifferent beak could let her drop?

1924

Sailing to Byzantium

1

That is no country for old men. The young
In one another's arms, birds in the trees
—Those dying generations—at their song,

LEDA AND THE SWAN. **Title:** In Greek myth, Leda, a mortal, is loved by Zeus, who visits her in the form of a swan. From their union are born two daughters: Helen, wife of Menelaus, and Clytemnestra, wife of Agamemnon. It was the abduction of Helen that led to the Trojan War (lines 9–10). SAILING TO BYZANTIUM. **Title:** Now Istanbul (Constantinople), Byzantium was the capital of Eastern Christendom, famous for its mosaics and its stylized and non-naturalistic art; for Yeats a symbol of the abstract intellect and skilled artifice, aloof from the natural world of process and decay. **1. That:** the ordinary sensuous world.

The salmon-falls, the mackerel-crowded seas,
Fish, flesh, or fowl, commend all summer long
Whatever is begotten, born, and dies.
Caught in that sensual music all neglect
Monuments of unaging intellect.

2

An aged man is but a paltry thing,
A tattered coat upon a stick, unless
Soul clap its hands and sing, and louder sing
For every tatter in its mortal dress,
Nor is there singing school but studying
Monuments of its own magnificence;
And therefore I have sailed the seas and come
To the holy city of Byzantium.

3

O sages standing in God's holy fire
As in the gold mosaic of a wall,
Come from the holy fire, perne in a gyre,
And be the singing-masters of my soul.
Consume my heart away; sick with desire
And fastened to a dying animal
It knows not what it is; and gather me
Into the artifice of eternity.

4

Once out of nature I shall never take
My bodily form from any natural thing,
But such a form as Grecian goldsmiths make
Of hammered gold and gold enameling
To keep a drowsy Emperor awake;
Or set upon a golden bough to sing
To lords and ladies of Byzantium
Of what is past, or passing, or to come.

1927

17–18. sages . . . wall: like the mosaic figures in the Church of St. Sophia in Constantinople. **19. perne . . . gyre:** A perne is a spool formed by the meeting of two gyres (see note to "Second Coming," line 1). The poet asks the sages to whirl down from their timeless world to this moment in time. **27–29. goldsmiths . . . awake:** In the palace of one of the Byzantine Emperors, said Yeats, "was a tree made of gold and silver, and artificial birds that sang."

Two Songs from a Play

1

I saw a staring virgin stand
Where holy Dionysus died,
And tear the heart out of his side,
And lay the heart upon her hand
And bear that beating heart away;
And then did all the Muses sing
Of Magnus Annus at the spring,
As though God's death were but a play.

Another Troy must rise and set,
Another lineage feed the crow,
Another Argo's painted prow
Drive to a flashier bauble yet.
The Roman Empire stood appalled:
It dropped the reins of peace and war
When that fierce virgin and her Star
Out of the fabulous darkness called.

2

In pity for man's darkening thought
He walked that room and issued thence
In Galilean turbulence;
The Babylonian starlight brought
A fabulous, formless darkness in;
Odor of blood when Christ was slain
Made all Platonic tolerance vain
And vain all Doric discipline.

Everything that man esteems
Endures a moment or a day.
Love's pleasure drives his love away,
The painter's brush consumes his dreams;
The herald's cry, the soldier's tread
Exhaust his glory and his might:
Whatever flames upon the night
Man's own resinous heart has fed.

1927

TWO SONGS FROM A PLAY. **Title:** The play is *The Resurrection* (1931). **2. Dionysus:** Greek god of wine and revelry. **7. Magnus Annus:** "The Great Year" (in Yeats's system a period of 26,000 years). **11. Argo:** the ship that carried Jason and his fellow Argonauts in search of the Golden Fleece. **19. Galilean turbulence:** the Christian religion. **23. Platonic tolerance:** the open mindedness of ancient Greek philosophy. **24. Doric:** pertaining to the early Greeks, especially the Spartans, who were noted for discipline.

Among School Children

1

I walk through the long schoolroom questioning;
A kind old nun in a white hood replies;
The children learn to cipher and to sing,
To study reading-books and histories,
To cut and sew, be neat in everything
In the best modern way—the children's eyes
In momentary wonder stare upon
A sixty-year-old smiling public man.

2

I dream of a Ledaean body, bent
Above a sinking fire, a tale that she
Told of a harsh reproof, or trivial event
That changed some childish day to tragedy—
Told, and it seemed that our two natures blent
Into a sphere from youthful sympathy,
Or else, to alter Plato's parable,
Into the yolk and white of the one shell.

3

And thinking of that fit of grief or rage
I look upon one child or t'other there
And wonder if she stood so at that age—
For even daughters of the swan can share
Something of every paddler's heritage—
And had that color upon cheek or hair,
And thereupon my heart is driven wild:
She stands before me as a living child.

4

Her present image floats into the mind—
Did Quattrocento finger fashion it
Hollow of cheek as though it drank the wind
And took a mess of shadows for its meat?
And I though never of Ledaean kind
Had pretty plumage once—enough of that,
Better to smile on all that smile, and show
There is a comfortable kind of old scarecrow.

AMONG SCHOOL CHILDREN. **1. questioning:** As an Irish Senator, one of Yeats's tasks was to visit schools. **9. Ledaean body:** a body like Leda's (see "Leda and the Swan"). **15. Plato's parable:** In Plato's *Symposium,* there is a parable that human beings were originally both male and female and were then divided into halves, each of which longs to be reunited with its original half. **26. Quattrocento finger:** the skill of a fifteenth-century Italian painter.

5

What youthful mother, a shape upon her lap
Honey of generation had betrayed,
And that must sleep, shriek, struggle to escape
As recollection or the drug decide,
Would think her son, did she but see that shape
With sixty or more winters on its head,
A compensation for the pang of his birth,
Or the uncertainty of his setting forth?

6

Plato thought nature but a spume that plays
Upon a ghostly paradigm of things;
Solider Aristotle played the taws
Upon the bottom of a king of kings;
World-famous golden-thighed Pythagoras
Fingered upon a fiddle-stick or strings
What a star sang and careless Muses heard:
Old clothes upon old sticks to scare a bird.

7

Both nuns and mothers worship images,
But those the candles light are not as those
That animate a mother's reveries,
But keep a marble or a bronze repose.
And yet they too break hearts—O Presences
That passion, piety or affection knows,
And that all heavenly glory symbolize—
O self-born mockers of man's enterprise;

8

Labor is blossoming or dancing where
The body is not bruised to pleasure soul,
Nor beauty born out of its own despair,
Nor blear-eyed wisdom out of midnight oil.
O chestnut-tree, great-rooted blossomer,

33. shape: baby. **34. Honey of generation:** pleasure of sexual intercourse. **41–42. Plato . . . things:** The ultimate reality for Plato consists of ideal forms (paradigms), the natural world being a mere flux that plays upon them. **43–44. Solider Aristotle . . . kings:** "Solider" because, as contrasted with Plato, he believed that reality consisted not of ideal forms but in the union of form with matter. He was tutor to Alexander the Great ("king of kings") when Alexander was a boy, and is said to have had to thrash his pupil with a leather strap ("taws"). **45. Pythagoras:** Greek philosopher who taught that the universe, like music, was harmoniously ordered in a mathematical way. He was said to have had a golden thigh. **49. Both . . . images:** Nuns worship before images of saints; mothers before images of their children. **56. mockers:** The images mock us because we can never reach the ideal they represent.

Are you the leaf, the blossom or the bole?
O body swayed to music, O brightening glance,
How can we know the dancer from the dance?

1927

Byzantium

The unpurged images of day recede;
The Emperor's drunken soldiery are abed;
Night resonance recedes, night-walkers' song
After great cathedral gong;
A starlit or a moonlit dome disdains
All that man is,
All mere complexities,
The fury and the mire of human veins.

Before me floats an image, man or shade,
Shade more than man, more image than a shade;
For Hades' bobbin bound in mummy-cloth
May unwind the winding path;
A mouth that has no moisture and no breath
Breathless mouths may summon;
I hail the superhuman;
I call it death-in-life and life-in-death.

Miracle, bird or golden handiwork,
More miracle than bird or handiwork,
Planted on the starlit golden bough,
Can like the cocks of Hades crow,
Or, by the moon embittered, scorn aloud
In glory of changeless metal
Common bird or petal
And all complexities of mire or blood.

At midnight on the Emperor's pavement flit
Flames that no faggot feeds, nor steel has lit,
Nor storm disturbs, flames begotten of flame,
Where blood-begotten spirits come
And all complexities of fury leave,
Dying into a dance,
An agony of trance,
An agony of flame that cannot singe a sleeve.

62. bole: trunk. BYZANTIUM. **Title:** See note to "Sailing to Byzantium." **11–12. Hades' bobbin . . . path:** The soul, in the realm of the dead, is like a spool ("bobbin"). It is wrapped around with the mummy cloth of its experience in life, but it may unwind that cloth and find a path to a more purified existence in a timeless world. **14. Breathless mouths:** the mouths of poets breathless with inspiration. **20. cocks of Hades:** heralds of rebirth carved on Roman tombs. **26. Flames:** of the imagination.

Astraddle on the dolphin's mire and blood,
Spirit after spirit! The smithies break the flood,
The golden smithies of the Emperor!
Marbles of the dancing floor
Break bitter furies of complexity,
Those images that yet
Fresh images beget,
That dolphin-torn, that gong-tormented sea.

1932

Crazy Jane Talks with the Bishop

I met the Bishop on the road
And much said he and I.
"Those breasts are flat and fallen now,
Those veins must soon be dry;
Live in a heavenly mansion,
Not in some foul sty."

"Fair and foul are near of kin,
And fair needs foul," I cried.
"My friends are gone, but that's a truth
Nor grave nor bed denied,
Learned in bodily lowliness
And in the heart's pride.

"A woman can be proud and stiff
When on love intent;
But Love has pitched his mansion in
The place of excrement;
For nothing can be sole or whole
That has not been rent."

1933

Crazy Jane and Jack the Journeyman

I know, although when looks meet
I tremble to the bone,
The more I leave the door unlatched
The sooner love is gone,
For love is but a skein unwound
Between the dark and dawn.

A lonely ghost the ghost is
That to God shall come;
I—love's skein upon the ground,

CRAZY JANE AND JACK THE JOURNEYMAN. **7. ghost:** spirit.

My body in the tomb—
Shall leap into the light lost
In my mother's womb.

But were I left to lie alone
In an empty bed,
The skein so bound us ghost to ghost
When he turned his head
Passing on the road that night,
Mine must walk when dead.

1932

After Long Silence

Speech after long silence; it is right,
All other lovers being estranged or dead,
Unfriendly lamplight hid under its shade,
The curtains drawn upon unfriendly night,
That we descant and yet again descant
Upon the supreme theme of Art and Song:
Bodily decrepitude is wisdom; young
We loved each other and were ignorant.

1932

Under Ben Bulben

1

Swear by what the sages spoke
Round the Mareotic Lake
That the Witch of Atlas knew,
Spoke and set the cocks a-crow.

Swear by those horsemen, by those women
Complexion and form prove superhuman,
That pale, long-visaged company

UNDER BEN BULBEN. **Title:** mountain in County Sligo, West Ireland. Beneath it is Drumcliffe Churchyard, where Yeats is buried. **2–3. Mareotic . . . Atlas:** In "The Witch of Atlas," a poem by Shelley, the witch's journey takes her past the Mareotic Lake in Egypt, near Alexandria, the center of the ancient Neoplatonic philosophers. The witch for Yeats was a symbol of timeless beauty, hence what she wrote "Set the cocks a-crow," summoning us to a spiritual rebirth. **5. horsemen:** superhuman beings; the "sidhe" in Irish legend who were thought to ride around Ben Bulben. The poem is saying: Swear by those who are superhuman. The second part then gives "the gist of what they mean" about the existence of an afterlife.

That air in immortality
Completeness of their passions won;
Now they ride the wintry dawn
Where Ben Bulben sets the scene.

Here's the gist of what they mean.

2

Many times man lives and dies
Between his two eternities,
That of race and that of soul,
And ancient Ireland knew it all.
Whether man die in his bed
Or the rifle knocks him dead,
A brief parting from those dear
Is the worst man has to fear.
Though gravediggers' toil is long,
Sharp their spades, their muscles strong,
They but thrust their buried men
Back in the human mind again.

3

You that Mitchel's prayer have heard,
"Send war in our time, O Lord!"
Know that when all words are said
And a man is fighting mad,
Something drops from eyes long blind,
He completes his partial mind,
For an instant stands at ease,
Laughs aloud, his heart at peace.
Even the wisest man grows tense
With some sort of violence
Before he can accomplish fate,
Know his work or choose his mate.

4

Poet and sculptor, do the work,
Nor let the modish painter shirk
What his great forefathers did,
Bring the soul of man to God.
Make him fill the cradles right.

25. Mitchel: John Mitchel, Irish patriot. Yeats quotes his remark: "Give us war in our time, O Lord."

Measurement began our might:
Forms a stark Egyptian thought,
Forms that gentler Phidias wrought.
Michael Angelo left a proof
On the Sistine Chapel roof,
Where but half-awakened Adam
Can disturb globe-trotting Madam
Till her bowels are in heat,
Proof that there's a purpose set
Before the secret working mind:
Profane perfection of mankind.

Quattrocento put in paint
On backgrounds for a God or Saint
Gardens where a soul's at ease;
Where everything that meets the eye,
Flowers and grass and cloudless sky,
Resemble forms that are or seem
When sleepers wake and yet still dream,
And when it's vanished still declare,
With only bed and bedstead there,
That heavens had opened.
Gyres run on;
When that greater dream had gone
Calvert and Wilson, Blake and Claude,
Prepared a rest for the people of God,
Palmer's phrase, but after that
Confusion fell upon our thought.

5

Irish poets, learn your trade,
Sing whatever is well made,
Scorn the sort now growing up
All out of shape from toe to top,
Their unremembering hearts and heads
Base-born products of base beds.
Sing the peasantry, and then

42–44. Measurement . . . Egyptian . . . Phidias: Mathematics ("measurement") began Western art and architecture in Egypt; this developed further in the "gentler," more humanistic art of the Greeks typified by Phidias, the great sculptor of fifth-century Athens. **46–48. Sistine . . . Adam . . . Madam:** In the Sistine Chapel, Michelangelo's painting of the creation shows the naked Adam coming alive; the picture, says Yeats, can arouse the lady tourist. **53. Quattrocento:** fifteenth-century Italian art. **64. Calvert . . . Claude:** four artists who influenced Yeats and provided images for his poetry: Edward Calvert, a nineteenth-century engraver; Richard Wilson, an eighteenth-century landscape painter; William Blake; and Claude Lorraine, the seventeenth-century artist. **65–66. people of God . . . Palmer:** Yeats quotes from a remark by the artist Samuel Palmer (1805–1881) about Blake's illustrations: They provide glimpses that saints have had "of the rest which remains to the people of God."

Hard-riding country gentlemen,
The holiness of monks, and after
Porter-drinkers' randy laughter;
Sing the lords and ladies gay
That were beaten into the clay
Through seven heroic centuries;
Cast your mind on other days
That we in coming days may be
Still the indomitable Irishry.

6

Under bare Ben Bulben's head
In Drumcliff churchyard Yeats is laid.
An ancestor was rector there
Long years ago, a church stands near,
By the road an ancient cross.
No marble, no conventional phrase;
On limestone quarried near the spot
By his command these words are cut:
Cast a cold eye
On life, on death.
Horseman, pass by!

1939

Ernest Dowson

(1867–1900)

A typical English poet of the 1890s, Dowson was strongly influenced by French culture and also by classical poetry in Latin. He was the victim of an erotic obsession, and worshipped a young woman named Adelaide, whom he thought "cold" and inaccessible until, some years having passed, she married a waiter in her father's restaurant. Dowson was tubercular, and further shortened his life by dissipation. His lyrics dwelt on themes—the frustration of love, the brevity of life, the allure of the grave—that arose naturally from his experience, although they were equally suggested by the classical and contemporary

80. seven . . . centuries: the period since the Norman Conquest of Ireland in the twelfth century. **86. ancestor:** John Yeats (1774–1846). **92–94. Cast . . . pass by:** The last three lines of the poem are carved on Yeats's tombstone.

French poetry he greatly admired. He wrote his famous lyric on Cynara in a bar. It has been thought the most complete expression in English of the so-called "Decadent strain" in literature at the end of the nineteenth century.

Vitae Summa Brevis Spem nos Vetat Incohare Longam

They are not long, the weeping and the laughter,
    Love and desire and hate:
I think they have no portion in us after
        We pass the gate.

They are not long, the days of wine and roses:
    Out of a misty dream
Our path emerges for a while, then closes
        Within a dream.

1896

Non Sum Qualis Eram Bonae sub Regno Cynarae

Last night, ah, yesternight, betwixt her lips and mine
There fell thy shadow, Cynara! thy breath was shed
Upon my soul between the kisses and the wine;
And I was desolate and sick of an old passion,
  Yea, I was desolate and bowed my head:
I have been faithful to thee, Cynara! in my fashion.

All night upon mine heart I felt her warm heart beat,
Night-long within mine arms in love and sleep she lay;
Surely the kisses of her bought red mouth were sweet;
But I was desolate and sick of an old passion,
  When I awoke and found the dawn was gray:
I have been faithful to thee, Cynara! in my fashion.

VITAE SUMMA BREVIS. **Title:** The Latin title is from Horace, *Odes,* I. 4: "The shortness of life forbids us to consider a long hope." NON SUM QUALIS. **Title:** Like the preceding title, the Latin sentence is quoted from Horace, *Odes,* IV. 1: "I am not as I was under the reign of the good Cynara."

I have forgot much, Cynara! gone with the wind,
Flung roses, roses riotously with the throng,
Dancing, to put thy pale, lost lilies out of mind;
But I was desolate and sick of an old passion,
  Yea, all the time, because the dance was long:
I have been faithful to thee, Cynara! in my fashion.

I cried for madder music and for stronger wine,
But when the feast is finished and the lamps expire,
Then falls thy shadow, Cynara! the night is thine;
And I am desolate and sick of an old passion,
  Yea hungry for the lips of my desire:
I have been faithful to thee, Cynara! in my fashion.

1896

EDWIN ARLINGTON ROBINSON

(1869–1935)

Growing up in a small town in Maine, Robinson found almost no one to share his interest in poetry during his early years. He formed his highly original style by himself. The sort of contemporary American poetry Robinson would have been familiar with in his teens and twenties was printed in the serious magazines. This poetry usually expressed personal feelings of a conventionally edifying kind in beautiful, melodious words and images. It was the opposite of realistic. Poems of Robinson's such as "Richard Cory," "Reuben Bright," and "Miniver Cheevy," on the other hand, present characters and social environments of the kind found in the realistic novels of the nineteenth century, although almost never in its poetry.

To its first readers, "Miniver Cheevy" would have seemed especially surprizing because its subject—someone who is a failure in life—would have seemed so "unpoetic." The mingling of tenderness and irony in this and many other poems was also unusual at a time when most poetry still maintained the undeviating seriousness that was conventional in the nineteenth century. In its use of Yankee rural character and setting, "Mr. Flood's Party" represents the side of Robinson that Robert Frost caught and made his own.

Richard Cory

Whenever Richard Cory went down town,
We people on the pavement looked at him:
He was a gentleman from sole to crown,
Clean favored, and imperially slim.

And he was always quietly arrayed,
And he was always human when he talked;
But still he fluttered pulses when he said,
"Good-morning," and he glittered when he walked.

And he was rich—yes, richer than a king—
And admirably schooled in every grace:
In fine, we thought that he was everything
To make us wish that we were in his place.

So on we worked, and waited for the light,
And went without the meat, and cursed the bread;
And Richard Cory, one calm summer night,
Went home and put a bullet through his head.

1896

Reuben Bright

Because he was a butcher and thereby
Did earn an honest living (and did right),
I would not have you think that Reuben Bright
Was any more a brute than you or I;
For when they told him that his wife must die,
He stared at them, and shook with grief and fright,
And cried like a great baby half that night,
And made the women cry to see him cry.

And after she was dead, and he had paid
The singers and the sexton and the rest,
He packed a lot of things that she had made
Most mournfully away in an old chest
Of hers, and put some chopped-up cedar boughs
In with them, and tore down the slaughter-house.

1897

Miniver Cheevy

Miniver Cheevy, child of scorn,
  Grew lean while he assailed the seasons;
He wept that he was ever born,
  And he had reasons.

Miniver loved the days of old
  When swords were bright and steeds were prancing;
The vision of a warrior bold
  Would set him dancing.

Miniver sighed for what was not,
  And dreamed, and rested from his labors;
He dreamed of Thebes and Camelot,
  And Priam's neighbors.

Miniver mourned the ripe renown
  That made so many a name so fragrant;
He mourned Romance, now on the town,
  And Art, a vagrant.

Miniver loved the Medici,
  Albeit he had never seen one;
He would have sinned incessantly
  Could he have been one.

Miniver cursed the commonplace
  And eyed a khaki suit with loathing;
He missed the medieval grace
  Of iron clothing.

Miniver scorned the gold he sought,
  But sore annoyed was he without it;
Miniver thought, and thought, and thought,
  And thought about it.

Miniver Cheevy, born too late,
  Scratched his head and kept on thinking;
Miniver coughed, and called it fate,
  And kept on drinking.

1910

MINIVER CHEEVY. **11–12. Thebes . . . Camelot . . . Priam:** The city of Thebes was the setting of many Greek legends; Camelot was the site of King Arthur's court; and Priam was the last King of Troy ("neighbors" included Helen, Hector, and Aeneas). **17. Medici:** family of Renaissance merchants who ruled Florence, famous for their brilliance and help to the arts.

Mr. Flood's Party

Old Eben Flood, climbing alone one night
Over the hill between the town below
And the forsaken upland hermitage
That held as much as he should ever know
On earth again of home, paused warily.
The road was his with not a native near;
And Eben, having leisure, said aloud,
For no man else in Tilbury Town to hear:

"Well, Mr. Flood, we have the harvest moon
Again, and we may not have many more;
The bird is on the wing, the poet says,
And you and I have said it here before.
Drink to the bird." He raised up to the light
The jug that he had gone so far to fill,
And answered huskily: "Well, Mr. Flood,
Since you propose it, I believe I will."

Alone, as if enduring to the end
A valiant armor of scarred hopes outworn,
He stood there in the middle of the road
Like Roland's ghost winding a silent horn.
Below him, in the town among the trees,
Where friends of other days had honored him,
A phantom salutation of the dead
Rang thinly till old Eben's eyes were dim.

Then, as a mother lays her sleeping child
Down tenderly, fearing it may awake,
He set the jug down slowly at his feet
With trembling care, knowing that most things break;
And only when assured that on firm earth
It stood, as the uncertain lives of men
Assuredly did not, he paced away,
And with his hand extended paused again:

"Well, Mr. Flood, we have not met like this
In a long time; and many a change has come
To both of us, I fear, since last it was
We had a drop together. Welcome home!"
Convivially returning with himself,
Again he raised the jug up to the light;
And with an acquiescent quaver said:
"Well, Mr. Flood, if you insist, I might.

MR. FLOOD'S PARTY. **1. bird . . . poet:** a quotation from *The Rubáiyát of Omar Khayyam,* 7:4. **20. Roland . . . horn:** In the French medieval epic, *The Song of Roland,* the hero is supposed to blow his horn as a signal for help from Charlemagne's army. But when Roland is surrounded by the enemy, he refuses to blow his horn until he is dying.

"Only a very little, Mr. Flood—
For auld lang syne. No more, sir; that will do."
So, for the time, apparently it did,
And Eben evidently thought so too;
For soon amid the silver loneliness
Of night he lifted up his voice and sang,
Secure, with only two moons listening,
Until the whole harmonious landscape rang—

"For auld lang syne." The weary throat gave out,
The last word wavered; and the song was done.
He raised again the jug regretfully
And shook his head, and was again alone.
There was not much that was ahead of him,
And there was nothing in the town below—
Where strangers would have shut the many doors
That many friends had opened long ago.

1920

PAUL LAURENCE DUNBAR

(1872–1906)

The first black poet to win a wide audience in the United States, Dunbar usually sentimentalized the lives and characters of black people in a dialect borrowed from the minstrel shows. A realistic representation of the experience of blacks would not have been accepted in Dunbar's time. He suffered morally and psychologically from the necessity of this "accommodation," however, and "We Wear the Mask" has a particular application to his own situation, although of course it also speaks for that of most blacks in his time. He wrote many other poems in conventional English, such as "The Colored Soldiers" and "Black Sampson of Brandywine," but they made little impression on the audience of his day.

We Wear the Mask

We wear the mask that grins and lies,
It hides our cheeks and shades our eyes—
This debt we pay to human guile;
With torn and bleeding hearts we smile,
And mouth with myriad subtleties.

Why should the world be over-wise,
In counting all our tears and sighs?
Nay, let them only see us, while
    We wear the mask.

We smile, but, O great Christ, our cries
To thee from tortured souls arise.
We sing, but oh the clay is vile
Beneath our feet, and long the mile;
But let the world dream otherwise,
    We wear the mask!

1896

Walter de la Mare

(1873–1956)

Walter de la Mare is one of those rare poets who have inspired devotion both from the general reader and from the most sophisticated of their fellow poets. W. H. Auden, for example, greatly admired de la Mare and edited a selection of his work, even though Auden's own poetry was of an utterly different kind. De la Mare is the greatest writer in English of poems for children, although most of his poems are not for children and none of them are for children only. All his writing is pervaded by feelings of mystery and wonder. He brooded on ultimate issues—the nature of time, of identity, of dreams, of death—and whatever he thought about dissolved into uncertainty, although it is an uncertainty shot with intimations. The riddle was among his favorite poetic forms, as in "Old Shellover," and he was also fond of seeming-nonsense verses, as in the lovely "Song of the Mad Prince." The famous "The Listeners" may be a poem on the familiar theme of a quest; if so, the quester receives no answer, although there are "listeners."

Napoleon

"What is the world, O soldiers?
      It is I:
I, this incessant snow,
   This northern sky;
Soldiers, this solitude
   Through which we go
      Is I."

1906

The Listeners

"Is there anybody there?" said the Traveler,
  Knocking on the moonlit door;
And his horse in the silence champed the grasses
  Of the forest's ferny floor:
And a bird flew up out of the turret,
  Above the Traveler's head:
And he smote upon the door again a second time;
  "Is there anybody there?" he said.
But no one descended to the Traveler;
  No head from the leaf-fringed sill
Leaned over and looked into his gray eyes,
  Where he stood perplexed and still.
But only a host of phantom listeners
  That dwelt in the lone house then
Stood listening in the quiet of the moonlight
  To that voice from the world of men:
Stood thronging the faint moonbeams on the dark stair,
  That goes down to the empty hall,
Hearkening in an air stirred and shaken
  By the lonely Traveler's call.
And he felt in his heart their strangeness,
  Their stillness answering his cry,
While his horse moved, cropping the dark turf,
  'Neath the starred and leafy sky;
For he suddenly smote on the door, even
  Louder, and lifted his head:—
"Tell them I came, and no one answered,
  That I kept my word," he said.
Never the least stir made the listeners,
  Though every word he spake
Fell echoing through the shadowiness of the still house
  From the one man left awake:
Ay, they heard his foot upon the stirrup,
  And the sound of iron on stone,
And how the silence surged softly backward,
  When the plunging hoofs were gone.

1912

Old Susan

When Susan's work was done, she'd sit,
With one fat guttering candle lit,
And window opened wide to win
The sweet night air to enter in.
There, with a thumb to keep her place,
She'd read, with stern and wrinkled face,

Her mild eyes gliding very slow
Across the letters to and fro,
While wagged the guttering candle flame
In the wind that through the window came.
And sometimes in the silence she
Would mumble a sentence audibly,
Or shake her head as if to say,
"You silly souls, to act this way!"
And never a sound from night I'd hear,
Unless some far-off cock crowed clear;
Or her old shuffling thumb should turn
Another page; and rapt and stern,
Through her great glasses bent on me,
She'd glance into reality;
And shake her round old silvery head,
With—"You!—I thought you was in bed!"—
Only to tilt her book again,
And rooted in Romance remain.

1912

Miss Loo

When thin-strewn memory I look through,
I see most clearly poor Miss Loo;
Her tabby cat, her cage of birds,
Her nose, her hair, her muffled words,
And how she'd open her green eyes,
As if in some immense surprise,
Whenever as we sat at tea
She made some small remark to me.
It's always drowsy summer when
From out the past she comes again;
The westering sunshine in a pool
Floats in her parlour still and cool;
While the slim bird its lean wires shakes,
As into piercing song it breaks;

Till Peter's pale-green eyes ajar
Dream, wake; wake, dream, in one brief bar.
And I am sitting, dull and shy,
And she with gaze of vacancy,
And large hands folded on the tray,
Musing the afternoon away;
Her satin bosom heaving slow
With sighs that softly ebb and flow,
And her plain face in such dismay,
It seems unkind to look her way:

Until all cheerful back will come
Her gentle gleaming spirit home:
And one would think that poor Miss Loo
Asked nothing else, if she had you.

1912

The Song of the Mad Prince

Who said, "Peacock Pie"?
  The old King to the sparrow:
Who said, "Crops are ripe"?
  Rust to the harrow:
Who said, "Where sleeps she now?
  Where rests she now her head,
Bathed in eve's loveliness"?—
  That's what I said.

Who said, "Ay, mum's the word";
  Sexton to willow:
Who said, "Green dusk for dreams,
  Moss for a pillow"?
Who said, "All Time's delight
  Hath she for narrow bed;
Life's troubled bubble broken"?—
  That's what I said.

1906

Old Shellover

"Come!" said Old Shellover.
"What?" says Creep.
"The horny old Gardener's fast asleep;
The fat cock Thrush
To his nest has gone;
And the dew shines bright
In the rising Moon;
Old Sallie Worm from her hole doth peep:
Come!" said Old Shellover.
"Ay!" said Creep.

1913

ROBERT FROST

(1874–1963)

Although he will always be identified with the New England countryside, Frost was born in San Francisco, where he lived for eleven years until his father died and his mother returned to Lawrence, Massachusetts. Frost attended high school, married, and after two years in college bought a farm in New Hampshire, where he lived with the help of a small legacy from his grandfather. For years his poems were mostly rejected by magazines and no book of his was published. In desperation Frost moved to England in 1912. An English publisher brought out his first volume of lyrics, and this was quickly followed by *North of Boston* (1914), which contained such famous poems as "The Death of the Hired Man," "Mending Wall," and "After Apple-Picking." Frost's success in England quickly spread to the United States, and when he returned home in 1915 he was recognized as one of the leading new poets of the age. He did not always thereafter enjoy the esteem of critics, but he continued to be widely read. He supported himself and his family by college teaching, public readings of his poetry, lectures, and royalties. In his middle and later years he was assailed by domestic sorrows—the insanity of his sister, the death of a daughter and of his wife, and the suicide of his son. In old age he received more and greater honors than had ever before been conferred on a poet in the United States, and he became something of a celebrity. He hoped the recognition given to him might lead to more support for poets generally. As he said in another connection, although poetry "must remain a theft to retain its savour . . . it does seem as if it could be a little more connived at than it is."

Frost's poetic style formed itself by a radical self-limitation. He chose the landscape, people, and spoken idiom of rural New England for his boundaries. His poetry could have, therefore, no grand rhetoric, hypnotic melody, witty conceits, or learned symbolism and allusion, because people did not think or talk that way in the New England countryside. They did not, of course, talk exactly like a Frost poem either, but when we read in Frost's "Birches," "Earth's the right place for love:/ I don't know where it's likely to go better," the lines have the poetic quality that is usually called "voice." In other words, the style of speech or "sound of the sentence" (as Frost would have put it) characterize the speaker. The effect results from a combination of many fine touches. The slightly roughened rhythm seems conversational, and so do the elisions of

"Earth's" and "it's" and the contraction in "don't." The first clause is short, declarative, and monosyllabic, suggesting a speaker whose mind is downright and firmly made up. But the second clause, an indirect question, reveals a slightly humorous, teasing trait of the speaker's character. Such phrases as "right place" and "likely to go better" are generally typical of Frost's colloquial diction, but here, in conjunction with the subject of love, they are surprizing. If someone said, "Farming is likely to go better in the Midwest," the words would sound pleasantly idiomatic but not unusual, but when said of love, "go better" seems strangely understated and practical, especially in a poem. In short, the lines characterize a forthright yet teasingly argumentative and ironical person, one who keeps actualities in mind and refuses to be sentimental.

The attitude of the speaker in "Birches" has enhanced meaning and poetic effect if we are mindful, as Frost was, of the contrast it makes with Romantic attitudes. His poems repeatedly invoke a familiar theme of Romantic poetry in order to develop it in a way that opposes Romanticism. He was a poet in the Romantic tradition who sought to criticize and correct Romantic emotions from a standpoint that seemed to him more realistic. Frost's "The Most of It," for example, interplays with the Wordsworthian theme of a consciousness in nature answering to human consciousness. "Come In" must be read against the background of Keats's "Ode to a Nightingale," for both poems express the allure of the woods, the dark, and the bird singing from within them. "Birches" comments on the Romantic hope to commune with a reality that transcends mortal life. The Romantic poets often expressed this hope in metaphors of ascent, as in Shelley's "To a Skylark," and Frost echoes this in a reduced, gently mocking form by speaking of climbing up a birch tree. Because they state that love does not transcend earth and mortal life, the lines we quoted from "Birches" in the previous paragraph deny a premise or hope of much Romantic love poetry. But unless he had felt strongly pulled toward Romantic beliefs and emotions, Frost would not have been motivated to deny them. Consequently, his poems express ambivalence and self-doubt as much as they do a resolved state of mind.

As is true with every great poet, Frost's achievement had many aspects, and critics have differed in describing it. He is an extremely subtle artist, as we see not only in his manipulation of syntax, diction, and meter, but also in the complex counterpoint of different suggested meanings his lyrics weave. These suggestions are typically quite elusive. In the second line of "After Apple-Picking," for example—"My long two-pointed ladder's sticking through a tree/ Toward heaven still"—we cannot help but wonder how much more than the literal "sky" may be meant by "heaven," and we cannot answer this question definitely. Also, his style reflects the tendencies to "local color" and "poetic realism" that flourished around the turn of the century. "Love, the moon, and murder have poetry in them by common consent," Frost said, "but it's in other places. It's in the axe-handle of a French Canadian woodchopper." The literature of local color often dwelled too fondly on the realities it presented and became sentimental. Frost shared this temptation, but excessive sentimentalism was usually checked by his hard knowledge of life's bleakness. In "Provide, Provide" the speaker advises us to seek money and power so we can buy "friendship" when we need to. The irony is savage, but it would be wrong to think that the poem is merely ironic. It drives us to a shocked recognition of the minimal lives, the dismaying choices to which people are brought. This "dark" awareness in Frost was only gradually recognized and can be emphasized too strongly, but he is certainly among the more pessimistic of the major American poets.

Frost is the finest narrative poet of the twentieth century; "The Death of the Hired Man" and "The Hill Wife" present their stories by different narrative methods, but both are vivid and authentic in setting and psychologically shrewd. Frost was deeply versed in the classics, and his best poems remind many readers of the Roman poet Horace. He has a similar balance and poise of attitude, a mingled sympathy and irony, tenderness, detachment, and uneluded vision. Such poems as "The Road Not Taken" and "Stopping by Woods on a Snowy Evening" are classical in a more general sense. With economy, grace, and perfectly developed metaphor, they express feelings all human beings share. If poetry is read five hundred years from now, Frost is the poet of our time most likely to be remembered.

Mending Wall

Something there is that doesn't love a wall,
That sends the frozen-ground-swell under it,
And spills the upper boulders in the sun;
And makes gaps even two can pass abreast.
The work of hunters is another thing:
I have come after them and made repair
Where they have left not one stone on a stone,
But they would have the rabbit out of hiding,
To please the yelping dogs. The gaps I mean,
No one has seen them made or heard them made,
But at spring mending-time we find them there.
I let my neighbor know beyond the hill;
And on a day we meet to walk the line

And set the wall between us once again.
We keep the wall between us as we go.
To each the boulders that have fallen to each.
And some are loaves and some so nearly balls
We have to use a spell to make them balance:
"Stay where you are until our backs are turned!"
We wear our fingers rough with handling them.
Oh, just another kind of outdoor game,
One on a side. It comes to little more:
There where it is we do not need the wall:
He is all pine and I am apple orchard.
My apple trees will never get across
And eat the cones under his pines, I tell him.
He only says, "Good fences make good neighbors."
Spring is the mischief in me, and I wonder
If I could put a notion in his head:
"*Why* do they make good neighbors? Isn't it
Where there are cows? But here there are no cows.
Before I built a wall I'd ask to know
What I was walling in or walling out,
And to whom I was like to give offense.
Something there is that doesn't love a wall,
That wants it down." I could say "Elves" to him,
But it's not elves exactly, and I'd rather
He said it for himself. I see him there
Bringing a stone grasped firmly by the top
In each hand, like an old-stone savage armed.
He moves in darkness as it seems to me,
Not of woods only and the shade of trees.
He will not go behind his father's saying,
And he likes having thought of it so well
He says again, "Good fences make good neighbors."

1914

After Apple-Picking

My long two-pointed ladder's sticking through a tree
Toward heaven still,
And there's a barrel that I didn't fill
Beside it, and there may be two or three
Apples I didn't pick upon some bough.
But I am done with apple-picking now.
Essence of winter sleep is on the night,
The scent of apples: I am drowsing off.
I cannot rub the strangeness from my sight
I got from looking through a pane of glass
I skimmed this morning from the drinking trough
And held against the world of hoary grass.

It melted, and I let it fall and break.
But I was well
Upon my way to sleep before it fell,
And I could tell
What form my dreaming was about to take.
Magnified apples appear and disappear,
Stem end and blossom end,
And every fleck of russet showing clear.
My instep arch not only keeps the ache,
It keeps the pressure of a ladder-round.
I feel the ladder sway as the boughs bend.
And I keep hearing from the cellar bin
The rumbling sound
Of load on load of apples coming in.
For I have had too much
Of apple-picking: I am overtired
Of the great harvest I myself desired.
There were ten thousand thousand fruit to touch,
Cherish in hand, lift down, and not let fall.
For all
That struck the earth,
No matter if not bruised or spiked with stubble,
Went surely to the cider-apple heap
As of no worth.
One can see what will trouble
This sleep of mine, whatever sleep it is.
Were he not gone,
The woodchuck could say whether it's like his
Long sleep, as I describe its coming on,
Or just some human sleep.

1914

The Death of the Hired Man

Mary sat musing on the lamp-flame at the table
Waiting for Warren. When she heard his step,
She ran on tiptoe down the darkened passage
To meet him in the doorway with the news
And put him on his guard. "Silas is back."
She pushed him outward with her through the door
And shut it after her. "Be kind," she said.
She took the market things from Warren's arms
And set them on the porch, then drew him down
To sit beside her on the wooden steps.

"When was I ever anything but kind to him?
But I'll not have the fellow back," he said.
"I told him so last haying, didn't I?

If he left then, I said, that ended it.
What good is he? Who else will harbor him
At his age for the little he can do?
What help he is there's no depending on.
Off he goes always when I need him most.
He thinks he ought to earn a little pay,
Enough at least to buy tobacco with,
So he won't have to beg and be beholden.
'All right,' I say, 'I can't afford to pay
Any fixed wages, though I wish I could.'
'Someone else can.' 'Then someone else will have to.'
I shouldn't mind his bettering himself
If that was what it was. You can be certain,
When he begins like that, there's someone at him
Trying to coax him off with pocket money,—
In haying time, when any help is scarce.
In winter he comes back to us. I'm done."

"Sh! not so loud: he'll hear you," Mary said.

"I want him to: he'll have to soon or late."

"He's worn out. He's asleep beside the stove.
When I came up from Rowe's I found him here,
Huddled against the barn door fast asleep,
A miserable sight, and frightening, too—
You needn't smile—I didn't recognize him—
I wasn't looking for him—and he's changed.
Wait till you see."

"Where did you say he'd been?"

"He didn't say. I dragged him to the house,
And gave him tea and tried to make him smoke.
I tried to make him talk about his travels.
Nothing would do: he just kept nodding off."

"What did he say? Did he say anything?"

"But little."

"Anything? Mary, confess
He said he'd come to ditch the meadow for me."

"Warren!"

"But did he? I just want to know."

"Of course he did. What would you have him say?
Surely you wouldn't grudge the poor old man
Some humble way to save his self-respect.
He added, if you really care to know,
He meant to clear the upper pasture, too.
That sounds like something you have heard before?
Warren, I wish you could have heard the way

He jumbled everything. I stopped to look
Two or three times—he made me feel so queer—
To see if he was talking in his sleep.
He ran on Harold Wilson—you remember—
The boy you had in haying four years since.
He's finished school, and teaching in his college.
Silas declares you'll have to get him back.
He says they two will make a team for work:
Between them they will lay this farm as smooth!
The way he mixed that in with other things.
He thinks young Wilson a likely lad, though daft
On education—you know how they fought
All through July under the blazing sun,
Silas up on the cart to build the load,
Harold along beside to pitch it on."

"Yes, I took care to keep well out of earshot."

"Well, those days trouble Silas like a dream.
You wouldn't think they would. How some things linger!
Harold's young college boy's assurance piqued him.
After so many years he still keeps finding
Good arguments he sees he might have used.
I sympathize. I know just how it feels
To think of the right thing to say too late.
Harold's associated in his mind with Latin.
He asked me what I thought of Harold's saying
He studied Latin, like the violin,
Because he liked it—that an argument!
He said he couldn't make the boy believe
He could find water with a hazel prong—
Which showed how much good school had ever done him.
He wanted to go over that. But most of all
He thinks if he could have another chance
To teach him how to build a load of hay—"

"I know, that's Silas' one accomplishment.
He bundles every forkful in its place,
And tags and numbers it for future reference,
So he can find and easily dislodge it
In the unloading. Silas does that well.
He takes it out in bunches like big birds' nests.
You never see him standing on the hay
He's trying to lift, straining to lift himself."
"He thinks if he could teach him that, he'd be
Some good perhaps to someone in the world.
He hates to see a boy the fool of books.
Poor Silas, so concerned for other folk,
And nothing to look backward to with pride,
And nothing to look forward to with hope,
So now and never any different."

Part of a moon was falling down the west,
Dragging the whole sky with it to the hills.
Its light poured softly in her lap. She saw it
And spread her apron to it. She put out her hand
Among the harp-like morning-glory strings,
Taut with the dew from garden bed to eaves,
As if she played unheard some tenderness
That wrought on him beside her in the night.
"Warren," she said, "he has come home to die:
You needn't be afraid he'll leave you this time."

"Home," he mocked gently.

"Yes, what else but home?
It all depends on what you mean by home.
Of course he's nothing to us, any more
Than was the hound that came a stranger to us
Out of the woods, worn out upon the trail."

"Home is the place where, when you have to go there,
They have to take you in."

"I should have called it
Something you somehow haven't to deserve."

Warren leaned out and took a step or two,
Picked up a little stick, and brought it back
And broke it in his hand and tossed it by.
"Silas has better claim on us you think
Than on his brother? Thirteen little miles
As the road winds would bring him to his door.
Silas has walked that far no doubt to-day.
Why doesn't he go there? His brother's rich,
A somebody—director in the bank."

"He never told us that."

"We know it though."

"I think his brother ought to help, of course.
I'll see to that if there is need. He ought of right
To take him in, and might be willing to—
He may be better than appearances.
But have some pity on Silas. Do you think
If he had any pride in claiming kin
Or anything he looked for from his brother,
He'd keep so still about him all this time?"

"I wonder what's between them."

"I can tell you.
Silas is what he is—we wouldn't mind him—
But just the kind that kinsfolk can't abide.
He never did a thing so very bad.
He don't know why he isn't quite as good

As anybody. Worthless though he is,
He won't be made ashamed to please his brother."

"*I* can't think Si ever hurt anyone."

"No, but he hurt my heart the way he lay
And rolled his old head on that sharp-edged chair-back.
He wouldn't let me put him on the lounge.
You must go in and see what you can do.
I made the bed up for him there tonight.
You'll be surprised at him—how much he's broken.
His working days are done; I'm sure of it."

"I'd not be in a hurry to say that."

"I haven't been. Go, look, see for yourself.
But, Warren, please remember how it is:
He's come to help you ditch the meadow.
He has a plan. You mustn't laugh at him.
He may not speak of it, and then he may.
I'll sit and see if that small sailing cloud
Will hit or miss the moon."

It hit the moon.
Then there were three there, making a dim row,
The moon, the little silver cloud, and she.

Warren returned—too soon, it seemed to her,
Slipped to her side, caught up her hand and waited.
"Warren?" she questioned.

"Dead," was all he answered.

1914

The Road Not Taken

Two roads diverged in a yellow wood,
And sorry I could not travel both
And be one traveler, long I stood
And looked down one as far as I could
To where it bent in the undergrowth;

Then took the other, as just as fair,
And having perhaps the better claim,
Because it was grassy and wanted wear;
Though as for that, the passing there
Had worn them really about the same,

And both that morning equally lay
In leaves no step had trodden black.
Oh, I kept the first for another day!
Yet knowing how way leads on to way,
I doubted if I should ever come back.

I shall be telling this with a sigh
Somewhere ages and ages hence:
Two roads diverged in a wood, and I—
I took the one less traveled by,
And that has made all the difference.

1916

Birches

When I see birches bend to left and right
Across the lines of straighter darker trees,
I like to think some boy's been swinging them.
But swinging doesn't bend them down to stay
As ice-storms do. Often you must have seen them
Loaded with ice a sunny winter morning
After a rain. They click upon themselves
As the breeze rises, and turn many-colored
As the stir cracks and crazes their enamel.
Soon the sun's warmth makes them shed crystal shells
Shattering and avalanching on the snow-crust—
Such heaps of broken glass to sweep away
You'd think the inner dome of heaven had fallen.
They are dragged to the withered bracken by the load,
And they seem not to break; though once they are bowed
So low for long, they never right themselves:
You may see their trunks arching in the woods
Years afterwards, trailing their leaves on the ground
Like girls on hands and knees that throw their hair
Before them over their heads to dry in the sun.
But I was going to say when Truth broke in
With all her matter-of-fact about the ice-storm,
I should prefer to have some boy bend them
As he went out and in to fetch the cows—
Some boy too far from town to learn baseball,
Whose only play was what he found himself,
Summer or winter, and could play alone.
One by one he subdued his father's trees
By riding them down over and over again
Until he took the stiffness out of them,
And not one but hung limp, not one was left
For him to conquer. He learned all there was
To learn about not launching out too soon
And so not carrying the tree away
Clear to the ground. He always kept his poise
To the top branches, climbing carefully
With the same pains you use to fill a cup
Up to the brim, and even above the brim.
Then he flung outward, feet first, with a swish,

Kicking his way down through the air to the ground.
So was I once myself a swinger of birches.
And so I dream of going back to be.
It's when I'm weary of considerations,
And life is too much like a pathless wood
Where your face burns and tickles with the cobwebs
Broken across it, and one eye is weeping
From a twig's having lashed across it open.
I'd like to get away from earth awhile
And then come back to it and begin over.
May no fate willfully misunderstand me
And half grant what I wish and snatch me away
Not to return. Earth's the right place for love:
I don't know where it's likely to go better.
I'd like to go by climbing a birch tree,
And climb black branches up a snow-white trunk
Toward heaven, till the tree could bear no more,
But dipped its top and set me down again.
That would be good both going and coming back.
One could do worse than be a swinger of birches.

1916

The Hill Wife

I. Loneliness

Her Word

One ought not to have to care
  So much as you and I
Care when the birds come round the house
  To seem to say good-bye;

Or care so much when they come back
  With whatever it is they sing;
The truth being we are as much
  Too glad for the one thing

As we are too sad for the other here—
  With birds that fill their breasts
But with each other and themselves
  And their built or driven nests.

II. House Fear

Always—I tell you this they learned—
Always at night when they returned
To the lonely house from far away
To lamps unlighted and fire gone gray,

They learned to rattle the lock and key
To give whatever might chance to be
Warning and time to be off in flight:
And preferring the out- to the in-door night,
They learned to leave the house-door wide
Until they had lit the lamp inside.

III. The Smile

Her Word

I didn't like the way he went away.
That smile! It never came of being gay.
Still he smiled—did you see him?—I was sure!
Perhaps because we gave him only bread
And the wretch knew from that that we were poor.
Perhaps because he let us give instead
Of seizing from us as he might have seized.
Perhaps he mocked at us for being wed,
Or being very young (and he was pleased
To have a vision of us old and dead).
I wonder how far down the road he's got.
He's watching from the woods as like as not.

IV. The Oft-Repeated Dream

She had no saying dark enough
  For the dark pine that kept
Forever trying the window-latch
  Of the room where they slept.

The tireless but ineffectual hands
  That with every futile pass
Made the great tree seem as a little bird
  Before the mystery of glass!

It never had been inside the room,
  And only one of the two
Was afraid in an oft-repeated dream
  Of what the tree might do.

V. The Impulse

It was too lonely for her there,
  And too wild,
And since there were but two of them,
  And no child,

And work was little in the house,
  She was free,
And followed where he furrowed field,
  Or felled tree.

She rested on a log and tossed
  The fresh chips,
With a song only to herself
  On her lips.

And once she went to break a bough
  Of black alder.
She strayed so far she scarcely heard
  When he called her—

And didn't answer—didn't speak—
  Or return.
She stood, and then she ran and hid
  In the fern.

He never found her, though he looked
  Everywhere,
And he asked at her mother's house
  Was she there.

Sudden and swift and light as that
  The ties gave,
And he learned of finalities
  Besides the grave.

1916

Fire and Ice

Some say the world will end in fire,
Some say in ice.
From what I've tasted of desire
I hold with those who favor fire.
But if it had to perish twice,
I think I know enough of hate
To say that for destruction ice
Is also great
And would suffice.

1923

Nothing Gold Can Stay

Nature's first green is gold,
Her hardest hue to hold.
Her early leaf's a flower;
But only so an hour.

Then leaf subsides to leaf.
So Eden sank to grief,
So dawn goes down to day.
Nothing gold can stay.

1923

Stopping by Woods on a Snowy Evening

Whose woods these are I think I know.
His house is in the village, though;
He will not see me stopping here
To watch his woods fill up with snow.

My little horse must think it queer
To stop without a farmhouse near
Between the woods and frozen lake
The darkest evening of the year.

He gives his harness bells a shake
To ask if there is some mistake.
The only other sound's the sweep
Of easy wind and downy flake.

The woods are lovely, dark and deep,
But I have promises to keep,
And miles to go before I sleep,
And miles to go before I sleep.

1923

The Need of Being Versed in Country Things

The house had gone to bring again
To the midnight sky a sunset glow.
Now the chimney was all of the house that stood,
Like a pistil after the petals go.

The barn opposed across the way,
That would have joined the house in flame
Had it been the will of the wind, was left
To bear forsaken the place's name.

No more it opened with all one end
For teams that came by the stony road
To drum on the floor with scurrying hoofs
And brush the mow with the summer load.

The birds that came to it through the air
At broken windows flew out and in,
Their murmur more like the sigh we sigh
From too much dwelling on what has been.

Yet for them the lilac renewed its leaf,
And the aged elm, though touched with fire;
And the dry pump flung up an awkward arm;
And the fence post carried a strand of wire.

For them there was really nothing sad.
But though they rejoiced in the nest they kept,
One had to be versed in country things
Not to believe the phoebes wept.

1923

Acquainted with the Night

I have been one acquainted with the night.
I have walked out in rain—and back in rain.
I have outwalked the furthest city light.

I have looked down the saddest city lane.
I have passed by the watchman on his beat
And dropped my eyes, unwilling to explain.

I have stood still and stopped the sound of feet
When far away an interrupted cry
Came over houses from another street,

But not to call me back or say good-by;
And further still at an unearthly height
One luminary clock against the sky

Proclaimed the time was neither wrong nor right.
I have been one acquainted with the night.

1928

Spring Pools

These pools that, though in forests, still reflect
The total sky almost without defect,
And like the flowers beside them, chill and shiver,
Will like the flowers beside them soon be gone,
And yet not out by any brook or river,
But up by roots to bring dark foliage on.

The trees that have it in their pent-up buds
To darken nature and be summer woods—
Let them think twice before they use their powers
To blot out and drink up and sweep away
These flowery waters and these watery flowers
From snow that melted only yesterday.

1928

Neither Out Far nor In Deep

The people along the sand
All turn and look one way.
They turn their back on the land.
They look at the sea all day.

As long as it takes to pass
A ship keeps raising its hull;
The wetter ground like glass
Reflects a standing gull.

The land may vary more;
But wherever the truth may be—
The water comes ashore,
And the people look at the sea.

They cannot look out far.
They cannot look in deep.
But when was that ever a bar
To any watch they keep?

1936

Design

I found a dimpled spider, fat and white,
On a white heal-all, holding up a moth
Like a white piece of rigid satin cloth—
Assorted characters of death and blight
Mixed ready to begin the morning right,
Like the ingredients of a witches' broth—
A snow-drop spider, a flower like a froth,
And dead wings carried like a paper kite.

What had that flower to do with being white,
The wayside blue and innocent heal-all?
What brought the kindred spider to that height,

Then steered the white moth thither in the night?
What but design of darkness to appall?—
If design govern in a thing so small.

1936

Provide, Provide

The witch that came (the withered hag)
To wash the steps with pail and rag,
Was once the beauty Abishag,

The picture pride of Hollywood.
Too many fall from great and good
For you to doubt the likelihood.

Die early and avoid the fate.
Or if predestined to die late,
Make up your mind to die in state.

Make the whole stock exchange your own!
If need be occupy a throne,
Where nobody can call *you* crone.

Some have relied on what they knew,
Others on being simply true.
What worked for them might work for you.

No memory of having starred
Atones for later disregard
Or keeps the end from being hard.

Better to go down dignified
With boughten friendship at your side
Than none at all. Provide, provide!

1936

Come In

As I came to the edge of the woods,
Thrush music—hark!
Now if it was dusk outside,
Inside it was dark.

Too dark in the woods for a bird
By sleight of wing
To better its perch for the night,
Though it still could sing.

The last of the light of the sun
That had died in the west
Still lived for one song more
In a thrush's breast.

Far in the pillared dark
Thrush music went—
Almost like a call to come in
To the dark and lament.

But no, I was out for stars;
I would not come in.
I meant not even if asked,
And I hadn't been.

1942

Never Again Would Birds' Song Be the Same

He would declare and could himself believe
That the birds there in all the garden round
From having heard the daylong voice of Eve
Had added to their own an oversound,
Her tone of meaning but without the words.
Admittedly an eloquence so soft
Could only have had an influence on birds
When call or laughter carried it aloft.
Be that as may be, she was in their song.
Moreover her voice upon their voices crossed
Had now persisted in the woods so long
That probably it never would be lost.
Never again would birds' song be the same.
And to do that to birds was why she came.

1942

The Most of It

He thought he kept the universe alone;
For all the voice in answer he could wake
Was but the mocking echo of his own
From some tree-hidden cliff across the lake.
Some morning from the boulder broken beach
He would cry out on life, that what it wants
Is not its own love back in copy speech,
But counter-love, original response.

And nothing ever came of what he cried
Unless it was the embodiment that crashed
In the cliff's talus on the other side,
And then in the far distant water splashed,
But after a time allowed for it to swim,
Instead of proving human when it neared
And someone else additional to him,
As a great buck it powerfully appeared,
Pushing the crumpled water up ahead,
And landed pouring like a waterfall,
And stumbled through the rocks with horny tread,
And forced the underbrush—and that was all.

1942

The Gift Outright

The land was ours before we were the land's.
She was our land more than a hundred years
Before we were her people. She was ours
In Massachusetts, in Virginia,
But we were England's, still colonials,
Possessing what we still were unpossessed by,
Possessed by what we now no more possessed.
Something we were withholding made us weak
Until we found out that it was ourselves
We were withholding from our land of living,
And forthwith found salvation in surrender.
Such as we were we gave ourselves outright
(The deed of gift was many deeds of war)
To the land vaguely realizing westward,
But still unstoried, artless, unenhanced,
Such as she was, such as she would become.

1942

Adelaide Crapsey

(1878–1914)

Adelaide Crapsey, who died of tuberculosis at thirty-five, was already in her twenties an accomplished scholar of versification, meter, and phonetics. She is remembered for her invention of the short lyric form she called the "cinquain," which, as she herself used it, often permits a suggestive, beautifully austere condensation. A cinquain consists of two syllables in the first line, four in the second, six in the third, eight in the fourth, and a drop back to two again in the last. American poets at this time, such as Ezra Pound and Amy Lowell, were becoming familiar with short, concentrated Japanese poems, such as the *haiku,* with three lines, or the *tanka,* with five lines. Although Crapsey invented the cinquain independently, most of her cinquains were written after she had studied the Japanese forms. Her finest poems date from her last months, when she was a patient in a tuberculosis sanatorium at Saranac Lake, New York.

Triad

These be
Three silent things:
The falling snow . . . the hour
Before the dawn . . . the mouth of one
Just dead.

1915

The Warning

Just now,
Out of the strange
Still dusk . . . as strange, as still . . .
A white moth flew. Why am I grown
So cold?

1915

November Night

Listen . . .
With faint dry sound,
Like steps of passing ghosts,
The leaves, frost-crisp'd, break from the trees
And fall.

1918

John Masefield

(1878–1967)

One of the most popular English poets before the First World War, Masefield impressed his contemporaries especially by realistic narrative poems in which he drew on Chaucer for example and inspiration. The following poems, however, represent him as a lyricist; in them he resembles Robert Bridges and the early Yeats in melodious beauty and nostalgic emotion. Like Yeats, Masefield wished to break away from this Romantic style, which to him seemed bookish, in favor of lyrics which expressed active, energetic life. "Sea-Fever" and "Cargoes" were examples of this. He believed that poets since the Romantic period had written "with a restricted sense of what is poetical" and in a "language which the multitudes seldom spoke and often could not understand." As a result, the audience for poetry had been greatly narrowed. If poets wished to recapture the large readership that once existed, they had to reflect the feelings of ordinary men and women, and they had to write for the ear. Masefield was greatly interested in the public performance of poetry, for he believed that in public readings there is a direct contact between the poet and the audience, and that the emotion of the audience is deepened because it is shared.

Sea-Fever

I must go down to the seas again, to the lonely sea and the sky,
And all I ask is a tall ship and a star to steer her by,
And the wheel's kick and the wind's song and the white sail's
    shaking,
And a grey mist on the sea's face and a grey dawn breaking.

I must go down to the seas again, for the call of the running tide
Is a wild call and a clear call that may not be denied;
And all I ask is a windy day with the white clouds flying,
And the flung spray and the blown spume, and the sea-gulls
    crying.

I must go down to the seas again to the vagrant gypsy life,
To the gull's way and the whale's way where the wind's like
    a whetted knife;
And all I ask is a merry yarn from a laughing fellow-rover,
And quiet sleep and a sweet dream when the long trick's over.

1902

Cargoes

Quinquireme of Nineveh from distant Ophir,
Rowing home to haven in sunny Palestine,
With a cargo of ivory,
And apes and peacocks,
Sandalwood, cedarwood, and sweet white wine.

Stately Spanish galleon coming from the Isthmus,
Dipping through the Tropics by the palm-green shores,
With a cargo of diamonds,
Emeralds, amethysts,
Topazes, and cinnamon, and gold moidores.

Dirty British coaster with a salt-caked smoke-stack,
Butting through the Channel in the mad March days,
With a cargo of Tyne coal,
Road-rails, pig-lead,
Firewood, iron-ware, and cheap tin trays.

1910

On Growing Old

Be with me Beauty for the fire is dying,
My dog and I are old, too old for roving,
Man, whose young passion sets the spindrift flying
Is soon too lame to march, too cold for loving.

I take the book and gather to the fire,
Turning old yellow leaves; minute by minute,
The clock ticks to my heart; a withered wire
Moves a thin ghost of music in the spinet.

I cannot sail your seas, I cannot wander
Your cornland, nor your hill-land nor your valleys,
Ever again, nor share the battle yonder
Where the young knight the broken squadron rallies.

Only stay quiet while my mind remembers
The beauty of fire from the beauty of embers.

1919

Carl Sandburg

(1878–1967)

The son of Swedish immigrants, Sandburg worked his way through college and became a journalist. His first volume, *Chicago Poems* (1916), shocked readers who were used to a more formal and genteel type of poetry, for as in "Chicago," he celebrated the city as a strong, sweating worker. In style his poems amalgamated the tradition of Whitman with the new "Imagist" movement created by Ezra Pound. Like most young poets in America at this time he accepted the "Imagist" plea for free verse and for presentation through concrete images, but he was less strict in pursuing the condensed language that was, for Pound, the most important of the Imagist ideals. In subsequent volumes Sandburg dwelt on the lives of midwestern farmers and Pennsylvania steelworkers. All his books were imbued with a strong democratic faith, as one sees in the title of his *The People, Yes* (1936); he also spent fourteen years (1926–39) writing a huge biography of Abraham Lincoln. Throughout his career Sandburg also composed lyrics, such as "Grass" and "Cool Tombs," on ultimate themes.

Chicago

Hog Butcher for the World,
Tool Maker, Stacker of Wheat,
Player with Railroads and the Nation's Freight Handler;
Stormy, husky, brawling,
City of the Big Shoulders:

They tell me you are wicked and I believe them, for I have seen your painted women under the gas lamps luring the farm boys.
And they tell me you are crooked and I answer: Yes, it is true I have seen the gunman kill and go free to kill again.
And they tell me you are brutal and my reply is: On the faces of women and children I have seen the marks of wanton hunger.
And having answered so I turn once more to those who sneer at this my city, and I give them back the sneer and say to them:
Come and show me another city with lifted head singing so proud to be alive and coarse and strong and cunning.
Flinging magnetic curses amid the toil of piling job on job, here is a tall bold slugger set vivid against the little soft cities;
Fierce as a dog with tongue lapping for action, cunning as a savage pitted against the wilderness,

Bareheaded,
Shoveling,
Wrecking,
Planning,
Building, breaking, rebuilding,
Under the smoke, dust all over his mouth, laughing with white teeth,
Under the terrible burden of destiny laughing as a young man laughs,
Laughing even as an ignorant fighter laughs who has never lost a battle,
Bragging and laughing that under his wrist is the pulse, and under his
ribs the heart of the people,
Laughing!
Laughing the stormy, husky, brawling laughter of Youth, half-naked,
sweating, proud to be Hog Butcher, Tool Maker, Stacker of Wheat,
Player with Railroads and Freight Handler to the Nation.

1916

Grass

Pile the bodies high at Austerlitz and Waterloo.
Shovel them under and let me work—
I am the grass; I cover all.

And pile them high at Gettysburg
And pile them high at Ypres and Verdun.
Shovel them under and let me work.
Two years, ten years, and passengers ask the conductor:
What place is this?
Where are we now?

I am the grass.
Let me work.

1918

Cool Tombs

When Abraham Lincoln was shoveled into the tombs, he forgot the
copperheads and the assassin . . . in the dust, in the cool tombs.

GRASS. **1. Austerlitz . . . Waterloo:** At Austerlitz, in Czechoslovakia, Napoleon won a great victory (1805), and at Waterloo, in Belgium, he was decisively defeated by the British under the Duke of Wellington (1815). **4–5. Gettysburg . . . Ypres . . . Verdun:** The three day Battle of Gettysburg was fought July 1–3, 1863. In 1917, during World War I, the terrible Battle of Ypres, in Belgium, was considered a fruitless waste of lives. In the long Battle of Verdun (1916–17), the Allies were successful—but at the cost of over half a million casualties. COOL TOMBS. **1. copperheads:** nickname for northerners who sympathized with the South in the Civil War.

And Ulysses Grant lost all thought of con men and Wall Street, cash
and collateral turned ashes . . . in the dust, in the cool tombs.

Pocahontas' body, lovely as a poplar, sweet as a red haw in November
or a pawpaw in May, did she wonder? does she remember? . . .
in the dust, in the cool tombs?

Take any streetful of people buying clothes and groceries, cheering a
hero or throwing confetti and blowing tin horns . . . tell me
if the lovers are losers . . . tell me if any get more than the
lovers . . . in the dust . . . in the cool tombs.

1918

WALLACE STEVENS

(1879–1955)

A lawyer for an insurance firm, Stevens composed poetry in his spare time, often while walking to work in the morning. His famous first volume, *Harmonium* (1923), included poems of quite different kinds written over the previous eight years, when his art and vision were changing rapidly. In later years Stevens wrote in relative independence from contemporary trends, but during these formative years he was much influenced by recent developments in literature and the arts: the poetic impressionism of the 1890s, the interest in the poetry of Japan and China, the Imagism advocated by Ezra Pound, and Impressionism, Fauvism, Cubism, and other tendencies in modern painting.

In style "Sunday Morning" reflected his early love for Keats, but the ideas informing the poem owed much to the German philosopher, Nietzsche. The poem affirms the value of life in a world in which God—or belief in Him—is absent. Precisely because we are not "sponsored" by heaven, the poem argues, we are "free" to live as natural beings in harmony with nature. Moreover, to accept the finality of death makes us respond more vividly to things, since we feel we have only a limited time in which to do so. Death is the "mother of beauty." But "The Snow Man" reveals a different attitude and a remarkably abstract imagination. The lyric does not describe a snowman—there is no mention of coals for eyes, a carrot nose, and the like—but instead evokes the snowman only in the title as a metaphor of a metaphor. The snowman symbolizes what

2. Grant . . . Wall Street: As President, Grant was exploited by unscrupulous financiers.

Stevens calls a "mind of winter," and this more abstract metaphor expresses in its turn something still more abstract: a way of perceiving in which one "beholds/ Nothing that is not there and the nothing that is." The lines express a state of mind in which there is absolute realism and zero activity of imagination. "Thirteen Ways of Looking at a Blackbird" explored still another form and vision. The poem is a suite of brief, economical, precisely expressed scenes, each including a blackbird as one of its components. The blackbird may represent a reality that is constant and unchanging in itself, although it appears in different contexts and relations, and can be viewed with different attitudes. No poem better illustrates the wit, freshness, inventiveness, and intelligence that pervades *Harmonium* as a whole.

Yet *Harmonium* attracted little attention when it first appeared. For twelve years Stevens published little more; then, in his fifties, he began to bring out the other volumes that with *Harmonium* made him one of the greatest American poets. Many of these poems are too long to be represented in an anthology—*Notes Toward a Supreme Fiction* (1942), *Esthétique du Mal* (1945), *The Auroras of Autumn* (1950)—but their type of poetry is partially illustrated and described in "Of Modern Poetry." Like "Sunday Morning" and "The Snow Man," this is a poetry of "meditative" form: The sequence of statements enacts a process of thinking that is taking place immediately. In such poems formal effects are located especially in syntax, which embodies such qualities of the motion of thought as suspension and temporary resolution, repetition with variation and incremental development, and—overriding everything else—urgent onward momentum. Meditative form displays the power of the mind to proceed by its own inherent forms of logic, association, and amplification, in relative independence from external stimuli.

The general theme of all Stevens' later poetry is the difference between reality as it is in itself and as it is perceived imaginatively. But the illustrations of this theme vary enormously from poem to poem, as does the balance of Stevens' allegiance between "reality" and "imagination." He sometimes defines "reality" as the world seen without imagination. If so, he may ask himself, is "imagination" the world seen without reality? This would be a bitter truth. But perhaps what the imagination adds to "reality" is itself, paradoxically, a part of "reality." The black, harsh "crow is realist," as Stevens says in one poem, but the gaudy, musical "oriole, also, may be realist." Perhaps the snow man beholds "nothing" only because he is "nothing himself." If Stevens could not finally resolve such questions and their endless permutations, the verve of his meditation celebrated the dynamism of the human mind, our capacity of absorbed attention and continuing interest despite the "poverty" of our reality or experience.

The Snow Man

One must have a mind of winter
To regard the frost and the boughs
Of the pine-trees crusted with snow;

And have been cold a long time
To behold the junipers shagged with ice,
The spruces rough in the distant glitter

Of the January sun; and not to think
Of any misery in the sound of the wind,
In the sound of a few leaves,

Which is the sound of the land
Full of the same wind
That is blowing in the same bare place
For the listener, who listens in the snow,
And, nothing himself, beholds
Nothing that is not there and the nothing that is.

1923

The Emperor of Ice-Cream

Call the roller of big cigars,
The muscular one, and bid him whip
In kitchen cups concupiscent curds.
Let the wenches dawdle in such dress
As they are used to wear, and let the boys
Bring flowers in last month's newspapers.
Let be be finale of seem.
The only emperor is the emperor of ice-cream.

Take from the dresser of deal,
Lacking the three glass knobs, that sheet
On which she embroidered fantails once
And spread it so as to cover her face.
If her horny feet protrude, they come
To show how cold she is, and dumb.
Let the lamp affix its beam.
The only emperor is the emperor of ice-cream.

1923

Sunday Morning

1

Complacencies of the peignoir, and late
Coffee and oranges in a sunny chair,
And the green freedom of a cockatoo
Upon a rug mingle to dissipate
The holy hush of ancient sacrifice.
She dreams a little, and she feels the dark
Encroachment of that old catastrophe,
As a calm darkens among water-lights.
The pungent oranges and bright, green wings
Seem things in some procession of the dead,
Winding across wide water, without sound.
The day is like wide water, without sound,
Stilled for the passing of her dreaming feet
Over the seas, to silent Palestine,
Dominion of the blood and sepulchre.

2

Why should she give her bounty to the dead?
What is divinity if it can come
Only in silent shadows and in dreams?
Shall she not find in comforts of the sun,
In pungent fruit and bright, green wings, or else
In any balm or beauty of the earth,
Things to be cherished like the thought of heaven?
Divinity must live within herself:
Passions of rain, or moods in falling snow;
Grievings in loneliness, or unsubdued
Elations when the forest blooms; gusty
Emotions on wet roads on autumn nights;
All pleasures and all pains, remembering
The bough of summer and the winter branch.
These are the measures destined for her soul.

3

Jove in the clouds had his inhuman birth.
No mother suckled him, no sweet land gave
Large-mannered motions to his mythy mind.
He moved among us, as a muttering king,
Magnificent, would move among his hinds,
Until our blood, commingling, virginal,
With heaven, brought such requital to desire
The very hinds discerned it, in a star.
Shall our blood fail? Or shall it come to be

SUNDAY MORNING. **35. hinds:** shepherds.

The blood of paradise? And shall the earth
Seem all of paradise that we shall know?
The sky will be much friendlier then than now,
A part of labor and a part of pain,
And next in glory to enduring love,
Not this dividing and indifferent blue.

4

She says, "I am content when wakened birds,
Before they fly, test the reality
Of misty fields, by their sweet questionings;
But when the birds are gone, and their warm fields
Return no more, where, then, is paradise?"
There is not any haunt of prophecy,
Nor any old chimera of the grave,
Neither the golden underground, nor isle
Melodious, where spirits gat them home,
Nor visionary south, nor cloudy palm
Remote on heaven's hill, that has endured
As April's green endures; or will endure
Like her remembrance of awakened birds,
Or her desire for June and evening, tipped
By the consummation of the swallow's wings.

5

She says, "But in contentment I still feel
The need of some imperishable bliss."
Death is the mother of beauty; hence from her,
Alone, shall come fulfillment to our dreams
And our desires. Although she strews the leaves
Of sure obliteration on our paths,
The path sick sorrow took, the many paths
Where triumph rang its brassy phrase, or love
Whispered a little out of tenderness,
She makes the willow shiver in the sun
For maidens who were wont to sit and gaze
Upon the grass, relinquished to their feet.
She causes boys to pile new plums and pears
On disregarded plate. The maidens taste
And stray impassioned in the littering leaves.

6

Is there no change of death in paradise?
Does ripe fruit never fall? Or do the boughs

74. disregarded plate: Stevens wrote in a letter: "Plate is used in the sense of so-called family plate. 'Disregarded' refers to the disuse into which things fall that have been possessed for a long time."

Hang always heavy in that perfect sky,
Unchanging, yet so like our perishing earth,
With rivers like our own that seek for seas
They never find, the same receding shores
That never touch with inarticulate pang?
Why set the pear upon those river-banks
Or spice the shores with odors of the plum?
Alas, that they should wear our colors there,
The silken weavings of our afternoons,
And pick the strings of our insipid lutes!
Death is the mother of beauty, mystical,
Within whose burning bosom we devise
Our earthly mothers waiting, sleeplessly.

7

Supple and turbulent, a ring of men
Shall chant in orgy on a summer morn
Their boisterous devotion to the sun,
Not as a god, but as a god might be,
Naked among them, like a savage source.
Their chant shall be a chant of paradise,
Out of their blood, returning to the sky;
And in their chant shall enter, voice by voice,
The windy lake wherein their lord delights,
The trees, like serafin, and echoing hills,
That choir among themselves long afterward.
They shall know well the heavenly fellowship
Of men that perish and of summer morn.
And whence they came and whither they shall go
The dew upon their feet shall manifest.

8

She hears, upon that water without sound,
A voice that cries, "The tomb in Palestine
Is not the porch of spirits lingering.
It is the grave of Jesus, where he lay."
We live in an old chaos of the sun,
Or old dependency of day and night,
Or island solitude, unsponsored, free,
Of that wide water, inescapable.
Deer walk upon our mountains, and the quail
Whistle about us their spontaneous cries;
Sweet berries ripen in the wilderness;
And, in the isolation of the sky,
At evening, casual flocks of pigeons make
Ambiguous undulations as they sink,
Downward to darkness, on extended wings.

1923

Anecdote of the Jar

I placed a jar in Tennessee,
And round it was, upon a hill.
It made the slovenly wilderness
Surround that hill.

The wilderness rose up to it,
And sprawled around, no longer wild.
The jar was round upon the ground
And tall and of a port in air.

It took dominion everywhere.
The jar was gray and bare.
It did not give of bird or bush,
Like nothing else in Tennessee.

1923

Thirteen Ways of Looking at a Blackbird

1

Among twenty snowy mountains,
The only moving thing
Was the eye of the blackbird.

2

I was of three minds,
Like a tree
In which there are three blackbirds.

3

The blackbird whirled in the autumn winds.
It was a small part of the pantomime.

4

A man and a woman
Are one.
A man and a woman and a blackbird
Are one.

5

I do not know which to prefer,
The beauty of inflections
Or the beauty of innuendoes,
The blackbird whistling
Or just after.

6

Icicles filled the long window
With barbaric glass.
The shadow of the blackbird
Crossed it to and fro.
The mood
Traced in the shadow
An indecipherable cause.

7

O thin men of Haddam,
Why do you imagine golden birds?
Do you not see how the blackbird
Walks around the feet
Of the women about you?

8

I know noble accents
And lucid, inescapable rhythms;
But I know, too,
That the blackbird is involved
In what I know.

9

When the blackbird flew out of sight,
It marked the edge
Of one of many circles.

10

At the sight of blackbirds
Flying in a green light,
Even the bawds of euphony
Would cry out sharply.

11

He rode over Connecticut
In a glass coach.
Once, a fear pierced him,
In that he mistook
The shadow of his equipage
For blackbirds.

THIRTEEN WAYS. **25. Haddam:** town in Connecticut. Stevens wrote that it had no significance. "I just like the name." Since it was "an old whaling town . . . it has a completely Yankee sound."

12

The river is moving.
The blackbird must be flying.

13

It was evening all afternoon.
It was snowing
And it was going to snow.
The blackbird sat
In the cedar-limbs.

1923

The Idea of Order at Key West

She sang beyond the genius of the sea.
The water never formed to mind or voice,
Like a body wholly body, fluttering
Its empty sleeves; and yet its mimic motion
Made constant cry, caused constantly a cry,
That was not ours although we understood,
Inhuman, of the veritable ocean.

The sea was not a mask. No more was she.
The song and water were not medleyed sound
Even if what she sang was what she heard,
Since what she sang was uttered word by word.
It may be that in all her phrases stirred
The grinding water and the gasping wind;
But it was she and not the sea we heard.

For she was the maker of the song she sang.
The ever-hooded, tragic-gestured sea
Was merely a place by which she walked to sing.
Whose spirit is this? we said, because we knew
It was the spirit that we sought and knew
That we should ask this often as she sang.

If it was only the dark voice of the sea
That rose, or even colored by many waves;
If it was only the outer voice of sky
And cloud, of the sunken coral water-walled,
However clear, it would have been deep air,
The heaving speech of air, a summer sound
Repeated in a summer without end
And sound alone. But it was more than that,
More even than her voice, and ours, among
The meaningless plungings of water and the wind,

Theatrical distances, bronze shadows heaped
On high horizons, mountainous atmospheres
Of sky and sea.
                    It was her voice that made
The sky acutest at its vanishing.
She measured to the hour its solitude.
She was the single artificer of the world
In which she sang. And when she sang, the sea,
Whatever self it had, became the self
That was her song, for she was the maker. Then we,
As we beheld her striding there alone,
Knew that there never was a world for her
Except the one she sang and, singing, made.

Ramon Fernandez, tell me, if you know,
Why, when the singing ended and we turned
Toward the town, tell why the glassy lights,
The lights in the fishing boats at anchor there,
As the night descended, tilting in the air,
Mastered the night and portioned out the sea,
Fixing emblazoned zones and fiery poles,
Arranging, deepening, enchanting night.

Oh! Blessed rage for order, pale Ramon,
The maker's rage to order words of the sea,
Words of the fragrant portals, dimly-starred,
And of ourselves and of our origins,
In ghostlier demarcations, keener sounds.

1935

Of Modern Poetry

The poem of the mind in the act of finding
What will suffice. It has not always had
To find: the scene was set; it repeated what
Was in the script.
                    Then the theater was changed
To something else. Its past was a souvenir.
It has to be living, to learn the speech of the place.
It has to face the men of the time and to meet
The women of the time. It has to think about war
And it has to find what will suffice. It has
To construct a new stage. It has to be on that stage

THE IDEA OF ORDER. **43. Ramon Fernandez:** "Not intended to be anyone at all," said Stevens. The two common Spanish names were picked simply for their suggestiveness.

And, like an insatiable actor, slowly and
With meditation, speak words that in the ear,
In the delicatest ear of the mind, repeat,
Exactly, that which it wants to hear, at the sound
Of which, an invisible audience listens,
Not to the play, but to itself, expressed
In an emotion as of two people, as of two
Emotions becoming one. The actor is
A metaphysician in the dark, twanging
An instrument, twanging a wiry string that gives
Sounds passing through sudden rightnesses, wholly
Containing the mind, below which it cannot descend,
Beyond which it has no will to rise.
It must
Be the finding of a satisfaction, and may
Be of a man skating, a woman dancing, a woman
Combing. The poem of the act of the mind.

1942

To an Old Philosopher in Rome

On the threshold of heaven, the figures in the street
Become the figures of heaven, the majestic movement
Of men growing small in the distances of space,
Singing, with smaller and still smaller sound,
Unintelligible absolution and an end—

The threshold, Rome, and that more merciful Rome
Beyond, the two alike in the make of the mind.
It is as if in a human dignity
Two parallels become one, a perspective, of which
Men are part both in the inch and in the mile.

How easily the blown banners change to wings . . .
Things dark on the horizons of perception,
Become accompaniments of fortune, but
Of the fortune of the spirit, beyond the eye,
Not of its sphere, and yet not far beyond,

The human end in the spirit's greatest reach,
The extreme of the known in the presence of the extreme
Of the unknown. The newsboys' muttering
Becomes another murmuring; the smell
Of medicine, a fragrantness not to be spoiled . . .

TO AN OLD PHILOSOPHER IN ROME. **Title:** The old philosopher was George Santayana (1863–1952), who had taught Stevens at Harvard and had long lived in retirement in Rome. His influence on Stevens' thought was profound.

The bed, the books, the chair, the moving nuns,
The candle as it evades the sight, these are
The sources of happiness in the shape of Rome,
A shape within the ancient circles of shapes,
And these beneath the shadow of a shape

In a confusion on bed and books, a portent
On the chair, a moving transparence on the nuns,
A light on the candle tearing against the wick
To join a hovering excellence, to escape
From fire and be part only of that of which

Fire is the symbol: the celestial possible.
Speak to your pillow as if it was yourself.
Be orator but with an accurate tongue
And without eloquence, O, half-asleep,
Of the pity that is the memorial of this room,

So that we feel, in this illumined large,
The veritable small, so that each of us
Beholds himself in you, and hears his voice
In yours, master and commiserable man,
Intent on your particles of nether-do,

Your dozing in the depths of wakefulness,
In the warmth of your bed, at the edge of your chair, alive
Yet living in two worlds, impenitent
As to one, and, as to one, most penitent,
Impatient for the grandeur that you need

In so much misery; and yet finding it
Only in misery, the afflatus of ruin,
Profound poetry of the poor and of the dead,
As in the last drop of the deepest blood,
As it falls from the heart and lies there to be seen,

Even as the blood of an empire, it might be,
For a citizen of heaven though still of Rome.
It is poverty's speech that seeks us out the most.
It is older than the oldest speech of Rome.
This is the tragic accent of the scene.

And you—it is you that speak it, without speech,
The loftiest syllables among loftiest things,
The one invulnerable man among
Crude captains, the naked majesty, if you like,
Of bird-nest arches and of rain-stained-vaults.

The sounds drift in. The buildings are remembered.
The life of the city never lets go, nor do you
Ever want it to. It is part of the life in your room.

47. afflatus: inspiration.

Its domes are the architecture of your bed.
The bells keep on repeating solemn names

In choruses and choirs of choruses,
Unwilling that mercy should be a mystery
Of silence, that any solitude of sense
Should give you more than their peculiar chords
And reverberations clinging to whisper still.

It is a kind of total grandeur at the end,
With every visible thing enlarged and yet
No more than a bed, a chair and moving nuns,
The immensest theater, the pillared porch,
The book and candle in your ambered room,

Total grandeur of a total edifice,
Chosen by an inquisitor of structures
For himself. He stops upon this threshold,
As if the design of all his words takes form
And frame from thinking and is realized.

1954

E. J. Pratt

(1883–1964)

Edwin John Pratt was born in a Newfoundland fishing village, the son of a minister. He attended Victoria College, University of Toronto, and then, as a graduate student, specialized in theology and psychology. He decided after much hesitation not to become a clergyman, and made his career teaching English literature in Victoria College. His first book, *Newfoundland Lyrics* (1923), presented the landscape and people of his native region. These were vivid, effective poems, but from them no one could have predicted the verve, imaginativeness, and individuality of Pratt's next phase, when he started writing long, narrative poems in octosyllabic couplets. *The Witches' Brew* (1925) was a fantasia on the theme of alcohol. "The Cachalot" (in *Titans*, 1926), perhaps Pratt's finest single poem, described a sperm whale, its fight with a giant squid, and its final combat with a whaling ship. Pratt's absorption in the narrative, sympathy with the hugely powerful whale, and battle-joy combine in this original poem with a comic perspective. For the rest of his life Pratt continued to publish both lyrics and narrative poems, but the latter especially established his popularity. The extent to which his poetry draws on Canadian history and landscape has been important to readers and other writers in that country. As a stylist Pratt rejected the various Modernist developments of his time; they moved, as he said, "away from clarity of expression into obscurity, which I think is a bad drift." Among the lyrics printed here, "The Highway" directly expresses religious views which, as Northrop Frye says, are never obtrusive in Pratt but "organize all his poetry." "Come Away, Death" was first published in April, 1941. The "bolt" of the last stanza refers primarily to a bomb exploding during the air attacks of the Second World War.

The Highway

What aeons passed without a count or name,
Before the cosmic seneschal,
Succeeding with a plan
Of weaving stellar patterns from a flame,
Announced at his high carnival
An orbit—with Aldebaran!

And when the drifting years had sighted land,
And hills and plains declared their birth
Amid volcanic throes,
What was the lapse before the marshal's hand
Had found a garden on the earth,
And led fourth June with her first rose?

And what the gulf between that and the hour,
Late in the simian-human day,
When Nature kept her tryst
With the unfoldment of the star and flower—
When in her sacrificial way
Judaea blossomed with her Christ!

But what made *our* feet miss the road that brought
The world to such a golden trove,
In our so brief a span?
How may we grasp again the hand that wrought
Such light, such fragrance, and such love,
O star! O rose! O Son of Man?

1932

THE HIGHWAY. **2. seneschal:** medieval term for a steward in a noble household. **6. Aldebaran:** one of the brightest stars in the sky.

The Prize Cat

Pure blood domestic, guaranteed,
Soft-mannered, musical in purr,
The ribbon had declared the breed,
Gentility was in the fur.

Such feline culture in the gads
No anger ever arched her back—
What distance since those velvet pads
Departed from the leopard's track!

And when I mused how Time had thinned
The jungle strains within the cells,
How human hands had disciplined
Those prowling optic parallels;

I saw the generations pass
Along the reflex of a spring,
A bird had rustled in the grass,
The tab had caught it on the wing.

Behind the leap so furtive-wild
Was such ignition in the gleam,
I thought an Abyssinian child
Had cried out in the whitethroat's scream.

1937

Come Away, Death

Willy-nilly, he comes or goes, with the clown's logic,
Comic in epitaph, tragic in epithalamium,
And unseduced by any mused rhyme.
However blow the winds over the pollen,
Whatever the course of the garden variables,
He remains the constant,
Ever flowering from the poppy seeds.

There was a time he came in formal dress,
Announced by Silence tapping at the panels
In deep apology.
A touch of chivalry in his approach,
He offered sacramental wine,
And with acanthus leaf
And petals of the hyacinth
He took the fever from the temples
And closed the eyelids,

THE PRIZE CAT. **5. gads:** claws. **20. whitethroat's:** sparrow's.

Then led the way to his cool longitudes
In the dignity of the candles.

His mediaeval grace is gone—
Gone with the flame of the capitals
And the leisured turn of the thumb
Leafing the manuscripts,
Gone with the marbles
And the Venetian mosaics,
With the bend of the knee
Before the rose-strewn feet of the Virgin.
The *paternosters* of his priests,
Committing clay to clay,
Have rattled in their throats
Under the gride of his traction tread.

One night we heard his footfall—one September night—
In the outskirts of a village near the sea.
There was a moment when the storm
Delayed its fist, when the surf fell
Like velvet on the rocks—a moment only;
The strangest lull we ever knew!
A sudden truce among the oaks
Released their fratricidal arms;
The poplars straightened to attention

As the winds stopped to listen
To the sound of a motor drone—
And then the drone was still.
We heard the tick-tock on the shelf,
And the leak of valves in our hearts.
A calm condensed and lidded
As at the core of a cyclone ended breathing
This was the monologue of Silence
Grave and unequivocal.

What followed was a bolt
Outside the range and target of the thunder,
And human speech curved back upon itself
Through Druid runways and the Piltdown scarps,
Beyond the stammers of the Java caves,
To find its origins in hieroglyphs
On mouths and eyes and cheeks
Etched by a foreign stylus never used
On the outmoded page of the Apocalypse.

1941

COME AWAY, DEATH. **27. paternosters:** prayers (Our Fathers). **52–53. Druid . . . Java:** The Druids were ancient Celtic priests; Piltdown (in England) and Java refer to sites where bones of extinct species of man were discovered. The Piltdown Man was not yet known to be a hoax when Pratt wrote this poem.

WILLIAM CARLOS WILLIAMS

(1883–1963)

A New Jersey doctor, Williams was a friend and also a rival of Ezra Pound, and in both relations was much influenced by him. As a busy professional man he had relatively little time to read or write, and he was obliged to stay in the United States rather than moving to Europe as Pound and T. S. Eliot had done. Over a period of time he managed to convert these handicaps into advantages. Since he had little time for writing—sometimes composing his poems between patients—he developed a theory of poetry which emphasized the value of rapid immediacy in composition. Only so, he argued, could a poem make contact with "life." To revise and perfect a work would make it "dead."

Williams could hardly have produced the erudite allusions we find in the poetry of Pound and Eliot, but he also rejected them on principle. Such "cosmopolitan" allusions to the literature and culture of the past aligned a poem, he thought, with the traditions of Europe and the Old World rather than the new sensibility Williams sensed developing in the United States. He believed that to express this new sensibility was far more difficult, challenging, and important than anything Eliot and Pound had attempted. Therefore, an American poet should stay where he was—in Williams' case, in Rutherford, New Jersey—and seek to make "contact" with that place. He should share and express the life there—the character and sensibility of the people, the things they saw and how they perceived them, and their emotions and the ways in which they expressed or did not express them.

All that he wrote is imbued with the desire to break with poetic tradition. The poem entitled "Spring and All" reveals this in the second and third words of the title. Spring is of course a traditional theme of poetry; "and All" deflates it. The poem corrects poetic notions of spring—those we find, for example, in Chaucer's famous opening of the *Canterbury Tales,* in which he describes the "sweet" season of flowers, bird songs, and balmy zephyrs. This and virtually all Williams' lyrics also illustrate his unremitting effort to develop in poetry the rhythm, diction, and syntax of the language actually spoken in Rutherford. His versification typically achieves a remarkably swift, weightless line that permits his lyrics to move forward with clean economy. Directness and speed expressed, he believed, the modern American sensibility, while formality and cluttering associations would align a poem with the past and with

Europe. The opening of Milton's "Lycidas," for example, is "Yet once more, O ye laurels and once more . . . I come to pluck your berries harsh and crude"—a way of saying that Milton is about to compose another poem. Williams might have written, "Here I go again."

Many of his lyrics are about poetry—what it is, how to write it—but a poem about poetry is also, for Williams, about how to live, for poetry is essentially the direct "contact"—the fresh perceiving and feeling—by which life becomes worth living. "The Red Wheelbarrow" shows him discovering an aesthetic pattern and sensory pleasure in an utterly ordinary sight. The poem—or the moment of perception it reports—evokes no cultural traditions or literary associations. The absence of these is strongly noticed, however, for if the poem is an immediate experience, it is also a demonstration and argument. "So much depends," it says, on the object being there; but it also means that so much depends on us, on our response to what we see. If our response is dull, the world takes on this quality for us, and the converse is also true. Thus, although Williams believed that the American environment offered a new challenge and possibility to poetry, his deeper meaning was that anything, however familiar or even drab, would become significant and moving when met with a full response. In "The Young Housewife," for example, the woman and her actions seem banal in the extreme, but she arouses in Williams an astonishing nexus of sympathy and eroticism. The fineness of his "emotional equipment," as Pound called it, is also evident in "To Waken an Old Lady." In this metaphor of old age, every detail is part of a complex, mobile-like balance of perceptions. It is winter, and life is diminished to a "shrill piping." The poem is not in the least sentimental. But neither, on the other hand, does it exaggerate the adversity and pathos of old age. Winter is not an unchanging condition but a varied one which includes times of relative content. As the birds settle on the weedstalks,

> the snow
> is covered with broken
> seedhusks
> and the wind tempered
> by a shrill
> piping of plenty.

Throughout most of his career, Williams was not widely known. He felt that he had been eclipsed by T. S. Eliot, who in style and interpretation of life differed completely from Williams. Moreover, Eliot had inspired a whole generation of critics. In the 1930s and 1940s their opinions prevailed in the literary world, and while they did not attack

Williams, they mostly ignored him. When the inevitable reaction came in the 1950s, young poets turned with new appreciation to Williams, and his work was a major influence on the poetry of the 1960s.

El Hombre

It's a strange courage
you give me ancient star:

Shine alone in the sunrise
toward which you lend no part!

1917

The Young Housewife

At ten A.M. the young housewife
moves about in negligee behind
the wooden walls of her husband's house.
I pass solitary in my car.

Then again she comes to the curb
to call the ice-man, fish-man, and stands
shy, uncorseted, tucking in
stray ends of hair, and I compare her
to a fallen leaf.

The noiseless wheels of my car
rush with a crackling sound over
dried leaves as I bow and pass smiling.

1917

To Waken an Old Lady

Old age is
a flight of small
cheeping birds
skimming
bare trees
above a snow glaze.
Gaining and failing

they are buffeted
by a dark wind—
But what?
On harsh weedstalks
the flock has rested,
the snow
is covered with broken
seedhusks
and the wind tempered
by a shrill
piping of plenty

1921

Spring and All

By the road to the contagious hospital
under the surge of the blue
mottled clouds driven from the
northeast—a cold wind. Beyond, the
waste of broad, muddy fields
brown with dried weeds, standing and fallen

patches of standing water
the scattering of tall trees
All along the road the reddish
purplish, forked, upstanding, twiggy
stuff of bushes and small trees
with dead, brown leaves under them
leafless vines—

Lifeless in appearance, sluggish
dazed spring approaches—

They enter the new world naked,
cold, uncertain of all
save that they enter. All about them
the cold, familiar wind—

Now the grass, tomorrow
the stiff curl of wildcarrot leaf
One by one objects are defined—
It quickens: clarity, outline of leaf

But now the stark dignity of
entrance—Still, the profound change
has come upon them: rooted, they
grip down and begin to awaken

1923

To Elsie

The pure products of America
go crazy—
mountain folk from Kentucky

or the ribbed north end of
Jersey
with its isolate lakes and

valleys, its deaf-mutes, thieves
old names
and promiscuity between

devil-may-care men who have taken
to railroading
out of sheer lust of adventure—

and young slatterns, bathed
in filth
from Monday to Saturday

to be tricked out that night
with gauds
from imaginations which have no

peasant traditions to give them
character
but flutter and flaunt

sheer rags—succumbing without
emotion
save numbed terror

under some hedge of choke-cherry
or viburnum—
which they cannot express—

Unless it be that marriage
perhaps
with a dash of Indian blood

will throw up a girl so desolate
so hemmed round
with disease or murder

that she'll be rescued by an
agent—
reared by the state and

TO ELSIE. **1. pure products:** descendants of old families in isolated communities; "pure" because often inbred as well as unmixed with later American strains.

sent out at fifteen to work in
some hard-pressed
house in the suburbs—

some doctor's family, some Elsie—
voluptuous water
expressing with broken

brain the truth about us—
her great
ungainly hips and flopping breasts

addressed to cheap
jewelry
and rich young men with fine eyes

as if the earth under our feet
were
an excrement of some sky

and we degraded prisoners
destined
to hunger until we eat filth

while the imagination strains
after deer
going by fields of goldenrod in

the stifling heat of September
Somehow
it seems to destroy us

It is only in isolate flecks that
something
is given off

No one
to witness
and adjust, no one to drive the car

1923

The Red Wheelbarrow

so much depends
upon

a red wheel
barrow

glazed with rain
water

beside the white
chickens.

1923

The Yachts

contend in a sea which the land partly encloses
shielding them from the too-heavy blows
of an ungoverned ocean which when it chooses

tortures the biggest hulls, the best man knows
to pit against its beatings, and sinks them pitilessly.
Mothlike in mists, scintillant in the minute

brilliance of cloudless days, with broad bellying sails
they glide to the wind tossing green water
from their sharp prows while over them the crew crawls

ant-like, solicitously grooming them, releasing,
making fast as they turn, lean far over and having
caught the wind again, side by side, head for the mark.

In a well guarded arena of open water surrounded by
lesser and greater craft which, sycophant, lumbering
and flittering follow them, they appear youthful, rare

as the light of a happy eye, live with the grace
of all that in the mind is fleckless, free and
naturally to be desired. Now the sea which holds them

is moody, lapping their glossy sides, as if feeling
for some slightest flaw but fails completely.
Today no race. Then the wind comes again. The yachts

move, jockeying for a start, the signal is set and they
are off. Now the waves strike at them but they are too
well made, they slip through, though they take in canvas.

Arms with hands grasping seek to clutch at the prows.
Bodies thrown recklessly in the way are cut aside.
It is a sea of faces about them in agony, in despair

until the horror of the race dawns staggering the mind,
the whole sea become an entanglement of watery bodies
lost to the world bearing what they cannot hold. Broken,

beaten, desolate, reaching from the dead to be taken up
they cry out, failing, failing! their cries rising
in waves still as the skillfull yachts pass over.

1935

The Dance

In Breughel's great picture, The Kermess,
the dancers go round, they go round and
around, the squeal and the blare and the
tweedle of bagpipes, a bugle and fiddles
tipping their bellies (round as the thick-
sided glasses whose wash they impound)
their hips and their bellies off balance
to turn them. Kicking and rolling about
the Fair Grounds, swinging their butts, those
shanks must be sound to bear up under such
rollicking measures, prance as they dance
in Breughel's great picture, The Kermess.

1944

SARA TEASDALE

(1884–1933)

A follower of such nineteenth-century poets as Christina Rossetti and A. E. Housman, Sara Teasdale was widely read and admired in her time. Her best lyrics voice directly a universal human feeling. Often they are carried by a simple, apt metaphor, as in "The Long Hill." Their mood is melancholy, but as in the poetry of Housman, the elegant formality and brevity of her expression keep her from seeming sentimental. Strong emotion is present, but it is under control.

I Shall Not Care

When I am dead and over me bright April
Shakes out her rain-drenched hair,
Tho' you should lean above me broken-hearted,
I shall not care.

I shall have peace, as leafy trees are peaceful
When rain bends down the bough,
And I shall be more silent and cold-hearted
Than you are now.

1915

The Long Hill

I must have passed the crest a while ago
  And now I am going down—
Strange to have crossed the crest and not to know,
  But the brambles were always catching the hem of my gown.

All the morning I thought how proud I should be
  To stand there straight as a queen,
Wrapped in the wind and the sun with the world under me—
  But the air was dull, there was little I could have seen.

It was nearly level along the beaten track
  And the brambles caught in my gown—
But it's no use now to think of turning back,
  The rest of the way will be only going down.

1920

D. H. Lawrence

(1885–1930)

A great novelist and critic as well as poet, Lawrence was a powerfully liberating force in every sphere of his activity. His views on poetic form were strongly influenced by his fascination with Walt Whitman. In his Preface to the American edition of his *New Poems* (1918), he described and advocated a new type of poetry, "the poetry of that which is at hand: the immediate present." Such poetry would not be "of the present" by its subject matter, however, but by having the character of immediate experience. The present, he explained, is always a moment in transition. It cannot have a final, perfected form. So in the poetry "of the present" there "must be mutation, swifter than irridescence, haste, not rest, come-and-go, not fixity, inconclusiveness, immediacy, the quality of life itself, without dénouement or close." This was an argument for composing spontaneously, since a poem created in a moment was of that moment. It was also an argument for using free verse, since Lawrence believed that only free verse could embody immediate impulse. In free verse a poem was like a bird "on the wing in the winds, flexible to every breath." Poetry was to be the "insurgent naked throb of the instant moment," "direct utterance from the instant, whole man."

The following poems reflect these ideas, but they also reflect Lawrence's preoccupation with the mythical. Like many twentieth-century writers, he felt that primitive or ancient myth expressed profound intuitions. Such intuitions are no longer possessed by modern man, either because rational and conscious thought has been too exclusively valued, with a consequent loss of access to the unconscious sources from which myths emerge, or because we no longer think in the symbolic or mythical terms in which alone such intuitions can be expressed. In "Bavarian Gentians" Lawrence recreates with uncanny power what one might call the myth-believing state of mind. Lawrence was dying when he wrote the poem, and he identifies his death with the journey to the underworld of the mythical Persephone. The terrific repetitions of the poem enable Lawrence to establish a sense of descending deeper and deeper into a realm that is, at the same time, undifferentiated, being mere darkness. And the myth unites—as the conscious, logical mind never could—the idea of death with that of sexual consummation. The conjunction of these ideas underlies the emotions felt in the journey—the pathos, awe, mystery, and total lack of fear. In "Snake," a more complicated poem, the educated, conscious mind struggles with the unconscious, myth-believing one. In the struggle, which is played out in the speaker's changing attitudes toward the snake, the snake is gradually seen as a mythical being from the world of death, the erotic, and the divine.

Snake

A snake came to my water-trough
On a hot, hot day, and I in pajamas for the heat,
To drink there.

In the deep, strange-scented shade of the great dark carob-tree
I came down the steps with my pitcher
And must wait, must stand and wait, for there he was at the trough
        before me.

He reached down from a fissure in the earth-wall in the gloom
And trailed his yellow-brown slackness soft-bellied down, over the edge of
        the stone trough
And rested his throat upon the stone bottom,
And where the water had dripped from the tap, in a small clearness,
He sipped with his straight mouth,
Softly drank through his straight gums, into his slack long body,
Silently.

Someone was before me at my water-trough,
And I, like a second comer, waiting.

He lifted his head from his drinking, as cattle do,
And looked at me vaguely, as drinking cattle do,
And flickered his two-forked tongue from his lips, and mused a moment,
And stooped and drank a little more,
Being earth-brown, earth-golden from the burning bowels of the earth
On the day of Sicilian July, with Etna smoking.

The voice of my education said to me
He must be killed,
For in Sicily the black, black snakes are innocent, the gold are venomous.

And voices in me said, If you were a man
You would take a stick and break him now, and finish him off.

But must I confess how I liked him,
How glad I was he had come like a guest in quiet, to drink at my
    water-trough

And depart peaceful, pacified, and thankless,
Into the burning bowels of this earth?

Was it cowardice, that I dared not kill him?
Was it perversity, that I longed to talk to him?
Was it humility, to feel so honored?
I felt so honored.

And yet those voices:
If you were not afraid, you would kill him!

And truly I was afraid, I was most afraid,
But even so, honored still more
That he should seek my hospitality
From out the dark door of the secret earth.

He drank enough
And lifted his head, dreamily, as one who has drunken,
And flickered his tongue like a forked night on the air, so black;
Seeming to lick his lips,
And looked around like a god, unseeing, into the air,
And slowly turned his head,
And slowly, very slowly, as if thrice adream,
Proceeded to draw his slow length curving round
And climb again the broken bank of my wall-face.

And as he put his head into that dreadful hole,
And as he slowly drew up, snake-easing his shoulders, and entered
    farther,
A sort of horror, a sort of protest against his withdrawing into that horrid
    black hole,
Deliberately going into the blackness, and slowly drawing himself after,
Overcame me now his back was turned.

I looked round, I put down my pitcher,
I picked up a clumsy log
And threw it at the water-trough with a clatter.

I think it did not hit him,
But suddenly that part of him that was left behind convulsed in undignified haste,
Writhed like lightning, and was gone
Into the black hole, the earth-lipped fissure in the wall-front,
At which, in the intense still noon, I stared with fascination.

And immediately I regretted it.
I thought how paltry, how vulgar, what a mean act!
I despised myself and the voices of my accursed human education.

And I thought of the albatross,
And I wished he would come back, my snake.

For he seemed to me again like a king,
Like a king in exile, uncrowned in the underworld,
Now due to be crowned again.

And so, I missed my chance with one of the lords
Of life.
And I have something to expiate;
A pettiness.

1923

Bavarian Gentians

Not every man has gentians in his house
in Soft September, at slow, sad Michaelmas.

Bavarian gentians, big and dark, only dark
darkening the daytime, torch-like with the smoking blueness of Pluto's gloom,
ribbed and torch-like, with their blaze of darkness spread blue
down flattening into points, flattened under the sweep of white day
torch-flower of the blue-smoking darkness, Pluto's dark-blue daze,
black lamps from the halls of Dis, burning dark blue,
giving off darkness, blue darkness, as Demeter's pale lamps give off light,
lead me then, lead the way.

Reach me a gentian, give me a torch!
let me guide myself with the blue, forked torch of this flower
down the darker and darker stairs, where blue is darkened on blueness
even where Persephone goes, just now, from the frosted September
to the sightless realm where darkness is awake upon the dark

SNAKE. **65. albatross:** in Coleridge's "Rhyme of the Ancient Mariner." BAVARIAN GENTIANS. **Title:** Gentians are flowering plants, the roots of which are used as a gastrointestinal tonic. **2. Michaelmas:** feast of the archangel Michael, Sept. 29. **8. Dis:** another name for Pluto, ruler of the underworld, who abducted Persephone (line 14), daughter of Demeter, or Ceres (line 9), to be his queen there.

and Persephone herself is but a voice
or a darkness invisible enfolded in the deeper dark
of the arms Plutonic, and pierced with the passion of dense gloom,
among the splendor of torches of darkness, shedding darkness on the
    lost bride and her groom.

1932

Ezra Pound

(1885–1972)

Pound grew up in the suburbs of Philadelphia, attended Hamilton College and the University of Pennsylvania, and taught very briefly in Wabash College in Indiana. But he was resolved to be a poet, and moved in 1908 to London. At first he was dazzled by contemporary English poetry, but as time passed he began to think it weakly "diluted" and too reliant on "abstract" terms, such as "love," "wonder," "beauty," or "sorrow."

One day in 1912 Pound was having tea with two other poets, Hilda Doolittle and Richard Aldington, and told them to their bewilderment that they were "Imagistes." Having invented this school of poetry on the spur of the moment, he went on to establish it with a brilliant campaign of publicity. He and his allies referred frequently to this "school" in mysterious hints that roused curiosity; he persuaded Doolittle to sign her poems "H. D. Imagiste"; and he put together an anthology entitled *Des Imagistes* (1914), spelling the term in French for avant-garde aura. In March, 1913, *Poetry* magazine published the most important of the many explanations of Imagism that were produced at the time. The statement had been written by Pound, although it was signed by a friend, F. S. Flint, who said he had obtained it by interviewing an Imagist. The principles of Imagism were said to be threefold:

1. Direct treatment of the "thing," whether subjective or objective.
2. To use absolutely no word that did not contribute to the presentation.
3. As regarding rhythm: to compose in sequence of the musical phrase, not in sequence of a metronome.

Poetry should present images, but this key term was defined only vaguely: an image "presents an intellectual and emotional complex in an instant of time."

The Imagist movement (the term was quickly Anglicized) had a large influence on modern poetry in the United States. We can see its impact in such different poets as Carl Sandburg, William Carlos Williams, Hilda Doolittle, Marianne Moore, Archibald MacLeish, and E. E. Cummings. For Pound the fundamental principle of Imagism was the second one, advocating utmost economy of language. His two-line poem "In a Station of the Metro," for example, was pared down from an original version containing thirty lines.

Meanwhile, in 1913 and 1914, Pound had been studying the ancient poetry of China and Japan. For his guide in this subject he relied on manuscripts left by Ernest Fenollosa (1853–1908), an American who had taught in Japan. Studying Fenollosa, he found that a line of Chinese poetry might be a sequence of images. Line three, for example, of the poem Pound translated as "Lament of the Frontier Guard" appeared in Fenollosa's notebook as (omitting the Chinese characters),

tree fall autumn grass yellow,

and meant, as Fenollosa explained, "The tree leaves fall, and autumn grass is yellow." To Pound it appeared that Chinese poetry always presented images and that its impact was not weakened by terms that merely indicate syntax. There were not, in other words, the parts of speech, such as conjunctions and prepositions, that in English indicate how the elements of a sentence are related to each other. Hence Chinese poetry was rapid, terse, suggestive, and concrete, and Pound struggled to achieve an equivalent style in English. As part of this effort he made versions of ancient Chinese poems which he published as *Cathay* (1915). "The Lament of the Frontier Guard" was one of these. Composed in 1915, the poem reflected Pound's revulsion from the First World War.

Meanwhile, in 1914 Pound met T. S. Eliot, and was enormously impressed with his poetry. The two poets greatly influenced each other, especially in technique, and both learned from Joyce, whose great novel, *Ulysses,* they were reading in manuscript installments. Pound's methods in *Hugh Selwyn Mauberley* (1920) were formed in response to the work of Eliot and Joyce. This suite of poems presents an imagined poet and his career. The attitude of the narrator (we may call him "Pound") to Mauberley himself is impossible to establish definitely, because although the poem suggests much sympathy with Mauberley and his ideals of style, it also views him ironically and portrays him as a failure.

After 1920 Pound's effort as a poet was devoted almost exclusively to the *Cantos*. He worked on this long poem through a life of much misfortune. From 1924 until the end of the Second World War, he lived in Rapallo, Italy. He admired the Italian dictator, Mussolini, as a ruler who got necessary jobs accomplished, and he sympathized with Italian Fascism. When war broke out between the United States and Italy, he broadcast in English over the Italian radio. These broadcasts roved over topics that had always interested Pound, and they revealed that his mind was now highly eccentric, distractible, and at times even paranoiac. Some of his remarks on the radio were treasonable. Indicted for this crime, he was arrested in Italy at the end of the war and placed in a U.S. Army prison camp. He expected to be hanged, and composed in prison the moving though extraordinarily difficult Pisan Cantos, which he conceived as a final, testamentary statement of his ideals. He was brought back to the United States for trial, but a committee of psychiatrists reported that he was not mentally competent to cooperate in his own defense. Because he could not legally be tried, he was placed in St. Elizabeth's hospital for the insane in Washington, where he spent the next thirteen years. Finally, after much lobbying by his fellow poets, the government agreed to dismiss the indictment against him, and he returned to live in Italy in 1958.

The Return

See, they return; ah, see the tentative
        Movements, and the slow feet,
        The trouble in the pace and the uncertain
        Wavering!

See, they return, one, and by one,
With fear, as half-awakened;
As if the snow should hesitate
And murmur in the wind,
                and half turn back;
These were the "Wing'd-with-Awe,"
                Inviolable.
Gods of the wingèd shoe!
With them the silver hounds,
                sniffing the trace of air!

THE RETURN. **1. they return:** probably meant to be indistinct, but may partly refer to the pagan gods. **12. Gods of the wingèd shoe:** Hermes, the messenger of the gods, wore winged shoes.

Haie! Haie!
These were the swift to harry;
These the keen-scented;
These were the souls of blood.

Slow on the leash,
pallid the leash-men!

1912

Lament of the Frontier Guard

By the North Gate, the wind blows full of sand,
Lonely from the beginning of time until now!
Trees fall, the grass goes yellow with autumn.
I climb the towers and towers
to watch out the barbarous land:
Desolate castle, the sky, the wide desert.
There is no wall left to this village.
Bones white with a thousand frosts,
High heaps, covered with trees and grass;
Who brought this to pass?
Who has brought the flaming imperial anger?
Who has brought the army with drums and with kettle-drums?
Barbarous kings.
A gracious spring, turned to blood-ravenous autumn,
A turmoil of wars-men, spread over the middle kingdom,
Three hundred and sixty thousand,
And sorrow, sorrow like rain.
Sorrow to go, and sorrow, sorrow returning.
Desolate, desolate fields,
And no children of warfare upon them,
No longer the men for offence and defence.
Ah, how shall you know the dreary sorrow at the North Gate,
With Rihoku's name forgotten,
And we guardsmen fed to the tigers.

By Rihaku

1915

In a Station of the Metro

The apparition of these faces in the crowd;
Petals on a wet, black bough.

1916

from Hugh Selwyn Mauberley

Life and Contacts

I. *E. P. Ode Pour L'Election de son Sépulchre*

For three years, out of key with his time,
He strove to resuscitate the dead art
Of poetry; to maintain "the sublime"
In the old sense. Wrong from the start—

No, hardly, but seeing he had been born
In a half savage country, out of date;
Bent resolutely on wringing lilies from the acorn;
Capaneus; trout for factitious bait;

Ἴδμεν γάρ τοι πάνθ' ὅσ' ἐνὶ Τροίῃ
Caught in the unstopped ear;
Giving the rocks small lee-way
The chopped seas held him, therefore, that year.

His true Penelope was Flaubert,
He fished by obstinate isles;
Observed the elegance of Circe's hair
Rather than the mottoes on sundials.

Unaffected by "the march of events,"
He passed from men's memory in *l'an trentuniesme*
De son eage; the case presents
No adjunct to the Muses' diadem.

II

The age demanded an image
Of its accelerated grimace,
Something for the modern stage,
Not, at any rate, an Attic grace;

Not, not certainly, the obscure reveries
Of the inward gaze;
Better mendacities
Than the classics in paraphrase!

HUGH SELWYN MAUBERLEY. **Epigraph:** "Ode Concerning the Choice of his Tomb": the title of a poem by the French poet Pierre Ronsard (1524–1585), in his *Odes* IV.4. SECTION I. **6. half savage country:** the United States. **8. Capaneus:** In Greek myth, Capaneus was one of seven warriors who tried to conquer Thebes. As he climbed the walls, he hurled defiance at Zeus and in return was struck by a thunderbolt. **factitious:** artificial. **9. Greek quotation:** "For we know all the things that in Troy" were suffered by the Greeks and Trojans; from the Sirens' song in *Odyssey* XII, lines 184ff. **13. Penelope:** the faithful wife of Odysseus who waited for years for his return from Troy. **Flaubert:** Gustave Flaubert (1821–1880), French novelist, author of *Madame Bovary,* famous for painstaking skill in craftsmanship. **15. Circe:** enchantress in Greek myth, who lured men to her island and turned them into swine. Odysseus was able to resist her spells with the help of the god Hermes. **18–19. *l'an . . . eage:*** in the thirty-first year of his age. Adapted from a line in *Le grande testament* (1461) by the fifteenth-century French poet François Villon. Pound was thirty-one when his book *Lustra* was published. SECTION II. **4. Attic:** Athenian.

The "age demanded" chiefly a mold in plaster,
Made with no loss of time,
A prose kinema, not, not assuredly, alabaster
Or the "sculpture" of rhyme.

III

The tea-rose tea-gown, etc.
Supplants the mousseline of Cos,
The pianola "replaces"
Sappho's barbitos.

Christ follows Dionysus,
Phallic and ambrosial
Made way for macerations;
Caliban casts out Ariel.

All things are a flowing,
Sage Heracleitus says;
But a tawdry cheapness
Shall outlast our days.

Even the Christian beauty
Defects—after Samothrace;
We see *τὸ καλὸν*
Decreed in the market place.

Faun's flesh is not to us,
Nor the saint's vision.
We have the press for wafer;
Franchise for circumcision.

All men, in law, are equals.
Free of Pisistratus,
We choose a knave or an eunuch
To rule over us.

O bright Apollo,
τίν ἄνδρα, τίν ἥρωα, τίνα θεὸν,
What god, man, or hero
Shall I place a tin wreath upon!

11. kinema: Greek word for motion (hence our word "cinema" for motion pictures). SECTION III. **2. Cos:** Greek island, famous for its muslin. **4. Sappho's barbitos:** the lyre (barbitos) of the Greek poet Sappho. **5. Dionysus:** early Greek god of revelry and wine (later Bacchus). **7. macerations:** wasting away through fasting. **8. Caliban . . . Ariel:** In Shakespeare's *The Tempest,* Caliban is a monster, typifying the animal creation, and Ariel is a sprite, typifying the spiritual. **10. Heracleitus:** Greek philosopher (535–475 B.C.), who taught that everything was in constant flux and change. **14. Samothrace:** Greek island where the famous statue "The Winged Victory" was found. **15. Greek phrase:** *To Kalon,* "the beautiful." **19–20. press . . . circumcision:** In our modern secular society we have the newspaper instead of the wafer used in Holy communion (to represent the body of Christ), and the vote in place of circumcision (among the ancient Jews, a sign that one was committed to God). **22. Pisistratus:** Athenian tyrant, or dictator, of the sixth century B.C. **26. Greek phrase:** *tin andra, tin heroa, tina theon,* "What man, what hero, what god." From *Olympian Odes* II of the sixth-century Greek poet Pindar.

IV

These fought in any case,
and some believing,
pro domo, in any case . . .

Some quick to arm,
some for adventure,
some from fear of weakness,
some from fear of censure,
some for love of slaughter, in imagination,
learning later . . .
some in fear, learning love of slaughter;

Died some, pro patria,
non "dulce" non "et decor" . . .
walked eye-deep in hell
believing in old men's lies, then unbelieving
came home, home to a lie,
home to many deceits,
home to old lies and new infamy;
usury age-old and age-thick
and liars in public places.

Daring as never before, wastage as never before.
Young blood and high blood,
fair cheeks, and fine bodies;

fortitude as never before

frankness as never before,
disillusions as never told in the old days,
hysterias, trench confessions,
laughter out of dead bellies.

V

There died a myriad,
And of the best, among them,
For an old bitch gone in the teeth,
For a botched civilization,

Charm, smiling at the good mouth,
Quick eyes gone under earth's lid,

For two gross of broken statues,
For a few thousand battered books.

. . .

SECTION IV. **3.** ***pro domo:*** for [one's] home. **11–12.** ***pro patria . . . decor:*** Pound echoes a famous line of Horace, *Dulce et decorum est pro patria mori,* "Sweet and fitting it is to die for one's country" (*Odes* III, verse 2, line 13).

Envoi (1919)

Go, dumb-born book,
Tell her that sang me once that song of Lawes:
Hadst thou but song
As thou hast subjects known,
Then were there cause in thee that should condone
Even my faults that heavy upon me lie,
And build her glories their longevity.

Tell her that sheds
Such treasure in the air,
Recking naught else but that her graces give
Life to the moment,
I would bid them live
As roses might, in magic amber laid,
Red overwrought with orange and all made
One substance and one color
Braving time.

Tell her that goes
With song upon her lips
But sings not out the song, nor knows
The maker of it, some other mouth,
May be as fair as hers,
Might, in new ages, gain her worshipers,
When our two dusts with Waller's shall be laid,
Siftings on siftings in oblivion,
Till change hath broken down
All things save Beauty alone.

1920

The *Cantos*

The *Cantos* grew ultimately into an uncompleted work of approximately 23,000 lines. A primary technique of the poem is the elliptical juxtaposition of fragments of writing, including fragments in quite different styles. Many of these fragments are quoted or translated from literary works, letters, diaries, memoirs, account books, and other written records from past ages; through these and other types of allusion, Pound presents in brief space the beliefs, values, and sensibilities characteristic of different historical cultures. Since much of the *Cantos* is not

ENVOI. **2. Lawes:** Henry Lawes (1596–1662), an English composer who put to music Edmund Waller's "Go, lovely rose," a poem Pound echoes here. See also line 23.

less difficult than *The Waste Land*, which has only 433 lines, the poem obviously requires a formidable commitment of time and attention, and critical opinion is still very divided about it. The least one could claim for it is that many passages have startling power and beauty; along with much that is dross or worse, there is a moving quest for values and insight. The density of Pound's language and the intricate interweaving of his motifs is such that the poem is inexhaustible.

Canto 13 shows Confucius teaching in ancient China. This Canto uses a narrative method somewhat like that of the Gospels; it is as though tradition had passed down disconnected sayings and actions of the teacher, which a scribe had then compiled. Canto 47 recreates the mentality of the ancient Mediterranean littoral, in which human beings interpreted their lives and that of the natural world in terms of myth. Believing in such myths, men and women felt themselves to be part of nature, and felt also that in nature the divine was everywhere present. The states of mind recreated in these two Cantos are different in many respects, but for Pound both represented ideals, especially in comparison with the modern world.

from the Cantos

XIII

Kung walked
        by the dynastic temple
and into the cedar grove,
        and then out by the lower river,
And with him Khieu, Tchi
        and Tian the low speaking
And "we are unknown," said Kung,
"You will take up charioteering?
        Then you will become known,
"Or perhaps I should take up charioteering, or archery?
"Or the practice of public speaking?"
And Tseu-lou said, "I would put the defences in order,"
And Khieu said, "If I were lord of a province
I would put it in better order than this is."
And Tchi said, "I would prefer a small mountain temple,
"With order in the observances,
        with a suitable performance of the ritual,"
And Tian said, with his hand on the strings of his lute

CANTO XIII. **1. Kung:** Confucius (551–479 B.C.), Chinese philosopher. **5–6. Khieu, Tchi . . . Tian:** disciples of Confucius. **12. Tseu-lou:** disciple of Confucius.

The low sounds continuing
        after his hand left the strings,
And the sound went up like smoke, under the leaves,
And he looked after the sound:
        "The old swimming hole,
"And the boys flopping off the planks,
"Or sitting in the underbrush playing mandolins."
        And Kung smiled upon all of them equally.
And Thseng-sie desired to know:
        "Which had answered correctly?"
And Kung said, "They have all answered correctly,
"That is to say, each in his nature."
And Kung raised his cane against Yuan Jang,
        Yuan Jang being his elder,
For Yuan Jang sat by the roadside pretending to
        be receiving wisdom.
And Kung said
        "You old fool, come out of it,
Get up and do something useful."
        And Kung said
"Respect a child's faculties
"From the moment it inhales the clear air,
"But a man of fifty who knows nothing
        Is worthy of no respect."
And "When the prince has gathered about him
"All the savants and artists, his riches will be fully employed."
And Kung said, and wrote on the bo leaves:
        If a man have not order within him
He can not spread order about him;
And if a man have not order within him
His family will not act with due order;
        And if the prince have not order within him
He can not put order in his dominions.
And Kung gave the words "order"
and "brotherly deference"
And said nothing of the "life after death."
And he said
        "Anyone can run to excesses,
It is easy to shoot past the mark,
It is hard to stand firm in the middle."

And they said: If a man commit murder
        Should his father protect him, and hide him?
And Kung said:
        He should hide him.

27. Thseng-sie: another name for the disciple Tain. **31. Yuan Jang:** an old friend of Confucius.

And Kung gave his daughter to Kong-Tch'ang
        Although Kong-Tch'ang was in prison.
And he gave his niece to Nan-Young
        although Nan-Young was out of office.

And Kung said "Wang ruled with moderation,
        In his day the State was well kept,
And even I can remember
A day when the historians left blanks in their writings,
I mean for things they didn't know,
But that time seems to be passing."
And Kung said, "Without character you will
        be unable to play on that instrument
Or to execute the music fit for the Odes.
The blossoms of the apricot
        blow from the east to the west,
And I have tried to keep them from falling."

1924

XLVII

Who even dead, yet hath his mind entire!
This sound came in the dark
First must thou go the road
                                        to hell
And to the bower of Ceres' daughter Proserpine,
Through overhanging dark, to see Tiresias,
Eyeless that was, a shade, that is in hell
So full of knowing that the beefy men know less than he,
Ere thou come to thy road's end.
        Knowledge the shade of a shade,
Yet must thou sail after knowledge
Knowing less than drugged beasts. *phtheggometha*
thasson
φθεγγώμεθα θᾶσσον
        The small lamps drift in the bay
And the sea's claw gathers them.

63. Kong-Tch'ang: disciple of Confucius. **65. Nan-Young:** another disciple. **67. Wang:** Wu Wang (1169–1115 B.C.), first emperor of the Chou dynasty. CANTO XLVII. **1–9. Who . . . end:** The enchantress Circe is speaking to Odysseus. When Odysseus, in Homer's *Odyssey,* was staying with Circe, she spoke to him in the dark, and told him that before he would be able to return to his home on the island of Ithaca, he would first have to go down into the underworld (Hell), where Proserpine, daughter of Ceres, reigned as queen. In the underworld Odysseus was to seek out the blind prophet Tiresias, to whom line 1 of this canto refers. **8. beefy men:** living men, as opposed to the shades who dwell in the underworld. **12–13. phtheggometha thasson:** a transliteration of the Greek words in line 14, "Let us raise our voices without delay." **15. small lamps:** In Rapallo, Italy, where Pound was living when he wrote this Canto, the local women set votive lights adrift in the Mediterranean in honor of the Virgin Mary. Pound associated this custom with ceremonies in the ancient Mediterranean world commemorating the death of the mythical youth, Adonis, beloved of the goddess Aphrodite (the Roman Venus).

Neptunus drinks after neap-tide.
Tamuz! Tamuz!!
The red flame going seaward.
        By this gate art thou measured.
From the long boats they have set lights in the water,
The sea's claw gathers them outward.
Scilla's dogs snarl at the cliff's base,
The white teeth gnaw in under the crag,
But in the pale night the small lamps float seaward
                                        Τυ Δκώνα
                                        TU DIONA
Και Μοῖραι' Ἄδονιν
Kai MOIRAI' ADONIN
The sea is streaked red with Adonis,
The lights flicker red in small jars.
Wheat shoots rise new by the altar,
        flower from the swift seed.
Two span, two span to a woman,
Beyond that she believes not. Nothing is of any importance.
To that is she bent, her intention
To that art thou called ever turning intention,
Whether by night the owl-call, whether by sap in shoot,
Never idle, by no means by no wiles intermittent
Moth is called over mountain
The bull runs blind on the sword, *naturans*
To the cave art thou called, Odysseus,
By Molü hast thou respite for a little,
By Molü art thou freed from the one bed
        that thou may'st return to another
The stars are not in her counting,
        To her they are but wandering holes.
Begin thy plowing
When the Pleiades go down to their rest,

17. Neptunus: Roman god of the sea. **18. Tamuz:** In the ancient Near East the mythological equivalent of Adonis was Tammuz, beloved of the goddess Ishtar. Both Tammuz and Adonis died and were resurrected annually. They are often interpreted as myths of vegetation and agricultural crops. **20. this gate:** the gate into the underworld, death. **23. Scilla:** In Greek mythology Scylla is a monster with six heads, each with three rows of teeth. She barks like a dog, and is dangerous to mariners. Scylla is identified with a rock on the coast of southern Italy. **26. Greek words:** "You, Dione"; the Greek is transliterated in line 27. Dione is the goddess Aphrodite (see line 15). **28. Greek words:** "And the fates Adonis," transliterated in line 29. The phrase is a fragmentary quotation from the "Lament for Adonis" by the ancient Greek poet, Bion (second century B.C.). The complete line in Bion is "The fates cry over Adonis." **30. sea . . . Adonis:** The swollen streams in spring carry the red-colored earth into the Mediterranean. Ancient peoples interpreted this red color as the blood of Adonis. **31. jars:** the lamps of lines 15 and 19. **41. *naturans*:** "naturing," that is, according to its nature. **42. cave:** Circe's. **43. Molü:** The god Hermes gave the magic herb Molü to Odysseus so that with it he might be able to resist the seductions of Circe. **48–60. Begin . . . stone:** Except for lines 56–57, this is a very free translation of a passage in the *Works and Days* of the ancient Greek poet Hesiod (eighth century B.C.). **49. Pleiades:** cluster of seven stars.

Begin thy plowing
40 days are they under seabord,
Thus do in fields by seabord
And in valleys winding down toward the sea.
When the cranes fly high
        think of plowing.
By this gate art thou measured
Thy day is between a door and a door
Two oxen are yoked for plowing
Or six in the hill field
White bulk under olives, a score for drawing down stone,
Here the mules are gabled with slate on the hill road.
Thus was it in time.
And the small stars now fall from the olive branch,
Forked shadow falls dark on the terrace
More black than the floating martin
        that has no care for your presence,
His wing-print is black on the roof tiles
And the print is gone with his cry.
So light is thy weight on Tellus
Thy notch no deeper indented
Thy weight less than the shadow
Yet hast thou gnawed through the mountain,
        Scylla's white teeth less sharp.
Hast thou found a nest softer than cunnus
Or hast thou found better rest
Hast'ou a deeper planting, doth thy death year
Bring swifter shoot?
Hast thou entered more deeply the mountain?

The light has entered the cave. Io! Io!
The light has gone down into the cave,
Splendour on splendour!
By prong have I entered these hills:
That the grass grow from my body,
That I hear the roots speaking together,
The air is new on my leaf,
The forked boughs shake with the wind.
Is Zephyrus more light on the bough, Apeliota
more light on the almond branch?
By this door have I entered the hill.
Falleth,
Adonis falleth.
Fruit cometh after. The small lights drift out with the tide,
sea's claw has gathered them outward,

57. door . . . door: the door by which one enters life and the door by which one enters the realm of death. **69. Tellus:** Roman goddess of the earth. **72. Scylla:** See line 23. **74. cunnus:** female sex organ (Latin). **79. Io!:** "Hail!" (Greek). **87. Zephyrus:** west wind. **Apeliota:** east wind. **91. Adonis falleth:** see lines 15 and 26.

Four banners to every flower
The sea's claw draws the lamps outward.
Think thus of thy plowing
When the seven stars go down to their rest
Forty days for their rest, by seabord
And in valleys that wind down toward the sea
        Και Μοῖραι' Ἄδονιν
        KAI MOIRAI' ADONIN
When the almond bough puts forth its flame,
When the new shoots are brought to the altar,
        Τυ Διώνα, Και Μοῖραι
        TU DIONA, KAI MOIRAI
Και Μοῖραι' Ἄδονιν
KAI MOIRAI' ADONIN
        that hath the gift of healing,
that hath the power over wild beasts.

1937

Hilda Doolittle

(1886–1961)

A college friend of Ezra Pound and William Carlos Williams, Doolittle renewed her acquaintance with Pound on a trip to Europe in 1911, which led to the founding of the Imagist movement (see Introduction to Pound). Pound later said that he had invented Imagism in order to get Doolittle's poems into print. She stayed in England, was briefly married, and later moved to Switzerland, where she lived most of the time. In the first phase of her career Doolittle expressed a sensibility and vision of life she identified with that of classical Greece. Her style was widely admired for its hard, cold intensity. In later years her style changed, and between 1944 and 1956 she wrote a remarkable series of long poems contemplating occult myths and symbols. She also wrote a memorable account of her psychoanalysis with Freud. She always signed her work "H. D."

97. seven stars: Pleiades, as in line 49. **100–101. Greek words:** as in lines 28–29. **104–107. Greek words:** as in lines 26–29. **109. beasts:** Adonis–Tammuz is here identified with the god Dionysus of Greek mythology.

Sea Rose

Rose, harsh rose,
marred and with stint of petals,
meager flower, thin,
sparse of leaf,

more precious
than a wet rose
single on a stem—
you are caught in the drift.

Stunted, with small leaf,
you are flung on the sand,
you are lifted
in the crisp sand
that drives in the wind.

Can the spice-rose
drip such acrid fragrance
hardened in a leaf?

1916

Oread

Whirl up, sea—
whirl your pointed pines,
splash your great pines
on our rocks,
hurl your green over us,
cover us with your pools of fir.

1924

The Pool

ARE you alive?
I touch you.
You quiver like a sea-fish.
I cover you with my net.
What are you—banded one?

1924

OREAD. **Title:** a mountain nymph.

Rupert Brooke

(1887–1915)

One of the promising young English poets of his generation, Brooke volunteered for service in the First World War. His sonnets, of which "The Soldier" is the most famous, contemplated the war with high-minded idealism. The emotion was widely shared in the first years of the war, and when Brooke died of fever in 1915, he represented to his countrymen the brilliant youth of England sacrificed in the fighting. He became almost legendary, and his war sonnets were prized even by people who otherwise read no poetry at all.

The Soldier

If I should die, think only this of me,
  That there's some corner of a foreign field
That is forever England. There shall be
  In that rich earth a richer dust concealed,
A dust whom England bore, shaped, made aware,
  Gave, once, her flowers to love, her ways to roam,
A body of England's, breathing English air,
  Washed by the rivers, blest by suns of home.

And think, this heart, all evil shed away,
  A pulse in the Eternal mind, no less
    Gives somewhere back the thoughts by England given,
Her sights and sounds; dreams happy as her day;
  And laughter, learnt of friends; and gentleness,
    In hearts at peace, under an English heaven.

1915

Robinson Jeffers

(1887–1962)

In 1914 Jeffers settled in Carmel, California, with which he was henceforth to be identified. His poetry had the vast, wild landscape of that part of California for its setting, and his long, narrative poems, such as *Tamar* (1924) and *The Women at Point Sur* (1927), depicted the harsh lives of the early ranchers. A reader of Freud and of Nietzsche, Jeffers explored the irrational depths of human nature. The actions and emotions of his protagonists are violent and frequently cruel. They reject compassion and struggle for dominance. Jeffers sought to recreate the stark, tragic terror and grandeur of classical Greek drama. He identified much more with the cliffs and the sea than with human beings, and regarded mankind as ultimately little more than an ephemeral pollution of the landscape.

Hurt Hawks

1

The broken pillar of the wing jags from the clotted shoulder,
The wing trails like a banner in defeat,
No more to use the sky forever but live with famine
And pain a few days: cat nor coyote
Will shorten the week of waiting for death, there is game without talons.
He stands under the oak-bush and waits
The lame feet of salvation; at night he remembers freedom
And flies in a dream, the dawns ruin it.
He is strong and pain is worse to the strong, incapacity is worse.
The curs of the day come and torment him
At distance, no one but death the redeemer will humble that head,
The intrepid readiness, the terrible eyes.
The wild God of the world is sometimes merciful to those
That ask mercy, not often to the arrogant.
You do not know him, you communal people, or you have forgotten him;
Intemperate and savage, the hawk remembers him;
Beautiful and wild, the hawks, and men that are dying, remember him.

2

I'd sooner, except the penalties, kill a man than a hawk; but
    the great redtail
Had nothing left but unable misery
From the bone too shattered for mending, the wing that trailed under
    his talons when he moved.
We had fed him six weeks, I gave him freedom,
He wandered over the foreland hill and returned in the evening,
    asking for death,
Not like a beggar, still eyed with the old
Implacable arrogance. I gave him the lead gift in the twilight. What
    fell was relaxed,
Owl-downy, soft feminine feathers; but what

Soared: the fierce rush: the night-herons by the flooded river cried fear at its rising
Before it was quite unsheathed from reality.

1928

The Purse-Seine

Our sardine fishermen work at night in the dark of the moon; daylight or moonlight
They could not tell where to spread the net, unable to see the phosphorescence of the shoals of fish.
They work northward from Monterey, coasting Santa Cruz; off New Year's Point or off Pigeon Point
The look-out man will see some lakes of milk-color light on the sea's night-purple; he points, and the helmsman
Turns the dark prow, the motorboat circles the gleaming shoal and drifts out her seine-net. They close the circle
And purse the bottom of the net, then with great labor haul it in.

I cannot tell you
How beautiful the scene is, and a little terrible, then, when the crowded fish
Know they are caught, and wildly beat from one wall to the other of their closing destiny the phosphorescent
Water to a pool of flame, each beautiful slender body sheeted with flame, like a live rocket
A comet's tail wake of clear yellow flame; while outside the narrowing
Floats and cordage of the net great sea-lions come up to watch, sighing in the dark; the vast walls of night
Stand erect to the stars.

Lately I was looking from a night mountain-top
On a wide city, the colored splendor, galaxies of light: how could I help but recall the seine-net
Gathering the luminous fish? I cannot tell you how beautiful the city appeared, and a little terrible.
I thought, We have geared the machines and locked all together into interdependence; we have built the great cities; now
There is no escape. We have gathered vast populations incapable of free survival, insulated
From the strong earth, each person in himself helpless, on all dependent. The circle is closed, and the net
Is being hauled in. They hardly feel the cords drawing, yet they shine already. The inevitable mass-disasters

THE PURSE-SEINE. **Title:** a fishing net. **2. shoals:** schools. **3. Monterey . . . Pigeon Point:** places in the Monterey Bay area of California, where Jeffers lived.

Will not come in our time nor in our children's, but we and our
children
Must watch the net draw narrower, government take all powers—or
revolution, and the new government
Take more than all, add to kept bodies kept souls—or anarchy, the
mass-disasters.

These things are Progress;
Do you marvel our verse is troubled or frowning, while it keeps its
reason? Or it lets go, lets the mood flow
In the manner of the recent young men into mere hysteria, splintered
gleams, crackled laughter. But they are quite wrong.
There is no reason for amazement: surely one always knew that
cultures decay, and life's end is death.

1937

Marianne Moore

(1887–1972)

One of the most original and brilliant of the Modernist poets, Moore attended Bryn Mawr College, taught for a few years, and then moved to New York City. Between 1926 and 1929 she edited the *Dial,* perhaps the most important literary magazine of the time. Many poets of her generation strove for an especially close, exact rendering of objects, and Moore developed this to an extreme degree. The implicit moral suggestion was that a close grasp of particular reality is essential.

She created a type of versification (syllabic verse), new in English or American poetry, based on counting the number of syllables in a line and ignoring quantity and accent. She was one of the first modern poets to end lines and even to rhyme on words that have no emphasis *(and, the);* she also created rhymes by hyphenating words (" . . . *ac-/* cident—*lack* . . . "). In general her versification reflected a liking for arbitrary, self-imposed difficulties, and for making things hard. She wished to refuse herself and her readers easy satisfactions—regular rhythm, harmony of verse forms with syntactical forms—to which they had been accustomed. She also wished to bring forward the prose sense of the words.

She inserted into her verses extracts from prose sources such as the *National Geographic Magazine,* surrounding these passages with quotation marks that kept them at an ironic distance. Like other Modernist poets she cultivated the poetic possibilities of the vocabulary and word order of colloquial speech and of prose, and the interplay of her line breaks, enjambments, and caesuras enacts the motions and pauses of the thinking mind or speaking voice, although she could also be extremely elliptical. In all she wrote, her sharp intelligence and wit resulted in swift, unexpected associations, comparisons, and distinctions. When in "The Steeple-Jack," for example, we are told that the student named Ambrose liked "an elegance of which/ the source is not bravado," we are forced to think what kind of elegance this might be, and what the other kind motivated by bravado might be, and whether the latter kind is in some sense false or less admirable. The sensitive and very firm morality underlying the observation is typical of Moore.

Poetry

I, too, dislike it: there are things that are important beyond all this
 fiddle.
Reading it, however, with a perfect contempt for it, one discovers in
it after all, a place for the genuine.
Hands that can grasp, eyes
that can dilate, hair that can rise
if it must, these things are important not because a

high-sounding interpretation can be put upon them but because they
 are
useful. When they become so derivative as to become unintelligible,
the same thing may be said for all of us, that we
do not admire what
we cannot understand: the bat
holding on upside down or in quest of something to

eat, elephants pushing, a wild horse taking a roll, a tireless wolf under
a tree, the immovable critic twitching his skin like a horse that feels
a flea, the base-
ball fan, the statistician—
nor is it valid
to discriminate against "business documents and

school-books"; all these phenomena are important. One must make a
 distinction

POETRY. **17–18. business documents . . . school books:** In a note Moore quotes a remark from Leo Tolstoy's *Diary:* "Where the boundary between prose and poetry lies, I shall never be able to understand. The question is raised in manuals of style, yet the answer to it lies beyond me. Poetry is verse: prose is not verse. Or else poetry is everything with the exception of business documents and school books."

however: when dragged into prominence by half poets, the result is
not poetry,
nor till the poets among us can be
"literalists of
the imagination"—above
insolence and triviality and can present

for inspection, "imaginary gardens with real toads in them," shall we
have
it. In the meantime, if you demand on the one hand,
the raw material of poetry in
all its rawness and
that which is on the other hand
genuine, you are interested in poetry.

1921

The Steeple-Jack

Dürer would have seen a reason for living
in a town like this, with eight stranded whales
to look at; with the sweet air coming into your house
on a fine day, from water etched
with waves as formal as the scales
on a fish.

One by one in two's and three's, the seagulls keep
flying back and forth over the town clock,
or sailing around the lighthouse without moving their wings—
rising steadily with a slight
quiver of the body—or flock
mewing where

a sea the purple of the peacock's neck is
paled to greenish azure as Dürer changed
the pine green of the Tyrol to peacock blue and guinea
gray. You can see a twenty-five-
pound lobster; and fishnets arranged
to dry. The

whirlwind fife-and-drum of the storm bends the salt
marsh grass, disturbs stars in the sky and the
star on the steeple; it is a privilege to see so
much confusion. Disguised by what
might seem the opposite, the sea-
side flowers and

21–22. literalists . . . imagination: a quote from a discussion of Blake in Yeats's *Ideas of Good and Evil* (1903). THE STEEPLE-JACK. **1. Dürer:** Albrecht Dürer (1471–1528), German painter and engraver. **15. Tyrol:** mountain district in western Austria. **15–16. guinea gray:** the gray plumage of the guinea fowl.

trees are favored by the fog so that you have
the tropics at first hand: the trumpet-vine,
fox-glove, giant snapdragon, a salpiglossis that has
spots and stripes; morning-glories, gourds,
or moon-vines trained on fishing-twine
at the back

door: cattails, flags, blueberries and spiderwort,
stripped grass, lichens, sunflowers, asters, daisies—
yellow and crab-claw ragged sailors with green bracts—toad-plant,
petunias, ferns; pink lilies, blue
ones, tigers; poppies; black sweet-peas.
The climate

is not right for the banyan, frangipani, or
jack-fruit trees; or an exotic serpent
life. Ring lizard and snake-skin for the foot, if you see fit;
but here they've cats, not cobras, to
keep down the rats. The diffident
little newt

with white pin-dots on black horizontal spaced-
out bands lives here; yet there is nothing that
ambition can buy or take away. The college student
named Ambrose sits on the hillside
with his not-native books and hat
and sees boats

at sea progress white and rigid as if in
a groove. Liking an elegance of which
the source is not bravado, he knows by heart the antique
sugar-bowl shaped summerhouse of
interlacing slats, and the pitch
of the church

spire, not true, from which a man in scarlet lets
down a rope as a spider spins a thread;
he might be part of a novel, but on the sidewalk a
sign says C. J. Poole, Steeple Jack,
in black and white; and one in red
and white says

Danger. The church portico has four fluted
columns, each a single piece of stone, made
modester by whitewash. This would be a fit haven for
waifs, children, animals, prisoners,
and presidents who have repaid
sin-driven

58. C. J. Poole: an actual steeplejack, says Moore, who removed the spire of the Lafayette Avenue Presbyterian Church in New York.

senators by not thinking about them. The
place has a schoolhouse, a post-office in a
store, fish-houses, hen-houses, a three-masted
schooner on
the stocks. The hero, the student,
the steeple-jack, each in his way,
is at home.

It could not be dangerous to be living
in a town like this, of simple people,
who have a steeple-jack placing danger signs by the church
while he is gilding the solid-
pointed star, which on a steeple
stands for hope.

1935
(revised 1961)

The Mind Is an Enchanting Thing

is an enchanted thing
like the glaze on a
katydid-wing
subdivided by sun
till the nettings are legion.
Like Gieseking playing Scarlatti;

like the apteryx-awl
as a beak, or the
kiwi's rain-shawl
of haired feathers, the mind
feeling its way as though blind,
walks along with its eyes on the ground.

It has memory's ear
that can hear without
having to hear.
Like the gyroscope's fall,
truly unequivocal
because trued by regnant certainty,

it is a power of
strong enchantment. It
is like the dove-
neck animated by
sun; it is memory's eye;
it's conscientious inconsistency.

THE MIND IS AN ENCHANTING THING. **6. Gieseking:** Walter Gieseking (1895–1956), pianist. **Scarlatti:** Domenico Scarlatti (1685–1757), Italian composer. **7. apteryx:** a bird of New Zealand, also called the kiwi (line 9).

It tears off the veil; tears
the temptation, the
mist the heart wears,
from its eyes—if the heart
has a face; it takes apart
dejection. It's fire in the dove-neck's

iridescence; in the
inconsistencies
of Scarlatti.
Unconfusion submits
its confusion to proof; it's
not a Herod's oath that cannot change.

1944

Edwin Muir

(1887–1959)

As a child Muir lived on his father's farm in the remote and primitive Orkney Islands. When he was thirteen, his family moved to the city of Glasgow, where they were miserable. Within five years both his parents were dead, and Muir was supporting himself with a job in a boneyard which filled him with horror. In later years the contrast between the Orkneys and Glasgow and the transition from one to another became archetypal for Muir. In his own life he saw a pattern that repeated the story of the garden of Eden, the fall of man, and the wandering in the desert that followed. A happy marriage, psychoanalysis, and writing poetry helped him to gradually overcome the trauma of his adolescent years. Leaving Glasgow, he made his living by literary journalism and by teaching. His poems contemplate archetypal symbols.

36. Herod's oath: Herod Antipas, ruler of Galilee in Roman Palestine from 4 B.C. to 39 A.D., swore to Salome that in return for her dancing before him and his guests he would give her whatever she might request. She asked for the head of John the Baptist, and Herod reluctantly ordered John to be beheaded, although it was against his wishes (Mark 6:22–26), because he could not break his oath.

"One Foot in Eden" is in part an effort to find a redeeming moral value in the "shapes of terror and of grief" that had assailed him since leaving the Eden of childhood. Among poems that refer to nuclear war "The Horses" is extremely unusual because it assumes that history will continue afterwards. Nuclear war is, for Muir, the final stage of man's fall from the pre-industrial, agricultural world he had known in the Orkneys; it will be followed by a return of that pastoral Eden. The calm assurance with which Muir expresses his vision arises from his faith in the reality and controlling power of the archetypal pattern he has discerned.

One Foot in Eden

One foot in Eden still, I stand
And look across the other land.
The world's great day is growing late,
Yet strange these fields that we have planted
So long with crops of love and hate.
Time's handiworks by time are haunted,
And nothing now can separate
The corn and tares compactly grown.
The armorial weed in stillness bound
About the stalk; these are our own.
Evil and good stand thick around
In the fields of charity and sin
Where we shall lead our harvest in.
Yet still from Eden springs the root
As clean as on the starting day.
Time takes the foliage and the fruit
And burns the archetypal leaf
To shapes of terror and of grief
Scattered along the winter way.
But famished field and blackened tree
Bear flowers in Eden never known.
Blossoms of grief and charity
Bloom in these darkened fields alone.
What had Eden ever to say
Of hope and faith and pity and love
Until was buried all its day
And memory found its treasure trove?
Strange blessings never in Paradise
Fall from these beclouded skies.

1956

The Horses

Barely a twelvemonth after
The seven days war that put the world to sleep,
Late in the evening the strange horses came.
By then we had made our covenant with silence,
But in the first few days it was so still
We listened to our breathing and were afraid.
On the second day
The radios failed; we turned the knobs; no answer.
On the third day a warship passed us, heading north,
Dead bodies piled on the deck. On the sixth day
A plane plunged over us into the sea. Thereafter
Nothing. The radios dumb;
And still they stand in corners of our kitchens,
And stand, perhaps, turned on, in a million rooms
All over the world. But now if they should speak,
If on a sudden they should speak again,
If on the stroke of noon a voice should speak,
We would not listen, we would not let it bring
That old bad world that swallowed its children quick
At one great gulp. We would not have it again.
Sometimes we think of the nations lying asleep,
Curled blindly in impenetrable sorrow,
And then the thought confounds us with its strangeness.
The tractors lie about our fields; at evening
They look like dank sea-monsters couched and waiting.
We leave them where they are and let them rust:
"They'll moulder away and be like other loam."
We make our oxen drag our rusty ploughs,
Long laid aside. We have gone back
Far past our fathers' land.
                                        And then, that evening
Late in the summer the strange horses came.
We heard a distant tapping on the road,
A deepening drumming; it stopped, went on again
And at the corner changed to hollow thunder.
We saw the heads
Like a wild wave charging and were afraid.
We had sold our horses in our fathers' time
To buy new tractors. Now they were strange to us
As fabulous steeds set on an ancient shield
Or illustrations in a book of knights.
We did not dare go near them. Yet they waited,
Stubborn and shy, as if they had been sent
By an old command to find our whereabouts
And that long-lost archaic companionship.
In the first moment we had never a thought
That they were creatures to be owned and used.

Among them were some half-a-dozen colts
Dropped in some wilderness of the broken world,
Yet new as if they had come from their own Eden.
Since then they have pulled our ploughs and borne our loads,
But that free servitude still can pierce our hearts.
Our life is changed; their coming our beginning.

1956

T. S. ELIOT

(1888–1965)

A shy, sheltered, bird-watching, and bookish child, Eliot came from a genteel family in St. Louis. He went to private schools in Missouri and Massachusetts, and then to Harvard. Since his school-days he had been writing verse in late Romantic styles. In his junior year in college, however, he read the poetry of Jules Laforgue (1860–1887), a French poet of brilliant, ironic pessimism. Laforgue also deployed stock Romantic themes and emotions, but he presented them with irony or parody. As, for example, the lady in a moonlit scene waits for the tender, conventional avowals, the Laforguean lover may launch into a philosophic lecture. This is incongruous and amusing, of course, and it strikes a pose of intellectual superiority. But at a deeper level of meaning the "lover" is retreating from an erotic relation in which he would feel anxious and inadequate. Eliot identified strongly, though briefly, with Laforgue or with such Laforguean protagonists, and this influence freed him from the naively Romantic styles in which he had been working.

The most important of Eliot's early poems was "The Love Song of J. Alfred Prufrock," which he finished in 1911. To its first readers, such as Ezra Pound, this poem seemed highly original and "modernized." That Prufrock's mind is filled with the particulars of urban life—"one-night cheap hotels/ And sawdust restaurants with oyster shells"—was one of the reasons, as we discuss in the headnote to *The Waste Land.* Another reason was the vision of human nature and life embodied in Prufrock. He is completely unlike the typical protagonist of Romantic poetry, such as the poet in Wordsworth's lyrics, Coleridge's Ancient Mariner, or Tennyson's Ulysses. These Romantic protagonists are felt to be greater than the reader in emotion, imagination, experience or quest; Prufrock, on the other hand, is futile, empty, anxious, and trapped.

In genre "The Love Song of J. Alfred Prufrock" develops from Browning's dramatic monologues (see the Introduction to Browning), but Prufrock is not speaking to anyone except himself, and the poem takes us more directly into his inner life of self-conflict and escapist fantasy than Browning would have. Some of the images (for example, in lines 73–74) seem to erupt from Prufrock's unconscious; in this the poem anticipates Eliot's later poetry, which also reflects the depth psychology of Freud and his followers.

As in all of Eliot's later poems, the language of the poem is directed toward expressive function only. With the possible exception of lines 15–22—a passage Eliot had written earlier and could not resist including—nothing is in the poem for the sake of its beauty or for any other purpose except that of exposing Prufrock's character and plight. This is the function, for example, of the description of the sunset at the start of the poem: "the evening is spread out against the sky/ Like a patient etherized upon a table." To compare a sunset to a naked, prone, pink body would have seemed strangely far-fetched and lacking in beauty to most readers in 1911. More important, the comparison does not describe the sunset from the poet's point of view, but tells us how Prufrock sees it, thus expressing his state of mind. It suggests that Prufrock feels like a patient on an operating table—exposed, passively helpless, and frightened. That he sees the outer world in terms of his own anxiety indicates how greatly this anxiety dominates him. The last six lines of the poem are an even more striking example. In thinking of the mermaids, Prufrock invokes traditional symbols of beauty and seduction, and his language acquires the melodious assonance and rhythmic beauty of Romantic poetry at its loveliest. But such beauty of language is not here pursued as an end in itself, as it might have been in the poetry of Keats or Tennyson. It is used to render Prufrock's emotions in this moment of fantasied escape and to reinforce the unreality. That this kind of beauty is Romantically conventional further characterizes Prufrock. Even in fantasizing he cannot escape from himself. As he envisions the mermaids "combing the white hair of the waves blown back," he is still preoccupied with his "bald spot in the middle of my hair."

Eliot completed "The Love Song of J. Alfred Prufrock" while he was at Harvard, where he became a graduate student in Philosophy. In England, while working on his doctoral thesis, he met Pound in 1914. Pound's enthusiasm for his poetry may have given him new confidence. In 1915 he married Vivien Haigh-Wood, an Englishwoman; he decided at the same time to abandon his intended career as a university teacher of philosophy and to live in England rather than the United States. His family vigorously disapproved of these decisions, and his wife proved to be seriously ill and also mentally unstable. The next few years were deeply unhappy, and Eliot's wretchedness was further aggravated by remorse in relation to his wife, for whose troubles he seems to have thought himself at least partly to blame. In order to earn a living he taught briefly, then took a job in a London bank.

"Sweeney Among the Nightingales" illustrates the development of Eliot's attitudes and poetic style during the early years of his marriage. The characters it portrays are repellent compared with Prufrock, and they are viewed with an animosity barely controlled by the tautness of the versification and the strict objectivity of the narrative method. Eliot had revealed Prufrock's mind from within, but Sweeney is seen from without and from a long distance. Other techniques of the poem were suggested to Eliot by Joyce's *Ulysses* (1922). In a way that anticipates *The Waste Land,* "Sweeney Among the Nightingales" includes widely different styles—the first stanza, for example, is realistic and satiric, while the second is Romantic and *symboliste*—and swiftly contrasts images of beauty and extreme sordidness. Eliot uses allusions to open sudden vistas of meaning, as when the poem compares the death of Sweeney, which possibly is being plotted, with that of Agamemnon in classical Greek tragedy.

In 1921 and 1922 Eliot completed *The Waste Land* while recovering in Switzerland from a psychological breakdown or near breakdown. When published in 1922, the poem, which is discussed later in a separate head-note, aroused violent opposition among more conservative readers, but was quickly championed by younger intellectuals and poets. In the same year Eliot founded a journal of literature and ideas, *Criterion,* which he continued to edit until 1939. In 1925 he quit his employment in the bank and joined the publishing firm of Faber and Gwyer (later Faber and Faber), where he worked for the rest of his life. In 1927 he became a naturalized English citizen, announced his religious conversion, and became a member of the Anglican Church. The formal acts of naturalization and baptism expressed his resolve, at the age of thirty-nine, to make final commitments, determining who he was and would be in the future. Five years later he separated from his wife. Such poems as *The Hollow Men* (1925), *Ash-Wednesday* (1930), and the *Four Quartets* (1936–42) reflect his exhausting inward turmoil in making these fundamental decisions and in living with them.

By the 1930s Eliot's poetry and criticism had raised him to a position of eminence in the literary world unrivaled by any author since Samuel Johnson. Except for the *Four Quartets,* he wrote no more significant poems, although he continued the experiments with poetic drama he had begun in the 1920s. In 1957, his first wife having died, he married

Valerie Fletcher. Although he was troubled with ill health, his last years must have been among his happiest.

"Burnt Norton," the first of the *Four Quartets,* explores the situation of human beings living in time yet fleetingly in touch with the eternal or haunted by symbols of it, and the poem tries to grasp the meaning given in such experiences or symbols. It expresses a struggle for religious faith and for an understanding of the human condition in terms of faith. It is very different from *The Waste Land,* and measures the enormous development in Eliot's emotions and beliefs that had taken place over the intervening years. The main difference is of course that in *Burnt Norton* Eliot writes from within a religious commitment. The attitude of the poem is finally much less ambiguous and more positive than *The Waste Land,* and the state of mind *The Waste Land* expresses is now understood as a possible phase in religious life. Stylistically the *Four Quartets* develop further the use of *leitmotifs* that was already fundamental to *The Waste Land;* in the *Four Quartets* a nexus of growing meanings attends recurrent images of roses, fire, traveling, dancing, light and dark, and many others, as well as such terms as "end," "beginning," and "word." But the most important stylistic development in the *Four Quartets* was the use of discursive speech, the language of meditation and generalization that had been excluded from *The Waste Land.* In terms of literary history, the *Four Quartets* represent a partial retreat from the high Modernist style of the 1920s and a return to poetry of a more traditional type.

The Love Song of J. Alfred Prufrock

S'io credesse che mia risposta fosse
A persona che mai tornasse al mondo,
Questa fiamma staria senza più scosse.
Ma perciocche giammai di questo fondo
Non tornò vivo alcun, s'i'odo il vero,
Senza tema d'infamia ti rispondo.

Let us go then, you and I,
When the evening is spread out against the sky
Like a patient etherized upon a table;
Let us go, through certain half-deserted streets,

THE LOVE SONG OF J. ALFRED PRUFROCK. **Epigraph:** From Dante's *Inferno,* XXVII, 61–66. Here Dante and his guide Virgil are in the circle of Hell that contains the "False Counsellors," the spirit of each of which is wrapped in a tall flame. One of them is Guido da Montefeltro, whom they ask to identify himself, and who replies in these words of the epigraph: "If I believed my reply would be given to anyone who would return to the world, this flame [through which he had to speak] would stop shaking. But since nobody has ever come back from this place, if what I hear is true, I answer you without fear of infamy."

The muttering retreats
Of restless nights in one-night cheap hotels
And sawdust restaurants with oyster-shells:
Streets that follow like a tedious argument
Of insidious intent
To lead you to an overwhelming question . . .
Oh, do not ask, "What is it?"
Let us go and make our visit.

In the room the women come and go
Talking of Michelangelo.

The yellow fog that rubs its back upon the window-panes,
The yellow smoke that rubs its muzzle on the window-panes
Licked its tongue into the corners of the evening,
Lingered upon the pools that stand in drains,
Let fall upon its back the soot that falls from chimneys,
Slipped by the terrace, made a sudden leap,
And seeing that it was a soft October night,
Curled once about the house, and fell asleep.

And indeed there will be time
For the yellow smoke that slides along the street,
Rubbing its back upon the window-panes;
There will be time, there will be time
To prepare a face to meet the faces that you meet;
There will be time to murder and create,
And time for all the works and days of hands
That lift and drop a question on your plate;
Time for you and time for me,
And time yet for a hundred indecisions,
And for a hundred visions and revisions,
Before the taking of a toast and tea.

In the room the women come and go
Talking of Michelangelo.

And indeed there will be time
To wonder, "Do I dare?" and, "Do I dare?"
Time to turn back and descend the stair,
With a bald spot in the middle of my hair—
[They will say: "How his hair is growing thin!"]
My morning coat, my collar mounting firmly to the chin,
My necktie rich and modest, but asserted by a simple pin—
[They will say: "But how his arms and legs are thin!"]
Do I dare
Disturb the universe?
In a minute there is time
For decisions and revisions which a minute will reverse.

29. works and days: title of a poem by the Greek Hesiod (eighth century B.C.) on farming and rural life.

For I have known them all already, known them all—
Have known the evenings, mornings, afternoons,
I have measured out my life with coffee spoons;
I know the voices dying with a dying fall
Beneath the music from a farther room.
  So how should I presume?

And I have known the eyes already, known them all—
The eyes that fix you in a formulated phrase,
And when I am formulated, sprawling on a pin,
When I am pinned and wriggling on the wall,
Then how should I begin
To spit out all the butt-ends of my days and ways?
  And how should I presume?

And I have known the arms already, known them all—
Arms that are braceleted and white and bare
[But in the lamplight, downed with light brown hair!]
Is it perfume from a dress
That makes me so digress?
Arms that lie along a table, or wrap about a shawl.
  And should I then presume?
  And how should I begin?

. . . . .

Shall I say, I have gone at dusk through narrow streets
And watched the smoke that rises from the pipes
Of lonely men in shirt-sleeves, leaning out of windows? . . .

I should have been a pair of ragged claws
Scuttling across the floors of silent seas.

. . . . .

And the afternoon, the evening, sleeps so peacefully!
Smoothed by long fingers,
Asleep . . . tired . . . or it malingers,
Stretched on the floor, here beside you and me.
Should I, after tea and cakes and ices,
Have the strength to force the moment to its crisis?
But though I have wept and fasted, wept and prayed,
Though I have seen my head [grown slightly bald] brought in
    upon a platter,
I am no prophet—and here's no great matter;
I have seen the moment of my greatness flicker,
And I have seen the eternal Footman hold my coat, and
    snicker,
And in short, I was afraid.

82. head . . . platter: alluding to John the Baptist, whose head, cut off by King Herod, was brought to Salome on a platter (Matthew 14:1–12).

And would it have been worth it, after all,
After the cups, the marmalade, the tea,
Among the porcelain, among some talk of you and me,
Would it have been worth while,
To have bitten off the matter with a smile,
To have squeezed the universe into a ball
To roll it toward some overwhelming question,
To say: "I am Lazarus, come from the dead,
Come back to tell you all, I shall tell you all"—
If one, settling a pillow by her head,
  Should say: "That is not what I meant at all.
  That is not it, at all."

And would it have been worth it, after all,
Would it have been worth while,
After the sunsets and the dooryards and the sprinkled streets,
After the novels, after the teacups, after the skirts that trail
    along the floor—
And this, and so much more?—
It is impossible to say just what I mean!
But as if a magic lantern threw the nerves in patterns on a
    screen:
Would it have been worth while
If one, settling a pillow or throwing off a shawl,
And turning toward the window, should say:
  "That is not it at all,
  That is not what I meant, at all."

. . . . .

No! I am not Prince Hamlet, nor was meant to be;
Am an attendant lord, one that will do
To swell a progress, start a scene or two,
Advise the prince; no doubt, an easy tool,
Deferential, glad to be of use,
Politic, cautious, and meticulous;
Full of high sentence, but a bit obtuse;
At times, indeed, almost ridiculous—
Almost, at times, the Fool.

I grow old . . . I grow old . . .
I shall wear the bottoms of my trousers rolled.

Shall I part my hair behind? Do I dare to eat a peach?
I shall wear white flannel trousers, and walk upon the beach.
I have heard the mermaids singing, each to each.

I do not think that they will sing to me.

92. squeezed . . . ball: an allusion to Andrew Marvell's poem, "To His Coy Mistress," lines 41–42: "Let us roll all our strength and all/ Our sweetness up into one ball." **94. Lazarus:** raised from the dead by Christ (John 11:1–44). **113. swell a progress:** help swell out a state procession.

I have seen them riding seaward on the waves
Combing the white hair of the waves blown back
When the wind blows the water white and black.

We have lingered in the chambers of the sea
By sea-girls wreathed with seaweed red and brown
Till human voices wake us, and we drown.

1917

Whispers of Immortality

Webster was much possessed by death
And saw the skull beneath the skin;
And breastless creatures under ground
Leaned backward with a lipless grin.

Daffodil bulbs instead of balls
Stared from the sockets of the eyes!
He knew that thought clings round dead limbs
Tightening its lusts and luxuries.

Donne, I suppose, was such another
Who found no substitute for sense,
To seize and clutch and penetrate;
Expert beyond experience,

He knew the anguish of the marrow
The ague of the skeleton;
No contact possible to flesh
Allayed the fever of the bone.

. . . . .

Grishkin is nice: her Russian eye
Is underlined for emphasis;
Uncorseted, her friendly bust
Gives promise of pneumatic bliss.

The couched Brazilian jaguar
Compels the scampering marmoset
With subtle effluence of cat;
Grishkin has a maisonette;

The sleek Brazilian jaguar
Does not in its arboreal gloom
Distil so rank a feline smell
As Grishkin in a drawing room.

WHISPERS OF IMMORTALITY. **1. Webster:** John Webster, seventeenth-century poet and dramatist. **9. Donne:** John Donne, the seventeenth-century poet. **22. marmoset:** Central and South American monkey. **24. maisonette:** small house or apartment.

And even the Abstract Entities
Circumambulate her charm;
But our lot crawls between dry ribs
To keep our metaphysics warm.

1919

Sweeney Among the Nightingales

ὤμοι, πέπληγμαι καιρίαν πληγὴν ἔσω.

Apeneck Sweeney spreads his knees
Letting his arms hang down to laugh,
The zebra stripes along his jaw
Swelling to maculate giraffe.

The circles of the stormy moon
Slide westward toward the River Plate,
Death and the Raven drift above
And Sweeney guards the hornèd gate.

Gloomy Orion and the Dog
Are veiled; and hushed the shrunken seas;
The person in the Spanish cape
Tries to sit on Sweeney's knees

Slips and pulls the table cloth
Overturns a coffee-cup,
Reorganized upon the floor
She yawns and draws a stocking up;

The silent man in mocha brown
Sprawls at the window-sill and gapes;
The waiter brings in oranges
Bananas figs and hothouse grapes;

The silent vertebrate in brown
Contracts and concentrates, withdraws;
Rachel *née* Rabinovitch
Tears at the grapes with murderous paws;

SWEENEY AMONG THE NIGHTINGALES. **Epigraph:** From *The Agamemnon* by Aeschylus, line 1343, when Agamemnon is struck by his wife Clytemnestra: "Oh, I have been struck a deadly blow." **4. maculate:** spotted, stained. **6. River Plate:** Rio de la Plata, between Argentina and Uruguay. **7. Raven:** Corvus, a constellation seen in the Southern sky; sometimes considered a symbol of death or ill omen. **8. hornèd gate:** in Greek myth, a gate of Hades through which true dreams come (whereas untrue dreams come through the ivory gate). **9. Orion . . . Dog:** Near the constellation Orion (the Hunter) is his dog, Sirius (the Dog Star). **10. shrunken seas:** The tide is out.

She and the lady in the cape
Are suspect, thought to be in league;
Therefore the man with heavy eyes
Declines the gambit, shows fatigue,

Leaves the room and reappears
Outside the window, leaning in,
Branches of wistaria
Circumscribe a golden grin;

The host with someone indistinct
Converses at the door apart,
The nightingales are singing near
The Convent of the Sacred Heart,

And sang within the bloody wood
When Agamemnon cried aloud,
And let their liquid siftings fall
To stain the stiff dishonored shroud.

1919

35–40. nightingales . . . shroud: Conflating the murder of Orpheus with that of Agamemnon, Eliot implies that the nightingales sang while these murders were taking place, and are still singing in this modern scene.

The Waste Land

The Waste Land may be introduced separately because of its importance and complexity. Although Eliot had long had it in mind, most of this famous poem was composed in 1921 during a time when Eliot was ill and feared psychological collapse. After he had completed a draft of the poem, Eliot gave it to Ezra Pound, who went through it suggesting revisions and deletions. (A facsimile of the original manuscript with Pound's marginal comments and excisions in the text was published in 1971.) Pound hailed *The Waste Land* as "the justification of our modern experiment," and it remains the greatest single poem of the Modernist period.

One of the many reasons why *The Waste Land* struck its first readers as arrestingly modern was its urban setting. In the poetry of the nineteenth century the commonest source of imagery had been nature. Although there were profound reasons for this around 1800, the use of nature had weakened to a poetic convention over the next century. By Eliot's time it entailed at least two liabilities. The imagery of nature isolated poetry from the contemporary urban milieu and therefore made it seem escapist. Moreover, because nature was felt to be refreshing, consoling, or beautiful, it imposed these qualities upon poetry, and thus limited the range of emotion poetry could express. The sights and sounds of the modern city—honking automobiles, barges on the polluted river, a crowd of people crossing London Bridge on their way to work—were far from unprecedented but still very unusual in English or American poetry. Eliot's achievement, moreover, was not merely to present the urban milieu but to do so with imaginative power—and to use it to express a vision of life. In one aspect *The Waste Land* resembles a documentary film as it cuts from one shot of the city to another, but these vignettes are also phantasmagoric, and their total effect is inexpressibly doleful. The lives of Eliot's city dwellers are sordid, empty, incoherent, and meaningless.

Amid its images of the modern city, the poem interfuses allusions to the historical past and to the literature, art, and myths of many languages and cultures. Many of these allusions are brief quotations, often in the original language. Usually they present parallels and contrasts to the contemporary material; in both aspects the allusions bring complex meanings to bear rapidly and suddenly. One general effect of the allusions is to locate the present moment of history within a vast temporal perspective, extending to ancient India and the prehistoric world whose vegetation myths the poem invokes. Whether the poem suggests that the condition of man has always and everywhere been essentially the same, or that in the past mankind was in touch with spiritual values now lost, may be argued; but however it is interpreted, the panoramic effect of the allusions is powerful.

One strand of allusions refers to primitive vegetation myths, which explained the annual withering of nature in the fall and its revival in spring as the death and rebirth of a god or gods. Following sources he indicated in his footnotes, Eliot conflated these myths with the medieval legends of the quest for the Holy Grail. According to the composite myth invoked in the poem, the land is waste (a desert) because its king is ill or dead. If he can be restored, the rain will return to the land and it will again be fertile. The myth of the dead and resurrected king also alludes to Christ.

Both the imagery of being in a desert and that of the modern city express the psychological and spiritual state that is the poem's subject. But the symbolism of the desert additionally suggests at least the possibility of relief from this condition. Relief would be obtained through finding a spring of water or by the coming of rain. The vegetation and Grail myths similarly posit that the dead god may be revived or the king healed. Many of the other allusions in the poem may also suggest a truth or faith that could save if the protagonists of *The Waste Land* were able to understand or accept it.

Eliot's style in *The Waste Land* was deliberately impersonal, concrete, fragmentary, and discontinuous. Thanks partly to the prestige of *The Waste Land*, these methods characterize much modern poetry. *Impersonality* means that an author does not express his own experience and emotion. At least, he does not voice it as his own, but describes things, invents characters, or creates dramatic scenes, and thus embodies emotion objectively in the particulars he renders. These particulars are *concrete* in the sense that they render sensations and actions as opposed to general ideas. But in *The Waste Land* such concrete particulars are only *fragments*. The poem does not give complete descriptions, quotations, conversations, or actions, but only bits and pieces of them. The words of Marie, for example, at the start of the poem are clearly part of a longer conversation, but we cannot know the context of this conversation or anything else about Marie. Such fragments are juxtaposed in unpredictable ways, and since each presents a different voice, action, emotion, and style, their sequence is at first disorienting. Gradually one finds interrelations within this *discontinuity*, but the interrelations are not the older, simpler ones of a continuing story, logical argument, or exposition of a character. One method of interrelation is by *leitmotifs*. This term, which is borrowed from the musical theories of Richard Wagner, refers to the use in separate passages of a poem of the same or similar images, allusions, or themes. Because we associate the different contexts in which a leitmotif appears, a web of leitmotifs throughout a work helps us to sense that it is an interconnected whole. In *The Waste Land* the images of water and of a desert are leitmotifs. Among the many more particular ones are the several allusions to Shakespeare's *The Tempest.* In the course of the poem a leitmotif acquires a dense cluster of associations and becomes a symbol. Fragmentation and discontinuity make *The Waste Land* difficult to read and interpret, but for Eliot they mirrored the reality of our experience.

The Waste Land

'Nam Sibyllam quidem Cumis ego ipse oculis meis vidi in ampulla pendere, et cum illi pueri dicerent: Σίβυλλα τί θέλεις; *respondebat illa:* ἀποθανεῖν θέλω.'

For Ezra Pound
il miglior fabbro.

I. The Burial of the Dead

April is the cruellest month, breeding
Lilacs out of the dead land, mixing
Memory and desire, stirring
Dull roots with spring rain.
Winter kept us warm, covering
Earth in forgetful snow, feeding
A little life with dried tubers.
Summer surprised us, coming over the Starnbergersee
With a shower of rain; we stopped in the colonnade,
And went on in sunlight, into the Hofgarten,
And drank coffee, and talked for an hour.

THE WASTE LAND. **Epigraph:** "For with my own eyes I saw the Sibyl hanging in a jar at Cumae, and when the boys said to her, 'Sibyl, what do you want?' she replied, 'I want to die.'" The quotation is from the *Satyricon* of Petronius (first century A.D.). The Sibyl, a famous prophetess, had been granted immortal life by the god Apollo. But she had forgotten to ask for immortal youth; hence she aged perpetually and her shriveled form was kept in a jar in the temple of Hercules at Cumae. **Dedication:** Ezra Pound helped Eliot revise *The Waste Land.* The phrase in Italian means "the better craftsman" and is a quotation from Dante's *Purgatorio,* XXVI, 117. Dante meets the poet Guido Guinizelli, who tells Dante that the Provençal poet Arnaut Daniel was a better craftsman than himself. I. THE BURIAL OF the dead. **Title:** a phrase from the Anglican burial service. **8. Starnbergersee:** a resort lake near Munich, in southern Germany. **10. Hofgarten:** court garden (German). A palace formerly occupied by King Ludwig II of Bavaria stands on the Starnbergersee.

Bin gar keine Russin, stamm' aus Litauen, echt deutsch.
And when we were children, staying at the arch-duke's,
My cousin's, he took me out on a sled,
And I was frightened. He said, Marie,
Marie, hold on tight. And down we went.
In the mountains, there you feel free.
I read, much of the night, and go south in the winter.

What are the roots that clutch, what branches grow
Out of this stony rubbish? Son of man,
You cannot say, or guess, for you know only
A heap of broken images, where the sun beats,
And the dead tree gives no shelter, the cricket no relief,
And the dry stone no sound of water. Only
There is shadow under this red rock,
(Come in under the shadow of this red rock),
And I will show you something different from either
Your shadow at morning striding behind you
Or your shadow at evening rising to meet you;
I will show you fear in a handful of dust.
Frisch weht der Wind
Der Heimat zu.
Mein irisch Kind,
Wo weilest du?
"You gave me hyacinths first a year ago;
"They called me the hyacinth girl."
—Yet when we came back, late, from the hyacinth garden,
Your arms full, and your hair wet, I could not
Speak, and my eyes failed, I was neither
Living nor dead, and I knew nothing,
Looking into the heart of light, the silence.
Oed' und leer das Meer.

12. Bin . . . deutsch: "I'm not Russian, I come from Lithuania, true German" (German). **13. arch-duke:** title of central European nobility. Eliot said the voice speaking here is that of a woman who had been a countess in the Austro-Hungarian empire, which collapsed at the end of the First World War. **20. Son . . . man:** Cf. Ezekiel 2:1 [Eliot's note]; God is speaking to Ezekiel. **23. cricket . . . relief:** Cf. Ecclesiastes 12:5 [Eliot's note]. The passage Eliot cites dwells on old age, "when the grasshopper [an aphrodisiac] shall be a burden, and desire shall fail." **26. red rock:** Isaiah, 22:2: a man shall be "as rivers of water in a dry place, as the shadow of a great rock in a weary land." ***31–34. Frisch . . . du:*** V. *Tristan und Isolde*, I, verses 5–8 [Eliot's note]. The quotation from Wagner's opera means, "Fresh blows the wind to the homeland; my Irish child, where do you tarry," and is sung by a sailor who is thinking of a girl left behind. ***42. Oed' . . . Meer:*** Id. [the same] III, verse 24 [Eliot's note]. The German words mean, "waste and empty the sea." In Wagner's opera they are sung by a shepherd as Tristan lies dying; Isolde, with whom Tristan is in love, is supposed to be coming, but the shepherd, looking out over the sea for the sails of her ship, can only report that no sails can be seen.

Madame Sosostris, famous clairvoyante,
Had a bad cold, nevertheless
Is known to be the wisest woman in Europe,
With a wicked pack of cards. Here, said she,
Is your card, the drowned Phoenician Sailor,
(Those are pearls that were his eyes. Look!)
Here is Belladonna, the Lady of the Rocks,
The lady of situations.
Here is the man with three staves, and here the Wheel,
And here is the one-eyed merchant, and this card,
Which is blank, is something he carries on his back,
Which I am forbidden to see. I do not find
The Hanged Man. Fear death by water.
I see crowds of people, walking round in a ring.
Thank you. If you see dear Mrs. Equitone,
Tell her I bring the horoscope myself:
One must be so careful these days.

Unreal City,
Under the brown fog of a winter dawn,
A crowd flowed over London Bridge, so many,
I had not thought death had undone so many.
Sighs, short and infrequent, were exhaled,
And each man fixed his eyes before his feet.
Flowed up the hill and down King William Street,
To where Saint Mary Woolnoth kept the hours

46. cards: I am not familiar with the exact constitution of the Tarot pack of cards, from which I have obviously departed to suit my own convenience. The Hanged Man, a member of the traditional pack, fits my purpose in two ways: because he is associated in my mind with the Hanged God of Frazer, and because I associate him with the hooded figure in the passage of the disciples to Emmaus in Part V. The Phoenician Sailor and the Merchant appear later; also the 'crowds of people,' and Death by Water is executed in Part IV. The Man with Three Staves (an authentic member of the Tarot pack) I associate, quite arbitrarily, with the Fisher King himself [Eliot's note]. The Tarot pack of cards is used for playing and for fortune-telling, and some of the figures on the cards are said to descend from ancient vegetation myths, such as those of which Eliot had read in Sir James Frazer (*The Golden Bough*, 1890–1915) and Jessie Weston (*From Ritual to Romance*, 1920). **47. Phoenician Sailor:** See Part IV. **48. Those . . . eyes:** quoted from Shakespeare's *The Tempest*, I, ii, 398. At this point in Shakespeare's play Ferdinand has been shipwrecked with his father on an island. A song, from which Eliot quotes, tells him, falsely as it turns out, that his father has drowned. The song describes the drowning, however, as though it were not dreadful, but a peaceful and magical change of being. **60. Unreal City:** Cf. Baudelaire: "Fourmillante cité, cité pleine de rêves,/ Où le spectre en plein jour raccroche le passant" [Eliot's note]. From *Les Sept Vieillards* ("The Seven Old Men") of Charles Baudelaire (1821–1867), the lines may be translated, "Swarming city, city full of dreams,/ Where the specter in broad daylight accosts the passerby." **63. I . . . many:** Cf. Dante's *Inferno* III, 55–57 [Eliot's note]. Eliot goes on in the note to quote the Italian: "so long a train of people, that I would never have believed death had undone so many." Dante is describing souls who lived "without infamy and without praise." **64. Sighs . . . exhaled:** Cf. Dante's *Inferno* IV, 25–27 [Eliot's note]. The note continues by quoting the passage in Italian: "Here, to my hearing, there was no weeping, but sighs which caused the eternal air to tremble."

With a dead sound on the final stroke of nine.
There I saw one I knew, and stopped him, crying: "Stetson!
"You who were with me in the ships at Mylae!
"That corpse you planted last year in your garden,
"Has it begun to sprout? Will it bloom this year?
"Or has the sudden frost disturbed its bed?
"Oh keep the Dog far hence, that's friend to men,
"Or with his nails he'll dig it up again!
"You! hypocrite lecteur!—mon semblable,—mon frère!"

II. A Game of Chess

The Chair she sat in, like a burnished throne,
Glowed on the marble, where the glass
Held up by standards wrought with fruited vines
From which a golden Cupidon peeped out
(Another hid his eyes behind his wing)
Doubled the flames of sevenbranched candelabra
Reflecting light upon the table as
The glitter of her jewels rose to meet it,
From satin cases poured in rich profusion;
In vials of ivory and colored glass
Unstoppered, lurked her strange synthetic perfumes,
Unguent, powdered, or liquid—troubled, confused
And drowned the sense in odors; stirred by the air
That freshened from the window, these ascended
In fattening the prolonged candle-flames,
Flung their smoke into the laquearia,
Stirring the pattern on the coffered ceiling.
Huge sea-wood fed with copper

68. dead . . . nine: A phenomenon which I have often noticed [Eliot's note]. Eliot worked in a bank in the financial district of London, known as the City, where the church of St. Mary Woolnoth is located. **70. Mylae:** sea battle in the first Punic war between the Romans and the Carthaginians (260 B.C.). **74–75. Dog . . . again:** Cf. the Dirge in Webster's *White Devil.* [Eliot's note]. Eliot refers to a song in IV. iv of the play by John Webster (*c.* 1580–1625). The song includes the lines: "But keep the wolf far thence, that's foe to men,/ For with his nails he'll dig them up again." **76. hypocrite . . . frère!:** V. Baudelaire, Preface to *Fleurs du Mal* [Eliot's note]: "Hypocrite reader!— my likeness,— my brother!" The reference is to "*Au Lecteur*" ("To the Reader"), in which Baudelaire lists a number of man's sins and concludes with ennui, which, he says, "You, reader, know." II. A GAME OF CHESS. **Title:** Suggests the title of a play by Thomas Middleton (1570?–1627), *A Game of Chess*, but also alludes to a scene in another play of Middleton's, *Women Beware Women.* In this play a woman is seduced in the next room while her mother is distracted by a game of chess; the movements in the game correspond to moves in the seduction. **77–78. Chair . . . marble:** Cf. *Antony and Cleopatra,* II, ii, l. 190 [Eliot's note]. In a famous passage in Shakespeare's play, Enobarbus describes Cleopatra: "The barge she sat in, like a burnished throne,/ Burned on the water . . . " **92. laquearia:** V. *Aeneid*, I, 726 [Eliot's note]. The note goes on to quote two lines in Latin, in which Virgil describes a feast given by Dido for Aeneas: "blazing torches hang from the golden paneled ceiling (*laquearibus aureis*), and the torches conquer the night with flames." Aeneas and Dido are lovers, but he is compelled by his destiny to leave her.

Burned green and orange, framed by the colored stone,
In which sad light a carvèd dolphin swam.
Above the antique mantel was displayed
As though a window gave upon the sylvan scene
The change of Philomel, by the barbarous king
So rudely forced; yet there the nightingale
Filled all the desert with inviolable voice
And still she cried, and still the world pursues,
"Jug Jug" to dirty ears.
And other withered stumps of time
Were told upon the walls; staring forms
Leaned out, leaning, hushing the room enclosed.
Footsteps shuffled on the stair.
Under the firelight, under the brush, her hair
Spread out in fiery points
Glowed into words, then would be savagely still.

"My nerves are bad to-night. Yes, bad. Stay with me.
"Speak to me. Why do you never speak. Speak.
  "What are you thinking of? What thinking? What?
"I never know what you are thinking. Think."

I think we are in rats' alley
Where the dead men lost their bones.

"What is that noise?"
                    The wind under the door.
"What is that noise now? What is the wind doing?"
                    Nothing again nothing.
                                        "Do
"You know nothing? Do you see nothing? Do you remember
"Nothing?"

    I remember
Those are pearls that were his eyes.
"Are you alive, or not? Is there nothing in your head?"
                                        But
O O O O that Shakespeherian Rag—
It's so elegant
So intelligent
"What shall I do now? What shall I do?"

98. sylvan scene: V. Milton, *Paradise Lost,* IV. 140. [Eliot's note]. In the Milton passage Satan is looking at Eden. **99. change . . . Philomel:** V. Ovid, *Metamorphoses,* VI, Philomela [Eliot's note]. King Tereus raped Philomela and cut out her tongue. Nevertheless she was able to tell her sister, Procne, the wife of Tereus, what had happened. In revenge Procne killed her son Itys and served his flesh to Tereus. The gods changed Philomela into the nightingale and Procne into the swallow. **100. nightingale:** Cf. Part III, l. 204 [Eliot's note]. **103. "Jug Jug":** in Elizabethan poetry a way of representing the nightingale's song; also obscene slang. **115. rats' alley:** Cf. Part III, l. 195 [Eliot's note]. **118. The . . . door:** Cf. Webster: "Is the wind in that door still?" [Eliot's note]. The reference is to John Webster's play, *The Devil's Law Case,* III, ii, 162.

"I shall rush out as I am, and walk the street
"With my hair down, so. What shall we do tomorrow?
"What shall we ever do?"
The hot water at ten.
And if it rains, a closed car at four.
And we shall play a game of chess,
Pressing lidless eyes and waiting for a knock upon the door.

When Lil's husband got demobbed, I said—
I didn't mince my words, I said to her myself,
HURRY UP PLEASE ITS TIME
Now Albert's coming back, make yourself a bit smart.
He'll want to know what you done with that money he gave you
To get yourself some teeth. He did, I was there.
You have them all out, Lil, and get a nice set,
He said, I swear, I can't bear to look at you.
And no more can't I, I said, and think of poor Albert,
He's been in the army four years, he wants a good time,
And if you don't give it him, there's others will, I said.
Oh is there, she said. Something o' that, I said.
Then I'll know who to thank, she said, and give me a straight look.
HURRY UP PLEASE ITS TIME
If you don't like it you can get on with it, I said.
Others can pick and choose if you can't.
But if Albert makes off, it won't be for lack of telling.
You ought to be ashamed, I said, to look so antique.
(And her only thirty-one.)
I can't help it, she said, pulling a long face,
It's them pills I took, to bring it off, she said.
(She's had five already, and nearly died of young George.)
The chemist said it would be all right, but I've never been the same.
You *are* a proper fool, I said.
Well, if Albert won't leave you alone, there it is, I said,
What you get married for if you don't want children?
HURRY UP PLEASE ITS TIME
Well, that Sunday Albert was home, they had a hot gammon,
And they asked me in to dinner, to get the beauty of it hot—
HURRY UP PLEASE ITS TIME
HURRY UP PLEASE ITS TIME
Goonight Bill. Goonight Lou. Goonight May. Goonight.
Ta ta. Goonight. Goonight.
Good night, ladies, good night, sweet ladies, good night, good night.

137–38. And . . . door: Cf. the game of chess in Middleton's *Women Beware Women* [Eliot's note]. See note to the title of this part of the poem. **139. demobbed:** demobilized from the army after the First World War. **152. Hurry . . . time:** the barkeeper's call at closing time in a London pub. **161. chemist:** druggist. **166. gammon:** ham. **172. Good . . . night:** Ophelia's words just before drowning herself in Shakespeare's *Hamlet*, IV, v. 72.

III. The Fire Sermon

The river's tent is broken; the last fingers of leaf
Clutch and sink into the wet bank. The wind
Crosses the brown land, unheard. The nymphs are departed.
Sweet Thames, run softly, till I end my song.
The river bears no empty bottles, sandwich papers,
Silk handkerchiefs, cardboard boxes, cigarette ends
Or other testimony of summer nights. The nymphs are departed.
And their friends, the loitering heirs of City directors;
Departed, have left no addresses.
By the waters of Leman I sat down and wept . . .
Sweet Thames, run softly till I end my song,
Sweet Thames, run softly, for I speak not loud or long.
But at my back in a cold blast I hear
The rattle of the bones, and chuckle spread from ear to ear.

A rat crept softly through the vegetation
Dragging its slimy belly on the bank
While I was fishing in the dull canal
On a winter evening round behind the gashouse
Musing upon the king my brother's wreck
And on the king my father's death before him.
White bodies naked on the low damp ground
And bones cast in a little low dry garret,
Rattled by the rat's foot only, year to year.
But at my back from time to time I hear
The sound of horns and motors, which shall bring
Sweeney to Mrs. Porter in the spring.
O the moon shone bright on Mrs. Porter
And on her daughter
They wash their feet in soda water
Et O ces voix d'enfants, chantant dans la coupole!

III. THE FIRE SERMON. **Title:** In the *Fire Sermon* Buddha says that all existing things are burning with desire, and that this desire must be renounced. **176. Sweet . . . song:** V. Spenser, *Prothalamion* [Eliot's note]. Spenser's Elizabethan poem from which the line is quoted celebrates marriage with high-minded idealism. **180. City directors:** directors of businesses in London's financial district; their sons would be wealthy. **182. By . . . wept:** alludes to Psalms 137:1. **191. Musing . . . wreck:** Cf. *The Tempest,* I, ii [Eliot's note]. See line 48. **196. But . . . hear:** Cf. Marvell, *To His Coy Mistress* [Eliot's note]. The lines in Andrew Marvell's poem go, "But at my back I always hear/ Time's winged chariot hurrying near." See also line 185. **197–98. sound . . . spring:** Cf. Day, *Parliament of Bees*: "When of the sudden listening, you shall hear,/ A noise of horns and hunting, which shall bring/ Actaeon to Diana in the spring,/ Where all shall see her naked skin . . . " [Eliot's note]. The reference is to John Day (*c.* 1574–1640), an Elizabethan dramatist. Actaeon saw Diana, goddess of chastity, bathing; she changed him into a stag and he was hunted to death by his own dogs. **199–201. O . . . water:** I do not know the origin of the ballad from which these lines are taken: it was reported to me from Sydney, Australia [Eliot's note]. **202. *Et . . . coupole!*:** V. Verlaine, *Parsifal* [Eliot's note]. The line is from the sonnet "Parsifal" by Paul Verlaine (1844–1896): "And O these voices of children singing in the dome!"

Twit twit twit
Jug jug jug jug jug jug
So rudely forc'd.
Tereu

Unreal City
Under the brown fog of a winter noon
Mr. Eugenides, the Smyrna merchant
Unshaven, with a pocket full of currants
C.i.f. London: documents at sight,
Asked me in demotic French
To luncheon at the Cannon Street Hotel
Followed by a weekend at the Metropole.

At the violet hour, when the eyes and back
Turn upward from the desk, when the human engine waits
Like a taxi throbbing waiting,
I Tiresias, though blind, throbbing between two lives,
Old man with wrinkled female breasts, can see
At the violet hour, the evening hour that strives
Homeward, and brings the sailor home from sea,
The typist home at teatime, clears her breakfast, lights
Her stove, and lays out food in tins.
Out of the window perilously spread
Her drying combinations touched by the sun's last rays,
On the divan are piled (at night her bed)
Stockings, slippers, camisoles, and stays.
I Tiresias, old man with wrinkled dugs
Perceived the scene, and foretold the rest—
I too awaited the expected guest.
He, the young man carbuncular, arrives,

204. Jug . . . jug: See line 103. **206. Tereu:** alluding to Tereus, see line 99; also, in Elizabethan poetry "tereu" was, like "jug, jug," a way of representing the nightingale's song. **210–11. currants . . . sight:** The currants were quoted at a price "carriage and insurance free to London"; and the Bill of Lading etc. were to be handed to the buyer upon payment of the sight draft [Eliot's note]. **218. Tiresias:** Tiresias, although a mere spectator and not indeed a "character," is yet the most important personage in the poem, uniting all the rest. Just as the one-eyed merchant, seller of currants, melts into the Phoenician Sailor, and the latter is not wholly distinct from Ferdinand Prince of Naples, so all the women are one woman, and the two sexes meet in Tiresias. What Tiresias *sees*, in fact, is the substance of the poem [Eliot's note]. Continuing his note, Eliot quotes a long passage from Ovid's *Metamorphosis*, III, 316–38, which, Eliot says, is of "great anthropological interest." The passage tells how Tiresias saw two snakes copulating and struck them. For this he was turned into a woman, and eight years later, the same thing happening again, he was turned back into a man. Tiresias was then called upon by the gods to decide whether men or women had more pleasure in sexual intercourse. When he said women did, the goddess Juno was angry and blinded him. The god Jove then granted him the gift of prophecy in recompense. **221. sailor . . . sea:** This may not appear as exact as Sappho's lines, but I had in mind the "longshore" or "dory" fisherman, who returns at nightfall [Eliot's note]. Eliot refers to Fragment 149 of Sappho (seventh century B.C.), but he is closer to the allusion to this Fragment in the "Requiem" of Robert Louis Stevenson (1850–1894): "Home is the sailor, home from sea,/ And the hunter home from the hill."

A small house agent's clerk, with one bold stare,
One of the low on whom assurance sits
As a silk hat on a Bradford millionaire.
The time is now propitious, as he guesses,
The meal is ended, she is bored and tired,
Endeavours to engage her in caresses
Which still are unreproved, if undesired.
Flushed and decided, he assaults at once;
Exploring hands encounter no defence;
His vanity requires no response,
And makes a welcome of indifference.
(And I Tiresias have foresuffered all
Enacted on this same divan or bed;
I who have sat by Thebes below the wall
And walked among the lowest of the dead.)
Bestows one final patronising kiss,
And gropes his way, finding the stairs unlit . . .

She turns and looks a moment in the glass,
Hardly aware of her departed lover;
Her brain allows one half-formed thought to pass:
'Well now that's done: and I'm glad it's over.'
When lovely woman stoops to folly and
Paces about her room again, alone,
She smoothes her hair with automatic hand,
And puts a record on the gramophone.

"This music crept by me upon the waters"
And along the Strand, up Queen Victoria Street.
O City city, I can sometimes hear
Beside a public bar in Lower Thames Street,
The pleasant whining of a mandoline
And a clatter and a chatter from within
Where fishmen lounge at noon: where the walls
Of Magnus Martyr hold
Inexplicable splendour of Ionian white and gold.

234. Bradford millionaire: Manufacturers in the Yorkshire town of Bradford were said to have made large profits out of the war. As a newly rich person, a Bradford millionaire would not be used to wearing a silk hat. **245. Thebes:** Tiresias (see line 218) prophesied in the market place of Thebes, next to the city's wall. **253. When . . . folly:** V. Goldsmith, the song in the *Vicar of Wakefield* [Eliot's note]. See Oliver Goldsmith. **257. "This . . . waters":** V. *The Tempest*, as above [Eliot's note]. See lines 48 and 125. **264–65. Magnus . . . gold:** The interior of St. Magnus Martyr is to my mind one of the finest among Wren's interiors . . . [Eliot's note]. The reference is to Sir Christopher Wren, architect, 1632–1723.

The river sweats
Oil and tar
The barges drift
With the turning tide
Red sails
Wide
To leeward, swing on the heavy spar.
The barges wash
Drifting logs
Down Greenwich reach
Past the Isle of Dogs.
Weialala leia
Wallala leialala

Elizabeth and Leicester
Beating oars
The stern was formed
A gilded shell
Red and gold
The brisk swell
Rippled both shores
Southwest wind
Carried down stream
The peal of bells
White towers
Weialala leia
Wallala leialala

"Trams and dusty trees.
Highbury bore me. Richmond and Kew
Undid me. By Richmond I raised my knees
Supine on the floor of a narrow canoe."

266. The river sweats: The Song of the (three) Thames-daughters begins here. From line 292 to 306 inclusive they speak in turn. V. *Götterdämmmerung* III, i: the Rhine-daughters [Eliot's note]. In the opera of Richard Wagner (1813–1883) the Rhine maidens try to seduce the hero, Siegfried, but also lament the theft of the gold of the Niebelungs, which has destroyed the beauty of the river, and foresee the destruction of the gods. The verse form here is imitated from Wagner, and the refrains at lines 276–77 and 290–91 are from the song in the opera. **274–75. Greenwich . . . Dogs:** Greenwich reach is a bend in the river, near the London borough of Greenwich; it forms a peninsula called the Isle of Dogs. **279. Elizabeth and Leicester:** V. Froude, *Elizabeth*, Vol. I, ch. iv, letter of De Quadra to Philip of Spain: "In the afternoon we were in a barge, watching the games on the river. (The queen) was alone with Lord Robert and myself on the poop, when they began to talk nonsense, and went so far that Lord Robert at last said, as I was on the spot there was no reason why they should not be married if the queen pleased" [Eliot's note]. Eliot's reference is to a passage about Queen Elizabeth I and her favorite, Lord Robert Dudley, Earl of Leicester, in the *History of England*, Vol. VII, p. 349, by J. A. Froude (1818–1894). **293–94. Highbury . . . me:** Cf. *Purgatorio*, V, 135 [Eliot's note]. Eliot then quotes in Italian the speech of La Pia, whom Dante meets in purgatory: "Remember me, who am La Pia;/ Sienna made me, Maremma undid me." Highbury is a suburb of London; Richmond and Kew are places on the Thames river for boating.

"My feet are at Moorgate, and my heart
Under my feet. After the event
He wept. He promised 'a new start.'
I made no comment. What should I resent?"

"On Margate Sands.
I can connect
Nothing with nothing.
The broken fingernails of dirty hands.
My people humble people who expect
Nothing."

To Carthage then I came

Burning burning burning burning
O Lord Thou pluckest me out
O Lord Thou pluckest

burning

IV. Death by Water

Phlebas the Phoenician, a fortnight dead,
Forgot the cry of gulls, and the deep sea swell
And the profit and loss.
A current under sea
Picked his bones in whispers. As he rose and fell
He passed the stages of his age and youth
Entering the whirlpool.
Gentile or Jew
O you who turn the wheel and look to windward,
Consider Phlebas, who was once handsome and tall as you.

V. What the Thunder Said

After the torchlight red on sweaty faces
After the frosty silence in the gardens
After the agony in stony places

296. Moorgate: slum area of London. **300. Margate Sands:** seaside resort. **307. Carthage . . . came:** V. St. Augustine's *Confessions*: "to Carthage then I came, where a cauldron of unholy loves sang all about mine ears" [Eliot's note]. **308. Burning . . . burning:** Eliot's note observes that "The complete text of the Buddha's Fire Sermon . . . corresponds in importance to the Sermon on the Mount." See note to the title of Part III. **309. O . . . out:** From St. Augustine's *Confessions* X, 34 again. The collocation of these two representatives of eastern and western asceticism, as the culmination of this part of the poem, is not an accident [Eliot's note]. V. WHAT THE THUNDER SAID. **Title:** In the first part of Part V three themes are employed: the journey to Emmaus, the approach to the Chapel Perilous (see Miss Weston's book) and the present decay of Eastern Europe [Eliot's note]. In Luke 24:13–31, after Christ's resurrection two disciples are journeying along the road to Emmaus and are joined by Jesus, whom they do not recognize. The Chapel Perilous is encountered in the final stage of the quest for the Holy Grail. **322–28. After . . . dead:** allusions to the agony of Jesus in the Garden of Gethsemane, his arrest, questioning before Pilate, and crucifixion.

The shouting and the crying
Prison and palace and reverberation
Of thunder of spring over distant mountains
He who was living is now dead
We who were living are now dying
With a little patience

Here is no water but only rock
Rock and no water and the sandy road
The road winding above among the mountains
Which are mountains of rock without water
If there were water we should stop and drink
Amongst the rock one cannot stop or think
Sweat is dry and feet are in the sand
If there were only water amongst the rock
Dead mountain mouth of carious teeth that cannot spit
Here one can neither stand nor lie nor sit
There is not even silence in the mountains
But dry sterile thunder without rain
There is not even solitude in the mountains
But red sullen faces sneer and snarl
From doors of mudcracked houses
                                                    If there were water
    And no rock
    If there were rock
    And also water
    And water
    A spring
    A pool among the rock
    If there were the sound of water only
    Not the cicada
    And dry grass singing
    But sound of water over a rock
    Where the hermit-thrush sings in the pine trees
    Drip drop drip drop drop drop drop
    But there is no water

Who is the third who walks always beside you?
When I count, there are only you and I together
But when I look ahead up the white road
There is always another one walking beside you
Gliding wrapt in a brown mantle, hooded
I do not know whether a man or a woman
—But who is that on the other side of you?

357–58. hermit-thrush . . . drop: . . . which I have heard in Quebec Province . . . . Its "water-dripping song" is justly celebrated [Eliot's note]. **360. Who . . . beside you:** The following lines were stimulated by the account of one of the Antartic expeditions (I forget which, but I think one of Shackleton's): it was related that the party of explorers, at the extremity of their strength, had the constant delusion that there was *one more member* than could actually be counted [Eliot's note].

What is that sound high in the air
Murmur of maternal lamentation
Who are those hooded hordes swarming
Over endless plains, stumbling in cracked earth
Ringed by the flat horizon only
What is the city over the mountains
Cracks and reforms and bursts in the violet air
Falling towers
Jerusalem Athens Alexandria
Vienna London
Unreal

A woman drew her long black hair out tight
And fiddled whisper music on those strings
And bats with baby faces in the violet light
Whistled, and beat their wings
And crawled head downward down a blackened wall
And upside down in air were towers
Tolling reminiscent bells, that kept the hours
And voices singing out of empty cisterns and exhausted wells

In this decayed hole among the mountains
In the faint moonlight, the grass is singing
Over the tumbled graves, about the chapel
There is the empty chapel, only the wind's home.
It has no windows, and the door swings,
Dry bones can harm no one.
Only a cock stood on the rooftree
Co co rico co co rico
In a flash of lightning. Then a damp gust
Bringing rain

Ganga was sunken, and the limp leaves
Waited for rain, while the black clouds
Gathered far distant, over Himavant.
The jungle crouched, humped in silence.
Then spoke the thunder
DA

367–77. What is . . . Unreal: In his note to these lines Eliot quotes in German from Hermann Hesse's *Blick ins Chaos* (1920): "Already half of Europe, already at least half of Eastern Europe is on the way to Chaos, drives drunkenly in sacred madness along the edge of the abyss and, moreover, sings, sings drunken hymns as Dimitri Karamasoff sang. The offended bourgeois laughs at these songs, the saint and seer hears them with tears." Dimitri Karamazov is a character in Dostoievski's novel, *The Brothers Karamazov* (1879–80). **396. Ganga:** the sacred river Ganges in India. **398. Himavant:** the Himalayan mountains. **401. Da:** the sound of the thunder. Eliot's note translates the subsequent words in Sanskrit at lines 402, 412, and 419 as "Give, sympathise, control" respectively, and adds that "The fable of the meaning of the Thunder is found in the *Brihadaranyaka-Upanishad*, 5, 1." In this fable the gods, men, and demons each in turn ask the Creator to speak to them. To each order of being in turn the Creator says "Da." Each hears in it a different word or command.

Datta: what have we given?
My friend, blood shaking my heart
The awful daring of a moment's surrender
Which an age of prudence can never retract
By this, and this only, we have existed
Which is not to be found in our obituaries
Or in memories draped by the beneficent spider
Or under seals broken by the lean solicitor
In our empty rooms
DA
Dayadhvam: I have heard the key
Turn in the door once and turn once only
We think of the key, each in his prison
Thinking of the key, each confirms a prison
Only at nightfall, aethereal rumours
Revive for a moment a broken Coriolanus
DA
Damyata: The boat responded
Gaily, to the hand expert with sail and oar
The sea was calm, your heart would have responded
Gaily, when invited, beating obedient
To controlling hands

I sat upon the shore
Fishing, with the arid plain behind me
Shall I at least set my lands in order?
London Bridge is falling down falling down falling down
Poi s'ascose nel foco che gli affina

408. spider: Cf. John Webster, *The White Devil*, V, vi: " . . . they'll remarry/ Ere the worm pierce your winding-sheet, ere the spider/ Make a thin curtain for your epitaphs" [Eliot's note]. **411–12. Da *Dayadhvam*:** See line 401. **key:** Cf. Dante's *Inferno*, XXXIII, 46 [Eliot's note]. Eliot quotes in Italian, "and I heard below me the door of the horrible tower being locked." The words are spoken by Ugolino, who was locked into a tower with his children to starve to death. Eliot's note continues, "Also F. H. Bradley, *Appearance and Reality* [1893], p. 346. 'My external sensations are no less private to myself than are my thoughts or my feelings. In either case my experience falls within my own circle, a circle closed on the outside; and, with all its elements alike, every sphere is opaque to the others which surround it . . . In brief, regarded as an existence which appears in a soul, the whole world for each is peculiar and private to that soul.'" The English philosopher F. H. Bradley was the subject of Eliot's Ph.D. thesis. **417. Coriolanus:** Roman general, subject of Shakespeare's play, whose haughty pride led him to lead an army against Rome. Before the city he was encountered by his mother, whose arguments and pleas broke his will. **419. *Damyata*:** see line 401. **425. Fishing:** V. Jessie Weston, *From Ritual to Romance*; chapter on the Fisher King [Eliot's note]. **426. set . . . order:** Isaiah, 38:1: "Thus saith the Lord, Set thine house in order: for thou shalt die, and not live." **427. London . . . down:** quoted from a nursery rhyme. **428. *Poi . . . affina*:** V. Dante's *Purgatorio*, XXVI, 148 [Eliot's note]. Eliot goes on to quote four lines in Italian: "'Now I pray you by that virtue/ that guides you to the top of the stair [where Dante will leave purgatory],/ be mindful in time of my suffering.'/ Then he hid himself in the fire that refines them." The speaker is the Provençal poet Arnaut Daniel; the last line of the passage is the one quoted by Eliot.

Quando fiam uti chelidon—O swallow swallow
Le Prince d'Aquitaine à la tour abolie
These fragments I have shored against my ruins
Why then Ile fit you. Hieronymo's mad againe.
Datta. Dayadhvam. Damyata.
Shantih shantih shantih

1922

Burnt Norton

τοῦ λόγου δ'ἐόντος ξυνοῦ ζώουσιν οἱ πολλοί
ὡς ἰδίαν ἔχοντες φρόνησιν.
I. p. 77. Fr. 2.

ὁδὸς ἄνω κάτω μία καὶ ὡυτή.
I. p. 89. Fr. 60.

Diels: *Die Fragmente der Vorsokratiker* (Herakleitos).

I

Time present and time past
Are both perhaps present in time future,
And time future contained in time past.
If all time is eternally present
All time is unredeemable.
What might have been is an abstraction
Remaining a perpetual possibility
Only in a world of speculation.
What might have been and what has been
Point to one end, which is always present.
Footfalls echo in the memory

429. *Quando . . . chelidon*: V. *Pervigilium Veneris*. Cf. Philomela in Parts II and III [Eliot's note]. The Latin means, "When shall I be like the swallow." The *Pervigilium Veneris*, a late Latin poem, refers in its last two stanzas to the myth of Tereus, Philomela, and Procne. See line 99 above. **430. *Le Prince . . . abolie*:** V. Gérard de Nerval, Sonnet *El Desdichado* [The Disinherited] [Eliot's note]. The French means, "The Prince of Aquitaine at the ruined tower." **432. Why . . . againe:** V. Kyd's *Spanish Tragedy* [Eliot's note]. In the play by Thomas Kyd (*c.* 1558–1594) Hieronymo's son is murdered. Asked to write a play, Hieronymo replies, "Why then Ile fit [accommodate] you." Acting in the play, he carries out his revenge. The subtitle of Kyd's drama is "Hieronymo's mad again." **434. Shantih . . . shantih:** Repeated as here, a formal ending to an Upanishad. "The Peace which passeth understanding" is our equivalent to this word [Eliot's note]. The Upanishads are poetic dialogues that comment on the ancient Hindu scriptures or Vedas. BURNT NORTON. **Epigraph.** The Greek philosopher Heracleitus (*c.*535–475 B.C.) taught that all reality is in flux. The four elements of fire, air, water, and earth were constantly transforming themselves one into another. The first quotation says, "But though the word is common, the many live as though they had a wisdom of their own"; and the second, "The way up and the way down are one and the same."

Down the passage which we did not take
Towards the door we never opened
Into the rose-garden. My words echo
Thus, in your mind.
But to what purpose
Disturbing the dust on a bowl of rose-leaves
I do not know.
Other echoes
Inhabit the garden. Shall we follow?
Quick, said the bird, find them, find them,
Round the corner. Through the first gate,
Into our first world, shall we follow
The deception of the thrush? Into our first world.
There they were, dignified, invisible,
Moving without pressure, over the dead leaves,
In the autumn heat, through the vibrant air,
And the bird called, in response to
The unheard music hidden in the shrubbery,
And the unseen eyebeam crossed, for the roses
Had the look of flowers that are looked at.
There they were as our guests, accepted and accepting.
So we moved, and they, in a formal pattern,
Along the empty alley, into the box circle,
To look down into the drained pool.
Dry the pool, dry concrete, brown edged,
And the pool was filled with water out of sunlight,
And the lotos rose, quietly, quietly,
The surface glittered out of heart of light,
And they were behind us, reflected in the pool.
Then a cloud passed, and the pool was empty.
Go, said the bird, for the leaves were full of children,
Hidden excitedly, containing laughter.
Go, go, go, said the bird: human kind
Cannot bear very much reality.
Time past and time future
What might have been and what has been
Point to one end, which is always present.

II

Garlic and sapphires in the mud
Clot the bedded axle-tree.
The trilling wire in the blood

16. rose-leaves: rose petals. **32. box:** shrub used for borders and hedges. **37. heart of light:** see *The Waste Land,* I, line 41. **47. Garlic . . . mud:** Garlic suggests the coarse gluttony, and sapphires the avarice and greed for possessions of the human animal, who is made, like Adam, from the "dust of the ground." **48. Clot . . . tree:** These "clot" the center of the wheel ("axle-tree") embedded within the world of matter.

Sings below inveterate scars
Appeasing long forgotten wars.
The dance along the artery
The circulation of the lymph
Are figured in the drift of stars
Ascend to summer in the tree
We move above the moving tree
In light upon the figured leaf
And hear upon the sodden floor
Below, the boarhound and the boar
Pursue their pattern as before
But reconciled among the stars.

At the still point of the turning world. Neither flesh nor fleshless;
Neither from nor towards; at the still point, there the dance is,
But neither arrest nor movement. And do not call it fixity,
Where past and future are gathered. Neither movement from nor towards,
Neither ascent nor decline. Except for the point, the still point,
There would be no dance, and there is only the dance.
I can only say, *there* we have been: but I cannot say where.
And I cannot say, how long, for that is to place it in time.
The inner freedom from the practical desire,
The release from action and suffering, release from the inner
And the outer compulsion, yet surrounded
By a grace of sense, a white light still and moving,
Erhebung without motion, concentration
Without elimination, both a new world
And the old made explicit, understood
In the completion of its partial ecstasy,
The resolution of its partial horror.
Yet the enchainment of past and future
Woven in the weakness of the changing body,
Protects mankind from heaven and damnation
Which flesh cannot endure.

Time past and time future
Allow but a little consciousness.
To be conscious is not to be in time
But only in time can the moment in the rose-garden,
The moment in the arbour where the rain beat,
The moment in the draughty church at smokefall
Be remembered; involved with past and future.
Only through time time is conquered.

52–54. dance . . . stars: The mysterious and ordered movement of blood and lymph is, in miniature, a reflection of the larger order of the stars and the cosmos. **74. *Erhebung:*** elevation.

III

Here is a place of disaffection
Time before and time after
In a dim light: neither daylight
Investing form with lucid stillness
Turning shadow into transient beauty
With slow rotation suggesting permanence
Nor darkness to purify the soul
Emptying the sensual with deprivation
Cleansing affection from the temporal.
Neither plenitude nor vacancy. Only a flicker
Over the strained time-ridden faces
Distracted from distraction by distraction
Filled with fancies and empty of meaning
Tumid apathy with no concentration
Men and bits of paper, whirled by the cold wind
That blows before and after time,
Wind in and out of unwholesome lungs
Time before and time after.
Eructation of unhealthy souls
Into the faded air, the torpid
Driven on the wind that sweeps the gloomy hills of London,
Hampstead and Clerkenwell, Campden and Putney,
Highgate, Primrose and Ludgate. Not here
Not here the darkness, in this twittering world.

Descend lower, descend only
Into the world of perpetual solitude,
World not world, but that which is not world,
Internal darkness, deprivation
And destitution of all property,
Desiccation of the world of sense,
Evacuation of the world of fancy,
Inoperancy of the world of spirit;
This is the one way, and the other
Is the same, not in movement
But abstention from movement; while the world moves
In appetency, on its metalled ways
Of time past and time future.

IV

Time and the bell have buried the day,
The black cloud carries the sun away.
Will the sunflower turn to us, will the clematis

90. place: In Part III, the London subway provides an introductory image for the theme of descent into darkness. **99. plenitude:** fullness and variety. **103. tumid:** swollen. **108. Eructation:** belching forth. **111–12. Hampstead . . . Ludgate:** districts of London. **119. Desiccation:** dryness, aridity. **125. appetency:** craving or appetite. **metalled ways:** referring to the rails of the subway trains.

Stray down, bend to us; tendril and spray
Clutch and cling?
  Chill
Fingers of yew be curled
Down on us? After the kingfisher's wing
Has answered light to light, and is silent, the light is still
At the still point of the turning world.

V

Words move, music moves
Only in time; but that which is only living
Can only die. Words, after speech, reach
Into the silence. Only by the form, the pattern,
Can words or music reach
The stillness, as a Chinese jar still
Moves perpetually in its stillness.
Not the stillness of the violin, while the note lasts,
Not that only, but the co-existence,
Or say that the end precedes the beginning,
And the end and the beginning were always there
Before the beginning and after the end.
And all is always now. Words strain,
Crack and sometimes break, under the burden,
Under the tension, slip, slide, perish,
Decay with imprecision, will not stay in place,
Will not stay still. Shrieking voices
Scolding, mocking, or merely chattering,
Always assail them. The Word in the desert
Is most attacked by voices of temptation,
The crying shadow in the funeral dance,
The loud lament of the disconsolate chimera.

    The detail of the pattern is movement,
As in the figure of the ten stairs.
Desire itself is movement
Not in itself desirable;
Love is itself unmoving,
Only the cause and end of movement,
Timeless, and undesiring
Except in the aspect of time
Caught in the form of limitation
Between un-being and being.

155. Word: Christ. **160. ten stairs:** St. John of the Cross, a sixteenth-century Spanish mystic, describes a ladder of "contemplation" consisting of ten steps by which we can ascend to union with God. **161–64. Desire . . . movement:** Desire itself is not an object, but a movement toward an object; whereas Love is both the original cause and the object to which we aspire, as God is prior to all movement toward Him and is also the end.

Sudden in a shaft of sunlight
Even while the dust moves
There rises the hidden laughter
Of children in the foliage
Quick now, here, now, always—
Ridiculous the waste sad time
Stretching before and after.

1936

John Crowe Ransom

(1888–1974)

After studying as a Rhodes Scholar at Oxford, Ransom returned as a teacher to Vanderbilt University in Tennessee. He was associated with the Fugitives, a group of writers who advocated traditional values of the agrarian South in opposition to the unrooted, industrial society of the North. At Vanderbilt Ransom and other young teachers and students, including Allen Tate and Robert Penn Warren, met regularly to read and discuss each other's poems. These discussions were minute, analytic, and devoted especially to formal aspects of poems, such as logic, syntax, versification, figures of speech, and image patterns. The method of studying poems by close "reading," which became widespread in the 1940s, had one of its sources in these discussions. Ransom invented the term, the "New Criticism," that is still used to refer to this method.

Poetic values advocated by the New Critics—such as formality, density of implication, and irony—were illustrated in Ransom's poetry. He was especially sympathetic to the poetry of Thomas Hardy, and he was also influenced by the Metaphysical style of Donne and by poems of Edwin Arlington Robinson, such as "Richard Cory," which present a speaker and a social milieu with humorous irony and pathos. In 1937 Ransom moved to Kenyon College in Ohio, where he founded and edited an important literary magazine, the *Kenyon Review*. He had stopped writing poetry ten years earlier, but he remained one of the leading critics of his generation.

Bells for John Whiteside's Daughter

There was such speed in her little body,
And such lightness in her footfall,
It is no wonder her brown study
Astonishes us all.

Her wars were bruited in our high window.
We looked among orchard trees and beyond
Where she took arms against her shadow,
Or harried unto the pond

The lazy geese, like a snow cloud
Dripping their snow on the green grass,
Tricking and stopping, sleepy and proud,
Who cried in goose, Alas,

For the tireless heart within the little
Lady with rod that made them rise
From their noon apple-dreams and scuttle
Goose-fashion under the skies!

But now go the bells, and we are ready,
In one house we are sternly stopped
To say we are vexed at her brown study,
Lying so primly propped.

1924

Here Lies a Lady

Here lies a lady of beauty and high degree.
Of chills and fever she died, of fever and chills,
The delight of her husband, her aunt, an infant of three,
And of medicos marveling sweetly on her ills.

For either she burned, and her confident eyes would blaze,
And her fingers fly in a manner to puzzle their heads—
What was she making? Why, nothing; she sat in a maze
Of old scraps of laces, snipped into curious shreds—

Or this would pass, and the light of her fire decline
Till she lay discouraged and cold, like a stalk white and blown,
And would not open her eyes, to kisses, to wine;
The sixth of these states was her last; the cold settled down.

Sweet ladies, long may ye bloom, and toughly I hope ye may
thole,
But was she not lucky? In flowers and lace and mourning,
In love and great honor we bade God rest her soul
After six little spaces of chill, and six of burning.

1924

Dead Boy

The little cousin is dead, by foul subtraction,
A green bough from Virginia's aged tree,
And none of the county kin like the transaction,
Nor some of the world of outer dark, like me.

A boy not beautiful, nor good, nor clever,
A black cloud full of storms too hot for keeping,
A sword beneath his mother's heart—yet never
Woman bewept her babe as this is weeping.

A pig with a pasty face, so I had said,
Squealing for cookies, kinned by poor pretense
With a noble house. But the little man quite dead,
I see the forbears' antique lineaments.

The elder men have strode by the box of death
To the wide flag porch, and muttering low send round
The bruit of the day. O friendly waste of breath!
Their hearts are hurt with a deep dynastic wound.

He was pale and little, the foolish neighbors say;
The first-fruits, saith the Preacher, the Lord hath taken;
But this was the old tree's late branch wrenched away,
Grieving the sapless limbs, the shorn and shaken.

1927

Claude McKay

(1890–1948)

McKay was born in Jamaica and emigrated to the United States, where he lived in Harlem. His poems were usually romantic and rhetorical in style. They boldly expressed his racial self-consciousness and his ambivalent feelings about white culture, and had a liberating impact on black poets of the next generation. "If We Must Die" was written in response to the race riots of 1919, which were terrifying to the black community. McKay later settled in France and turned out prose fiction. Believing in Communism, he was deeply disillusioned and depressed by the development of the Russian state. He later became a convert to Roman Catholicism. He spent his last years in poverty and obscurity, teaching in Catholic schools in Chicago. He wrote little after 1932.

DEAD BOY. **15. bruit:** news.

If We Must Die

If we must die, let it not be like hogs
Hunted and penned in an inglorious spot,
While round us bark the mad and hungry dogs,
Making their mock at our accursed lot.
If we must die, O let us nobly die,
So that our precious blood may not be shed
In vain; then even the monsters we defy
Shall be constrained to honor us though dead!
O kinsmen! we must meet the common foe!
Though far outnumbered let us show us brave,
And for their thousand blows deal one deathblow!
What though before us lies the open grave?
Like men we'll face the murderous, cowardly pack,
Pressed to the wall, dying, but fighting back!

1922

Hugh MacDiarmid (C. M. Grieve)

(1892–1978)

A Scotch Nationalist and Communist, Grieve went to Edinburgh University, served in World War I, and worked as a journalist. He took the pseudonymn of Hugh MacDiarmid, by which he is now known, in 1922, when he started composing in Scots rather than English. The Scots in his poetry is not spoken anywhere in Scotland, but is a language synthesized out of several different dialects, and it also includes archaic words. Not all his later poetry is in Scots, but he is the best poet in this language since Robet Burns.

Parley of Beasts

Auld Noah was at hame wi' them a',
The lion and the lamb,
Pair by pair they entered the Ark
And he took them as they cam'.

PARLEY OF BEASTS. **1.Auld:** old. **hame:** home. **a':** all. **4. cam':** came.

If twa o' ilka beist there is
Into this room sud come,
Wad I cud welcome them like him,
And no' staun' gowpin' dumb!

Be chief wi' them and they wi' me
And a' wi' ane anither
As Noah and his couples were
There in the Ark thegither.

It's fain I'd mell wi' tiger and tit,
Wi' elephant and eel,
But noo-a-days e'en wi' ain's se
At hame it's hard to feel.

1926

O Wha's the Bride?

O wha's the bride that cairries the bunch
O' thistles blinterin' white?
Her cuckold bridegroom little dreids
What he sall ken this nicht.

For closer than gudeman can come
And closer to'r than hersel',
Wha didna need her maidenheid
Has wrocht his purpose fell.

O wha's been here afore me, lass,
And hoo did he get in?
—A man that deed or was I born
This evil thing has din.

And left, as it were on a corpse,
Your maidenheid to me?
—Nae lass, gudeman, sin' Time began
'S hed ony mair to gi'e.

But I can gi'e ye kindness, lad,
And a pair o' willin' hands,
And you sall ha'e my breists like stars,
My limbs like willow wands.

5. twa o' ilka beist: two of every beast. **6. sud:** should. **7. Wad:** would. **cud:** could. **8. no' staun' gowpin':** not stand gaping. **9. chief wi':** friendly with. **10. ane anither:** one another. **12. thegither:** together. **13. mell wi':** mix with. **tit:** titmouse. **15. e'en wi' ain's se:** even with one's self. O WHA'S THE BRIDE? **1. wha's:** who is. **2. blinterin':** gleaming. **3. dreids:** dreads. **4. sall ken:** shall know. **5. gudeman:** husband. **8. wrocht:** worked. **10. hoo:** how. **11. deed:** died. **12. din:** done. **15. sin':** since. **16. 'S:** Has. **ony . . . gi'e:** any more to give. **19. sall:** shall. **breists:** breasts.

And on my lips ye'll heed nae mair,
And in my hair forget,
The seed o' a' the men that in
My virgin womb ha'e met. . . .

1926

ARCHIBALD MACLEISH

(1892–1982)

In 1923 MacLeish abandoned a promising career as a lawyer and moved with his family to France to study and write poetry. He studied the styles of Eliot and Pound and was greatly influenced by them. But he combined their methods with the elegiac emotion and musical cadence of the nineteenth century, and this combination makes such lyrics as "You, Andrew Marvell" haunting and distinctive. Returning to the United States in 1928, MacLeish worked for *Fortune* magazine. Engaged politically in the struggle against Fascism, he experimented with radio plays designed to reach and warn a large audience. He was a speech writer for President Roosevelt, and held many important posts in the federal government, including that of Librarian of Congress. In 1949 he became a professor in the English department of Harvard University. Through all these activities he continued to write prolifically. Many of his later lyrics were in an intellectually intense, prophetic mode he caught from Yeats and handled with enormous skill.

Ars Poetica

A poem should be palpable and mute
As a globed fruit,

Dumb
As old medallions to the thumb,

Silent as the sleeve-worn stone
Of casement ledges where the moss has grown—

A poem should be wordless
As the flight of birds.

23. o' a': of all. **24. ha'e:** have.

A poem should be motionless in time
As the moon climbs,

Leaving, as the moon releases
Twig by twig the night-entangled trees,

Leaving, as the moon behind the winter leaves,
Memory by memory the mind—

A poem should be motionless in time
As the moon climbs.

A poem should be equal to:
Not true.

For all the history of grief
An empty doorway and a maple leaf.

For love
The leaning grasses and two lights above the sea—

A poem should not mean
But be.

1926

You, Andrew Marvell

And here face down beneath the sun
And here upon earth's noonward height
To feel the always coming on
The always rising of the night:

To feel creep up the curving east
The earthy chill of dusk and slow
Upon those under lands the vast
And ever climbing shadow grow

And strange at Ecbatan the trees
Take leaf by leaf the evening strange
The flooding dark about their knees
The mountains over Persia change

And now at Kermanshah the gate
Dark empty and the withered grass
And through the twilight now the late
Few travelers in the westward pass

YOU, ANDREW MARVELL. **Title:** MacLeish is developing the theme expressed in the lines from Marvell's poem "To His Coy Mistress," "But at my back I always hear/ Time's wingèd chariot hurrying near." The poem follows the course of the sun from East to West, symbolizing the rise and fall of civilizations from Persia and the Near East through Sicily and then Spain to the western hemisphere. **9. Ecbatan:** once a captial of ancient Persia. **13. Kermanshah:** also in Persia.

And Baghdad darken and the bridge
Across the silent river gone
And through Arabia the edge
Of evening widen and steal on

And deepen on Palmyra's street
The wheel rut in the ruined stone
And Lebanon fade out and Crete
High through the clouds and overblown

And over Sicily the air
Still flashing with the landward gulls
And loom and slowly disappear
The sails above the shadowy hulls

And Spain go under and the shore
Of Africa the gilded sand
And evening vanish and no more
The low pale light across that land

Nor now the long light on the sea:
And here face downward in the sun
To feel how swift how secretly
The shadow of the night comes on . . .

1930

Winter Is Another Country

If the autumn would
End! If the sweet season,
The late light in the tall trees would
End! If the fragrance, the odor of
Fallen apples, dust on the road,
Water somewhere near, the scent of
Water touching me; if this would end
I could endure the absence in the night,
The hands beyond the reach of hands, the name
Called out and never answered with my name:
The image seen but never seen with sight.
I could endure this all
If autumn ended and the cold light came.

1948

21. Palmyra: city in ancient Syria, once a famous center of trade. Among its ruins is only a small Arab village.

EDNA ST. VINCENT MILLAY

(1892–1950)

Associated with the American literary bohemia of the 1920s, Millay defied middle-class moral convention by speaking of love and sex frankly and from a woman's point of view. *Fatal Interview* (1931), from which one of our selections is taken, was a sequence of fifty-two Shakespearean sonnets on the course of a love affair. Her style was rhetorical and Romantic in ways that were then somewhat out of fashion but still cherished by many readers. Her appeal lay precisely in this combination of traditionally "poetic" high style with a direct intimacy or frankness that seemed contemporary, adventurous, and liberating.

What Lips My Lips Have Kissed, and Where, and Why

What lips my lips have kissed, and where, and why,
I have forgotten, and what arms have lain
Under my head till morning; but the rain
Is full of ghosts tonight, that tap and sigh
Upon the glass and listen for reply,
And in my heart there stirs a quiet pain
For unremembered lads that not again
Will turn to me at midnight with a cry.
Thus in the winter stands the lonely tree,
Nor knows what birds have vanished one by one,
Yet knows its boughs more silent than before:
I cannot say what loves have come and gone,
I only know that summer sang in me
A little while, that in me sings no more.

1922

from Fatal Interview

XXX

Love is not all: it is not meat nor drink
Nor slumber nor a roof against the rain;
Nor yet a floating spar to men that sink

And rise and sink and rise and sink again;
Love can not fill the thickened lung with breath,
Nor clean the blood, nor set the fractured bone;
Yet many a man is making friends with death
Even as I speak, for lack of love alone.
It well may be that in a difficult hour,
Pinned down by pain and moaning for release,
Or nagged by want past resolution's power,
I might be driven to sell your love for peace,
Or trade the memory of this night for food.
It well may be. I do not think I would.

1931

Wilfred Owen

(1893–1918)

The greatest English poet of the First World War, Owen served as an officer in the trenches. He was appalled at the suffering of the soldiers and at the waste of their lives. Filled with compassion and seared in conscience, he composed poems to show what the war was like and to attack the safe patriots at home who tolerated its continuation. His poems presented vivid and often grisly, realistic details, but his strong pity for the common soldiers and his idealization of them expressed a Romantic strain in his character, and this also manifested itself in his poetic imagery and diction. He was the first important poet in English to use "off" or "slant" rhyme, in which the same consonants surround different vowels (escaped/ scooped). The complexity and power of his poetry is such that, had he lived, he would have become one of the major poets of the twentieth century. He was killed a week before the war ended.

Greater Love

Red lips are not so red
  As the stained stones kissed by the English dead.
Kindness of wooed and wooer
Seems shame to their love pure.
O Love, your eyes lose lure
  When I behold eyes blinded in my stead!

GREATER LOVE. **Title:** A reference to the sentence in the Bible: "Greater love hath no man than this, that a man lay down his life for his friends" (John 15:13).

Your slender attitude
  Trembles not exquisite like limbs knife-skewed,
Rolling and rolling there
Where God seems not to care;
Till the fierce love they bear
  Cramps them in death's extreme decrepitude.

Your voice sings not so soft,—
  Though even as wind murmuring through raftered loft,—
Your dear voice is not dear,
Gentle, and evening clear,
As theirs whom none now hear,
  Now earth has stopped their piteous mouths that coughed.

Heart, you were never hot
  Nor large, nor full like hearts made great with shot;
And though your hand be pale,
Paler are all which trail
Your cross through flame and hail:
  Weep, you may weep, for you may touch them not.

1920

Strange Meeting

It seemed that out of battle I escaped
Down some profound dull tunnel, long since scooped
Through granites which titanic wars had groined.
Yet also there encumbered sleepers groaned,
Too fast in thought or death to be bestirred.
Then, as I probed them, one sprang up, and stared
With piteous recognition in fixed eyes,
Lifting distressful hands as if to bless.
And by his smile, I knew that sullen hall,
By his dead smile I knew we stood in Hell.
With a thousand pains that vision's face was grained;
Yet no blood reached there from the upper ground,
And no guns thumped, or down the flues made moan.
"Strange friend," I said, "here is no cause to mourn."
"None," said that other, "save the undone years,
The hopelessness. Whatever hope is yours,
Was my life also; I went hunting wild
After the wildest beauty in the world,
Which lies not calm in eyes, or braided hair,
But mocks the steady running of the hour,
And if it grieves, grieves richlier than here.
For of my glee might many men have laughed,
And of my weeping something had been left,
Which must die now. I mean the truth untold,
The pity of war, the pity war distilled.
Now men will go content with what we spoiled,

Or, discontent, boil bloody, and be spilled.
They will be swift with swiftness of the tigress.
None will break ranks, though nations trek from progress.
Courage was mine, and I had mystery,
Wisdom was mine, and I had mastery:
To miss the march of this retreating world
Into vain citadels that are not walled.
Then, when much blood had clogged their chariot-wheels,
I would go up and wash them from sweet wells,
Even with truths that lie too deep for taint.
I would have poured my spirit without stint
But not through wounds; not on the cess of war.
Foreheads of men have bled where no wounds were.
I am the enemy you killed, my friend.
I knew you in this dark: for so you frowned
Yesterday through me as you jabbed and killed.
I parried; but my hands were loath and cold.
Let us sleep now. . . . "

1920

Anthem for Doomed Youth

What passing-bells for these who die as cattle?
  Only the monstrous anger of the guns.
  Only the stuttering rifles' rapid rattle
Can patter out their hasty orisons.
No mockeries now for them; no prayers nor bells,
  Nor any voice of mourning save the choirs,—
The shrill, demented choirs of wailing shells;
  And bugles calling for them from sad shires.

What candles may be held to speed them all?
  Not in the hands of boys, but in their eyes
Shall shine the holy glimmers of good-byes.
  The pallor of girls' brows shall be their pall;
Their flowers the tenderness of patient minds,
And each slow dusk a drawing-down of blinds.

1920

E. E. Cummings

(1894–1962)

The son of a minister, Cummings attended Harvard College. Perhaps because of his genteel background he was attracted to Bohemian revolt, and he delighted in shocking conventional readers by sexual frankness, by satires on American culture, and by the peculiarities of his grammar and typography. At a time when this was still unusual, he arranged the words of a poem on the page to indicate how they should be read, jamming them together for speed or spacing them at wide intervals to indicate a pause. Sometimes he spilled the letters of a word down the page. He manipulated line breaks and the spacing between lines for similar effects, and he also used punctuation and capitalization idiosyncratically for expressive purposes. Freely violating grammar, he deployed verbs, adverbs, or adjectives as though they were nouns and similarly distorted parts of speech in other ways. In the 1920s, when these devices were new, he seemed one of the most inventive and delightful of modern poets. But in the 1930s a more intellectual type of modern poetry prevailed, and Cummings lyrical emotions seemed old-fashioned and lacking in depth. He was for a while greatly undervalued.

All in green went my love riding

All in green went my love riding
on a great horse of gold
into the silver dawn.

four lean hounds crouched low and smiling
the merry deer ran before.

Fleeter be they than dappled dreams
the swift sweet deer
the red rare deer.

Four red roebuck at a white water
the cruel bugle sang before.

Horn at hip went my love riding
riding the echo down
into the silver dawn.

four lean hounds crouched low and smiling
the level meadows ran before.

Softer be they than slippered sleep
the lean lithe deer
the fleet flown deer.

Four fleet does at a gold valley
the famished arrow sang before.

Bow at belt went my love riding
riding the mountain down
into the silver dawn.

four lean hounds crouched low and smiling
the sheer peaks ran before.

Paler be they than daunting death
the sleek slim deer
the tall tense deer.

Four tall stags at a green mountain
the lucky hunter sang before.

All in green went my love riding
on a great horse of gold
into the silver dawn.

four lean hounds crouched low and smiling
my heart fell dead before.

1923

in Just-

in Just-
spring   when the world is mud-
luscious the little
lame balloonman

whistles   far   and wee

and eddieandbill come
running from marbles and

          thou answerest

them only with

                    spring)

1923

the Cambridge ladies who live in furnished souls

the Cambridge ladies who live in furnished souls
are unbeautiful and have comfortable minds
(also, with the church's protestant blessings
daughters, unscented shapeless spirited)
they believe in Christ and Longfellow, both dead,
are invariably interested in so many things—
at the present writing one still finds
delighted fingers knitting for the is it Poles?
perhaps. While permanent faces coyly bandy
scandal of Mrs. N and Professor D
. . . . the Cambridge ladies do not care, above
Cambridge if sometimes in its box of
sky lavender and cornerless, the
moon rattles like a fragment of angry candy

1923

Buffalo Bill's

Buffalo Bill's
defunct
who used to
ride a watersmooth-silver
stallion
and break onetwothreefourfive pigeonsjustlikethat
Jesus
he was a handsome man
and what i want to know is
how do you like your blueeyed boy
Mister Death

1923

THE CAMBRIDGE LADIES. **Title:** Referring to the genteel ladies of Cambridge, Massachusetts, in the early 1900s, whose lives are confined to a polite but narrow world. **5. Longfellow:** Henry Wadsworth Longfellow (1807–1882), poet and college professor, who lived in Cambridge. BUFFALO BILL'S. **Title:** An enormously popular American hero, Buffalo Bill (1846–1917), whose actual name was William F. Cody, was a famous scout who in 1883 organized "Buffalo Bill's Wild West Show," which toured throughout the country for over thirty years. The "pigeons" at which he shot were made of clay, and put in rows at a distance of eighty feet or more so that he could display his marksmanship.

anyone lived in a pretty how town

anyone lived in a pretty how town
(with up so floating many bells down)
spring summer autumn winter
he sang his didn't he danced his did.

Women and men (both little and small)
cared for anyone not at all
they sowed their isn't they reaped their same
sun moon stars rain

children guessed (but only a few
and down they forgot as up they grew
autumn winter spring summer)
that noone loved him more by more

when by now and tree by leaf
she laughed his joy she cried his grief
bird by snow and stir by still
anyone's any was all to her

someones married their everyones
laughed their cryings and did their dance
(sleep wake hope and then) they
said their nevers they slept their dream

stars rain sun moon
(and only the snow can begin to explain
how children are apt to forget to remember
with up so floating many bells down)

one day anyone died i guess
(and noone stooped to kiss his face)
busy folk buried them side by side
little by little and was by was

all by all and deep by deep
and more by more they dream their sleep
noone and anyone earth by april
wish by spirit and if by yes.

Women and men (both dong and ding)
summer autumn winter spring
reaped their sowing and went their came
sun moon stars rain

1940

my father moved through dooms of love

my father moved through dooms of love
through sames of am through haves of give,
singing each morning out of each night
my father moved through depths of height

this motionless forgetful where
turned at his glance to shining here;
that if (so timid air is firm)
under his eyes would stir and squirm

newly as from unburied which
floats the first who, his april touch
drove sleeping selves to swarm their fates
woke dreamers to their ghostly roots

and should some why completely weep
my father's fingers brought her sleep:
vainly no smallest voice might cry
for he could feel the mountains grow.

Lifting the valleys of the sea
my father moved through griefs of joy;
praising a forehead called the moon
singing desire into begin

joy was his song and joy so pure
a heart of star by him could steer
and pure so now and now so yes
the wrists of twilight would rejoice

keen as midsummer's keen beyond
conceiving mind of sun will stand,
so strictly (over utmost him
so hugely) stood my father's dream

his flesh was flesh his blood was blood:
no hungry man but wished him food;
no cripple wouldn't creep one mile
uphill to only see him smile.

MY FATHER MOVED THROUGH DOOMS OF LOVE. **Title:** Reverend Edward Cummings, a Unitarian minister who lived in Cambridge, Massachusetts.

Scorning the pomp of must and shall
my father moved through dooms of feel;
his anger was as right as rain
his pity was as green as grain

septembering arms of year extend
less humbly wealth to foe and friend
than he to foolish and to wise
offered immeasurable is

proudly and (by octobering flame
beckoned) as earth will downward climb,
so naked for immortal work
his shoulders marched against the dark

his sorrow was as true as bread:
no liar looked him in the head;
if every friend became his foe
he'd laugh and build a world with snow.

My father moved through theys of we,
singing each new leaf out of each tree
(and every child was sure that spring
danced when she heard my father sing)

then let men kill which cannot share,
let blood and flesh be mud and mire,
scheming imagine, passion willed,
freedom a drug that's bought and sold

giving to steal and cruel kind,
a heart to fear, to doubt a mind,
to differ a disease of same,
conform the pinnacle of am

though dull were all we taste as bright,
bitter all utterly things sweet,
maggoty minus and dumb death
all we inherit, all bequeath

and nothing quite so least as truth
—i say though hate were why men breathe—
because my father lived his soul
love is the whole and more than all

1940

Jean Toomer

(1894–1967)

In 1923 Toomer published *Cane,* a collection of short stories, dramatic sketches, and poems dealing with the lives of black people in the rural south. Toomer himself did not come from this background. He was a highly educated, avant-garde writer, who had discovered this material during three years of teaching school in Sparta, Georgia. That a light-skinned, urban sophisticate who had lived, as he said, "equally amid the two race groups" and been "now white, now colored," should have written such a book, confronting a racial and historical past he could easily have ignored, was obviously a fact of much psychological significance. *Cane* was a brilliant book, and much was expected of Toomer in the future, but he disappointed his admirers. He became a follower of George Gurdjieff, a Russian philosopher and mystic, and his later writings expounded and defended this system of thought. The following poems are from *Cane.*

Song of the Son

Pour O pour that parting soul in song,
O pour it in the sawdust glow of night,
Into the velvet pine-smoke air to-night,
And let the valley carry it along.
And let the valley carry it along.

O land and soil, red soil and sweet-gum tree,
So scant of grass, so profligate of pines,
Now just before an epoch's sun declines
Thy son, in time, I have returned to thee,
Thy son, I have in time returned to thee.

In time, for though the sun is setting on
A song-lit race of slaves, it has not set;
Though late, O soil, it is not too late yet
To catch thy plaintive soul, leaving, soon gone,
Leaving, to catch thy plaintive soul soon gone.

O Negro slaves, dark purple ripened plums,
Squeezed, and bursting in the pine-wood air,
Passing, before they stripped the old tree bare
One plum was saved for me, one seed becomes

An everlasting song, a singing tree,
Caroling softly souls of slavery,
What they were, and what they are to me,
Caroling softly souls of slavery.

1923

Georgia Dusk

The sky, lazily disdaining to pursue
  The setting sun, too indolent to hold
  A lengthened tournament for flashing gold,
Passively darkens for night's barbecue,

A feast of moon and men and barking hounds,
  An orgy for some genius of the South
  With blood-hot eyes and cane-lipped scented mouth,
Surprised in making folksongs from soul sounds.

The sawmill blows its whistle, buzz-saws stop,
  And silence breaks the bud of knoll and hill,
  Soft settling pollen where plowed lands fulfill
Their early promise of a bumper crop.

Smoke from the pyramidal sawdust pile
  Curls up, blue ghosts of trees, tarrying low
  Where only chips and stumps are left to show
The solid proof of former domicile.

Meanwhile, the men, with vestiges of pomp,
  Race memories of king and caravan,
  High-priests, an ostrich, and a juju-man,
Go singing through the footpaths of the swamp.

Their voices rise . . the pine trees are guitars,
  Strumming, pine-needles fall like sheets of rain . .
  Their voices rise . . the chorus of the cane
Is caroling a vesper to the stars . .

O singers, resinous and soft your songs
  Above the sacred whisper of the pines,
  Give virgin lips to cornfield concubines,
Bring dreams of Christ to dusky cane-lipped throngs.

1923

GEORGIA DUSK. **19. juju-man:** witch doctor.

Robert Graves

(born 1895)

After serving in the First World War, Graves studied at Oxford, but soon withdrew from the university in order to devote all his time to writing. He admired the poetry of John Crowe Ransom, as one sees in "Richard Roe and John Doe," and through Ransom he became acquainted in 1926 with the American poet Laura Riding, whose intellectuality, irony, and close, analytic attention to the meanings of words greatly influenced his work. Graves also participated in the contemporary revival of interest in the Metaphysical poets of the seventeenth century. His poetry was intellectual and impassioned; his phrasing, although compact, was colloquial and easily followed; his awareness and emotions were always complex and often sardonic. Like "Sick Love," his poems were imbued with an undersense of fearful and horrible aspects of human nature and life.

At the end of the 1920s Graves went with Riding to Majorca, Spain, where Graves spent the rest of his life. In the 1940s he became deeply interested in ancient myths that testified, as he believed, to the existence of matriarchal communities and religions in the Mediterranean world prior to the Greek city states. He worked out his mythological beliefs in *The White Goddess* (1948), a work of immense, eccentric scholarship in which the Goddess is presented in her triple character as the mother, the beautiful woman, and the terrible witch or crone associated with death. "To Juan at the Winter Solstice" draws on Graves' mythology. Graves lives by his pen, publishing novels, autobiographies, translations, criticisms, and mythological studies as well as poetry.

Richard Roe and John Doe

Richard Roe wished himself Solomon,
Made cuckold, you should know, by one John Doe:
Solomon's neck was firm enough to bear
Some score of antlers more than Roe could wear.

Richard Roe wished himself Alexander,
Being robbed of house and land by the same hand:
Ten thousand acres or a principal town
Would have cost Alexander scarce a frown.

Richard Roe wished himself Job the prophet,
Sunk past reclaim in stinking rags and shame—
However ill Job's plight, his own was worse
He knew no God to call on or to curse.

He wished himself Job, Solomon, Alexander,
For patience, wisdom, power to overthrow
Misfortune; but with spirit so unmanned
That most of all he wished himself John Doe.

1922

Sick Love

O Love, be fed with apples while you may,
And feel the sun and go in royal array,
A smiling innocent on the heavenly causeway,

Though in what listening horror for the cry
That soars in outer blackness dismally,
The dumb blind beast, the paranoiac fury:

Be warm, enjoy the season, lift your head,
Exquisite in the pulse of tainted blood,
That shivering glory not to be despised.

Take your delight in momentariness,
Walk between dark and dark—a shining space
With the grave's narrowness, though not its peace.

1938

To Juan at the Winter Solstice

There is one story and one story only
That will prove worth your telling,
Whether as learned bard or gifted child;
To it all lines or lesser gauds belong
That startle with their shining
Such common stories as they stray into.

Is it of trees you tell, their months and virtues,
Or strange beasts that beset you,
Of birds that croak at you the Triple will?
Or of the Zodiac and how slow it turns
Below the Boreal Crown,
Prison of all true kings that ever reigned?

Water to water, ark again to ark,
From woman back to woman:
So each new victim treads unfalteringly
The never altered circuit of his fate,
Bringing twelve peers as witness
Both to his starry rise and starry fall.

Or is it of the Virgin's silver beauty,
All fish below the thighs?
She in her left hand bears a leafy quince;
When with her right she crooks a finger, smiling,
How may the King hold back?
Royally then he barters life for love.

Or of the undying snake from chaos hatched,
Whose coils contain the ocean,
Into whose chops with naked sword he springs,
Then in black water, tangled by the reeds,
Battles three days and nights,
To be spewed up beside her scalloped shore?

Much snow is falling, winds roar hollowly,
The owl hoots from the elder,
Fear in your heart cries to the loving-cup:
Sorrow to sorrow as the sparks fly upward.
The log groans and confesses:
There is one story and one story only.

Dwell on her graciousness, dwell on her smiling,
Do not forget what flowers
The great boar trampled down in ivy time.
Her brow was creamy as the crested wave,
Her sea-blue eyes were wild
But nothing promised that is not performed.

1945

STEPHEN VINCENT BENÉT

(1898–1943)

As a boy Benét fell in love with American history. His great ambition was to put into poetry American legends and American historical characters and incidents. He supported himself largely by writing novels and short stories. One of the latter, "The Devil and Daniel Webster" (1937), has become a minor American classic, and has been turned into a play, a film, and even an opera. His major work is his long poem, or rather group of poems, *John Brown's Body* (1928), about the beginning of the Civil War. Of his shorter poems, the most famous is "American Names" (1927), which he wrote in France during a period of homesickness for his native land.

American Names

I have fallen in love with American names,
The sharp names that never get fat,
The snakeskin-titles of mining-claims,
The plumed war-bonnet of Medicine Hat,
Tucson and Deadwood and Lost Mule Flat.

Seine and Piave are silver spoons,
But the spoonbowl-metal is thin and worn,
There are English counties like hunting-tunes
Played on the keys of a postboy's horn,
But I will remember where I was born.

I will remember Carquinez Straits,
Little French Lick and Lundy's Lane,
The Yankee ships and the Yankee dates
And the bullet-towns of Calamity Jane.
I will remember Skunktown Plain.

I will fall in love with a Salem tree
And a rawhide quirt from Santa Cruz,
I will get me a bottle of Boston sea
And a blue-gum nigger to sing me blues.
I am tired of loving a foreign muse.

AMERICAN NAMES. **4–5. Medicine . . . Flat:** Medicine Hat is in Alberta, Canada. **Tucson** ("dark spring") is in the Santa Cruz Valley, Arizona. At **Deadwood** in South Dakota, named for the dead timber of a forgotten forest fire, gold was discovered in 1876. **Lost Mule Flat** is an imagined name. **6. Seine . . . Piave:** rivers, the Seine in France, the Piave in Italy. **11–12. Carquinez . . . Lane:** Carquinez Straits (the name is Indian, not Spanish) comprise the outlet of the Sacramento and San Joaquin rivers in California. **Little French Lick**, in Indiana, was named for a salt deposit or "lick" where animals went to secure salt. **Lundy's Lane**, in Ontario, Canada, immediately across the U.S. border, was named for a Quaker farmer and the lane leading to his farm, where a small battle was fought between the Americans and British in 1814. **14–15. Calamity Jane . . . Plain:** "Calamity Jane" was the name given Martha Jane Burke (1852–1903), who wore cowboy clothes, was a well-known prostitute in frontier towns, and a crack shot with a gun. She was particularly associated with Deadwood (line 5). **Skunktown Plain** is near the Skunk River in Iowa. **16–17. Salem . . . Santa Cruz:** The great shade trees in the port of **Salem**, Massachusetts, were famous before being killed by elm and chestnut blights. **Santa Cruz** is on the north shore of Monterey Bay, California, and was originally founded as a Spanish mission in 1791.

Rue des Martyrs and Bleeding-Heart-Yard,
Senlis, Pisa, and Blindman's Oast,
It is a magic ghost you guard
But I am sick for a newer ghost,
Harrisburg, Spartanburg, Painted Post.

Henry and John were never so
And Henry and John were always right?
Granted, but when it was time to go
And the tea and the laurels had stood all night,
Did they never watch for Nantucket Light?

I shall not rest quiet in Montparnasse.
I shall not lie easy at Winchelsea.
You may bury my body in Sussex grass,
You may bury my tongue at Champmédy.
I shall not be there. I shall rise and pass.
Bury my heart at Wounded Knee.

1927

HART CRANE

(1899–1932)

One of the greatest modern American poets, Crane attributed his psychological ruin in his later years to the bitter, continual quarreling of his parents, which had overwhelmed him from childhood. As a boy he took his mother's side in the domestic battles, as she virtually compelled him to do, pursuing him with hysterical demands and collapses. In later life he rejected her. Lacking money, he took jobs in fac-

21–25. Rue . . . Post: Rue des Martyrs (street of the Martyrs) is in Paris; **Bleeding-Heart-Yard** in Sussex, southern England ("Bleeding-Heart" is a flower, and the yard is a term for the old coach yards at inns). **Senlis**, a town in northern France, is famous for its cathedral, and **Pisa**, in Italy, for its "Leaning Tower." **Blindman's Oast** is an inlet in Cornwall, once used by smugglers. **Harrisburg** is the capital of Pennsylvania, **Spartanburg** the seat of the Piedmont section in South Carolina, and **Painted Post** was a gathering place for the Iroquois Indians in upper New York state. **30–36. Nantucket . . . Knee:** Nantucket, the famous island off the southern coast of Massachusetts, was a center of whaling in the early nineteenth century. **Montparnasse** is a district of Paris, **Winchelsea** a port town in the county of Sussex, England. There is no place in France called "Champmédy." It could have been a printer's error, a slip on Benét's part for Champéry (in Switzerland), or, like "Lost Mule Flat," an invention for the sake of rhyme. **Wounded Knee**, South Dakota, was the site of a fierce 1890 massacre of hundreds of Indians by U.S. soldiers.

tories, newspapers, and advertising agencies, but these consumed time and energy needed for his work. His life included periods of towering joy, but gradually self-destructive phases of rage and despair predominated. Writing became more and more difficult. At the age of thirty four he committed suicide by jumping from a boat in the Caribbean.

Crane created his mature poetry by synthesizing dissimilar styles. As an adoloscent he had followed the course of contemporary Modernism by reading avant-garde magazines. These led him to study French poets of the nineteenth century such as Mallarmé and Rimbaud, and in some poems, such as the "Voyages" sequence, he developed Mallarmé's *symboliste* style, or some aspects of it, further than any other poet has yet done in English. In such poems he selected words much less for their denotative values than for connotative ones, and he wove dense interrelationships between the words. He hoped to interconnect all the words of a poem by innumerable threads of metaphor and association, and so to make the poem totally unified, as though, Crane said (echoing Mallarmé), it were a "single, *new* word." These poems are beautiful and difficult, and "Voyages" is the more difficult because in it Crane expressed himself through the medium of subjective impressions. He did not, as he put it, orient the reader "in factual terms" as to what was being narrated or described, but let this be inferred, for he did not want his poetry to "lose its impact" by becoming "simply categorical." He conceded that phrases such as "adagios of islands" (from "Voyages") may make "initial difficulties in understanding my poems," but believed that this was a "much more direct and creative statement than any more logical employment of words such as 'coasting slowly through the islands.'" "Adagios of islands" suggests "the motion of a boat through islands clustered thickly, the rhythm of the motion . . . besides ushering in a whole world of music."

Around the age of twenty Crane read the Elizabethan dramatists, and he caught from them a boldly emotional rhetoric. In, for example, "The seal's wide spindrift gaze toward Paradise," a line from "Voyages," the musical organization of obscure suggestion illustrates Crane's *symboliste* style, while the sweep and climax of the line recall the dramatic blank verse of Christopher Marlowe. There are many similar lines in *The Bridge*.

Both the *symboliste* poets of France and the Elizabethan dramatists also fascinated T. S. Eliot, and as Crane built his style on these sources, he partly followed Eliot and partly explored in the same places. Yet, although he enormously admired Eliot's technique, Crane dissented from Eliot's pessimistic vision; his great long poem, *The Bridge,* was intended as a counterstatement to Eliot's *The Waste Land.* To reject Eliot,

Crane invoked the third major source of his style—Walt Whitman (who, like Crane, had lived in Brooklyn and written about the Brooklyn Ferry and the East River). A hugely ambitious poem, *The Bridge* carried the optimistic, democratic, mystically ecstatic vision of Whitman into the twentieth century, expressing it in the imagery of the urban-industrial world Eliot had also used. Like Whitman, Crane presented the American landscape, people, and material civilization realistically; but he also saw them as symbols of spiritual meaning. And much more than Whitman, Crane also gathered American history into his poem. In line 10 of the "Proem," for example, the "multitudes bent toward some flashing scene" are, on one level, ordinary people at the movies, but they remind us of many other figures from the present and the historical past who are also described in the poem—Columbus, the pioneers, the sailors, the hoboes riding the rails, and the madman or "bedlamite" who jumps from the bridge. Although they may not know it, they are on a quest, and their quest is ultimately for mystical communion with the divine. As the poem repeats and interweaves its motifs, the "strange bird-wit" of the hoboes in "The River" recalls the madness of the bedlamite in the "Proem," and the river under Brooklyn Bridge into which the madman leaps becomes, in the later section, about the Mississippi, a symbol of time in its endless flow. Yet at the conclusion of "The River," the Mississippi, lifting itself and entering the Gulf of Mexico, reenacts the leap of the bedlamite. As the river unites with the Gulf, the imagery of the poem suggests an experience that is both ecstatic and religiously transcendent. It does so by evoking opposite meanings and fusing them. Ultimately the opposites reconciled in this passage are of time and eternity, the mortal and the divine. The bridge is the poem's central symbol of this uniting and transcending; the bridge is also *The Bridge,* the poem itself, a constructed work of art which embodies mystical aspiration and communion.

from Voyages

—And yet this great wink of eternity,
Of rimless floods, unfettered leewardings,
Samite sheeted and processioned where
Her undinal vast belly moonward bends,
Laughing the wrapt inflections of our love;

VOYAGES. **3. Samite:** silk cloth. **4. undinal:** from Undine, a water nymph in classical myth who could become human through love.

Take this Sea, whose diapason knells
On scrolls of silver snowy sentences,
The sceptered terror of whose sessions rends
As her demeanors motion well or ill,
All but the pieties of lovers' hands.

And onward, as bells off San Salvador
Salute the crocus lusters of the stars,
In these poinsettia meadows of her tides—
Adagios of islands, O my Prodigal,
Complete the dark confessions her veins spell.

Mark how her turning shoulders wind the hours,
And hasten while her penniless rich palms
Pass superscription of bent foam and wave—
Hasten, while they are true—sleep, death, desire,
Close round one instant in one floating flower.

Bind us in time, O Seasons clear, and awe.
O minstrel galleons of Carib fire,
Bequeath us to no earthly shore until
Is answered in the vortex of our grave
The seal's wide spindrift gaze toward paradise.

1926

from The Bridge

Proem: To Brooklyn Bridge

How many dawns, chill from his rippling rest
The seagull's wings shall dip and pivot him,
Shedding white rings of tumult, building high
Over the chained bay waters Liberty—

Then, with inviolate curve, forsake our eyes
As apparitional as sails that cross
Some page of figures to be filed away;
—Till elevators drop us from our day . . .

11. San Salvador: island in the Bahamas where Columbus first found land. **12. crocus lusters:** reflections of stars in the ocean. **13. poinsettia:** scarlet flowered plant of the southern U.S. and West Indies. **14. Adagios:** slow movements of musical compositions. **16. wind the hours:** the waves and tides mark the hours like a clock. **22. minstrel galleons . . . fire:** The sunlit islands are seen as "galleons" (the old Spanish ships) and also as producers of music. **Carib:** This may refer to the Caribbean sea, to the islands in it, and to the cannibal Indians that lived on these islands when the Spanish galleons were plying the sea. **Fire** may suggest among other things, the light on the sea and the cannibal fires of the Indians. THE BRIDGE. **Proem. 6–7. cross . . . figures:** cross the accounts being read or written by a clerk in an office.

I think of cinemas, panoramic sleights
With multitudes bent toward some flashing scene
Never disclosed, but hastened to again,
Foretold to other eyes on the same screen;

And Thee, across the harbor, silver-paced
As though the sun took step of thee, yet left
Some motion ever unspent in thy stride—
Implicitly thy freedom staying thee!

Out of some subway scuttle, cell or loft
A bedlamite speeds to thy parapets,
Tilting there momently, shrill shirt ballooning,
A jest falls from the speechless caravan.

Down Wall, from girder into street noon leaks,
A rip-tooth of the sky's acetylene,
All afternoon the cloud-flown derricks turn . . .
Thy cables breathe the North Atlantic still.

And obscure as that heaven of the Jews,
Thy guerdon . . . Accolade thou dost bestow
Of anonymity time cannot raise:
Vibrant reprieve and pardon thou dost show.

O harp and altar, of the fury fused,
(How could mere toil align thy choiring strings!)
Terrific threshold of the prophet's pledge,
Prayer of pariah, and the lover's cry—

Again the traffic lights that skim thy swift
Unfractioned idiom, immaculate sigh of stars,
Beading thy path—condense eternity:
And we have seen night lifted in thine arms.

Under thy shadow by the piers I waited;
Only in darkness is thy shadow clear.
The City's fiery parcels all undone,
Already snow submerges an iron year . . .

O Sleepless as the river under thee,
Vaulting the sea, the prairies' dreaming sod,
Unto us lowliest sometime sweep, descend
And of the curveship lend a myth to God.

14. took step: followed the lead. **16. thee:** Brooklyn Bridge. **18. bedlamite:** an insane person (from "Bedlam," or St. Bethlehem Hospital, the old London hospital for the insane). He "speeds" to the "parapets" of the bridge in order to commit suicide by jumping from them. **25. heaven . . . Jews:** The Jewish heaven was conceived in vague, uncertain terms, largely as a land of the dead. **26. guerdon:** reward. **29. fury fused:** combined together by the poetic fury of the imagination. **39. parcels:** buildings. **44. lend . . . God:** present a new mythological form of God.

The River

Stick your patent name on a signboard
brother—all over—going west—young man
Tintex—Japalac—Certain-teed Overalls ads
and lands sakes! under the new playbill ripped
in the guaranteed corner—see Bert Williams what?
Minstrels when you steal a chicken just
save me the wing for if it isn't
Erie it ain't for miles around a
Mazda—and the telegraphic night coming on Thomas
a Ediford—and whistling down the tracks
a headlight rushing with the sound—can you
imagine—while an EXPRESS makes time like
SCIENCE—COMMERCE and the HOLYGHOST
RADIO ROARS IN EVERY HOME WE HAVE THE NORTHPOLE
WALLSTREET AND VIRGINBIRTH WITHOUT STONES OR
WIRES OR EVEN RUNning brooks connecting ears
and no more sermons windows flashing roar
breathtaking—as you like it . . . eh?

. . . and past the din and slogans of the year—

So the 20th Century—so
whizzed the Limited—roared by and left
three men, still hungry on the tracks, ploddingly
watching the tail lights wizen and converge, slip-
ping gimleted and neatly out of sight.

. . .

The last bear, shot drinking in the Dakotas
Loped under wires that span the mountain stream.
Keen instruments, strung to a vast precision

THE RIVER. **Title:** The "River of Time," Crane said in explanation. At the start of the poem he presents the image of a subway, which then turns into the famous train of the 1920s and 1930s, "The Twentieth-Century Limited," from New York to Chicago. Crane discussed this in a letter written to Otto Kahn on September 12, 1927: "The subway is simply a figurative, psychological 'vehicle' for transporting the reader to the Middle West. He lands on the railroad tracks in the company of several tramps in the twilight. The extravagance of the first twenty-three lines of this section is an intentional burlesque on the cultural confusion of the present—a great conglomeration of noises analogous to the strident impression of a fast express [the 20th Century Limited] rushing by. The rhythm is jazz." **2. going . . . man:** an allusion to a famous saying of Horace Greeley (1811–1872), "Go West, young man, and grow up with the country." **3. Tintex . . . ads:** trade names for dye, varnish, and overalls. **5. Bert Williams:** popular entertainer in minstrel shows of the period 1910–20. **6–7. chicken . . . wing:** an echo of the hobo railroading song, "Railroad Bill": "Kill me a chicken,/ Save me the wing./ You think I'm workin'/ But I don't do a thing./ I just ride, ride, ride." **9. Mazda:** trade name for electric bulbs produced by the Edison Company. **9–10. Thomas a Ediford:** play on names of Thomas Alva Edison and Henry Ford in contrast to the medieval saint Thomas à Becket. **17–18. sermons . . . eh:** reference to Shakespeare's *As You Like It* (II, i, 16–17), in which nature is said to provide us with "books in the running brooks,/ Sermons in stones." **23. gimleted:** as though into a hole bored by a gimlet. **26. Keen instruments:** telephone and telegraph.

Bind town to town and dream to ticking dream.
But some men take their liquor slow—and count
—Though they'll confess no rosary nor clue—
The river's minute by the far brook's year.
Under a world of whistles, wires and steam
Caboose-like they go ruminating through
Ohio, Indiana—blind baggage—
To Cheyenne tagging . . . Maybe Kalamazoo.

to those whose addresses are never near

Time's rendings, time's blendings they construe
As final reckonings of fire and snow;
Strange bird-wit, like the elemental gist
Of unwalled winds they offer, singing low
My Old Kentucky Home and *Casey Jones,*
Some Sunny Day. I heard a road-gang chanting so.
And afterwards, who had a colt's eyes—one said,
"Jesus! Oh I remember watermelon days!" And sped
High in a cloud of merriment, recalled
"—And when my Aunt Sally Simpson smiled," he drawled—
"It was almost Louisiana, long ago."

"There's no place like Booneville though, Buddy,"
One said, excising a last burr from his vest,
"—For early trouting." Then peering in the can,
"—But I kept on the tracks." Possessed, resigned,
He trod the fire down pensively and grinned,
Spreading dry shingles of a beard. . . .

Behind
My father's cannery works I used to see
Rail-squatters ranged in nomad raillery,
The ancient men—wifeless or runaway
Hobo-trekkers that forever search
An empire wilderness of freight and rails.
Each seemed a child, like me, on a loose perch,
Holding to childhood like some termless play.
John, Jake or Charley, hopping the slow freight
—Memphis to Tallahassee—riding the rods,
Blind fists of nothing, humpty-dumpty clods.

Yet they touch something like a key perhaps.
From pole to pole across the hills, the states
—They know a body under the wide rain;
Youngsters with eyes like fjords, old reprobates
With racetrack jargon,—dotting immensity
They lurk across her, knowing her yonder breast
Snow-silvered, sumac-stained or smoky blue—
Is past the valley-sleepers, south or west.
—As I have trod the rumorous midnights, too.

but who have touched her, knowing her without name

And past the circuit of the lamp's thin flame
(O Nights that brought me to her body bare!)
Have dreamed beyond the print that bound her name.

Trains sounding the long blizzards out—I heard
Wail into distances I knew were hers.
Papooses crying on the wind's long mane
Screamed redskin dynasties that fled the brain,
—Dead echoes! But I knew her body there,
Time like a serpent down her shoulder, dark,
And space, an eaglet's wing, laid on her hair.

Under the Ozarks, domed by Iron Mountain,
The old gods of the rain lie wrapped in pools
Where eyeless fish curvet a sunken fountain
And re-descend with corn from querulous crows.
Such pilferings make up their timeless eatage,
Propitiate them for their timber torn
By iron, iron—always the iron dealt cleavage!
They doze now, below axe and powder horn.

nor the myths of her fathers . . .

And Pullman breakfasters glide glistening steel
From tunnel into field—iron strides the dew—
Straddles the hill, a dance of wheel on wheel.
You have a half-hour's wait at Siskiyou,
Or stay the night and take the next train through.
Southward, near Cairo passing, you can see
The Ohio merging,—borne down Tennessee;
And if it's summer and the sun's in dusk
Maybe the breeze will lift the River's musk
—As though the waters breathed that you might know

Memphis Johnny, Steamboat Bill, Missouri Joe.
Oh, lean from the window, if the train slows down,
As though you touched hands with some ancient clown,
—A little while gaze absently below
And hum *Deep River* with them while they go.

Yes, turn again and sniff once more—look see,
O Sheriff, Brakeman and Authority—
Hitch up your pants and crunch another quid,
For you, too, feed the River timelessly.
And few evade full measure of their fate;
Always they smile out eerily what they seem.
I could believe he joked at heaven's gate—
Dan Midland—jolted from the cold brake-beam.

80–81. serpent . . . eaglet: symbols of land and air as well as time and space. **83. gods . . . pools:** The old Indian gods are forgotten. **88. iron . . . cleavage:** the Industrial Revolution, which has cut off humankind from nature. **93. Siskiyou:** range of mountains in Oregon and northern California. **95. Cairo:** in southern Illinois, where the Ohio River joins the Mississippi. **107. quid:** piece of chewing tobacco. **112. Dan Midland:** hobo of folklore who died when he fell from a train. **brake-beam:** projecting brake on a freight car on which tramps used to ride.

Down down—born pioneers in time's despite,
Grimed tributaries to an ancient flow—
They win no frontier by their wayward plight,
But drift in stillness, as from Jordan's brow.

You will not hear it as the sea; even stone
Is not more hushed by gravity . . . But slow,
As loth to take more tribute—sliding prone
Like one whose eyes were buried long ago

The River, spreading, flows—and spends your dream.
What are you, lost within this tideless spell?
You are your father's father, and the stream—
A liquid theme that floating niggers swell.

Damp tonnage and alluvial march of days—
Nights turbid, vascular with silted shale
And roots surrendered down of moraine clays:
The Mississippi drinks the farthest dale.

O quarrying passion, undertowed sunlight!
The basalt surface drags a jungle grace
Ochreous and lynx-barred in lengthening might;
Patience! and you shall reach the biding place!

Over De Soto's bones the freighted floors
Throb past the City storied of three thrones.
Down two more turns the Mississippi pours
(Anon tall ironsides up from salt lagoons)

And flows within itself, heaps itself free.
All fades but one thin skyline 'round . . . Ahead
No embrace opens but the stinging sea;
The River lifts itself from its long bed,

Poised wholly on its dream, a mustard glow
Tortured with history, its one will—flow!
—The Passion spreads in wide tongues, choked and slow,
Meeting the Gulf, hosannas silently below.

1930

113. time's despite: though born too late to be real pioneers. **116. Jordan:** river in Palestine, celebrated in the old spirituals as a borderline between earth and heaven. **133. De Soto:** the Spanish explorer Hernando de Soto (1500–1542), who discovered the Mississippi and was secretly buried in it. **134. City . . . thrones:** New Orleans, held by the Spaniards, the French, and then the Americans. **136. ironsides:** the warships of the Union fleet that sailed up the Mississippi and captured New Orleans in the Civil War. **143–144. Passion . . . Gulf:** the river symbolizes, among other things, Christ's "passion" (crucifixion); the Gulf of Mexico, into which the river flows, symbolizes eternity.

Allen Tate

(1899–1979)

Tate's poetic style matured in 1922 and 1923 when he first assimilated the poetry of T. S. Eliot. But in "Ode to the Confederate Dead," which he wrote in 1926, he also drew on earlier traditions. In particular the ode recalls the formal, graveyard meditations of the eighteenth century, of which Thomas Gray's "Elegy in a Country Churchyard" is the greatest example. That Tate commemorated the Confederate dead expressed his regional identification. He was born in Kentucky and attended Vanderbilt University in Tennessee, where he became one of a group of young writers, also including John Crowe Ransom and Robert Penn Warren, who advocated Southern rural values, such as social community and rooted tradition. They contrasted their region with the industrial North, which created, they argued, an alienated, deracinated type of human being. Tate became one of the foremost literary critics of his generation, and his critical intelligence was active as he composed his poetry. It underlay the cerebral complexity of his work and it may have inhibited emotional spontaneity. The feelings Tate voiced were often intense, even violent and tortured, but they were strangely distant and frozen. In later life Tate befriended both Hart Crane and Robert Lowell, and his influence can be seen in their work.

Ode to the Confederate Dead

Row after row with strict impunity
The headstones yield their names to the element,
The wind whirrs without recollection;
In the riven troughs the splayed leaves
Pile up, of nature the casual sacrament
To the seasonal eternity of death;
Then driven by the fierce scrutiny
Of heaven to their election in the vast breath,
They sough the rumor of mortality.

ODE TO THE CONFEDERATE DEAD. **Title:** Tate said the poem is based on the Greek myth of Narcissus, who fell in love with his own image in a pool, leapt into the water to embrace the image, and was drowned. In other words, the poem, said Tate, "is 'about' solipsism, a philosophical doctrine which says that we create the world in the act of perceiving it; or about Narcissism, or any other *ism* that denotes the failure of the human personality to function objectively in nature and society" ("Narcissus as Narcissus," *Essays of Four Decades,* pages 595–96).

Autumn is desolation in the plot
Of a thousand acres where these memories grow
From the inexhaustible bodies that are not
Dead, but feed the grass row after rich row.
Think of the autumns that have come and gone!
Ambitious November with the humors of the year,
With a particular zeal for every slab,
Staining the uncomfortable angels that rot
On the slabs, a wing chipped here, an arm there:
The brute curiosity of an angel's stare
Turns you, like them, to stone,
Transforms the heaving air
Till plunged to a heavier world below
You shift your sea-space blindly
Heaving, turning like the blind crab.

Dazed by the wind, only the wind
The leaves flying, plunge

You know who have waited by the wall
The twilight certainty of an animal,
Those midnight restitutions of the blood
You know—the immitigable pines, the smoky frieze
Of the sky, the sudden call: you know the rage,
The cold pool left by the mounting flood,
Of muted Zeno and Parmenides.
You who have waited for the angry resolution
Of those desires that should be yours tomorrow,
You know the unimportant shrift of death
And praise the vision
And praise the arrogant circumstance
Of those who fall
Rank upon rank, hurried beyond decision—
Here by the sagging gate, stopped by the wall.

Seeing, seeing only the leaves
Flying, plunge and expire

10–24. Autumn . . . crab: Tate explained, "The structure of the Ode is simple. Figure to yourself a man stopping at the gate of a Confederate graveyard on a late autumn afternoon. The leaves are falling; his first impressions bring him the 'rumor of mortality'; and the desolation barely allows him, at the beginning of the second stanza, the conventionally heroic surmise that the dead will enrich the earth, 'where these memories grow.' From those quoted words to the end of that passage he pauses for a baroque meditation on the ravages of time, concluding with the figure of the 'blind crab.' This figure has mobility but no direction, energy but, from the human point of view, no purposeful world to use it in: in the entire poem there are only two explicit symbols for the locked-in ego; the crab is the first and less explicit symbol, a mere hint, a planting of the idea that will become overt in its second instance—the jaguar towards the end. The crab is the first intimation of the nature of the moral conflict upon which the drama of the poem develops: the cut-off-ness of the modern 'intellectual man' from the world." **30. immitigable:** unvarying. **33. Zeno . . . Parmenides:** Greek philosophers who maintained that the universe is a single whole.

Turn your eyes to the immoderate past,
Turn to the inscrutable infantry rising
Demons out of the earth—they will not last.
Stonewall, Stonewall, and the sunken fields of hemp,
Shiloh, Antietam, Malvern Hill, Bull Run.
Lost in that orient of the thick and fast
You will curse the setting sun.

Cursing only the leaves crying
Like an old man in a storm

You hear the shout, the crazy hemlocks point
With troubled fingers to the silence which
Smothers you, a mummy, in time.

The hound bitch
Toothless and dying, in a musty cellar
Hears the wind only.

Now that the salt of their blood
Stiffens the saltier oblivion of the sea,
Seals the malignant purity of the flood,
What shall we who count our days and bow
Our heads with a commemorial woe
In the ribboned coats of grim felicity,
What shall we say of the bones, unclean,
Whose verdurous anonymity will grow?

The ragged arms, the ragged heads and eyes
Lost in these acres of the insane green?
The gray lean spiders come, they come and go;
In a tangle of willows without light
The singular screech-owl's tight
Invisible lyric seeds the mind
With the furious murmur of their chivalry.

We shall say only the leaves
Flying, plunge and expire

We shall say only the leaves whispering
In the improbable mist of nightfall
That flies on multiple wing:
Night is the beginning and the end
And in between the ends of distraction
Waits mute speculation, the patient curse
That stones the eyes, or like the jaguar leaps
For his own image in a jungle pool, his victim.

47. Stonewall: Thomas J. ("Stonewall") Jackson (1824–1863), the famous Confederate general of the Civil War; Tate is one of his biographers. **48. Shiloh . . . Bull Run:** some of the great battles of the Civil War.

What shall we say who have knowledge
Carried to the heart? Shall we take the act
To the grave? Shall we, more hopeful, set up the grave
In the house? The ravenous grave?

Leave now
The shut gate and the decomposing wall:
The gentle serpent, green in the mulberry bush,
Riots with his tongue through the hush—
Sentinel of the grave who counts us all!

1928

LANGSTON HUGHES

(1902–1967)

The finest black poet of his generation, Hughes was born in Joplin, Missouri. In high school he was especially impressed by the lyrics of Carl Sandburg. His father, a businessman living in Mexico, was willing to send Hughes to college, but insisted on his becoming an engineer. Hughes rejected this, broke with his father, and supported himself as best he could. After his first volume, *The Weary Blues,* appeared in 1926, the story of his life is mainly a record of successive publications. He was enormously inventive and prolific. He composed fiction, drama, children's books, histories, opera librettos, radio scripts, essays, and much else besides poetry.

Although he could look deep into his own psyche, he mostly looked out at the world. He presented the lives and feelings of blacks, especially of those living in Harlem, and he used the diction and rhythm of their speech. His forms, moreover, were often based on types of music, such as the blues and jazz, that had been created by blacks. In composing poems he always had in mind a public recitation of them, an art in which he was extremely effective. Many of his poems were designed for musical accompaniment, and all of them can be understood immediately when heard. Unless the reader imagines Hughes' recitation—or, better

88. **serpent:** traditional symbol of time (and hence also of death). Tate says he placed the serpent in the mulberry tree (the leaves of which are the favorite food of the silkworm) in the "faint hope" that the image would also suggest the silkworm, which, in its spinning of silken thread, is associated with creativity.

still, listens to him on records—the poems do not have their full force. Moreover, no selection of poems can do Hughes justice, for his effect lies partly in the variety and scope of his representation.

The Weary Blues

Droning a drowsy syncopated tune,
Rocking back and forth to a mellow croon,
        I heard a Negro play.
Down on Lenox Avenue the other night
By the pale dull pallor of an old gas light
        He did a lazy sway. . . .
        He did a lazy sway. . . .
To the tune o' those Weary Blues.
With his ebony hands on each ivory key
He made that poor piano moan with melody.
        O Blues!
Swaying to and fro on his rickety stool
He played that sad raggy tune like a musical fool.
        Sweet Blues!
Coming from a black man's soul.
        O Blues!
In a deep song voice with a melancholy tone
I heard that Negro sing, that old piano moan—
        "Ain't got nobody in all this world,
        Ain't got nobody but ma self.
        I's gwine to quit ma frownin'
        And put ma troubles on the shelf."
Thump, thump, thump, went his foot on the floor.
He played a few chords then he sang some more—
        "I got the Weary Blues
        And I can't be satisfied.
        Got the Weary Blues
        And can't be satisfied—
        I ain't happy no mo'
        And I wish that I had died."
And far into the night he crooned that tune.
        The stars went out and so did the moon.
        The singer stopped playing and went to bed
        While the Weary Blues echoed through his head.
        He slept like a rock or a man that's dead.

1926

THE WEARY BLUES. **4. Lenox Avenue:** street in Harlem. THE NEGRO SPEAKS OF RIVERS. **4. Euphrates:** river in Mesopotamia, near which ancient Babylon was situated.

The Negro Speaks of Rivers

I've known rivers:
I've known rivers ancient as the world and older than the flow of human blood in human veins.

My soul has grown deep like the rivers.

I bathed in the Euphrates when dawns were young.
I built my hut near the Congo and it lulled me to sleep.
I looked upon the Nile and raised the pyramids above it.
I heard the singing of the Mississippi when Abe Lincoln went down to New Orleans, and I've seen its muddy bosom turn all golden in the sunset.

I've known rivers:
Ancient, dusky rivers.

My soul has grown deep like the rivers.

1926

Morning After

I was so sick last night I
Didn't hardly know my mind.
So sick last night I
Didn't know my mind.
I drunk some bad licker that
Almost made me blind.

Had a dream last night I
Thought I was in hell.
I drempt last night I
Thought I was in hell.
Woke up and looked around me—
Babe, your mouth was open like a well.

I said, Baby! Baby!
Please don't snore so loud.
Baby! Please!
Please don't snore so loud.
You jest a little bit o' woman but you
Sound like a great big crowd.

1942

Stevie Smith

(1902–1971)

Florence Margaret Smith (nicknamed "Stevie") was an office worker in London. Her poems should be read in the original publications, for they are delightfully illustrated with her own drawings. Especially in England, she has a large following. She expressed a stoic, somewhat embittered sense of life with tart, humorous intelligence and originality.

Not Waving but Drowning

Nobody heard him, the dead man,
But still he lay moaning:
I was much further out than you thought
And not waving but drowning.

Poor chap, he always loved larking
And now he's dead
It must have been too cold for him his heart gave way,
They said.

Oh, no no no, it was too cold always
(Still the dead one lay moaning)
I was much too far out all my life
And not waving but drowning.

1957

Thoughts about the Person from Porlock

Coleridge received the Person from Porlock
And ever after called him a curse,
Then why did he hurry to let him in?
He could have hid in the house.

THOUGHTS ABOUT THE PERSON FROM PORLOCK. **Title:** Coleridge said that the writing of his "Kubla Khan" was interrupted by "a person on business from Porlock," and that afterwards he could not remember the rest of the poem, which he had composed in a dream (see "Kubla Khan").

It was not right of Coleridge in fact it was wrong
(But often we all do wrong)
As the truth is I think he was already stuck
With Kubla Khan.

He was weeping and wailing: I am finished, finished,
I shall never write another word of it,
When along comes the Person from Porlock
And takes the blame for it.

It was not right, it was wrong,
But often we all do wrong.

May we enquire the name of the Person from Porlock?
Why, Porson, didn't you know?
He lived at the bottom of Porlock Hill
So had a long way to go,

He wasn't much in the social sense
Though his grandmother was a Warlock,
One of the Rutlandshire ones I fancy
And nothing to do with Porlock,

And he lived at the bottom of the hill as I said
And had a cat named Flo,
And had a cat named Flo.

I long for the Person from Porlock
To bring my thoughts to an end,
I am becoming impatient to see him
I think of him as a friend,

Often I look out the window
Often I run to the gate
I think, He will come this evening,
I think it is rather late.

I am hungry to be interrupted
For ever and ever amen
O Person from Porlock come quickly
And bring my thoughts to an end.

I felicitate the people who have a Person from Porlock
To break up everything and throw it away
Because then there will be nothing to keep them
And they need not stay.

Why do they grumble so much?
He comes like a benison
They should be glad he has not forgotten them
They might have had to go on.

16. Porson: Although there was a famous classical scholar of the time, Richard Porson (1759–1808) of Cambridge, Smith is presumably using the name to pun with "person."
21. Rutlandshire: county in central England.

These thoughts are depressing I know. They are depressing,
I wish I was more cheerful, it is more pleasant,
Also it is a duty, we should smile as well as submitting
To the purpose of One Above who is experimenting
With various mixtures of human character which goes best,
All is interesting for him it is exciting, but not for us.
There I go again. Smile, smile, and get some work to do
Then you will be practically unconscious without positively having to go.

1962

Countee Cullen

(1903–1946)

Cullen was the adopted son of a Methodist minister in Harlem. He started writing poetry in high school, and his gifts were recognized quickly. By the time he was twenty-four years old, he had published two books of poetry and was an assistant editor of *Opportunity,* a prominent magazine for blacks. But he now became embroiled in a war of criticism, for he offended many persons by arguing that black poets should not restrict themselves to racially relevant subjects and forms. He warned that to write for a particular group might make one less rigorous in literary standards. Yet Cullen's best work came in poems such as "Heritage" in which he wrote on racial themes. His last collection of poems appeared in 1929. In his final years he was a high-school teacher of French in Harlem.

Heritage

For Harold Jackman

What is Africa to me:
Copper sun or scarlet sea,
Jungle star or jungle track,
Strong bronzed men, or regal black
Women from whose loins I sprang
When the birds of Eden sang?
One three centuries removed
From the scenes his fathers loved,
Spicy grove, cinnamon tree,
What is Africa to me?

So I lie, who all day long
Want no sound except the song
Sung by wild barbaric birds
Goading massive jungle herds,
Juggernauts of flesh that pass
Trampling tall defiant grass
Where young forest lovers lie,
Plighting troth beneath the sky.
So I lie, who always hear,
Though I cram against my ear
Both my thumbs, and keep them there,
Great drums throbbing through the air.
So I lie, whose fount of pride,
Dear distress, and joy allied,
Is my somber flesh and skin,
With the dark blood dammed within
Like great pulsing tides of wine
That, I fear, must burst the fine
Channels of the chafing net
Where they surge and foam and fret.

Africa? A book one thumbs
Listlessly, till slumber comes.
Unremembered are her bats
Circling through the night, her cats
Crouching in the river reeds,
Stalking gentle flesh that feeds
By the river brink; no more
Does the bugle-throated roar
Cry that monarch claws have leapt
From the scabbards where they slept.
Silver snakes that once a year
Doff the lovely coats you wear,
Seek no covert in your fear
Lest a mortal eye should see;
What's your nakedness to me?
Here no leprous flowers rear
Fierce corollas in the air;
Here no bodies sleek and wet,
Dripping mingled rain and sweat,
Tread the savage measures of
Jungle boys and girls in love.
What is last year's snow to me,
Last year's anything? The tree
Budding yearly must forget
How its past arose or set—

HERITAGE. **47. corollas:** petals of the inner envelope of a flower. **52. last year's snow:** echo of the famous line, "Where are the snows of yesteryear?" in François Villon's *Grand Testament.*

Bough and blossom, flower, fruit,
Even what shy bird with mute
Wonder at her travail there,
Meekly labored in its hair.
One three centuries removed
From the scenes his fathers loved,
Spicy grove, cinnamon tree,
What is Africa to me?

So I lie, who find no peace
Night or day, no slight release
From the unremittent beat
Made by cruel padded feet
Walking through my body's street.
Up and down they go, and back,
Treading out a jungle track.
So I lie, who never quite
Safely sleep from rain at night—
I can never rest at all
When the rain begins to fall;
Like a soul gone mad with pain
I must match its weird refrain;
Ever must I twist and squirm,
Writhing like a baited worm,
While its primal measures drip
Through my body, crying, "Strip!
Doff this new exuberance.
Come and dance the Lover's Dance!"
In an old remembered way
Rain works on me night and day.

Quaint, outlandish heathen gods
Black men fashion out of rods,
Clay, and brittle bits of stone,
In a likeness like their own,
My conversion came high-priced;
I belong to Jesus Christ,
Preacher of Humility;
Heathen gods are naught to me.

Father, Son, and Holy Ghost,
So I make an idle boast;
Jesus of the twice-turned cheek,
Lamb of God, although I speak
With my mouth thus, in my heart
Do I play a double part.
Ever at Thy glowing altar
Must my heart grow sick and falter,

95. cheek: referring to Jesus' remark that, when one is struck on one cheek, one should turn the other to be struck rather than give a blow in return (Matthew 5:39).

Wishing He I served were black,
Thinking then it would not lack
Precedent of pain to guide it,
Let who would or might deride it;
Surely then this flesh would know
Yours had borne a kindred woe.
Lord, I fashion dark gods, too,
Daring even to give You
Dark despairing features where,
Crowned with dark rebellious hair,
Patience wavers just so much as
Mortal grief compels, while touches
Quick and hot, of anger, rise
To smitten cheek and weary eyes.
Lord, forgive me if my need
Sometimes shapes a human creed.
All day long and all night through,
One thing only must I do:
Quench my pride and cool my blood,
Lest I perish in the flood,
Lest a hidden ember set
Timber that I thought was wet
Burning like the dryest flax,
Melting like the merest wax,
Lest the grave restore its dead.
Not yet has my heart or head
In the least way realized
They and I are civilized.

1925

Cecil Day Lewis

(1904–1972)

As a college student Cecil Day Lewis composed poems strongly influenced by the contemporary revival of the "metaphysical" style of Donne. Like virtually all intellectuals in the 1930s, he was preoccupied with social and political issues, for this was the decade of the Great Depression, the growth of Fascism in Europe, and the increasing drift toward the Second World War. His poetry voiced his political emotions. *The Magnetic Mountain* (1933) was a long poem of social agitation and prophecy, ranging from doggerel satire to splendid revolutionary odes, such as "You That Love England." Two years later Day Lewis joined the Communist Party. Gradually, however, other emotions and commitments made politics less central for him. He was appointed Poet Laureate in 1968. His lyrics in his later years reflected his devotion to the poetry of Thomas Hardy, and he was buried, by his wish, in the same churchyard as Hardy.

You That Love England

You that love England, who have an ear for her music,
The slow movement of clouds in benediction,
Clear arias of light thrilling over her uplands,
Over the chords of summer sustained peacefully;
Ceaseless the leaves' counterpoint in a west wind lively,
Blossom and river rippling loveliest allegro,
And the storms of wood strings brass at year's finale:
Listen. Can you not hear the entrance of a new theme?

You who go out alone, on tandem or on pillion,
Down arterial roads riding in April,
Or sad beside lakes where hill-slopes are reflected
Making fires of leaves, your high hopes fallen:
Cyclists and hikers in company, day excursionists,
Refugees from cursed towns and devastated areas;
Know you seek a new world, a saviour to establish
Long-lost kinship and restore the blood's fulfilment.

You who like peace, good sorts, happy in a small way
Watching birds or playing cricket with schoolboys,
Who pay for drinks all round, whom disaster chose not;
Yet passing derelict mills and barns roof-rent
Where despair has burnt itself out—hearts at a standstill,
Who suffer loss, aware of lowered vitality;
We can tell you a secret, offer a tonic; only
Submit to the visiting angel, the strange new healer.

You above all who have come to the far end, victims
Of a run-down machine, who can bear it no longer;
Whether in easy chairs chafing at impotence
Or against hunger, bullies and spies preserving
The nerve for action, the spark of indignation—
Need fight in the dark no more, you know your enemies.
You shall be leaders when zero hour is signalled,
Wielders of power and welders of a new world.

1933

YOU THAT LOVE ENGLAND. **9. tandem:** bicycle for two riders. **pillion:** seat behind the saddle of a motorcycle for a second rider. **20. derelict mills:** abandoned factories. **24. visiting . . . healer:** Day Lewis had no one in particular in mind, but was here vaguely promising a rescuer and exhorting readers to be open to this saviour.

ROBERT PENN WARREN

(born 1905)

A novelist *(All the King's Men,* 1946) and critic as well as a poet, Warren has long been one of America's most distinguished men of letters. At Vanderbilt University in the early 1920s he was associated with John Crowe Ransom and Allen Tate. With Cleanth Brooks he wrote *Understanding Poetry* (1938), one of the most influential textbooks of our century; it taught students to read and criticize poetry by close analysis of the text. His first important poems were in the style of the so-called "Metaphysical Revival," and reflected his reading of seventeenth-century poets such as John Donne and Andrew Marvell. But in the 1940s he broke with this style, and, drawing on his formidable skills as a novelist, wrote a number of long narrative poems with a regional setting. In his next phase, beginning in 1954, he composed lyrics rooted in personal experiences. Usually, however, they were not conceived as individual lyrics but as parts of longer sequences. Around 1966 his poetry entered still another phase, and to most readers he seemed a greater poet than ever before, although the reasons for this were not easy to define. He was now using free verse, and this seems to have released a less rhetorical, more natural idiom. Perhaps the main reason was that the whole of his previous work now formed an enriching background to new poems.

In *Audubon* (1969), from which three of the following selections are printed, Warren presented a suite of poems on the life of the nineteenth-century naturalist, famous for his paintings of American birds. The sequence enacts a spiritual and psychological quest. After the introductory poem describing Audubon in the forest, there is a narrative (not printed here) of his near murder in a frontier cabin. In this episode Audubon discovers dark and terrible realities in life and in his own psyche. Moments of saving vision and self-definition come to him in the fourth poem of the sequence, and in the sixth poem Warren reflects on Audobon's life and expresses a meaning he finds in it.

The Dogwood

All right: and with that wry acceptance you follow the cow-track.
Yes, it's dark in the woods, as black as a peddler's pocket
Cobweb tangles, briar snatches. A sensible man would go back.
A bough finds your face, and one eye grieves in the socket.

Midnight compounds with the peeper. Now whippoorwills speak,
Far off. Then silence. What's that? And something blots star—
By your head velvet air-*whoosh,* a curdle and shudder of wing-creak.
It is only an owl. You go on. You can guess where you are.

For here is the gum-swamp, the slough where you once trapped the weasel.
Here the dead cow was dumped, and by buzzards duly divested.
All taint of mortality's long since wiped clean as a whistle.
Now love vine threads eyehole, God's peace is by violet attested.

The bones are long lost. In green grass the skull waits, has waited:
A cathedral for ants, and at noon, under white dome and transept,
They pass in green gloom, where sunlight's by leaf mitigated,
For leaf of the love vine shuts eyehole, as though the eye slept.

But now it's not noon, it is night, and ant-dark in that cow skull.
And man-dark in the woods. But go on, that's how men survive.
You went on in the dark, your heart tight as a nut in the hull.
Came back in the dark, and home, and throve as men thrive.

But not before you had seen it, sudden at a path-turn,
White-floating in darkness, the dogwood, white bloom in dark air.
Like an ice-break, broke joy; then you felt a strange wrath burn
To strike it, and strike, had a stick been handy in the dark there.

But one wasn't handy, so there on the path then, breath scant,
You stood, you stood there, and oh, could the poor heart's absurd
Cry for wisdom, for wisdom, ever be answered? Triumphant,
All night, the tree glimmered in darkness, and uttered no word.

1957

I
Was Not the Lost Dauphin

[A]

Was not the lost dauphin, though handsome was only
Base-born and not even able
To make a decent living, was only
Himself, Jean Jacques, and his passion—what
Is man but his passion?

AUDUBON. I. WAS NOT THE LOST DAUPHIN. **1. dauphin:** eldest son of the King of France. There was a false story that Audubon was the son of the dethroned king of France, Louis XVI (1754–1793) and his queen Marie Antoinette (1755–1793). **11. crank:** like a ship that is liable to heel over or capsize.

Saw,
Eastward and over the cypress swamp, the dawn,
Redder than meat, break;
And the large bird,
Long neck outthrust, wings crooked to scull air, moved
In a slow calligraphy, crank, flat, and black against
The color of God's blood split, as though
Pulled by a string.

Saw
It proceed across the inflamed distance.

Moccasins set in hoar frost, eyes fixed on the bird,
Thought: "On that sky it is black."
Thought: "In my mind it is white."
Thinking: "*Ardea occidentalis,* heron, the great one."

Dawn: his heart shook in the tension of the world.

Dawn: and what is your passion?

IV
The Sign Whereby he Knew

[A]

His life, at the end, seemed—even the anguish—simple.
Simple, at least, in that it had to be,
Simply, what it was, as he was,
In the end, himself and not what
He had known he ought to be. The blessedness!—

To wake in some dawn and see,
As though down a rifle barrel, lined up
Like sights, the self that was, the self that is, and there,
Far off but in range, completing that alignment, your fate.

Hold your breath, let the trigger-squeeze be slow and steady.

The quarry lifts, in the halo of gold leaves, its noble head.

This is not a dimension of Time.

[B]

In this season the waters shrink.

The spring is circular and surrounded by gold leaves
Which are fallen from the beech tree.

Not even a skitter-bug disturbs the gloss
Of the surface tension. The sky

Is reflected below in absolute clarity.
If you stare into the water you may know

That nothing disturbs the infinite blue of the sky.

[C]

Keep store, dandle babies, and at night nuzzle
The hazelnut-shaped sweet tits of Lucy, and
With the piratical mark-up of the frontier, get rich.

But you did not, being of weak character.

You saw, from the forest pond, already dark, the great trumpeter swan
Rise, in clangor, and fight up the steep air where,
At the height of last light, it glimmered, like white flame.

The definition of love being, as we know, complex,
We may say that he, after all, loved his wife.

The letter, from campfire, keelboat, or slum room in New Orleans,
Always ended, "God bless you, dear Lucy." After sunset,

Alone, he played his flute in the forest.

[D]

Listen! Stand very still and,
Far off, where shadow
Is undappled, you may hear

The tusked boar grumble in his ivy-slick.

Afterward, there is silence until
The jay, sudden as conscience, calls.

The call, in the infinite sunlight, is like
The thrill of the taste of—on the tongue—brass.

[F]

The world declares itself. That voice
Is vaulted in—oh, arch on arch—redundancy of joy, its end
Is its beginning, necessity
Blooms like a rose. Why,
Therefore, is truth the only thing that cannot
Be spoken?

It can only be enacted, and that in dream,
Or in the dream become, as though unconsciously, action, and he stood,

At dusk, in the street of the raw settlement, and saw
The first lamp lit behind a window, and did not know
What he was. Thought: "I do not know my own name."

He walked in the world. He was sometimes seen to stand
In perfect stillness, when no leaf stirred.

Tell us, dear God—tell us the sign
Whereby we may know the time has come.

IV. THE SIGN WHEREBY HE KNEW. **22. Lucy:** Audubon's wife.

VI
Love and Knowledge

Their footless dance
Is of the beautiful liability of their nature.
Their eyes are round, boldly convex, bright as a jewel,
And merciless. They do not know
Compassion, and if they did,
We should not be worthy of it. They fly
In air that glitters like fluent crystal
And is hard as perfectly transparent iron, they cleave it
With no effort. They cry
In a tongue multitudinous, often like music.

He slew them, at surprising distances, with his gun.
Over a body held in his hand, his head was bowed low,
But not in grief.

He put them where they are, and there we see them:
In our imagination.

What is love?

One name for it is knowledge.

1971

SIR JOHN BETJEMAN

(1906–1984)

Betjeman's witty and polished verses reflect his fascination with Victorian and Edwardian England, in other words, with England in the middle and end of the nineteenth century and the early years of the twentieth. He wrote and lectured often in explanation and defense of the architecture, furniture design, and other decorative arts of this period, and admired even its minor poets, if only because they expressed the atmosphere of their age. He contributed greatly to a revolution in taste in which the arts of this period were better understood and appreciated. In 1972 he was named Poet Laureate.

An Incident in the Early Life of Ebenezer Jones, Poet, 1828

The lumber of a London-going dray,
The still-new stucco on the London clay,
Hot summer silence over Holloway.

Dissenting chapels, tea-bowers, lovers' lairs,
Neat new-built villas, ample Grecian squares,
Remaining orchards ripening Windsor pears.

Hot silence where the older mansions hide
On Highgate Hill's thick elm-encrusted side,
And Pancras, Hornsey, Islington divide.

June's hottest silence where the hard rays strike
Yon hill-foot house, window and wall alike,
School of the Reverend Mr. Bickerdike,

For sons of Saints, blest with this world's possessions
(Seceders from the Protestant Secessions),
Good grounding in the more genteel professions.

A lurcher dog, which draymen kick and pass,
Tongue lolling, thirsty over shadeless grass,
Leapt up the playground ladder to the class.

The godly usher left his godly seat,
His skin was prickly in the ungodly heat,
The dog lay panting at his godly feet.

The milkman on the road stood staring in,
The playground nettles nodded "Now begin"—
And Evil waited, quivering, for sin.

He lifted it and not a word he spoke,
His big hand tightened. Could he make it choke?
He trembled, sweated, and his temper broke.

AN INCIDENT IN THE EARLY LIFE **Title:** Ebenezer Jones (1820–1860) was a minor poet who, discouraged by the poor reception of his book of poems, did not publish another. In his portrait of this gentle, idealistic man, Betjeman uses an incident from Jones's life at school. A stray dog had wandered into the schoolroom, and the tyrannical and hard-natured teacher dragged it to the top of the stairs and was about to hurl it down when the small Jones rushed forward in protest crying, "You shall not!" **3. Holloway:** district of London. **4. Dissenting chapels:** Dissenters were Protestants who were not members of the Church of England. Their houses of meeting were commonly called "chapels" rather than churches in the nineteenth century. Jones came from a dissenting family. **8–9. Highgate . . . Islington:** districts of London surrounding Holloway. **14. Seceders . . . Secessions:** seceders from the Church of England which earlier had itself seceded from the Catholic Church.

"YOU SHALL NOT!" clear across to Highgate Hill
A boy's voice sounded. Creaking forms were still.
The cat jumped slowly from the window sill.

"YOU SHALL NOT!" flat against the summer sun,
Hard as the hard sky frowning over one,
Gloat, little boys! enjoy the coming fun!

"GOD DAMNS A CUR. I AM, I AM HIS WORD!"
He flung it, flung it and it never stirred,
"You shall not!—shall not!" ringing on unheard.

Blind desolation! bleeding, burning rod!
Big, bull-necked Minister of Calvin's God!
Exulting milkman, redfaced, shameless clod,

Look on and jeer! Not Satan's thunder-quake
Can cause the mighty walls of Heaven to shake
As now they do, to hear a boy's heart break.

1940

WILLIAM EMPSON

(1906–1984)

As a student at the University of Cambridge, Empson was fascinated by the poetry of John Donne. What caught him was the combination of intense emotion with intellectual play, and especially the compression of Donne's phrasing, in which multiple meanings were presented simultaneously. In influential critical studies, of which *Seven Types of Ambiguity* (1930) was the most important, Empson argued that a good poem does not speak with just "one voice"; that is, it is not "univocal." It activates different meanings and connotations, and these are complexly interrelated with each other or sometimes even contradictory. Through much of his adult life Empson was a university teacher of English in China. "Villanelle" shows the rigorous standards he imposed on his poetry. Villanelles are exceptionally difficult to write because of their intricate rhyme scheme, and therefore most villanelles in English have been composed merely to display prosodic skill. Empson's "Villanelle" is very different, being packed with personal meaning and emotion.

38. Calvin's God: John Calvin (1509–1564), Protestant theologian, who preached the inherent sinfulness of man, and that salvation (the "elect") came only from the grace of God.

Villanelle

It is the pain, it is the pain, endures.
Your chemic beauty burned my muscles through.
Poise of my hands reminded me of yours.

What later purge from this deep toxin cures?
What kindness now could the old salve renew?
It is the pain, it is the pain, endures.

The infection slept (custom or change inures)
And when pain's secondary phase was due
Poise of my hands reminded me of yours.

How safe I felt, whom memory assures,
Rich that your grace safely by heart I knew.
It is the pain, it is the pain, endures.

My stare drank deep beauty that still allures.
My heart pumps yet the poison draught of you.
Poise of my hands reminded me of yours.

You are still kind whom the same shape immures.
Kind and beyond adieu. We miss our cue.
It is the pain, it is the pain, endures.
Poise of my hands reminded me of yours.

1935

Ignorance of Death

Then there is this civilising love of death, by which
Even music and painting tell you what else to love.
Buddhists and Christians contrive to agree about death

Making death their ideal basis for different ideals.
The Communists however disapprove of death
Except when practical. The people who dig up

Corpses and rape them are I understand not reported.
The Freudians regard the death-wish as fundamental,
Though "the clamour of life" proceeds from its rival "Eros."

Whether you are to admire a given case for making less clamour
Is not their story. Liberal hopefulness
Regards death as a mere border to an improving picture.

VILLANELLE. **Title:** A villanelle is a French form of five three-line stanzas followed by a four-line stanza (a quatrain). The same rhymes are kept throughout (except that the last stanza adds an *a*-rhyme to the tercet *aba*); and the first and third lines of the first stanza are repeated alternately throughout until the last stanza, when they are put together in the two final lines.

Because we have neither hereditary nor direct knowledge of death
It is the trigger of the literary man's biggest gun
And we are happy to equate it to any conceived calm.

Heaven me, when a man is ready to die about something
Other than himself, and is in fact ready because of that,
Not because of himself, that is something clear about himself.

Otherwise I feel very blank upon this topic,
And think that though important, and proper for anyone to bring up,
It is one that most people should be prepared to be blank upon.

1940

W. H. AUDEN

(1907–1973)

The son of a doctor, Auden intended as a schoolboy to become a mining engineer or a scientist. In college at Oxford he impressed his fellow students by analyzing his and their emotions with coldly clinical detachment. They were also struck by his intellectual sophistication, self-confidence, energy, and humor. He was preparing himself for a career as a poet—a "great" poet, as he insisted. On leaving Oxford, he spent a year in Germany and then, returning to England, taught school for several years. He published copiously throughout the 1930s, and young though he was, he was soon widely read.

One reason for his impact was that he created a style for other poets of his generation. When T. S. Eliot's *The Waste Land* was published in 1922, it aroused conflicting responses in younger poets. The techniques of Eliot's poem were so new and brilliant that to adopt them was almost irresistibly tempting. On the other hand, poets were very reluctant to do this, for they did not want to become mere followers of Eliot, they feared that the extreme difficulty of Eliot's style would narrow the audience for poetry, and they rejected, as needlessly pessimistic and defeated, the moral and spiritual vision of *The Waste Land.* Since the techniques of the poem had been created to express this vision, to use them seemed to commit poets to an interpretation of life that was not theirs. Young poets sought, therefore, a style that would incorporate Eliot's technical achievement, equal his excellence, and yet be different. Auden greatly admired the poetry of T. S. Eliot, but except perhaps for a few months at Oxford, he was never a disciple of Eliot, and he also learned his art from many other poets—Yeats, Hardy, Hopkins, Pope, Skelton—ranging back to poems in the Anglo-Saxon language. His style seemed hardly less brilliant, at least in its promise, than that of Eliot, but it was more traditional, and as time passed, his writing became easier to understand.

This last point was especially important in the 1930s. The overwhelming historical crises of the age—the economic depression, the rise of Fascism in Germany and Italy, and, toward the end of the decade, the approaching war—preoccupied all thinking persons, and poets wished to write about these political and social issues. Sometimes they pleaded in poetry for a particular cause, which of course necessitated a style that would be widely understood. For the most part, however, poets sought only to express their own perceptions and emotions with utmost honesty, but the fact that these pertained to the public crises meant that they were widely shared. To use a style so difficult that it excluded this large audience would have seemed irresponsible.

In rapid, vivid allusion Auden's poetry depicted the industrial paralysis and the social strife of the age. He voiced the anxious uncertainty and sense of doom that to many readers seemed the ground emotions of the time. He showed how this age of economic and political breakdown engendered utopian, apocalyptic, and elegiac states of mind, and he understood the longing of the period for a strong leader—a teacher, healer, and saviour. Auden was contemporary not only in the emotions he represented, but in the lore on which he drew. Fascinated by psychoanalytic doctrines, he explored, as in "A Free One," the contrast between the public image of a hero or leader and the psychological inner man. His poetry applied depth psychology to social analysis. Uniting Freudian with Marxist insights, he described, for example, the wealthy bourgeoisie as subject to neurotic death wishes. In a way that was witty, original, and sometimes profound, he combined the criteria of social, psychic, and religious good. In "Sir, No Man's Enemy" the prayer is typically for "power and light," terms that may suggest both rural electrification and spiritual illumination.

Essentially Auden was a moralist, and his lyrics enacted a process of formulating moral judgments or of reluctantly accepting moral truths. In "As I Walked Out One Evening" romantic love is exposed by parody as illusion; another voice then warns that it must be surrendered for a different mode of love, which we might call charity. "Lullaby" fights out a conflict between sentimental eroticism and clear, intelligent awareness of reality. Erotic emotion creates illusions that the beloved person is "entirely beautiful" and that heaven and earth sympathize with the lovers. But at the same time the speaker knows that his beloved is only mortal and therefore "guilty," and that the "certainty" and "fidelity" felt in this moment will quickly pass.

In 1939 Auden left England and settled in the United States; he became an American citizen in 1946. Through most of his later life he spent winters in New York City and summers in a house near Vienna in Kirchstetten, Austria. He committed himself to Anglican Christianity, and many of his poems were on religious themes. He supported himself by sales of his books, reviewing, and public readings of his poetry. At the end of his life he returned to Oxford. His poetry after the 1940s was conversational and reflective. Even when he was most serious, his pose was likely to be comic or semi-comic. As time passed his style became increasingly leisurely and perspicuous. Everything that was to be understood was said. A poem such as "In Praise of Limestone" is an entertaining play of wit and intelligence for sophisticated readers.

A Free One

Watch any day his nonchalant pauses, see
His dextrous handling of a wrap as he
Steps after into cars, the beggar's envy.

"There is a free one," many say, but err.
He is not that returning conqueror,
Nor ever the poles' circumnavigator.

But poised between shocking falls on razor-edge
Has taught himself this balancing subterfuge
Of an accosting profile, an erect carriage.

The song, the varied action of the blood,
Would drown the warning from the iron wood,
Would cancel the inertia of the buried:

Travelling by daylight on from house to house
The longest way to an intrinsic peace,
With love's fidelity and with love's weakness.

1930

Taller To-day

Taller to-day, we remember similar evenings,
Walking together in a windless orchard
Where the brook runs over the gravel, far from the glacier.

Nights come bringing the snow, and the dead howl
Under headlands in their windy dwelling
Because the Adversary put too easy questions
On lonely roads.

But happy now, though no nearer each other,
We see farms lighted all along the valley;
Down at the mill-shed hammering stops
And men go home.

Noises at dawn will bring
Freedom for some, but not this peace
No bird can contradict: passing but here, sufficient now
For something fulfilled this hour, loved or endured.

1930

Sir, No Man's Enemy

Sir, no man's enemy, forgiving all
But will his negative inversion, be prodigal:
Send to us power and light, a sovereign touch
Curing the intolerable neural itch,
The exhaustion of weaning, the liar's quinsy,
And the distortions of ingrown virginity.
Prohibit sharply the rehearsed response
And gradually correct the coward's stance,
Cover in time with beams those in retreat
That, spotted, they turn though the reverse were great;
Publish each healer that in city lives
Or country houses at the end of drives;
Harrow the house of the dead; look shining at
New styles of architecture, a change of heart

1930

As I Walked Out One Evening

As I walked out one evening,
  Walking down Bristol Street,
The crowds upon the pavement
  Were fields of harvest wheat.

And down by the brimming river
  I heard a lover sing
Under an arch of the railway:
  "Love has no ending.

SIR, NO MAN'S ENEMY. **2. will . . . inversion:** perverse will toward whatever is negative. **3. sovereign touch:** alluding to the old belief that the touch of the king would cure scrofula, a skin disease. **5. quinsy:** sore throat. **13. harrow . . . dead:** alluding to Christ's harrowing of hell (descending into the underworld) for the purpose of redeeming those worthy of salvation who had died before His coming.

"I'll love you, dear, I'll love you
  Till China and Africa meet,
And the river jumps over the mountain
  And the salmon sing in the street,

"I'll love you till the ocean
  Is folded and hung up to dry
And the seven stars go squawking
  Like geese about the sky.

The years shall run like rabbits,
  For in my arms I hold
The Flower of the Ages,
  And the first love of the world."

But all the clocks in the city
  Began to whirr and chime:
"O let not Time deceive you,
  You cannot conquer Time.

"In the burrows of the Nightmare
  Where Justice naked is,
Time watches from the shadow
  And coughs when you would kiss.

"In headaches and in worry
  Vaguely life leaks away,
And Time will have his fancy
  Tomorrow or today.

"Into many a green valley
  Drifts the appalling snow;
Time breaks the threaded dances
  And the diver's brilliant bow.

"O plunge your hands in water,
  Plunge them in up to the wrist;
Stare, stare in the basin
  And wonder what you've missed.

"The glacier knocks in the cupboard,
  The desert sighs in the bed,
And the crack in the teacup opens
  A lane to the land of the dead.

"Where the beggars raffle the banknotes
  And the Giant is enchanting to Jack,
And the Lily-white Boy is a Roarer,
  And Jill goes down on her back.

"O look, look in the mirror,
  O look in your distress;
Life remains a blessing
  Although you cannot bless.

"O stand, stand at the window
  As the tears scald and start;
You shall love your crooked neighbor
  With your crooked heart."

It was late, late in the evening,
  The lovers they were gone;
The clocks had ceased their chiming,
  And the deep river ran on.

1940

Lullaby

Lay your sleeping head, my love,
Human on my faithless arm;
Time and fevers burn away
Individual beauty from
Thoughtful children, and the grave
Proves the child ephemeral:
But in my arms till break of day
Let the living creature lie,
Mortal, guilty, but to me
The entirely beautiful.

Soul and body have no bounds:
To lovers as they lie upon
Her tolerant enchanted slope
In their ordinary swoon,
Grave the vision Venus sends
Of supernatural sympathy,
Universal love and hope;
While an abstract insight wakes
Among the glaciers and the rocks
The hermit's carnal ecstasy.

Certainty, fidelity
On the stroke of midnight pass
Like vibrations of a bell
And fashionable madmen raise
Their pedantic boring cry:
Every farthing of the cost,
All the dreaded cards foretell,
Shall be paid, but from this night
Not a whisper, not a thought,
Not a kiss nor look be lost.

Beauty, midnight, vision dies:
Let the winds of dawn that blow
Softly round your dreaming head

Such a day of welcome show
Eye and knocking heart may bless,
Find our mortal world enough;
Noons of dryness find you fed
By the involuntary powers,
Nights of insult let you pass
Watched by every human love.

1940

Musée des Beaux Arts

About suffering they were never wrong,
The Old Masters: how well they understood
Its human position; how it takes place
While someone else is eating or opening a window or just walking
    dully along;
How, when the aged are reverently, passionately waiting
For the miraculous birth, there always must be
Children who did not specially want it to happen, skating
On a pond at the edge of the wood:
They never forgot
That even the dreadful martyrdom must run its course
Anyhow in a corner, some untidy spot
Where the dogs go on with their doggy life and the torturer's horse
Scratches its innocent behind on a tree.

In Brueghel's *Icarus,* for instance: how everything turns away
Quite leisurely from the disaster; the ploughman may
Have heard the splash, the forsaken cry,
But for him it was not an important failure; the sun shone
As it had to on the white legs disappearing into the green
Water, and the expensive delicate ship that must have seen
Something amazing, a boy falling out of the sky,
Had somewhere to get to and sailed calmly on.

1940

MUSÉE DES BEAUX ARTS. **Title:** "Museum of Fine Arts." The reference is to the museum in Brussels, which contains the painting mentioned below. **14. Brueghel's *Icarus*:** "The Fall of Icarus," by Pieter Brueghel (1520–1569). Icarus was the son of Daedalus, a skillful Greek craftsman who built the famous Labyrinth for King Minos of Crete. Later imprisoned there with his son, he constructed wings of wax and feathers with which they flew away. But Icarus flew too close to the sun, the wax melted, and he fell into the sea.

In Memory of W. B. Yeats

(d. Jan. 1939)

I

He disappeared in the dead of winter:
The brooks were frozen, the airports almost deserted,
And snow disfigured the public statues;
The mercury sank in the mouth of the dying day.
What instruments we have agree
The day of his death was a dark cold day.

Far from his illness
The wolves ran on through the evergreen forests,
The peasant river was untempted by the fashionable quays;
By mourning tongues
The death of the poet was kept from his poems.

But for him it was his last afternoon as himself,
An afternoon of nurses and rumors;
The provinces of his body revolted,
The squares of his mind were empty,
Silence invaded the suburbs,
The current of his feeling failed; he became his admirers.

Now he is scattered among a hundred cities
And wholly given over to unfamiliar affections,
To find his happiness in another kind of wood
And be punished under a foreign code of conscience.
The words of a dead man
Are modified in the guts of the living.

But in the importance and noise of to-morrow
When the brokers are roaring like beasts on the floor of the Bourse,
And the poor have the sufferings to which they are fairly accustomed,
And each in the cell of himself is almost convinced of his freedom,
A few thousand will think of this day
As one thinks of a day when one did something slightly unusual.
What instruments we have agree
The day of his death was a dark cold day.

II

You were silly like us; your gift survived it all:
The parish of rich women, physical decay,
Yourself. Mad Ireland hurt you into poetry.
Now Ireland has her madness and her weather still,
For poetry makes nothing happen: it survives

IN MEMORY OF W. B. YEATS. **25. Bourse:** stock exchange. **32. silly:** referring to Yeats's interest in the occult. **33. rich women:** Lady Gregory and other wealthy women who befriended Yeats.

In the valley of its making where executives
Would never want to tamper, flows on south
From ranches of isolation and the busy griefs,
Raw towns that we believe and die in; it survives,
A way of happening, a mouth.

III

Earth, receive an honoured guest:
William Yeats is laid to rest.
Let the Irish vessel lie
Emptied of its poetry.

In the nightmare of the dark
All the dogs of Europe bark,
And the living nations wait,
Each sequestered in its hate;

Intellectual disgrace
Stares from every human face,
And the seas of pity lie
Locked and frozen in each eye.

Follow, poet, follow right
To the bottom of the night,
With your unconstraining voice
Still persuade us to rejoice;

With the farming of a verse
Make a vineyard of the curse,
Sing of human unsuccess
In a rapture of distress;

In the deserts of the heart
Let the healing fountain start,
In the prison of his days
Teach the free man how to praise.

1940

In Praise of Limestone

If it form the one landscape that we, the inconstant ones,
  Are consistently homesick for, this is chiefly
Because it dissolves in water. Mark these rounded slopes
  With their surface fragrance of thyme and, beneath,
A secret system of caves and conduits; hear the springs
  That spurt out everywhere with a chuckle,
Each filling a private pool for its fish and carving
  Its own little ravine whose cliffs entertain

47. dogs . . . bark: World War II was to begin that year (September, 1939).

The butterfly and the lizard; examine this region
  Of short distances and definite places:
What could be more like Mother or a fitter background
  For her son, the flirtatious male who lounges
Against a rock in the sunlight, never doubting
  That for all his faults he is loved; whose works are but
Extensions of his power to charm? From weathered outcrop
  To hill-top temple, from appearing waters to
Conspicuous fountains, from a wild to a formal vineyard,
  Are ingenious but short steps that a child's wish
To receive more attention than his brothers, whether
  By pleasing or teasing, can easily take.
Watch, then, the band of rivals as they climb up and down
  Their steep stone gennels in twos and threes, at times
Arm in arm, but never, thank God, in step; or engaged
  On the shady side of a square at midday in
Voluble discourse, knowing each other too well to think
  There are any important secrets, unable
To conceive a god whose temper-tantrums are moral
  And not to be pacified by a clever line
Or a good lay: for, accustomed to a stone that responds,
  They have never had to veil their faces in awe
Of a crater whose blazing fury could not be fixed;
  Adjusted to the local needs of valleys
Where everything can be touched or reached by walking,
  Their eyes have never looked into infinite space
Through the lattice-work of a nomad's comb; born lucky,
  Their legs have never encountered the fungi
And insects of the jungle, the monstrous forms and lives
  With which we have nothing, we like to hope, in common.
So, when one of them goes to the bad, the way his mind works
  Remains comprehensible: to become a pimp
Or deal in fake jewellery or ruin a fine tenor voice
  For effects that bring down the house, could happen to all
But the best and the worst of us . . .
                                        That is why, I suppose,
  The best and worst never stayed here long but sought
Immoderate soils where the beauty was not so external,
  The light less public and the meaning of life
Something more than a mad camp. 'Come!' cried the granite wastes,
  'How evasive is your humor, how accidental
Your kindest kiss, how permanent is death.' (Saints-to-be
  Slipped away sighing.) 'Come!' purred the clays and gravels.
'On our plains there is room for armies to drill; rivers

IN PRAISE OF LIMESTONE. **22. gennels:** Yorkshire dialect term for a passage between houses (here a passage between rocks).

Wait to be tamed and slaves to construct you a tomb
In the grand manner: soft as the earth is mankind and both
Need to be altered.' (Intendant Caesars rose and
Left, slamming the door.) But the really reckless were fetched
By an older colder voice, the oceanic whisper:
'I am the solitude that asks and promises nothing;
That is how I shall set you free. There is no love;
There are only the various envies, all of them sad.'
They were right, my dear, all those voices were right
And still are; this land is not the sweet home that it looks,
Nor its peace the historical calm of a site
Where something was settled once and for all: A backward
And dilapidated province, connected
To the big busy world by a tunnel, with a certain
Seedy appeal, is that all it is now? Not quite:
It has a worldly duty which in spite of itself
It does not neglect, but calls into question
All the Great Powers assume; it disturbs our rights. The poet,
Admired for his earnest habit of calling
The sun the sun, his mind Puzzle, is made uneasy
By these marble statues which so obviously doubt
His antimythological myth; and these gamins,
Pursuing the scientist down the tiled colonnade
With such lively offers, rebuke his concern for Nature's
Remotest aspects: I, too, am reproached, for what
And how much you know. Not to lose time, not to get caught,
Not to be left behind, not, please! to resemble
The beasts who repeat themselves, or a thing like water
Or stone whose conduct can be predicted, these
Are our Common Prayer, whose greatest comfort is music
Which can be made anywhere, is invisible,
And does not smell. In so far as we have to look forward
To death as a fact, no doubt we are right: But if
Sins can be forgiven, if bodies rise from the dead,
These modifications of matter into
Innocent athletes and gesticulating fountains,
Made solely for pleasure, make a further point:
The blessed will not care what angle they are regarded from,
Having nothing to hide. Dear, I know nothing of
Either, but when I try to imagine a faultless love
Or the life to come, what I hear is the murmur
Of underground streams, what I see is a limestone landscape.

1951

81. Common Prayer: The Book of Common Prayer standardized prayers for the Church of England.

Louis MacNeice

(1907–1963)

MacNeice was one of the young English poets who came to prominence in the 1930s and did his best work in that period. "The Sunlight on the Garden" is a lyric on the traditional themes of time, love, and death, but it also reflects the emotional atmosphere of the 1930s. The days of love and happiness are drawing to a close because a war is coming. The quotation from Shakespeare's *Antony and Cleopatra* brings to mind the impact in that play of history—in other words, of politics, empire, and war on a love affair. "Bagpipe Music" ominously forbodes the end of the corrupt society it satirizes.

The Sunlight on the Garden

The sunlight on the garden
Hardens and grows cold,
We cannot cage the minute
Within its nets of gold,
When all is told
We cannot beg for pardon.

Our freedom as free lances
Advances towards its end;
The earth compels, upon it
Sonnets and birds descend;
And soon, my friend,
We shall have no time for dances.

The sky was good for flying
Defying the church bells
And every evil iron
Siren and what it tells:
The earth compels,
We are dying, Egypt, dying

And not expecting pardon,
Hardened in heart anew,
But glad to have sat under

THE SUNLIGHT ON THE GARDEN. **18. dying, Egypt:** from Antony's speech to Cleopatra, "I am dying, Egypt, dying," in Shakespeare's *Antony and Cleopatra* (IV, xv, 41).

Thunder and rain with you,
And grateful too
For sunlight on the garden.

1938

Bagpipe Music

It's no go the merrygoround, it's no go the rickshaw,
All we want is a limousine and a ticket for the peepshow.
Their knickers are made of crêpe-de-chine, their shoes are made
of python,
Their halls are lined with tiger rugs and their walls with heads of bison.

John MacDonald found a corpse, put it under the sofa,
Waited till it came to life and hit it with a poker,
Sold its eyes for souvenirs, sold its blood for whisky,
Kept its bones for dumb bells to use when he was fifty.

It's no go the Yogi-man, it's no go Blavatsky,
All we want is a bank balance and a bit of skirt in a taxi.

Annie MacDougall went to milk, caught her foot in the heather,
Woke to hear a dance record playing of Old Vienna.
It's no go your maidenheads, it's no go your culture,
All we want is a Dunlop tire and the devil mend the puncture.

The Laird o' Phelps spent Hogmanay declaring he was sober,
Counted his feet to prove the fact and found he had one foot over.
Mrs. Carmichael had her fifth, looked at the job with repulsion,
Said to the midwife "Take it away; I'm through with over production."

It's no go the gossip column, it's no go the ceilidh,
All we want is a mother's help and a sugar-stick for the baby.

Willie Murray cut his thumb, couldn't count the damage,
Took the hide of an Ayrshire cow and used it for a bandage.
His brother caught three hundred cran when the seas were lavish,
Threw the bleeders back in the sea and went upon the parish.

It's no go the Herring Board, it's no go the Bible,
All we want is a packet of fags when our hands are idle.

It's no go the picture palace, it's no go the stadium,
It's no go the country cot with a pot of pink geraniums,
It's no go the Government grants, it's no go the elections,
Sit on your arse for fifty years and hang your hat on a pension.

BAGPIPE MUSIC. **9. Blavatsky:** Madame Helena Blavatsky (1831–1891), Russian spiritualist, whose ideas became popular again in Britain in the 1930s. **15. Hogmanay:** Scots for New Year's Eve. **19. Ceilidh:** Gaelic (pronounced "kaley") for a social evening of song and storytelling. **24. went . . . parish:** went on relief. **26. fags:** cigarettes.

It's no go my honey love, its no go my poppet;
Work your hands from day to day, the winds will blow the profit.
The glass is falling hour by hour, the glass with fall forever,
But if you break the bloody glass you won't hold up the weather.

1938

THEODORE ROETHKE

(1908–1963)

Roethke went to the University of Michigan and, as a graduate student, to Harvard, and made his living by teaching college courses in creative writing. He was on the faculty of the University of Washington for many years until his death. His poetry passed through three phases. At first he was a poet of formally tight, "well-made poems," as he called them, but by the end of the 1930s he was tiring of these. This restlessness led him to compose *The Lost Son* (1948), a famous volume that began with an extraordinary sequence based on memories of the employees and the greenhouses in the nursery florist business of his father. These poems included, among those printed below, "Cuttings," "Root Cellar," and "Frau Bauman, Frau Schmidt, and Frau Schwartze." Flowers and plants were a traditional topic of lyric poetry, but never before had they been endowed with such tremendous vitality.

In other poems of this and subsequent volumes, Roethke enacted a spiritual and psychological quest to identify with primordial being. His poetry entered imaginatively into primitive creatures such as lizards, minnows, and even lower watery forms—snails, worms, scum—"With these I would be./ And with water: the waves coming forward . . ." But his psychological stability, which was always fragile, seems to have been especially endangered by composing poems of this kind. By the end of the 1940s he had lived through three mental breakdowns. As if to withdraw from psychoanalytic inwardness and imaginative identification with the primitive, organic, and vital, he began to write poems of intellectual generalization in firm, traditional forms. Many of these were strongly and obviously influenced by the philosophical lyrics of Yeats. But in his last volume, *The Far Field* (1964), which included "Meditation at Oyster River," Roethke partially returned to the greater mode he had created in the 1940s.

Cuttings

(later)

This urge, wrestle, resurrection of dry sticks,
Cut stems struggling to put down feet,
What saint strained so much,
Rose on such lopped limbs to a new life?

I can hear, underground, that sucking and sobbing,
In my veins, in my bones I feel it,—
The small waters seeping upward,
The tight grains parting at last.
When sprouts break out,
Slippery as fish,
I quail, lean to beginnings, sheath-wet.

1948

Root Cellar

Nothing would sleep in that cellar, dank as a ditch,
Bulbs broke out of boxes hunting for chinks in the dark,
Shoots dangled and drooped,
Lolling obscenely from mildewed crates,
Hung down long yellow evil necks, like tropical snakes.
And what a congress of stinks!
Roots ripe as old bait,
Pulpy stems, rank, silo-rich,
Leaf-mold, manure, lime, piled against slippery planks.
Nothing would give up life:
Even the dirt kept breathing a small breath.

1948

Frau Bauman, Frau Schmidt, and Frau Schwartze

Gone the three ancient ladies
Who creaked on the greenhouse ladders,
Reaching up white strings

CUTTINGS. **Title:** Cuttings are young shoots of plants that have been cut off and planted to root in soil. This was the second or "later" of two poems called "Cuttings." FRAU BAUMAN, FRAU SCHMIDT, AND FRAU SCHWARTZE. **Title:** The names are those of employees in the greenhouses of Roethke's father, a florist in Saginaw, Michigan.

To wind, to wind
The sweet-pea tendrils, the smilax,
Nasturtiums, the climbing
Roses, to straighten
Carnations, red
Chrysanthemums; the stiff
Stems, jointed like corn,
They tied and tucked,—
These nurses of nobody else.
Quicker than birds, they dipped
Up and sifted the dirt;
They sprinkled and shook;
They stood astride pipes,
Their skirts billowing out wide into tents,
Their hands twinkling with wet;
Like witches they flew along rows
Keeping creation at ease;
With a tendril for needle
They sewed up the air with a stem;
They teased out the seed that the cold kept asleep,—
All the coils, loops, and whorls.
They trellised the sun; they plotted for more than themselves.

I remember how they picked me up, a spindly kid,
Pinching and poking my thin ribs
Till I lay in their laps, laughing,
Weak as a whiffet;
Now, when I'm alone and cold in my bed,
They still hover over me,
These ancient leathery crones,
With their bandannas stiffened with sweat,
And their thorn-bitten wrists,
And their snuff-laden breath blowing lightly over me in my
first sleep.

1953

My Papa's Waltz

The whiskey on your breath
Could make a small boy dizzy;
But I hung on like death:
Such waltzing was not easy.

29. whiffet: a small dog.

We romped until the pans
Slid from the kitchen shelf;
My mother's countenance
Could not unfrown itself.

The hand that held my wrist
Was battered on one knuckle;
At every step you missed
My right ear scraped a buckle.

You beat time on my head
With a palm caked hard by dirt,
Then waltzed me off to bed
Still clinging to your shirt.

1948

Elegy for Jane

My student, thrown by a horse

I remember the neckcurls, limp and damp as tendrils;
And her quick look, a sidelong pickerel smile;
And how, once startled into talk, the light syllables leaped for her,
And she balanced in the delight of her thought,
A wren, happy, tail into the wind,
Her song trembling the twigs and small branches.
The shade sang with her;
The leaves, their whispers turned to kissing;
And the mold sang in the bleached valleys under the rose.

Oh, when she was sad, she cast herself down into such a pure depth,
Even a father could not find her:
Scraping her cheek against straw;
Stirring the clearest water.

My sparrow, you are not here,
Waiting like a fern, making a spiny shadow.
The sides of wet stones cannot console me.
Nor the moss, wound with the last light.

If only I could nudge you from this sleep,
My maimed darling, my skittery pigeon.
Over this damp grave I speak the words of my love:
I, with no rights in this matter,
Neither father nor lover.

1953

The Waking

I wake to sleep, and take my waking slow.
I feel my fate in what I cannot fear.
I learn by going where I have to go.

We think by feeling. What is there to know?
I hear my being dance from ear to ear.
I wake to sleep, and take my waking slow.

Of those so close beside me, which are you?
God bless the Ground! I shall walk softly there,
And learn by going where I have to go.

Light takes the Tree; but who can tell us how?
The lowly worm climbs up a winding stair;
I wake to sleep, and take my waking slow.

Great Nature has another thing to do
To you and me; so take the lively air,
And, lovely, learn by going where to go.

This shaking keeps me steady. I should know.
What falls away is always. And is near.
I wake to sleep, and take my waking slow.
I learn by going where I have to go.

1953

Meditation at Oyster River

1

Over the low, barnacled, elephant-colored rocks,
Come the first tide-ripples, moving almost without sound, toward me,
Running along the narrow furrows of the shore, the rows of dead
clam shells;
Then a runnel behind me, creeping closer,
Alive with tiny striped fish, and young crabs climbing in and out of the
water.

No sound from the bay. No violence.
Even the gulls quiet on the far rocks,
Silent, in the deepening light,
Their cat-mewing over,
Their child-whimpering.

MEDITATION AT OYSTER RIVER. **Title:** Oyster River in British Columbia, Canada, near Vancouver.

At last one long undulant ripple,
Blue-black from where I am sitting,
Makes almost a wave over a barrier of small stones,
Slapping lightly against a sunken log.
I dabble my toes in the brackish foam sliding forward,
Then retire to a rock higher up on the cliff-side.
The wind slackens, light as a moth fanning a stone:
A twilight wind, light as a child's breath
Turning not a leaf, not a ripple.
The dew revives on the beach-grass;
The salt-soaked wood of a fire crackles;
A fish raven turns on its perch (a dead tree in the rivermouth),
Its wings catching a last glint of the reflected sunlight.

2

The self persists like a dying star,
In sleep, afraid. Death's face rises afresh,
Among the shy beasts, the deer at the salt-lick,
The doe with its sloped shoulders loping across the highway,
The young snake, poised in green leaves, waiting for its fly,
The hummingbird, whirring from quince-blossom to morning-glory—
With these I would be.

And with water: the waves coming forward, without cessation,
The waves, altered by sand-bars, beds of kelp, miscellaneous driftwood,
Topped by cross-winds, tugged at by sinuous undercurrents
The tide rustling in, sliding between the ridges of stone,
The tongues of water, creeping in, quietly.

3

In this hour,
In this first heaven of knowing,
The flesh takes on the pure poise of the spirit,
Acquires, for a time, the sandpiper's insouciance,
The hummingbird's surety, the kingfisher's cunning—
I shift on my rock, and I think:
Of the first trembling of a Michigan brook in April,
Over a lip of stone, the tiny rivulet;
And that wrist-thick cascade tumbling from a cleft rock,
Its spray holding a double rain-bow in early morning,
Small enough to be taken in, embraced, by two arms,—
Or the Tittebawasee, in the time between winter and spring,
When the ice melts along the edges in early afternoon.
And the midchannel begins cracking and heaving from the pressure
beneath,
The ice piling high against the iron-bound spiles,
Gleaming, freezing hard again, creaking at midnight—

42. Michigan: where Roethke was born and grew up. **47. Tittebawasee:** river in central Michigan.

And I long for the blast of dynamite,
The sudden sucking roar as the culvert loosens its debris of
branches and sticks,
Welter of tin cans, pails, old bird nests, a child's shoe riding a log,
As the piled ice breaks away from the battered spiles,
And the whole river begins to move forward, its bridges shaking.

4

Now, in this waning of light,
I rock with the motion of morning;
In the cradle of all that is,
I'm lulled into half-sleep
By the lapping of water,
Cries of the sandpiper.
Water's my will, and my way,
And the spirit runs, intermittently,
In and out of the small waves,
Runs with the intrepid shorebirds—
How graceful the small before danger!

In the first of the moon,
All's a scattering,
A shining.

1964

Stephen Spender

(born 1909)

Like Louis MacNeice and Cecil Day Lewis, Spender was prominent in the 1930s when he was still young. Some of his lyrics, including the two printed here, quickly became famous, partly because of their eloquence, and partly because they challenged accepted conventions of poetic or moral feeling. The symbol of the railroad train in "The Express" suggests, among other meanings, that industrial power is carrying mankind into an unknown future. The contemporary impact of the poem depended especially on its affirmative attitude to machinery. Pistons, bolts, and wheels had not traditionally been poetic subjects for Romantic enthusiasm. "I Think Continually of Those Who Were Truly Great" celebrated a kind of person most readers would have praised much more tepidly, if at all, and thus the poem rejected common moral assumptions and proposed new ones.

I Think Continually of Those Who Were Truly Great

I think continually of those who were truly great.
Who, from the womb, remembered the soul's history
Through corridors of light where the hours are suns
Endless and singing. Whose lovely ambition
Was that their lips, still touched with fire,
Should tell of the Spirit clothed from head to foot in song.
And who hoarded from the Spring branches
The desires falling across their bodies like blossoms.

What is precious is never to forget
The essential delight of the blood drawn from ageless springs
Breaking through rocks in worlds before our earth.
Never to deny its pleasure in the morning simple light
Nor its grave evening demand for love.
Never to allow gradually the traffic to smother
With noise and fog the flowering of the spirit.

Near the snow, near the sun, in the highest fields
See how these names are fêted by the waving grass
And by the streamers of white cloud
And whispers of wind in the listening sky.
The names of those who in their lives fought for life
Who wore at their hearts the fire's center.
Born of the sun they traveled a short while towards the sun,
And left the vivid air signed with their honor.

1933

The Express

After the first powerful, plain manifesto
The black statement of pistons, without more fuss
But gliding like a queen, she leaves the station.
Without bowing and with restrained unconcern
She passes the houses which humbly crowd outside,
The gasworks, and at last the heavy page
Of death, printed by gravestones in the cemetery.
Beyond the town, there lies the open country
Where, gathering speed, she acquires mystery,
The luminous self-possession of ships on ocean.
It is now she begins to sing—at first quite low
Then loud, and at last with a jazzy madness—
The song of her whistle screaming at curves,
Of deafening tunnels, brakes, innumerable bolts.

And always light, aerial, underneath,
Retreats the elate metre of her wheels.
Steaming through metal landscape on her lines,
She plunges new eras of white happiness,
Where speed throws up strange shapes, broad curves
And parallels clean like trajectories from guns.
At last, further than Edinburgh or Rome,
Beyond the crest of the world, she reaches night
Where only a low stream-line brightness
Of phosphorus on the tossing hills is light.
Ah, like a comet through flame, she moves entranced,
Wrapt in her music no bird song, no, nor bough
Breaking with honey buds, shall ever equal.

1933

CHARLES OLSON

(1910–1970)

After several years as a college teacher of English, Olson moved to Washington, D.C., and embarked on a successful career in the federal government. In 1945 he abandoned this for literature. Beginning in 1948 he taught at Black Mountain College in North Carolina, a school which emphasized the arts, where he served as rector from 1952 until the college closed in 1956. He then settled in Gloucester, Massachusetts, a seaport city where he had spent summers as a child.

Until the 1960s Olson had almost no audience, but he then had an influence on other poets. His reception depended partly on his ideas about poetry, which he expounded in letters, essays, and lectures. He was deeply interested in the writings of Ezra Pound and William Carlos Williams, from whom he both derived and dissented.

From 1950 until his death, Olson worked on his long sequence of "Maximus" poems. They resembled Pound's *Cantos* (as Olson viewed the *Cantos*) because as Olson wrote them he was continually "open" to whatever new impulses might enter. At no point, in other words, had he committed himself to a particular plan, subject matter, or form. For Olson this readiness to respond freshly in the moment, to begin anew in every instant, enacted a necessary "stance" in living. But the "Maximus" poems differed from the *Cantos* in that they have one particular locality, the city of Gloucester, for their setting. In this Olson was influenced by the argument of William Carlos Williams that poetry should be rooted in the "local conditions"—that is, in the place where the poet lives. Williams had observed this principle in most of his poetry and especially in his long poem, *Paterson* (1946–58), which was centered in the New Jersey city of that name. Like *Paterson,* Olson's "Maxies," as he called them, presented both the contemporary city and its past history. But Olson's vision of the past was much longer than that of either Pound or Williams; it extended back beyond human history to include the geological events that formed the land and its topography around Gloucester.

In keeping with his principle of "openness," Olson's style in the "Maximus" poems was extremely variable. Moreover, it changed over the twenty years in which he composed the unfinished sequence. The reader must be prepared for anything, including some things for which previous poetry offers little precedent. In "I, Maximus of Gloucester, to You," for example, there are unclosed parentheses. These indicate "openness," the orientation or projection of the mind toward the future. In a similar spirit the poem establishes no norm of diction, rhythm, or line length, but instead changes quickly and extremely in these respects. In "Letter 72" the expressive means include pointing arrows. There is also a prosaic list of facts, stating where the original settlers built their homes in the section of Gloucester called "Dogtown." The first eight lines of the poem use Pound's techniques of allusion and "ideogram" (assemblage of separate fragments) to suggest a pristine world, love, gardens, the garden of Eden, and the fall from this state of happiness. The latter part of the poem plots the location of the early houses, and we find that the map of early Dogtown suggests the spiritual cosmography of the seventeenth-century settlers. To them the hills where they lived represented heaven, and the swamp and lower road had an opposite connotation.

from The Maximus Poems

I, Maximus of Gloucester, to You

Off-shore, by islands hidden in the blood
jewels & miracles, I, Maximus
a metal hot from boiling water, tell you
what is a lance, who obeys the figures of
the present dance

THE MAXIMUS POEMS. **Title:** Maximus (Olson) is writing from the fishing port of Gloucester, Massachusetts, which he had known well since boyhood, and which he peoples with individuals he had known as well as characters he invents.

1

the thing you're after
may lie around the bend
of the nest (second, time slain, the bird! the bird!

And there! (strong) thrust, the mast! flight
(of the bird
o kylix, o
Antony of Padua
sweep low, o bless

the roofs, the old ones, the gentle steep ones
on whose ridge-poles the gulls sit, from which they depart,

And the flake-racks

of my city!

2

love is form, and cannot be without
important substance (the weight
say, 58 carats each one of us, perforce
our goldsmith's scale

feather to feather added
(and what is mineral, what
is curling hair, the string
you carry in your nervous beak, these

make bulk, these, in the end, are
the sum

(o my lady of good voyage
in whose arm, whose left arm rests
no boy but a carefully carved wood, a painted face, a schooner!
a delicate mast, as bow-sprit for

forwarding

3

the underpart is, though stemmed, uncertain
is, as sex is, as moneys are, facts!
facts, to be dealt with, as the sea is, the demand
that they be played by, that they only can be, that they must
be played by, said he, coldly, the
ear!

11. kylix: Greek drinking bowl. **12. Antony of Padua:** thirteenth-century Franciscan monk, who preached a sermon to the fish in the Brenta River near Padua, Italy, where he lived. **16. flake-racks:** racks for drying fish. **28. lady:** the Virgin Mary, who was traditionally the protector of voyagers. **30. no boy:** no Christ-child, as in most portraits of Mary, but a ship symbolic of the travelers she guarded.

By ear, he sd.
But that which matters, that which insists, that which will last,
that! o my people, where shall you find it, how, where, where
        shall you listen
when all is become billboards, when, all, even silence, is spray-gunned?
when even our bird, my roofs,
cannot be heard

when even you, when sound itself is neoned in?

when, on the hill, over the water
where she who used to sing,
when the water glowed,
black, gold, the tide
outward, at evening

when bells came like boats
over the oil-slicks, milkweed
hulls

And a man slumped,
attentionless,
against pink shingles

o sea city)

4

one loves only form,
and form only comes
into existence when
the thing is born

                born of yourself, born
                of hay and cotton struts,
                of street-pickings, wharves, weeds
                you carry in, my bird

                                of a bone of a fish
                                of a straw, or will
                                of a color, of a bell
                                of yourself, torn

5

love is not easy
but how shall you know,
New England, now
that pejorocracy is here, how
that street-cars, o Oregon, twitter
in the afternoon, offend
a black-gold loin?

73. pejorocracy: rule or government by what makes a thing worse. Olson coins the term from Latin *pejorare* (to make worse) plus the Greek *cracy* (rule).

how shall you strike,
o swordsman, the blue-red back
when, last night, your aim
was mu-sick, mu-sick, mu-sick
And not the cribbage game?

(o Gloucester-man,
weave
your birds and fingers
new, your roof-tops,
clean shit upon racks
sunned on
American
braid
with others like you, such
extricable surface
as faun and oral,
satyr lesbos vase
o kill kill kill kill kill
those
who advertise you
out)

6

in! in! the bow-sprit, bird, the beak
in, the bend is, in, goes in, the form
that which you make, what holds, which is
the law of object, strut after strut, what you are, what you must be, what
the force can throw up, can, right now hereinafter erect,
the mast, the mast, the tender
mast!

The nest, I say, to you, I Maximus, say
under the hand, as I see it, over the waters
from this place where I am, where I hear,
can still hear

from where I carry you a feather
as though, sharp, I picked up,
in the afternoon delivered you
a jewel,
it flashing more than a wing,
than any old romantic thing,
than memory, than place,
than anything other than that which you carry
than that which is,
call it a nest, around the head of, call it

92–93. faun . . . lesbos: Fauns and satyrs were classical spirits of woods and fields; Lesbos is a Greek island noted for vases and other objects of art.

the next second

than that which you
can do!

1953

from Maximus Poems, IV, V, VI

Letter 72

of love & hand-holding sweet flowers & drinking
waters) Hilton's & Davis', Davis' the

garden of Ann
↘ get back to
& Elizabeth & Eden
Nasir Tusi
& where I fall

man is the fallen angel

and after Davis' swamp—Joshua Elwell
sitting high in heaven

→Bennett placed himself
above 75′

Hilton above the trough between
(on the edge of 75′ too)
—& Sam'l Davis on the height of
the next rise, inside 125′
(100′ lying almost exactly the middle
of the 600 foot distance between his
& Hilton's houses); and Joshua Elwell
the other rise on the Commons Road,
or "to the wood-lots" (1727),
on the other

MAXIMUS POEMS, IV, V, VI: LETTER 72. **2. Hilton's & Davis':** William Hilton and Samuel Davis, sixteenth-century settlers in the Dogtown district of Gloucester, Massachusetts. **3. Ann:** wife of Samuel Davis. **4. slanting arrow:** perhaps for emphasis, perhaps to indicate a fall—for example, the fall of man in the persons of Adam and Eve in the garden of Eden. **5. Elizabeth:** name of Olson's wife. **6. Nasir Tusi:** Nasir of the city of Tus, a Mohammedan philosopher of the thirteenth-century who wrote a commentary on the fall of the angels. **9. Joshua Elwell:** born 1687, another settler in Dogtown. **11. Bennett:** Anthony Bennett (died 1691). **12. above 75′:** the height above sea level at which Bennett's house was located. The other heights given subsequently in the poem indicate the same information for the other settlers. **21. "to the wood-lots":** quoted from a 1727 document. The families living in Dogtown had rights to pasture cows and cut wood on certain lots of land in the area now known as the Dogtown Commons.

side of the 2nd trough, at
125′ Thus
three 'hills' or hogbacks
& two brooks
characterize the upper
road (as against the lower
or dog Town road proper,
where moraine, and the more
evident presence of rock-tumble
gives the road, & center, its
moor character—moonscape
and hell) the Commons is
garden, and manor, ground rose
                                        & candle
shapes of spruce & bayberry garden

1968

ELIZABETH BISHOP

(1911–1979)

Bishop spent her early childhood on the Nova Scotia farm of her grandparents. She then lived with other relatives in Massachusetts (her father was dead, and her mother incurably insane). She was frequently ill as she was growing up, and filled much of her time with books, but she was able to go to boarding school and then to Vassar. She lived thereafter for many years in Brazil. In the last phase of her career she taught at Harvard. She published only four small volumes of poetry, but her genius was recognized from the start.

Her work was often compared to that of Marianne Moore, mainly because both poets achieved an extraordinary closeness and exactness in description. Both occasionally composed, moreover, idyllic poems on goodness, as in Bishop's charming "Manners." But Bishop's poetry reflects a more speculative intelligence than Moore's, and she was either more exposed to emotional and metaphysical distresses or more willing to express them.

25. hogbacks: a long, sharply crested ridge. **30. moraine:** a ridge or mound composed of rocks, sand, gravel, and so on, which was carried by a glacier and left behind when the glacier melted. **34. Commons:** See line 21. **35. ground rose:** a wild rose. **37. bayberry:** a shrub common on seacoasts.

Bishop's early poems were more obviously intellectual and symbolic than the greater ones printed here, for after her first volume (1946) she developed a way of writing that seemed remarkably plain and circumstantial. In this transition the work of William Carlos Williams was an influence. Moreover, Bishop seems to have been suspicious of the selecting and unifying of details in which every artist must engage, for she felt that these acts necessarily involve an assertion of will and a distortion of reality. Her poems suggest an opposite moral and stylistic ideal of receptivity to whatever appears or happens. If life or reality is, so far as we can tell, aimless, contingent, and random, poetry must suggest this in its style as well as content. "All the untidy activity continues/ awful but cheerful," she says in describing "The Bight," and this is the sense of life her poetry typically conveys. The illusion of "untidy" aimlessness in her poetry is, needless to say, only an illusion, for she was an extraordinarily self-conscious, skillful artist.

The Fish

I caught a tremendous fish
and held him beside the boat
half out of water, with my hook
fast in a corner of his mouth.
He didn't fight.
He hadn't fought at all.
He hung a grunting weight,
battered and venerable
and homely. Here and there
his brown skin hung in strips
like ancient wallpaper,
and its pattern of darker brown
was like wallpaper:
shapes like full-blown roses
stained and lost through age.
He was speckled with barnacles,
fine rosettes of lime,
and infested
with tiny white sea-lice,
and underneath two or three
rags of green weed hung down.
While his gills were breathing in
the terrible oxygen
—the frightening gills,
fresh and crisp with blood,
that can cut so badly—
I thought of the coarse white flesh

packed in like feathers,
the big bones and the little bones,
the dramatic reds and blacks
of his shiny entrails,
and the pink swim-bladder
like a big peony.
I looked into his eyes
which were far larger than mine
but shallower, and yellowed,
the irises backed and packed
with tarnished tinfoil
seen through the lenses
of old scratched isinglass.
They shifted a little, but not
to return my stare.
—It was more like the tipping
of an object toward the light.
I admired his sullen face,
the mechanism of his jaw,
and then I saw
that from his lower lip
—if you could call it a lip—
grim, wet, and weaponlike,
hung five old pieces of fish-line,
or four and a wire leader
with the swivel still attached,
with all their five big hooks
grown firmly in his mouth.
A green line, frayed at the end
where he broke it, two heavier lines,
and a fine black thread
still crimped from the strain and snap
when it broke and he got away.
Like medals with their ribbons
frayed and wavering,
a five-haired beard of wisdom
trailing from his aching jaw.
I stared and stared
and victory filled up
the little rented boat,
from the pool of bilge
where oil had spread a rainbow
around the rusted engine
to the bailer rusted orange,
the sun-cracked thwarts,
the oarlocks on their strings,
the gunnels—until everything
was rainbow, rainbow, rainbow!
And I let the fish go.

1946

The Bight

On my birthday

At low tide like this how sheer the water is.
White, crumbling ribs of marl protrude and glare
and the boats are dry, the pilings dry as matches.
Absorbing, rather than being absorbed,
the water in the bight doesn't wet anything,
the color of the gas flame turned as low as possible.
One can smell it turning to gas; if one were Baudelaire
one could probably hear it turning to marimba music.
The little ocher dredge at work off the end of the dock
already plays the dry perfectly off-beat claves.
The birds are outsize. Pelicans crash
into this peculiar gas unnecessarily hard,
it seems to me, like pickaxes,
rarely coming up with anything to show for it,
and going off with humorous elbowings.
Black-and-white man-of-war birds soar
on impalpable drafts
and open their tails like scissors on the curves
or tense them like wishbones, till they tremble.
The frowsy sponge boats keep coming in
with the obliging air of retrievers,
bristling with jackstraw gaffs and hooks
and decorated with bobbles of sponges.
There is a fence of chicken wire along the dock
where, glinting like little plowshares,
the blue-gray shark tails are hung up to dry
for the Chinese-restaurant trade.
Some of the little white boats are still piled up
against each other, or lie on their sides, stove in,
and not yet salvaged, if they ever will be, from the last
        bad storm,
like torn-open, unanswered letters.
The bight is littered with old correspondences.
Click. Click. Goes the dredge,
and brings up a dripping jawful of marl.
All the untidy activity continues,
awful but cheerful.

1955

THE BIGHT. **7. Baudelaire:** Charles Baudelaire (1821–1867), French poet. **10. claves:** small sticks of wood. In Cuban dance bands a player holds one in his left hand and taps it with the other held in his right hand.

Manners

for a Child of 1918

My grandfather said to me
as we sat on the wagon seat,
"Be sure to remember to always
speak to everyone you meet."

We met a stranger on foot.
My grandfather's whip tapped his hat.
"Good day, sir. Good day. A fine day."
And I said it and bowed where I sat.

Then we overtook a boy we knew
with his big pet crow on his shoulder.
"Always offer everyone a ride;
don't forget that when you get older,"

my grandfather said. So Willy
climbed up with us, but the crow
gave a "Caw!" and flew off. I was worried.
How would he know where to go?

But he flew a little way at a time
from fence post to fence post, ahead;
and when Willy whistled he answered.
"A fine bird," my grandfather said,

"and he's well brought up. See, he answers
nicely when he's spoken to.
Man or beast, that's good manners.
Be sure that you both always do."

When automobiles went by,
the dust hid the people's faces,
but we shouted "Good day! Good day!
Fine day!" at the top of our voices.

When we came to Hustler Hill,
he said that the mare was tired,
so we all got down and walked,
as our good manners required.

1955

Irving Layton

(born 1912)

Born in Romania, Layton grew up in a Jewish community in Montreal, where his mother had a small grocery store. He attended McGill University, and after several other jobs, became a school teacher and eventually a professor of English at York University. Many of his poems deliberately violated middle-class proprieties, voiced social protest, and displayed him in the role of a rebel. These naturally shaped his reputation, and he became one of the more widely known poets in Canada. But his work also had a more inward and reflective dimension, which is illustrated in the poems printed here.

Berry Picking

Silently my wife walks on the still wet furze
Now darkgreen the leaves are full of metaphors
Now lit up is each tiny lamp of blueberry.
The white nails of rain have dropped and the sun is free.

And whether she bends or straightens to each bush
To find the children's laughter among the leaves
Her quiet hands seem to make the quiet summer hush—
Berries or children, patient she is with these.

I only vex and perplex her; madness, rage
Are endearing perhaps put down upon the page;
Even silence daylong and sullen can then
Enamor as restraint or classic discipline.

So I envy the berries she puts in her mouth,
The red and succulent juice that stains her lips;
I shall never taste that good to her, nor will they
Displease her with a thousand barbarous jests.

How they lie easily for her hand to take,
Part of the unoffending world that is hers;
Here beyond complexity she stands and stares
And leans her marvelous head as if for answers.

No more the easy soul my childish craft deceives
Nor the simpler one for whom yes is always yes;
No, now her voice comes to me from a far way off
Though her lips are redder than the raspberries.

1958

Keine Lazarovitch, 1870–1959

When I saw my mother's head on the cold pillow,
Her white waterfalling hair in the cheeks' hollows,
I thought, quietly circling my grief, of how
She had loved God but cursed extravagantly his creatures.

For her final mouth was not water but a curse,
A small black hole, a black rent in the universe,
Which damned the green earth, stars and trees in its stillness
And the inescapable lousiness of growing old.

And I record she was comfortless, vituperative,
Ignorant, glad, and much else besides; I believe
She endlessly praised her black eyebrows, their thick weave,
Till plagiarizing Death leaned down and took them for his mould.

And spoiled a dignity I shall not again find,
And the fury of her stubborn limited mind;
Now none will shake her amber beads and call God blind,
Or wear them upon a breast so radiantly.

O fierce she was, mean and unaccommodating;
But I think now of the toss of her gold earrings,
Their proud carnal assertion, and her youngest sings
While all the rivers of her red veins move into the sea.

1961

R. S. Thomas

(born 1913)

A Welsh country priest of the Anglican Church, Thomas usually wrote on directly religious themes. But in the 1940s and 1950s many of his poems described the region where he lived. Thomas' grim picture of rural life was not totally unprecedented in poetry, for in the descriptions by George Crabbe in *The Village* (1783) and other volumes there had been a similar harsh naturalism infused with anger, protest, and satire. But Crabbe still retained much of the emotional distance from his materials—the firm artistic control and elegance of poetry in the eighteenth century; Thomas arrests and shocks us by the intensity and conflict of his feelings.

"The Welsh Hill Country" is ostensibly directed against a tourist who harbors sentimental, idyllic notions about the countryside. But we sense that the tourist is a surrogate for Thomas himself, whose illusions are the real object of attack. In "A Peasant" the speaker is dismayed and repelled by the person he describes, and tends, moreover, to see in him a symbolic figure of ominous suggestion. In the last six lines of the poem, he struggles to view this "peasant" more positively and criticizes the "refined" reader for being repelled by him. Yet the guilt of this reader would lie only in sharing the revulsion that is obvious in the first part of the poem.

A Peasant

Iago Prytherch his name, though, be it allowed,
Just an ordinary man of the bald Welsh hills,
Who pens a few sheep in a gap of cloud.
Docking mangels, chipping the green skin
From the yellow bones with a half-witted grin
Of satisfaction, or churning the crude earth
To a stiff sea of clods that glint in the wind—
So are his days spent, his spittled mirth
Rarer than the sun that cracks the cheeks
Of the gaunt sky perhaps once in a week.
And then at night see him fixed in his chair
Motionless, except when he leans to gob in the fire.
There is something frightening in the vacancy of his
        mind.
His clothes, sour with years of sweat
And animal contact, shock the refined,
But affected, sense with their stark naturalness.
Yet this is your prototype, who, season by season
Against siege of rain and the wind's attrition,
Preserves his stock, an impregnable fortress
Not to be stormed even in death's confusion.
Remember him, then, for he, too, is a winner of wars,
Enduring like a tree under the curious stars.

1946

A PEASANT. **4. mangels:** large turnips used to feed cattle. **12. gob:** spit.

The Welsh Hill Country

Too far for you to see
The fluke and the foot-rot and the fat maggot
Gnawing the skin from the small bones,
The sheep are grazing at Bwlch-y-Fedwen,
Arranged romantically in the usual manner
On a bleak background of bald stone.

Too far for you to see
The moss and the mould on the cold chimneys,
The nettles growing through the cracked doors,
The houses stand empty at Nant-yr-Eira,
There are holes in the roofs that are thatched with
sunlight,
And the fields are reverting to the bare moor.

Too far, too far to see
The set of his eyes and the slow phthisis
Wasting his frame under the ripped coat,
There's a man still farming at Ty'n-y-Fawnog,
Contributing grimly to the accepted pattern,
The embryo music dead in his throat.

1952

ROBERT HAYDEN

(1913–1980)

Through most of his adult life, Hayden taught at Fisk University in Tennessee. He is a narrative poet in the sense that he relies heavily on the rendering of character, setting, or event. In "Those Winter Sundays" we build our image of the father and of the son's relation with him by inferring from the particular, circumstantial details that are reported. Similarly, in "The Ballad of Sue Ellen Westerfield" the large themes of the poem are embodied in the particular story of one woman. Not all Hayden's poetry centers on black experience in the United States, but this is his central subject. Although other poets, such

THE WELSH HILL COUNTRY. **2. fluke:** parasitic worm in the sheep. **maggot:** on the sheep. **14. phthisis:** tuberculosis of the lungs.

as Langston Hughes, have expressed this with more exuberant vitality and imagination, Hayden's direct, unostentatious art grows on readers steadily as they increasingly appreciate the depth of intelligence reflected in it.

The Ballad of Sue Ellen Westerfield

(For Clyde)

She grew up in bedeviled southern wilderness,
but had not been a slave, she said,
because her father wept and set her mother free.
She hardened in perilous rivertowns
and after The Surrender,
went as maid upon the tarnished Floating Palaces.
Rivermen reviled her for the rankling cold
sardonic pride
that gave a knife-edge to her comeliness.

When she was old, her back still straight,
her hair still glossy black,
she'd talk sometimes
of dangers lived through on the rivers.
But never told of him,
whose name she'd vowed she would not speak again
till after Jordan.
Oh, he was nearer nearer now
than wearisome kith and kin.
His blue eyes followed her
as she moved about her tasks upon the *Memphis Rose.*
He smiled and joshed, his voice quickening her.
She cursed the circumstance. . . .

The crazing horrors of that summer night,
the swifting flames, he fought his way to her,
the savaging panic, and helped her swim to shore.
The steamer like besieged Atlanta blazing,
the cries, the smoke and bellowing flames,
the flamelit thrashing forms in hellmouth water,
and he swimming out to them,
leaving her dazed and lost.
A woman screaming under the raddled trees—

THE BALLAD OF SUE ELLEN WESTERFIELD. **5. Surrender:** of the Confederate forces in the Civil War. **6. Floating Palaces:** the Mississippi steam boats. **16. after Jordan:** after passing the Jordan River into the "promised land" (that is, after death). **26. besieged Atlanta:** Atlanta was burned by General Sherman in his "march to the sea" during the Civil War.

Sue Ellen felt it was herself who screamed.
The moaning of the hurt, the terrified—
she held off shuddering despair
and went to comfort whom she could.
Wagons torches bells
and whimpering dusk of morning
and blankness lostness nothingness for her
until his arms had lifted her
into wild and secret dark.

How long how long was it they wandered,
loving fearing loving,
fugitives whose dangerous only hidingplace
was love?
How long was it before she knew
she could not forfeit what she was,
even for him—could not, even for him,
forswear her pride?
They kissed and said farewell at last.
He wept as had her father once.
They kissed and said farewell.
Until her dying-bed,
she cursed the circumstance.

1962

Those Winter Sundays

Sundays too my father got up early
and put his clothes on in the blueblack cold,
then with cracked hands that ached
from labor in the weekday weather made
banked fires blaze. No one ever thanked him.

I'd wake and hear the cold splintering, breaking.
When the rooms were warm, he'd call,
and slowly I would rise and dress,
fearing the chronic angers of that house,

Speaking indifferently to him,
who had driven out the cold
and polished my good shoes as well.
What did I know, what did I know
of love's austere and lonely offices?

1962

John Berryman

(1914–1972)

Berryman made his living as a college teacher of English, but the story of his life lies essentially in his brave, interminable struggle with obsessive griefs and guilts—including those connected with the suicide of his father and with his own love affairs and alcoholism—and in his effort to redeem his life through his achievement as a writer. His early poems were typical of the poetry of the 1940s—packed, formal, impersonal, intellectual—and his first important poem, *Homage to Mistress Bradstreet* (1956), both continued and broke away from this style.

But it was not until he wrote his "Dream Songs," of which the first installment appeared in 1964, that Berryman escaped from the academic limitations in which he had been confined. The "Dream Songs" are about a character named Henry, who is partly based on comic figures in the stage minstrel shows of the nineteenth century. Henry is an anti-hero—feckless, vulnerable, trapped, guilt-ridden, and absurd. But while the mode of the sequence is comic, the substance is woe, and although the poems are not literally autobiographical, they closely reflect Berryman's life and emotions. In poem after poem Henry's state is inventoried and found to be awful. Yet nothing very much is wrong in his life except his psyche. One context of these poems, we should remember, is the so-called "Confessional" poetry of the United States in the 1950s and 1960s, when poets such as Robert Lowell, Allen Ginsberg, and Sylvia Plath presented morbid fantasies and fears, of the sort all human beings have in some degree, with a new directness, frankness, and detail. In poetry of this type, evil and danger threaten not from external sources but from the mind itself, from the tensions and processes of human psychology. How much tact and art was involved in keeping to a comic mode and a feigned protagonist in the "Dream Songs," in transforming sorrow into rueful or wistful humor and horror into absurdity, can be seen from Berryman's last book, *Recovery* (1973). Although still fictionalized, this prose account of Berryman's final, ambivalent effort to overcome alcoholism wrings the heart with pity for the psychological dilemmas that tortured him. Berryman committed suicide by jumping off a bridge at the age of fifty-seven.

from The Dream Songs

16

Henry's pelt was put on sundry walls
where it did much resemble Henry and
them persons was delighted.
Especially his long & glowing tail
by all them was admired, and visitors.
They whistled: This is *it*!

Golden, whilst your frozen daiquiris
whir at midnight, gleams on you his fur
& silky & black.
Mission accomplished, pal.
My molten yellow & moonless bag,
drained, hangs at rest.

Collect in the cold depths barracuda. Ay,
in Sealdah Station some possessionless
children survive to die.
The Chinese communes hum. Two daiquiris
withdrew into a corner of the gorgeous room
and one told the other a lie.

1964

29

There sat down, once, a thing on Henry's heart
so heavy, if he had a hundred years
& more, & weeping, sleepless, in all them time
Henry could not make good.
Starts again always in Henry's ears
the little cough somewhere, an odor, a chime.

And there is another thing he has in mind
like a grave Sienese face a thousand years
would fail to blur the still profiled reproach of. Ghastly,
with open eyes, he attends, blind.
All the bells say: too late. This is not for tears;
thinking.

But never did Henry, as he thought he did,
end anyone and hacks her body up
and hide the pieces, where they may be found.
He knows: he went over everyone, & nobody's missing.
Often he reckons, in the dawn, them up.
Nobody is ever missing.

1964

DREAM SONGS. DREAM SONG 29 **8. Sienese:** from Sienna, Italy, famous for its painters in the Renaissance.

76

Henry's Confession

Nothin very bad happen to me lately.
How you explain that?—I explain that, Mr. Bones,
terms o' your bafflin odd sobriety.
Sober as man can get, no girls, no telephones,
what could happen bad to Mr. Bones?
—*If* life is a handkerchief sandwich,

in a modesty of death I join my father
who dared so long agone leave me.
A bullet on a concrete stoop
close by a smothering southern sea
spreadeagled on an island, by my knee.
—You is from hunger, Mr. Bones,

I offers you this handkerchief, now set
your left foot by my right foot,
shoulder to shoulder, all that jazz,
arm in arm, by the beautiful sea,
hum a little, Mr. Bones.
—I saw nobody coming, so I went instead.

1964

312

I have moved to Dublin to have it out with you,
majestic Shade, You whom I read so well
so many years ago,
did I read your lesson right? did I see through
your phases to the real? your heaven, your hell
did I enquire properly into?

For years then I forgot you, I put you down,
ingratitude is the necessary curse
of making things new:
I brought my family to see me through,
I brought my homage & my soft remorse,
I brought a book or two

only, including in the end your last
strange poems made under the shadow of death
Your high figures float
again across my mind and all your past
fills my walled garden with your honey breath
wherein I move, a mote.

1968

DREAM SONG 76 (HENRY'S CONFESSION) **2. Mr. Bones:** Henry's alter ego and interlocutor in the *Dream Songs*. **7–8. death . . . leave me:** Berryman's father committed suicide. DREAM SONG 312 **2. Shade:** the ghost of W. B. Yeats. **9. making . . . new:** referring to Ezra Pound's dictum, "Make It New."

Dylan Thomas

(1914–1953)

Thomas grew up in Wales and spent most of his life there. He was amazingly precocious, and had composed several of his famous poems by the time he was seventeen years old. His style combined the diction and rhythms of the Bible and of hymns with modes and traditions of poetry that also influenced most of his contemporaries—the Metaphysical "wit" of the early seventeenth century (to which T. S. Eliot had called favorable attention in his critical essays of the 1920s) and the extreme emphasis on suggestive and musical uses of words in modern poetry derived from French *Symbolisme*. His vision of the world was much influenced by contemporary depth psychology and by writers, such as D. H. Lawrence, who celebrated the life force and identified it with bodily (as opposed to mental) experience, especially with sexuality.

Thomas sought to possess and assert a quasi-mystical sense of life as something indestructible and omnipresent. As he puts it in the first line of a famous lyric, the same "force that through the green fuse" of a plant "drives the flower" also drives him. Within this vision of things individuality has little significance—it is merely a local and temporary event within the encompassing whole of life—and, more important still, death is not to be feared, for it is as natural as any other process of life; in fact, it is the return of the individual to the whole from which he emerged. To praise life is inevitably also to accept death. The same force, as Thomas says in the poem from which we just quoted, that "Drives my green age" is also "my destroyer."

Thomas' words frequently convey ambivalent emotions and ambiguous senses. The last line of "A Refusal to Mourn the Death, by Fire, of a Child in London" includes, among its several possible meanings, both that there is no death but only life and also an opposite implication that death is final. Thomas was a very honest writer, and it was not always possible for him to celebrate the life force that involved personal death. "Do Not Go Gentle into That Good Night" voices a revolt. The poem was addressed to his dying father, and it urges that from the point of view of the dying individual, the "light" itself is "dying"; every person who loves life must rage against death precisely because death is for him the end of the world.

Despite the complexity and subtlety of his lyrics, Thomas was one of the most popular poets of his generation. The reasons for this lie in the musical and rhythmic qualities of his verse and in his ambiguous but, on the whole, celebratory vision of life. Above all there was the powerful impact of his public readings. Thomas was the most effective reciter of poetry in his generation, and toward the end of his life the records of his readings and his radio performances reached millions. By this time, moreover, he was writing in a more accessible style, as one sees in "Fern Hill." But he was not now writing many new poems, for enormous and constant drinking had undermined his health. He died at the age of forty-nine in a New York City hospital.

The Force That Through the Green Fuse Drives the Flower

The force that through the green fuse drives the flower
Drives my green age; that blasts the roots of trees
Is my destroyer.
And I am dumb to tell the crooked rose
My youth is bent by the same wintry fever.

The force that drives the water through the rocks
Drives my red blood; that dries the mouthing streams
Turns mine to wax.
And I am dumb to mouth unto my veins
How at the mountain spring the same mouth sucks.

The hand that whirls the water in the pool
Stirs the quicksand; that ropes the blowing wind
Hauls my shroud sail.
And I am dumb to tell the hanging man
How of my clay is made the hangman's lime.

The lips of time leech to the fountain head;
Love drips and gathers, but the fallen blood
Shall calm her sores.
And I am dumb to tell a weather's wind
How time has ticked a heaven round the stars.

And I am dumb to tell the lover's tomb
How at my sheet goes the same crooked worm.

1934

And Death Shall Have No Dominion

And death shall have no dominion.
Dead men naked they shall be one
With the man in the wind and the west moon;

AND DEATH SHALL HAVE NO DOMINION. **Title:** from the words of St. Paul, "Death hath no more dominion" (Romans 6:19).

When their bones are picked clean and the clean bones gone,
They shall have stars at elbow and foot;
Though they go mad they shall be sane,
Though they sink through the sea they shall rise again;
Though lovers be lost love shall not;
And death shall have no dominion.

And death shall have no dominion.
Under the windings of the sea
They lying long shall not die windily;
Twisting on racks when sinews give way,
Strapped to a wheel, yet they shall not break;
Faith in their hands shall snap in two,
And the unicorn evils run them through;
Split all ends up they shan't crack;
And death shall have no dominion.

And death shall have no dominion.
No more may gulls cry at their ears
Or waves break loud on the seashores;
Where blew a flower may a flower no more
Lift its head to the blows of the rain;
Though they be mad and dead as nails,
Heads of the characters hammer through daisies;
Break in the sun till the sun breaks down,
And death shall have no dominion.

1936

A Refusal to Mourn the Death, by Fire, of a Child in London

Never until the mankind making
Bird beast and flower
Fathering and all humbling darkness
Tells with silence the last light breaking
And the still hour
Is come of the sea tumbling in harness

And I must enter again the round
Zion of the water bead
And the synagogue of the ear of corn
Shall I let pray the shadow of a sound
Or sow my salt seed
In the least valley of sackcloth to mourn

The majesty and burning of the child's death.
I shall not murder
The mankind of her going with a grave truth

Nor blaspheme down the stations of the breath
With any further
Elegy of innocence and youth.

Deep with the first dead lies London's daughter,
Robed in the long friends,
The grains beyond age, the dark veins of her mother,
Secret by the unmourning water
Of the riding Thames.
After the first death, there is no other.

1946

Fern Hill

Now as I was young and easy under the apple boughs
About the lilting house and happy as the grass was green,
The night above the dingle starry,
Time let me hail and climb
Golden in the heydays of his eyes,
And honored among wagons I was prince of the apple towns
And once below a time I lordly had the trees and leaves
Trail with daisies and barley
Down the rivers of the windfall light.

And as I was green and carefree, famous among the barns
About the happy yard and singing as the farm was home,
In the sun that is young once only,
Time let me play and be
Golden in the mercy of his means,
And green and golden I was huntsman and herdsman, the calves
Sang to my horn, the foxes on the hills barked clear and cold,
And the sabbath rang slowly
In the pebbles of the holy streams.

All the sun long it was running, it was lovely, the hay
Fields high as the house, the tunes from the chimneys, it was air
And playing, lovely and watery
And fire green as grass.
And nightly under the simple stars
As I rode to sleep the owls were bearing the farm away,
All the moon long I heard, blessed among stables, the night-jars
Flying with the ricks, and the horses
Flashing into the dark.

And then to awake, and the farm, like a wanderer white
With the dew, come back, the cock on his shoulder: it was all
Shining, it was Adam and maiden,
The sky gathered again
And the sun grew round that very day.

So it must have been after the birth of the simple light
In the first, spinning place, the spellbound horses walking warm
Out of the whinnying green stable
On to the fields of praise.

And honored among foxes and pheasants by the gay house
Under the new made clouds and happy as the heart was long,
In the sun born over and over,
I ran my heedless ways,
My wishes raced through the house high hay
And nothing I cared, at my sky blue trades, that time allows
In all his tuneful turning so few and such morning songs
Before the children green and golden
Follow him out of grace,

Nothing I cared, in the lamb white days, that time would take me
Up to the swallow thronged loft by the shadow of my hand,
In the moon that is always rising,
Nor that riding to sleep
I should hear him fly with the high fields
And wake to the farm forever fled from the childless land.
Oh as I was young and easy in the mercy of his means,
Time held me green and dying
Though I sang in my chains like the sea.

1946

In My Craft or Sullen Art

In my craft or sullen art
Exercised in the still night
When only the moon rages
And the lovers lie abed
With all their griefs in their arms,
I labor by singing light
Not for ambition or bread
Or the strut and trade of charms
On the ivory stages
But for the common wages
Of their most secret heart.

Not for the proud man apart
From the raging moon I write
On these spindrift pages
Nor for the towering dead
With their nightingales and psalms
But for the lovers, their arms
Round the griefs of the ages,
Who pay no praise or wages
Nor heed my craft or art.

1946

Do Not Go Gentle into That Good Night

Do not go gentle into that good night,
Old age should burn and rave at close of day;
Rage, rage against the dying of the light.

Though wise men at their end know dark is right,
Because their words had forked no lightning they
Do not go gentle into that good night.

Good men, the last wave by, crying how bright
Their frail deeds might have danced in a green bay,
Rage, rage against the dying of the light.

Wild men who caught and sang the sun in flight,
And learn, too late, they grieved it on its way,
Do not go gentle into that good night.

Grave men, near death, who see with blinding sight
Blind eyes could blaze like meteors and be gay,
Rage, rage against the dying of the light.

And you, my father, there on the sad height,
Curse, bless, me now with your fierce tears, I pray.
Do not go gentle into that good night.
Rage, rage against the dying of the light.

1952

GWENDOLYN BROOKS

(born 1917)

After working for several years in an office, Brooks became known for her poetry; this led to a career as a college teacher in Chicago, where she has lived since childhood. Most of her poems deal with black experience in the United States, especially in the Chicago ghettos. In form and style her work has great variety. Generally her later verse, which is represented here, has a more concentrated and difficult idiom than that for which she was first known. "Medgar Evers," for

DO NOT GO GENTLE. **Title:** Written while Thomas' father (D. J. Thomas, a schoolteacher in Swansea, Wales) was dying.

example, is far from being a surrealist poem, but draws effectively on the resources of that style. That both this poem and "Boy Breaking Glass" avoid direct political and social polemic is typical of Brooks. Her poems seek to understand and help us understand the social circumstances to which they refer, and in this sense she is a contemplative and reflective poet, although of course to imagine and describe poverty, suffering, and self-alienation is implicitly to protest.

Boy Breaking Glass

To Marc Crawford from whom the commission

Whose broken window is a cry of art
(success, that winks aware
as elegance, as a treasonable faith)
is raw: is sonic: is old-eyed première.
Our beautiful flaw and terrible ornament.
Our barbarous and metal little man.

"I shall create! If not a note, a hole.
If not an overture, a desecration."

Full of pepper and light
and Salt and night and cargoes.

"Don't go down the plank
if you see there's no extension.
Each to his grief, each to
his loneliness and fidgety revenge.

Nobody knew where I was and now I am no longer there."

The only sanity is a cup of tea.
The music is in minors.

Each one other
is having different weather.

"It was you, it was you who threw away my name!
And this is everything I have for me."

Who has not Congress, lobster, love, luau,
the Regency Room, the Statue of Liberty,
runs. A sloppy amalgamation.
A mistake.
A cliff.
A hymn, a snare, and an exceeding sun.

1968

Medgar Evers

For Charles Evers

The man whose height his fear improved he
arranged to fear no further. The raw
intoxicated time was time for better birth or
a final death.
Old styles, old tempos, all the engagement of
the day—the sedate, the regulated fray—
the antique light, the Moral rose, old gusts,
tight whistlings from the past, the mothballs
in the Love at last our man forswore.

Medgar Evers annoyed confetti and assorted
brands of businessmen's eyes.

The shows came down: to maxims and surprise.
And palsy.

Roaring no rapt arise-ye to the dead, he
leaned across tomorrow. People said that
he was holding clean globes in his hands.

1968

ROBERT LOWELL

(1917–1977)

Lowell came from a genteel family in Boston, Massachusetts. He attended Harvard for two years and then, having decided to be a poet, transferred to Kenyon College in Ohio in order to study with John Crowe Ransom. Other young writers of the time who were also associated with Ransom—such as Robert Penn Warren, Allen Tate, and Randall Jarrell—became his friends. His poems in the 1940s were metrical, often with elaborate rhyme schemes. Their phrasing was compressed, and the connotations of their imagery were intricately counterpointed. Generally his work was of a type advocated by the then influential New Critics, a group which included Ransom and Lowell's other friends.

MEDGAR EVERS. **Title:** Evers, a black civil rights leader in Mississippi, had been killed in 1963.

Lowell's major poem in this phase, "The Quaker Graveyard in Nantucket," is peculiarly characteristic of him. The poem is hugely, almost inconceivably, ambitious. Taking the drowning of a cousin for his subject, Lowell deliberately intended to rival Milton's "Lycidas," which may be the greatest lyric in English. At the same time his poem challenged Melville's famous novel, *Moby Dick,* by reinterpreting the same material. Like Milton and Melville, Lowell explored ultimate metaphysical and religious themes. He had converted to Roman Catholicism, but his religious vision in this poem was no more comforting or hopeful than it had been before his conversion or was to be later, when he was no longer a Christian believer. Life's evil and pain engrossed Lowell's imagination. To him the world seemed infinitely distant from God. Uncontrollable power, mystery, and terror were the attributes of the divine to which his emotions were magnetized. The violence and abrupt transitions of the poem were also typical of Lowell—as was the overwhelming grandeur, which was beyond the range of any other American poet then writing.

Impressive as the poem is, we must also keep in mind, if we are to understand Lowell's subsequent development, that its phrasing can seem artful in an undesirable way. When at line 46, for example, Lowell refers to the sea as the "harrowed brine," he typically condenses multiple implications: the sea is "harrowed"—both farmed and tortured—by man's ships, but remains unchangeably adverse to humanity. It is salt ("brine") and "fruitless." "Harrowed" also refers to Christ's harrowing of hell (descent into the underworld) in order to "recover" souls there. As we grasp the many implications of the phrase, we understand why Lowell wrote it, yet "harrowed brine" is very unnatural diction, remote from the spoken language. From the standpoint of Lowell's later poetry, virtually everything in "The Quaker Graveyard in Nantucket" might be criticized in a similar way.

The major transition in Lowell's style came in *Life Studies* (1959), from which "Memories of West Street and Lepke" and "Skunk Hour" are selected. This famous volume began when Lowell, who was subject to recurrent mental breakdowns, started writing out material about himself for his psychiatrist. In doing so, he created a new poetic mode. Poetry of this type, which is now usually called "confessional" or "personal," describes very intimate and sometimes even shocking experiences and emotions, and stresses that they are autobiographical. Such poetry was written after Lowell by many younger poets, most notably Sylvia Plath, and versions of the same mode were created before Lowell by Allen Ginsberg in the United States and, with more discretion, by Philip Larkin in England.

Yet in *Life Studies* Lowell had not really abandoned the intricate organization and subtle symbolic suggestion of his earlier style; he had, instead, combined these qualities with a way of speaking which seemed much more direct and natural. Moreover, the "confessional" poems of *Life Studies* also encompass larger, less personal themes. "Memories of West Street and Lepke" describes Lowell's experience in prison during the Second World War, when he was a conscientious objector. (He refused to serve in protest against the bombing of civilians.) As a personal memory the poem looks back to the early 1940s, but the aimlessness and futility it portrays represent the United States as a society at the end of the prosperous 1950s, when the poem was composed. We see big business in Lepke, the head of Murder Incorporated, and the tradition of radical protest is equally satirized in its representative. "Skunk Hour" is the personal utterance of a sick soul, but by implication the poem also compares the past of America with its present.

Under the impact of the war in Vietnam and the protest movement against it, Lowell's poetry in the 1960s became overtly political. "For the Union Dead" is, among other things, about the kind of society that created, used, and may again use the atomic bomb. "Waking Early Sunday Morning" explores and criticizes the imperial emotions that underlay, in Lowell's view, America's involvement in the "small" war in Vietnam. Yet in these poems—it is an element of their greatness—Lowell recognizes that whatever he deplores in American society exists within himself as well. As a result, there is no rhetorical denunciation. The poems are complex and tormented expressions in which introspection and social analysis illuminate each other.

In the last ten years of his life Lowell published a great many sonnets. Some of them dealt with his divorce from his second wife, Elizabeth Hardwick, and his remarriage. Others were on writers or on political and historical subjects. They were composed more spontaneously than his earlier work, and present themselves as detached observations, although Lowell also deepened their implications by arranging them in sequences. The "notebook" genre to which Lowell's final volumes belong was popular with American poets in the 1960s and 1970s; Lowell's use of it does not necessarily indicate that his powers or ambition were slackening.

The Quaker Graveyard in Nantucket

(For Warren Winslow, dead at sea)

Let man have dominion over the fishes of the sea and the fowls of the air and the beasts and the whole earth, and every creeping creature that moveth upon the earth.

1

A brackish reach of shoal off Madaket,-
The sea was still breaking violently and night
Had steamed into our North Atlantic Fleet,
When the drowned sailor clutched the drag-net. Light
Flashed from his matted head and marble feet,
He grappled at the net
With the coiled, hurdling muscles of his thighs:
The corpse was bloodless, a botch of reds and whites,
Its open, staring eyes
Were lusterless dead-lights
Or cabin-windows on a stranded hulk
Heavy with sand. We weight the body, close
Its eyes and heave it seaward whence it came,
Where the heel-headed dogfish barks its nose
On Ahab's void and forehead; and the name
Is blocked in yellow chalk.
Sailors, who pitch this portent at the sea
Where dreadnaughts shall confess
Its hell-bent deity,
When you are powerless
To sand-bag this Atlantic bulwark, faced
By the earth-shaker, green, unwearied, chaste
In his steel scales: ask for no Orphean lute
To pluck life back. The guns of the steeled fleet
Recoil and then repeat
The hoarse salute.

THE QUAKER GRAVEYARD IN NANTUCKET. **Subtitle:** Warren Winslow, who was in the Navy in World War II, was a cousin of Lowell, and died when his ship was sunk. **Epigraph:** from Genesis 1:26. **1. Madaket:** a village and bay on the western side of Nantucket Island. **4–12. Light . . . sand:** The images are from the first chapter ("The Shipwreck") of Henry David Thoreau's *Cape Cod* (1864). **10. dead-lights:** shutters over the portholes to keep out water. **15. Ahab:** Captain Ahab in Melville's *Moby Dick* (1841), who sailed from Nantucket in search of the white whale. **23–24. Orphean . . . back:** Orpheus, the musician, had so charmed Persephone, Queen of Hades, with his lute playing that he was given permission to bring his wife Eurydice back from the dead.

2

Whenever winds are moving and their breath
Heaves at the roped-in bulwarks of this pier,
The terns and sea-gulls tremble at your death
In these home waters. Sailor, can you hear
The Pequod's sea wings, beating landward, fall
Headlong and break on our Atlantic wall
Off 'Sconset, where the yawing S-boats splash
The bellbuoy, with ballooning spinnakers,
As the entangled, screeching mainsheet clears
The blocks: off Madaket, where lubbers lash
The heavy surf and throw their long lead squids
For blue-fish? Sea-gulls blink their heavy lids
Seaward. The winds' wings beat upon the stones,
Cousin, and scream for you and the claws rush
At the sea's throat and wring it in the slush
Of this old Quaker graveyard where the bones
Cry out in the long night for the hurt beast
Bobbing by Ahab's whaleboats in the East.

3

All you recovered from Poseidon died
With you, my cousin, and the harrowed brine
Is fruitless on the blue beard of the god,
Stretching beyond us to the castles in Spain,
Nantucket's westward haven. To Cape Cod
Guns, cradled on the tide,
Blast the eelgrass about a waterclock
Of bilge and backwash, roil the salt and sand
Lashing earth's scaffold, rock
Our warships in the hand
Of the great God, where time's contrition blues
Whatever it was these Quaker sailors lost
In the mad scramble of their lives. They died
When time was open-eyed,
Wooden and childish; only bones abide
There, in the nowhere, where their boats were tossed
Sky-high, where mariners had fabled news
Of IS, the whited monster. What it cost
Them is their secret. In the sperm-whale's slick
I see the Quakers drown and hear their cry:

31. Pequod: Captain Ahab's ship in *Moby Dick*. **33. 'Sconset:** Siasconset, a Nantucket town. **S-boats:** sailboats. **42. Quaker graveyard:** Many of the Nantucket inhabitants were Quakers. **45. Poseidon:** Greek god of the sea. **62. IS:** Meaning simply "It *is*." The whale is associated with the primal force of God, Who, when Moses asks His name, says "I am that I am" (Exodus 3:14).

"If God himself had not been on our side,
If God himself had not been on our side,
When the Atlantic rose against us, why,
Then it had swallowed us up quick."

4

This is the end of the whaleroad and the whale
Who spewed Nantucket bones on the thrashed swell
And stirred the troubled waters to whirlpools
To send the Pequod packing off to hell:
This is the end of them, three-quarters fools,
Snatching at straws to sail
Seaward and seaward on the turntail whale,
Spouting out blood and water as it rolls,
Sick as a dog to these Atlantic shoals:
Clamavimus, O depths. Let the sea-gulls wail

For water, for the deep where the high tide
Mutters to its hurt self, mutters and ebbs.
Waves wallow in their wash, go out and out,
Leave only the death-rattle of the crabs,
The beach increasing, its enormous snout
Sucking the ocean's side.
This is the end of running on the waves;
We are poured out like water. Who will dance
The mast-lashed master of Leviathans
Up from this field of Quakers in their unstoned graves?

5

When the whale's viscera go and the roll
Of its corruption overruns this world
Beyond tree-swept Nantucket and Wood's Hole
And Martha's Vineyard, Sailor, will your sword
Whistle and fall and sink into the fat?
In the great ash-pit of Jehoshaphat
The bones cry for the blood of the white whale,
The fat flukes arch and whack about its ears,
The death-lance churns into the sanctuary, tears
The gun-blue swingle, heaving like a flail,
And hacks the coiling life out: it works and drags
And rips the sperm-whale's midriff into rags,
Gobbets of blubber spill to wind and weather,

69. whaleroad: an ancient Anglo-Saxon word for the sea. **78. *Clamavimus:*** "We have cried." From Psalms 130:1 "Out of the depths I have cried unto thee, O Lord." **87. Leviathans:** Biblical name for the whale. **91. Wood's Hole:** on the southern coast of Massachusetts facing Martha's Vineyard, a neighboring island of Nantucket famed as a center for Marine biology. **94. Jehoshaphat:** where the Last Judgment is to take place (Joel 3), and where, according to some prophecies, the world is to end in fire. **98. swingle:** wooden stick for beating flax.

Sailor, and gulls go round the stoven timbers
Where the morning stars sing out together
And thunder shakes the white surf and dismembers
The red flag hammered in the mast-head. Hide,
Our steel, Jonas Messias, in Thy side.

6. Our Lady of Walsingham

There once the penitents took off their shoes
And then walked barefoot the remaining mile;
And the small trees, a stream and hedgerows file
Slowly along the munching English lane,
Like cows to the old shrine, until you lose
Track of your dragging pain.
The stream flows down under the druid tree,
Shiloah's whirlpools gurgle and make glad
The castle of God. Sailor, you were glad
And whistled Sion by that stream. But see:

Our Lady, too small for her canopy,
Sits near the altar. There's no comeliness
At all or charm in that expressionless
Face with its heavy eyelids. As before,
This face, for centuries a memory,
Non est species, neque decor,
Expressionless, expresses God: it goes
Past castled Sion. She knows what God knows,
Not Calvary's Cross nor crib at Bethlehem
Now, and the world shall come to Walsingham.

7

The empty winds are creaking and the oak
Splatters and splatters on the cenotaph,
The boughs are trembling and a gaff
Bobs on the untimely stroke
Of the greased wash exploding on a shoal-bell
In the old mouth of the Atlantic. It's well;
Atlantic, you are fouled with the blue sailors,
Sea-monsters, upward angel, downward fish:
Unmarried and corroding, spare of flesh

105. flag hammered: an echo of the end of *Moby Dick,* where the arm of Tashtego rises from the water and nails Ahab's flag to the sinking mast. **106. Jonas Messias:** Jonas (Jonah), swallowed by the whale in the Old Testament, is here merged with Christ, and the spear thrust into the side of the crucified Christ is associated with the harpoon piercing the whale's belly. **6. Our Lady of Walsingham:** a medieval shrine to the Virgin Mary existed at Walsingham, Norfolk, England. Images in this section of the poem are taken from a description of the shrine that Lowell read in E. I. Watkins, *Catholic Art and Culture.* **114–16. Shiloah . . . Sion:** Shiloah stream flowed by the Temple at Mount Sion, a hill in Jerusalem. **122. *Non . . . decor*:** There is no comeliness or charm. **128. cenotaph:** an empty tomb. **129. gaff:** spar.

Mart once of supercilious, wing'd clippers,
Atlantic, where your bell-trap guts its spoil
You could cut the brackish winds with a knife
Here in Nantucket, and cast up the time
When the Lord God formed man from the sea's slime
And breathed into his face the breath of life,
And blue-lung'd combers lumbered to the kill.
The Lord survives the rainbow of His will.

1946

Memories of West Street and Lepke

Only teaching on Tuesdays, book-worming
in pajamas fresh from the washer each morning,
I hog a whole house on Boston's
"hardly passionate Marlborough Street,"
where even the man
scavenging filth in the back alley trash cans,
has two children, a beach wagon, a helpmate,
and is a "young Republican."
I have a nine months' daughter,
young enough to be my granddaughter.
Like the sun she rises in her flame-flamingo infants' wear.

These are the tranquillized *Fifties,*
and I am forty. Ought I to regret my seedtime?
I was a fire-breathing Catholic C.O.,
and made my manic statement,
telling off the state and president, and then
sat waiting sentence in the bull pen
beside a Negro boy with curlicues
of marijuana in his hair.

Given a year,
I walked on the roof of the West Street Jail, a short
enclosure like my school soccer court,
and saw the Hudson River once a day
through sooty clothesline entanglements

143. rainbow: God made a covenant with Noah that humanity would never again be destroyed by flood, and put a rainbow in heaven as a sign of this (Genesis 9:11). MEMORIES OF WEST STREET AND LEPKE. **Title:** As a conscientious objector, Lowell in 1943 was sentenced for a year to West Street Jail, New York. One of the other prisoners there was Lepke Buchalter, who had been convicted of murder and was head of a crime syndicate, "Murder Incorporated." **4. "hardly . . . Street":** a phrase of William James about a street in Boston's Back Bay, a sedate residential district until a generation ago. Lowell moved to Marlborough Street on his return to Boston in the 1950s. **14. C.O.:** conscientious objector.

and bleaching khaki tenements.
Strolling, I yammered metaphysics with Abramowitz,
a jaundice-yellow ("it's really tan")
and fly-weight pacifist,
so vegetarian,
he wore rope shoes and preferred fallen fruit.
He tried to convert Bioff and Brown,
the Hollywood pimps, to his diet.
Hairy, muscular, suburban,
wearing chocolate double-breasted suits,
they blew their tops and beat him black and blue.

I was so out of things, I'd never heard
of the Jehovah's Witnesses.
"Are you a C.O.?" I asked a fellow jailbird.
"No," he answered, "I'm a J.W."
He taught me the "hospital tuck,"
and pointed out the T-shirted back
of *Murder Incorporated's* Czar Lepke,
there piling towels on a rack,
or dawdling off to his little segregated cell full
of things forbidden the common man:
a portable radio, a dresser, two toy American
flags tied together with a ribbon of Easter palm.
Flabby, bald, lobotomized,
he drifted in a sheepish calm,
where no agonizing reappraisal
jarred his concentration on the electric chair—
hanging like an oasis in his air
of lost connections. . . .

1959

Skunk Hour

(For Elizabeth Bishop)

Nautilus Island's hermit
heiress still lives through winter in her Spartan cottage;
her sheep still graze above the sea.
Her son's a bishop. Her farmer
is first selectman in our village;
she's in her dotage.

37. Jehovah's Witnesses: revivalist sect opposed to war and the right of the state to interfere with individual conscience. **40. "hospital tuck":** method of making beds in hospitals. SKUNK HOUR. **5. selectman:** title of elected administrators in New England towns.

Thirsting for
the hierarchic privacy
of Queen Victoria's century,
she buys up all
the eyesores facing her shore,
and lets them fall.

The season's ill—
we've lost our summer millionaire,
who seemed to leap from an L. L. Bean
catalogue. His nine-knot yawl
was auctioned off to lobstermen.
A red fox stain covers Blue Hill.

And now our fairy
decorator brightens his shop for fall;
his fishnet's filled with orange cork,
orange, his cobbler's bench and awl;
there is no money in his work,
he'd rather marry.

One dark night,
my Tudor Ford climbed the hill's skull;
I watched for love-cars. Lights turned down,
they lay together, hull to hull,
where the graveyard shelves on the town. . . .
My mind's not right.

A car radio bleats,
"Love, O careless Love. . . . " I hear
my ill-spirit sob in each blood cell,
as if my hand were at its throat. . . .
I myself am hell;
nobody's here—

only skunks, that search
in the moonlight for a bite to eat.
They march on their soles up Main Street:
white stripes, moonstruck eyes' red fire
under the chalk-dry and spar spire
of the Trinitarian Church.

I stand on top
of our back steps and breathe the rich air—
a mother skunk with her column of kittens swills the garbage pail.
She jabs her wedge-head in a cup
of sour cream, drops her ostrich tail,
and will not scare.

1959

15. L. L. Bean: mail order house, in Freeport, Maine, for sporting goods. **18. Blue Hill:** mountain near a summer place in Castine, Maine, where Lowell lived for a time; the "fox stain" is meant to suggest the reddish color of the leaves in early fall. **32. "Love . . . ":** from a popular song of the time, "Careless Love." **35. I . . . hell:** a quote from Satan's remark, "myself am hell," in *Paradise Lost,* IV, 75.

For the Union Dead

"Relinquunt Omnia Servare Rem Publicam."

The old South Boston Aquarium stands
in a Sahara of snow now. Its broken windows are boarded.
The bronze weathervane cod has lost half its scales.
The airy tanks are dry.

Once my nose crawled like a snail on the glass;
my hand tingled
to burst the bubbles
drifting from the noses of the cowed, compliant fish.

My hand draws back. I often sigh still
for the dark downward and vegetating kingdom
of the fish and reptile. One morning last March,
I pressed against the new barbed and galvanized

fence on the Boston Common. Behind their cage,
yellow dinosaur steamshovels were grunting
as they cropped up tons of mush and grass
to gouge their underworld garage.

Parking spaces luxuriate like civic
sandpiles in the heart of Boston.
A girdle of orange, Puritan-pumpkin colored girders
braces the tingling Statehouse,

shaking over the excavations, as it faces Colonel Shaw
and his bell-cheeked Negro infantry
on St. Gaudens' shaking Civil War relief,
propped by a plank splint against the garage's earthquake.

Two months after marching through Boston,
half the regiment was dead;
at the dedication,
William James could almost hear the bronze Negroes breathe.

Their monument sticks like a fishbone
in the city's throat.
Its Colonel is as lean
as a compass-needle.

FOR THE UNION DEAD. **Title:** Originally published as "Colonel Shaw and the Massachusetts 54th," the poem is concerned with a monument, in bronze relief, by the sculptor Augustus Saint-Gaudens (1848–1907) placed on the edge of Boston Common and dedicated in 1897. The monument is in honor of Robert Gould Shaw (1837–1863), who organized the first black regiment from the North in the Civil War and was killed at Fort Wagner, South Carolina, in 1863. See lines 21–23. **Epigraph:** "They left everything to serve the state." **16. underworld garage:** a large parking garage was being built underneath the Boston Common at the time Lowell wrote. **28. William James:** (1842–1910), Harvard professor of philosophy and psychology, who gave the oration when the monument was dedicated.

He has an angry wrenlike vigilance,
a greyhound's gentle tautness;
he seems to wince at pleasure,
and suffocate for privacy.

He is out of bounds now. He rejoices in man's lovely,
peculiar power to choose life and die—
when he leads his black soldiers to death,
he cannot bend his back.

On a thousand small town New England greens,
the old white churches hold their air
of sparse, sincere rebellion; frayed flags
quilt the graveyards of the Grand Army of the Republic.

The stone statues of the abstract Union Soldier
grow slimmer and younger each year—
wasp-waisted, they doze over muskets
and muse through their sideburns . . .

Shaw's father wanted no monument
except the ditch,
where his son's body was thrown
and lost with his "niggers."

The ditch is nearer.
There are no statues for the last war here;
on Boylston Street, a commercial photograph
shows Hiroshima boiling

over a Mosler Safe, the "Rock of Ages"
that survived the blast. Space is nearer.
When I crouch to my television set,
the drained faces of Negro school-children rise like balloons.

Colonel Shaw
is riding on his bubble,
he waits
for the blessèd break.

The Aquarium is gone. Everywhere,
giant finned cars nose forward like fish;
a savage servility
slides by on grease.

1964

50–51. ditch . . . thrown: his body was stripped and thrown into a trench with his black soldiers at Fort Wagner. **54. last war:** World War II. **55. Boylston Street:** a nearby street, adjoining Boston Common. **66. giant finned cars:** referring to the huge tail fins of cars built in the 1950s, now replacing the fish of the old Aquarium which had once been nearby.

Waking Early Sunday Morning

O to break loose, like the chinook
salmon jumping and falling back,
nosing up to the impossible
stone and bone-crushing waterfall—
raw-jawed, weak-fleshed there, stopped by ten
steps of the roaring ladder, and then
to clear the top on the last try,
alive enough to spawn and die.

Stop, back off. The salmon breaks
water, and now my body wakes
to feel the unpolluted joy
and criminal leisure of a boy—
no rainbow smashing a dry fly
in the white run is free as I,
here squatting like a dragon on
time's hoard before the day's begun!

Vermin run for their unstopped holes;
in some dark nook a fieldmouse rolls
a marble, hours on end, then stops;
the termite in the woodwork sleeps—
listen, the creatures of the night
obsessive, casual, sure of foot,
go on grinding, while the sun's
daily remorseful blackout dawns.

Fierce, fireless mind, running downhill.
Look up and see the harbor fill:
business as usual in eclipse
goes down to the sea in ships—
wake of refuse, dacron rope,
bound for Bermuda or Good Hope,
all bright before the morning watch
the wine-dark hulls of yawl and ketch.

I watch a glass of water wet
with a fine fuzz of icy sweat,
silvery colors touched with sky,
serene in their neutrality—
yet if I shift, or change my mood,

WAKING EARLY SUNDAY MORNING. **1–8. O . . . die:** Fish ladders have been built into the dams in rivers. The salmon force their way up these ladders and thus pass beyond the dams into the upper reaches of the rivers, where they spawn and die. **15–16. dragon . . . hoard:** in medieval romances dragons often guard treasure hoards. **28. goes . . . ships:** allusion to Psalms 107:23. **30. Bermuda:** resort island in the western Atlantic. **Good Hope:** Cape of Good Hope at the southern tip of Africa.

I see some object made of wood,
background behind it of brown grain,
to darken it, but not to stain.

O that the spirit could remain
tinged but untarnished by its strain!
Better dressed and stacking birch,
or lost with the Faithful at Church—
anywhere, but somewhere else!
And now the new electric bells,
clearly chiming, "Faith of our fathers,"
and now the congregation gathers.

O Bible chopped and crucified
in hymns we hear but do not read,
none of the milder subtleties
of grace or art will sweeten these
stiff quatrains shovelled out four-square—
they sing of peace, and preach despair;
yet they gave darkness some control,
and left a loophole for the soul.

No, put old clothes on, and explore
the corners of the woodshed for
its dregs and dreck: tools with no handle,
ten candle-ends not worth a candle,
old lumber banished from the Temple,
damned by Paul's precept and example,
cast from the kingdom, banned in Israel,
the wordless sign, the tinkling cymbal.

When will we see Him face to face?
Each day, He shines through darker glass.
In this small town where everything
is known, I see His vanishing
emblems, His white spire and flag-
pole sticking out above the fog,
like old white china doorknobs, sad,
slight, useless things to calm the mad.

Hammering military splendor,
top-heavy Goliath in full armor—
little redemption in the mass
liquidations of their brass,

47. "Faith . . . fathers": Protestant hymn. **59. dreck:** filth (German). **61. Temple:** at Jerusalem. **62. Paul's:** St. Paul the Apostle. **74. Goliath:** giant Philistine whom David killed in I Samuel 17:4.

elephant and phalanx moving
with the times and still improving,
when that kingdom hit the crash:
a million foreskins stacked like trash . . .

Sing softer! But what if a new
diminuendo brings no true
tenderness, only restlessness,
excess, the hunger for success,
sanity of self-deception
fixed and kicked by reckless caution,
while we listen to the bells—
anywhere, but somewhere else!

O to break loose. All life's grandeur
is something with a girl in summer . . .
elated as the President
girdled by his establishment
this Sunday morning, free to chaff
his own thoughts with his bear-cuffed staff,
swimming nude, unbuttoned, sick
of his ghost-written rhetoric!

No weekends for the gods now. Wars
flicker, earth licks its open sores,
fresh breakage, fresh promotions, chance
assassinations, no advance.
Only man thinning out his kind
sounds through the Sabbath noon, the blind
swipe of the pruner and his knife
busy about the tree of life . . .

Pity the planet, all joy gone
from this sweet volcanic cone;
peace to our children when they fall
in small war on the heels of small
war—until the end of time
to police the earth, a ghost
orbiting forever lost
in our monotonous sublime.

1967

77. elephant and phalanx: Elephants were used in warfare by the Carthaginians against the Romans; the phalanx was the military formation of the ancient Greeks in battle. **80. foreskins:** alluding to the custom of the ancient Israelites in warfare of cutting off the foreskins of their slain enemies. **91. President:** Lyndon Johnson. **95. nude:** President Johnson used to swim nude in the White House pool.

A. W. PURDY

(born 1918)

After growing up in a small farming community in Ontario, Alfred Purdy led a wandering life. He served during the Second World War in the Royal Canadian Air Force, became a scriptwriter for the Canadian Broadcasting Corporation, and later, having committed himself to poetry, built his home not far from where he had passed his boyhood. He is one of Canada's most respected and popular poets. His poetic personality somewhat resembles that of William Carlos Williams. In both writers poetry seems very close to natural talk, and the talk reveals a sensitive, engaging, humorous personality. Both poets have a strong love of life, and celebrate, as Purdy does in "Trees at the Arctic Circle," its power to persist amid adversity. But this is not Purdy's usual note. His imagination is magnetized to transience and death, although in many poems he also invokes a feeling of man's continuity with past generations.

Trees at the Arctic Circle

(Salix Cordifolia—Ground Willow)

They are 18 inches long
or even less
crawling under rocks
groveling among the lichens
bending and curling to escape
making themselves small
finding new ways to hide
Coward trees
I am angry to see them
like this
not proud of what they are
bowing to weather instead
careful of themselves
worried about the sky
afraid of exposing their limbs
like a Victorian married couple

I call to mind great Douglas firs
I see tall maples waving green
and oaks like gods in autumn gold
the whole horizon jungle dark
and I crouched under that continual night
But these
even the dwarf shrubs of Ontario
mock them
Coward trees

And yet—and yet—
their seed pods glow
like delicate gray earrings
their leaves are veined and intricate
like tiny parkas
They have about three months
to make sure the species does not die
and that's how they spend their time
unbothered by any human opinion
just digging in here and now
sending their roots down down down
And you know it occurs to me
about 2 feet under
those roots must touch permafrost
ice that remains ice forever
and they use it for their nourishment
they use death to remain alive

I see that I've been carried away
in my scorn of the dwarf trees
most foolish in my judgments
To take away the dignity
of any living thing
even tho it cannot understand
the scornful words
is to make life itself trivial
and yourself the Pontifex Maximus
of nullity
I have been stupid in a poem
I will not alter the poem
but let the stupidity remain permanent
as the trees are
in a poem
the dwarf trees of Baffin Island

1967

TREES AT THE ARCTIC CIRCLE. **51. Pontifex Maximus:** the high priest in ancient Rome. **58. Baffin Island:** lies between Greenland and mainland Canada.

Wilderness Gothic

Across Roblin Lake, two shores away,
they are sheathing the church spire
with new metal. Someone hangs in the sky
over there from a piece of rope,
hammering and fitting God's belly-scratcher,
working his way up along the spire
until there's nothing left to nail on—
Perhaps the workman's faith reaches beyond:
touches intangibles, wrestles with Jacob,
replacing rotten timber with pine thews,
pounds hard in the blue cave of the sky,
contends heroically with difficult problems of
gravity, sky navigation and mythopeia,
his volunteer time and labor donated to God,
minus sick benefits of course on a non-union job—

Fields around are yellowing into harvest,
nestling and fingerling are sky and water borne,
death is yodeling quiet in green woodlots,
and bodies of three young birds have disappeared
in the sub-surface of the new county highway—

That picture is incomplete, part left out
that might alter the whole Dürer landscape:
gothic ancestors peer from medieval sky,
dour faces trapped in photograph albums escaping
to clop down iron roads with matched grays:
work-sodden wives groping inside their flesh
for what keeps moving and changing and flashing
beyond and past the long frozen Victorian day.
A sign of fire and brimstone? A two-headed calf
born in the barn last night? A sharp female agony?
An age and a faith moving into transition,
the dinner cold and new-baked bread a failure,
deep woods shiver and water drops hang pendant,
double yolked eggs and the house creaks a little—
Something is about to happen. Leaves are still.
Two shores away, a man hammering in the sky.
Perhaps he will fall.

1968

WILDERNESS GOTHIC. **1. Roblin Lake:** in Ontario, where Purdy lives. **9. wrestles . . . Jacob:** Genesis 32:24–29. **22. Dürer:** Albrecht Dürer (1471–1528), German artist. Purdy was probably thinking of the reference to Dürer in Marianne Moore's poem, "The Steeple-Jack."

Robert Duncan

(born 1919)

Duncan grew up in California, where he still lives. He was the adopted child of a family named Symmes, and used this surname until he became an adult, when he reverted to the Duncan of his birth. In the 1950s he taught briefly at Black Mountain College with Charles Olson, with whom he shares many theories about poetry, especially the view that in composing a poet must not follow a preconceived form or idea, but must proceed spontaneously, always receptive to whatever new impulse may arise. He is deeply interested in ancient myth, and in Neoplatonic, gnostic, and hermetic writings.

The poems printed here are from a sequence entitled "Passages." "Up Rising" reflects Duncan's admiration for the so-called "Prophetic Books" of William Blake, and is especially comparable with Blake's *America* (1793). The poem was written during the war in Vietnam, conveys Duncan's fierce opposition to it, and sees the war as expressing and resulting from psychological traits that are characteristic of Americans. "The Fire," an unusually difficult poem, describes two paintings of the early Renaissance, and contrasts the vision of things they represent.

In "The Fire" the painting by Hieronymus Bosch (*c.* 1450–1516) seems especially relevant to our own age, so much so that Duncan conflates images from contemporary history with those in the painting. His description of the Bosch painting leads him into references to nuclear war and the destruction of the world. The painting by Piero di Cosimo also depicts catastrophic destruction, and it does this even more directly, since its subject is a forest fire. The animals in their burning world are fleeing in panic. Yet both the animals and the painting as a whole also suggest Edenic peace, stillness, and beauty. The reason for this, the poem suggests, is that Piero di Cosimo possessed the Orphic wisdom of the ancient, pagan, Mediterranean world. This lore, which had been passed down to the painter through esoteric traditions, taught that harmony is the ultimate principle of reality, reconciling conflict and prevailing over evil and destruction. Because the painting of Bosch seems prophetic of our present world, and that of Piero di Cosimo derives from the past, their conjunction might disclose changes that have taken place in human feeling and vision from the ancient world to the modern. But on the other hand, the two paintings were done at approximately the same time; this fact might suggest that in any age either vision of reality is possible. The deeper truth of Piero di Cosimo, in other words, need not be lost to us.

The poem begins and concludes with a block of thirty-six words arranged in vertical and horizontal rows. These blocks of words illustrate a theme of the poem because to some readers the words may seem merely random and senseless, while other readers may find in them an order and hidden meaning. The same thing may bc true of experience generally. We might also regard the words in these blocks as primordial elements out of which a more organized world emerges and to which it returns.

Up Rising

Now Johnson would go up to join the great simulacra of men,
    Hitler and Stalin, to work his fame
    with planes roaring out from Guam over Asia,
all America become a sea of toiling men
    stirrd at his will, which would be a bloated thing,
    drawing from the underbelly of the nation
    such blood and dreams as swell the idiot psyche
    out of its courses into an elemental thing
    until his name stinks with burning meat and heapt honors

And men wake to see that they are used like things
    spent in a great potlatch, this Texas barbecue
        of Asia, Africa, and all the Americas,
And the professional military behind him, thinking
    to use him as they thought to use Hitler
    without losing control of their business of war,

But the mania, the ravening eagle of America
    as Lawrence saw him "bird of men that are masters,
    lifting the rabbit-blood of the myriads up into . . ."
    into something terrible, gone beyond bounds, or
As Blake saw America in figures of fire and blood raging,
    . . . in what image? the ominous roar in the air,
the omnipotent wings, the all-American boy in the cockpit
    loosing his flow of napalm, below in the jungles

UP RISING. **1. Johnson:** President Lyndon Johnson. **simulacra:** shadowy or sham images. **3. Guam:** U.S. military base in the South Pacific. **11. potlatch:** formerly a type of feast of the Amerindians of the Northwest coast. Participants destroyed their own property in a competitive show of wealth. **13–14. military . . . Hitler:** The German generals at first thought they would be able to control and use Hitler, although the opposite turned out to be the case. **16. eagle:** symbol of the United States. **17–18. Lawrence . . . into:** D. H. Lawrence (1885–1930), English novelist and poet. Duncan quotes from Lawrence's poem, "The American Eagle." **20. Blake:** In *America* (1793) and other poems William Blake (1757–1827) depicted the American Revolution in these terms. In form Duncan's poem is modeled somewhat on Blake's.

"any life at all or sign of life" his target, drawing now
not with crayons in his secret room
the burning of homes and the torture of mothers and fathers and
children,
their hair a-flame, screaming in agony, but
in the line of duty, for the might and enduring fame
of Johnson, for the victory of American will over its victims,
releasing his store of destruction over the enemy,
in terror and hatred of all communal things, of communion,
of communism •
has raised from the private rooms of small-town bosses and
businessmen,
from the council chambers of the gangs that run the great cities,
swollen with the votes of millions,
from the fearful hearts of good people in the suburbs turning the
savory meat over the charcoal burners and heaping their barbecue
plates with more than they can eat,
from the closed meeting-rooms of regents of universities and sessions
of profiteers

—back of the scene: the atomic stockpile; the vials of synthesized
diseases eager biologists have developt over half a century dreaming
of the bodies of mothers and fathers and children and hated rivals
swollen with new plagues, measles grown enormous, influenzas
perfected; and the gasses of despair, confusion of the senses, mania,
inducing terror of the universe, coma, existential wounds, that
chemists we have met at cocktail parties, passt daily and with a
happy "Good Day" on the way to classes or work, have workt to
make war too terrible for men to wage—

raised this secret entity of America's hatred of Europe, of Africa, of
Asia,
the deep hatred for the old world that had driven generations of
America out of itself,
and for the alien world, the new world about him, that might have
been Paradise
but was before his eyes already cleard back in a holocaust of burning
Indians, trees and grasslands,
reduced to his real estate, his projects of exploitation and profitable
wastes,

this specter that in the beginning Adams and Jefferson feard and knew
would corrupt the very body of the nation
and all our sense of our common humanity,
this black bile of old evils arisen anew,

24. "any . . . life": It was said that United States pilots in Vietnam would fire on "any life at all," making no distinction between civilians and soldiers, friends and enemies. **50. Adams . . . Jefferson:** Presidents John Adams (1735–1826) and Thomas Jefferson (1743–1826). **57. Goldwater:** Senator Barry Goldwater, Republican presidential candidate who ran against Lyndon Johnson in 1964.

takes over the vanity of Johnson;
and the very glint of Satan's eyes from the pit of the hell of
America's unacknowledged, unrepented crimes that I saw in
Goldwater's eyes
now shines from the eyes of the President
in the swollen head of the nation.

1968

The Fire

jump stone hand leaf shadow sun
day plash coin light downstream fish
first loosen under boat harbor circle
old earth bronze dark wall waver
new smell purl close wet green
now rise foot warm hold cool

blood disk
horizon flame

The day at the window
the rain at the window
the night and the star at the window

Do you know the old language?
I do not know the old language.

Do you know the language of the old belief?

From the wood we thought burning
our animal spirits flee, seeking refuge wherever,
as if in Eden, in this panic
lion and lamb lie down, quail
heed not the eagle in flight before the flames high
over head go.
We see at last the man-faced roe and his

THE FIRE. **1–8. jump . . . flame:** The separate words perhaps represent elements that can be associated with each other in different ways to make different systems or orders. The last four words may represent the sun rising or setting. **14. old belief:** Neoplatonic, Orphic, occult, semi-magical beliefs; see lines 33–36. **15–33. From . . . magic:** a description of the painting mentioned in line 28 by Piero di Cosimo, also known as Pietro di Lorenzo (1462–1521).

gentle mate;   the wild boar too
turns a human face.   In whose visages no terror
but a philosophic sorrow shows.   The ox
is fierce with terror, his thick tongue
slavers and sticks out panting
to make the gorgoneion face.
(This is Piero di Cosimo's great painting *A Forest Fire,* dated 1490–
1500, preserved in the Ashmolean Museum at Oxford)
He inherits the *sfumato* of Leonardo da Vinci—
there is a softening of outline,   his color fuses.
A glow at the old borders makes
magic Pletho, Ficino, Pico della Mirandola prepared,
reviving in David's song,
Saul in his flaming rage heard,   music
Orpheus first playd,

chords and melodies of the spell that binds
the many in conflict in contrasts of one mind:

"For, since song and sound arise from the cognition of the mind,
and the impetus of the phantasy, and the feeling of the heart,
and, together with the air they have broken up and temperd,
strike the aerial spirit of the hearer, which is the junction of the
soul and the body, they easily move the phantasy, affect the
heart and penetrate into the deep recesses of the mind"

Di Cosimo's   featherd, furrd, leafy

boundaries where   even the Furies are birds
and blur   in higher harmonies Eumenides;
whose animals, entering a charmd field
in the light of his vision, a stillness,
have their dreamy glades and pastures.

27. gorgoneion: pertaining to the Gorgon, one of three sisters in Greek mythology who had serpents for hair. They were so terrible to look at that the beholder turned to stone. **30. *sfumato* . . . Vinci:** Leonardo (1452–1519) offers brilliant examples of this technique in which minute gradations of tones and colors are used in a painting to blur or veil the contours of forms. **33. Pletho . . . Mirandola:** Giorgius Gemisthus Pletho (*c.* 1355–1452), Marsilio Ficino (1433–1499), and Pico della Mirandola (1463–1494), early Renaissance humanists. They translated and commented on Plato and Neoplatonic philosophers, and were also interested in occult lore, such as that of the ancient Pythagoreans, the Orphic cults, Hermes Trismegistus, and the Jewish Cabalists. In Duncan's interpretation this ancient lore taught the ultimate oneness or harmony of all reality, and he believes that the revival of such ancient beliefs underlay the vision expressed in Piero di Cosimo's painting. **34–36. David . . . Orpheus:** In I Samuel 16:23 David plays the lyre before King Saul and calms his rage. In Greek mythology Orpheus was a poet and musician possessed of magic lore and power. **39–44. "For . . . mind":** "Ficino [see line 33], letter to Antonio Canisano, quoted in D. P. Walker, *Spiritual and Demonic Magic from Ficino to Campanella*" [Duncan's note]. **46. Furies:** In classical mythology the Furies were three goddesses who avenged unpunished crimes. **47. Eumenides:** another name for the Furies of line 46.

The flames, the smoke. The curious
sharp focus in a glow sight
in the Anima Mundi has.

Where in the North (1500) shown in Bosch's illumination:
Hell breaks out an opposing music.
The faces of the deluded leer, faint, in lewd praise,
close their eyes in voluptous torment,
enthralld by fear, avidly
following the daily news: the earthquakes, eruptions,
flaming automobiles, enraged lovers, wars against communism,
heroin addicts, police raids, race riots . . .
caught in the *lascivia animi* of this vain sound
And we see at last the faces of evil openly
over us,
bestial extrusions no true animal face knows.
There are rats, snakes, toads, Boehme tells us,
that are the Devil's creatures. There is
a Devil's mimic of man, a Devil's chemistry.
The Christ closes His eyes, bearing the Cross
as if dreaming. Is His Kingdom
not of this world, but a dream of the Anima Mundi,
the World-Ensouling?
The painter's *sfumato* gives His face.
pastoral stillness amidst terror, sorrow
that has an echo in the stag's face we saw before.
About Him, as if to drown sweet music out,
Satan looks forth from
men's faces:
Eisenhower's idiot grin, Nixon's
black jaw, the sly glare in Goldwater's eye, or
the look of Stevenson lying in the U.N. that our
Nation save face •
His face multiplies from the time of Roosevelt, Stalin,
Churchill, Hitler, Mussolini; from the dream
of Oppenheimer, Fermi, Teller, Vannevar Bush,

brooding the nightmare formulae—to win the war! the
inevitable • at Los Alamos
plotting the holocaust of Hiroshima •

53. Anima Mundi: soul of the world. **54. Bosch:** Hieronymus Bosch (*c.* 1450–1516), Dutch painter, known for his paintings of hell. **62. *lascivia animi*:** lust of the soul (Latin). **66. Boehme:** Jacob Böhme, 1575–1624, German mystical writer. **79–81. Eisenhower . . . Stevenson:** President Dwight Eisenhower; Richard Nixon, Eisenhower's Vice President and later himself President; Senator Barry Goldwater, known for his conservative views and advocacy of strong military forces; and Adlai Stevenson, U.S. Ambassador to the United Nations. **83–85. His . . . Bush:** His is Satan's; after the world leaders from Roosevelt to Mussolini, Duncan names scientists who helped develop the atomic bomb—J. Robert Oppenheimer, Enrico Fermi, Edward Teller, and Vannevar Bush. **87. Los Alamos:** in New Mexico, where the atom bomb was made.

Teller openly for the Anti-Christ
• glints of the evil that one sees in the power of this world,
"In the North and East, swarms of dough-faces, office-vermin, kept editors, clerks, attaches of ten thousand officers and their parties, aware of nothing further than the drip and spoil of politics—ignorant of principles . . . In the South, no end of blusterers, braggarts, windy, melodramatic, continually screaming, in falsetto, a nuisance to These States, their own just as much as any . . . and with the most incredible successes, having pistol'd, bludgeoned, yelled and threatend America, these past twenty years, into one long train of cowardly concessions, and still not through but rather at the commencement. Their cherished secret scheme is to dissolve the union of These States. . ."
(Whitman, 1856)

faces of Princes, Popes, Prime Usurers, Presidents,
Gang Leaders of whatever Clubs, Nations, Legions   meet

to conspire, to coerce, to cut down •
Now, the City, impoverisht, swollen, dreams again
the great plagues—typhus, syphilis, the black buboes
epidemics,   manias.

My name is Legion   and in every nation   I multiply.
Over those who would be Great Nations   Great Evils.

They are burning the woods, the brushlands, the
grassy fields razed;   their
profitable suburbs spread.

Pan's land, the pagan countryside, they'd
lay waste.

cool   green   waver   circle   fish   sun
hold   wet   wall   harbor   downstream   shadow
warm   close   dark   boat   light   leaf
foot   purl   bronze   under   coin   hand
rise   smell   earth   loosen   plash   stone
now   new   old   first   day   jump

1968

91–101. "In . . . States": As Duncan's parenthesis partially indicates, this prose passage comes from *The Eighteenth Presidency*, a pamphlet written by Walt Whitman in 1856, five years before the Civil War began. **106. buboes:** swellings of the lymph glands characteristic of bubonic plague. **108. Legion:** traditional name for the devil. **113. Pan:** Greek god of the countryside.

Richard Wilbur

(born 1921)

The son of a painter, Wilbur went to Amherst and Harvard and has taught at Wesleyan and Smith colleges. His first volume appeared when he was twenty-six. With poems that were playfully witty, elegant, kindly, and accessible, Wilbur captured his audience. He is a poet of dazzling technique, sophisticated intelligence, decent emotions, poise, and charm. While American poetry has gone through phases of Confessionalism, Beat and other rhetoric, Postmodernism, and Surrealism, Wilbur has continued to be an exemplar of civilized artistry and reasonableness.

The Beautiful Changes

One wading a Fall meadow finds on all sides
The Queen Anne's Lace lying like lilies
On water; it glides
So from the walker, it turns
Dry grass to a lake, as the slightest shade of you
Valleys my mind in fabulous blue Lucernes.

The beautiful changes as a forest is changed
By a chameleon's tuning his skin to it;
As a mantis, arranged
On a green leaf, grows
Into it, makes the leaf leafier, and proves
Any greenness is deeper than anyone knows.

Your hands hold roses always in a way that says
They are not only yours; the beautiful changes
In such kind ways,
Wishing ever to sunder
Things and things' selves for a second finding, to lose
For a moment all that it touches back to wonder.

1947

Ceremony

A striped blouse in a clearing by Bazille
Is, you may say, a patroness of boughs
Too queenly kind toward nature to be kin.
But ceremony never did conceal,
Save to the silly eye, which all allows,
How much we are the woods we wander in.

Let her be some Sabrina fresh from stream,
Lucent as shallows slowed by wading sun,
Bedded on fern, the flowers' cynosure:
Then nymph and wood must nod and strive to dream
That she is airy earth, the trees, undone,
Must ape her languor natural and pure.

Ho-hum. I am for wit and wakefulness,
And love this feigning lady by Bazille.
What's lightly hid is deepest understood,
And when with social smile and formal dress
She teaches leaves to curtsey and quadrille,
I think there are most tigers in the wood.

1950

Love Calls Us to the Things of This World

The eyes open to a cry of pulleys,
And spirited from sleep, the astounded soul
Hangs for a moment bodiless and simple
As false dawn.
Outside the open window
The morning air is all awash with angels.

Some are in bed-sheets, some are in blouses,
Some are in smocks: but truly there they are.
Now they are rising together in calm swells
Of halcyon feeling, filling whatever they wear
With the deep joy of their impersonal breathing;

Now they are flying in place, conveying
The terrible speed of their omnipresence, moving
And staying like white water; and now of a sudden
They swoon down into so rapt a quiet
That nobody seems to be there.
The soul shrinks

CEREMONY. **1. Bazille:** Frédéric Bazille (1841–1871), French Impressionist painter.

From all that it is about to remember,
From the punctual rape of every blessèd day,
And cries,
"Oh, let there be nothing on earth but laundry,
Nothing but rosy hands in the rising steam
And clear dances done in the sight of heaven."

Yet, as the sun acknowledges
With a warm look the world's hunks and colors,
The soul descends once more in bitter love
To accept the waking body, saying now
In a changed voice as the man yawns and rises,

"Bring them down from their ruddy gallows;
Let there be clean linen for the backs of thieves;
Let lovers go fresh and sweet to be undone,
And the heaviest nuns walk in a pure floating
Of dark habits,
keeping their difficult balance."

1956

Philip Larkin

(born 1922)

Most modern English poets never wholly accepted the Modernism of Eliot and Pound. To them it seemed somewhat foreign, a combination of American with French traditions. But even for English poets the brilliance of this Modernism temporarily eclipsed the poetry that had preceded it earlier in the twentieth century. With Larkin and his generation, however, this phase is over. Rejecting both the Modernism of Eliot and the Romantic mysticism of Dylan Thomas, who was extremely popular in the 1950s, Larkin looks back for predecessors and inspiration to Thomas Hardy and the "Georgian" poets of England in the 1910s.

Larkin writes a poetry of personal statement and dreary realism. His imagery helped give English poets a new language—of littered back yards, weedy pavements, plastic furniture, defaced posters, and dime-

LOVE CALLS US. **23. bitter love:** Wilbur states of this line: "Plato, St. Theresa, and the rest of us . . . have known that it is painful to return [from ideal things] . . . to the earth . . . Augustine says that it is love that brings us back. That is why the love of line 23 has got to be bitter." (*The Contemporary Poet as Artist and Critic,* page 18.)

store jewelry—to suggest the suburban boredom, drabness, and aimlessness of contemporary life. Such imagery could be found in T. S. Eliot's *The Waste Land,* of course, but in Eliot's poem it has a phantasmagoric intensity which Larkin deliberately avoids. "Wan unhope," to use a Hardyesque phrase, is his pervading emotional state; but the mood, though somewhat predictable, never seems sentimental, for it is expressed empirically. His poems describe an experience—entering an empty church ("Church Going") or visiting his old college ("Dockery and Son")—and explore his thoughts and emotions on the occasion. His responses are complicated and ambivalent, and the poems proceed by self-correctively weighing one consideration against another. They are searches to discover what he really feels and thinks. His power as a moralist lies especially in his scrupulous personal honesty.

Church Going

Once I am sure there's nothing going on
I step inside, letting the door thud shut.
Another church: matting, seats, and stone,
And little books; sprawlings of flowers, cut
For Sunday, brownish now; some brass and stuff
Up at the holy end; the small neat organ;
And a tense, musty, unignorable silence,
Brewed God knows how long. Hatless, I take off
My cycle-clips in awkward reverence,

Move forward, run my hand around the font.
From where I stand, the roof looks almost new—
Cleaned, or restored? Someone would know: I don't.
Mounting the lectern, I peruse a few
Hectoring large-scale verses, and pronounce
"Here endeth" much more loudly than I'd meant.
The echoes snigger briefly. Back at the door
I sign the book, donate an Irish sixpence,
Reflect the place was not worth stopping for.

Yet stop I did: in fact I often do,
And always end much at a loss like this,
Wondering what to look for; wondering, too,
When churches fall completely out of use
What we shall turn them into, if we shall keep
A few cathedrals chronically on show,
Their parchment, plate and pyx in locked cases,
And let the rest rent-free to rain and sheep.
Shall we avoid them as unlucky places?

CHURCH GOING. **25. pyx:** box holding communion wafers.

Or, after dark, will dubious women come
To make their children touch a particular stone;
Pick simples for a cancer; or on some
Advised night see walking a dead one?
Power of some sort or other will go on
In games, in riddles, seemingly at random;
But superstition, like belief, must die,
And what remains when disbelief has gone?
Grass, weedy pavement, brambles, buttress, sky,

A shape less recognizable each week,
A purpose more obscure. I wonder who
Will be the last, the very last, to seek
This place for what it was; one of the crew
That tap and jot and know what rood-lofts were?
Some ruin-bibber, randy for antique,
Or Christmas-addict, counting on a whiff
Of gown-and-bands and organ-pipes and myrrh?
Or will he be my representative,

Bored, uninformed, knowing the ghostly silt
Dispersed, yet tending to this cross of ground
Through suburb scrub because it held unspilt
So long and equably what since is found
Only in separation—marriage, and birth,
And death, and thoughts of these—for whom was built
This special shell? For, though I've no idea
What this accoutred frowsty barn is worth,
It pleases me to stand in silence here;

A serious house on serious earth it is,
In whose blent air all our compulsions meet,
Are recognized, and robed as destinies.
And that much never can be obsolete,
Since someone will forever be surprising
A hunger in himself to be more serious,
And gravitating with it to this ground,
Which, he once heard, was proper to grow wise in,
If only that so many dead lie round.

1955

The Whitsun Weddings

That Whitsun, I was late getting away:
   Not till about
One-twenty on the sunlit Saturday
Did my three-quarters-empty train pull out,

THE WHITSUN WEDDINGS. **Title:** Whitsunday, seventh Sunday after Easter, celebrates the descent of the Holy Ghost on the disciples. It is one of the British legal holidays ("bank holidays") providing long weekends.

All windows down, all cushions hot, all sense
Of being in a hurry gone. We ran
Behind the backs of houses, crossed a street
Of blinding windscreens, smelt the fish-dock; thence
The river's level drifting breadth began,
Where sky and Lincolnshire and water meet.

All afternoon, through the tall heat that slept
  For miles inland,
A slow and stopping curve southwards we kept.
Wide farms went by, short-shadowed cattle, and
Canals with floatings of industrial froth;
A hothouse flashed uniquely: hedges dipped
And rose: and now and then a smell of grass
Displaced the reek of buttoned carriage-cloth
Until the next town, new and nondescript,
Approached with acres of dismantled cars.

At first, I didn't notice what a noise
  The weddings made
Each station that we stopped at: sun destroys
The interest of what's happening in the shade,
And down the long cool platforms whoops and skirls
I took for porters larking with the mails,
And went on reading. Once we started, though,
We passed them, grinning and pomaded, girls
In parodies of fashion, heels and veils,
All posed irresolutely, watching us go,

As if out on the end of an event
  Waving goodbye
To something that survived it. Struck, I leant
More promptly out next time, more curiously,
And saw it all again in different terms:
The fathers with broad belts under their suits
And seamy foreheads; mothers loud and fat;
An uncle shouting smut; and then the perms,
The nylon gloves and jewelry-substitutes,
The lemons, mauves, and olive-ochers that

Marked off the girls unreally from the rest.
  Yes, from cafés
And banquet-halls up yards, and bunting-dressed
Coach-party annexes, the wedding-days
Were coming to an end. All down the line
Fresh couples climbed aboard: the rest stood round;
The last confetti and advice were thrown,
And, as we moved, each face seemed to define
Just what it saw departing: children frowned
At something dull; fathers had never known

Success so huge and wholly farcical;
  The women shared
The secret like a happy funeral;

While girls, gripping their handbags tighter, stared
At a religious wounding. Free at last,
And loaded with the sum of all they saw,
We hurried towards London, shuffling gouts of steam.
Now fields were building-plots, and poplars cast
Long shadows over major roads, and for
Some fifty minutes, that in time would seem

Just long enough to settle hats and say
I nearly died,
A dozen marriages got under way.
They watched the landscape, sitting side by side
—An Odeon went past, a cooling tower,
And someone running up to bowl—and none
Thought of the others they would never meet
Or how their lives would all contain this hour.
I thought of London spread out in the sun,
Its postal districts packed like squares of wheat:

There we were aimed. And as we raced across
Bright knots of rail
Past standing Pullmans, walls of blackened moss
Came close, and it was nearly done, this frail
Traveling coincidence; and what it held
Stood ready to be loosed with all the power
That being changed can give. We slowed again,
And as the tightened brakes took hold, there swelled
A sense of falling, like an arrow-shower
Sent out of sight, somewhere becoming rain.

1964

Dockery and Son

"Dockery was junior to you,
Wasn't he?" said the Dean. "His son's here now."
Death-suited, visitant, I nod. "And do
You keep in touch with——" Or remember how
Black-gowned, unbreakfasted, and still half-tight
We used to stand before that desk, to give
"Our version" of "these incidents last night"?
I try the door of where I used to live:

65. Odeon: chain of British movie theaters. DOCKERY AND SON. **5. Black-gowned:** referring to the gowns worn by students at Oxford and Cambridge. **8. door:** of his room while a student at Oxford.

Locked. The lawn spreads dazzlingly wide.
A known bell chimes. I catch my train, ignored.
Canal and clouds and colleges subside
Slowly from view. But Dockery, good Lord,
Anyone up today must have been born
In '43, when I was twenty-one.
If he was younger, did he get this son
At nineteen, twenty? Was he that withdrawn

High-collared public-schoolboy, sharing rooms
With Cartwright who was killed? Well, it just shows
How much . . . How little . . . Yawning, I suppose
I fell asleep, waking at the fumes
And furnace-glares of Sheffield, where I changed,
And ate an awful pie, and walked along
The platform to its end to see the ranged
Joining and parting lines reflect a strong

Unhindered moon. To have no son, no wife,
No house or land still seemed quite natural.
Only a numbness registered the shock
Of finding out how much had gone of life,
How widely from the others. Dockery, now:
Only nineteen, he must have taken stock
Of what he wanted, and been capable
Of . . . No, that's not the difference: rather, how

Convinced he was he should be added to!
Why did he think adding meant increase?
To me it was dilution. Where do these
Innate assumptions come from? Not from what
We think truest, or most want to do:
Those warp tight-shut, like doors. They're more a style
Our lives bring with them: habit for a while,
Suddenly they harden into all we've got

And how we got it; looked back on, they rear
Like sand-clouds, thick and close, embodying
For Dockery a son, for me nothing,
Nothing with all a son's harsh patronage.
Life is first boredom, then fear.
Whether or not we use it, it goes,
And leaves what something hidden from us chose,
And age, and then the only end of age.

1964

13. Anyone up: anyone at the university. **17. public-schoolboy:** In England, a "public" school is what in the U.S. is considered a private "preparatory" school. **21. Sheffield:** industrial city in the English "midlands."

JAMES DICKEY

(born 1923)

A novelist and critic as well as poet, Dickey was born in Atlanta, Georgia, and still lives in the South. He was in the U.S. Air Force during the Second World War and again during the Korean War, and between 1956 and 1961 he wrote copy for advertising agencies. Byron was his favorite poet as a child, and both his liking for Byron and his successful career in advertising suggest some of his qualities as a writer. His poems always make a strong impression. Their images or narratives are frequently violent and sensational, and frequently also dreamlike, surrealistic, and visionary. In "The Heaven of Animals" his phrasing typically remains direct and accessible despite the complexity of his thought and attitude. Dickey's themes are often metaphysical or mystical.

The Heaven of Animals

Here they are. The soft eyes open.
If they have lived in a wood
It is a wood.
If they have lived on plains
It is grass rolling
Under their feet forever.

Having no souls, they have come,
Anyway, beyond their knowing.
Their instincts wholly bloom
And they rise.
The soft eyes open.

To match them, the landscape flowers,
Outdoing, desperately
Outdoing what is required:
The richest wood,
The deepest field.

For some of these,
It could not be the place
It is, without blood.
These hunt, as they have done,
But with claws and teeth grown perfect,

More deadly than they can believe.
They stalk more silently,
And crouch on the limbs of trees,
And their descent
Upon the bright backs of their prey

May take years
In a sovereign floating of joy.
And those that are hunted
Know this as their life,
Their reward: to walk

Under such trees in full knowledge
Of what is in glory above them,
And to feel no fear,
But acceptance, compliance.
Fulfilling themselves without pain

At the cycle's center,
They tremble, they walk
Under the tree,
They fall, they are torn,
They rise, they walk again.

1962

Buckdancer's Choice

So I would hear out those lungs,
The air split into nine levels,
Some gift of tongues of the whistler

In the invalid's bed: my mother,
Warbling all day to herself
The thousand variations of one song;

It is called Buckdancer's Choice.
For years, they have all been dying
Out, the classic buck-and-wing men

Of traveling minstrel shows;
With them also an old woman
Was dying of breathless angina,

Yet still found breath enough
To whistle up in my head
A sight like a one-man band,

BUCKDANCER'S CHOICE. **Title:** Buckdancing ("the buck and wing") is a tap dance performed with wooden shoes.

Freed black, with cymbals at heel,
An ex-slave who thrivingly danced
To the ring of his own clashing light

Through the thousand variations of one song
All day to my mother's prone music,
The invalid's warbler's note,

While I crept close to the wall
Sock-footed, to hear the sounds alter,
Her tongue like a mockingbird's break

Through stratum after stratum of a tone
Proclaiming what choices there are
For the last dancers of their kind,

For ill women and for all slaves
Of death, and children enchanted at walls
With a brass-beating glow underfoot,

Not dancing but nearly risen
Through barnlike, theatrelike houses
On the wings of the buck and wing.

1965

DENISE LEVERTOV

(born 1923)

Born in England, Levertov moved to the United States in 1948. Up till then her writing had reflected the neoromantic influences that were then prominent in England, and her style changed greatly in the 1950s. The main source of her new mode was the poetry of William Carlos Williams, which she now read for the first time. Her poems centered on particular experiences of ordinary life—on "dailyness," as she put it—and were distinguished for their economy of means and sensitivity of feeling. In the 1960s she protested fiercely against the war in Vietnam, and her poetry denounced it, in doing so becoming rhetorically external, sensational in image, and emotionally violent. After the war ended she wrote of her personal life, adopting the direct, intimate frankness and the rapid spontaneity in composition that were then widespread in American poetry. But she always continued to compose the Williams-like poem she had mastered in the 1950s. This remains her best type, and is illustrated in poems such as "Triple Feature" which present a moment of actual experience—her's or someone's observed by her—with sympathy, realizing it by means of sensitive, particular details. Or they pursue apt yet surprizing comparisons, such as the metaphors she finds in "Illustrious Ancestors" for the kind of poetry she would wish to write.

Triple Feature

Innocent decision: to enjoy.
And the pathos
of hopefulness, of his solicitude:

—he in mended serape,
she having plaited carefully
magenta ribbons into her hair,
the baby a round half-hidden shape
slung in her rebozo, and the young son steadfastly
gripping a fold of her skirt,
pale and severe under a
handed-down sombrero—

all regarding
the stills with full attention, preparing
to pay and go in—
to worlds of shadow-violence, half-
familiar, warm with popcorn, icy
with strange motives, barbarous splendors!

1959

Illustrious Ancestors

The Rav
of Northern White Russia declined,
in his youth, to learn the
language of birds, because
the extraneous did not interest him; nevertheless
when he grew old it was found
he understood them anyway, having
listened well, and as it is said, "prayed
with the bench and the floor." He used
what was at hand—as did

ILLUSTRIOUS ANCESTORS. **1. Rav:** Rabbi. Rabbi Schneour Zaimon, on Levertov's father's side, and Angel Jones of Mold, on her mother's side, were ancestors who were religious mystics.

Angel Jones of Mold, whose meditations
were sewn into coats and britches.
                    Well, I would like to make,
thinking some line still taut between me and them,
poems direct as what the birds said,
hard as a floor, sound as a bench,
mysterious as the silence when the tailor
would pause with his needle in the air.

1958

O Taste and See

The world is
not with us enough.
O taste and see

the subway Bible poster said,
meaning The Lord, meaning
if anything all that lives
to the imagination's tongue,

grief, mercy, language,
tangerine, weather, to
breathe them, bite,
savor, chew, swallow, transform

into our flesh our
deaths, crossing the street, plum, quince,
living in the orchard and being

hungry, and plucking
the fruit.

1964

11. Mold: town in Wales. O TASTE AND SEE. **1–2. world . . . enough:** an echo of the opening of Wordsworth's sonnet, "The World Is Too Much with Us."

A. R. AMMONS

(born 1926)

Ammons grew up on a farm in North Carolina, was a businessman for many years, and now teaches at Cornell University. In many ways he is a poet in the Romantic tradition. His poetry deals with ultimate metaphysical or religious questions, and presents the poet alone in nature, reflecting on its forms and drawing his symbols from them. On the other hand, the universe disclosed to his meditations reflects the lore of modern science, and is therefore different from that intuited by Wordsworth or Emerson. In the relation of Emerson to nature there was already, as compared to Wordsworth, a standoffishness—and this coolness is much greater in Ammons, although it is still combined with a close description of natural objects.

Ammons is also a meditative poet in the mode of Wallace Stevens. If we imagine a typical Ammonsian meditation, we might begin with the poet looking at puddles in his driveway, or (as in "Corsons Inlet") walking along the sea, or watching a bird in a tree. What he observes is ordinary and familiar, and would not engage the mind of most persons. Yet in the object or event he sees a potentially infinite number of forms, details, and processes. How, then, he asks himself, can the mind's paradigms ever correspond to the multiplicity of reality? Is there a unity, an "Overall" (as he puts it in "Corsons Inlet," punning on Emerson's Oversoul), or a center where all these particulars meet? If so, would one wish to be at this center or on the circumference amid the particulars? Thus he reflects on what he sees, but depends very little on what he sees to sustain his train of thought, which proceeds by the inherent fertility of the mind in itself.

Corsons Inlet

I went for a walk over the dunes again this morning
to the sea,
then turned right along
  the surf
            rounded a naked headland
            and returned

  along the inlet shore:

CORSONS INLET. **Title:** inlet in southern New Jersey.

it was muggy sunny, the wind from the sea steady and high,
crisp in the running sand,
    some breakthroughs of sun
  but after a bit

continuous overcast:

the walk liberating, I was released from forms,
from the perpendiculars,
    straight lines, blocks, boxes, binds
of thought
into the hues, shadings, rises, flowing bends and blends
        of sight:

                I allow myself eddies of meaning:
yield to a direction of significance
running
like a stream through the geography of my work:
  you can find
in my sayings
            swerves of action
            like the inlet's cutting edge:
        there are dunes of motion,
organizations of grass, white sandy paths of remembrance
in the overall wandering of mirroring mind:

but Overall is beyond me: is the sum of these events
I cannot draw, the ledger I cannot keep, the accounting
beyond the account:

in nature there are few sharp lines: there are areas of
primrose
    more or less dispersed;
disorderly orders of bayberry; between the rows
of dunes,
irregular swamps of reeds,
though not reeds alone, but grass, bayberry, yarrow, all . . .
predominantly reeds:

I have reached no conclusions, have erected no boundaries,
shutting out and shutting in, separating inside
        from outside: I have
        drawn no lines:
        as

manifold events of sand
change the dune's shape that will not be the same shape
tomorrow,

so I am willing to go along, to accept
the becoming
thought, to stake off no beginnings or ends, establish
        no walls:

by transitions the land falls from grassy dunes to creek
to undercreek: but there are no lines, though
      change in that transition is clear
      as any sharpness: but "sharpness" spread out,
allowed to occur over a wider range
than mental lines can keep:

the moon was full last night: today, low tide was low:
black shoals of mussels exposed to the risk
of air
and, earlier, of sun,
waved in and out with the waterline, waterline inexact,
caught always in the event of change:
      a young mottled gull stood free on the shoals
      and ate
to vomiting: another gull, squawking possession, cracked a crab,
picked out the entrails, swallowed the soft-shelled legs, a ruddy
turnstone running in to snatch leftover bits:

risk is full: every living thing in
siege: the demand is life, to keep life: the small
white blacklegged egret, how beautiful, quietly stalks and spears
            the shallows, darts to shore
                        to stab—what? I couldn't
      see against the black mudflats—a frightened
      fiddler crab?

            the news to my left over the dunes and
reeds and bayberry clumps was
            fall: thousands of tree swallows
            gathering for flight:
            an order held
            in constant change: a congregation
rich with entropy: nevertheless, separable, noticeable
      as one event,
               not chaos: preparations for
flight from winter,
cheet, cheet, cheet, cheet, wings rifling the green clumps,
beaks
at the bayberries
   a perception full of wind, flight, curve,
   sound:
   the possibility of rule as the sum of rulelessness:
the "field" of action
with moving, incalculable center:

in the smaller view, order tight with shape:
blue tiny flowers on a leafless weed: carapace of crab:
snail shell:
         pulsations of order
         in the bellies of minnows: orders swallowed,
broken down, transferred through membranes

to strengthen larger orders: but in the large view, no
lines or changeless shapes: the working in and out, together
and against, of millions of events: this,
so that I make
no form
formlessness:

orders as summaries, as outcomes of actions override
or in some way result, not predictably (seeing me again
the top of a dune,
the swallows
could take flight—some other fields of bayberry
could enter fall
berryless) and there is serenity:

no arranged terror: no forcing of image, plan,
or thought:

no propaganda, no humbling of reality to precept:

terror pervades but is not arranged, all possibilities
of escape open: no route shut, except in
the sudden loss of all routes:

I see narrow orders, limited tightness, but will
not run to that easy victory:
still around the looser, wider forces work:
I will try
to fasten into order enlarging grasps of disorder, widening
scope, but enjoying the freedom that
Scope eludes my grasp, that there is no finality of vision,
that I have perceived nothing completely,
that tomorrow a new walk is a new walk.

1965

ROBERT BLY

(born 1926)

Robert Bly grew up on a farm in Minnesota and eventually returned to live in this region. He founded a literary magazine, and in it he championed irrationalist poets of Europe and South America such as Georg Trakl and Pablo Neruda. Bly argued that a poet must escape from the controls of the rational self or "ego" and release the deeper, less conscious levels of the mind. Alluding to Ezra Pound's "In a Station of the Metro," Bly explained the difference between

Pound's Imagism (see the introduction to Pound) and what Bly called the "deep image": "To Pound an image meant 'petals on a wet, black bough.' To us an image is 'death on the wet deep roads of the guitar.'" Bly's best poems, however, are closer to Pound's Imagist ones than to the Surrealism Bly advocated and often practiced. In these poems wide, empty fields, solitary human figures, or oncoming twilight or snow suggest the loneliness and evanescence of human beings in nature or the cosmos. During the Vietnam war, Bly composed a great many poems in protest against it. "Driving through Minnesota during the Hanoi Bombings" represents this side of his work, and is also typical of poems of war protest written by many other American poets at this time.

Waking from Sleep

Inside the veins there are navies setting forth,
Tiny explosions at the water lines,
And seagulls weaving in the wind of the salty blood.

It is the morning. The country has slept the whole winter.
Window seats were covered with fur skins, the yard was full
Of stiff dogs, and hands that clumsily held heavy books.

Now we wake, and rise from bed, and eat breakfast!—
Shouts rise from the harbor of the blood,
Mist, and masts rising, the knock of wooden tackle in the sunlight.

Now we sing, and do tiny dances on the kitchen floor.
Our whole body is like a harbor at dawn;
We know that our master has left us for the day.

1962

Driving toward the Lac Qui Parle River

1

I am driving; it is dusk; Minnesota.
The stubble field catches the last growth of sun.
The soybeans are breathing on all sides.
Old men are sitting before their houses on carseats
In the small towns. I am happy,
The moon rising above the turkey sheds.

DRIVING TOWARD THE LAC QUI PARLE RIVER. **Title:** "River of the Lake that Speaks"; a river and lake in southern Minnesota.

2

The small world of the car
Plunges through the deep fields of the night,
On the road from Willmar to Milan.
This solitude covered with iron
Moves through the fields of night
Penetrated by the noise of crickets.

3

Nearly to Milan, suddenly a small bridge,
And water kneeling in the moonlight.
In small towns the houses are built right on the ground;
The lamplight falls on all fours in the grass.
When I reach the river, the full moon covers it;
A few people are talking low in a boat.

1962

After Drinking All Night with a Friend, We Go Out in a Boat at Dawn To See Who Can Write the Best Poem

These pines, these fall oaks, these rocks,
This water dark and touched by wind—
I am like you, you dark boat,
Drifting over water fed by cool springs.

Beneath the waters, since I was a boy,
I have dreamt of strange and dark treasures,
Not of gold, or strange stones, but the true
Gift, beneath the pale lakes of Minnesota.

This morning also, drifting in the dawn wind,
I sense my hands, and my shoes, and this ink—
Drifting, as all of this body drifts,
Above the clouds of the flesh and the stone.

A few friendships, a few dawns, a few glimpses of grass,
A few oars weathered by the snow and the heat,
So we drift toward shore, over cold waters,
No longer caring if we drift or go straight.

1962

9. Willmar . . . Milan: towns in Minnesota.

Driving through Minnesota during the Hanoi Bombings

We drive between lakes just turning green;
Late June. The white turkeys have been moved
To new grass.
How long the seconds are in great pain!
Terror just before death,
Shoulders torn, shot
From helicopters, the boy
Tortured with the telephone generator,
"I felt sorry for him,
And blew his head off with a shotgun."
These instants become crystals,
Particles
The grass cannot dissolve. Our own gaiety
Will end up
In Asia, and in your cup you will look down
And see
Black Starfighters.
We were the ones we intended to bomb!
Therefore we will have
To go far away
To atone
For the sufferings of the stringy-chested
And the small rice-fed ones, quivering
In the helicopter like wild animals,
Shot in the chest, taken back to be questioned.

1967

DRIVING THROUGH MINNESOTA DURING THE HANOI BOMBINGS. **Title:** referring to the bombings during the Vietnam War of Hanoi, capital of North Vietnam. **17. Black Starfighters:** combat airplanes of the United States.

Robert Creeley

(born 1926)

Creeley grew up in Massachusetts, went to Harvard, and then lived for three years on a farm in New Hampshire before moving to Majorca. Through an exchange of letters he struck up a friendship with Charles Olson, and Olson invited Creeley to join the faculty of Black Mountain College in North Carolina, where Olson was rector. Creeley left there in 1956, but since then has generally made his living by teaching college. His style is often described as "minimal," in reference to his plain diction and terse, muted, colorless lines. You cannot, Creeley pointed out, "derail a train by standing directly in front of it," but "a tiny piece of steel, properly placed . . . " His lyrics were frequently comic in mode, but the states of mind they exposed were painful. Creeley's elliptical statements opened precisely calculated gaps, within which uncertainty, nervousness, doubt, mistrust, bitterness, or panic might be revealed. The poems printed here are of this type, for which Creeley is especially known. But towards the end of the 1960s his poetry changed. He began to present fragments as spontaneous jottings in long poetic notebooks or journals. He has also experimented with poems accompanied by photographs.

The Business

To be in love is like going out-
side to see what kind of day

it is. Do not
mistake me. If you love

her how prove she
loves also, except that it

occurs, a remote chance on
which you stake

yourself? But barter for
the Indian was a means of sustenance.

There are records.

1957

I Know a Man

As I sd to my
friend, because I am
always talking,—John, I

sd, which was not his
name, the darkness sur-
rounds us, what

can we do against
it, or else, shall we &
why not, buy a goddamn big car,

drive, he sd, for
christ's sake, look
out where yr going.

1957

Naughty Boy

When he brings home a whale,
she laughs and says, that's not for real.

And if he won the Irish sweepstakes,
she would say, where were you last night?

Where are you now, for that matter? Am
I always (she says) to be looking

at you? She says,
if I thought it would get any better I

would shoot you, you
nut, you. Then pats her hair

into place, and waits
for Uncle Jim's deep-fired, all-fat, real gone

whale steaks.

1959

Allen Ginsberg

(born 1926)

Ginsberg first recited *Howl,* his most famous poem, at a public reading in San Francisco in 1955. This reading is often said to mark the beginning of the "Beat" movement in poetry. His poem denounced American society as oppressive and visionless. The power of the poem lay partly in its unrestrained emotion, partly in its shocking details, and partly in its bold challenge to conventional ideas of morality. Ginsberg celebrated hipsters as heroes. Morever, he was himself living by the ideals he preached. Without this proof of sincerity, his transvaluation of American values could not have been impressive. There was also much humor in *Howl,* and if this somewhat undermined its moral insistence, it further aided its acceptance, since it allowed middle-class readers to view Ginsberg as a clown as well as a prophet. Moreover, although his hipsters were endowed with heroic and even mythical stature, they were also presented as victims—their Dada gestures of protest seemed futile. American society could readily tolerate a radicalism couched in these terms.

Howl expressed and gave further impetus to several contemporary tendencies in American poetry. It was "Confessional" in the sense that it revealed emotions and actions that most readers would have kept hidden, and it did so in a spirit of human solidarity and liberation from taboo. Readers found that sexual lusts, bodily humiliations, fears of death, grandiose imaginations of power, and the like were common, even commonplace, and could be openly discussed. (Nakedness is a powerful symbol for Ginsberg, who occasionally takes off his clothes at public readings of his poetry.) *Howl* rejected the formal craftsmanship of much American poetry in the 1940s in favor of rapid spontaneity in composition, because poetry written in this way seemed to Ginsberg more vital as well as more sincere. The poem was, as we stressed, morally and politically committed to a nexus of social ideals. Both in its protest against the dominant culture and also in its advocacy, *Howl* set precedents for black and feminist poetry, and also for the poetry of the 1960s that denounced the Vietnam war. In terms of literary history *Howl* marked the returning authority of Walt Whitman, whose prestige had been suppressed for thirty years by that of T. S. Eliot, as a predecessor for American poets. It equally indicated the growing influence of William Carlos Williams.

Ginsberg grew up in Paterson, New Jersey, where his father taught school. His idealistic, politically radical mother was increasingly hysterical and delusional, and when Ginsberg was twelve, she became insane. While a student at Columbia University, Ginsberg began to write poetry. He met Jack Kerouac and William Burroughs, writers who influenced his tendency to romanticize the reckless life of the hipster. By 1948 he had formed his literary program, which was to present his feelings and way of life with unflinching realism, while at the same time accusing the social order. But he had as yet no literary form or method, and he did not find what he needed until he read *On the Road,* the well-known prose work composed by Jack Kerouac in 1951 in three weeks of spontaneous outpouring.

Meanwhile, Ginsberg had been employed in the field of market research, wearing a business suit and carrying a briefcase. In sessions with a psychiatrist he gradually decided instead to follow his own ideal of life, which was to "do nothing but write poetry and have leisure . . . [to] cultivate the visionary thing in me. Just a literary and quiet city-hermit existence." When *Howl* was published in 1956, legal proceedings were initiated against it on the grounds of obscenity. Controversy rose, and the famous—or notorious—poem was read more and more widely. By 1959 the Beat poets were topics of discussion in popular magazines such as *Time.*

Henceforth a public figure, Ginsberg continued to write prolifically; *Kaddish* (1961), a powerful lament at the death of his mother, *Reality Sandwiches* (1963), and *Planet News* (1968) were among his better volumes. He also contributed his energies to movements of protest and reform. He opposed the war in Vietnam, the arms race, and nuclear reactors, and testified against authority before United States Senate committees and in Czechoslovakia, from which he was expelled. He visited the Far East and became a devotee of Buddhism and Hinduism. All his poetry entertained through its wit and its picaresque, confessional realism, but his major contribution was made in *Howl.*

Howl

For Carl Solomon

I

I saw the best minds of my generation destroyed by madness, starving
hysterical naked,
dragging themselves through the negro streets at dawn looking for an
angry fix,
angelheaded hipsters burning for the ancient heavenly connection to
the starry dynamo in the machinery of night,
who poverty and tatters and hollow-eyed and high sat up smoking in
the supernatural darkness of cold-water flats floating across the
tops of cities contemplating jazz,
who bared their brains to Heaven under the El and saw Moham-
medan angels staggering on tenement roofs illuminated,
who passed through universities with radiant cool eyes hallucinating
Arkansas and Blake-light tragedy among the scholars of war,
who were expelled from the academies for crazy & publishing obscene
odes on the windows of the skull,
who cowered in unshaven rooms in underwear, burning their money
in wastebaskets and listening to the Terror through the wall,
who got busted in their pubic beards returning through Laredo with
a belt of marijuana for New York,
who ate fire in paint hotels or drank turpentine in Paradise Alley,
death, or purgatoried their torsos night after night
with dreams, with drugs, with waking nightmares, alcohol and cock
and endless balls,
incomparable blind streets of shuddering cloud and lightning in the
mind leaping toward poles of Canada & Paterson, illuminating
all the motionless world of Time between,
Peyote solidities of halls, backyard green tree cemetery dawns, wine
drunkenness over the rooftops, storefront boroughs of teahead
joyride neon blinking traffic light, sun and moon and tree vibra-
tions in the roaring winter dusks of Brooklyn, ashcan rantings and
kind king light of mind,
who chained themselves to subways for the endless ride from Battery
to holy Bronx on benzedrine until the noise of wheels and chil-

HOWL. **Subtitle.** Solomon (born 1928) was a fellow patient of Ginsberg's at the Columbia Psychiatric Institute in 1949. Ginsberg, who described him as "an intuitive Bronx Dadaist and prose-poet," incorporated in *Howl* many of the adventures Solomon told him, "compounded," said Solomon later, "partly of truth, but for the most [part] raving self-justification, crypto-bohemian boasting . . . and esoteric aphorisms." **3. hipsters:** beats who went on the road. **5. El:** Elevated railway in New York. **6. Blake-light:** referring to an hallucination Ginsberg had in 1948 of the poet William Blake (see Index) reciting two of his poems. **9. Laredo:** city in Texas on the Mexican border. **10. Paradise Alley:** tenement courtyard in New York's East Side. **12. Paterson:** Ginsberg's hometown in New Jersey, celebrated in William Carlos Williams's poem *Paterson.* **14. Battery . . . Bronx:** the southern and northern ends of a New York subway line. **Zoo:** Bronx Zoo.

dren brought them down shuddering mouth-wracked and battered
bleak of brain all drained of brilliance in the drear light of Zoo,
who sank all night in submarine light of Bickford's floated out and
sat through the stale beer afternoon in desolate Fugazzi's, listen-
ing to the crack of doom on the hydrogen jukebox,
who talked continuously seventy hours from park to pad to bar to
Bellevue to museum to the Brooklyn Bridge,
a lost battalion of platonic conversationalists jumping down the stoops
off fire escapes off windowsills off Empire State out of the moon,
yacketayakking screaming vomiting whispering facts and memories
and anecdotes and eyeball kicks and shocks of hospitals and jails
and wars,
whole intellects disgorged in total recall for seven days and nights
with brilliant eyes, meat for the Synagogue cast on the pavement,
who vanished into nowhere Zen New Jersey leaving a trail of ambig-
uous picture postcards of Atlantic City Hall,
suffering Eastern sweats and Tangerian bone-grindings and migraines
of China under junk-withdrawal in Newark's bleak furnished
room,
who wandered around and around at midnight in the railroad yard
wondering where to go, and went, leaving no broken hearts,
who lit cigarettes in boxcars boxcars boxcars racketing through snow
toward lonesome farms in grandfather night,
who studied Plotinus Poe St. John of the Cross telepathy and bop
kaballa because the cosmos instinctively vibrated at their feet in
Kansas,
who loned it through the streets of Idaho seeking visionary indian
angels who were visionary indian angels,
who thought they were only mad when Baltimore gleamed in super-
natural ecstasy,
who jumped in limousines with the Chinaman of Oklahoma on the
impulse of winter midnight streetlight smalltown rain,
who lounged hungry and lonesome through Houston seeking jazz or
sex or soup, and followed the brilliant Spaniard to converse about
America and Eternity, a hopeless task, and so took ship to Africa,
who disappeared into the volcanoes of Mexico leaving behind nothing
but the shadow of dungarees and the lava and ash of poetry
scattered in fireplace Chicago,
who reappeared on the West Coast investigating the F.B.I. in beards
and shorts with big pacifist eyes sexy in their dark skin passing
out incomprehensible leaflets,

15. Bickford's: a chain of all-night cafeterias, at one of which Ginsberg had worked as a college student. **Fugazzi's:** bar immediately north of Greenwich Village in New York. **16. Bellevue:** mental hospital in New York. **21. Tangerian . . . China:** drugs from Tangiers, Morocco, and China. **24. Plotinus . . . St. John:** regarded as "visionaries" by Ginsberg—the Neoplatonist philosopher Plotinus (205–70); Edgar Allan Poe (1809–1849), because of his supernatural tales; and the Spanish mystic St. John of the Cross (1542–1591), author of *The Dark Night of the Soul.* **bop kaballa:** bop was a jazz style of the 1940s; the Kaballa, a mystical Hebraic interpretation of the Bible, emphasizes the supremacy of spirit over the bodily senses.

who burned cigarette holes in their arms protesting the narcotic tobacco haze of Capitalism,
who distributed Supercommunist pamphlets in Union Square weeping and undressing while the sirens of Los Alamos wailed them down, and wailed down Wall, and the Staten Island ferry also wailed,
who broke down crying in white gymnasiums naked and trembling before the machinery of other skeletons,
who bit detectives in the neck and shrieked with delight in policecars for committing no crime but their own wild cooking pederasty and intoxication,
who howled on their knees in the subway and were dragged off the roof waving genitals and manuscripts,
who let themselves be fucked in the ass by saintly motorcyclists, and screamed with joy,
who blew and were blown by those human seraphim, the sailors, caresses of Atlantic and Caribbean love,
who balled in the morning in the evenings in rosegardens and the grass of public parks and cemeteries scattering their semen freely to whomever come who may,
who hiccupped endlessly trying to giggle but wound up with a sob behind a partition in a Turkish Bath when the blonde & naked angel came to pierce them with a sword,
who lost their loveboys to the three old shrews of fate the one eyed shrew of the heterosexual dollar the one eyed shrew that winks out of the womb and the one eyed shrew that does nothing but sit on her ass and snip the intellectual golden threads of the craftsman's loom,
who copulated ecstatic and insatiate with a bottle of beer a sweetheart a package of cigarettes a candle and fell off the bed, and continued along the floor and down the hall and ended fainting on the wall with a vision of ultimate cunt and come eluding the last gyzym of consciousness,
who sweetened the snatches of a million girls trembling in the sunset, and were red eyed in the morning but prepared to sweeten the snatch of the sunrise, flashing buttocks under barns and naked in the lake,
who went out whoring through Colorado in myriad stolen night-cars, N. C., secret hero of these poems, cocksman and Adonis of Denver—joy to the memory of his innumerable lays of girls in empty lots & diner backyards, moviehouses' rickety rows, on mountaintops in caves or with gaunt waitresses in familiar roadside lonely petticoat upliftings & especially secret gas-station solipsisms of johns, & hometown alleys too,

32. Union Square: a New York square frequented by radical speakers in the 1930s. **Los Alamos:** in New Mexico, where the atom bomb was developed. **Wall:** Wall Street; also the "Wailing Wall" in Jerusalem, where public laments were made. **43. N. C.:** Neal Cassady, beat figure and companion of Jack Kerouac. **solipsisms:** beliefs that all truth is subjective (solely in the mind).

who faded out in vast sordid movies, were shifted in dreams, woke on a sudden Manhattan, and picked themselves up out of basements hungover with heartless Tokay and horrors of Third Avenue iron dreams & stumbled to unemployment offices,
who walked all night with their shoes full of blood on the snowbank docks waiting for a door in the East River to open to a room full of steamheat and opium,
who created great suicidal dramas on the apartment cliff-banks of the Hudson under the wartime blue floodlight of the moon & their heads shall be crowned with laurel in oblivion,
who ate the lamb stew of the imagination or digested the crab at the muddy bottom of the rivers of Bowery,
who wept at the romance of the streets with their pushcarts full of onions and bad music,
who sat in boxes breathing in the darkness under the bridge, and rose up to build harpsichords in their lofts,
who coughed on the sixth floor of Harlem crowned with flame under the tubercular sky surrounded by orange crates of theology,
who scribbled all night rocking and rolling over lofty incantations which in the yellow morning were stanzas of gibberish,
who cooked rotten animals lung heart feet tail borsht & tortillas dreaming of the pure vegetable kingdom,
who plunged themselves under meat trucks looking for an egg,
who threw their watches off the roof to cast their ballot for Eternity outside of Time, & alarm clocks fell on their heads every day for the next decade,
who cut their wrists three times successively unsuccessfully, gave up and were forced to open antique stores where they thought they were growing old and cried,
who were burned alive in their innocent flannel suits on Madison Avenue amid blasts of leaden verse & the tanked-up clatter of the iron regiments of fashion & the nitroglycerine shrieks of the fairies of advertising & the mustard gas of sinister intelligent editors, or were run down by the drunken taxicabs of Absolute Reality,
who jumped off the Brooklyn Bridge this actually happened and walked away unknown and forgotten into the ghostly daze of Chinatown soup alleyways & firetrucks not even one free beer,
who sang out of their windows in despair, fell out of the subway window, jumped in the filthy Passaic, leaped on negroes, cried all over the street, danced on broken wineglasses barefoot smashed phonograph records of nostalgic European 1930's German jazz finished the whiskey and threw up groaning into the

44. Tokay: a sweet Hungarian wine. **47. Bowery:** southern part of Third Avenue, New York, traditionally frequented by alcoholics and derelicts. **56. Madison Avenue:** center of advertising firms in New York; "flannel suits" were associated in the 1950s with aspiring business executives there, as in Sloan Wilson's satiric novel *The Man in the Gray Flannel Suit* (1955). **58. Passaic:** a river that flows past Paterson, New Jersey.

bloody toilet, moans in their ears and the blast of colossal steam-
whistles,
who barreled down the highways of the past journeying to each other's
hotrod-Golgotha jail-solitude watch or Birmingham jazz incar-
nation,
who drove crosscountry seventytwo hours to find out if I had a vision
or you had a vision or he had a vision to find out Eternity,
who journeyed to Denver, who died in Denver, who came back to
Denver & waited in vain, who watched over Denver & brooded &
loned in Denver and finally went away to find out the Time, &
now Denver is lonesome for her heroes,
who fell on their knees in hopeless cathedrals praying for each other's
salvation and light and breasts, until the soul illuminated its hair
for a second,
who crashed through their minds in jail waiting for impossible crim-
inals with golden heads and the charm of reality in their hearts
who sang sweet blues to Alcatraz,
who retired to Mexico to cultivate a habit, or Rocky Mount to tender
Buddha or Tangiers to boys or Southern Pacific to the black
locomotive or Harvard to Narcissus to Woodlawn to the daisy
chain or grave,
who demanded sanity trials accusing the radio of hypnotism & were
left with their insanity & their hands & a hung jury,
who threw potato salad at CCNY lecturers on Dadaism and subse-
quently presented themselves on the granite steps of the mad-
house with shaven heads and harlequin speech of suicide, de-
manding instantaneous lobotomy,
and who were given instead the concrete void of insulin metrasol
electricity hydrotherapy psychotherapy occupational therapy
pingpong & amnesia,
who in humorless protest overturned only one symbolic pingpong
table, resting briefly in catatonia,
returning years later truly bald except for a wig of blood, and tears
and fingers, to the visible madman doom of the wards of the
madtowns of the East,
Pilgrim State's Rockland's and Greystone's foetid halls, bickering
with the echoes of the soul, rocking and rolling in the midnight
solitude-bench dolmen-realms of love, dream of life a nightmare,
bodies turned to stone as heavy as the moon,
with mother finally ******, and the last fantastic book flung out of
the tenement window, and the last door closed at 4 AM and the
last telephone slammed at the wall in reply and the last furnished

59. Golgotha: site of the crucifixion of Christ. **63. Alcatraz:** formerly a federal prison on an island in San Francisco Bay. **66. CCNY:** City College of New York, now City University (CUNY). **Dadaism:** artistic cult of absurdity and accident (1916–20). **70. Pilgrim . . . Greystone's:** three mental hospitals near New York. Carl Solomon was a patient at Pilgrim State and Rockland. Ginsberg's mother, Naomi, was permanently institutionalized at Greystone. **dolmen-realms:** a dolmen, or "table-stone," is a prehistoric structure of two stones capped by a third, possibly used as an early tomb.

room emptied down to the last piece of mental furniture, a yellow
paper rose twisted on a wire hanger in the closet, and even that
imaginary, nothing but a hopeful little bit of hallucination—
ah, Carl, while you are not safe I am not safe, and now you're really
in the total animal soup of time—
and who therefore ran through the icy streets obsessed with a sudden
flash of the alchemy of the use of the ellipse the catalog the meter
& the vibrating plane,
who dreamt and made incarnate gaps in Time & Space through images
juxtaposed, and trapped the archangel of the soul between 2
visual images and joined the elemental verbs and set the noun
and dash of consciousness together jumping with sensation of
Pater Omnipotens Aeterna Deus
to recreate the syntax and measure of poor human prose and stand
before you speechless and intelligent and shaking with shame,
rejected yet confessing out the soul to conform to the rhythm of
thought in his naked and endless head,
the madman bum and angel beat in Time, unknown, yet putting down
here what might be left to say in time come after death,
and rose reincarnate in the ghostly clothes of jazz in the goldhorn
shadow of the band and blew the suffering of America's naked
mind for love into an eli eli lamma lamma sabacthani saxophone
cry that shivered the cities down to the last radio
with the absolute heart of the poem of life butchered out of their own
bodies good to eat a thousand years.

1956

James Merrill

(born 1926)

Although he has traveled a good deal and taught briefly in colleges, for the most part Merrill has lived in Stonington, Connecticut, and devoted himself with steadily growing power to the writing of poetry. His first volumes, which appeared in 1946 and 1951, belonged to the condensed, formal, witty style that was then admired, and his latest poems are still metrical and still stuffed with puns, connota-

74. Pater . . . Deus: "All-powerful Father, eternal God." Applied by the French Impressionist painter Paul Cezanne (1839–1906) to the sensations he felt in painting objects of nature. Ginsberg said that his own method of juxtaposing images was an attempt to apply, in poetry, Cezanne's method of foreshortening perspective in painting. **77. eli . . . sabacthani:** Hebrew for "My God, my God, why has thou forsaken me?"—the last words spoken by Christ on the cross (Matthew 26:46).

tions, and allusions in intricate interplay. But he wished also to explore aspects of life or literature which could best be developed in long, narrative works—time and the changes it brings, the interaction of events and of character with events, the threading and permutations of a theme through a great multiplicity of materials. He has also published two novels.

His poems, moreover, were autobiographical in the sense that most of them referred with relative immediacy to his own experience. Their autobiographical dimension was less clearly evident in the earlier poems, however, for the poetic mode of the period when he wrote them did not favor personal utterance, and Merrill expressed himself indirectly through symbol and metaphor. But changes in literary style and in society since the 1960s made it possible for him to write in a more openly personal and autobiographical way. The latter point contributes importantly to the effect of his work, for poems written at different times throughout his career may refer to the same personal experiences. As we recognize these experiences, we associate the poems based on them, and each poem adds resonance to the others.

These three elements—formal wit, narrative, and autobiography—are present in all Merrill's greatest poems and in combination make up his inimitable style. In the poems printed here, both "A Broken Home" and "Lost in Translation" deal with experiences in Merrill's childhood and their psychological aftermath in his later life. As they express this material, the poems also use it to suggest wider, more general themes. In "Lost in Translation," for example, the jigsaw puzzle is both an event in the narrative and a complex metaphor for the effort, which the poem enacts, of reconstructing and trying to understand our own past lives and the lives of others. The greatest of Merrill's poems—*The Changing Light at Sandover* (1982)—cannot be represented in an anthology, for it is a poem of five hundred and sixty pages, and extracts from it lose much of their brilliance when read out of context. *The Changing Light at Sandover* is certainly the most ambitious and original long poem written in the United States over the last twenty years. In it Merrill and his friend David Jackson converse by means of a ouija board with spirits and dead persons. The revelations from beyond the grave are intertwined with the stories of the writing of the poem and of the life together of Merrill and Jackson.

A Renewal

Having used every subterfuge
To shake you, lies, fatigue, or even that of passion,
Now I see no way but a clean break.
I add that I am willing to bear the guilt.

You nod assent. Autumn turns windy, huge,
A clear vase of dry leaves vibrating on and on.
We sit, watching. When I next speak
Love buries itself in me, up to the hilt.

1959

The Broken Home

Crossing the street,
I saw the parents and the child
At their window, gleaming like fruit
With evening's mild gold leaf.

In a room on the floor below,
Sunless, cooler—a brimming
Saucer of wax, marbly and dim—
I have lit what's left of my life.

I have thrown out yesterday's milk
And opened a book of maxims.
The flame quickens. The word stirs.

Tell me, tongue of fire,
That you and I are as real
At least as the people upstairs.

My father, who had flown in World War I,
Might have continued to invest his life
In cloud banks well above Wall Street and wife.
But the race was run below, and the point was to win.

Too late now, I make out in his blue gaze
(Through the smoked glass of being thirty-six)
The soul eclipsed by twin black pupils, sex
And business; time was money in those days.

THE BROKEN HOME. **15. father:** Charles E. Merrill (1885–1956), investment banker and founding partner of the brokerage and investment company, Merrill Lynch Pierce Fenner & Smith.

Each thirteenth year he married. When he died
There were already several chilled wives
In sable orbit—rings, cars, permanent waves.
We'd felt him warming up for a green bride.

He could afford it. He was "in his prime"
At three score ten. But money was not time.

When my parents were younger this was a popular act:
A veiled woman would leap from an electric, wine-dark car
To the steps of no matter what—the Senate or the Ritz Bar—
And bodily, at newsreel speed, attack

No matter whom—Al Smith or José Maria Sert
Or Clemenceau—veins standing out on her throat
As she yelled *War mongerer! Pig! Give us the vote!*,
And would have to be hauled away in her hobble skirt.

What had the man done? Oh, made history.
Her business (he had implied) was giving birth,
Tending the house, mending the socks.

Always that same old story—
Father Time and Mother Earth,
A marriage on the rocks.

One afternoon, red, satyr-thighed
Michael, the Irish setter, head
Passionately lowered, led
The child I was to a shut door. Inside,

Blinds beat sun from the bed.
The green-gold room throbbed like a bruise.
Under a sheet, clad in taboos
Lay whom we sought, her hair undone, outspread,

And of blackness found, if ever now, in old
Engravings where the acid bit.
I must have needed to touch it
Or the whiteness—was she dead?
Her eyes flew open, startled strange and cold.
The dog slumped to the floor. She reached for me. I fled.

Tonight they have stepped out onto the gravel.
The party is over. It's the fall
Of 1931. They love each other still.
She: Charlie, I can't stand the pace.
He: Come on, honey—why, you'll bury us all!

30. veiled woman: a suffragette, a woman campaigning for the right to vote for women.
33–35. Al Smith . . . Sert . . . Clemenceau: Alfred E. Smith (1873–1944), Governor of New York; José Maria Sert (1876–1945), Spanish painter; Georges Clemenceau (1841–1929), Premier of France during World War I.

A lead soldier guards my windowsill:
Khaki rifle, uniform, and face.
Something in me grows heavy, silvery, pliable.

How intensely people used to feel!
Like metal poured at the close of a proletarian novel,
Refined and glowing from the crucible,
I see those two hearts, I'm afraid,
Still. Cool here in the graveyard of good and evil,
They are even so to be honored and obeyed.

. . . Obeyed, at least, inversely. Thus
I rarely buy a newspaper, or vote.
To do so, I have learned, is to invite
The tread of a stone guest within my house.

Shooting this rusted bolt, though, against him,
I trust I am no less time's child than some
Who on the heath impersonate Poor Tom
Or on the barricades risk life and limb.

Nor do I try to keep a garden, only
An avocado in a glass of water—
Roots pallid, gemmed with air. And later,

When the small gilt leaves have grown
Fleshy and green, I let them die, yes, yes,
And start another. I am earth's no less.

A child, a red dog roam the corridors,
Still, of the broken home. No sound. The brilliant
Rag runners halt before wide-open doors.
My old room! Its wallpaper—cream, medallioned
With pink and brown—brings back the first nightmares,
Long summer colds, and Emma, sepia-faced,
Perspiring over broth carried upstairs
Aswim with golden fats I could not taste.

The real house became a boarding school.
Under the ballroom ceiling's allegory
Someone at last may actually be allowed
To learn something; or, from my window, cool
With the unstiflement of the entire story,
Watch a red setter stretch and sink in cloud.

1966

77. Poor Tom: in Shakespeare's *King Lear* Edgar, who has been disowned by his father, pretends to be Poor Tom, a mad beggar living on the heath.

Lost in Translation

for Richard Howard
Diese Tage, die leer dir scheinen
und wertlos für das All,
haben Wurzeln zwischen den Steinen
und trinken dort überall.

A card table in the library stands ready
To receive the puzzle which keeps never coming.
Daylight shines in or lamplight down
Upon the tense oasis of green felt.
Full of unfulfillment, life goes on,
Mirage arisen from time's trickling sands
Or fallen piecemeal into place:
German lesson, picnic, see-saw, walk
With the collie who "did everything but talk"—
Sour windfalls of the orchard back of us.
A summer without parents is the puzzle,
Or should be. But the boy, day after day,
Writes in his Line-a-Day *No puzzle.*

He's in love, at least. His French Mademoiselle,
In real life a widow since Verdun,
Is stout, plain, carrot-haired, devout.
She prays for him, as does a curé in Alsace,
Sews costumes for his marionettes,
Helps him to keep behind the scene
Whose sidelit goosegirl, speaking with his voice,
Plays Guinevere as well as Gunmoll Jean.
Or else at bedtime in his tight embrace
Tells him her own French hopes, her German fears,
Her—but what more is there to tell?
Having known grief and hardship, Mademoiselle
Knows little more. Her languages. Her place.
Noon coffee. Mail. The watch that also waited
Pinned to her heart, poor gold, throws up its hands—
No puzzle! Steaming bitterness
Her sugars draw pops back into his mouth, translated:
"Patience, chéri. Geduld, mein Schatz."
(Thus, reading Valéry the other evening
And seeming to recall a Rilke version of "Palme,"

LOST IN TRANSLATION. **Epigraph:** "These days that seem empty to you/ and worthless for the cosmos,/ have roots between the stones/ and there drink everywhere." From a translation by the Austrian poet Rainer Maria Rilke (1875–1926) of "Palme" ("Palm"), a poem by Paul Valéry (1871–1945). **15. Verdun:** battle in the First World War. **17. Alsace:** Now part of France, Alsace has also belonged to Germany, and is of mixed French and German culture. **21. Guinevere:** consort of King Arthur in the legends of the Round Table. **31. "Patience . . . Schatz":** "Patience, dear" (French); "Patience, my treasure" (German). **32–33. Valéry . . . "Palme":** See note to epigraph.

That sunlit paradigm whereby the tree
Taps a sweet wellspring of authority,
The hour came back. Patience dans l'azur.
Geduld im . . . Himmelblau? Mademoiselle.)

Out of the blue, as promised, of a New York
Puzzle-rental shop the puzzle comes—
A superior one, containing a thousand hand-sawn,
Sandal-scented pieces. Many take
Shapes known already—the craftsman's repertoire
Nice in its limitation—from other puzzles:
Witch on broomstick, ostrich, hourglass,
Even (surely not just in retrospect)
An inchling, innocently branching palm.
These can be put aside, made stories of
While Mademoiselle spreads out the rest face-up,
Herself excited as a child; or questioned
Like incoherent faces in a crowd,
Each with its scrap of highly colored
Evidence the Law must piece together.
Sky-blue ostrich? Likely story.
Mauve of the witch's cloak white, severed fingers
Pluck? Detain here. The plot thickens
As all at once two pieces interlock.

Mademoiselle does borders—(Not so fast.
A London dusk, December last.
Chatter silenced in the library
This grown man reenters, wearing grey.
A medium. All except him have seen
Panel slid back, recess explored,
An object at once unique and common
Displayed, planted in a plain tole
Casket the subject now considers
Through shut eyes, saying in effect:
"Even as voices reach me vaguely
A dry saw-shriek drowns them out,
Some loud machinery—a lumber mill?
Far uphill in the fir forest
Trees tower, tense with shock,
Groaning and cracking as they crash groundward.
But hidden here is a freak fragment
Of a pattern complex in appearance only.

36–37. **Patience . . . Mademoiselle:** Patience in the blue (in French and then in German).

What it seems to show is superficial
Next to that long-term lamination
Of hazard and craft, the karma that has
Made it matter in the first place.
Plywood, Piece of a puzzle." Applause
Acknowledged by an opening of lids
Upon the thing itself. A sudden dread—
But to go back. All this lay years ahead.)

Mademoiselle does borders. Straight-edge pieces
Align themselves with earth or sky
In twos and threes, naive cosmogonists

Whose views clash. Nomad inlanders meanwhile
Begin to cluster where the totem
Of a certain vibrant egg-yolk yellow
Or pelt of what emerging animal
Acts on the straggler like a trumpet call
To form a more sophisticated unit.
By suppertime two ragged wooden clouds
Have formed. In one, a Sheik with beard
And flashing sword hilt (he is all but finished)
Steps forward on a tiger skin. A piece
Snaps shut, and fangs gnash out at us!
In the second cloud—they gaze from cloud to cloud
With marked if undecipherable feeling—
Most of a dark-eyed woman veiled in mauve
Is being helped down from her camel (kneeling)
By a small backward-looking slave or page-boy
(Her son, thinks Mademoiselle mistakenly)
Whose feet have not been found. But lucky finds
In the last minutes before bed
Anchor both factions to the scene's limits
And, by so doing, orient
Them eye to eye across the green abyss.
The yellow promises, oh bliss,
To be in time a sumptuous tent.

Puzzle begun I write in the day's space,
Then, while she bathes, peek at Mademoiselle's
Page to the curé: ". . . cette innocente mère,
Ce pauvre enfant, que deviendront-ils?"
Her azure script is curlicued like pieces
Of the puzzle she will be telling him about.
(Fearful incuriosity of childhood!
"Tu as l'accent allemand," said Dominique.
Indeed. Mademoiselle was only French by marriage.
Child of an English mother, a remote

112–13. cette . . . ils: "this innocent mother, this poor child, what will become of them?"
117. "Tu . . . allemand": "You have a German accent."

Descendant of the great explorer Speke,
And Prussian father. No one knew. I heard it
Long afterwards from her nephew, a UN
Interpreter. His matter-of-fact account
Touched old strings. My poor Mademoiselle,
With 1939 about to shake
This world where "each was the enemy, each the friend"
To its foundations, kept, though signed in blood,
Her peace a shameful secret to the end.)
"Schlaf wohl, chéri." Her kiss. Her thumb
Crossing my brow against the dreams to come.

This World that shifts like sand, its unforeseen
Consolidations and elate routine,
Whose Potentate had lacked a retinue?
Lo! it assembles on the shrinking Green.
Gunmetal-skinned or pale, all plumes and scars,
Of Vassalage the noblest avatars—
The very coffee-bearer in his vair
Vest is a swart Highness, next to ours.

Kef easing Boredom, and iced syrups, thirst,
In guessed-at glooms old wives who know the worst
Outsweat that virile fiction of the New:
"Insh'Allah, he will tire—" "—or kill her first!"

(Hardly a proper subject for the Home,
Work of—dear Richard, I shall let *you* comb
Archives and learned journals for his name—
A minor lion attending on Gérôme.)

While, thick as Thebes whose presently complete
Gates close behind them, Houri and Afreet
Both claim the Page. He wonders whom to serve,
And what his duties are, and where his feet,

And if we'll find, as some before us did,
That piece of Distance deep in which lies hid
Your tiny apex sugary with sun,
Eternal Triangle, Great Pyramid!

Then Sky alone is left, a hundred blue
Fragments in revolution, with no clue
To where a Niche will open. Quite a task,
Putting together Heaven, yet we do.

120. Speke: John Hanning Speke (1827–1864), African explorer who discovered the source of the Nile. **129. "Schlaf . . . chéri":** "Sleep well, dear" (the first two words are German, the third French). **139. Kef:** marijuana. **146. Gérôme:** Jean Léon Gérôme (1824–1904), French painter, sculptor, and engraver. **147. Thebes:** ancient capital of Upper Egypt, in Homer called "hundred-gated" Thebes, with a pun on "thieves." **148. Houri . . . Afreet:** A houri is a beautiful woman of the Moslem paradise; an afreet is an evil demon in Arabic mythology.

It's done. Here under the table all along
Were those missing feet. It's done.

The dog's tail thumping. Mademoiselle sketching
Costumes for a coming harem drama
To star the goosegirl. All too soon the swift
Dismantling. Lifted by two corners,
The puzzle hung together—and did not.
Irresistibly a populace
Unstitched of its attachments, rattled down.
Power went to pieces as the witch

Slithered easily from Virtue's gown.
The blue held out for time, but crumbled, too.
The city had long fallen, and the tent,
A separating sauce mousseline,
Been swept away. Remained the green
On which the grown-ups gambled. A green dusk.
First lightning bugs. Last glow of west
Green in the false eyes of (coincidence)
Our mangy tiger safe on his bared hearth.

Before the puzzle was boxed and readdressed
To the puzzle shop in the mid-Sixties,
Something tells me that one piece contrived
To stay in the boy's pocket. How do I know?
I know because so many later puzzles
Had missing pieces—Maggie Teyte's high notes
Gone at the war's end, end of the vogue for collies,
A house torn down; and hadn't Mademoiselle
Kept back her pitiful bit of truth as well?
I've spent the last days, furthermore,
Ransacking Athens for that translation of "Palme."
Neither the Goethehaus nor the National Library
Seems able to unearth it. Yet I can't
Just be imagining. I've seen it. Know
How much of the sun-ripe original
Felicity Rilke made himself forego
(Who loved French words—verger, mûr, parfumer)
In order to render its underlying sense.
Know already in that tongue of his
What Pains, what monolithic Truths
Shadow stanza to stanza's symmetrical
Rhyme-rutted pavement. Know that ground plan left
Sublime and barren, where the warm Romance
Stone by stone faded, cooled; the fluted nouns

172. sauce mousseline: hollandaise sauce with whipped cream added. **183. Maggie Teyte:** English soprano (1888–1976). **188. "Palme":** See note to epigraph. **189. Goethehaus:** German library in Athens. **193. Rilke:** See note to epigraph. **194. verger . . . parfumer:** orchard, ripe, to perfume (French).

Made taller, lonelier than life
By leaf-carved capitals in the afterglow.
The owlet umlaut peeps and hoots
Above the open vowel. And after rain
A deep reverberation fills with stars.

Lost, is it, buried? One more missing piece?

But nothing's lost. Or else: all is translation
And every bit of us is lost in it
(Or found—I wander through the ruin of S
Now and then, wondering at the peacefulness)
And in that loss a self-effacing tree,
Color of context, imperceptibly
Rustling with its angel, turns the waste
To shade and fiber, milk and memory.

1976

FRANK O'HARA

(1926–1966)

O'Hara spent his childhood and youth in the exurbia of Boston, Massachusetts. He served in the U.S. Navy during the Second World War and, after college and graduate school, found a job in New York City selling books and postcards in the Museum of Modern Art, where eventually he became an associate curator. Amid a short life filled in every moment with work, parties, concerts, art galleries, movies, gay bars, and all-night conversations, he composed more than five hundred pages of poetry. He wrote at incredible speed, and could turn out one or more poems during a lunch hour. They were written spontaneously, and reported personal feelings and experiences.

"Poem" is typical of O'Hara's light, bright, ebullient style. Its frivolousness is amusing, but it is also defiant, a stance chosen in challenge to more conventional ones. The tone announces itself in the opening line with the chatty and personal "the right day." The phrase makes the public event of Khrushchev's coming seem less portentous. For O'Hara the state visit is just one more stimulating item in a morning that is already delightful. Even in the phrase "Khrushchev is coming" the rhythm dances, announcing the light joyousness of the poem.

"The Day Lady Died" illustrates what O'Hara called his "I do this I do that" poems. In a flatly factual voice such poems tell O'Hara's ordinary actions over some short period of time. They give an impression of the randomness of existence, although this poem ends in a moment of intense feeling. The "I do this I do that" poems usually refer by name to friends of O'Hara. His pose, in other words, is intimate, for this is the way we would talk to friends who knew our friends; but since we know nothing about these persons, the effect is deliberately the opposite of what the pose would suggest. Our impression is of being not on the inside but on the outside of a busy social circle, and we are reminded how superficial and external our acquaintances are with other people's lives. But this is merely one example of a more general impression O'Hara conveys in a great many ways. All our experience is, for him, essentially superficial, rapid, and random. But he does not find this depressing. His poetry expresses a life lived in high speed and continual excitement.

Poem

Khrushchev is coming on the right day!
the cool graced light
is pushed off the enormous glass piers by hard wind
and everything is tossing hurrying on up
this country
has everything but *politesse,* a Puerto Rican cab driver says
and five different girls I see
look like Piedie Gimbel
with her blonde hair tossing too,
as she looked when I pushed
her little daughter on the swing on the lawn it was also windy

last night we went to a movie and came out,
Ionesco is greater
than Beckett, Vincent said, that's what I think, blueberry blintzes
and Khrushchev was probably being carped at
in Washington, no *politesse*
Vincent tells me about his mother's trip to Sweden
Hans tells us
about his father's life in Sweden, it sounds like Grace Hartigan's
painting *Sweden*

POEM. **Khrushchev:** Nikita Khrushchev (1894–1971), leader of the USSR. **6. *politesse*:** politeness (French). **13. Ionesco:** Eugène Ionesco (b. 1912), Franco-Rumanian dramatist. **14. Beckett:** Samuel Beckett (b.1906), playwright. **19. Grace Hartigan:** contemporary New York painter.

so I go home to bed and names drift through my head
Purgatorio Merchado, Gerhard Schwartz and Gaspar Gonzales, all
unknown figures of the early morning as I go to work

where does the evil of the year go
when September takes New York
and turns it into ozone stalagmites
deposits of light
so I get back up
make coffee, and read François Villon, his life, so dark
New York seems blinding and my tie is blowing up the street
I wish it would blow off
though it is cold and somewhat warms my neck
as the train bears Khrushchev on to Pennsylvania Station
and the light seems to be eternal
and joy seems to be inexorable
I am foolish enough always to find it in wind

1960

The Day Lady Died

It is 12:20 in New York a Friday
three days after Bastille day, yes
it is 1959 and I go get a shoeshine
because I will get off the 4:19 in Easthampton
at 7:15 and then go straight to dinner
and I don't know the people who will feed me

I walk up the muggy street beginning to sun
and have a hamburger and a malted and buy
an ugly NEW WORLD WRITING to see what the poets
in Ghana are doing these days
I go on to the bank
and Miss Stillwagon (first name Linda I once heard)
doesn't even look up my balance for once in her life
and in the GOLDEN GRIFFIN I get a little Verlaine
for Patsy with drawings by Bonnard although I do

29. François Villon: French poet (1431–1465). THE DAY LADY DIED. **Title:** "Lady Day" was the popular name for Billie Holliday (1915–1959), famous black singer of jazz and the blues. **2. Bastille day:** July 14, French Independence Day, celebrating the storming of the Bastille in 1789. **4. Easthampton:** in eastern Long Island, frequented by artists in summer. **14. Golden Griffin:** New York bookstore near the Museum of Modern Art, where O'Hara worked as a curator. **Verlaine:** Paul Verlaine (1844–1896), French symbolist poet. **15. Patsy:** Patsy Southgate, who kept the bookshop. **Bonnard:** Pierre Bonnard (1867–1947), French Impressionist painter.

think of Hesiod, trans. Richmond Lattimore or
Brendan Behan's new play or *Le Balcon* or *Les Nègres*
of Genet, but I don't, I stick with Verlaine
after practically going to sleep with quandariness

and for Mike I just stroll into the PARK LANE
Liquor Store and ask for a bottle of Strega and
then I go back where I came from to 6th Avenue
and the tobacconist in the Ziegfeld Theatre and
casually ask for a carton of Gauloises and a carton
of Picayunes, and a NEW YORK POST with her face on it

and I am sweating a lot by now and thinking of
leaning on the john door in the 5 SPOT
while she whispered a song along the keyboard
to Mal Waldron and everyone and I stopped breathing

1964

JOHN ASHBERY

(born 1927)

A Quiz-Kid at the age of fourteen, Ashbery went to Harvard and then, as a graduate student, to Columbia University in New York City. Here he became enthusiastic for contemporary music and painting, both of which influenced his technique in poetry. In 1955 Ashbery traveled to France and stayed there for ten years, writing poems, translating, and publishing art criticism in newspapers and magazines. Returning to the United States in 1965, he settled in New York City and worked as executive editor of *Art News* magazine. Later he became a professor of English at Brooklyn College, where he still teaches. At first readers associated his poetry with that of Frank O'Hara and other poets of New York City and spoke of a "New York School," but Ashbery's development has been so brilliant and idiosyncratic that he resembles no one else, not even his many imitators.

Our constant experience in reading Ashbery is of losing the thread of his meaning. We think we are following, and then discover that we are

16–18: Hesiod . . . Genet: Richmond Lattimore translated classical works, including the Greek poet Hesiod. Plays by the Irish dramatist Brendan Behan and the French writer Jean Genet were currently being performed in New York. **24–25. Gauloises . . . Picayunes:** cigarettes. **29. Mal Waldron:** Billie Holliday's accompanist.

astray. His poems produce neither meaning nor mere meaninglessness, but a continual expectation of meaning which is continually frustrated. Thus his poems enact our situation, as Ashbery conceives it, as we try to perceive and understand.

Most of Ashbery's writing is more or less ironical. He adopts or alludes, for example, to styles of contemporary journalism, advertising, bureaucracy, business memos, academic textbooks, scientific reports, and the like. A similar irony resides in Ashbery's use of stock ideas and cliché phrases. When, for example, in "Evening in the Country" we read that "these things eventually take care of themselves/ With rest and fresh air and the outdoors," the clichés tell us that the speaker does not really believe these assurances.

But the main single difficulty in interpreting Ashbery is that his texts simultaneously undermine what they assert. His sentences involve us in logical self-contradictions. Or their subjects cannot be connected with their predicates in a way that makes sense. Or their grammar suddenly lapses. A verb is in the wrong person, tense, or number, or a pronoun confuses by being "you" or "it" when it should have been "I." His metaphors transform themselves as we read, so that we are constantly forming new hypotheses to interpret them.

Yet the difficulty of Ashbery's poetry can easily be overstated. We register Ashbery's vision and emotion. Though the intellectual challenge of reading him is undoubtedly one reason for his appeal, readers of poetry would not enjoy his work if it were merely a puzzle. Ashbery grips us by the profundity of his scepticism, by the degree, in other words, to which he makes us conscious of intellectual and therefore emotional anxieties shared to some degree by all thinking persons in the modern world. He delights by his brilliant inventiveness, by his high spirits and wit, and by innumerable striking insights and aphorisms. Although he usually avoids climax, he is capable of moments of grandeur, as at the conclusion of "Evening in the Country." His attitudes and emotions are indescribably gallant as he mingles humor with pathos, resignation and elegiac feeling with hope, always maintaining his relaxed, equable, fluent, wonderfully imaginative utterance despite premises that might have led to despair and silence.

Evening in the Country

I am still completely happy.
My resolve to win further I have
Thrown out, and am charged by the thrill
Of the sun coming up. Birds and trees, houses,
These are but the stations for the new sign of being
In me that is to close late, long
After the sun has set and darkness come
To the surrounding fields and hills.
But if breath could kill, then there would not be
Such an easy time of it, with men locked back there
In the smokestacks and corruption of the city.
Now as my questioning but admiring gaze expands
To magnificent outposts, I am not so much at home
With these memorabilia of vision as on a tour
Of my remotest properties, and the eidolon
Sinks into the effective "being" of each thing,
Stump or shrub, and they carry me inside
On motionless explorations of how dense a thing can be,
How light, and these are finished before they have begun
Leaving me refreshed and somehow younger.
Night has deployed rather awesome forces
Against this state of affairs: ten thousand helmeted footsoldiers,
A Spanish armada stretching to the horizon, all
Absolutely motionless until the hour to strike
But I think there is not too much to be said or be done
And that these things eventually take care of themselves
With rest and fresh air and the outdoors, and a good view
        of things.
So we might pass over this to the real
Subject of our concern, and that is
Have you begun to be in the context you feel
Now that the danger has been removed?
Light falls on your shoulders, as is its way,
And the process of purification continues happily,
Unimpeded, but has the motion started
That is to quiver your head, send anxious beams
Into the dusty corners of the rooms
Eventually shoot out over the landscape
In stars and bursts? For other than this we know nothing
And space is a coffin, and the sky will put out the light.
I see you eager in your wishing it the way
We may join it, if it passes close enough:
This sets the seal of distinction on the success or failure of
        your attempt.
There is growing in that knowledge
We may perhaps remain here, cautious yet free

On the edge, as it rolls its unblinking chariot
Into the vast open, the incredible violence and yielding
Turmoil that is to be our route.

1966

Soonest Mended

Barely tolerated, living on the margin
In our technological society, we were always having to be rescued
On the brink of destruction, like heroines in *Orlando Furioso*
Before it was time to start all over again.
There would be thunder in the bushes, a rustling of coils,
And Angelica, in the Ingres painting, was considering
The colorful but small monster near her toe, as though wondering whether forgetting
The whole thing might not, in the end, be the only solution.
And then there always came a time when
Happy Hooligan in his rusted green automobile
Came plowing down the course, just to make sure everything was O.K.
Only by that time we were in another chapter and confused
About how to receive this latest piece of information.
Was it information? Weren't we rather acting this out
For someone else's benefit, thoughts in a mind
With room enough to spare for our little problems (so they began to seem),
Our daily quandary about food and the rent and bills to be paid?
To reduce all this to a small variant,
To step free at last, minuscule on the gigantic plateau—
This was our ambition: to be small and clear and free.
Alas, the summer's energy wanes quickly,
A moment and it is gone. And no longer
May we make the necessary arrangements, simple as they are.
Our star was brighter perhaps when it had water in it.
Now there is no question even of that, but only
Of holding on to the hard earth so as not to get thrown off,
With an occasional dream, a vision: a robin flies across
The upper corner of the window, you brush your hair away
And cannot quite see, or a wound will flash
Against the sweet faces of the others, something like:

SOONEST MENDED. **3. *Orlando Furioso*:** Italian epic poem by Ludovico Ariosto (1474–1533). Its heroine Angelica (see line 6) is constantly being rescued from monsters and other perils. **6. Ingres painting:** "Roger Delivering Angelica," based on Ariosto's poem, by the French artist Jean A. D. Ingres (1780–1867). **10. Happy Hooligan:** a simple-minded character in a comic strip of the same name during the 1920s and 1930s.

This is what you wanted to hear, so why
Did you think of listening to something else? We are all talkers
It is true, but underneath the talk lies
The moving and not wanting to be moved, the loose
Meaning, untidy and simple like a threshing floor.
These then were some hazards of the course,
Yet though we knew the course *was* hazards and nothing else
It was still a shock when, almost a quarter of a century later,
The clarity of the rules dawned on you for the first time.
They were the players, and we who had struggled at the game
Were merely spectators, though subject to its vicissitudes
And moving with it out of the tearful stadium, borne on shoulders,
at last.
Night after night this message returns, repeated
In the flickering bulbs of the sky, raised past us, taken away from us,
Yet ours over and over until the end that is past truth,
The being of our sentences, in the climate that fostered them,
Not ours to own, like a book, but to be with, and sometimes
To be without, alone and desperate.
But the fantasy makes it ours, a kind of fence-sitting
Raised to the level of an esthetic ideal. These were moments,
years,
Solid with reality, faces, namable events, kisses, heroic acts,
But like the friendly beginning of a geometrical progression
Not too reassuring, as though meaning could be cast aside some day
When it had been outgrown. Better, you said, to stay cowering
Like this in the early lessons, since the promise of learning
Is a delusion, and I agreed, adding that
Tomorrow would alter the sense of what had already been learned,
That the learning process is extended in this way, so that from this
standpoint
None of us ever graduates from college,
For time is an emulsion, and probably thinking not to grow up
Is the brightest kind of maturity for us, right now at any rate.
And you see, both of us were right, though nothing
Has somehow come to nothing; the avatars
Of our conforming to the rules and living
Around the home have made—well, in a sense, "good citizens"
of us,
Brushing the teeth and all that, and learning to accept
The charity of the hard moments as they are doled out,
For this is action, this not being sure, this careless
Preparing, sowing the seeds crooked in the furrow,
Making ready to forget, and always coming back
To the mooring of starting out, that day so long ago.

1970

35. threshing floor: where, after harvest, wheat is separated from the chaff. **60. emulsion:** in chemistry, the suspension of particles of one liquid in a second liquid, where they do not actually mix (for example, milk fats in milk).

Worsening Situation

Like a rainstorm, he said, the braided colors
Wash over me and are no help. Or like one
At a feast who eats not, for he cannot choose
From among the smoking dishes. This severed hand
Stands for life, and wander as it will,
East or west, north or south, it is ever
A stranger who walks beside me. O seasons,
Booths, chaleur, dark-hatted charlatans
On the outskirts of some rural fete,
The name you drop and never say is mine, mine!
Some day I'll claim to you how all used up
I am because of you but in the meantime the ride
Continues. Everyone is along for the ride,
It seems. Besides, what else is there?
The annual games? True, there are occasions
For white uniforms and a special language
Kept secret from the others. The limes
Are duly sliced. I know all this
But can't seem to keep it from affecting me,
Every day, all day. I've tried recreation,
Reading until late at night, train rides
And romance.
                    One day a man called while I was out
And left this message: "You got the whole thing wrong
From start to finish. Luckily, there's still time
To correct the situation, but you must act fast.
See me at your earliest convenience. And please
Tell no one of this. Much besides your life depends on it."
I thought nothing of it at the time. Lately
I've been looking at old-fashioned plaids, fingering
Starched white collars, wondering whether there's a way
To get them really white again. My wife
Thinks I'm in Oslo—Oslo, France, that is.

1975

WORSENING SITUATION. **8. chaleur:** warmth, animation, vivacity (French). **32. Oslo:** capital of Norway.

W. S. Merwin

(born 1927)

The son of a Pennsylvania clergyman, W. S. Merwin went to Princeton. After a year in graduate school, he quit academic life and lived in Europe, supporting himself by tutoring and translating. In the 1950s his poetry exemplified the impersonality and formal control that readers then admired, but these qualities had a special implication for Merwin, for the subjects he wrote about were often charged with intense emotion. Hence there was a tension between the form and the subject, in which the form was exhibited as mastering, controlling, and distancing the emotion invoked by the subject matter. Merwin's attitude toward this was ambiguous. On the one hand, the emotions were often of a disturbing, fearful kind, and strict form was a defense against them. On the other hand, obvious formal control implied artifice or unreality, and he desired to break out of it.

"The Isaiah of Souillac" is one of several poems that explore these problems. It describes a dancing figure of the prophet Isaiah carved in stone on the facade of a medieval church in France. The poem dwells on the paradox that dithyrambic activity and emotion are expressed in stone. In presenting its subject, this work of art miniatures and freezes it, yet the work of art also, at the end of the poem, allows the spectator not merely to contemplate but at least partly to share the prophet's emotion, his mystical sense of union with God.

After 1956 Merwin struggled to change his style. He wrote poems that tried variously to be rowdy, prosy and realistic, open and spontaneous in form, or surrealistic. Surrealism was especially effective in expressing feelings of alienation and revolt, and prevailed in *The Lice* (1967), an important volume in the poetry of political and social protest that characterized the 1960s. Thereafter Merwin cultivated a poetry of naive affirmation. At the very start of his career he had written dreamy, contemplative, remote poems that recalled those of Tennyson and D. G. Rossetti; his later style again emphasized these qualities, although in a new way that did not closely resemble nineteenth-century predecessors. Even in love poems such as "Summer Doorway," he and his girlfriend seem figures in a painting. When he falls to his knees and clasps her thighs, the erotic gesture is frozen as an artistic image for contemplation.

The Isaiah of Souillac

Why the prophet is dancing the sculptor knew. If
The prophet is dancing. Or even if it is only
Wind, a wind risen there in the doorway
Suddenly as a fish leaps, lifting his garments
His feet, like music, a whirling of breath carved
There in the narrow place that is enough for a man.
You see a wind in its signs but in itself not.
You hear a spirit in its motion, in its words, even
In its stillness, but in itself not. Know it here in the stance
Of a prophet, and his beard blown in a doorway.
His words stream in the stoney wind; woe
Unto the dust that is deaf, for even stones
Can rise as with feet when the spirit passes
Upon the place where they are. But they are all gone away
Backward; from the soles of their feet to their heedless heads
There is no measure nor soundness in them. His fingers,
Frail as reeds making the music they move to,
Embody a lightness like fire. They shall be moved
With burning whom this breath moves not, who have refused
The waters of Shiloah that go softly shall the river
Rise over, out in the sunlight, roaring
Like the sea, like lions, spreading its wings like a wind.
And yet will the wind of heaven wear the shape of a man,
Be mortal as breath, before men, for a sign, and stand
Between good and evil, the thieves of the left and right hand.
And the sign of a wind is dancing, the motion
Of a sign is dancing and ushered with words beating
And with dancing. So there is terrible gentleness
Unleashed in the stone of his eyes, so
The words dance as a fire, as a clapping
Of hands, as the stars dance, as the mountains
Leap swelling, as the feet of the prophet, faithful
Upon them, dance, dance, and still to the same song.

1956

THE ISAIAH OF SOUILLAC. **Title:** Sculptured figure of the prophet in the twelfth-century church in the town of Souillac, France. **20. Shiloah:** brook in Jerusalem, whose waters were used in the Hebrew Tabernacles. In Isaiah 8:5–8 the prophet fortells the conquest of Israel by Assyria: "Because this people have refused the waters of Shiloah that flow gently . . . therefore, behold, the Lord is bringing up against them the waters of the River . . . the king of Assyria and all his glory." **23–25. man . . . hand:** verses towards the end of the book of Isaiah are often interpreted as fortelling the coming of Christ, who was crucified between two thieves.

Summer Doorway

I come down from the gold mountains
each of them the light of many years
high up the soughing of cold pines among stones
the whole way home dry grass seething
to these sounds I think of you already there
in the house all my steps lead to

you have the table set to surprise me
you are lighting the two candles
I come to the door quickly to surprise you
but you laugh we laugh you run toward me
under the long skirt your feet are bare
I drop to my knees in the doorway and catch you
holding the backs of your thighs I watch the candle flames
over my head you watch the birds flying home from the sea

1977

James Wright

(1927–1980)

Wright was born in an Ohio industrial town where his father worked in a factory. After serving in the army he went to Kenyon College in Ohio and, as a graduate student, to the University of Washington. He made his living thereafter by teaching literature in various colleges and universities. In his first two volumes (1957 and 1959), his style derived from traditional poets of the nineteenth and twentieth centuries, and was little touched by Modernist or contemporary developments. But his subject matter was more distinctively individual, for he was fascinated by social outcasts such as drunks, murderers, prostitutes, and police informers. As he presented these persons, he identified with their feelings of helplessness, bewilderment, loneliness, humiliation, criminality, and defeat. In many ways President Harding, in Wright's "Two Poems About President Harding," is such a figure. Wright's objective yet compassionate view of Harding is typical of these earlier poems, as is his tendency to view Harding as an expression and victim of American culture.

Early in the 1960s Wright felt that he had reached a dead end. Unable to continue in his former style, he found suggestions toward a new development in the work of European poets such as the Austrian Georg Trakl (1887–1914), whose lyrics might be called either Expressionist or Surrealist.At the same time he met Robert Bly, who was also enthusiastic for these poets, and was greatly encouraged by Bly's friendship. These influences were evident in *The Branch Will Not Break* (1963), which remains Wright's finest volume. "The Blessing" appeared in it and became one of the most widely loved of contemporary American lyrics. It expresses a moment of shy, intense emotion. The final Surrealist image conveys Wright's poetically traditional longing to become part of an innocent, Edenic nature. The poem is somewhat sentimental, but if we read further in Wright we understand the psychological necessity that impelled him to this. He was appalled by the brutality and sordidness of modern urban life, and idealized animals and nature in compensation. In the last ten years of his life Wright's poetry reflected, on the whole, a resolve to be affirmative. In this he succeeded, but at a cost, for his imagination was more greatly stimulated by the vision of human suffering he was now seeking to reject. What was best in Wright recalls Thomas Hardy in sensitivity to the darker sides of human nature and experience, direct honesty, seriousness, essentialism, and compassion.

Two Poems About President Harding

One: His Death

In Marion, the honey locust trees are falling.
Everybody in town remembers the white hair,
The campaign of a lost summer, the front porch
Open to the public, and the vaguely stunned smile
Of a lucky man.

"Neighbor, I want to be helpful," he said once.
Later, "You think I'm honest, don't you?"
Weeping drunk.

I am drunk this evening in 1961,
In a jag for my countryman,
Who died of crab meat on the way back from Alaska.
Everyone knows that joke.

TWO POEMS ABOUT PRESIDENT HARDING: ONE: HIS DEATH. **1. Marion:** town in Ohio, home of president Warren G. Harding (1865–1923). **7. honest:** During Harding's presidency (1921–23) members of his cabinet were involved in political corruption and scandal. Harding was probably innocent of personal wrongdoing. **11. Alaska:** In 1923 Harding took a political trip that went as far as Alaska. He died soon after his return.

How many honey locusts have fallen,
Pitched rootlong into the open graves of strip mines,
Since the First World War ended
And Wilson the gaunt deacon jogged sullenly
Into silence?
Tonight,
The cancerous ghosts of old con men
Shed their leaves.
For a proud man,
Lost between the turnpike near Cleveland
And the chiropractors' signs looming among dead mulberry trees,
There is no place left to go
But home.

"Warren lacks mentality," one of his friends said.
Yet he was beautiful, he was the snowfall
Turned to white stallions standing still
Under dark elm trees.

He died in public. He claimed the secret right
To be ashamed.

Two: His Tomb in Ohio

" . . . he died of a busted gut."
—Mencken, on Bryan.

A hundred slag piles north of us,
At the mercy of the moon and rain,
He lies in his ridiculous
Tomb, our fellow citizen.
No, I have never seen that place,
Where many shadows of faceless thieves
Chuckle and stumble and embrace
On beer cans, stogie butts, and graves.

One holiday, one rainy week
After the country fell apart,
Hoover and Coolidge came to speak
And snivel about his broken heart.
His grave, a huge absurdity,
Embarrassed cops and visitors.
Hoover and Coolidge crept away
By night, and women closed their doors.

14. strip mines: Wright believed present-day policy with regard to strip mining was analogous to the corruption in Harding's administration. **16. Wilson:** President Woodrow Wilson (1856–1924), a Presbyterian, suffered a stroke in 1919 and was incapacitated thereafter. TWO: HIS TOMB IN OHIO. **4. Tomb:** ostentatious and in classical style. **11. Hoover and Coolidge:** Calvin Coolidge (1872–1933) and Herbert Hoover (1874–1964), the presidents who succeeded Harding.

Now junkmen call their children in
Before they catch their death of cold;
Young lovers let the moon begin
Its quick spring; and the day grows old;
The mean one-legger who rakes up leaves
Has chased the loafers out of the park;
Minnegan Leonard half-believes
In God, and the poolroom goes dark;

America goes on, goes on
Laughing, and Harding was a fool.
Even his big pretentious stone
Lays him bare to ridicule.
I know it. But don't look at me.
By God, I didn't start this mess.
Whatever moon and rain may be,
The hearts of men are merciless.

1963

A Blessing

Just off the highway to Rochester, Minnesota,
Twilight bounds softly forth on the grass.
And the eyes of those two Indian ponies
Darken with kindness.
They have come gladly out of the willows
To welcome my friend and me.
We step over the barbed wire into the pasture
Where they have been grazing all day, alone.
They ripple tensely, they can hardly contain their happiness
That we have come.
They bow shyly as wet swans. They love each other.
There is no loneliness like theirs.
At home once more,
They begin munching the young tufts of spring in the darkness.
I would like to hold the slenderer one in my arms,
For she has walked over to me
And nuzzled my left hand.
She is black and white,
Her mane falls wild on her forehead,
And the light breeze moves me to caress her long ear
That is delicate as the skin over a girl's wrist.
Suddenly I realize
That if I stepped out of my body I would break
Into blossom.

1963

THOM GUNN

(born 1929)

Gunn was born in England, went to Cambridge University, and then moved to California, where he now lives. In "On the Move," a relatively early poem, Gunn described the goalless but somehow splendid onrush of a motorcycle gang. The leather-jacketed cyclists were a many-sided symbol of the poet or poetry, of technological civilization divorced from nature, and of modern man existentially affirming himself in a universe that in itself is without values or meaning. Psychologically speaking, the poem expressed a side of Gunn that inclines, partly out of mistrust, to aggressive thrust, keeping other people at a distance. The theme of touch, of touching, and being touched by others has much resonance for him; it is something he both fears and desires.

"From the Wave" was written more than ten years later, and contrasts directly with "On the Move." In doing so, it expresses both an opposite side of Gunn's nature and also a change in his attitudes over time. Here again we see riders in black uniforms, but instead of the leather-jacketed motorcyclists of the earlier poem, they are surfers in rubber suits. The motorcyclists were unrelated to nature, if not aggressive toward it, but the surfers merge with the wave and its rhythm. The final lines of "From the Wave" suggest an attitude altogether different from the restless, assertive ethos of "On the Move." Through the course of his career Gunn has written in different styles, but the themes and attitudes we have touched on run through all his work.

On the Move

'Man, you gotta Go.'

The blue jay scuffling in the bushes follows
Some hidden purpose, and the gust of birds
That spurts across the field, the wheeling swallows,
Have nested in the trees and undergrowth.
Seeking their instinct, or their poise, or both,
One moves with an uncertain violence
Under the dust thrown by a baffled sense
Or the dull thunder of approximate words.

On motorcycles, up the road, they come:
Small, black, as flies hanging in heat, the Boys,
Until the distance throws them forth, their hum
Bulges to thunder held by calf and thigh.
In goggles, donned impersonality,
In gleaming jackets trophied with the dust,
They strap in doubt—by hiding it, robust—
And almost hear a meaning in their noise.

Exact conclusion of their hardiness
Has no shape yet, but from known whereabouts
They ride, direction where the tires press.
They scare a flight of birds across the field:
Much that is natural, to the will must yield.
Men manufacture both machine and soul,
And use what they imperfectly control
To dare a future from the taken routes.

It is a part solution, after all.
One is not necessarily discord
On earth; or damned because, half animal,
One lacks direct instinct, because one wakes
Afloat on movement that divides and breaks.
One joins the movement in a valueless world,
Choosing it, till, both hurler and the hurled,
One moves as well, always toward, toward.

A minute holds them, who have come to go:
The self-defined, astride the created will
They burst away; the towns they travel through
Are home for neither bird nor holiness,
For birds and saints complete their purposes.
At worst, one is in motion; and at best,
Reaching no absolute, in which to rest,
One is always nearer by not keeping still.

1957

From the Wave

It mounts at sea, a concave wall
  Down-ribbed with shine,
And pushes forward, building tall
  Its steep incline.

Then from their hiding rise to sight
  Black shapes on boards
Bearing before the fringe of white
  It mottles towards.

Their pale feet curl, they poise their weight
  With a learn'd skill.
It is the wave they imitate
  Keeps them so still.

The marbling bodies have become
  Half wave, half men,
Grafted it seems by feet of foam
  Some seconds, then,

Late as they can, they slice the face
  In timed procession:
Balance is triumph in this place,
  Triumph possession.

The mindless heave of which they rode
  A fluid shelf
Breaks as they leave it, falls and, slowed,
  Loses itself.

Clear, the sheathed bodies slick as seals
  Loosen and tingle;
And by the board the bare foot feels
  The suck of shingle.

They paddle in the shallows still;
  Two splash each other;
Then all swim out to wait until
  The right waves gather.

1971

Adrienne Rich

(born 1929)

After graduating from Radcliffe College, Rich married and had three children. Her early volumes of poetry, which appeared in 1951 and 1955, were in the tight, formal, impersonal style of the period. In *Snapshots of a Daughter-in-Law* (1963) she found her distinctive subject matter in her immediate experience as a woman. She rendered with powerful honesty and realism the tensions she felt between, on the one hand, the feminine roles of wife and mother our society supports, and, on the other hand, her human need for a fully individual development of her own person. Simultaneously she abandoned her earlier style and composed, instead, in a looser prosody and with a more personal voice. This change in her poetry reflected emotional and intellectual crises through which she was going, but it also participated in wider movements in American poetry—the so-called "confessional" writing of the late 1950s, the politically engaged poetry of the 1960s, which included expressions of feminist consciousness and protest, and the general tendency of the period to write in more open forms. She began to write more rapidly and spontaneously, and she took for granted that the conflicts she felt in herself were, in large degree, socially induced and therefore expressive of contemporary American culture. This assumption was validated by the response of many readers, who found that in exploring her own inner and outer experience, Rich was also highlighting theirs. As time passed Rich became increasingly more convinced, outspoken, and angry in voicing her sense of women's victimization.

Snapshots of a Daughter-in-Law

1

You, once a belle in Shreveport,
with henna-colored hair, skin like a peachbud,
still have your dresses copied from that time,
and play a Chopin prelude
called by Cortot: *"Delicious recollections*
float like perfume through the memory."
Your mind now, mouldering like wedding-cake,
heavy with useless experience, rich
with suspicion, rumor, fantasy,
crumbling to pieces under the knife-edge
of mere fact. In the prime of your life.

Nervy, glowering, your daughter
wipes the teaspoons, grows another way.

2

Banging the coffe-pot into the sink
she hears the angels chiding, and looks out
past the raked gardens to the sloppy sky.
Only a week since They said: *Have no patience.*

SNAPSHOTS OF A DAUGHTER-IN-LAW. **1. Shreveport:** city in northern Louisiana. **4–5. Chopin . . . Cortot:** Frédéric Chopin (1810–1849), the famous Polish composer for the piano. Alfred Cortot (1877–1962), a French pianist, was noted for his interpretations of Chopin.

The next time it was: *Be insatiable.*
Then: *Save yourself; others you cannot save.*
Sometimes she's let the tapstream scald her arm,
a match burn to her thumbnail,

or held her hand above the kettle's snout
right in the woolly steam. They are probably angels,
since nothing hurts her any more, except
each morning's grit blowing into her eyes.

3

A thinking woman sleeps with monsters.
The beak that grips her, she becomes. And Nature,
that sprung-lidded, still commodious
steamer-trunk of *tempora* and *mores*
gets stuffed with it all: the mildewed orange-flowers,
the female pills, the terrible breasts
of Boadicea beneath flat foxes' heads and orchids.

Two handsome women, gripped in argument,
each proud, acute, subtle, I hear scream
across the cut glass and majolica
like Furies cornered from their prey:
The argument *ad feminam,* all the old knives
that have rusted in my back, I drive in yours,
ma semblable, ma soeur!

4

Knowing themselves too well in one another:
their gifts no pure fruition, but a thorn,
the prick filed sharp against a hint of scorn . . .
Reading while waiting
for the iron to heat,
writing, *My Life had stood—a Loaded Gun—*
in that Amherst pantry while the jellies boil and scum,
or, more often,
iron-eyed and beaked and purposed as a bird,
dusting everything on the whatnot every day of life.

29. *tempora . . . mores*: times . . . manners. Rich echoes the opening of Cicero's First Oration against Cataline: *"O tempora, O mores"* ("Oh, these times; oh, these manners"). **32. Boadicea:** queen of a British tribe (first century A.D.) that rebelled against the Romans. When defeated, she took poison. **35. majolica:** Italian Renaissance pottery, enameled and glazed. **36. Furies:** in Greek myth, three avenging deities. **37. *ad feminam*:** literally "to the woman," varying the more common phrase, *ad hominem,* that refers to an argument addressed to an individual's particular situation. **39. *ma semblable, ma soeur*:** "my fellow [one like me], my sister." Rich alludes to Baudelaire's poem "Au Lecteur," which concludes by addressing the "hypocrite reader" as "mon semblable,—mon frère" ("my fellow—my brother"), and also alludes to T. S. Eliot's *The Waste Land,* line 76, which quotes the line from Baudelaire. **45. My Life . . . Gun:** a quotation from Emily Dickinson, *Complete Poems,* ed. T. H. Johnson (1960), p. 369. **46. Amherst:** the city of Amherst, Massachusetts, site of Amherst College.

5

Dulce ridens, dulce loquens,
she shaves her legs until they gleam
like petrified mammoth-tusk.

6

When to her lute Corinna sings
neither words nor music are her own;
only the long hair dipping
over her cheek, only the song
of silk against her knees
and these
adjusted in reflections of an eye.

Poised, trembling and unsatisfied, before
an unlocked door, that cage of cages,
tell us, you bird, you tragical machine—
is this *fertilisante douleur?* Pinned down
by love, for you the only natural action,
are you edged more keen
to prise the secrets of the vault? has Nature shown
her household books to you, daughter-in-law,
that her sons never saw?

7

"To have in this uncertain world some stay
which cannot be undermined, is
of the utmost consequence."
Thus wrote
a woman, partly brave and partly good,
who fought with what she partly understood.
Few men about her would or could do more,
hence she was labelled harpy, shrew and whore.

8

"You all die at fifteen," said Diderot,
and turn part legend, part convention
Still, eyes inaccurately dream
behind closed windows blankening with steam.
Deliciously, all that we might have been,
all that we were—fire, tears,

50. ***Dulce ridens, dulce loquens*:** "sweetly laughing, sweetly speaking." **53. When . . . sings:** the first line of a lyric by Thomas Campion (1567–1620). **63.** ***fertilisante douleur*:** fertilizing grief. **69–71. To have . . . consequence:** from Mary Wollstonecraft [1759–1797], *Thoughts on the Education of Daughters*, London, 1787 [Rich's note]. **76. Diderot:** from the *Lettres à Sophie Volland,* quoted by Simone de Beauvoir in *Le Deuxième Sexe* [*The Second Sex*], vol. II, pp. 123–4 [Rich's note]; Denis Diderot (1713–84), French philosopher.

wit, taste, martyred ambition—
stirs like the memory of refused adultery
the drained and flagging bosom of our middle years.

9

Not that it is done well, but
that it is done at all? Yes, think
of the odds! or shrug them off forever.
This luxury of the precocious child,
Time's precious chronic invalid,—
would we, darlings, resign it if we could?
Our blight has been our sinecure:
mere talent was enough for us—
glitter in fragments and rough drafts.

Sigh no more, ladies.
                    Time is male
and in his cups drinks to the fair.
Bemused by gallantry, we hear
our mediocrities over-praised,
indolence read as abnegation,
slattern thought styled intuition,
every lapse forgiven, our crime
only to cast too bold a shadow
or smash the mould straight off.

For that, solitary confinement,
tear gas, attrition shelling.
Few applicants for that honor.

10

                              Well,
she's long about her coming, who must be
more merciless to herself than history.
Her mind full to the wind, I see her plunge
breasted and glancing through the currents,
taking the light upon her
at least as beautiful as any boy
or helicopter,
              poised, still coming,
her fine blades making the air wince
but her cargo
no promise then:
delivered
palpable
ours.

1963

94. Sigh . . . ladies: the opening of a song in Shakespeare's *Much Ado about Nothing.* The second line of the song is "Men were deceivers ever." **106–19. Well . . . ours:** Rich states that she here translates *Le Deuxième Sexe,* Vol. II, p. 574.

A Marriage in the 'Sixties

As solid-seeming as antiquity,
you frown above
the *New York Sunday Times*
where Castro, like a walk-on out of *Carmen,*
mutters into a bearded henchman's ear.

They say the second's getting shorter—
I knew it in my bones—
and pieces of the universe are missing.
I feel the gears of this late afternoon
slip, cog by cog, even as I read.
"I'm old," we both complain,
half-laughing, oftener now.

Time serves you well. That face—
part Roman emperor, part Raimu—
nothing this side of Absence can undo.
Bliss, revulsion, your rare angers can
only carry through what's well begun.

When
I read your letters long ago
in that half-defunct
hotel in Magdalen Street
every word primed my nerves.
A geographical misery
composed of oceans, fogbound planes
and misdelivered cablegrams
lay round me, a Nova Zembla
only your live breath could unfreeze.
Today we stalk
in the raging desert of our thought
whose single drop of mercy is
each knows the other there.
Two strangers, thrust for life upon a rock,
may have at last the perfect hour of talk
that language aches for; still—
two minds, two messages.

Your brows knit into flourishes. Some piece
of mere time has you tangled there.
Some mote of history has flown into your eye.
Will nothing ever be the same,
even our quarrels take a different key,
our dreams exhume new metaphors?
The world breathes underneath our bed.
Don't look. We're at each other's mercy too.

A MARRIAGE IN THE 'SIXTIES. **4. Castro:** Fidel Castro (born 1926), dictator of Cuba. **14. Raimu:** Jules Mauraire Raimu (1883–1946), French actor. **26. Nova Zambla:** two islands off the coast of Russia in the Arctic Sea.

Dear fellow-particle, electric dust
I'm blown with—ancestor
to what euphoric cluster—
see how particularity dissolves
in all that hints of chaos. Let one finger
hover toward you from There
and see this furious grain
suspend its dance to hang
beside you like your twin.

1961

from Ghazals: Homage to Ghalib

7/14/68: ii

Did you think I was talking about my life?
I was trying to drive a tradition up against the wall.

The field they burned over is greener than all the rest.
You have to watch it, he said, the sparks can travel the roots.

Shot back into this earth's atmosphere
our children's children may photograph these stones.

In the red wash of the darkroom, I see myself clearly;
when the print is developed and handed about, the face is
nothing to me.

For us the work undoes itself over and over:
the grass grows back, the dust collects, the scar breaks open.

7/17/68

Armitage of scrapiron for the radiations of a moon.
Flower cast in metal, Picasso-woman, sister.

Two hesitant Luna moths regard each other
with the spots on their wings: fascinated.

To resign *yourself*—what an act of betrayal!
—to throw a runaway spirit back to the dogs.

When the ebb-tide pulls hard enough, we are all starfish.
The moon has her way with us, my companion in crime.

FROM GHAZALS: HOMAGE TO GHALIB. **Title:** This poem began to be written after I read Aijaz Ahmad's literal English versions of the work of the Urdu poet Mirza Ghalib, 1797–1869. While the structure and metrics used by Ghalib are much stricter than mine, I have adhered to his use of a minimum five couplets to a *ghazal,* each couplet being autonomous and independent of the others. The continuity and unity flow from the associations and images playing back and forth among the couplets in any single *ghazal* . . . I have left the *ghazals* dated as I wrote them [Rich's note].

At the Aquarium that day, between the white whale's loneliness
and the groupers' mass promiscuities, only ourselves.

7/26/68: i

Last night you wrote on the wall: Revolution is poetry.
Today you needn't write; the wall has tumbled down.

We were taught to respect the appearance behind the reality.
Our senses were out on parole, under surveillance.

A pair of eyes imprisoned for years inside my skull
is burning its way outward, the headaches are terrible.

I'm walking through a rubble of broken sculpture, stumbling
here on the spine of a friend, there on the hand of a brother.

All those joinings! and yet we fought so hard to be unique.
Neither alone, nor in anyone's arms, will we end up sleeping.

TED HUGHES

(born 1930)

Hughes grew up in Yorkshire, England, the son of a carpenter. From childhood he was fascinated by and identified with animals, which have provided his most expressive poetic symbols. After two years in the National Service, Hughes went to Pembroke College, Cambridge, and after graduating in 1954, worked at odd jobs in Cambridge and London. In 1956 he met the American poet, Sylvia Plath, who was at Cambridge on a Fulbright scholarship, and the two were married. But strains developed between them, and they were living apart when Plath committed suicide in 1963. Hughes married again in 1970. He has composed radio plays and short stories as well as verse, and has produced several notable volumes in collaboration with the American artist Leonard Baskin, the poems and drawings mutually illustrating each other.

The animals in Hughes's poems seem alien from the human, yet may ominously image the essence of man's nature and situation. "Hawk Roosting," a hawk's monologue, expresses murderous instinct and manic egoism. "Crow's First Lesson" and "That Moment" are from a famous volume entitled *Crow* (1970) in which the poems resemble primitive myths. Several of the poems in *Crow* explain how a feature of existence originated. "Crow's First Lesson" tells how sex came about through God's ill-advised effort to teach Crow to say "Love," a word which Crow did not have within him. In several other poems in the sequence, God is similarly well-meaning but ineffective, and powers other than God have contributed to create a world which God himself deplores. The world depicted in *Crow* is one of harsh natural necessities and instincts. Physical pain and suffering are common in Crow's life, and he also experiences moments of guilt. So far as we see in him an image of human nature, we may find the recognition appalling. He embodies such qualities as egoism, suspicious alertness, aggressive violence, limited imagination, insensitivity, and low-minded, scavenging practicality. But however unlovable they may be, these are qualities that enable life to persist—and, as in "That Moment," Crow is a survivor. Although he is stunned, scorched, chopped to pieces, and hung up by one claw, he is never wholly killed. For this reason we may even harbor a certain affection for him. There is reassurance in his scrawny, sinewy body, his ability to digest anything, his tenacity and indestructibility.

Hawk Roosting

I sit in the top of the wood, my eyes closed.
Inaction, no falsifying dream
Between my hooked head and hooked feet:
Or in sleep rehearse perfect kills and eat.

The convenience of the high trees!
The air's buoyancy and the sun's ray
Are of advantage to me;
And the earth's face upward for my inspection.

My feet are locked upon the rough bark.
It took the whole of Creation
To produce my foot, my each feather:
Now I hold Creation in my foot

Or fly up, and revolve it all slowly—
I kill where I please because it is all mine.
There is no sophistry in my body:
My manners are tearing off heads—

The allotment of death.
For the one path of my flight is direct
Through the bones of the living.
No arguments assert my right:

The sun is behind me.
Nothing has changed since I began.
My eye has permitted no change.
I am going to keep things like this.

1957

Wodwo

What am I? Nosing here, turning leaves over
Following a faint stain on the air to the river's edge
I enter water. What am I to split
The glassy grain of water looking upward I see the bed
Of the river above me upside down very clear
What am I doing here in mid-air? Why do I find
this frog so interesting as I inspect its most secret
interior and make it my own? Do these weeds
know me and name me to each other have they
seen me before, do I fit in their world? I seem
separate from the ground and not rooted but dropped
out of nothing casually I've no threads
fastening me to anything I can go anywhere
I seem to have been given the freedom
of this place what am I then? And picking
bits of bark off this rotten stump gives me
no pleasure and it's no use so why do I do it
me and doing that have coincided very queerly
But what shall I be called am I the first
have I an owner what shape am I what
shape am I am I huge if I go
to the end on this way past these trees and past these trees
till I get tired that's touching one wall of me
for the moment if I sit still how everything
stops to watch me I suppose I am the exact centre
but there's all this what is it roots
roots roots roots and here's the water
again very queer but I'll go on looking

1967

Crow's First Lesson

God tried to teach Crow how to talk.
"Love," said God. "Say, Love."
Crow gaped, and the white shark crashed into the sea
And went rolling downwards, discovering its own depth.

"No, no," said God, "Say Love. Now try it. LOVE."
Crow gaped, and a bluefly, a tsetse, a mosquito
Zoomed out and down
To their sundry flesh-pots.

WODWO. **Title:** Middle English for "wild man of the woods" or "wood demon."

"A final try," said God. "Now, LOVE."
Crow convulsed, gaped, retched and
Man's bodiless prodigious head
Bulbed out onto the earth, with swivelling eyes,
Jabbering protest—

And Crow retched again, before God could stop him.
And woman's vulva dropped over man's neck and tightened.
The two struggled together on the grass.
God struggled to part them, cursed, wept—

Crow flew guiltily off.

1970

That Moment

When the pistol muzzle oozing blue vapour
Was lifted away
Like a cigarette lifted from an ashtray

And the only face left in the world
Lay broken
Between hands that relaxed, being too late

And the trees closed forever
And the streets closed forever

And the body lay on the gravel
Of the abandoned world
Among abandoned utilities
Exposed to infinity forever

Crow had to start searching for something to eat.

1970

Widdop

Where there was nothing
Somebody put a frightened lake.

Where there was nothing
Stony shoulders
Broadened to support it.

A wind from between the stars
Swam down to sniff at the trembling.

WIDDOP. **Title:** a reservoir in the Calder Valley in West Yorkshire.

Trees, holding hands, eyes closed,
Acted at world.

Some heath-grass crept close, in fear.

Nothing else
Except when a gull blows through

A rip in the fabric

Out of nothingness into nothingness

1979

Gary Snyder

(born 1930)

Snyder grew up in the Northwest on a dairy farm surrounded by woods. "From a very early age," he says, "I found myself standing in an undefinable awe before the natural world," feeling "gratitude, wonder, and a sense of protection." He attended Reed College and then, planning to become an anthropologist, went as a graduate student for one semester to Indiana University. At this point, however, his interest in the cultures and religions of the Far East became primary, and he moved to the University of California at Berkeley in order to learn oriental languages. Needing money, he worked occasionally in the mountains as a fire lookout or as a member of a crew clearing trails; many of his poems reflect experiences in these jobs and in backpacking. For twelve years, from 1956 to 1968, he spent most of his time in Japan, at first as a novice in a Zen monastery and later as a member of a small island community. When he returned to the United States, he moved with his Japanese wife to a home in the California mountains. Wishing to live in relative independence from modern civilization, he cut his own wood for heating, grew vegetables, and hunted. For many readers his way of life, knowledge of Zen Buddhism, and ecological philosophy gave his poetry a special authority, as that of a spiritual teacher.

"Trail Crew Camp . . ." illustrates the type of lyric for which Snyder is best known. The poem describes a day spent clearing trails in the Yosemite National Park. The day, as the poem presents it, has a natural, archetypal rhythm of effort and culmination—the view for hundreds of miles—followed by rest at sundown. The poem is influenced by Zen Buddhism, as can be seen, for example, in the way it concentrates wholly on the immediate experience, without expatiating in thought about it or relating it to anything else. As Snyder once explained his Zen ideal, if you are sweeping the floor and thinking of Hegel, your mind is not focussed with your body. But if you are sweeping the floor and thinking of sweeping the floor, you are unified in the moment, and "sweeping the floor becomes, then, the most important thing in the world. Which it is." The poem also reflects Snyder's idealization of a timeless, nontechnological lifestyle recalling that of primitive humanity. The small group of the trail crew does physical work that men and women have always done, rides horses, lives in tents, and has only a few simple belongings.

Mid-August at Sourdough Mountain Lookout

Down valley a smoke haze
Three days heat, after five days rain
Pitch glows on the fir-cones
Across rocks and meadows
Swarms of new flies.

I cannot remember things I once read
A few friends, but they are in cities.
Drinking cold snow-water from a tin cup
Looking down for miles
Through high still air.

1959

Trail Crew Camp at Bear Valley, 9,000 Feet. Northern Sierra—White Bone and Threads of Snowmelt River

Cut branches back for a day—
trail a thin line through willow
            up buckbrush meadows,
            creekbed for twenty yards
   winding in boulders
            zigzags the hill
into timber, white pine.

gooseberry bush on the turns.
hooves clang on the riprap

TRAIL CREW CAMP AT BEAR VALLEY. **9. riprap:** loose stone.

dust, brush, branches.
a stone
cairn at the pass—
strippt mountains hundreds of miles.

sundown went back
the clean switchbacks to camp.
bell on the gelding,
stew in the cook tent,
black coffee in a big tin can.

1959

Meeting the Mountains

He crawls to the edge of the foaming creek
He backs up the slab ledge
He puts a finger in the water
He turns to a trapped pool
Puts both hands in the water
Puts one foot in the pool
Drops pebbles in the pool
He slaps the water surface with both hands
He cries out, rises up and stands
Facing toward the torrent and the mountain
Raises up both hands and shouts three times!

1970

Derek Walcott

(born 1930)

Walcott was born on the Caribbean island of St. Lucia, attended the University of the West Indies in Jamaica, and then moved to Trinidad. He writes plays and literary criticism as well as poetry, and has taught frequently in colleges in the United States. Despite (or perhaps because of) his island background, he is a poet in a modern, eclectic, international style. "Europa," for example, recalls Yeats's "Leda and the Swan" in its sexual-mythical subject matter and in the directness with which it expresses this. But Walcott's is very different from the rapt

12. cairn: pile of stones marking a trail.

attitude of Yeats—and the reason lies not only in his personal temperament but also in the general development of English and American poetry since the 1950s. After the bald plain-speaking of Philip Larkin (as in "you yield to human horniness," in line 7 of Walcott's poem), and Robert Lowell's powerful rendering of the sickness of the psyche in his "confessional" poetry, no poet could express himself on such a subject in the way that Yeats did.

Codicil

Schizophrenic, wrenched by two styles,
one a hack's hired prose, I earn
my exile. I trudge this sickle, moonlit beach for miles,

tan, burn
to slough off
this love of ocean that's self-love.

To change your language you must change your life.

I cannot right old wrongs.
Waves tire of horizon and return.
Gulls screech with rusty tongues

Above the beached, rotting pirogues,
they were a venomous beaked cloud at Charlotteville.

Once I thought love of country was enough,
now, even I chose, there's no room at the trough.

I watch the best minds root like dogs
for scraps of favour.
I am nearing middle-

age, burnt skin
peels from my hand like paper, onion-thin,
like Peer Gynt's riddle.

At heart there's nothing, not the dread
of death. I know too many dead.
They're all familiar, all in character,

even how they died. On fire,
the flesh no longer fears that furnace mouth
of earth,

CODICIL. **11. pirogues:** canoes made of hollowed logs. **12. Charlotteville:** town on the island of Tobago, near Trinidad, in the West Indies. **20. Peer Gynt's riddle:** In Henrik Ibsen's *Peer Gynt* (1867), peeling an onion, one layer after another, and finding no core, Peer says life is like that: all layers and no real core.

that kiln or ashpit of the sun,
nor this clouding, unclouding sickle moon
whitening this beach again like a blank page.

All its indifference is a different rage.

1965

Europa

The full moon is so fierce that I can count the
coconuts' cross-hatched shade on bungalows,
their white walls raging with insomnia.
The stars leak drop by drop on the tin plates
of the sea almonds, and the jeering clouds
are luminously rumpled as the sheets.
The surf, insatiably promiscuous,
groans through the walls; I feel my mind
whiten to moonlight, altering that form
which daylight unambiguously designed,
from a tree to a girl's body bent in foam;
then, treading close, the black hump of a hill,
its nostrils softly snorting, nearing the
naked girl splashing her breasts with silver.
Both would have kept their proper distance still,
if the chaste moon hadn't swiftly drawn the drapes
of a dark cloud, coupling their shapes.

She teases with those flashes, yes, but once
you yield to human horniness, you see
through all that moonshine what they really were,
those gods as seed-bulls, gods as rutting swans—
an overheated farmhands' literature.
Who ever saw her pale arms hook his horns,
her thighs clamped tight in their deep-plunging ride,
watched, in the hiss of the exhausted foam,
her white flesh constellate to phosphorous
as in salt darkness beast and woman come?
Nothing is there, just as it always was,
but the foam's wedge to the horizon-light,
then, wire-thin, the studded armature,
like drops still quivering on his matted hide,
the hooves and horn-points anagrammed in stars.

1981

EUROPA. **Title:** In Greek myth, Europa was a maiden abducted by Zeus, who appeared in the form of a bull.

GEOFFREY HILL

(born 1932)

Born in Worcestershire, England, Hill attended Keble College, Oxford, and now teaches English Literature. He has published critical essays as well as poetry. His poems dwell on the evil of man's nature with ruthless awareness and cold intensity. Because he so deeply suspects the human heart, Hill inevitably has qualms of conscience about writing poetry at all. The motives for writing may be morally condemnable—vanity, for example—and even if this were not the case, to express evil and suffering artistically may belie their reality. Yet the same mistrust of human nature leads him to write with scrupulous deliberation and in rigorously controlled forms. He would have little confidence in whatever might come forth spontaneously. Because of his alertness to the twists and intertwining of motives and emotions, and his mistrust of their moral character, his poetry is extremely ambivalent and ironical.

"Funeral Music" is a sequence of sonnets in which the subjects and speakers are drawn from the medieval Wars of the Roses—the English civil war between the Yorkists and Lancastrians. "In this sequence," Hill said, "I was attempting a florid grim music broken by grunts and shrieks . . . [an] ornate and heartless music punctuated by mutterings, blasphemies and cries for help." But the style of the sonnets is less dramatic than this might imply, because although Hill was modifying his art in them, they are still highly reflective and formal when compared with most other contemporary poetry. They present and meditate upon violence and suffering, upon the motives by which people act, and upon the meaning and possibility of religious faith. Hill is not a Christian believer, but his vision of things has affinities with Christian interpretations of man's fallen nature, and Hill can therefore express himself within this traditional vocabulary and imagery.

Ovid in the Third Reich

non peccat, quaecumque potest peccasse negare,
solaque famosam culpa professa facit.
(Amores, III, xiv)

I love my work and my children. God
Is distant, difficult. Things happen.
Too near the ancient troughs of blood
Innocence is no earthly weapon.

I have learned one thing: not to look down
So much upon the damned. They, in their sphere,
Harmonize strangely with the divine
Love. I, in mine, celebrate the love-choir.

1968

September Song

Born 19·6·32—Deported 24·9·42

Undesirable you may have been, untouchable
you were not. Not forgotten
or passed over at the proper time.

As estimated, you died. Things marched,
sufficient, to that end.
Just so much Zyklon and leather, patented
terror, so many routine cries.

(I have made
and elegy for myself it
is true)

OVID IN THE THIRD REICH. **Title:** The Roman poet Ovid (43 B.C.–17 A.D.) was exiled by Emperor Augustus because, it was said, of his poems about love. The "Third Reich" (German for "kingdom") was the term Hitler applied to his rule in Germany from 1933 to 1945. **Epigraph:** "Any woman has not sinned who denies having sinned, and only a confession of guilt makes her guilty." ***Amores*** is a long poem by Ovid about famous loves.
SEPTEMBER SONG. **Title:** In the poem, which is about the killing of the Jews by gas in German concentration camps, the dates are meant to apply to the birth and death dates ("deported" used ironically for death) of a ten-year-old Jewish child. **6. Zyklon:** Hydrocyanic acid (Zycklon B) used in the Nazi gas chambers.

September fattens on vines. Roses
flake from the wall. The smoke
of harmless fires drifts to my eyes.

This is plenty. This is more than enough.

1968

Funeral Music

William de la Pole, Duke of Suffolk: beheaded 1450
John Tiptoft, Earl of Worcester: beheaded 1470
Anthony Woodville, Earl Rivers: beheaded 1483

1

Processionals in the exemplary cave,
Benediction of shadows. Pomfret. London.
The voice fragrant with mannered humility,
With an equable contempt for this World,
"In honorem Trinitatis." Crash. The head
Struck down into a meaty conduit of blood.
So these dispose themselves to receive each
Pentecostal blow from axe or seraph,
Spattering block-straw with mortal residue.
Psalteries whine through the empyrean. Fire
Flares in the pit, ghosting upon stone
Creatures of such rampant state, vacuous
Ceremony of possession, restless
Habitation, no man's dwelling-place.

2

For whom do we scrape our tribute of pain—
For none but the ritual king? We meditate
A rueful mystery; we are dying
To satisfy fat Caritas, those

FUNERAL MUSIC. **Dedication:** Pole (1396–1450), Tiptoft (*c.*1427–1470), and Woodville (*c.*1442–1483), were prominent in the English Wars of the Roses (1453–1497), which were fought for possession of the monarchy by the rival parties of Lancastrians and Yorkists. All three were poets and scholars as well as political and military leaders, and Woodville was also known for his piety. Tiptoft was infamous for the cruelty of his sentences as a judge. SONNET 1. **2. Pomfret:** Pontefract, in Yorkshire, where Woodville was executed. **London:** where Tiptoft was executed. **5. "In honorem Trinitatis":** At his execution Tiptoft conducted himself with great dignity, and asked the headsman to kill him with three blows "in honor of the Trinity." **8. Pentecostal:** pertaining to Pentecost. In the Christian church calendar the day of Pentecost commemorates the descent in tongues of flame of the Holy Spirit on the disciples of Jesus on the fiftieth day after Easter. **10. Psalteries:** the Book of Psalms used in religious services. SONNET 2. **4. Caritas:** the Christian virtue of charity or love.

Wiped jaws of stone. (Suppose all reconciled
By silent music; imagine the future
Flashed back at us, like steel against sun,
Ultimate recompense.) Recall the cold
Of Towton on Palm Sunday before dawn,
Wakefield, Tewkesbury: fastidious trumpets
Shrilling into the ruck; some trampled
Acres, parched, sodden or blanched by sleet,
Stuck with strange-postured dead. Recall the wind's
Flurrying, darkness over the human mire.

3

They bespoke doomsday and they meant it by
God, their curved metal rimming the low ridge.
But few appearances are like this. Once
Every five hundred years a comet's
Over-riding stillness might reveal men
In such array, livid and featureless,
With England crouched beastwise beneath it all.
"Oh, that old northern business . . . " A field
After battle utters its own sound
Which is like nothing on earth, but is earth.
Blindly the questing snail, vulnerable
Mole emerge, blindly we lie down, blindly
Among carnage the most delicate souls
Tup in their marriage-blood, gasping "Jesus."

4

Let mind be more precious than soul; it will not
Endure. Soul grasps its price, begs its own peace,
Settles with tears and sweat, is possibly
Indestructible. That I can believe.
Though I would scorn the mere instinct of faith,
Expediency of assent, if I dared,
What I dare not is a waste history
Or void rule. Averroes, old heathen,
If only you had been right, if Intellect
Itself were absolute law, sufficient grace,
Our lives could be a myth of captivity
Which we might enter: an unpeopled region
Of ever new-fallen snow, a palace blazing
With perpetual silence as with torches.

9. Towton: the battle of Towton, fought in a snow storm on Palm Sunday, 1461, during the Wars of the Roses. **10. Wakefield, Tewkesbury:** Battles in the Wars of the Roses: Wakefield (1460) was a Lancastrian victory; Tewkesbury (1471), a Yorkist victory. SONNET 3. **8. "Oh . . . business":** The battle of Towton was fought in the north of England. **14. Tup:** come into heat and copulate. SONNET 4. **8. Averroes:** Mohammedan philosopher (1126–1198), who taught that intellect is abstract and immaterial, and knows eternal ideas.

5

As with torches we go, at wild Christmas,
When we revel in our atonement
Through thirty feasts of unction and slaughter,
What is that but the soul's winter sleep?
So many things rest under consummate
Justice as though trumpets purified law,
Spikenard were the real essence of remorse.
The sky gathers up darkness. When we chant
"Ora, ora pro nobis" it is not
Seraphs who descend to pity but ourselves.
Those righteously-accused those vengeful
Racked on articulate looms indulge us
With lingering shows of pain, a flagrant
Tenderness of the damned for their own flesh:

6

My little son, when you could command marvels
Without mercy, outstare the wearisome
Dragon of sleep, I rejoiced above all—
A stranger well-received in your kingdom.
On those pristine fields I saw humankind
As it was named by the Father; fabulous
Beasts rearing in stillness to be blessed.
The world's real cries reached there, turbulence
From remote storms, rumour of solitudes,
A composed mystery. And so it ends.
Some parch for what they were; others are made
Blind to all but one vision, their necessity
To be reconciled. I believe in my
Abandonment, since it is what I have.

7

"Prowess, vanity, mutual regard,
It seemed I stared at them, they at me.
That was the gorgon's true and mortal gaze:
Averted conscience turned against itself."
A hawk and a hawk-shadow. "At noon,
As the armies met, each mirrored the other;
Neither was outshone. So they flashed and vanished
And all that survived them was the stark ground
Of this pain. I made no sound, but once
I stiffened as though a remote cry
Had heralded my name. It was nothing . . . "
Reddish ice tinged the reeds; dislodged, a few
Feathers drifted across; carrion birds
Strutted upon the armour of the dead.

SONNET 5. **7. Spikenard:** aromatic substance used in perfumes and ointments. **9. "Ora . . . nobis":** "pray, pray for us," a traditional Christian prayer.

8

Not as we are but as we must appear,
Contractual ghosts of pity; not as we
Desire life but as they would have us live,
Set apart in timeless colloquy:
So it is required; so we bear witness,
Despite ourselves, to what is beyond us,
Each distant sphere of harmony forever
Poised, unanswerable. If it is without
Consequence when we vaunt and suffer, or
If it is not, all echoes are the same
In such eternity. Then tell me, love,
How that should comfort us—or anyone
Dragged half-unnerved out of this worldly place,
Crying to the end "I have not finished."

1968

SYLVIA PLATH

(1932–1963)

After graduating from Smith College, Plath received a Fulbright scholarship to study in Cambridge, England, where she met and married Ted Hughes. They lived for two years in the United States, then returned to England, where they settled in a rural village in Devon, and had two children. In the final three years of her life Plath created a poetry of immense force and somewhat appalling fascination, for she explored and laid bare deep psychological conflicts (for example, her feelings about her father, as in "Daddy") that were leading her toward suicide. Reading the poems of her last months, one can watch her impulse toward death growing. Yet their deeply troubling content is not what makes these poems powerful, but rather the union of this with brilliantly imaginative phrasing and artistic intelligence.

In terms of literary history Plath united two traditions. On the one hand, she derived from the poetry of the 1940s and the 1950s that had been written under the influence of the so-called New Criticism. This poetry was dense in phrasing and intricately complex in its implications, usually ironical and impersonal, and metrically traditional or formal. On the other hand, the "confessional" poetry of the 1950s and 1960s usually created the illusion of a more rapid and spontaneous way of speaking, and of course it was personal and psychoanalytic in its subject matter. In

"The Colossus," Plath presented and explored a central, "objective" symbol—the colossus—as a poem of the New Critical type might have done. But the phrasing and syntax have a headlong force and vigor that suggests spontaneity, and the symbol represents her father. Although the development of psychoanalysis has made most people alert to recognize emotions of the type Plath expresses regarding her father, few, even now, would be willing to admit to harboring them. The reference to the Oresteia in "The Colossus" suggests, for example, an impulse to murder. The other poems printed here were written later than "The Colossus" and not published until after Plath's death. Although it is irrelevant to "Daddy" as a work of art, it may be of some interest for revealing Plath's state of mind to remark that Otto Plath, her father, immigrated to the United States from Poland and taught at Boston University. He seems to have been a person of normally decent life and feeling. If the image of him in Plath's poem has any objective basis in reality, no one has revealed it.

The Colossus

I shall never get you put together entirely.
Pieced, glued, and properly jointed.
Mule-bray, pig-grunt and bawdy cackles
Proceed from your great lips.
It's worse than a barnyard.

Perhaps you consider yourself an oracle,
Mouthpiece of the dead, or of some god or other.
Thirty years now I have labored
To dredge the silt from your throat.
I am none the wiser.

Scaling little ladders with gluepots and pails of lysol
I crawl like an ant in mourning
Over the weedy acres of your brow
To mend the immense skull plates and clear
The bald, white tumuli of your eyes.

A blue sky out of the Oresteia
Arches above us. O father, all by yourself
You are pithy and historical as the Roman Forum.
I open my lunch on a hill of black cypress.
Your fluted bones and acanthine hair are littered

COLOSSUS. **16. Oresteia:** A trilogy of plays by the Greek dramatist Aeschylus (525–456 B.C.), concerned with the revenge by Electra and Orestes of the murder of their father, Agamemnon, by their mother, Clytemnestra.

In their old anarchy to the horizon-line.
It would take more than a lightning-stroke
To create such a ruin.
Nights, I squat in the cornucopia
Of your left ear, out of the wind,

Counting the red stars and those of plum-color.
The sun rises under the pillar of your tongue.
My hours are married to shadow.
No longer do I listen for the scrape of a keel
On the blank stones of the landing.

1960

Lady Lazarus

I have done it again.
One year in every ten
I manage it—

A sort of walking miracle, my skin
Bright as a Nazi lampshade,
My right foot

A paperweight,
My face a featureless, fine
Jew linen.

Peel off the napkin
O my enemy.
Do I terrify?—

The nose, the eye pits, the full set of teeth?
The sour breath
Will vanish in a day.

Soon, soon the flesh
The grave cave ate will be
At home on me

And I a smiling woman.
I am only thirty.
And like the cat I have nine times to die.

This is Number Three.
What a trash
To annihilate each decade.

LADY LAZARUS. **Title:** Lazarus was raised from the dead by Christ (John 11:44). **5. Nazi lampshade:** From the skins of some of the Jews they killed, the more brutal officials of Nazi concentration camps made lampshades.

What a million filaments.
The peanut-crunching crowd
Shoves in to see

Them unwrap me hand and foot—
The big strip tease.
Gentleman, ladies,

These are my hands,
My knees.
I may be skin and bone,

Nevertheless, I am the same, identical woman.
The first time it happened I was ten.
It was an accident.

The second time I meant
To last it out and not come back at all.
I rocked shut

As a seashell.
They had to call and call
And pick the worms off me like sticky pearls.

Dying
Is an art, like everything else.
I do it exceptionally well.

I do it so it feels like hell.
I do it so it feels real.
I guess you could say I've a call.

It's easy enough to do it in a cell.
It's easy enough to do it and stay put.
It's the theatrical

Comeback in broad day
To the same place, the same face, the same brute
Amused shout:

"A miracle!"
That knocks me out.
There is a charge

For the eyeing of my scars, there is a charge
For the hearing of my heart—
It really goes.

And there is a charge, very large charge,
For a word or a touch
Or a bit of blood

Or a piece of my hair or my clothes.
So, so, Herr Doktor.
So, Herr Enemy.

I am your opus,
I am your valuable,
The pure gold baby

That melts to a shriek.
I turn and burn.
Do not think I underestimate your great concern.

Ash, ash—
You poke and stir.
Flesh, bone, there is nothing there—

A cake of soap,
A wedding ring,
A gold filling.

Herr God, Herr Lucifer,
Beware
Beware.

Out of the ash
I rise with my red hair
And I eat men like air.

1965

Elm

For Ruth Fainlight

I know the bottom, she says. I know it with my great tap root:
It is what you fear.
I do not fear it: I have been there.

Is it the sea you hear in me,
Its dissatisfactions?
Or the voice of nothing, that was your madness?

Love is a shadow.
How you lie and cry after it.
Listen: these are its hooves: it has gone off, like a horse.

All night I shall gallop thus, impetuously,
Till your head is a stone, your pillow a little turf,
Echoing, echoing

Or shall I bring you the sound of poisons?
This is rain now, this big hush.
And this is the fruit of it: tin-white, like arsenic.

ELM. **Dedication:** Fainlight, an American poet, lived in England at the same time as Plath.

I have suffered the atrocity of sunsets.
Scorched to the root
My red filaments burn and stand, a hand of wires.

Now I break up in pieces that fly about like clubs.
A wind of such violence
Will tolerate no bystanding: I must shriek.

The moon, also, is merciless: she would drag me
Cruelly, being barren.
Her radiance scathes me. Or perhaps I have caught her.

I let her go. I let her go
Diminished and flat, as after radical surgery.
How your bad dreams possess and endow me.

I am inhabited by a cry.
Nightly it flaps out
Looking, with its hooks, for something to love.

I am terrified by this dark thing
That sleeps in me;
All day I feel its soft, feathery turnings, its malignity.

Clouds pass and disperse.
Are those the faces of love, those pale irretrievables?
Is it for such I agitate my heart?

I am incapable of more knowledge.
What is this, this face
So murderous in its strangle of branches?—

Its snaky acids kiss.
It petrifies the will. These are the isolate, slow faults
That kill, that kill, that kill.

1965

Daddy

You do not do, you do not do
Any more, black shoe
In which I have lived like a foot
For thirty years, poor and white,
Barely daring to breathe or Achoo.

Daddy, I have had to kill you.
You died before I had time—
Marble-heavy, a bag full of God,
Ghastly statue with one gray toe
Big as a Frisco seal

And a head in the freakish Atlantic
Where it pours bean green over blue
In the waters off beautiful Nauset.
I used to pray to recover you.
Ach, du.

In the German tongue, in the Polish town
Scraped flat by the roller
Of wars, wars, wars.
But the name of the town is common.
My Polack friend

Says there are a dozen or two.
So I never could tell where you
Put your foot, your root,
I never could talk to you.
The tongue stuck in my jaw.

It stuck in a barb wire snare.
Ich, ich, ich, ich,
I could hardly speak.
I thought every German was you.
And the language obscene

An engine, an engine
Chuffing me off like a Jew.
A Jew to Dachau, Auschwitz, Belsen.
I began to talk like a Jew.
I think I may well be a Jew.

The snows of the Tyrol, the clear beer of Vienna
Are not very pure or true.
With my gypsy ancestress and my weird luck
And my Taroc pack and my Taroc pack
I may be a bit of a Jew.

I have always been scared of *you,*
With your Luftwaffe, your gobbledygoo.
And your neat moustache
And your Aryan eye, bright blue.
Panzer-man, panzer-man, O You—

Bit my pretty red heart in two.
I was ten when they buried you.
At twenty I tried to die
And get back, back, back to you.
I thought even the bones would do.

DADDY. **15. Ach, du:** "Ah, you" (German). **16. Polish town:** Grabow, birthplace of Sylvia Plath's father, Otto. **27. Ich:** German for "I." **42. Luftwaffe:** "Air force" in German.

But they pulled me out of the sack,
And they stuck me together with glue,
And then I knew what to do.
I made a model of you,
A man in black with a Meinkampf look

And a love of the rack and the screw.
And I said I do, I do.
So daddy, I'm finally through.
The black telephone's off at the root,
The voices just can't worm through.

If I've killed one man, I've killed two—
The vampire who said he was you
And drank my blood for a year,
Seven years, if you want to know.
Daddy, you can lie back now.

There's a stake in your fat black heart
And the villagers never liked you.
They are dancing and stamping on you.
They always *knew* it was you.
Daddy, daddy, you bastard, I'm through.

1965

AMIRI BARAKA

(born 1934)

Baraka published for several years as LeRoi Jones (his original name) before becoming a Muslim and changing his name. He went to Howard University, served in the U.S. Air Force, attended Columbia University as a graduate student, and edited *Yugen,* a magazine specializing in poetry. In New York City he was associated with Beat writers, with whom he shared a radical protest against American society—but he was especially a spokesman for feelings of black alienation. His dramas and poems on themes of racial relations were expressed in plots and rhetoric of violence. He was a leader in establishing several artistic and social institutions within the black community around New York City. Despite its title, "Notes for a Speech" is an inward and personal poem. "A Poem for Black Hearts" is typical of Baraka's public voice.

55. Meinkampf: *My Battle,* Hitler's 1924 autobiography.

With its direct, colloquial diction, uncomplicated emotion, and effective repetitions, it could easily move a crowd when recited aloud. One should note Baraka's management of line length in this poem. The lines get gradually longer, conveying a growing emotion, until the last line breaks off, as though words were suddenly to be replaced by action.

Notes for a Speech

African blues
does not know me. Their steps, in sands
of their own
land. A country
in black & white, newspapers
blown down pavements
of the world. Does
not feel
what I am.
Strength
in the dream, an oblique
suckling of nerve, the wind
throws up sand, eyes
are something locked in
hate, of hate, of hate, to
walk abroad, they conduct
their deaths apart
from my own. Those
heads, I call
my "people."
(And who are they. People. To concern
myself, ugly man. Who
you, to concern
the white flat stomachs
of maidens, inside houses
dying. Black. Peeled moon
light on my fingers
move under
her clothes. Where
is her husband. Black
words throw up sand
to eyes, fingers of
their private dead. Whose
soul, eyes, in sand. My color
is not theirs. Lighter, white man
talk. They shy away. My own
dead souls, my, so called

people. Africa
is a foreign place. You are
as any other sad man here
american.

1961

A Poem for Black Hearts

For Malcolm's eyes, when they broke
the face of some dumb white man, For
Malcolm's hands raised to bless us
all black and strong in his image
of ourselves, For Malcolm's words
fire darts, the victor's tireless
thrusts, words hung above the world
change as it may, he said it, and
for this he was killed, for saying,
and feeling, and being/change, all
collected hot in his heart, For Malcolm's
heart, raising us above our filthy cities,
for his stride, and his beat, and his address
to the gray monsters of the world, For Malcolm's
pleas for your dignity, black men, for your life,
black man, for the filling of your minds
with righteousness, For all of him dead and
gone and vanished from us, and all of him which
clings to our speech black god of our time.
For all of him, and all of yourself, look up,
black man, quit stuttering and shuffling, look up,
black man, quit whining and stooping, for all of him,
For Great Malcolm a prince of the earth, let nothing in us rest
until we avenge ourselves for his death, stupid animals
that killed him, let us never breathe a pure breath if
we fail and white men call us faggots till the end of
the earth.

1967

A POEM FOR BLACK HEARTS. **1. Malcolm:** Malcolm X (1925–1965), activist black leader who was assassinated.

Margaret Atwood

(born 1939)

A Canadian novelist and poet, Atwood is read with enthusiasm by a growing number of persons in her own country and in the United States. Her poems render things observed or moments of experience in exact, simple language, bringing them vividly before the mind. And they reflect with sharp intelligence on what they render, although the reflection is expressed glancingly and is often only implied. In her earlier poems she—or the "I" speaking the poems—was especially appealing and remarkable for the direct, clear, strong sense of reality that inclined her to look beneath the surface of what she encountered, to question and puncture. She was not usually a satiric poet, but maintained an undertone of tartness and occasionally bitterness.

Both formally and in content her later poems, which are represented here, are more ambitious; they are also more philosophical in theme and kindlier or tenderer in emotion. "There is Only One of Everything" activates consideration of the relation of words to existence and also of the unique character of each particular, fleeting moment. The poem manages the difficult literary feat of conveying a moment of happiness without seeming sentimental. "Book of Ancestors" uses in an original way the Modernist technique of juxtaposing scenes of the present with others in the historical past. The doubts implied in this poem as to whether the past can be known and whether it has any relevance to the present are widespread in contemporary poetry. The poem's juxtaposition of a scene of Amerindian ritual sacrifice and of twentieth-century lovers is potentially explosive, because the cruelty of the "ancestral" scene contrasts starkly with the trust and tenderness of the modern one, yet the display of both scenes in the same poem also suggests that there is a resemblance and continuity between them. The art of the poem lies very largely in managing the complex emotional suggestions thus activated.

There is Only One of Everything

Not a tree but the tree
we saw, it will never exist, split by the wind
                    and bending down
like that again. What will push out of the earth

later, making it summer, will not be
grass, leaves, repetition, there will
have to be other words. When my

eyes close language vanishes. The cat
with the divided face, half black half orange
nests in my scruffy fur coat, I drink tea,

fingers curved around the cup, impossible
to duplicate these flavours. The table
and freak plates glow softly, consuming themselves,

I look out at you and you occur
in this winter kitchen, random as trees or sentences,
entering me, fading like them, in time you will disappear

but the way you dance by yourself
on the tile floor to a worn song, flat and mournful,
so delighted, spoon waved in one hand, wisps of
roughened hair

sticking up from your head, it's your surprised
body, pleasure I like. I can even say it,
though only once and it won't

last: I want this. I want
this.

1974

Book of Ancestors

i

Book of Ancestors: these brutal, with curled
beards and bulls' heads · these flattened,
slender with ritual · these contorted
by ecstacy or pain · these bearing
knife, leaf, snake

and these, closer to us,
copper hawkman arched on the squat rock
pyramid, the plumed and beak-
nosed priests pressing his arms and feet
down, heart slashed from his opened
flesh, lifted to where
the sun, red and dilated
with his blood, glows in the still hungry sky

Whether he thinks this is
an act of will:

BOOK OF ANCESTORS. **7–13. hawkman . . . sky:** The lines describe ritual human sacrifice among the Aztec Indians of Mexico in the sixteenth century.

the life set free
by him alone, offered, ribs expanding
by themselves, bone petals,
the heart released and flickering in the
taloned hand, handful of liquid
fire joined to that other fire
an instant before the sacrificed eyes
burst like feathered stars in the darkness

of the painted border.

ii

So much for the gods and their
static demands · our demands, former
demands, death patterns
obscure as fragments of an
archeology, these frescoes
on a crumbling temple
wall we look at now and can scarcely
piece together

History
is over, we take place
in a season, an undivided
space, no necessities

hold us closed, distort
us. I lean behind you, mouth touching
your spine, my arms around
you, palm above the heart,
your blood insistent under
my hand, quick and mortal

iii

Midwinter, the window
is luminous with blown snow, the fire
burns inside its bars

On the floor your body curves
like that: the ancient pose, neck slackened, arms
thrown above the head, vital
throat and belly lying
undefended · light slides over you,
this is not an altar, they are not
acting or watching

You are intact, you turn
towards me, your eyes opening, the eyes
intricate and easily bruised, you open

yourself to me gently, what
they tried, we
tried but could never do

before · without blood, the killed
heart · to take
that risk, to offer life and remain

alive, open yourself like this and become whole

1974

SEAMUS HEANEY

(born 1939)

The finest of living Irish poets, Heaney attended Queen's University in Belfast, but later moved to the vicinity of Dublin. He has taught at colleges and universities in Ireland and the United States. Some of his poetry has for its theme the struggle between Protestants and Catholics in Northern Ireland, which he observes from an independent and personal point of view. Like many Irish poets in the twentieth century, including Yeats, he also takes Ireland itself for one of his subjects—the nature of the land, its tragic history, the character and ways of life of its people. But although he is firmly identified with Ireland, Heaney, again like Yeats, also transcends this national identification, and is read throughout the world for reasons that have to do not with Ireland but with the quality of his art and vision.

In the poems printed here the bogland of Ireland, a skunk, and a bow of straw respectively are played on by Heaney's reflective subtlety and imagination so that they become many-sided symbols. Heaney's poetry is not pastoral or idyllic, for he is deeply sensitive to the darker side of human existence; but he shows a great deal of compassion, affection, humor, and pleasure, particularly in the rural and earthy things. All this is somewhat unexpected in a sophisticated modern poet, for the Modernist and post-Modernist writing of the twentieth century is, in some aspects, one of the great pessimistic literatures in history.

Bogland

for T. P. Flanagan

We have no prairies
To slice a big sun at evening—
Everywhere the eye concedes to
Encroaching horizon,

Is wooed into the cyclops' eye
Of a tarn. Our unfenced country
Is bog that keeps crusting
Between the sights of the sun.

They've taken the skeleton
Of the Great Irish Elk
Out of the peat, set it up
An astounding crate full of air.

Butter sunk under
More than a hundred years
Was recovered salty and white.
The ground itself is kind, black butter

Melting and opening underfoot,
Missing its last definition
By millions of years.
They'll never dig coal here,

Only the waterlogged trunks
Of great firs, soft as pulp.
Our pioneers keep striking
Inwards and downwards,

Every layer they strip
Seems camped on before.
The bogholes might be Atlantic seepage.
The wet centre is bottomless.

1969

BOGLAND. **5. cyclops' eye:** In Homer's *Odyssey,* the Cyclopes are giants with one eye. **10. Great Irish Elk:** a gigantic, prehistoric deer.

North

I returned to a long strand,
the hammered shod of a bay,
and found only the secular
powers of the Atlantic thundering.

I faced the unmagical
invitations of Iceland,
the pathetic colonies
of Greenland, and suddenly

those fabulous raiders,
those lying in Orkney and Dublin
measured against
their long swords rusting,

those in the solid
belly of stone ships,
those hacked and glinting
in the gravel of thawed streams

were ocean-deafened voices
warning me, lifted again
in violence and epiphany.
The longship's swimming tongue

was buoyant with hindsight—
it said Thor's hammer swung
to geography and trade,
thick-witted couplings and revenges,

the hatreds and behindbacks
of the althing, lies and women,
exhaustions nominated peace,
memory incubating the spilled blood.

It said, 'Lie down
in the word-hoard, burrow
the coil and gleam
of your furrowed brain.

Compose in darkness.
Expect aurora borealis
in the long foray
but no cascade of light.

Keep your eye clear
as the bleb of the icicle,
trust the feel of what nubbed treasure
your hands have known.'

1976

NORTH. **2. shod:** heel tip. **22. Thor:** Norse god of thunder and war. **26. althing:** the whole assembly in Norse society; the Icelandic parliament. **38. bleb:** air bubble.

The Skunk

Up, black, striped and damasked like the chasuble
At a funeral mass, the skunk's tail
Paraded the skunk. Night after night
I expected her like a visitor.

The refrigerator whinnied into silence.
My desk light softened beyond the verandah.
Small oranges loomed in the orange tree.
I began to be tense as a voyeur.

After eleven years I was composing
Love-letters again, broaching the word 'wife'
Like a stored cask, as if its slender vowel
Had mutated into the night earth and air

Of California. The beautiful, useless
Tang of eucalyptus spelt your absence.
The aftermath of a mouthful of wine
Was like inhaling you off a cold pillow.

And there she was, the intent and glamorous,
Ordinary, mysterious skunk,
Mythologized, demythologized,
Snuffing the boards five feet beyond me.

It all came back to me last night, stirred
By the sootfall of your things at bedtime,
Your head-down, tail-up hunt in a bottom drawer
For the black plunge-line nightdress.

1979

The Harvest Bow

As you plaited the harvest bow
You implicated the mellowed silence in you
In wheat that does not rust
But brightens as it tightens twist by twist
Into a knowable corona,
A throwaway love-knot of straw.

Hands that aged round ashplants and cane sticks
And lapped the spurs on a lifetime of game cocks
Harked to their gift and worked with fine intent
Until your fingers moved somnambulant:
I tell and finger it like braille,
Gleaning the unsaid off the palpable,

THE SKUNK. **14. eucalyptus:** a tree with aromatic leaves, imported to California from Australia.

And if I spy into its golden loops
I see us walk between the railway slopes
Into an evening of long grass and midges,
Blue smoke straight up, old beds and ploughs in hedges,
An auction notice on an outhouse wall—
You with a harvest bow in your lapel,

Me with the fishing rod, already homesick
For the big lift of these evenings, as your stick
Whacking the tips off weeds and bushes
Beats out of time, and beats, but flushes
Nothing: that original townland
Still tongue-tied in the straw tied by your hand.

The end of art is peace
Could be the motto of this frail device
That I have pinned up on our deal dresser—
Like a drawn snare
Slipped lately by the spirit of the corn
Yet burnished by its passage, and still warm.

1979

APPENDIX

VERSIFICATION

The most important element in all versification is *rhythm.* Rhythm was originally an ancient Greek word meaning a motion that recurs in a pattern—that is, motion that is "measured." This measured or patterned recurrence appeals deeply to all of us, and to all animals (and even, biologists tell us, to all plants). Recurring pattern is built into all living phenomena. Habits in animals or in plants reflect this. Rhythm also gives pleasure and reassurance. Babies can be soothed or lulled by the regular rocking of a cradle, and infants are pleased as we bounce them on our knee and recite nursery rhymes. All music, of whatever kind, depends on rhythm, and dancing is, by definition, a movement in rhythmic ways.

In poetry, as in music, there is an alteration between something *emphasized* and something that is not. A simple example is the opening line of Gray's "Elegy Written in a Country Churchyard":

The cúr / few tólls / the knéll / of párt / ing dáy.

Here every second syllable is given a strong accent. And the syllable before each of these strong accents is "weak." The rhythm goes de-*dúm,* de-*dúm,* de-*dúm,* de-*dúm,* de-*dúm.*

Meter

Meter, which comes from the Greek word for *measure,* is the term given to rhythm in verse that is "regular"—meaning a rhythm that keeps repeating the same pattern.

In English verse, almost all rhythm is **accentual**—that is, it consists of a pattern of **accented** or **stressed** syllables in relation to syllables that are not accented or stressed (as in the preceding line from Gray's "Elegy").

The basic unit of meter is the **foot**. There are several kinds of feet: for example, **iambic**, **trochaic**, **dactylic**, **anapestic**, and (used as an occasional variation of any of the previous four kinds) **pyrrhic** and **spondaic**.

Iambic Meter The most common foot is the *iambic foot*—a light syllable, followed by a stressed syllable. There may be *two* iambic feet in a line (**dimeter**):

Who's there? / It's I

Or *three* feet (**trimeter**):

Who said, / Where sleeps / she now?

Or *four* feet (**iambic tetrameter**):

If I / and you / were here / alone.

Or, by far the most common line in serious English verse, *five* feet, as in the line from Gray's "Elegy":

The cur / few tolls / the knell / of part / ing day

This line is called **iambic pentameter**. Pentameter comes from the Latin word *penta* (five) and the Greek and Latin word *meter* (measure). Over half of the poems in this anthology, written before the twentieth century, are written in this iambic pentameter.

Chaucer, who had so much influence on all later poetry, established iambic pentameter as the normal rhythm for English verse, especially for longer poems. In fact, this is so much the standard line in English poetry from Chaucer to the early 1900s, that it was called the *heroic line* for centuries, meaning that it was the line used for verse-plays (it is the standard line in Shakespeare's plays), epics (like Milton's *Paradise Lost*), and various other longer kinds of poems.

When it is rhymed in pairs (couplets), it is therefore called the *heroic couplet.* When it alternates, with rhymes going *abab,* it is the *heroic quatrain.*

Unrhymed iambic pentameter is called *blank verse.* It is important to remember that blank verse is not "free verse," which is discussed below.

Longer lines are also made of iambic meter. The most frequent of these longer lines is the *six* foot line (*hexameter,* sometimes called an *Alexandrine*), as in the opening sonnet of Sidney's *Astrophel and Stella,* where a typical line is

Oft turn / ing oth / er's leaves, / to see / if thence /
would flow.

Comparatively few poems in English are written in iambic hexameter. Instead, hexameter lines are used mainly as a **variation** in iambic pentameter. John Dryden, for example, often inserts an Alexandrine for the sake of variety in his heroic couplets. To a lesser extent, other poets (such as Pope) who use the heroic couplet, also insert an Alexandrine for the same purpose. Another common use of the Alexandrine is as the final line in the **Spenserian stanza**, first used in Spenser's *Faerie Queene* and then by other poets, such as Keats in "The Eve of St. Agnes."

Finally, we occasionally find—although rarely—still longer lines: **heptameter** (seven feet), sometimes called "fourteeners" from the number of syllables, and even **octometer** (eight feet).

Other feet used in **metered** (regularly rhythmed verse):

(1) the **trochee** (**trochaic** verse), in which the strong syllable comes first and the light syllable after it

Dark be / hind it / rose the / water.

Poets in English who use this meter frequently omit the final, weak syllable, so that the line ends as well as begins with an accented syllable. Most of the lines in Milton's "L'Allegro" have this form, as in

Come and / trip it / as you / go

Iambic meter, in contrast to trochaic meter, is a graver, more solemn rhythm. It is also more flexible and can be used for a wider variety of effects. Trochaic meter tends to have a tripping, dancing quality, with a perpetual falling effect. It is best adapted for short lyric poems, and can become tedious when it is used for long poems.

(2) **Spondees** (**spondaic** feet): two strong, accented syllables, as in:

But when / *loud surg* / es lash / the sound / ing shore
The hoarse / *rough verse* / should like / the tor / rent
roar

(3) **Pyrrhic feet**: two light syllables per foot, as in:

Like pi / ous in / *cense from* / a cens / er old.

Here the third foot is pyrrhic (two unstressed syllables).

Note: Whole lines of verse are not written in either spondees or pyrrhic feet. It is virtually impossible to do! Instead, spondees and/or pyrrhic feet are used almost solely for variation in either iambic, trochaic, or dactylic and anapestic meter.

(4) The **dactyl** (**dactylic feet**) is patterned after the old Greek and Latin *epic* meter, used in Homer's *Iliad* and *Odyssey* and Virgil's *Aeneid.* It consists of three syllables: one stressed, followed by two light or unstressed syllables, as in (except for the last foot—a trochee):

This is the / forest pri / meval, the / murmuring / pines
and the / hemlocks

The dactyl does not suit English verse very well, despite its effectiveness in Latin and Greek. In English it has a light, dancing effect, like a waltz. Hence not many poems are written in it. It is used mainly as a form of variation within iambic or trochaic verse.

(5) This is also true of **anapests**, or **anapestic feet** (the opposite of the dactyl). The **anapest** has three syllables—two light (unstressed) followed by a strong (or stressed) syllable:

˘ ˘ ´ / ˘ ˘ ´ / ˘ ˘ ´ / ˘ ˘ ´
The Assyr / ian came down / like a wolf / on the fold

Variation of Meter in Iambic Feet

Very few poets keep strictly to the normal iambic meter (or any other meter). The verse would become intolerably monotonous if they did! So, roughly speaking, a third of the lines are varied by replacing an iambic foot with, say, a trochee, a spondee, a pyrrhic, and so on. Thus, in the opening of Keats's "On First Looking into Chapman's Homer," the first foot is *inverted* (that is, changed into a trochee, with the first syllable accented instead of the second), and the third foot is a pyrrhic (two unstressed syllables):

´ ˘ / ˘ ´ / ˘ ˘ / ˘ ´ / ˘ ´
Much have / I trav / elled in / the realms / of gold

Or, in the "Eve of St. Agnes," the second foot is a spondee (two stressed syllables) followed by a pyrrhic:

˘ ´ / ´ ´ / ˘ ˘ / ˘ ´ / ˘ ´
The hare / *limped tremb* / ling through / the froz / en grass

A third common variation in meter is the use of *trisyllabic* (three-syllable) feet in place of the normal two-syllable iamb, as in the second foot of this line from Keats's "Ode to a Nightingale":

˘ ´ / ˘ ˘ ´ / ˘ ´ / ˘ ´ / ˘ ´
Through verd / *urous glooms* / and wind / ing moss / y ways

Caesura (or **pause**) In almost every line that is longer than two or three syllables, there is a natural **pause**. It is called a **caesura** (from the Latin word for "cut"), as in the opening line of one of Shakespeare's songs:

Fear no more (x) the heat of the sun.

The caesura is not always, by any means, in the exact middle of the line, any more than it is in the preceding line. If it were, then a series of several lines, with one half of each line equalling the other half, would become monotonous. So it tends to vary from line to line.

Enjambment (or **run-on** lines) When the natural sense in a phrase or clause comes at the close of a line (usually marked with a period, comma, or semicolon) the line is called **end-stopped**, as in the following two lines:

> When, in disgrace with fortune and men's eyes,
> I all alone beweep my outcast state.

But almost as common as end-stopped lines are **run-on** lines in which, without any significant pause, the sense continues immediately into the next line, as in

> My heart aches, and a drowsy numbness pains
> My sense, as though of hemlock I had drunk.

For run-on lines, we frequently use a French term, **enjambment**, which means "a striding on." Enjambment is especially frequent in longer poems, as in Shakespeare's plays, where a continual use of end-stopped lines would produce a wooden and monotonous effect. Similarly, Milton, in *Paradise Lost,* uses enjambment in 70 percent of all the lines, starting with the very opening of the poem:

> Of man's first disobedience, and the fruit
> Of that forbidden tree, whose mortal taste
> Brought death into the world, and all our woe,
> With loss of Eden, till one greater man
> Restore us . . .

Alliteration Alliteration occurs when two or more words close together begin with or contain the same consonant, as in these lines from a sonnet of Shakespeare:

> When I do *c*ount the *c*lock that *t*ells the *t*ime.

Or:

> And summer's *g*reen all *g*irded up in sheaves.

Alliteration was a special feature of Old English or Anglo Saxon poetry. It is in imitation of this early poetry that Gerard Manley Hopkins uses alliteration with special richness:

> I caught this morning morning's minion, king-
>
> dom of daylight's dauphin, dapple-dawn drawn falcon . . .
>
> Fall, gall themselves, and gash gold vermilion.

Assonance This term is applied to the repetition of the same vowel sound, as in Pope's "Rape of the Lock":

> Or alum st*y*pt*i*cs w*i*th contract*i*ng power
> Shr*i*nk h*i*s th*i*n essence like a r*i*veled flower.

The most lavish use of assonance in English is found in some of the poems of Keats, Swinburne, and Hopkins.

In Keats, the repetition of vowels can become rather elaborate, as in these lines from "The Eve of St. Agnes":

> And diamonded with panes of quaint device.
>
> A shielded scutcheon blush'd with blood of queens and kings.
>
> And still she slept an azure-lidded sleep

Rhyme The term is applied to the repetition of the closing sound of a word, as in *down/town, dawn/fawn, fill/mill.* When just one syllable is repeated—for example the sound "ill" in *fill/mill*—the rhyme is called a *masculine rhyme.* When the rhyme consists of *two* syllables (as in *master/faster,* or *filling/milling*), the first syllable of which is strong and the second weak, it is called a *feminine rhyme.*

Longer rhymes, involving three syllables (as in *Thackeray/quackery,* or *take of it/make of it*) are so unusual that they often make the reader laugh, and are therefore usually used only in comic verse, as when Byron, in *Don Juan,* writes:

> He learned the arts of riding, fencing, gunnery,
> And how to scale a fortress—or a nunnery.

Rhyme in poetry is found in many primitive languages, including ancient Chinese and ancient Indian poetry. It was never common in Greek or Latin poetry. But it was common in Arabic poetry, and brought into Spain by the Moors. Provençal poetry in medieval France took it over, and from France it was carried over into "Middle English," where we find it in songs, ballads, and longer forms of poetry. Chaucer used it constantly, and in different ways, in everything he wrote.

Principal Forms

Couplet This is the simplest of all forms that use rhyme. It is a rhyme in simple "pairs" (a "couple"). Couplets can be made of lines of any length, from one foot to ten feet. But the most common couplets are either those of **four** feet (tetrameter) or **five** feet (pentameter). A beautiful example of tetrameter (four-feet) couplets is Andrew Marvell's "To His Coy Mistress," which begins:

> Had we but world enough, and time,
> This coyness, Lady, were no crime.

The **heroic couplet** is the term applied to five-feet iambic lines (iambic pentameter), as in a couplet from Dryden's "Mac Flecknoe":

The rest to some faint meaning make pretence;
But Shadwell never deviates into sense.

The heroic couplet is given this name not because there is anything particularly "heroic" about the sound. It is only because the five-foot iambic line had by 1600 become the standard or "heroic" line for poetry in drama or in the epic.

After the Restoration in 1660, John Dryden established the heroic couplet as the standard form for much of the longer poetry. It was especially good for satire, since the poet could condense words into a sharp, epigram-like statement.

Quatrain (and **Ballad**) A **quatrain** (from the Latin word *quattuor,* meaning "four") is a stanza of four lines. A **stanza** is a collection of lines arranged in some regular fashion. The simplest of all stanzas is the quatrain.

All that is required in the **ballad stanza** is that its second and its fourth (or last) line rhyme: *abcb.* We find this not only in the early ballads but sometimes in later imitations of the ballad, as in Keats's "La Belle Dame sans Merci":

O what can ail thee, Knight at arms,
  Alone and palely loitering?
The sedge has withered from the Lake,
  And no birds sing!

A stricter form of the quatrain rhymes the first line with the third and the second line with the fourth: *abab.* In English, quatrains of this kind usually tend to be four-foot (tetrameter quatrains), as in Blake's "London":

I wander thro' each charter'd street,
Near where the charter'd Thames does flow,
And mark in every face I meet
Marks of weakness, marks of woe.

or else five-foot (pentameter quatrains), as in Gray's "Elegy Written in a Country Churchyard." The latter is called the **heroic quatrain,** because it uses the five-foot "heroic meter."

There are other forms of quatrains. One example is Tennyson's "In Memoriam," in which the rhyme scheme is *abba:*

Thy voice is on the rolling air;
  I hear thee where the waters run;
  Thou standest in the rising sun,
And in the setting thou art fair.

Another is that of Fitzgerald's "The Rubáiyát of Omar Khayyám," in which the rhyme scheme is *aaba:*

A Book of Verses underneath the Bough,
A Jug of Wine, a Loaf of Bread—and Thou
  Beside me singing in the Wilderness—
Oh, Wilderness were Paradise enow!

Sonnet The sonnet, used by many of the greatest poets in our language, was first developed as a form in Italy, where the great exemplar for later poets was the Italian poet, Petrarch. The sonnet, which consisted of fourteen lines, was divided by Petrarch into two sections: an *octave* (the first eight lines), and then a *sestet* (a six-line close). For the octave the rhyme scheme was *abba, abba;* the sestet might then be *cde, cde,* or *cdcdcd,* or some other combination. In Elizabethan England, Sir Thomas Wyatt introduced the *Petrarchan* (or Italian) *sonnet.* Soon afterwards, the Earl of Surrey modified the fourteen-line poem into something a little different: three alternate-rhyming quatrains *(abab, cdcd, efef)* followed by a couplet *(gg).* This is the form used by most English Elizabethan writers of the sonnet. Hence it is called the *English sonnet* or the *Shakespearean sonnet* (because Shakespeare chose the form for his sonnets).

Spenserian Stanza For his epic, *The Faerie Queene,* Edmund Spenser invented a nine-line stanza. It consisted of two alternate-rhyming quatrains, *abab, bcbc,* and then, after these eight lines, a *c*-rhyming Alexandrine, or six-foot line. In the quatrains *abab, bcbc,* notice that the *b*-rhyme, in the second and fourth line of the first quatrain, becomes the rhyme in the first and third lines of the second quatrain. There is a resonant unity to the stanza because the interlocked *b*-rhyme, recurring throughout *ababbcbcc,* serves as a sounding board; the long, six-foot line at the close is like a wave that completes the stanza at the end. This is called **interlocking rhyme**. (Spenser also used interlocking rhyme in his sonnets, in which the rhyme-scheme is *abab, bcbc, cdcd, ee.*) The Spenserian stanza was widely imitated, especially in the Romantic period, as, for example, in Keats's "Eve of St. Agnes."

Blank Verse The standard epic and dramatic line for English drama and English epic, and for many other kinds of poems, is **unrhymed** iambic pentameter. Established by the great examples of Shakespeare and Milton, no poet using the language has ever been able completely to forget it. Either it begins to creep back into unrhymed poems, or else the poet seems to have to fight to keep it out of mind and write a kind of unrhymed verse that differs from it.

Free Verse (not to be confused with the unrhymed iambic pentameter called *blank verse*) disregards regular meter, and uses any number of syllables in a line in various ways. Although there are notable examples before 1900 (for example, Whitman), free verse becomes particularly common in the twentieth century.

Other Terms for Poetic Forms or Versification

(Arranged Alphabetically)

Elision: Running together of words for the purpose of omitting a syllable in order to maintain a regular rhythm, as in "th'art of poetry."

Epic: A long narrative poem, originally on some subject of large public interest, as, for example, Homer's *Iliad* and *Odyssey,* Virgil's *Aeneid,* or Milton's *Paradise Lost.* Now it is used more loosely for lengthy poems that also have some range or sweep of subject.

Madrigal: Elizabethan term for a short lyric or song. Originally the madrigal had a very strict musical form.

Ode: Originally a Greek term for a *hymn,* or an exalted lyric. In time it came to imply, in English, not a strict form as it had in Greece, but any short poem with a serious purpose and tone.

Onomatopoeia: A term used for the attempted poetic imitation of a sound, as in Tennyson's line, "The murmuring of innumerable bees."

Ottava rima: Eight lines (usually of iambic pentameter) rhyming *ababab cc,* as in Byron's *Don Juan* or Yeats's "Among School Children."

Quantitative meter: The conventional kind of meter used in Greek and Latin, in which the difference between *major* syllables and *minor* ones is not by *stress* (or accent) but by *length of time* in which the syllable is pronounced. Many attempts have been made in English to duplicate this. None has been wholly successful. Some of the poems of Thomas Campion are the nearest approach to it.

Rhyme Royal: A stanza of seven lines rhyming *ababbcc*; frequently used by Chaucer.

Sprung rhythm: Hopkins' term for the meter that he often (but not always) used. In contrast to the *regular* kinds of feet (iambic, trochaic, and so on) a metrical foot here consists of a unit in which there is *one* strong, accented syllable, whereas the number of "light" or unaccented syllables can vary from 1 or 2 to 4, 5, or even more.

For example, in the start of "The Windhover":

I caught / this morn / ing morn / ing's min / ion, king-
dom of day / light's dauph / in, dap / ple-dawn-drawn
falcon, / in his riding
Of the roll / ing level / underneath him stead / y air, /
and striding

Syllabic meter: Verse distinguished by number of syllables in a line rather than by number of stresses or (as in *quantitative* verse) the length of time in which syllables are pronounced. "Stress," or accent, is of course inevitable in English speech, although in syllabic verse it is not the determining factor. The most notable example of syllabic verse in modern poetry is that of Marianne Moore.

Terza rima: Lines in groups of three with interlocking rhymes, *aba, bcb, cdc, ded,* and so on. The form was used by Dante in his *Divine Comedy,* and introduced into English in the Elizabethan period. Perhaps the most famous English poem using it is Shelley's "Ode to the West Wind."

Reading Poetry Aloud

Most people make one of two mistakes when they read or recite verse aloud: (1) They do it in a sing-song way, pausing at the end of every line, whether or not it is a line that runs on in sense into the next line; or (2) they read it as though it were prose, the way most Shakespearean actors have tended to recite since the 1940s. Whatever the advantages—or disadvantages—this may have in Shakespearean acting, this second way of reading is not the proper way to read lyric poetry. When poetry is read this way the student may legitimately ask why the poet bothers to use individual lines at all instead of simply writing his poem as though it were prose.

The traditional way to avoid these two extremes is, in *rhymed* verse, to pause at the end of a line *only* if there is a comma, semicolon, or period (in other words, a "natural" pause).

If the line of poetry is a run-on line (that is, if the sentence runs directly on into the next line), what you should do is drag out slightly the vowel of the rhyme word (the last word) and make the vowel a bit longer (do not *stress* it unduly, or change the pitch). Just let it be pronounced *more slowly;* immediately after that, do not pause, but go on at once with the next line.

So, in Keats's "Ode to a Nightingale":

My heart aches, and a drowsy numbness PAINS →
(Drag out the length and proceed at once to the next line without pause)
  My sense, as though of hemlock I had drunk,
Or emptied some dull opiate to the DRAINS →
  One minute past, and Lethe-wards had sunk.

Or, in the opening of the last stanza of the same poem:

Forlorn! the very word is like a BELL→
  To toll me back from thee to my sole self!
Adieu! the fancy cannot cheat so WELL→
  As she is famed to do, deceiving elf!

Once you learn to do this (as one easily can with five to ten minutes practice), half the battle is won.

This procedure was taught in the English public schools from the seventeenth century until the early years of our own century. It was also the procedure taught to American students in the traditional classes in oratory and elocution in the eighteenth and nineteenth centuries. Then it became lost. Only now is the practice being recovered.

A second suggestion, almost as important: Observe all possible pauses *extravagantly*. Not just the caesura (the natural *main* pause that is in every line), but pause after each phrase. *Read aloud slowly,* and look for every possible pause. A famous professor, who taught in the days when students studied elocution, used to say: "Silence never makes a mistake."

For example, to take the lines of Keats just quoted, the sign (x) means a smaller pause, the (xx) signifies a longer pause (the *caesura*):

My heart aches, (xx) and a drowsy numbness (x) PAINS
  My sense, (xx) as though of hemlock (x) I had drunk
Or emptied (x) some dull opiate (xx) to the DRAINS
  One minute past, (xx) and Lethe-wards (x) had sunk.

Or:

Forlorn! (xx) the very word (x) is like a BELL
  To toll me back (xx) from thee (xx) to my sole self!
Adieu! (xx) the fancy (x) cannot cheat so WELL
  As she is famed (x) to do, (xx) deceiving elf!

Once you have done these two things, which will establish the fact that it is verse you are reading aloud, combine with them a third rule, which has two parts:

(1) **Accent** the syllables and words just as you would in reading prose well: That is, *stress* the syllables (or whole words) as you would *if* you were giving a speech in public to a sizeable audience. We say here an audience of some size because there one has to speak slowly and distinctly in order to be understood.

The poet (if the poet is a good poet) has already seen to it that this "prose emphasis" on key words or key syllables will also take care of the "poetic" sound, with the result that the prose sense operates against the background of the meter, both counterpointing with each other (playing a match, as in tennis):

> ´ ´ ´´ ˘ ˘ ´ ˘ ´ ˘ ´
> My heart *aches,* (x) and a drowsy numbness PAINS→
> ˘ ´
> My sense . . .

Scurry over light syllables (such as "and a" in the preceding quote).

(2) Do this extravagantly, excessively, at first, until you have had a few minutes of practice every day or so for a week, and you then have much of the secret of reading verse aloud. Only after you have done this *extravagantly* for a while should you pull back; your own ear will tell you how to modify this a bit.

One final suggestion: It has to do with what is called "pitch." Pitch does not mean *stress* or "*accent,*" but whether the voice is "high" or "low." Americans find it difficult to vary pitch when reading aloud. Compared with the English—especially the Scots, Irish, and Welsh—we tend to keep the same flat level of tone ("monotone") except when we ask a question, or become angry and shout. *If you can do so,* without feeling affected, try—as you read aloud—to vary the pitch in any way you think you can get away with. Otherwise—despite pauses, stresses, and all of the preceding suggestions—verse can get monotonous. Go up and down in pitch with stress (or emphasis) on certain syllables, and with the natural meaning.

For example, to go back to the Keats quote:

> ´ ´ ´´
> My heart aches (*pause*)
> (*Stress* all *three syllables, and without worrying about pitch, unless you wish*)
> ˘ ˘ ´ ˘ ´ ˘
> and a drowsy numbness
> (*stress "numbness"—a key word—and, if you can, raise your voice—pitch—as you stress it)*
> and a drowsy *numbness* (x) PAINS→

Do not raise the pitch on "pains." Just drag out the syllable before hurrying on to the next line. However, varying the pitch, which may seem too difficult to do without feeling embarassment, is not entirely necessary. Do it only as much as you feel you can do easily.

Bibliography of Critical and Biographical Works

The following list is intended for students who may wish to pursue further their study of particular poets. Since the course for which the present anthology is planned is a general course in poetry, the list of works is naturally selective. Titles are included, as a rule, only when they are actual books. Articles in journals with which the student is not likely to be familiar are not included, nor are specialized monographs.

General Works

Chaucer to 1500

The new standard work is Derek Pearsall, *Old and Middle English Poetry* (1977), although A. C. Baugh, " The Middle English Period," in *A Literary History of England,* ed. A. C. Baugh (1948; rev. 1967) is still useful, as are relevant sections of H. J. C. Grierson and J. A. Smith, *A Critical History of English Poetry* (rev. 1947). For the ballads, a recent general treatment is James Reed, *The Border Ballads* (1975).

The English Renaissance (1500–1660)

Douglas Bush, *Mythology and the Renaissance Tradition* (1932; rev. 1963), goes beyond the implications of its title and offers suggestive criticism of most of the poets. Still useful as a summary is Tucker Brooke, " The Renaissance," in *A Literary History of England,* ed. A. C. Baugh (1948; rev. 1967), and, for intellectual background, E. M. W. Tillyard, *The Elizabethan World Picture* (1943; rev. 1956). Helpful for the sixteenth century is Douglas Peterson, *The English Lyric from Wyatt to Donne* (1966); and, for the seventeenth century, two books by Earl Miner, *The Metaphysical Mode from Donne to Cowley* (1969) and *The Cavalier Mode from Jonson to Cotton* (1971); and two by Louis Martz, *The Poetry of Meditation* (1954) and *The Paradise Within* (1964). For religious background, see Barbara Lewalski, *Protestant Poetics* (1979).

The Enlightenment (1660–1800)

James Sutherland, *A Preface to Eighteenth Century Poetry* (1948) is still the best general introduction. Help may also be found in Roger Lonsdale (ed.), *Dryden to Johnson* (1971). Good observations may be found in the chapters on poetry in George Sherburn, "The Restoration and Eighteenth Century," in *A Literary History of England,* ed. A. C. Baugh (1948; rev. 1967). More specialized discussions are Ian Jack, *Augustan Satire* (1952), Rachel Trickett, *The Honest Muse: A Study in Augustan Verse* (1967), and, for psychological motivations in the rise of Neoclassical and, later, Romantic poetry, W. J. Bate, *The Burden of the Past and the English Poet* (1970).

Romantic and Nineteenth Century

Douglas Bush, *Mythology and the Romantic Tradition* (1937; rev. 1957) offers perceptive critical discussions of most poets from 1800 to World War I. Romantic symbolism is discussed in David Perkins, *The Quest for Permanence* (1959). Collections of modern critical essays are *English Romantic Poets,* ed. M. H. Abrams (1960) and *Romanticism and Consciousness* (1970). Helpful insights are given in Northrop Frye, *A Study of English Romanticism* (1968), and, for the Victorians, in Robert Langbaum, *The Poetry of Experience* (1957) and E. D. H. Johnson, *The Alien Vision of Victorian Poetry* (1975). For the American poets, see especially Roy Harvey Pearce, *The Continuity of American Poetry* (1961) and Hyatt Waggoner, *American Poets from the Puritans to the Present* (1968).

Modern (1900 to the Present)

A general history is provided by David Perkins, *A History of Modern Poetry: From the 1890s to the High Modernist Mode* (1976). A second volume, from the 1930s to the present, is in preparation. Cleanth Brooks, *Modern Poetry and the Tradition* (1939) is still valuable for the major earlier Moderns, although it neglects "popular Modernism" in favor of the tradition of Yeats, Pound, and Eliot. For the more recent moderns, see John Press, *Rule and Energy: Trends in British Poetry Since the Second World War* (1963); M. L. Rosenthal, *The Modern Poets, A Critical Introduction* (1960) and *The New Poets* (1967); Calvin Bedient, *Eight Contemporary Poets* (1974); Hugh Kenner, *A Homemade World: The American Modernist Writers* (1975); Arthur Oberg, *The Modern American Lyric: Lowell, Berryman, Creeley, and Plath* (1978); P. R. King, *Nine Contemporary Poets* (1979); and Helen Vendler, *Part of Nature, Part of Us* (1980).

Versification, Poetic Forms, and Technical Terms

A standard work is Paul Fussell, *Poetic Meter and Poetic Form* (1966). Also helpful are Robert Hillyer, *First Principles of Verse* (rev. 1950) and Karl Shapiro and Robert Beum, *A Prosody Handbook* (1965). Technical terms are given alphabetically in M. H. Abrams (ed.), *A Glossary of Literary Terms* (rev. 1971) and the more detailed and general *Princeton Encyclopedia of Poetry and Poetics,* ed. Alex Preminger (1965). A complete bibliography of works on every aspect of the subject is T. V. Brogan, *English Versification: A Reference Guide* (1981).

Works on Individual Poets

Ammons, A. R.

Alan Holder, *A. R. Ammons* (1978), and discussion in Richard Howard, *Alone with America* (1969).

Anonymous Lyrics, 1400–1600

Lyrics, 1400–1600 For further selections see in *The Oxford Book of Mediaeval Verse,* ed. C. and K. Sisam (1970), *One Hundred Middle English Poems* (1964), ed. R. D. Stevick, and *Elizabethan Lyrics,* ed. Norman Ault (1949).

Ballads The great ballad collection is that of F. J. Child (ed.), *The English and Scottish Popular Ballads* (1883–98), abridged by H. C. Sargent and G. L. Kittredge (1904). Standard discussions are in F. B. Gummere, *The Popular Ballad* (1907), G. H. Gerould, *The Ballad of Tradition* (1932), and M. J. C. Hodgart, *The Ballads* (1950).

Arnold, Matthew

Biography: Park Honan, *Matthew Arnold: A Life* (1981). **Critical:** Lionel Trilling, *Matthew Arnold* (1949); G. Robert Stange, *The Poet as Humanist* (1967); Douglas Bush, *Matthew Arnold* (1971); Kenneth Allott, *Matthew Arnold* (1975).

Ashbery, John

David Shapiro, *John Ashbery: An Introduction* (1979); David Lehman, *Beyond Amazement: New Essays on John Ashbery* (1980). Discussions are included in David Kalstone, *Five Temperaments* (1977), and, by Harold Bloom, in *Contemporary Poetry in America,* ed. Robert Boyers (1973).

Atwood, Margaret

Margaret Atwood: A Symposium, ed. Linda Sandler (1977).

Auden, Wystan Hugh

Edward Mendelson, *Early Auden* (1981); a volume on the later years is being finished by Mendelson. A briefer treatment is Humphry Carpenter, *W. H. Auden: A Biography* (1981). Samuel Hynes, *The Auden Generation* (1976), discusses Auden and his contemporaries as a group. Specific critical studies include Richard Hoggart, *Auden: An Introductory Essay* (1951); Monroe Spears, *The Poetry of W. H. Auden* (1963); Barbara Everett, *Auden* (1964); John Fuller, *A Reader's Guide to Auden* (1970).

Baraka, Amiri (Le Roi Jones)
Critical and biographical: Werner Sollors, *Amiri Baraka/Le Roi Jones: The Quest for a Populist Modernism* (1978). See also K. W. Benston (ed.), *Baraka: A Collection of Critical Essays* (1978).

Benét, Stephen Vincent
Biography: Charles Fenton, *S. V. Benét* (1958). **Critical:** Parry Stroud, *S. V. Benét* (1962).

Berryman, John
Biography: Joel Canarroe, *John Berryman* (1977); John Haffenden, *Life of John Berryman* (1982). **Critical:** Essay on Berryman in Martin Dodsworth, *The Survival of Poetry* (1970); John Haffenden, *John Berryman* (1980), and, on *Dream Songs,* a chapter in Helen Vendler, *Part of Nature, Part of Us* (1980).

Betjeman, John
Critical biography: M. L. Stapleton; *Sir John Betjeman* (1975).

Bishop, Elizabeth
Biography: Anne Stevenson, *Elizabeth Bishop* (1966), which also provides critical discussion. See also David Kalstone, *Five Temperaments* (1977) and Helen Vendler, *Part of Nature, Part of Us* (1980).

Blake, William
Biography: Alexander Gilchrist, *Life of William Blake* (1863; rev. 1945). **Critical:** Northrop Frye, *Fearful Symmetry* (1947) and his edition of critical essays (1966); David Erdman, *William Blake: Prophet Against Empire* (1954); Hazard Adams, *William Blake: A Reading of the Shorter Poems* (1963); E. D. Hirsch, *Innocence and Experience: An Introduction to Blake* (1964); M. K. Nurmi, *William Blake* (1976).

Bly, Robert
Critical: Ingegord Friborg, *Moving Inward: A Study of Robert Bly's Poetry* (1977); and a collection, *Of Solitude and Silence: Writings on Robert Bly,* ed. K. Daniels and Richard Jones (1982).

Bogan, Louise
Critical biography: Wiliam J. Smith, *Louise Bogan* (1971).

Bradstreet, Anne
Josephine Piercy, *Anne Bradstreet* (1965). **Critical:** Elizabeth White, *Anne Bradstreet: The Tenth Muse* (1971); Ann Stanford, *Anne Bradstreet: The Worldly Puritan* (1974).

Bridges, Robert
Biography: Edward Thompson, *Robert Bridges* (1944). **Critical:** Albert Guerard, *Bridges: A Study of Traditionalism in Poetry* (1942).

Brontë, Emily
Biography: Winifred Gerin, *Emily Brontë* (1971). Several essays discuss the poetry in the collection, *The Art of Emily Brontë,* ed. Anne Smith (1977).

Brooke, Rupert
Robert B. Pearsall, *Rupert Brooke: Man and Poet* (1974).

Brooks, Gwendolyn
Autobiography: *Report from Part One* (1972). Critical discussion is given in Houston Baker, *Singers of Daybreak: Studies in Black American Literature* (1975).

Browning, Elizabeth Barrett

Critical biography: Gardner Taplin, *Life of E. B. Browning* (1957); Alethea Hayter, *E. B. Browning* (1965); Virginia Radley, *E. B. Browning* (1972).

Browning, Robert

Biography: William Irvine and Park Honan, *The Book, The Ring, and the Poet* (1974). **Critical:** G. K. Chesterton, *Robert Browning* (1903); W. C. DeVane, *A Browning Handbook* (rev. ed., 1955); R. A. King, *The Bow and the Lyre* (1957) and *The Focusing Artifice* (1969), which discusses the monologues; Ian Jack, *Browning's Major Poetry* (1973), and Robert Langbaum, *The Poetry of Experience* (1957).

Bryant, William Cullen

Critical biography: Charles H. Brown, *William Cullen Bryant* (1971).

Burns, Robert

Biography: F. B. Snyder, *Life of Robert Burns* (1932). A brilliant portrait, less detailed than Snyder's, is John Ferguson, *Pride and Passion* (1939). **Critical:** Thomas Crawford, *Burns: A Study of the Poems and Songs* (1960); David Daiches, *Robert Burns and His World* (1971); Catarina Ericson-Roos, *The Songs of Robert Burns* (1977).

Byron, George Gordon, Lord

The standard biography, quite detailed, is that of Leslie Marchand, 1957, who also wrote a condensed one-volume version (1970). Two readable shorter lives are those by Peter Quennell (1934) and Elizabeth Longford (1976). **Critical:** Leslie Marchand, *Byron's Poetry* (1965); Jerome McGann, *Fiery Dust* (1968); Michael Cooke, *The Blind Man Traces the Circle* (1969); and *Byron: A Collection of Critical Essays,* ed. Paul West (1963).

Campion, Thomas

The two best general discussions are: Miles Kastendieck, *England's Musical Poet* (1938), and Edward Lowbury, *et al., Thomas Campion, Poet, Composer, Physician* (1970).

Chaucer, Geoffrey

Biography: Derek Brewer, *Chaucer and His Time* (1963). The best critical introduction to Chaucer is still G. L. Kittredge, *Chaucer and His Poetry* (1915; and later reprintings) supplemented by Brewer's book. Somewhat more advanced are: John L. Lowes, *Geoffrey Chaucer and the Development of His Genius* (1934), J. S. P. Tatlock, *The Mind and Art of Chaucer* (1950), and, among later works, *Chaucer: Modern Essays in Criticism,* ed. E. C. Wagenknecht (1959), and *Speaking of Chaucer,* ed. E. T. Donaldson (1970; and later reprintings).

Coleridge, Samuel Taylor

Critical biography: W. J. Bate, *Coleridge* (1968); and, among studies devoted specifically to the poetry, those of Humphry House (1953), George Watson (1966), and Reeve Parker (1975). A fascinating account of Coleridge's literary sources is the classic book, John L. Lowes, *The Road to Xanadu* (1927; and later reprintings).

Collins, William

E. G. Ainsworth, *Poor Collins* (1937) is both biography and criticism. More specifically critical is Richard Wendorf, *William Collins and Eighteenth-Century Poetry* (1981).

Cowley, Abraham

Biography: A. H. Nethercot, *Abraham Cowley* (1931). **Critical:** David Trotter, *The Poetry of Abraham Cowley* (1979). Never outdated is the short, critical life in Samuel Johnson's *Lives of the Poets,* ed. G. B. Hill (1905), Vol. I.

Cowper, William

Biography: Maurice Quinlan, *William Cowper* (1953). **Critical:** Norman Nicholson, *Cowper* (1951); Morris Golden, *In Search of Stability* (1960).

Crane, Hart

Biography: Brom Weber, *Hart Crane* (1948); and especially John Unterecker, *Voyager: A Life of Hart Crane* (1969). **Critical:** Allen Tate's essay on Crane in *Reactionary Essays*

(1936); Monroe Spears, *Hart Crane* (1965); R. W. B. Lewis, *The Poetry of Hart Crane* (1967); R. W. Butterfield, *The Broken Arc* (1969).

Crapsey, Adelaide

Mary E. Osborn, *Adelaide Crapsey* (1933); and the short but perceptive Introduction by Susan Sutton to her edition of *The Complete Poems and Letters of Adelaide Crapsey* (1977).

Creeley, Robert

Critical: Cynthia Edelberg, *Robert Creeley's Poetry: A Critical Introduction* (1978); Arthur L. Ford, *Robert Creeley* (1978).

Cullen, Countee

Critical studies, with some biographical interest as well, are Helen Dinger, *A Study of Countee Cullen* (1953); Stephen Bronz, *Three Harlem Renaissance Authors* (1954); Blanche Ferguson, *Countee Cullen and the Negro Renaissance* (1966).

Cummings, E. E.

Biography: Charles Norman, *The Magic Maker* (1958) is by a personal friend and includes interesting first-hand information. More detailed and recent is Richard Kennedy, *Dreams in the Mirror* (1979). **Critical:** Norman Friedman, *E. E. Cummings: The Art of His Poetry* (1960) and *E. E. Cummings: The Growth of a Writer* (1964). Other works, all entitled with the name of the poet, are by Robert Wagner (1965) and Bethany Dumas (1974), and a collection of essays, ed. Norman Friedman (1972).

Daniel, Samuel

Joan Rees, *Samuel Daniel: A Critical and Biographical Study* (1964); Cecil Seronsy, *Samuel Daniel* (1967).

Day Lewis, Cecil

Joseph Riddel, *Day Lewis* (1971); Derek Stanford, *Spender, MacNeice, Day Lewis* (1969).

de la Mare, Walter

Critical biography: R. L. Mégroz, *Walter de la Mare* (1972). Critical studies, all entitled with the name of the poet, are by Kenneth Hopkins (1957), Doris McGrosson (1966), and Forrest Reid (1970).

Dickey, James

Critical: Richard Calhoun (ed.), *James Dickey: The Expansive Imagination* (1973); Patricia de la Fuente, *et al.* (ed.), *James Dickey: Splintered Sunlight* (1979).

Dickinson, Emily

Biography: Thomas H. Johnson, *Emily Dickinson* (1955), and, more detailed, Richard Sewall, *Life of Emily Dickinson* (1974). **Critical:** George Whicher, *This Was a Poet* (1939), and three general studies by Richard Chase (1951), Charles Anderson (1960), and John Pickard (1967). Albert Gelpi, *Emily Dickinson* (1965), concentrates on her mind and inner life, and Brita Lindberg-Seyerstad, *The Voice of the Poet* (1968), on her poetic style. See also Robert Weisbuck, *Emily Dickinson's Poetry* (1975).

Dobson, Austin

Alban Dobson, Edmund Gosse, and George Saintsbury, *Austin Dobson* (1928).

Donne, John

Biography: R. C. Bald, *John Donne: A Life* (1970), and, on a smaller scale, Richard E. Hughes, *The Progress of the Soul* (1968). **Critical:** Of foremost importance are the influential essays on the "metaphysical" poets by T. S. Eliot in *Selected Essays* (1932). Also helpful for the beginning student are collections of essays edited by Theodore Spencer (1931), Helen Gardner (1962), and Frank Kermode (1962). For the more advanced student, there [illegible] George Williamson, *The Donne Tradition* (1930); Leonard Unger, *Donne's* [illegible] *Criticism* (1950); and Clay Hunt, *Donne's Poetry* (1954).

Doolittle, Hilda ("H. D.")

Biography: Barbara Guest, *Herself Defined: The Poet H. D. and Her* [illegible]

cal studies: Thomas Swann, *The Classical World of H. D.* (1962); Vincent Quinn, *Hilda Doolittle* (1967).

Dowson, Ernest

Critical biographies: J. M. Longaker, *Ernest Dowson* (1944); T. B. Swann, *Ernest Dowson* (1965).

Drayton, Michael

B. H. Newdigate, *Michael Drayton and His Circle* (1941); R. F. Hardin, *Michael Drayton and the Passing of Elizabethan England* (1973).

Dryden, John

Biography: Charles E. Ward, *Life of John Dryden* (1961). Important critical works include: Mark Van Doren, *John Dryden* (1920) and T. S. Eliot's essays in *Homage to John Dryden* (1924) and *John Dryden the Poet, the Dramatist, the Critic* (1932); Earl Miner, *Dryden's Poetry* (1967); Paul Ramsey, *The Art of John Dryden* (1969). Still classic is Samuel Johnson's "Dryden" in *Lives of the Poets* ed. Hill (1905), Vol. I.

Dunbar, Paul

Jean Wagner, *Black Poets of the United States: From Paul Dunbar to Langston Hughes* (1973).

Duncan, Robert

Robert J. Bertholf and I. A. Reid (ed.), *Robert Duncan: Scales of the Marvelous* (1979).

Eliot, Thomas Stearns

For biography, see Peter Ackroyd, *T. S. Eliot* (1984) and Allen Tate's collection of short memoirs, *T. S. Eliot: The Man and His Work* (1967); Herbert Howarth, *Notes on Some Figures Behind T. S. Eliot* (1965) and Lyndall Gordon, *Eliot's Early Years* (1977). Critical: F. O. Matthiessen, *The Achievement of T. S. Eliot* (rev. 1947); Elizabeth Drew, *T. S. Eliot, the Design of His Poetry* (1950); George Williamson, *A Reader's Guide to T. S. Eliot* (1953); Northrop Frye, *T. S. Eliot* (1963), Hugh Kenner, *The Invisible Poet* (1965), and Ronald Bush, *T. S. Eliot* (1983).

Emerson, Ralph Waldo

Biography: Van Wyck Brooks, *Life of Emerson* (1932), remains a fine introduction. More detailed is the *Life* by Ralph Rusk (1949).

Critical works are mainly concerned with Emerson's prose, but some touch on the poetry: Sherman Paul, *The Angle of Vision* (1952); Hyatt Waggoner, *Emerson as Poet* (1974); and relevant sections in F. O. Matthiessen, *American Renaissance* (1941) and Roy H. Pearce, *The Continuity of American Poetry* (1961).

Empson, William

John H. Willis, *William Empson* (1969) and Roma Gill (ed.), *William Empson: The Man and His Work* (1974).

Fitzgerald, Edward

Of both biographical and critical interest: A. M. Terhune, *Life of Edward Fitzgerald* (1947) and A. J. Arberry, *The Romance of the Rubáiyát* (1959).

Freneau, Philip

Critical biography: Lewis Leary, *That Rascal Freneau* (1941). More specifically critical: Richard Vitzhum, *Land and Sea: The Lyric Poetry of Philip Freneau* (1978).

Frost, Robert

Biography: The three volume work by Lawrance Thompson (1966–1976) is standard, although at times somewhat needlessly grudging; a corrective view is William Pritchard, *Frost: A Literary Life Reconsidered* (1984). Critical studies include Reginald Cook, *The Dimensions of Robert Frost* (1958); Elizabeth Isaacs, *An Introduction to Robert Frost* (1972). A study of Frost as a regional poet is John Kemp, *Robert Frost and New England* (1979). Three collec-ions of critical essays are those ed. by Robert Greenberg and James Hepburn (1961), nes Cox (1962) and Richard Thornton (1970).

Ginsberg, Allen
Of general interest is Jane Kramer, *Allen Ginsberg in America* (1969). **Critical:** Paul Portugés, *The Visionary Poetics of Allen Ginsberg* (1978); Helen Vendler, *Part of Nature, Part of Us* (1980).

Goldsmith, Oliver
The standard biography is Ralph Wardle, *Oliver Goldsmith* (1957). A general critical survey is Ricardo Quintana, *Goldsmith* (1967).

Graves, Robert
Critical biography: J. M. Cohen, *Robert Graves* (1960). Other critical studies, all entitled with the name of the poet, are by Douglas Day (1963), Michael Kirkham (1969), and James Mehoke (1975).

Gray, Thomas
R. W. Ketton–Cremer, *Thomas Gray* (1955), is the best recent biography, For good critical essays, see those included in *From Sensibility to Romanticism,* ed. F. W. Hilles and H. Bloom (1965), *Fearful Joy,* ed. James Downey and B. Jones (1974), and *Twentieth Century Interpretations of Gray's "Elegy"*, ed. Herbert Starr (1968).

Gunn, Thom
Critical: John Press, *Rule and Energy* (1963); *British Poetry Since 1960,* ed. Michael Schmidt and Grevel Lindop (1972); Alan N. Bold, *Gunn and Hughes* (1976); Neil Powell, *Carpenters of Light: Some Contemporary English Poets* (1980).

Hardy, Thomas
Biography: Robert Gittings, *Young Thomas Hardy* (1975) and *Thomas Hardy's Later Years* (1978). **Critical:** *Hardy: A Collection of Critical Essays,* ed. Albert Guerard (1963); Donald Davie, *Thomas Hardy and British Poetry* (1973); John Bayley, *Essay on Hardy* (1978).

Hayden, Robert
Critical discussion is almost wholly in magazine articles. Some material is available in *Modern Black Poets,* ed. D. B. Gibson (1973) and John O'Brien, *Interviews with Black Writers* (1973).

Heaney, Seamus
Robert Buttel, *Seamus Heaney* (1975); Blake Morrison, *Seamus Heaney* (1982). Some discussion is also in Douglas Dunn, *Two Decades of Irish Writing* (1975).

Henley, William Ernest
Critical: Jerome H. Buckley, *W. E. Henley* (1945); Joseph M. Flora, *W. E. Henley* (1970).

Herbert, George
Biography: Marchette Chute, *Two Gentle Men* (1959); and, more detailed, Amy Charles, *Life of George Herbert* (1977). **Critical:** Margaret Bottrall, *George Herbert* (1954), largely helpful as an introduction; and, at a more advanced level, J. H. Summers, *George Herbert, His Religion and Art* (1954); Arnold Stein, *George Herbert's Lyrics* (1968); and especially Helen Vendler, *The Poetry of George Herbert* (1975).

Herrick, Robert
Biographical: Marchette Chute, *Two Gentle Men* (1959). **Critical:** Sidney Musgrove, *The Universe of Herrick* (1950); and John Press, *Robert Herrick* (1961); Robert Deming, *Ceremony and Art: Robert Herrick's Poetry* (1974).

Hill, Geoffrey
Critical: Harold Bloom wrote an Introduction to the collection of Hill's poems, *Somewhere Is Such a Kingdom* (1975). Essays are also found in *British Poetry Since 1960,* ed. by M. Schmidt and G. Lindop (1972), and in *Donald Davie, C. Tomlinson, and Geoffrey Hill,* ed. by G. Martin, *et al.* (1976).

Holmes, Oliver Wendell
Critical biography: Eleanor Tilton, *Amiable Autocrat* (1947).

Hopkins, Gerard Manley

Biography: The most complete accounts are those of W. H. Gardner (rev. ed., 1949) and especially Eleanor Ruggles (1944). **Critical:** John Pick, *G. M. Hopkins: Priest and Poet* (1942); the section on Hopkins in Geoffrey Hartman, *The Unmediated Vision* (1954); Allison Sulloway, *G. M. Hopkins and the Victorian Temper* (1972); and two collections of essays, *Immortal Diamond,* ed. Norman Weyand (1949) and *Hopkins: A Collection of Critical Essays,* ed. Geoffrey Hartman (1966).

Housman, A. E.

Biography: George L. Watson, *A. E. Housman: A Divided Life* (1957); and especially Norman Page, *A. E. Housman: A Critical Biography* (1983). **Critical:** B. J. Leggett, *Housman's Land of Lost Content* (1970) and excellent discussion in *A. E. Housman: A Collection of Critical Essays,* ed. Christopher Ricks (1968).

Hughes, Langston

Biography: Milton Meltzer, *Langston Hughes* (1968); C. Rollins, *Black Troubador* (1970); James Haskins, *Always Movin' On* (1976). The best critical introduction is still probably that of James Emmanuel (1967) followed by that of Richard Barksdale (1977). For a collection of essays, see Therman O'Daniel (ed.), *Langston Hughes, Black Genius* (1972).

Hughes, Ted

Critical: John Press, *Rule and Energy* (1963); Calvin Bedient, *Eight Contemporary Poets* (1974); Keith Sagar, *The Art of Ted Hughes* (1978); Ekbert Faas, *Ted Hughes: The Unaccommodated Universe* (1980).

Jeffers, Robinson

Critical biography: Lawrence Powell, *Robinson Jeffers: The Man and His Work* (1940). Two more recent critical discussions, both bearing the name of the poet, are by Arthur Coffin (1971) and Robert Brophy (1973).

Johnson, Samuel

Biography: James Boswell's monumental *Life,* ed. G. B. Hill (1934–50); John Wain, *Samuel Johnson* (1975); W. Jackson Bate, *Samuel Johnson* (1977).

Critical writing that deals with the poetry includes W. Jackson Bate, *The Achievement of Samuel Johnson* (1955) and discussions of the poems in *Samuel Johnson* (1977); Ian Jack, *Augustan Satire* (1952), pp. 135–45.

Jones, David

David Blamires, *David Jones: Artist and Writer* (1972); Roland Mathias (ed.), *David Jones: Eight Essays on His Work* (1976); Samuel Rees, *David Jones* (1978). Critical discussions are also found in chapters devoted to Jones in John Johnston, *English Poetry of the First World War* (1964); Bernard Bergonzi, *Heroes' Twilight* (1965); Jon Silkin, *Out of Battle* (1972).

Jonson, Ben

Biography: J. B. Bamborough, *Ben Jonson* (1970). **Critical:** Wesley Trimpi, *Ben Jonson's Poems* (1962); *Ben Jonson* ed. Jonas Barish (1963); and George Parfitt, *Ben Jonson: Public Poet and Private Man* (1976).

Keats, John

Concerned with both biography and criticism: W. Jackson Bate, *John Keats* (1963). Focussing more specifically on biography are Aileen Ward (1963) and Robert Gittings (1968). A short and distilled critical biography is that of Douglas Bush (1966). **Critical:** Richard Fogle, *The Imagery of Keats and Shelley* (1949); David Perkins, *The Quest for Permanence* (1959); Stuart Sperry, *Keats the Poet* (1973); Helen Vendler, *The Odes of John Keats* (1983).

King, Henry

Ronald Berman, *Henry King and the Seventeenth Century* (1964).

Kipling, Rudyard

Biography: Two in particular are recommended—those of Philip Mason (1975) and, more psychologically probing, Angus Wilson (1978). **Critical:** A penetrating essay by T. S. Eliot was prefixed to his *Choice of Kipling's Verse* (1941), and others are written by Edmund Wilson in *The Wound and the Bow* (1941), George Orwell in *Critical Essays* (1946), and Lionel Trilling in *The Liberal Imagination* (1950). See also the collection of essays in *Rudyard Kipling*, ed. John Gross (1972).

Landor, Walter Savage

Biography: R. H. Super, *Landor* (1954). **Critical:** Malcolm Elwin, *Landor* (1958); Robert Pinsky, *Landor's Poetry* (1968).

Larkin, Philip

Critical: David Timms, *Philip Larkin* (1973); a section in Calvin Bedient, *Eight Contemporary Poets* (1974); Alan Brownjohn, *Philip Larkin* (1975); Bruce Martin, *Philip Larkin* (1978).

Lawrence, D. H.

Biography: Harry T. Moore, *The Intelligent Heart* (1954). **Critical:** H. M. Daleski, *The Forked Flame* (1965); David Cavitch, *D. H. Lawrence* (1969); and Frank Kermode, *D. H. Lawrence* (1971). Like most of the other commentary, these writers inevitably concentrate primarily on the prose fiction but indirectly throw light on the verse. A good chapter specifically on poetry is in Graham Hough, *The Dark Sun* (1956).

Levertov, Denise

Linda Wagner, *Denise Levertov* (1967) and also Wagner's edition of essays, *Denise Levertov: In Her Own Province* (1979).

Longfellow, Henry Wadsworth

Biography: Edward Wagenknecht, *Longfellow: A Full-Length Portrait* (1955) and, for the early years, Lawrance Thompson, *Young Longfellow* (1938). The best critical discussion as a whole is Newton Arvin, *Longfellow* (1963).

Lovelace, Richard

Manfred Weidhorn, *Richard Lovelace* (1970).

Lowell, Robert

Biography: Ian Hamilton, *Robert Lowell* (1982). **Critical:** Jerome Mazzaro, *The Poetic Themes of Robert Lowell* (1965); Steven Axelrod, *Robert Lowell: Life and Art* (1978); Alan Williamson, *Pity the Monsters: The Political Vision of Robert Lowell* (1974); the discussion in Helen Vendler, *Part of Nature, Part of Us* (1980); and *Robert Lowell: A Collection of Critical Essays*, ed. Thomas Parkinson (1968).

MacDiarmid, Hugh

Biography: Gordon Wright, *MacDiarmid: An Illustrated Biography* (1977). **Critical:** Kenneth Buthlay, *Hugh MacDiarmid* (1964); and a collection of essays ed. by Duncan Glen (1972).

MacLeish, Archibald

A biography is now being completed by Roy Winnick. Critical studies are those of Signi Falk (1965) and Grover Smith (1971).

McKay, Claude

Addison Gayle, *Claude McKay: The Black Poet at War* (1972). Max Eastman gives a short biography in McKay's *Selected Poems* (1953). A critical introduction by Wayne Cooper is in his selection from McKay entitled *The Passion of Claude McKay* (1973).

MacNeice, Louis

Varieties of Parable (1967) is an unfinished autobiography. **Critical:** William McKinnon, *Apollo's Blended Dream* (1971); Terence Brown, *Louis MacNeice* (1975). A collection of essays and recollections is *Time Was Away*, ed. Terence Brown (1974).

Marlowe, Christopher

Biography: Frederick S. Boas, *Christopher Marlowe* (1940; rev. 1964). **Critical:** Harry Levin, *The Overreacher* (1953); J. B. Steane, *Marlowe: A Critical Study* (1964).

Marvell, Andrew

Aside from the classic essay on Marvell by T. S. Eliot in *Selected Essays* (1932), general works include: M. C. Bradbrook and Lloyd Thomas, *Andrew Marvell* (1962); Ann Berthoff, *The Resolved Soul* (1970); Rosalie Colie, *My Echoing Song* (1970).

Masefield, John

Constance B. Smith, *John Masefield* (1978).

Melville, Herman

Biography: Leon Howard, *Herman Melville* (1951). **Critical:** William B. Stein, *The Poetry of Melville's Later Years* (1970).

Meredith, George

Biography: J. B. Priestley, *George Meredith* (1926); Lionel Stevenson, *The Ordeal of George Meredith* (1953). **Critical:** G. M. Trevelyan, *The Poetry and Philosophy of Meredith* (1912); Norman Kelvin, *A Troubled Eden* (1961); and John Lucas, "Meredith as a Poet," in *Meredith Now,* ed. Ian Fletcher (1961).

Merrill, James

Critical: David Kalstone, *Five Temperaments* (1977); the discussion in Helen Vendler, *Part of Nature, Part of Us* (1980); Judith Moffett, *James Merrill: An Introduction to the Poetry* (1984).

Merwin, W. S.

Cheri Davis, *W. S. Merwin* (1981). Critical discussion is also given in Richard Howard, *Alone with America* (1969) and in Helen Vendler, *Part of Nature, Part of Us* (1980).

Millay, Edna St. Vincent

Biography: Jean Gould, *The Poet and Her Book* (1969); Miriam Gurko, *Restless Spirit* (1957). Critical introductions to the poet are by Norman Brittin (1967) and James Gray (1967).

Milton, John

Biography: William R. Parker, *Milton* (1968), supersedes older biographies and is now standard. One of the best introductions is David Daiches, *Milton* (1961). A critically perceptive handbook is E. M. W. Tillyard, *Milton* (1930), which is not outdated. Somewhat pedestrian but full of fact is J. H. Hanford, *A Milton Handbook* (5th ed., 1970). Among dozens of general studies, we should mention those of A. E. Barker (1942), Douglas Bush (1964), and, on more specific subjects, Anne Ferry, *Milton's Epic Voice* (1963); Helen Gardner, *A Reading of Paradise Lost* (1964); John Reesing, *Milton's Poetic Art* (1965); and, on "Lycidas," collections of essays edited by C. A. Patrides (1961) and Scott Elledge (1966).

Moore, Marianne

Commentary is almost entirely critical rather than biographical. Book length studies include those by George Nitchie (1969), Pamela Hadas (1977), and Bonnie Costello (1981). Five critical essays by poets and well-known critics are those by T. S. Eliot, prefixed to Moore's *Selected Poems* (1935); R. P. Blackmur, in *Double Agent* (1935); Kenneth Burke, in *A Grammar of Motives* (1945); Randall Jarrell, in *Poetry and the Age* (1953); and Hugh Kenner, in *A Homemade World* (1975). Collections of critical essays are edited by M. J. Tambimuttu (1964) and by Charles Tomlinson (1969).

Moore Thomas

Critical biography: Howard M. Jones, *The Harp That Once* (1937).

Muir, Edwin

Biography: P. H. Butter, *Edwin Muir, Man and Poet* (1962). Muir's *Autobiography* (1954) is also of interest, as is the memoir by his wife, Willa Muir, *Belonging* (1968). **Critical:** E. L.

Huberman, *The Poetry of Edwin Muir* (1971); D. Hoffman, *Barbarous Knowledge: Myth in the Poetry of Yeats, Graves, and Muir* (1967).

Nashe, Thomas

G. R. Hibbard, *Thomas Nashe: A Critical Introduction (1962).*

O'Hara, Frank

Critical: Marjorie Perloff, *Frank O'Hara: Poet Among Painters* (1977); Alan Feldman, *Frank O'Hara* (1979); and the discussion in Helen Vendler, *Part of Nature, Part of Us* (1980). Recollections of O'Hara are given in the collection *Homage to Frank O'Hara,* ed. Bill Berkson and Joe Le Sueur (1978).

Olson, Charles

Biography: Charles Boer, *Charles Olson in Connecticut* (1975). **Critical:** Two books on the Maximus poems are those of George Buttrick (1978) and Don Byrd (1980). General studies, the title of all of which bear the name of the poet, are those of Sherman Paul (1978), Robert Von Halberg (1978) and Paul Christenson (1979).

Owen, Wilfred

Biography: Jon Stallworthy, *Wilfred Owen* (1974). Helpful critical studies, all entitled *Wilfred Owen,* are by Gertrude White (1969), Dominic Hibberd (1975), and especially D. S. R. Welland (2nd ed., 1978).

Plath, Sylvia

Biography: Doris Eder, *Life and Poetry of Sylvia Plath* (1974); Barry Kyle, *Slyvia Plath: A Dramatic Portrait* (1976). **Critical:** *The Art of Sylvia Plath,* ed. Charles Newman (1970); John Rosenblatt, *Sylvia Plath: The Poetry of Initiation* (1979); and M. D. Vroff, *Sylvia Plath and Ted Hughes* (1979); Alan Williamson, *Introspection and Contemporary Poetry* (1984).

Poe, Edgar Allan

Arthur H. Quinn, *Edgar Allan Poe: A Critical Biography* (1941); *Poe: A Collection of Critical Essays,* ed. Robert Regan (1967); Floyd Stovall, *Edgar Poe the Poet* (1969).

Pope, Alexander

Biography: Samuel Johnson's "Pope," in *Lives of the Poets* is still a treasure of insight, and has been called the finest short "life" of any poet. For whatever reason, no complete modern life has been attempted. Already classic is George Sherburn, *Early Career of Alexander Pope* (1934), which covers only the period up to 1727. Brilliant critical studies abound. An ideal introduction is Geoffrey Tillotson, *On the Poetry of Pope* (1938). Other helpful interpretations include Austin Warren, *Alexander Pope as Critic and Humanist* (1929); Reuben Brower, *Alexander Pope: The Poetry of Allusion* (1959); *Essential Articles for the Study of Pope,* ed. Maynard Mack (1964); G. Wilson Knight, *The Poetry of Alexander Pope* (1965); John Paul Russo, *Alexander Pope: Tradition and Identity* (1972); and David Morris, *Alexander Pope: The Genius of Sense* (1985).

Pound, Ezra

Full length biographies are those by Charles Norman (1960), Noel Stock (1970), and C. David Hayman (1976), the last of which deals especially with Pound's political beliefs and adventures. Two good critical introductions are Donald Davie, *Pound* (1975) and M. L. Rosenthal, *A Primer of Ezra Pound* (1960). More advanced are Noel Stock, *Reading the Cantos* (1967); Walter Bauman, *The Rose in the Steel Dust* (1967); Daniel Pearlman, *The Barb of Time: The Unity of Pound's Cantos* (1969); and Ronald Bush, *The Genesis of Pound's Cantos* (1976). Collections of essays on Pound are edited by Walter Sutton (1963), Eva Hesse (1969), and Eric Homberger (1972). For background, see Hugh Kenner, *The Pound Era* (1971).

Ralegh, Sir Walter

W. F. Oakeshott, *The Queen and the Poet* (1960) is concerned primarily with the poetry. Of general interest is S. J. Greenblatt, *Sir Walter Ralegh* (1973).

Ransom, John Crowe

Biography: Thomas Young, *Gentleman in a Dustcoat* (1976). Critical studies include those by John Stewart (1962), Thornton Parsons (1969), Miller Williams (1972), and *John Crowe Ransom: Critical Essays,* ed. Thomas Young (1968).

Rich, Adrienne

Critical: *Adrienne Rich's Poetry,* ed. Barbara and Albert Gelpi (1975); and the discussions in Richard Howard, *Alone with America* (1969), and in Helen Vendler, *Part of Nature, Part of Us* (1980).

Robinson, Edwin Arlington

Biography: The two standard biographies, each entitled *Edwin Arlington Robinson,* are those by Hermann Hagedorn (1938) and especially Emery Neff (1948). Four earlier critical studies, each entitled with the name of the poet, are by Mark Van Doren (1927), Charles Cestre (1930), Yvor Winters (1946), and, what is still the best introduction to the poetry, Ellsworth Barnard (1952). Later studies, with the same title, are by Wallace Anderson (1967), Louis Coxe (1969), and *E. A. Robinson: A Collection of Critical Essays,* ed. Francis Murphy (1970).

Roethke, Theodore

Biography: Some material is given in Allan Seager, *The Glass House* (1968). **Critical:** Karl Malkoff, *Theodore Roethke: An Introduction to the Poetry* (1966); Rosemary Sullivan, *The Garden Master* (1975); George Wolff, *Theodore Roethke* (1981).

Rossetti, Christina

Of both biographical and critical interest are Lona Packer, *Christina Rossetti* (1963), Ralph Bellas, *Christina Rossetti* (1977), and the fine essay in Virginia Woolf, *The Second Common Reader* (1932).

Rossetti, Dante Gabriel

Biography: Oswald Doughty, *D. G. Rossetti: A Victorian Romantic* (1960). Critical discussion is given in Lionel Stevenson, *The Pre-Raphaelite Poets* (1973) and Brian and Judy Dobbs, *D. G. Rossetti: An Alien Victorian* (1977).

Sandburg, Carl

In addition to the biographies by Karl Detzer (1941) and North Callahan (1970), there is Sandburg's own autobiography, *Always the Young Strangers* (1952). The best general critical studies are those by Richard Crowder (1964) and Gay W. Allen (1972).

Scott, Sir Walter

Biography: J. G. Lockhart's classic, *Memoirs of Scott* (1937–38). More recent books include the critical biographies of John Buchan (1932), Edgar Johnson (1970), and David Daiches (1971).

Shakespeare, William

Biography: Gerald E. Bentley, *Shakespeare* (1961); Samuel Schoenbaum, *Shakespeare's Lives* (1970). For the sonnets and other poems, critical discussions include: G. W. Knight, *The Mutual Flame* (1955); Stephen Booth, *An Essay on Shakespeare's Sonnets* (1969); *New Essays on Shakespeare's Sonnets* (1976), ed. Hilton Landry. Extensive material on facts, readings, and interpretations of the sonnets is contained in Hyder E. Rollins' Variorum edition of *The Sonnets* (1944), which still remains the standard edition, although a more recent one, almost as elaborate, is that ed. by Stephen Booth (1977). A shorter edition that may be recommended is that by J. C. Maxwell (1966).

Shelley, Percy Bysshe

Biography: Richard Holmes, *Shelley: The Pursuit* (1975) has replaced the former standard biography by Newman White (1940), although the latter is useful. **Critical:** Carlos Baker, *Shelley's Major Poetry* (1948); Richard Fogle, *The Imagery of Keats and Shelley* (1949); David Perkins, *The Quest for Permanence* (1959); Earl Wasserman, *The Subtler Language* (1959); and a collection of critical essays, *Shelley,* ed. George Ridenour (1965).

Sidney, Sir Philip

Biography: Mona Wilson, *Sir Philip Sidney* (1931); James Osborn, *Young Philip Sidney*

(1972). **Critical:** David Kalstone, *Sidney's Poetry* (1965), Neil Rudenstine, *Sidney's Poetic Development* (1967), and Richard McCoy, *Sir Philip Sidney* (1979).

Skelton, John

Arthur Heiserman, *Skelton and Satire* (1961); Maurice Pollst, *John Skelton, Poet of Tudor England* (1971).

Smith, Stevie

Critical: Calvin Bedient, *Eight Contemporary Poets* (1974). Personal reminiscence and conversations are given in Kay Dick, *Ivy and Stevie: Ivy Compton-Burnett and Stevie Smith* (1971).

Snyder, Gary

Howard McCord, *Some Notes to Gary Snyder's Myths and Texts* (1971); Bob Stending, *Gary Snyder* (1976).

Spender, Stephen

H. B. Kulkarni, *Stephen Spender: Poet in Crisis* (1970); A. K. Weatherhead, *Stephen Spender and the Thirties* (1975).

Spenser, Edmund

Biography: B. E. C. Davis, *Edmund Spenser* (1933). Modern interest in Spenser has been overwhelmingly critical rather than biographical. A few of the main critical works are relevant sections in C. S. Lewis, *The Allegory of Love* (1936) and his *Spenser's Images of Life* (1967); Paul Alpers, *The Poetry of The Faerie Queene* (1967); A. B. Giammatti, *Play of Double Senses* (1975), Helena Shire, *A Preface to Spenser* (1975).

Stevens, Wallace

Biography: Samuel F. Morse, *Wallace Stevens* (1970). Peter Brazeau, *Parts of a World: Wallace Stevens Remembered* (1982) contains interesting details and anecdotes obtained in extensive interviews with people who knew Stevens. **Critical:** Joseph Riddle, *The Clairvoyant Eye* (1965); Helen Vendler, *On Extended Wings: Wallace Stevens' Longer Poems* (1969); Walton Litz, *Introspective Voyager* (1972); Harold Bloom, *Wallace Stevens: The Poems of Our Climate* (1977); and Helen Vendler, *Wallace Stevens: Words Chosen Out of Desire* (1984).

Stevenson, Robert Louis

Biography: J. A. Stewart, *Stevenson: A Critical Biography* (1926). Critical studies concentrate almost solely on Stevenson's prose fiction. A good essay on the poetry is in H. W. Garrod, *The Profession of Poetry* (1929).

Suckling, Sir John

Joseph H. Summers, *The Heirs of Donne and Jonson* (1972).

Surrey, Henry Howard, Earl of

Edwin Casaday, *Henry Howard* (1938).

Swift, Jonathan

The standard biography is long and detailed: that of Irwin Ehrenpreis (3 vols., 1962–83). His shorter work may be recommended: *The Personality of Jonathan Swift* (1958). Most of the critical discussion is naturally concerned with his prose satire. More relevant to the poetry are Maurice Johnson, *The Sin of Wit* (1950) and Nora Jaffe, *The Poet Swift* (1977).

Swinburne, Algernon Charles

Biography: Philip Henderson, *Swinburne: Portrait of a Poet* (1974). **Critical:** Jean O. Fuller, *Swinburne* (1968); Jerome McGann, *Swinburne: An Experiment in Criticism* (1972).

Tate, Allen

Critical Biography: Radcliffe Squires, *Allen Tate* (1971). Some critical discussion is in John Bradbury, *The Fugitives* (1958).

Taylor, Edward

Donald Stanford, *Edward Taylor* (1965). Critical essays are given in *The Poetical Works of Taylor*, ed. T. H. Johnson (1939) and in Austin Warren, *Rage for Order* (1948).

Teasdale, Sara
Critical biographies, both bearing the name of the poet, are those by Margaret Carpenter (1960) and William Drake (1979).

Tennyson, Alfred, Lord
Biography: Sir Charles Tennyson, *Alfred Tennyson* (1949). **Critical:** Sir Harold Nicolson, *Tennyson* (1923), although spotty, is still considered full of insights. Later works include: *Critical Essays on the Poetry of Tennyson,* ed. John Kilham (1960); Jerome H. Buckley, *Tennyson: The Growth of a Poet* (1961); Christopher Ricks, *Tennyson* (1972); A. Dwight Culler, *The Poetry of Tennyson* (1977).

Thomas, Dylan
Biography: Constantine Fitzgibbon, *Life of Dylan Thomas* (1965); Paul Ferris, *Dylan Thomas* (1977). **Critical:** Elder Olson, *The Poetry of Dylan Thomas* (1954); and, perhaps more helpful, Ralph Maud, *Entrances to Dylan Thomas' Poetry* (1963).

Toomer, Jean
For critical comment, see the discussions in *Anger and Beyond,* ed. Herbert Hill (1968), Edward Margolies, *Native Sons* (1968), and Jean Wagner, *Black Poets of the United States* (1973).

Traherne, Thomas
K. W. Salter, *Thomas Traherne* (1965) remains standard as a critical biography. More recent discussions are A. L. Clements, *Mystical Poetry of Thomas Traherne* (1969) and Stanley Steward, *Expanded Voice* (1970).

Vaughan, Henry
Biography: F. E. Hutchinson, *Henry Vaughan* (1947). For critical discussion, see E. C. Pettet, *Of Paradise and Light* (1960); R. A. Durr, *Of the Mystical Poetry of Henry Vaughan* (1962); and in Louis Martz, *The Paradise Within* (1964).

Walcott, Derek
Edward Baugh, *Derek Walcott: Memory as Vision* (1979); Robert D. Hamner, *Derek Walcott* (1981).

Waller, Edmund
Jack G. Gilbert, *Edmund Waller* (1979); and critical discussion in Earl Miner, *The Cavalier Mode from Jonson to Cotton* (1971).

Warren, Robert Penn
Critical: Victor Strandberg, *The Poetic Vision of R. P. Warren* (1977); James Justus, *The Achievement of R. P. Warren* (1982); and *Critical Essays on R. P. Warren,* ed. William B. Clark (1981).

Watts, Isaac
Thomas Wright, *Isaac Watts and Contemporary Hymn Writers* (1914).

Webster, John
Most of the commentary is naturally on Webster as a dramatist. Of general interest is the collection of essays edited by G. K. and S. K. Hunter, *John Webster, A Critical Anthology* (1969).

Wheatley, Phillis
Critical biography: Shirley Graham, *The Story of Phillis Wheatley* (1969).

Whitman, Walt
Biography: Gay W. Allen, *The Solitary Singer* (rev. ed., 1967); Justin Kaplan, *Walt Whitman, A Life* (1980). **Critical:** Edwin H. Miller, *Walt Whitman's Poetry* (1968); Gay W. Allen, *New Walt Whitman Handbook* (1975). Many of the finest critical essays are included in the three following collections: *The Presence of Walt Whitman,* ed. R. W. B. Lewis (1962); *Whitman,* ed. Roy H. Pearce (1962); *Whitman the Poet,* ed. John Broderick (1962).

Whittier, John Greenleaf

Biography: Two fairly recent biographies are those of John A. Pollard (1949) and especially John B. Pickard (1961). A general guide to Whittier is Donald C. Freeman, *et al., Whittier and Whittierland: Portrait of a Poet and His World* (1976).

Wilbur, Richard

Critical: Donald Hill, *Richard Wilbur* (1967).

Williams, William Carlos

Biography: Reed Whittemore, *W. C. Williams: Poet from Jersey* (1975). **Critical:** The best general introduction is probably still James Breslin, *W. C. Williams: An American Artist* (1970). Other critical works include those of Linda Wagner (1964), Alan Ostrom (1966), Thomas Whitaker (1968), and Jerome Mazzaro (1973); Joseph Riddel, *The Inverted Bell* (1974); and the chapter on Williams in Hugh Kenner, *A Homemade World* (1975).

Wordsworth, William

The standard biography is Mary Moorman, *William Wordsworth* (1957–65). Briefer and more suggestive is H. N. M. Margoliouth, *Wordsworth and Coleridge* (1953). For criticism, an indispensable start may be made from one of the greatest texts in the history of criticism, Coleridge's *Biographia Literaria* (any edition; there are a dozen), in which Chapters 17–22 concentrate on Wordsworth. Also of perennial value is Matthew Arnold's essay, "Wordsworth," in *Essays in Criticism, Second Series* (1888, or later editions). For recent criticism, see especially David Ferry, *The Limits of Mortality* (1959); David Perkins, *The Quest for Permanence* (1959) and *Wordsworth and the Poetry of Sincerity* (1964); Geoffrey Hartman, *Wordsworth's Poetry, 1787–1814* (1964); and *Wordsworth: A Collection of Critical Essays,* ed. M. H. Abrams (1972).

Wright, James

A useful introduction is included in Richard Howard, *Alone with America* (1969). See also Dave Smith (ed.), *The Pure Clear Word: Essays on the Poetry of James Wright* (1982).

Wyatt, Sir Thomas

Biography: Kenneth Muir, *Life and Letters of Wyatt* (1963) and Patricia Thomson, *Sir Thomas Wyatt and His Background* (1965). For critical interpretation, see E. M. W. Tillyard, *The Poetry of Sir Thomas Wyatt* (1929) and the discussion in J. W. Lever, *The Elizabethan Love Sonnet* (1956).

Yeats, William Butler

Biography: Joseph Hone, *W. B. Yeats* (2nd ed., 1962); Richard Ellmann, *Yeats: The Man and the Masks* (1948); Frank Tuohy, *Yeats* (1976). **Critical:** For general discussion, especially Richard Ellmann, *The Identity of Yeats* (2nd ed., 1964); T. R. Henn, *The Lonely Tower* (2nd ed., 1965); and three collections of essays, *The Permanence of Yeats,* ed. James Hall and Martin Steinman (1950); *Yeats,* ed. John Unterecker (1963), and *In Excited Reverie,* ed. A. N. Jaffares and K. Cross (1965). More specialized studies include: Jon Stallworthy, *Between the Lines . . . Yeats's Poetry in the Making* (1963; rev. 1965) and A. N. Jaffares, *A Commentary on the Collected Poems of . . . Yeats* (1968). For discussion of particular poems, see Harold Bloom, *Yeats* (1970).

Copyrights and Acknowledgments

The authors are grateful to the following publishers and copyright holders for permission to use the selections reprinted in this book:

ATHENEUM PUBLISHERS, INC. James Merrill, "Lost in Translation" from *Divine Comedies,* copyright © 1976 by James Merrill. W. S. Merwin, "The Isaiah of Souillac" from *The First Four Books of Poems,* copyright © 1975 by W. S. Merwin. W. S. Merwin, "Summer Doorway" from *The Compass Flowers,* copyright © 1977 by W. S. Merwin. The preceding reprinted by permission of Atheneum Publishers, Inc.

ROBERT BLY "Waking from Sleep," "Driving Toward the Lac Qui Parle River," and "After Drinking All Night . . . " reprinted from *Silence in the Snowy Fields,* Wesleyan University Press, 1962, copyright 1961, 1962 by Robert Bly, reprinted by permission of Robert Bly.

GEORGES BORCHARDT, INC. John Ashberry, "Soonest Mended" and "Evening in the Country" from *Double Dream of Spring.* Reprinted by permission of Georges Borchardt, Inc. and the author. Copyright © 1970 by John Ashenberry.

JOHNATHAN CAPE LTD. Robert Bly, "Waking from Sleep," "Driving Toward the Lac Qui Parle River," and "After Drinking All Night with a Friend We Go Out in a Boat at Dawn to See Who Can Write the Best Poem" reprinted from *Silence in the Snowy Fields* by permission of Robert Bly and Jonathan Cape Ltd. C. Day Lewis, "You that Love England . . . " reprinted from *Collected Poems 1954* by permission of the Executors of the Estate of C. Day Lewis, Hogarth Press, and Jonathan Cape Ltd. Derek Walcott, "Codicil" reprinted from *The Castaway* by permission of Derek Walcott and Jonathan Cape Ltd.

CHATTO & WINDUS LTD. William Empson, "Villanelle" and "Ignorance of Death" from *Collected Poems of William Empson.* Reprinted by permission of the Literary Estate of William Empson and Chatto & Windus.

CITY LIGHTS BOOKS. Allen Ginsberg, "Howl" from *Howl & Other Poems,* copyright © 1956, 1959 by Allen Ginsberg. Frank O'Hara, "The Day Lady Died" from *Lunch Poems,* copyright © 1964 by Frank O'Hara. The preceding reprinted by permission of City Lights Books.

ANDRE DEUTSCH LTD. Geoffrey Hill, "Ovid in the Third Reich," "September Song," and "Funeral Music" from *King Log* (1968). Reprinted by permission of Andre Deutsch Ltd.

DOUBLEDAY & COMPANY, INC. Rudyard Kipling, "Recessional" and "Danny Deever" from *Rudyard Kipling's Verse: Definitive Edition.* Reprinted by permission of Doubleday & Company and the National Trust. Theodore Roethke, "Cuttings (Later)," "Elegy for Jane," "Frau Bauman, Frau Schmidt, and Frau Schwartze," and "The Walking" copyright 1948, 1950, 1952, 1953 by Theo dore Roethke. "Root Cellar" copyright 1943 by Modern Poetry Association, Inc. "My Papa's Waltz" by Hearst Magazines, Inc. "Meditation at Oyster River" copyright © 1960 by Beatrice Roethke, Administratrix of the Estate of Theodore Roethke. From the book *The Collected Poems of Theodore Roethke* by Theodore Roethke. Reprinted by permission of Doubleday & Company Inc.

FABER AND FABER LTD. W. H. Auden, "Sir, No Man's Enemy, Forgiving All," from *The English Auden: Poems, Essays and Dramatic Writings 1927–1957* by W. H. Auden. "A Free One," "Taller Today," "As I Walked Out One Evening," "Lullaby," "Musée des Beaux Arts," and "In Memory of W. B. Yeats" from *Collected Poems* by W. H. Auden. T. S. Eliot, "The Love Song of J. Alfred Prufrock," "Whispers of Immortality," "Sweeney Among the Nightingales," "The Waste Land," and "Burnt Norton" from *Collected Poems 1909–1962* by T. S. Eliot. Ted Hughes, "Crow's First Lesson" and "That Moment" from *Crow: From the Life and Songs of Crow* by Ted Hughes. "Hawk Roosting" from *Lupercal* by Ted Hughes. "Widdop" from *Remains of Elmet* by Ted Hughes. "Wodwo" from *Wodwo* by Ted Hughes. David Jones, "In Parenthesis" from *In Parenthesis* by David Jones. Philip Larkin, "The Whitsun Weddings" and "Dockery and Son" from *The Whitsun Weddings* by Philip Larkin. Louis MacNeice, "Sunlight on the Garden" and "Bagpipe Music" from *The Collected Poems of Louis MacNeice.* Edwin Muir, "One Foot in Eden" and "The Horses" from *The Collected Poems of Edwin Muir.* Stephen Spender, "I Think Continually of Those Who Were Truly Great" and "The Express" from *Collected Poems* by Stephen Spender. The preceding reprinted by permission of Faber and Faber Ltd.

FARRAR, STRAUS & GIROUX, INC. John Berryman, "Dream Songs #16, 29, 76, and 312" from *The Dream Songs* by John Berryman. Copyright © 1959, 1962, 1963, 1964, 1969 by John Berryman. Elizabeth Bishop, "The Fish," "The Bight," and "Manners" from *The Complete Poems 1927–1979* by Elizabeth Bishop. Copyright © 1983 by Alice Helen Methfessel. Copyright © 1940, 1949, 1955, 1969 by Elizabeth Bishop. Copyright renewed © 1976 by Elizabeth Bishop. Louise Bogan, "Song for the Last Act" from *The Blue Estuaries: Poems 1923–1968* by Louise Bogan. Copyright © 1949, 1969 by Louise Bogan. This poem first appeared in *The New Yorker.* Thom Gunn, "On the Move" and "From the Wave" from *Selected Poems 1950–1975* by Thom Gunn. Copyright © 1957, 1958, 1961, 1967, 1971, 1973, 1974, 1975, 1976, 1979 by Thom Gunn. Seamus Heaney, "Bogland" and "North" from *Poems 1965–1975* by Seamus Heaney. Copyright © 1966, 1969, 1972, 1975, 1980 by Seamus Heaney. "The Harvest Bow" and "The Skunk" from *Field Work* by Seamus Heaney. Copyright © 1976, 1979 by Seamus Heaney. Robert Lowell, "Memories of West Street and Lepke" and "Skunk Hour" from *Life Studies* by Robert Lowell. Copyright © 1956, 1959 by Robert Lowell. "For the Union Dead" from *For the Union Dead* by Robert Lowell. Copyright © 1956, 1960, 1961, 1962, 1963, 1964 by Robert Lowell. "Waking Early Sunday Morning" from *Near the Ocean* by Robert Lowell. Copyright © 1963, 1965, 1966, 1967 by Robert Lowell. Allen Tate, "Ode to the Confederate Dead" from *Collected Poems 1919–1976* by Allen Tate. Copyright © 1952, 1953, 1970, 1977 by Allen Tate. Copyright 1931, 1932, 1937, 1948 by Charles Scribner's Sons. Copyright renewed © 1959, 1960, 1965 by Allen Tate. Derek Walcott, "Codicil" from *The Gulf* by Derek Walcott. Copyright © 1965, 1970 by Derek Walcott. "Europa" from *The Fortunate Traveller* by Derek Walcott. Copyright © 1980, 1981 by Derek Walcott. The preceding reprinted by permission of Farrar, Straus & Giroux, Inc.

GRANADA PUBLISHING LIMITED R. S. Thomas, "The Welsh Hill Country" and "A Peasant" from *Song at the Year's Turning* by R. S. Thomas. Reprinted by permission of Granada Publishing Limited.

G. K. HALL & CO. PUBLISHERS Claude McKay, "If We Must Die" from *The Selected*

DAVID HIGHAM ASSOCIATES LIMITED Dylan Thomas, "The Force That Through the Green Fuse Drives the Flower," "And Death Shall Have No Dominion," "A Refusal to Mourn the Death, by Fire, of a Child in London," and "Fern Hill" from *Collected Poems* by Dylan Thomas, reprinted by permission of David Higham Associates Limited.

HOLT, RINEHART AND WINSTON, PUBLISHERS Stephen Vincent Benét, "American Names" from *Ballads and Poems* by Stephen Vincent Benét, copyright 1931 by Stephen Vincent Benét, copyright © 1959 by Rosemary Carr Benét. A. E. Housman, "Loveliest of Trees, the Cherry Now," "Reveille," "To an Athlete Dying Young," "On Wenlock Edge," "With Rue My Heart Is Laden," and "Terence, This Is Stupid Stuff . . . " from "A Shropshire Lad"—Authorised Edition—from *The Collected Poems of A. E. Housman*, copyright 1939, 1940 © 1965 by Holt, Rinehart and Winston. Copyright © 1967, 1968 by Robert E. Symons. The preceding reprinted by permission of Holt, Rinehart and Winston, Publishers.

HOUGHTON MIFFLIN COMPANY Archibald MacLeish, "Ars Poetica," "You, Andrew Marvell," and "Winter Is Another Country" from *New and Collected Poems 1917–1976* by Archibald MacLeish, copyright © 1976 by Archibald MacLeish. Reprinted by permission of Houghton Mifflin Company.

OLWYN HUGHES Sylvia Plath, "The Colossus" from *The Colossus* by Sylvia Plath, published by Faber & Faber, London, copyright Ted Hughes 1967. "Lady Lazarus," "Elm," and "Daddy" from *Ariel,* published by Faber & Faber, copyright Ted Hughes 1965. Reprinted by permission of Olwyn Hughes.

PHOEBE LARMORE Margaret Atwood, "There Is Only One of Everything" and "Book of Ancestors" from *You Are Happy* by Margaret Atwood. Reprinted by permission of Phoebe Larmore.

LITTLE, BROWN AND COMPANY Emily Dickinson, "After Great Pain, a Formal Feeling Comes" from *The Complete Poems of Emily Dickinson* edited by Thomas H. Johnson. Copyright 1929 by Martha Dickinson Bianchi; copyright renewed © 1957 by Mary L. Hampson. By permission of Little, Brown and Company.

LIVERIGHT PUBLISHING CORPORATION Hart Crane, "Voyages," "Proem" (from *The Bridge*), and "The River" from *The Complete Poems and Selected Letters and Prose of Hart Crane,* edited by Brom Weber. Copyright 1933, © 1958, 1966 by Liveright Publishing Corporation. E. E. Cummings, "All in green went my love riding," "in Just-," "Buffalo Bill's," "the Cambridge ladies who live in furnished souls" from *Tulips & Chimneys* by E. E. Cummings. Copyright 1923, 1925 and renewed 1951, 1953 by E. E. Cummings. Copyright © 1973, 1976 by the Trustees for the E. E. Cummings Trust. Copyright © 1973, 1976 by George James Firmage. Robert Hayden, "The Ballad of Sue Ellen Westerfield" and "Those Winter Sundays" from *Angel of Ascent, New and Selected Poems* by Robert Hayden. Copyright © 1975, 1972, 1970, 1966 by Robert Hayden. Jean Toomer, "Georgia Dusk" and "Song of the Sun" from *Cane* by Jean Toomer. Copyright 1923 by Boni & Liveright. Copyright renewed 1951 by Jean Toomer. The preceding by permission of Liveright Publishing Corporation.

MACMILLAN ACCOUNTS AND ADMINISTRATION LTD. E. J. Pratt, "The Highway," "The Prize Cat," and "Come Away Death" from *Collected Poems of E. J. Pratt.* Reprinted by permission of Macmillan, London and Basingstoke.

MACMILLAN PUBLISHING CO., INC. John Masefield, "Sea-Fever" and "Cargoes" from *Poems* by John Masefield (New York: Macmillan, 1953). "On Growing

Old" from *Poems* by John Masefield. Copyright 1920, and renewed 1948, by John Masefield. Marianne Moore, "Poetry" from *Collected Poems* by Marianne Moore. Copyright 1935 by Marianne Moore, renewed 1963 by Marianne Moore and T. S. Eliot. "The Mind Is an Enchanting Thing" from *Collected Poems* by Marianne Moore. Copyright 1944, and renewed 1972, by Marianne Moore. "The Steeple-Jack" from *Collected Poems* by Marianne Moore. Copyright 1951 by Marianne Moore, renewed 1979 by Lawrence E. Brinn and Louise Crane. Edwin Arlington Robinson, "Mr. Flood's Party" from *Collected Poems* by Edwin Arlington Robinson; copyright 1921 by Edwin Arlington Robinson, renewed 1949 by Ruth Nivison. Sara Teasdale, "I Shall Not Care" from *Collected Poems* by Sara Teasdale. Copyright 1915 by Macmillan Pupblishing Co., Inc., renewed 1943 by Mamie T. Wheless. "The Long Hill" from *Collected Poems* by Sara Teasdale; copyright 1920 by Macmillan Publishing Co., Inc., renewed 1948 by Mamie T. Wheless. W. B. Yeats, "The Magi" copyright 1916 by Macmillan Publishing Co., Inc., renewed 1944 by Bertha Georgie Yeats. "The Wild Swans at Coole," "The Scholars," and "A Deep-Sworn Vow" copyright 1919 by Macmillan Publishing Co., Inc., renewed 1947 by Bertha Georgie Yeats. "Easter 1916" and "The Second Coming" copyright 1924 by Macmillan Publishing Co., Inc., renewed 1952 by Bertha Georgie Yeats. "Leda and the Swan," "Sailing to Byzantium," "Two Songs from a Play," and "Among School Children" copyright 1928 by Macmillan Publishing Co., Inc., renewed 1956 by Georgie Yeats. "Byzantium," "Crazy Jane Talks with the Bishop," "Crazy Jane and Jack the Journeyman," and "After Long Silence" copyright 1933, 1961 by Macmillan Publishing Co., Inc., renewed 1961 by Bertha Georgie Yeats. "Under Ben Bulben" copyright 1940 by Georgie Yeats, renewed 1968 by Bertha Georgie Yeats, Michael Butler Yeats, and Anne Yeats. "The Lake Isle of Innisfree," "When You Are Old," and "The Song of Wandering Aengus" (New York: Macmillan, 1983). All selections from W. B. Yeats from *The Poems of W. B. Yeats* edited by Richard J. Finneran. The preceding reprinted with permission of Macmillan Publishing Company.

MARTIN BRIAN & O'KEEFE LTD Hugh MacDiarmid, "Parley of Beasts" and "O Wha's the Bride" from *The Complete Poems of Hugh MacDiarmid 1920–1976.* Reprinted by permission of Martin Brian & O'Keefe Ltd and Mrs. Valda Grieve.

THE MARVELL PRESS Philip Larkin, "Church Going" from *The Less Deceived* by permission of The Marvell Press, England.

MCCLELLAND AND STEWART LIMITED Irving Layton, "Berry Picking" and "Keine Lazarovitch 1870–1959" from *The Darkening Fire.* Al Purdy, "Wilderness Gothic" and "Trees at the Arctic Circle" from *Being Alive, 1958–78.* The preceding used by permission of The Canadian Publishers, McClelland and Stewart Limited, Toronto.

NORMA MILLAY (ELLIS) Edna St. Vincent Millay, "What Lips My Lips Have Kissed" and "Love Is Not All" from *Collected Poems,* Harper & Row. Copyright 1923, 1931, 1951, 1958 by Edna St. Vincent Millay and Norma Millay Ellis. Reprinted by permission of Norma Millay (Ellis), Literary Executor.

WILLIAM MORROW & COMPANY, INC. Amiri Baraka, "A Poem for Black Hearts" copyright © 1969, 1979 by Amiri Baraka. LeRoi Jones, "Notes for a Speech" copyright © 1961 by LeRoi Jones. Both from *Selected Poetry of Amiri Baraka/LeRoi Jones.* By permission of William Morrow & Company.

JOHN MURRAY (PUBLISHERS) LTD. John Betjeman, "An Incident in the Early Life of Ebenezer Jones, Poet, 1828" from *Collected Poems* by John Betjeman. Reprinted by permission of John Murray (Publishers) Ltd.

NEW DIRECTIONS PUBLISHING CORPORATION Robert Duncan, "The Fire" and "Up Rising" from *Bending the Bow* by Robert Duncan, copyright © 1965, 1968 by Robert Duncan, "The Fire" was first published in *Poetry* in 1965. Hilda Doolittle, "Sea Rose," "Dread," and "The Pool" from *Collected Poems 1912–1944* by Hilda Doolittle, copyright © 1982 by the Estate of Hilda Doolittle. Denise Levertov, "Triple Feature" and "Illustrious Ancestors" from *Collected Earlier Poems 1940–1960* by Denise Levertov, copyright © 1958 by Denise Levertov Goodman. "O Taste and See" from *Poems 1960–1967* by Denise Levertov, copyright © 1964 by Denise Levertov Goodman. Wilfred Owen, "Greater Love," "Strange Meeting," and "Anthem for a Doomed Youth" from *Collected Poems* by Wilfred Owen, copyright © 1963 by Chatto & Windus, Ltd. Ezra Pound, "Canto XIII" and "Canto XLVII" from *The Cantos of Ezra Pound* by Ezra Pound. Copyright 1934, 1948 by Ezra Pound. "The Return," "Lament of the Frontier Guard," "In a Station of the Metro," "Envoi," "There Died a Myriad," "E. P. Ode Pour L'Election de Son Sepulchre," "The Age Demanded an Image," "The Tea-rose Tea-gown," and "These Fought in Any Case" from *Personae* by Ezra Pound, copyright 1926 by Ezra Pound. Stevie Smith, "Thoughts about the Person from Porlock" and "Not Waving but Drowning" from *Collected Poems* by Stevie Smith, copyright 1972 by Stevie Smith. New Directions Publishing Corporation Agents for the estate of Stevie Smith. Gary Snyder, "Trail Crew Camp at Bear Valley" from *The Back Country* by Gary Snyder, copyright © 1970 by Gary Snyder. "Meeting the Mountains" from *Regarding Wave* by Gary Snyder, copyright © 1970 by Gary Snyder. Dylan Thomas, "The Force That Through The Green Fuse Drives the Flower," "And Death Shall Have No Dominion," "A Refusal to Mourn the Death by Fire . . . ," "Fern Hill," "In My Craft or Sullen Art," and "Do Not Go Gentle into that Good Night" from *The Poems of Dylan Thomas* by Dylan Thomas, copyright 1939, 1943, 1946 by New Directions, 1945 by the Trustees for the Copyrights of Dylan Thomas, 1952 by Dylan Thomas. William Carlos Williams, "El Hombre," "The Young Housewife," "To Waken an Old Lady," "Spring and All," "To Elsie," "The Red Wheelbarrow," and "The Yachts" from *Collected Earlier Poems* by William Carlos Williams, copyright 1938 by New Directions Publishing Corporation. "The Dance" from *Collected Later Poems* by William Carlos Williams, copyright 1944 by William Carlos Williams. The preceding reprinted by permission of New Directions Publishing Corporation.

W. W. NORTON & COMPANY, INC. A. R. Ammons, "Corsons Inlet" from *Collected Poems 1951–1971* by A. R. Ammons, copyright © 1972 by A. R. Ammons. Adrienne Rich, "A Marriage in the 'Sixties" and "Snapshopts of a Daughter-in-Law" from *Poems, Selected and New, 1950–1974* by Adrienne Rich, copyright © 1975, 1973, 1971, 1969, 1966 by W. W. Norton & Company, Inc., copyright © 1967, 1963, 1962, 1961, 1960, 1959, 1958, 1957, 1956, 1955, 1954, 1953, 1952, 1951 by Adrienne Rich. "Ghazals: Homage to Ghalib" from *The Fact Of a Doorframe, Poems Selected and New, 1950–1984,* copyright © 1984 by Adrienne Rich, copyright © 1975, 1978 by W. W. Norton & Company, Inc., copyright © 1981 by Adrienne Rich. Reprinted by permission of the author. The preceding reprinted by permission of W. W. Norton & Company, Inc.

OXFORD UNIVERSITY PRESS, INC. Edwin Muir, "One Foot in Eden" and "Horses" from *Collected Poems* by Edwin Muir, copyright © 1960 by Willa Muir. Reprinted by permission of Oxford University Press, Inc.

A D PETERS & CO LTD C. Day Lewis, "You That Love England" from *The Poems of C. Day Lewis* edited by Ian Parsons. Reprinted by permission of A. D. Peters & Co Ltd.

RANDOM HOUSE, INC. W. H. Auden, "Sir, No Man's Enemy" copyright 1934 and renewed 1962 by W. H. Auden. Reprinted from *The English Auden: Poems, Essays and Dramatic Writings 1927–1939* by W. H. Auden, edited by Edward Mendelson, by permission of Random House, Inc. "A Free One" and "Taller To-day, We Remember Similar Evenings" copyright 1934 and renewed 1962 by W. H. Auden. "As I Walked Out One Evening" and "Lullaby" copyright 1940 and renewed 1968 by W. H. Auden. "Musée des Beaux Arts," "In Memory of W. B. Yeats," and "In Praise of Limestone" copyright 1951 by W. H. Auden. Reprinted from *W. H. Auden: Collected Poems* edited by Edward Mendelson, by permission of Random House, Inc. Langston Hughes, "The Negro Speaks of Rivers," "Morning After," and "The Weary Blues" copyright 1926 by Alfred A. Knopf, Inc. and renewed 1954 by Langston Hughes, copyright 1942 by Alfred A. Knopf, Inc. and renewed 1970 by Arna Bontemps and George Houston Bass. Reprinted from *Selected Poems of Langston Hughes,* by permission of Alfred A. Knopf, Inc. Robinson Jeffers, "Hurt Hawks" and "The Purse-Seine" copyright 1928 and renewed 1956 by Robinson Jeffers, copyright 1937 and renewed 1965 by Donnan Jeffers and Garth Jeffers. Reprinted from *The Selected Poetry of Robinson Jeffers,* by permission of Random House, Inc. Frank O'Hara, "Poem" (Khrushchev is coming on the right day!) copyright © 1960 by Maureen Granville-Smith, Administratrix of the Estate of Frank O'Hara. Reprinted from *The Collected Poems of Frank O'Hara* edited by Donald Allen, by permission of Alfred A. Knopf, Inc. Sylvia Plath, "The Colossus" copyright © 1961 by Sylvia Plath. Reprinted from *The Colossus and Other Poems* by Sylvia Plath, by permission of Alfred A. Knopf, Inc. John Crowe Ransom, "Bells for John Whiteside's Daughter," "Dead Boy," and "Here Lies a Lady" copyright 1924, 1927 and renewed 1952, 1955 by John Crowe Ransom. Reprinted from *Selected Poems, Third Edition, Revised and Enlarged* by John Crowe Ransom, by permission of Alfred A. Knopf, Inc. Stephen Spender, "I Think Continually of Those Who Were Truly Great" and "The Express" copyright 1934 and renewed 1962 by Stephen Spender. Reprinted from *Selected Poems* by Stephen Spender, by permission of Random House, Inc. Wallace Stevens, "The Snow Man," "The Emperor of Ice-Cream," "Sunday Morning," "Anecdote of the Jar," and "Thirteen Ways of Looking at a Blackbird" copyright 1923 and renewed 1951 by Wallace Stevens. "The Idea of Order at Key West" copyright 1936 by Wallace Stevens and renewed 1964 by Holly Stevens. "Of Modern Poetry" copyright 1942 by Wallace Stevens and renewed 1970 by Holly Stevens. "To an Old Philosopher in Rome" copyright 1952 by Wallace Stevens. Reprinted from *The Collected Poems of Wallace Stevens,* by permission of Alfred A. Knopf, Inc. Robert Penn Warren, "The Dogwood" from "Dark Woods" copyright © 1957 by Robert Penn Warren. "Was Not the Lost Dauphin," "The Sign Whereby He Knew," and "Love and Knowledge" copyright © 1969 by Robert Penn Warren. Reprinted from *Selected Poems 1923–1975* by Robert Penn Warren, by permission of Random House, Inc.

GARY SNYDER Gary Snyder, "Mid-August at Sourdough Mountain Lookout" from *Riprap and Cold Mountain Poems,* copyright © 1965 by GS. Reprinted by permission of Gary Snyder.

THE SOCIETY OF AUTHORS LTD. Walter de la Mare, "The Listeners," "Old Susan," "Napoleon," "Miss Loo," "Old Shellover," and "Song of the Mad Prince." Reprinted by permission of The Literary Trustees of Walter de la Mare and The Society of Authors as their representative. A. E. Housman, "Loveliest of Trees, the Cherry Now," "Reveille," "To an Athlete Dying Young," "On Wenlock Edge the Wood's in Trouble," "With Rue My Heart Is Laden," and "Terrence, This Is Stupid Stuff . . . ." Reprinted by permission of The Society of Authors as the literary representative of the Estate of A. E. Housman and Jonathan Cape Ltd., publishers of A. E. Housman's *Collected Poems.*

STATE UNIVERSITY OF NEW YORK PRESS Adelaide Crapsey, "The Warning," "November Night," and "Triad" from *The Complete Poems & Collected Letters of Adelaide Crapsey* edited by Susan S. Smith. Reprinted by permission of State University of New York Press.

THE UNIVERSITY OF CALIFORNIA PRESS Robert Creeley, "I Know a Man," "The Business," and "Naughty Boy" from *The Collected Poems of Robert Creeley* (1982). Charles Olson, "I, Maximus of Gloucester, to You" and "Letter 72" from *The Maximus Poems* edited by George F. Butterick. The preceding reprinted by permission of the University of California Press.

VIKING PENGUIN INC. John Ashberry, "Worsening Situation" from *Self-Portrait In a Convex Mirror* by John Ashberry. Copyright © 1972, 1973, 1974, 1975 by John Ashberry. This poem originally appeared in *The New Yorker.* D. H. Lawrence, "Bavarian Gentians" and "Snake" from *The Complete Poems of D. H. Lawrence* edited by Vivian de Sola Pinto and Warren Roberts, copyright © 1964 by Angelo Ravagli and C. M. Weekley, Executors of the Estate of Freida Lawrence Ravagli. The preceding reprinted by permission of Viking Penguin Inc.

A P WATT LTD. Robert Graves, "Richard Roe and John Doe," "Sick Love," and "To Juan at the Winter Solstice" from *Collected Poems 1975* by Robert Graves. Reprinted by permission of Robert Graves. Rudyard Kipling, "Recessional" and "Danny Deever" from *The Definitive Edition of Rudyard Kipling's Verse.* Reprinted by permission of The National Trust for Places of Historic Interest or Natural Beauty and Macmillan London Ltd. W. B. Yeats, "The Lake Isle of Innisfree," "When You Are Old," "The Song of Wandering Aengus," "The Magi," "Easter 1916," "The Wild Swans at Coole," "The Scholars," "A Deep Sworn Vow," "Among School Children," "Byzantium," "Crazy Jane Talks with the Bishop," "Crazy Jane and Jack the Journeyman," "After Long Silence," "Under Ben Bulben," "The Second Coming," "Leda and the Swan," "Sailing to Byzantium," and "Two Songs from a Play" from *The Collected Poems of W. B. Yeats.* Reprinted by permission of Michael B. Yeats and Macmillan London, Ltd.

WESLEYAN UNIVERSITY PRESS James Dickey, "The Heaven of Animals" copyright © 1981 by James Dickey. Reprinted from *The Early Motion.* "Buckdancer's Choice" copyright © 1965 by James Dickey. Reprinted from *Buckdancer's Choice.* "Buckdancer's Choice" first appeared in *The New Yorker.* James Wright, "Two Poems About President Harding/One: His Death" and "Two: His Tomb in Ohio" copyright © 1961, 1962 by James Wright. "A Blessing" copyright © 1961 by James Wright. Reprinted from *Collected Poems.* The preceding reprinted by permission of Wesleyan University Press.

Index of First Lines

Index of Authors and Titles